Warm Regards Dougherty
July 2, 2003

D0881685

MANDARIN CHINESE DICTIONARY

Chinese-English

Fred Fangyu Wang

DOVER PUBLICATIONS, INC.
Mineola, New York

Published in the United Kingdom by David & Charles, Brunel House, Forde Close, Newton Abbot, Devon TQ12 4PU.

Bibliographical Note

This work was developed pursuant to a contract between the United States Office of Education and Seton Hall University.

This Dover edition, first published in 2002, is an unabridged republication of the work first published by Seton Hall University Press, South Orange, New Jersey, in 1967.

NOTE: Broken type and other instances of less-than-clear print are part of the original 1967 edition. Dover apologizes for these flaws, but felt it important that the work be made available to the public despite them.

Library of Congress Cataloging-in-Publication Data

Wang, Fangyu, 1913–
    Mandarin chinese dictionary : Chinese-English / Fred Fangyu Wang.
      p. cm.
    Originally published: South Orange, N.J. : Seton Hall University Press, 1967.
    ISBN 0-486-42477-4 (pbk.)
     1. Chinese language-Dictionaries—English.

PL1455 .W15 2002
495.1'321—dc21

2002067741

Manufactured in the United States of America
Dover Publications, Inc., 31 East 2nd Street, Mineola, N.Y. 11501

Table of Contents

Foreword

The teaching of Chinese in the United States has developed very rapidly in the last few years in colleges as well as high schools. As this foreword is written, there are nearly 120 colleges and universities, and 135 high schools in the United States which are teaching Chinese to more than 2500 students. Despite the enormous number of students who are studying Chinese, there has not been, until now, a pocket size, structure-oriented dictionary helpful to elementary students of Chinese for both comprehension and reproduction of the Chinese language.

The need for such a dictionary was publicly recognized when the Modern Language Association of America conducted a survey in 1962 of instructional materials for the neglected languages. Teachers of Chinese who attended Seton Hall's NDEA language institutes also expressed the want of such a dictionary.

In view of this urgent need and the pioneering work done by Seton Hall in promoting the teaching of Chinese on the secondary school level, where most students are beginners, the University asked Prof. Fred Fangyu Wang, who has joined Seton Hall from Yale University, to undertake the compilation of this dictionary with financial support from the U. S. Office of Education. This dictionary is designed, therefore, for students of elementary Chinese in both colleges and high schools.

Prof. Wang taught Chinese at Yale University for nearly twenty years. He has compiled a large number of Chinese textbooks among Yale's Far Eastern Publications. He was the Chairman of the Committee on Applied Linguistics and the Chairman of the Editorial Committee at the Institute of Far Eastern Languages, Yale University. He also served as the principal investigator of Chinese-language study for photocomposing machines in the Applied Research Department of the Radio Corporation of America. He acted as a consultant for International Business Machines on Chinese-English machine translation.

Prof. Wang is one of the few Chinese lexicographers in the United States who is experienced in Chinese language teaching and in compiling dictionaries for students who want to learn Chinese as a second language. He was one of the compilers of the Dictionary of Spoken Chinese(TM 30-033), published by the War Department in 1945, and he served as Chairman of the Dictionary Committee at Yale University's Institute of Far Eastern Languages where the War Department's dictionary was revised. The revised edition of the Dictionary of Spoken Chinese was published by Yale University Press this year.

Seton Hall's dictionary is a two-way dictionary, with one section from Chinese to English and one section from English to Chinese. The present work is the Chinese-English section of the dictionary. The dictionary is being compiled in the light of contemporary linguistics, psychology, and language teaching and draws upon the best traditions in Chinese and English lexicography. The compiler always puts himself in the position of the student in selecting vocabulary words, in forming sample sentences and in analyzing the structures. Special attention has been paid to the basic problems in Chinese that are faced by English-speaking students. Particular emphasis has been given to syntactical structure, functional elements such as particles, and idiomatic expressions. The dictionary will play the role of a friendly guide, pointing out the safe and well-travelled roads to students who have just begun to learn Chinese.

This dictionary had to be completed within a limited time and the compiler worked diligently and painstakingly. Nevertheless, his meticulousness, his precision, his thoroughness, his scholarship and his accuracy have not suffered and deserve high commendation. In compiling this dictionary, Prof. Fred Fangyu Wang was assisted by Mr. Ned Owyang, Mr. Kenny Huang and Mr. Michael Metallo, who worked laboriously on the project. They deserve both praise and thanks. Mr. Kenny Huang was one of the compilers of the revised Dictionary of Spoken Chinese, having worked on that project from beginning to end. He has contributed to this work in various aspects based on his experience. Appreciation should also be extended to Dr. John DeFrancis, Professor of Chinese at Seton Hall University and compiler of Seton Hall's first three sets of Chinese textbooks. Prof. DeFrancis, who served as consultant to the dictionary, has given many valuable suggestions in substantive and technical matters. Prof. William Wang of the University of California at Berkeley also gave much assistance and advice. Thanks should also be given to Dr. Simon Chang, who did all of the calligraphical work in this dictionary.

Deep thanks must be given to The Most Rev. Bishop John J. Dougherty, President of Seton Hall University, the Very Rev. Monsignor Edward Fleming, Ph. D., Executive Vice President and the Rev. Thomas Fahy, Ph. D., Vice President for Academic Affairs, for all the assistance and academic freedom they gave to the project. Utmost appreciation should be accorded to the Rev. Albert Hakim, Ph. D., Dean of the College of Arts and Sciences, Mr. John Cole, Director of Research and Projects, and Mr. Michael Jackieme, University comptroller, for all their support and assistance throughout the project.

One cannot close this foreword without thanking Mrs. Margaret Chiang, who did all of the typing for this dictionary. Last, but not least, appreciation must be given to Mrs. Fred Fangyu Wang, who not only encouraged Prof. Wang in compiling this dictionary, but also rendered all the help needed during the process of compilation.

The compiler will feel the greatest satisfaction if the student can improve his study of Chinese through the use of this dictionary.

John B. Tsu, Ph. D.
Director, Institute of
Far Eastern Studies,
Seton Hall University.

September, 1966
South Orange, N. J.

Introduction

There are many different kinds of dictionaries. Each has its own specific objective and the method of compilation will depend upon that objective. In learning a second language, the nature and structure of a bilingual dictionary, say Chinese-English, will be totally different, depending on whether it is designed for a Chinese student learning English or an English-speaking student learning Chinese. This dictionary is designed primarily for English-speaking students who are learning spoken Mandarin Chinese as a second language.

The gap between spoken and written Chinese is greater than that between the spoken and written forms of other languages. With the audio-lingual method of teaching, used by the great majority of schools currently teaching Chinese, it is preferable to teach spoken Chinese to elementary students through romanized forms rather than Chinese characters. Therefore, a dictionary of spoken Chinese and one of written Chinese will be different both in form and content. Some dictionaries can be used only for reading comprehension; that is, to find out the meaning of a word which one does not know in reading a passage. This is not the purpose of this dictionary.

In the broader sense, a dictionary is not only a reference book for checking the meaning of one word but it can also be used to help learn the language. When learning a language, particularly spoken, the production of certain sentences with certain words is important. However, at this stage of knowledge of the structure of a language, we do not have enough structural rules to produce sentences without mistakes. The way for a learner to produce sentences using a new word is to follow the pattern of a model sentence. The examples given in this dictionary are designed not only to show the precise meanings of the words being learned, but can also be used as model sentences to be copied in producing new sentences.

Theoretically, the scope of a dictionary should include every aspect of the language, including the structure of the language and the cultural situation in which the language is used. In this small dictionary the number of entries is limited but the structure of the language and the cultural situation are both taken into account. Since the number of entries is limited, only the basic vocabulary, especially the grammatical function words, has been selected and analyzed thoroughly. With only about 6,000 entries, it is easy to find certain seemingly very common words missing, but there is a matter of degree of importance which was the decisive factor in the selection of the entries. Despite the relatively small number of entries, the following important points have been considered in the formulation of each example: 1) the sentence pattern is commonly used; 2) words in the sentence are commonly used and are included in this dictionary; 3) the cultural situation in which the sentence is used is a common situation in Chinese culture.

The structure of a language is very complicated. A detailed analysis of the structure is useful for language teachers to control for leading the way in language learning but is not feasible for students who want to gain command of the language. The structure of Chinese language shown through the parts of speech in this dictionary is not refined, but it is useful to a certain extent. "One day" in Chinese is not "yíge-tiān" 一 個 天 but "yìtiān" 一 天 , simply because tiān 天 is a measure and not a noun when it means "day". Why is "open your mouth" zhāng-zuǐ 張 嘴 but not kāi-zuǐ 開 嘴 ? This can only be answered by a deeper study of structure. In this dictionary, instead of going into complicated structural forms, information is supplied by explanation or by showing the associated words through examples.

Very few Chinese words have quite the same range of meaning as English words. When the Chinese expression is more specific than the English, the meaning of the English expression is specifically described. For example: tóufa 頭髮 (N) hair on the top of human's head. (M:gēn 根).When the meaning of the Chinese expression is wider than the English, a general description of the meaning is given and different English words are supplied for the translation in specific situations. For example: bǐ 筆 (N) writing instrument, such as pen, pencil, brush, etc. (M: zhī 枝).

The romanization used in this dictionary is the Pinyin system, which is the official romanized form of Chinese promulgated by the People's Republic of China. It is used in certain types of magazines and periodicals published in Mainland China. In addition, books and bi-lingual dictionaries newly-published in Mainland China use Pinyin to give phonetic value when it is needed.

As far as teaching Chinese as a second language is concerned, the Pinyin system is not only used in books published in China but also in those published in Japan, the Soviet Union and European countries. In this country Seton Hall University has already published a series of three sets of Chinese textbooks in eleven volumes, by John DeFrancis, which are written in Pinyin. Two dictionaries in Pinyin have been published in the United States. They are: Modern Chinese-English Technical and General Dictionary, McGraw Hill, 1963; and Chinese-English Dictionary, U. S. Department of Commerece, 1963.

The Pinyin system used in this dictionary has tried to follow the original system without change. However, two entries, Ss and Tsk, do not follow the spelling system. Information on these entries can be found in the section on Sounds. There have also been two additional marks. One has been to provide stress marks to the syllables which receive the chief stress; that is, those which are spoken most loudly. The second has been insertion of hyphens between syllables which are spoken without a pause. Blank spaces are used to mark places where it is possible in slow-speech to hesitate briefly or stop to catch one's breath.

This is a dictionary of spoken Chinese. A spoken language may be written down using different writing systems. In this dictionary, the spoken Chinese is written down primarily by romanized forms in Pinyin system. The characters are used only for identification. Therefore, all of the romanized syllables are followed by the appropriate characters, but variant and simplified forms are not used.

In most cases, the difference in meaning between two or more similar words is difficult to pin down. There are no absolute synonyms in any language, but there are words which can be used interchangeably in most situations. These shades of difference raise questions in the elementary student's mind, for he is anxious to know the difference between certain words. While the great majority of these questions could be answered only by detailed structural and semantic analysis, some information about the differences between words with similar meanings is given in this dictionary through the use of cross-references. The types of cross-references used are explained in detail in the cross-reference guide.

ABBREVIATIONS

AD	Adverb	NU	Number
AV	Auxiliary Verb	ONO	Onomatopoetic (pertaining to imitation of sounds)
B	Bound Form		
B-	Bound chiefly to a following syllable or syllables	opp.	opposite or antonym
		P	Particle
-B	Bound chiefly to a preceding syllable or syllables	Peip.	localism of Peiping
		PR	Pronoun
con.	contraction	PV	Post-Verb
CV	Co-Verb	PW	Place Word
dial.	dialect(s), dialectal	RE	Resultative Ending
fig.	figurative(ly)	RV	Resultative Verb
I	Interjection	S	Structure
IV	Intransitive Verb	SP	Specifier
L	Localizer	SV	Stative Verb
lit.	literal(ly)	syn.	synonym(ous)
M	Measure	TV	Transitive Verb
MA	Movable Adverb	TW	Time Word
N	Noun	VO	Verb-Object Compound

CROSS-REFERENCE GUIDE

| A | see | B | | All the information is in | B | -entry. |

| A | or | B | | A and B are interchangeable. |

| A | ... (opp. | B |) | B is the antonym of A . |

| A | ... (syn. | B |) | A and B are close in meaning and usually are interchangeable. |

| A | ... (cf. | B |) | A and B can be compared. |

| A | ... (See: | B |) | There is more information in B . |

| A | ... (con. | B |) | A is a contracted form of B and can usually be used interchangeably. |

| A | No. | The number found at the bottom-right of the entry indicates the suggested order of learning. |

SOUNDS

Most of the Chinese syllables can be divided into two parts; the initial and the final. The initial is the initial consonant. The final is the rest of the syllable, either a vowel, a diphthong or a vowel with nasal ending. It should be noticed that the following charts are meant simply as guides and that the Chinese and English sounds will not correspond in every case. For a detailed description of the Pinyin system, consult the sound description in Beginning Chinese by John DeFrancis.

THE INITIALS

Chinese Phonetic Alphabet	Approximate English Equivalent
b	spy
p	peak
m	man
f	fan
d	style
t	team
n	no
l	law
g	sky
k	kill
h	hard
j	jeer
q	cheer
x	ship
z	reads
c	that's
s	sound
zh	large (tip of tongue curved back, and voiceless)
ch	chew (tip of tongue curved back)
sh	shrub (tip of tongue curved back)
r	leisure (tip of tongue curved back)
y	you
w	way

THE FINALS

a	father
o	saw
e	her (r being silent, or e in French le)
i	machine
u	rude
ü	as German ü (or i and u pronounced simultaneously).
er	err (tongue slightly curled)

Note: 1. When i, u and ü are used as separate syllables they are written as yi, wu and yu respectively.
   2. After j, q, x, the umlaut on ü is omitted.
   3. i after the initials zh, ch, sh, r,z, c and s is not pronounced as i but indicates that the preceding initial is prolonged and vocalized in pronunciation.

ai	I
ao	now
an	close to an in English hand
ang	close to ang in English gang
ei	eight
en	omen
eng	close to ung in sung
ou	old
ong	oo ng
ia	yah (or Asia)
ie	yes
iao	yowl
iu	you
ian	yen
in	in
iang	young
ing	sing
iong	y oong

Note: When iu is used as a separate syllable, it is written as you — y + ou.

ua	waft
uo	woman
uai	wife
ui	way
uan	oo ahn (or close to one)
un	went
uang	oo ahng
üe	ü eh
üan	ü an
ün	ü n

Note: 1. When finals starting with ü are used as separate syllables, ü is written as yu.

   2. Two entries, Ss 嘶 and Tsk 嘖 , do not follow the normal Pinyin sound system. Ss, a voiceless dental fricative with air sucked in, is used to indicate discomfort from cold, sudden pain or the process of thinking. Tsk, a sound created by clicking of the tongue, is usually used in English to indicate that something has gone wrong.

THE TONES

Each Chinese vowel has a certain tone of voice. In the sound system of Pekinese, which is the standard sound system of Mandarin, there are four tones. The first one, marked - , is called level tone. It is spoken in a high pitch and neither rises nor falls. The second, ´ , is called rising tone. It starts with the voice lower but ends up high. The third, ˇ , is called low tone. The voice is dropped at first and then rises. And the fourth, ` , is called falling tone. The voice falls from high to low. There are also syllables which are slight in sound. They are called toneless and are not marked.

Stress marks are used on the syllables which receive the chief stress when the syllable is not the last one with a tone marking. Hyphens are used between syllables which are spoken without a pause.

When the suffix r 兒 is used, r is not pronounced as a separate syllable but indicates that the sound of r should be added to the final of the preceding syllable. Some finals are changed when r is added. The following chart shows the change of the sound value.

Original finals plus r:	Actual sound is changed into:
ai(r)	ar
an(r)	ar
ei(r)	er
en(r)	er
i(r) (after y, x, q, j)	ier
i(r) (after z, c, s, zh, ch, sh, r)	er
in(r)	ier
ü(r)	üer
ün(r)	üer

PARTS OF SPEECH

Parts of speech are form classes. The classes are defined by syntactical forms. A detailed analysis of sentences may produce numerous classes and sub-classes, which are difficult to use for language study. The classes used in this dictionary are limited to the general classes.

The meaning of a lexical item can be narrowed down by the classes in which it belongs. And also, based on the syntactical forms which define the classes, with reasonable application, sentences may be produced.

The following descriptions are meant to serve only as a general guide in the usage of this lexicon. For a thorough and more scientific description, consult A Grammar of Spoken Chinese by Yuen Ren Chao.

AD-Adverb

Adverbs are bound forms which cannot be used independently but appear before a verb.

Tā-hěn-máng.	他很忙.	He is very busy.
'Tā-qù, 'wǒ-yě-qù.	他去我也去.	He'll go, I'll go also.

Some adverbs may be used before a number-measure structure.

cái-'wǔkuai-qián	才五塊錢	only five dollars.

In very idiomatic speech they may appear at the end of a sentence.

Tā-zuò-'shì hái.	他作事還.	He is working, besides.

AV-Auxiliary Verb

An auxiliary verb is used before a verb phrase. In Chinese, the auxiliary verb is actually the main verb. It may be used to form a choice-type question by repeating itself with the negative bu 不 or it may be used by itself as the predicate of a sentence.

Wǒ-xǐhuan-qù.	我喜歡去.	I like to go.
Tā-kěn-qù-bu-ken?	他肯去不肯?	Is he willing to go?
Tā-kěn.	他肯.	He is willing.

An auxiliary verb or a verb phrase with an auxiliary verb functions in a way similar in two aspects to a stative verb:

1. It may be preceded by certain adverbs, such as duóma 多麼 how, to what degree; hěn 很 very; tài 太 too; etc.; or followed by certain particles indicating degree, such as jíle 極了 extremely; dehěn 得很 very much; etc.

Tā-hěn-ài-shuō-huà.	他很愛說話.	She likes to talk very much.
Tā-néng-chī-jíle.	他能吃極了.	He can eat a lot.

2. It may be used as the main verb in the bǐ-structure.

Tā-bǐ-nǐ-ài-kàn-diànyǐngr.	他比你愛看電影兒.	He likes to go to the movies more than you.

When the particle le 了 is used at the end of a sentence containing an auxiliary verb, a change of status is indicated.

Tā-<u>yuànyi</u>-qù-le.　他願意去了.　He is willing to go now. (Previously he was unwilling.)

B-Bound Form

A bound form can neither be used independently nor as the subject or predicate of a sentence. There are many kinds of bound forms, and their function will depend upon their behavior in a structure. Some of them are denoted as one class, such as: adverb, co-verb, localizer, measure, particle and resultative ending.

The bound forms listed as entries are those which are productive. The ones which are bound to a following element are marked (B-) as jīn 金 in jīnzi 金子 gold. Those which are bound to a preceding element are marked (-B) as huà 化 in jiǎndanhuà 簡單化 simplify.

CV-Co-Verb

A co-verb is a verb followed by a noun which, together with the noun, precedes and modifies the main verb. When a verb is used in this position and function, and its meaning is distinctively changed from its meaning when used as a main verb, it is a co-verb.

Wǒ-<u>gěi</u>-ta-mǎi.　我給他買.　I'll buy it for him.
Wǒ-<u>gēn</u>-ta-qu.　我跟他去.　I'll go with him.

I-Interjection

An interjection is used independently or for introducing a sentence. Precisely speaking, the tones of interjections may not exactly coincide with the tones of ordinary syllables, but in this dictionary tone marks are used on interjections to show that the tone is close to one of the four tones of ordinary syllables.

Ōu, wǒ-míngbai-le.　喔,我明白了.　Oh, now I understand.
Óu, wǒ-méi-tīngshuōguo.　喔,我沒聽説過.　Oh, I've never heard it.

IV-Intransitive Verb

The characteristics of an intransitive verb may lie in any one of the following three categories.

1. No noun can be used to follow it, as in tǎng 躺 lie down; zuì 醉 get drunk; xǐng 醒 awake.

2. Only a noun which indicates place can be used to follow it.
   Tā-dàole-zhèr-le.　他到了這兒了.　He has arrived here.

3. The noun following it is the actor of the action described by the verb.
   Lái-kè-le.　來客了.　Some guests are here.
   Sǐle-hěn-duō-rén.　死了很多人.　A lot of people died.

L-Localizer

The following items are marked as localizers:

shàng 上 above; xià 下 underneath; qián 前 front; hòu 後 back;

lǐ 裏 inside; wài 外 outside; dōng 東 east; nán 南 south; xī 西 west;
bēi 北 north; zuǒ 左 left; yòu 右 right. Their functions are as follows:

1. They may be followed by biānr 邊兒 , miàn 面, tóu 頭 or bù
   部 , or preceded by yǐ 以 , to form place words.
   lǐbianr 裏邊兒 the area inside; shàngtou 上頭 the area
   above; qiánmian 前面 the area in front; yǐdōng 以東 east of.

2. They may be added to nouns to form place words.
   lóushàng 樓上 upstairs; guówài 國外 outside of a country.

3. They may be used before nouns to modify them.
   hòupái 後排 back row; qiánfāng 前方 front.

4. They may be used after co-verbs, such as wǎng 往 , wàng 望 ,
   xiàng 向 , cháo 朝 , chùng 衝 , etc. wàng-qián-zǒu 望前
   走 go ahead; xiàng-dōng-fēi 向東飛 fly toward the east.

M-Measure

A measure is an item which is used after a number to form a unit,
either to measure the noun which in most cases follows it, such as
zhāng 張 in sānzhang(-zhǐ) 三張 (紙) three sheets of paper; or
the occurrence of the action indicated by the verb which precedes it,
such as cì 次 in shuō-sāncì 説三次 say three times. A measure
is a definite requirement in forming a NU-M N unit, even though some
of the measures do not carry a definite meaning, as ge 個 in liǎngge-
rén 兩個人 two persons.

The number yi 一 one, used before a measure, may be dropped if
it is preceded by a specifier or a verb, as: Zhèi(yi)ge. 這(一)個.
This one. Wǒ-yǒu-(yi)ge-péngyou. 我有(一)個朋友. I have a
friend.

A measure may be reduplicated to indicate the meaning of every,
as in tiāntian 天天 every day.

A measure may be immediately preceded by certain stative verbs,
such as dà 大 , xiǎo 小 , zhěng 整 , etc., as in yídàkuài-miànbāo
大塊麵包 a big piece of bread.

Certain measures may be followed by r 兒 or zi 子 to form a noun,
as kuàir 塊兒 size; gèr 個兒 size.

Certain nouns which can be used as a container may be used as a
borrowed measure, such as yìwūzi-tǔ 一屋子土 a roomful of
dirt; yìzhuōzi-cài 一桌子菜 a tableful of food. In such cases, the
nouns are not marked as measures.

MA-Movable Adverb

Movable adverbs may stand before or after the subject of a sentence.
Wǒ-dāngrán-zhīdao. 我當然知道. or Dāngran-wǒ-zhīdao. 當
然我知道. Of course I know.

N-Noun

A noun may be used after a number-measure structure, as in wǔkuai-
qián 五塊錢 five dollars. It may modify another noun or be modified
by another noun, as in zhuōzi-tuǐ 桌子腿 leg of a table or mùtou-
zhuōzi 木頭桌子 wooden table.

A noun may be used either as the subject or predicate of a sentence. But when it is used as the predicate, in most cases the verb shì 是 is dropped, as: Tā-Zhōngguo-ren. 他 中 國 人 . (a contraction of Tā-shi-Zhōngguo-ren. 他 是 中 國 人 .) He is a Chinese. It is similar in structure to the idiomatic English, "Finders keepers, losers weepers."

NU-Number

A number may be used between a specifier and a measure. While bǎi 百 hundred; qiān 千 thousand; wàn 萬 ten thousand; and yì 億 hundred thousand are marked as numbers, they have certain characteristics and they must take another number before them to qualify as complete numbers, as in zhèi-èrbǎi-zhāng-zhǐ 這 二 百 張 紙 these two hundred sheets of paper.

Numbers are free forms only in counting, in reading digits or in a mathematical context. In other cases they are bound to measures or nouns.

Cardinal and ordinal numbers in Chinese cannot be identified by themselves (except for liǎng 兩 two, which is always a cardinal number) but they can be identified with other elements in certain structures. Some specifiers such as dì 第 , lǎo 老 , etc., may indicate an ordinal number, as in dìsānge 第 三 個 the third one. When certain nouns, such as lóu 樓 , yuè 月 , etc., are used after the numbers, the numbers become ordinal, as in sānlóu 三 樓 third floor; èryuè 二 月 the second month of a year, February.

ONO-Onomatopoetic

There are two common ways of using Onomatopoetic words in Chinese.

1. They may be used independently.

   Pūtōng, diàozai-shuǐli-le. 撲通.掉在水裏了. Splash, it fell into the water.

2. They may be reduplicated and followed by de 的 to modify a verb or a noun or to be used independently as a predicate.

   Pūtōng-pūtong-de-xiǎng. 撲通撲通的響. It sounds like something fell.

P-Particles

Particles are grammatical function words which are used in certain positions in the structure of a sentence or a phrase. Some can be used only at the end of a sentence while others may be used with a verb or with certain structures of a phrase. The usage and the grammatical meaning of each one are described under each entry.

PR-Pronoun

Pronouns are substitutes for nouns, usually for personal nouns. Personal pronouns are made plural by adding the suffix men 們 . They are used as subjects or objects of sentences and as modifiers of nouns.

PV-Post-Verb

A post-verb is a verb which is used immediately after the main verb and before a noun or a place word. There are only five verbs which may be used this way. They are: zài 在 , gěi 給 , dào 到 , chéng 成 and zuò 作 . Usages and examples are listed under each entry.

PW-Place Word

Place words are basically nouns. Like time words, they may be used after zài 在 or dào 到 but, unlike time words, they may be used between dào...qù 到 ...去 go to...; cóng...lái 從 ... 來 come from ...; etc. They may also function as adverbs. Any noun plus a localizer or any localizer plus the suffix biānr 邊兒 , miàn 面 , tóu 頭 , bù 部 , etc., will form a place word.

lǐtou	裏頭	inside.
wūzili	屋子裏	inside the room.
Měiguo hěn-dà.	美國很大.	America is very big.
Shū-zài-zhuōzishang.	書在桌子上.	The books are on the table.
Jiāli méi-you-rén.	家裏沒有人.	There isn't anyone at home.
Tā-dào-nǎr-qu-le?	他到那兒去了?	Where has he gone?

RE-Resultative Ending

All resultative endings are verbs, usually stative verbs or intransitive verbs. A resultative ending indicates the result obtained from the action of the verb or the state of the stative verb which precedes it. However, certain verbs used as resultative endings carry a meaning which is different from the meaning of the verb when it is used as the main verb of a sentence. qǐ 起 used as a main verb can never mean "afford", but used as a resultative ending it may mean "can or cannot afford" in the potential forms. All the verbs which carry different meanings when used as resultative endings are listed and noted. All stative verbs which carry the same meaning as when used as resultative endings are not listed.

    xǐbugānjing   洗不乾淨 cannot wash clean.

Since gānjing 乾淨 means clean and the meaning does not change when it is used as a resultative ending, gānjing 乾淨 is not listed as a resultative ending.

RV-Resultative Verb

A resultative verb is formed by a verb, either a stative verb, transitive verb or intransitive verb, and a resultative ending. Generally, there are four transformational forms of each resultative verb. These four forms are divided into two groups: actual forms and potential forms.

Actual forms:

V - RE - le	chībǎo-le	吃飽了	have enough to eat and be satisfied.
méi-V-RE	méi-chībǎo	沒吃飽	didn't eat enough.

Potential forms:

V- de - RE	chīdebǎo	吃得飽	can be satisfied.
V- bu - RE	chībubǎo	吃不飽	cannot be satisfied.

The potential forms indicate whether the result indicated by the resultative ending can or cannot be achieved.

S-Structure

When two or more items are often used discontinuously in sentence formation, they are marked as a structure. That is, under a certain structure, the items may be used and carry the meaning listed. No detailed description of the structure is given; however, the illustrative sentences will serve as examples.

SP-Specifier

Specifiers are bound forms and are used before number-measure structures. They are used to point to a definite person or thing. However, the specifiers zhèi 這 , nèi 那 and nĕi 那 may be used as subjects of a sentence. When the number is yī 一 , the number may be dropped. Then, the specifier looks the same as when it is used before a measure.

> Zhèi(yi)ge.　　這 (一) 個 .　　This one.

SV-Stative Verb

Stative verbs are in the same class as verbs because they may be preceded by bù 不 and followed by le 了 . They are different from other verbs, however, since they may be used before a noun to modify it, instead of taking the noun as an object.

They may, as auxiliary verbs, be preceded by certain adverbs, such as duóma 多麼 , hĕn 很 , tài 太 , etc. They may also be followed by certain particles indicating degree, such as tòule 透了 , jíle 極了 , dehĕn 的很 , etc.

They may be used as the main verb of the bī-structure, followed by certain complements, such as the number-measure structure.

> Tā-bī-wŏ-gāo-liăngcùn.　　他比我高兩寸.　　He is two inches taller than I am.

They may be used as resultative endings.

> Tā-zhăngdà-le.　　他長大了.　　He is grown up now.

They may be reduplicated plus de 的 to form expressions which may be used to modify a noun or a verb which may be omitted. When they are reduplicated, the last syllable may be changed into level tone and an r 兒 sound added.

If the SV has two syllables, such as AB, the reduplicated form is AABB.

> kuàikuăirde-zŏu　　快快兒的走　　walk fast.
>
> qīngqingchuchūde-yijiu-huà　　清清楚楚的一句話　　a clear sentence.

TV-Transitive Verb

Transitive verbs are verbs which may take a noun, verb or a clause as an object.

> tīng-xì　　聽戲　　listen to opera.
>
> tìng-chàng　　聽唱　　listen to singing.
>
> tīng-chàng-xì　　聽唱戲　　listen to operatic singing.
>
> tīng-ta-chàng-xì　　聽他唱戲　　listen to him singing opera.

Transitive verbs may be reduplicated. The reduplicated form of a transitive verb, as V V, is a contractional form of V-yiV, which is a transformation of V-yihuǐr V- 一 會 兒　do something for a little while or V-yixiàr V- 一 下 兒 do something a little bit. If the TV has two syllables, such as AB, the reduplicated form is ABAB.

kànkan-shū　　看 看 書　　read for a while

shōushi-shōushi-wūzi 收 拾 收 拾 clean up the room a little
　　　　　　　　 屋 子

TW-Time Word

Time words are basically nouns but they may be used after zài or dào 到 , and they may also function as adverbs.

Wǒ-yízhí-xiědao-shídian-　我 一 直 寫 到　I wrote all the way
　zhong.　　　　　十 點 鐘　　　until ten o'clock.

Kāi-huì-de-shíjiān gāizai-　開 會 的 時 間　The time of the meeting
　xiàwu-le.　　　　 改 在 下 午 了.　was changed to the
　　　　　　　　　　　　　　　afternoon.

Jīntian shi-lǐbàiyī.　今 天 是 禮 拜 一.　Today is Monday.

Jīntiande-bào lái-le.　今 天 的 報 來 了.　Today's newspaper has
　　　　　　　　　　　　　　　come.

Jīntian wo-bu-qù.　今 天 我 不 去.　I am not going today.

VO-Verb-Object Structure

A verb-object structure is formed by either a transitive verb or an intransitive verb plus a nominal word. In most cases, the nominal word is a noun, but in other cases it is a measure, as in dǎle-sānzhēn 打 了 三 針 got three shots.

Verb-object structures can produce many transformational forms which are very useful and common, some of which are shown below.

They may be used with a NU-M structure or a modifier of the noun, as in chī-sānwan-fàn 吃 三 碗 飯 eat three bowls of rice; chī-Zhōngguo-fàn 吃 中 國 飯 eat Chinese food.

The object may be transposed to a position before the verb, as in Fàn nǐ-chīle-meiyou? 飯 你 吃 了 沒 有 ? Have you eaten? Yǒu-fàn-chī. 有 飯 吃 . There is food to eat. They may be followed by de 的 to form a noun phrase, as in mài-bào-de 賣 報 的 newspaper seller.

The verb may be reduplicated to make the action casual, as in sàn-san-bu 散 散 步 take a stroll.

A verb-object structure can never take another object. To show the relation with another noun, either a co-verb is used with the noun or the noun is used between the VO, as in gēn-ta-jié-hūn 跟 他 結 婚 marry her; shēng-wǒde-qì 生 我 的 氣 mad at me.

The relation between the action of the verb and the object is not always the relation of action-receiver, but is sometimes rather loose and may produce various types of relationships.

chī-fàn　　　　　吃 飯　　　eat or eat rice.

chī-fànguǎnr　　　吃 飯 館 兒　　eat in a restaurant.

chī-nǚzhāodài　　　吃 女 招 待　　eat the food served by a
　　　　　　　　　　　　　　　waitress.

chī-jiào　　　　　吃 教　　　make a living from religion.

A

A₁ 啊 (P) (1) used at the end of interrogative sentences. Shéi-a? 誰啊? Who is it? (2) used at the end of exclamatory sentences. Zhēn-hǎo-a! 真好啊! It is really good. (3) used at the end of sentences which indicate irritation or impatience. Búyòng-'gàosong-wo, wǒ-zhīdao-a! 不用告訴我，我知道啊! Don't tell me, I know it! (4) used at the end of sentences which are mild commands. Nǐ-děngzhe-a! 你等着啊! You wait, eh! (5) used to indicate a pause either after the subject or at the end of a clause. Wǒ-a, bu-yào. 我啊,不要. As far as I am concerned, I don't want it. Wǒ-kàn-a, tā-bú-qù. 我看哪,他不去. The way I see it, he won't go. (cf:NE 哪, MA 嗎). (6) used after items which are enumerated. Shū-a, bào-a, wǒmen-dōu-yǒu. 書啊,報啊,我們都有. Books, paper, we have them all. (cf: LE 了). (7) used after the name of a person one is addressing directly. 'Lǐ-xiansheng-a, nín-gàosong-ta-ba. 李先生啊,您告訴他吧. Mr. Li, tell him. The sound a may be changed according to the final sound of the syllable which immediately precedes it. a may be changed into ya, when after e, i, ü, ua or uo; into wa, when after u or ao; into na, when after n; into nga, when after ng; and into ra, when after zhi, chi, shi or ri. However, if a final e in the preceding syllable is in the neutral tone, it often links with the initial of the preceding syllable, such as: zhe a becomes zha; le a becomes la; de a becomes da.

Ā₂ 啊 (I) (1) used for a firmly admitted answer, yes. A: Shì-'nǐ-shuōde-ma? B: Ā! Zěnmale? A: 是你説的嗎? B: 啊!怎麼了? A: Is that what you said? B: Yes! What's wrong? (2) or À 啊 indicates satisfaction. Ā! 'Zhè-jiu-'duì-le. 啊!這就對了. Ah! this way is right. (3) used at the end of sentences which are mild commands or suggestions to which the hearer is expected to agree. Bié-zài-cuò-le, ā! 別再錯了,啊! Don't make mistakes again, all right? Hǎohǎorde-shuìjiào-ba, ā! 好好兒的睡覺吧,啊! Sleep tight, will you? Zài-jiàn, lái-wánr, ā! 再見，來玩

兒啊! (lit. See again, come to have a nice time, will you?) Goodbye! Come again, will you?

Á₂ 啊 (I) indicates doubt or surprise, What? Á? Nǐ-shuō-shénma? 啊? 你説甚麼? What? What did you say? Á? Zhè-shi-'shéi-xiěde? 啊? 這是誰寫的? What? Who wrote this? Á? Nǐ-gǎn? 啊? 你敢? What? How dare you?

À₂ 啊 see Ā 啊 (I) 2.

ÀGĒNTÍNG₂ 阿根廷 (PW) Argentina.

ĀI₂ 哎 or EI 哎 (I) (1) used informally to get someone's attention. Āi! Nǐ-děi-zǒu-le. 哎! 你得走了. Hey! You must go now. Āi Āi Āi! shuō-nǐ-ne. 哎哎哎! 説你哪. Hey! You! (2) used to introduce a statement of agreement. Āi, jiù-nènma-bàn-ba. 哎, 就那麼辦吧. O. K. let's do it that way. (3) used to answer a call or a request. A: Lǎo-Zhāng! B: Āi, 'shénma-shì? A: 老張! B: 哎, 甚麼事? A: Chang! B: Yes, what is it? A: 'Gěi-wǒ-yìzhī-'bǐ. B: Āi. A: 給我一枝筆. B: 哎. A: Give me a pen. B: Yes. (4) used to express surprise at a coincidence. Āi, wǒmen-zhèng-shuō-ni, ni-jiù-lái-le. 哎, 我們正説你, 你就來了. We were just talking about you, and here you are.

ĀI₂ 挨 (TV) adjacent, next to, close to, touching. Yíge-āi-yígè. 一個挨一個. One is next to the other or one after another. Zhèi-liǎngge-qìchē āishangle. 這兩個汽車挨上了. These two cars are touching each other. Nǐ-āizhe-'wǒ-zuò-ba. 你挨着我坐吧. You sit next to me. Fànguǎnr-gēn-shū-pù jǐn-āizhe. 飯館兒跟書鋪緊挨着. The restaurant is right next to the bookstore.

ĀI₂ 挨 or ÁI 挨 (TV) suffer (a beating, hunger, etc.), receive (a scolding). Tā-āi-dǎ-le. 他挨打了. He was beaten up. Tā-āile-yidun-shuō. 他挨了一頓説. He got a talking to. Wǒ-āile-ta-yidun-mà. 我挨了他一頓罵. I got a scolding from him. Tā-āile-yidāo. 他挨了一刀. He was cut by a knife.

ĀI₅ 挨 (TV) Peip. for zài 在 be at as a main verb or co-verb but not as a post-verb. Tā-āi-nǎr-ne? 他挨那兒哪? Where is he? Nǐ-āi-'nǎr-chī-'fàn? 你挨那兒吃飯? Where do you eat? (cf: ZÀI 在).

ĀI₂ 哎 or EI 哎 (I) (1) indicates surprise. Āi! Zhèi-shi-shénma? 哎! 這是甚麼? Eh! What is this? (2) indicates disagreement. Āi! bié-'zènma-bàn. 哎! 別這麼辦.

No, don't do it this way.

ÁI₅ 捱 (TV) put off, procrastinate with no or little intention to act. yì'tiān-yitiān-de-wàng-hòu-'ái 一天一天的往後捱 put off from one day to the next.

ÁI₂ 挨 see ÁI 挨 .

ĂI₂ 哎 or ĔI 哎 (I) (1) used to introduce a different opinion. Ăi! 'Nà-jiu-bu-'duì-le. 哎 ! 那就不對了 . Get off it, that won't be right. Ăi! Bié-'nènma-shuō. 哎 ! 別那麼說 . No, don't talk like that. (2) used to show annoyance. Ăi! 'Yòu-cuò-le. 哎 ! 又錯了 . Nuts! It's wrong again.

ĂI₁ 矮 (SV) short (of stature), low in grade, position, pitch. (opp. gāo 高). Tā-bu-ăi. 他不矮 . He is not short. Zhèige-zhuōzi tài-ăi. 這個桌子太矮 . This table is too low. Tā-bǐ-wǒ-ăi-yibǎn. 他比我矮一班 . He is one grade lower than I am. (cf: DĪ 低).

ÀI₂ 哎 (I) used as an expression of disappointment. Ài, 'zhè-zěnma-bàn-a? 哎 , 這怎麼辦呢 ? Tch-Tch, what can be done? Ài, méi-fázi. 哎 , 沒法子 . Too bad, there is no way out.

ÀI₁ 愛 (TV) love, be fond of, like. Nǐ-hái-ài-ta-ma? 你還愛他麼 ? Do you still love her? Wǒ-hěn-ài-zhèige-dìfang 我很愛這個地方 I am very fond of this place. (AV) love to, like to. Wǒ-ài-

chī Zhōngguo-fàn. 我愛吃中國飯 . I like (to eat) Chinese food. (AD) easily, often. Tā-ài-tóuteng. 他愛頭疼 . He gets headaches easily. Tā-hēle-jiǔ, ài-shuìjiào. 他喝了酒，愛睡覺 . After he drinks, he often goes to sleep. (S) Ài...Bu...愛 ... 不 ... or not... as you like. Nǐ-ài-chī-bu-chī , wǒ-buguǎn. 你愛吃不吃，我不管. You can eat it or not as you please, I don't care. Ài-xìn-bu-xìn. 愛信不信 . Believe it or not. Ài-yào-bu-yào. 愛要不要 . Take it or leave it.

'ÁIBĂN₄ 呆板 (SV) inflexible in thinking or doing things. Zhèige-rén zhēn-'áibǎn. 這個人真呆板 . This person is inflexible.

ÁI-'E₃ 挨餓 or ÁI-'E 挨餓 (VO) endure or suffer hunger. Wǒ-méi-āiguo-è. 我沒挨過餓 . I have never suffered hunger.

ÁI-'E₃ 挨餓 see ÁI-'E 挨餓 .

ÀI'ĚRLÁN₂ 愛爾蘭 (PW) Ireland.

ĂIGER₅ 矮個兒 (N) a short person.

ÀI-GUÓ₁ 愛國 (VO) love (one's) country. Nǐ-ài-'guó-bu-ài? 你愛國不愛 ? Do you love your country? (SV) patriotic. Tā-hěn-ài-guó. 他很愛國 . He is very patriotic.

A

A

ˋAIHÀO₃ 愛好 (TV) like something as a hobby. àihào-yīnyue 愛好音樂 like music. àihào-yìshu 愛好藝術 like art.

ˋAIHÙ₃ 愛護 (TV) love and protect. àihù-zìjǐde-házi 愛護自己的孩子 love and protect (one's) own children.

ĀIJI₂ or YĪJI 埃及 (PW) Egypt.

ÀIKÈSĪGUĀNG₂ 愛克斯光 (N) X-ray. zhào-àikesiguāng 照愛克斯光 take an x-ray or have an x-ray taken.

ĀI-MÉNR₄ 挨門(兒)(AD) from door to door. āi-ˈménr-mài-ˈdōngxi 挨門兒賣東西 sell things from door to door.

ˋAIQÍNG₁ 愛情 (N) love, affection (between a man and a woman) Tāmende-àiqíng-hěn-shēn. 他們的愛情很深. They have a deep love for each other.

ĀIQIÚ₅ 哀求 (TV) beg for mercy or favor, plead.

ˋAIRÉN₃ 愛人 (N) (1) lover, beloved, sweetheart. (2) used in mainland China as lover, husband or wife.

ÀI-RÉN₂ 愛人 (VO) love people. ài-rén-rújǐ 愛人如己. love others as oneself.

ÀI-SHÌ₁ 礙事 (VO) block one's way. Wǒ-pà-ˈài-nǐde-ˈshì. 我怕礙你的事. I am afraid that I am in your way. (SV) be in someone's way. Zhuōzi-fàngzai-zhèr, hen-àishì. 桌子放在這兒, 很礙

事. The table placed here will be in the way. Bú-àishì. 不礙事. It doesn't matter. or No bother.

ĀIYĀ₁ 哎呀 see ĀIYŌU 哎唷 (I) (2).

ĀIYŌU₁ 哎唷 (I) (1) indicating pain or suffering, ouch! Aiyōu! hǎo-téng. 哎唷! 好疼. Ouch! It's very painful. (2) or ĀIYĀ 哎呀 indicating surprise, gosh, oh my. Āiyōu!zhěn-bù-deliǎo. 哎唷!真不得了. Gosh! It's terrific.

ĂIZI₁ 矮子 (N) a short person, a dwarf.

ÀLĀBÓ₂ 阿拉伯 (PW) Arabia.

ÀLĀSĪJIĀ₂ 阿拉斯加 (PW) Alaska.

ÀMÓNÍYÀ₃ 阿摩尼亞 (N) ammonia.

ĀN₂ 安 (TV) install, set up. ān-diàndēng 安電燈 install the lights. ān-yá 安牙 install a dental plate or bridge. ān-jiā 安家 set up a family or home. Wǒmen-bǎ-diànhuà ānzai-nǎr-ne? 我們把電話安在那兒呢? Where should we install the telephone?

ĀN₄ 安 (SV) at ease, peaceful. Tā-xīnli-ˈān-bu-ān? 他心裏安不安? Is his mind at ease?

ÀN₂ 岸 (N) shore, bank, coast. Tāmen-dou-zài-ànshang děngzhe-ne. 他們都在岸上等着哪. They are all waiting on the shore. Tā-zài-chuánshang-ne, hái-méi-shàng-àn-ne. 他在

A

船上哪，還沒上岸哪．He is on the boat and has not yet disembarked. Dōngxi-liǎng'àn 東西兩岸 East and West coast.

ÀN₄ 暗 (SV) dim. (opp. liàng 亮). Dēng-guāng tài-àn. 燈光太暗．The light is too dim. Lǐ-tou-hěn-àn, wàitou-hěn-liàng. 裏頭很暗，外頭很亮．It is very dim inside, but outside it is very bright.

ÀN₂ 按 see ÈN 按．

AN(ZHE)₁ 按着 or 'ÀN ZHÀO 按照 (CV) according to an opinion, method, plan, schedule, etc. Wǒmen-jiu-àn(zhe)-'tāde-yìsi-'bàn-ba. 我們就按着他的意思辦吧．Let's do it according to his idea. An(zhe)-zhèige-fázi-zuò, yídìng-méi-wèntí. 按着這個法子作，一定沒問題．If we do it according to this method, there won't be any trouble. Wǒmen-děi-àn(zhe)-'shíhou-zuòwán. 我們得按着時候作完．We have to finish it according to schedule. Tā-shuō-yíqiè dōu-děi-àn(zhe) guīju zuò. 他說一切都得按着規矩作．He said that everything must be done according to regulations.

'ANDI(LI)₄ 暗地(裏)(MA) stealthily, in the dark, slyly, furtively. Tā-àndì(li) zuòle-xiē-bu-néng-Gàosong-'rén-de-shì. 他暗地(裏)作了些不能告訴人的事．

He did something stealthily which cannot be told to anybody.

'ĀNDÌNG₂ 安定 (SV) peaceful and stable (situation). Xiànzài tāde-'dìwèi-hen-'āndìng. 現在他的地位很安定．His position is very stable now. Wǒmen-dou-xīwang you-yige-'āndìngde-shēnghuo. 我們都希望有一個安定的生活．We all hope that we have a peaceful and stable life.

ĀNGZANG₅ 骯髒 (SV) dial. dirty, filthy. (opp. gānjing 乾淨), (syn. Peip. āza 骯髒 zāng 髒).

ANHAO(R)₃ 暗號(兒)(N) cryptic sign, cryptic signal.

ĀNHUĪ₂ 安徽 (PW) Anhwei province.

'ÀNJIÀN₅ 案件 (N) case (at law).

ĀNJÌNG₁ 安靜 (SV) quiet. (opp. rènao 熱鬧). Zhèige-dìfang hěn-ānjìng. 這個地方很安靜．It is very quiet here. Qǐng-nǐmen-ānjìng-yidianr. 請你們安靜一點兒．Please make less noise.

ÀN- LǏ₃ 按理 (AD) according to principle or reason. Àn-'lǐ-shuō ta-'bù-yīngdāng-bu-gěi-nǐ-'qián. 按理說，他不應當不給你錢．According to principle, he ought to give you money.

ÀNMÅR₃ 暗碼兒 (N) crypti-cal or special code signal for letters, words or Chinese char-acters. (opp. míngmǎr 明碼兒), (syn. mìmǎr 密碼兒).

A

ĀNMIÁNYÀO₂ 安眠藥 (N)
sleeping pill. (M: piàn 片,
lì 粒).

ÀNMÓ₂ 按摩 (TV) massage.

'ĀNPÁI₁ 安排 (TV) arrange
matters. Nèixiē-shìqìng wǒ-dou-
ānpai-le. 那些事情我都
安排了. I have arranged
all those matters.

ÀNQĪ₃ 按期 (AD) according to a
predetermined timetable, on
schedule. Zhèige-gōngzuo wǒ-
men-bìxu-ànqī-wánchéng. 這個
工作我們必須按
期完成. We must com-
plete this job on schedule.

'ĀNQUÁN₁ 安全 (SV) safe.
(opp. 'wēixiǎn 危險). Zài-
zhèili-zhù-ānquán-ma? 在這
裏住安全嗎? Is it
safe to live here?

ĀNQUÁNDÀI₃ 安全帶 (N)
seat belt. (M: tiáo 條).

ÀNSHĀ₁ 暗殺 (TV) assassinate.
Tā-jiào-rén-gei-ànshāle. 他叫
人給暗殺了. He was
assassinated.

ÀNSHÌ₄ 暗室 (N) photographic
darkroom. (M: jiān 間).

ÀNSHÌ₂ 暗示 (TV) imply, hint.
Tā-ànshì-wo-nènma-bàn. 他暗
示我那麼辨. He
implied that I should do it that
way.
(N) implication, hint. Nà-shi-
yizhǒng-ànshì, ni-bu-míngbai-
ma? 那是一種暗示,
你不明白嗎? That
is a hint, don't you understand?

ÀN...SHUŌ₂ 按...說 (S) ac-
cording to,... àn-(dào)lǐ-shuō 按
(道) 理說 (lit. speak ac-
cording to logic) logically. An-
'bàoshang-shuō, jīntian-bu-xiàjǔ.
按報上說, 今天不
下雨. According to what the
newspaper said, it will not rain
today.

ÀNSHUŌ₂ 按說 (AD) logically.
Ànshuō bu-yīngdang-zènma-bàn.
按說不應當這麼
辨. Logically, it shouldn't be
done this way.

ĀNWEI₁ 安慰 (TV) console,
comfort someone. Nǐ-qu-'ānwei-
ānwei-ta-ba. 你去安慰安
慰他吧. You'd better go
to comfort him.
(N) consolation, pleasure derived
from human consolation. Tā-
méi-dézhao-shénma-ānwei. 他
沒得着甚麼安慰.
He didn't get any consolation.

ĀNWEN₂ 安穩 (SV) steady,
peaceful, calm. Nèrde-qíngxing
hen-ānwen. 那兒的情形
很安穩. The situation
there is very peaceful. Tā-
'shuìde-hen- ānwen. 他睡的
很安穩. He sleeps very
soundly.

ĀN-XĪN₂ 安心 (VO) (1) have a
calm mind. Tā-bu-néng-ānxīn.
他不能安心. He
can't calm his mind. (2) set
one's mind to. Tā-bu-néng-
ānxīn-zuò-shì. 他不能安
心作事. He can't set his
mind to work. (3) (lit. set an
intent) have intentions. Tā-méi-

ān-hǎo-xīn. 他 没 安 好 心.
He did not have good intentions.
(AD) on purpose, purposely, intentionally. (syn. chéngxīn 成
心). Tā-ān'xīn-bu-hǎohāorde-
'zuò. 他 安 心 不 好 好
兒 的 作. He intentionally
doesn't do it properly.

ÀNYUÈ₃ 按月 (AD) according to
month, monthly, by the month.
ànyuè-gěi-qián 按月 給錢
pay monthly.

'ÀNZHÀO₁ 按照 see ÀN(ZHE)
按(着).

'ÀNZHÌ₂ 安置 (TV) arrange
things or persons. Wǒmen bǎ-
jiā-ānzhihǎole, zài-shuō. 我們
把家安置好了,再
説. We'll see about it after
we have set up our home.

'ÀNZHŌNG₃ 暗中 (PW) in dark-
ness, secretly. Zhèijian-shìqing
tāmen-shì-zài-'ànzhong-zuòde,
méi-ràng-women-zhǐdao. 這件
事情他們是在暗
中作的,没讓我們
知道. They did this se-
cretly, and did not inform us.

ĀNZI₄ 鞍子 (N) saddle for riding animals.

ÀNZI₂ 案子 (N) case (lawsuit).
(M: jiàn 件).

ĀO₄ 熬 (TV) stew certain food.
āo-báicài 熬白菜 stew cab-
bage or stewed cabbage.

ĀO₅ 熬 (SV) Peip. unhappy,
sad. Tā-xīnli hěn-āo. 他心
裏很熬. He is very un-
happy (in his heart).

ĀO₃ 熬 (TV) (1) decoct, boil or
prepare something in a watery
fluid for a long period to extract
its virtues. áo-tāng 熬湯 make
soup. áo-yào 熬藥 brew med-
icine. (2) fig. work patiently for
a long period. Tā-áole-shínián,
cái-áoshang-yige-xiàozhǎng.
他熬了十年才熬
上一個校長. He
worked for ten long years, then
got the position of a principal.
Nǐde-háizi-yǐjing-dàle, suàn-
áochulaile. 你的孩子已
經大了,算熬出來
了. Your child has grown up,
a long period of hard work has
ended for you.

ÀODÀLÌYÀ₂ 奧大利亞 (PW)
Australia.

ÀODÌLÌ₂ 奧地利 (PW) Austria.

ÀOGUO₂ 奧國 (PW) Austria.

'ÀOHUǏ₅ 懊悔 (SV) regretful.
Nǐ-zhèiyàngr-zuò ke-bié-'àohuǐ.
你這樣兒作可別
懊悔. If you do it this way
don't be regretful.

ÀOLÍNPǏKÈ₂ 奧林匹克
(N) Olympic.

'ÀOMÀN₄ 傲慢 (SV) haughty.
Tāde-tàidu-'àomàn. 他的態
度傲慢. His attitude is
haughty.

'ÀOMIÀO₂ 奧妙 (SV) intriguing,
inspiring interest. 'Zhèngzhi-
'wèntí fēichang-'àomiào. 政治
問題非常奧妙.
Political problems are very
intriguing (because they are not
easily understood).

A

A

ʾÀONǍO₅ 懊惱 (SV) sad, grievous, despondent. Tā-tàitai-sǐle-yǐhòu, ta-xīnli-fēichang-ʾàonǎo. 他太太死了以後他心裏非常懊惱. After his wife died, he was very despondent.

ÁO-YÈ₂ 熬夜 (VO) stay awake at night. Wǒ-zuótian-áole-yiyè. 我昨天熬了一夜. I stayed up all night last night.

ÀOZHOU₂ 澳洲 (PW) Australia (continent).

ÀSĪPǏLÍNG₁ 阿斯匹靈 (N) aspirin. (M: lì 粒). chī-àsī-pǐlíng 吃阿斯匹靈 take aspirin.

ÀYÍ₅ 阿姨 (N) dial. aunt (mother's sister).

ĀZA₅ 骯髒 (SV) Peip. dirty, filthy. (opp. gānjing 乾淨), (syn. dial. āngzang 骯髒, zāng 髒).

B

BA₄ 巴 (B) (1) a nominal suffix. yǐba or wěiba 尾巴 tail. (2) used after numbers, bǎi 百 hundred, qiān 千 thousand, wàn 萬 ten thousand, to indicate approximate amount. wànba- kwai-qián 萬巴塊錢 about ten thousand dollars.

BA₁ 吧 (P) (1) used at the end of a sentence, indicates a suggestion or a mild command, had better.. Nǐ-xiān-zǒu-ba. 你先走吧. You had better go first. Suànle- ba! 算了吧! Forget it! (2) used at the end of a sentence, indicates a tentative statement or a mild question, ... I sup- pose. Nǐ-shi-'Zhōngguo-rén-ba. 你是中國人吧 You are Chinese, I suppose. or Are you Chinese? (3) used to mark a pause after a suppositional phrase. Búlun-nǐ-zěnma-shuō- ba, fǎnzheng-bu-duì. 不論你 怎麼説吧,反正不 對. It doesn't matter how you say it, it's still not right. Yào- shi-wo-'bú-qù-ba, bu-hǎo; 'qù- ba, 'yě-bu-hǎo. 要是我不 去吧,不好;去吧,也 不好. If I don't go, it is no good, if I go, it is also no good. (4) used at the end of an interrogative sentence to force

an answer. Nǐ-qù-bu-qù-ba? 你 去不去吧? Are you going or not?

BĀ₁ 八 (NU) eight, eighth. bālóu 八 樓 eighth floor. The tone of bā 八 may be changed into rising tone when it is followed by a syllable with a falling tone, as in 'bákwài, 八塊 eight pieces, eight dollars. 'básuì 八歲 eight years old.

BÁ₁ 八 see BĀ 八.

BÁ₂ 拔 (TV) pull up or out some- thing long and thin that offers considerable resistance, ex- tract by pulling. bá-tóufa 拔 頭髮 pull hair. bá-yá 拔牙 extract a tooth.

BǍ₃ 把 (TV) (1) hold something with the hand. Tā-yòng-shǒu- bǎzhe-bu-fàng. 他用手把 着不放. He is holding it with his hand and won't re- lease it. or fig. He is monopo- lizing it and won't let anyone else do it. Wǒ-bǎzhe-tāde-shǒu jiāo-ta-xiě-zì. 我把着他 的手教他寫字. I hold his hand to teach him how to write. (2) guard. Nǐ-bǎ- 'qiánmén, wǒ-bǎ-'hòumén. 你 把前門,我把後門. You guard the front door, and I will guard the back door. (3) be

B

located at <u>a corner of a street,</u> <u>adjacent to a door way or at the</u> <u>mouth of a river.</u> Nèige-pùzi, bǎzhe-lù-kǒur. 那 個 鋪 子 把 着 路 口 兒. That store is located at the corner of the street. (4) <u>hold a baby in</u> <u>position to help it defecate and/</u> <u>or urinate.</u> Nǐ-'bába-háizi. 你 把 把 孩 子. Hold the baby so that he can <u>urinate.</u>

BǍ₁ 把 or BǍI 把 (CV) <u>used to</u> <u>bring the direct object of the</u> <u>sentence before the verb, which</u> <u>must be followed by a comple-</u> <u>ment in all but a few cases; may</u> <u>be accompanied by the adverb</u> gěi 給 <u>which precedes the main</u> <u>verb.</u> (1) (<u>with</u> le 了 <u>as a com-</u> plement). Wǒ-bǎ-qìchē (gěi)- màile. 我 把 汽 車 (給) 賣 了. I sold the car. (2) (<u>with</u> zhe 着). Bǎ-zhèige-qián názhe ba. 把 這 個 錢 拿 着 吧. Take this money. (3) (<u>with</u> zài 在 <u>plus a PW</u>). Qǐng-nǐ-bǎ-shū (gěi)-fàngzai-zhèr. 請 你 把 書 (給) 放 在 這 兒. Please put the book here. (4) <u>with</u> zuò 作 <u>plus a N</u>). Tā-bǎ-nèige- háizi dàngzuo-tāde-nǚer. 他 把 那 個 孩 子 當 作 他 的 女 兒. He treated that child as if she were his own daughter. (5) (<u>with</u> chéng 成 <u>plus a N</u>). Wǒ-yào-bǎ-nèiben-shū (gěi)- fāncheng-Fǎwén. 我 要 把 那 本 書 (給) 翻 成 法 文. I want to translate that book into French. (6) (<u>with an indirect</u>

object). Nǐ-bǎ-qián-gěi wo. 你 把 錢 給 我. (You) give me that money. (7) (<u>with</u> gěi 給 <u>plus an indirect object</u>). Tā- 'méi-bǎ-qìchē-'sònggei-wo. 他 沒 把 汽 車 送 給 我. He didn't give me the car. (8) (<u>with</u> RE). Tā-bǎ-wǒde- dōngxi '(gei)-ná-zǒule. 他 把 我 的 東 西 (給) 拿 走 了. He took my things away. Qǐng-nǐ- bǎ-qìchē (gei)-kāichulai. 請 你 把 汽 車 (給) 開 出 來. Please drive the car out (here). Tā-bǎ-zhuōzi (gei)-bānshang-lóu- que. 他 把 桌 子 (給) 搬 上 樓 去 了. He carried the table upstairs. (9) (<u>with</u> dào 到 <u>plus a PW</u>). Ta-bǎ-yǐzi (gei)-bāndao-wàitou-que. 他 把 椅 子 (給) 搬 到 外 頭 去 了. He moved the chair outside. (10) (<u>with a NU-M</u>). Tā- bǎ-nèiběn-shū kànle-'sāncì. 他 把 那 本 書 看 了 三 次. He read that book three times. Bǎ-zhuōzi (gei)-'bān-yibān. 把 桌 子 (給) 搬 一 搬. Move the table a little. (11) (<u>with</u> de 的 <u>plus a manner complement</u>). Bǎ- wǒ-(gei)-xiàode zhànbuqilái-le. 把 我 (給) 笑 的 站 不 起 來 了. I laughed so much that I could not stand up. (12) (<u>with a N</u>). Tā-bǎ-zhǐ dōu-(gei)- bāo-le-dōngxi-le. 他 把 紙 都 (給) 包 了 東 西 了. He used all the paper to wrap things. (13) (<u>with no complement,</u> <u>only a few polysyllabic verbs can</u>

be used). Nǐ-'néng-bu-néng bǎ-zhèi-jian-'shìqing-jiǎndan'huà? 你 能 不 能 把 這 件 事 情 簡 單 化? Can you simplify this matter? (14) (with no complement in the yi.... jiu ....一.... 就....structure). Tā-bǎ-mén-yi-guān, jiu-chūqu-le. 他 把 門 一 關, 就 出 去 了. As soon as he closed the door, he went out.

BĂ₁ 把 (M) (1) for things with handles, such as knives, scissors, etc. yìbǎ-dāozi 一 把 刀 子 a knife. yìbǎ-jiǎnzi 一 把 剪 子 a pair of scissors. yìbǎ-yǐzi 一 把 椅 子 a chair. (2) handful of. yìbǎ-mǐ 一 把 米 a handful of rice. (3) for a helping hand, for describing a person's performance on the job. yìbǎ-'hǎo-shǒu 一 把 好 手 a good worker. (4) for a card player. Yàoshi-dǎ-pái, wǒmen-děi-zài-zhǎo-yìbǎ-shǒur. 要 是 打 牌 我 們 得 再 找 一 把 手 兒. If we want to play cards we have to find another player. (5) do something once with the hand. Wǒ-'lāle-ta-yìbǎ, yīnwei-ta-'shuō-de-tài-'duō-le. 我 拉 了 他 一 把, 因 為 他 說 的 太 多 了. I gave him a tug, because he talked too much. Nǐ-xǐ-bǎ-liǎn-ba. 你 洗 把 臉 吧. You'd better give your face a washing.

BĂ(R)₂ 把 兒 (M) bunch of.

yìbǎ(r)-huār 一 把 兒 花 兒 a bunch of flowers. yìbǎ(r)-kuàizi 一 把 兒 筷 子 a bunch of chopsticks.

BÀBA₁ 爸 爸 (N) papa.

BĀBUDE₄ 巴 不 得 (AV) dial. anxious to do something.

BĀCHÉNG(R)₃ 八 成 兒 (NU-M) eighty per cent. Wǒ-néng-cāi-ge-'bāchéng(r). 我 能 猜 個 八 成 兒. I can guess eighty per cent of it. (AD) most likely. Wǒ- shuō-de-bāchéng(r)-bu-duì. 我 說 的 八 成 兒 不 對. What I said is most likely not right.

BÀDAO₃ 霸 道 (SV) unreasonable, ornery. Nǐ-shuō-ta-'bàdao-bu-bàdao? 你 說 他 霸 道 不 霸 道? Would you say that he is unreasonable or not?

BÀ-GŌNG₂ 罷 工 (VO) go on strike (for laborers only).

BĀI₂ 掰 (TV) open, separate or break something apart forcibly by holding it between the thumb and other fingers and twisting outwards. Tā-bāile-yikuai-miàn-bāo. 他 掰 了 一 塊 麵 包. He broke off a piece of bread.

BÁI₁ 白 (SV) (1) white (color). (opp. hēi 黑). Zhèige-shì-báide. 這 個 是 白 的. This is white. (2) fair (of complexion). Tā-liǎn-hěn-bái. 他 臉 很 白. He has a fair complexion. (3) plain. bái-shuǐ 白 水 plain water. (4) blank. bái-zhǐ 白 紙 blank paper or white paper.

B

B

BAI₁ 白 (AD) (1) free of charge. bái-gěi 白給 give free of charge. (2) in vain, without desired results. bái-lái 白來 come in vain. Many cases are ambiguous, as bái-chī 白吃 eat without charge or eat without filling up.

(TV) Peip. fail to pay. Nǐ-zuò-zhèijian-shì, wǒmen-báibu'liǎo-nǐ. 你作這件事，我們白不了你. If you work on this, we will not let you do it for nothing.

BÁI₃ 白 (SV) colloquial. (opp. wén 文). Tā-xiě-de-wénzhang hěn-bái. 他寫的文章很白. The articles he wrote are very colloquial. (cf: BÁI HUÀ 白話). (RE) (1) wrong or colloquial pronunciation of a character. "Hái" jiushi-bǎ "huán"-zi niànbáile. "Hái" 就是把"還"字念白了. The pronunciation of " 還 " as "hái" is to read the character " 還 huán" in a colloquial way. (2) wrong in writing a character in place of another which represents the same or similar pronunciation (comparable to a misspelled word in English). Nà-shì-bǎ-zì xiěbáile. 那是把字寫白了. That is the character that was written wrong. (See: BÁIZÌ 白字).

BǍI₂ 擺 (TV) (1) arrange things in order. Wūzili-de-zhuōyǐ dou-bǎihǎole. 屋子裏的桌椅都擺好了. The

furniture in the room is all arranged well. (2) display. 'Zhuōzìshang-de-dōngxi bǎide-hen-hǎokàn. 桌子上的東西擺的很好看. The things on the table are beautifully displayed. Zhèige jiùshi-bǎi-'yàng-zi-yòngde. 這個就是擺樣子用的. This is just for the purpose of putting on a display. (3) dial. place, put. Shū bǎizai-zhèli. 書擺在這裏. Put the books here.(cf: FÀNG 放).(4) play board games chess, especially the game of "go". bǎi-yipán-qí 擺一盤棋 play a game of go.

BǍI₃ 擺 (TV) swing, wave. bǎilai-bǎiqù 擺來擺去 swing to and fro or fig. uncertain. (N) pendulum. Zhèige-zhōngde-bǎi huài-le. 這個鐘的擺壞了. The pendulum of the clock is broken.

BǍI₁ 把 see BǍ 把.

BǍI₁ 百 (NU) hundred. bǎiwàn 百萬 (lit. one hundred ten thousand) million. (B) indicates a numerous amount. bǎixìng 百姓 (lit. numerous surnames) common people.

BÀI₁ 拜 (TV) bow deeply to pay respects.

BÀI₃ 敗 (IV) suffer defeat, be defeated. 'Shéi-bàile? 誰敗了? Who was defeated? (RE) (1) be defeated, defeat. Wǒ-men-dǎbàile-tamen-yǐhòu, 'hái-shi-yǒu-hěn-duō-máfan. 我們打敗了他們以後，

還 是 有 很 多 麻 煩.
After we defeated them, there
were still many problems.

BÀIBĪNG₄ 敗兵 (N) defeated
soldiers.

BÁICÀI₃ 白菜 (N) Chinese cabbage, celery cabbage. (M: kē
棵).

BÁIDĀ₄ 白搭 (IV) do something
in addition without any result.
Nǐ-gēn-tā-shuō yě-báidā. 你跟
他 說 也 白 搭. Even
if you talk to him, it will not get
any results, it is useless.

BÁIFÁN₅ 白礬 (N) alum. (M:
kuài 塊).

'BÀIFĂNG₂ 拜訪 (TV) pay a
visit. Tā-yào-lái-'bàifăng-nǐ.
他要來拜訪你. He
wants to pay you a visit.

BÁIFÈI₂ 白廢 (TV) (1) waste.
Bié-báifèi-shíhou. 別 白 廢
時 候. Don't waste time. (2)
useless, in vain. Nǐ-jiùshi-qǐng-
ta-chī-fàn, nà-yě-shi-báifèi. 你
就是請他吃飯那
也 是 白 廢. Even if you
invite him for dinner, it is still
useless.

BÁIFĒNBǏ₄ 百分比 or BÁI-
FĒNLǙ 百分率 (N) percen-
tage.

BÁIFĒNLǙ₄ 百分率 see
BÁIFĒNBǏ 百分比.

BĂIFĒNSHÙ₃ 百分數 (N) per-
centage (in number). Bǎifenshù
shi-duōshao? 百 分 數 是
多 少 ? What is the per-
centage?

BĂIFĒNZHĪ₁ 百分之 (B-) per
cent. bǎifēnzhiwǔ 百分之五
five per cent. bǎifenzhijǐ 百分
之 幾 what per cent.

BÁIGĀNR₂ 白乾兒 (N) Chinese
white liquor (similar to Russian
Vodka). (M: jīn 斤, hú 壺).

BÁIGĚI₁ 白給 (TV) (1) give
something free. 'Shéi-báigěi?
誰 白 給 Who will give it
free? (2) give something away
without desired results.

BÁIGŌNG₂ 白宮 (N) White
House.

BĂIHE₄ 百合 (N) lily. (M: duǒr
朵兒 , kē 棵).

BÁIHOU₅ 白喉 (N) diphtheria.

BÁIHUÀ(R)₁ 白話(兒)(N) colloquial language. (opp. wényán
文言). báihua(r)-xiǎoshuō(r)
白話(兒)小說(兒)
novels written in colloquial language.

BÁIHUÀWÉN₂ 白話文 (N)
Chinese writings in vernacular
style.

BÀI-HUǑ₃ 敗火 (VO) relieve
indigestion, sore throat, headache or some other discomfort
caused by spicy and very rich
food. (opp. shàng-huǒ 上火).
Chī-liángde bài-huǒ. 吃 涼 的
敗火 . Eating cold things will
relieve the discomfort.

BÁIHUÒGŌNGSI₄ 百貨公司
(N) department store.

BÀI-JIÀZI₃ 擺架子 (VO) put on
airs in order to seem important.
Tā-jiào-ni děng, bú-shì-yīnwei-

B

B

mǎng, nà-shì-ta-yào-bǎi-jiàzi. 他叫你等不是因為忙,那是他要擺架子. He told you to wait not because he is busy, but because he wants to put on airs.

BÀIJIĀZĬR₄ 敗家子兒 (N) profligate son who ruins the family financially.

BÁIJĪN₄ 白金 (N) platinum.

BÁIJŬANR₂ 白卷兒 (N) blank examination paper. Bié-jiāo-báijǔanr. 別交白卷兒. Don't turn in a blank examination paper.

BÁIKEQUÁNSHŪ₄ 百科全書 (N) encyclopedia.(M: bù 部). Dàyīng-bǎikēquán'shū 大英百科全書 Encyclopedia Britannica.

BÁILÁNDÌ₅ 白蘭地 (N) cognac, brandy. (M: píng 瓶).

BÀI-NIÁN₁ 拜年 (VO) wish a happy New Year, happy New Year. Gěi-nin-bàinián. 給您拜年. I wish you a happy New Year. Bàinián-bàinián. 拜年拜年. Happy New Year.

BǍI-SHŎU₃ 擺手 (VO) wave the hand from left to right with the palm open and outward, indicating a negative statement. Wǒ-wèn-ta-qù-bu-qu, tā-bǎile-bai-shŏu. 我問他去不去,他擺了擺手. I asked him whether he was going or not, and he said no by waving his hand.

BÀI-SHÒU₂ 拜壽 (VO) give

birthday greetings, happy birthday.

BÁISHŬ₃ 白薯 (N) sweet potato. (M: kuài 塊).

BǍISHŬ₅ 柏樹 (N) cypress tree. (M: kē 棵).

BÁITIAN₁ 白天 (TW) daytime. in broad daylight.

BÁITÁNG₃ 白糖 (N) sugar.

BÀITUŌ₁ 拜托 (TV) (1) ask someone to do something as a favor. Wǒ-xiǎng-'bàituō-nín-yijiàn-'shì 我想拜托您一件事. I want to ask you a favor. (2) used after asking someone to do something as a favor, thank you. Qǐng-nín-tì-wo-gēn-ta-shuō-yixia. Bàituō-bàituō. 請您替我跟他説一下,拜托拜托 Please speak to him for me. Thank you.

BǍIWÀN₂ 百萬 (NU) million. yìbǎiwàn 一百萬 one million.

BǍIWÀNFÙWŌNG₄ 百萬富翁 (N) millionaire.

BÁIXIÓNG₄ 白熊 (N) polar bear. (M: jī 隻).

BǍI-YÀNGZI₃ 擺樣子 (VO) put on display without any practical use. Bǎ-zhèige-fàngzai-zhèr bǎibǎi-yàngzi. 這個放在這兒擺擺樣子. Put it here for display.

BǍIYÓULÙ₂ 柏油路 (N) asphalt street. (M: tiáo 條).

BÀIZHÀNG₃ 敗仗 (N) a lost battle. Tā-méi-dǎguo-bàizhàng. 他没打過敗仗. He has never lost a battle.

BÁIZÌ₃ 白字 _or_ BIÉZÌ 別字 (N) wrong character <u>used in place of another which has the same pronunciation</u>. Tā-cháng-xiě-báizì, rén-dou-jiào-ta-báizì-lǎo-xiānsheng. 他常寫白字，人都叫他白字老先生. He often uses wrong characters, so everyone calls him old Mr. Wrong Character.

BĀJIĀO₅ 芭蕉 (N) banana tree (not the fruit). (cf: XIĀNGJIĀO 香蕉).

BÀ-JIÀO₄ 罷教 (VO) strike <u>against the school by refusing to teach.</u>

BĀJĪSĪTǍN₃ 巴基斯坦 (PW) Pakistan.

BÀ-KÈ₄ 罷課 (VO) strike <u>a-gainst the school by refusing to attend classes.</u>

BĀLA₃ 疤癩 (N) scar. Tā-liǎnshang yǒu-yige-bāla. 他臉上有了一個疤癩. He has a scar on his face.

BĀLA₄ 扒拉 (TV) move <u>some-thing with stick or finger.</u> Ná-kuàizi 'bāla-bāla. 拿筷子扒拉扒拉. Use the chopsticks to move it.

BÀLE₂ 罷了 (P) <u>used at the end of a sentence with</u> búguo 不過 jiùshi 就是 , zhǐshi 只是 etc.,that's all. (<u>syn</u>. éryǐ 而已 Wǒ-buguò-'shuōshuo-bàle. 我不過說說罷了. I only talk about it, that's all.

BÀLE₂ 罷了 (IV) call off, cancel, forget it. (<u>syn</u>. suàn le

算了). Nǐ-bu-kěn jiu-bàle. 你不肯就罷了. If you are not willing, then call it off.

BĀLÉIWǓ₄ 巴蕾舞 (N) ballet.

BĀLÍ 巴黎 (PW) Paris.

BÀLIĂO₂ 罷了 (SV) (1) all right, acceptable, passable, will do. Tāde-zhōngwén hái-bàliǎo. 他的中文還罷了. His Chinese is O.K. (2) all right, that's enough. Bàliǎo-bàliǎo, shi-wǒde-'yùnqi bu-hǎo. 罷了罷了. 是我的運氣不好. All right, all right, it is my bad luck.

BĀN₁ 班 (M) (1) class <u>of students.</u> Wǒmen-zài-yibān. 我們在一班. We are in the same class. Nǐ-jiāo-'jǐbān? 你教幾班? How many classes do you teach? (2) <u>for scheduled trains, flights, ships, etc.</u> Yìtiān-you-'jǐbān-fēijī? 一天有幾班飛機? How many flights are there in one day? (3) squad of <u>soldiers.</u>

BĀN(R)₂ 班兒 (N) turn <u>to do something</u>, shift. Wǒmen-āizhe-bān(r)-jìnqu. 我們挨着班兒進去. We take turns going in. Nǐmen-'shénma-shíhou-huàn-bān(r)? 你們甚麼時候換班? When are you going to change shifts?

BĀN₁ 搬 (TV) (1) lift <u>or</u> move <u>something heavy with both palms up, not above the head.</u> Qǐng-bǎ-zhuōzi-bānlai. 請把桌子搬來. Please move the

B

table here. Tā-bǎ-shíou- bān-
qilai, you-fàngxiale. 他把石
頭 搬 起 來 ， 又 放 下
了 . He lifted the stone and
then put it down. (2) move house
or an organization. Nèige-xuéxiào bān-le. 那 個 學 校 搬
了 . That school has moved.

BĀN₃ 扳 (TV) pull with the hand,
without the fingers being wrapped
around the object. Bié-'bān-
nèige-shù-'zhīzi. 別 扳 那
個 樹 枝 子 . Don't pull
the branches of that tree.

BĀN₂ 板 (N) printing plate.
(M) edition. Zhèige-shū yìnle-
shíjibǎn. 這 個 書 印 了
十 幾 板 . More than ten
editions of this book have been
printed. dìyībǎn 第 一 板 first
edition.
(B) (1) board, slab, sheet. hēi-
bǎn 黑 板 blackboard. tiěbǎn
鐵 板 sheet of iron. (2) edition. Sòngbǎn-shū 宋 板 書
edition of the Sung period.
(SV) stiff, wooden, lifeless. Zhèizhang-huàr tài-bǎn. 這 張 畫
兒 太 板 . This painting is
lifeless.

BÀN₁ 辦 (TV) (1) do, take care of
or carry out some matter. Wǒ-
jīntian-'bànle hǎoxiē-'shìqing.
我 今 天 辦 了 好 些
事 情 . Today I have done a
lot of things. Nǐ-kànzhe-bàn-ba.
你 看 着 辦 吧 . See
what you can do. Jiu-nènma-
bàn. 就 那 麼 辦 . Let's
do it that way. Méi-fázi-bàn. 沒

法 子 辦 . There is no way
to do it. Tāmen-gāng-bànwán-
xǐshì. 他 們 剛 辦 完 喜
事 . They just finished
taking care of the wedding. Nǐ-
zài-shénma dìfang-bàn- gōng?
你 在 甚 麼 地 方 辦
公 ? Where do you work?
Zhèige-ànzi shi-shéi-bànde? 這
個 案 子 是 誰 辦 的 ?
Who handled this case at law?
(2) investigate or punish someone
in a law suit. Wǒmen-děi-bàn
ta. 我 們 得 辦 他 . We
must investigate him. (3) buy
merchandise for retail. Tā-qu-
bàn-huò-qule. 他 去 辦 貨
去 了 . He went to buy some
goods. (4) operate, run an
organization. Tā-bànguo-bào.
他 辦 過 報 . He ran a
newspaper (at lease once). (5)
start, establish an organization.
Zhèige-xuéxiào shì-'shéi-bànde?
這 個 學 校 是 誰 辦
的 ? Who founded this school?

BÀN₂ 拌 (TV) mix things (at least
one of which is solid) with chopsticks, spoon, fork, etc. Qǐng-
nǐ-bǎ-nèige-cài bàn-yiban. 請
你 把 那 個 菜 拌 一
拌 . Please mix that salad a
little.

BÀN₁ 半 (NU) half of something.
bànnián 半 年 half a year.
bànge 半 個 one half (of a
whole). liǎngge-bànzhāng 兩 個
半 張 two half-sheets.
added to a NU-M, indicates a
half more than the whole amount

specified by the NU-M. sānge-bàn-zhōngtóu 三個半鐘頭 three hours and a half. sāndian-bàn 三點半 three-thirty. (B) mid-, semi-, half. bànyè 半夜 midnight. bànpíngcù 半瓶醋 (lit. half a bottle of vinegar) half-baked. (S) (1) bàn...bàn... 半...半... half...and half...bàn-zhēn-bàn-jiǎ 半真半假 half true and half false. (2) bàn...bu... 半...不...half...and half not...bàn-xìn-bu-xìn 半信不信. (lit. believe half and disbelieve half) doubt, be uncertain about (something).

BÀN₄ 絆 (TV) trip.

BĀNÁMǍ₃ 巴拿馬 (PW) Panama.

BÀNBÈIZI₃ 半輩子 (NU-M) half of a person's life. Wǒ-huóle-bànbèizi-le, nǐ-xiǎng wǒ-bu-zhīdao-zhèige ma? 我活了半輩子了，你想我不知道這個嗎? I have lived half of my life, don't you think I know this?

BǍNCĀR₂ 板擦兒 (N) black-board eraser.

BÀNDǍO₃ 半島 (N) peninsula.

BÀNDÀOR₃ 半道兒 (PW) half-way. Tā-zǒudao-bàndàor you-huílaile. 他走到半道兒又回來了. He went half-way and then returned.

BǍNDÈNG₂ 板凳 (N) wooden stool.

BÀNFA₁ 辦法 (N) (1) method, way. Wǒ-gěi-nǐ-xiǎng-ge-bànfa.

我給你想個辦法. I will think up a way for you. Nǐ-'zhēn-yǒu-bànfa. 你真有辦法. You really can get things done. Lǎo-jiè-qián bu-shì-ge-bànfa. 老借錢不是個辦法. Borrowing money all the time is not a good way to do things. (2) regulation, rule. Zhè-shi-zhèngfǔ-'dìngde-bànfa. 這是政府定的辦法. These are the regulations that the government has passed.

BÀNFĒNGR₄ 半瘋兒 (N) half crazy.

BĀNG₁ 幫 (TV) help, aid, assist. Wǒ-bāng-ni. 我幫你. I'll help you. Nǐ-bāngzhe-wo ná-yidianr. 你幫着我拿一點兒. Help me to carry some. Bāng-rén-bāngdao-dǐ. 幫人幫到底. If you help people, help them all the way through. 'Shéi-bāng-nide-'máng? 誰幫你的忙? Who is helping you? (cf: BĀNG-MÁNG 幫忙).

BĀNG₂ 幫 (M) group of people. Zhèi-yibāng-háizi zhēn-nào. 這一幫孩子真鬧. This group of children is very disturbing.

BǍNG₂ 綁 (TV) (1) tie, fasten. Bǎ-xiāngzi bǎngzai-qìchē-shang. 把箱子綁在汽車上. Tie the suitcase to the car. (2) kidnap. Yǒu-rén-bǎ-ta-bǎng-qu-le. 有人把他綁去了. Someone kid-

B

napped him.

BÀNG₂ 棒 (B) bat, stick. bīngbàng 冰棒 popsicle. bàngqiú 棒球 (lit. bat ball) baseball. (SV) (Peip.) (1) strong. Tāde-shēnti-hěn-bàng. 他的身體很棒. (lit. His body is very strong.) He is very strong. (2) terrific. Tā-'shénma-dōu-'bàng. 他甚麼都棒. He is terrific in everything.

BÀNG₁ 磅 (M) (1) pound (weight). yíbàng-niú-ròu 一磅牛肉 a pound of beef. (2) pound (English money). sānbàng-qián 三磅錢 three pounds. (N) scale, weighing machine. Yòng-bàng-chēng-cheng. 用磅稱稱. Weigh it on the scale. guòguo-bàng 過過磅 (lit. pass through the scale). weigh. (TV) weigh. Qu-'bàng-yixiàr. 去磅一下兒. Go and weigh it.

BĀNGJIĀO₂ 邦交 (N) friendship between countries. Tāmende-bāngjiāo-duàn-le. 他們的邦交斷了. They broke off relations.

BĀNG-MÁNG₁ 幫忙 (VO) help, aid, assist. Wǒ-gěi-nǐ-bāng-máng. 我給你幫忙. I will help you. 'Bāng-wo-dianr-máng. 幫我點兒忙. Help me a little. Tā-'méi-bāng-guo-wode-máng. 他沒幫過我的忙. He has never helped me. Zhèi-yidiǎnr-xiǎo-máng ni-dou-bu-bāng-wo. 這

一點兒小忙你都不幫我. You don't even give me this little bit of help. Nǐ-'búyòng-bāng'máng-le, nǐ-yuè-bāng, wǒ-yuè-máng. 你不用幫忙了, 你越幫我越忙. It's no use for you to help. The more you help, the busier I get. (cf: BĀNG 幫)

BÀN-GŌNG₁ 辦公 (VO) do office work, work in an office. Nín-zài-nǎr bàn-gōng? 您在那兒辦公 ? Where do you work? Tā-bànle-yitiande-gōng. 他辦了一天的公. He worked for a whole day.

BÀNGŌNGCHÙ₃ 辦公處 (N) office (referring to a large one).

BÀNGŌNGSHÌ₂ 辦公室 (N) office (referring to one which has one room). (M: jiān 間). (cf: BÀNSHÌCHÙ 辦事處).

BĂNG-PIÀOR₄ 綁票兒 (VO) kidnap. Tāmen-yao-bǎng-nide-piàor. 他們要綁你的票兒. They want to kidnap you.

BĀNGQIĀNG₄ 幫腔 (VO) (1) speak for someone, help someone by speaking for him. (2) accompanying voices for solo singing.

BÀNGQIÚ₂ 棒球 (N) (lit. bat ball) baseball. (M: chǎng 場). Dǎ-yìchǎng-bàngqiú, 'hǎo-bu-hao? 打一場棒球, 好不好 ? Let's play a game of baseball, O.K. ?

BĂNGYANG₂ 榜樣 (N) model,

example. Nǐ-kéyi-gěi-tāmen-zuò-ge-bǎngyang. 你 可 以 給 他 們 作 個 榜 樣. You can be a model for them.

BĀNGZHU₁ 幫 助 (TV) help, assist. Qǐng-ni-bāngzhu-wo. 請 你 幫 助 我. Please help me.

(N) help, assistance. Wǒ-lái-qiú-bāngzhu-lai-le. 我 來 求 幫 助 來 了. I came for help.

BǍNGZI₃ 膀 子 (N) (1) arm (of a human). (M: zhī 隻). (2) wing (of a bird). (M: zhī 隻).

BÀNGZI₃ 棒 子 (N) (1) club, bat, heavy stick. (M: gēn 根) (2) corn, maize.

BĀN-JIĀ₁ 搬 家 (VO) move house or organization, change one's residence.

BÀNJIÉR₃ 半 截 兒 (PW) lit. or fig. half-way. Tā-zǒudao-bànjiér jiu-'huílaile. 他 做 到 半 截 兒 就 回 來 了. He walked half-way there and then came back. Tā-jiu-zuòle-bànjiér. 他 就 做 了 半 截 兒. He only did half (of the work).

(NU-M) half of something long. bànjiér-qiānbǐ 半 截 兒 鉛 筆 half a pencil.

BÀNLǍ₅ 半 拉 (N) Peip. one half of a whole object.

BÀNLÁNG₄ 伴 郎 (N) grooms-man, bestman. (M: wèi 位).

'BÀNLǏ₄ 辦 理 (TV) manage, carry out a temporary plan or project. Zhèige-shì wǒ-méi-fázi-bànlǐ. 這 個 事 我 沒 法 子 辦 理. I have no way to carry out this matter.

BǍN-LIǍN₄ 板 臉 (VO) make a serious face. (syn. běng-liǎn 繃 臉). Tā-yi-bǎn-liǎn, shéi-dou-pà. 他 一 板 臉 誰 都 怕. Once he makes a serious face, everyone will be scared.

BÀNNIÁNG₄ 伴 娘 (N) brides-maid, maid of honor. (M: wèi 位).

BÀNPÍNGCÙ₂ 半 瓶 醋 (N) (lit. half a bottle of vinegar) (1) half-baked, half-educated. Tā-xuéde shénma-dōu-shi-bàn-píngcù. 他 學 的 甚 麼 都 是 半 瓶 醋. Everything he learned was only half-understood. (2) half-baked person. Tā-shì-ge-bànpíngcù. 他 是 個 半 瓶 醋 He is a half-baked person.

BÀNR₂ 伴 兒 (N) mate, companion, partner. lǎobànr 老 伴 兒 wife or husband(in elder age). Wǒ-dei-jǎo-ge-bànr yíkuàir-qù. 我 得 找 個 伴 兒 一 塊 兒 去 I have to find a companion so that we can go together.

BÀNR₃ 瓣 兒 (N) petal. (M: bànr 瓣 兒 piànr 片 兒). yibànr-huābànr 一 瓣 兒 花 瓣 兒 flower petal. Huār diào-bànr-le. 花 兒 掉 瓣 了. The petals fell from the flowers.

(M) (1) section of (orange, grape-fruit, etc.). (2) petal.

BÀN-SHÌ₁ 辦 事 (VO) attend to

B

B

business, do work. Tā-chūqu-bàn-shì-qu-le. 他 出 去 辦 事 去 了. He went out to attend to some business.

BÀNSHÌCHÙ₂ 辦 事 處 (N) office (referring to a large one). (cf: BÀNGŌNGSHÌ 辦公室).

BÀNTIĀNR₁ 半 天 兒 (NU-M) half a day. Wǒ-jiu-zuò-'bàn-tiānr-shì. 我 就 作 半 天 兒 事. I only work half-days.

BÀNYÈ₁ 半 夜 (TW) mid-night. Tā-bànyè cai-huílaide. 他 半 夜 才 回 來 的. He didn't come back until mid-night.

BĀNYÙN₃ 搬 運 (TV) move, transport (items which are large in size and/or quantity).

BĀNZHǍNG₁ 班 長 (N) (1) leader of a class. (2) leader of a squad of soldiers.

BÀNZÒU₃ 伴 奏 (TV) accompany (with a musical instrument).

BÀN-ZUǏ₂ 拌 嘴 (VO) quarrel, argue. Wǒmen-bànle-bàntiān-zuǐ. 我 們 拌 了 半 天 嘴. We quarreled for quite a while.

BĀO₁ 包 (TV) (1) wrap, cover completely. Yòng-zhǐ bǎ-zhèige-bāoshang. 用 紙 把 這 個 包 上. Wrap this in paper. (2) take on an entire job under contract. Zhèige-gōngzuo shì-tā bāoxialai-de. 這 個 工 作 是 他 包 下 來 的. He took on the entire job under contract. (3) take full responsibility for some job. Zhèijian-shì bāo-zai-wǒ-shēnshang-le. 這 件 事

包 在 我 身 上 了. I will take full responsibility for that matter. (4) hire for one's exclusive use (for a certain per-iod of time or a defined course) the services of a person, a vehi-cle, an establishment, etc., that is normally serving the public on a piece rate basis. Tā-qǐng-kè-de-shíhou, bǎ-nèige-fànguǎnr-bāo-le. 他 請 客 的 時 候 把 那 個 飯 館 兒 包 了. When he was entertaining guests, he took over the entire restaurant for his exclusive use. Wǒmen-'bāo-yijia-fēijī, 'hǎo-bu-hǎo? 我 們 包 一 架 飛 機, 好 不 好? How about chartering a plane?

(N) bump, swelling. Tā-tóushang pèngle-yíge-bāo. 他 頭 上 碰 了 一 個 包. He hit his head and got a bump.

(M) for package or bundle. Tā-názhe-yibāo-dōngxi. 他 拿 着 一 包 東 西. He is holding a package.

BĀO₂ 剝 (TV) remove the outer covering of fruit, nuts, animals, etc., peel, shell, skin. bāo-pí 剝 皮 take the skin off. bāo-júzi 剝 橘 子 peel the orange. bāo-huāshēng 剝 花 生 shell the peanuts. bāo-tùzide-pí 剝 兔 子 的 皮 skin a rabbit.

BÁO₂ 薄 (SV) (1) thin (in dimen-sion). (opp. hòu 厚). Děi-yòng-báo-zhǐ. 得 用 薄 紙. (You) must use thin paper. (2) poor (in quality or cost of a gift).

Tā-sòng-de-lǐ hěn-báo. 他 送 的 禮 很 薄. His gift is very cheap. (3) weak (referring to mutual concern among people). Xiànzai rénqíng-hen-báo. 現 在 人 情 很 薄. Mutual concern among people is weak in these times. (4) stingy in treating people. Wǒ-dài-ni-bu-báo. 我 待 你 不 薄. I didn't treat you poorly. (5) weak (referring to taste or flavor). Jiǔ-hěn-báo. 酒 很 薄. The wine is weak.

BǍO₁ 保 (TV) (1) hold on, keep. Tāde-xìngming-nán-bǎo. 他 的 性 命 難 保. (lit. His life is difficult to hold on to.) It will be hard for him to stay alive. 'Nèige-chéng yě-bǎobuzhù-le. 那 個 城 也 保 不 住 了. That city cannot be held either. (2) assure someone that something will happen. Wǒ-bǎo-ni-chīle-zhèige-yào jiu-hǎo. 我 保 你 吃 了 這 個 藥 就 好. I assure you that you will recover after taking this medicine. (3) guarantee someone's proper behavior or something's proper performance. Wǒ-bǎ-ta-bǎochulai-le. 我 把 他 保 出 來 了. He was released in my custody. Wǒ-kéyi-bǎo-ta. 我 可 以 保 他. I can vouch for him. Zhèige-biǎo tāmen-bǎo-yinián. 這 個 表 他 們 保 一 年. They guarantee this watch for one year. (4) insure, as in an in-

surance policy. Zhèige-fángzi wǒ-bǎole-'sānwankuai-qián. 這 個 房 子 我 保 了 三 萬 塊 錢. I insured this house for thirty thousand dollars. (N) guarantor. Nǐ-děi-zhǎo-yige-bǎo. 你 得 找 一 個 保. You must find a guarantor.

BǍO₁ 飽 (SV) be full (stomach), satisfied by having fulfilled the need or desire for food. (opp. è 餓). Wǒ-bǎo-le. 我 飽 了. I am full.

(RE) satisfied by having fulfilled the need or desire for something. Wǒ-chībǎo-le. 我 吃 飽 了. I have eaten my fill. Wǒ-kànbǎo-le. 我 看 飽 了. I've seen a lot, I'm satisfied.

BÀO₁ 報 (N) newspaper. (M: fèr 份兒 , zhāng 張). (TV) declare, report. bào-shuì 報 稅 declare value for tax or duty purposes. bào-jǐngchájú 報 警 察 局 report to the police office.

BÀO₂ 抱 (TV) (1) hold, carry in the arm or arms as a baby or a package. bào-háizi 抱 孩 子 hold the baby. (2) embrace, put one's arms around something or someone. Tāmen-bào-tóu-dà-kū. 他 們 抱 頭 大 哭. They embraced each other and cried. (3) adopt a child. Tāde-háizi shi-bàode. 他 的 孩 子 是 抱 的. His child was adopted. (4) embrace a doctrine, a point of view or attitude. Nǐ-bié-bào-'zhèizhong-tàidu. 你 別 抱

B

B

這種態度. Don't take this kind of attitude.

(M). armful of. yìbào-yīshang 一抱衣裳 an armful of clothes.

BÀO₄ 鉋 (TV) plane, smooth off with a plane. Bǎ-zhèikuai-'mùtou yòng-bàozi-bàobao. 把這塊木頭用鉋子鉋鉋. Smooth off this piece of wood with a plane.

BĀOBÀN₂ 包辦 (TV) take care of everything involved in some job. Suǒ'yǒude-shì ta-'yíge-rén bāo'bàn-le. 所有的事他一個人包辦了. He takes care of the whole thing (business).

BǍOBEI₂ 寶貝 (N) (1) valuable or precious thing. (2) used to refer to babies or children, darling, dear, precious thing.

'BÀOBING₂ 暴病 (N) sudden violent illness. (M: chǎng 場).

'BǍOCHÍ₂ 保持 (TV) maintain (an attitude, situation, point of view). Tā hái-bǎochí-yuánláide-tàidu. 他還保持原來的態度. He's still maintaining his original attitude.

BÀOCHOU₂ 報酬 (N) compensation, remuneration, payment for service (money or otherwise) salary. Wǒmen-zhèr gěi-nín-de-bàochou hěn-dī. 我們這兒給您的報酬很低. The remuneration for your (services) at our place is not high.

(TV) compensate. Wǒ-bu-zhī-dào zěnma-bàochou-nín. 我不知道怎麼報酬您. I don't know how to compensate you.

BǍOCÚN₃ 保存 (TV) preserve, keep something in a safe place. Zhèizhang-huàr děi-bǎocúnqi-lai. 這張畫兒得保存起來. This painting must be preserved.

'BÀODÁ₃ 報答 (TV) return, repay someone for a favor or kindness. Nǐ-yīngdāng-'bàodá-tade-hǎoyì. 你應當報答他的好意. You must repay him for his kindness.

BǍODĀN₄ 保單 (N) document of guarantee or insurance. (M: zhāng 張).

BÀO-DÀO₃ 報到 (VO) (1) report for work or duty. (2) check in (as in a dormitory). Nǐ-shì-shénma-shíhou-bàode- dào? 你是甚麼時候報的到? When did you first report for work? or What time did you check in?

BÀOFĀ₃ 爆發 (IV) break out, burst out, start suddenly (usually of something explosive or violent in nature). Shìjie-dàzhàn bàofā-le. 世界大戰爆發了. World-wide war broke out.

BĀO-FÀN₂ 包飯 (VO) board, provide board. Wǒ-zài-tāmen-jiā-bāo-fàn. 我在他們家包飯. I board at their house.

(N) meal provided for the board-er. chī-bāofàn 吃包飯 eat

meals (provided for the boarders).

BĀOFU₃ 包袱 (N) (1) cloth wrapper. (M: kuài 塊). (2) bundle wrapped in cloth. (3) fig. burden. Tā-xǐhuan-mǎi-huàr. Tāde-bāofu tài-zhòng. 他喜歡買畫兒. 他的包袱太重. He likes to buy paintings, he is heavily burdened by them.

'BÀOFU₃ 報復 (TV) take revenge, avenge.

BÀOGÀO₁ 報告 (TV) report. Wǒ-bàogào-nín-yijiàn-shìqing. 我報告您一件事情. I want to report one thing to you. Bàogào-zhǔxí, kāihuì-shíjiān-dàole. 報告主席開會時間到了. May I report to you, Mr. Chairman, that it is now time to start the meeting. (N) report. Tāde-bàogào xiěde-hěn-hǎo. 他的報告寫的很好. His report is very well written.

BÀOGUĂN₂ 報館 (N) newspaper (the organization). (syn. bàoshè 報社).

'BĂOGUÌ₂ 寶貴 (SV) precious, valuable. Nínde-yìjian hěn-bǎoguì. 您的意見很寶貴. Your opinion is very valuable.

BĀOGUǑ₃ 包裹 (N) parcel, package. (M: jiàn 件). jì-bāoguǒ 寄包裹 mail a package.

BĀOHAN₄ 包含 (TV) (1) include, contain (of something abstract).

Tāde-huà bāohan-hěn-duōde-yìsi. 他的話包含很多意思. What he said has many meanings. (2) (lit. enlarge one's capacity to allow for mistakes) excuse. Qǐng-nín-bāohan-dianr. 請您包含點兒. Please excuse the errors.

BÁOHÒU₃ 薄厚 (N) thickness. (syn. hòubáo 厚薄).

BĂOHÙ₁ 保護 (TV) protect (by providing shelter, care, etc.).

BĀOJIN₄ 包金 (VO) cover with gold. bāo-yicéng-jīn 包一層金 cover it with a layer of gold. (N) gold-plated. Nèige-biǎo-shi-bāojīn-de. 那個表是包金的. That watch is gold-plated.

BĂOJUÀN₂ 寶眷 (N) (your) family (a polite form, used when referring to the family of the person spoken to). Nínde-bǎo-'juàn-zài-nǎr? 您的寶眷在那兒? Where is your family?

'BĀOKUÒ₂ 包括 (TV) include, contain (of something concrete or abstract). Wǒde-bàogào bāo-kuò-'sāndiǎn. 我的報告包括三點. My report contains three points. Měiyuè-fángzū-'bāshikuai-qián, diàn-shuǐ dou-bāokuò-zàinèi. 每月房租八十塊錢, 電水都包括在内. Each month's rent is eighty dollars, electricity and water included.

B

B

BÀOLU₃ 暴露 (TV) uncover, reveal, expose. Bié-bă-zhèi-jiàn-shì bàoluchulai. 別 把 這件事 暴露 出去 Don't allow this affair to be exposed.

BÀO-MÍNG₂ 報名 (VO) (lit. report the name) send in application, apply in writing to a school, for membership in some society, for an examination, etc. Tā-yǐjing-zai-nèige-xuéxiào bàomíng-le. 他 已 經 在 那 個 學 校 報 名 了 . He has already applied to that school.

BĂOMŬ₄ 保姆 (N) governess (a woman entrusted with the care and management of a child, but not with his education). (M: wèi 位).

BÀOPÍQI₃ 暴脾氣 (N) hot temper, violent temper.

BÀOQIÀN₁ 抱歉 (SV) regret or be sorry for not fulfilling one's own social or other responsibilities. Wǒ-méi-zuòhǎo, fēichang-bàoqiàn. 我 没 作 好 , 非 常 抱 歉 . I didn't do it well, I am sorry.

BĂOREN₁ 保人 (N) guarantor. (M: wèi 位). Nǐ-qiānwàn·bié-gěi-ta dāng- bǎoren. 你 千 萬 別 給 他 當 保 人 . Be sure that you don't become a guarantor for him.

BÀOSHÈ₃ 報社 (N) newspaper (the organization). (syn. bàoguǎn 報館). (M: jiā 家). Tā-zài-bàoshè-zuò-shì. 他 在 報 社 作 事 . He works for a newspaper.

BĂOSHÍ₂ 寶石 (N) precious stone. (M: kuài 塊).

'BĂOSHŎU₂ 保守 (SV) conservative (in thought and ideas). Tāde-'sīxiang-hen-'bǎoshǒu. 他 的 思 想 很 保 守 . His thinking is very conservative. (TV) keep secret, conceal. Wǒ-men-dei-bǎoshǒu-mìmì. 我 們 得 保 守 秘 密 . We must keep it a secret.

BĂOWÉI₂ 包圍 (TV) surround, blockade, hem in. 'Díren-bǎ-chéng gei-bāowéile. 敵人把 城 給 包 圍 了 . The enemy surrounded the city. fig. Biérende-huà tā-bu-xìn. Tāmen-bǎ-ta-gei-bāowéi le. 別 人 的 話 他 不 信 , 他 們 把 他 給 包 圍 了 . He does not believe what others say. They influenced him exclusively.

'BĂOWÈI₄ 保衛 (TV) protect by guarding. 'Rénren-dōu-yào-bǎowèi-tāmende-guójiā. 人 人 都 要 保 衛 他 們 的 國 家 . Everybody wants to guard his country.

BĂO-XIĂN₁ 保險 (VO) protect by insurance, insure. bǎo-'huǒ-xiǎn 保火險 protect against losses by fire by insurance. Nǐde-qìchē pǎoxiǎnle-meiyou? 你 的 汽 車 保 險 了 没 有 ? Is your car insured? (TV) guarantee (be sure of some future occurrence). Wǒ-bu-néng-bǎo'xiǎn-ta yidìng-'lái. 我 不 能 保 險 他 一 定 來 .

I cannot guarantee that he'll come for sure.

(N) insurance. mǎi-bǎoxiǎn 買保險 buy insurance. mài-bǎoxiǎn-de 賣保險的 insurance salesman.

(SV) be safe. bǎoxiǎnxiāng 保險箱 a safe, safe deposit box, strong box. Wǒ-xiǎng qián-dou-fàngzai-jiāli, bu-bǎoxiǎn. 我想錢都放在家裏，不保險. I think that it is not safe to keep all your money in your home.

'BĀOXIĀO₄ 剝削 or 'BŌXUĒ 剝削 (TV) exploit, take advantage of. Tāmen-zǒngshi-'bāoxiāo-biéren. 他們總是剝削別人. They always exploit others.

BÀOYING₄ 報應 (N) retribution, due punishment (in a spiritual sense). Zhèi-shì-'huài-rén yīngdāng-'déde-bàoying. 這是壞人應當得的報應. This is the due punishment for a bad person.

(IV) get paid back spiritually for some evil deed. Tā-lǎo-zuò-'huài-shì; nǐ-kàn, xiànzài-bào-yingle. 他總作壞事，你看，現在報應了. He always does bad things; look, now he has been paid back.

BĀOYOU₅ 保佑 (TV) protect and help (by a spiritual being). Qiú-Shàngdì-bǎoyou. 求上帝保佑. Ask God to protect and help.

BÀOYǓ₂ 暴雨 (N) sudden rain-storm, squall. (M: cháng 場, zhèn 陣). Xiàle-yizhen-bàoyǔ. 下了一陣暴雨. There was a heavy downpour for a while.

BÀOYUAN₁ 抱怨 (TV) (lit. hold a fault against someone or something) (1) blame. Tā-bàoyuan-wǒ. 他抱怨我. He blames me. (2) complain. Bié-bàoyuan, shuō-diǎnr-biéde. 別抱怨，說點別的. Don't complain, talk about something else.

BĀO-YUÈ₅ 包月 (VO) hire a rickshaw, a limousine, a prostitute for one's exclusive use by the month.

'BǍOZHÈNG₂ 保証 (TV) guarantee, go bond for, vouch for a person. Wǒ-kéyi-'bǎozhèng ta-shì-hǎo-rén. 我可以保証他是好人. I can guarantee that he is a good person.

(N) guarantee (in any form). Nǐ-děi-gěi-wǒ-yige-'bǎozhèng. 你得給我一個保証. You must give me a guarantee.

BÀOZHǏ₁ 報紙 (N) (1) newspaper. (M: fèr 份, zhāng 張). (2) newsprint. (M: zhāng 張).

BĀOZI₄ 包子 (N) a certain kind of steamed pastry, made with a dough covering filled with meat, vegetables or sweets, characterized by its semi-spherical shape.

BÁOZI₄ 雹子 (N) (1) hailstone. (2) hailstorm. (M: cháng 場, zhèn 陣). Xià-báozi-le. 下

B

雹子了 . It's hailing now.

BÀOZI₅ 鉋子 (N) carpenter's plane. (M: bǎ 把).

BǍWO₁ 把握 (N) grasp. yǒu-bǎwo 有把握 (lit. have grasp) be certain (about a result). Tā-zuò-zhèi-zhong-shì hěn-yǒu-bǎwo. 他作這種事很有把握. He is certain that he can do this kind of job.

(TV) take hold of, control completely. Wǒmen-dei-bǎwo-jīhui. 我們得把握機會. We must take hold of each opportunity.

BĀXĪ₃ 巴西 (PW) Brazil.

BǍXÌ₃ 把戲 (N) (1) act of skill. shuǎ-bǎxi 耍把戲 perform an act of skill. (2) practical joke or trick. Tā-wánr-de-shi-shénma-bǎxì? 他玩兒的是甚麼把戲? What kind of trick is he playing?

BǍXIONGDI₃ 把兄弟 (N) sworn brothers.

BĀYUE₁ 八月 see BÁYUE 八月 .

BĀYUE₁ 八月 or BÁYUE 八月 (TW) (lit. the eighth month of the year) August.

BÀZHAN₄ 霸佔 (TV) seize and control a territory, position, property or time exclusively and by might or force. Nǐ-bu-néng-bàzhan-bié-ren-de- dōngxi. 你不能霸佔別人的東西. You cannot take other people's things by force.

BĒI₃ 揹 (TV) carry on the back. Bēizhe-háizi. 揹着孩子. Carry the child (on the back).

BĒI₂ 杯 (N) small vessel for drinking, cup, glass, tumbler, goblet, mug, etc. jiǔbēi 酒杯 small vessel for drinking alcoholic beverages. chábēi 茶杯 tea cup.

(M) cup, glass, etc. Lái, hē-bei-jiǔ. 來, 喝杯酒. Come, have a drink.

BĒI₁ 北 (L) north. běifáng 北方 north room. běibànqiú 北半球 northern hemisphere. Wàng-běi-zǒu. 往北走. Go north.

BĒI₂ 背 (N) back (part of a body or certain objects). shǒubèi 手背 back of the hand. dāobèi 刀背 blunt edge of the knife. Wǒ-'bèi-téng. 我背疼. My back aches.

(TV) (1) have one's back toward something. Tā-bèizhe-yángguāng kàn-shū. 他背着陽光看書. He is reading with his back to the sun. Bié-bèizhe shǒu-zǒu. 別背着手走. Don't walk with your hands clasped behind your back. (2) keep secret from someone, behind one's back. Wǒmen-shuō-huà bu-bèi-rén. 我們説話不背人. (lit. When we talk, we don't turn our back toward others.) We don't keep secrets from the others when we talk. Háizimen bèizhe-fùmǔ-chōu-yān. 孩子們背着父母抽

煙 . (lit. Children smoke and have their back toward their parents.) Children smoke behind their parents' backs. (3) repeat lines of a book verbally from memory. Jīntian xiānsheng-jiào-wo-bèi-shū, wǒ-méi-bèiguolái. 今天先生叫我背書，我没背過來. Today the teacher asked me to recite the lines from memory, but I couldn't remember them. (4) do something from memory. Nèige-zì shi-ta-'bèizhe-xiě-de. 那個字是他背着寫的 . That character was written by him from memory. (5) do something against what should be obeyed, such as good conscience. Bié-bèizhe-liángxin-shuō-huà. 别背着良心説話 . Don't talk against good conscience.

BÈI₃ 背 (SV) (1) hard of hearing. Tā ěrduo-bèi. 他耳朵背 He is hard of hearing. (2) unlucky. Wǒ-xiànzài zǒu-bèi-yùn. 我現在走背運. I am going through an unlucky period. (3) off the beaten track, out of the way. Nèige-dìfang hěn-bèi. 那個地方很背 . That place is off the beaten track.

BÈI₂ 倍 (M) times (as in one and a half times as much), fold (as in two-fold). usually used in two basic structures. (1) X shì Y de NU-bèi. X 是 Y 的 NU 倍. Liù shì-sānde-liǎngbèi. 六是三的兩倍. Six is two

times three. But when the NU preceding bèi 倍 is yī 一 , yí-bèi 一倍 may mean double. Therefore, it is commonly acceptable to say: Liù shì-sānde-yíbèi. 六是三的一倍. Six is two times three. (2) X bǐ Y ... NU bèi. X 比 Y ...NU 倍 . When the NU is yī 一 in this structure, yíbèi 一倍 can only mean double. Liù-bǐ-sān dà-yíbèi. 六比三大一倍 . Six is two times bigger than three. Dōngxi jīnnian-bǐ-qùnian guì-yíbèi. 東西今年比去年貴一倍. The prices of things this year are two times more expensive than last year. When the NU is higher than yī 一 , this meaning is ambiguous. Zhèrde-rénkou bǐ-nèr duō-liǎngbèi. 這兒的人口比那兒多兩倍 . The population here is two times more than there. or The population here is three times more than there. Tāde-xīnshui jīnnian-bǐ-qùnian jiāle-sānbèi. 他的薪水今年比去年加了三倍 . His salary of this year has increased by three times over last year's. or His salary of this year has increased by four times over last year's. However, when the NU is ten or a multiple of ten, the ambiguity is ruled out. Tāde-qián-bǐ-wǒde duō-yibǎibèi. 他的錢比我的多一百倍 . He has one hundred

B

B

times more money than I do.
(cf: YĪBÈI 一倍).

BÈI₂被 (CV) by (marking the
agent). colloquially, often accompanied by the adverb gěi 給.
Lǐ-xiansheng bèi-biéren-gei-
qǐngqule. 李先生被別
人給請去了. Mr. Li
was invited away by others. (cf:
BǍ 把, JIÀO 叫, RÀNG 讓).
(AD) followed by a TV serves to
translate the TV in the passive
voice. Nǐ-bèi-qǐng-le-ma? 你
被請了嗎? Were you
invited?

'BÈI' ĀI₄ 悲哀 (SV) sad. (opp.
kuàile 快樂). Tā-xīnli hen-
'bēi'āi. 他心裏很悲哀.
He is very sad (in his heart).

'BĒIBǏ₄ 卑鄙 (SV) low in de-
meanor, unprincipled. (opp.
gāoshàng 高尚). Zhèige-rén-
hěn-'bēibǐ. Tā-qīpiàn gū'ér-
guǎfu. 這個人很卑鄙.
他欺騙孤兒寡婦.
This person is unprincipled, he
cheats orphans and widows.

BĚIBIANR₁ 北邊兒 (PW)
north side, northern part, north
of. Niǔyuē-zai-Měiguode-běi-
bianr. 紐約在美國的
北邊兒. New York is in
the northern part of America.
Jiānádà z'ai-Měiguode-běibianr.
加拿大在美國的
北邊兒. Canada is north
of America.

BĚIBĪNGYÁNG₂ 北冰洋 (PW)
Arctic Ocean.

BÈIDĀNR₄ 被單兒 (N) sheet

(bedding). (M: chuáng 床).

BÈIDÒNG₄ 被動 (AD) do some-
thing which one is asked or
forced to do, involuntarily. (opp.
zìdòng 自動). Wǒ-zuò-zèige-
shì-bèidòng-de, búshi-'zìdòng-
de. 我作這個是被
動的, 不是自動
的 I did this thing because I
was forced to, it wasn't voluntary.

BĚIFĀNG₂ 北方 (PW) north,
north side.

BĒIGUĀN₃ 悲觀 (SV) pessimistic. (opp. lèguān 樂觀).
(N) pessimism. bào-bēiguān 抱
悲觀 have a pessimistic attitude.

BÈIHÒU₂背後 (PW) (1) behind
someone's back. Bié-zài-rén-
bèihòu 'pīping-rén. 別在人
背後批評人. Don't
criticize people behind their
backs. (2) behind. Bié-'gēnzhe-
wo-bèihòu-'zǒu. 別跟着
我背後走. Don't walk
behind me.

BĚIJÍ₃ 北極 (PW) The Arctic,
North pole.

BÈIJÌNG₃ 僻靜 (SV) secluded
and quiet. Zhèitiao-jiē hěn-
bèijing. 這條街很僻靜.
This is a very quiet street.

BĚIJĪNG₁ 北京 (PW) Peking.

BĚIMĚIZHŌU₂ 北美洲 (PW)
North America.

BĚIPÍNG₁ 北平 (PW) Peiping.

BÈI-SHŪ₃ 背書 (VO) repeat
some lines from a book verbally
from memory.

BÈIXĪN₂ 背心 (N) (lit. back
and chest) sleeveless garment
covering upper part of the trunk,
such as sleeveless sweater, undershirt, waistcoat. vest, etc.
(M: jiàn 件).

BĒIZI₁ 杯子 (N) small vessel
for drinking, cup, glass, tumbler, etc. (See: BĒI 杯).

BĚN₁ 本 (M) volume, tome.
yiběn-shū 一 本 書 one book.
yiběn-xiǎoshuōr 一 本 小 説
a (volume of) novel, a tome of
a multi-volume novel. Zhè-zhǐ-
shi-zhèibu-'shū-de-yi'běn. 這
只 是 這 部 書 的 一
本. This is only one tome of
the book.
(B) booklet. běnzi 本子 paper
in book form.
(N) (1) trunk of a tree or main
stem of a plant. Zhèige-shù-běn-
hěn-cū. 這 個 樹 本 很
粗. This tree trunk is very thick.
(2) base, root, Bié-wàng-běn.
别 忘 本. Don't forget your
roots.
(CV) using something as a basis
for something else, according to.
Běnzhe-tāde-yìsi-shuō. 本 着
他 的 意 思 説. Talk about
it using his idea as a basis.
(B-) this, the same. běnxiào 本
校 this school. běnlǐbài 本 禮
拜 this week.

BÈN₄ 奔 (TV) Peip. be in a hurry
and strive (for a certain goal).
Wǒ-děi-chūqu-bèn-qu. 我 得
出 去 奔 去. I have to go
out to earn a living.

(CV) toward some direction for
a goal. Tā-bèn-'nèibiānr-qù-le.
他 奔 那 邊 兒 去 了.
He went toward that direction.

BÈN₁ 笨 (SV) (1) stupid, dull, slow
(in learning, of a person or an
animal). (opp. cōngming 聰 明).
Tā-tài-bèn, xuébuhuì. 他 太
笨, 學 不 會. He is too
stupid, he cannot learn it. (2)
clumsy (of a person, an animal
or an object). (opp. líng 靈).
Wǒde-shǒu hěn-bèn. 我 的
手 很 笨 I'm clumsy with
my hands. Zhèige-zhuōzi you-
dà-you-bèn. 這 個 桌 子
又 大 又 笨. This table is
big and clumsy.

BĚNDÌ₂ 本 地 (PW) local place.
Tā-jiù-zài-běndì. 他 就 在
本 地. He is just in this locality.

BĒNG₅ 繃 (TV) (1) baste(sewing).
(2) stretch taut, such as tight-
ening the skin of a drum.

BÉNG₁ 甭 (AV) Peip.(con. bú-
yong 不 用). no need to, don't.
Nǐ-'béng-qù. 你 甭 去. You
need not go.

BÈNG₄ 蹦 (IV) Peip. jump, hop.

BĒNGDÀI₃ 繃 帶 (N) bandage.

BĒNG-LIǍN₄ 繃 臉 (VO) (lit.
tighten the face) make a serious
face. (syn. bǎn-liǎn 板 臉).
Tā-bǎ-liǎn-yi-běng, shénma-dou-
méi-shuō. 他 把 臉 一 繃,
甚 麼 都 没 説. He made
a serious face and said nothing.

BĚNLÁI₁ 本 來 (AD) (1) originally, at the outset. Zhèige

B

běnlái-shì-wǒde; hòulai wǒ-gěi-tā-le. 這個本來是我的；後來我給他了. Originally, this belonged to me; later I gave it to him. (2) naturally, of course. Zhèige-běn'lái-shì-wǒde-ma. 這個本來是我的麼. Of course, it is mine.

BĚNLĬBÀI₁ 本禮拜 (TW) the current week. (syn. běnxīngqī 本星期).

'BĚNLĬNG₁ 本領 (N) ability. (syn. běnshi 本事). Tāde-'běnlǐng-hěn-'dà. 他的本領很大. He is very capable.

BĚNQIAN₂ 本錢 (N) (lit. base money) (1) capital, money invested for making profit. (2) money used at the start of gambling. (cf: BĚNR 本兒).

BĚNR₁ 本兒 (N) (1) or BĚNZI 本子 booklet, something in book form. rìjiběnr 日記本兒 diary book. (2) capital, money invested for making profit. (3) money used at the start of gambling. Wǔkuai-qián-de-běr yíngle-shí-kuai. 五塊錢的本兒贏了十塊. I started with five dollars and I won ten. (cf: BĚNQIAN₂ 本錢).

BĚNRÉN₂ 本人 (PR) (1) oneself, one's own. Zhè-shi wǒ-běnrén-de-yìjian. 這是我本人的意見. This is my own opinion. Wǒ-bǎ-dōngxi jiāogei-běnrén-le. 我把東西交

給本人了. I handed the things over to the person himself. (2) used in a speech or other formal situation, I, me. Běnren-dàibiǎo-wǒmen-xuéxiào jiǎng-jijiu-huà. 本人代表我們學校講幾句話. I will say a few words on behalf of our school.

BĚNSHI₁ 本事 (N) ability. (syn. 'běnlǐng 本領). Tā-běnshi-bu-xiǎo. 他本事不小. He has quite a bit of ability.

BĚNXĪNGQĪ₁ 本星期 (TW) the current week. (syn. běnlǐbài 本禮拜).

BĚNYUÈ₁ 本月 (TW) the current month.

'BÈNZHÒNG₃ 笨重 (SV) clumsy and heavy (physical objects).

BĚNZI₁ 本子 or BĚNR 本兒 (N) booklet, something in book form. diànhua-běnzi 電話本子 phone book. (cf: BÙZI 簿子).

BĪ₁ 逼 (TV) compel, press, force someone to do something. Nǐ-bù-bī-ta, tā-bu-gěi nǐ-qián. 你不逼他，他不給你錢. If you don't press him, he won't pay you. Tā-ná-qiāng-bī-zhe-wo, wǒ bu-néng-bu-gěi-ta. 他拿鎗逼着我，我不能不給他. He forced me at gun point, I had no choice but to give it to him.

BĬ₁ 筆 (N) writing instrument, such as pen, pencil, brush, etc. (M: zhī 枝). gāngbǐ 鋼筆 pen. máobǐ 毛筆 brush pen. zìlai-shuǐbǐ 自來水筆 fountain

pen. fěnbǐ 粉筆 chalk.
(M) (1) stroke of a pen in writing
or a brush in painting. Zhèige-
zì 'jǐbǐ? 這個字幾筆?
How many strokes does this character have? (2) hand (in writing).
Tā-nèibi-zì bu-zěnmayàng. 他
那筆字不怎麼樣.
His handwriting is not very good.
(3) for a sum of money. Tā-shóuli-
yǒu-wǒ-yibǐ-qián. 他手裏
有我一筆錢. There
is a sum of my money in his hand.
(4) for a financial account or a
debt. Zhèibǐ-zhàng tā-hái-méi-
huán. 這筆賬他還没
還. He·hasn't yet paid off this
debt.

BǏ₁ 比 (TV) compare. Wǒmen-
'bǐ-yibǐ, kàn-shéi-gāo. 我們
比一比,看誰高.
Let's compare and see who is
taller. Wǒmen-bu-néng-ná-
'nèige-bǐ. 我們不能拿
那個比. We cannot use
that to compare. Yàoshi-bǐ-
běnshi, nàshi-'Zhāng-xiānsheng-
hǎo. 要是比本事,那
是張先生好. If we
compare their ability, Mr. Chang
is better. Wǒ-gēn-'tā-zhànzai
yikuàir, bǎ-wǒ-'bǐde-gèng-nán-
'kàn-le. 我跟他站在
一塊兒,把我比得
更難看了. When we
stand together, I look even uglier
by comparison.
(CV) more...than... (1) followed
by a SV. Zuò-fēijī bu-bǐ-zuò-
huǒchē-kuài. 坐飛機不

比坐火車快. Going
by plane is not faster than going
by train. Tāde-qián bǐ-wǒde-
duōdeduō 他的錢比我
的多的多. He has much
more money than I do. (2) followed by an AV. Tā-bǐ-'shéi
dou-ài-shuō-huà. 他比誰都
愛說話. He likes to talk
more than anyone else. (3) followed by certain adverbs, such
as zǎo 早, wǎn 晚, duō 多,
shǎo 少, etc. and a TV or IV.
Wǒ-bǐ-ta zǎo-lái-yíge-zhōngtóu.
我比他早來一個
鐘頭. I came one hour ear-
lier than he did.
(S) yìtiān-bǐ-yitiān 一天比
一天 getting more...and
more... everyday. Tāde-Zhōngwén yitiān-bǐ-yitiān-hǎo. 他的
中文一天比一天
好. His Chinese is getting
better and better everyday.

BǏ₂ 比 (TV) (1) use something as a
guide, an example or a model to
do something. Wǒmen-kéyi-bǐ-
zhe-zhèige lìngwài-zuò-yige. 我
們可以比著這個
另外作一個. We can
make another one using this one
as a model. Yòng chǐ-bǐzhe-huà.
用尺比著畫. Use a
ruler as a guide to draw. (2)
measure by comparison with
something. Tā-yòng-shǒu-bǐle-
bǐ-dàxiǎo. 他用手比了比
大小. He measured the size
with his hand. (3) aim or point
a gun. Tā-ná-qiāng bǐzhe-wo.

B

B

他拿鎗比着我. He is pointing a rifle at me. (4) used between two numbers for keeping score of a game, to. A: Duōshao-le? B:Wǔ-bǐ-sān. A: 多少了? B: 五比三. A: What's the score? B: Five to three.

BÌ₃ 閉 (TV) (1) shut (usually used for the eyes and mouth, but also used in a limited number of other compounds, such as a meeting, a curtain of a stage, etc.). Tā-xiàode bibushang-zuǐ. 他笑得閉不上嘴. (lit. He laughed so hard he couldn't even keep his mouth shut.) He couldn't stop laughing. (2) hold back breath. bì-yikǒu-qì. 閉一口氣 hold a breath. (cf: GUĀN 關, HÉ 合).

BÌ₃ 避 (TV) dodge, avoid, stay away from. Yǔ-tài-dà-le, wǒmen-bì-yibi-ba. 雨太大了. 我們避一避吧. The rain is too heavy, let's take shelter.

BIĀN₃ 編 (TV) (1) weave, plait, braid. Biān-yige-cǎomàor. 編一個草帽兒. Weave a straw hat. (2) compile, edit, write a story or play, compose a song. biān-bào 編報 edit a newspaper. biān-yichū-xì 編一齣戲 write a play. (3) fabricate a story, make up a lie. Tā-biānle-jijiù-xiāhuà. 他編了幾句瞎話. He made up a lie.

BIǍN₃ 扁 (SV) flat (in the sense that vertical dimension is smaller than the horizontal dimension). Bǐnggān-shi-biǎnde. 餅乾是扁的. Cookies are flat. (RE) (1) make something flat by some action. Bǎ-qiú-yābiǎnle. 把球壓扁了. The ball was squashed flat. (2) fig. consider someone small in ability. Tā-zhēn-ba-wo-kànbiǎnle. 他真把我看扁了. He really underestimated me.

BIÀN₁ 變 (TV) change, turn into, become. Zhèige-dìfang biànle-yàngzi-le. 這個地方變了樣子了. This place has changed in appearance. 'Yèzi dōu-biàn-yánse-le. 葉子都變顏色了. The leaves have all changed color. Tā-biàncheng-lǎo-tàitai le. 她變成老太太了. She changed into an old lady. (cf: GǍI 改, HUÀN 換).

BIÀN₃ 遍 (M) time (occurrence of some action or happening). Nǐ-zài-niàn-yibian, wǒ-tīngting. 你再念一遍, 我聽聽. Read it once more, let me hear it. (cf: CÌ 次, HUÍ 回).

BIÀN₃ 遍 (AD) throughout, everywhere. Wǒ-'biàn-zhǎo, méi-yǒu. 我遍找沒有. I have looked everywhere, but I can't find it. (RE) indicates that the action of the verb that precedes it covers every place and every spot. Zǒu-biàn-tiānxià. 走遍天下. Go everywhere in the world.

BIǍNDAN₅ 扁担 (N) pole (for

carrying things on one's shoulder).
(M: gēn 根).

'BIÀNDÒNG₂ 變動 (TV) change.
Nǐ-ānpaide-bucuò, bu-bì-'biàn-
dòng-le. 你 安 排 的 不 錯,
不 必 變 動 了. Your
arrangement is not bad, there is
no need to change it.

(N) change. Zhèng'fǔ-lǐde-'rénshì
'méi-you-shénma-'biàndòng. 政
府 裏 的 人 事, 沒 有
甚 麼 變 動. There is not
much change of personnel in the
government. (cf:'BIÀNHUÀ 變
化).

BIĂNDÒU₄ 扁 豆 (N) string bean.
(M; jīn 斤).

BIÀNFÀN₂ 便 飯 (N) informal
meal, usual meal. jiācháng-biàn-
fàn 家 常 便 飯 ordinary
daily home-cooked meal.

(IV) have an ordinary meal. Lǐ-
bàiliù qǐng-guòlai-biànfàn, 'hǎo-
bu-hǎo? 禮 拜 六 請 過 來,
便 飯, 好 不 好? How
about coming to have supper with
me on Saturday?

BIÀN-GUÀ₃ 變 卦 (VO) change
one's mind, ideas, plans, etc.
'Zuótian-ta-shuō-ta-'qù, 'jīntian-
ta-biànle-'guà-le. 昨 天 他
說 他 去; 今 天 他 變
了 卦 了. Yesterday he
said he would go; today he has
changed his mind.

'BIÀNHUÀ₁ 變 化 (N) change.
'Biànhuà-hěn-dà. 變 化 很 大.
The change has been very great.
(cf: 'BIÀNDÒNG 變 動).

BIĀNJI₂ 編 輯 (TV) compile,
edit.

(N) compiler, editor. Tā-zài-
bào'guǎn-zuò-biānji. 他 在 報
館 作 編 輯. He is an
editor for the newspaper.

BIÀN-LIĂN₃ 變 臉 (VO) change
one's facial expression suddenly,
because of anger. Tā-méi-gēn-
wo-biànguo-liǎn. 他 沒 跟 我
變 過 臉. He has never
made his anger visible to me
(by changing his facial expression).

BIÀNLÙN₂ 辯 論 (TV) debate,
argue. Tāmen-zai-diàn'shì-shang
biànlùn. 他 們 在 電 視 上
辯 論. They debated on television.

BIĀNR₁ 邊 兒 (N) (1) edge.
zhuōzi-biānr 桌 這 邊 兒 the
edge of a table. Bié-fàngzai-
biānrshang. 別 放 在 邊 上.
Don't put it on the edge. (2) side.
hébiānr 河 邊 兒 riverside.
suffix to localizer to form PW,
side. lǐbianr 裏 邊 兒 inside.
zuǒbianr 左 邊 兒 left side.
(M) side. zhèibianr 這 邊 兒
this side. Liǎngbiānr-dou-yuànyi.
兩 邊 兒 都 願 意. Both
sides are willing.

BIÀN-XĪN₂ 變 心 (VO) change
loyalties, break faith (toward
people). Wǒ-méi-xiǎngdào ta-
huì-biànle-xīn-le. 我 沒 想
到 他 會 變 了 心 了.
I didn't expect him to change his
loyalty.

BIĀNZI₃ 鞭 子 (N) whip. (M:
gēn 根).

BIÀNZI₄ 辮 子 (N) braid. (M:

B

B

gēn 根). biān-biànzi 編 辮 子 make pigtails, braid.

BIÀNZHÈNGFǍ₃ 辯 證 法 (N) dialectical method.

BIǍO₁ 表 (N) (1) watch (timepiece). shǒubiǎo 手表 wrist watch. (2) meter, gauge. shuǐbiǎo 水 表 water meter. (3) table, chart, form. shíjiānbiǎo 時 間 表 time-table.

BIǍO₄ 表 (B-) indicates second-degree relatives outside of one's family. biǎoqīn 表親 second-degree relatives.

BIǍODÌ₅ 表弟 (N) younger male cousin (on the maternal side or on the paternal aunt's side).

BIǍOGĒ₅ 表哥 or BIǍOXIŌNG 表兄 (N) older male cousin (on the maternal side or on the paternal aunt's side).

BIǍOGÉ₃ 表格 (N) form, blank (to be filled out). (M: zhāng 張).

BIǍOJIĚ₅ 表姐 (N) older female cousin (on the maternal side or the paternal aunt's side).

BIǍOJIĚMÈI₅ 表姐妹 or BIǍOZǏMÈI 表姊妹 (N) female cousin (daughter of father's sister or mother's sister or brother). (cf: TÁNGJIĚ-MÈI 堂姐妹).

BIǍOJUÉ₂ 表決 (TV) reach a decision by voting. Wǒmen-xiàn-zài-biǎojué. 我們現在 表決 . Let's take a vote.

BIǍOMÈI₅ 表妹 (N) younger female cousin (on the maternal side or on the paternal aunt's side).

'BIǍOMIÀN₂ 表面 (N) (1) superficiality, surface appearance, veneer. Tā-biǎomiàn duì-rén hen-hǎo. 他表面對人 很好 . On the surface, he is very nice to people. (2) exterior, outside. Zhè-dou-shì-biǎomiàn-'gōngzuò. 這都是表面 工作 . All of this is outside of the really important work.

BIǍOSǍO₅ 表嫂 (N) older cousin's wife (wife of biǎogē 表哥).

'BIǍOSHÌ₁ 表示 (TV) express, show, make clear. biǎoshì-yì-jian 表示意見 express (one's) opinion. biǎoshichulai 表示出來 express outwardly. biǎoshì-tàidu 表示 態度 make clear (one's) attitude.

BIǍOXIAN₃ 表現 (N) achievement or performance (of a job). Tā-zài-zhèr-zuò-shì-yǐlái, gōng-zuode- biǎoxian hěn-hǎo. 他在 這兒作事以來, 工 作的表現很好. Since he has worked here, his performance has been very good. (TV) express, show, demonstrate one's capability, reaction, feelings or thoughts by action. Tā-de-sīxiang dou-zài-tāde-gōngzuo-shang biǎoxian-chulai-le. 他的 思想都在他的工 作上表現出來了. All of his ideas are reflected in his work.

BIǍOXIŌNG₅ 表兄 see BIǍOGĒ 表哥 .

BIǍOXIŌNGDÌ₅ 表兄弟 (N)

male cousin (son of father's
sister or mother's sister or
brother). (cf: TÁNGXIŌNGDÌ
堂兄弟).

'BIĂOYĂN₁ 表演 (TV) perform,
act, give a demonstration (before an audience).
(N) performance (of a show).

'BIĂOYÁNG₄ 表揚 (TV) praise
openly.

BIĀOYŬ₂ 標語 (N) slogan, watch-
word (in writing). (M: jù 句).
tiē-biāoyŭ 貼標語 paste up
a slogan.

'BIĀOZHÌ₅ 標誌 (N) sign or
mark to show a route, sea-lane.

BIĀOZHUN₁ 標準 (N) standard,
criterion. méi-biāozhun 没標
準 no standard.

BIĂOZĬMÈI₄ 表姊妹 see
BIĂOJIĚMÈI 表姐妹 .

BÌBÀO₃ 壁報 (N) newspaper
(put on the wall for the public).

BĬCĬ₂ 彼此 (AD) each other,
mutually. Wŏmen-bĭcĭ-bāngmáng.
我們彼此幫忙 . We
help each other. Tāmen-bĭcĭ-
bu-shuō-huà. 他們彼此
不說話 . They don't speak
to each other.
used as a polite expression, usually is repeated, it (the feeling)
is mutual. A: Nín-duō-zhĭjiào.
B: Bĭcĭ-bĭcĭ. A: 您多指教
B: 彼此彼此 A: (lit.
Please give me more instructions.) Please feel free to give
me as much advice as you can.
B: (lit.The feeling is mutual.)
You know as much about it as I

do. (cf: HÙXIĀNG 互相).

BÌDĚI₂ 必得 (AV) must, have to.
Nĭ-bìděi-gàosong-wo. 你必
得告訴我 . You must tell
me.

BÌDÌNG₃ 必定 (AD) certainly,
must be, must have. Tā-bìdìng-
zhīdao. 他必定知道 .
He must have known it.

BIĒ₄ 憋 (TV) (1) restrain, hold
back, restrict something that
will result in inner pressure.
biē-yikou-qì 憋一口氣
hold one's breath or fig. hold
one's temper. Bié-bă-huà biē-
zai-xīnli. 別把話憋在
心裏 . Don't keep things
inside of you. Wŏmen-dou-biē-
zhe bu-xiào. 我們都憋着
不笑 . We all held ourselves
from laughing. Bié-lăo-zài-
jiāli-biēzhe. 別老在家裏
憋着 . Don't stay home all
the time (let yourself go once in
a while). (2) ponder, contem-
plate under inner pressure caused
by eagerness or anxiousness.
Tā-biēchu-'zhèiyàng-yíge-zhúyi-
lai. 他憋出這樣一
個主意來 . He pondered
it and then got this idea. (3)
keep watch on someone or something in anticipation of some
expected activity or behavior.
Wŏ-zhèr-biēzhe-ni-ne. 我這
兒憋着你呢 . I am
watching you. (4) be destroyed
by inner pressure. Băoxiănsī-
piē-le. 保險絲憋了 .
The fuse has blown out.

B

B

BIE₁ 別 (AV) (con. bú-yào 不要). don't (used as a command), had better not.... Nǐ-'bié-qù. 你別去. Don't go. Nín-'qiān-wàn-bié-'kèqi. 您千萬別客氣. Be sure not to be overly polite. 'Míngtian ke-bié-xià-yǔ. 明天可別下雨. It had better not rain tomorrow.

BIÉ₃ 別 (TV) (1) fasten or attach something long as a stick or pin onto something. Tā-bǎ-zhēn bié-zai-yīshangshang-le. 他把針別在衣裳上了. She fastened the needle on her clothes. (2) fasten or attach things to-gether with a pin, a clip, or a safety pin. Bǎ-zhǐ biézai-yí-kuàir. 把紙別在一塊兒. Clip these papers together.

BIĚ₂ 癟 (SV) be flattened, flat. (opp. gǔ 鼓). Chē-dài-biě-le. 車帶癟了. The tire of the car is flat. (IV) dent, be pushed in. Qìchē-biějin-yikuai-qu. 汽車癟進一塊去. The car is dented in one spot.

BIÉCHUR₁ 別處兒 (PW) an-other place. Tā-dào-biéchur-qu-le. 他到別處去了. He went to another place.

BIÉDE₁ 別的 (N) other things or objects. Wǒ-bu-yào-biéde. 我不要別的. I don't want another thing.

BIĒMEN₃ 憋悶 (SV) depressed (caused by lack of emotional out-let). (opp. tòngkuai 痛快). Wǒ-xīnli-hen-biēmen. 我心裏很憋悶. I am very depressed.

BIÈNIU₃ 彆扭 (SV) (1) frustrated because of a contrary or disa-greeable situation. (opp. tòng-kuai 痛快). Wǒ-juéde-xīnli hěn-bièniu. 我覺的心裏很彆扭. I feel very frus-trated (because of a disagreeable situation). (2) contrary, dis-agreeable (persons). 'Zhèige-rén zhēn-bièniu. 這個人真彆扭. This person is really contrary. (3) contrary, disa-greeable (situations). (opp. shùndang 順當). Shìqing lǎo-shi-zhèiyàngr bièniu. 事情老是這樣彆扭. (lit. Things are always so disagreeable) Things never seem to go smoothly. (N) disagreement, frustration. Nǐ-bié-jǎo-bièniu. 你別找彆扭. Don't look for points of disagreement.

BIÉREN₁ 別人 (N) other person, others. Biéren-kǒngpa-'bú-zhèiyang-kàn. 別人恐怕不這樣看. The others probably won't look at it this way.

BIÉSHI₂ 別是 (AD) (hope) it better not be.... 'Biéshi-shuō-'cuòle. 別是說錯了. (I) hope it was not said wrong.

BIÉZHĒNR₃ 別針兒 (N) safe-ty pin.

BIÉZÌ₃ 別字 see BÁIZÌ 白字.

BĪFANG₁ 比方 (TV) describe with some kind of gesture. Tā yòng-shǒu-bǐfang. 他用手比方. He described it with his hands.

(AD) for example. bǐfang-shuō 比方説 (lit. verbally explaining with an example) for example.

(N) example. Ná-zhèige zuò-ge-bǐfang. 拿這件事作個比方. Use this as an example. Wǒ-gěi-nǐ-dǎ-ge-bǐfang. 我給你打個比方. I'll give you an example.

BǏGUO₃ 比國 (PW) Belgium.

BǏJÌ₂ 筆記 (N) notes (taken down for future reference).

'BǏJIǍO₁ 比較 (TV) compare. Yì-bǐjiao jiu-zhīdao-nèige-hǎo. 一比較就知道那個好. Once you compare them you will know which is better.

(AD) comparatively. Zhèige-bǐjiao-kuài. 這個比較快. Comparatively this is faster.

BǏJIBĚNR₁ 筆記本兒 (N) notebook. (M: běn 本).

BÌMÁZǏYÓU₅ 蓖麻子油 (N) castor oil.

'BÌMIǍN₂ 避免 (TV) avoid, evade, elude (difficulties, troubles, etc.). 'Zhèiyangr kéyi-bìmiǎn-hěn-duō-máfan. 這樣兒可以避免很多麻煩. This way we may avoid a lot of trouble.

BǏMÍNG₃ 筆名 (N) pen name.

BÌ-MÙ₂ 閉幕 (VO) close the curtain, close a performance. fig. adjourn a meeting, end some occasion.

BĪNG₁ 兵 (N) (1) enlisted men of armed forces. (2) troops. pài-bīng 派兵 send troops.

BĪNG₁ 冰 (N) ice. (M: kuài 塊). Dòng-bīng-le. 凍冰了. It is frozen. or It is freezing. Bīng-huà-le. 冰化了. The ice has melted.

(TV) (1) chill something on ice or in a refrigerator. Bǎ-shuǐguǒ-bīngshang. 把水果冰上. Chill the fruit. (2) chilled by touching something very cold. Wàitou-yídìng-hěn-lěng. Zhèige chuānghu-bīng-shǒu. 外頭一定很冷. 這個窗戶冰手. It must be very cold outside. This window chills (my) hand (when I touch it).

BǏNG₁ 餅 (N) something round and flat made of dough with or without other ingredients. (B) something round and flat. tiěbǐng 鐵餅 discus.

BÌNG₂ 病 (N) illness, sickness. Tā-yǒu-bìng. 他有病. He is ill. Tāde-bìng hǎole-meiyou? 他的病好了沒有? Has he recovered?

(IV) become sick, sick, ill. Tā-yòu-bìng-le. 他又病了. He is sick again. Tā-bìngde-hěn-lìhai. 他病得很厲害. He is very sick.

BÌNG₃ 並 (TV) combine. Bǎ-zhèi-liǎngge bìngzai-yíkuàir. 把這兩個並在一塊兒. Combine these two together.

B

B

BÌNG₁ 並 (AD) used only with bu
不 or méi 没 to strongly negate
someone's affirmative statement,
actually, definitely. Tā-yǐwei-
ta-zhǐdao, ta-bìng-'bù-zhǐdào.
他 以 為 他 知 道, 他
並 不 知 道. He thought
he knew, but actually he doesn't
know. Tāmen-shuō wo-shuōle,
wǒ-bìng-'méi-shuō. 他 們 説
我 説 了, 我 並 没 説.
They said that I said it, but actually I didn't say it. Tā-lǎo-shuō-
ta-mǎi, qíshí tā-bìng-mǎibuqǐ.
他 老 説 他 買, 其 實
他 並 買 不 起. He al-
ways talks about buying it, but
as a matter of fact he cannot afford to buy it.

BÌNGBÁO₅ 冰雹 (N) hail.

BÌNGFĒI₂ 並非 (AD) used as an
emphatic negative, it isn't that...
Bìngfēi wǒ-bú-yào, shì-tā-bù-
gěi. 並 非 我 不 要, 是
他 不 給. It is not that I
don't want it; it is that he doesn't
want to give.

BÌNGGĀN₁ 餅乾 (N) cookies,
biscuits. (M: kuài 塊).

BÌNGGÙNR₁ 冰棍兒 (N)
popsicle. (M: gēn 根).

BÌNGJILÍNG₁ 冰激凌 (N) icecream.

BÌNGLIÁNG₄ 冰涼 (SV) ice-
cold.

BÌNGPÁIR₄ 並排兒 (AD) side
by side.

BÌNGQIĚ₁ 並且 (MA) more-
over, and. Zhèige-xuéxiào hěn-
dà, bìngqiě hěn-yǒumíng. 這個
學 校 很 大, 並 且 很

有 名. That school is very
large and moreover it is very
famous. (cf: ÉRQIĚ 而且).
(S) búdàn ... bìngqiě ... 不 但
... 並 且 ... not only ... but
also ... Tā-búdàn-cōngming,
bìngqiě-yònggōng. 他 不 但
聰 明, 並 且 用 功. He
is not only intelligent but also
studious.

BÌNGQIÚ₂ 冰球 (N) ice hockey.
(M: chǎng 場).

BÌNGREN₂ 病人 (N) (1) sick
person. (2) patient.

BÌNGTÁNG₄ 冰糖 (N) rock candy.
(M: kuài 塊).

BÌNGXIĀNG₁ 冰箱 (N) ice box,
refrigerator.

BÌNGYUÀN₃ 病院 (N) hospital,
clinic. (M: jiā 家).

BÍQI₅ 荸薺 (N) water chestnut.

BǏRU₂ 比如 (AD) for example.
bǐru-shuō 比如説 (lit. ver-
bally explaining with an example)
for example.

BǏSÀI₁ 比賽 (N) race, contest,
competition.
(TV) race, compete. Wǒ-bù-
néng-gēn-ta-bǐsài. 我 不 能
跟 他 比 賽. I cannot
compete against him.

BǏSHÌ₃ 筆試 (IV) give or take a
written examination.
(N) written examination.

BÌ-SHǓ₃ 避暑 (VO) go on vacation to escape from the heat.

BÍTI₄ 鼻涕 (N) mucous (dis-
charge from the nose).

BǏTǑNG₅ 筆筒 (N) writing-brush holder (in the form of a cylinder).

BÌXÌNG₃ 敝 姓 (TV) my (humble) surname is. Bìxìng-Zhāng. 敝 姓 張. My last name is Chang.

BÌXŪ₁ 必 須 (AV) must, have to, it's necessary to. Wŏmen bìxū-zhèiyàngr-zuò. 我 們 必 須 這 樣 兒 作. We must do it this way.
(N) need, necessity. (syn. bìyào 必 要). Méiyou-bìxū. 沒 有 必 須. There isn't any need.

BÌ-YĂN₂ 閉 眼 (VO) close the eyes.

BÌYÀO₁ 必 要 (N) necessity, need. (syn. bìxū 必 須). 'Méi-yŏu-bìyào. 沒 有 必 要. There is no necessity. Zài-zhōng-xué-jiāo-shū, dàxué-bìyè shì-bìyàode tiáojian. 在 中 學 敎 書, 大 學 畢 業 是 必 要 的 條 件. To teach in high school, it is necessary to be a college graduate.

BÌ-YÈ₁ 畢 業 (VO) graduate. Nĭ-shi-nĕinian-bìde-yè? 你 是 那 年 畢 的 業? Which year did you graduate? Tā-dà-xué hái-méi-bìyè-ne. 他 大 學 還 沒 畢 業 呢. He has not yet graduated from college.

BÌYU₃ 比 喻 (N) parable, meta-phor. Wŏ-gĕi-nĭmen-shuō-yige-bĭyu. 我 給 你 們 說 一 個 比 喻. I'll tell you a story to show you.

BÍZI₂ 鼻 子 (N) nose.

BŌ₂ 撥 (TV) (1) move something

with something long and thin, such as a stick or a finger. bō-diànhuà 撥 電 話 dial a tele-phone. (2) adjust or turn a knob which operates an indicator. bō-biāo 撥 表 set a watch. (3) transfer personnel or funds. Bă-ta-bōdao-xiàozhăngshì-qu-dă-zì-qu. 把 他 撥 到 校 長 室 去 打 字 去. Transfer her to the president's office to do typing. Tā-gĕi-wŏ bōle-yibĭ-qián-lai. 他 給 我 撥 了 一 筆 錢 來. He trans-ferred some money to me.

BŌBO₅ 餑 餑 (N) Peip. baked goods (cake, cookies, etc., but not bread).

BÓCÀI₄ 菠 菜 (N) spinach. (M: jīn 斤).

BÓFÙ₃ 伯 父 (N) uncle (father's elder brother).

BÒHE₄ 薄 荷 (N) mint (plant), mint-flavor.

BŌLÁN₃ 波 蘭 (PW) Poland.

'BŌLÀNG₄ or 'PŌLÀNG 波 浪 (N) ripple, wave (in any body of water).

BÓLĂNHUÌ₃ 博 覽 會 (N) commer-cial exhibit on a large scale , exposition. Shìjiè-bólănhuì. 世 界 博 覽 會. World's Fair.

BŌLI₂ 玻 璃 (N) (1) glass(mate-rial). (2) plastic. bōli-píbāo 玻 璃 皮 包 plastic hand-bag.

BÓLÍN₂ 柏 林 (PW) Berlin.

BŌLUÓ₃ 菠 蘿 (N) pineapple.

BÓMŬ₃ 伯 母 (N) aunt (wife of

B

father's elder brother).

'BŌNÒNG₅ 撥弄 (TV) (1) manipulate with a stick or finger. (2)
stir up, agitate, incite.

BÒQI₄ 簸箕 (N) dust pan.

'BÓRUÒ₄ 薄弱 (SV) weak in
willpower or determination.

BÓSHI₁ 博士 (N) (1) doctoral
degree, doctorate. niàn-bóshi
念博士 study for a doctoral
degree. dé-bóshi 得博士
receive a doctorate. (2) holder
of a doctorate. Tā-shì-yiwéi-bó-
shi. 他是一位博士.
(lit. He is a person holding a
doctorate) He has a doctorate.
(3) title given to a person holding
a doctorate. Zhāng-Bóshi 張
博士 Dr. Chang.

BŌSÒNG₃ 播送 (TV) broadcast.

BÓWÙGUǍN₂ 博物館 (N)
museum.

BÓWÙYUÀN₂ 博物院 (N)
museum.

'BŌXUĒ₄ 剝削 see 'BĀOXIĀO
剝削.

BŌ-ZHÒNG₄ 播種 (VO) sow.

BÓZI₄ 脖子 (N) neck.

BǓ₂ 補 (TV) (1) patch, repair.
bǔ-yīshang 補衣裳 patch
the clothes. (2) fill (a vacant
position or a hole). Shéi-bǔ-tā-
nèige-quē? 誰補他那個
缺 ? Who will take over his
position? Wǒde-yá bǔle-liǎngge-
dòng. 我的牙補了兩
個洞. I had two cavities
filled. (3) make up (class or
examination). Jīntian wǒ-gei-

xuésheng-bǔ-le-yitáng-kè. 今天
我給學生補了一
堂課. Today I made up a
class for the students. (4) pay
more money to make up the difference. Wǒ-búgei-ni-'liǎngkuai-
qián. 我補給你兩塊
錢. I will pay you two dollars
more to make up the difference.

BÙ₂ 布 (N) cloth (made of any kind
of material except silk).

BÙ₁ 部 (M) (1) set for books. yíbù-
shū 一部書 a set of a multi-
ple volume work.
(B) (1) part of. nánbù 南部
southern part. (2) department,
section. wàijiāobù 外交部
foreign affairs department.

BÙ₁ 步 (M) (1) step, stride. yíbù-
yíbù-de-zǒu 一步一步的
走 walk step by step. (2) fig.
step, degree, level of advancement or progress. yíbù-yíbù-de-
zuò 一步一步的作
do things one step at a time.
Zhè-shi di'yíbù. 這是第
一步. This is the first step.
'Yàoshi néng-zuòdao-'zhèi-bù,
yǐjing-hěn-hǎo-le. 要是能
作到這步,已經很
好了. If we can work up to
this point, it will be very good.
(3) move (in a board game). zǒu-
yíbu-qí 走一步棋 make
one move.

BÙ₁ 不 (AD) a negative form
which may be used before any
verbal expression except yǒu 有,
not, don't, won't, didn't want to.

The tone of bù 不 may be changed into rising tone when it is followed by a syllable with a falling tone. búqù 不 去 don't want to go. bú-mài 不 賣 won't sell. Tā-bú-shì-xuésheng. 他 不 是 學生 . He is not a student. Wǒ-bú-huì. 我 不 會 . I don't know how. Tā-cóngqián bù-hē-jiǔ. 他 從前 不 喝 酒 . He didn't drink before. Tā-zuótian-bù-mǎi, jīntian gǎi-le-zhúyi-le. 他 昨天 不 買, 今天 改了 主意 了 . He didn't want to buy yesterday, but today he changed his mind.

used by itself or with a particle, no. A: Qù-shuì-jiào-qu. B: Bù. A: 去 睡 覺 去 . B: 不 . A: Go to sleep. B: No. A: Tā-shì-Zhōngguo-ren. B: Bù-ba. A: 他 是 中國 人 . B: 不 吧 . A: He is a Chinese. B: No, I doubt it. A: Nín-zài-chī-yidiǎnr-ba. B: Bù-le, xièxie. A: 您 再 吃 一 點 兒 吧 . B: 不 了, 謝謝 . A: How about having some more? B: No more, thanks.

used as an infix between a verb and a RE, produces the negative potential form of RV, cannot, could not. Yàoshi-ni-xiànzai bú-jìnqu, děng-yihuǐr jiu-jìnbuqù-le. 要 是 你 現 在 不 進 去, 等 一 會 兒 就 進 不 去 了 . If you don't go in now, you cannot go in later.

(S) bù.. bù. 不 .. 不 .. (1) (con.

yě-bu.. yě-bù.. 也 不 .. 也 不 ..). when two expressions which are opposite in meaning are introduced by bu 不 , with or without a pause after the first phrase, neither... nor... bù-cháng bù-duǎn 不 長 不 短 neither long nor short. bù-zhōng-bùxī 不 中 不 西 neither Chinese nor Western. bù-nán-bù-nǚ 不 男 不 女 neither like a man nor like a woman. Tā-bu-chī-fàn, bu-hē-jiǔ. 他 不 吃 飯 不 喝 酒 . He neither eats nor drinks. (2) (con. yàoshi-bù... jiu-bù... 要 是 不 ... 就 不 ...). when a heavy stress is put on the last full tone syllable of the first bu-phrase with no pause after it, if not..., then won't.... Tā-bu-chī-'fàn-bù-hē-jiǔ. 他 不 吃 飯 不 喝 酒 . If he is not eating, then he won't drink.

BÚBÌ₁ 不 必 (AV) need not, don't have to. Nǐ-búbì-gàosong-ta. 你 不 必 告 訴 他 . You need not tell him.

BÚBIÀN₃ 不 便 (AV) (lit. not convenient) no value to, be disadvantageous to. Wǒmen-bubiàn-gàosong-ta. 我 們 不 便 告 訴 他 . There is no advantage for us to tell him.

BǓCHŌNG₂ 補 充 (TV) supplement, increase, add. Wǒ-gěi-ta-'bǔchōng-liǎngju. 我 給 他 補 充 兩 句 . I will add a couple of remarks to what he said. Hái-bu-gòu, hái-dei-bǔchōng.

B

還不夠，還得補充·
It's still not enough, I have to add some more.

BÚCUÒ₁ 不錯 (SV) not bad. 'Zhèige-búcuò, nǐ-mǎi-'zhèige-·ba. 這個不錯，你買 這個吧· This one is not bad, you had better buy it. (See: CUÒ 錯).

BÚDA₂ 不大 (AD) (syn. bùzěnma 不怎麼). (1) not very. bù-da-hǎokàn 不大好看 not very good-looking. (2) not often, not much. Wǒ-búda-chūqu. 我 不大出去· I don't go out very often. (See: DÀ 大).

BÚDÀN₁ 不但 (AD) not only. used in a clause which is followed by another clause containing érqiě 而且, bìngqiě 並 且 , hái 還 , etc., not only. Tā-budàn-zhǐdao, hái-zhǐdaode-hěn-qīngchu. 他不但知 道，還知道的很清 楚· He not only knew it, but knew it very clearly.

BÚDAO₂ 不到 used before a NU-M, less than. búdao-wǔkuai-qián 不到五塊錢 less than five dollars.

BÙDĀYING₃ 不答應 (TV) not let someone get away with something by continually demanding satisfaction. Nǐ-bù-gěi-ta-qián, tā-yídìng-budāying. 你不給 他錢，他一定不答 應· If you won't pay him, he certainly will not let you get away with it. (See: DĀYING 答應).

BÙDÉBU₁ 不得不 (AD) cannot help but... , must. Tā-zhèi-yàngr-yi-shuō, wǒ-bùdébu-gào-song-ta. 他這樣兒一說， 我不得不告訴他· When he says it this way, I must tell him.

BÙDÉLIǍO₁ 不得了 (SV) (lit. cannot get to an end) (1) extreme Wǒ-lèide-bùdéliǎo. 我累得 不得了· I am extremely tired. (2) terrific or with pejorative sense, no end of trouble. Yàoshi-zhèiyang-zuò, nà-ke-bùdéliǎo. 要是這樣作， 那可不得了· If you do it this way, it would be terrific. or If you do it this way, the trouble will never end. Zhèige-rén zhēn-bùdéliǎo. 這個人真 不得了· This person is really terrific. (3) used for introducing some astounding happening. Bùdeliǎo shuǐ-dou-jìn-lai-le. 不得了，水都進 來了· My goodness, all the water is coming in. (cf: 'LIAO-BUDÉ 了不得).

BÙDÉYǏ₂ 不得已 (SV) be forced to do so, no other choice, having no alternative. Wǒ-'nèi-yàngr-zuò, shì-yīnwei-bùdéyǐ. 我那一樣作是因為 不得已· I did it that way because I had no choice. 'Wàn-budéyǐ-de-shíhou, wǒ-cai-zuò-fēijī. 萬不得已的時 候，我才坐飛機· If there is absolutely no alternative, then, and only then, will I fly.

BǓDING₄ 補釘 (N) patch. dǎbǔding 打補釘 _or_ bǔ-bǔding 補補釘 make a patch.

BÚDUÀN₃ 不斷 (AD) continuously, unceasingly. Tāmen-búduàn-tōng-xìn. 他們不斷通信. They correspond continuously. (See: DUÀN 斷).

BÙDUÌ₃ 部隊 (N) troops (military).

BÙ'ĚRQIÁOYÀ₄ 布爾喬亞 (N) bourgeoisie.

BÙFÁNG₂ 不妨 (AV) no harm to.

BÙFEN₁ 部分 (M) (1) part of, portion of. Tā-bǎ-tade-qián fēncheng-sānbùfen. 他把他的錢分成三部分. He divided his money into three portions. (2) section of an organization. Nǐ-zài-'něibùfen-gōngzuo? 你在那部分工作? Which section do you work in?
(AD) partially. Nèige-gōngzuo yǐjing-bùfen-wánchéng. 那個工作己經部分完成. That job is already partially completed.

BÙFÚ₃ 不符 (TV) not in accord with. Tā-shuō-de gēn-shìshí-bùfú. 他說的跟事實不符. What he said is not in accord with the facts.

BÙGǍNDĀNG₁ 不敢當 polite form which is used in answering a compliment or a complimentary gesture, (lit. I dare not accept it.) I am flattered. A: Nín-Zhōngguohuà shuōde-zhēn-hǎo. B: Bùgǎndāng. A: 您中國話說的真好. B: 不敢當. A: You speak Chinese very well. B: I'm flattered. A: Qǐng-'shàng-zuò. B: Bùgǎndāng. A: 請上坐. B: 不敢當. A: Please sit in the position reserved for the honored guests. B: I'm flattered. (cf: QǏGǍN 豈敢).

BÙGÀO₂ 布告 (N) posted official notice. (M: zhāng 張). Chū-bùgào-le. 出布告了. A notice was put out.

BÙGUǍN₁ 不管 (AD) (1) regardless of, no matter (whether), it doesn't matter (whether). (syn. búlùn 不論 , wúlùn 無論). Bùguǎn-'shéi-qù dou-xíng. 不管誰去都行. It doesn't matter who goes, it will be all right. (2) don't care. (syn. buzàihu 不在乎). Wǒ-bù-guǎn nǐ-yǒu-qián-mei-you, fǎn-zhèng-nǐ-děi-gěi-wǒ-mǎi. 我不管你有錢沒有, 反正你得給我買. I don't care whether you have any money or not, you must buy it for me. (See: GUǍN 管).

BÚGUÒ₁ 不過 (MA) but, however. (syn. kěshi 可是 , dànshi 但是). Nèige-hěn-hǎo, búguò-wǒ-bu xǐhuan. 那個很好, 不過我不喜歡. That is very good, but I don't like it. (See: GUÒ 過).

BÙHǍOYÌSI₁ 不好意思 (SV) embarrassed. Tā-yi-buhǎoyìsi liǎn-jiu-hóng-le. 他一不好意思臉就紅了. As soon as he feels embarrassed, his face gets red.

B

B

(AD) embarrassingly. Wǒ-bù-hǎo yìsi-gēn-ta-shuō. 我不好意思跟他說. I'm embarrassed to talk to him.

BÙHÉ₄ 不和 (IV) not get along well. Tāmen-liǎngge-ren-bùhé. 他們兩個人不和. Those two don't get along.

BÚJIÀNDE₂ 不見得 (AV) not necessarily, cannot be sure. Tā-bújiànde-gàosong-ni. 他不見得告訴你. He will not necessarily tell you. A: Zhèige-hěn-hǎo. B: Bújiànde. A: 這個很好. B: 不見得. A: This is very good. B: Not necessarily so.

BÙJĪNG₃ 布景 (N) stage or motion picture set.

BÚJIÙSHI...MA₃ 不就是...嗎 (S) isn't it only... Bújiushi-yìbǎikuai-qián-ma? 不就是一百塊錢嗎? Isn't it only a matter of one hundred dollars?

BÙJŪ₄ 不拘 (MA) (lit. not limited to) no matter (whether). Bùjū-něitian dōu-xíng. 不拘那天都行. It doesn't matter which day, any day will do.

BÙKĚ₃ 不可 (AV) (con. bù-kéyi 不可以). may not, cannot. Nǐ-bùkě-suíbiàn-shuō-huà. 你不可隨便說話. You cannot say whatever you wish. (See: FĒI(DEI)...BÙKĚ 非得...不可).

BÙKĚBU₃ 不可不 (AD) cannot afford not to do something, should, have to, must. Zhèige-

dìfang bùkěbu-qù. 這個地方不可不去. You have to go to that place.

BÚKÈQI₁ 不客氣 (SV) used to respond to some polite remarks. A: Xièxie. B: Búkèqi. A: 謝謝. B: 不客氣. A: Thanks. B: Don't mention it. A: Duìbuqǐ. B: Búkèqi. A: 對不起. B: 不客氣. A: Excuse me. B: It's nothing. (See: KÈQI 客氣).

BÚLÌ₂ 不利 (SV) unfavorable, disadvantageous. (opp. yǒulì 有利). Zhèiyàngr-bàn duì-wǒmen búlì. 這樣兒辦對我們不利. If it's done this way, it is disadvantageous to us.

BÙLIE₄ 不咧 (P) Peip. that's not much, that isn't anything special. Tā-shì-ge-jǐngchá-bù-lie. 他是個警察不咧. He is a policeman, that's not much.

BÚLÙN₂ 不論 (AD) regardless of, no matter (whether), it doesn't matter (whether). (syn. bùguǎn 不管, wúlùn 無論). Búlùn-ta-'lái-bu-lái, wǒmen-yě-děi-zuò. 不論他來不來, 我們也得作. It does not matter whether he comes or not, we'll have to do it. Búlùn-zěnma-bàn dōu-xíng. 不論怎麼辦都行. Regardless of how it is done, it will be all right.

BÙMĂN₂ 不滿 (SV) (con. bù-mǎnyì 不滿意). unhappy about something, dissatisfied.

Tā-duì-zhèijian-shì, fēichang-bùmǎn. 他對這件事, 非常不滿. He is very unhappy about this matter. (See: MǍN 滿).

BÙMÉN₂ 部門 (N) department, section of an organization. Zhèige-jīguan bùmen-hěn-duō. 這個機關部門很多. There are many departments in this organization.

BÙMIǍN₂ 不免 (AV) cannot help but, cannot avoid. Yàoshi-'zhèi-yangr-bàn, nà-jiu-bumiǎn-guì-yidianr. 要是這樣辦,那就不免貴一點兒. If it is done like this, it cannot help but be a little more expensive.

BÚNÀIFÁN₃ 不耐煩 (SV) can't stand the annoyance, impatient. Wǒ-děng-a-děng-a děng-de-bu-nàifán-le. 我等啊等啊等得不耐煩了. I waited and waited and became impatient. Tā-lǎo-shuō-nèi-yijian-shì, wǒ-zhēn-bunàifán-le. 他老說那一件事,我真不耐煩了. He is always talking about that matter, I really can't stand it anymore.

BÙNÉNGBU₁ 不能不 (AD) cannot help but, have to. Wǒ-bùnéngbu-gěi-ta. 我不能不給他. I cannot help but give it to him.

BÚPÈI₁ 不配 (AV) shouldn't do certain things because they don't fit someone's situation, not qualified, not good enough to have

something. Tā-búpèi-dài-zhèige-biǎo. 他不配帶這個表. He shouldn't be wearing this watch.

'BÙPǏ₃ 布匹 (N) cotton cloth (generic term). (M: zhǒng 種). Zhèr-chūchan-bùpǐ. 這兒出產布匹. Cotton cloth is produced here.

BÙPÍNG₂ 不平 (SV) (1) (con. bu-gōngping 不公平). unfair. Wǒ-juéde zhèijian-shì tā-bànde-bùpíng. 我覺得這件事他辦得不平. I feel that he was unfair in this matter. (2) uneasy, troubled. Tā-xīnli qì-bùpíng. 他心裏氣不平. He feels uneasy (in his heart). (See: PÍNG 平).

BÙQIĀNG₄ 步鎗 (N) infantry rifle. (M: gǎn 桿, zhī 枝).

BÙRÁN₃ 不然 (IV) it is not so. Tā-shi-nènma-shuō, kěshi-wǒ-kàn-bùrán. 他是那麼說,可是我看不然. He said it that way, but I don't think it's so.

BÙRÚ₁ 不如 (TV) (1) be not as good as... Zhèige-bùrú-nèige. 這個不如那個. This is not as good as that. (2) followed by a SV, be not as... as... Jīntian-bùrú-zuótian-shū-fu. 今天不如昨天舒服. Today is not as comfortable as yesterday. (cf:MÉI(YOU) (没有)).
(AD) it would be better. Bùrú-búqù. 不如不去. It would be better not to go.

B

BÚSHI₃ 不是 (N) error, fault. Tā-shuō dou-shì-nǐde-búshi. 他說都是你的不是. He said that it is all your fault.

'BÚSHÌ₁ 不是 (V) (1) be not. Néige-shì-wǒde-'búshì? 那個是我的不是? Is that mine or not? Zhèige-shénma-dou-búshì. 這個甚麼都不是. This isn't anything. (2) it is not the fact that... Wǒ-búshì-'yuànyiqù, shì-'děi-qù. 我不是願意去，是得去. It is not the fact that I want to go, I have to go. (3) not right. Bùzhīdao-zěnmayàngr-hǎo, zuòzheye-'búshì, zhànzhe-ye-'búshì. 不知道怎麼樣兒好，坐着也不是站着也不是. I don't know how to act; sitting is not right, standing is not right either. Zhèige-cài-búshì-wèir. 這個菜不是味兒. The taste of this dish is not right. Wǒ-lái-de-búshì-shíhour. 我來的不是時候. I didn't come at the right time. (4) used to negate a question, no. A: Shì-hóngde-ma? B: 'Búshì. Shì-lǜde. A: 是紅的嗎? B: 不是，是綠的. A: Is it red? B: No, it is green.

(S) (1) (hái)-búshì...ma (還) 不是....嗎 as usual, as always done in the past. Tā-(hái)-búshì-gēn-ni-yào-qiánr-ma? 他(還)不是跟你要錢嗎? Won't he ask for money from you as he did before? (2) (yě) búshì... (也) 不是... used in a question of puzzlement where no answer is expected,... I wonder? Tā-(yě)-búshì-zai-'nǎr-mǎide? 他(也)不是在那兒買的? Where did he buy it, I wonder? Tā-(yě)-búshì-zěnma-zhīdao-de? 他(也)不是怎麼知道了? How did he find out about it, I wonder? (3) búshì... jiùshì... 不是...就是... if it isn't...then it is... Búshì-guāfēng jiùshì-xiàyǔ 不是颳風就是下雨. If it isn't windy, then it's raining. (cf: SHÌ 是).

BÙSHŪFU₂ 不舒服 (SV) not feel well. Tā-yǒu-diǎnr-bushūfu. 他有點兒不舒服. He doesn't feel very well.

BÚSÒNG₃ 不送 (TV) (1) don't bother to accompany me farther (said by the guest at the door of the host's house). (2) excuse me for not accompanying you any farther (said by the host at the door of his house).

BÙTÓNG₂ 不同 (SV) different, not the same. Zhèi-liǎngge-bùtóng. 這兩個不同. These two are not the same.

BÚXIÀNGHUÀ₂ 不像話 (SV) beyond the limits of acceptability, unacceptable. Wǒ-sāndian-zhōng cái-shuì-jiào, tài-búxiànghuà-le. 我三點鐘才睡覺太不像話了. I can't

go to sleep until three o'clock.
This is going too far. Tā-lián-
zhèige-zì dōu-bu-rènshi, zhēn-
búxiànghuà. 他 連 這 個
字 都 不 認 識 真 不
像 話. He doesn't know
even this character, that's really too much.

BÚXÌNG₃ 不 幸 (SV) unfortunate.
(MA) unfortunately.

BÚYÀO₁ 不 要 (AV) don't.(syn.
bié 別). Nǐ-búyào-shuō. 你
不 要 説. Don't say it.
(See: YÀO 要).

BÚYÀOJǏN₁ 不 要 緊 used
to respond to someone's apology.
A: Duìbuqǐ. B: Búyàojǐn. A: 對
不 起. B: 不 要 緊 A: I
am sorry. B: That's all right.

BÙYǏ₄ 不 依 (TV) not let someone get away with something by
continually demanding satisfaction. (See: BÙDÀYING 不 答
應).

BÚYONG₁ 不 用 (AV) no need
to, not necessary to. (syn. béng
甭). Nín-búyòng-gěi-qián. 您
不 用 給 錢. You don't
need to pay. (See: YÒNG 用).

BÚYUÀNYÌ₃ 不 願 意 (AV) feel
offended. Wǒ-yí-quàn-ta bié-hē-
jiǔ, tā-búyuànyì-le. 我 一 勸
他 别 喝 酒, 他 不 願
意 了. As soon as I advised
him not to drink, he felt offended.

BÚZÀIHU₁ 不 在 乎 (TV) (1)
not depend on. Hǎo-rén-huài-
rén buzàihu-yǒu-xuéwen-méi-
xuéwen. 好 人 壞 人 不 在
乎 有 學 問 没 學 問.

Whether a person is good or bad
does not depend on whether he
has knowledge or not. Wǒ-xǐhuan-
zuò cai-zuò, búzàihu-'qián-duō-
shǎo. 我 喜 歡 作 才 作,
不 在 乎 錢 多 少. I'll
do it only when I like to do it, it
doesn't depend on how much
money (is involved). Búzàihu-
yìliǎngkuai-qián. 不 在 乎
一 兩 塊 錢. It doesn't
depend on one or two dollars.
(2) not care about, unconcerned.
Wǒ-búzàihu-qián. 我 不 在
乎 錢. I am unconcerned
about money. Tā-'mǎn-bu-zàihu.
他 滿 不 在 乎. He doesn't
care at all.

BÙZÉNMA₂ 不 怎 麼 (AD) (syn.
búda 不 大). (1) not very. bù-
zěnma-guì 不 怎 麼 貴 not
very expensive. (2) not often, not
much. Tā-bùzěnma-shuō-huà.
他 不 怎 麼 説 話. He
doesn't talk much.

BÙZÉNMAYÀNG₁ 不 怎 麼 樣
(IV) it doesn't amount to much,
nothing special. Tāde-qìchē bù-
zěnmayàng. 他 的 汽 車 不
怎 麼 樣. His car is nothing
special.

BÙZHǍNG₃ 部 長 (N) secretary,
minister, head or chief of a
government department. (M:
wèi 位). Zhāng-bùzhǎng 張
部 長 Secretary Chang.

BÙZHI₂ 布 置 (TV) arrange, put
in order. Tā-zhèngzai-bùzhi-
xīn-fángzi. 他 正 在 布 置
新 房 子. He is in the midst

B

B

of putting the new house in order.
Wǒ-děi-bǎ-gōngshifángde-shìqing
bùzhi-bùzhi. 我 得 把 公 事
房 的 事 情 布 置 布 置.
I must put the office's business
in order.

BÙZHǏ₃ 不 只 (MA) (lit. not
within certain limits) (1) more
than. Zhèige-bùzhǐ-wǔkuai-qián.
這 個 不 只 五 塊 錢.
This is more than five dollars.
(2) not only. Tā-buzhǐ-bu-gěi-
qián, hái-shuō-bu-hǎotīngde-huà.
他 不 只 不 給 錢, 還
說 不 好 聽 的 話. He
not only didn't pay, but also said
some unpleasant things.

BÙZHǏBUJUÉ₁ 不 知 不 覺
(AD) without realizing it, without being conscious of it. Nèi-
yibǎikuai-qián wǒ-buzhǐbujuéde
yòngwán-le. 那 一 百 塊
錢, 我 不 知 不 覺 的
用 完 了. I have used up
that $100 without realizing it.

BÚZHÌYU₁ 不 至 於 (AD) (1)

not... to the extent of..., not...
so far as... Tā-búzhìyu-zìshā-
ba. 他 不 至 於 自 殺 吧.
He won't go so far as to commit
suicide. (2) it cannot be (to a
certain extent). Tā-buzhìyu-
lián-zhèige-dōu-bu-zhīdào. 他
不 至 於 連 這 個 都
不 知 道. It cannot be that
he doesn't even known this. Qìchē-
búzhìyu-nènma-guì. 汽 車 不
至 於 那 麼 貴. The
cars cannot be that expensive.

BÙZI₂ 簿 子 (N) paper bound into
book form, such as booklets,
notebooks, record books, accounting books, etc. (M: běn 本).
diànhuà-bùzi 電 話 簿 子
telephone book. (cf: BĚNZI 本
子).

'BÙZÒU₂ 步 驟 (N) step, procedure (in doing something). Wǒ-
men-děi-ànzhe-'bùzòu-zuò. 我
們 得 按 着 步 驟 作.
We must work according to procedure.

C

CĀ₁ 擦 (TV) action requiring wiping or rubbing such as wipe, rub, polish, erase, apply (ointments), etc. cāca-hàn 擦擦汗 wipe off perspiration. cā-hēibǎn 擦黑板 erase the blackboard. cā-píxié 擦皮鞋 polish shoes. cā-dianr-tóuyóu 擦點兒頭油 put on some hair oil. fig. pass close by (almost touching). Feījǐ-cāzhe-fǎng fēiguoqu-le. 飛機擦着房飛過去了. The airplane flew past almost touching the roof (of the house).

CĀI₁ 猜 (TV) guess. Nǐ-cāi ta-shuō-shénma? 你猜他說甚麼? Guess what he said? Cāicai-kàn. 猜猜看. Guess and see. Wǒ-cāibuzháo. 我猜不着. I cannot guess it.

CÁI₃ 裁 (TV) (1) cut something flat in the form of a sheet. cái-zhǐ 裁紙 cut paper. cái-yīshang 裁衣裳 cut materials for making clothes. (2) lay off, cut down personnel or offices in an organization. cáile-sānge-rén 裁了三個人 lay off three persons. Zhèngfǔ cáile-hǎoxiē-jīguan. 政府裁了好些機關 The government eliminated quite a few offices.

CÁI₄ 才 (N) talent, gift (endowment of special powers and faculties). Tā-yǒu-cái, kěshì -bu-ai-niàn-shū. 他有才,可是不愛念書. He has the talent, but doesn't like to study.

CÁI₁ 才 (AD) (1) just (an action completed or started a moment ago). (syn. gāng 剛). Wǒ-'cái-lái. 我才來. I just came (a moment ago). Wǒmen-'cái-chī. 我們才吃. We just started eating. Tā-'cái-zuòxia, jiu-yào-zǒu. 他才坐下,就要走. He just sat down, now he wants to leave. (2) followed by a NU-M expression or a period of time, indicates less than what was expected, only. (syn. gāng 剛). Tā-xuéle-cái-'bànnián. 他學了才半年. He has studied only half a year. Xiànzài cái-'bādiǎn-zhōng, tài-zǎo. 現在才八點鐘太早. Now it is only eight o'clock, it's too early. (cf: DŌU 都).(3) preceded by an expression of time or condition, not until, not unless, then and only then. Tā-'jiǔdiǎn-zhōng cai-láide. 他九點鐘才來的. He didn't come until nine o'clock. Tā-zǒule-'liǎngge-zhōngtóu cai-dào. 他走了兩個鐘頭才到.

C

He didn't arrive until he had traveled for two hours. 'Tā-shuō-xíng cai-xíng. 他說行才行. It won't do unless he says so. Zhǐyǒu-zhèiyàngr-bàn cai-bàndeliǎo. 只有這樣辦才辦的了. It cannot be done unless it is done this way. Chúfēi-nǐ-gěi-wǒ-qián wǒ-cai-néng-qù. 除非你給我錢我才能去. I cannot go unless you give me money. (cf: ZÀI 再). (4) indicates the contradiction of a previous statement by stressing the expression that comes before cái 才. A: Nǐ-guǎn-ma? B: 'Wǒ-cai-bu-guǎn-ne. A: 你管嗎? B: 我才不管呢. A: Do you take care of it? B: Not me, I don't. A: Wǒ-xiǎng tā-lái. B: Tā-'lái cai-guài-ne. A: 我想他來. B: 他來才怪呢. A: I think he'll come. B: It'll be awfully strange if he comes.

CĂI₂ 踩 (TV) step on, press down (with the foot). Yòng-jiǎo 'cǎi-yicǎi. 用腳踩一踩. Press it down a little with your foot. Nǐ-'cǎile-wǒde-'jiǎo-le. 你踩了我的腳了. You stepped on my foot.

CÀI₁ 菜 (1) vegetables. qíngcài 青菜 green vegetables. zhòng-cài 種菜 grow vegetables. (2) groceries, provisions (other than staples such as rice, flour, bread, etc.). Wǒ-qu-mǎi-cài-qu. 我去買菜去. I am going to buy groceries. (3) dish (food) to be eaten in small portions to accompany the staple foods to make the meal more palatable and to enhance the appetite. Tā-zuò-de-cài hǎochī. 他作的菜好吃. The dishes he cooked are delicious. Wǒ-bu-huì-diǎn-cài. 我不會點菜. I don't know how to order (in a restaurant).

CÁICHAN₂ 財產 (N) property (of considerable value).

CÀIDĀNR₂ 菜單兒 (N) menu (M: zhāng 張).

CÁIFÁ₅ 財閥 (N) plutocrat.

CÁIFENG₃ 裁縫 (N) tailor.

CÁIJŪN₃ 裁軍 (IV) disarm (of nations), reduce the size of armed forces. (N) disarmament.

CÁILIAO₁ 材料 (N) (1) materials. (2) data.

'CÁINÉNG₄ 才能 (N) gifted ability.

CÁIPÀN₄ 裁判 (TV) judge, render a decision, referee.

CÀIPIÀO₃ 彩票 (N) lottery ticket. (M: zhāng 張).

'CǍIQǓ₃ 採取 (TV) selectively adopt, take material things as well as an attitude, a position, method, etc. Tā-wèi-shénma cǎiqǔ-'zhèizhong-tàidu? 他為甚麼採取這種態度? Why has he adopted this kind of attitude?

CǍISÈ₄ 彩色 (B) colorful, colored. cǎisè-diànyǐngr 彩色電影兒 colored movie.

'CĀIXIĂNG₂ 猜 想 (TV) surmise, presume, guess, suspect. Wǒ-'cāixiǎng ta-bu-yuànyi-qù. 我 猜 想 他 不 願 意 去. I suspect that he doesn't want to go.

'CĂIYÒNG₃ 採 用 (TV)selectively apply (principles, ideas, methods, etc.). Zhèimén-gōng-ke, xiānsheng-cǎiyòng-něiben-shū? 這 門 功 課, 先 生 採 用 那 本 書? Which book did the teacher select to be used in this course?

'CĂIZHÈNG₃ 財 政 (N) (1) finance (management of monetary affairs). cáizhèngbù 財 政 部 treasury department. (2) financial situation, financial position.

CÁIZHU₃ 財 主 (N) wealthy person.

CÁN₅ 蠶 (N) silk worm. (M: tiáo 條).

CĂN₂ 慘 (SV) (1) tragic. Tāmende-fángzi-zháo-huǒ, sānge-háizi-dou-shāosi-le, zhēn-cǎn. 他 們 的 房 子 着 火, 三 個 孩 子 都 燒 死 了, 真 慘. Their house caught fire and all three children died, it was really tragic. (2) cruel. Tā-men-bǎ-ta-dǎcheng zhèiyangr, nǐ-kàn duó-cǎn. 他 們 把 他 打 成 這 樣 兒. 你 看 多 慘. They beat him like this, look how cruel it is. (3) used by students to indicate something bad or poor. Wǒde-lìshǐ kǎode-cǎnjíle. 我 的 歷

史 考 得 慘 極 了. My history test was really terrible.

CĂN' ÀN₄ 慘 案 (N) tragic event.

CÁNFEI₃ 殘 廢 (IV) disable,cripple. Tā-cánfei-le. 他 殘 廢 了. He became cripped. (N) disabled or cripped person. Tā-shì-yige-cánfei. 他 是 一 個 殘 廢. He is a disabled person.

CĀNG₄ 艙 (N) (1) hold (in a ship). (2) ship's cabin. tóuděng-cāng 頭 等 艙 first class cabin.

CÁNG₃ 藏 (TV) (1) hide. Tā-cáng-qilai-le. 他 藏 起 來 了. He hid himself. (2) collect and keep. Tā-cáng-shū hen-duō. 他 藏 書 很 多. He collects a lot of books.

CÁNGKÙ₃ 倉 庫 (N) any large storage facility, such as warehouse, storehouse, etc.

CĀNGUĀN₂ 參 觀 (TV) visit (a public place as an observer or a spectator). cānguān-xuéxiào 參 觀 學 校 visit a school.

CĀNGYING₃ 蒼 蠅 (N) common housefly.

CĀNJIĀ₂ 參 加 (TV) participate in.

CĀNKĂO₂ 參 考 (TV) refer, use something to compare. Wǒmen-kànkan-byéren-zěnma-zuò, 'cān-kao-cānkao. 我 們 看 看 別 人 怎 麼 作. 參 考 參 考. Let's see how the others do it and compare it.

CĀNKAOSHŪ₃ 參 考 書 (N) reference book. (M: běn 本).

'CÁNKÙ₃ 殘 酷 (SV) cruel, bru-

C

C

tal (implying tyrannical extremity).

(See: 'CÁNRĚN 殘 忍).

CÁNKUI₂ 慚 愧 (SV) ashamed, embarrassed. Nín-shuō-wo-zuòde-hǎo, wǒ-juéde-hěn-cánkui. 您 説 我 作 的 好, 我 覺 得 很 慚 愧. When you said that I did it well, I felt very embarrassed.

'CÁNRĚN₂ 殘 忍 (SV) cruel, brutal (implying cruelty without restraint).

(See: CÁNKÙ 殘 酷).

CĀNTĪNG₃ 餐 廳 (N) dining room. (M: jiān 間).

CĀNYÌYUÁN₄ 參 議 員 (N) senator.

CĂO₁ 草 (N) (1) grass, straw, hay. cǎodì 草 地 grass land or lawn.

CĂO₃ 草 (B) (1) rough (something done without caring to details). liǎocǎo 了 草 not neat (in external appearance). cǎocǎo-liǎo-shì 草 草 了 事 finish up roughly (without bothering about details). cǎogǎor 草 稿 兒 rough draft. (2) (con. cǎogǎor 草 稿 兒) rough draft. gǐ-cǎo 起 草 make the rough draft.

CĂO₂ 草 (SV) cursively written. cǎozì 草 字 cursive writing. Zhèixiē-xì tài-cǎo, wǒ-bu-rèn-shi. 這 些 字 太 草, 我 不 認 識. These words are too cursively written, I cannot read them.

CĂO'ÀN₃ 草 案 (N) temporary draft, first draft of an official document.

CĀOCHǍNG₂ 操 場 (N) athletic field, drill field.

CĂOLIÀO₅ 草 料 (N) hay (for feeding animals), fodder.

CĂOMÀOR₂ 草 帽 兒 (N) straw hat. (M: dǐng 頂).

CÁOR₄ 槽 兒 (N) (1) groove. (M: dào 道). Chuānghu chū-'cáor-le, suóyi-'kāibukāi. 窗 户 出 槽 兒 了, 所 以 開 不 開 . The window is out of its groove, so it cannot be opened. (2) space or slot into which something is fitted.

CǍOXIÉ₃ 草 鞋 (N) straw sandals. (M: shuāng 雙).

'CĀOZÒNG₂ 操 縱 (TV) manipulate (control by artful management of influential factors). Xué-xiàode-zhèngce, jiu-shi ji'gè-ren-'cāozòng. 學 校 的 政 策, 就 是 幾 個 人 操 縱 . The policies of the school are manipulated by just a few people.

CÈLIÁNG₂ 測 量 (TV) survey (in order to determine position, dimensions, shape, etc. of land).

CÉNG₂ 層 (M) (1) story, floor (of a building). 'liǎngcéng-lóu 兩 層 樓 two stories (of a building). di'èrcéng 第 二 層 second floor. (2) layer, coat (of paint). qiāncénggāo 千 層 糕 thousand layer cake (a Chinese pastry). (3) phase, aspect. 'hái-yǒu-yicéng 還 有 一 層 (lit. There is still another aspect) furthermore. Zhèi-yicéng, wǒ-méi-xiǎngdào. 這 一 層, 我

没想到. I didn't think about this aspect of it.

CÈNG₃ 蹭 (TV) (1) brush (act of one surface in moving contact with another). Tāde-qìchē-gēn-wŏde-cèngshang-le. 他的汽車跟我的蹭上了. His car sideswiped mine. Tā-de-yīshang-tài-cháng, cèng-dì-le. 他的衣裳太長, 蹭地了. Her clothes are too long, they drag on the floor. (2) rub, polish a surface in deliberate strokes. Zhèi-pízi zhēn-hăo. Shàng-dianr-yóu, yí-cèng-jiu-liàng. 這皮子真好上點兒油一蹭就亮. This leather is really good. With a little polish and a little rubbing it shines. (3) remove or transfer some substance from one surface to another, by brushing contact. Wŏ-zài-chēfáng cèngle-yishēn-yóu. 我在車房蹭了一身油. I was in the garage and got grease (through brushing contact) all over me. Nĭ-bă-xié-shangde-ní cènggānjing-le zai-jìnlai. 你把鞋上的泥, 蹭乾淨了再進來. Rub off the mud on your shoes and then come in. (4) walk, travel or do something very slowly. Kuài-diănr-zuò, bié-cèng. 快點兒作, 別蹭. Do it faster, don't take so long.

CÉNG(JING)...GUO₃ 曾 (經)... 過 (S) have experienced. Wŏ-céng(jing)-qùguo-yici. 我曾

(經) 去過一次. (lit. I have experienced going once.) I have been there once.

CÈSUŎ₂ 厠所 (N) outhouse, privy, watercloset.

CÈZI₂ 冊子 (N) booklet, album. (M: bĕn 本).

CHĀ₁ 插 (TV) insert. Bă-huār chāzai-píngzi-litou. 把花兒插在瓶子裏頭. Put the flowers in the vase. Tāde-tóufa-shang chāzhe-yiduŏ-huār. 他的頭髮上插着一朵花兒. She wears a flower in her hair.

CHÁ₁ 茶 (N) tea. (M: wăn 碗, hú 壺). Zhèige-dìfang chăn-chá. 這個地方產茶. Tea is produced here. Qĭng-nĭ-gĕi-wŏ-dào-wăn-chá. 請你給我倒碗茶. Please pour me a cup of tea.

CHÁ₁ 查 (TV) (1) investigate (a case at law). Tāmen-zhèngzai-'chá-zhèige-'shì-ne. 我們正在查這個事呢. They are investigating this case. (2) inspect, examine, check. Tā-men-mĕige-yuè chá-yicì-zhàng. 他們每個月查一次賬. They audit accounts every month. Jìn-'mén-de-shí-hou, yŏu-rén-chá-piào. 進門的時候, 有人查票. When you go in, someone will check your ticket. (3) look up information in a dictionary, directory, reference book, etc. Nĭ-huì-chá-zìdiăn-ma? 你會查字典嗎? Do you know

C

how to look up characters in a dictionary? Nǐ-'cháchá-diǎnhuà-'běnzi. 你查查電話本子. (You) look it up in the telephone directory.

CHÀ₄ 岔 (TV) go into a different course, in speech, train of thought or activity. Wǒ-yòng-'biéde-huà chàkai-le. 我用別的話岔開了. I used other words to change the subject.

CHÀ₁ 差 (TV) (1) differ by. Zhèi-liǎngge chàde-hěn-yuǎn. 這兩個差的很遠. (lit. These two differ very far.) These two are very different. Zhèige-bǐ gen-'nèige-bǐ chà-wǔkuai-qián. 這個筆跟那個筆差五塊錢. (lit. This pen and that pen differ by five dollars.) There is a difference of five dollars between the price of this pen and that. Dàzhì bu-chà. 大致不差. (lit. Generally not different from the ordinary.) Generally it is all right. (2) short of. Wǒmen-shénma-dou-yǒu-le, jiu-chà-qián. 我們甚麼都有了就差錢. We have everything except that we are short of money. Cháli chà-dianr-táng. 茶裏差點兒糖. (lit. The tea is short of a little sugar.) The tea needs more sugar. (cf: DUǍN 短, QUĒ 缺, SHǍO 少). (3) lack a certain amount from a specified whole. Chà-shífēn-liǎngdiǎn. 差十分兩點. Ten minutes of

two. Chà-yíkuai-qián yi'bǎikuai-qián. 差一塊錢一百塊錢. It lacks one dollar to be one hundred dollars. (4) owe. Wǒ-chà-ta-wǔkuai-qián. 我差他五塊錢. I owe him five dollars.

(SV) inferior, poor in quality. Cáiliao-tài-chà. 材料太差. The material is too poor. Zhèige-bucuò, nèige-jiu-chà-le. 這個不錯,那個就差了. This is not bad, the other one is no good.

CHÀ-BĀN₃ 插班 (VO) (lit. insert into a class) enter the appropriate grade or level in a school, other than the first.

CHÁBĒI₂ 茶杯 (N) teacup.

CHÀBIE₃ 差別 (N) difference. Méiyou-chābie. 沒有差別. There is no difference.

CHÀBUDUŌ₁ 差不多 (RV) (1) doesn't differ much, almost the same. (con. chàbuduō-yíyàng 差不多一樣). Zhèi-liǎngge chàbuduō (yíyàng). 這兩個差不多一樣. These two are almost the same. (2) not bad, almost all right (implies acceptability without great enthusiasm). A: Nèrde-tiānqi-hǎo-bu-hǎo? B: Chàbuduō. A: 那兒的天氣好不好? B: 差不多. A: Is the weather good there? B: Not bad. (3) almost at the desired point, just about. A: Fàn-zěnma-yàng? B: Chàbuduō-le. A: 飯怎麼樣? B: 差不多了. A:

How about the food? B: Almost ready.

(AD) almost, about. Chàbuduō-shíkuai-qián. 差 不 多 十 塊 錢 . Almost ten dollars. Xìnzhǐ chàbuduō-kuai-yòngwán-le.信紙差不多快用完了 . The writing paper is almost all used up.

CHÁCHÍ₅ 茶 匙 (N) teaspoon. (M: bǎ 把).

CHÀDÀO₄ 盆 道 (N) (l) branch road, side road. (M: tiáo 條). (2) wrong course of action.

CHÁDIǍN₁ 茶 點 (N)(lit. tea and cake) refreshments. (M: fènr 份).

CHÀ(YI)DIANR₁ 差 (一) 點 兒 (SV) (lit. lack a little). infe-rior. Zhèige-chà(yi)dianr. 這 個差 (一) 點 兒 . This one is not as good (as it should be).

CHÀ(YI)DIÀNR₁ 差 (一) 點 兒 (MA) (1) almost. (syn. 'jǐ(ji)hū 幾 (幾) 乎).Wǒ-chà(yi)diǎnr-gàosong-ta. 我 差 (一) 點 兒告 訴 他 . I almost told him. Tā-chà(yi)diǎnr-bu-géi-wo. 他差 (一) 點 兒 不 給 我 . He almost didn't give it to me. Wǒ-chà(yi)diǎnr láibuliǎo. 我 差 (一) 點 兒 來 不 了 . I almost couldn't come. (2) used with an unstressed méi 沒 , the negative meaning of méi 沒 , is lost, almost. Wǒ chà(yi)diǎnr mei-gàosong-ta. 我差 (一) 點 兒 没 告 訴 他 . I almost told him. Wǒ-chà(yi)diǎnr mei-'shuōchulai.我 差 (一) 點 兒 没 説 出

來 . I almost said it. (3) used with a stressed méi 沒 , the negative meaning of méi 沒 remains. Wǒ-chà(yi)diǎnr 'méi-shuōchu'lái.我 差 (一) 點 兒 没 説 出 來 . I almost didn't say it.

CHÁFÁNG₃ 茶 房 (N) waiter in a teahouse or restaurant, one whose job is mainly to serve tea in railroad trains,hotels and other places of public accomoda-tion).

CHÁFÉNG₅ 查 封 (TV) seal a property, to prevent fraudulent removal of contents or evidences, as part of a judicial investigation.

CHÁGUǍNR₁ 茶 館 兒 (N) tea house. (M: jiā 家).

CHÁHÚ₂ 茶 壺 (N) teapot. (M: bǎ 把).

CHÁHUA₅ 茶 花 (N) camellia. (M: duǒ 朶 , kē 棵).

CHAHUAHUI₁ 茶 話 會 (N) tea party.

CHĀI 拆 (TV) (1) take something apart, disassemble, demolish. Tāmen-bǎ-fángzi-chāile. 他 們 把 房 子 拆 了 . They demolished the house. (2)open a sealed letter or package. Xìn-gāng-lái, hái-méi-chāi-ne. 信 剛 來 , 還 没 拆 呢. The letters have just arrived and have not yet been opened.

CHÁIHUO₃ 柴 火 (N) firewood, kindling.

CHÁISHÌ₃ 差 事 (N) position, job. Tā-bǎ-chāishi diū-le. 他 把 差 事 丢 了 . He lost his

C

job.

CHĀI-TÁI₃ 拆台 (VO) (1) tear down a stage. (2) fig. upset a person's position by a deliberate or accidental act, pull the rug out from under someone. Nǐ-zhè-bú shi-chāi-wǒde-tái-ma? 你 這 不 是 拆 我 的 台 嗎 ? Aren't you pulling the rug out from under me?

CHÀ-JÌN₃ 差勁 (VO) (1) lack strength. Zhèige-jiǔ 'dōu-hǎo, jiushi-chà-diǎnr-jìn. 這 個 酒 都 好，就 是 差 點 兒 勁 . Everything about this wine is good, except that it lacks strength. (2) Peip. lack of character (describing a person). Zhèige-rén zhēn-chà-jìn. 這 個 人 真 差 勁 . This person really lacks character.

CHĀN₃ 攙 (TV) support, uphold a person by the arm, like supporting a cripple, a debilitated person, etc. Nǐ-chānzhe-lǎo-tàitai. 你 攙 着 老 太 太 .(You) hold the old lady's arm.

CHĀN₃ 攙 (TV) mix in, mix together. Bié-bǎ-zhèixiē-shū dou-chānzai-yikuàir. 别 把 這 些 書 都 攙 在 一 塊 兒 . Don't mix all these books together. Zhèige-jiúli chānle-hěn-duō-shuǐ. 這 個 酒 裏 攙 了 很 多 水 . There is a lot of water mixed in this wine.

CHÁN₃ 纏 (TV) (1) wrap around. Tāde-shǒu yòng-bù-chánshangle. 他 的 手 用 布 纏 上 了 . His hand is wrapped with a bandage. fig. Tā-ràng-nèige-nǚren gei-chánzhule. 他 讓 那 個 女 人 給 纏 住 了 . He is wrapped around that girl's finger. (2) roll up (as a string). Bǎ-xiàn cháncheng-yí-ge-qiú. 把 線 纏 成 一 個 球 . Roll the string up into a ball. (3) bother, annoy (people constantly). 'Zhèige-háizi chán-rén. 這 個 孩 子 纏 人 . This child bothers people.

CHÁN₄ 饞 (SV) crave for or indulge in oral pleasures, such as eating only savory food for pleasure of the mouth rather than sustenance, like a child indulging in candy. 'Zhèige-rén zhēn-chán, guāng-chī-ròu, bu-chī-fàn. 這 個 人 真 饞，光 吃 肉 不 吃 飯 . This person is given to indulgence of his taste. He eats only meat, but not rice.

CHÀN₃ 顫 (SV) quiver, shake, tremble. Tā-hěn-jǐnzhang, shǒu-zhi-chàn. 他 很 緊 張，手 直 顫 . He is very tense, his hands keep shaking. Tā-shuō-'huà-de-shíhou, shēngyin yǒu-yi-diǎnr-chàn. 他 說 話 的 時 候 聲 音 有 一 點 兒 顫 . When he talks, his voice quivers a little.

'CHÀNÀ₅ 剎那 (M) split-second, in a flash.

CHǍNDÌ₄ 產地 (N) place of production or origin.

CHÁNG₁ 嚐 (TV) taste. Nǐ-cháng-chang-zhèige-yú. 你 嚐 嚐 這 個 魚 . Taste this fish.

Wŏ-chángbuchūlái shì-shénma-wèir. 我 嚐 不 出 來 是 甚 麼 味. I cannot make out (by tasting) what flavor it is.

CHÁNG₁ 長 (SV) long (in extent or duration). (opp. duăn 短). Shí-hou-tài-cháng le. 時 候 太 長 了. The time is too long. 'Zhuōzi-hĕn-cháng. 桌 子 很 長. The tables are very long. Tiān-cháng-le. 天 長 了. The days are longer now. Tā-men-suírán jiéhūn-le, kĕshi-wŏ-kàn chángbuliăo. 他 們 雖 然 結 婚 了, 可 是 我 看 長 不 了. Although they are married, I don't think it will last long. Wŏmen-dei-wàng-'cháng-li-kàn, bu-néng-jiù-kàn-xiànzài. 我 們 得 往 長 裏 看, 不 能 就 看 現 在. We have to look at it for the long run, not just for now. Nèige-wūzi yŏu-'shíchĭ-cháng. 那 個 屋 子 有 十 尺 長. That room is about ten feet long.

(N) length. Nèige-wūzi-de-cháng shì-'shíchĭ. 那 個 屋 子 的 長 是 十 尺. The length of that room is ten feet.

(B) good point or strong point, a good quality. (opp. duăn 短). chángchu 長 處 strong point. Gè-yŏu-suŏ-cháng. 各 有 所 長. Each one has his own good points.

CHÁNG₁ 常 (AD) (1) often. Tā-'cháng-lái. 他 常 來. He comes often. Tā-'cháng-ài-zhèiyàngr-shuō. 他 常 愛 這

樣 兒 說. He likes to say this very often. Wŏ-bù-cháng-chūqu. 我 不 常 出 去. I don't go out often. (cf: 'CHÁNG-CHÁNG 常 常). (2) always. Dōngxià-cháng-qīng. 冬 夏 常 青. Winter or summer, it is always green. Chī'kuīde cháng-'zài. 吃 虧 的 常 在. The one who can take a loss will always be around.

(B) regular, usual. chánghuì 常 會 regular meeting.

CHĂNG₃ 場 see CHĂNG 場.

CHĂNG₄ 廠 (N) factory. Tā-xiăng-bàn-yíge-chăng. 他 想 辦 一 個 廠. He wants to establish a factory.

CHĂNG₃ 場 or CHÁNG 場 (M) (1) for a performance of a play, opera, movie, etc. Kàn-yichăng-diànyĭngr. 看 一 場 電 影 兒. See a movie. (2) for a contest, real or sporting. dă-yichăng-guānsi 打 一 場 官 司 bring a lawsuit. dă-yichăng-qiú 打 一 場 球 play a game of ball. dă-yichăng-pái 打 一 場 牌 play a game of cards. (3) for an event, natural or human, possessing unpredictable or dramatic qualities. 'bìngle-yichăng 病 了 一 場 or déle-yichăng-bìng 得 了 一 場 病 be sick once. zuò-yichăng-mèng 作 一 場 夢 have a dream. zuò-yichăng-quān 作 一 場 官 serve as an official. zháo-yichăng-huŏ 着 一 場 火 have a fire. (4) act of an opera or play. Dìyī-chăng. 第一 場 . The first act:

CHĂNG₃ 場 (-B) (1) an open space, field, or court. kōngchăng 空 場 a vacant lot. yùndòngchăng 運動場 athletic field. qiú-chăng 球場 ball park. (2) an activity or a circle of activities. guānchăng 官場 official or political circle. shìchăng 市 場 the market (activity). zài-chăng 在場 to be present during an activity. dāngchăng 當 場 right at or during the activity.

CHĂNG₁ 唱 (TV) (1) sing (songs, operas etc.). Tā-ài-chàng-gēr. 他愛唱歌兒. He likes to sing. Nǐ-chàng-yíduànr-xì-ba. 你唱一段兒戲吧. Sing an aria from an opera. (2) call out the ballots. 'Shéi-chàng-piào? 誰唱票? Who will call out the ballots?

CHÁNGCHANG₁ 常常 (AD) often, frequently. Wǒ-chángchang-gēn-ta-xué. 我常常跟他學. I learn from him very often.

CHÁNGCHÉNG₃ 長城 (N) (con. Wànlǐ-chángchéng 萬里長 城). the Great Wall of China.

CHÁNGCHONG₅ 長蟲 (N) snake. (M: tiáo 條).

CHÁNGCHU₂ 長處 (N) good point, strong point, a good quality. (M: diǎn 點). Tā-yǒu-ji-diǎn-chángchu. 他有幾點 長處. He has several good points.

CHÁNGCHŪN₃ 長春 (PW) Ch'ang-

ch'un (capital of Kirin province).

CHÁNGDUĂN₂ 長短 (N) (1) length. Nèige-zhuōzi chángduǎn 'duó-cháng? 那個桌子長短 多長? What is the length of that table? (2) unfortunate happening. Yàoshì-tā-yǒu-ge-cháng-duǎn, zěnma-bàn? 要是他 有個長短,怎麼辦? If something unfortunate happens to him, what can be done?

CHÁNGFĀNGR₅ 長方兒 (N) rectangle.

CHÁNGGŌNG₅ 長工 (N) (1) long-term laborious job. Tā-dǎ-chánggong. 他打長工. He has a long-term job. (2) laborer who is engaged in a long-term job in agriculture. Tā-shì-wǒmende-chánggōng. 他是我 們的長工. He is our worker.

CHĂNGJIĀ₄ 廠家 (N) factory (referring to the establishment).

CHÁNGJIĀNG₁ 長江 (N) Yangtze River.

CHÁNGJIŬ₄ 長久 (SV) for a long time.

CHĂNGKĀIR₄ 敞開兒 (AD) Peip. without restriction. Tā-chǎngkāir-wánr. 他敞開兒 玩兒. He plays as much as he wants.

CHÀNGKUAI₄ 暢快 (SV) happy (implies freedom from restraint).

CHĂNGLIANG₅ 敞亮 (SV) spacious and bright (of a room).

CHĂNGMIAN₃ 場面 (N) (1) stage setting (including the set, costumes, props, music and sup-

porting cast). Táishangde-chǎng-
mian hěn-jīngcai. 台 上 的 場
面 很 精彩 . The stage
setting is wonderful. (2) act in a
grandiose or spectacular manner,
mainly for appearance, either by
a person or an organization. Tā-
qǐng-kè-de-shíhou, chǎngmian-
hěn-dà. 他 請 客 的 時 候
場 面 很 大 . When he
gives a party, he does it in a
spectacular manner.

CHÀNGPIĀNR₁ 唱 片 兒 (N)
phonograph record. (M: zhāng 張).

CHÁNGQĪ₃ 長 期 (B-) long-term.
(opp. duǎnqī 短期).

CHÁNGSHĀ₃ 長 沙 (PW) Ch'ang-
sha (capital of Hunan province).

CHÁNGSHÌ₂ 常 識 (N) general
knowledge that everyone should
have. 'Zhèige-rén méi-yǒu-
'chángshì. 這 個 人 沒 有
常 識. This man has very little
general knowledge. Lián-'shísuì-
de-háizi bǐ-tā-zhīdao-de-'chángshì dou-duō. 連 十 歲 的
孩 子 比 他 知 道 的
常 識 都 多.A ten year old
child has more general knowledge than he does.

CHÁNGTÚ₂ 長 途 (N) long-distance. chángtú-diànhuà 長 途
電 話 long-distance telephone
call. chángtú-qìchē 長 途 汽
車 long-distance bus.

CHÁNGYÒNG₂ 常 用 (IV) use
frequently. chángyòngzì 常 用
字 frequently used characters.
Zhèiju-huà bu-chángyòng. 這 句

話 不 常 用 . This sentence
isn't frequently used.

'CHÁNGYUÀN₅ 場 院 (N) a big
open yard, threshing court.

CHÁNGZI₃ 腸 子 (N) (1) intes-
tines. (M: tiáo 條 , gēn 根).
(2) sausage.

CHǍNLIÀNG₄ 產 量 (N) quantity
(of production).

CHǍNSHĒNG₂ 產 生 (TV) cause
to grow out, make arise (in the
sense of to spring forth, appear,
issue or originate), create (certain reactions). Yīnwei-rénkǒu-
tài-duō, suóyi-'chǎnshēngle-hen-
duō-'wènti. 因 為 人 口 太
多 所 以 產 生 了 很
多 問 題.Because of our
population, many problems have
arisen.

CHǍNYE₁ 產 業 (N) property.

CHǍNZI₃ 鏟 子 (N) spade, shovel.
(M: bǎ 把).

CHĀO₁ 抄 (TV) copy in writing or
drawing. Nǐ-bǎ-tāde-diànhuà-
hàomǎr chāoxialaile-ma? 你 把
他 的 電 話 號 碼 兒
抄 下 來 了 嗎? Have
you copied down his telephone
number?

CHÁO₃ 潮 (N) tide. zhǎng-cháo
長 潮 rising tide. tuì-cháo
退 潮 receding tide.
(SV) damp. Zhèi-wūzi hěn-cháo.
這 屋 子 很 潮.This room
is very damp.

CHÁO₂ 朝 (TV) face toward. Nèige
'pùzi cháo 'nán. 那 個 鋪 子
朝 南.That store faces south.

C

C

CHÁO₂ 朝 (N) imperial or royal court. shàng-cháo 上朝 attend the imperial court. (M) dynasty. 'Něi-cháo? 那朝? Which dynasty?

CHÁO₂ 吵 (SV) noisy. Háizimen tài-chǎo. 孩子們太吵. The children are too noisy. (TV) (1) make noise. Háizi-bǎ-wo-chǎoxǐng-le. 孩子把我吵醒了. The children made a lot of noise and woke me up. (2) quarrel, argue (noisily). Bié-gēn-wo-chǎo. 別跟我吵. Don't quarrel with me.

CHǍO₁ 炒 (TV) sauté in very hot fat or roast in a pan while continuously turning over and mixing the ingredients. chǎo-cài 炒菜 fry vegetables or fried vegetables. chǎo-fàn 炒飯 fry rice or fried rice. chǎo-huāshēng 炒花生 roast peanuts or roasted peanuts.

'CHĀOBĚN₃ 抄本 (N) copy, facsimile duplication.

'CHÁODÀI₂ 朝代 (N) dynasty (period).

CHĀO'É₄ 超額 (AD) over and above the assigned quota. chāo'é-wánchéng 超額完成 finished over and above the assigned quota.

CHĀOGUÒ₃ 超過 (TV) surpass, exceed.

CHǍO-JIÀ₂ 吵架 (VO) quarrel, engage in a verbal brawl. Wǒmen-méi-chǎoguo-jià. 我們沒吵過架. We have never quarreled. (cf: CHǍO-ZUǏ 吵嘴).

CHĀO-JÌNR₂ 抄近兒 (VO) lit.

or fig. take a short cut. (opp. rào-yuǎnr 繞遠兒). Niàn-shū bu-néng-chāo-jìnr. 念書不能抄近兒. You cannot take a short cut in studying.

'CHÁOLIÚ₂ 潮流 (N) trend of changes. Wǒ-gēnbushàng-'cháoliú. 我跟不上潮流. I cannot catch up with the trend.

CHǍONÀO₄ 吵鬧 (TV) (1) quarrel. (2) make noise.

CHĀOPIÀO₁ 鈔票 (N) paper money, bank note. (M: zhāng 張). Měiguo-chāopiào dou-shi-zhèng'fǔ-fāxíngde. 美國鈔票都是政府發行的. All American paper money is issued by the government.

CHÁOQÌ₃ 潮氣 (N) dampness.

CHǍORANG₄ 吵嚷 (TV) shout, yell.

CHÁOSHI₃ 潮濕 (SV) damp. (opp. gānzào 乾燥).

CHÁOXIĀN₁ 朝鮮 (PW) Korea (used for North Korea). (cf: HÁNGUO 韓國

CHÁOXIÀO₅ 嘲笑 (TV) laugh jeeringly at.

CHĀOXIĚ₃ 抄寫 (TV) copy in writing. Shéi-tì-nǐ-chāoxiě? 誰替你抄寫? Who will copy it for you?

CHǍO-ZUǏ₃ 吵嘴 (VO) (lit. quarrel with mouth) quarrel. (cf: CHǍO-JIÀ 吵架).

CHÁQIAN₂ 茶錢 (N) (1) payment for tea (at a teahouse). (2) (lit. tea money) tips, gratuities.

CHÁR₄ 碴兒 (N) (1) fragment.

bōlichár 玻璃碴兒 glass fragments. wănchár 碗碴兒 fragments of a bowl. tóufachár 頭髮碴兒 fragments (clippings) of hair. (2) flaw on glassware or pottery. Zhèige-píngzi yŏu-chár. 這個瓶子有碴兒.This vase has flaws. (3) flaw in inter-personal relationship caused by some incident. Tāmen-yŏu-chár. 他們有碴兒. There is some flaw in their relationship. (4) faults of a person. Nĭ-bié-zhăo-wŏde-chár. 你別找我的碴兒. Don't find faults in me. (5) relevant material that fits in a conversation. Tā-shuō-huà wŏ-méi-dā-chár. 他説話我沒答碴兒. When he spoke about it, I didn't speak a word (connected with what he said). Tā-zuótian-shuō-de gen-jīntian shuō-de duìbushang-chár. 他昨天説的跟今天説的對不上碴兒. What he said yesterday and what he said today don't correlate.

CHĀTÚ₂ 插圖 (N) illustrations in a book.

CHÁWĂN₁ 茶碗 (N) teacup.

CHÁYÈ₁ 茶葉 (N) processed tea leaves.

'CHĀYÌ₅ 差異 (N) difference.

CHÀYÌ₃ 詫異 (SV) surprised, astonished. Tā-tīngjian-zhèige-huà juéde-hen-chàyi. 他聽見這個話覺得很詫異. When he heard this he was very surprised.

CHĀZI₁ 义子 (N) (1) fork. (M: bă 把). (2) an X to indicate a check mark. dă-chāzi 打义子 draw a check mark.

CHÀZI₃ 岔子 (N) accident, mishap. chū-chàzi 出岔子 have an accident.

CHĀ-ZUĬ₂ 插嘴 (VO) interject. Wŏmen-shuō-huà tā-chāle-yiju-zuĭ. 我們説話, 他插了一句嘴. He interjected his comments into our conversation.

CHĒ₁ 車 (N) wheeled vehicle, automobile, bus, bicycle, cart, etc. (M: liàng 輛). (M) (1) for a load of a wheeled vehicle. yìchē-shū 一車書 a cartful of books. (2) a lot of. Tā-shuōde-shì-yi'chēde-'fèihuà. 他説的是一車的廢話. What he said was a lot of idle talk.

CHĔ₃ 扯 (TV) (1) pull, drag (a person). Tā-chĕ-zhe-wo, bu-xú-wo-zŏu. 他扯着我不許我走. He is pulling me and won't let me go. (2) tear something by pulling. (syn. sĭ 撕). Tā-bă-zhĭ chĕ-le. 他把紙扯了. He tore the paper. (3) speak on random topics without objective. Tā-jìng-xiā-chĕ. 他竟瞎扯. He always talks nonsense.

CHĒCHUÁNG₄ 車床 (N) lathe.

CHĔ-DÀN₂ 扯淡 (VO) talk nonsense, shoot the bull. Bié-chĕ-dàn, shuō-zhèngjǐng-de. 別扯淡,説正經的.Don't shoot

C

C

the bull, let's talk seriously.

CHÈDǏ₂ 澈底 (SV) thorough, complete. Tā-zuòde bu-chèdǐ. 他作的不澈底. He is not thorough in doing that. (AD) thoroughly, completely. Děi-chèdǐ-jiějué. 得澈底解決.(We) must resolve it completely.

CHÉFÁNG₁ 車房 (N) garage. (M: jiān 間).

CHĒFU₅ 車夫 (N) chauffeur, driver, a person operating, driving or pulling a wheeled vehicle (a term gradually becoming obsolete). (See: SIJI 司機).

CHEJIĀN₂ 車間 (N) room for machine tools, lathes, milling machines, etc.

CHĒLÚNZI₃ 車輪子 (N) wheel (of a vehicle).

CHĒMǍFÈI₂ 車馬費 (N) travelling expenses.

CHĒN₃ 抻 (TV) stretch, pull a rope, string, thread straight, pull cloth to smooth out wrinkles.

CHÉN₁ 沈 (SV) heavy (in weight). (syn. zhòng 重, opp. qīng 輕). (IV) sink. Chuán-chén-le. 船沈了. The ship sank.

CHÈN₁ 趁 (CV) while (at an opportune moment). Chèn-ta-'zài-zhèr-de-shíhou gēn-ta-shuō. 趁他在這兒的時候跟他説. Speak to him while he is here. Wǒmen-chèn-zhèige-jīhui mǎi-yige-pi ányide. 我們趁這個機會買一個便宜的. We'll use

this opportunity and buy a cheap one.

CHĒNG₃ 撐 (TV) (1) propel with a pole. chēng-chuán 撐船 pole a boat. (2) prop up with a pole. chēng-liánzi 撐簾子 prop up a curtain. Bǎ-sǎn chēngqilai. 把傘撐起來. Open the umbrella. (3) prop up or support spiritually, morally, financially or otherwise, a weak person or organization to make it appear strong. Rúguǒ-méi-you-ta-tì-women-chēngzhe, wǒmende-gōngsī zǎo-pòchǎn-le.如果沒有他替我們撐着, 我們的公司早破產了. Were it not for his propping it up for us, our company would have gone bankrupt long ago. (SV)uncomfortable in the stomach due to overeating. stuff oneself to the point of feeling uncomfortable. Bu-néng-zài-chī-le, wǒ-chēng-le. 不能再吃了,我撐了 I can't eat any more, I feel stuffed. (RE) stuff oneself to the point of feeling uncomfortable. Wǒ-chī-chēng-le. 我吃撐了. I feel uncomfortable because I stuffed myself.

CHĒNG₁ 稱 (TV) weigh. Bǎ-zhèige chēng-yicheng. 把這個稱一稱. Weigh this.

CHÉNG₁ 成 (SV) (1) satisfactory, OK. (syn. xíng 行). 'Zhèiyangr-bàn, 'chéng-bu-chéng?這樣兒辦成不成? Is it OK to do it this way? (2) capable. Tā-zìjǐ-juéde-tā-chéng. 他自己覺得他成. He himself feels that he is capable.

(IV) accomplish, succeed, become a reality, materialize. Tā-qùle-yi-shuō jiu-chéng. 他去了一說就成. It will succeed by his going there to talk for it. 'Zhèizhong-rén bù-néng-'chéng-shénma-'dà-shì. 這種人不能成甚麼大事. This kind of person isn't able to accomplish anything big.

(RE) accomplish, succeed. Tā-xiǎng-mǎi-de-nèijian-dōngxi méi-mǎi-chéng. 他想買的那件東西沒買成. He didn't succeed in buying the thing he wanted to buy.

(TV) become, turn into. Nì-nèi-yàngr-shuō-huà, chéngle-háizi-le. 你那樣兒説話, 成了孩子了. When you talk like that, you turn into a child. Bù-chéng-huà. 不成話. (lit. It doesn't become a sentence) It doesn't look like anything.

(PV) as (when combined with certain verbs such as write, read, draw, etc.); into (when combined with certain verbs such as grow, translate, etc.). Tā-bǎ-DÀ-zi xiěcheng-TÀI-zi-le. 他把大字寫成太字了. He wrote the character "dà" 大 as "tài" 太. Tā-yǐjing-zhǎngcheng-dàren-le. 他已經長成大人了. He has already grown into an adult. (See: BǍ 把).

CHÉNG₁ 城 (N) city, center of a town. (M: zuò 座). Jìn-chéng qu-kànkan. 進城去看看. Go into the city and look around.

CHÉNG₂ 盛 (TV) (1) contain, hold (in a container). Zhèige-wǎn shì-chéng-shénma-de? 這個碗是盛甚麼的? What is this bowl for (holding)? (2) put something into a vessel. Wǒ-zài-gěi-nín-chéng-dianr-fàn. 我再給您盛點兒飯. I'll give you a little more rice.

CHÉNG₂ 乘 (TV) multiply. Èr-chéng-sān dé-liù. 二乘三得六. Two times three equals six.

CHÈNG₄ 秤 (N) steelyard, a weighing machine. (M: gǎn 桿).

CHÉNGBĚN₃ 成本 (N) cost.

CHÉNGDU₁ 程度 (N) extent, level, degree (of moral, intellectual, educational elevation). Méixiǎngdào tā-daole-zhèige-chéngdu. 沒想到他到了這個程度. I didn't think that he had reached this level. Tāde-Zhōngwén chéngdu-hěn-hǎo. 他的中文程度很好. His (level of) Chinese is very good. Kǒngpà-wǒ-bú-gòu-chéngdu. 恐怕我不夠程度. I am probably not qualified. Nǐmen-zuòdao-'shénma-chéngdu-le? 你們作到甚麼程度了? What level have you worked up to?

CHÉNGDŪ₃ 成都 (PW) Ch'eng-tu (capital of Szechwan pro-

C

C

vince).

'CHĚNGFÁ₃ 懲罰 (TV) punish, impose a penalty, prison sentence, fine.

(N) punishment. Nà-ta-děi-shòu-'chěngfá. 那他得受懲罰. In that case he must be punished.

CHĚNGGĀNRTIÀO₂ 撐竿兒跳 (N) pole vault.

CHÉNG-GŌNG₁ 成功 (VO) complete a task successfully.

(SV) successful. (opp. shībài 失敗). Tā-bànde hěn-chénggōng. 他辦的很成功. He did it quite successfully.

CHĒNGHU₃ 稱呼 (TV) address someone in a special polite way. Wǒmen-zěnma-chēnghu-ta? Shì-Zhāng-ˈtàitai háishi-Zhāng-ˈxiáo-jie? 我們怎麼稱呼他?是張太太還是張小姐? How should we address her? Mrs. Chang or Miss Chang?

CHÉNGJI₁ 成績 (N) evidence of achievement or work done (such as school grades, awards, citations, publications, etc.). Wǒmen-děi-zuòchu-yìdiǎnr-chéngji-lai. 我們得作出一點兒成績來. We have to show some achievement.

CHÉNG-JIĀ₄ 成家 (VO) get married. (This is an old fashioned term, jiéhūn 結婚 is now more commonly used.)

CHÉNGJIU₂ 成就 (N) achievement. Wǒ-zuòle-zènma-duō-nián, yě-méi-shénma-chéngjiu. 我作

了這麼多年,也没甚麼成就. I have worked for many years without any achievement.

(TV) bring to satisfactory completion.

'CHÉNGKĚN₁ 誠懇 (SV) sincere. Tā-ˈtàidu-hen-ˈchéngkěn.他態度很誠懇. His attitude is very sincere.

CHÉNGLI₂ 成立 (TV) (1) set up, establish. Tāmen-yào-chénglì-yige-xuéxiào. 他們要成立一個學校. They want to establish a school. (2) stand up, hold true. Nǐde-lǐlun bu-néng-chénglì. 你的理論不能成立. Your theory won't hold true.

CHÈNG-LIÁNG₅ 乘涼 (VO) cool oneself in the shade or in the breeze.

CHĚNG-NÉNG₄ 逞能 (VO) show off one's ability.

CHÉNGQIÁNG₂ 城牆 (N) city wall. (M: duàn 段).

CHÉNGQUAN₂ 成全 (TV) give the kind of help without which something could not be accomplished. Tā-jiègei-wo-qián, wǒ-cái-bǎ-dàxué-niànwán-le. Tā-bǎ-wǒ-chéngquan-le.他借給我錢,我才把大學念完了. 他把我成全了. He lent me money, only then could I finish college. He helped me attain my objective.

CHÉNGR₃ 成兒 (M) tenth. liù-chéngr 六成兒 six-tenths.

CHÉNGRÈN₁ 承認 (TV) admit,

confess. Tā-zuò-de-shì, ta-bu-chéngrèn. 他 作 的 事, 他 不 承 認. He won't admit what he did.

CHÉNGSHÌ₂ 城 市 (N) city, town. (opp. xiāngcūn 鄉 村).

CHÉNGSHÍ₁ 誠 實 (SV) honest.

'CHÉNGSHÚ₂ 成 熟 (SV) mature.

CHÉNGTIĀN₂ 成 天 (AD) all the time, always. Tā-chéngtiān-niàn shū. 他 成 天 念 書. He studies all the time.

CHÉNGXĪN₁ 成 心 (AD) on purpose, intentionally. (syn. gùyì 故 意, ānxīn 安 心). Tā-chéngxīn-zuòcuò-le. 他 成 心 作 錯 了. He intentionally made it wrong.

(IV) do something on purpose. Duìbuqǐ, wǒ-bu-shi-chéngxīn. 對 不 起, 我 不 是 成 心. I am sorry, but I didn't do it on purpose.

CHÉNGXU₅ 程 序 (N) sequence, procedure in formal activities. kāikuìde-chéngxu 開 會 的 程 序 the procedure of the meeting.

CHÉNGYǓR₄ 成 語 兒 (N) an adage.

CHÉNGZAN₂ 稱 讚 (TV) praise, commend. Wǒ-'chēngzanle-ta-jijiù. 我 稱 讚 了 他 幾 句. I praised him with a couple of words.

CHÉNGZI₂ 橙 子 (N) orange.

CHÉNGZI₃ 呈 子 (N) petition. shàng-yige-chéngzi 上 一 個 呈 子 present a petition.

CHÉNJING₃ 沈 靜 (SV) calm and quiet (of a person).

CHÉNLIE₃ 陳 列 (TV) display, exhibit (as in a showcase or museum).

CHÈNSHĀN₁ 襯 衫 (N) shirt. (M: jiàn 件).

CHÉNSHE₄ 陳 設 (N) decorative objects, knick-knacks. (M: jiàn 件).

CHÉNTǓ₃ 塵 土 (N) dust.

CHÈN-XĪN₃ 稱 心 (VO) be in accord with one's wishes. 'Zhèi-yàngr suàn-'chènle-tade-'xīn-le. 這 樣 算 稱 了 他 的 心 了. This way made him happy.

CHÈN-ZǍOR₂ 趁 早 兒 (VO) (lit. Take advantage of being early, otherwise it will be too late.) it's better now, the sooner...the better.

(AD) immediately, at once. Nǐ-chènzǎor-shuō. 你 趁 早 兒 說. You better say it, and the sooner the better.

CHĒPIÀO₂ 車 票 (N) ticket for riding on any kind of wheeled vehicle. (M: zhāng 張).

CHĒTÓU₂ 車 頭 (N) locomotive. (syn. huǒchētóu 火 車 頭), (M: liàng 輛).

CHÈTUI₂ 撤 退 (TV) withdraw, retreat (referring to military action). Dírén-chètuì-le. 敵 人 撤 退 了. The enemy retreated.

CHĒZHÀN₁ 車 站 (N) train station, bus stop, bus depot.

CHĪ₁ 吃 (TV) (1) eat something. Chī-fàn-le-meiyou? 吃 飯 了 沒 有? Have you eaten? or

C

may be used as a greeting, How are you? Wǒ-bu-chī-táng. 我不吃糖. I don't eat candy. (2) eat in a restaurant. Tā-cháng-chī-fànguǎnr. 他常吃飯館兒. He often eats in a restaurant. (3) eat the food prepared by a certain chef or served by a certain waiter. chī-nǔzhāodài 吃女招待 eat the food served by a certain waitress. (4) eat food provided or paid for by someone else. Tā-zìjǐ-bu-qǐngkè, lǎo-chī-byéren. 他自己不請客老吃別人. He himself does not treat anybody, but always eats when treated by someone else. (5) make a living from. Tā-shì-chī-jiàode. 他是吃教的. He makes a living from religion. (6) take medicine. chī-àsīpǐlíng 吃阿斯匹靈 take aspirin. (7) dial. drink. Wǒ-bu-huì-chī-jiǔ. 我不會吃酒. I cannot drink. (8) Peip. smoke a pipe, a cigarette, etc. Nín-chī-shénma-yān? 您吃甚麼烟? What do you smoke? (9) absorb. chīmòzhǐ 吃墨紙 (lit. ink absorbing paper) blotter. (10) accept, suffer, take. Wǒ-bu-chī-zhèi-yitào. 我不吃這一套. I won't accept this kind of treatment. Tā-chīguo-liǎngcì-bàizhàng. 他吃過兩次敗仗. He has suffered two defeats.

(N) food. Wǒmen-zài-zhèr yǒu-chī-yǒu-hē. 在這兒有吃有喝. We have food and drink here.

CHǏ$_1$ 尺 (M) a unit of measure for length, equivalent to about 13 inches, Chinese foot, foot. gōngchǐ 公尺 meter. yīngchǐ 英尺 foot. (N) yardstick, tape measure, ruler. (M: gēn 根).

CHĪBǍNG$_2$ 翅膀 (N) wing (of birds).

CHĪBUXIĀO$_2$ 吃不消 (RV) cannot endure it, can't take it. Lǎo-zhèiyang-máng wǒ-chībuxiāo. 老這樣忙我吃不消. If we were always this busy, I couldn't take it.

CHǏCUN$_3$ 尺寸 (N) measurement (length and size). Liángliang-chǐcun. 量量尺寸. Get the measurement.

CHÍDÀO$_1$ 遲到 (IV) (lit. arrive late) tardy.

'CHÍHUǍN$_5$ 遲緩 (SV) slow. (opp. xùnsu 迅速). Tāde-dòngzuo hěn-'chíhuǎn. 他的動作很遲緩. His movements are very slow.

CHĪ-JĪNG$_2$ 吃驚 (VO) (lit. receive surprise) be startled. Wǒ-chīle-yijǐng. 我吃了一驚. I was startled.

CHĪ-KǓ$_2$ 吃苦 (VO) endure hardship. Tā-bu-néng-chī-kǔ. 他不能吃苦. He cannot endure hardship.

CHĪ-KUĪ$_1$ 吃虧 (VO) sustain a loss, be at a disadvantage. (opp. zhàn-piányi 佔便宜). Nǐ-zhèiyang-zuò, chībuliǎo-kuī.

你這樣作, 吃 不 了
虧. If you do it this way, you
will not sustain a loss.

CHĪLÌ₂ 吃 力 (SV) require
strength, be strenuous. Wǒ-
juéde hen-chīlì. 我 覺 的 很
吃 力. I feel it is very strenuous.

CHǏLÚN₄ 齒 輪 (N) cogwheel,
gear.

CHĪMÒZHǏ₁ 吃 墨 紙 (N) (lit.
ink absorbing paper) blotter.
(M: zhāng 張).

CHÍTÁNG₄ 池 塘 (N) pond.

CHĪXIĀNG₂ 吃 香 (SV) be in a
favorable situation. Xiànzài tā-
men-zhèi-yiháng hěn-chīxiāng.
現 在 他 們 這 一 行
很 吃 香. Nowadays people
in their profession are in demand.

CHÍYÍ₅ 遲 疑 (SV) hesitate. Wǒ-
kàn, nín-buyòng-chíyi-le. 我
看 您 不 用 遲 疑 了.
I don't think that you should hesitate any more.

'CHÍZǍO₃ 遲 早 (MA) sooner or
later. (syn. 'zǎowǎn 早 晚).

CHĪ-ZHĀI₅ 吃 齋 (VO) observe
the rules of religious fasting,
be on a vegetable diet. Tā-xìn-
fó chūyī-shíwǔ tā-chī-zhāi. 他
信 佛, 初 一 十 五 他
吃 齋. He believes in
Buddha, on the first and the 15th
of the month he is on a vegetable
diet.

CHÍZI₃ 匙 子 (N) spoon. (M:
bǎ 把).

CHÍZI₃ 池 子 (N) pond, pool.

CHŌNG₃ 衝 (TV) crash or dash

ahead, pushing obstacles aside.
Tā-bǎ-mén dǎpuòle, 'chōngjin-
qu-le. 他 把 門 打 破 了,
衝 進 去 了. He broke the
door open and dashed in. Zài-
hóng-dēng-de-shíhou tā-kāizhe-
chē chōngguoqu-le. 在 紅 燈
的 時 候 他 開 着 車
衝 過 去 了. (lit. When
the light was red he drove his
car crashing through). He crashed
the light.

CHŌNG₃ 沖 (TV) (1) wash out, flush
away, rinse (the act of water
crashing into something). Xià-
yǔ bǎ-qiáng-gei-chōnghuài-le.
下 雨 把 牆 給 沖 壞
了. The rain pouring on the
wall ruined it. Dàshuǐ-bǎ-qiáo-
chōngzǒu-le. 大 水 把 橋
沖 走 了. The flood washed
the bridge away. (2) pour water
onto something, flush, rinse,
infuse, etc., with water. Yòng-
wánle-mǎtǒng bié-wàngle-chōng.
用 完 了 馬 桶 別 忘 了 沖.
Don't forget to flush after using
the toilet. Chōng-yiwan-kāfēi.
沖 一 碗 咖 啡. Make
a cup of (instant) coffee. Yòng-
shuǐ-chōngchong jiu-gānjing-le.
用 水 沖 沖 就 乾 淨
了. Rinse it and then it will
be clean.

CHÓNG₂ 重 (TV) repeat, do something once again. chóngyàngrde
重 樣 兒 的 (lit. repeated
kind) duplicate. Zhèige-chóng-le.
這 個 重 了. This one
is repeated. Wǒ-pà-ta-bu-zhùyì,

C

suóyi wǒ-'chónglе-yijù. 我 怕 他 不 注意, 所 以 我 重 了 一 句. I was afraid that he wasn't paying attention, so I repeated it.

(RE) repeated (with the same action expressed by the preceding verb). Zhèige-zì nǐ-xiěchóng-le. 這 個 字 你 寫 重 了. You wrote this word twice.

(AD) once again, over again. Jiào-ta-chóng-zuò. 叫 他 重 作. Ask him to do it all over again.

CHÒNG₂ 衝 (TV) face towards. Nǐ-liǎn chòng-něibianr? 你 臉 衝 那 邊 兒? Which direction are you facing? Tāde-fángzi chòngzhe-hé. 他 的 房 子 衝 着 河. His house faces the river. Tāmen-chòng-wǒmen-lái-le. 他 們 衝 我 們 來 了. They are coming toward us.

CHÒNG₃ 衝 (SV) (1) strong to the taste or smell. Nǐ-wénwen, wèir-duóma-chòng. 你 聞 聞, 味 兒 多 麼 衝. Smell how strong the odor is. (2) strong (of a hand of cards). Tā-shǒu-hěn-chòng. 他 手 很 衝. He has a very strong hand. (3) blunt. Tā-shuō-huà hěn-chòng. 他 說 話 很 衝. He speaks very bluntly.

CHÒNG₅ 沖 (M) for a deck of cards. yichòng-pái 一 沖 牌 a deck of cards.

CHŌNG-FĒNG₂ 衝 鋒 (VO) charge (as in a battle).

CHÓNGFU₂ 重 複 (TV) repeat.

Qǐng-nǐ-zài-chóngfu-yicì. 請 你 再 重 複 一 次. Please repeat it once more.

CHŌNG-GŌNG₃ 充 公 (VO) con- fiscate someone's property.

CHÓNGQÌNG₂ 重 慶 (PW) Chung- king (city in Szechuan province).

CHŌNGTU₁ 衝 突 (IV) conflict. Wǒmen-dìngde-shíjiān gēn-kāi-huì-chōngtu. 我 們 定 的 時 間 跟 開 會 衝 突. The time we decided on conflicts with the time of the meeting. Tāmen-liǎngge-rén chōngtu-qi-lai-le. 他 們 兩 個 人 衝 突 起 來 了. These two people are in conflict with each other.

(N) conflict. Méi-yǒu-shénma-chōngtu. 沒 有 甚 麼 衝 突. There is no conflict.

CHÓNGXĪN₁ 重 新 or CÓNGXĪN 從 新 (MA) all over again. Guānyú-'zhèijiàn-shì, tāmen-yào-chóngxīn-'shāngliang-shāngliang. 關 於 這 件 事, 他 們 要 重 新 商 量 商 量. As for this matter, they want to discuss it again.

CHÓNGYÁNG₅ 重 陽 (N) a festi- val on the ninth day of the ninth month of the lunar calendar.

CHÓNGZI₁ 蟲 子 (N) (1) worm. (M: tiáo 條). (2) insect.

CHŌNGZU₄ 充 足 (SV) sufficient (for reason, quantity of some- thing in storage, etc.).

CHŌU₃ 抽 (TV) whip. Wǒ-'chōule-ta-yidùn. 我 抽 了 他 一 頓. I gave him a whipping.

CHŌU₂ 抽 (TV) (1) draw or pull out something that offers little resistance. (2) draw or suck liquid or air. chōu-shuǐ 抽水 draw the water. chōu-qì 抽氣 draw the air out. chōu-yān 抽烟 (lit. draw the smoke) smoke. (3) take out time from a busy schedule. chōuchu-diǎnr-gōngfu-lai 抽出點兒工夫來 make some time. (4) draw from the people by the government. chōu-shuì 抽稅 levy taxes. chōu-zhuàngdīng 抽壯丁 draft.

CHŌU₃ 抽 (TV) shrink. Zhèizhong-bù yi-xià-shuǐ jiu-chōu. 這種布一下水就抽. This cloth shrinks as soon as it is put in the water.

CHÒU₂ 臭 (SV) (1) smell bad, have a bad odor, stink. (opp. xiāng 香). (2) used before a noun has a bad connotation. Tā-buguò-yǒu-jǐge-chòu-qián. 他不過有幾個臭錢. All he has is some stinking money. (3) Peip. conceited, proud. Tā-nèige-yàngr chòujíle. 他那個樣兒臭極了. That manner of his is really conceited. (AD) has a bad connotation, heavily, severely. Wǒ-bǎ-ta-chòu-'màle-yidùn. 我把他臭罵了一頓. I gave him a severe bawling out.

CHÓUBEI₂ 籌備 (TV) make preparation for some occasion or project.

CHÒUCHONG₅ 臭蟲 (N) bed bug.

CHÓUDUÀN₄ 綢緞 (N) (lit. thin silk and satin) silk material (yard goods).

CHŌU-FĒNG₂ 抽瘋 (VO) (1) have an epileptic attack. (2) have spasms.

'CHÓUHUÀ₃ 籌畫 (TV)(con. chóubei 籌備 and jìhua 計畫). make plans.

CHŌULĚNGZI₅ 抽冷子 (MA) Peip. all of a sudden, unexpectedly.

'CHÓUMÌ₄ 稠密 (SV) thick, dense (referring to population, etc.). 'Rénkǒu-'chóumì. 人口稠密. The population is dense.

CHÓUREN₂ 仇人 (N) enemy (personal). Shéi-shi-nǐde-chóu-ren? 誰是你的仇人? Who is your enemy?

'CHÓUSHÌ₄ 仇視 (TV) regard as an enemy.

CHŌUTI₂ 抽屜 (N) drawer.

CHŌUXIÀNG₂ 抽象 (SV) abstract. (opp. jùtǐ 具體).

CHŌU-YĀN₁ 抽烟 (VO) smoke a pipe, a cigar, a cigarette, etc.

CHÓUZI₃ 綢子 (N) plain weave silk. (M: chǐ 尺).

CHŪ₁ 出 (IV) (1) exit, egress, come or go out of a place. chū-chéng 出城 come or go out of the city. chū-guó 出國 come or go abroad, depart from(one's own)country. (2) go or come out to a place or to do something. chū-shì 出世 (lit. come out to the world) be born. chū-chāi 出差 go out on business, go on an official trip. (3) appear in a

C

place. chū-xí 出席 attend a meeting. chū-chǎng 出場 appear in the scene, come out on the stage. (4) appear (of something), happen (of something), come out. chū-tàiyang 出太陽 the sun comes out. chū-shì 出事 something happens, have an accident. (5) eruption on the skin of certain diseases. chū-tiānhuār 出天花兒 get smallpox. (6) produce. Zhèige-dìfang chū-shénma? 這個地方出甚麼? What is produced here? Tā-yòu-chū-le-yiběn-shū. 他又出了一本書. (lit. He produced a book again) He has brought out another book. (7) put forth, put up, contribute for a cause. Nǐ-bié-chū-zhúyi. 你別出主意. Don't give your ideas. Nǐ-kěn-chū-'duōshao-qián? 你肯出多少錢? How much money are you willing to put up? (8) exceed. Chūle-yi'bǎikuai-qián wǒ-jiu-bu-yào-le. 出了一百塊錢我就不要了. If it exceeds one hundred dollars then I don't want it. Tā-shuō-de-huà, chūle wǒ-men-tǎolunde-fànwéi-le. 他說的話, 出了我們討論的範圍了. What he said is beyond the limits of our discussion.

(B) used after CV, such as wàng 往, xiàng 向, etc., out. Nèige-shíhou, ta-zhèng-wàng-'chū-zǒu. 那個時候他正往出走. At that time he was just going out.

(RE) followed by a noun or in potential forms. Dàgài-tā-néng-náchu-'duōshao-qián? 大概他能拿出多少錢? Approximately how much money can he put up? Wǒ-'kànbuchū ta-yǒu-'nènma-duō-qián. 我看不出他有那麼多錢. I can't see that he has that much money.

CHŪ₂ 初 (B) (1) used before NU from one to ten for dates of the month in the lunar calendar. chū'èr 初二 the second day (of a month). (2) used after an expression of period of time, the early part of... èryuechū 二月初 the early part of February. (AD) at the beginning, at first. 'chū-xué 初學 just beginning to learn. Wǒ-'chū-dào-zhèr-de-shíhou, shénma-dou-bu-shú. 我初到這兒的時候, 甚麼都不熟. When I first arrived here, I wasn't familiar with anything at all.

CHŪ₃ 齣 (M) for play, drama, opera, etc. yìchū-xì 一齣戲 one play.

CHÚ₂ 除 (TV) divide (arithmetic). Er-chú-shí dé-wǔ. 二除十得五. Two divided into ten is five. Shí-bèi-èr-chú de-wǔ. 十被二除得五. Ten divided by two is five.

CHÚ₃ 除 (TV) remove something evil. Tāde-bìng méi-chú-gēn.

他的病没除根. The evil roots of his illness have not been removed.

CHÚ(LE)₁ 除了 (CV) (1) except, besides, aside from. (syn. chúqu 除去). Chú(le)-tā, méi-you-hé'shìde-rén. 除了他,没有合适的人. There is no suitable person except him. (2) unless. (syn. chúfēi 除非). Tā-chú(le)-bu-kěn-zuò, yàoshi-zuò jiu-zuòde-hen-hǎo. 他除了不肯作,要是作就作得很好. Unless he's not willing to do it, he will do it very well if he does it.

CHÙ₂ 處 (M) for a place. Wǒ-děi-qu-sānchu-dìfang. 我得去三處地方. I have to go to three places.

CHUĀI₄ 揣 (TV) Peip. carry something in a pocket or in one's clothes near the chest. Tā-bǎ-xìn chuāizai-kǒudàirli-le. 他把信揣在口袋兒裏了. He put the letter in his pocket. Tā-chuāizhe-shǒu-zuǒ. 他揣着手走. He walks with his hands in his sleeves. (Old-fashioned Chinese gowns had wide sleeves so that the left hand could be put into the right sleeve and vice-versa, at the bosom, to keep the hands warm.)

CHUĀI₅ 踹 (TV) Peip. kick, stamp.

CHUĀIMO₃ 揣摩 (TV) think over a problem.

CHUĀN₁ 穿 (TV) wear clothes, footgear. (opp. tuō 脫). Bǎ-xié-chuānshang. 把鞋穿上.

Put on your shoes. (cf: DÀI 戴).
(2) pass through, have something passed through, thread a needle, pierce something, string something. chuān-zhūzi 穿珠子 string pearls or beads. Wǒmen-cóng-gōngyuán chuānguoqu. 我們從公園穿過去. Let's go through this park.
(RE) reveal (by stating verbally or sense (see through) some secret thoughts. Wǒ-bǎ-ta-xīnli-'xiǎngde-shì gei-shuōchuān-le. 我把他心裏想的事給説穿了. I told him (revealed) what he had in mind. Wǒ-bǎ-ta-kànchuān-le. 我把他看穿了. I saw through him (knew what he had in mind).

CHUÁN₁ 船 (N) boat, ship. (M: zhǐ 隻, tiáo 條).

CHUÁN₂ 傳 (TV) (1) pass something on to someone. Tā-bǎ-tade-xué-wen dou-chuángei-ta-érzi-le. 他把他的學問都傳給他兒子了. He passed all his knowledge on to his son. Wǒ-qǐng-nǐ-chuán-yi-jiu-huà. 我請你傳一句話. I want you to please pass the word on (to convey a message). Tā-zài-Zhōngguo-chuán-jiào. 他在中國傳教. He is preaching religion in China. (2) conduct electricity, heat, light, etc. Shuǐ yě-chuán-rè-ma? 水也傳熱嗎? Does water also conduct heat?

CHUÁN₄ 傳 (TV) summon. Bǎ-ta-

C

C

chuánlai. 把他傳來 Summon him.

CHUĂN₄ 喘 (TV) breathe quickly, pant. Tā-păode-zhí-chuǎn. 他 跑 得 直 喘. He is panting because he was running. Tā-chuǎn shi-yīnwei-yǒu-bìng. 他 喘 是 因 為 有 病. He breathes quickly because he is sick. (cf: CHUĂN-QÌ 喘氣).

CHUÀN₃ 串 (M) (1) string. yichuàn-zhūzi 一 串 珠 子 a string of pearls. (2) for a sequence of events.
(TV) thread one's way. Wǒmen-zài-zhèi-jitiao-jiēshang lái'huíde-chuàn. 我 們 在 這 幾 條 街 上 來 回 的 串. We threaded our way back and forth through these several streets.

CHUÁNCĀNG₃ 船 艙 (N) cabin, quarters, hold (in a ship).

CHUÁNDÁCHÙ₃ 傳 達 處 (N) (lit. place for conveying messages) an area, generally near the entrance of a large operation, where visitors state their purpose or whom they wish to see and wait for the message to be conveyed, reception area.

CHUÁNDĀN₂ 傳 單 (N) hand-bill. (M: zhāng 張). Tāmen-sā-chuán-dān-ne. 他 們 撒 傳 單 呢. They are passing out hand-bills.

CHUÁNG₃ 瘡 (N) boil. zhǎng-chuāng 長 瘡 have a boil.

CHUÁNG₁ 牀 (N) bed. (M: zhāng 張).
(B) certain machine tools. chē-chuáng 車 牀 lathe.

(M) for bedding which covers the length of the bed. yichuáng-dānzi 一 牀 單 子 a bed sheet.

'CHUÁNGBĀ₅ 瘡 疤 (N) scar or scab of a boil.

CHUÁNGBÀN₂ 創 辦 (TV) start, establish, found (implies being the original).

CHUÁNGHU₁ 窗 户 (N) window. (M: shàn 扇).

CHUÁNGHULIÁNR₂ 窗 户 簾 兒 (N) window curtain.

CHUĂNG-HUÒ₂ 闖 禍 (VO) cause trouble by brusque action, make a bad mess of things. Wǒ-kāi-qìchē méi-chuǎng-guò-huò. 我 開 汽 車 没 闖 過 禍. I have never had any accidents since I have been driving a car.

CHUĂNGLIAN₄ 闖 練 (TV) gain experience by doing. Nǐ-chūqu-'chuǎnglian-yixià. 你 出 去 闖 練 一 下. Go out and get some experience.

'CHUĂNGZÀO₂ 創 造 (TV) create (objects).
(N) creation.

'CHUĂNGZUÒ₂ 創 作 (N) creation (literature and other fine arts). Zhèiben-xiǎoshuōr shi-tāde-'chǎngzuò. 這 本 小 説 兒 是 他 的 創 作. This novel is his own creation.

CHUÁN-JIÀO₂ 傳 教 (VO) (lit. spread the religion) preach the gospel, do missionary work.

CHUÁNPIÀO₁ 船 票 (N) boat ticket. (M: zhāng 張).

CHUĂN-QÌ₃ 喘 氣 (VO) catch

breath. Wǒ-chuǎnbuguo-chì-lai-le. 我 喘 不 過 氣 來 了. I cannot catch my breath. Děng-wǒ-chuǎn-yichuǎn-qì. 等 我 喘 一 喘 氣. Wait, let me catch my breath. (cf: CHUĂN 喘).

CHUÁNRǍN₁ 傳 染 (IV) conta-gious. Zhèizhong-bìng chuánrǎn. 這 種 病 傳 染. This disease is contagious.

CHUÁNSHUŌ₂ 傳 説 (N) hearsay. Zhèi-buguò-shi-chuánshuō, bu zhǐ'dào-shì-bu-shi-zhēnde. 這 不 過 是 傳 説, 不 知 道 是 不 是 真 的. This is only hearsay, it is not known whether it is true or not. (TV) pass <u>from person to person by speech.</u> Rén-dou-zènma-chuán-shuō. 人 都 這 麼 傳 説. Everybody passed it on this way.

CHUÁNTǑNG₂ 傳 統 (N) tradi-tion.

CHUÀNTŌNG₃ 串 通 (TV) con-spire. Tāmen-chuàntōng-le zài-yikuàir-zuò-hēishì-de-mǎimai. 他 們 串 通 了 在 一 塊 兒 作 黑 市 的 買 賣. They conspired together to carry on black market busi-ness.

CHŪBǍN₂ 出 版 (TV) publish (printing). Nèiben-shū shi-'něi-nian-chūbǎn-de? 那 本 書 是 那 年 出 版 的? In what year was that book published?

CHŪBÙ₃ 初 步 (N) initial step.

CHŪCHǍN₁ 出 產 (TV) produce. (N) production.

CHŪ-CHǍNG₄ 出 場 (VO) come

on stage (<u>of an actor</u>).

CHŪ-CHǑU₄ 出 醜 (VO) have something shameful exposed.

CHÙCHU₁ 處 處 (PW) every-where.

CHÚCǏYǏWÀI₃ 除 此 以 外 (MA) besides this, in addition to this.

'CHÚDIÀO₃ 除 掉 (TV) (1) elim-inate. Bǎ-'zhèiju-huà 'chúdiào. 把 這 句 話 除 掉. Elim-inate this sentence. (2) besides, except, aside from. Chúdiao-tā jiu-'méi-yǒu-biérén-le. 除 掉 他 就 沒 有 別 人 了. Except for him there is nobody else. Chúdiao= tā hái-you-'sānge-rén. 除 掉 他 還 有 三 個 人. Besides him there are three other people. (See: CHÚ(LE) 除 (了), CHÚQU 除 去).

CHŪFĀ₂ 出 發 (IV) set off, start a journey, start (<u>from a point of reference</u>). Wǒmen-'bādian-zhōng-chūfā. 我 們 八 點 鐘 出 發. We are leaving at eight o'clock.

CHǓFÁ₃ 處 罰 (TV) punish.

CHÚFÁNG₁ 廚 房 (N) kitchen. (M: jiān 間).

CHÚFĒI₁ 除 非 (MA) (1) unless. (syn. chú(le) 除 (了)). Chúfei-piányi, yàoburán wǒ-bu-mǎi. 除 非 便 宜 要 不 然 我 不 買. I won't buy it unless it is cheap. Wǒ-kéyi-zuò, chúfēi-nǐ-bu-yuànyi-ràng-wo-zuò. 我 可 以 作, 除 非 你 不 願 意 讓 我 作. I can do it, unless you don't want me to

C

do it. (2) only when. Chúfēi-tā-
zuòbuliǎo, ta-cái-jǎo-wǒ-bāng-
máng-ne. 除非他作不
了，他才找我幫忙
呢. Only when he can't do it
does he ask me for help.

CHŪ-FĒNGTOU₂ 出風頭 (VO)
be in the limelight, gain publicity or notoriety. Tā-zǒngshi-
xiǎng-chū-fēngtou. 他總是
想出風頭. He always
wants to be in the limelight. Tā-
zhèicì-lái, hěn-chū-fēngtou. 他
這次來，很出風頭.
He gained a lot of publicity when
he came this time.

CHŪ-GUǏ₃ 出軌 (VO) (1) derail.
(2) fig. deviate. Tāmen-zuò-de-
shì chūle-zhèng-guǐ-le. 他們
作的事出了正軌
了. What they are doing de-
viates from the right way.

CHŪ-GUÓ₂ 出國 (VO) go abroad.

CHŪ-HÀN₂ 出汗 (VO) perspire,
sweat.

CHUĪ₁ 吹 (TV) (1) blow. Bǎ-huǒ-
chuīmiè-le. 把火吹滅了.
Blow the fire out. (2) Peip. fall
through (of plans), peter out, end
(of friendship). Nèige-jìhua-chuī-
le. 那個計劃吹了.
That plan fell through. (3) play
a musical wind instrument. chuī-
hào 吹號 play a bugle. (4)
(con. chuī-niú 吹牛). boast,
brag. Tā-bu-zuò-shì, jìng-chuī.
他不作事，竟吹. He
doesn't work, he just bluffs. Bié-
gēn-women-chuī. 別跟我們
吹. Don't boast to us.

CHUĪ₃ 垂 (IV) droop, hang down.
Guǒzi-tài-zhòng, shù-zhīzi dou-
chuí-xialai-le. 果子太重，
樹枝子都垂下來
了. The fruit was too heavy,
all the branches of the tree droop-
ed.

CHUĪ-NIÚ₃ 吹牛 (VO) boast,
brag. Nǐ-gēn-wǒ chuī-shénma-
niú? 你跟我吹甚麼
牛 ? Why do you boast to me?
(cf: CHUĪ 吹).

CHUĪXU₄ 吹噓 (IV) say things
to promote the interest of, say
a good word for. Tā-zǒngshi-
tì-ni-chuīxu. 他總是替
你吹噓. He always puts
in a good word for you.

CHUÍZI₂ 鎚子 (N) hammer,
mallet. (M: bǎ 把).

'CHŪJÍ₂ 初級 (B-) lower level,
lower grade. (opp. gāojí 高級).
chūjízhōngxué 初級中學
junior high school.

CHŪ-KǑU₂ 出口 (VO) (1) export.
Zhèizhong-huò bu-xǔ-chūkǒu. 這
種貨不許出口. This
type of goods is not allowed to be
exported. (2) (lit. out of the mouth)
speak, say. Wǒ-xiǎng-gēn-ta-
jiè-qián, kěshi bu-hǎo-chū-kǒu.
我想跟他借錢可
是不好出口. I intend
to borrow money from him, but
it is embarrassing (not easy to
say).

CHŪKǑU₃ 出口 (N) exit.

CHŪLAI₁ 出來 (RV) come out.
Wūzili chūlai-yige-rén. 屋子
裏出來一個人. A

person came out of the room.
Nǐ-míngtian 'chūdelái-chūbulái?
你 明 天 出 得 來 出
不 來? Can you come out or
not tomorrow?

(RE) (1) out (here). Bǎ-qìchē kāi-
chulai. 把 汽 車 開 出 來
Drive the car out (here). Tā
dǎsuan-náchu-wǔkuài- qián-lai.
他 打 算 拿 出 五 塊
錢 來. He plans to put out
five dollars. Wǒ-xiǎng 'wǔkuài-
qián nábuchu-shǒu-lai. 我 想
五 塊 錢 拿 不 出 手
來. (lit. I think five dollars
cannot be handed out.) I think
five dollars is an embarrassingly
small sum. (2) make out what
something is. Wǒ-yǐjing-bǎ-ta-
de-yìsi kànchulai-le. 我 已
經 把 他 的 意 思 看
出 來 了. I saw (made out)
what he meant. Shì-hóngde shì-
lüde, ta kànbuchulái. 是 紅
的 是 綠 的 他 看 不
出 來. He can't make out
(by looking) whether it is red or
green. Wǒ-chībuchulái shì-shén-
ma- wèir. 我 吃 不 出 來
是 甚 麽 味 兒. I cannot
make out (by eating) what it
tastes like. (3) complete, succeed in a task. Nèifeng-xìn nǐ-
dǎchulai-le-ma? 那 封 信
你 打 出 來 了 嗎?
Have you finished typing that
letter?

CHÚLE...YĬWÀI₁ 除 了 ... 以
外 (S) besides. Chúle-nǐmen-
yǐwài, jiu-méi-you-biéren-le.

除 了 你 們 以 外 就
沒 有 別 人 了. Besides
you, there is nobody else.

'CHŬLI₂ 處 理 (TV) take care of,
manage, handle (an affair).
Zhèijian-shì zěnma-'chŭlǐ? 這
件 事 怎 麽 處 理? How
shall we handle this affair?

CHŪ-MÁOBING₁ 出 毛 病 (VO)
develop difficulties or problems.

CHŪ-MÍNG₁ 出 名 (VO) (lit.
have the name out) famous. 'Nèi-
shíhou ta-yǐjing-chū-míng-le.
那 時 候 他 已 經 出
名 了. At that time he had already made his name.

CHŬN₂ 蠢 (SV) stupid, clumsy (of
people).

CHÚNCUÌ₂ 純 粹 (SV) pure. Tā-
shuō-de shi-chúncuìde-Běijing-
huà. 他 説 的 是 純 粹
的 北 京 話. What he
speaks is pure Pekinese.

CHŪNJIÀ₁ 春 假 (N) Spring vacation.

CHŪNJIÉ₃ 春 節 (N) Spring Festival (New Year's Day according
to the lunar calendar).

'CHÚNJIÉ₃ 純 潔 (SV) pure and
clean, chaste. Tāde-sīxiang hěn-
'chúnjié. 他 的 思 想 很
純 潔. His thought is very
pure and clean.

CHŪNTIAN₁ 春 天 (N) Spring.

CHUŌZI₃ 戳 子 (N) seal, stamps
(for making an imprint). Dǎ-yige-
'chuōzi. 打 一 個 戳 子.
Put a stamp (make an impression)
on it.

CHŪQU₁ 出 去 (RV) go out. Tā-

C

C

chūqu-le. 他出去了. He
went out.

(RE) out (there). Bǎ-zhuōzi bān-
chuqu. 把桌子搬出去.
Move the table out (there). Zhèiyàngrde-huà shuōbuchūqù. 這樣
兒的話說不出去. This
kind of statement cannot be said
to the outside world.

CHÚQU₃ 除去 (CV) except, besides, aside from. (syn. chú(le)
除(了)).
(TV) eliminate. (See: CHÚDIÀO
除掉).

CHŪSÈ₃ 出色 (SV) stand out,
be prominent among one's equals.
Zhèige-rén hěn-chūsè. 這個人
很出色. This person is
outstanding.

CHŪSHĒN₂ 出身 (N) upbringing,
background (of a person). Tā-
shi-shénma-chūshēn? 他是甚
麼出身? What is his back-
ground?

CHŪ-SHÉN₃ 出神 (VO) (lit.
spirit has gone out) lost in thought.
Tā-'zuòzai-nèr chū-shén. 他坐
在那兒出神. He is sit-
ting there, his mind is far away.

CHŪSHENG₃ 畜生 (N) (1) domestic animal. (2) a brute (when
applied to a person, a derogatory
term).

CHŪ-SHÌ₁ 出事 (VO) have something go wrong, have an accident.
Wǒ-kāi-chē méi-chūguo-shì. 我
開車沒出過事. I
have never had an accident driving a car.

CHÚSHIFU₂ 廚師傅 (N) chef,

cook (a polite form of chúzi 廚
子).

CHÚTOU₅ 鋤頭 (N) hoe. (M: bǎ
把).

CHŪ-XÍ₂ 出席 (VO) be present
at a meeting. Zuótian-kāi-kuì
ta-méi-chū-xí. 昨天開會
他沒出席. He was
absent from yesterday's meeting.

CHÚXÌ₂ 除夕 (TW) New Year's
eve.

'CHÙXÙ₂ 儲蓄 (TV) save, ac-
cumulate. Nǐ-méi-chùxù-yi-
diǎnr-qián ma? 你沒儲蓄
一點兒錢嗎? Didn't
you save a little money?
(N) savings. Wǒ-jiù-yǒu-zhèi-
yidiǎnr-'chùxù. 我就有這
一點兒儲蓄. I only
have this little bit in savings.

CHŪ-YÁNG₂ 出洋 (VO) go
abroad.

CHŪ-ZHĚN₃ 出診 (VO) (lit.
go out to give medical treatment)
make a house call (of a medical
doctor).

CHŪZHŌNG₁ 初中 (N) (con.
chūjí-zhōngxué 初級中學).
junior high school.

CHŪ-ZHÚYI₁ 出主意 (VO)
suggest a plan.

CHÚZI₂ 廚子 (N) cook. (cf:
CHÚSHIFU 廚師傅).

CHŪZŪ₂ 出租 (TV) rent some-
thing to someone, for rent.

CÍ₄ 詞 (N) a form of Chinese poem
(characterized by lines of une-
qual length as opposed to poems,
shī 詩, which have the same
number of syllables in each line).

(M: shǒu 首).

CÍ₂ 辭 (TV) refuse, decline <u>an invitation or a request</u>. Tā-qǐng-wǒ-chī-fàn, wǒ-cí-le. 他 請 我 吃 飯, 我 辭 了. He invited me for dinner, I declined. (2) resign. Wǒ-bǎ-shìqing-cí-le. 我 把 事 情 辭 了. I resigned from my job. (3) re-lease, discharge <u>someone from a job</u>. Wǒmen-děi-cí-jige-rén. 我 們 得 辭 幾 個 人. We have to let several people go.

CÌ₃ 刺 (TV) (1) stab, pierce, punc-ture. Tā-ná-dāozi-yào-cì-wo. 他 拿 刀 子 要 刺 我. He grabbed a knife and wanted to stab me. (2) assassinate. Tā-bèi-ren-cì-le. 他 被 人 刺 了. He was assassinated. (N) (1) thorn, splinter. (2) fish bone. (See: CÌR 刺兒).

CÌ₁ 次 (M) time (<u>a case of occur-rence and recurrence</u>). (<u>syn.</u> huí 回). liǎngcì 兩 次 twice. dìsāncì 第 三 次 the third time. yicì-yòu-yicì 一 次 又 一 次 over and over again. (SV) (1) be of poor quality(<u>ap-plied to objects</u>). cì-huò 次 貨 goods of second quality, seconds. (2) be of poor character, dis-honorable (<u>applied to a person</u>). Zhèige-ren tài-cì. 這 個 人 太 次. This person is very low.

CÌDĀO₄ 刺 刀 (N) bayonet, dag-ger. (M: bǎ 把).

CÍDIǍN₁ 詞 典 (N) dictionary.

(M: běn 本 , bù 部). (cf: ZÌ-DIǍN 字典).

CÌHOU₂ 伺 候 (TV) serve, take care of, attend to <u>someone's personal needs, as a servant, nurse, etc.</u> cìhou-bìngrén 伺 候 病 人 take care of the patients.

CÍHUÌ₂ 詞 彙 (N) vocabulary, glossary.

CÌJI₁ 刺 激 (TV) sting, provoke to cause an emotional reaction. Bié-cìji-ta. 別 刺 激 他. Don't provoke him. (N) emotional shock. Tā-shòule-hěn-dàde-cìji. 他 受 了 很 大 的 刺 激. He received a great shock.

CÍLÈI₅ 詞 類 (N) parts of speech.

CÍQI₃ 瓷 器 (N) porcelain, china-ware. (M: jiàn 件).

CÍR₁ 詞 兒 (N) word, expression (<u>uttered saying</u>).

CÌR₃ 刺 兒 (N) (1) thorn, splinter, barb (<u>on a plant, board or wire</u>). Huārshang-yǒu-cìr. 花 兒 上 有 刺 兒. That flower has thorns. (2) pique. Tā-shuō-huà dài-cìr. 他 說 話 帶 刺 兒 He speaks with pique.

'CÍSHÀN₅ 慈 善 (SV) <u>formal</u>. kind, benevolent.

CÍSHÍ₃ 磁 石 (N) magnet.

CÌSHU₂ 次 數 (N) number of times (<u>of occurrence</u>). cìshu-tài-duō-le 次 數 太 多 了 too many times.

CÌWÀI₂ 此 外 (MA) besides this, beyond this. Cǐwài jiu-méiyou-biéde-le. 此 外 就 沒 有

C

别 的 了. There are no others besides this.

CÍ-XÍNG₂ 辭行 (VO) say good-bye, bid farewell (by a person going far away). Wǒ-lái-gēn-nín-cí-xíng. 我來跟您辭行. I have come here to bid you farewell (because I am going far away).

CÌXU₁ 次序 (N) sequence, proper order. Bǎ-nèitao-shū àn-cì-xu-fànghǎo. 把那套書按次序放好. Put the set of books in order.

CÍ-ZHÍ₂ 辭職 (VO) resign from a job.

CŌNG₃ 蔥 (N) onion, scallion.

CÓNG₁ 從 (CV) (1) from (a time or a place). Wǒ-cóng-bādiǎn-zhōng jiu-zài-zhèr-děng-ta. 我從八點鐘就在這兒等他. I have been waiting here for him since eight o'clock. Nǐ-cóng-nǎr-lái? 你從那兒來? Where have you come from? Wǒmen-cóng-dìyíkè-niàn-ba. 我們從第一課念吧. Let's read from lesson one. (2) from (a point of view). Nǐ-děi-cóng-gè-fāngmian-kàn. 你得從各方面看. You must look at it from different angles. Túng-jīngjishang-shuō, tāde yìjian-bu-cuò. 從經濟上說,他的意見不錯. Speaking from the point of view of economics, his opinion is right. (3) via, through or past a place. Wǒmen shi-cóng-ʼzhèige-mén jìnlaide.

我們是從這個門進來的. This is the door that we came in through. (cf: DǍ 打, YÓU 由).

CÓNGCǏ₃ 從此 (MA) from this time on. Wǒ-cóngcǐ-bu-hē-jiǔ-le. 我從此不喝酒了. From this time on, I will not drink (liquor) any more.

CÓNG...DÀO...₁ 從...到... (S) from...to... cóng-zǎo-dào-wǎn 從早到晚 from morning to evening. Cóng-zhèr zǒu-dao-nèr. 從這兒走到那兒. Walk from here to there.

CÓNGLÁI₁ 從來 (MA) always (in the past), from the beginning. Tā-cónglái jiu-zài-zhèr-zhù. 他從來就在這兒住. He has always lived here. Wǒ-cónglái bu-chàng-gēr. 我從來不唱歌兒. I never sing.

CŌNGMING₁ 聰明 (SV) smart, brilliant, intelligent. (opp. bèn 笨).

CÓNG...QǏ₁ 從...起 (S) starting from..., from...on. cóng-xiàn-zài-qǐ 從現在起 from now on. cóng-zhèitiao-xiàn-qǐ 從這條線起 from this line on.

CÓNGQIÁN₁ 從前 (TW) formerly, before. Nà-shì-cóngqiánde-shì. 那是從前的事. That is a past event. Cóngqián wǒ-bu-zhīdào. 從前我不知道. I didn't know before.

CÓNGRONG₂ 從容 (SV) be at leisure because there is enough time. Hái-yǒu-liǎngge-zhōngtóu

feī̆jǐ-cái-kāi-ne. Wǒmen-kéyi-
hen-cóngrong. 還 有 兩 個
鐘 頭 飛 機 才 開 呢.
我 們 可 以 很 從 容.
There is still two hours before
the plane departs. We can take
our time.
(AD) at ease. Bú-yào-máng,
cóngrong-yidiǎnr-zuò. 不 要
忙, 從 容 一 點 兒 作.
Don't rush, do it leisurely.

CÓNGTÓUR₂ 從 頭 兒 (AD)
from the very beginning. Cóng-
tóur-zuò-chǐ. 從 頭 兒 作 起.
Do it from the very beginning.

CÓNG...WÀNG...₂ 從 ... 往 ...
(S) from...to... Cóng-zuǒ-wàng-
yòu-xiě. 從 左 往 右 寫.
Write from left to right.

CÓNGXIǍOR₂ 從 小 兒 (AD)
since childhood. Tā-cóngxiǎor-
jiu-xǐhuan-'Lǐ-xiáojie. 他 從
小 兒 就 喜 歡 李 小
姐. He loved Miss Li since
his childhood.

CÓNGXĪN₁ 從 新 see CHÓNG-
XĪN 重 新.

CÒU₃ 湊 (TV) (1) gather together,
collect or piece together, make
up. Tāmen-còuzai-yíkuair-guò-
nián. 他 們 湊 在 一 塊 兒
過 年 They all gather together
to celebrate New Year's. Zhèi-
xie-jiāju bú-shi-yítào, shì còu-
qilai-de. 這 些 家 具 不
是 一 套, 是 湊 起 來
的. This furniture is not an
ensemble, they are pieced together. Wǒ-zuǒ-jiè-yòu-jiè,
cái-còuchengle-yìbǎikuai-qián.

我 左 借 右 借 才 湊
成 了 一 百 塊 錢. I
borrowed left and right and finally made up a hundred dollars.
(2) join in (a group for fun or
merriment). Wǒmen-còucou-rè-
nao-qu. 我 們 湊 湊 熱 鬧
去. Let's go and join in the
excitement. (3) move gradually
toward a place Bié-wàng-nèi-
bianr-còu. 別 往 那 邊 兒
湊 Don't get close to that side.

CÒUHE₃ 湊 合 (TV) (1) move
gradually toward a certain place
or point. Bié-wàng-nèibianr-còu-
he. 別 往 那 邊 湊 合.
lit. or fig. Don't move toward
that side. (2) compromise(accept something less than what
was originally desired), put up
with, make things do. (syn. jiāngjiu 將 就). Wǒ-lǎo-còuhe-nǐ,
wèi-shénma-nǐ-bu-néng-còuhe-
wǒ-ne? 我 老 湊 合 你 為
甚 麼 你 不 能 湊 合
我 呢 ? I always compromise
for you, why can't you compromise for me? Zhèige-suírán-
bu-hǎo, kěshi hái-néng-còuhe.
這 個 雖 然 不 好, 可
是 還 能 湊 合. Though
this isn't any good, it will do.
Méi-yǒu-hǎode, nǐ-jiu-còuhezhe-
yòng-zhèige-ba. 沒 有 好 的,
你 就 湊 合 着 用 這
個 吧. There aren't any good
ones. Try to put up with this one.

CÒUQIǍO₃ 湊 巧 (SV) just right,
coincidentally. Nǐ-lái-de zhēn-
còuqiǎo. 你 來 的 真 湊

C

C

巧 . You came just at the right time (coincidentally). (MA) by coincidence. Còuqiǎo wǒ-nèitian-bìng-le. 湊巧我那天病了. By coincidence I was sick that day.

CŪ$_1$ 粗 (SV) (1) coarse. cū-rén 粗人 coarse person. cū-bù 粗布 coarse cloth. yímiàn-guāng, yímiàn-cū 一面光, 一面粗 one side is smooth, the other side is coarse. (2) thick (large in crossection). (opp. xì 細). Xiàn-tai-cū. 線太粗. The thread is too thick.or The line is too thick.

CÙ$_2$ 醋 (N) vinegar.

'CŪBÀO$_5$ 粗暴 (SV) crude, rough, unrefined (of a person).(opp. 'wényǎ 文雅).

'CŪCĀO$_5$ 粗糙 (SV) coarse, rough (of things).

CUĪ$_2$ 催 (TV) rush someone to do something. Bié-cuī-wo. 別催我 . Don't rush me.

CUĪ$_4$ 呼 (TV) spit.

CUÌ$_2$ 脆 (SV) (1) crisp, brittle, (materials or voice). (2) quick and easy, snappy (in doing something), just like that (with the snap of fingers). Zhèijian-shì ta-bànde-hěn-cuì. 這件事他辦的很脆. He did this easily and quickly.

'CÙJÌN$_5$ 促進 (TV) urge, press forward, stimulate, spur on.

'CŪLǓ$_5$ 粗魯 (SV) coarse, crude (of a person).

CÚN$_1$ 存 (TV) (1) store. Tā-jiāli-cúnzhe-hěn-duō-liángshi. 他家

裏存着很多糧食. He has a lot of provisions stored in his home. (2) check (as baggage), deposit money in a bank. Bǎ-màozi cúnzai-zhèr. 把帽子存在這兒. Check your hat here. (3) keep, hold on to. Tā-cúnbuzhù-qián. 他存不住錢 . He can't keep money. Nǐ-cún-'shénma-xīn? 你存甚麼心 ? What intentions do you have in mind?

CÙN$_1$ 寸 (M) a Chinese measure of length equivalent to about 1.3 inches, Chinese inch. gōngcùn 公寸 decimeter. yīngcùn 英寸 , inch.

CÚN-HUÒ$_2$ 存貨 (VO) (lit. hoard goods) stock up. Wǒmen-děi-chèn-zhèige-jīhui cún-yidiǎnr-huò. 我們得趁這個機會存一點兒貨 We ought to take this opportunity to stock up.

(N) stock (merchandise), inventory. Méi-yǒu-cúnhuò-le. 没有存貨了 . There is no stock left.

CÚN-KUǍN$_2$ 存款 (VO) deposit money. Wǒ-zài-yínháng-cúnle-yibǐ-kuǎn. 我在銀行存了一筆款 . I deposited a sum of money in the bank.

(N) deposited money. Wǒ-yǒu-yibǐ-cúnkuǎn. 我有一筆存款 . I have a sum of money deposited.

CÚNR$_3$ 村兒 see CÚNZI 村子.

CÚNZÀI$_3$ 存在 (IV) exist. 'Zhèi-jǒng-rén bu-yāngdāng cúnzài.

這種人不應當存在 . This kind of person should not exist.

CŪNZHǍNG4 村長 (N) head of a village. (M: wèi 位).

CÚNZHÉ4 存摺 (N) bank book. (M: běn 本).

CŪNZHUĀNGR4 村莊兒 (N) village.

CŪNZI2 村子 or CŪNR 村兒 (N) village.

CUŌ3 搓 (TV) (1) rub with the palm of the hand. Tā-lěngde zhí-cuō-shǒu. 他冷得直搓手. He is so cold that he is rubbing his hands. Yòng-hǒujiǔ-cuōcuo. 用火酒搓搓. Rub it with alcohol. (2) roll a cylindrical object between two palms or between the palm and another surface to twist it or to make it tight. xuō-xiàn 搓線 twist a thread (a process of making thread).

CUÒ1 錯 (IV) make a mistake. Wǒ-men-cuòle-bu-shǎo. 我們錯了不少. We made quite a few mistakes. Tā-jiù-cuòle-'yí-ge-zì. 他就錯了一個字. He was mistaken on only one word.

(SV) wrong. (opp. duì 對). Wǒ-shuōle-yijiu-cuò-huà. 我說了一句錯話. I said some wrong words. Nǐ-cuò-le. 你錯了 . You are wrong. (cf: BU-CUÒ 不錯).

(RE) wrong. Duìbu'qǐ, wo shuō-

'cuòle. 對不起，我說錯了 . I am sorry, I said it wrong. (cf: CUÒR 錯兒 , BUCUÒ 不錯).

CUÒ3 錯 (N) file, rasp (tool). (M: bǎ 把).

(TV) (1) file. Yòng-cuò cuòcuo. 用錯錯錯. Use the file to file it. (2) move past one another. cuò-chē 錯車 two trains pass by each other.

CUÒCHU2 錯處 (N) mistake, fault.

CUŌHE5 撮合 (TV) make people get together. Wàng-yikuàir-gěi-tamen-'cuōhe cuōhe. 往一塊兒給他們撮合撮合. Make them get together.

CUÒR1 錯兒 (N) Peip. mistake, error, fault. (syn. cuòwu 錯誤). Méi-cuòr. 沒錯兒 . No mistakes. Tā-lǎo-ai-fàn-zhèi-yàngrde-cuòr. 他老愛犯這樣兒的錯兒. He always makes this kind of mistake. Shì-wǒde-cuòr. 是我的錯兒. It is my fault.

'CUÒSHI3 措施 (N) steps, measures in dealing with a certain situation.

CUÒWU1 錯誤 (N) mistakes, errors. (syn. cuòr 錯兒).

CUÒZÌ1 錯字 (N) wrong character, wrong word.

'CŪRÉN3 粗人 (N) crude person.

CÙXĪN2 粗心 (SV) careless. (syn. dàyi 大意). (opp. xìxīn 細心).

D

DĀ₃ 搭 (TV) (1) lay across. Bǎ-yīshang dāzai-shéngzishang. 把衣裳搭在繩子上. Hang the clothes on the clothes line. (2) build something for temporary use, as scaffolding, platform, a temporary bridge, etc. Tāmen-zài-yuànzili dāle-yige-tái. 他們在院子裏搭了一個台. They built a platform in the yard.

DĀ₃ 搭 (TV) lift or carry something, by two or more persons. Bǎ-zhuōzi-dāguolai. 把桌子搭過來. Move the table here.

DĀ₂ 搭 (TV) travel by or take a train, bus, boat, airplane, etc. Nǐ-dā-něibān-fēijī? 你搭那班飛機? Which flight are you going to take?

DĀ₃ 搭 (TV) add, plus. Sānkuai-dā-liǎngkuai shì-wǔkuai. 三塊搭兩塊是五塊. Three dollars plus two dollars are five dollars.

DǍ₁ 打 (M) dozen.

DǍ₃ 打 (CV) Peip. (1) from (a time, a place or a point of view). (2) via, through. (See: CÓNG 從).

DǍ₁ 打 (TV) (1) strike, beat, hit. Bié-dǎ-rén. 別打人. Don't hit people. Tā-āile-yídùn-dǎ. 他挨了一頓打. He was beaten up. (2) fight. Tāmen-dáqilai-le. 他們打起來了. They started to fight. (3) break. Tā-bǎ-wǎn-dǎ-le. 他把碗打了. He broke the bowl. (4) strike, beat, play a percussion instrument. dǎ-zhōng 打鐘 strike the bell. (5) gather and fetch. dǎ-chái 打柴 fetch firewood. (6) buy something in liquid form. dǎ-yóu 打油 buy oil. dǎ-jiǔ 打酒 buy wine. (7) dip up liquids with a dipper. dǎ-shuǐ 打水 get water (from a well, river or lake). (8) play a game (of competition or with hitting action). dǎ-pái 打牌 play cards. dǎ-qiú 打球 play a ball game. (9) send a message. dǎ-diànhuà 打電話 make a phone call. (10) fish or hunt. dǎ-yú 打魚 fish. dǎ-lǎohǔ 打老虎 hunt for a tiger. (11) inject. dǎ-zhēn 打針 inject (medicine). (12) fire (firearms). dǎ-qiāng 打鎗 fire a gun. (13) make a mark. dǎ-túzhāng 打圖章 make an imprint with a seal. (14) make sudden uncontrollable physical actions. dǎ-tìfen 打嚏噴 sneeze. (15) hold aloft. dǎ-sǎn 打傘 hold an umbrella. (16) knit, crochet, tat. dǎ-máoyī 打

毛衣 knit a sweater. (17) plan, originate. dǎ-gǎozi 打稿子 make a draft. dǎ-zhúyi 打主意 make plans. (18) give a discount. dǎ-zhékou 打折扣 give a discount or discredit (as a story). (19) have something made. dǎ-shǒushi 打首飾 have jewelry made. (20) (con. dǎkai 打開). open packages. Zhèixie-bāoguǒ-gāng-dào, hái-méi-dǎ-ne. 這些包裹剛到還沒打呢. These parcels which have just arrived haven't been opened yet. (21) pack. Kuài-yidiǎnr-dǎ-xíng-li, wǒmen-děi-zǒu-le. 快一點兒打行李, 我得走了. Hurry up and pack, we have to go. (22) make a knot. dǎ-lǐngdài 打領帶 tie a necktie. (23) drill a hole. dǎ-jǐng 打井 drill a well. (24) estimate a certain amount for something. Lián chī-dài-zhù yígòng-dǎ-sānshi-kuai-qián. 連吃帶住一共打三十塊錢 Including food and lodging, we can estimate thirty dollars.

DÀ₁ 大 (SV) (opp. xiǎo 小). (1) big, large (in size, capacity). Tāde-háizi dou-dà-le. 他的孩子都大了. His children have all grown up. 'Shēngyin-hěn-dà. 聲音很大. The noise is very loud. Wǒ-mei-you-nènma-dà-gōngfu. 我沒有那麼大工夫. I don't have that much time. Tāde-guān hěn-dà, míngqi yě-hen-dà. 他的官

很大, 名氣也很大. His rank is very high and he is very famous. Guā-'dà-fēng, xià-'dà-yǔ. 颳大風, 下大雨. The wind is blowing hard and it is raining hard. Wù-hěn-dà. 霧很大. It is very foggy. Tāde-pàitóur hěn-dà. 他的派頭兒很大. He is very imposing. Tā-yí-kànjian-bu-duì, qì-jiu-dà-le. 他一看見不對, 氣就大了. As soon as he saw that it wasn't right, he got very angry. Wàng-dàli-xiě. 往大裏寫. Write big. (2) old (referring to a person's age). Tā-suìshu tài-dà-le. 他歲數太大了 He is too old. Tā-bǐ-nǐ dà-yísuì. 他比你大一歲. He is one year older than you.

(TV) make something big, large, great. Nǐ-dàzhe-dǎnzi-jìnqu. 你大着膽子進去. Get your courage up and go in.

(B) first, oldest. Tā-shi-lǎodà. 他是老大. He is the oldest one. Zhèi-shi-wǒ-'dàʼérzi 這是我大兒子. This is my oldest son.

(AD) on a large scale, greatly. Tāmen-dà-chī-dà-hē. 他們大吃大喝. They eat and drink a lot. Tā-dà-kū-yízhèn. 他大哭一陣. She cried hard for a while. (See: BÚDA 不大).

DÁʼÀN₃ 答案 (N) answer, solution to a problem (especially in writing). Zhèige-wèntí méi-you-

D

dá'àn. 這 個 問 題 没 有 答 案 . There is no answer for this question.

DÁBAN₃ 打 扮 see DǍBAN 打 扮.

DÁBAN₃ 打 扮 or DÁBAN 打 扮 (TV) (1) dress up, make up, adorn a person. Nǐ-děi-'dǎban-dǎban. 你 得 打 扮 打 扮 . You have to dress up (or make up) a little. (2) disguise a person. Tā-dǎbancheng-yíge-nǚren. 他 打 扮 成 一 個 女 人 . He disguised himself as a woman.

DǍ-BĀO₃ 打 包 (VO) (1) wrap a package. (2) unwrap a package.

DÀBIÀN₃ 大 便 (IV) (lit. great convenience) have a bowel movement, defecate. Wǒ-liǎngtiān méi-dàbiàn-le. 我 兩 天 没 大 便 了 . I haven't moved my bowels for two days. (N) human feces.

DÀBÙFEN₂ 大 部 分 (N) most part, greater part.

DǍ-CHÀ₂ 打 岔 (VO) (1) misinterpret as a result of not hearing clearly. (2) break into someone's conversation, interrupt someone's speech. Duìbuqǐ, wǒ-dǎ-ge-chà. 對 不 起 , 我 打 個 岔 . Excuse me for interrupting.

DǍ-CHÁR₃ 嗒 喳 兒 (VO) (1) say something related to what was said before by somebody else. Tā-shuō-huà, nǐ-bié-dǎ-chár. 他 説 話 , 你 别 嗒 喳 兒 . When he is talking, don't say anything related to

what he says. (2) verbally acknowledge someone's speech. Wǒ-gēn-nǐ-shuō-huà-ne. Nǐ-zěnma bù-dā-chár? 我 跟 你 説 話 哪 , 你 怎 麽 不 嗒 喳 兒 啊 ? I am talking to you, why don't you say something?

DÀ-DǍN₂ 大 胆 (VO) (lit. make courage big) bold, daring, fearless. Nǐ-zhēn-dà-dǎn. 你 真 大 胆 . You are really bold.

DÁDAO₂ 達 到 (TV) arrive at, reach, attain (objective, level, point, etc.). Wǒmen-zuò-de yǐjing-dádao xiāngdāngde-chéngdu-le, kěshi hái-méi dádao-mùdi. 我 作 的 已 經 達 到 相 當 的 程 度 了 , 可 是 還 没 達 到 目 的 . What we have done has reached a certain point, but we still haven't reached our objective.

DǍDǍO₂ 打 倒 (RV) knock down, overthrow. Dǎdǎo-dìguozhǔyì! 打 倒 帝 國 主 義 ! Down with imperialism! Tāmen-bǎ-Lǎo-Lǐ dǎdǎo-le. 他 們 把 老 李 打 倒 了 . lit. or fig. They knocked old Li down.

DǍ-DIÀNBÀO₁ 打 電 報 (VO) send a telegram.

DǍ-DIÀNHUÀ₁ 打 電 話 (VO) make a telephone call.

DÀDÒU₄ 大 豆 (N) soybean.

DǍ-DǓ₃ 打 賭 (VO) bet, make a friendly wager (with or without money). Míngtian-yídìng-xià-yǔ. Wǒ-gǎn-gēn-ní-dǎ-dǔ. 明 天 一 定 下 雨 我 敢

跟 你 打 賭. I will
bet you that tomorrow it definitely will rain. (cf: DŬ-QIÁN
賭 錢).

DĂ-DÙNR₃ 打 盹 兒 (VO) doze
off, take a nap.

DÀDUŌSHÙ₂ 大 多 數 (N) the
great majority.

DĂFA₂ 打 發 (TV) (1) send someone on an errand. Wŏ-dăfa-ta-
qù-măi-yidiănr dōngxi. 我 打
發 他 去 買 一 點 兒
東 西 . I sent him to buy
something. (2) dismiss with
proper justification or compensation. Wŏ-bă-gōngren-dăfa-
zŏu-le. 我 把 工 人 打
發 走 了 . I have dismissed
the worker.

DÀFANG₁ 大 方 (SV) act in a
manner befitting a gentleman,
lady or person of high status,
generous, dignified, poised. (opp.
xiăoqi 小 氣). Tā-yòng-qián
hen-dàfang. 他 用 錢 很 大
方 . He is very generous with
his money. 'Hēi-yīshang kànzhe-
hen-dàfang. 黑 衣 裳 看 着
很 大 方 .Black clothes make
people look very dignified. Tā-
shuō-huà zŏngshi-hĕn-'dàfangde-
yàngzi. 他 説 話 總 是 很
大 方 的 樣 子 . When he
speaks he is always very poised.

DÁFU₃ 答 覆 (TV) reply formally.
(N) formal reply. Xiàlibài-yi-
qián, nĭ-dei-gĕi-wŏ-yige-dáfu.
下 禮 拜 以 前, 你 得
給 我 一 個 答 覆 .
Before next week, you must give
me a reply.

DÀGÀI₁ 大 概 (AD) (1) probably.
Tā-dàgài-bu-zhīdào. 他 大 概
不 知 道 . Probably he does
not know. (2) approximately. Nĭ-
dàgài-yŏu-duōshao-qián? 你 大
概 有 多 少 錢 ? How
much money do you have, approximately?

DÀGÀI₁ 大 概 (AD) generally
(without going into detail). Wŏ-
dàgàide-shuōle-shuo. 我 大 概
的 説 了 説 I spoke gener-
ally.
(N) general idea. Qĭng-nĭ-xiān-
gàosong-wo-ge-dàgài. 請 你
先 告 訴 我 個 大 概 .
Please tell me the general idea
first.

DĂ-GÉR₅ 打 嗝 兒 (VO) (1)
hiccup. (2) belch.

DĂ-GŬ₃ 打 鼓 (VO) beat a drum,
play a drum. fig. worry, fear.
Wŏ-xīnli zhí-dă-gŭ. 我 心 裏
直 打 鼓 .My heart is beat-
ing like a drum.

DĂ-GUĀNSI₂ 打 官 司 (VO) engage
in a law suit.

DĂ-HĀCHI₃ 打 哈 欠 (VO) yawn.

'DÀHÒUNIAN₂ 大 後 年 (TW)
three years hence from this
year.

'DÀHÒUTIAN₂ 大 後 天 (TW)
three days hence from today.

DÀHUÀ₂ 大 話 (N) big talk,
boasting. shuō-dàhuà 説 大
話 talk big, exaggerate.

DÀHUÌ₃ 大 會 (N) general meeting, plenary assembly.

DÀHUŎ₂ 搭 夥 (IV) form a part-

D

D

nership, do <u>something</u> jointly.
Wǒ-gēn-ta dāhuǒ-zuò-mǎimai.
我 跟 他 搭 彩 作 買
賣. He and I became business
partners.
DǍHUŎJĪ₂ 打 火 機 (N) ciga-
rette lighter. (<u>syn.</u> zìlaihuǒ 自
來 火).
DĀI₁ 待 (IV) stay, remain. Tā-
zài-jiāli dāizhe-ne. 他 在 家
裏 待 着 呢.He is staying
home (doing nothing). Wǒ-zài-
nèr dāide-gōngfu-bu-dà. 我 在
那 兒 待 的 工 夫 不
大. I didn't stay there for
long. (cf: ZHÙ 住).
DǍI₂ 逮 <u>or</u> DĚI 逮 (TV) catch <u>a</u>
<u>person, a bird or an animal</u>.Tā-
men-dǎizhao-yige-zéi. 他 們
逮 着 一 個 賊.They
caught a thief. Xiǎo-háizi yào-
dǎi-niǎor.小 孩 子 要 逮
鳥 兒. The children want to
catch a bird.
DÀI₁ 帶 (TV) (1) carry along with,
bring <u>or</u> take along. Nǐ-dài-
qián-meiyou? 你 帶 錢 沒
有? Do you have money with
you? (2) include, be with. Nèige-diànyǐngr dài-'yánse-bu-dài?
那 個 電 影 兒 帶 顏
色 不 帶?Is that movie in
color? (3) lead <u>someone</u>. Qǐng-
nǐ-dàizhe-wo qu-jiàn-ta.請 你
帶 着 我 去 見 他.
Please take me to see him. Wǒ-
dài-ni-kànkan.我 帶 你 看
看. I will take you along to
show you around.
DÀI₁ 戴 (TV) wear <u>on the head or</u>

hand, such as glasses, ear muffs,
gloves; or somewhere else on
the body, such as jewelry, flowers or other adornment. (cf:
CHUĀN 穿, ZHĀI 摘).
DÀI₂ 待 (TV) treat, deal with
people. (<u>syn.</u> duì 對). Tā-dài-
péngyou hen-hǎo. 他 待 朋
友 很 好. He treats his
friends very nicely.
DÀIBIǍO₁ 代 表 (TV) represent.
Wǒ-dàibiǎo-ta-qu-kāi-kuì. 我
代 表 他 去 開 會. I
will go to the meeting repre-
senting him. Gāngde-chǎnliang
kéyi-dàibiǎo-gōngye-jìnbude-
chéngdu. 鋼 的 產 量 可
以 代 表 工 業 進 步
的 程 度. Steel production
may represent the level of industrial progress.
(N) representative. Wǒ-qǐng-ta-
dāng-wǒde-dàibiǎo. 我 請 他
當 我 的 代 表. I will
ask him to act as my representative.
DÀIBǓ₄ 逮 捕 (TV) arrest (<u>law</u>
<u>enforcement</u>).
DÀIFU₁ 大 夫 (N) doctor (<u>medi-</u>
<u>cal</u>). (<u>syn.</u> yīsheng 醫 生).
'DÀILǏ₃ 代 理 (TV) (1) act on
someone's behalf <u>while that per-</u>
<u>son is absent or unable to per-</u>
<u>form his duties</u>. Tā-jiào-wo-
'dàilǐ-ta. 他 叫 我 代 理
他. He asked me to take his
place. (2) act as an agent. Wǒ-
men-'dàilǐ-nèige-gōng'sī-de-shì-
qing.我 們 代 理 那 個
公 司 的 事 情. We take

care of that company's business.
(N) agent.

(B-) acting. dàilǐzǒngtǒng 代
理 總 統 acting president
(of a country).

DÀIMÀN₃ 待 慢 (TV) (lit. I have
treated you shabbily.) said by
the host to his guests when they
leave.

DÀISHǑUR₄ 帶 手 兒 (AD)
while (when the circumstance or
time is convenient). Nǐ-dàishǒur-
guānshang-mén. 你 帶 手 兒
關 上 門 . Close the door
while you are there.

DÀITÌ₃ 代 替 (TV) substitute for
someone or something, be a
substitute. Wǒmen-kéyi-yòng-
zhèige-dàiti. 我 們 可 以
用 這 個 代 替 . We can
use this as a substitute.

DÀI-YIHUIR₁ 待 一 會 兒 (MA)
after awhile, later. Dāi-yihuir
zai-shuō. 待 一 會 兒 再
說 . I'll talk about it later.

DÀIYU₃ 待 遇 (N) treatment
(usually refers to pay or salary).
Zhèige-xuéxiàode-dàiyu-bu-cuò.
這 個 學 校 的 待 遇
不 錯 . The salary this school
pays is not bad.

DÀIZI₂ 帶 子 (N) strap, belt,
ribbon, tape. (M: gēn 根 , tiáo
條).

DǍJI₃ 打 擊 (N) mental blow,
shock. Tāde-'háizi-sǐle, tā-
shòule-hěn-'dàde-dǎji. 他 的
孩 子 死 了 , 他 受 了
很 大 的 打 擊 . Her
child died, she received a tre-

mendous shock.
(TV) strike a blow. dǎji-díren
打 擊 敵 人 strike a blow
at the enemy.

DǍ-JIÀ₂ 打 架 (VO) (1) fight
(personal), come to blows. (2)
argue violently. dǎ-'zuǐ-jià 打
嘴 架 argue, dispute.

DÀJIĀ₁ 大 家 (PR) everybody.
Dàjiā-xiǎoxin. 大 家 小 心 .
Everybody be careful. Wǒmen-
dàjiā-dōu-qù. 我 們 大 家
都 去 . All of us will go.

DǍJIǍO₂ 打 攪 (TV) (1) disturb
someone. Bié-dǎjiǎo-ta. 別 打
攪 他 . Don't disturb him. (2)
used as a polite phrase, usually
said by a visitor when leaving.
Dǎjiǎo-dǎjiǎo. 打 攪 打 攪 .
Thank you for all your trouble.

DǍKAI₁ 打 開 (RV) (1) open. dǎ-
kai-mén 打 開 門 open the
door. (2) turn on a valve, a television set, a radio, etc. dǎkai-
wúxiàndiàn 打 開 無 線 電
turn on the radio.

DǍ-LÉI₁ 打 雷 (VO) thunder.
DǍ-LIÈ₂ 打 獵 (VO) hunt for
game.

DÀLǏTÁNG₂ 大 禮 堂 (N) au-
ditorium.

DÀLÙ₂ 大 陸 (N) (1) continent.
Měizhou-dàlù 美 洲 大 陸
continent of America. (2) mainland. Měiguo-dàlù 美 國 大
陸 American Mainland.

DÀMÀI₅ 大 麥 (N) barley (grain).

DÀMÉN₁ 大 門 (N) (1) big door
or doorway. (2) main gate or
main entrance.

D

D

DÀMǏ₃ 大米 (N) rice (hulled and uncooked.

DǍMO₅ 打磨 (TV) polish, sand, rub to make smooth.

DĀN₃ 擔 (TV) (1) carry with a pole on one's shoulder. (2) fig. shoulder a responsibility. dān-búshi 擔不是 take the blame. Wǒ-bu-néng-dān-zhèige-zéren. 我不能擔這個責任. I cannot take responsibility for this.

DĀN₃ 單 (AD) (1) particularly. Tā-wèi-shénma dān-yào-zhèige? 他為甚麼單要這個? Why did he want this particularly? (2) solely, alone. Wǒ-men-dān-zǒu-ba. 我們單走吧. Let's go by ourselves. (B-) (1) single. 'dānrenfáng 單人房 single room. (2) something in the form of a sheet.

DǍN₅ 撣 (TV) dust (with a duster).

DÀN₂ 淡 (SV) weak in concentration, diluted. (1) weak or light in taste (of wine, cigarettes, etc.). (opp. chòng 衝). (2) not salty, tasteless. (opp. xián 鹹). Cài-tài-dàn. 菜太淡. The food is tasteless. (3) light, pale (of a color). (opp. shēn 深). Yánse-hěn-dàn. 顏色很淡. The color is very light. (4) fig. slow (of business). (opp. hǎo 好). Zhèige-yuè shì-'dàn-yuè. 這個月是淡月. This month is the month when business is slow.

DÀN₅ 石 (M) (1) a picul, a weight measure équivalent to 100 catties or 133-1/2 lbs. (2) a volume measure recently standardized to contain 100 liters. yídàn-mǐ 一石米 a picul of rice or 100 liters of rice.

DĀNCHUN₂ 單純 (SV) simple (not involved with other affairs). Zhèijian-shìqing bu-dānchun. 這件事情不單純. This affair is not simple.

DĀNG₁ 當 (TV) serve as, be (in the role of). dāng-xuésheng 當學生 be a student. dāng-bīng 當兵 serve as a soldier. dāng-tàitai 當太太 be a (house) wife. Zài-nèichu-xìli, nǐ-dāng-shéi? 在那齣戲裏你當誰? Which role do you have in that play? (cf: DÀNG(ZUO) 當(作)).

DĀNG₂ 當 (CV) in the presence of someone. Tā-bu-gǎn-dāngzhe-ta fùmǔ-chōu-yān. 他不敢當着他父母抽烟 He doesn't dare smoke in front of his parents.

DǍNG₃ 當 (TV) think (mistakenly) that... Wǒ-dǎng-ta-shì-Zhōng-guo-ren-ne. 我當他是中國人呢. I thought he was a Chinese (but I was wrong). (cf: 'YǏWÉI 以為).

DǍNG₂ 黨 (N) party (political). rù-dǎng 入黨 enter the party, become a member of a party.

DǍNG₃ 擋 (TV) block the way, light or view. Bié-dǎngzhe-wo, ràng-wo-guòqu. 別擋着我, 讓我過去. Don't block my way, let me pass. Nǐ-dǎng-

zhe-wo, wǒ-kànbujiàn. 你擋
着我，我看不見. You
are blocking my view, I cannot
see.

DÀNG₄ 當 (TV) pawn.
(N) things to be pawned. dàng-
dàng 當當 pawn things. dàng-
pu 當鋪 pawn shop.

DÀNG(ZUO)₁ 當作 (TV) as, take
for. Nǐ-kéyi ná-zhèige dàng(zuo)-
chǐ-yong. 你可以拿這
個當作尺用. You may
take this to be used as a ruler.
Wǒ-ná-tā dàng(zuo)-hǎo-ren-le.
我拿他當作好人
了. I took him for a good man.

DÀNGĀO₂ 蛋糕 (N) cake (such
as a birthday or wedding cake).
(M: kuài 塊).

DĀNG-BĪNG₂ 當兵 (VO) enlist
as a soldier or be a soldier.

DĀNGCHŪ₂ 當初 (1) in the beginning. (2) in the past.

DĀNG... DE-SHÍHOU₂ 當...的
時候 (S) at the time when...
Dāng-wǒmen-'zài-nèr-de-
shíhou, tā-méi-shuō-huà. 當
我們在那兒的時
候，他沒説話. When
we were there, he didn't say
anything.

DĀNGE₃ 耽擱 (TV) (1) put off,
delay. Bù-máng, zhèifēng-xìn
dānge-liǎngtian-zai-xiě yě-kéyi.
不忙,這封信耽擱
兩天再寫也可以.
No hurry, it is all right to delay
the writing of this letter for a
couple of days. (2) waste time,
spend idle time. (syn. dānwu

耽誤). Děng-huǒchē tài-
dānge-shíhou. 等火車太
耽擱時候. Waiting for
the train wastes too much time.
(N) stay. Wǒ-'méi-you-jitiande-
dānge. 我沒有幾天的
耽擱. I will not stay long,
perhaps just a few days. (cf:
DĀNWU 耽誤).

DĀNGJIÀNR₂ 當間兒 (PW)
Peip. (1) middle. Zhànzai-dāng-
jiànr. 站在當間兒.
Stand in the middle. (cf: DĀNG-
ZHŌNG 當中). (2) space in
between. Nèi-liǎng-ge-qìchē-
dāngjiànr hái-kéyi-tíng-yíge-qì-
chē. 那兩個汽車當
間兒,還可以停一
個汽車. You are still able
to park another car between those
two cars.

DĀNG-MIÀN₃ 當面 (VO) in front
of someone, face to face. Bié-
dāng-tāde-'miàn-shuō. 別當
他的面説. Don't talk in
front of him. Wǒ-gēn-ta-dāng-
miàn-shuō. 我跟他當面
説. I'll speak to him face to
face.

DĀNGPÀI₃ 黨派 (N) clique,
group (social or political). Dǎng-
pài-hěn-duō. 黨派很多.
There are many cliques.

DĀNGRAN₁ 當然 (SV) natural.
Nàshi-dāngrande-shìqing.那是
當然的事情. That's
a natural thing.
(AD) of course, naturally. Tā-
dāngran-qù. 他當然去
Of course he'll go.

D

DĀNGSHÍ₁ 當時 (TW) at the very same time. Wǒ-dāngshí-méi-xiángchilái. 我 當 時 没 想 起 來. At that moment I did not think of it.

DĀNGTIĀN₃ 當天 (TW) the same day. Wǒ-dāngtiān-qù, dāngtiān-huílai. 我 當 天 去，當 天 回 來. I go and come back on the same day.

DĀNGXUǍN₄ 當選 (TV) be e-lected. Tā-dāngxuǎn-zǒngtǒng. 他 當 選 總 統. He was elected president.

DĀNGYUÁN₄ 黨員 (N) political party member.

DÀNGZI₄ 擋子 (M) for an event, affair, etc. (syn. jiàn 件). Wǒ-pèngjian-'zènma yidàngzi-shì. 我 碰 見 這 麽 一 擋 子 事. I ran into this kind of affair.

DĀNGZHŌNG₁ 當中 (PW) (1) middle. Fàngzai-dāngzhōng. 放 在 當 中. Put it in the middle. (cf: DĀNGJIÀNR 當間兒). (2) space in between. Liǎngbǎ-yǐzi-dāngzhōng yǒu yizhāng-zhuō-zi. 雨 把 椅 子 當 中 有 一 張 桌 子. There is a table in between those two chairs. (3) among, between. Wǔge-rén-dāngzhōng yǒu-yíge-shi-wàiguo-ren. 五 個 人 當 中 有 一 個 是 外 國 人. Among those five people, there is one foreigner.

DĀNJÙ₃ 單據 (N) simple documentary proof, receipt, invoice, shipping ticket, etc.

(M: zhāng 張).

DĀNMÀI₂ 丹麥 (PW) Denmark.

DĀNREN₂ 担任 (TV) assume a position or responsibilities. Tā-dānren-fùxiàozhǎng. 他 担 任 副 校 長. He assumes the position of vice president of the school. Nǐ-dānren-shénma-kè? 你 担 任 甚 麽 課? (lit. For which courses are you as-suming responsibility?) What courses are you teaching?

DÀNSHI₁ 但是 (AD) but, how-ever. Wǒ-tīngshuōle, dànshi-wǒ bu-xìn. 我 聽 説 了，但 是 我 不 信. I have heard it but I don't believe it. (cf: KĚSHI 可 是, BÚGUÒ 不 過).

DĀNWÈI₃ 單位 (N) unit (of meas-urement, of an organization, etc.).

DĀNWU₂ 耽誤 (TV) (1) let an opportunity go by, cause some-thing to be missed by delaying. Bié-dānwu-háizi-niàn-shū-de-jīhui. 別 耽 誤 孩 子 念 書 的 機 會. Don't let the opportunity for the children to study go by. Kuài-qǐng-dàifu, bié-bǎ-bìng-dānwu-le. 快 請 大 夫，別 把 病 耽 誤 了. Call the doctor fast, don't delay the treatment of the illness. (2) waste time, spend idle time. (syn. dānge 耽擱). Zhèiyangr-zuò tài-dānwu-shíhou. 這 樣 兒 作 太 耽 誤 時 候. Doing it this way wastes too much time. (3) delay, procrastinate. Yīnwei-xià-xuě dānwule-yitian. 因 為 下 大 雪 耽 誤

了 一 天. Because of heavy snow it was delayed a day. (cf: DǍNGE 耽 擱).

DǍNXIǍO₄ 膽 小 (SV) timid.

DĀN-XĪN₄ 擔 心 (VO) worry. Wǒ-zhēn-tì-ni-dānxīn. 我 真 替 你 擔 心 . I am really worried for you.

DĀNZI₃ 單 子 (1) list of items. kāi-dānzi 開 單 子 make out a list or itemize. (M: zhāng 張). (2) sheet (bedding).

DǍNZI₅ 膽 子 (N) fearlessness.

DǍNZI₅ 撢 子 (N) an implement for dusting made of feathers or strips of cloth tied to a handle, duster. (M: bǎ 把). Yòng-dǎzi dǎn-yidǎn-tǔ. 用 撢 子 撢 一 撢 土 . Use the duster to dust.

DÀNZI₄ 担 子 (N) load carried by a pole across the shoulders. Dànzi-hěn-zhòng. 担 子 很 重. (lit. or fig.) The load is very heavy. (cf: TIĀOZI 挑 子).

DĀO₁ 刀 (N) knife. (M: bǎ 把). (M) stroke of a knife. Tā-āile-yidāo. 他 挨 了 一 刀 . He got a cut (from the slash of a knife).

DÁO₅ 捯 (TV) pull in something like string or rope, an arm-length at a time alternating each arm. Bǎ-'fēngzheng-'dáoxia-lai. 把 風 箏 捯 下 來. Pull the kite down.

DǍO₁ 倒 (IV) (1) turn something from upright to postrate position, topple. Fángzi-dǎo-le. 房 子 倒 了 . The house fell over.

(2) fail (financially, of a store or business). Pùzi-dǎo-le. 鋪 子 倒 了 . The store failed.

(RE) fall over, topple. Tā-bǎ-dēng-pèngdǎo-le.他 把 燈 碰 倒 了 . He bumped the lamp and it fell over.

DǍO₂ 倒 (TV) (1) change or switch things around. Bǎ-zhèi-liǎngge-dǎo-yidao.把 這 兩 個 倒 一 倒 . Change these two around. (2) buy or sell a store or business, change hands. Tā-bǎ-pùzi dáogei-wǒ-le. 他 把 鋪 子 倒 給 我 了. He sold the store to me.

DǍO₃ 島 (N) island.

DÀO₁ 到 (IV) reach, arrive. Tā-lái-le, kěshi-hái-méi-dào-ne. 他 來 了, 可 是 還 沒 到 呢 . He started to come, but has not arrived yet. Wǒmen-dàole-nǎr-le? 我 們 到 了 那 兒 了 ? (lit.Where have we reached?) Where are we now? Tā-dàoguo-Zhōngguo. 他 到 過 中 國 . (lit. He has reached China.) He has been in China. Jīntian-kāikuì dàole-duōshao-ren? 今 天 開 會 到 了 多 少 人 ? How many came to the meeting today? Qián-yi-dào-shǒu jiu-huā-le. 錢 一 到 手 就 花 了 . (lit. As soon as the money reached the hand, it was spent.) As soon as he got the money, he spent it. Búlùn-shénma-shì yí-dào-tā-ner, jiu-máfan-le.不 論 甚 麼 事 一 到 他 那 兒 就 麻

D

D

煩了. It doesn't matter what it is, as soon as it gets to him there's trouble with it. Shíhou-dàole-ma? 時候到了嗎? Is the time up? Dàole-shíhou zai-mǎi. 到了時候再買. When the time comes then (we) will buy it.

(CV) move or travel to a place. Dào-xuéxiào-lái. 到學校來. Come to the school. Tā-dào-pùzi-qu-mǎi-dōngxi-qule. 他到鋪子去買東西去了. He went to the store to buy something.

(PV) to a place, a certain time or degree. Nádao-lóushang-qu. 拿到樓上去. Take it upstairs (there). Zhèiben-shū nǐ-niàndao-dì'jǐkè-le? 這本書你念到第幾課了? What lesson are you up to in this book? Tā-zuòdao-'wǔdiǎn-zhong jiu-bú-zuò-le. 他作到五點鐘就不作了. He'll work only until five o'clock. Zhèr-xiàtian yǒu-shíhou-rèdao-yíbǎidù. 這兒夏天有時候熱到一百度. In the summer here, sometimes the temperature goes up to one hundred degrees.

(RE) arrive at a place, reach a point. Wǒ-yào-zǒudao-ta-jiā, kěshi-méi-zǒudào. 我要走到他家,可是沒走到. I wanted to walk to his house, but didn't get there by walking. Nèijian-shìqing wo-bàn-budào. 那件事情我

辦不到. (lit. I cannot reach the result of that affair.) I can't do that. 'Tā-láile, wo-méi-xiǎngdào. 他來了,我沒想到. (lit. I didn't extend my thinking that far to reach the fact that he came.) I didn't expect him to come.

DÀO₁ 倒 (TV)(1) invert. Bǎ-huàr-dàoguolai. 把畫兒倒過來. Turn the picture upside down. Shùmude-cìxu dào-le. 數目的次序倒了. The order of the numbers is inverted. (2) pour out. dào-chá 倒茶 pour tea. Bǎ-yàopiàr cóng-píng-zili-dàochulai. 把藥片兒從瓶子裏倒出來. Pour the pills out of the bottle. (3) discard something by turning its container upside down. Tā-bǎ-fàn dou-dào-le. 他把飯都倒了. He threw out all the rice.

(RE) be inverted. Tā-bǎ-bào nádào-le. 他把報拿倒了. He held the newspaper upside down.

(AD) in reverse or inverse order or position. Tā-'dào-shǔ-dìyī. 他倒數第一. (lit. He is the number one, counting backwards.) He is the last one.

DÀO₂ 倒 (TV) go backward. Bǎ-qìchē dàochulai. 把汽車倒出來. Back the car out. Dào, dào, dào, hǎo-le. 倒,倒,倒,好了. Back up, back up, back up, O.K.

DÀO₃ 倒 (AD) but, yet. Zhèige-zì 'wǒ-bu-rènshi, nèige-Měiguo-ren dào-rènshi. 這 個 字 我 不 認 識, 那 個 美 國 人 倒 認 識. I don't recognize this character but that American does. Tā-bu-jiào-'wǒ-shuō, ta-zì'jǐ-dào-'shuō-le. 他 不 叫 我 説, 他 自 己 倒 説 了. He told me not to talk about it and yet he himself talked about it. (cf: FĂN(DAO) 反(倒)).

DÀO(SHI)₁ 倒 (是) (1) admittedly, it is(followed by a phrase with or and yet). 'Hǎo-dào(shi)-hǎo, kěshi-guì. 好 倒 (是) 好, 可 是 貴. It's good all right, but it's expensive. 'Hǎo-dào(shi)-bù-hǎo, kěshi piányi. 好 倒 (是) 不 好, 可 是 便 宜. Sure it isn't good, but it's cheap. (2) at least. Nǐ-dào(shi)-xiǎng-yixiang-a! 你 倒 (是) 想 一 想 啊! At least (you) think about it a little! Tā-suíran-bu-cōngming, dào(shi)-hái-kěn-niàn-shū. 他 雖 然 不 聰 明, 倒 (是) 還 肯 念 書. Although he is not bright, at least he is willing to study. (3) (con. dào-dǐ(shi)到底(是)). used for pressing for an exact answer, actually, really, indeed. Nǐ-dào(shi)-yào-shénma? 你 倒 (是) 要 甚 麼? What do you really want?

DÀO₂ 道 (M) (1) for objects that are long and narrow. yídao-hé 一 道 河 one river. (2) for questions in examinations. Zuò-le-jǐdao-tí? 作 了 幾 道 題? How many problems did you answer? (3) for commands or orders. Tā-xiàle-yídào-mìngling. 他 下 了 一 道 命 令. He gave an order. (4) beam of light. yídao-húng-guāng 一 道 紅 光. a beam of red light. (5) time (occurrence). Guòle-háoji'dào-shǒu-le. 過 了 好 幾 道 手 了. It has changed hands several times. (6) for doorway or passageway. Wǒmen-děi-guò-liǎngdao-mén. 我 們 得 過 兩 道 門. We have to pass two doorways. (7) for food or drink served. yí-dao-cài 一 道 菜 one course of a meal. yídao-jiǔ 一 道 酒 a round of drinks. (8) for levies of taxes, customs, duties, etc. Děi-shàng-liǎngdao-shuì. 得 上 兩 道 税. We must pay two kinds of taxes. (9) for stages in procedure. yídao-shǒu-xu 一 道 手 續 one step of the procedure. (10) coat of paint. Shàngle-sāndao-yóu. 上 了 三 道 油. It has been given three coats.

DÀO₂ 道 (N) (1) road, way. huǒ-chē-dào 火 車 道 railway. (2) way, doctrine, gospel. Tā-ài-jiǎng-dào. 他 愛 講 道 He likes to preach (the gospel).

DÀOBÌ₄ 倒 閉 (IV) close down a business due to insolvency. Yínháng-dǎobì-le. 銀 行 倒 閉 了 The bank has closed down.

DÀOCHĀ₁ 刀 叉 (N) knife and fork.

D

D

DÀOCHU₃ 到 處 (PW) every-
where. Wǒ-'dàochu-zhǎo-ta.
我 到 處 找 他. I looked
everywhere for him.

DÀODE₃ 道 德 (N) morals, vir-
tue. Tā-dàodé-hěn-gāo. 他 道
德 很 高. His morals are
very high.

DÀODǏ 到 底 (MA) (1) used for
pressing for an exact answer,
actually, really, indeed. (syn.
dào(shi) 倒 (是)). Nǐ-dàodǐ-qù-
bu-qu? 你 到 底 去 不 去 ?
Are you really going? (2) after
all, finally. Dàodǐ-hái-shi-'wǒ-
gěide-qián. 到 底 還 是 我
給 的 錢. It was I who fi-
nally paid. Dàodǐ-wǒmen-shì-
lǎo-péngyou. 到 底 我 們
是 老 朋 友. After all, we
are old friends. (cf: JIŪJING 究竟).
(VO) reach the bottom. Píngzili-
de-yóu jǐjing-dàole-dǐ-le. 瓶子
裏 的 油 巳 經 到 了
底 了. (lit. The oil in the
bottle has reached the bottom.)
The oil has been all used up.
(RE) to the end. Bāng-rén bāng-
daodǐ. 幫 人 幫 到 底. If
you help someone, help him until he has completed his job.
Wǒ-yào-bǎ-zhèijian-shì wèndao-
dǐ. 我 要 把 這 件 事 問
到 底. I want to ask and get
to the bottom of this affair.

DÀOLI₂ 道 理 (N) (1) principle,
reason. Bié-shuō-méi-yǒu-
'dàolide-huà. 別 說 没 有
道 理 的 話. Don't say
unreasonable things. (2) doc-

trine, gospel. .Zhè-shi-'Kǒngzǐ-
jiǎngde-dàolǐ. 這 是 孔 子
講 的 道 理. This is the
doctrine preached by Confucius.

DÀOLU₃ 道 路 (N) road, way.

DǍO-LUÀN₂ 搗 亂 (VO) make
trouble, cause trouble, stir up
a disturbance. Nǐ-bié-gēn-wo-
dǎo-luàn. 你 別 跟 我 搗
亂. Don't make trouble for me.

DǍO-MÉI₃ 倒 霉 (VO) have bad
luck. Tā-dǎole-yiniánde-méi.
他 倒 了 一 年 的 霉.
He has had bad luck for a year.
(SV) unlucky. Wǒ-zhēn-dǎoméi.
我 真 倒 霉. I am really
unlucky.

DÀOR₂ 道 兒 (N) (1) road, way.
(syn. lù 路). zǒu-dàor 走 道
兒 walk, travel on foot. Dàor-
hen-yuǎn. 道 兒 很 遠. The
road is very long. fig. Huā-qián-
de-dàor tài-duō. 花 錢 的 道
兒 太 多. There are
too many ways to spend money.
(2) line. huà-dàor 畫 道 兒
draw a line.

DÀOTUÌ₃ 倒 退 (TV) (lit. or
fig.) go backward. Wǒmen-děi-
wàng-qián-jìn, bu-néng-dàotuì.
我 們 得 往 前 進, 不
能 倒 退. We have to go
forward, not backward. dàotuì-
èrshinián 倒 退 二 十
年. go back twenty years.

DÀO-XǏ₁ 道 喜 (VO) congratulate.
Dàoxǐ-dàoxǐ. 道 喜 道 喜.
I wish you happiness. Wǒmen-
qù-gěi-ta-dào-ge-xǐ. 我 們
去 給 他 道 個 喜. Let's

go to congratulate him.

DÀO-XIÈ₁ 道 謝 (VO) thank. Wǒ-
hái-méi-gei-nín-dàoxiè-ne. 我
還 没 給 您 道 謝 呢.
I haven't thanked you yet.

DǍOYǍN₃ 導 演 (TV) direct a
play.
(N) director of a play.

DÀOZI₁ 刀 子 (N) knife. (M: bǎ
把).

DÀOZI₅ 稻 子 (N) rice (plant).

DǍ-PÁI₂ 打 牌 (VO) play cards
or mah-jong.

DÀPÀO₃ 大 砲 (N) (1) big gun,
cannon. (M: mén 門). fàng-
dàpao 放 大 砲 fire the big
gun or fig. brag. (2) person who
brags. Tā-shì-ge-dàpào. 他 是
個 大 砲 . He is a braggart.

DǍPÒ₂ 打 破 (RV) (1) break by
striking or knocking against or
upon something. Wǒ-bǎ-yǎnjìngr
dǎpò-le. 我 把 眼 鏡 兒
打 破 了 . I broke my glasses.
Tā-bǎ-fànwǎn dǎpò-le. 他 把
飯 碗 打 破 了 . He broke
the rice bowl.or fig. He lost his
job. (2) break a precedent . dǎ-
pò-shìjiè-jìlù 打 破 世 界
記 錄 break the world's record.
(3) dispel a belief, disprove a
theory. Zhèige-lǐlùn méi-fázi-
dǎpò. 這 個 理 論 没 法
子 打 破 . This theory can-
not be disproved.

DǍ-QÌ₃ 打 氣 (1) pump air into
something, such as a tire. Qiú-
děi-dǎ-qì-le. 球 得 打 氣
了 . The ball needs some air
(to be pumped in). (2) encourage,

boost morale or spirit. Tāde-
'jīngshen-bu-hǎo, wǒmen-děi-
gei-ta-dǎ-qì. 他 的 精 神
不 好 , 我 們 得 給 他
打 氣 . His spirits are low,
we must give him encouragement.

'DÀQIÁNNIAN₃ 大 前 年 (TW)
three years ago from this year.

'DÀQIÁNTIAN₃ 大 前 天 (TW)
three days ago from today.

DǍ-QIÚ₁ 打 球 (VO) play a ball
game (of any kind), play ball.

DÀREN₂ 大 人 (N) adults, grown-
ups.

DÁSAO₄ 打 掃 (TV) clean up a
place.

DǍ-SHǍN₁ 打 閃 (VO) flash (of
lightning).

DÀSHǏ₂ 大 使 (N) ambassador.
(M: wèi 位). zhù-Měi dàshǐ
駐 美 大 使 the ambassa-
dor stationed in America. 'Měi-
guo-dàshǐ 美 國 大 使
American ambassador.

DǍSUAN₁ 打 算 (AV) plan to.
Nǐ-dǎsuan-zěnma-bàn? 你 打
算 怎 麼 辦 ? How do you
plan to do it?
(TV) plan, think over. Nǐ-'dǎ-
suan-dǎsuan. 你 打 算 打
算 . You think it over.
(N) plan. Tā-méi-yǒu-ge-dǎsuan.
他 没 有 個 打 算 . He
doesn't have a plan.

DǍ-SUÀNPAN₃ 打 算 盤 (VO)
(1) calculate on an abacus. (2)
plan, scheme for profit.

DǍTING₁ 打 聽 (TV) inquire.
Méi-dìfang-dǎting-qu. 没 地
方 打 聽 去 . There is no

D

place to inquire.

DÀTÓNG₃ 大同 (PW) Ta-t'ung (city in Shensi province).

DĂ-TÓUR₃ 打頭兒 (VO) be first to do something. Shéi-dă-tóur? 誰打頭兒? Who is the first one?
(AD) from the beginning. Wŏmen-dă-tóur-shŭ. 我們打頭兒數. Let's count from the very beginning.

DĂ-WŌ₅ 搭窩 (VO) build a nest (of a bird).

DÀXIĂO₂ 大小 (N) size, dimensions. Zhèige-wūzide-dàxiăo bu-gòu-dà. 這個屋子的大小不夠大. The (size of this) room is not large enough.

DÀXĪYÁNG₂ 大西洋 (PW) Atlantic Ocean.

DÀXUÉ₁ 大學 (N) university, college. niàn-dàxué 念大學 study in college.

DÀXUÉSHĒNG₂ 大學生 (N) college student. Note, however, that when the final syllable is toneless. dà-xuésheng 大學生 big student.

DÀYĀN₅ 大烟 (N) opium. chōu-dàyān 抽大烟 smoke opium.

DÀYÀN₅ 大雁 (N) wild goose. (M: zhĭ 隻).

DÀYI₂ 大意 (SV) careless in having overlooked or neglected something. (syn. xìxīn 細心) (opp. cūxīn 粗心). Wŏ-dàyi-le. 我大意了. I was careless.

DÀYĪ₃ 大衣 (N) overcoat, topcoat. (M: jiàn 件).

DÀYÌ₂ 大意 (N) outline, general idea of some statement, story, etc.

DĀYING₂ 答應 (1) answer. Wŏ-jiào-ni, ni-zĕnma-bu-dāying? 我叫你, 你怎麽不答應? I called you, why didn't you answer me? (2) agree to, promise. 'Zhèryàngrde-tiáo-jian wŏmen bu-néng-dāying. 這樣的條件我們不能答應. We cannot agree to this kind of terms. Wŏ-dāying-ta gĕi-ta-bàn. 我答應他給他辦. I promised to do it for him. (cf: BUDĀYING 不答應).

DĂ-YÚ₂ 打魚 (VO) catch fish.

DÀYUĒ₃ 大約 (MA) in a person's rough estimate. Dàyuē-ta-bu-zhidào. 大約他不知道. In my estimation he doesn't know. Dàyuē-'shífēn-zhōng. 大約十分鐘. Roughly ten minutes.

DĂ-ZÁR₃ 打雜兒 (VO) do odd jobs.

DÁZI₅ 疊子 (M) stack of paper. yídázi-piàozi 一疊子票子 a pile of bank notes.

DÀZHÀN₃ 大戰 (N) (1) major war, big war. (M: cì 次) shìjiè-dàzhàn 世界大戰 world war. (2) big battle. (M: chăng 場)

DĂ-ZHÀNG₁ 打仗 (VO) fight (by armed forces).

DĂ-ZHĀOHU₂ 打招呼 (VO) (1) make a gesture to someone to say hello. Tā-kànjian-wo, méi-gēn-wo-dă-zhāohu. 他看見我沒跟我打招呼. He saw me, but he didn't say hel-

lo. (2) tell <u>someone</u> about <u>some-</u>
<u>thing.</u> Nǐ-xiān-gēn-ta-dǎ-ge-
zhāohu. 你 先 跟 他 打 個
招 呼. You tell him about it
first.

DAZHE₄ 搭着 (MA) moreover.
Nèige-bu-tài-hǎo, yòu-dazhe-guì,
suóyi-wǒ-méi-mǎi. 那 個 不
太 好，又 搭着 貴，所
以 我 没 買. That thing
is not too good, moreover it is
expensive, so I didn't buy it.

DǍ...ZHÉ₂ 打...折 (S) give
a certain discount. <u>The Chinese</u>
<u>way of expressing the idea of</u>
<u>"giving a discount" is to state</u>
<u>the percentage of the original</u>
<u>price which is to be paid rather</u>
<u>than the percentage taken off the</u>
<u>original price.</u> dǎ-bāzhé 打
八 折 20% off (80% needs to be
paid). (cf: ZHÉ 折).

DǍ-ZHÉKOU₂ 打 折 扣 (VO)
(1) give a discount. Tā-bu-kěn-
dǎ-zhékou. 他 不 肯 打 折
扣. He is not willing to give a
discount. (2) discredit (<u>as a</u>
<u>story</u>). Tā-shuō-de-huà, děi-dǎ-
zhékou. 他 説 的 話，得 打
折 扣. What he said can-
not be completely believed. (See:
DǍ..ZHÉ 打...折).

DǍ-ZHĒN₁ 打 針 (VO) have <u>or</u>
give an injection. Tā-gěi-wǒ-
dǎle-yizhēn. 他 給 我 打 了
一 針. He gave me an injec-
tion. <u>or fig.</u> He gave me a shot
in the arm.

DÀZHÌ₁ 大 致 (MA) on the whole,
in general. Tā-shuōde dàzhì-hěn-

duì. 他 説 的 大 致 很
對. On the whole, what he said
is correct.

DǍ-ZHÚYI₂ 打 主 意 (VO) make
plans. Tā-dǎdìngle-zhúyi-le.
他 打 定 了 主 意 了.
He has decided.

DǍ-ZÌ₁ 打 字 (VO) type (<u>words</u>).
Tā-yìfēn-zhōng néng-dǎ-wǔshige-
zì. 他 一 分 鐘 能 打 五
十 個 字. He is able to type
fifty words a minute.

DÀZIJĪ₁ 打 字 機 (N) type-
writer. (M: jià 架).

DE₁ 的 (1) <u>used after an expres-</u>
<u>sion, X, and followed by a noun,</u>
<u>X-de N, the expression X-de</u>
<u>serves as a modifier of the noun;</u>
<u>it may be rendered in English as</u>
<u>the N that X. When the noun af-</u>
<u>ter de</u> 的 <u>is omitted, the ex-</u>
<u>pression X-de is nominal and</u>
<u>may be translated as the one(s)</u>
<u>that X. (a) after a pronoun, a</u>
<u>noun of person or other nouns,</u>
<u>indicates a possessive.</u> wǒde-
shū 我 的 書 the book that is
mine, my book. Shū-shi-wǒde.
書 是 我 的. The books
are mine. wūzide-mén 屋 子
的 門 the door which belongs
to the room, the door of the
room. (b) <u>after a noun to form</u>
<u>another noun</u> mùtoude-zhuōzi 木
頭 的 桌 子 the table which
is made of wood, wooden table.
Zhuōzi-shi-mùtoude. 桌 子 是
木 頭 的. Tables are made
of wood. (c) <u>after a PW or TW.</u>
Zhōngguode-rén 中 國 的 人

D

D

the people who are in China. shàngtoude-huàr 上 頭 的 畫 兒 the picture that is on the top. Wǒ-yào-shàngtoude. 我要上 頭 的. I want the one that is on the top. jīntiande-bào 今 天 的 報 today's newspaper. Zhèige-zázhì shì-shànglibàide. 這 個 雜 誌 是 上 禮 拜 的. This is last week's magazine. (d) after NU-M. yì-tiānde-gōngfu 一 天 的 工 夫 one day's time. yíkuai-qiánde-táng 一 塊 錢 的 糖 the candy that sells for one dollar or one dollar's worth of candy. Géi-wo-liǎngzhang wǔ-kuai-qiánde (-piàozi). 給 我 兩 張 五 塊 錢 的 (票 子). Give me two fives. yìzhuōzide-cài 一 桌 子 的 菜 a tableful of food. (e) after SV (when the SV is one syllable, an AD is required to precede it). hěn-dàde-zhuōzi 很 大 的 桌 子 the table that is very big. (hěn) cōngmingde-háizi (很) 聰 明 的 孩 子 the child that is brilliant. Wǒ-xǐhuan-cōngmingde. 我 喜 歡 聰 明 的. I like the bright ones. (f) after a verbal expression. màile-de-fángzi 賣 了 的 房 子 the house that was sold. wǒ-mǎi-de-dōngxi 我 買 的 東 西 the things that I bought. Tā-mǎi-de wo-dōu-xǐhuan. 他 買 的 我 都 喜 歡. I like all of the ones that he bought. Zhèige-shi-màide, nèige-shi-búmàide.

這 個 是 賣 的, 那 個 是 不 賣 的. This is the one for sale, that is not. Zhèi-shì-wǒ-mǎi-fángzi-de-qián. 這 是 我 買 房 子 的 錢. This is the money that I'll use to buy a house. (g) after VO. mài-bào-de-nèixie-rén 賣 報 的 那 些 人 those people who sell newspapers. Tā-shi-mài-bào-de. 他 是 賣 報 的. He is a newspaper seller. Zhèige-shi-chī-fàn-de-zhuōzi. 這 個 是 吃 飯 的 桌 子. This table is used for eating. mài-bào-de-háizi 賣 報 的 孩 子 the child who sells newspapers or the child who belongs to the newspaper seller. (2) used with certain AD. dàgàide-shuō 大 概 的 説 generally speaking. Tā-hěn-xiǎoxinde wàng-qián-zǒu. 他 很 小 心 的 往 前 走. He walked forward very carefully. (3) when added to a reduplicated SV, NU-M, ONO or certain combinations of opposites, forms expressions which may be used to modify a noun or a verb, which may be omitted. In reduplicated SV, the last syllable may be changed into level tone and an r 兒 sound added. mànmānrde-zǒu 慢 慢 兒 的 走 walk slowly. kuàikuāirde 快 快 兒 的 hurry up. yíge-xiǎoxiǎode-huāyuánr 一 個 小 小 的 花 園 兒 a small garden. āiyou-āiyoude-jiào 哎 喲 哎

唷的叫 shout ouch. yìnián-yìniánde guòde-hěn-kuài 一年一年的過得很快 passes very fast year by year. Dǎ-ge-diànhuà-suàn-le. Shěngde-zǒulái-zǒuqù-de. 打個電話算了,省得走來走去的 Make a phone call to save running around. (4) used after a verb or VO, or between a verb and its object which is preceded by the element in the sentence to be stressed, such as a subject or an expression of time, place or manner. Shì 是 or búshi 不是 often precedes the stressed element. De 的 indicates that the action of the verb is completed. Shì-'tā gěide-qián. 是他給的錢. It was he who paid. Wǒ-búshì-'qùnian-bì-yède. 我不是去年畢業的. It wasn't last year that I graduated. Nì-shì-zuò-fēi'jī-láide-ma? 你是坐飛機來的嗎? Was it by plane that you came? Tā-shi-'jīnnian-xuǎnde-zhǔxí. 他是今年選的主席. It was this year that he voted for the chairman. or It was this year that he was elected chairman. or He is the chairman who voted this year. or He is the chairman who was elected this year. (5) used after a pronoun or personal noun and followed by a noun, PR-de N is a contraction of PR-dāng-de N or PR-zuò-de N, the N is played by PR. Nèicì-

yǎn-xì shì 'Lǐ-tàitaide nǚzhǔjuér. 那次演戲是李太太的女主角兒. In that performance the main female role was played by Mrs. Li. (6) used after a verbal phrase and before a SV, indicates using a course of action which has been suggested. Wǒ-xiǎng-shi-gào-song-ta-de duì. 我想是告訴他的對. I think (the course of action of) telling him is right. (7) used at the end of a sentence, indicates a certain category to which the subject belongs. Zhèifēng-xìn shi-yào-jìdao-Zhōngguo-qu-de. 這封信是要寄到中國去的. This is the letter which will be sent to China. (8) used at the end of a sentence, that's what it is. Nǐ-háishi-dei-gěi-ta-qián-de. 你還是得給他錢的. You still have to pay him, that's what it is. (9) used between two NU-M, plus, and. Liǎngge-de-sānge shi-wǔge. 兩個的三個是五個. Two plus three are five. (See: SHÌ 是).

(S) (1) X de-X, Yde-Y, X 的-X, Y 的-Y. some...some... Nèi-xie-rén gāode-gāo ǎide-ǎi. 那些人高的高矮的矮. Some of those people are tall, some are short. Háizimen jié-hūnde-jié-hūn, shàng-xuéde-shàng-xué, dōu-zǒu-le. 孩子們結婚的結婚,上學的上學,都走了.

D

D

Some of the children got married, some went to school. They are all gone. (2) <u>with</u> yŏu 有 <u>or</u> méi 没, yŏude-V 有 的 - V <u>or</u> méide-V 没 有 -V, have <u>or</u> there is something to... <u>or</u> haven't <u>or</u> there isn't anything to... Wŏ-hái-yŏude-yòng-ne. 我 還 有 的 用 呢. I still have something to use.

DE₃ 的 Peip. <u>used for</u> dào 到 <u>or</u> zài 在 <u>as a PV</u>. Tā-pǎode-qián-tou-qu-le. (<u>for</u> dào 到) 他 跑 的 前 頭 去 了. He ran ahead to the front. Nǐ-zhùde-nǎr-le? (<u>for</u> zài 在) 你 住 的 那 兒 了 ? Where did you stay? (See: DÀO 到, ZÀI 在).

DE₁ 得 (1) <u>used as an infix in a RV, Vde RE, to form the affirmative potential RV, able to do something.</u> kàndejiàn 看 得 見 able to see. zūde-chūqù 租 得 出 去 able to rent out. (2) <u>used after a verb to indicate some phenomenon caused by the action of the verb, so... that, because... so much.</u> Tā-xiàode-zhànbuqilái-le. 他 笑 得 站 不 起 來 了. He laughed so much that he couldn't stand up. A: Tā-wèi-shénma-zènma-lèi-a? B: Niàn-shū-niànde. A: 他 為 甚 麼 這 麼 累 啊 ? B: 念 書 念 得. A: Why is he so tired? B: Because he studies so much. (3) <u>used after SV and followed by an expression which describes the</u> degree of the SV, so... that... Tā-gāoxìng-de 'shénma-dou-wàng-le. 他 高 興 得 甚 麼 都 忘 了. He is so happy that he forgot everything. (RE) <u>in potential RV only. In the affirmative form the infix</u> de <u>is dropped.</u> (1) fit to, safe to. Zhèige-huà shuōde-shuōbude? 這 個 話 説 得 説 不 得 ? Is it fit to say this? (2) able to. Nǐ-rènde-rènbude? 你 認 得 認 不 得 ? Are you able to recognize? Wŏ-jì-bude-le. 我 記 不 得 了. I cannot remember.

DÉ₁ 得 (TV) obtain, acquire, get. Tā-déde-shi-'shénma-bìng? 他 得 的 是 甚 麼 病 ? What kind of sickness does he have? Nǐ-shi-'nĕinián-déde-'bóshi? 你 是 那 年 得 的 博 士 ? In which year did you receive your doctorate? Wŏ-kàn-xiǎo-shuōr déle-bushǎo-zhīshi. 我 看 小 説 兒 得 了 不 少 知 識. I acquired a lot of knowledge from reading novels. Zhèiyangr-zuò kŏngpa-débuzháo-jiéguo. 這 樣 作 恐 怕 得 不 着 結 果. If we do it this way, I am afraid we cannot get any results. Èr-jiā-sān dé-wŭ. 二 加 三 得 五. Two plus three is five.

(IV) ready. Yìhuĭr-jiu-dé. 一 曾 兒 就 得. It will be ready in a minute. Fàn shénma-shíhou-dé? 飯 甚 麼 時 候 得 ? When will dinner be ready? Yíge-

zhōngtóu-'dédeliǎo-ma? 一個
鐘 頭 得 得 了 嗎? Can
it be ready in one hour?
(RE) ready. Yīshang míngtian-
xǐde'dé-xǐbudé? 衣裳 明天
洗 得 得 洗 不 得? Can
these clothes be washed and
ready by tomorrow?
used by itself. (1) that does it.
Dé, nǐ-kàn, zhè-zěnma-bàn?
得, 你看, 這怎麼辦?
That does it! Look, what are you
going to do now? Nǐ-yi-shuō-ta-
chàngde-hǎo, dé, tā-'yòu-chàng-
qilai-le. 你一説他唱得
好, 得, 他又唱起來
了. As soon as you say that he
sings well, that does it, he starts
to sing again. (2) O.K.   Dé, jiù-
zènma-bàn. 得, 就這麼辦.
O.K.! we'll do it that way.
DÉDAO₁ 得到 (RV) obtain, get.
Tā-qu-jiāoshe-le, kěshi méi-dé-
dao-jiéguo. 他去交涉了,
可是没得到結果.
He went to negotiate but didn't
get any results.
DEDUŌ₁ 得多 (-B) used after
SV or expression with AV in bǐ-
construction, much more. Zhèige dàdeduō. 這個大得多.
This is much bigger. Tā-bǐ-nǐ-
ài-shuō-huà-deduō. 他比你
愛説話得多. He is
much more talkative than you
are.
DÉGUO₁ 德國 (PW) Germany.
DEHĔN₂ 得很 (-B) (1) used after
SV, very. guìdehěn 貴得很
very expensive. (2) used after

expression with AV, very much.
Tā-xǐhuan-qùdehěn. 他喜歡
去得很. He likes to go
very much.
DEHENG₄ 得哼 or DEHUANG
得慌 (-B) used after SV im-
plies that the condition stated is
causing discomfort or irritation.
Wǒ-zhèiliangtian lèideheng. 我
這兩天累得哼. I
have been tired these couple of
days.
DEHUÀ₁ 的話 (-B) used at the
end of suppositional phrases,
with or without adverbs, such as
yàoshi 要是, ruòshi 若是,
rúguǒ 如果, etc., if. (Yàoshi)
tā-kěn-dehuà, nà-jiu-hǎo-le.
(要是) 他肯的話, 那
就好了. If he is willing,
that will be good.
DEHUANG₄ 得慌 see DEHENG
得哼.
DĚI₁ 得 (AV) (1) must, have to.
Wǒ-děi-zǒu-le. 我得走了.
I must leave now. (2) certainly
will be. Yàoshi-nǐ-bu-chuān-dà-
yī, míngtian-děi-shāngfēng. 要
是你不穿大衣, 明
天得傷風. If you don't
wear your overcoat you will
certainly catch cold tomorrow.
followed by numerical expression,
need. Mǎi-zhèige-qìchē děi-sì-
qiānkuai-qián. 買這個汽
車得四千塊錢. To
buy this car you need four thousand dollars.
DĚI₁ 逮 see DĀI 逮.
DÉ-JÌNR₄ 得勁兒 (VO) feel

D

D

right (<u>physically, morally or
emotionally</u>). 'Zhèiyàngr-ná cái
dé-jìnr. 這 樣 拿 才 得
勁 兒. Holding it this way will
feel right. 'Xīnli-búda-dé-jìnr.
心 裏 不 大 得 勁 兒·
I don't feel right inside.

DÉLE₁ 得 了 <u>used at the beginning of some remarks</u>. (1) that's
enough: Déle-déle, bié-shuō-le.
得 了 得 了, 別 說 了·
That's enough, don't say any
more. Déle-ba, nǐ. 得 了 吧,
你. That's enough, you. (2)
everything is all right now. Déle, fángzi-ye-mǎile, qìchē-ye-
mǎile, hái-yao-zěnmayàng? 得
了, 房 子 也 買 了, 汽
車 也 買 了, 還 要 怎
麼 樣? All right, you have
bought the house and also the car,
what else do you want?

<u>used at the end of sentences indi-
cates a suggestion</u>. (1) that'll
be all right. Ài, jiù-zhènma-
bàn-déle. 哎, 就 這 麼 辦
得 了. Say, let's do it this
way (that'll be all right). (2)
that's all. Wǒ-gěi-nǐ-qián jiu-
déle. 我 給 你 錢 就 得
了. I'll pay you, that's all.

DÈN₅ 挗 (TV) pull suddenly, jerk,
yank.

DĒNG₁ 燈 (N) lamp, lantern. (M:
zhǎn 盞).

DĒNG₂ 登 (IV) (1) publish (<u>in a
newspaper or periodical</u>). Nèijian-shì dēng-bào-le. 那 件 事
登 報 了. That event was
published in the newspaper. Zài-

bàoshang dēngle-yige-guǎnggào.
在 報 上 登 了 一 個
廣 告. He put an advertise-
ment in the newspaper. (2)
mount, ascend. Dēngzhe-yǐzi-
guà-huàr. 登 着 椅 子 掛
畫 兒. Stand on the chair to
hang up the pictures. (3) press
down <u>with the foot</u>.

DĚNG₁ 等 (TV) wait, wait for.
'Děng-yihuǐr. 等 一 會 兒·
Wait a moment. Nǐ-děngzhe-wo.
你 等 着 我. Wait for me.

DĚNG₂ 等 (M) class of, degree of,
grade of. Zhōngguo-huǒchē fēn-
'sānděng. 中 國 火 車 分
三 等. Chinese train accom-
modations are divided into three
classes.

DÈNG₄ 瞪 (TV) (1) stare, look
intently. (2) give <u>someone</u> a
dirty look.

DĒNG-BÀO 登 報 (VO) appear
in the newspaper.

DĚNG... CAI..₂ 等 ... 才 ...(S)
wait until... then and only then...
Děng-ta-huílai wǒmen-cai-zǒu-
ne. 等 他 回 來 我 們 才
走 哪. We are not leaving
until he comes back.

DĚNGDĚNG₁ 等 等 (N) and the
like, etc.

DĒNG-GUANGGAO₂ 登 廣 告
(VO) put an advertisement in the
newspaper.

DĒNG-JÌ₃ 登 記 (VO) register
(<u>used generally except when
there is a specific term applica-
ble</u>). (cf: GUA-HÀO 掛 號,
ZHEI-CÈ 註 冊).

DĒNGLONG₂ 燈籠 (N) lantern. (M: zhǎn 盞). dǎ-dēnglong 打燈籠 hold a lantern.

DĒNGPÀOR₄ 燈炮兒 (N) light bulb.

'DĚNGYÚ₁ 等於 (TV) (1) equal to, be an equivalent. Sān-jiā-èr děngyu-wǔ. 三加二等於五 . Three plus two equal five. (2) followed by a verbal expression, same as. Nèiyàngr-zuò děngyu-zìshā. 那樣兒作等於自殺. Doing that is the same as committing suicide.

DĚNG...ZAI...₁ 等...再...(S) wait until...then... Děng-ta-huí-lai wǒmen-zai-zǒu-ba. 等他回來我們再走吧. Wait until he comes back, then we'll leave.

DĒNGZHÀOR₄ 燈罩兒 (N) lampshade.

DÈNGZI₃ 凳子 (N) stool.

DÉWÉN₁ 德文 (N) German language.

DÉXING₄ 德行 (N) (1) morals. Tāde-déxing-hěn-gāo. 他的德行很高 . His morals are very high. (2) Peip. disgusting appearance or behavior of a person. Nǐ-kàn-ta-nèige-déxing. 你看他那個德行 . How disgusting he looks.

DÉYÌ₃ 得意 (SV) feel proud of someone or something. Tā-shi-wǒ-zuì-dé'yìde-xuésheng. 他是我最得意的學生 . He is the student I'm proudest of. Tā-huà-de-zhèizhāng-huàr, ta-

hen-déyì. 他畫的這張畫兒, 他很得意 . He is very proud of the painting that he did.

DÉZUI₂ 得罪 (TV) offend. Wǒ-buzhǐbujuéde jiu-ba-rén-dézui-le. 我不知不覺的就把人得罪了 . I offended people without realizing it.

DĪ₃ 滴 (IV) drip. Wàng-yán-li dī-yǎnyào. 往眼裏滴眼藥 . Put eye drops in the eyes. (M) drop of liquid. Wǒ-lián-yi'dī-shuǐ dou-méi-hē. 我連一滴水都沒喝 . I didn't even drink a drop of water.

DĪ₁ 低 (SV) low. (opp. gāo 高). dìwei hěn-dī 地位很低 the position is very low. Tāmen-de-qùwei hěn-dī. 他們的趣味很低 . Their taste is very bad. Shēngyin hěn-dī. 聲音很低 . The sound is very low. (cf: ǍI 矮).

DÌ₁ 地 (N) (1) earth, ground, floor. Dì-dǐxia yǒu-shuǐ. 地底下有水 . There is water underground. Zhǐ zai-dìxia-ne. 紙在地下呢 . The papers are on the floor. (2) land, ground. (M: kuài 塊 , mǔ 畝). zhòng-dì 種地 (lit. plant on the land) do farm work. Wǒ-mǎile-yikuai-dì. 我買了一塊地 . I bought a piece of land. (3) earth (vs. heaven). "Tiān-bu-pà, dì-bu-pà." "天不怕, 地不怕." "Neither afraid of Heaven nor of Earth" (an adage describing a fearless person).

D

(M) ground, floor. Yídì-shuǐ. 一地水. The water is all over the floor.

DÌ₃ 遞 (TV) hand over. Qǐng-nǐ-dìgei-wo-yige-bǐ. 請你遞給我一個筆. Please hand me a pen.

DÌ₁ 第 used before NU to form ordinal numbers. dì'èrtiān 第二天 the second day or the next day. Tā-dìyī, nǐ-dìjǐ? 他第一, 你第幾? He is the first one, which one are you?

DIĂN₅ 掂 (TV) Peip. estimate the weight of something by holding or lifting it. Nǐ-diāndian, duóchén? 你掂掂, 多沉? Pick it up and guess how much it weighs? or Pick it up and see how heavy it is!

DIĂN₁ 點 (TV) touch something with something long and pointed.

(1) dot (make a dot). diǎn-diǎnr 點點兒 make dots. (2) make punctuation marks. diǎn-shū 點書 make punctuation marks in the book. (Traditional Chinese books and writing were not punctuated; the reader or the teacher punctuated them with red ink). (3) apply medicine with small stick-like instrument. diǎn-yǎnyào 點眼藥 apply medicine into the eye, put eye drops in one's eye. (4) apply fire with a stick, ignite, light. diǎn-yān 點烟 light a cigarette. diǎn-huǒ 點火 light a fire. diǎn-yánghuǒ 點洋火 strike a match. (5) point out something by touching it with a finger or a pointer. Tā-yòng-shǒu zài-dìtú-shang diǎnle-yidian. 他用手在地圖上點了一點. He used his hand (finger) to point to something on the map. (6) point out or indicate the key to understanding something. Wǒ-yi-diǎn, ta-jiu-míngbai-le. 我一點, 他就明白了. As soon as I pointed it out to him, he understood. (7) indicate what is wanted, order by selecting from a list of items. diǎn-cài 點菜 order food (in a restaurant). (8) check one by one. diǎn-shùr 點數兒 check the number, diǎn-míng 點名 (lit. check names) roll call. (9) count. Nǐ-bǎ-qián diǎn-yidian. 你把錢點一點. You better count this money. (10) move one's hand or head up and down to indicate some message. Tā-gēn-wo-diǎn- shǒu. 他跟我點手. He beckoned me to come by waving his hand.(The Chinese way of beckoning someone to come toward you is similar to the American way of waving good-bye.)

DIĂN₁ 點 (N) (1) dot, point. Wǒ-men-yào-cóng- diǎn fāzhǎn-dao-miàn. 我們要從點發展到面. We want to develop from small points into large areas. (2) time (specified point). Huǒ'chē-méi wù-'diǎn. 火車沒誤點. The train is on time.

(M) (1) for o'clock or hour. 'liǎng-diǎn-zhōng 兩 點 鐘 two o'clock or two hours. (2) point, matter. Wǒ-yào-'shuō-de-yǒu-'sāndiǎn. 我 要 説 的 有 三 點. There are three points that I want to talk about.

DIÀN₁ 電 (N) electricity.

DIÀN₃ 墊 (TV) (1) put something underneath. Dì-bu-píng, zhuō-zi-tuǐ-dǐxia dei-diàn-dianr-dōng-xi. 地 不 平，桌 子 腿 底 下 得 墊 點 兒 東 西. The floor is not even, you have to put something under the leg of the table. (2) put forth money for someone temporarily. Nǐ-xiān-tì-wo-diànshang, míngtian-wo-zai-huán-ni. 你 先 替 我 墊 上 明 天 我 再 還 你. Pay it for me, and I'll pay you back tomorrow.

DIÀNBÀO₁ 電 報 (N) telegram. dǎ-diànbào 打 電 報 send a telegram.

DIǍN-CÀI₂ 點 菜 (VO) order food (in a restaurant). Wǒmen-hái-méi-diǎn-cài-ne. 我 們 還 沒 點 菜 呢. We have not yet ordered the food (in a restaurant).

DIÀNCHĒ₅ 電 車 (N) trolley car. (M: liàng 輛).

DIÀNCHĒZHÀN₅ 電 車 站 (N) trolley car stop.

DIÀNCHÍ₂ 電 池 (N) electric cell or battery.

DIÀNDĒNG₁ 電 燈 (N) electric light. (M: zhǎn 盞). kāi-diàn-dēng 開 電 燈 turn on the light. guān-diàndēng 關 電 燈 turn off the light.

DIÀNDÒNGJĪ₅ 電 動 機 (N) electric motor.

DIÀNHÀN₅ 電 銲 (TV) weld electrically. (N) electric welding.

DIÀNHU₅ 佃 户 (N) tenant farmer.

DIÀNHUÀ₁ 電 話 (N) telephone. ān-diànhuà 安 電 話 install a telephone. Wǒ-gěi-ta-dǎ-diàn-huà, méi-rén-jiē. 我 給 他 打 電 話 沒 人 接. I phoned him, nobody answered.

DIÀNJI₂ 惦 記 (TV) be concerned about a person or matter. Wǒ-lǎo-diànjizhe-wǒde-háizi. 我 老 惦 記 着 我 的 孩 子. I am always concerned about my children.

DIǍNLǏ₄ 典 禮 (N) ceremony. jiéhūndiǎnlǐ 結 婚 典 禮 wedding ceremony.

DIÀNLÍNGR₂ 電 鈴 兒 (N) electric bell. èn-diànlíngr 按 電 鈴 兒 press the electric bell.

DIÀNLIÚ₄ 電 流 (N) electric current.

DIÀNMÉN₁ 電 門 (N) (lit. electric door) electric switch. kāi-diànmén 開 電 門 (lit. open electric door to allow flow of electricity) switch on (electric). guān-diànmén 關 電 門 (lit. close electric door to cut off flow of electricity) switch off (electric).

DIǍN-MÍNG₂ 點 名 (VO) roll call.

D

DIÀNQÌ₅ 電氣 (N) electricity.

DIǍNR₃ 點兒 (N) (1) point (decimal), period (punctuation mark). Sì-diǎnr-'wǔ-de-jìng'tóu 四點兒五的鏡頭 4.5 lens. xiǎoshu-diǎnr 小數點兒 decimal point. jù-diǎnr 句點兒 period. (2) beat (music). gǔ-diǎnr 鼓點兒 drum beat. gǎnbushang-diǎnr 趕不上點兒 cannot keep up with the beat. fig. cannot keep up with the speed. (3) rain-drop. Diào (yǔ)-diǎnrle. 掉(雨)點兒了. It is starting to rain. (M) (1) for drops of rain or tears. Méi-xiàqilái, jiu-diàole-jidiǎnr. 沒下起來, 就掉了幾點兒. It didn't really rain, just a few drops came down. (2) dots on the faces of dice. 'Jǐ diǎnr? 幾點兒? What number (did you throw)?(See: YĪ-DIǍNR一點兒).

DIÀNSHÀN₂ 電扇 (N) electric fan.

DIÀNSHÌ₂ 電視 (N) television. kāi-diànshì 開電視 turn on the television.

DIÀNTÁI₃ 電台 (N) broadcasting station.

DIÀNTĪ₃ 電梯 (N) elevator. zuò-diàntī 坐電梯 ride an elevator. kāi-diàntī 開電梯 operate the elevator.

DIÀNTǑNG₁ 電筒 (N) flashlight.

DIǍN-TÓU₂ 點頭 (VO) nod one's head. Wǒ-wèn-ta qù-bu-qu, ta-diǎnle-dian-tóu. 我問他去不去, 他點了點頭. I asked him whether he was going or not, he said yes by nodding his head. Tā-kànjian-wo, lián'tóu-dou-méi-diǎn. 他看見我, 連頭都沒點. When he saw me he didn't even nod his head.

DIÀNXIÀN₂ 電線 (N) electric wire or cable. (M: gēn 根).

DIÀNXIN₁ 點心 (N) (1) pastry, cake, cookies. (M: kuài 塊).(2) snack. (M: dùn 頓). (3) breakfast. (M: dùn 頓).

DIǍNXÍNG₅ 典型 (N) model, example.

DIÀNYǏNGR₁ 電影兒 (N) movie. (M: chǎng 場). yǎn-diànyǐngr 演電影 show the movie or act in a movie.

DIÀNYǏNGYUÀN₂ 電影院 (N) movie theater. (M: jiā 家).

DIÀNYUÁN₄ 店員 (N) salesman or clerk in a store.

DIǍN(...)ZHŌNG₁ 點(...)鐘 (M...N) o'clock, hour. yìdian-zhōng 一點鐘 one o'clock or one hour. yìdian'bàn-zhōng 一點半鐘 one thirty or one hour and a half.

DIǍNZHUI₄ 點綴 (TV) do or add something extra to something which is already satisfactory to make it more interesting or attractive. Fángzi-wàitou zài-zhòng-jikē-shù, diǎnzhui-yixia. 房子外頭再種幾棵樹, 點綴一下. A few more trees will be planted outside the house to make it even more attractive. Tā-jié-hūn, Wǒ-

men-děi-sòng-dianr-lǐ, 'diǎnzhui-diǎnzhui. 他 結 婚, 我 們 得 送 點 兒 禮, 點 綴 點 綴. He is getting married, we will have to give some gifts to make the occasion even happier.
(N) something extra added to make things more interesting or attractive. Zhèige-méi-you-yòngchu, jiu-shi-yìzhǒng-diǎn-zhui.這 個 沒 有 用 處, 就 是 一 種 點 綴. This has no practical use, it's just a kind of decoration.

DIÀNZI₃ 墊 子 (N) pad or cushion used underneath something or a person, a seat cushion.

DIĀO₃ 叼 (TV) (1) carry things with the beak or mouth (of birds or animals). Niǎor diāozhe-yi-tiao-chóngzi. 鳥 兒 叼 着 一 條 蟲 子. The bird is carrying a worm (with his beak).
(2) hold something, such as a cigarette, cigar, pencil, etc., between one's lips or teeth. Tā-diāozhe-yān. 他 叼 着 烟. He has a cigarette in his mouth.

DIÀO₂ 掉 (IV) (1) fall, drop. Shù-yèzi dou-diào-le. 樹 葉 子 都 掉 了. All the leaves fell off the tree. Shū diàozai-dìxia-le. 書 掉 在 地 下 了. The book dropped on the ground.
(2) lose color, fade. Diào-yán-se-le. 掉 顏 色 了. The color faded. (3) be removed (stain, dirt). Zhèizhong-mòshuǐ yi-xǐ jiu-diào. 這 種 墨 水

一 洗 就 掉. As soon as (you) wash it the ink will be removed.
(4) dial. lose. Wǒde-bǐ-diào-le. 我 的 筆 掉 了. I lost my pen.
(RE) be removed from object. Chuānghu-shangde-tǔ cābudiào. 窗 戶 上 的 土 擦 不 掉. The dirt on the window can not be removed by wiping it.

DIÀO₃ 吊 (TV) lift, suspend or hang with string, rope, cable, etc. Bǎ-qìchē diàoqilai. 把 汽 車 吊 起 來. Suspend the car. Tāmen-bǎ-ta 'diàoqilai-'dǎ-ta. 他 們 把 他 吊 起 來 打 他. They hung him up with a rope and beat him.

DIÀO₂ 調 (TV) transfer, shift, deploy, transpose. Bǎ-bīng diào-dao-wàiguo-qu-le. 把 兵 調 到 外 國 去 了. The troops were moved to a foreign country. Bǎ-shàngkède-shíjian diào-yidiao. 把 上 課 的 時 間 調 一 調. Shift the class hour around. Jiē-tài-zhǎi, qìchē-diào-tóu diàobuguolái. 街 太 窄, 汽 車 調 頭 調 不 過 來. The street is too narrow, the car isn't able to turn around in it.

DIÀO₁ 釣 (TV) catch fish with a line and hook. Tā-lián-'yìtiao-yú ye-méi-diàoshanglái.他 連 一 條 魚 也 沒 釣 上 來. He didn't even catch one fish.

DIÀOCHÁ₂ 調 查 (TV) investigate. Wǒmen-pài-rén-qu-diào-

D

cha-qu-le. 我們派人去調查去了. We have sent people to investigate.

DIÀODONG₃ 調動 (TV) move, shift. Bǎ-gōngkebiǎo 'diàodong-diàodong. 把功課表調動調動. Let's shift the teaching schedule around.

DIÀO(YU)GĀNR₃ 釣(魚)竿兒 (N) fishing rod. (M: gēn 根).

DIĀOKÈ₃ 雕刻 (TV) sculpt, engrave, carve. (N) sculpture, carving.

DIĀONAN₄ 刁難 (TV) make difficulties intentionally, harass.

DIÀOR₂ 調兒 (N) melody, tune.

DIÀO-SĀNG₅ 弔喪 (VO) attend a funeral.

DIÀO-YÚ₂ 釣魚 (VO) fish (with a pole and line).

DÌBĂN₁ 地板 (N) wooden floor.

DÌDAO₂ 地道 (SV) (1) genuine, real, true. Zhè-shi-dìdaode Zhōngguo-fàn. 這是地道的中國飯. This is genuine Chinese food. (2) good (in quality). Zhèige-zhuōzide-shǒugong zhēn-dìdao. 這個桌子的手工真地道. The workmanship of this table is of good solid quality. (3) true, honorable, upright, trustworthy. Zhèige-rén bu-dìdao. 這個人不地道. This person is not trustworthy.

DÌDÀO₃ 地道 (N) underground tunnel.

DÌDI₁ 弟弟 (N) younger brother.

DÌDIĂN₂ 地點 (N) location, address.

DIĒ₁ 爹 (N) daddy.

DIĒ₃ 跌 (IV) dial. (1) stumble and fall down. Tā-diéle-yijiāo. 他跌了一交. He fell down. (2) drop (of price). Jiàqian-dié-le. 價錢跌了. The price has dropped.

DIĒZI₁ 碟子 (N) plate, saucer.

DÍFANG₃ 提防 (TV) be on the alert against, be on guard against. Nǐ-dei-dīfangzhe-ta. 你得提防著他. You must be on guard against him.

DÌFANG₁ 地方 (PW) (1) place. Zhèige-dìfang hen-hǎo. 這個地方很好. This place is very good. (2) room, space. Méi-dìfang-fàng-dōngxi. 沒地方放東西. There is no room to put things. (3) characteristics. 'Zhèixie-dìfang shi-tāde-chángchu. 這些地方是他的長處. These several characteristics are his strong points.

DǏGĂOR₃ 底稿兒 (N) original draft, first draft, manuscript. (M: zhāng 張).

DÍGU₄ 啾咕 (IV) (1) be preoccupied by questions about one's actions. Yǐjing-juédìngle, xīnli-jiu-bié-dígule. 已經決定了，心裏就別啾咕了. Since it is already decided, don't think about it anymore. (2) discuss a matter quietly or secretly. Wǒ-bù-zhīdào-tamen-dígu-shénma-ne. 我不知道他們啾咕甚麼呢. I don't know what they are secretly discussing.

DÌGUÓZHǓYÌ₁ 帝國主義 (N) imperialism.

DÌJǏ₁ 第幾 (SP-NU) which one (in a sequence)? number what? Tā-dìyī, nǐ-dìjǐ? 他第一, 你第幾 ? He is the first, what number are you? Dìjǐtiān? 第幾天 ? Which day (in a sequence)?

'DÍKÀNG₂ 抵抗 (TV) resist, oppose.

DÌLÉI₃ 地雷 (N) land mine (explosive).

DÌLǏ₁ 地理 (N) (1) geography (as a branch of learning). Xiàwu yǒu-yitáng-dìlǐ. 下午有一堂 地理 . There is a geography class this afternoon. (2) area, geographical location. Wǒ-zhèr-de-dìlǐ-bu-shú. 我這兒的 地理不熟 . I am not familiar with this area.

DÍLIU₃ 提溜 (TV) carry a hanging or dangling object by a string or handle. Tā-dílíuzhe-yíge-pí-bāo. 他提溜着一個 皮包 . He is carrying a suitcase.

DÌMÍNGR₁ 地名兒 (N) name of a place, such as New York. Nǐ-bǎ-dìmíngr gàosong-wo. 你把 地名兒告訴我 . Tell me the name of the place.

DÌNG₂ 釘 (TV) (1) hammer a nail, put a nail or screw into something. Zài-zhèr dìng-ge-dìngzi. 在這兒釘個釘子 . Put a nail here. 'Dìng-liǎngxià-zi jiu-jiēshi-le. 釘兩下子

就結實了 . After you hammer it a little, it will be fastened. (2) sew. 'dìng-le-jizhēn 釘了幾針 sew several stitches. (3) bind a book. dìng-shū 釘書 bind a book. Bǎ-bào-zhǐ dìngcheng-běnzi. 把報紙 釘成本子 . Bind the newspaper together in book form. (4) look at someone or something with special attention, stare at. Wǒ-'dìngle-ta-yiyǎn. 我釘了 他一眼 . I stared at him once. (5) make sure by repeating what was said before. Wǒ-'dìngle-ta-yijiù. 我釘了他 一句 . I said it once more to make sure. (6) keep an eye on (some operation). Wǒ-zǒu-le, nǐ-dìngzhe. 我走了, 你釘 着 . I am leaving, you keep an eye on it. Wǒ-dìngbuzhù-le. 我 釘不住了 . (lit. I cannot keep an eye on it any more.) I cannot stand it any more.

DĪNG₅ 疔 (N) a small boil. Tā-zhǎngle-ge-dīng. 他長了個 疔 . He got a small boil.

DĬNG₃ 頂 (TV) (1) carry something on one's head. Tā-bǎ-shū dǐngzai-tóushang. 他把書 頂在頭上 . He is carrying the books on his head. fig. Tā-shi-dǐngzhe-'yǔ-lái-de. 他 是頂着雨來的 . It was raining when he came. Dà-shì yǒu-'fùchin-dǐngzhe-ne. 大 事有父親頂着呢 . The father will take care of important affairs. (2) ram or push

D

against <u>with the head</u>. 'Xiǎoxīn, nèige-yáng-dǐng-rén. 小 心 , 那 個 羊 頂 人. Be careful, that goat rams people. <u>fig.</u> Wǒ-bǎqiántoude-chē gěi-dǐngchu-hěn-yuǎn-qu. 我 把 前 頭 的 車 給 頂 出 很 遠 去 . I rammed into the car in front of me and pushed it a long distance. Tā-'yíju-huà jiu-bǎ-wǒ-dǐnghuilai-le. 他 一 句 話 就 把 我 頂 回 來 了 . With one sentence he stopped me from saying anything. (3) push <u>something</u> against <u>something</u>. Chuán-dǐngzhe-fēng-zǒu. 船 頂 着 風 走 . The boat is travelling against this wind. Yòng-yǐzi bǎ-mén-dǐngshang. 用 椅 子 把 門 頂 上. Push the chair against the door. (4) substitute, take the place of. Wǒmen-kéyi-ná zhèige dǐng-nèige. 我 們 可 以 拿 這 個 頂 那 個. We can substitute this for that. Nèige-pùzi bǎ-wǒmen-gei-dǐng-le. 那 個 鋪 子 把 我 們 給 頂 了 . That shop has taken business away from us.

(AD) most. Tā-dǐng niánqīng. 他 頂 年 青 . He is the youngest.

(M) (1) <u>for headgear of any kind</u>. yidǐng-màozi 一 頂 帽 子 one hat. (2) <u>for sedan chairs.</u>

DÌNG₁ 定 (TV) (1) fix, set, make <u>something</u> definite. dì-hétong 定 合 同 (<u>lit</u>. make the contract definite)sign a contract. dìng-hūn

定 婚 become engaged (to marry). Tāmen-jiéhūnde-rìzi dìngle-ma? 他 們 結 婚 的 日 子 定 了 嗎 ? Did they set a date for their wedding? Wǒmen-děi-dìng-yige-guīju. 我 們 得 定 一 個 規 矩 . We must make a rule. (2) order <u>something, either specially made or to be delivered later</u>. dìng-huò 定 貨 order goods. dìng-niú-nǎi 定 牛 奶 order milk to be delivered(at regular intervals). dìng-bào 定 報 subscribe to a newspaper. Wǒ-dìngle-jige-cài. 我 定 了 幾 個 菜 . I ordered several dishes (beforehand). (3) reserve, make reservations. Nǐ-zài-fàngguǎnr-dìng-zuòr-le meiyou?你 在 飯 館 兒 定 坐 兒 了 沒 有 ? Did you make reservations in the restaurant?

(IV) congeal, coagulate. Xiě-yǐ-jing-dìng-le. 血 已 經 定 了 . The blood has already congealed.

(RE) make <u>something</u> definite. Nǐmen-shuōdìngle-ma? 你 們 說 定 了 嗎 ? Did they come to a definite agreement? Tā-hái-méi-dǎdìng-zhǔyi-ne. 他 還 沒 打 定 主 意 呢 . He has not yet made up his mind.

(AD) (<u>con</u>.yídìng 一 定).certainly, must be. Tā-dìng-bu-shi-hǎo-rén. 他 定 不 是 好 人 . He must be a bad man.

DÌNGGUI₄ 定 規 (TV) decide. Wǒmen-dìngguī-míngtian-qù. 我 們 定 規 明 天 去 . We decided to go tomorrow.

DÌNG-JIÀ₂ 定價 (VO) decide the price, establish the price. Zhèi-xie-huò hái-méi-dìng-jià-ne. 這些貨還沒定價呢. The price of these goods still hasn't been decided. (N) fixed price, established price, Zhèige bǐ dìngjia-yíkuai-qián. 這個筆定價一塊錢. The marked price of this pen is one dollar.

DÌNGQIAN₃ 定錢 (N) deposit (given as evidence of intention to purchase or rent something).

DÌNG-SHÉNR₄ 定神兒 (VO) compose oneself. Wǒ-gāng-pǎo-huilai, hái-méi-dìngshénr-ne, ta-jiu-lái-le. 我剛跑回來還沒定神兒呢,他就來了. I just ran back, and had not yet composed myself, and he came.

DÌNGZI₂ 釘子 (N) nail (for fastening). dìng-dìngzi 釘釘子 pound a nail. qǐ-dìngzi 起釘子 pull the nail out. (See: PÈNG-DÌNGZI 碰釘子).

DÌNG-ZUǏ₄ 頂嘴 (VO) talk back, argue back. Nǐ-gǎn-gen-wo-dǐng-zhǐ? 你敢跟我頂嘴 ? How dare you talk back to me?

DÌNGZUÒ₂ 定作 (TV) made to order. Zhèitao-yīshang shi-dìngzuòde. 這套衣裳是定作的 These clothes are made to order.

DÌPǏ₄ 地痞 (N) local scoundrel.

DÌQIÚ₂ 地球 (N) (1) globe (map).

(2) earth. (3) bowling. dǎ-dìqiú 打地球 bowl.

DÌQŪ₃ 地區 (N) region, section (of territory).

DÍQUE₁ 的確 (AD) in fact, really. Tāde-Zhōngwén díque-bucuò. 他的中文的確不錯. His Chinese is in fact not bad.

DÍREN₂ 敵人 (N) enemy, adversary.

DÌTǍN₃ 地毯 (N) rug, carpet. (M: zhāng 張).

DĪ-TÓU₃ 低頭 (VO) bow one's head.

DÌTÚ₂ 地圖 (N) map. (M: zhāng 張).

DIŪ₁ 丟 (IV) lose (except for losses incurred in contests, gambling, battles or business). Wǒ-diūle-yibǎikuai-qián. 我丟了一百塊錢. I lost one hundred dollars (by misplacing it or having it stolen). (RE) lost caused by the action indicated by the verb which precedes it. Wǒ-zǒu-diū-le. 我走丟了. I have lost my way. (cf: SHŪ 輸 , PÉI 賠).

DIŪ-LIǍN₂ 丟臉 (VO) lose face, suffer disgrace. (syn. diū-rén 丟人).

DIŪ-RÉN₂ 丟人 (VO) lose face, suffer disgrace. (syn. diū-liǎn 丟臉).

DÌWEI₂ 地位 (N) position. Zhǎo-ge-héshìde-dìwei fàng-zhèige. 找個合適的地位放這個. Find a suitable place to put this. Tāde-dìwei hěn-gāo. 他的地位很

D

高. His position is very high.

DĬXI₄ 底細 (N) detailed back-ground (of a person or matter). Tāde-dǐxi wǒmen-buda-qīngchu. 他 的 底 細 我 們 不 大 清 楚. We are not very clear on his background. shì-qingde-dǐxi 事 情 的 底 細 detailed causes affecting a mat-ter.

DĬXIA₁ 底下 (PW) (1) underneath something. Xié-zai-zhuōzi-dǐxia. 鞋 在 桌 子 底 下. The shoes are under the table. (2) that which follows. Tā-shuōdao-zhèr, dǐxia ta-bu-shuō-le. 他 說 到 這 兒，底 下 他 不 說 了. He talked up to this point, after which he stopped talking. (cf: XIÀBIANR 下邊兒)

DÌXIONG₃ 弟兄 (N) (1) brothers. Nǐmen-dìxiong-jǐge? 你 們 弟 兄 幾 個？ How many broth-ers are there in your family? (2) brethren (members of a brotherhood). Zánmen-dìxiong bié-kèqi. 咱 們 弟 兄 別 客 氣. Brethren, let us not be formal.

DÌYU₃ 地獄 (N) hell. xià-dìyu 下 地 獄 go down to hell.

DÌZHǏ₂ 地址 (N) address (place of residence, business, etc.).

DÌZHŌNGHǍI₂ 地中海 (PW) Mediterranean Sea.

DÌZHǓ₄ 地主 (N) land-owner, land-lord (of land).

DÍZI₄ 笛子 (N) a wind instrument made of bamboo similar to a flute. chuī-dízi 吹 笛 子 (lit.

blow a flute) play the flute.

DǏZI₂ 底子 (N) (1) original draft, copy for preservation as record. Wǒ-méi-liú-dǐzi. 我 沒 留 底 子. I didn't keep a copy (to be preserved). (2) foundation (of learning). Tāde-dǐzi hěn-hǎo. 他 的 底 子 很 好. His foundation (of learning) is very good. (3) sole of a shoe.

DŌNG₁ 東 (L) east. dōngbù 東 部 eastern part. wàng-dōng-fēi 往 東 飛 fly to the east. (N) host. Ràng-wo-zuò-dōng-ba. 讓 我 作 東 吧. Let me pay the check. fángdōng 房 東 landlord (of a house).

DǑNG₁ 懂 (TV) understand, 'com-prehend. Wǒ-shuō-de-huà ta-bu-dǒng. 我 說 的 話 他 不 懂. He doesn't understand what I said. Nǐ-dǒng-zhèige-yìsi-ma? 你 懂 這 個 意 思 嗎？ Do you understand this idea? Tā-hěn-dǒng-zuò-mǎimai. 他 很 懂 作 買 賣. He understands very well how to do business.

DÒNG₂ 洞 (N) hole. shāndòng 山 洞 mountain cave or tunnel.

DÒNG₁ 動 (IV) (1) move (be in motion). Nǐ-zhànhǎole, bié-dòng. 你 站 好 了，别 動. Stand properly, don't move. (2) move (mentally). Tā-dòngle-xīn-le. 他 動 了 心 了. (lit. His heart has moved.) He is inter-ested. (RE) move physically or mentally. Wǒ-zǒubudòng le. 我 走 不

動了．I can't move(by walking) any further. Wǒ-qǐngbudòng-ta. 我請不動他．I am unable to invite him.

DÒNG₁ 動 (TV) (1) touch, handle something. Bié-dòng-zhèige. 別動這個．Don't touch this. Tā-yān-jiǔ-bu-dòng. 他烟酒不動．He never touches cigarettes or liquor. (2) use, apply. Wǒmen-děi-dòngdong-nǎojīn. 我們得動動腦筋．We have to use our minds. (IV) move (change position).

DÒNG₂ 凍 (IV) freeze. Shuǐ dòng-cheng-bīng-le. 水凍成冰了．The water has turned to ice. Zhèr dòngsi-liǎngge-rén. 這兒凍死兩個人．Two people froze to death here. Wǒ-shǒu-dòng-le. 我手凍了．My hands are frozen.

DŌNGBĚI₂ 東北 (L) northeast (PW) Manchuria. (cf: DŌNGSĀN SHĚNG 東三省).

DŌNGBIANR₁ 東邊兒 (PW) east, east side, east part of. Tàiyang-cóng-dōngbianr-chūlai. 太陽從東邊兒出來．The sun comes up in the east. Niǔyue-zai-Měiguo-dōng-bianr. 紐約在美國東邊兒．New York is in the eastern part of America. Rìběn-zài-Zhōngguo-dōngbianr. 日本在中國東邊兒．Japan is to the east of China.

'DÒNGBUDÒNG₂ 動不動 (AD) at the slightest provocation or excuse, very often. Tā-'dòng-budòng-jiu-shēn-qì. 他動不動就生氣．He gets angry at the slightest provocation.

DǑNGDE₁ 懂得 (TV) understand.

DŌNGFĀNG₂ 東方 (PW) the Orient.

DÒNG-GŌNG₂ 動工 (VO) start construction. Zhèige-lóu shén-ma-shíhou-dòngde-gōng? 這個樓甚麼時候動的工？When did construction start on this building?

DŌNGGUA₅ 冬瓜 (N) winter melon (a variety of melon eaten as a vegetable).

DŌNGJIA₄ 東家 (N) host.

DÒNGJINGR₃ 動靜兒 (N) light noises indicating some activity, rustling sound. Wǒ-tīng-jian wàitou-you-dòngjingr. 我聽見外頭有動靜兒．heard some activity outside.

DŌNGNÁN₂ 東南 (L) southeast.

DŌNGNÁNXĪBĚI₁ 東南西北 (L) north, east, south, west.

DÒNGR₄ 凍兒 (N) jelly-like substance. Jītāng dìngcheng-dòngr-le. 雞湯定成凍兒了．The chicken soup set (into a jelly-like substance).

DŌNGSĀNSHĚNG₄ 東三省 (PW) (lit. the three provinces in the east) Manchuria. (cf: DŌNGBĚI 東北).

DÒNG-SHĒN₂ 動身 (VO) set off on a journey. Nǐ-něitian-dòng-shēn? 你那天動身？On which day are you leaving?

DǑNGSHÌ₄ 董事 (N) member of board of directors or trustees.

D

D

(M: wèi 位).

DŎNGSHÌ₃ 懂 事 (SV) (lit. understand things) sensible, understanding. Zhèige-háizi hěn-dŏngshì. 這 個 孩 子 很 懂 事. This child is very sensible.

DÒNG-SHŎU₂ 動 手 (VO) (1) take action. Nǐ-xián-bié-dòng-shŏu. 你 先 別 動 手. You better not take action now. (2) take violent action with the hands, fight. Shì-tā xiān-dòngde-shŏu. 是 他 先 動 的 手. He was the first one who started to fight. (cf: XIÀ-SHŎU 下 手).

DŌNGTIAN₁ 冬 天 (N) winter.

DÒNGWU₁ 動 物 (N) animal.

DÒNGWÙYUÁN₃ 動 物 園 (N) zoo.

DŌNGXI₁ 東 西 (N) things, objects. mǎi-dōngxi 買 東 西 buy things. (2) a derogative when applied to a person or animals. 'Zhèi-dōngxi, zhēn-hùnzhàng. 這 東 西, 真 混 張. This dope is really a damn fool.

DŌNGXINÁNBĚI₁ 東 西 南 北 (L) north, east, south, west.

DŌNGYÀ₂ 東 亞 (PW) East Asia.

'DÒNGYÁO₃ 動 搖 (IV) be swayed, rocked, shaken, etc. Tāde-yìjian ye-'dòngyáo-le. 他 的 意 見 也 動 搖 了. His opinion was also swayed.

DŌNGZHÌ₅ 冬 至 (N) winter solstice.

DÒNGZUO₃ 動 作 (N) motion, movement, action. Tāde-dòngzuo-hen-kuài. 他 的 動 作 很 快. His movements are very quick.

DŌU₁ 都 (AD) all. (1) totalizes and adds up the items specified before it. Tāmen-dou-lái-le. 他 們 都 來 了. They all came. Nèixie-shū wǒ-dōu-yào. 那 些 書 我 都 要. I want all of those books. Nèibenshū tāmen-dou-yào. 那 本 書 他 們 都 要. All of them want that book. Nèixie-shū tāmen-dou-yào. 那 些 書 他 們 都 要. They want all of those books. or All of them want all of those books. or All of them want those books.

(2) totalizes the items expressed by a question word which is used after dōu 都 and a verb. Tā-dou-mài-shénma? 他 都 賣 甚 麼? What are all the things he sells? Nǐ-dou-qǐngshéi? 你 都 請 誰! Whom are all the ones you want to invite? (3) used after a nominal expression with a stressed question word, the nominal expression with dōu 都 means every-, any-. 'Shéi-dou-zhīdao. 誰 都 知 道. Everybody knows it. 'Shénma-dōngxi-dou-guì. 甚 麼 東 西 都 貴. Anything is expensive. or Everything is expensive. Wǒ-'nǎr-dou-bugù. 我 那 兒 都 不 去. I am not going anywhere. (4) used after a verbal expression with a stressed question word, the verbal expression with dōu 都 means no matter, it doesn't

matter. Tā-gěi-wǒ-'shénma wǒ-dou-bu-yào. 他給我甚麼我都不要. No matter what he gives me I don't want it. Nǐ-gěi-wǒ-'duōshao-qián wǒ-dou-bu-mài. 你給我多少錢我都不賣. It doesn't matter how much money you pay me I won't sell it. (5) used before the predicate of a sentence ending in le 了 and/or at the end of such a sentence, already. Jīntian dou-lǐbaisì-le (dou). 今天都禮拜四了(都). or Jīntian (dou-) lǐbaisì-le-dou. 今天(都)禮拜四了都. Today is Thursday already.(6) used after a verbal or nominal expression with or without lián 連 or jiùshi 就是, even. (Lián-) wǒ dou-bu-zhīdào. (連)我都不知道. Even I don't know it. Yìdiǎnr-dōu-bu-cuò. 一點兒都不錯. Not even a little bit is wrong. (cf: YĚ 也).

DǑU(LOU)₃ 抖(擻)(TV) shake off (dust, particles, etc.). Dǒu(lou)-dou(lou)-zhuōbù. 抖(擻)抖(擻)桌布. Shake the tablecloth. Bǎ-yīshang-shang-de-xuě dǒu(lou)-xiaqu. 把衣裳上的雪抖(擻)下去. Shake the snow off your clothes.

DǑU₃ 抖 (IV) quiver, shake, shiver. Tā-lěngde zhí-dǒu. 他冷的直抖 He is shivering from cold. Tā-hēle-jiǔ shǒu-jiu-dǒu. 他喝了酒手就抖. When he drinks his hands shake.

(cf: DUŌSUO 哆嗦).

DǑU₅ 斗 (M) a Chinese form of measurement for quantity, similar to a bushel. yidǒu-mǐ 一斗米 one dǒu of rice. (N) the container which holds one dǒu.

DÒU₄ 逗 (TV) (1) tease. Bié-'dòunèige-háizi. 別逗那個孩子. Don't tease that child. Wǒ-bǎ-ta-dòuxiàole. 我把他逗笑了. I teased him into laughter. (2) incite, provoke someone intentionally. dòu-qìr. 逗氣兒 provoke anger. dòuxiàor 逗笑兒 provoke laughter.

DÒUFU₂ 豆腐 (N) bean curd. (M: kuài 塊). chǐ-dòufu 吃豆腐 tease a woman by acting as her lover would. Tā-nà-shi-chǐ-nǐde-dòufu. 他那是吃你的豆腐. He is teasing you.

DÒU-GÉN(R)₄ 逗哏(兒)(VO) incite mirth.

DÒUR₅ 兜兒 (N) Peip. pocket.

DÒUSHĀ₄ 豆沙 (N) mashed black or red beans with sugar used for pastry filling.

DÒUYÁR₄ 豆芽兒 (N) bean sprout.

DÒUYÓU₅ 豆油 (N) soybean oil.

DÒUZHĒNG₂ 鬥爭 (TV) (1) fight or struggle against. Shēnghuo jiu-shi-dòuzhēng. 生活就是鬥爭. To live is to struggle. (2) Communist Chinese terminology used to signify struggle against capitalists and landlords.

D

D

jiējí-dòuzhēng 階級鬥爭 class struggle.

DÒUZI₃ 豆子 (N) beans.

DÚ₂ 毒 (N) poison, venom. dúyào 毒藥 poison. yǒu-dú 有毒 poisonous.

(TV) poison. Bǎ-gǒu-gei-dúsi-le. 把狗給毒死了. The dog was poisoned and died.

(SV) lit. and fig. venomous. Zhèi-ge-rénde-shǒuduan hen-dú. 這個人的手段很毒. This man's schemes are venomous. Tàiyang hěn-dú. 太陽很毒. (lit. The sun is venomous.) The sun is very strong and hot.

DǓ₂ 賭 (TV) gamble, bet. dǔ-qián 賭錢 bet money.

(N) bet. Wǒ-gēn-ni-dǎ-ge-dǔ. 我跟你打個賭. I will make a bet with you.

DǓ₂ 堵 (TV) plug up or stop up a hole or a gap. Yòng-tǔ dǔshang-nèige-dòng. 用土堵上那個洞. Plug up that hole with dirt.

DǓ₄ 堵 (M) for wall. yìdǔ-qiáng 一堵牆 one wall.

DÙ₁ 度 (M) (1) degree (in temperature or unspecified units). Jīntian duōshao-dù? 今天多少度? What is the temperature today? zhuànle-yibai-bāshi-dù 轉了一百八十度 made a one hundred eighty degree turn. (2) time (occurrence of doing something).Tā-yídù-zài-nèr-jiāo-shū. 他一度在那兒教書. He taught there once.

DUÀN₂ 端 (TV) raise up or hold something with the hand, keeping it level. Tā-duānqi-jiǔbēi-lai shuō, "nín-qǐng." 他端起酒杯來說,"您請". He raised the wine cup and said: "Please drink." Wǒ-duānzhe-tāng-ne. 我端着湯呢. I am carrying the soup.

DUÀN₁ 短 (SV) short (in length). (opp. cháng 長). Zhèitiao-hé bu-duǎn. 這條河不短. This river is not short. Shíhou-tài-duǎn. 時候太短. Time is too short. (See: AI 矮).

(TV) (1) owe. (syn. qiàn 欠, gāi 該). Wǒ-duǎn-ta-quán. 我短他錢. I owe him money. (2) lack. (syn. quē 缺, quàn 欠). Zhèi-wūli hǎoxiang-duǎn-dianr-shenma. 這屋裏好像短點兒甚麼. There seems to be something lacking (missing) in this room. (AD) infrequently. Wǒ-méi-duǎn-gàosong-ta. 我沒短告訴他. I told him, not infrequently.

DUÀN₁ 斷 (IV) break, cut off. Xiàn-duàn-le. 線斷了. The thread (or wire) is broken. 'Xiāo-xi-yì'zhíde-méi-'duàn. 消息一直的沒斷. All the way through the years, communications did not stop. Tāmende-guānxi zǎojiu-duàn-le. 他們的關係早就斷了. Their relationship ended a long time ago.

(TV) cut out a habit. Nǐ-děi-duàn-yān. 你得斷烟. You must

cut out smoking.

(AD) definitely. Nǐ-'duàn-bu-néng-zài-zhèiyangr-zuòle. 你 斷 不 能 再 這 樣 兒 作 了. You definitely cannot do it this way anymore.

DUÀN₁ 段 (M) a stretch, a section, a segment. yíduàn-lù 一 段 路 a stretch of road. yí-duàn-gùshi 一 段 故 事 a story. yíduàn-wénzhāng 一 段 文 章 a composition (literary) or a paragraph. chàng-yíduàn-xì 唱 一 段 戲 a part of a musical play or an opera.

DUÀNCHU₂ 短 處 (N) shortcomings, weak points. (M: diǎn 點).

DUÀNGŌNG₅ 短 工 (N) (1) short term or temporary labor. (2) short term or temporary laborer.

DUÀNPIĀN₅ 短 篇 (B) short (for written compositions). duǎnpiān xiǎoshuōr 短 篇 小 說 兒 a short novel.

DUÀNQI₃ 短 期 (B) short term. (opp. chángqī 長 期).

DUĀNWǓJIÉ₄ 端 午 節 or DUĀNYÁNGJIÉ 端 陽 節 (N) a festival occurring on the fifth day of the fifth month of the lunar calendar.

DUĀNYÁNGJIÉ₄ 端 陽 節 see DUĀNWǓJIÉ 端 午 節.

DUÀNZI₃ 緞 子 (N) satin. (M: pǐ 匹 , chǐ 尺).

DÚBĚN(R)₃ 讀 本 (兒) (N) reader (as a book). (M: běn 本).

DUĪ₂ 堆 (TV) pile. Dōngxi-zai-zhuōzi-shang-duīzhe 東 西 在

桌 子 上 堆 着. The things are piled up on the table. Shū-dou-duīcheng-shān-le. 書 都 堆 成 山 了. The books are all piled up like a mountain. Shìqing-dōu-duīqilai-le. 事 情 都 堆 起 來 了. The work has piled up.

(M) pile of. yiduī-tǔ 一 堆 土 a pile of dirt.

DUÌ₄ 兌 (TV) exchange money. duì-wǔkuai-qián 兌 五 塊 錢 exchange five dollars.

DUÌ₂ 對 (TV) (1) check for accuracy. Nǐ-duìdui-biǎo. 你 對 對 表. Check your watch. Wǒ-duìbushàng-zhàng-le. 我 對 不 上 賬 了. I have checked, but the accounts don't balance. (2) face, point toward, aim at. Zhèige-fángzi zhèng-duìzhe-nèige-shān. 這 個 房 子 正 對 着 那 個 山. This house directly faces that mountain. Bǎ-qiāng-duìzhǔnle-nèige-niǎor zai-fàng. 把 鎗 對 準 了 那 個 鳥 兒 再 放. Don't shoot until you have properly aimed at the bird with the gun. (3) match, agree with. Zhèige-cài bu-duì-wèir. 這 個 菜 不 對 味 兒. (lit. This food does not match the taste that I expected.) This food doesn't taste right. Tāmen-liǎngge-rénde-yìjian bu-duì. 他 們 兩 個 人 的 意 見 不 對. Their opinions don't match. (4) treat someone. (syn. dài 待). Tā-duì-wo bu-cuò. 他

D

D

對我不錯. He treats me very well. (5) direct attention to. Wǒmen-shi-duì-shì, bú-shi duì-rén. 我們是對事，不是對人. We were to direct attention to the business, not the individuals.

DUÌ₁ 對 (CV) (1) for someone's advantage or disadvantage. Zhèi-yangr duì-shéi dou-méi-hǎochu. 這樣兒對誰都沒好處. In this manner there is no benefit for anybody. Tā-lái kǒng-pà-duì-women-búlì. 他來恐怕對我們不利. His coming, I am afraid, would be harmful for us. (2) towards. Nǐ-qu-duì-ta-shuō-qu-ba. 你去對他說去吧. You go to speak to him. (3) or DUÌYU 對於 concerning, with regard to. Wǒ-duì(yu)-zhèi-jian-shì méi-you-yìjian. 我對於這件事沒有意見. I have no opinion concerning this affair. (cf: GUĀNYU 關於).

DUÌ₁ 對 (SV) correct, accurate, right. Tā-zuòde hen-duì. 他作的很對. His work is very accurate. Nǐ-juéde nǐ-duì-ma? 你覺得你對嗎? Do you think you are right? (RE) correctly, accurately, properly. Wǒ-lǎo-shuōbuduì. 我老說不對. I can never say it correctly. (AD) to or at each other. Tāmen-bǐcǐ-duì-mà. 他們彼此對罵. They curse each other.

DUÌ(R)₂ 對 (兒) (M) pair. Zhèi-liǎngbǎ-yǐzi shi-yíduì(r). 這兩把椅子是一對(兒). These two chairs are a pair. (cf: SHUĀNG 雙).

DUÌ₂ 隊 (M) for an organized group of people. yíduì-bīng 隊兵 a body of soldiers (in formation). (B) team, an organized group of people. yīnyuèduì 音樂隊 band (music).

DUÌBUQĬ₁ 對不起 or DUÌBU-ZHÙ 對不住 (RV) an expression of apology, excuse me, pardon me, I'm sorry.

DUÌBUZHÙ₃ 對不住 see DUÌ-BUQĬ 對不起.

DUÌFU₂ 對付 (TV) (1) handle a person or an affair. Zhèige-rén bu-róngyi-duìfu. 這個人不容易對付. This person is not easy to handle. (2) be compromising towards a person. Nǐ-yuè-duìfu-ta, ta-yuè-bu-kěn. 你越對付他, 他越不肯. The more you compromise the more he refuses. (3) do or accept something as a compromise. Wǒmen-duìfuzhe-zuò. 我們對付着作. We do the best we can (under compromising conditions). Ná-zhèi-ge-duìfu-duìfu-ba. 拿那個對付對付吧. Take this as a compromising substitute. (See: CÒUHE 湊合, JIĀNGJIU 將就).

DUÌGUÒR₃ 對過兒 (PW) a place opposite. Pùzi-jiu-zài-duì-

guòr. 鋪子就在對過
兒. The store is just across
the way.

DUÌMIÀN(R)₃ 對面兒 (PW)
opposite (place). Pùzi jiù-zài-
women-jiāde-duìmiàn(r). 鋪子
就在我們家的對
面兒. The store is just opposite our house.

(AD) face to face. Duìmiàn(r)-
shuō bǐ-xiě-xìn-hǎo. 對面
兒說比寫信好. Talk-
ing face to face is better than
by correspondence.

DUÌTOU₅ 對頭 (N) (1) opponent.
(2) personal enemy.

DUÌXIÀNG₂ 對象 (N) person or
object of one's attention, interests, study. Tā-xiǎng-jiéhūn,
kěshi méi-yǒu-duìxiàng. 他想
結婚,可是没有對
象. He wishes to get married,
but there isn't anyone he cares
that much for. Zhèi-shi-wǒ-yán-
jiude-duìxiàng. 這是我研
究的對象. This is the
subject for my study.

DUÌYU₁ 對於 see DUÌ 對 (CV).

DUÌYUÁN₃ 隊員 (N) member of
a team.

DUÌZHǍNG₃ 隊長 (N) (1) leader
or captain of a team. (2) commander or leader of a military
unit. (3) a form of address for
a leader or commander. Zhāng-
duìzhang 張隊長 leader
Chang.

DUÌZHENG₃ 對証 (N) proof (to
check with some written records
or someone). Tā-sǐle jiu-méi-

you-duìzheng-le. 他死了
就没有對証了.
After his death, there will be no
proof.

DÚLÌ₂ 獨立 (IV) independent
(countries or organizations).

DŪN₃ 蹲 (TV) squat, sit on one's
haunches. Nǐ-dūnxia. 你蹲下.
Squat down.

DŪN₁ 噸 (M) ton.

DŪN₄ 躉 (TV) buy in wholesale
quantities for resale purposes.

DÙN₃ 燉 (TV) stew. dùn-niúròu
燉牛肉 stew beef or beef-
stew.

DÙN₂ 頓 (M) (1) for an action of
attack. Wǒ-'dǎle-ta-yidùn. 我
打了他一頓. I gave him
a beating. (2) for a meal. Yìtiān-
chī-sāndùn-fàn. 一天吃三
頓飯. Eat three meals a
day.

DŪNANG₅ 嘟嚷 (TV) mumble
(particularly complaints). Bié-
dūnang-le. 别嘟嚷了.
Stop mumbling.

DUŌ₁ 多 (SV) many, much. (opp.
shǎo 少). Duō, kuài, hǎo,
shěng. 多,快,好,省.
More, faster, better and more
economical (a slogan used in
Mainland China concerning production). Rén-hen-duō. 人很
多. There are many people.
Bù-duō-bù-shǎo. 不多不少.
Not too much, not too little.
When used to modify a noun, an
adverb must precede it. Tā-yǒu-
hěn-duō-péngyou. 他有很
多朋友. He has a lot of

D

D

friends.

(RE) much, many. Zhèige-bǐ-nèige hǎoduō-le. 這個比那個好多了. This is much better than the other. Tā-bǐ-wǒ gāodeduō. 他比我高得多. He is much taller than I am. Zhèrde-rén bǐ-yǐqián duódeduō. 這兒的人比以前多得多. There are many more people here than before.

(TV) have something or some number of things extra. Zěnma-duōchu-wǔkuai-qián-lai? 怎麼多出五塊錢來? How come there are five dollars extra?

(NU) (1) many, much (may or may not take a M). Tā-yǒu-hěn-duō(zhang)-huàr. 他有很多(張)畫兒. He has a lot of paintings. Wǒ-yǐjing-chīle-hěn-duō(kuài)-le. 我已經吃了很多(塊)了. I already ate many (pieces). (2) a fraction of the unit which precedes it, more. Sānshi-duō(ge)-rén. 三十多(個)人. More than thirty people (but less than forty), thirty some people. Sāngeduō-yuè. 三個多月. More than three months (but less than four).

(AD) more, much or many. Nǐ-yīnggāi duō-chī-yidianr. 你應該多吃一點兒. You ought to eat a little more. Wǒ-bǐ-nǐ duō-gěile-wǔkuai qián. 我比你多給了五塊

錢. I gave him five dollars more than you did. Wǒ-duō-gěile-ta wǔkuai-qián. 我多給了他五塊錢. I gave him five dollars more. or I gave him five dollars too many. Bié-duō-shuō-huà. 別多說話. Don't talk much. Duō-xiè. 多謝. Many thanks.

DUÓ₃ 奪 (TV) take something by force from someone. Bié-gēn-nèige-háizi-duó. 別跟那個孩子奪. Do not take it by force from the child. Tā-cóng-wǒ-shóuli bǎ-bǐ-duóguoqu-le. 他從我手裏把筆奪過去了. He took my pen out of my hand. fig. Tā-'lǎo-xiǎng duó-wǒde-dìwei. 他老想奪我的地位. He always tries to get my position.

DUÓ(MA)₁ 多(麼) (AD) used before a SV or AV, how (to what extent). (1) used in interrogative sentences. Zhèitiao-hé 'duó(ma)-cháng? 這條河多(麼)長? How long is this river? (2) used in exclamatoŕy sentences. Zhèi-huār duó(ma)-hǎokàn! 這花兒多(麼)好看! How beautiful this flower is! (3) used after a vocally stressed negative expression, very. Nèige-dìfang ye-'búhui-you-duó(ma)rè.那個地方也不會有多(麼)熱. That place cannot be very hot. Tā-zǒule-'méi-duó(ma)-jiǔ. 他走了沒多(麼)久. He wasn't gone for very long. (4) when vocally stressed and followed by a phrase with dōu 都 or yě 也, it doesn't matter how. Wǒ-zuò-de 'duó-(ma)-hǎo, tā-dōu-shuō bù-xíng. 我 作 的 多 (麼) 好, 他 都 說 不 行. It doesn't matter how well I have done it, he will say that it's not good enough. (5) used in two phrases repeatedly, as... as... 'Nǐ-pǎo-duó(ma)-kuài 'wǒ-yě-pǎo-duó(ma)-kuài. 你 跑 多 (麼) 快 我 也 跑 多 (麼) 快. I will run as fast as you. Nǐ-'yào-duó(ma)-dà, jiu-'zuò-duó (ma)-dà. 你 要 多 (麼) 大, 就 作 多 (麼) 大. It can be made as big as you want. (6) used in reduplication, how. Tā-'cháng-shuō ta-nǚpéngyou duóma-duóma-kǎokàn. 他 常 說 他 的 女 朋 友 多 (麼) 多 (麼) 好 看. He often says how pretty his girl friend is.

DUǑ₂ 躲 (TV) (1) avoid, keep away from a person, situation, danger, harm, etc. Nǐ-'duǒzhe-ta-diǎnr. 你 躲 着 他 點 兒. You better avoid that person. Yǔ-tài-dà-le, wǒmen-dào-pùzili qu-duǒ-yixia-ba. 雨 太 大 了, 我 們 到 铺 子 裏 去 躲 一 下 吧. It's raining hard, let's go into the shop to keep out of it. Nǐ-duǒkai-wo. 你 躲 開 我. You keep away from me. (2) hide. Tā-zài-lóushang duǒzhe-ne. 他 在 樓 上 躲 着 呢. He is up-stairs hiding. Tā-duóqilai-le.

他 躲 起 來 了. He is hiding. (cf: BI 避).

DUǑ₃ 朵 (M) for a flower. Dài-yiduǒ-huār. 帶 一 朵 花 兒 Wear a flower.

DUÒ₅ 跺 (TV) stamp one's foot. Nǐ-bǎ-jiǎoshangde-xuě duòxiaqu. 你 把 脚 上 的 雪 跺 下 去. Stamp your feet and get the snow off of them.

DUŌ(YI)BANR₃ 多 (一) 半 兒 (N) more than half. Tāde-dōngxi duō(yi)bànr-dou-diū-le. 他 的 東 西 多 (一) 半 兒 都 丟 了. More than half of his things are lost. (MA) most likely. Tā-duō(yi)-bànr-bu-qù. 他 多 (一) 半 兒 不 去. Most likely he won't go.

DUŌHUIR₄ 多 會 兒 or DUŌ-ZAN 多 喒 (TW) Peip. when, what time. (syn. shénma-shí-hou 甚 麼 時 候).

DUÒ-JIǍO₄ 跺 脚 (VO) stamp one's feet.

DUŌSHAO₁ 多 少 (NU) used with or without a M, how many, how much. (1) used in interrogative sentences. Nèr-yǒu-'duōshao(ge)-rén? 那 兒 有 多 少 (個) 人? How many persons are there? Nǐ-qùle-'duōshao-shíhou? 你 去 了 多 少 時 候? How long have you been away? 'Duōshao-qián? 多 少 錢? How much? (2) used in exclam-atory sentences, how much, how many. Nǐ-kàn! Wèi-nǐ-niàn-shū, nǐ-fùchin-huāle-'duōshao-qián!

D

你看!為你念書,你
父親花了多少錢!
Look at how much money your
father has spent for your education! (3) used after a vocally
stressed negative expression,
(not) much, (not) many. Wǒ-
'méi-you-duōshao-qián. 我沒
有多少錢. I don't have
much money. 'Chàbuliǎo-duō-
shǎo. 差不了多少. (lit.
It cannot differ much.) It's about
right. (4) when vocally stressed
and followed by a phrase with
dōu 都 or yě 也, whatever
amount, no matter how much.
Zhèige-biǎo nǐ-gěi-wǒ-'duōshao-
qián wǒ-dōu-bu-mài. 這個表
你給我多少錢我
都不賣. No matter how
much money you give me for
this watch, I won't sell it. (5)
repeated in two phrases, whatever amount, no matter how
much. Nǐ-'yào-duōshao, wǒ-
'gěi-nǐ duōshao. 你要多少,
我給你多少. I'll give
you whatever amount you want.
(6) used in reduplication, such
amount, so many, so much. Tā-
'lǎo-ài-shuō ta-yǒu-duōshao-
duōshao-péngyou. 他老愛
說他有多少多少
朋友. He always likes to say
that he has so many friends. (cf:
JǏ 幾).
DUŌSHĂO₃ 多少 (MA) followed
by yidiǎnr 一點兒 or ji-M
indicates the quantity is not considered. Wǒ-duōshǎo huì-shuō-

jijiu-Zhōngguohuà. 我多少
會說幾句中國話.
I can speak a few sentences in
Chinese (not considering how
much). (cf: SHĀOWĒI 稍微.
DUŌSHU₂ 多數 (N) the majority.
DUŌSUO₃ 哆嗦 (IV) Peip. quiver,
shake, shiver. Tāde-shǒu zhí-
(dǎ)-duōsuo. 他的手直(打)
哆嗦. His hand shakes.(cf:
DǑU 抖).
DUŌXIÈ₁ 多謝 (TV) many
thanks.
DUŌ-XĪN₂ 多心 (VO) get the
wrong idea because of being
over-suspicious. Wǒ-yi-shuō-
nèijian-shì, tā-duōle-xīn-le. 我
一說那件事他多
了心了. When I mentioned
that, he got the wrong idea(because of being over-suspicious).
DUŌYÚ₂ 多餘 (N) superfluous,
unnecessary. Nà-shì-duōyú. 那
是多餘. That is super-
fluous.
DUŌZAN₄ 多喒 see DUŌHUIR
多會兒.
DŬ-QÌ₄ 賭氣 (VO) vexed and
angered. Wǒ-gen-ta-dǎ-guānsì,
jiu-wèideshì-dǔ-zheikou-qì. 我
跟他打官司就為
的是賭這口氣. I
am taking him to court just because I am vexed and angered.
Wǒ-yi-dǔ-qì chūqu-le. 我一賭
氣出去了. Vexed and
angered, I walked out.
DŬ-QIÁN₃ 賭錢 (VO) bet, wager
for money. (cf: DǍ-DŬ 打賭).
DÙSHÌ₃ 都市 (N) a major city,

metropolis.

DÚ-SHŪ₂ 讀書 (VO) (1) study.
(2) read books <u>aloud or silently.</u>
(cf: NIÀN-SHŪ 念書, KAN-

SHŪ 看書).

DÚZHĔ₅讀者 (N) reader <u>of a</u>
<u>publication.</u> (M: wèi 位).

DÙZI₃ 肚子 (N) stomach, belly.

D

E

E₂ 哦 (I) sound of hesitation, uh..., er... Tā-ya, e, bié-tí-le. 他 呀，哦，别 提 了. Him, uh, don't talk about him.

É₄ 鵝 (N) domesticated goose. (M: zhī 隻).

É₃ 訛 (TV) cheat someone out of money. Bié-é-wo. 别 訛 我. Don't cheat me. Tā-shuō-wǒ-qiàn-ta-qián. Nà-shi-ta-é-wo. 他 說 我 欠 他 錢. 那 是 他 訛 我. He said that I owed him money. He's just trying to cheat me.

È₁ 餓 (SV) hungry. (opp. bǎo 飽). Wǒ dùzi-è-le. 我 肚子 餓 了. (lit. As far as I am concerned, stomach is hungry).I am hungry.

(I V) suffer from hunger. È-ta-liǎngtian tā-jiu-kěn-zuò-le. 餓 他 兩 天 他 就 肯 作 了. Make him suffer from hunger for a couple of days, then he will be willing to do it.

ÈBÀ₅ 惡 霸 (N) vicious bully, local tyrant.

ÈGUO₁ 俄 國 (PW) Russia.

ĒI₂ 哎 see ĀI 哎.

ÉI₂ 哎 see ÁI 哎.

ĚI₂ 哎 see ǍI 哎.

ÈI₂ 哎 see ÀI 哎.

ÈLIÈ₄ 惡 劣 (SV) bad, poor, foul. Tiānqi-hen-'èliè. 天氣 很 惡 劣. The weather is bad.

ĒMITUÓFÓ₅ 阿 彌 陀 佛 (N) Amitabba Buddha, short for "Amitabba Buddha, the Immeasurable, Buddha of Boundless light." Worshipped by the "Pureland" sect and used as an incantation repeated by the faithful.

(I) used as an exclamation similar to the English "My God."

EN₂ 嗯 or NG 哼 (I) (1) uh-huh, um-hum, yeah. A: Nǐ-chī-a! B: En. A: 你 吃 啊! B: 嗯. A: Go ahead and eat! B: Uh-huh. (2) when pronounced in a long, drawn-out manner, well...er...

En, děng-wǒ-xiángxiang. 嗯, 等 我 想 想. Uh, wait, let me think.

ÈN₃ 按 or ÀN 按 (TV) press with the finger or palm. èn-(diàn)-língr 按 (電) 鈴 兒 ring a (small) bell (by pressing a button).

ĒNDIAN₅ 恩 典 (N) a great benefaction, favor.

ĒNREN₄ 恩 人 (N) benefactor or benefactress.

ÉR₂ 而 (B) used between two verb phrases. (1) both... and... cōngming-ér-'měilì 聰 明 而 美 麗 . both clever and pretty. (2) but, while on the other hand. cōngming-ér-bu-ˈměilì 聰 明 而 不 美 麗 clever but not pretty.

ÈR₁ 二 (NU) two. (1) an independent numeral in counting. yī, èr, sān 一 , 二 , 三 one, two, three. (2) a digit in a number when it is read off. bā-èr-èr-sān 八 二 二 三 8223.èr-diǎnr-èr 二 點 兒 二 2.2. èrfēnzhiyī 二 分 之 一 1/2. (3) the last element in compound numerals. yìbǎi'èr 一 百 二 one hundred and twenty. yìbǎi-líng-èr 一 百 零 二 one hundred and two. (4) the only form before and/or after the numeral shí 十 . èrshi'èr 二 十 二 twenty-two. (5) the only form before the measure liǎng 兩 . èrliǎng-jīnzi 二 兩 金 子 two ounces of gold. (6) an alternate to liǎng 兩 before the numerals bǎi 百 , qiān 千 , and wàn 萬 . (7) an alternate to liǎng 兩 before a number of measures of distance, time and weight, and before certain other measures. èrlǐ 二 里 two (Chinese) miles. èrkè 二 刻 (lit. two quarters of an hour) half an hour. èrjīn 二 斤 two catties. èrwèi 二 位 two people. èrmáowǔ 二 毛 五 twenty-five cents. (8) the only form in expressing ordinal numbers, second. dì'èr 第 二 the second. èryuè 二 月 (lit. the second

month of the year) February. (cf: LIǍNG 兩).

ÈRBǍDĀO₅ 二 把 刀 (N) (1) dial. second cook. (2) Peip. a person lacking professional skill.

ÈRBǍIWǓ₅ 二 百 五 (N) Peip. half-crazy person, nut.

ÈRDUO₁ 耳 朵 (N) ear (on the head). (M: zhī 隻).

É-RÉN₃ 訛 人 (VO) cheat people out of money. Tā-zuòle-'shífēn-zhōng jiu-yào-wǔkuai-qián, zhè-bú-shi-é-rén-ma? 他 作 了 十 分 鐘 就 要 五 塊 錢,這 不 是 訛 人 嗎 ? He worked only ten minutes and asked for five dollars, isn't this cheating?

ĚRHUÁNZI₃ 耳 環 子 (N) earring. dài-ěrhuánzi 戴 耳 環 子 wear earrings. (M: duèi 對).

ÉRNǓ₃ 兒 女 (N) son and daughter. Tāde-érnǔ dōu-dà-le. 他 的 兒 女 都 大.了 . His sons and daughters are all grown up.

ĚRPÁNGFĒNG₅ 耳 旁 風 (N) (lit. wind passing by the ears of a listener) words which have no effect on the listener. Tā-bǎ-wǒde-huà dàngzuo-ěrpángfēng. 他 把 我 的 話 當 作 耳 旁 風 . My words have no effect on him.

ÉRQIĚ₁ 而 且 (MA) and also, moreover. Zhèige-piányi érqiě-hǎokàn. 這 個 便 宜 而 且.好 看 . This is cheap and also good looking. (cf:

E

E

BÌNGQIĚ 並且).

ĔRSHĒNG₄ 耳生 (SV) unfamiliar to the listener in sound or in expression. Zhèijiu-huà tīng-zhe-ĕrshēng. 這句話聽着耳生 . This statement doesn't sound familiar.

ĔRSHÓU₄ 耳熟 see ĔRSHÚ 耳熟.

ĔRSHÚ₄ 耳熟 or ĔRSHÓU 耳熟 (SV) familiar sounding. Zhèige-gēr hĕn-ĕrshú. 這個歌兒很耳熟 . This song sounds familiar.

'ÉRTÓNG₃ 兒童 (N) child (in general). értóng-jiàoyù 兒童教育 child education.

ÉRYĬ₂ 而已 (P) used at the end of a sentence with búguò 不過, jiùshi 就是 , zhǐshi 只是 etc. , that's all. (syn. bàle 罷了). Zhèige zhǐshi-yíge-lìzi-éryǐ. 這個只是一個例子而已 . This is only an example, that's all.

ÉRYUÈ₁ 二月 (TW) (lit. the second month of a year) February.

ÉRZI₁ 兒子 (N) son.

ÈSHÀO₅ 惡少 (N) a villainous young man, juvenile delinquent.

ÉSHU₄ 額數 (N) a predetermined fixed number, quota.

ÉWÀI₃ 額外 (AD) extra, over and above the quota. Wŏ-éwài-gĕi-ta-yibăikuài-qián. 我額外給他一百塊錢 I gave him an extra $100.

ÉWÉN₁ 俄文 (N) Russian language.

ĔXIN₄ 惡心 (SV) lit. or fig. nauseated.

ÈYÀO₃ 阨要 (SV) hit important points (in writing or speaking). Tā-shuō-de-huà hĕn-èyào. 他說的話很阨要 . What he said hit the important points.

'ÈYÌ₄ 惡意 (N) bad intention. (opp. 'hăoyì 好意). Wŏ-shuō-nèiju-huà, méi-yŏu-'èyì. 我說那句話沒有惡意. When I said it, I didn't have any bad intentions.

ÈYÚ₅ 鰐魚 (N) alligator, crocodile. (M: tiáo 條).

ÉZHÀ₄ 訛詐 (TV) cheat, defraud.

F

FĀ₁ 發 (B-) (1) when used with expressions indicating colors, certain tastes and textures, appears to be, suggestive of. fāhuáng 發黃 yellowish. Niúnǎi-huài-le. Yǒu-yidiǎnr-fāsuān. 牛奶壞了. 有一點兒發酸. The milk is spoiled, it tastes a little sour. (2) when used with expressions indicating certain discomforts, feel certain discomforts (emanating from a certain part of the body). fāyǎng 發痒 feel itchy. Wǒ-zuǐ fāgān. 我嘴發乾. My mouth feels dry. (3) when used with expressions indicating certain emotional states or symptoms, be in certain emotional states or display certain emotional symptoms. fāzào 發躁 feel irritable, easily provoked. fājí 發急 feel anxious.

FĀ₁ 發 (TV) (1) send out (troops, letters, invitations, etc.). fā-bīng 發兵 send troops. fāle-yifēng-xìn 發了一封信 sent out a letter, mailed a letter. Diànbào-fā-le-ma? 電報發了嗎? Has the telegram been sent out? Tā-fāle-wǔshige-qǐngtiě. 他發了五十個請帖. He sent out fifty invitations. (2) fire, shoot

arrow, gun, etc. fāle-yipào 發了一炮 shot a round from a cannon. Zhèige-jīguānqiāng měi-miǎo-zhōng néng-fā-shígezǐdàn. 這個機關鎗每秒鐘能發十個子彈. This machine gun can shoot ten bullets per second. (3) distribute, hand out. fā-chuándān 發傳單 distribute handbills. Gāi-shéi-fā-pái-le? 該誰發牌了? Whose turn to deal (playing cards)? (4) distribute money, particularly the payroll, pay. fā-xīnshui 發薪水 pay the salaries. (5) issue by the government, an authority, or a superior, orders, documents, money, tools, materials, clothing, food, etc. fā-mìngling 發命令 issue an order. fā-xǔkězhèng 發許可証 issue a permit. Kāiwánle-huì tāmenfāle-yíge-gōngbào. 開完了會他們發了一個公報. After the meeting they issued a communique. Měiyige-bīng fā-yizhī-qiāng. 每一個兵發一枝鎗. Each soldier is issued a gun. (6) send forth, emanate, radiate. Tàiyang-néng-fā-guāng. 太陽能發光. The sun can radiate light. Zhèige-kuòyīnqì fāchulai-

de-shēngyin bu-hǎo. 這個擴音器發出來的聲音不好. The sound of this amplifier is not good. (7) break out with a disease, be afflicted with symptoms or illness. fāzhǒng 發腫 be swollen. fā-yàozi 發瘧子 have malaria. (8) germinate, grow. fā-yár 發芽兒 germinate, sprout. fā-jiào 發酵 ferment. (9) make something grow, raise dough, with leaven, puff up dried or dehydrated food by soaking in water. fā-dòuyár 發豆芽兒 make bean sprouts. Xiān-bǎ-mógu yòng-shuǐ-fā-le. 先把蘑菇用水發了. First soak the dried mushrooms in water. (10) express, state. fā-yán 發言 make a statement. fā-wèn(ti) 發問(題)ask a question.
(M) round of ammunition. Měi-ge-rén lǐngle-yibǎifā-zǐdàn. 每個人領了一百發子彈. Each person received 100 rounds of ammunition.

FĀ₃ 乏 (SV) (1) tired. Wǒ-fá-le. 我乏了. I am tired. (2) weak (physically). Nǐ-zhēn-fá, lián-zhèige-dōu-bānbudòng. 你真乏,連這個都搬不動. You are really weak, you cannot even move this.

FĀ₂ 罰 (TV) fine, penalize, impose a penalty, make someone pay as a consequence. Tāmen-fále-wo-wǔkuai-qián. 他們罰了我五塊錢. They

fined me five dollars. Tāmen-fá-ta, fáde-hěn-zhòng. 他們罰他, 罰得很重. They imposed a heavy penalty on him. Wǒ-děi-fá-ni-hē-sānbei-jiǔ. 我得罰你喝三杯酒. As a consequence I have to make you drink three drinks. (Drinking is considered a penalty or consequence).

FĀ₁ 法 (-B) (1) or FAR 法兒 with TV to form a noun, way of. xiě-fǎ or xiéfar 寫法兒 way of writing. 'kànfǎ or kànfar 看法兒 way of looking at. (2) with certain nouns to form another noun, technique of. 'dāofǎ 刀法 technique of the knife. 'bǐfǎ 筆法 technique of the brush-pen.

FĂ₄ 法 (B) law. jūnfǎ 軍法 military law. guójìgōngfǎ 國際公法 international law.

FĀ-BĂNG₄ 發榜 (VO) publicly post the list of successful candidates of an examination.

FĀBIĂO₁ 發表 (TV) (1) express opinion. Tā-bù-xǔ-wo-fābiǎo-wǒde-yìjian. 他不許我發表我的意見. He does not allow me to express my opinion. (2) publish an article. Wǒ-zài-zázhishang fābiǎole-yipian-wénzhang. 我在雜誌上發表了一篇文章. I published an article in a magazine. (3) announce, make something public. Zhèijiàn-shì ni-xiān-bié-shuō, hái-mei-fābiǎo-ne.這件事你先別說,還沒發表.

還 沒 發 表 呢. Don't mention this matter yet, as it hasn't been announced.

FĀ-CÁI₁ 發 財 (VO) (1) make a fortune, become wealthy, get rich. 'Shéi-dōu-xiǎng-fā-cái. 誰 都 想 發 財. Everybody wants to get rich (quickly). Zuò-zhèiyàngrde-shì fābuliao-dà-cái. 作 這 樣 兒 的 事 發 不 了 大 財. It's impossible to make a fortune doing this kind of work. (2) wish you wealth (a New Year's greeting). Gōngxǐ-fācái. 恭 喜 發 財. Wish you happiness and wealth. Fācái-fācái. 發 財 發 財. Wish you wealth.

FĀ-CHÁO₄ 發 潮 (VO) damp ('atmosphere or a place). Zhèige-dìfang xiàtian-fā-cháo, hěn-bu-shūfu. 這 個 地 方 夏 天 發 潮, 很 不 舒 服. This place is damp in the summer, it's very uncomfortable.

FĀ-CHÓU₂ 發 愁 (VO) worry, be worried (implies sadness). Nǐ-fā-shénma-chóu? 你 發 甚 麼 愁? Why should you worry? or What worries you? Tā-zhěngtian-fā-chóu. 他 整 天 發 愁. He worries all day long.

FĀ-CHÙ₃ 發 怵 (VO) afraid, uneasy. 'Xiāngxia-rén shuō-huà fā-chù. 鄉 下 人 說 話 發 怵. When a country man speaks he is uneasy. Tā-zuò-fēijǐ yǒu-yidianr-fā-chù. 他 坐 飛 機 有 一 點 兒 發

怵. He is a little afraid of going by airplane.

FĀDA₂ 發 達 (SV) flourishing, well-developed (business, industry, education, communications, etc.). Zhèige-dìfangde-jiāotōng hěn-fāda. 這 個 地 方 的 交 通 很 發 達. This place has a well-developed transportation system. Rìběnde-gōngye hěn-fāda. 日 本 的 工 業 很 發 達. Japan's industry is well-developed.

FĀ-DĀI₃ 發 呆 (VO) be in a daze, not alert. Wǒ-èle-de-shi-hou, zǒngshi fā-dāi. 我 餓 了 的 時 候, 總 是 發 呆. When I am hungry, I am not alert.

FĀ-DIÀN₃ 發 電 (VO) generate electricity.

FĀDIÀNCHǍNG₃ 發 電 廠 (N) electric generating plant, power plant.

FĀDIÀNJĪ₂ 發 電 機 (N) electric generator.

FĀDIÀNZHÀN₄ 發 電 站 (N) electric distribution station, power substation.

FĀDÒNGJĪ₄ 發 動 機 (N) motor, engine.

FĀ-DǑU₃ 發 抖 (VO) tremble shake. Tā-qìde-zhí-fā-dǒu. 他 氣 得 直 發 抖. He was shaking from anger.

FĀ-FĒNG₃ 發 瘋 (VO) be crazy.

FĀ-FÚ₃ 發 福 (VO) (lit. grow with blessings) gain weight, a complimentary way of saying that a person is fat. Nín-fā-fú-le. 您

F

發福了. You have gained weight (a compliment).

FĂGUĀN₂ 法官 (N) a judge.

FÀGUO₁ 法國(PW) France.

FĀ-HÁNG₃ 發行 (VO) sell wholesale, distribute goods or merchandise. Wŏmende-huò wŏmen-zìjĭ-fā-háng, bu-líng-mài. 我們的貨我們自己發行,不零賣. We distribute our merchandise ourselves, but we don't retail it.

FĀ-HUÀ₃ 發話 (VO) give orders. Shàngbianr bù-fā-ḥuà, wŏ-bu-găn-géi-ni. 上邊兒不發話我不敢給你. If the superior doesn't give the order, I dare not give it to you.

FĀ-HUÀI₃ 發壞 (VO) have malicious or naughty thoughts. Wŏ-kàn-ta-yănjing-zhí-zhuàn, jiu-zhídao-ta-fā-huài-ne. 我看他眼睛直轉, 就知道他發壞呢. When I saw that his eyes kept turning, I knew that he was having malicious thoughts.

FĀHUĀNG₃ 發慌 (SV) be in a state of nervous agitation. Wŏ-ède-fāhuāng. 我餓的發慌. I am so hungry that it makes me nervous.

'FĀHUĪ₂ 發揮 (TV) (1) develop and express one's ideas or opinion. Qĭng-nĭ-bă-nĭde-yì-jian zai-'fāhuĭ-yixia. 請你把你的意見再發揮一下. Please express your idea some more. (2) develop and fully utilize one's ability. Huánjing-bu-hăo méi-you-fázi fāhuĭ-tade-néngli. 環境不好沒有法子發揮他的能力. The environment was not good, there was no way to fully utilize his ability.

FĀHŪN₃ 發昏 (SV) (1) be dizzy. (2) feel dullness (not sharp).

FĀ-HUŎR₃ 發火兒 (VO)burst into anger.

FĀJUÉ₂ 發覺 (TV) discover by sense something unknown to the subject, become aware of, realize. Wŏ-fājué-wŏ-cóngqiánde-cuòchu. 我發覺我從前的錯處. I became aware of my past errors. (cf: FĀXIÀN 發現).

FĀ-KUÁNG₃ 發狂 (VO) lit. or fig. go berserk.

FĀ-LÁOSAO₃ 發牢騷 (VO) express one's grievances. Tā-gen-wo fāle-bàntiānde-láosao. 他跟我發了半天的牢騷. He talked to me for a long while about his unpleasant situation.

FĀLÈNG₃ 發愣 (VO) (1) be in a daze, not alert. Tā-gāng-qĭlai-de-shihou cháng-zuòzai-nèr-fā-lèng. 他剛起來的時候常生在那兒發愣. As soon as he gets up, he often sits there in a daze. (2) dumfounded. Tā-tīngshuō-tā-háizi-sĭle, fāle-bàntian-lèng. 他聽說他孩子死了,發了半天愣.When he heard that his child died, he was dumfounded for a long time.

'FĂLÌNG₅ 法令 (N) law and decree.

'FĂLǛ₃ 法律 (N) law. (M: tiáo 條).

FĀ-MÁ₃ 發麻 (VO) feel numb. Wǒde-shǒu fā-má. 我的手發麻. My hand feels numb.

FĀ-MÁO₃ 發毛 (VO) (1) feel uneasy, apprehensive. Tā-xīnli fā-máo. 他心裏發毛. He feels a little afraid. (2) worth less than before (of currency). Qián fā-máo-le. 錢發毛了. The value of money is worth less now.

FĀ-MÉI₃ 發霉 (VO) become moldy.

FĀMÈN₃ 發悶 (SV) feel unhappy (caused by oppression in the mind). Yàoshi-ni-xīnli-fāmèn, nǐ-kéyi-dào-gōngyuán-qu-sàn-san-bù. 要是你心裏發悶，你可以到公園去散散步. If you feel unhappy, you may go for a stroll in the park.

FĀMÍ₃ 發迷 (SV) be infatuated.

FĀ-MIÀN₃ 發麵 (VO) leaven dough. (N) leavened dough. Miànbāo-shì-fāmian-zuòde. 麵包是發麵作的. Bread is made of leavened dough.

FĀMÍNG₁ 發明 (TV) invent. Tā-fāmíngle-yīge-xīn-jīqi. 他發明了一個新機器. He invented a new machine. (N) invention. Zhè-shi-wǒde-xīn-fāmíng. 這是我的

新發明. This is my new invention.

FĀMÍNGJIĀ₃ 發明家 (N) inventor.

FĀN₂ 翻 (IV) (1) reverse, turn over. Zhèijian-dàyī kéyi-'fān-zhe chuān. 這件大衣可以翻着穿. This coat may be worn in reverse (inside out). Nǐ-bǎ-pái fānguolai-kàn-kan. 你把牌翻過來看看. Turn over the card and let us see it. (2) turn pages of a book, flip through. Zhèiben-shū wǒ-jiu-fānle-jiyè, méi-'xì-kàn. 這本書我就翻了幾頁沒細看. I flipped through a few pages of this book, I did not read it carefully. (3) turn over things in order to search for something. Tāmen-bǎ-wǒ-xiāngzili-de-dōng-xi dou-fān-le. 他們把我箱子裏的東西都翻了. They turned over everything I had in my trunk. Bǎ-zhèige-bǐ fānchulai-le. 把這個筆翻出來了. This pen was discovered in the search. (4) turn one's attitude from "pro" to "con," from friendly into unfriendly. Tā-fān-le. 他翻了. He became angry. (5) (con. fān-yìn 翻印). reprint, reproduce (of a book, painting, photograph, etc.). (6) go up and over the top of something. Fān-guo-nèige-shān-qu jiu-dào-le. 翻過那個山去就到了. Once we go over that

F

F

mountain we will be there.
(RE) (1) upset, upturn, over-
turn. Tā-bă-qìchē kāifān-le.

他 把 汽 車 開 翻 了.

He drove the car and overturned
it. (2) indicates the attitude is
turned. Tāmen-liǎngge-rén nào-
fān-le. 他 們 兩 個 人
鬧 翻 了. Their (friendly)
attitude has changed into enmity.
(AD) in reverse (inside out). Tā-
fān-chuānzhe-dàyī. 他 翻 穿
着 大 衣. He is wearing
the overcoat in reverse.

FĀN₂ 翻 (TV) (con. fānyì 翻 譯).
translate. Zhèiju-huà, wǒ-bu-
hui-fān. 這 句 話 我 不
會 翻. I don't know how to
translate this sentence.

FĀN₄ 帆 (N) sail. Bă-fān-lāqilai.
把 帆 拉 起 來. Raise
the sails. Fān-shi-'bù-zuò-de.
帆 是 布 作 的. Sails
are made of cloth.

FĀN₃ 煩 (SV) be disturbed, troubled, annoyed, vexed. Wǒ-xīnli hěn-fán. 我 心 裏 很 煩.
I am very much distrubed.
(RE) be disturbed or annoyed by
doing something. Tā-lǎo-shuō,
zhēn-bă-wǒ-shuōfán-le. 他 老
説, 真 把 我 説 煩 了.
He is always talking; it really
annoys me.
(TV) trouble someone to do
something, used in a request.
Wǒ-fán-nin-géi-wo-bàn-diǎnr-
shì, xíng-bu-xíng? 我 煩 您
給 我 辦 點 兒 事 行
不 行? May I trouble you

to do something for me?

FĀN(SHI)₁ 凡 (是) used at the
beginning of a sentence followed
by dōu 都, quán 全 or quán-
dōu 全 都, whatever, all,
every. Fán(shi)-hǎode dōu-guì.
凡 (是) 好 的 都 貴. All
the good ones are expensive.
Fán-zuò-yíjiàn-shì, jiu-děi-zuò-
hǎole. 凡 作 一 件 事, 就
得 作 好 了. Whatever
job you want to do, you must do
it well.

FĂN₁ 反 (IV) (1) reverse (with
wrong side out or up). Bǎ-zhǐ-
fǎnguolai-xiě. 把 紙 反 過
來 寫. (lit. reverse thè paper
and write) Write on the other
side of the paper. (2) oppose.
Tāde-yìsi lǎo-gen-wo-fǎnzhe.
他 的 意 思 老 跟 我
反 着. His opinion is always
opposed to mine. (3) rebel.
Zhèngfǔ bu-hǎo, rénmín-jiu-
dōu-fǎn-le. 政 府 不 好 人
民 就 都 反 了. If the
government is bad, the people
will rebel. (4) behave boister-
ously, make a disturbance (of
children). Bié-zài-zhèr-fǎn. 別
在 這 兒 反. Don't make
a disturbance here.
(RE) reverse. Bǎ-nèige-zì xiě-
fǎnle. 把 那 個 字 寫 反
了. That character was written in reverse.

FĂN(DAO)₂ 反 (倒) or FĂN'ÉR 反
而 (AD) showing the opposite of
what was expected, and yet, but.
Wǒ-yǒu-gōngfu-de-shihou, tā-bu-

lái, jīntian-zènma-máng tā-
fǎn(dao)-lái-le. 我 有 功 夫
的 時 候 他 不 來, 今
天 這 麼 忙 他 反 倒
來 了. When I had time he
wouldn't come but he comes today, when I'm so busy. Shì-tāde-
cuòr, tā-fǎn(dao)-shuō wǒ-bu-
duì. 是 他 的 錯 兒 他
反 倒 說 我 不 對. It's
his fault, yet he said I did wrong.

FÀN₁ 飯 (N) (1) meal. (M: dùn
頓). chī-yidun-fàn 吃 一 頓
飯 eat a meal. (2) cooked rice.
(M: wǎn 碗). Zài-gěi-nín-tiān-
diǎnr-fàn. 再 給 您 添 點
兒 飯. Let me give you an-
other serving of rice. (3) living.
Zhèi-wǎn-fàn zhēn-bu-róngyi
chī. 這 碗 飯 真 不 容
易 吃. This is a hard way to
make a living.

FÀN₂ 犯 (TV) (1) transgress, commit an offense, sin, crime, etc.
fàn-zuì 犯 罪 commit a crime
or a sin. fàn-fǎ 犯 法 commit
an offense (law). fàn-cuòr 犯 錯
兒 commit an error. (2) be
afflicted with chronic illness,
faults or emotional upset. fàn-
bìng 犯 病 be afflicted with
chronic illness. fàn-bièniu 犯
彆 恆 be contrary.

FÀN₄ 犯 (B) criminal (person).
zuìfàn 罪 犯 culprit.

FÀN-ÀNZI₄ 犯 案 子 (VO)
commit a major crime or offense
that has become a court or police case. Tā-fànguo-hěn-duō-
ànzi, qiǎng-yínháng, shā-rén,

fàng-huǒ, 'děngděng. 他 犯
過 很 多 案 子, 搶 銀
行, 殺 人, 放 火 等 等.
He commited many crimes; bank
robbery, murder, arson, etc.

FÀN-BǍN₄ 翻 板 (VO) repro-
duce (by printing).
(N) reproduced copy.

FÀN-BÌNG₂ 犯 病 (VO) be afflicted
with chronic illness. Wǒde-dù-
zi-bu-hǎo, chīduōle-jiu-fàn-
bìng. 我 的 肚 子 不 好,
吃 多 了 就 犯 病. My
stomach is not good, when I eat
too much I get sick.

FÀNBÙ₄ 帆 布 (N) sailcloth,
canvas, duck.

FÀNBUSHÀNG₂ 犯 不 上 or
FÀNBUZHÁO 犯 不 着 (RV)
not worth doing. Zhèi-dianr-
xiǎo-shì, fànbushàng gēn-jīnglǐ-
shuō. 這 點 兒 小 事 犯
不 上 跟 經 理 說. Such
a minor matter, it's not worth
taking to the manager.

FÀNBUZHÁO₃ 犯 不 着 see
FÀNBUSHÀNG 犯 不 上.

FÀNCÀI₅ 蕃 菜 (N) western
style meal.

FÀNCHÁO₄ 反 潮 (SV) damp
(caused by nature). Jīntian yǒu-
dianr-fǎncháo. 今 天 有 點
兒 反 潮. It is a little damp
today.

FÀNCHĒ₃ 飯 車 (N) dining car.
(M: liàng 輛).

FÀNCHUÁN₃ 帆 船 (N) wind-
propelled ship, sailboat, a junk.
(M: tiáo 條 , zhī 隻).

FÀN-CUÒR₂ 犯 錯 兒 (VO)

F

F

commit an error <u>or</u> mistake, be at fault. Tā-zuò-shì-bu-xiǎoxin, chángchang-fàn-cuòr. 他 作 事 不 小 心 , 常 常 犯 錯 兒 . He is careless in his work; he often makes errors.

FÀNDIÀN₃ 飯店 (N) hotel. (<u>syn.</u> lǚguan 旅館). (M: jiā 家).

FǍNDÒNG₃ 反動 (SV) reactionary. fǎndòng-fènzǐ 反動份子 a reactionary. Tāmen-shuō-nǐ-fǎndòng. 他們說你反動. They say you are reactionary.

FǍNDUÌ₁ 反對 (TV) oppose, be against. (<u>opp.</u> zànchéng 贊成). Tāmen-dōu-fǎnduì-wo. 他們都反對我. They are all against me. Wǒ-fànduì-jiā-shuì. 我反對加稅. I am against raising t xes.

FǍN'ÉR₂ 反而 <u>see</u> FǍN(DAO) 反(倒)

FÀN-FǍ₂ 犯法 (VO) commit an offense (<u>law</u>). Zài-zhèli-tìng-chē fàn-fǎ. 在這裏停車犯法. To park here is against the law.

FǍNFU₅ 反復 (IV) recur. Tā-de-bìng-fǎnfu-le. 他的病反復了. His illness has recurred.

(AD) over and over again. Tā-fǎnfude-shuōle hǎoxiēcì. 他反復的說了好些次. He said it over and over again (many times).

FĀNG₁ 方 (B) (1) square (<u>par-allelogram)</u> <u>or nearly so.</u> sìfāng 四方 square. zhèngfāng 正方 perfect square. chángfāng

長方 rectangular, oblong. fāngzhuān 方磚 square brick. fāngtáng 方糖 sugar cube. Zhèige-zhuōzi shì-fāngde. 這個桌子是方的. This table is square. Tāde-liǎn shi-fāngde, nǐde-liǎn shi-yuánde. 他的臉是方的,你的臉是圓的 His face is square, your face is round. (2) <u>used before measurements to</u> <u>form M</u>, square (<u>measurement</u> <u>of area)</u>. yìfāngmǎ 一方碼 a square yard. sìfāngcùn 四方吋 four square inches. (3) square. (<u>mathematics</u>). píngfāng 平方 square. Sānde-píngfāng-shi-jiǔ. 三的平方是九. The square of three is nine. lìfāng 立方 cube. Bā-shi-èrde-lì-fāng. 八是二的立方. Eight is the cube of two. (N) (1) (<u>con.</u> píngfāng 平方). square (<u>mathematics</u>). (M: cì 次). X-fāng-jiā-Y-fāng. X 方加 Y 方 . $X^2 + Y^2$. (2) power (<u>mathe-matics</u>). Erde-sìcì-fāng děngyu-shílliù. 二的四次方等於十六. Two to the fourth power is equal to sixteen.

FĀNG₁ 方 (B) <u>added to L to form</u> <u>PW,</u> area <u>in certain direction.</u> dōngfāng 東方 the East, the Orient. xīfāng 西方 the West, the Occident. qiánfāng 前方 the front (in battle). hòufāng 後方 the rear (in battle).

FÁNG₄ 防 (TV) guard against, prevent. Wǒmen-děi-fángzhe-ta. 我們得防著他. We have to guard against him. Zhèige-shi-fáng-huǒ-yòng-de. 這 個 是 防 火 用 的 . This is used for preventing fire.

FÁNG(ZI)₁ 房 子 (N) (1) house, building. (M: suǒ 所). (2) dial. room. (M: jiān 間).

FǍNG₄ 紡 (TV) spin. fǎng-xiàn 紡線 spin thread. fǎng-mián-hua 紡綿花 spin cotton.

FǍNG₄ 仿 (TV) imitate, copy (art work). Nǐ-děi-chuàngzuo, bú-yao-fǎng-biéren. 的 得 創 作, 不 要 仿 別 人 . You have to create, don't copy from others.

FÀNG₁ 放 (TV) (1) release, set free, let go. Tā-lāzhe-wo bu-fàng. 他 拉 着 我 不 放 . He grabbed hold of me and wouldn't let me go. Bǎ-gǒu-fàngchuqu. 把 狗 放 出 去 . Let the dog out. Tā-zuòle-sān-nian-jiān, xiànzài-fàngchulai-le. 他 坐 了 三 年 監 , 現 在 放 出 來 了 . He was in prison for three years, now he is released. (2) place, put. Nèiben-shū nǐ-fàngzai-nǎr-le? 那 本 書 你 放 在 那 兒 了 ? Where did you put that book? (3) tend grazing animals. fàng-niú 放 牛 tend cows. (4) lend money for interest. Tā-bǎ-qián-dōu-fàngchu-qu-le. 他 把 錢 都 放 出 去 了 . All his money was lent out for interest. (5) fire a weapon. fàng-qiāng 放 鎗 shoot a gun. (6) light fireworks.

fàng-huā 放 花 light fireworks (for display). fàng-huǒjiàn 放 火 箭 launch a missile. (7) make something longer, bigger, wider, etc. Tāde-yīshang-duǎn-le, děi-fàngchu-yidianr-lai. 他 的 衣 裳 短 了, 得 放 出 一 點 兒 來 . His clothes are short now, they must be lengthened a little. (8) send forth, radiate. Tāde-shǒushi zhí-fàng-guāng. 他 的 首 飾 直 放 光 . Her jewelry is sparkling.

FÁNG'AI₄ 妨 礙 (TV) hinder. Wǒ-fáng'aibuzháo-ni. 我 妨 礙 不 着 你 . I am not hindering you. (N) hindrance. Tā-zài-zhèr méi-shénma-fáng'ai. 他 在 這 兒 沒 甚 麼 妨 礙 . His being here is not any hindrance.

'FÁNGBEI₃ 防 備 (TV) be on guard (against). Děi-fángbeizhe-ta. 得 防 備 着 他 . (You) must be on guard against him. Tā-yi-bu-fángbei wǒmen-jiu-pǎo. 他 一 不 防 備 我 們 就 跑 . When he is not on guard we will run. (N) precaution. Díren-yǒule-fángbei-le. 敵 人 有 了 防 備 了 . The enemy has already taken precautions.

FĀNGBIAN₁ 方 便 (SV) convenient. (TV) (1) relieve oneself. Wǒ-děi-qu-fāngbian-fāngbian. 我 得 去 方 便 方 便 . I have to go to the bathroom. (2) make

F

convenient <u>for someone</u>. Wǒ-
fèile-hǎo-dàde-jìn, duì-wǒ-méi-
shénma-yòng dàoshì-fāngbianle-
tā-le. 我費了好大的
勁，對我沒甚麼用
倒是方便了他了．
I spent a great deal of effort.
It was not much use to me, but
it made it convenient for him.

FÁNGCHǍN₃ 房產 (N) house <u>as</u>
<u>property</u>, real estate (<u>house</u>).

FÁNGDǏNG₄ 房頂 (N) (1) roof.
(2) ceiling.

FÁNGDŌNG₂ 房東 (N) landlord
(<u>of a building</u>).

FĀN-GĒNTOU₃ 翻跟頭 (VO)
turn a somersault.

'FĀNGFǍ₁ 方法 (N) method,
way. kēxué-fāngfǎ 科學方
法 scientific method. (cf:
FÁZI 法子).

FÀNG-FĒNGZHENG₄ 放風箏
(VO) fly a kite.

FǍNGFU₃ 彷彿 (MA) seemingly,
it seems that. Tā-fǎngfu-bu-
yuànyì-qù. 他彷彿不願
意去 . It seems that he does
not want to go.

FÀNG-HUǑ₂ 放火 (VO) set
afire maliciously.

FÀNG-JIÀ₁ 放假 (VO) have a
vacation. Xuéxiào fàng-sāntiān-
jià. 學校放三天假．
The school is having a three day
vacation.

FÁNGJIĀN₃ 房間 (N) (1) <u>dial.</u>
room. (2) room (<u>in a hotel</u>). zài-
lǚguǎn kāi-fángjiān 在旅館
開房間 take a room in the

hotel.

FÁNGKÈ₂ 房客 (N) tenant.

FÁNGKŌNG₃ 防空 (B) air de-
fense. fángkōngdòng 防空洞
air-raid shelter (in the form of
a cave or tunnel). fángkōng-shè-
bèi 防空設備 air defense
installation. Zhèixiē-dōngxi dōu-
shi-fángkōng-yòng-de. 這些
東西都是防空用
的． These things are all used
for air defense.

FÀNG-KUǍN₃ 放款 (VO) lend
money (<u>for interest</u>). Zhèige-
yínháng-fàngde-kuǎn-bu-duō. 這
個銀行放的款不
多． This bank doesn't lend
much money.

FĀNGMIAN₂ 方面 (M) (1) side,
party (<u>person or group of persons</u>).
Yàoshi-liǎngfāngmian-bu-tóngyì,
zai-xiǎng-biéde-fázi. 要是
兩方面不同意，再
想別的法子． If both
sides won't agree, then we will
think of some other way. 'Wǒ-
zhèifāngmiàn méi-wèntí. 我這
方面沒問題． There
is no problem on my side. (2)
side, angle. Wǒ-bu-néng-jiù-
cóng-zhèifāngmian-kàn. 我不
能就從這方面看．
I can't look at it only from this
angle.

FÀNG-PÀO₂ 放炮 (VO) (1) shoot
large caliber weapons. fàngle-
sānsheng-pào 放了三聲
炮 shoot three rounds from the
cannon. (2) blow, burst (<u>as a</u>

tire). Pídài fàng-pào-le. 皮帶
放砲了 . The tire blew.
(3) talk big, bluff. (4) light fire-
crackers.

FÀNG-PÌ₃ 放屁 (VO) (1) give
off gas (from the rectum). (2)
what rot, nonsense.

FÁNGQIAN₁ 房錢 (N) (lit. house
money) (1) rent for a house or
for space in a building. (syn.
fángzū 房租). (2) money for
purchasing a house.

FĀNGR₃ 方兒 see FĀNGZI 方
子 .

FĂNGSHĀCHĂNG₄ 紡紗廠
(N) spinning mill. (M: jiā 家).

FĀNGSHÌ₃ 方式 (N) way, style,
form, format or method of
doing something. shēnghuo-
fāngshì 生活方式 way of
living. Wǒmen-yòng-'shénma-
fāngshì gěi-ta-dàoxiè? 我們
用甚麼方式給他
道謝? How shall we ex-
press our thankfulness to him?

FÀNGSI₃ 放肆 (SV) behave
without regard to rules of pro-
priety. Tā-shuò-huà tài-fàngsi-
le. 他說話太放肆了.
He speaks without regard to
others.

FÀNGSŌNG₄ 放鬆 (TV) loosen
something tight, slacken, relax
grip, hold or control. Bǎ-xié-
dài-fàngsōng-le. 把鞋帶
放鬆了. Loosen up the
shoe-strings. Bié-bǎde-nènma-
jǐn, fàngsōng-dianr. 別把得
那麼緊,放鬆點兒.
lit. or fig. Don't hold it that

tight, loosen your grip a bit.

FÀNGUĂNR₁ 飯館兒 (N)
restaurant.(M: jiā 家).

FÀN-GUĪ(JU)₃ 犯規(矩)(VO)
commit an offense (rules or
regulations. Nǐ-qiántian-wǎn-dào,
zuótian-zài-kèshì-chī-dōngxi,
jīntian-you-dǎ-jià. Nǐ-zěnma-
lǎo-fàn-guī(ju)-a? 你前天
晚到,昨天在課室
吃東西,今天又打
架,你怎麼老犯規
(矩)啊? Day before yester-
day you were late; yesterday
you were eating in class; today
you were fighting; why are you
always breaking the rules?

'FĀNGWÈN₃ 訪問 (TV) (lit.
visit and inquire) (1) interview
by a visiting reporter. Yǒu-yi-
ge-jìzhě-lai-fǎngwen-ni. 有一
個記者來訪問你.
A reporter is here to interview
you. (2) visit a foreign country
on official business. Zhèici-bù-
zhǎng dào-Nánměi-qu-fǎngwèn-
le-sānge guójiā. 這次部
長到南美去訪問
了三個國家. When
the chief went to South America
this time, he visited three countries.

FÁNGWŪ₄ 房屋 (N) house,
buildings.

FĀNGXIANG₂ 方向 (N) (lit. or
fig.) direction. Wǒmen-wàng-
něige-fāngxiang-xuǒ-ne?我們
往那個方向走呢?
lit. or fig. In which direction
are we going?

F

F

FÀNG-XĪN₁ 放 心 (VO) set
one's mind at ease, not to be
worried or deeply concerned.
Nín-fàng-xīn! 您 放 心!
Set your mind at ease! Wǒ-
fàngbuxia-xīn-qu. 我 放 不
下 心 去. I can't set my
mind at ease (I'm worried).
(TV) not to be worried. Búyong-
bu-fàngxīn-wo. 不 用 不 放
心 我. Dont worry about me.
Nǐ-fàngxīn-qu-zuò-ba. 你 放
心 去 作 吧. You go ahead
and do it, don't worry.

FÀNG-XUÉ₁ 放 學 (VO) (1) let
out of school. Wǒmende-xiān-
sheng-bìng-le, suóyi-'yìdian-
zhōng jiu-fàng-xué-le. 我 們
的 先 生 病 了, 所 以
一 點 鐘 就 放 學 了.
Our teacher is sick, so we were
let out of school at one o'clock.
(2) temporary closing of a
school. Míngtian-fàng-xué. 明
天 放 學. School is closed
tomorrow.

FĀNGYÁN₄ 方 言 (N) dialect.
FĀNGZHĒN₃ 方 針 (N) objective
or general direction indicating
course of action. Tā-zuò-shì
méi-you-yídìngde- fāngzhēn. 他
作 事 没 有 一 定 的
方 針. His work doesn't
have a definite objective.

'FÁNGZHǏ₅ 防 止 (TV) prevent,
check or stop an activity.

'FĂNGZHǏ₄ 紡 織 (B) spin and
weave. fǎngzhichǎng 紡 織 廠
spinning and weaving mill. fǎng-
zhīgōngyè 紡 織 工 業 the

textile industry.

FĀNGZI₃ 方 子 or FĀNGR 方
兒 (N) prescription (medical).
kāi-fāngzi 開 方 子 prescribe
(a prescription).

FÁNGZŪ₂ 房 租 (N) rent for a
house or space in building. (cf:
FÁNGQIAN 房 錢).

'FĂNKÀNG₃ 反 抗 (TV) oppose,
resist an enemy, higher authority, power. Tāde-yìsi méi-ren-
gǎn-'fǎnkàng. 他 的 意 思
没 人 敢 反 抗. Nobody
dares to oppose his opinion.

FĂN-LIĂN₄ 翻 臉 (VO) show
anger on the face to bring an
issue to a head forcibly. Wǒ-
yì-gēn-ta-yào-zhàng, tā-jiu-
fān-liǎn-le. 我 一 跟 他
要 賬, 他 就 翻 臉 了.
As soon as I asked for his
payment, he became very unfriendly. Hǎohāor-de-gen-ta-
shuō, bié-fān-liǎn. 好 好 兒
的 跟 他 説, 别 翻 臉
Talk to him nicely, don't show
anger.

FÀN-MÁOBING₂ 犯 毛 病
(1) develop or show certain
faults chronically. Yí-dào-
dōngtian zhèige-qìchē jiu-fàn-
máobing. 一 到 冬 天 這
汽 車 就 犯 毛 病.
As soon as winter comes, this
car will develop some faults.
(2) commit minor errors chronically. (3) be afflicted with
chronic illness. Tā-cháng fàn-
zhèige-máobing. 他 常 犯
這 個 毛 病 了. He often

commits this error. or He is often afflicted with illness.

FǍNMIÀNR₂ 反面兒 (N) (1) reverse or wrong side of any flat thing with two sides. Zhèi-shi₇fǎnmianr, bú-shi-zhèng-mianr. 這是反面兒，不是正面. This is the wrong side, not the right side. (2) opposite side. Tā-shuō-de shi-fǎnmiànrde-lǐ. 他說的是反面兒的理. What he said was the opposite side's argument.

FÁNNAO₄ 煩惱 (SV) vexed, unhappy, disturbed, Zhèizhŏng-shì ràng-rén-hěn-fánnao. 這種事讓人很煩惱. This kind of thing made people feel unhappy. (N) vexation. Tāde-fánnao dōu-shi-zìjǐ-zhǎode. 他的煩惱都是自己找的. His unhappiness is all created by himself.

FÀN-PÍQÌ₂ 犯脾氣 (VO) be angry, throw a tantrum. Tā-guò-liǎngtian jiu-fàn-yici-píqi. 他過兩天就犯一次脾氣. His temper is out of control every couple of days.

FĀNQIÉ₄ 番茄 (N) tomato.

'FÁNRÓNG₄ 繁榮 (SV) prosperous (referring to a place with a great deal of bustling, flourishing activities.) Rìběnde-shāngyè hěn-fánróng. 日本的商業很繁榮. Japan's commerce is very prosperous.

(N) a bustling prosperity.

FĀN-SHĒN₃ 翻身 (VO) (1) turn oneself over. Nèige-chuáng-tài-zhǎi wǒ-yi-fān-shēn jiu-diào-dìxia-le. 那個牀太窄我一翻身就掉地下了. That bed was too narrow, I turned over and fell on the floor. (2) fig. change one's economic or social status for the better. Bàoshang-shuō, xiànzài 'qióng-rén-dou-fān-shēn-le. 報上說，現在窮人都翻身了. The newspaper said that the poor people are no longer poor.

FÁNSHÌLÍN₄ 凡士林 (N) petroleum jelly (a transliteration of Vaseline).

FĀNTENG₅ 翻騰 (TV) turn things over (in a disorderly manner). Bié-fānteng-wǒ-zhuōzi-shangde-dōngxi. 別翻騰我桌子上的東西. Don't turn over things on my desk.

FÀNTĪNG₁ 飯廳 (N) dining room, dining hall. (M: jiān 間).

FÀNTŎNG₄ 飯桶 (N) (1) bucket for holding cooked rice. (2) fig. a person who eats a great deal but can't do anything else, a useless person. Tā-shì-ge-fàn-tŏng. 他是個飯桶. He is useless.

FÀNWǍN₂ 飯碗 (N) (1) rice bowl. (2) fig. job for making a living. tiě-fànwǎn 鐵飯碗 (lit. iron rice bowl) a permanent job. Wǒ-bǎ-fàn'wǎn-dǎ-le.

F

我把飯碗打了. I broke the rice bowl. *or fig.* I lost my job.

FÀNWEI₂ 範圍 (N) scope. Tā-yánjiu-de-fànwei hěn-guǎng. 他 研究 的 範圍 很 廣. The scope of his research is very broad. Nǐ-wèn-de-wènti bu-zài-wǒ-tǎolun-de-fànwei-yǐneì. 你 問 的 問題 不 在 我 討論 的 範圍 以 內. The question you asked is not within the scope of what I have discussed.

FÀNXING₃ 反省 (IV) examine oneself, attain self-realization. Nǐ-zìjǐ-zuòcuò-le, děi-fǎnxing. 你 自己 作 錯 了, 得 反省. If you do something wrong, you have to examine yourself.

FÀNYI₁ 翻譯 (TV) translate. Qǐng-nǐ-bǎ-zhèiben-shū fānyi-cheng-Yīngwén. 請 你 把 這 本 書 翻 譯 成 英文. Please translate this book into English.
(N) (l) translation. Tāde-fānyi-hěn-hǎo, kěshi-tài-màn. 他的 翻 譯 很 好 可是 太 慢. His translation is very good, but he is too slow. (2) translator, interpreter. Tā-gěi-wǒ-dāng-fānyi. 他 給 我 當 翻 譯. He acts as interpreter for me.

FÀNYIN₃ 翻印 reproduce a book or printed matter. Zhèiběn-shū, bunéng-suíbiàn-fānyìn. 這 本 書 不 能 隨便 翻

印. This book can't be re-produced at will.

FÀNYING₃ 反應 (N) reaction, response. Wǒ-gēn-dàjiā-tán-huà-yǐhòu, tāmende-fǎnying-zěnmayàng? 我 跟 大家 談 話 以 後, 他 們 的 反 應 怎 麼 樣? After I talked to everybody, what was their response? Dǎ-zhèizhǒng-zhēn-de-fǎnying jiushi-fāshāo. 打 這 種 針 的 反 應 就 是 發 燒. The reaction from this injection is fever.

FÀNYING₃ 反映 (TV) reflect thoughts, opinions, etc. Tāde-zhèiben-shū kéyi-fǎnying tāde-sīxiang. 他 的 這 本 書 可 以 反 映 他 的 思 想. This book of his may reflect his thinking. Wǒmen-děi-bǎ-tade-yìjian fǎnyingshangqu. 我 們 得 把 他 的 意 見 反 映 上 去. We must reflect his opinion to the superior.

'FÀNZHÈNG₁ 反正 (MA) anyway, in any case. Wǒ-bu-guǎn-'nǐ-qù-bu-qu, fǎnzhèng-'wǒ-bu-qù. 我 不 管 你 去 不 去. 反 正 我 不 去. I don't care whether you go or not, I am not going in any case.

FÀNZI₄ 販子 (N) peddler, vendor.

FÀN-ZUÌ₂ 犯罪 (VO) commit a crime *or* a sin. Shā-rén-shi-fàn-zuì. 殺 人 是 犯 罪. To kill a person is a crime. Yǒu-rén-rènwei-chī-ròu fàn-zuì. 有 的 人 認 為 吃 肉 犯

F

罪 . There are some people who consider eating meat a sin.

FĀPÀNG₄ 發 胖 (SV) be fat, become fat. Nǐ-lǎo-chī-nènma-duō, zěnma-néng-bu-fāpàng-ne? 你 老 吃 那 麼 多, 怎 麼 能 不 發 胖 呢? You always eat so much, how could you help from becoming fat?

FĀPIÀO₃ 發 票 (N) invoice, bill of goods, bill of lading. kāi-fā-piào 開 發 票 make or send an invoice.

FĀ-PÍQI₂ 發 脾 氣 (VO) loose one's temper, throw a tantrum. Tā-zhēn-wěn, cónglái-méi-fā-guo-píqi. 他 真 穩, 從 來 沒 發 過 脾 氣 . He is really steady, he has never lost his temper.

FĀQǏ₃ 發 起 (TV) originate, initiate, found a project or an organization. Zhèige-gōngsī, shì-tāmen-sānge-rén-fāqǐ-de. 這 個 公 司 是 他 們 三 個 人 發 起 的 . This company was founded by those three persons.

FĀQǏRÉN₄ 發 起 人 (N) originator, initiator or founder (of a project or an organization). Zhèige-xuéxiàode-fāqírén shì-shéi? 這 個 學 校 的 發 起 人 是 誰 ? Who is the founder of this school?

FĀ-QIÚ₃ 發 球 (VO) serve a ball in a game. Gāi-shéi-fā-qiú-le? 該 誰 發 球 了? Whose turn to serve?

FAR₁ 法 兒 see FĀ 法 (-B) (1).

FĀR₂ 法 兒 see FÁZI 法 子 .

FĀ-RÈ₂ 發 熱 (VO) (1) feel hot. shēnshang-fā-rè 身 上 發 熱 feel hot (in the body). (2) have a fever.(syn. fā-shāo 發 燒).

FĀRUǍN₃ 發 軟 (SV) feel weak. Tā-bìng-gāng-hǎo, tuǐ-hai-fā-ruǎn. 他 病 剛 好, 腿 還 發 軟 . He just recovered (from illness), his legs still feel weak.

FĀ-SHĀO₂ 發 燒 (VO) have a fever. (syn. fā-rè 發 熱). Tā-fā-shāo fāde-hěn-gāo. 他 發 燒 發 的 很 高 . He has a high temperature (fever).

FĀSHÈ₅ 發 射 (TV) shoot a gun, arrow, missile, etc.

FĀSHĒNG₁ 發 生 (TV) happen, occur, arise, come into prominence. Jīntian-zài-bānshang fāshēngle-yijian shìqing. 今 天 在 班 上 發 生 了 一 件 事 情 . An incident occurred today in the office. Nǐ-yi-zǒu zhǔn-fāsheng-kùnnan. 你 一 走, 準 發 生 困 難 · As soon as you leave, some trͦ ble will happen, I'm sure. Tīngle-tāde-huà, wǒ-fāsheng-hěn-duō-de-yíwèn. 聽 了 他 的 話, 我 發 生 很 多 的 疑 問 . After hearing him speak, many doubts arose in my mind. Nǐ-jiu-zhàozhe-ta-gàosong-nide nèiyangr-zuò, jué-bu-huì-fāsheng-wèntí. 你 就 照 著 他 告 訴 你 的 那 樣 兒 作, 決 不 會 發 生 問

F

F

題. You just do it as he told you, I am sure there will be no problem.

FĀ-SHÌ₃ 發誓 (VO) swear, make an oath. Wǒ-fā-shì, jué-bu-zài-zuò-le. 我發誓,決對不再作了. I swear I absolutely won't do it again.

FĀ-SHUǏ₃ 發水 (VO) flood. Yàoshi-zài-xià-yǔ kǒngpà-jiu-yào-fā-dà-shuǐ-le. 要是再下雨恐怕就要發大水了. If it rains some more, I am afraid there will be a flood.

FÀTIÁO₅ 發條 (N) mainspring of a time piece, or a similar kind of spring. Nǐde-biǎo fàtiáo-duàn-le. 你的表的發條斷了. The mainspring of your watch is broken.

FǍTÍNG₂ 法庭 (N) court (law, general). Zhèi ge-děi-zai-fǎ-tíng jiějué. 這個得在法庭解決. This will have to be decided in court.

FĀ-WĒIFENG₅ 發威風 (VO) radiate or display a majestic, awe-inspiring appearance (of a person). Nǐ-búbi-gen-wǒ fā-wēifeng. 你不必跟我發威風. You don't have to put on appearances for me.

FÀWÉN₁ 法文 (N) French language.

FĀXIÀN₁ 發現 (TV) discover. Tā-zài-Tàipingyáng-fāxiàn-yíge-dǎo. 他在太平洋發現一個島. He discovered an island in the Pacific Ocean.

(cf: FĀJUÉ 發覺).

(N) discovery. Zhèi-shi-xīn-fānxiàn. 這是新發現. This is a new discovery.

FĀXIĒ₃ 發洩 (TV) release certain pent-up emotions. Wǒ-yi-dùzide-qì méi-fázi-fāxiè. 我一肚子的氣沒法子發洩. I have a belly-full of anger with no way to release it. Dǎ-tàitai yě-shi-yizhǒng-fāxiède-bànfa. 打太太也是一種發洩的辦法. Wife beating is also a way of releasing emotions.

FĀXÍNG₃ 發行 (TV) issue, circulate bonds, banknotes, money or printed matter, such as periodicals, books etc. Zhè-shi-Zhōngguoyínháng-fāxíngde-chāo-pào. 這是中國銀行發行的鈔票. This is a banknote issued by the Bank of China. Wǒ-zhǐ-néng-zuò-biānji, yìnshuā, chūbǎn, fāxíng, dou-dei-zhǎo-'biéren-zuò. 我只能作編輯,印刷,出版,發行都得找別人作. I can be the editor, but you must find other people to do the printing, publishing and circulating.

FĀ-YÁN₃ 發炎 (VO) have an inflammation. Wǒ-sǎngzi-yǒu-yidianr-fā-yán. 我嗓子有點兒發炎. I have a slight inflammation in my throat.

FĀ-YÁN₃ 發言 (VO) make a statement, speak up. Kāi-huì-de-shíhou, ta-méi-fāguo-yán.

開 會 的 時 候 他 沒 發 過 言. When the meeting was in session, he never spoke up at all.

FĀYÁNG₄ 發 揚 develop, spread. fāyáng-Zhōngguo-wénhuà 發 揚 中 國 文 化 spread Chinese culture.

FĀYÁNQUÁN₃ 發 言 權 (N) right to speak. Fēihuìyuán-ké-yi-pángtīng, méi-you-fāyánquán. 非 會 員 可 以 旁 聽 沒 有 發 言 權. Non-members may stay in the meeting as observers, but they do not have the right to speak.

FĀYÁNRÉN₃ 發 言 人 (N) spokesman. Tā-shi-zhèngfǔde-fāyánrén. 他 是 政 府 的 發 言 人. He is the spokes-man for the government.

FĀ-YÁR₃ 發 芽 兒 (VO) ger-minate, sprout. Shù fā-yár-le. 樹 發 芽 兒 了. The tree is sprouting.

FĀ-YĪN₃ 發 音 (VO) pronounce (vocalization). Zhèige-zì wǒ-bu-huì-fā-yīn. 這 個 字 我 不 會 發 音. I don't know how to pronounce this character. (N) pronunciation. Tāde-fāyin hěn-qingchu. 他 的 發 音 很 清 楚. His pronuncia-tion is very clear.

FĀYU₃ 發 育 (IV) develop, grow into maturity (of body organs). Zài-shēnti-fāyude-shihou, chī-de-duō. 在 身 體 發 育 的 時 候, 吃 得 多. While the body is growing into maturity,

one eats a lot.

FĀYUÀN₂ 法 院 (N) law court (establishment). Zhèige-ànzi yìzhí-dǎdao-zuìgāo-fǎyuàn. 這 個 案 子 一 直 打 到 最 高 法 院. This case was fought all the way to the Supreme Court.

FĀYUĀNDÌ₄ 發 源 地 (N) (1) place of origin (of a culture). Hénán, Shāndōng, shì-Zhōngguo-wénhuàde fāyuāndì. 河 南、山 東、是 中 國 文 化 的 發 源 地. Honan and Shan-tung are the places of origin of Chinese culture. (2) source, place of origin (of a river). Huánghéde-fāyuāndì-zài-shénma-dìfang? 黃 河 的 發 源 地 在 甚 麼 地 方? Where is the place of origin of the Yellow River?

FĀ-YÙN₃ 發 暈 (VO) feel dizzy.

FĀZHAN₁ 發 展 (TV) extend, ex-pand, develop, make grow, cer-tain powers, interests, indus-tries, etc. fāzhan-zhòng-gōngyè 發 展 重 工 業 develop heavy industries. fāzhan-wényì-de-huódong 發 展 文 藝 的 活 動 expand activities in art and literature. fāzhan-rénminde-zìyóu 發 展 人 民 的 自 由 extend people's freedom. (N) expansion, growth. Wǒ-zài-zhèlide-dìwei dào-tóur-le. Yǐ-hòu-bu-huì-yǒu-tài-dàde-zāzhan-le. 我 在 這 裏 的 地 位 到 頭 兒 了; 以 後 不 會 有 太 大 的 發 展 了.

F

My position here has reached the top. From now on there won't be much growth(potential).

FĀ-ZHŎNG₃ 發腫 (SV) be swollen. Wŏ-zŏule-yìtiān, jiăo-dou-fāzhŏng-le. 我走了一天, 腳都發腫了. I walked a whole day, my feet are swollen.

FĀZHUĀNG₅ 發莊 (N) wholesaler, distributor (vs. retailer). Wŏmen-shi-fāzhuāng, bù-líng-mài. 我們是發莊, 不零賣. We are wholesalers; we don't sell retail.

FĂZI₁ 法子 (N) or FĂR 法兒 method, way (of doing something). Méi-fázi. 沒法子. There's no way out (of a situation). Wŏmen-děi-xiăng-fázi. 我們得想法子. We must figure out a way. Méi-fá-zi-bàn. 沒法子辦. There is no way of handling it.

FĀZUO₅ 發作 erupt, come to the surface (of an illness or emotional feeling that has been arrested, but not eliminated). Tāde-bìng-yòu-fāzuole. 他的病又發作了. He is sick again.

FĒI₁ 飛 (IV) (1) fly (as a bird). Fēijinlai-yizhī-niăor. 飛進來一隻鳥兒. A bird flew in. (2) fly (travel by plane). Tā-míngtian jiu-fēidao-Rìběn-qule. 他明天就飛到日本去了. Tomorrow he will fly to Japan. (3) fly, float in the air. Chuándān-măn-tiān-fēi. 傳單滿天飛.

Handbills are flying all over. Tŭ dou-fēiqilai-le. 土都飛起來了. Dust is flying. (4) evaporate. Qìyóu-dou-fēi-le. 汽油都飛了. The gasoline has evaporated.

(AD) do something fast as flying. Qìchē zŏude-fēi-kuài. 汽車走得飛快. The car went as fast as flying.

FĒI₄ 非 (B-) non-, in-, un-, etc. fēizhèngshi 非正式 informal, unofficial.

FĒI(DEI)₁ 非(得) (AD) (1) insist on doing something. Wŏ-jiào-ta-lái tā-fēi(dei)-bu-lái. 我叫他來他非(得)不來. I told him to come but he insists on not coming. Tā-fēi(dei) yào-gěi-qián. 他非(得)要給錢. He insisted on paying. (2) absolutely have to, absolutely must. Wŏ-fēi(dei)-qu-jiàn-ta. 我非得去見他. I absolutely must go to see him.

FĒI₃ 肥 (SV) (1) fat (of animals). Zhū-hěn-féi. 猪很肥. The pig is very fat. (2) fertile (land). Dì-bú-gòu-féi. 地不夠肥. The land is not fertile enough. (3) loose, big (clothes). Zhèi-tiao-kùzi tài-féi. 這條褲子太肥. These pants are too loose. (cf: PÁNG 胖).

FĒI₄ 匪 (B) bandit. tŭfěi 土匪 (local) bandit.

(SV) roguish. Tā-chuān-de-yī-shang yàngzi-hěn-fěi. 他穿的衣裳樣子很匪. The style of his clothes is very roguish.

FÈI₂ 費 (TV) (1) consume, expend, use up. (opp. shěng 省). Yào-mǎi-piányi-dōngxi, děi-fèi-shí-hou-qu-zhǎo. 要 買 便 宜 東 西 , 得 費 時 候 去 找 . To buy bargains one has to take time to look for them. Zhèiyangr-zuò tài-fèishì. 這 樣 兒 作 太 費 事. It's too much work to do it this way. Zhèiyàngrde-yīshang hěnfèi-cáiliao. 這 樣 兒 的 衣 裳 很 費 材 料 . This kind of dress takes a lot of material to make. (2) use up in excessive quantities or in a shorter time than expected. Zhèige-qìchē fèi-yóu. 這 個 汽 車 費 油 . This car uses too much gasoline. Zhèi-háizi fèi-xié. 這 孩 子 費 鞋 . This child wore out his shoes (sooner than expected). (3) waste. Chū-mén-guān-dēng, bié-fèi-diàn. 出 門 關 燈 , 別 費 電 . Turn off the light when you go out; don't waste electricity. Zhè-bú-shì(-bái)fèi-qián-ma? 這 不 是 (白) 費 錢 嗎 ? Isn't this a waste of money? (SV) wasteful. (opp.shěng 省). Nǐ-zhèiyàng-yòng-dōngxi tài-fèi. 你 這 樣 用 東 西 太 費 . The way you use things is wasteful.

FÈI₃ 費 (B) fee, expense. xuéfèi 學 費 tuition. yīyàofèi 醫 藥 費 medical expenses.

FÈI₄ 肺 (N) lung.

FÈIBÌNG₃ 肺 病 (N) tuberculosis of the lung, lung illness. (M: chǎng 場).

FĒI(DEI)...BU...₁ 非 (得)....不 ... (S) not... unless... Zhūròu-fēi(dei)-shúle-bu-néng-chī. 豬 肉 非 (得) 熟 了 不 能 吃 . Pork shouldn't be eaten unless cooked. Fēi(dei)-yòng-féizào xǐbugānjing. 非 (得) 用 肥 皂 洗 不 乾 淨 . Unless you use soap you can't wash it clean. (cf: CHÚFĒI 除 非).

FĒI(DEI)...BÙKÈ₁ 非 (得)....不 可 (S) unless... won't do, cannot do. Nǐ-fēi-'qù-bùkě. 你 非 去 不 可 . It won't do unless you go (stress on go). Fēi-'nǐ-qù bùkě. 非 你 去 不 可 . It won't do unless you go (stress on you). Fēi-zuò-shì bu-néng-chī-fàn. 非 作 事 不 能 吃 飯 . Unless one works one can't eat.

FĒI(DEI)...CÁI...₁ 非 (得)...才 ... (S) only... by... then, and only then. :., not... unless... Zhèi-bìng fēi(dei)-dòng-shǒushu cái-néng-hǎo. 這 病 非 得 動 手 術 才 能 好 . This illness can only be cured by operating. Wǒ-bànbuliǎo. Zhèi-shì-fēi(dei)-'tā-qù cái-xíng. 我 辦 不 了 . 這 事 非 得 他 去 才 行 . I can't do it. This matter can only be accomplished by his going. (cf: CHÚ-FĒI 除 非).

FĒICHANG₁ 非 常 (AD) extra-ordinarily, extremely. Nèige-

F

gùshi-fēichang-yǒu-yìsi. 那個 故事非常有意思. That story is extremely interesting.

FÈICHENG₂ 費城 (PW) Philadelphia.

FÈI-HUÀ₂ 費話 (VO) make a meaningless statement or question. Bié-fèi-huà. 別費話. Don't make meaningless statements. Fèi-shénma-huà-ne! 費甚麼話呢! Why even bother to say it! (N) useless talk. Bié-shuō-fèihuà. 別說費話. Don't make useless talk.

FĒIJĪ₁ 飛機 (N) aircraft, airplane. (M: jià 架).

FĒIJĪCHǍNG₂ 飛機場 (N) airfield, airport.

FÈI-JÌN₃ 費勁 (VO) (1) expend energy or effort. Wǒ-zài-zhèijian-shìshang, fèile-hěn-dàde-jìn. 我在這件事上,費了很大的勁. I spent a great deal of effort on this matter. (2) waste energy or effort. Béng-fèi-na-jìn méiyòng. 甭費那勁,沒用. Don't waste that kind of effort. It's useless.

FÈIKUÀI₄ 飛快 (SV) as fast as flying.

FÉILIÀO₄ 肥料 (N) fertilizer.

FĒILÜBĪN₂ 菲律賓 (PW) the Philippines.

FĒIPǍO₃ 飛跑 (IV) (lit. fly run) run as fast as flying, dash.

FÈI-SHÉN₃ 費神 (VO) (1) exert

mental effort with particular concentration. Kāi-chē-hěn-fèishén. 開車很費神. Driving (motor vehicles) requires a great deal of concentration. (2) a polite expression of appreciation for service requiring concentration of the mind, thank you, I appreciate it. Ràngnín-fèi-shén. 讓您費神 I appreciate your help. (cf: FÈI-XĪN 費心).

FÈI-SHÌ₁ 費事 (VO) (1) do something that requires considerable work effort, take trouble. Zuò-Zhōngguo-fàn bǐ-zuò-xīcān-fèi-shì. 作中國飯比作西餐費事. To prepare a Chinese meal is more work than to prepare a Western meal. (2) waste work effort. Zuòle-bàntiān yidiǎnr-dou-bu hǎochī, wǒ-bú-zài-fèi-na-shì-le. 作了半天一點兒都不好吃,我不再費那事了. I spent a lot of time to prepare it, and it doesn't taste good at all, I'm not going to waste that kind of effort again.

FÉITIÁNFĚN₅ 肥田粉 (N) fertilizer (chemical).

FÈIWU₃ 廢物 (N) (1) useless thing. (2) waste material. (3) useless person. Tā-shi-ge-fèi-wu. 他是個廢物. He is useless.

FEI-XĪN₃ 費心 (VO) exert mental effort with particular

thoughtfulness. Zhèixie-lǐwu dou-shi-ta-fèile-bushǎode-xīn-xuǎn-de. 這 些 禮 物 都 是 他 費 了 不 少 的 心 選 的. These gifts were all selected by him with great thoughtfulness. (2) used to express appreciation for some-one's anticipated or completed service requiring mental effort, I'll appreciate it, thank you. Nín-bāngbang-máng-ba. Fèi-xīn-fèi-xīn. 您 幫 幫 忙 吧. 費 心 費 心. Please help me. Thank you. (cf: FÈI-SHÉN 費 神).

FÈI-YĂN₄ 費 眼 (VO) strenuous on the eyes. Shūde-zì tai-xiǎo, guāng-bu-gòu, fèi-yǎn. 書 的 字 太 小, 光 不 够, 費 眼. The letters in the book are too small; the light is insufficient; it's strenuous on the eyes.

FÉIZÀO₃ 肥皂 (N) soap. (syn. yízi 胰 子). (M: kuài 塊).

FĒIZHǍNG₄ 飛 漲 (IV) sudden rise in prices. Jiàqian yìtian-yitiānde-fēizhǎng. 價 錢 一 天 一 天 的 飛 漲. The price goes up every day.

FĒIZHŌU₂ 非 洲 (PW) Africa.

FÈIZI₅ 痱 子 (N) prickly heat. zhǎng-fèizi 長 痱 子 have prickly heat.

FĒN₁ 分 (TV) (1) share, give something as someone's share or get as one's own share. Zhèi wǔkuai-qián nǐmen-liǎngge-rén-fēn. 這 五 塊 錢 你 們

兩 個 人 分. You two share these five dollars. Tā-bǎ-táng fēngei-wo-yíbàn. 他 把 糖 分 給 我 一 半. He gave me half of the candy as my share. Tā-fēn(dao)le-yìsuo-fángzi. 他 分 到 了 一 所 房 子. He got a house (as his share). (2) divide. Qǐng-nǐ-bǎ-zhèixie-fēncheng-wǔfènr. 請 你 把 這 些 分 成 五 分 兒. Please divide these into five shares. Wǒmen-fēn-biānr-dǎ-qiú-ba. 我 們 分 邊 兒 打 球 吧. Let's split up into two teams and play ball. (3) separate something. Qǐng-nǐ-ba-hóngde-gen-lǜde-fēn-yifen. 請 你 把 紅 的 跟 綠 的 分 一 分. Please separate the red ones from the green ones. Tāde-tóu-fa zài-yòubianr-fēn. 他 的 頭 髮 在 右 邊 兒 分. He parts his hair on the right side. (4) distinguish. Lánde-gen-lǜde ta-fēnbuqīng(chu). 藍 的 跟 綠 的 他 分 不 清 楚. He cannot distinguish clearly between blue and green. (5) it makes a difference how, what, whether, etc. Huà-fēn-zěnma-shuō. 話 分 怎 麼 說. It makes a difference how you say it. Wǔkuai-qián-yíge, bù-fēn-dàxiǎo. 五 塊 錢 一 個 不 分 大 小. Each one is five dollars, it doesn't make any difference whether it is large or small.

F

FĒN₁ 分 (M) (1) a tenth of certain larger units, such as a dime, a Chinese inch, acre, etc. yìmáo-wǔfēn-qián 一毛五分錢 (lit. a dime and five cents) fifteen cents. Shífēn-děngyu-yícùn. 十分等於一寸. Ten fēn are equal to one Chinese inch. (2) sixtieth of an hour, a degree. sānfēn-zhōng 三分鐘 three minutes. sāndiǎn-wǔshifēn 三點五十分 3:50. (3) 1% interest. niánlì-sìfēn 年利四分 four per cent annual interest. (See: FĒNR 分兒).

FĒN₅ 分 (B-) branch of an organization. Wǒmen-fēnxiào zài-nèr. 我們分校在那兒. Our branch school is there.

FÉN₃ 墳 (N) grave, tomb, sepulcher. (M: zuò 座). shàngfén 上墳 go to visit a tomb. Zhèi-shi-wǒ-fùqinde-fén. 這是我父親的墳. This is my father's grave.

FĒN₂ 粉 (N) face powder. Tā-liǎn-shang méi-cá-fěn. 他臉上沒擦粉. She didn't put on any powder.
(B) (1) something in powder form. yàofěn 藥粉 powdered medicine. (2) something made from flour of rice, beans, or other materials. mǐfěn 米粉 rice flour or noodles made of rice. fěnsī 粉絲 or fěntiáor 粉條兒 noodles made of beans.

FĚN₂ 粉 (B) pink. fěn-yánse 粉顏色 or fěnhóng 粉紅

pink color. Tāde-yīshang-shi-fěnde. 他的衣裳是粉的. Her dress is pink.

FÈN₄ 糞 (N) excrement, stools, dung, feces. (M: duī 堆). niú-fèn 牛糞 cow manure.

FĚNBǏ₁ 粉筆 (N) chalk (for writing). (M: zhī 枝).

FĒNBIE₁ 分別 (N) difference. Yǒu-shénma-fēnbie-ne? 有甚麼分別哪? What is the difference?
(TV) distinguish, make out the difference. Něige-shì-gēge, něige-shì-dìdi, wǒ-fēnbiebuchu-lái. 那個是哥哥, 那個是弟弟, 我分別不出來. I can't make out which one is the older brother and which one is the younger brother.
(AD) separately. Zhèi-liǎngjian-shì děi fēnbie-bànlǐ. 這兩件事得分別辦理. We have to handle these two things separately.

FĒNBIÉ₄ 分別 (TV) leave someone, say farewell. Tāmen-liǎng-ge-rén yào-fēnbié-le. 他們兩個人要分別了. They two are going to say goodbye (to each other). (cf: FĒN-SHǑU 分手).

FĒNCUN₄ 分寸 (N) judgment of relative value, weight or importance, etc., against a situation for proper behavior. Shuǒ-huà, zuò-shì, dōu-dei-yǒu-fēn-cun. 說話, 作事, 都得有分寸. In talking and doing things, you must have proper judgment.

'FÈNDÒU₂ 奮鬭 (TV) struggle. Wǒmen-yào-fèndòu-dàodǐ. 我 們要奮鬭到底. We must struggle to the end.

FĒNFU₃ 吩咐 (TV) leave or give instructions to someone (usually verbal). Yǒu-shénma-shì nín-jiu-fēnfu-ba. 有甚 麼事您就吩咐吧. If there is anything I can do, just tell me. (N) instruction. Nín-you-shén-ma-fēnfu? 您有甚麼吩 咐? Do you have any instructions?

FĒNG₁ 風 (N) wind, breeze. (M: zhèng 陣). Xiànzài-qǐ-fēng-le. 現在起風了. The wind has begun to blow. Guāle-yizhèn-dà-fēng. 颳了一 陣大風. The strong wind blew for awhile. Fēng-zhù-le. 風住了. The wind stopped.

FĒNG₂ 瘋 (SV) (1) insane, mad, crazy. Tā-'fēngle-shìde-gēn-wo-dǎ. 他瘋了似的跟 我打. He fought with me just as if he were insane. (2) unbefitting behavior, crazy, wild. Yǒuxie-nǚháizi fēngde-lìhai. 有些女孩子瘋的 利害. Some of the young girls are very wild. (AD) wildly. fēng-pǎo 瘋跑 run wildly.

FĒNG₄ 封 (TV) (1) seal. Bǎ-xìn-fēngshang. 把信封上.

Seal the letter. Tāde-shāng yǐ-jing-fēng-kǒur-le. 他的傷 已經封口兒了. His wound has already closed. (2) bestow honors, titles, etc. Shéi-fēngde-ta? 誰封的他? Who gave him the title? (sarcastically). (M) for something with an envelope. yìfeng-xìn 一封信 a letter. yifēng-diànbào 一封 電報 a telegram.

FĒNG₄or FÉNG 逢 (TV) meet, encounter. Tā-fēng-ren jiu-shuō. 他逢人就說. He talks about it when he sees someone. (See: MÉIFÉNG 每 逢).

FÉNG₄ 逢 see FÉNG 逢.

FÉNG₃ 縫 (TV) sew. Nǐ-gěi-wǒ-féngshang. 你給我縫 上. You sew it for me. Dàifu-gěi-wǒ-féngle-jizhen. 大夫 給我縫了幾針. The doctor sewed a couple of stitches on me.

FĒNGBŌ₃ 風波 or FĒNGPŌ 風波.

FĒNGCHÁO₃ 風潮 (N) (lit. wind tide) unrest, agitation caused by dissatisfaction against a government or authority. Yīnwei-dǎ-zhàng hěn-duō-dàxuéli nào-fēng-cháo. 因為打扙很多 大學裏鬧風潮. Because of war, many universities are troubled with unrest.

FĒNGCHĒ₅ 風車 (N) (1) wind-mill. (2) winnowing machine.

FÈNGCHÉNG₅ 奉承 (TV) flatter,

F

F

pay court to, compliment.
praise. Nǐ-děi-fèngcheng-ta-
jijiu. 你 得 奉 承 他 幾
句. You must give him a
couple of words of praise. (See:
GŌNGWÉI 恭 維).

'FÈNGCÌ₃ 諷 刺 (TV) ridicule.
Bié-'fèngcì-ta-le. 別 諷 刺
他 了. Don't ridicule him.
(N) ridicule. Wǒ-shòubuliao-
zhèzhongde-'fèngcì. 我 受 不
了 這 種 的 諷 刺. I
can't stand this kind of ridicule.

FĒNGFU₂ 豐 富 (SV) plenty,
rich in content, broad. Nínde-
cài tài-fēngfu-le. 您 的 菜
太 豐 富 了. You've pre-
pared too many dishes. Tāde-
zhīshi hen-fēngfu. 他 的 知
識 很 豐 富. He has a
broad knowledge.
(TV) broaden experience. Wǒ-
men-bìxū-fēngfu-wǒmende-jīng-
yan. 我 們 必 須 豐 富
我 們 的 經 驗. We must
broaden our experience.

'FĒNGJIÀN₁ 封 建 (SV) feu-
dalistic. fēngjianzhǔyì 封 建
主 義 feudalism. Tāde-sī-
xiang tài-'fēngjiàn. 他 的 思
想 太 封 建. His thinking
is too feudalistic.

'FĒNGJǏNG₁ 風 景 scenery.
Táiwānde-'fēngjǐng hěn-hǎo. 台
灣 的 風 景 很 好.
Taiwan has some very good
scenery. (cf: JǏNGZHÌ 景 緻).

'FĒNGLIÚ₃ 風 流 (SV) deport-
ment characterized by gaiety,
romanticism, attractiveness to
the opposite sex, etc., romantic,
sentimental, dreamy. Zhèige-
rén-hěn-fēngliu, cháng-gěi-nǚ-
péngyou-zuò-shī. 這 個 人
很 風 流,常 給 女 朋
友 作 詩. This fellow is
really romantic. He often writes
poems for his girl friend.

FĒNGPŌ₃風 波 or FĒNGBŌ風 波.
(N) (lit. wind ripples) troubles
(generally of a social nature).
(M: chǎng 場). Tāmen-lǐle-
hūn-le. Zhèi-chǎng-fēngpō ké-
yi-shuō yǐjing-guòqu-le. 他 們
離 了 婚 了,這 場 風
波 可 以 説 己 經 過
去 了. They are divorced.
One could say that the trouble is
already over.

FĒNGQI₃風 氣 (N) (lit. wind
air) (1) atmosphere of an organization. Zhèige-xuéxiàode-fēng-
qi-bu-hǎo, tài-zhùzhòng-tǐyu.
這 個 學 校 的 風 氣
不 好,太 注 重 體 育.
This school has a bad atmosphere;
it overemphasizes sports. (2)
taste of the times, fashion.
Chuān-duǎn-dàyī shì-xìanzàide-
fēngqi.穿 短 大 衣 是 現
在 的 風 氣. To wear a
short overcoat is the present
fashion.

FĒNGQÍN₃風 琴 (N) organ (musical instrument). (M: jià 架).
èn-fēngqín or tán-fēngqín 按
風 琴 or 彈 風 琴 play an
organ.

FĒNGR₃縫 兒 (N) (1) seam. (M:
dào 道 , tiáo 條). féng-yidao-

fèngr 縫 一 道 縫兒 sew
a seam. (2) parting line of the
hair. Tā-tóufashang fēn-yidao-
fèngr. 他 頭 髮 上 分 一
道 縫兒. His hair has a part.
(3)crack. Qiáng-lièle-yídao-fèngr.
牆 裂 了 一 道 縫兒.
There is a crack in the wall.(4)
a narrow opening, a crevice.
mén-fèngr 門 縫兒 narrow
opening of the door. (5) fig.
fault. Tāde-huà yìdiǎn-fèngr-
dou-méi-yǒu. 他 的 話 一
點 縫兒 都 沒 有. His
statements are unassailable.
(6) fig. opportunity. Tā-jiàn-
fèngr-jiu-zuān. 他 見 縫兒 就
鑽. Whenever he sees an
opportunity he bores in.
FÉNGRÈNJĪ₄ 縫 紉 機 (N)
sewing machine. (M: jià 架).
FĒNGSĀO₄ 風 騷 (SV) bewitching (of a woman). Tā-xiézhe-
yǎn-xiàozhe-kàn-wo xiǎnchu-
hěn-fēngsāode-yàngzi. 他 斜
着 眼 笑 着 看 我, 顯
出 很 風 騷 的 樣 子.
She looked at me from the corner of her eyes with a smiling
face, exposing a very bewitching
manner.
FĒNGSHŌU₅ 豐 收 (TV) rich
harvest. Jīnnian fēngshōu. 今
年 豐 收. This year we
had a rich harvest.
FĒNGSHÙ₃ 楓 樹 (N) maple tree.
(M: kē 棵).
FĒNGSU₁ 風 俗 (N) custom.
fēngsu-xíguàn 風 俗 習 慣

customs and habits. Yíge-dìfang
yǒu-yíge-dìfangde-fēngsu. 一
個 地 方 有 一 個 地
方 的 風 俗. Each place
has its local customs.
FĒNGTÀOR₅ 封 套 兒 (N) en-
velope.
FĒNGXIANG₅ 風 箱 (N) wind
box, bellows.
FĒNGYǓBIĂO₄ 風 雨 表 (N)
barometer.
FĒNGZHENG₃ 風 箏 (N) kite.
fàng-fēngzheng 放 風 箏 fly
a kite.
FĒNGZI₂ 瘋 子 (N) crazy person, maniac, madman.
FĒNHÁNG₄ 分 行 (N) branch
office (of a bank), branch (of a
business establishment).
FĒNHÀO₄ 分 號 (N) branch
store.
FĒN-HÓNG₄ 分 紅 (VO) declare,
pay or receive dividends or bonus. Zhèige-gōngsī wǔnián-méi-
fēn-hóng-le. 這 個 公 司
五 年 沒 分 紅 了. This
company hasn't declared a divi-
dend in five years. Niándǐ wǒ-
kéyi-fēn-dianr-hóng. 年 底 我
可 以 分 點兒 紅. I
will get a little bonus at the end
of the year.
FĒNHÓNG₃ 粉 紅 (N) pink.
FĒN-JIĀ₃ 分 家 (VO) separate,
divide family property (as between husband and wife or among
brothers and sisters).
FĒNLÁN₃ 芬 蘭 (PW) Finland.
FĒN-LÈI₂ 分 類 (VO) divide by

F

category <u>or</u> type. Zhèizhǒng-
zhǐ fēn-sānlèi. 這 種 紙 分
三 類 . This kind of paper
is divided into three types.
(N) classification. Zhèige-tú-
shuguánli shūde-fēnlèi bú-tài-
qīngchu. 這 個 圖 書 館
裏 書 的 分 類 不 太
清 楚 . In this library, the
classification of books is not
very clear.

FĒNLIANG₂ 分 量 (N) weight.
Fēnliang-shi-duōshao? 分 量
是 多 少 ? What is the
weight? Chēngcheng-fēnliang.
稱 稱 分 量 . Weigh it.
fig. Tā-shuō-de-huà yǒu-fēn-
liang. 他 說 的 話 有 分
量 . What he says carries
weight.

FĒNPÈI₄ 分 配 (TV) distribute,
allocate, assign. fēnpei-liáng-
shi 分 配 糧 食 distribute
the provisions. fēnpei-gōngzuo
分 配 工 作 assign work.
(N) distribution, allocation,
assignment. gōngzuòde-fēnpèi
工 作 的 分 配 the dis-
tribution of work.

FĒNR₂ 分 兒 (M) <u>for point in</u>
<u>the scoring of a game or test.</u>
Zhèiduì déle-duōshao-fēnr? 這
隊 得 了 多 少 分 兒?
How many points did this team
get? Tā-kǎoshì-méi-kǎoguo-
yibǎifēnr. 他 考 試 沒 考
過 一 百 分 兒 . He has
never received 100 on a test.
(N) <u>or</u> FĒNSHUR 分 數 兒 point
(in the scoring of a game or

test). Xiānsheng-gěi-ta-de-fēnr
bu-gōngping. 先 生 給 他
的 分 兒 不 公 平.
The score which the teacher
gave him is unfair.

FĒNR₂ 份 兒 (M) (1) share, portion. fēn-sānfēnr 分 三 份 兒
divide into three shares. (2) <u>for</u>
<u>a newspaper or magazine.</u> dìng-
yifēnr-zázhì 訂 一 份 兒 雜
誌 subscribe to a magazine.
(3) <u>for a gift.</u> sòng-yifēnr-lǐ 送
一 份 兒 禮 give a gift.
(N) a share, a portion, a part.
Tāmen-fēn-qián, méi-wǒde-fēnr.
他 們 分 錢 沒 我 的
份 兒. They're dividing the
money, no share for me.

FĒNSHÀN₄ 風 扇 (N) fan (<u>me-</u>
<u>chanical</u>).

FĒNSHĪBING₅ 風 濕 病 (N)
rheumatism.

FĒN-SHǑU₃ 分 手 (VO) leave
<u>someone,</u> say farewell. Wǒmen-
jiù-yào-fēn-shǒu-le. 我 們
就 要 分 手 了 . We are
just about to say farewell. (cf:
FĒNBIÉ 分 別).

FĒNSHUDĀNR₃ 分 數 單 兒
(N) report card, transcript (<u>of</u>
<u>grades</u>). (M: zhāng 張).

FĒNSHUR₂ 分 數 兒 <u>see</u> FĒNR
分 兒 (N).

FĒNSĪ₅ 粉 絲 <u>see</u> FĒNTIÁOR
粉 條 兒 .

'FĒNSUÌ₃ 粉 碎 (SV) (<u>lit.</u> pul-
verize) break into small pieces.
Tā-bǎ-nèige-píngzi dǎde-'fēnsuì.
他 把 那 個 瓶 子 打

得 粉 碎 · He smashed that vase into pieces.

FĒNTIÁOR₅ 粉 條 兒 or FĔN-SĪ 粉 綠 (N) noodles (made of bean flour).

FĒNTÓU₄ 分 頭 (AD) each person taking part of the same job in different places. Nǐ-qu-jiàn-lüshǐ, wǒ-qu-zhǎo-jǐngchá. Wǒ-men-fēntóu-qu-bàn. 你 去 見 律 師, 我 去 找 警 察 · 我 們 分 頭 去 辦 · You go to see the lawyer, I will go to find the policeman. We'll each handle a different aspect to take care of this matter.

FĒNXI₂ 分 析 (TV) analyze. Nǐ-bǎ-zhèige-wèntí fēnxi-fenxi. 你 把 這 個 問 題 分 析 分 析 · (You) analyze this problem. (N) analysis.

FĒNZHI₁ 分 之 (-B-) used in between two numbers in giving fractions. A fēnzhi B. A 分 之 B. B parts of A. sìfēnzhiyī 四 分 之 一 one-fourth.

FĒNZǏ₄ 分 子 (N) molecule. Yǎngqìde-yíge-fēnzǐ yǒu-liǎng-ge-yuánzǐ. 氧 氣 的 一 個 分 子 有 兩 個 原 子 · A molecule of oxygen has two atoms.

FÈNZI₅ 份 子 (N) monetary gifts for wedding, birthday, birth of a child or death. chū-fenzi 出 份 子 put out money as a gift. sòng-fènzi 送 份 子 present money as a gift. suí-fenzi 隨 份 子 follow others

in making monetary gifts.

FÈNZǏ₄ 份 子 (N) part of, an element of a society. zhīshi-fèn-zǐ 知 識 份 子 the learned. dǎoluàn-fènzǐ 搗 亂 份 子 the ones who make trouble.

FÓ₃ 佛 (N) Buddha, a buddha. Tā-chéng-fó-le. 他 成 佛 了 · He became a buddha. Yǒu-hěn-duō-rén xìn-fó. 有 很 多 人 信 佛 · There are many people who believe in Buddha.

FÓJIÀO₃ 佛 教 (N) Buddhism.

'FÓUDÌNG₄ 否 定 (TV) negate, deny.

'FÓUJUÉ₄ 否 決 (TV) (1) decide against, vote against. Kāi-huì-de-shihou, bǎ-tāde-tíyì-fǒujué-le. 開 會 的 時 候, 把 他 的 提 議 否 決 了 · At the meeting his motion was voted down. (2) veto. Nèitiao-fǎlü, guóhuì-tōngguò-le. Kěshi-zǒngtǒng-gei-fóujué-le. 那 條 法 律 國 會 通 國 了 · 可 是 總 統 給 否 決 了 · Congress passed it, but the act was vetoed by the President.

FÓUJUÉQUÁN₅ 否 決 權 (N) veto power.

'FǑURÈN₃ 否 認 (TV) deny. Nǐ-búbi-fóurèn-nǐ-zuòcuò-le. 你 不 必 否 認 你 作 錯 了 · You don't have to deny that you were wrong.

'FÓUZÉ₃ 否 則 (MA) otherwise. (syn. yàoburán 要 不 然). Nǐ-děi-qù, fóuzé-wo-bu-qù. 你 得 去, 否 則 我 不 去 ·

F

You must go, otherwise I won't go.

FÓXIÀNG₅ 佛像 (N) statue or portrait of a buddha.

FŪ₄ 孵 (TV) hatch. fū-jīdàn 孵難蛋 hatch chicken eggs fū-xiǎojīr 孵小難兒 hatch little chicks.

FÚ₄ 浮 (IV) float, surface from underwater. zài-shuǐshang fú-zhe 在水上浮着 floating in water. Yìhuǐr jiu-fú-shanglai-le. 一會兒就浮上來了. In a moment it will come up to the surface. (SV) unstable, unsettled (characterized by desire for change or fun). Tā-xìngqing-tài-fú. 他性情太浮. He has an unstable nature.

FÚ₃ 扶 (TV) (1) put the hand against something for support. Nǐ-fúzhe-qiáng-zǒu. 你扶着牆走. Put your hand against the wall to help in your walking. (2) support something or someone by holding. Fúzhe-wo-dianr, wǒ-hūran-tóuyùn. 扶着我點兒,我忽然頭暈. Hold me, I suddenly feel dizzy. Fúzhe-zhèige-gùnzi,bié-ràng-ta-dǎo-le. 扶着這個棍子,別讓他倒了. Hold this stick, don't let it fall.

FÚ₃ 服 (TV) submit to or admit superior forces,intellect, judgment, ability, etc. Wǒ-fúle-ni-le. 我服了你了. I have to hand it to you. Nǐ-fú-bu-fú? Bù-fú-wǒ-dá-ni. 你服不

服? 不服我打你. Do you submit? If not I'll beat you up.

(RE) make someone submit to or admit the superiorty of someone. Tā-bǎ-wǒ-shuōfú-le. 他把我說服了. He talked me into agreeing with him.

FÚ₃ 服 (B) clothes.lǐfú禮服 formal clothes. xīfú 西服 Western clothes.

FÚ₃ 幅 (M) for paintings. yìfú-huàr一幅畫兒 one painting.

FÙ₂ 付 (TV) pay. Shéi-fù-qián? 誰付錢? Who is going to pay? Wǒ-xiànzài-fùbuchulái, fēnqī-fù,kéyi-ma? 我現在付不出來,分期付,可以嗎? I can't pay now, can I pay it in installments?

FÙ₃ 副 (M) a set, a pair. yìfù-kuàizi 一副筷子 a pair of chopsticks. yìfù-pái 一副牌 a set of cards. Zhèifu-shǒu-shi yígòng-sānjian. 這一副首飾一共三件. This set of jewelry consists of three items.

FÙ₃ 副 (B-) vice (second rank subordinate to the top rank). fùxiàozhǎng 副校長 vice principal (of a school). Tā-shì-fùde. 他是副的. He is of the "vice" rank (vice president, vice chairman, etc.).

FŬBÀI₃ 腐敗 (SV) corrupt, decadent. Qīngchao-'mònian-de-shíhou, Zhōngguo-zhèngfǔ-hěn-fǔbài. 清朝末年的時候中國政府很腐

敗. In the later part of Ch'ing dynasty the Chinese government was very corrupt.

FÚCÓNG₃ 服從 (TV) obey. fúcóng-mìngling 服從命令 obey an order.

FÙDÀI₂ 附帶 (TV) bring, take, get _or_ send along something of lesser importance, be accompanied by something. Wǒ-gěi-ta-jìle-yiben-shū, bìngqiě-fùdai-yizhāng-xiàngpiānr. 我給他寄了一本書, 並且附帶一張像片兒. I mailed him a book, and along with it, a photograph.

(AD) doing something less important along with some main activity. Nín-qu-Rìběn-kāi-huì-de-shihou, fùdàizhe-tì-wo-dàidianr-dōngxi-qu, xíng-bu-xing? 您去日本開會的時候,附帶着替我帶點兒東西去,行不行? When you go to Japan for the meeting, could you take something along for me?

FÙDÀN₂ 負擔 (TV) shoulder responsibility. Zhèige-zéren wǒ-fùdan-buqǐlái. 這個責任我負擔不起來. I can't take this responsibility.

(N) responsibility, mostly financial. Tā-jiāli-rén-duō, fùdan-hen-zhòng. 他家裏人多, 負擔很多. His family is large, he has very heavy financial responsibilities.

'FŪFÙ₂ 夫婦 (N) husband and wife. (M: duì 對). Nèidui-fūfu-

lái-le. 那對夫婦來了. That couple came. (cf: FŪQĪ 夫妻).

FÚHÀOR₂ 符號兒 (N) symbol, emblem. Wénzì-shi-yǔyánde-fúhàor. 文字是語言的符號兒. Written words are symbols of language. Nèige-bīng méi-dai-fúhàor. 那個兵沒帶符號兒. That soldier didn't wear an emblem.

'FÚHÉ₄ 符合 (TV) agree with something, fit in, tally. Wǒ-shìyan-de-jiéguǒ gēn-ta-suànchulai-de-'fúhé. 我試驗的結果跟他算出來的符合. The result of my experiment agrees with the result of his computations.

FŬHUÀ₅ 腐化 (IV) changed into a corrupted state. Yíge-zǔzhi-hěn-róngyi-fǔhuà. 一個組織很容易腐化. An organization is very easily corrupted.

FÚJIÀN₂ 福建 (PW) Fukien province.

FÙJÌN₂ 附近 (PW) nearby, vicinity. Zhèr-fùjìn-méi-yǒu-xué xiào. 這兒附近沒有學校. There is no school in this vicinity.

FÙKĒ₃ 婦科 (N) gynecologist.

FÚLÌ₃ 福利 (N) welfare, benefit. Zhè-shì-tóngxué-dà'jiāde-fúlì. 這是同學大家的福利. This is for the benefit of the student body.

FÚLŬ₃ 俘虜 or FÚLUŎ 俘虜 (N) prisoners of war, captive

F

(person). 'dǎile-hěn-duō-fúlǔ 逮了很多俘虜 brought in many prisoners.

FÚLUǑ₃ 俘虜 see FÚLǓ 俘虜.

FÙMǓ₁ 父母 (N) (lit. father and mother) parents.

'FÙNǙ₃ 婦女 (N) woman. fùnǚ-huì 婦女會 women's club. 'Fùnǚ-bu-néng-cānjiā. 婦女不能參加. Women cannot join.

FÚQÌ₂ 福氣 (N) blessing. Wǔge-háizi-dou-dàxue-bì-yè-le, nín-zhēn-yǒu-fúqi. 五個孩子都大學畢業了,您真有福氣. You are really blessed; five children all graduated from college.

(SV) be blessed. Nǐ-kàn, rénjia-duó-fúqi! 你看人家多福氣! Look at how blessed they are!

FŪQĪ₃ 夫妻 (N) husband and wife. Tāmen-shi-fūqī. 他們是夫妻. They are husband and wife. (cf: FŪFÙ 夫婦).

FÚQIĀN₃ 浮淺 see FÚQIAN 膚淺.

FÚQIĀN₃ 膚淺 or FÚQIAN 浮淺 shallow, superficial in thinking. Tā-shuō-de-huà tài-fúqian. 他說的話太膚淺. What he said is too shallow.

FÙQIN₁ 父親 (N) father.

FŪREN₃ 夫人 (N) (1) wife (a polite form for the wife of another person). Nín-fúren hǎo? 您夫人好? How is your wife? Tāde-fūren láile-ma? 他的夫人來了嗎? Has his wife come? (2) Madam, Mrs. Zhāng-Fūren 張夫人 Madam Chang.

FÙREN₃ 婦人 (N) woman.

FÚRONG₄ 芙蓉 (N) hibiscus. (M: duǒ 朵, kē 棵).

FÚ-RUǍNR₅ 服軟兒 (VO) give up fighting a superior force and become submissive. Nǐ-zěnma-dǎ-ta, tā-dou-bu-fú-ruǎnr. 你怎麼打他,他都不服軟兒. No matter how you beat him he won't give up.

FǓSHANG₂ 府上 (N) home (a polite form referring to the home of another person). Nín-fǔshang (zài-shénma-dìfang)? 您府上(在甚麼地方)? Where is your home?

FÙSHǓ₄ 附屬 (IV) dependent upon, belong to some larger and more important organization. Zhèige-yǔyán-xuéxiào shì-fù-shǔzai-zhèige-dàxué-litou. 這個語言學校是附屬在這個大學裏頭. This language school is an extension of this university.

FÚ-SHUǏ₄ 浮水 (VO) swim. (syn. yóuyǒng 游泳).

FÙWŌNG₃ 富翁 (N) a wealthy man. bǎiwàn-fùwōng 百萬富翁 a millionaire.

FÚWÙ₂ 服務 (TV) render service, work (generally in a public institution). fùwù-shèhuì 服務社會 render service to society. Wǒ-zài-yīyuàn-fúwù. 我在醫院服務.

我 在 醫 院 服 務 · I
work in the hospital.

FÚWUYUÁN₅ 服 務 員 (N)
worker (generally in a public
institution).

FÚXIĚZHǏ₃ 複 寫 紙 (N) car-
bon paper. (M: zhāng 張).

FÚYAN₃ 敷 衍 (TV) (1) deceive
by covering up some deficiency.
Yàoshi-méi-zuòwán jiu-gēn-wo-
shuō, búyong-fūyan-wo. 要 是
沒 作 完 就 跟 我 説,
不 用 敷 衍 我 · If it
isn't finished, then tell me so,
don't pull the wool over my eyes.
(2) do a job or deal with a problem superficially and then cover up the deficiency. Zuòcuòle,
jiu-děi-cóng-zuò, bù-néng-fū-
yan. 作 錯 了 就 得 從
作. 不 能 敷 衍 · If an
error is made, it has to be done
over again. We can't do a superficial job and cover up. Bǎ-
nèijian-shìqing fūyan-guoqu-le.
把 那 件 事 情 敷 衍
過 去 了. That matter got by
by being covered up.

'FÙYÈ₃ 副 業 (N) A secondary
job or profession. Zhè-shi-wǒ-
de-'fùyè. 這 是 我 的 副
業. This is my second pro-
fession.

FÚYĪN₅ 輔 音 (N) consonant.

FÙYU₂ 富 裕 (SV) abundant,
have more than enough. Zài-
Zhongguo rúguǒ-yinián-yǒu-
liǎngqiankuai-Měijǐnde-shōurù
jiu-hěn-fùyu-le. 在 中 國 如
果 一 年 有 兩 千 塊

美 金 的 收 入 就 很
富 裕 了. In China, if
one has an income of two thousand American dollars a year it
will be much more than enough.

FÙYU₂ 富 餘 (TV) have some-
thing left over. Zhè-shi-wǒmen-
fùyuchulai-de. 這 是 我 們
富 餘 出 來 的. This is
what we have left over.
(N) extra, more than necessary.
Méi-you-fùyu. 沒 有 富 餘 .
There is no extra.

FÙYUÁN₃ 復 原 (SV) recuperate
(health, strength, vigor). Tā-
bìng-gāng-hǎo, hái-méi-fùyuán.
他 病 剛 好, 還 沒 復
原 . He just recovered from an
illness and has not yet recuper-
ated.

'FÙZÁ₂ 複 雜 (SV) complicated.
(opp.'jiǎndān 簡 單). Wǒ-
cónglái-méi-kànjianguo zènma-
fǔzáde-jīqi. 我 從 來 沒 看
見 過 這 麼 複 雜 的
機 器 . I have never seen such
complicated machinery.

FÙ-ZE(REN)₂ 負 責 (任) (VO)
shoulder the responsibility. Wǒ-
bú-yuànyi-fù zhèige-zé(ren). 我
不 願 意 負 這 個 責 任
I don't want to take this responsibility.

FÙ-ZHÀI₃ 負 債 (VO) be in debt,
owe money. Tā-fùle-hěn-duōde-
zhài. 他 負 了 很 多 的
債 . He is very deeply in debt.

FÚZHÓU₂ 福 州 (PW) Foochow
(capital of Fukien province).

F

'FÚZHÙ₅ 扶助 (TV) help, assist, aid.

(N) assistance.

FǓZI₄ 斧子 (N) ax, hatchet. (M: bǎ 把).

G

GĀI₂ 該 (TV) owe. (syn. qiàn 欠).
Tā-gāi-wǒ-qián bu-huán. 他該
我錢不還. He owes me
money but does not pay me.

GĀI₁ 該 (AV) (1) (con. yīnggāi
應該) should, ought. Nǐ-bu-
gāi-nèiyàng-bàn. 你不該
那樣辦.You should not take
that course of action. (2) it's
time to do something or something will happen. Gāi-chī-fàn-le.
該吃飯了. Time to eat.
Xiàyue yòu-gāi-rè-le. 下月
又該熱了. Next month
it will be hot again. (3) it's
someone's turn. Gāi-nǐ-le. 該
你了. Your turn. Xiànzài
gāiˌnǐ-shuō-le. 現在該你
説了. Now it is your turn
to speak. (4) deserved punishment. Gāi! Hái-dei-dǎ. 該！
還得打. He deserves it,
he has got to be beaten some
more. Huó-gāi. 活該. Serves
you right.

GĀI₁ 改 (TV) change, alter, correct. Wǒ-gǎi-zhúyi-le. 我改
主意了. I changed my
mind. Zhèi-yīshang děi-gǎi. 這
衣裳得改. This clothing
has to be altered. Qǐng-nín-gěi-
wǒ gǎi-yigai, hǎo-ma? 請您
給我改一改,好嗎? Will
you please correct me? Zhèige-

máobing ta-lǎo-gǎibuguolái. 這
個毛病他老改不
過來. He is not able to correct this defect. Xiānsheng-gěi-
wo-gǎi-wénzhang. 先生給
我改文章. The teacher
corrects my essay.

GÀI₂ 蓋 (TV) (1) build, construct.
Wǒmen-gàile-yisuǒ-fángzi. 我
們蓋了一所房子.
We built a house. (2) imprint.
gài-túzhang 蓋圖章 imprint
a seal. (3) place a lid on. Bǎ-
'guō-gàishang. 把鍋蓋上.
Cover the pot.

'GǍIBIÀN₂ 改變 (TV) change,
vary. gǎibiàn-jìhua 改變計
劃 change plans.
(N) a change. 'Méi-shénma-
'gǎibiàn. 沒甚麼改變.
There is no change.

GǍIGÉ₃ 改革 (TV) reform.
(N) reformation, reform. wén-
zì-gǎigé 文字改革 (written)
language reform.

GǍIJÌN₄ 改進 (TV) improve
and go forward.

GǍILIÁNG₁ 改良 (TV) (lit.
change to the better) improve.

GÀIR₃ 蓋兒 or GÀIZI 蓋子
(N) cover, lid. cháhú-gàir 茶
壺蓋兒 cover of a teapot.

GǍISHÀN₅ 改善 (TV) change for
the better, improve.

G

GĂITIAN₁ 改天 (TW) some other day. Wŏ-'găitian-zai-'lái. 我 改 天 再 來 . I will come some other day. Găitian-jiàn. 改天見 . See you some other day.

GÀIYÀO₃ 概要 (N) general important points, outline.

GĂIZÀO₂ 改造 (TV) (1) reform (of a person). Sīxiang shi-kéyi-găizào-de. 思想是可以改造的. It is possible for thinking to be reformed. (2) rebuild (of a machine). găizào-jīqi 改造機器 rebuild a machine. (N) reform.

GĂIZHÈNG₅ 改正 (TV) correct.

GÀIZI₄ 蓋子 see GÀIR 蓋兒 .

GĀLÁR₄ 旮旯 (N) Peip. a comparatively inaccessible place, a corner.

GĀN₁ 乾 (SV) dry(desiccated). (opp. shī 濕). (B-) used before a kinship term indicates an adoptive relationship without legal action. gānmā 乾媽 adoptive mother (no legal action involved).

GĂN₄ 桿 (M) for a long and thin cylindrical object. yìgăn-qiāng 一桿鎗 a gun or a spear.

GĂN₂ 趕 (TV) (1) chase, run after. Tā-zài-qiántou-păo, wŏ-zài-hòutou-găn. 他在前頭跑, 我在後頭趕 . He runs ahead and I chase after him. lit. or fig. Wŏ-gănbushàng-ta. 我趕不上他 . I can't keep pace with him. (2) work fast on something to finish it in a certain time, rush a job. Wŏmen-'jīntian-dei-bă-zhèijian-shìqing gănwánle. 我們今天得把這件事情趕完了 . We must rush to finish this job today. (3) drive (animals with a whip). găn-niú 趕牛 drive cattle. găn-chē 趕車 drive a cart (which is pulled by some kind of animal).

GĂN₁ 敢 (AV) dare. Nĭ-bu-găn. 你不敢.You don't dare. Nĭ-găn-jìnqu-ma? 你敢進去嗎 ? Do you dare go in? Wŏ-găn-shuō, ta-bu-lái.我敢說他不來 . I dare say that he won't come.

GÀN₁ 幹 (TV) (1) accept certain conditions or terms. (2) undertake a job. Tā-gànbuxiqù-le. 他幹不下去了 . He can't go on working. Péi-qián, wŏ-bu-gàn. 賠錢我不幹. If I'll lose money, I won't accept. or If I'll lose money, I won't do it.

GĀN-BĒI₂ 乾杯 (VO) (lit. make the cup dry) bottoms up.

'GÀNBÙ₄ 幹部 (N) the core of a political unit, cadres.

GĀNCUÌ₃ 乾脆 (MA) simply, straightforward, clear-cut. Gāncuì-suànle. 乾脆算了 . Let us simply drop the matter.

GĂNDONG₃ 感動 (TV) move someone emotionally. shòu-găndòng 受感動 be moved emotionally. Zhèige-gùshi zhēn-găndong-rén. 這個故事真

感動人. This story is very moving.

GĀN'ĒNJIÉ$_3$ 感恩節 (N) Thanksgiving.

GĀNÉRZI$_4$ 乾兒子 (N) adoptive son (no legality involved).

GĀNFÀN$_4$ 乾飯 (N) cooked rice (in its common form, not gruel).

GĀNG$_2$ 鋼 (N) steel.

GĀNG$_4$ 缸 (N) large, wide-mouthed jar. (M: kǒu 口).

GĀNG$_1$ 剛 or GĀNGGĀNG 剛剛 (AD) (1) just (immediately preceding in time). Tā-'gāng(gāng) zǒu nǐ-jiu-lái-le. 他剛(剛)走, 你就來了. He left just as you came. (cf: CÁI 才). (2) a moment ago. Tā-gāng(gāng)-'zài-zhèr-laizhe. 他剛(剛)在這兒來着. He was here a moment ago. (cf: GĀNGCÁI 剛才). (3) just (precise in quantity or quality). 'gāng(gāng)-héshì 剛(剛)合適 fit just right.

GÀNG$_5$ 虹 (N) rainbow. Chū-gàng-le. 出虹了. A rainbow has appeared.

GĀNGBǏ$_1$ 鋼筆 (N) pen. (M: guǎn 管, zhī 枝).

GĀNGCÁI$_1$ 剛才 (MA) a moment ago. Gāngcái-wǒ-kànjian-ta-le. 剛才我看見他了. I saw him a moment ago. (cf: GĀNG 剛).

GĀNGGĀNG$_1$ 剛剛 (MA) see GĀNG 剛.

GĀNGQÍN$_2$ 鋼琴 (N) piano. tán-gāngqín 彈鋼琴 play the piano.

GĀNGTIĚ$_3$ 鋼鐵 (N) (lit. steel and iron) ferrous metals.

GǍNGWÈI$_4$ 崗位 (N) (1) guard post. (2) fig. proper position for carrying out one's duties. Gèren-zhànhǎo-zìjǐde-gǎngwèi. 各人站好自己的崗位. Everybody should be at his own post. or Everybody should do his own job.

GĀNGYÀO$_3$ 綱要 (N) outline (of a subject).

GǍNJI$_2$ 感激 (TV) grateful. Wǒ-hěn-gǎnji. 我很感激. I am very grateful.

GǍNJǏN$_2$ 趕緊 (AD) hurriedly, fast.

GĀNJING$_1$ 乾淨 (SV) clean. (opp. zāng 髒, āngzang 骯髒, āza 骯髒).

GǍNJUE$_1$ 感覺 (TV) feel (one's physical condition or ideas). Nǐ-gǎnjue-zěnmayàng? 你感覺怎麼樣? How do you feel? Wǒ-yǒu-yizhong-gǎnjue. 我有一種感覺. I have a kind of feeling. (cf: MŌ 摸).

GǍNKUÀI$_2$ 趕快 (AD) hurry. Nǐ-gǎnkuai-zuò. 你趕快作. Hurry up and do it.

GĀNMĀ$_4$ 乾媽 (N) adoptive mother (no legal action involved).

GÀN-MÁ$_2$ 幹麼 (VO) do what. Tā-zài-jiā-gàn-má-ne? 他在家幹麼呢? What is he doing at home?
(SV) used to describe something without finding the right word, something or other. Nà-zhēn-gàn-má. 那真幹麼 That's

really something or other.
(AD) why. Wǒ-gànmá-qù? 我 幹
麼去 ? Why. should I go?
GĀNMAO₂ 感冒 (N) common
cold.
(TV) catch cold. Wǒ-gǎnmao-le.
我 感 冒 了. I caught a cold.
GĂNQING₂ 感 情 (N) (1) emo-
tion, sentiment, emotional at-
tachment, emotional involvement. (syn. 'qínggǎn 情 感).
Bié-dòng- gǎnqing. 別 動 感
情. Don't get emotionally involved. Tāmen-fāshēng- gǎn-
qing-le. 他 們 發 生 感
情 了 . They became emo-
tionally attached (to each other).
Nà-shi- gǎnqing-zuòyong. 那 是
感 情 作 用 . That is an
emotional effect. (2) friendly
relationship. Tāmende-gǎnqing
hěn-hǎo. 他 們 的 感 情
很 好. Their relationship is
very good.
GĂNQING₃ 敢 情 (AD) (1) it turns
out that... after all. Tā-
gǎnqing-shi-Měiguo-rén. 他 敢
情 是 美 國 人 . So he
is an American! Gǎnqing-shi-
'zènma-hui-shì. 敢 情 是
這 麼 回 事 . So that's
what it is! (2) of course (indi-
cative of relief). 'Nǎ-gǎnqing-hǎo.
那 敢 情 好 . That would
be fine, of course.
GĀNSHE₄ 干 涉 (TV) interfere.
Nǐ-bu-yào-gǎnshe-wo. 你 不
要 干 涉 我 . Don't inter-
fere with me.
(N) mutual concern. Wǒ-gēn-ni

méi-you-gǎnshe. 我 跟 你
沒 有 干 涉 . I have no
concern with you.
GĀNSU₂ 甘 肅 (PW) Kansu province.
'GĀNTÀN₅ 感 嘆 (TV) lament.
'GĂNXIĂNG₂ 感 想 (N) thoughts
or feelings caused by impres-
sions of an event. Wǒ-tīngle-
zhèige-gùshi-yihòu, 'gǎnxiǎng-
hen-duō. 我 聽 了 這 個
故 事 以 後, 感 想 很
多 . After I heard this story,
it made me think a lot.
'GĂNXIÈ₂ 感 謝 (TV) thank.
Wǒmen-fēichang-'gǎnxiè-nín.
我 們 非 常 感 謝 您.
We thank you very much.
GĀNXIN₃ 甘 心 (SV) accept
certain conditions without bitterness. Zhèiyang-bàn kǒngpà-
ta-bu-gānxin. 這 樣 辦 恐
怕 他 不 甘 心 . If it's
done this way, I'm afraid he
won't accept.
(AD) willing without hard feelings.
Wǒ-gānxīn-gěi-ta. 我 甘 心
給 他 I am willing to give him.
GĀNZÀO₃ 乾 燥 (SV) (1) dry
(not wet). (opp. cháoshi 潮 濕).
(2) boring, dull.
GĀNZHE₅ 甘 蔗 (N) sugar cane.
GĀO₃ 糕 (N) raised, generally
sweet pastry, cake.(M: kuài 塊).
GĀO₁ 高 (SV) tall, high. (opp.
ǎi 矮 , dī 低). Tā-bi-wǒ-gāo.
他 比 我 高 . He is taller
than I. Huàr-guàde-tài-gāo.
畫 兒 掛 得 太 高. The
painting is hung too high. Tā-

de-dìwei-gāo. 他的地位高 . His position is high. Zhèr-wēndù-gāo. 這兒溫度高. The temperature here is high. Nǐ-shuō-de-duì, gāo. 你説的對, 高 . You are right, it's great. Tā-cái-'wǔchǐ-gāo. 他才五尺高. He is only five feet tall. (N) height. Cháng shi-'èrcùn, gāo shi-yícùn. 長是二寸, 高是一寸 . The length is two inches, the height is one inch.

GĂO₁ 搞 (TV) do <u>something or</u> work on <u>something in an involved manner</u> (used very often in main-land China). Tā-gǎo-shénma? 他搞甚麼 ? What is he in-volved in? Bié-hú-gǎo. 別胡搞 . Don't do anything fool-ishly. Wǒmen-děi-gǎo-shēng-chan. 我們得搞生産. We must work on production. Tā-hái-gǎo-duìxiàng-ne. 他還搞對象呢. He is still looking for someone to marry. Bié-zài-gǎo-liàn'ài-le. 別再搞戀愛了 . Don't get involved in a love affair again.

GÀO₄ 告 (TV) sue.

GĀO'ĂI₃ 高矮 (N) height. (<u>see:</u> GĀODĪ 高低).

GĀOCHÁO₅ 高潮 (N) (1) high tide. (2) climax.

GÀOCÍ₃ 告辭 (IV) bid <u>one's</u> leave. Wǒ-yào-gēn-nín-gàocí-le. 我要跟您告辭了 . I want to say good-bye to you (said by the person depart-ing).

GĀODÀ₅ 高大 (SV) tall and big.

'GĀODĔNG₃ 高等 (B) (1) high class. (2) higher level. gāo-dĕng-jiàoyu 高等教育 higher education.(cf: 'GĀOJI 高級).

GĀODĔNGXUÉXIÀO₃ 高等學校 (N) school of higher learn-ing.

GĀODĪ₂ 高低 (N) (<u>lit.</u> high low) height, quality level, rank. Fángzide-gāodĭ yǒu-duó-gāo? 房子的高低有多高 ? What is the height of the house? (cf: GĀO'ĂI 高矮). (MA) under any circumstances. Tā-gāodĭ-bu-kĕn. 他高低不肯 . He will not consent under any circumstances.

GĀO'ĔRFÚQIÚ₄ 高爾夫球 (N) golf.

GĀOFÈI₄ 稿費 (N) remunera-tion <u>to the author for his manu-scripts for publication.</u>

GĀOGĒNRXIÉ₅ 高跟兒鞋 (N) high heel shoes. (M: shuāng 雙).

'GĀOJÍ₂ 高級 (B) (1) high class. (2) higher grade, higher level. (<u>opp.</u> chūjí 初級). gāojíde-xuésheng 高級的學生 students of the higher grades. gāojí-zhōngxué 高級中學 senior high school. (cf: 'GĀO-DĔNG 高等).

GÀO-JIÀ₁ 告假 (VO) ask for leave. Wǒ-dèi-gào-sāntiān-jià. 我得告三天假 . I have to ask for a three-day leave.

G

GĀOLIANG5 高粱 (N) sorghum.

GĂOR3 稿兒 see GĂOZI 稿子

GÀO-RÁOR4 告饒兒 (VO) ask, plead, beg for mercy. Nǐ-bu-gào-ráor, wǒ-hái-dá-ni. 你不告饒兒，我還打你. If you don't plead for mercy, I will continue to beat you.

GĀOSHÈPÀO4 高射炮 (N) anti-aircraft gun. (M: jià 架).

GÀOSONG1 告訴 or GÀOSU 告訴 (TV) tell, inform. Nǐ-bié-bǎ-zhèijian-shì gàosong-ta. 你別把這件事告訴他. Don't tell him about this.

GÀOSU1 告訴 see GÀOSONG 告訴.

GĀOXIĂO2 高小 (N) (con. gāo-jíxiǎoxué 高級小學). the higher grades in primary school (5th and 6th grades).

GĀOXĪNG1 高興 (AV) like to do certain things without the best reasons. Tā-gāoxìng-nèiyangr-zuò. 他高興那樣兒作. He likes to do it that way. (cf: YUÀNYÌ 願意, XǏHUAN 喜歡). (SV) happy, elated, delighted. Nèitiān-tā-zhēn-gāoxìng. 那天他真高興. He was really happy that day.

GĀOYAO5 膏藥 (N) medicine plaster. (M: tiē 貼).

GĀOZHŌNG2 高中 (N) (con. gāojízhōngxué 高級中學). senior high school (upper grades of secondary school,10th, 11th and 12th grades).

GÀO-ZHUÀNG4 告狀 (VO) (1) sue. (2) fig. report someone's behavior to a superior.

GĂOZI3 稿子 or GĂOR 稿兒 (N) first draft. qǐ-gǎozi 起稿子 make a draft.

GĒ1 擱 (TV) Peip. place, put. (syn. fàng 放). Bǎ-dōngxi-gē-xia. 把東西擱下. Put the things down. Ròu gēzai-nǎr? 肉擱在那兒? Where should the meat be placed?

Gē3 割 (TV) cut. gē-cǎo 割草 cut the grass.

GÈ1 各 (B-) each, various. gèguó 各國 various countries. gè-ren 各人 each person.

GÈ1 個 (M) general measure applicable to all individual nouns. (1) used after a NU. liǎngge-yuè 兩個月 two months. (2) used after a SP, the-NU yī 一 is implied. zhèi(yi)ge 這(一)個 this one. Tā-jiù shì-zènma-(yi)ge-rén. 他就是這麼一個人. He is just such a person. Nǐ- zhèi-(yí) ge-xiǎo-dōngxi. 你這(一)個小東西. You little thing. (3) used after a modifier before a noun, the NU yī 一 is implied. hěn-cōngmingde-(yi)ge-háizi 很聰明的(一)個孩子a very bright child. (4) used after a verb but before a noun, the NU yī 一 is implied. Wǒ-xiǎng-xǐ-(yi)ge-zǎo. 我想洗(一)個澡. I wish to take a bath. (5) used after a verb and before an approximate number. Wǒmenxiǎn-zuò-ge-liǎngsāntiān zai-shuō. 我們先作個兩三天再説. Let us first work on it for (a period of) two or three days, then we will talk about it. (6) used after a verb with or without le 了 or de 得 before a SV or a descriptive expression. Ràng-tāmen-kànle-ge-gòu. 讓他們看了個够. Let them look to their heart's content. Tā-zài-wǒde-shūshang huàle-ge-luànqibazāo. 他在我的書上畫了個亂七八糟. He drew a mess (of lines) on my paper. Tāde-huà shuōde-ge-kuài. 他的話説得個快. He spoke very fast. (7) used after an indirect object, mostly tā 他, before a descriptive expression. Wǒ-gěi-ta-ge-bulǐ. 我給他個不理. I pay no attention to him.

GĒBEI₃ 胳臂 (N) arm (part of a body).

GÉBÌ₃ 隔壁 (N) (lit. separated by a wall) next door neighbor.

'GÈCHÙ₃ 各處 (PW) various places, everywhere. Wǒ-gèchu dou-zhǎo-le. 我各處都找了. I searched everywhere.

GĒDA₃ 疙瘩 (N) Peip. (1) a kind of turnip. xiáncài-gēda 鹹菜疙瘩 a kind of pickled turnip. (2) growth, lump, pimple, boil. Shǒusheng zhǎngle-yige-gēda. 手上長了一個疙瘩. I have a lump (growth) on my hand. (3) knot (in a string or

rope). Shéngzi jìle-yíge-gēda. 繩子繫了一個疙瘩. This rope has a knot. (4) knotty problem. Wǒ-xīn-litou yǒu-yige-gēda. 我心裏頭有一個疙瘩. I have a knotty problem on my mind.

GÈGE₁ 哥哥 (N) older brother.

GÈGE₂ 各個 (N) each one, every one.

GÈ...GÈDE₄ 各...各的 (S) each one does his own... gè-shuō-gède 各説各的 each one does his own talking.

GĚI₁ 給 (TV) (1) give someone something. Wǒ-gěile-ta-yiběn-shū. 我給了他一本書. I gave him a book. Tā-gěi-wǒ-'qián-huā. 他給我錢花. He gives me money to spend. Tā-'gěile-wo-yixiàzi. 他給了我一下子. He gave me a blow. (2) give someone the chance to do something, allow one to do something. Wǒ-yào-kàn, tā-jiu-gěi wǒ-kàn. 我要看,他就給我看. If I wish to look, he will let me look. (CV) (1) the object of it may be dropped,for the benefit of, for the sake of. Wǒ-gěi-nǐ-'jièshao-jièshao. 我給你介紹介紹. Let me introduce you. Tā-'méi-gěi-wǒ-dǎ-diànhuà. 他沒給我打電話. He did not telephone me. Wǒ-bǎ-tā-xīnlide-huà gěi-(ta-)shuōchulai-le. 我把他心裏的話給他説出來了. I

G

spoke out for him about what was on his mind. (2) used to bring the direct object before the verb, same as bǎ 把. Tā-men-gěi-nèiběn-shū názǒu-le. 他們給那本書拿走了. They took away that book. (3) by (marking the agent), same as ràng 讓 or jiào 叫. Jīnyú-gei-māo-chī-le. 金魚給貓吃了. The goldfish was eaten by the cat.

(AD) used before the main verb in the bǎ-construction or jiào-or-ràng-construction. Tā-bǎ-wǒde-biǎo gei-diū-le. 他把我的表給丢了. He lost my watch. Wǒde-biǎo ràng-tā-gei-diū-le. 我的表讓他給丢了. My watch was lost by him.

(PV) to someone. Wǒ-sònggei-ta-yige-bǐ. 我送給他一個筆. I give (as a gift) him a pen.

GÉLI₅ 蛤蜊 (N) shell-fish (of the clam family).

GĒLÚNBǏYÀ₂ 哥倫比亞 (PW) Colombia.

(N) Columbia University.

GÉMÌNG₁ 革命 (N) (lit. remove a mandate) revolution. Fàguo-dà-gémìng 法國大革命 the great French Revolution. Zhèngfǔ-shuō tāmen-shì-zàofǎn, tāmen-zì'jǐ-shuō tāmen-shì-gémìng. 政府説他們是造反,他們自己説他們是革命. The government says they are in

rebellion. They themselves say they are making a revolution. Tāmen-guónèi qǐle-gémìng-le. 他們國內起了革命了. A revolution started in their country.

(VO) revolt against political authority. Zhèngfǔ-bu-hǎo, rén-mín-jiu-yào-gémìng. 政府不好,人民就要革命. If the government is not good the people will rise in revolution. Wǒmen-dei-gé-tade-mìng. 我們得革他的命. We must revolt against him.

GÉMO₃ 隔膜 (N) mental or emotional barrier, due to lack of understanding, that prevents people from dealing with each other. Tāmende-gémo hen-shēn. 他們的隔膜很深. They have a great barrier between them.

(SV) unfamiliar with an affair or a job. Tā-duì-zhèijiàn-shì hěn-gémo. 他對這件事很隔膜. He is unfamiliar with this matter.

GĒN₁ 跟 (TV) (1) follow. Jǐngchá-gēnle-ta-sāntiān-le. 警察跟了他三天了. The police followed him for three days. (2) become part of an entourage of. 'Hòulai-tā-gēnle-yi-ge-zuò-guān-de. 後來他跟了一個作官的. Later, he followed (to become part of an entourage) an official.

(CV) to, from, with, at, etc. Wǒ-yào-gēn-ta-shuō-huà. 我要

跟 他 説 話. I want to talk to him. Bié-gēn-tā-xué. 別 跟 他 學. Don't learn from him. Gēn-nǐ-méi-guānxi. 跟 你 没 關 係. It has no connection with you. Tā-yòu-gēn-wo-jiè-qián. 他 又 跟 我 借 錢. He again borrowed money from me. Bié-gēn-wo-shēng-qì. 別 跟 我 生 氣. Don't be angry with me. (cf:SHÌDE似的, YÍYÀNG一樣). used to join coordinate expressions and. Wǒ-yào-bǐ gēn-zhǐ. 我 要 筆 跟 紙. I want pencil and paper. (cf: HÉ 和).

GĒN₅ 跟 (TV) Peip. for zài 在 be at as a main verb or a coverb but not a post-verb. Tā-gēn-jiā-ne. 他 跟 家 呢. He is at home. Tā-gēn-nǎr-chī-fàn? 他 跟 那 兒 吃 飯? Where does he eat? (cf: ZÀI 在).

GĒN(R)₁ 根 (兒) (N) root. shù-gēn(r) 樹 根 (兒) tree root. cǎo-gēn(r) 草 根 (兒) grass root. (M) for something relatively long and thin. yìgēn(r)-tóufa 一 根 (兒) 頭 髮 a strand of hair. yìgēn(r)-cǎo 一 根 (兒) 草 a blade of grass.

GĒN₄ 哏 (N) mirth, laughter. Tā-huì-dòu-gén. 他 會 鬥 哏. He knows how to provoke mirth. (SV) comical. Xiǎoháir-génjíle. 小 孩 兒 哏 極 了. Children are very comical.

GĒNBEN₂ 根 本 (N) (lit. root and trunk of a tree) origin, foundation, basis. Tā-ye-méi-you-'gēnben-bànfa. 他 也 没 有 根 本 的 辦 法. He doesn't have a fundamental course of action. Zài-gēnben-shang yǒu-hěn-'dàde-fēnbie. 在 根 本 上 有 很 大 的 分 別. Fundamentally there is a great difference. (MA) (1) used before a negative expression, absolutely, just (indicating for some very simple and understood reasons). Tā-'gēnben-méi-'bànfa. 他 根 本 没 辦 法. He just doesn't have any way. (2) from the very beginning. Tā-gēnben-zhīdao. 他 根 本 知 道. He knew it from the very beginning.

GĒNG₄ 耕 (TV) till. gēng-dì 耕 地 till the land.

GÈNG₁ 更 (AD) even more, still more. 'Zhèige-bǐ-nèige 'gèng-hǎo. 這 個 比 那 個 更 好. This is even better than that. (See: BÙDÀN...GÈNG... 不 但 ... 更 ..., JÌ...GÈNG... 既 ... 更 ...).

'GÈNGJIĀ₃ 更 加 (AD) even more. Nà-jiu-'gèngjiā-'fāngbian-le. 那 就 更 加 方 便 了. Then it would be even more convenient.

GÈNGZHÈNG₅ 更 正 (TV) correct.

GĒNJU₂ 根 據 (TV) according to, based upon. Zhè-shi-gēnju 'bào-shang-shuō-de. 這 是 根 據 報 上 説 的. This is based upon what was said in the newspapers.

G

G

(N) basis. Tā-shuō-de-huà méi-you- gēnju. 他 説 的 話 没 有 根 據. His words have no basis.

GĒNSUÍ₅ 跟 隨 (TV) follow.

GĒN...YÍYÀNG₁ 跟 ... 一 樣 (S) same as.... Zhèige-gēn-nèige-yíyàng. 這 個 跟 那 個 一 樣. This is the same as the other.

GĒQŬ₃ 歌 曲 (N) song.

GĒR₁ 歌 兒 (N) song. chàng-gēr 唱 歌 兒 sing a song.

GÉR₄ 格 兒 (N) (1) sections, segments. Hézi-li-fēn-wŭge-gér. 盒 子 裏 分 五 個 格 兒. The box is divided into five segments. (2) ruled lines dividing a surface into sections. Zài-zhǐshang dǎ-gér. 在 紙 上 打 格 兒. Make ruled lines on paper. (3) acceptable level. Zhèizhòng-shū bu-gòu-gér. 這 種 書 不 够 格 兒. This kind of book is un-acceptable.

GÉR₅ 個 兒 see GÈZI 個 子

GÈREN₂ 各 人 (N) each person. Gèren-you-gèrende-yìjian. 各 人 有 各 人 的 意 見. Each person has his own opinion.

'GÈRÉN₂ 個 人 (PR) oneself, one's own. Zhèi-buguò-shi-wǒ 'gèrénde-kànfa. 這 不 過 是 我 個 人 的 看 法. This is merely my personal point of view.

GÉSHI₂ 格 式 (N) standard form, generally accepted format.

GÈSHIGEYÀNGR₃ 各 式 各 樣 兒 (N) various kinds.

GÉWÀI₂ 格 外 (AD) extra, additional. Tā-qǐng-nín-géwài-bāng-máng. 他 請 您 格 外 幫 忙. He begs you to give extra help.

GÈYÀNGR₃ 各 樣 兒 (N) various kinds.

GÈZAO₅ 虼 蚤 or GÈZI 虼 子 (N) flea.

'GÈZHŎNG₂ 各 種 (N) various kinds. gèzhŏng-de-dōngxi 各 種 的 東 西 various kinds of objects.

GÈZHONGGEYÀNGR₃ 各 種 各 樣 兒 (N) various kinds.

GÈZI₅ 鴿 子 (N) pigeon. (M: zhī 隻).

GÈZI₅ 虼 子 see GÈZAO 虼 蚤.

GÈZI₄ 個 子 or GÉR 個 兒 (N) physical size or stature. Zhèige-rén gèzi-hěn-dà. 這 個 人 個 子 很 大. This fellow is physically enormous.

'GÈZÌ₅ 各 自 (AD) each individual by or for himself. Wǒmen-děi gèzì-xiǎoxin. 我 們 得 各 自 小 心. We must each be careful.

GŌNG₂ 工 (N) (1) work, labor. gōngren 工 人 workman, laborer, servant. zuò-gōng 作 工 do work (labor). (2) workmanship, craftsmanship. gōng-hěn-xì 工 很 細 fine craftsmanship.

GŌNG₄ 弓 (N) bow (archery). (M: zhāng 張).

GŌNG₄ 公 (B) male (for animals only), (opp. mǔ 母). gōnggǒu 公狗 male dog.

GŌNG₃ 公 (B-) used before measures of length, surface, weight, etc., forms names of the units in the metric system. gōngchǐ 公尺 meter.
(B) public or belonging to an organization, but not to an individual. (opp. sī 私). Tā-gōng-sī-bufēn. 他公私不分. He makes no distinction between private and public.
(AD) among everybody. Dàjiā-gōng-fēn. 大家公分. Divide it among everybody.

GŌNGBÀO₅ 公報 (N) announcement, proclamation, public report. zhèngfǔ-gōngbào 政府公報 government announcement.

GŌNGBÙ₃ 公布 (TV) (con. gōngkāi-xuānbù 公開宣布). announce openly, make information public. Shìqing-yǐjing-dìngle, kěshi hái-méi-gōngbù-ne. 事情已經定了, 可是還沒公布呢. The matter has been settled, but not yet made public.

GÒNGCHǍNDǍNG₁ 共產黨 (N) Communist party.

GŌNGCHǍNG₁ 工廠 (N) factory. (M: jiā 家).

GÒNGCHǍNZHǓYÌ₁ 共產主義 (N) Communism.

GŌNGCHÉNG₂ 工程 (N) (1) engineering. Tā-shi-xué-gōng-chéng-de. 他是學工程的. He is studying engineering. (2) engineering project, construction project. Gōngcheng-hen-dà. 工程很大. The project is very large.

GŌNGCHÉNGSHĪ₃ 工程師 (N) engineer.

GŌNGCHǏ₃ 公尺 (M) meter (the length measure of the metric system).

GŌNGDAO₂ 公道 (SV) just, fair. Zhè-shi-hěn-gōngdaode-bànfa. 這是很公道的辦法. This is a very just course of action. Jiàqian-hěn-gōngdao. 價錢很公道. The price is very fair.

GŌNGDÌ₅ 工地 (N) work place, site or location.

GŌNGFĒN₂ 公分 (M) centimeter.

GŌNGFU₁ 工夫 (N) (1) period of time. Wǒ-jīntian-méi-you-gōngfu. 我今天沒有工夫. I don't have the time today. (2) time and effort spent towards an accomplishment. Yào-chàng-de-hǎo, děi-xià-gōngfu. 要唱的好得下工夫. If one wishes to sing well, one must spend time and effort in training. (3) skills, artistry or accomplishments, acquired through much practice. liàn-gōngfu 練工夫 training for a certain skill.

GŌNGGONG₃ 公公 (N) father's father or husband's father.

GŌNGGÒNG₂ 公共 (B-) public. gōnggòng-diànhuà 公共電

G

話 public telephone.

GŌNGGÒNGQÌCHĒ₂ 公共汽車 (N) public bus. (M: liàng 輛).

GǑNGGÙ₄ 鞏固 (IV) consolidate, secure. Tāmende-dìwei yǐjing-gǒnggu-le. 他們的地位已經鞏固了. Their position has already been consolidated.

GÒNGHÉGUÓ₄ 共和國 (N) republic.

GŌNGHUÌ₂ 工會 (N) labor union.

GŌNGJĪ₃ 公雞 (N) rooster, cock. (M: zhī 隻).

GŌNGJĪ₂ 攻擊 (TV) attack.

'GŌNGJǏ₄ 供給 (TV) supply, support by supplying funds. Tā-jiù-yào-gōngjǐ-tāde-háizi-niàn-shū. 他就要供給他的孩子念書 He just wants to support his children's studies (education).
(N) supplies. Yīnwei-gōngjǐ-bu-gòu, suóyi-dǎbài-le. 因為供給不够所以打敗了. Because of insufficient supplies the battle was lost.

GŌNGJĪN₂ 公斤 (M) kilogram.

GŌNGJÙ₂ 工具 (N) instrument, tool.

GŌNGKĀI₃ 公開 (AD) openly, publicly. Nǐ gōngkāide-shuō-shuō. 你公開的説説. Speak about it publicly.
(TV) open to the public. Nèijian-shì yǐjing-gōngkāi-le. 那件事已經公開了. That matter has already been made public.

GŌNGKE₁ 功課 (N) (1) course of study. (M: mén 門). Nǐ-xuǎn-le-'jǐmen-gōngke? 你選了幾門功課? How many courses did you select? (2) scholastic accomplishment. Tā-de-gōngke-kěn-hǎo. 他的功課很好. His scholastic accomplishment is very good.
(3) study assignment. zuò-gōng-ke 作工課 work on study assignments.

GŌNGKEBIĀO₂ 功課表 (N) class schedule.

GŌNGLAO₃ 功勞 (N) merito-rious contribution of service. Tāde-gōnglao-hen-dà. 他的功勞很大. His contrib-ution (of service) was very great.

GŌNGLǏ₂ 公里 (M) kilometer.

GŌNGLÌ₂ 公立 (B-) public. (opp. sīlì 私立). gōnglixuéxiào 公立學校 public school.

GŌNGLÙ₂ 公路 (N) highway. (M: tiáo 條).

GŌNGNÓNG₄ 工農 (N) laborers and farmers.

GŌNGPÍNG₂ 公平 (SV) just, fair. Tāde-huà bu-gōngping. 他的話不公平. What he said is not fair.
(AD) fairly, justly. gōngping-jiāoyì 公平交易 trade fairly.

GŌNGPÓ₅ 公婆 (N) husband's parents.

GŌNGQIAN₁ 工錢 (N) wages.

GŌNGREN₁ 工人 (N) laborer, worker.

GŌNGSHÈ₂ 公社 (N) commune.

GŌNGSHĒNG₂ 公升 (M) liter.

GŌNGSHÌ₂ 公事 (N) (1) official business. (2) official document.

GŌNGSĪ₁ 公司 (N) company, corporation. (M: jiā 家).

GÒNGTÓNG₄ 共同 (AD) together. gòngtóng-nǔlì 共同努力 work hard together. (B-) common. gòngtóng-xìngqu 共同興趣 common interest.

GŌNGWEI₄ 恭維 (TV) compliment. Wǒ-gōngweile-ta-jiju. 我恭維了他幾句. I complimented him (with a few words). Tāde-Zhōngwén, wǒ-bu-gǎn-gōngwei. 他的中文我不敢恭維. I can't compliment him on his Chinese.

GŌNGXǏ₂ 恭喜 (TV) (1) congratulations. (2) Happy New Year.

'GÒNGXIÀN₁ 貢獻 (TV) contribute (money, time, effort, etc.). (N) contribution.

'GŌNGYÈ₁ 工業 (N) industry.

GŌNGYÈHUÀ₂ 工業化 (TV) industrialize.

GŌNGYUÁN₁ 公園 (N) public park.

GŌNGYUĒ₅ 公約 (N) treaty.

GŌNGZĪ₅ 工資 (N) wages.

GŌNGZUO₁ 工作 (IV) do work. Tā-zhèngzai-gōngzuo. 他正在工作. He is working. (N) work, job. Tā-yào-zhǎo-yige-héshìde-gōngzuo. 他要找一個合適的工作. He wants to find a suitable job.

GŌU₄ 溝 (N) (1) ditch. (2) groove. (M: dào 道).

GŌU₃ 鉤 (TV) (1) hook. Yòng-gōu-zi gōuzhu. 用鉤子鉤住. Use a hook to hold it. (2) be in cahoots. Tāmen-jige-rén gōu-qilai-fǎndui-wo. 我們幾個人鉤起來反對我. Several of them are in cahoots against me. (3) make a check mark. Bǎ-nǐ-xiǎng-mǎi-de-nèijiyangr, zài-dānzishang-gōu-yigou. 把你想買的那幾樣兒, 在單子上鉤一鉤. Make check marks on the items which you want to buy. (4) delete, cancel, write off by making a check mark. Nèibi-zhàng-yǐjing-gōu-le. 那筆賬已經鉤了. That account has already been cancelled. (5) remind someone of some unpleasant past event. Wǒ-yishuō, gōuqi-tade-xīnshi-lai-le. 我一說, 鉤起他的心事來了. When I mentioned it, it reminded him of past events.

GŌU₁ 狗 (N) dog. (M: zhǐ 隻, tiáo 條).

GÒU₁ 够 (SV) enough, sufficient. Shíhou-bu-gòu. 時候不够. It is not enough time. (AD) enough, sufficiently. Fàn bu-gòu-chī-de. 飯不够吃的. There is not enough food to eat. (TV) enough to reach a certain standard. gòu-biāozhun 够標準 reached the standard. (RE) enough. Wǒ-chīgòule. 我吃够了. I ate enough.

G

G

GŌUCHUÀN₅ 鈎串 (TV) be in cahoots.

GŌUDANG₅ 勾當 (N) business (with implication of surreptitiousness). Bù-zhīdào tāmen-yǒu-shénma-gōudang. 不知道他們有甚麼勾當. I don't know what kind of (surreptitious) business they have.

GŌUR₃ 鈎兒 see GŌUZI 鈎子.

GŌUXIĀO₅ 勾消 (TV) delete.

GÒUZÀO₂ 構造 (N) construction, structure.

GŌUZI₃ 鈎子 or GŌUR 鈎兒 (N) (1) hook. (2) stinger (of a bee).

GÒU-ZĪGE₂ 够資格 (VO) be qualified.

GǓ₂ 古 (SV) ancient, archaic.

GǓ₄ 股 (B) (1) share, portion. gǔzi 股子 share. gǔpiào 股票 stock. (2) section of an organization. kuàijigǔ 會計股 accounting section.

GǓ₃ 股 (M) (1) puff, column of smoke, air, steam, etc. yìgǔ-yān 一股烟 a puff of smoke. (2) for odors, whiff. yìgǔ-chòu-wèir 一股臭味 a whiff of foul odor. (3) band or skein of hair, rope, string, wool thread, etc. yìgǔ-máoxiàn 一股毛線 a skein of yarn. (4) band of robbers. yìgǔ-tǔfěi 一股土匪 a band of robbers. (5) for a sudden drive of strength, energy. yìgǔ-jìnr 一股勁兒 a surge of strength. yìgǔ-rèqì 股熱氣 a surge of enthu-

siasm or a puff of hot air. (6) share of stock. yìgǔ-gǔpiào 一股股票 one share of stock.

GǓ₂ 鼓 (N) drum. (M: miàn 面). (SV) (1) convex, bulging. (opp. biě 癟). Píbāo hěn-gǔ. 皮包很鼓. The purse is bulging. (2) hard or firm (because of the amount of air inside). Píqiú hěn-gǔ. 皮球很鼓. The ball is firm. (TV) bulge, stick out. Bǎ-dùzi-gúqilai. 把肚子鼓起來. Stick out your stomach.

GÙ₂ 雇 (TV) hire, employ (used with reference to the laboring class). gù-yíge-duǎngōng 雇一個短工 hire a temporary worker. gù-yíliang-qìchē 雇一輛汽車 hire a car (with a driver). gù-yipi-mǎ 雇一匹馬 hire a horse (with a driver). (cf: QǏNG 請).

GÙ₃ 顧 (TV) (1) take care of, look after. Tā-bu-gù-jiā. 他不顧家. He doesn't take care of his family. (2) take into consideration. Tā-bu-gù-yiqiè. 他不顧一切. He disregards everything.

GUĀ₄ 瓜 (N) melon. xīgua 西瓜 watermelon. Guā hěn-tián. 瓜很甜. The melon is very sweet.

(B) fruit or plant of the gourd family, including melon, cucumber, pumpkin, etc. huánggua 黃瓜 cucumber. sīgua 絲瓜 sponge gourd.

GUĀ₃ 刮 (TV) (1) scrape, shave. guā-húzi 刮鬍子 shave one's whiskers. Yòng-dāo-guā-le-qu-le. 用刀刮了去了. Scrape it off. (2) fig. exploit (people). Tā-guā-dìpí, guā-le-bushǎode-qián. 他刮地皮刮了不少的錢. He made money by exploitation.

GUÀ₁ 掛 (TV) (1) hang. (opp. zhāi 摘). guà-yīshang 掛衣裳 hang up the garments. Huàr zài-qiángshang-guàzhe-ne. 畫兒在牆上掛着呢. The painting is hanging on the wall. (2) hitch on (connection of vehicles or machinery). Zuò-'chē-de-rén tài-duō, děi-zài-guà-yiliàng-chē. 坐車的人太多,得再掛一輛車. There are too many passengers, another car must be hitched on. (3) fly a flag. guà-guóqí 掛國旗 fly a national flag.

(M) string of. yíguà-zhūzi 一掛珠子 a string of pearls.

GUÀ-CĂI₅ 掛彩 (VO) (1) put up decorations for some festive event. (2) (lit. be decorated with blood) be wounded. Tā-'gāng-dào-qiánxiàn jiu-guàle-cǎi-le. 他剛到前線,就掛了彩了. As soon as he arrived at the front lines he was wounded.

GUĀ-FĒNG₁ 颱風 (VO) wind blows.

GUĂFU₄ 寡婦 (N) widow.

GUÀ-HÀO₃ 掛號 (VO) (lit. hang a number) register (used primarily for mail or at a hospital, but not for courses in school, voting, etc.). Zhèifēng-xìn děi-guà-hào. 這封信得掛號. This letter must be (sent by) registered(mail). Zài-yīyuan-kànbìng děi-xiān-guà-hào. 在醫院看病得先掛號. To be treated at a hospital one must first register. (cf: DĒNGJÌ 登記, ZHÙCÈ 註冊).

GUĀI₃ 乖 (SV) well-behaved and endearing. guāi-háizi 乖孩子 well-behaved, endearing child.

(N) well-behaved, endearing child. Shéi-shi-xiǎo-guāi? 誰是小乖? Who is the little dear?

GUĂI₁ 拐 (TV) (1) turn in direction of travel. Wàng-zuǒ-yi-guǎi, jiu-kànjian-le. 往左一拐,就看見了. Turn to the left, then you will see it. (2) kidnap (usually a child), abscond with money belonging to others. Tā-guǎi'zuǒ-le yibǐ-qián. 他拐走了一筆錢. He absconded with a sum of money.

GUĂI₅ 拐 (N) crutch. Tā-jiàzhe-'guǎi-zǒu. 他架着拐走. He walks on crutches.

GUÀI₂ 怪 (SV) strange, odd (in the sense of being peculiar). Guài-a! 'Tā-zhěnma-zhīdao-le? 怪啊,他怎麼知道了? It's strange! How did he

know? 'Zhèige-rén hěn-guài.
這 個 人 很 怪 . This
person is very odd. Tā-bu-lái
cái-guài-ne. 他 不 來 才
怪 呢 . It would be very odd
if he doesn't come.
(TV) blame. Nà-bié-guài-wǒ.
那 別 怪 我 . Don't blame
me for that.
(AD) rather. Guài-buhǎoyìsi-de.
怪 不 好 意 思 的 . It
is rather embarrassing.
(M) a strange one. Tā-shi-zhèr-
de-yiguài. 他 是 這 兒 的
一 怪 . He is one of the 'pe-
culiarities" of this locale.

GUÀIBUDE₂ 怪 不 得 (RV) can-
not blame, cannot be blamed.
Nà-jiu-guàibude-ta-le. 那 就
怪 不 得 他 了 . In that
case, he cannot be blamed.
(MA) no wonder. Guàibude-ta-
zhǐdao-le, yuánlái-shi-'nǐ-gào-
song-ta-de. 怪 不 得 他 知
道 了 , 原 來 是 你 告
訴 他 了 . No wonder he
knew! It was you who told him.

GUǍIGÙNR₅ 拐 棍 兒 (N) Peip.
walking cane. (M: gēn 根).
(cf: GUǍI ZHÀNG 拐 扙).

GUǍIJIǍOR₅ 拐 角 兒 (N) cor-
ner of a street or passageway.

GUÀISHÌ₄ 怪 事 (N) strange happening, event, affair, etc.

GUǍI-WÀNR₂ 拐 彎 兒 (VO)
make a turn (in travel). Nǐ-
guǎi-yige-dà-wǎnr jiu-dào-le.
你 拐 一 個 大 彎 兒
就 到 了 . (You) make a
big turn, then you will get there.

GUÀIWU₄ 怪 物 (N) (1) strange
being, monster. Wǒ-huà-yige-
guàiwu. Shēnzi-xiàng-rén, tóu-
xiàng-mǎ, hái-huì-fēi. 我 畫
一 個 怪 物 , 身 子 像
人 , 頭 像 馬 , 還 會 飛
I painted a monster. His body
is like a man, his head like a
horse and he can fly. (2) hideous
person. Nǐ-kàn zhèige-lǎo-guài-
wu! 你 看 這 個 老 怪
物 ! Look at this old monster!

GUǍIZHÀNG₅ 拐 杖 (N) walking
cane, staff. (M: gēn 根). (cf:
GUǍI GÙNR 拐 棍 兒).

GUĀ-LIǍN₁ 刮 臉 (VO) shave
one's face.

GUĀN₁ 關 (TV) (1) shut, close. '(opp.
kāi 開). guān-mén 關 門 shut
the door. guān-diànmén 關 電
門 (lit. shut the gate of the electricity) turn off the electric
switch. guān-wúxiàndiàn 關 無
線 電 turn (shut) off the radio.
Bǎ-diàndēng guānshang. 把 電
燈 關 上 . Turn (shut) off the
light. Bǎ-gǒu guānzai-wàitou-le.
把 狗 關 在 外 頭 了 .
The dog was shut outside.
(2) close down, be out of business. Nèige-pùzi guān-le. 那 個
鋪 子 關 了 . That shop
closed down. (cf: BÌ 閉 , HÉ 合).
(N) guarded passage through a
barrier. hǎiguān 海 關 (lit.
guarded sea passage) customs
office. guò-guān 過 關 go
through the barrier or guarded
pass or fig. overcome the difficulty.

G

(M) barrier, difficulty (<u>to be overcome</u>). Kǎoshì-shì-yìguān. 考試是一關. The examination is a barrier (to be passed).

GUĀN₁ 官 (N) (1) government official. Tā-zuòguo-'shénma-guān? 他作過甚麼官? What kind of official positions has he held? (2) official rank Tā-yòu-shēng-guānle. 他又升官了. He was promoted in rank again. Tāde-guān hěn-dà. 他的官很大. His rank is very high. (B) governmental. guānfèi 官費 expenses paid by the government.

GUĂN₁ 管 (TV) (1) control, govern, regulate. Tā-fùqin guǎn-de-hěn-jǐn. 他父親管得很緊. His father is very strict (in control and regulation). (2) manage, take charge, take care of. Zhèr-de-shìqing 'shéi-guǎn? 這兒的事情誰管? Who takes care of the business affairs here? (3) care for, care about. Nǐ-ài-qu-bu-qù, wo-bu-guǎn. 你愛去不去,我不管. Go or not as you like, I don't care. (4) provide for <u>or</u> with. Tāmen-guǎn-jiē bu-guǎn-sòng. 他們管接不管送. They provide transportation to come, but not to go. 'Gōngqián, měiyuè-yìbǎikuai-qián, bu-guǎn-fàn. 工錢每月一百塊錢,不管飯. The wage is $100 per

month, meals are not provided. (5) used in a rhetorical question, why should...care. Nǐ-'guǎn-ta-shì-shéi-ne? 你管他是誰呢? Why should you care who he is? Nǐ-'guǎn-wǒ-ne? 你管我呢? Why should you care about me? (cf: BUGUǍN 不管).

GUǍN₃ 管 (M) <u>for writing instruments</u>. yìguǎn-bǐ 一管筆 a writing instrument (pen, pencil <u>or</u> writing brush). (B) tube. shuǐguǎnzi 水管子 water pipe.

GUǍN₂ 館 (-B) building, establishment. kēxuéguǎn 科學館 science museum. túshuguǎn 圖書館 library.

GUÀN₃ 灌 (TV) (1) direct the flow of liquid <u>into something</u>. guàn-diǎnr-qìyóu 灌點兒汽油 put a little gas in the tank. Tā-men-yǐjing-guànle-wo sānbēi-le. 他們已經灌了我三杯了. He made me drink three drinks. (2) <u>fig.</u> record (<u>sound, music,etc.</u>). Wǒ-qu-quàn-yīn-qu. 我去灌音去. I am on my way to do a recording (sound).

GUÀN₃ 慣 (TV) (1) be overly permissive. Bié-lǎo-'guànzhe-hái-zi, kǒngpà-bǎ-ta-guànhuài-le. 別老慣着孩子,恐怕把他慣壞了. Don't be overly permissive with the child, I'm afraid he will be spoiled. (2) accustomed to. 'Zhèiyàngr-zuò wǒ-bu-guàn. 這

G

樣兒作我不慣. I
am not accustomed to doing it
this way.
(RE) accustomed to. Nǐ-shuō-
guànle jiu-bu-róngyi-gǎi-le. 你
說慣了就不容易
改了. Once you become
accustomed to saying it, it will
be difficult to change.

GUĂNBĂO₂ 管保 (TV) guarantee
that. Wǒ-guǎnbǎo ta-bu-lái. 我
管保他不來. I guar-
antee that he won't come.

GUĀNCAI₄ 棺材 (N) coffin, cas-
ket. (M: kǒu 口).

'GUĀNCHÁ₃ 觀察 (TV) observe.
Zhèi-shi-wo-'guānchá-chulaide.
這是我觀察出來
的. This came from my ob-
servation.

GUĀN-DĒNG₁ 關燈 (VO) turn
off the light.

GUĀNDIĂN₃ 觀點 (N) point of
view.

GUĀNG₂ 光 (N) (1) light, luminos-
ity, beam. (M: dào 道). tài-
yangguāng 太陽光 sunlight.
Tāde-jīnbiǎo fàng-guāng. 他的
金表放光. His gold
watch is glittering. Zhèige-dǐ-
piàn jiànle-guāng-le. 這個底
片見了光了. This
negative(photographic) has been
exposed (to light). (2) glory.
Nín-you-'zhèiyàngrde-chéngjiu,
wǒmende-liǎnshang-ye-yǒu-
guāng. 您有這樣兒的
成就, 我們的臉上
也有光. (lit. You have
such accomplishments that the

glory is reflected even in our
face.) You have such accomplishments that we can share in
your glory. Wǒ-zhānle-nín-bu-
shǎode-guāng. 我沾了您不
少的光. I have shared a
great deal of your glory. or fig.
I have gotten a great deal because
of you.

GUĀNG₂ 光 (SV)(1) smooth, glossy
(surface). Zhèngmiànr-shi-
guāngde. 正面兒是光
的. The right surface is
smooth. (2) dispose of something completely, all gone. Tāde-
qián dou-guāng-le. 他的錢
都光了. All his money is
gone.
(RE) (1) smooth, glossy (surface).
(2) all gone. Zhǐ màiguāng-le. 紙
賣光了. All the paper is
sold.

GUĀNG₃ 光 or GUĂNG 廣 (AD)
only. Tā-guāng-huì-chī. 他光
會吃. He only knows how to
eat. Guāng-shi-wǒ-'yíge-rén-
zhèiyàngr-xiǎng. 光是我一
個人這樣想. I am
the only one who thinks this way.

GUĂNG₄ 廣 (SV) broad (of something abstract). (opp. zhǎi 窄).
'Fànwéi-hěn-guǎng. 範圍很
廣. The scope is very broad.

GUĂNG₃ 廣 see GUĀNG 光.

GUÀNG₄ 逛 (TV) look around
leisurely, take in the sights.
Wǒmen-dào-chéng-lǐtou-qu-
quàngguang. 我們到城裏
頭去逛逛. Let's go
rambling around in the city

(leisurely implied).

GUǍNGBŌ₃ 廣播 (TV) broadcast (radio, television). guǎngbo-xīn-wén 廣播新聞 broadcast the news. tīng-guǎngbō 聽廣播 listen to a broadcast.

GUǍNGBŌDIÀNTÁI₃ 廣播電台 (N) broadcasting station.

'GUǍNGCǍI₄ 光彩 (N) (1) glitter, sparkle. (2) glory. Nǐ-'yíge-rén-chénggōng, nǐmen-quán-'jiā dou yǒu-'guǎngcǎi. 你一個人成功，你們全家都有光彩. You alone being successful (bring) glory to your whole family.

GUǍNGCHǍNG₄ 廣場 (N) (lit. a large empty ground area) (1) large field (generally for rallies). (2) square, plaza. Tiān'ānmén-guǎngchǎng 天安門廣場 Tien An Men Square.

GUǍNGDÀ₅ 廣大 (SV) vast, broad. guǎngdàde-qúnzhòng 廣大的群眾 the broad masses.

GUǍNGDŌNG₂ 廣東 (PW) Kwang-tung province.

GUǍNGGÀO₂ 廣告 (N) adver-tisement. (M: duàn 段). Tā-zài-bàoshang dēngle-yiduàn-guǎnggào. 他在報上登了一段廣告. He in-serted an advertisement in the papers.

GUǍNGGÙNR₅ 光棍兒 (N) bachelor. dǎ-guǎnggùnr 打光棍兒 be single (of a man).

GUǍNGHUA₃ 光滑 (SV) smooth,

glossy (surface). Zhèige-zhuōzi-miànr hěn-guānghua. 這個桌子面兒很光滑. The surface of this table is very smooth.

GUǍNGJING₃ 光景 (N) time, situation, circumstances. Tā-jìnlái-guāngjing-zěnmayàng? 他近來光景怎麼樣? (lit. How is his recent time?) What is his present situation? used after a NU-M indicates an approximation, about. yìbǎi-kuai-qián-de-guāngjing 一百塊錢的光景 about one hundred dollars.

(AD) anyway, after all. Wǒ-kàn guāngjing-dei-zhèyangr-bàn. 我看光景得這樣兒辦. I think it has to be done this way after all.

'GUĀNGMÍNG₃ 光明 (SV) (opp. 'hēi'àn 黑暗). (1) bright(pro-spectively). Wǒmen-yǒu-'guāng-míngde-'yuǎnjǐng. 我們有光明的遠景. We have a bright future. (2) aboveboard. Tā-zuò-de-shì dōu-bu-'guāng-míng. 他作的事都不光明. Nothing he does is aboveboard.

'GUĀNGRÓNG₂ 光榮 (SV) glo-rious. Tā-juéde hen-'guāngróng. 他覺得很光榮. He feels glorious.

(N) glory. Zhè-shi-wǒmen-'guó-jiāde-'guāngróng. 這是我們國家的光榮. This is the glory of our nation.

G

G

GUĂNGXĪ₂ 廣西 (PW) Kwangsi province or autonomous region.

GUĂNGXIÀN₂ 光線 (N) light, illumination. Zhèi-wūzi guāngxiàn-bu-gòu. 這屋子光線不夠. There is not enough light in this room.

GUĂNGYĪN₃ 光陰 (N) time (expendable for a certain task). Wŏmen-bu-néng-bă-yŏu'yòngde guāngyīn-fèizai-'zhèizhong shì-qingshang. 我們不能把有用的光陰癈在這種事情上. We can not waste useful time on such matters.

GUĂNGZHOU₂ 廣州 (PW) Canton (capital of Kwangtung province).

GUĀNHUÀ₅ 官話 (N) (1) Mandarin language (a term gradually becoming obsolete). (syn. guóyŭ 國語). (2) speech used in referring to government regulations. dă-guānhuà 打官話 speak in the perfunctory manner of officialdom.

GUĀNJIÀ₄ 官價 (N) official price or value established by the government.

'GUĀNJIÀN₃ 關鍵 (N) key to the solution of a problem or in a situation. Zhèige-wèntíde-'guānjiàn shì-qián. 這個問題的關鍵是錢 Money is the key to this problem.

GUĂNJIAO₄ 管教 (TV) teach by rules and disciplinary action. Tā-bu-huì-guănjiao-tade-háizi. 他不會管教他的孩子. He does not know how to discipline his children.

GUĂN JIÀO₂ 管 ... 叫 ... (S) Peip. address someone, or call something as (title or name). Wŏmen-guăn-ta-jiào-Zhāng-Xiansheng. 我們管他叫張先生. We address him as Mr. Chang. Yŏuren-guăn-gémìng jiào-zàofăn. 有人管革命叫造反. Some people call revolution, rebellion.

'GUĀNJŪN₃ 冠軍 (N) winner of the highest award in a competition.

'GUĂNLĬ₂ 管理 (TV) manage, control.

(N) management, control. 'gōng-shāng-guănlĭ 工商管理 industrial and commercial management.

GUĀNLIÁO₄ 官僚 (N) bureaucracy, bureaucrat.

'GUĀNNIÀN₂ 觀念 (N) concept, notion, view.

GUĀNSI₃ 官司 (N) lawsuit. (M: chăng 場). dă-guānsi 打官司 sue, be involved in a lawsuit.

GUÀNTOU₄ 罐頭 (N) can (preserve). (M: guàn 罐).

GUĀNXI₁ 關係 (N) (1) relationship, connection. Tāmen-liăng-ge-ren shi-'shénma-guānxi? 他們兩個人是甚麼關係? What is the relationship between the two of them? Zhèiben-shū gēn-tā yŏu-shénma-guānxi? 這本書跟他有甚麼關係? What is the relationship between this book

and him? (2) influence, effect.
Diūle-yíkuai-qián 'wǒ-kàn méi-
guānxi, kěshi-'tā-juéde guānxi-
hěn-dà. 丢 了 一 塊 錢
我 看 沒 關 係, 可 是
他 覺 得 關 係 很 大.
I feel that losing a dollar is not
important, but he feels the effect is great. Wǒ-méi-mǎi shì-
yīnwei méi-'qián-de-quānxi. 我
沒 買 是 因 為 沒 錢
的 關 係. I didn't buy it
because (of the effect) of not
having money. (cf: MÉIGUĀNXÌ
沒 關 係).

GUĀNXĪN₂ 關 心 (TV) concerned
about someone or something.
Tāmen dou-hěn-guānxīn-nèijian-
shìqing. 他 們 都 很 關
心 那 件 事 情. They
are all very much concerned
about that matter.

GUÀN-YĪN₄ 灌 音 (VO) record
sound.

GUĀNYU₁ 關 於 (CV) in reference to, regarding, concerning.
Guānyu-zhèijiàn-shì wǒ-yìdiǎnr
dou-bu-zhīdào. 關 於 這 件
事 我 一 點 兒 都 不
知 道. I don't know the least
thing concerning this affair.
Zhèige-diànyǐngr shì-guānyu-
yíge-Měiguo-ren-zài-Zhōngguo-
de-shìqing. 這 個 電 影 兒
是 關 於 一 個 美 國
人 在 中 國 的 事 情.
This movie is about an American who is in China.

GUĀN-ZHĀNG₃ 關 張 (VO) go
out of business. (opp. kāizhāng

開 張).

GUĀNZHAO₂ 關 照 (TV) (1) inform, tell someone what to do.
Qǐng-'guānzhao-ta-yixia. 請 關
照 他 一 下. Please inform
him. Wǒ-guānzhao-ren qu-lìkè
tōngzhi-ta. 我 關 照 人 去
立 刻 通 知 他. I will
tell someone to go to notify him
immediately. (2) help by telling
what to do, look after (a polite
expression used upon meeting a
co-worker or a superior).Wǒ-dìdi-
méi-you-zuò-shì-de-jīngyan
qǐng-nín-guānzhao-guanzhao.
我 弟 弟 沒 有 作 事
的 經 驗, 請 您 關 照
關 照. This young brother of
mine has no work experience,
please help him by telling him
what to do.

GUĀNZHÒNG₃ 觀 眾 (N) viewing
audience. (cf:TĪNGZHÒNG 聽 眾).

GUǍNZI₄ 管 子 (N) pipe, tube,
tubing.(M:gēn 根). shuǐ-guǎnzi
水 管 子 water pipe.

GUÀ-XĪN₅ 掛 心 (VO) (lit. hang
on the mind) be concerned about.
Nèijian-shì nín-bu-bì-guà-xīn.
那 件 事 您 不 必 掛
心. You don't have to be concerned about that affair.

GUĀZǏR₅ 瓜 子 兒 (N) edible
melon seeds and sunflower seeds.

GǓBĀ₂ 古 巴 (PW) Cuba.

GǓBAN₅ 古 板 (SV) old fashioned
(implying certain old fashioned
stiffness).

GÙBUDE₃ 顧 不 的 (RV) too
preoccupied with one thing to

G

G

consider _or_ to take care of something else. Tā-mángde gù-bude-chī-fàn. 他 忙 得 顧 不 得 吃 飯. He was so busy that he didn't think of eating.

GŬDÀI₂ 古 代 (TW) ancient times.

GÙDE₃ 顧 得 (RV) take into consideration, pay attention to. Tā-jìng-qùde-shuō-huà, bǎ-shíhou-wàng-le. 他 竟 顧 得 說 話. 把 時 候 忘 了. All he paid attention to was talking, he even forgot the time.

GŪDŌNG₅ 咕 咚 (ONO) _sound of swallowing some liquid, something heavy falling down, thunder or a cannon being shot._ Dàpào-gūdōng-gūdōngde-xiǎng. 大 炮 咕 咚 咕 咚 的 響. The cannon makes booming sounds.

GŬDŌNG₃ 股 東 (N) owner _of a share of a business_, shareholder.

GŬDŎNG₃ 古 董 (N) (1) antique. (2) _fig._ old fashioned person.

GŬDÒNG₄ 鼓 動 (TV) incite.

GŬDUOR₄ 骨 朵 兒 (N) bud (flower).

'GŪ'ER₄ 孤 兒 (N) orphan.

GŬFEN₃ 股 份 (N) shares _in a business_.

GŪFÙ₃ 辜 負 (TV) neglect _or_ be unappreciative of someone's good will or efforts to help. Bié-gūfù-tade-hǎoyì. 別 辜 負 他 的 好 意. Don't neglect his good will.

GŪGU₅ 姑 姑 (N) aunt (sister of the father).

GŬGUÀI₄ 古 怪 (SV) strange, odd.

GUĪ₂ 歸 (TV) (1) put _things where they belong._ Bǎ-dōngxi-guī-yiqi. 把 束 西 歸 一 歸. Put the things back in order. (2) gather _things together._ Bǎ-dōngxi guīzai-yikuàir. 把 束 西 歸 在 一 塊 兒. Gather the things together. (3) be a possession of _someone._ Zhèiběn-shū guī-tā-le. 這 本 書 歸 他 了. This book became his possession. (CV) it is _someone's_ responsibility to... Nèige-xuésheng guī-shéi-guǎn? 那 個 學 生 歸 誰 管? Under whose jurisdiction is that student?

GUĬ₃ 鬼 (N) supernatural beings, such as ghosts, devils, demons, etc. Wǒ-bu-xìn-yǒu-guǐ. 我 不 信 有 鬼. I do not believe that there are ghosts. Tā-xīnli yǒu-guǐ. 他 心 裏 有 鬼. (lit. He has the devil in his heart.) He has something sly in mind. Zhèi-guǐ-dìfang. 這 鬼 地 方. This dammed place! (SV) smart, sly. Tā-zhēn-guǐ. 他 真 鬼. He is really a sly one. (-B) addict. dǔguǐ 賭 鬼 gambling addict.

GUÌ₃ 櫃 (N) (1) cupboard, cabinet, bureau, wardrobe, showcase, etc. (2) strong box _or_ safe.

GUÌ₂ 跪 (IV) kneel. guìxia 跪 下 kneel down. Tā-guìzai-ner buqǐlai. 他 跪 在 那 兒 不 起 來. He knelt there and wouldn't get up.

GUÌ₁ 貴 (SV) expensive (opp. jiàn 賤, piányi 便宜).
(RE) expensive. Wǒ-mǎi-guì-le. 我 買 貴 了. (lit. I bought it expensively.) I paid too much for it.
(B-) high in social rank, an exultation used for forming polite forms referring to the person spoken to or a third person, honorable. (opp. jiàn 賤, bǐ 鄙). Guìguó shi-něiguó? 貴 國 是 那 國? What country are you from?

GUÌBĪN₄ 貴 賓 (N) honorable guest.

GUÌCHÙ₂ 貴 處 (N) (1) polite form for place of origin (city, district or province). Wǒ-méidào-guìchu-qùguo. 我 沒 到 貴 處 去 過. I have never been to your city. (2) polite form for department. Guìchu-chùzhǎng shì-shéi? 貴 處 處 長 是 誰? Who is the head of your department? (See: GUÌ 貴).

GUĬDÀO₃ 軌 道 (N) (1) tracks, railroad tracks. (2) orbit (of a satellite). (3) proper course of doing things. shàng-guǐdào 上 軌 道 be on the (right) track, have a determined course of action.

GUĪDÌNG₃ 規 定 (N) ruling (decision). Zhè-shi-wǒmen-zherde-guīdìng. 這 是 我 們 這 兒 的 規 定. This is our ruling.
(TV) render a decision, decide. Wǒmen-guīdìng yíge-rén chūwǔkuai-qián. 我 們 規 定 一 個 人 出 五 塊 錢. We have decided that each person will contribute five dollars.

GUÌFÁNGR₅ 櫃 房 兒 (N) office (of a store).

GUǏGUǏSUÌSUÌ₄ 鬼 鬼 祟 祟 (SV) demoniacal, devilish (implying tendency to hide something). Zhèige-ren guǐguǐsuìsuìde, yí-kànjian-wǒ jiu-pǎo. 這 個 人 鬼 鬼 祟 祟 的, 一 看 見 我 就 跑. This man is behaving in a devilish manner, as soon as he sees me he runs away.

GUǏHUÀ₅ 鬼 話 (N) dishonest talk.

GUÌHUĀ₅ 桂 花 (N) cassia or cinnamon blossom. (M: kē 棵).

GUǏJÌ₄ 詭 計 (N) crafty way (of accomplishing something).

GUĪJU₁ 規 矩 (N) (lit. compass and square) (1) rules of proper behavior, social etiquette, manners. Zhèige-háizi méi-guīju. 這 個 孩 子 沒 規 矩. This child has no manners. (2) rules of a community or organization. shǒu-guīju 守 規 矩 abide by rules. Qiānzì-bìxūyòng-mòshuǐ, zhè-shì-wǒmengōngzī-de-guīju. 簽 字 必 須 用 墨 水, 這 是 我 們 公 司 的 規 矩. It is a rule of our company that signatures must be in ink.

G

(SV) proper (in behavior, implying conformity to certain tradition). Zhèige-rén hěn-guī-ju, tā-bu-zuò-bu-yīngdāng zuò-de-shì. 這個人很規矩,他不作不應當作的事. This person abides closely by the rules; he never does anything one should not do. Nǐ-guīji-yidiǎnr.你規距一點兒. (lit. Abide by the rules a bit more.) Behave properly.

GUĬLIĂNR₅ 鬼臉兒 (N) (1) demoniacal-looking mask. dài-guǐliǎnr 戴鬼臉兒 wear a demoniacal-looking mask. (2) a face (as in make a face). Zuò-guǐliǎnr. 作鬼臉兒. Make a face.

GUĪLÜ₅ 規律 (N) regulation, rule.

GUĪMO₃ 規模 (N) scope, sphere (extent covered by an activity). Nèige-gōngsīde-guīmo hen-dà. 那個公司的規模很大. The scope of that company is very extensive.

GUĪNÜ₄ 閨女 (N) unmarried young woman, maiden, girl.

GUÌXÌNG₁ 貴姓 (N) (con. guì-xìng-shi-shénma? 貴姓是甚麼?). polite form of asking for surname of the person spoken to or a third person. Nín-guìxìng? 您貴姓? May I ask your name? (See: GUÌ 貴).

GUÌYÁNG₂ 貴陽 (PW) Kweiyang (capital of Kweichow province).

GUÌZHONG₃ 貴重 (SV) valuable. Tā-sòngle-yifènr-guìzhòngde-lǐwu. 他送了一份兒貴重的禮物. He gave a valuable present.

GUÌZHOU₂ 貴州 (PW) Kweichow province.

GUÌZI₃ 鬼子 (N) (lit. the sly ones) foreigner.

GUÌZI₃ 櫃子 (N) cupboard, closet.

GŪJI₃ 估計 (TV) estimate (numbers). (N) estimation (of numbers).

GŬLI₂ 鼓勵 (TV) encourage. (N) encouragement.

GŪLU₄ 咕嚕 (ONO) a gurgling sound. Dùzi-li-gūlu-gūlude-xiǎng. 肚子裏咕嚕咕嚕的響. There is a gurgling sound in the belly.

GÙLÜ₂ 顧慮 (TV) concerned (anxiety implied). Nǐ-bu-yào-gùlü-zhèixie-xiǎo-shì. 你不要顧慮這些小事. Don't be concerned over these small matters.

GŪMO₄ 估摸 (TV) Peip. estimate. Wǒ-gūmo děi-'èrshikuai-qián. 我估摸得二十塊錢. I estimate that it would take twenty dollars.

GŬN₃ 滾 (TV)(1) roll. Gǔn-xuěqiú shi-yuè-gǔn-yuè-dà. 滾雪球是越滾越大. In rolling a snow ball, the more it is rolled the bigger it gets. (2) scram (a term of extreme rudeness). Nǐ-gěi-wǒ-gǔn. 你給我滾. Scram! (for my sake). (3) boil.

G

gǔn-rè 滾熱 boiling hot. Shuǐ-gǔn-le. 水滾了. The water is boiling.

GŪNIANG₁ 姑娘 (N) girl.

GŬNKAI₅ 滾開 (RV) Get away from here! (a term of extreme rudeness).

GÙNR₃ 棍兒 see GÙNZI 棍子.

GÙNZI₃ 棍子 or GÙNR 棍兒 (N) rod, stick.(M: gēn 根).

GUO₁ 過 (P) used after a verb (1) indicates that an action has been experienced, in a question, have ... ever, in a negative with méi 沒, have never. Nǐ-qùguo-Zhōngguo-ma? 你去過中國嗎? Have you ever been to China? Wǒ-méi-qùguo. 我沒去過. I have never been there. Wǒ-chīguo-'liǎngcì-Zhōngguo-fàn. 我吃過兩次中國飯. I have eaten Chinese meals twice. (2) used with le 了, indicates completed action. A: Nín-chīguo-fàn-méi-you? B: Chīguole. A: 你吃過飯沒有? B: 吃過了. A: Have you eaten? B: Yes, I have eaten. (3) do over again. Zhèige děi-cóngxīn-zuò-guo. 這個得從新作過. This has to be done once again.

GUŌ₄ 鍋 (N) cooking vessel, pot, deep cooking pan. (M) a potful. yìguō-fàn 一鍋飯 a pot of rice.

GUÓ₁ 國 (N) country, nation, state. 'Měiguó-shì-yige-'dàguó. 美國是一個大國. America is a big country. (M) country, nation, state. Tā-huì-shuō-háoji'guó-huà. 他會說好幾國話. He can speak several languages. (B) (1) national. guóhuā 國花 national flower. (2) Chinese, domestic. (opp. yáng 洋). guó-chǎn 國產 Chinese or domestic products. guóhuò 國貨 Chinese or domestic goods. Měiguode-'guóhuò dàole-Zhōng-guo jiu-shi-'yánghuò. 美國的國貨到了中國就是洋貨. American domestic goods imported to China become foreign goods.

GUÒ₁ 過 (IV) (1) cross, go or come through or over. guò-jiē 過街 cross the street. guò-guān 過關 go through a guarded pass. Wǒmen-yi-guò-hé jiu-dào. 我們一過河就到. As soon as we cross the river, we will be there. (2) pass by. Wǒ-tiāntiān cóng-nǐ-men-jiā-ménkǒur-guò. 我天天從你們家門兒過. I pass by your home every day. Wàitou-guò-dàbīng-ne. 外頭過大兵呢. Soldiers are passing by outside. (3) pass an object, particularly money, from one person to another. Tāmen-mǎi-fáng guò-qián-le-ma? 他們買房過錢了嗎? In their purchase of the house was the financial transaction completed? (4) pass over the eye, inspect, look over. 'Qǐng-nín-guòguo-yǎn. 請您過過眼. Please look it over. (5) pass through <u>hands</u>. Zhéige-qìchē yǐjing-guòle-liǎngci-shǒu-le. 這個汽車己經過了兩次手了. This car has changed hands twice. (6) go beyond <u>a certain point of time, place or number</u>. Nǐde-bǎoxiǎn guò-qī-le. 你的保險過期了. Your insurance has elapsed. Guòle-dōngtian zài-shuō-ba. 過了冬天再說吧. (We'll) see about it after the winter. Yàoshi-guò-'shíkuai-qián, wo-jiu-bu-yào-le. 要是過十塊錢, 我就不要了. If it is over ten dollars then I don't want it. (7) exchange <u>of acts as indication of degree of friendship</u>. Wǒmen-liǎngge-ren bu-guò-huà. 我們兩個人不過話. (<u>lit</u>. We two do not exchange words.) We don't talk to each other. Tāmen-guò-wánxiào. 他們過玩笑. They joke with each other. (<u>They're good friends to the extent of accepting jokes on each other</u>). (8) spend <u>or</u> live a period of time. Nǐ-zuótian-wǎnshang zài-'nǎr-guòde-yè? 你昨天晚上在那兒過的夜? Where did you spend the night last night? Tā-jìnlái guòde-hěn-hǎo. 他近來過得很好. Recently he is having an easy

time. Zhè-'rìzi zěnma-guò? 這日子怎麼過? What kind of life are we leading? (9) celebrate, observe <u>a certain occasion</u>. Nín-jīnnian-shēngri zai-'nǎr-guò? 你今年生日在那兒過? Where are you going to celebrate your birthday? (SV) go beyond <u>what is accepta-ble or necessary</u>. Nǐde-huà shuōde-tài-guò-le. 你的話說得太過了. What you said was much beyond necessity.

GUÒ[2] 過 (RE) <u>in potential forms only, indicates an ability to win in competition</u>. Wǒ-pǎobuguò-ta. 我跑不過他. I cannot win over him in running. Shéi-shuōdeguò-tā? 誰說的過他? Who can win over him in talking?

GUÒBUQÙ[2] 過不去 (RV) (1) cannot cross, cannot go over <u>or</u> through. Qiántou chē-tài-duō, wǒmen-guòbuqù. 前頭車太多, 我們過不去. There are too many cars in front, we can't pass through. (2) <u>fig</u>. inability to go through a difficult event <u>or</u> period. Méi-yǒu-guò-buqùde-shì. 没有過不去的事. There isn't any event that won't blow over. (3) delib-erate unfriendly <u>or</u> hostile acts to frustrate a person. Tā-lǎo-gēn-wo-guòbuqù. 他老跟我過不去. He is always deliberately frustrating me.

GUÒDEQÙ₂ 過得去 (RV) passable, fairly good. Tāde-Zhōngwén hái-guòdeqù. 他的中文還過得去. His Chinese is fairly good.

GUÓDŪ₂ 國都 (N) national capital.

GUÒDÙ₅ 過渡 (B) (lit. crossing on a ferry) transition. guòdù-shíqī 過渡時期 period of transition.

GUÓFÁNG₄ 國防 (N) national defense.

GUÓFÁNGBÙ₃ 國防部 (N) department of defense.

GUÒFÈN₃ 過份 (SV) go beyond what is acceptable or necessary. Nǐ-tài-guòfèn-le. 你太過份了. You are going way beyond necessity. (cf: GUÒ 過). (AD) overly. Bú-yào-guòfènde-jǐnzhang. 不要過份的緊張. Don't be overly tense.

GUÓFÙ₂ 國父 (N) father of the country.

GUÓGĒ₁ 國歌 (N) national anthem.

GUÒHÒU₃ 過後 (TW) after an event has passed, afterwards. Dāngshí-hěn-qīngchu, guòhòu-jiu-wàng-le. 當時很清楚, 過後就忘了. At the time it was very clear, afterwards it was forgotten. Chī-le-fàn-guòhòu-zài-shuō. 吃了飯過後再說. We'll talk about it after eating.

GUÓHUÌ₃ 國會 (N) a national meeting or assembly, the Chinese National Assembly, Congress, Parliament, Diet, Chamber of Deputies.

GUÓHUÒ₂ 國貨 (N) domestic or Chinese products.

GUÓJÌ₂ 國際 (B-) international. guójì-guānxi 國際關係 international relations.

GUÓJIĀ₁ 國家 (N) country, nation, state. (B-) national. guójia-yínháng 國家銀行 a national government bank.

GUÒJIĂNG₂ 過獎 (IV) (lit. overly praised) You flatter me. A: Nínde-guóyǔ shuō-de-zhēn-hǎo. B: Guòjiang-guojiǎng. A: 你的國語説的真好. B: 過獎過獎. A: You speak Mandarin very well. B: You flatter me.

GUÒ-JIÉ₂ 過節 (VO) (1) (lit. pass the festival) after the festival. Děng-guòle-jié zai-qù. 等過了節再去. You better not go until after the festival. (2) celebrate the festival.

GUÒLAI₁ 過來 (RV) (1) come over. Qǐng-nǐ-guòlai bāngbang-máng. 請你過來幫幫忙. Please come over to give us a hand. Wǒ-yi-xià-chē, guò-lai-yíge-jǐngchá. 我一下車, 過來一個警察. As soon as I got out of the car a policeman came over. Nǐ-néng-bu-neng guò-zhèibiar-'lái-yixiàr? 你能不能過這邊兒來一下兒?

G

Could you come over for a while? (2) pass through certain experiences. Wǒmen-dou-shì-'guòlai-rén-le. 我們都是過來人了. We are all people who have come through it (experiences).

(RE) (1) indicates a movement from there to here. náguolai 拿過來 bring it over (here). (2) indicates a change from an undesirable to a desirable condition. Tā-shuō-le, wǒ-cái-míngbai-guolai. 他說了，我才明白過來. After he said it, then I began to understand it. Tāde-huài-xíguan-gǎi-buguolái-le. 他的壞習慣改不過來了. His bad habits can never be changed. (3) indicates to get all around to do something. Shì-tài-duō, wǒ-zuòbu-guolái. 事太多，我作不過來. There are too many things, I can't get around to all of them.

'GUÓLÌ₂ 國立 (B-) that which is established and operated by the national government. 'guólì-dàxué 國立大學 a national government university.

GUÓMÍN₂ 國民 (N) citizen of a nation. (cf: RENMÍN 人民).

GUÓMÍNDǍNG₂ 國民黨 (N) Kuomintang (Chinese Nationalist Party).

GUÓMINZHÈNGFǓ₂ 國民政府 (N) national government.

GUÓNÈI₃ 國內 (PW) within the country, internal, domestic (of

a country).

GUÒ-NIÁN₁ 過年 (VO) (1) pass into a New Year. Wǒ-guòle-nián-yǐ'hòu-qù. 我過了年以後去. I will go after New Year's. Nín-guò-nián-hǎo. 您過年好. (lit. How are you after passing into the New Year?) Happy New Year. (2) celebrate the New Year holiday period. Hěnduō-Zhōngguo-ren háishi guò-yīnlinián. 很多中國人還是過陰歷年. Many Chinese still celebrate the lunar calendar New Year.

GUÓQÍ₁ 國旗 (N) national flag.

GUÓQÌNGRÌ₁ 國慶日 (N) national holiday(such as Independence Day in the United States).

GUÒQU₁ 過去 (RV)(1) go over. Nǐ-guòqu-kànkan. 你過去看看. Go over to take a look. Gāng-guòqu-liǎngjia-fēijī. 剛過去兩架飛機. Two airplanes have just gone over. Nǐ-guò-'nèibianr-qù-ba. 你過那邊兒去吧. You go over to that side. Zhèige-qiáo, nǐ-kàn wǒmende-chē 'guòdequ-guòbuqù. 這個橋你看我們的車過得去過不去. Do you think our car can cross this bridge? (2) pass by. Yǔ-xiànzài-xiàde-hěn-dà, yìhuǐr-jiu-guòqu. 雨現在下得很大．一會兒就過去. It is raining heavily now, but it will be over in a while. (3) pass

away, die. Méi-xiăngdào tā-
zènma-niánqĭng jiu-guòqu-le.

没 想 到 他 這 麼 年
青 就 過 去 了 . I never
thought it could happen. He
died so young.

(RE) (1) indicates a movement
from here to there. Bă-qìchē-
kāiguoqu. 把 汽 車 開 過
去 . Drive the car over (there).

(2) indicates a change from a
conscious to an unconscious
state. Tā-hūnguoqu-le. 他 昏
過 去 了 . He fainted. (3)
indicates acceptability. Tā-
zhèizhong-zuòfa, wŏ-zhēn-kàn-
buguoqù. 他 這 種 作 法,
我 真 看 不 過 去 . I
cannot let pass his way of doing
it. Zhèiyàngrde-huà nĭ-shuōde-
guoqù-ma? 這 樣 兒 的 話
你 說 得 過 去 嗎 ? Can
you get by with this kind of
statement?

GUÒQÙ₂ 過 去 (TW) in the past.
Guòqù-wŏ-méi-'jiànguo-ta. 過
去 我 沒 見 過 他 . I
have never seen him before.
Zhè-dou-shi-guòqùde-shìqing.
這 都 是 過 去 的 事
情 . These are all events of
the past.

(RV) pass, be over. Shìqing-yĭ-
jing-guòqùle. 事 情 已 經
過 去 了 . The matter is
over.

GUŎRAN₁ 果 然 (MA) (lit. result right) as expected or anticipated (proving a correct opinion). Guŏrán-ni-shuōduìle. 果

然 你 說 對 了 . As an-
ticipated, what you said proved
to be correct. Nĭ-shuō-nèige-
shì-hóngde, wŏ-yí-kàn, guŏrán.
你 說 那 個 是 紅 的,
我 一 看, 果 然 . You
said that it is red. I looked, and
you are right.

GUÓTUI₅ 裹 腿 (N) leggings.

GUÓWÀI₃ 國 外 (PW) outside
the country, external, foreign
(of a country).

GUÓWÁNG₃ 國 王 (N) king.

GUÓWÉN₂ 國 文 (N)(1) Chinese
written language. Tā-guówén-
hĕn-hăo. 他 國 文 很 好 .
His Chinese (writing and/or
reading) is very good. (2) Chinese written language (as a
course in school). (M: táng 堂).
Jīntian wŏ-yŏu-yìtáng-guówén.
今 天 我 有 一 堂 國
文 . Today I have a class of
Chinese.

GUÓWÙYUÀN₃ 國 務 院 (N) (1)
State Department (U. S.) (2)
State Council (People's Republic
of China).

GUÓYŬ₁ 國 語 (N) Chinese national language, Mandarin (as
opposed to local dialects).

GUŎZI₁ 果 子 (N) fruit.

GUŎZIJIANG₃ 果 子 醬 (N)
jam, marmalade.

GÙRAN₁ 固 然 (MA) though of
course, naturally .   Nà-
gùrán-hăo, dàshi-tài-máfan. 那
固 然 好, 但 是 太 麻
煩 . (Though) of course that is
good, it is too much trouble.

G

G

GÙSHI₁ 故事 (N) story. Wǒ-gěi-háizimen shuō-gùshi. 我給孩子們說故事. I tell stories to children.

GÚTOU₃ 骨頭 (N) (1) bone. (M: kuài 塊). (2) strength in character. Tā-zhēn-you-gútou, dǎ-ta-yě-bu-shuō. 他真有骨頭，打他也不說. He really has guts, couldn't beat him into talking.

GŬWÉN₄ 古文 (N) (1) ancient literature. (2) writings in the style of ancient literature. (3) ancient forms of written characters.

GÙXIĀNG₄ 故鄉 (N) home (a person's place of origin).

GÙYI₅ 估衣 (N) second-hand clothing.

GÙYI₁ 故意 (MA) on purpose, intentionally. (syn. chéngxīn 成心, ān-xīn 安心). Tā-gùyì ràng-wo-shēngqì. 他故意讓我生氣. He made me angry on purpose. (IV) do something on purpose. Tā-nà-shi-gùyìde. 他那是故意的. He did it on pur-pose.

GÙYǑU₄ 固有 long established, inherent. Zhè-shì-Zhōngguo gùyǒude-fēngsu. 這是中國固有的風俗. This is a long established Chinese custom.

GŬZHǍNG₄ 股長 (N) head of a section, section chief.

GŬ-ZHǍNG₂ 鼓掌 (VO) clap hands, applaud. Dà-'jiā gǔle-yízhèn-zhǎng. 大家鼓了一陣掌. Everybody applauded.

GÙZHI₃ 固執 (SV) stubborn, unyielding, inflexible.

GŬZI₅ 骨子 (N) (1) framework, skeleton or internal structure. shàn-gŭzi 扇骨子 skeleton or framework of a fan. (2) reasons behind certain actions. Bù-zhīdào-gǔzi-lǐtou shì-zěnma-huí-shì. 不知道骨子裏頭是怎麼回事. I don't know what the reasons were behind such actions.

GŬZI₅ 穀子 (N) (1) grain (plant or seed). (2) millet (unhulled).

H

HĀCHI₄ 呵欠 (N) yawn. Tā-
zhí-dǎ-hāchi. 他直打呵
欠. He kept yawning.

HĀ'ĒRBĪN₃ 哈爾濱 (PW)
Harbin (city in Kirin province).

HĀI₂ 咳 or HĒI 嘿 (I) (1) used
informally to get someone's
attention. Hāi! Nǐ-shàng-nǎr?
咳！你上那兒? Hey!
Where are you going? Kàn-zhèi-
ge, hāi! 看這個，咳！
Look at this! Hey! (2) used to
show surprise, huh, what. Hāi!
Méi-xiǎngdào. 咳！没想到.
What! I didn't think of it.

HĀI₁ 還 (AD) (1) still as before.
Nǐ-hái-yào-qù-ma? 你還要
去嗎? Do you still want to
go? (2) again. Nǐ²zài-bu-tīng-
huà, wǒ-'hái-dǎ-ni. 你再不
聽話，我還打你.
If you don't obey again, I'll beat
you again. (cf: ZÀI 再). (3)
still more, more. Nǐ-hái-you-
duōshao? 你還有多少?
How much more do you have?
Wǒ-hái-děi-qù-sānci. 我還
得去三次. I still have to
go three more times. (4) rather,
fairly. Zhèige-ren hái-kéyi. 這
個人還可以. This
person is fairly good. (5) used
before a SV in comparison, even
(more). Tā-bǐ-wo-hái-qióng.

他比我還窮. He is
even poorer than I. (6) and also,
but also. Děi-hǎo, hái-děi-pián-
yi. 得好，還得便宜.
It has to be good, and it also has
to be cheap. Búdàn-kuài, hái-
fāngbian. 不但快，還方
便. It is not only fast but also
convenient. Chúle-niàn-shū, tā-
hái-zuò-shì. 除了念書，
他還作事.He not only
studies, but also works. (7) used
with or without ma 嗎 at the end
of a rhetorical question, why is
it necessary. Nà-hái-yòng-shuō
(-ma)哪還用説(嗎)?
Why is it necessary to say it?
Yǒu-qián hái-pà-mǎibuzháo(-ma)?
有錢還怕買不着
(嗎)? If one has money why
is it necessary to worry about
not being able to buy it? (cf:
HÁI...NE 還...呢, HÁISHI
還是).

HǍI₁ 海 (N) sea, ocean. (M: piàn
片). yipiàn-dà-hǎi 一片大
海 a sea, an ocean.
(B) large, vast. hǎiwǎn 海碗
large bowl.

HÀI₃ 害 (TV) (1) murder. Tā-
yào-ná-dúyào bǎ-nèige-rén hài-
le.他要拿毒藥把那
個人害了. He wanted to
murder that man with poison.

H

(2) harm someone. Bié-hài-ren. 别害人 . Don't harm people. or Don't murder people. (3) be affected by, suffer from. hài-xiū 害羞 (lit. be affected by shame) feel ashamed. (N) harm. Wǒ-shòule-tade-hàile. 我受了他的害了 . I have been caused harm by him.

HÀI₂ 咳 (I) indicates discouragement, regret, disgust, dismay, nuts, darn it. Hài! 'Yòu-cuò-le. 咳！又錯了 . Nuts! Wrong again. Hài! Zhè-zěnma-bàn? 咳！這怎麼辦 ? Darn it! What can be done now?

HǍI'ÀN₂ 海岸 (N) seashore, coast.

HǍIBIĀNR₂ 海邊兒 (N) seashore, beach.

HÀI-BÌNG₂ 害病 (VO) affect or contract an illness. Tā-qùnian hàile-yìchǎng-bìng. 他去年 害了一場病 . He had a period of illness last year.

HÁIBUSHI₂ ...(MA) 還不是 ... (嗎) used in a rhetorical question, isn't it still (as before). Háibu-shi-děi-wǒ-gěi-qián(-ma)? 還 不是得我給錢 (嗎)? Isn't it the same as before that I pay the money? Háibushi-àn-zhe-(lǎo)-fázi-bàn(-ma)? 還不 是按着老法子辦 (嗎)? Isn't it that it'll be done according to the old method?

HÀICHU₂ 害處 (N) harm. Zhèi-yàngr-bàn, méi-you-hàichu. 這 樣兒辦没有害處 . There is no harm in doing this

way.

HǍIDÀI₅ 海帶 (N) kelp (a kind of edible seaweed).

HǍIGUĀN₂ 海關 (N) (lit. sea-pass) (1) customhouse. (2) customs.

HǍIJŪN₂ 海軍 (N) navy.

'HǍILIÀNG₄ 海量 (N) (lit. capacity as big as sea) big capacity (for holding liquor or for accepting faults in others).

HǍINÁNDǍO₃ 海南島 (PW) Hai-nan Island.

HÁI...NE₂ 還 ... 呢 (S) (1) still going on. Tā-hái-shuì-jiào-ne. 他還睡覺呢 . He is still sleeping. (2) even to a certain extent. Tā-hái-huì-shuō-Ewén-ne. 他還會說俄 文呢 . He can even speak Russian. (Lián) 'wǒ-hái-xiǎng-mǎi-ne. (連) 我還想買 呢 . Even I want to buy it.(3) when hái 還 is stressed and used in a rhetorical question, how can you say that... 'Hái-bu-nánkàn-ne? 還不難看 呢 ? How can you say that it's not ugly? (4) used in a negative sentence, (not)yet. Hái-méi-ne. 還没呢 . Not yet. Wǒ-hái-bù-chī-fàn-ne. 我還不 吃飯呢 . I don't want to eat yet. Wǒ-hái-měi-gěi-qián-ne. 我還没給錢呢 . I have not paid yet. (cf: HÁI 還).

HÀI-PÀ₁ 害怕 (VO) be afraid, scared. Tā-yi-tīng, jiu-hàile-pà-le. 他一聽，就害了 怕了 . As soon as he heard,

he became afraid.
(SV) be scared, fearful. Wǒ-hěn-
hàipà. 我 很 害 怕 . I am
very scared.

HÀI-SÀO₃ 害 臊 (VO) shy. Nǐ-
hài-shénma-sào ne? 你 害
甚 麼 臊 呢 ? Why are you
so shy?

HÁISHEN₅ 海 參 (N) sea cucumber (a kind of sea food).

HÁISHI₁ 還 是 (AD) (1) still as
before. Tā-háishi-nàyàngr. 他
還 是 那 樣 兒 . He is
still the same as before. (2) do
what was originally suggested
after considering other possi-
bilities, had better. Wǒ-háishi-
qu-ba. 我 還 是 去 吧 . I
had better go. (3) used in the
second of two parallel clauses
to mark a choice type question,
or (in a question). 'Nǐ-qù háishi-
wǒ-qù? 你 去 還 是 我
去 ? Will you go or will I go?
(cf: HÁI 還).

HÁISHI...(HÁI)SHI...₁ 還 是 ...
(還) 是 ... (S) or (in a question) or shì...(hái)shi... 是 ...
(還) 是 ... Nǐ-háishi-qù-(hái)
shi-bú-qù? 你 還 是 去 (還)
是 不 去 ? Are you going or
not?

HÁITÁNG₅ 海 棠 (N) crab-apple,
cherry-apple (flower, fruit or
plant).

HÁIWÀI₂ 海 外 (PW) abroad. Tā-
zài-hǎiwài zhùle-hěn-duōnián.
他 在 海 外 住 了 很
多 年 . He lived abroad for
many years.

HĂIWÈI₃ 海 味 (N) (lit. sea
taste) sea food.

HĂIXIÁ₄ 海 峽 (N) strait (between two pieces of land).

HÀI-XIŪ₂ 害 羞 (VO) feel a-
shamed.

HĂIYÁ₃ 海 牙 (PW) The Hague.

HÀI-YĂN₄ 害 眼 (VO) have an
eye illness.

HÁIYOU₁ 還 有 (MA) further-
more, there is another thing.
Bié-pǎo, háiyou, xiǎoxin-qìchē.
别 跑 . 還 有 , 小 心 汽
車 . Don't run, another thing,
be careful of cars.

HÁIZI₁ 孩 子 (N) child.

HĂIZHÉ₅ 海 蜇 (N) sea blubber
(a kind of edible jellyfish).

HÁMA₄ 蛤 蟆 (N) frog, toad.

HÁN₄ 含 (TV) (1) or HÉN 含 hold
something completely in one's
mouth or hold back tears. Tā-
zuǐli-hánzhe-yikuai-táng. 他
嘴 裏 含 着 . 一 塊 糖 .
He is holding a piece of candy in
his mouth. Tā-hánzhe-yǎnlèi.
他 含 着 眼 淚 . He is
holding back the tears. (2) contain (ideas, meanings, etc.).
Zhèjiu-huà hánzhe-hěn-duō-yìsi.
這 句 話 含 着 很 多
意 思 . This sentence has
many meanings.

HĂN₁ 喊 (TV) (1) shout. (syn.
jiào 叫 , rǎng 嚷). Bié-hǎn.
别 喊 . Don't shout. (2) call
someone. (syn. jiào 叫). Tā-
hǎn-nǐ-ne. 他 喊 你 呢 .
He is calling you.

H

HÀN₂ 汗 (N) sweat, perspiration. Wǒ-chū-hàn-le. 我 出 汗 了. I am perspiring.

HÀN₄ 銲 (TV) weld, solder.

HÀN₂ 漢 (B-) (1) China. Hànmín-zú 漢 民 族 Chinese race. (2) Han dynasty. Hànhuà 漢 畫 paintings of the Han dynasty.

HÀN₂ 和 see HÉ 和.

HÀNCHAO₂ 漢 朝 (TW) Han dynasty.

HÁNCHEN₄ 寒 磣 (SV) Peip. (1) ugly. (2) shameful.

HÀNDÀO₅ 旱 道 (N) road, land route.

HÁNG₂ 行 (M) (1) line, row, column. Nèige-zì zài-dì'erháng. 那 個 字 在 第 二 行. The character is in the second line. Zhòng-yiháng-shù. 種 一 行 樹. Plant a row of trees. (2) line of business or study. Wǒ-men-zhèi-yiháng, rén-bu-shǎo. 我 們 這 一 行 , 人 不 少 . There are many people in our line.

(N) trade, profession. Tā-gǎi-háng-le. 他 改 行 了. He changed his profession.

(-B) firm, business establishment. qìchēháng 汽 車 行 an automobile dealer, a garage. yángháng 洋 行 a western type of business establishment. yín-háng 銀 行 bank.

HÁNG₃ 行 (SP) used before a number to indicate the sequence of brothers and/or sisters. Wǒ-háng-èr. 我 行 二 . I am the

second one (among our brothers and/or sisters). (cf: PÁI 排).

HÁNGHUÀ₄ 行 話 (N) language peculiar to a particular trade or profession, jargon.

HÁNGJIA₄ 行 家 (N) member of a special trade or profession, a specialist.

HÁNGKŌNG₂ 航 空 (B) aviation, aeronautical. hángkōngxìn 航 空 信 airmail letter. háng-kōng-yóupiào 航 空 郵 票 airmail stamp.

HÁNGKŌNGXIǍOJIĚ₃ 航 空 小 姐 (N) airline stewardess.

HÁNGKŌNGXÌN₃ 航 空 信 (N) airmail letter.(M: fēng 封).

HÁNGSHI₂ 行 市 (N) market price (value as determind by the supply and demand in the market). méi-hángshi 沒 行 市 no true market value.

HÁNGUO₃ 韓 國 (PW) Korea (used for South Korea). (cf: CHÁO-XIǍO 朝 鮮).

HÁNGZHOU₁ 杭 州 (PW) Hang-chow (city in Chekiang province).

HÁNHU₃ 含 糊 (SV) (1) vague. Tāde-huà shuōde-hěn-hánhu. 他 的 話 説 得 很 含 糊 . What he said is pretty vague. (2) hesitant. Yīnwèi-tài-guì, suóyi-wǒ-yǒu-yidianr-hánhule. 因 為 太 貴 , 所 以 我 有 一 點 兒 含 糊 了 . I'm a little hesitant because it's too expensive.

HÁNJIÀ₂ 寒 假 (N) winter vacation (in school).

ˈHĂNJIÀO₅ 喊叫 (TV) shout, scream.

HÀNKOU₁ 漢口 (PW) Hankow (city in Hupeh province).

HÁNLĚNG₅ 寒冷 (SV) cold (weather).

HÁNMAO₄ 汗毛 (N) soft hairs of the human body (hair on top of the head, eyebrows, eyelashes, whiskers, beard; underarm hair and pubic hair excluded).

HÀNREN₃ 漢人 (N) Chinese people.

HÀNSĂN₅ 旱傘 (N) parasol.

HÀNSHĂN₄ 汗衫 (N)(1) shirt. (2) underwear. (M: jiàn 件).

HÁNSHŬBIĂO₃ 寒暑表 (N) thermometer (for the weather).

HÁNYANG₅ 涵養 (N) cultivated or natural ability to face troubles or take abuse without being upset emotionally. Zhèige-rén zhēn-yǒu-hányang. 這個人真有涵養. He is not easily upset.

HÀNYŬ₃ 漢語 (N) Chinese language (technical term).

HÀNZĀI₄ 旱災 (N) drought. Nèr-nào-hànzāi. 那兒鬧旱災. There is a drought there.

HÀNZÌ₃ 漢字 (N) Chinese character.

HĂO₁ 好 (SV) (1) good, well, nice. (opp. huài 壞). Tiānqi-hěn-hǎo. 天氣很好. The weather is good. Míngtian-qú hǎo. 明天去好. It's good to go tomorrow. (2) used as a greeting. Nín-hǎo! 您好!

How are you!

(IV)(1) ready, done. Fàn-hǎo-le. 飯好了. The food is ready. (2) get well, repaired. Děng-ta hǎole-bìng zàishuō-ba. 等他好了病再說吧. Let's talk about it after he recovers. (RE) (1) good, well, Yàoshi-zuò jiu-zuòhǎo-le. 要是作就作好了. If you do it, do it well. (2) get well, recovered, repaired. Wǒ-bǎ-tāde-dìng zhì-hǎo-le. 我把他的病治好了. I cured his sickness. (3) finish something satisfactorily. Nèifeng-xìn nǐ-xiěhǎo-le-ma? 那封信你寫好了嗎? Have you finished (writing) that letter?

(AD) (1) used in the last of a series of clauses, so that it will be possible to... Nǐ-gěi-wǒ-qián, wǒ-hǎo-qu-mǎi. 你給我錢,我好去買. (You) give me money so that it will be possible for me to buy it. (2) followed by a SV, to express unexpected or unusual excess, very, quite, so. Jīntian hǎo-lěng. 今天好冷. Today is quite cold. Nǐ-hǎo-dà-dǎnzi. 你好大胆子. You are so daring. (3) used before an unstressed bu 不 and followed by certain SV, the negative sense is lost. If bu 不 is stressed, the negative sense remains, very, quite. Wǒ-xīnli-hǎo(-bu)-gāoxìng. 我心裏好(不)高興. I am very happy (in my heart). Tā-hǎo-

H

'bùgāoxing. 他 好 不 高 興 .
He is so unhappy.

(I) (1) used at the beginning of a
sentence to agree to a suggestion, good; or when spoken in a
lower pitch and with a hoarse
quality to show surprise, gosh.
Hǎo, jiù-nènma-bàn. 好 , 就
那 麼 辦 . Good, let's do it
that way. Hǎo! Nà-dèi-duōshao-
qián! 好 ! 那 得 多 少 錢 !
Gosh! How much money will that
cost! (2) used between two independent clauses to show surprise, gosh. Wǒ-yikàn, hǎo,
dōu-zǒu-le. 我 一 看 , 好 ,
都 走 了 . I took a look,
gosh, everybody has left. (3)
Peip. used at the end of a sentence with a low pitch to indicate
doubtfulness, I don't believe it.
Nǐ-bu-zhīdào,(ke-) hǎo. 你 不
知 道 (可) 好 . You don't
know. I don't believe it.
(B) used with TV or IV to form
SV. (opp. nán 難).(1) good to.
hǎotīng 好 聽 good to listen to.
(2) easy to. hǎomài 好 賣 easy
to sell.

used before an indefinite number,
quite a few. hǎoxiē 好 些 quite
a few. hǎojitiān 好 幾 天
quite a few days.

HÀO₂ 好 (AV) be fond of, be addicted to. Tā-hào-hē-jiǔ. 他
好 喝 酒 . He likes to drink.
HÀO₁ 號 (M) (1) one of a series,
number, as in No. 2. Nǐ-diàn-
huà duōshaohào? 你 電 話
多 少 號 ? What is your

telephone number? (2) date of
the month. èryuè-wǔhào 二 月
五 號 February 5th.
HÀO₄ 號 (N) bugle. chuī-hào 吹
號 blow a bugle.
HǍOBÀN₁ 好 辦 (SV) easy to
manage, easy to do. Zhèijian-
shì bu-hǎobàn. 這 件 事 不
好 辦 .This is difficult to do.
HǍOBÀNTIĀN₅ 好 半 天 (N)
(lit. a good half a day) quite a
long while (less than a few hours).
HǍOBUHAO₂ 好 不 好 used at
the end of a sentence to ask for
agreement, how about it? Zhèiyangr bobuhao? 這 樣 兒
好 不 好 ? How about this
way?
HǍOCHĪ₁ 好 吃 (SV) (1) good to
eat, palatable, delicious. (2)
easy to eat.
HǍOCHU₁ 好 處 (N) (opp. huài-
chu 壞 處).(1) good point,
strong point, desirable quality.
Tāde-hǎochu hěn-duō. 他 的 好
處 很 多 . He has a lot of
good points. (2) benefit. Zuò-
zhèige-shì méi-hǎochu. 作 這
個 事 沒 好 處 . There
is no benefit in doing this.
HǍODǍI₃ 好 歹 (N) (1) or HǍO-
HUÀI 好 壞 good and bad.
Zhèi-háizi bu-zhīdao-hǎodǎi. 這
孩 子 不 知 道 好 歹 .
This child can't differentiate between good and bad. Tā-mǎi-de
huàr hǎodǎi-dōu-yǒu. 他 買
的 畫 兒 好 歹 都 有 .
There are good ones and bad ones
in the paintings he bought. (2)

hold quality as of little importance, anyway. Nǐ-hǎodǎi-gěi-
ta-yidiǎnr jiu-xíng-le. 你 好
歹 給 他 一 點 兒 就
行 了 . Disregard whether
it's good or bad, give him a
little, anyway.

HĂODE₂ 好 的 used to agree to
a suggestion or accept an order,
all right.

HĂODUŌ₂ 好 多 (N) used with
or without a M, very many,
very much. Tā-mǎile-hǎoduō
(zhāng)-huàr. 他 買 了 好
多 (張) 畫 兒 He bought a
lot of paintings.

HĂOFEI₃ 耗 費 (TV) waste.
hàofei-jīngshen 耗 費 精 神
waste(mental) energy.

HĂOHUÀI₃ 好 壞 see HĂODĂI 好
歹 (N) (1).

HĂOJǏ₁ 好 幾 (NV) several (a
little more than jǐ 幾). hǎojǐ-
gè 好 幾 個 several (units).
hǎojǐbǎi 好 幾 百 several
hundreds. hǎojǐtiān 好 幾 天
several days.

'HÁOJIÉ₄ 豪 傑 (N) hero.

HĂOKÀN₁ 好 看 (SV) (1) pretty,
good looking, beautiful. (2) easy
to look, see or read.

HĂOLÁIWÙ₂ 好 萊 塢 (PW)
Hollywood.

HÀOMĂR₂ 號 碼 兒 (N) numer-
als assigned for identification,
such as a telephone number, motor's serial number, etc.

HÀOQÍ₃ 好 奇 (SV) curious
(person).

HÀOQÍXĪN₃ 好 奇 心 (N) curiousity.

HÀOR₂ 號 兒 (M) size which is
standard, as for shoes, clothes,
etc., or for things which are
classified small, medium and
large. Nǐde-xié-jǐhàor? 你 的
鞋 幾 號 兒 ? What size are
your shoes?

HĂO(BU)RÓNGYI₃ 好 (不) 容 易
(AD) not easy to, difficult. Nín-
hǎo(bu)róngyi-lái-yicì, duō-
wánr-yihuir zài-zǒu. 你 好 (不)
容 易 來 一 次 , 多 玩
兒 一 會 兒 再 走 .It's
not easy for you to come, enjoy
yourself a little longer before
you go. Tā-hǎo(bu)-róngyi-xué-
huì-le.他 好 (不) 容 易 學
會 了 . It's difficult for him
to learn it.

'HĂOSHŎU₃ 好 手 (N) (lit. good
hand) (1) good worker. (M: bǎ
把). Zuò-shì, ta-shi-yibǎ-
hǎoshǒu. 作 事 他 是 一
把 好 手 . At work, he is a
good hand. (2) skilled craftsman,
accomplished artist, master.
Zhèi-huàr yídìng-shi-hǎoshǒu-
huà-de. 這 畫 兒 一 定
是 好 手 畫 的 . This
painting must have been done by
a master.

HĂOSHUŌ₁ 好 說 (IV) (1) a polite
reply to praise, you flatter me.
A: Nínde-huàr huàde-zhēn-hǎo.
B: 'Hǎoshuō-hǎoshuō. A: 您 的
畫 兒 畫 得 真 好 . B: 好
說 好 說 . A: Your paintings
are very good. B: Thank you for
your commendation. (2) talk
over, discuss or negotiate a

H

problem nicely. Yǒu-huà-hǎo-
shuō, bié-shēng-qì. 有話好
說別生氣. If you have
something to talk about, talk
nicely and don't get angry.

HǍOTING₁ 好聽 (SV) (1) pleasant
to listen to. Tāde-huà hǎotīng.
他的話好聽. His
words are pleasant to listen to.
(2) easy to hear.

HǍOXIANG (...SHIDE)₂ 好像
(...似的) (MA) it seems
that, appears to be. Tā-hǎo-
xiàng-bu-zhīdào(shide). 他好
像不知道(似的). It
seems that he did not know. Tā-
hàoxiang Fàguoren-(shide). 他
好像法國人(似的).
He appears to be a Frenchman.

HǍOXIE₁ 好些 (NU) used with
or without M, a good many, a
great deal of. Tā-yǒu-hǎo'xiē
(ge)-péngyou. 他有好些
(個)朋友. He has a good
many friends. Wǒde-Zhong-
guo-zì wàngle-hǎoxiē. 我的
中國字忘了好些.
I forgot a great deal of my
Chinese characters. (See: XIE
些).

HǍOYÌ₃ 好意 (N) kindness, good
intention. Xièxie-nínde-hǎoyì.
謝謝您的好意 Thank
you for your good intention.
(AD) with good intention. Wǒ-
hǎoyì-gàosong-ta, ta-bu-zhīqing.
我好意告訴他,他
不知情. I told him with
good intention, but he doesn't
appreciate it.

HǍOZAI₃ 好在 (MA) fortunately.
(syn. xìngkui 幸虧). Wǒ-bǎ-
pí'pāo-diū-le. Hǎozai-lǐtou qián-
bu-duō.我把皮包丟了.
好在裏頭錢不多.
I lost my wallet. Fortunately
there was not much money in it.

HǍOZHAO₄ 號召(TV) attract a fol
lowing through incitement of certain emotions,incite. Tā-kéyi-
'hàozhào-yiqì. 他可以號
召一氣. He can attract a
following. Tā-dǎzhe-mínzhǔde-
qízi, wèi-zìjǐde-lìyi-hàozhao.他
打著民主的旗子,為
自己的利益號召.
Waving the flag of democracy he
incites a following for his own
private benefit.

HǍOZI₄ 耗子 (N) Peip. rat,
mouse. (syn. lǎoshǔ 老鼠).

HE₂喝 or HUO 嚄 (I) indicates
surprise at some happening,
wow, gee. Hē! Zěnma-zènma-
guì! 喝! 怎麽這麽貴!
Wow! How come it is so expensive!

HE₁ 喝 (TV) (1) drink. Nǐ-hē-chá-
hē-kāfēi? 你喝茶喝咖
啡? Do you drink tea or coffee?
(2) drink something provided or
paid for by someone else. Bié-
ren-chī-ta-hē-ta, ye-bu-shuō-
ta-hǎo.別人吃他喝他,
也不説他好. The peo-
ple who were dined and wined by
him won't say nice things about
him either.
(N) something to drink. Yǒu-chī-
you-hē zhāo-shenma-jí? 有吃

有 喝,着 甚 麼 愁? There are food and drink, why should you worry?

HÉ₁ 河 (N) river. (M: tiáo 條). Héli yú-hěn-duō. 河 裏 魚 很 多. There are plenty of fish in the river.

HÉ₃ 合 (TV) (1) be in accord with, agree with. Tāmende-yìjian bu-hé. 他 們 的 意 見 不 合. Their opinions are not in accord. hé-lǐ 合 理 in accord with principle or reason, reasonable. hé-lóji 合 邏 選 in accord with logic, logical. hé-shíjì 合 實 際 in accord with reality, practical. hé-shēnfen 合 身 份 in accord with one's status. Tāde-sīxiang bù-hé-shí-dài. 他 的 思 想 不 合 時 代. His thought is not in accord with the trend. (2) combine. Bǎ-zhèi-liǎngbān hézai-yīkuàir. 把 這 兩 班 合 在 一 塊 兒. Combine these two classes (together). Wǒmen-héqilai lìliang-jiu-dà-le. 我 們 合 起 來 力 量 就 大 了. If we combine (our forces), our strength will be greater. (3) close (usually the eyes, books, or something with two flat pieces). hé-yǎn 合 眼 close eyes. héshang-shū 合 上 書 close books (physically). (cf: BI 閉 GUAN 關). (4) total up to, equal to, be equivalent to. Lián-gōng-dài-liào yígòng-hé-wǔshikuai-qián. 連 工 帶 料 一 共 合 五 十 塊

錢. Labor and materials altogether total fifty dollars. Yí-kuài-Měijīn hé-sānbǎi-liùshikuai Rìběn-qián. 一 塊 美 金 合 三 百 六 十 塊 日 本 錢. One American dollar is equal to three hundred and sixty Japanese Yen.

(AD) in joint action, together. Tāmen-liǎngjia hé-mǎile-yìsuǒ-fángzi. 他 們 兩 家 合 買 了 一 所 房 子. The two families bought a house together.

HÉ₃ 和 (IV) (1) make peace during a war. Yǒuren-yào-jìxu-dǎ, yǒu-ren-yòu-hé. 有 人 要 繼 續 打, 有 人 要 和. Some people want to continue to fight, some want to make peace. (2) come to a draw (in a board game). Nèipan-qí hé-le. 那 盤 棋 和 了. That chess game was a draw. (See: BUHÉ 不 和).

HÉ₂ 和 or HÀN 和 (CV) with. Bié-hé-ta-kāi-wánxiào. 别 和 他 開 玩 笑. Don't joke with him. Nǐ-hé-ta-yòng-Zhōng-guo-hua-shuō. 你 和 他 用 中 國 話 说. (You) speak with him in Chinese. Zhè-jiu-hé-fàng-jià-yiyàng. 這 就 和 放 假 一 樣. This is the same as having a vacation.

used to join coordinate expressions, and. Tā-jiu-huì-chī-fàn, shuì-jiào, hé-shēng-qì. 他 就 會 吃 飯, 睡 覺 和 生 氣. She only knows how to eat, sleep and get mad. (cf: GEN 跟).

H

'HÉ'ĀI₅ 和藹 (SV) amiable.

HÉBÀ₄ 河壩 (N) dam (across a river). (M: dào 道).

HÉBAOR₅ 荷包兒 (N)small purse.

HÉBĚI₂ 河北 (PW) Hopeh province.

HÉBÌ₃ 何必 (AD) why must it be so (an indirect request to stop certain actions). Nà-hébì-ne? 那何必呢? Why is it necessary? Nín-hébì-kèqi? 您何必客氣? Why be so formal? (Please don't be so formal).

HÉBÌNG₃ 合併 (TV) combine. Běnlái-shì-liǎngge-gōngsī,xiàn-zài-hébìng-le. 本來是兩個公司.現在合併了. Originally they were two companies, but now they have merged.

HÉBULÁI₃ 合不來 (RV) be unable to get along with someone. Wǒ-gen-ta-hébulái.我跟他合不來. I cannot get along with him.

HÉBUZHÁO₃ 合不着 (RV) be not worthwhile.

HÉ-CǍI₄ 喝采 (VO) shout of applause, such as to shout Bravo!

HÉCHÀNG₃ 合唱 (N) song sung by more than one voice. (TV) sing together, sing in chorus.

HÉDUI₃ 核對 (TV) check over item by item.

HÉ'ĚRMÉNG₄ 荷爾蒙 (N) hormone.

HÉ-FǍ₃ 合法 (VO) be within the confines of law, legal.

HÉ-GÉ₃ 合格 (VO) meet an acceptable standard, qualify.

HÉHUĀ₄ 荷花 (N) lotus plant or flower. (M: duǒ 朵).

HÉ-HUǑ₃ 合夥 (VO) in partnership in an undertaking or venture. Wǒmen-héhuǒ-zuò-mǎimai. 我們合夥作買賣. We are in business together.

HĒI₂ 嘿 see HĀI 咳.

HĒI₁ 黑 (SV) (1) black. (opp. bái 白). hēi-yánse 黑顏色 black color. (2) dark (opposite of fair). (opp. bái 白).Tā-bǐ-wǒ-hēi. 他比我黑. He is darker than I am. (3) dark (opposite of bright). (opp. liàng 亮). Tiān-hái-méi-hēi-ne. 天還沒黑呢. It (the sky) isn't dark yet. (N) black spot. Nǐ-liǎnshang yǒu-yikuài-hēi. 你臉上有一塊黑. There is a black spot on your face.

HĒI'ÀN₂ 黑暗 (SV) lit. or fig. dark (opposite of bright). (opp. guāngming 光明). hēi'àn-shídài 黑暗時代 the Dark Ages.

HĒIBÁI₃ 黑白 (N) black and white. Nèige-diànyǐngr shi-hēi-bái-de-shì-cǎisè-de? 那個電影兒是黑白的是彩色的? Is that picture in black and white or in color? (2) right or wrong. Tā-bu-fēn-hēibái, bǎ-háizi-dou-dǎ-le. 他不分黑白把孩

子 都 打 了 . He doesn't distinguish right or wrong, he spanks all the children.

HEIBĂN₂ 黑 板 (N) blackboard (M: kuài 塊).

HEIDÒU₅ 黑 豆 (N) black bean.

HEILÓNGJIANG₂ 黑 龍 江 (PW) Heilungkiang province.

HEIMÙ₄ 黑 幕 (N) (lit. behind a dark curtain) a covert, sinister act.

HEISHÌ₃ 黑 市 (N) black market.

HEI-XĪN₅ 黑 心 (VO) betray moral obligations. Tā-hēile-xīn-le. 他 黑 了 心 了 . He is a betrayer. Wǒ-bu-zuò-hēixīn-shì. 我 不 作 黑 心 事 . I don't do anything which betrays my obligations.

HÉKŬ₃ 何 苦 (AD) (lit. why suffer) why. Nǐ-hékŭ-ràng-ta-zhāo-jí? 你 何 苦 讓 他 着 急 ? Why do you make him worry? Nǐ-zhè-shi-hékŭ? 你 這 是 何 苦 ? Why are you doing this (and making yourself suffer)?

HÉLÁN₂ 荷 蘭 (PW) Holland.

HÉ-LǏ₂ 合 理 (VO) (lit. coincide with reason or logic) reasonable, logical.

HÉLIÚ₄ 河 流 (N) river (in general).

HĚN₂ 狠 (IV) hardened in feeling, callous. Tā-xīn-hěn. 他 心 狠 . He is callous. Wǒ-yi-hěn-xīn, 'dǎle-ta-yidùn. 我 一 狠 心 , 打 了 他 一 頓 . I hardened my feelings and gave him a beating.

HĚN₁ 很 (AD) used before a SV or AV, exceedingly, extremely, very, very much. Fángzi-hěn-dà. 房 子 很 大 . The house is very big. Tā-hěn-yǒuyìsi. 他 很 有 意 思 . He is very interesting. Wǒ hěn 'yuànyi qù. 我 很 顧 意 去 . I like to go very much.

used before yǒu 有 and an indefinite number, quite a number or quantity of. Tā-hěn-yǒu-ji-suǒr-'fángzi. 他 很 有 幾 所 兒 房 子 . He has quite a number of houses. Tā-hěn-yǒu-yidianr-qián. 他 很 有 一 點 兒 錢 . He has quite a bit of money.

used after de 得 at the end of a sentence, very, very much. Fēi-jī kuàidehěn. 飛 機 快 得 很 . Airplanes are very fast. (See: DEHEN 得 很).

HÈN₂ 恨 (TV) hate. Méi-rén-hèn-ta. 沒 人 恨 他 . Nobody hates him.

HÉNAN₂ 河 南 (PW) Honan province.

HÈNBUDE₂ 恨 不 得 (AV) wish to do something which cannot be done right now. Wǒ-hènbude-lì-kè-jiu-qù. 我 恨 不 得 立 刻 就 去 . I wish I could go immediately.

HÉNEI₂ 河 内 (PW) Hanoi.

HENG₃ 哼 (I) (1) indicates contempt or disapproval, humph, bah. Heng, bié-tí-le. 哼 , 別 提 了 . Humph, don't bring that (subject) up. Heng, suànle-

H

ba. 哼，算了吧. Humph,
forget about it. (2) implies a
slightly superior attitude, ha,
aha, ahem. Heng, tā-zhīdao-
shénma? 哼，他知道甚
麼? Aha, what does he know?
Heng, tā-gǎn! 哼，他敢!
Ha, how could he dare!

HĒNG₄ 哼 (ONO) hum. Tā-bǎ-
nèige-gēr hēngle-heng. 他把
那個歌兒哼了哼.
He hummed a little bit of that
song. (cf: HĒNGHENG 哼哼).

HÉNG₃ 橫 (IV) place something
crosswise or horizontally (a-
cross the long or vertical axis).
(opp. shù 豎). Bǎ-zhèige-zhuō-
zi héngguolai. 把這個桌
子橫過來. Turn this
table and place it crosswise.
Zhūngwén yě-néng-héngzhe-xiě.
中文也能橫着寫.
Chinese can also be written a-
cross the page.

HÈNG₃ 橫 (SV) overbearing, tyrannical. Zhèige-ren zhēn-
hèng. 這個人真橫.
This person is really tyrannical.

HÉNGBĪN₃ 橫濱 (PW) Yokoha-
ma.

HĒNGHENG₄ 哼哼 (ONO)groan,
moan. Tā-lèide zhí-hēngheng.
他累得直哼哼. He
was so tired that he groaned.
(cf: HĒNG 哼).

HÉNGSHI₃ 橫是 (MA) Peip.
most likely, must be, must have.
Héngshi-tā-qùle. 橫是他
去了. He must have gone,
I think.

HÉNGSHÙ₃ 橫豎 (MA) (lit.
horizontal and vertical) in any
case.

HÈNIÁNPIÀNR₂ 賀年片兒
(N) New Year greeting card.
(M: zhāng 張).

HÉNJI₃ 痕跡 (N) mark, trace.
Tōu-'dōngxi-de-shíhou, qiānwàn-
bié-liú-hénji. 偷東西的
時候，千萬別留痕
跡. When you steal, never
leave any trace.

'HÉPÍNG₂ 和平 (N) peace. shì-
jiè-hépíng 世界和平 world
peace.
(SV) peaceful. Wǒ-xīnli-hěn-'hé-
píng. 我心裏很和平.
I feel very peaceful (in my heart).
(AD) peacefully. Yòngbuzháo-dǎ,
kéyi-hépíng-jiějué. 用不着
打，可以和平解決.
There is no need to fight, it can
be peacefully settled.

HÉQI₂ 和氣 (SV) agreeable,
friendly, congenial (of a person
or his manner). Tā-duì-rén hen-
héqi. 他對人很和氣.
He is very friendly to people.

HÉR₃ 盒兒 or HÉZI 盒子
(N) box. zhǐhér 紙盒兒 pa-
per box.
(M) box of. yìhér-bǐnggān 一盒
兒餅乾 a box of cookies.

HÉSHANG₄ 和尚 (N) Buddhist
monk. (M: wèi 位).

HÉSHÌ₂ 合適 (SV) suitable, fit-
ting. Zhèisuo-fángzi wǒmen-zhù
zhèng-héshì. 這所房子
我們住正合適.
This house is just right for us to

live in. Zhèiyangr-bàn yǒu-méi-
you-shénma-bu-hé'shìde-dìfang?

這 樣 兒 辦 有 沒 有 甚
麼 不 合 適 的 地 方?
Is there anything wrong in doing
it this way? Wǒ-dùzi yǒu-yi-
diǎnr-bu-héshì. 我 肚 子 有
一 點 兒 不 合 適.
There is something wrong with
my stomach.

(VO) suit (a person's wish or a
certain situation). Hǎoxiàng-
'zěnma-bàn yě-bu-néng-hé-nǐ-
de-shì. 好 像 怎 麼 辦
也 不 能 合 你 的 適.
It seems that no matter how it
is done it won't suit you.

HÉSUÀN₃ 合 算 (SV) gain, profit by exchange, barter or business transaction.   Wǔkuai-qián mǎi-zhèige bu-hé-
suàn. 五 塊 錢 買 這 個
不 合 算. Buying this at
five dollars is no bargain. Zhèi-
yangr-huàn, tā-hésuàn. 這 樣
換, 他 合 算. If we ex-
change it like this, it will be to
his benefit.

HÉTAO₄ 核 桃 (N) walnut.

HÉTONG₂ 合 同 (N) contract.
dìng-hétong 訂 合 同 agree
on the terms of a contract. lì-
hétong 立 合 同 draw up a
contract. qiān-hétong 簽 合
同 sign a contract.

HÉXĪN₅ 核 心 (N) core (of a
problem or idea). Zhèi-shi-wèn-
tíde-héxīn. 這 是 問 題 的
核 心. This is the core of
the problem.

HÉZI₃ 盒 子 see HÉR 盒 兒.

HÉZI₃ 核 子 (N) nucleus. hézǐ-
néng 核 子 能 nuclear energy.
hézǐwǔqì 核 子 武 器 nuclear
weapons. hézǐ-zhànzhēng 核
子 戰 爭 nuclear war.

HÉZÒU₄ 合 奏 (IV) play musical
instruments together. èr-rén-
gāngqín-hézòu 二 人 鋼 琴
合 奏 a piano duet.

HÉZUÒ₂ 合 作 (TV) work together, co-operate. Nǐ-děi-gēn-wo-
hézuò. 你 得 跟 我 合 作.
You must co-operate with me.
Zhèijian-shì wǒmen-kéyi-hézuò.
這 件 事 我 們 可 以
合 作. We can work together
on this.

(SV) co-operative. Tā-hěn-hé-
zuò. 他 很 合 作. He is
very co-operative.

HÉZUÒSHÈ₃ 合 作 社 (N) a co-
operative enterprise.

HŌNG₃ 閧 (TV) shoo, drive away.
hōng-cāngying 閧 蒼 蠅 shoo
the flies away. Bǎ-ta-hōngchuqu.
把 他 閧 出 去. Chase him
out.

HŌNG₄ 轟 (TV) bombard, bomb.
yòng-pào-hōng 用 炮 轟 bom-
bard with a cannon.

HŌNG₄ 烘 (TV) heat something by
placing it near a fire or stove.
Bǎ-shī-yīshang zai-huǒshang-
hōnghong, yǐhuǐr-jiu-hōnggānle.
把 濕 衣 裳 在 火 上
烘 烘, 一 會 兒 就
烘 乾 了. Put the wet clo-
thes near the fire and they will
be dry in a little while. (cf: KǍO

H

烤).

HÓNG₁ 紅 (SV) (1) red (color).
Yánse-shi-hóng-de. 顏色是
紅的. The color is red.
Shù-yèzi dou-hóng-le. 樹葉
子都紅了. The tree
leaves have all turned red. (2)
red (communist). Wǒmen-shi
yòu-hóng-yòu-zhuān. 我們
是又紅又專. We are
both red and expert. (3) be ac-
claimed or be celebrated by the
public, be a favorite. Tā-chàng-
le-zènma-duō-nián yě-méi-hóng.
他唱了這麼多年
也沒紅. He sang for so
many years and never was celebrated. Zhèige-bùzhǎng zài-
zǒngtǒng-nèr zuì-hóng. 這個
部長在總統那兒
最紅. This department chief
is the President's fair-haired
boy.
(N) (con. hónglì 紅利). dividends, bonus. Dàjiā-dōu-děi-
fēn-diǎr-hóng. 大家都得
分點兒紅. Everybody
has to share some dividends
(or bonus).

HÓNG₃ 哄 (TV) pacify or please
a person by coddling, pampering,
coaxing, tact or deception. Tā-
hǒng-háizi-wár. 他哄孩子
玩兒. He is playing with the
child. Nǐ-bié-hǒng-wǒ-le. 你
別哄我了. Don't try to
cheat me. Bǎ-ta-hǒnggāoxìng-
le. 把他哄高興了.
He was made happy by coddling.

'HONGDÒNG₄ 轟動 (TV) arouse
attention, cause excitement (by
a person, event, achievement,
etc.). hōngdòng-quánqiú 轟動
全球 arouse attention all
over the world. hōngdòng-yishí
轟動一時 cause excite-
ment for awhile.

HÓNGJŪN₂ 紅軍 (N) The Red
Army.

HÓNGLÌ₃ 紅利 (N) dividends,
bonus. Měi-bànnián wǒ-kéyi-dé-
wǔbǎikuai-qiánde-hónglì. 每半
年我可以得五百
塊錢的紅利. Every six
months I can get $500 in divi-
dends (or bonus). (See: HÓNG
紅).

HÓNG-LIǍN₃ 紅臉 (VO) (lit.
cause the face to get red) angry,
embarrassed. Wǒmen-xiànglái-
méi-hóngguo-liǎn. 我們向
來沒紅過臉. We have
never gotten angry at each other.
Yàoshi-wǒ-shuōchulai, nǐ-ke-bié-
hóng-liǎn. 要是我說出
來, 你可別紅臉. If
I tell it don't be embarrassed.

HÓNGLǙDĒNG₂ 紅綠燈 (N)
traffic light.

HÓNGTÁNG₅ 紅糖 (N) brown
sugar.

HÓNGYÙN₃ 紅運 (N) good luck.
Tā-zhèng-zǒu-hóngyùn-ne. 他
正走紅運呢. He is
going through a lucky period.

H

HŌNGZHÀ₃ 轟炸 (TV) bombard, bomb.

HŌNGZHÀJĪ₃ 轟炸機 (N) bomber (aircraft).

HÒU₁ 厚 (SV) (opp. báo 薄). (1) thick (in dimension). sāncùn-hòu 三寸厚 three inches thick. Zhèijiàn-dàyī-hěn-hòu. 這件大衣很厚. This overcoat is very thick. liǎnpí-hòu 臉皮厚 (lit. thick face skin) difficult to embarrass, thick-skinned. (2) strong (referring to mutual concern among people). Jiāoqing-hěn-hòu. 交情很厚. The bond of friendship is very strong. (3) strong (referring to taste or flavor). Wèir-hěn-hòu. 味兒很厚. The taste is very strong. (4) generous in treating people. Tā-dài-ren-hěn-hòu. 他待人很厚. He is very generous in treating people. (5) good in quality or costly. Tā-sòng-de-lǐ hěn-hòu. 他送的禮很厚. His gifts are very costly. (N) thickness. Hòu shi-sāncùn. 厚是三寸. The thickness is three inches.

HÒU₁ 後 (L) (opp. qián 前). (1) back, behind. hòutou 後頭 in the back. hòuyuànr 後院兒 back yard. (2) after. wǔhòu 午後 afternoon. zhànhòu 戰後 post-war. sāntian-hòu 三天後 after three days. used after CV, such as wàng 往, chòng 衝, xiàn 向, etc. (1) back, rear. wàng-hòu-tuì 往

後退 retreat towards the rear. Zhèige-chuānghu-chòng-hòu. 這個窗户衝後. The window faces the back. (2) future. Nǐ-děi-wàng-hòu-xiáng-xiang. 你得往後想想. You have to think about the things in the future. (SP) (opp. qián 前). (1) last (in a series). hòuliǎngjù 後兩句 last two sentences. (2) second, next. hòubannián 後半年 the second half of the year. (AD) later, afterwards. (opp. xiān 先). Měiguo-ren xiān-hē-tāng, Zhōngguo-ren hòu-hē-tāng. 美國人先喝湯中國人後喝湯. Americans have soup first, Chinese have soup afterwards.

(B-) (1) used with terms denoting mother or father, step. hòumā 後媽 stepmother. (2) later. hòu-bèi 後輩 later generation.

¹HÒUBÀNTIĀNR₃ 後半天兒 (TW) Peip. afternoon.

HÒUBÁO₄ 厚薄 (N) thickness. (syn. báohou 薄厚).

HÒUBIĀNR₁ 後邊兒 or HÒUTOU 後頭 (PW) (1) the back or the back part. Tā-zai-hòubianr. 他在後邊兒. He is in the back. Fángzi-hòubianr yǒu-shù. 房子後邊兒有樹. There are trees in the back of the house. Tā-zài-fàngguǎr-hòubianr. 他在飯館兒後邊兒. He is in the back of the restaurant. or He is back of the restaurant.

H

H

fig. Yŏu-rén-zài-hòubianr-chū zhúyi. 有人在後邊兒出主意. There are people suggesting ideas behind his back. (2) the back side. Zhài-zhǐ-hòubianr-xiě-liǎngge-zì. 在紙後邊兒寫兩個字. Write several words on the back side of this paper. (cf: HÒU-MIANR 後面兒).

HÒUDAO₅ 厚道 (SV) generous (in nature). Tā-dài-rén hěn-hòu-dao. 他待人很厚道. He is very generous towards others.

HÒUDIĒ₄ 後爹 (N) stepfather.

HÒUFĀNG₃ 後方 the rear (battle field). Hòufāng-bù-néng-gōngjǐ qiánfāng-méi-fázi-dǎ-zhàng. 後方不能供給前方沒法子打仗. If the rear can't supply, the front can't wage a battle.

HÒU-HUǏ₁ 後悔 (VO) be remorseful, regret, repent. Tā-zuòwánle hòule-bàntian-huǐ. 他作完了後了半天悔. After he did it he was remorseful for a long time. Nèige-shíhou, hòu-huǐ kě-láibují-le. 那個時候,後悔可來不及了. At that time it would be too late to be sorry about it.

HÒULAI₁ 後來 (TW) used for past events, later on, afterwards. Tā-xiān-bu-dǒng, hòulai-dǒng-le. 他先不懂後來懂了. At first he didn't understand, later he understood.

HÓULONG₄ 喉嚨 (N) throat.

HÒUMĀ₄ 後媽 (N) stepmother.

HÒUMIANR₁ 後面兒 (PW)(1) the back side. Zài-zhīpiào-hòu-mianr-qiān-zì. 在支票後面兒簽字. Sign on the back of the check. (2) the back. Zhèi-qiáng-hòumianr jiu-shi-wŭshìsì-jiē. 這牆後面兒就是五十四號. In back of this wall is 54th Street. (cf: HÒUBIANR 後邊兒, HÒUTOU 後頭).

HÒUNIAN₁ 後年 (TW) year after next.

HÒUPÁI₃ 後排 (N) rear seats (in theater or auditorium).

HÓUR₂ 猴兒 or HÓUZI 猴子 (N) monkey. (M: zhī 隻).

HÒUTÁI₂ 後台 (N) (1) backstage. Bié-shàng-hòutái. 別上後台. Don't go backstage. (2) back-up, backing (financial, political, moral, etc.). Méi-you-hòutái nǐ-méi-fár-xuǎndeshàng. 沒有後台你沒法兒選得上. You won't be elected without backing.

HÒUTIAN₁ 後天 (TW) day after tomorrow. Nà-shi-hòutian-de-shì. 那是後天的事. That's a thing for day after tomorrow.

HÒUTOU₁ 後頭 see HÒUBIANR 後邊兒.

HOUXUANREN₄ 候選人 (N) election candidate.

HÓUZI₂ 猴子 see HÓUR 猴兒.

HÚ₄ 糊 (TV) plaster. Yòng-ní-hūshang. 用泥糊上. Plaster it with mud.

HÚ₃ 壺 (N) kettle, pot <u>with a spout, like a teapot</u>.

HÚ₃ 煳 (IV) be burned <u>in cooking</u>, charred. Fàn-hú-le. 飯 煳 了. The rice is burned. (RE) burned, charred. Shāohú-le. 燒 煳 了. It's charred.

HÚ₂ 湖 (N) lake, pond.

HÚ₃ 糊 (TV) (1) paste. Yòng-zhǐ-hú-qiáng. 用 紙 糊 牆. Paste the wall with paper. Hú-shang-yìzhangzhǐ. 糊 上 一 張 紙. Paste on a sheet of paper. (2) use paste to make <u>something with paper, cloth, etc</u>. Hù-yíge-zhǐ-hézi. 糊 一 個 紙 盒子. Make a box with paste and paper.

HÚ₂ 胡 (AD) blindly. (<u>syn</u>. xiā 瞎). Bié-hú-huā-qián. 別 胡 花 錢. Don't spend money blindly.

HǓ₃ 虎 (B) tiger. (TV) buffalo, bamboozle. Nǐ-bié-hǔ-wǒ. 你 別 虎 我. Don't buffalo me. Wǒ-jiào-tā-gěi-hǔzhu-le. 我 叫 他 給 虎 住 了. He's got me buffaloed.

HUĀ₁ 花 (TV) spend. huā-qián 花 錢 spend money. huā-shí-jian 花 時 間 spend time.

HUĀ₃ 花 (SV) (1) extravagantly fancy (<u>of colors</u>). Tāde-lǐngdài tài-huā. 他 的 領 帶 太 花. His necktie is extravagantly fancy. (2) blotched (<u>of color</u>). Zhèizhong-bù yì-xǐ-jiu-huā. 這 種 布 一 洗 就 花. Once you wash this kind

of fabric its colors become blotched. (3) fancy (<u>of certain skills</u>). Tā-dǎ-gǔ dǎde-hěn-huā. 他 打 鼓 打 得 很 花. He plays a fancy beat on the drum.

(IV) blurred (<u>of vision</u>), be farsighted. Wǒde-yǎn-huā-le. 我 的 眼 花 了. My vision is blurred. <u>or</u> I'm farsighted now. (N) fireworks (<u>for display</u>). fàng-huā 放 花 set off fireworks.

HUÁ₂ 滑 (SV) <u>lit. or fig</u>. slippery. Bīng-hěn-huá. 冰 很 滑. The ice is very slippery. Zhèige-rén hěn-huá. 這 個 人 很 滑. This person is very slippery.

(TV) slip. huá-bīng 滑 冰 skate. huá-xuě 滑 雪 ski. Tā-huádǎo-le. 他 滑 倒 了. He slipped and fell.

HUÀ₁ 話 (N) spoken language, speech, verbal expression, dialects. (M: jiù 句). Fàguo-huà 法 國 話 French language. Shànghai-huà 上 海 話 Wu <u>or</u> Shanghai dialect. Lái, wǒ-gēn-ni-shuō-jiu-huà. 來, 我 跟 你 說 句 話. Come here, I want to have a word with you. Tā-jiǎng-de shì-něiguo-huà? 他 講 的 是 那 國 話 ? What (country's) language is he speaking? Xiàng "duìbuqǐ" "xièxie" zhèileide 'huà, dou hěn yǒu'yòng. 像 "對 不 起" "謝 謝" 這 類 的 話. 都 很 有 用. Expressions such as "excuse me", "thank you" are all very useful.

H

Huà-yòu-shuōhuílai-le. 話又說回來了. Now, back to what we were talking about. Zhè-shi-shénma-huà?! 這是甚麼話?! What kind of talk is this? Tāde-huàli-yǒu-huà. 他的話裏有話. What he says implies something else.

HUÀ₁ 畫 (TV) draw, paint. huà-huàr 畫畫兒 paint pictures. huà-yitiáo-xiàn 畫一條線 draw a line. huà-yizhāng-dìtú 畫一張地圖 draw a map. Tā-huì-huà-liǎngbǐ-huàr. 他會畫兩筆畫兒. He knows how to paint a little. Tāde-méimao-shì-huà de. 他的眉毛是畫的. Her eyebrows are painted on.

(B) painting, picture. yóuhuà 油畫 oil painting. huàláng 畫廊 picture gallery.

HUÀ₃ 化 (IV) change in state, melt, evaporate, dissolve. huà-dòng 化凍 defrost. Táng fàngzai-shuǐli jiu-huà. 糖放在水裏就化. The sugar dissolves when put into water. Bīng-huà-le. 冰化了. The ice melted. Nèijia-shì huà-le. 那件事化了. That matter evaporated.

(-B) similar meaning to -ize, -fy, etc. gōngyehuà 工業化 industrialize. jiǎndanhuà 簡單化 simplify. yǎnghuà 氧化 oxidize.

HUÀBÀO₂ 畫報 (N) pictorial magazine. (M: fènr 份兒, běn 本).

HUÁ-BĪNG₂ 滑冰 (VO) skate. (syn. liū-bīng 溜冰).

HUÀCHÁR₅ 話碴兒 (N) fragmentary information from one's speech. Tīng-tāde-huàchár hǎoxiàng-tā-yào-cízhí. 聽他的話碴兒好像他要辭職. I gathered from what he said that apparently he wants to resign.

HUÁ-CHUÁN₃ 划船 (VO) row a boat.

HUÀ-DÀO₅ 畫到 (VO) (lit. draw the character dào 到, "arrive") sign in (in an office).

HUÀFĒN₄ 劃分 (TV) separate something by drawing a dividing line. Zhèi-liǎnglèide-jièxiàn bu-róngyi-huàfēn. 這兩類的界線不容易劃分. The line between these two species is not easy to draw.

HUÀHÓNG₃ 花紅 (N) bonus. fēn-huāhóng 分花紅 give or receive a bonus.

HUÀI₁ 壞 (SV) (opp. hǎo 好). (1) bad. Zhèige-dìfang bu-huài. 這個地方不壞. This place is not bad. (2) poor in character (person or animal). Zhèige-rén zhēn-huài, jìng-chū-huài-zhúyi. 這個人真壞竟出壞主意. This person is really crafty. He is always proposing sly ideas. (3) spoiled (as of food). Ròu-huài-le. 肉壞了. The meat is spoiled. (4) out of order. Diànhuà huài-le. 電話壞了. The telephone is out of order.

(TV) ruin, spoil. Bíe-huài-wǒ-de-shì. 別 壞 我 的 事. Don't ruin my affair.

HUÀICHU₂ 壞 處 (N) bad point, bad feature, drawback, short-coming. (opp. hǎochu 好 處).

HUÁIHÉ₃ 淮河 (N) the Huai River.

HUÁISHU₄ 槐 樹 (N) locust tree. (M: kē 棵).

'HUÁIYÍ₃ 懷 疑 (TV) suspect, doubt. Wǒ-huáiyí-ta-shuōde-huà. 我 懷 疑 他 說 的 話 . I doubt what he said.

HUÁJI₂ 滑 稽 (SV) comical.

HUÀJIĀ₃ 畫 家 (N) painter, art-ist.

HUÀJÙ₃ 話 劇 (N) a dialogue play (vs. musical plays). (M: chū 齣).

HUÁN₂ 還 (TV) return something owed or borrowed, do something in return of something. huán-zhàng 還 賬 pay a debt (mon-ey). huán-lǐ 還 禮 return the salute. Jiègei-wo-yíkuai-qián, wǒ-míngtian-huángei-ni. 借 給 我 一 塊 錢, 我 明 天 還 給 你 . Lend me a dollar, I'll pay you back tomorrow.

HUÀN₁ 換 (TV) change, exchange. Wǒ-xiǎng-bānban-jiā huàn-huan-huánjing. 我 想 搬 搬 家 換 換 環 境. I would like to move to change the environ-ment. Huàn-yíjian-yīshang zai-chūqu. 換 一 件 衣 裳 再 出 去 . Change clothes before going out. Tā-huàngei-wo-yíge-dàde. 他 換 給 我 一 個

大 的 . He exchanged with me giving me a big one. Zài-nǎr-huàn-chē? 在 這 兒 換 車 ? Where do we change trains? Wǒ-děi-huàn-qián. 我 得 換 錢. I have to exchange some money. Nèr-huànle-rén-le. 那 兒 換 了 人 了 . (lit. The people there have changed.) There are different people there now.

HUÀNDĒNG₄ 幻 燈 (N) lantern slide projector.

HUĀNG₃ 荒 (IV) (1) fallow, un-cultivated. Dì-méi-ren-guǎn zhǐhǎo-huāngzhe. 地 沒 人 管 只 好 荒 著 . There is nobody to take care of the land, so it just has to lie fallow. (2) barren. huāngshān 荒 山 wild mountain.

HUĀNG₃ 慌 (SV) (1) nervous, un-easy. Kàn-wo-yi-shēng-qì, tā-jiu-huāng-le. 看 我 一 生 氣, 他 就 慌 了 . As soon as he saw me get angry, he became nervous. (2) in a hurry. Tā-zuò-shi tài-huāng, suóyi-cháng-cuò. 他 作 事 太 慌, 所 以 常 錯 . He does things in a hurry, so he often makes mistakes.

HUÁNG₁ 黃 (SV) yellow, yellow-ish or brown. 'huáng-zhǒng-rén 黃 種 人 a person of the yel-low race. huáng-píxié 黃 皮 鞋 brown shoes.

HUÁNG₅ 黃 (IV) come to nothing, fail, fall through. Nèijian-shì huáng-le. 那 件 事 黃 了 .

H

H

That matter fell through.

HUĂNG₃ 謊 (N) (1) a lie. sā-huăng 撒謊 tell a lie. Biéshuō-huăng. 別説謊. Don't lie. (2) a higher selling price quoted in anticipation of bargaining. Wŏ-méi-yào-huăng. 我没要謊. I did not ask for a price higher than the regular price.

HUÀNG(YOU) 晃 (搖) or YÁO-SHUANG₃ 搖晃 (TV) (1) wave in sideway motion, rock. Tā-bă-qízi huàng(you)le-liăngxiàzi. 他把旗子晃(搖)了兩下子. He waved the flag a couple of times. (2) shake back and forth. Bă-píngzi-huàng(you)-huang(you). 把瓶子晃(搖)晃(搖). Shake the bottle. Zhèige-zhōzi-bu-jiēshi, yí-pèng jiu-huàng(you). 這個桌子不結實一碰就晃(搖). This table is not strong, everytime you touch it, it shakes back and forth.

HUÁNGCHONG₅ 蝗蟲 (N) locust (insect). guò-huángchong 過蝗蟲 (lit. locusts are passing) a locust attack.

'HUÁNGDÌ₃ 皇帝 (N) The Emperor, emperor. (cf: HUÁNG-SHANG 皇上).

HUÁNGDÒU₄ 黄豆 (N) soybean.

HUĂNGFÈI₄ 荒廢 (TV) wasted through lack of usage. Bă-shíjian dou-huāngfèi-le. 把時間都荒廢了. The time has all been wasted. Wŏde-xuéwen yǐjing-huāngfèi-le. 我的

學問已經荒廢了. What I learned has already been forgotten through lack of usage.

HUÁNGGŌNG₄ 皇宮 (N) the imperial palace.

HUÁNGGUA₄ 黄瓜 (N) cucumber. (M: tiáo 條).

HUÁNGHÉ₁ 黄河 (N) the Yellow River.

HUÁNGHÒU₄ 皇后 (N) The Empress, empress.

HUĂNGHUÀ₄ 謊話 (N) a lie. (syn. xiāhuà 瞎話). shuō-huănghuà 説謊話 tell a lie. (See: HUĂNG 謊).

HUÁNGHŪN₃ 黄昏 (TW) twilight.

HUÁNGJĪN₃ 黄金 (N) gold.

'HUĀNGMÁNG₅ 慌忙 (AD)'in a hurry. Tā-huāngmáng-zŏukai-le. 他慌忙走開了. He walked away in a hurry.

HUÁNGMÉITIĀN₅ 黄梅天 (N) the monsoon season.

'HUĀNGNIÁN₅ 荒年 (N) year of bad crops, year of famine.

HUÁNGR₄ 黄兒 (N) yolk. (opp. qīngr 清兒). jīdàn-huángr 鷄蛋黄兒 the yolk of an egg.

HUÁNGSHANG₄ 皇上 (N) emperor. (cf: 'HUÁNGDÌ 皇帝).

HUÁNGTAIHÒU₅ 皇太后 (N) The Empress Dowager.

HUĀNGTANG₂ 荒唐 (SV) used to describe a person who acts without forethought, hare-brained. Xiăngxiang-zai-shuō, bié-nènma-huāngtang. 想想再説, 别那麼荒唐. Think before you talk, don't be hare-brained. Zhèijian-shì tā-bànde tài-huāng-

tang-le. 這件事他辦
的太荒唐了. In this
matter he acted without much
forethought.

HUÁNGTÓNG₅ 黄銅 (N) yellow
brass.

HUĂNG-YĂN₃ 晃眼 (VO) be
glaring to the eyes. Tàiyang-
huăng-wŏde-yăn. 太陽晃
我的眼. The sun is glar-
ing in my eyes. Dēng-hĕn-
huăng-yăn. 燈很晃眼.
The light is very glaring.

HUÁNGYĪNG₄ 黄鶯 (N) canary.
(M: zhī 隻).

HUÁNGYÓU₂ 黄油 (N) butter.

HUÁNGZHANG₅ 慌張 (SV) ner-
vous agitation. Tāde-yàngzi
hĕn-huāngzhang. 他的樣
子很慌張. He looks
very nervous.

HUĂNGZI₄ 幌子 (1) sign for a
shop, indicating the nature of
its business, such as the three
balls of a pawn shop. (2) something fake, used for display purposes. (cf: ZHĀOPAI 招牌).

'HUĂNHÉ₃ 緩和 (SV) go easy,
loosen up. Huănhe-yidianr, bié-
bă-ta-bĭde-cí-zhí-le. 緩和
一點兒,別把他逼
得辭職了.Go easy on him,
don't force him into quitting. Nĭ-
ràng-yidiănr-bù, shìqing-jiu-
'huănhé-le. 你讓一點兒
步,事情就緩和了.
If you give in a little, it will
loosen up.

HUÁNJING₁ 環境 (N) enviro-
ment (physical or financial).

Tā-zhù-de-dìfang huánjing-bu-
cuò. 他住的地方環
境不錯. The environment
where he lives is not bad. Tā-
jiāli-de-huánjing hĕn-hăo. 他
家裏的環境很好.
The environment in his home is
very good.

HUÁN-LĬ₄ 還禮 (VO) return a
salute.

'HUÁNRÀO₄ 環繞 (TV) circums-
cribe, go around. Tāmen-zŏng-
shi huánrào-zhèige-wènti-tăolun
méi-tándao-wèntide-zhōngxīn.
他們總是環繞這
個問題討論沒談
到問題的中心.They
always discuss around this problem and never talk about the
core.

HUÁN-SHŎU₃ 還手 (VO) fight
in return, return a blow. (syn.
huí-shŏu 回手). Tā-dăle-wo-
sānxia wŏ-cái-huán-shŏu. 他
打了我三下我才
還手. He hit me three times
before I returned a blow.

HUĀNSÒNG₄ 歡送 (TV) send off
someone with joy. Tā-chū-guó-
de-shíhou wŏmen-qu-huānsòng-
ta. 他出國的時候
我們去歡送他.When
he leaves for abroad we shall go
to send him off.

HUĀNXI₄ 歡喜 see XĬHUAN
喜歡.

'HUÀNXIĂNG₃ 幻想 (N) fantasy,
illusion. Nà-shi-'huànxiăng, bu-
néng-shíxiàn. 那是幻想

H

H

不能實現. That is only an illusion, it cannot come true. (TV) imagine. Tā-huànxiang nèijian-shì kéyi-chénggōng. 他幻想那件事可以成功. He imagines that that affair could be successful.

HUĀNYÍNG₁ 歡迎 (TV) welcome. Wǒmen-dōu-huānyíng-ta-lái. 我們都歡迎他來. We all welcome him to come. Huānyíng-huānyíng. 歡迎歡迎. Welcome, welcome (as a greeting).

HUÁN-YUÀN₄ 還願 (VO) fulfill a vow. 'Xǔle-yuàn jiu-dei 'huán-yuàn. 許了願就得還願. If a vow is made it must be fulfilled.

HUĀPÍNG(R)₃ 花瓶兒 (N) (1) flower vase. (2) female office worker who was chosen for looks rather than ability. Nèige-nǔshūji shì tāmen-gōngshifángde-huāpíng(r). 那個女書記是他們公事房的花瓶(兒). That secretary is a decoration in their office.

HUÁQIÁO₂ 華僑 (N) Chinese living abroad, overseas Chinese.

HUĀQUĀN₃ 花圈 (N) wreath.

HUÁ-QUÁN₃ 划拳 (VO) play a finger-guessing game.

HUĀR₁ 花兒 (N) (1) flower, flower bush. (M: duǒr 朵, zhī 枝, kē 棵). Tā-dàizhe-yi-duǒr-huār. 他帶着一朵花兒. He is wearing a flower. (2) (con. tiānhuār 天花兒). smallpox. chū-huār 出

花兒 get smallpox. zhòng-huār 種花兒 inoculate for smallpox or plant a flower bush. (3) design, pattern. Bùshang yìn-zhe-you-huār. 布上印着有花兒. There is a design printed on the cloth.

(B) things resembling a flower. xuěhuār 雪花兒 snowflake.

HUÀR₁ 畫兒 (N) picture, painting. (M: zhāng 張). huà-huàr 畫畫兒 paint or draw. Qiáng-shang guàzhe-huàr. 牆上掛着畫兒. The wall is hung with pictures.

HUÁSHĀ₃ 華沙 (PW) Warsaw.

HUÁSHAO₃ 花稍 (SV) colorful, flowery, fancy. Tāde-yīshang hen-huāshao. 他的衣裳很花稍. Her clothes are very colorful.

HUĀSHĒNG₃ 花生 or LUÒHUA-SHĒNG 落花生 (N) peanut. bāo-huāsheng 剝花生 shell a peanut.

HUÁSHÈNGDÙN₁ 華盛頓 (PW) Washington.

HUÁSHÌ₄ 華氏 (B) Fahrenheit. Huáshibiāo 華氏表 Fahrenheit thermometer. Huáshi-sìshi-dù 華氏四才度 forty degrees Fahrenheit.

HUÁTĪ₄ 滑梯 (N) slide (for children).

HUÁTÓU₃ 滑頭 (SV) (lit. slippery head) elusive, cunning, crafty (of a person or animal). Tā-yě-bu-shuō-hǎo, ye-bu-shuō 'bù-hǎo, zhēn-huátóu. 他也不說好, 也不說不

好, 真 滑 頭. He doesn't say it's good, nor say it's bad, he is really cunning.

(N) an elusive, cunning, crafty person. Tā-shì-ge-dà-huátóu. 他 是 個 大 滑 頭. He is an elusive person.

HUĀWÉN₅ 花 紋 (N) linear pattern or design.

HUÀXUÉ₂ 化 學 (N) (1) chemistry. niàn-huàxué 念 化 學 study chemistry. (2) plastic. Zhèi-shi-huàxué-zuò-de. 這 是 化 學 作 的. This is made of plastic.

HUÁ-XUĚ₃ 滑 雪 (VO) ski.

HUĀYANGR₃ 花 樣 兒 (N) (1) decorative pattern, design, style. (2) variant or fancy way of doing things. Tā-zuò-shì huāyangr-hěn-duō. 他 作 事 花 樣 兒 很 多. In doing things he has a lot of fancy ways. Tā-yòu-biànle-huāyangr-le. 他 又 變 了 花 樣 兒 了. He again changed his way (method).

HUĀYUÁNR₂ 花 園 兒 see HUĀYUÁNZI 花 園 子.

HUĀYUÁNZI 花 園 子 or HUĀYUÁNR 花 園 兒 (N) garden. gài-huāyuánzi 蓋 花 園 子 build a garden.

HUÀZHUĀNG₃ 化 裝 (TV) (1) masquerade as. huàzhuāng-tiào-wǔ 化 裝 跳 舞 masquerade ball. Tā-huàzhuāng-yíge-nǚde. 他 化 裝 一 個 女 的. He masqueraded as a woman. (2) put on make-up (for a theatrical production or for decoration). Tā-qu-huàzhāng-qu-le. 他 去 化 裝 去 了. He went to put on make-up.

HUÀZHUĀNGPǏN₃ 化 裝 品 (N) make-up, cosmetics.

HUÁZI₅ 划 子 (N) rowboat, dinghy. (M: tiáo 條, zhǐ 隻).

HÚBĚI₂ 湖 北 (PW) Hupei province.

HÚDU₂ 糊 塗 or HÚTU 糊 塗 (SV) be muddled in the mind, foolish. Rèn-tài-lǎo-le, jiu-húdu-le. 人 太 老 了. 就 糊 塗 了. When a person grows too old he becomes senile. Zhèi-yi-dianr-dōu-nòngbuqīngchu, nǐ-zěnma-nènma-húdu! 這 一 點 兒 都 弄 不 清 楚, 你 怎 麼 那 麼 糊 塗! You can't even clear up this little thing. How foolish!

HUĪ₃ 灰 (N) ashes, dust. yānhuī 烟 灰 ashes of cigar or tobacco. (SV) gray. huīsè 灰 色 gray color.

HUÍ₁ 回 (IV) (1) return, come or go back. Tā-huída-zìjǐ-wūzili-qu-le. 他 回 到 自 己 屋 子 裏 去 了. He went back to his own room. Nín-shénma-shíhou huí-guó? 你 甚 麼 時 候 回 國? When are you returning to your native country? Wǒ-huí-xuéxiào, nǐ-ne? 我 回 學 校, 你 呢? I'm going back to the school, how about you? (2) answer a letter Nǐ-huí-ta-yìfēng-xìn-ba. 你 回 他 一 封 信 吧. You

H

write him a reply (letter). (3)
cancel a theatrical performance.
Jīntiande-xì-huí-le. 今 天 的
戲 回 了 . Today's perform-
ance is cancelled.
used after the CV wàng 往,
xiàng 向,etc., back. Bié-wàng-
huí-zǒu. 別 往 回 走 .Don't
go back.
HUÍ₁ 回 (M) (1) times of occurrence. (syn. cì 次). Wǒ-qù-
guo-liǎnghuí. 我 去 過 兩
回 . I have been there twice.
(2) for affairs, matters of business, matters in general. (syn.
jiàn 件). Zhè-shì-zěnma(yi)-
huí-shì? 這 是 怎 麼 (一)
回 事 ? What kind of a matter
is this? Òu, shì-zènma(yi) huí-
shì. 喔,是 這 麼 (一) 回
事 . Oh, this is how it is.
Kànzhe xiàng-nènma(yi)huí-shì.
看 着 像 那 麼 (一) 回
事 . It looks like that kind of a
matter. 'Tāmen-liǎngge-rén
shuōde-shì-'yìhuí-shì. 他 們
兩 個 人 說 的 是 一
回 事 . The two of them are
talking about the same thing. (3)
a chapter in a novel. Zhèiben-
xiǎoshuor yígòng-yǒu-èrshi-huí.
這 本 小 說 一 共 有
二 十 回 This novel has a
total of twenty chapters.
HUÍ₃ 毀 (TV) ruin, destroy. Hái-
zǐ-bǎ-wányìr-huí-le. 孩 子 把
玩 藝 兒 毀 了. The
children ruined the toys. Zhèige-rén, huí-le. 這 個 人 毀
了 . This person is ruined.

HUÌ₁ 會 (AV) (1) know how to,
have the skill to. Nǐ-huì-yòng-
kuàizi-ma? 你 會 用 筷 子
嗎 ? Do you know how to use
chopsticks? Tā-bu-huì-shuō-
Yīngwén. 他 不 會 說 英
文 . He does not (know how to)
speak English. (2) able to derive
pleasure or enjoyment from
something, know how to appreciate. Wǒ-bu-huì-hē-jiǔ. 我 不
會 喝 酒 .I don't know how to
appreciate drinking. Wǒ-bu-huì-
tīng-xì. 我 不 會 聽 戲 .
I don't know how to appreciate
opera. Tā-huì-xiǎng-fú. 他 會
享 福. He knows how to enjoy
life. (3) likely, apt to, liable to.
Nǐ-kàn-huì-xià-yǔ-ma? 你 看
會 下 雨 嗎? Do you think
(it is likely that) it will rain?
Wǒ-xiǎng-ta-bu-huì-lái. 我 想
他 不 會 來 . I think he is
not likely to come.
(TV) know how to do certain
things. Nǐ-huì-Yīngwén-ma?
你 會 英 文 嗎？
Do you know English? Wǒ-jiù-
hui-jǐjù. 我 就 會 幾 句 .
I only know a couple sentences.
(RE) have acquired a knowledge
or a skill through the action
shown by the verb which precedes it. Shì-yige-Zhōngguo-
rén bǎ-wǒ-jiāohuì-le-de. 是 一
個 中 國 人 把 我 教
會 了 的 . It was a Chinese
who taught me how (and I learned
it). Nǐ-cháng-liàn jiu-liànhuì-le.
你 常 練 就 練 會 了 .

If you practice often, you will learn it. (cf: NÉNG 能).

HUÌ₄ 會 (TV) pay a bill for treating somebody. Jīntiande-fànqian Lǐ-xiansheng-huì-le. 今天的 飯錢李先生會了. Mr. Li paid the bill for today's meal.

HUÌ₁ 會 (N) meeting. Wǒmen-kāi-ge-huì, tǎolun-taolun. 我們 開個會, 討論討論. Let's hold a meeting to discuss it. Huì shi-shénma-shíhou-sàn-de? 會是甚麼時候 散的 ? When did the meeting end?

(TV) meet with. Tā-zhèng-huì-zhe-kè-ne. 他正會着客 呢. He is meeting with a guest. Zài-huì. 再會. (lit. again meet) Good-bye.

(-B) (1) A body of persons associated for some purpose or for social intercourse, association, club, fraternity, union, lodge, etc. qīngniánhuì 青年會 YMCA or YWCA. xiōngdìhuì 兄 弟會 fraternity. (2) meeting, assembly, congregation, rally, convention, conference, etc. yuēhuì 約會 an appointment, date. yùndonghuì 運動會 athletic meet. zhǎnlǎnhuì 展 覽會 exhibition.

HUÌ₃ 匯 (TV) remit money. Wǒ-děi-gěi-ta huì-diǎnr-qián-qu. 我得給他匯點兒 錢去. I have to send him some money. (cf: DUÌ 兌).

HUÍBÀI₄ 回拜 (TV) pay a return visit. Tā-lai-huíbài-lai-le. 他來回拜來了. He came to pay a return visit.

HUÍBÀO₅ 會報 (N) report in a meeting.

HUÌCHǍNG₂ 會場 (PW) place of a meeting, convention, etc. Wǒmen-huìchǎng-jiàn. 我們 會場見. We'll see each other at the convention.

'HUÌCHÉN₄ 灰塵 (N) dust.

HUÍDÁ₃ 回答 (TV) reply, answer.

(N) a reply, an answer. Zhèi-'shi-tāde-huídá. 這是他的 回答. This is his reply.

HUÌDUÌ₃ 匯兌 (N) remittance and exchange of money. huìduì-bu-tōng 匯兌不通 remittances cannot reach there.

HUÌFÈI₃ 會費 (N) dues.

HUĪFU₂ 恢復 (TV) (1) return to original state. Nèige-dìfang you-huīfule-cóngqiánde-yàngzi. 那 個地方又恢復了 從前的樣子. That place once again has returned to its original state. (2) recover. Tāde-jiànkāng huīfule-meiyou? 他的健康恢復了 沒有 ? Has he recovered his health?

HUÌGUǍN₄ 會館 (N) a club, a clubhouse.

HUÍ-GUÓ₂ 回國 (VO) go back to one's own country.

HUÍ-HUÀ₃ 回話 (VO) reply, report (verbally). Wǒ-huí-nín-yi-jiù-huà. 我回您一句

話. I'll make a report(verbal) to
you.

(N) reply. Tā-méi-gěi-wǒ-huí-
huà. 他 没 給 我 回 話 .
He did not give me a reply.

HUÌHUÀ₃ 會 話 (N) conversation
(used for teaching or learning
foreign languages). Tāmen-jiāo-
Zhōngwen bu-zhùzhòng-huìhuà.
我 們 教 中 文 不 注
重 會 話. They teach Chinese
but do not emphasize conversation.

'HUĬHUÀI₄ 毁 壞 (TV) ruin, destroy. Tāmen-huǐhuài-nǐde-míng-
yu. 他 們 毁 壞 你 的
名 譽 . They ruined your reputation.

HUÍHUI₃ 回 回 (N) a Mohammed-
an, a Moslem. (cf: HUÍZI 回 子).

HUÍ-JIĀ₁ 回 家 (VO) return
home.

HUÍJIÀO₃ 回 教 (N) Mohammedanism. xìn-huíjiào 信 回 教
believe in Mohammedanism.

HUÌKÈSHÌ₃ 會 客 室 (N) room
for meeting visitors a reception
room.

HUÍLAI₁ 回 來 (RV) come back,
return. Wǒ-yìhuǐr jiu-huílai. 我
一 會 兒 就 回 來. I'll
be back in a little while. Nǐ-
yīngdāng-huí-jiā-lai-kànkan. 你
應 當 回 家 來 看 看.
You should come home to take
a look. Qùle-'wǔge-rén jiu-
huílai-yíge. 去 了 五 個 人
就 回 來 一 個. Five
persons went, only one came
back.

(RE) back (here). náhuilai 拿
回 來 bring it back here. Huà
you-shuōhuílai-le. 話 又 説
回 來 了 . Now, back to the
same thing that was said. Mài-
le-yǐhòu jiu-mǎibuhuílái-le. 賣
了 以 後 就 買 不 回
來 了 . After it's sold you
won't be able to buy it back.

(MA) later. (syn. huítóu 回 頭).
Búyàojǐn, huílai-wǒ-gěi-nǐ-mǎi-
yíge. 不 要 緊, 回 來 我
給 你 買 一 個 . It doesn't
matter, I'll buy you another one
later.

HUÌLU₃ 賄 賂 or HUÌLUO 賄
賂 (TV) bribe. Tā-xiǎng-huì-
lu-nèige-jǐngchá. 他 想 賄
賂 那 個 警 察. He in-
tended to bribe the policeman.

(N) bribe. shòu-huìlu 受 賄
賂 take a bribe.

HUÌLUO₃ 賄 賂 see HUÌLU 賄
賂.

HUÌMIÈ₅ 毁 滅 (TV) destroy.

HUÌPIÀO₂ 匯 票 (N) bank draft,
money order. (M: zhāng 張).

HUÍQǏNG₃ 回 請 (TV) treat
someone in return. Wǒmen-hái-
méi-huíqǐng-ta-ne. 我 們 還
沒 回 請 他 呢. We have
not treated him in return.

HUÍQU₁ 回 去 (RV) go back, return. Duìbuqǐ, wǒ-xiān-huíqu-le.
對 不 起, 我 先 回 去
了 . Excuse me, I'm going
back first. Nǐ-jīntian-huíbuqù-
le. 你 今 天 回 不 去 了.
You cannot go back today.

(RE) back (there). Tā-bǎ-zhuō-zi-bānhuíqu-le. 他 把 桌 子 搬 回 去 了 . He moved the table back. or He took back the table.

HUÍR₂ 會 兒 (M) moment, a short period of time. Zuò-(yi) huǐr-ba, 'máng-shénma? 坐 一 會 兒 吧，忙 甚 麼 啊 ? Stay for a while, what's the hurry? A: Láile-bàntiān-le-ba? B: Méi-duóda-huǐr. A: 來 了 半 天 了 吧? B: 沒 多 大 會 兒 A: Have you been here a long time? B: Just a short while. (See: YI-HUÍR 一 會 兒).

HUÍSHĒNG₅ 回 聲 (N) echo.

HUÍ-SHǑU₃ 回 手 (VO) return a blow, fight in retaliation. (syn. huan-shǒu 還 手).

(AD) reach back. Tā-huíshou-ong-shūjiàshang-ná-le-yiben-shū. 他 回 手 從 書 架 上 拿 了 一 本 書. He reached back and took a book from the shelf.

HUÍ-TÓU₂ 回 頭 (VO) (1) turn back one's head. Wǒ-huí-tóu-yí-kàn, yuánlái-shì-tā. 我 回 頭 一 看，原 來 是 他. I turned back and looked. It was him. (2) return. Tā-yi-qù-bu huí-tóu-le. 他 一 去 不 回 頭 了 . He left and never returned. (3)repent. Yàoshi-ni-zǎo-yidiǎnr-huí-tóu, hái-yǒu-xīwang. 要 是 你 早 一 點 兒 回 頭 還 有 希 望. If you

repent soon, there is still hope. (MA) later. (syn. huílai 回 來). Wǒ-huí-tóu-gàosong-ni. 我 回 頭 告 訴 你 . I'll tell you later. Huí-tóu-jiàn. 回 頭 見. See you later.

HUĪTǓ₅ 灰 土 (N) dust.

'HUÍXIǍNG₃ 回 想 (TV) recall, remember. huíxiǎng-cóngqiánde-shì 回 想 從 前 的 事 recall matters of the past.

HUĪ-XĪN₂ 灰 心 (VO)disheartened. Tā-shìle-sānci dou-méi-chéng, suóyi-huīxīn-le. 他 試 了 三 次 都 沒 成，所 以 灰 心 了. He tried three times, all without success. Therefore he is disheartened.

HUÍ-XÌN₂ 回 信 (VO) write a letter in reply. Wǒ-děi-huí-ta-yifeng-xìn. 我 得 回 他 一 封 信 . I have to write him a letter in reply.

(N) reply (letter). Wǒ-méi-jiē-zhou-tade-huíxìn. 我 沒 接 着 他 的 回 信 . I have not received his reply.

HUÌYÌ₄ 會 議 (N) a meeting. (TV) confer, have a meeting. Děng-tamen-huìyìwánle zai-shuō-ba. 等 他 們 會 議 完 了 再 說 吧. We'll talk about it after they have conferred.

HUÌYUÁN₂ 會 員 (N) members of a club, association, etc.

HUÌZHǍNG₂ 會 長 (N) head of an organization.

HUÌ-ZHÀNG₄ 會 賬 (VO) pay a bill (generally a bill for food or lodgings).

H

HUÍZI₄ 回子 (N) Peip. a Moham-
medan, a Moslem. (cf: HUÍHUI
回回).

HUÍ-ZUÍ₄ 回嘴 (VO) talk back.
Bùguǎn-ta-shuō-shénma nǐ-bié-
huí-zuǐ. 不管他說甚
麼你別回嘴. No matter
what he says, don't talk back.

HUKOU₃ 户口 (N) number of
people in a household. Tā-chá-
kùkou-lai-le. 他查户口
來了 . He came to check the
number of people in the household (a police method used to
control undesirable transients).

HÚLI₄ 狐狸 (N) fox. (M: zhī
隻).

HÚLU₅ 葫蘆 (N) Chinese bottle
gourd.

HÚLU₄ 胡嚕 (TV) move the
hand palm down in a wiping back
and forth motion, push aside
things on a surface. Yòng-shǒu
'húlu-húlu. 用手胡嚕胡
嚕 . Wipe back and forth with
the hands. Zhèi-háizi bǎ-wo-
zhuōzishang-de-dōngxi dōu-hú-
lu-luàn-le. 這孩子把我
桌子上的東西都
胡嚕亂了 . This child
messed up the things on my desk
by pushing them aside.

HÚN₄ 昏 (SV) dizzy. Wǒ-tóu-hūn.
我頭昏.I feel dizzy (in my
head).
(IV) faint. Tā-hūnguoqu-le. 他
昏過去了 . He fainted.

HÚN₃ 渾 (SV) (1) muddy. Huáng-
héde-shuǐ hěn-hún. 黃河的
水很渾. The water of the
Yellow River is very muddy. (2)
muddled. Jīntian wǒde-nǎozì-
hěn-hún, xiǎngbu-chulái-shi-
zěnma-hui-shì. 今天我的
腦子很渾，想不出
來是怎麼回事. My
mind is muddled today, I can't
figure out why. (3) unreasonable
(of a person). Zhèi-rén-zhēn-
hún. Gāi-ren-qián bu-huán, hái-
yào-dǎ-rén. 這人真渾，
該人錢不還還要
打人 . This fellow is really
unreasonable. He owes people
money, won't pay it back, and
still wants to beat people up.

HÙN₃ 混 see HÙN 混 (TV) (4),
(RE).

HÙN₃ 混 (TV) (1) fool around and
obtain something, pass by or
through by taking advantage of a
confused state. hùn-'fàn-chī 混
飯吃 make a living without
taking the work seriously. Tā-
bu-zhèngjing-niàn-shū, jiùshi-
xiǎng-hùn-yizhāng-wénpíng. 他
不正經念書，就是
想混一張文憑. He
doesn't study seriously, all he
wants to do is to get a diploma
somehow. Tā-méi-yǒu-ménpiào
ye-hùnjinqu-le. 他沒有門
票也混進去了. He
didn't have a ticket, but sneaked
in anyway. (2) let time go by but
do nothing worthwhile. hùn-shí-
hou 混時候 kill time. (3)
mix (with certain people). Bié-
gēn-tamen zài-yíhuàir-hùn. 別
跟他們在一塊兒

混. Don't get mixed up with them. (4) or HÙN 混, mix together. Yǒu-gēn-shuǐ bu-néng-hùnzai-yíhuàir. 油 跟 水 不 能 混 在 一 塊 兒. Oil and water can't be mixed together.

(RE) or HÙN 混, mix up. Tā-ba-Zhōngwén-gen-Rìwén-nòng-hùn-le. 他 把 中 文 跟 日 文 弄 混 了. He got the Chinese and Japanese languages mixed up.

(AD) confusedly, disorderly. Bié-hùn-chū zhúyi. 別 混 出 主 意. Don't make suggestions foolishly.

HÚNÁN₂ 湖 南 (PW) Hunan province.

HÚNÀO₂ 胡 鬧 (IV) make a disturbance without good reason or basis. Tā-hē-jiǔ hēduō-le, húnào. 他 喝 酒 喝 多 了, 胡 鬧. When he drinks too much he makes trouble. Bié-húnào-le. 別 胡 鬧 了. Don't make trouble.

HÚNDÀN₃ 渾 蛋 (N) damn fool. Nǐ-húndàn. 你 渾 蛋. You damn fool. Tā-shì-ge-húndàn. 他 是 個 渾 蛋. He is a damn fool.

(SV) be a damn fool. Zhèi-rén-zhēn-húndàn. 這 人 真 渾 蛋. This person is really a damn fool.

HǓNHÉ₄ 混 合 (TV) mix, combine. Zhèige-yào shi-sānzhong-yuánliào hǔnhé-qilai-zuò-de. 這 個 藥 是 三 種 原

料 混 合 起 來 作 的. This medicine is made by mixing three kinds of ingredients together.

HÚNLǏ₂ 婚 禮 (N) wedding ceremony.

HÙNONG₄ 糊 弄 (TV) (1) kid, deceive with a joke. Tā-lǎo-ài-hùnong-rén. 他 老 愛 糊 弄 人. He likes to kid people. (2) fool around with serious work. Tā-bu-zhèngjing-zuò, lǎo-xiǎng-hùnongguoqu jiu-suàn-le. 他 不 正 經 作. 老 想 糊 弄 過 去 就 算 了. He doesn't work seriously. He is always trying to get away with fooling around.

HÚNRÉN₄ 渾 人 (N) (1) unreasonable person. Méi-fázi-gen-húnrén-shuō-huà. 沒 法 子 跟 渾 人 說 話. You can't talk to an unreasonable person. (2) muddle-headed person.

HÚNSHĒN₄ 渾 身 (AD) all over one's body. Dǎde-ta-húnshēn-dōu-shi-shāng. 打 得 他 渾 身 都 是 傷. (They) beat him, wounding him all over his body. fig. Wǒ-húnshēn-shì-zhàng. 我 渾 身 是 賬. I am full of debts.

HÚNTUN₄ 餛 飩 (N) wonton (a small lump of meat wrapped in a thin sheet of dough, generally cooked and served in clear broth).

HÚNYĪN₂ 婚 姻 (N) marriage. hūnyin-wèntí 婚 姻 問 題 the problem of marriage. Hūn-yin-bu-shi-xiǎo-shì, nǐ-děi-

H

zǐxi-xiángxiang zai-juédìng. 婚
姻 不 是 小 事, 你 得
仔 細 想 想 再 決 定.
Marriage is not a small matter.
You must think carefully before
deciding.

HÙNZHÀNG₃ 混 帳 (N) damn
fool (same as HÚNDÀN 混蛋
but milder.)
(SV) be a damn fool.

HUO₃ 和 (-B) added to SV which
are sensory in nature, comfortably. nuǎnhuo 暖 和 comfortably warm. rǎnhuo 軟 和 nice
and soft.

HUŌ₂ 嚄 see HĒ 喝 (I).

HUŌ₄ 和 see HUÒ 和 (TV) (2).

HUÓ₁ 活 (IV) (1) be alive, live.
(opp. sǐ 死). Tā-hái-huózhe-ne.
他 還 活 着 呢. He is
still alive. Nǐ-lián-'zhèige-dou-
bu-zhīdào, zhēnshi-bái-huóle-
sìshi-duōsuì. 你 連 這 個
都 不 知 道, 真 是 白
活 了 四 十 多 歲. You
don't even know this? Really,
you have lived in vain for over
forty years. Wǒmen-hái-dei-
huóxiaqu-ne. 我 們 還 得
活 下 去 呢. We still have
to keep alive. Nǐ-zhòng-de-shù
huóle-mei-you? 你 種 的 樹
活 了 沒 有? Did the tree
that you planted live or not? (2)
live on. Tā-yì'tiān-yòng-de-
qián, gòu-wo-huó-yíge-yuè-de.
他 一 天 用 的 錢, 够
我 活 一 個 月 的.
What he spends in one day is
enough for me to live on for a
month.

(SV) (opp. sǐ 死). (1) active,
lively. Tāde-nǎozi hen-huó. 他
的 腦 子 很 活. His mind
is very alert. (2) (con. huódong
活 動). loose. Zhèige-zhuōzi-
tuǐr huó-le. 這 個 桌 子 腿
兒 活 了. This leg of the
table is loose. Tā-zhèiyangr-yi-
shuō, wǒ-de-xīn you-huóle. 他
這 樣 兒 一 説 我 的
心 又 活 了. When he said
it like this my previous decision
was not so firm. (3) movable,
detachable. Zhèige-bǐtóur-shi-
huóde, kéyi-náxialai. 這 個
筆 頭 兒 是 活 的 可
以 拿 下 來. This pen point
is detachable, it can be removed.
(AD) (1) alive. huó-shòu-zuì 活
受 罪 suffer a living hell. (2)
flexibly. Tā-xuéle-hěn-duō-huà,
kěshi-bu-huì-'huó-yòng. 他 學
了 很 多 話 可 是 不
會 活 用. He has learned
many sentences, but doesn't
know how to apply them in practice.

(N) (1) work (result of production,
generally referring to manual
work). xìhuó 細 活 fine work.
Wǒ-děi-gǎn-yidiǎnr-huó. 我 得
趕 一 點 兒 活. I have
to rush out some work. (2) needle work. zuò-huó 作 活 do
work or do needle work.

HUǑ₁ 火 (N) (1) fire. diǎn-huǒ
點 火 light a fire. fàng-huǒ
放 火 set a fire (incendiary).
Zháo-huǒ-le. 着 火 了. It's

on fire. Yòng-huǒ-shāo. 用 火 燒. Use the fire to burn it. (2) heat. shēng-huǒ 生 火 make a fire or start the heat. Wūzi-li méi-yǒu-huǒ. 屋 子 裏 沒 有 火. There's no heat in the room. (3) a physical condition, such as indigestion, sore throat, headache, etc., caused by spicy and very rich food. Tā-tóuteng shàng-huǒ-le. 他 頭 痛、上 火 了. He has a head-ache, he ate too much spicy food.

HUÒ₄ 和 (TV) (1) (con. huòlong 和 攏). stir thick liquid with something long. huò-yánse 和 顏 色 mix colors. Yòng-kuài-zi-huòhuo. 用 筷 子 和 和. Stir it with chopsticks. (2) or HUÓ 和 mix liquid with solid substances. huó-miàn 和 麵 make dough with water and flour. huó-ní 和 泥 make mud.

HUÒ₂ 貨 (N) goods, merchandise. (M: pī 批). Měiguohuò 美 國 貨 American goods. Wǒ-dìng-le-yipī-huò. 我 定 了 一 批 貨. I contracted for a batch of goods. Xiànzài-quē-huò. 現 在 缺 貨. There is a short-age of this merchandise.

HUÒ₄ 禍 (N) trouble, disaster, calamity. Nǐ-bié-rě-huò. 你 別 惹 禍. Don't court dis-aster. or Don't cause trouble. Qìchē-chuǎng-huò-le. 汽 車 闖 禍 了. The automobile caused a disaster. Wǒ-yě-bu-zhīdào-shi-fú háishi-huò. 我

也 不 知 道 是 福 還 是 禍. I don't know whether it's a blessing or a disaster.

HUǑBA₅ 火 把 (N) torch.

HUǑBÀNR₅ 夥 伴 兒 (N) part-ner.

HUǑCHÁI₄ 火 柴 (N) match. (syn. yánghuǒ 洋 火). (M: gēnr 根 兒, hé 盒, bāo 包).

HUǑCHĒ₁ 火 車 (N) railway train.

HUÒCHĒ₄ 貨 車 (N) freight car or truck.

HUǑCHĒTÓU₄ 火 車 頭 (N) locomotive. (M: liàng 輛).

HUǑCHĒZHÀN₁ 火 車 站 (N) railroad station.

HUÒCHUQU₄ 豁 出 去 (RV) be determined to do something, even at the risk of losing something or everything, go ahead regard-less. Wǒ-huòchu-sānniande-gōngfu-qu, yào-bǎ-bóshi niàn-wán-le. 我 豁 出 三 年 的 工 夫 去，要 把 博 士 念 完 了. I am determined to spend three years to get my doctorate degree. Wǒ-huòchuqu-le, fēi-gēn-ta-dǎ-guānsi-bu-kě. 我 豁 出 去 了，非 跟 他 打 官 司 不 可. I'm. determined to sue him, regard-less.

HUÓDONG₂ 活 動 (SV) (1) be loose. Zhèige-dīngzi huódong-le. 這 個 釘 子 活 動 了. This nail is loose. (2) be waver-ing. Tāde-tàidu yǒu-yidiǎnr-huó-dong. 他 的 態 度 有 一 點 兒 活 動. His attitude

H

is wavering somewhat. (3) active. Tā-zài-shèhuishang hěn-huódong. 他在社會上很活動. He is very active in society.

(TV) (1) loosen up one's body by exercise. Nǐ-děi-sànsan-bù, 'huódong-huódong. You must go take a walk to loosen up. (2) move about. move about. huó-dòng-diànyǐngr 活動電影兒 moving picture, movies. (3) lobby, pull strings. Yàoshi-nǐ-dào-zhèngfǔ-qu-huódong yixia, wǒ-xiǎng-zhèige-shìqing jiu-kéyi-jiějue. 要是你到政府去活動一下,我想這個事情就可以解決. I think this matter could be solved if you would go to the government to lobby. (N) activity. zhèngzhi-huódong 政治活動 political activity.

HUÓGÁI₃ 活該 (IV) it serves someone right. Fále-ta wǔkuai-qián, huógái. 罰了他五塊錢,活該. They fined him five dollars, it serves him right.

HUÒGEN₅ 禍根 (N) (lit. root of disaster) something or someone whomight cause great trouble later on. Zhèi-shi-nuògēn. 這是禍根. This is the one which will cause trouble later on.

HUǑHOUR₅ 火候兒 (N) proper timing in cooking food. Zhèi-ge-cài huǒhour-chàyidianr. 這

個菜火候兒差一點兒.This dish didn't cook long enough. Tā-suìshu-dà-le, huǒhour-ye-dào-le. 他歲數大了,火候兒也到了. He is old and mellowed in nature.

HUǑJI₂ 夥計 (N) waiter, salesman, clerk.

HUǑJĪ₃ 火雞 (N) turkey. (M: zhī 隻).

HUǑJIÀN₂ 火箭 (N) rocket. fàng-huǒjiang 放火箭 shoot a rocket.

HUǑJIǓ₂ 火酒 (N) alcohol (other than for drinking). (syn. jiǔjīng 酒精).

HUÒLONG₅ 和攏 (TV) stir thick liquid with something long. (See: HUÒ 和).

HUÒLUÀN₃ 霍亂 (N) cholera (disease or epidemic).

HUǑLÚZI₄ 火爐子 (N) stove.

HUÓPO₂ 活潑 (SV) lively, vivacious, spirited. Zhèige-háizi zhēn-huópo. 這個孩子真活潑.This child is really vivacious.

HUǑQI₃ 火氣 (N)(1) hot-headedness. Niánqīngde dōu-yǒu-huǒ-qi. 年青的都有火氣. Young people are all hot-headed. Tāde-huǒqi-tài-dà, lǎo ài shēng-qì. 他的火氣太大,老愛生氣. He is too hot-headed, he's always angry. (2) rather garish in color. Zhèige-huāpíng bu-cuò, kěshi-yǒu-dianr-huǒqi.這個花瓶不錯,可是有點兒火氣.

This vase is not bad except it is somewhat garish.

HUǑR₃ 火 兒 (N) (1) light <u>to ig-</u> <u>nite something</u>. Jiè-ge-huǒr shí-shi. 借 個 火 兒 使 使. Could I borrow a light? (2) anger. Nǎr-lái-de-zènma-dàde-huǒr-a? 那 兒 來 的 這 麼 大 的 火 兒 啊? (<u>lit</u>. Where did such big anger come from?) Why are you so angry? (IV) be angry, get mad. Wǒ-yi-shuō, ta-jiu-huǒr-le. 我 一 説, 他 就 火 兒 了. As soon as I said it he became angry.

HUǑSHI₄ 伙 食 (N) board (<u>food</u>). Nèrde-huǒshi-bu-cuò. 那 兒 的 伙 食 不 錯. The food there is not bad.

HUÒ(ZHE)SHI₁ 或 (者) 是 <u>or</u> HUÒZHE(SHI) 或 者 (是) <u>used</u> <u>to join coordinate expressions</u>, or. Gěi-wǒ-yizhī-gāngbǐ, huò (zhe) shi-qiānbǐ. 給 我 一 枝 鋼 筆 或 (者) 是 鉛 筆. Give me a pen or a pencil. Wǒ-jīntian huò(zhe)shi-míngtian-qù. 我 今 天 或 者 是 明 天 去. I will go today or tomorrow.

(MA) perhaps, maybe. (syn. yěxǔ 也 許, huòxǔ 或 許). Huòzhe(shi)-yǒu-diǎnr-cuòr. 或 者 有 點 兒 錯 兒. Perhaps there are some errors. Huò(zhe)shi wǒ-bú-qù. 或 者 是 我 不 去. Perhaps there is still another way, that is I don't go.

HUÒ(ZHE)SHI...HUÒ(ZHE)SHI...₁ 或 者 是 ... 或 者 是 ... (S) either... or... Huòshi-hóng-de huòshi-lüde dou-xíng. 或 是 紅 的 或 是 綠 的 都 行. Either red or green ones would do.

HUǑTUǏ₃ 火 腿 (N) cured ham.

HUÒWU₄ 貨 物 (N) goods, merchandise.

HUÓXIÀNG₅ 活 像 (TV) be a living image of, closely resemble. Tā-huóxiàng-tāde-fùqin. 他 活 像 他 的 父 親. He is a living image of his father.

HUǑXĪNGR₅ 火 星 兒 (N) sparks. mào-huǒxīngr 冒 火 星 兒 shoot off sparks.

HUÒXǓ₃ 或 許 (MA) maybe, perhaps. (<u>syn</u>. yěxǔ 也 許, huò (zhe)shi 或 者 是). Tā-huòxǔ-bu-zhīdào. 他 或 許 不 知 道. Maybe he doesn't know.

HUÓYÈ₄ 活 頁 (B) loose-leaf. Zhèige-bǐjìběnr shi-huóyède. 這 個 筆 記 本 兒 是 活 頁 的. This note book is loose-leaf.

HUÒZHÀN₄ 貨 棧 (N) warehouse.

HUÒZHE(SHI)₁ 或 者 (是) <u>see</u> HUÒ(ZHE)SHI 或 者 是.

HÚQINR₅ 胡 琴 兒 (N) a kind of two-stringed Chinese musical instrument. lā-húqinr 拉 胡 琴 兒 play the two-stringed Chinese musical instrument.

HÚR₄ 核 兒 (N) core, seed, pit <u>or</u> stone in a fruit. méi-húr-de-pútou 沒 核 兒 的 葡 萄 seedless grapes. líhúr 梨 核 兒 pear core. táohúr 桃 核

H

兒 peach pit.

HŪRAN₁ 忽然 (MA) suddenly. Tā-hūrán-shuō ta-bu-zuò-le. 他 忽然 説 他 不 作 了. He suddenly said that he quit.

HÙSHI₃ 護 士 (N) nurse.(syn. kānhu 看護).

HÚSHUŌ₂ 胡 説 (TV) talk irrele-vantly, talk nonsense, say some-thing without foundation. (syn. xiāshuō 瞎 説). Bié-húshuō. 別 胡 説. Don't talk nonsense.

HÚTIĚR₄ 蝴蝶兒(N) butterfly.

HÚTÒNGR₅ 胡 同兒 (N) Peip. a narrow street, a lane.

HÚTU₂ 糊 塗 see HÚDU 糊 塗 .

HŪXI₃ 呼 吸 (N) breathing. Tā-de-hūxī hěn-kuài. 他 的 呼 吸 很 快. His breathing is very fast.

(TV) breathe. hūxī-xīnxian-kōng-qì 呼 吸 新 鮮 空 氣 breathe the fresh air. Yòng-bízi-hūxī, bié-yòng-zuǐ. 用 鼻 子 呼 吸, 別 用 嘴 Breathe with the nose, not with the month.

HÙXIĀNG₂ 互 相 (AD) mutually, reciprocally, with each other. Wǒmen-hù'xiāng-tǎolun. 我 們 互 相 討 論. We will dis-cuss it with each other. (cf: BǏCǏ 彼 此).

HŪYUE₅ 呼 籲 (TV) make an appeal,cry out for justice or aid. Tā-cháng-tì-women-hūyue. 他 常 替 我 們 呼 籲. He often cries out for justice for us.

HÙZHÀO₂ 護 照 (N) passport. qǐng-hùzhào 請 護 照 apply for a passport. lǐng-hùzhào 領 護 照 receive a passport. fā-hùzhào 發 護 照 issue a passport.

HÙZHÙ₄ 互 助 (IV) (con. hù-xiāng-bāngzhu 互 相 幫 助). help each other. Wǒmen-děi-hùzhù. 我 們 得 互 助. We must help each other.

HÚZI₂ 鬍 子 (N) beard, mus-tache. liú-húzi 留 鬍 子 grow a beard. tì-húzi 剃 鬍 子 or guā-húzi 刮 鬍 子 shave a beard.

H

J

JĪ₁ 鶏 (N) chicken. (M: zhī 隻). gōngjī 公鶏 rooster. Jī-jiào-le. 鶏 叫 了 . The rooster crowed.

JĪ₂ 機 (-B) machine. dǎzìjī 打 字機 typewriter. jìsuànjī 計算機 computer. yìnshuā-jī 印刷機 printing machine.

JÍ₂ 急 (SV) (1) be excited, angry, anxious. Wǒ-yi-shuō-ta-bu-xíng, ta-jiu-jí-le. 我 一 説 他 不 行, 他 就 急 了. Whenever I said he was no good, he got excited. Wǒ-zhēn-jí-le. 我 真 急 了 . I really got angry. (2) quick-tempered. Tā-ìngqing-hen-jí. 他 性 情 很 急 . He's quick-tempered. (3) be hurried, urgent. Tā-qùde-hěn-jí. 他 去 的 很 急 . He went there in a hurry. Zhèige-diànbào-hěn-jí. 這 個 電 報 很 急 . This cable is urgent. (AD) urgently, anxiously. Tā-jí-děng-yǒng-qián. 他 急 等 用 錢 . He needs money urgently.

JĪ₂ 擠 (SV) be crowded. Chēli-tài-jǐ. 車 裏 太 擠 . It's too crowded in the car. (TV) (1) squeeze (out) something. jǐ-jiúzi-shuǐ 擠 橘 子 水 squeeze orange juice (out of an orange). jǐ-niúnǎi 擠 牛 奶

milk a cow. (2) jostle, push someone. Bié-jǐ-wǒ. 別 擠 我 . Don't jostle me.

JǏ₁ 幾 (NU) (1) how many (when less than ten is expected). 'jǐ-qiān 幾 千 how many thousands. Nǐ-yǒu-'jǐge-háizi? 你 有 幾 個 孩 子 ? How many children do you have? (2) which one (in a sequence)Lǐbàijǐ? 禮 拜 幾 ? Which day of the week? Nǐ-kàndao-dì-'jǐyè-le? 你 看 到 第 幾 頁 了 ? Which page did you read to? (3) several, odd. 'èrshíjige 二 十 幾 個 twenty-odd. (4) used after a stressed negative verb (not) many, (not) much. Wǒ-'méi-gěi-ta-jikwài-qián. 我 沒 給 他 幾 塊 錢 . I didn't give him much money. (5) repeated in two phrases, whatever amount, no matter how much. Nǐ-'gěi-wǒ-jige wo-yào-jige. 你 給 我 幾 個 我 要 幾 個 . Whatever amount you give me, I will take. (cf: DUŌSHAO 多 少).

JÌ₁ 寄 (TV) mail, send by mail. jì-qián 寄 錢 send money. jì-xìn 寄 信 mail a letter. Wǒ-jìgei-ta-yidiǎnr-dōngxi. 我 寄 給 他 一 點 兒 東 西 . I mailed him a little something.

JÌ₁ 記 (TV) (1) remember, keep

in mind. Nǐ jìzhe. 你記着 .
Remember this. Nǐ-jìdezhù-ma?
你 記 得 住 嗎? Can you
remember? (2) jot down, take
notes. Ná-bǐ-jì-yiji. 拿筆
記 一 記 . Jot it down with a
pen. Nǐ-jìxialaile-ma? 你 記
下 來 了 嗎 ? Have you
jotted it down?

Jì₃ 繫 (TV) tie. Bǎ-xiédàizi-jì-
shang. 把 鞋 帶 子 繫 上 .
Tie your shoelaces. Jì-yige-
kòur. 繫 一 個 扣 兒 . Tie
a knot.

Jì₃ 季 (-B) season. chūnjì 春季
spring season.
(M) season. yìnián-sìjì 一 年
四 季 four seasons in a year.

JIĀ₁ 家 (N) (1) home, hometown.
Wǒ-huí-jiā. 我 回 家 . I'll
go home. (2) family. Zhāngjia
張 家 the Chang family or the
Chang home. Tā-méi-yǒu-jiā.
他 沒 有 家 . He does not
have a family.
(-B) expert, -er, -ist. huàjiā
畫 家 painter (artist).
(M) (1) for business establishment. yìjiā-xìyuàn 一 家 戲
院 a theater. (2) for a family.
Zhèige-lóuli zhù-èrshiduōjiā.
這 個 樓 裏 住 二 十
多 家 . More than twenty families live in this building.

JIĀ₂ 加 (TV) (1) add, put together,
plus. Qǐng-nǐ-jiā-yijia zhèi-
liǎngge-shùr. 請 你 加 一
加 這 兩 個 數 兒. Please
add these two figures together.
Bǎ-zhèige yě-jiāzai-litou. 把

這 個 也 加 在 裏 頭 .
Add this in there. Èr-jiā-èr dé-
sì. 二 加 二 得 四 . Two
plus two is four. (2) increase.
jiā-yibèi 加 一 倍 (lit. in-
crease by one time) double. Jiā-
wǔkuai-qián. 加 五 塊 錢 .
Add five dollars.

JIĀ₃ 夾 (TV) (1) clamp with chopsticks, pincers, tongs, etc. Tā-
yòng-kùaizi bǎ-ròu jiāqilai. 他
用 筷 子 把 肉 夾 起
來 . He picked up the meat with
chopsticks. (2) put something
between two pressing objects.
Tā-bǎ-zhàopiàn jiāzai-rìjì-běnr-
li-le. 他 把 照 片 夾 在
日 記 本 兒 裏 了 . He
put the photo in his diary. Yòng-
liǎngkuai-bǎnzi-yì-jiā jiu-píng-le.
用 兩 塊 板 子 一 夾
就 平 了 . Put it between two
boards and then it will be flat.

JIĀ₂ 假 (SV) false, not real. (opp.
zhēn 真). Bié-shuō-jiǎ-huà.
別 說 假 話 Don't make
false statements. Tāde-zhèi-
zhang-huàr shì-jiǎde. 他 的
這 張 畫 兒 是 假 的 .
This picture of his is a fake.
Zhèige-ren tài-jiǎ. 這 個 人
太 假 . This person acts very
falsely.

JIÀ₂ 假 (N) vacation, leave. qǐng-
jià 請 假 ask for leave. fàng-
jià 放 假 give a vacation. Wǒ-
men-měi-nián yǒu-sānge-lǐbàide-
jià. 我 們 每 年 有 三 個
禮 拜 的 假 . We have
three weeks' vacation every year.

JIÀ₄ 架 (M) for machines. yíjia-
fēijī 一架飛機 one air-
plane.

JIÀ₃ 嫁 (TV) (1) marry, get married (of a girl). jià-rén 嫁人
marry (a husband). Tā-jiàgei-
shéi-le? 他嫁給誰了?
Whom did she marry? (2) give
a daughter in marriage. jià-
nǚ'er 嫁女兒 give a daugh-
ter in marriage. jiàbuchūqù 嫁
不出去 cannot get married
(of a girl) or cannot find a husband for one's daughter.

JIĀCHÁNGFÀN₄ 家常飯 (N)
ordinary home-cooked meal.
(M: dùn 頓).

JIĂDÌNG₃ 假定 (TV) suppose.
Wǒmen-jiǎdìng-ta-bu-Iái, kàn-
kan-zěnma-bàn? 我們假
定他不來, 看看怎
麼辦? Let us suppose that
he would not come, then, what
should we do?
(N) supposition. Zhè-zhǐ-shi-
yíge-jiǎdìng, hái-méi-zhèngshí-
ne. 這只是一個假
定, 還沒証實呢. This
is only a supposition which has
not yet been proved.

JIĀFÙ₄ 家父 (N) a polite form
referring to one's own father,
my father.

JIĀHUO₃ 傢伙 (N) (1) utensils.
(2) guy, fellow. Nèi-jiāhuo lǎo-
piàn-rén. 那傢伙老騙
人. That guy is always
cheating.

JIĀJĬN₃ 加緊 (AD) intensively.
Wǒmen-děi-jiājǐn-gōngzuò. 我

們得加緊工作. We
have to work intensively.

JIĀJU₂ 家俱 (N) furniture. (M:
jiàn 件, tào 套).

JIĀJUAN₃ 家眷 (N) members of
a family other than the husband,
wife and children. Tā-méi-dài-
jiājuan-lai. 他沒帶家眷
來. He didn't bring his family.

JIÀMĂR₅ 價碼兒 (N) price,
marked price.

JIĀMŬ₄ 家母 (N) a polite form
referring to one's own mother,
my mother.

JIĀN₄ 煎 (TV) (1) fry (with a small
amount of oil without mixing or
stirring). jiān-jīdàn 煎鷄蛋
fry an egg or fried egg. (2) boil
herb medicine. jiān-yào 煎藥
boil herb medicine.

JIĀN₂ 尖 (SV) (1) sharp (as a point).
Qiānbǐ bugòu-jiān. 鉛筆不
够尖. The pencil isn't sharp
enough. (2) sharp, acute. Tā-
ěrduo hen-jiān. 他耳朶很
尖. He has sharp ears. (3)
high in pitch, shrill (of sound or
voice). Tā-sǎngzi hen-jiān. 他
嗓子很尖. He has a
shrill voice.

JIĀN₂ 間 (M) for room. Zhèisuǒ-
fángzi yǒu-'jǐjiān-wūzi? 這所
房子有幾間屋子?
How many rooms are there in
this house?

JIĂN₄ 鹼 (N) (1) lye. (2) alkali.

JIĂN₂ 減 (TV) (1) subtract, minus.
Liù-jiǎn-sān dé-sān. 六減
三得三. Six minus three
leaves three. (2) decrease,

J

reduce. Nǐ-děi-jiǎn-yidianr-jià.
你 得 減 一 點 兒 價.
You must reduce the price a
little.

JIĂN₃ 剪 (TV) cut, clip <u>with scis-</u>
<u>sors or clipper</u>. Yòng-jiǎnzi-
'jiǎnxia-yikuài-qu. 用 剪 子
剪 下 一 塊 去. Cut off
a piece with the scissors. (cf:
JIĂO 铰).

JIĂN₂ 撿 (TV) (1) select, pick out.
(<u>syn</u>. tiāo 挑, xiǎn 選). Tā-
lǎo-jiǎn-hǎotīngde-shuō. 他 老 撿
好 聽 的 説. He always
chooses only the agreeable things
to say. Bǎ-hǎode jiǎnchulai. 把
好 的 撿 出 來. Pick out
the good ones. (2) pick up (<u>as</u>
<u>from the floor</u>). (<u>syn</u>. shí 拾).
Bǎ-shū-jiǎnqilai. 把 書 撿
起 來. Pick up the book. (3)
find <u>something</u> accidentally. (<u>syn</u>.
shí 拾). Wǒ-zhèige-bǐ shì-jiǎn-
de, bu-shì-mǎi-de. 我 這 個
筆 是 撿 的, 不 是 買
的. I found this pen, I didn't
buy it.

J JIÀN₁ 見 (TV) (1) meet <u>or</u> see
<u>someone</u>. Míngtiān-jiàn. 明 天
見. See you tomorrow. Wǒ-
děi-qu-jiànjian-xiàoshǎng. 我
得 去 見 見 校 長. I must
go to see the principal. Wǒ-qù-
le-sānci dou-méi-jiànzháo-ta.
我 去 了 三 次 都 没
見 着 他. I went there three
times but never got to see him.
Nà-wǒ-zěnma-jiàn-rén? 那 我
怎 麼 見 人? How then
can I face people? Tā-bu-jiàn-kè.

他 不 見 客. He
won't receive guests. (2) see
(<u>for the purpose of broadening</u>
<u>one's experience</u>). Zhèizhong-
dōngxi wǒ-méi-jiànguo. 這 種
東 西 我 没 見 過. I
have never seen this kind of
thing. (3) expose to, touch. jiàn-
guāng 見 光 expose to light.
Qìyóu jiàn-huǒ-jiu-zháo, jiàn-
fēng-jiu-huà. 汽 油 見 火
就 着, 見 風 就 化. Ga-
soline would burn as soon as it
is touched by fire; it would start
to evaporate as soon as it is
exposed to the air. (4) <u>used be-</u>
<u>fore a SV</u>, appear to be, seem.
Tāde-bìng jiàn-hǎo. 他 的 病
見 好. He seems to be getting
better. Tāde-tàitai zhèiliǎngnian
jiàn-lǎo. 他 的 太 太 這
兩 年 見 老. His wife has
appeared old these past two
years.
(RE) <u>indicates perception</u>. kàn-
jian 看 見 see. yùjian 遇 見
meet.

JIÀN₃ 賤 (SV) (1) cheap, inexpensive. (opp. guì 貴). Dōngxi hěn-
jiàn. 東 西 很 賤. Things
are very cheap. (2) cheap, low,
base. jiàn-gútou 賤 骨 頭 a
wretched character. Zhèige-rén
zhēn-jiàn. 這 個 人 真 賤.
This man is really cheap and low.
(AD) at a low price. jiàn-mǎi-
jiàn-mài 賤 買 賤 賣 buy
it at a low price and sell it a low
price. (cf: PIÁNYI 便 宜).

JIÀN₁ 件 (M) (1) <u>for clothing</u>. yījian-yīshang 一件衣裳 a garment. (2) piece of furni-ture, baggage. yíjian-jiāju 一件傢俱 a piece of furni-ture. (3) for affairs, matters in general. yíjian-shìqing 一件事情 an affair. (4) for official documents. yíjian-gōng-shì一件公事an official document.

JIÀN₅ 劍 (N) sword. (M: bǎ 把).

JIÀN₄ 箭 (N) arrow. (M: zhī 枝). shè-jiàn 射箭 shoot an arrow.

JIĀNÁDÀ₂ 加拿大 (PW) Ca-nada.

JIĀNBǍNGR₅ 肩膀兒 (N) shoulder.

JIĂNBIAN₄ 簡便 (SV) simple and convenient.

JIĂNCHÁ₂ 檢查 (TV) inspect, examine. jiǎnchá-xíngli 檢查行李 inspect the luggage (at a customs office). jiǎnchá-shēn-tǐ 檢查身體 physical ex-amination or examine the physi-cal state of a person. Dàfu jiǎn-chá-buchulái shi-shénma-bìng. 大夫撿查不出來是甚麼病. The physician examined the patient but could not make a diagnosis.

JIĀNCHI₃ 堅持 (TV) insist. Tā-jiānchi yào-nènma-bàn. 他堅持要那麼辦. He in-sisted on doing it that way.

JIĂNDAN₁ 簡單 (SV) simple. (opp.fùzá 複雜). Zhèige-shì-qing bu-jiǎndan. 這個事情不簡單. This is not a simple matter. (AD) briefly, simply. Wǒ-jiǎn-

dande-gēn-ni-shuō-yishuo. 我簡單的跟你說一說. I will tell you briefly about the matter.

JIĀNDIÉ₄ 間諜 (N) spy. (cf: JIĀNXI 奸細).

JIÀNDING₅ 鑑定 (TV) authenti-cate. Wǒde-huàr dōu-shì-tā-gěi-wǒ-jiànding-de. 我的畫兒都是他給我鑑定的. All the paintings in my collection have been authenti-cated by him.

JIĀNDU₄ 監督 (TV) supervise. Nǐ-jiāndu-tamen-zuò. 你監督他們作. You supervise them to do it. (N) supervisor. hǎiguān-jiāndu 海關監督 supervisor of customs.

JIĀNG₄ 江 (N) (1) river. (M: tiáo 條). Qiánmian-yǒu-yitiáo-dà-jiāng. 前面有一條大江. There is a big river in front. (2) Yangtze River. Tā-shi-jiāng-nán-rén. 他是江南人. His home town is in the region south of the Yangtze.

JIĀNG₅ 薑 (N) ginger. (M: kuài 塊).

JIĀNG₃ 僵 (SV) (1) unnatural, stiff, uncomfortable. Tā-zài-táishang shuō-huà-de-shihou, yàngzi-hěn-jiāng. 他在台上說話的時候,樣子很僵. When he speaks on the stage(or lecture platform), he seems to be very uncomfortable. (2) em-barrassing (of a situation). Nèige-qíngxing jiāng-jíle. 那個情

J

形僵極了 . That situation is extremely embarrassing. (RE) indicates a deadlock. Bié-bă-shìqing nòngjiăng-le. 別把事情弄僵了 . Don't drive the situation to a deadlock. (TV) dare someone. Nĭ-bié-jiāng-wo. 你別僵我 . Don't dare me.

JIĂNG₁ 講 (TV) (1) explain. (syn. jiĕshi 解釋). Tā-gĕi-wŏ-jiăngle-bàntiān wŏ-yĕ-bu-dŏng. 他給我講了半天我也不懂 . He explained it to me for a long time, but I still do not understand it. Zhèi-ge-zì zĕnma-jiăng? 這個字怎麼講 ? What is the meaning of this word? (2) speak, talk. (syn. shuō 説). Bú-yào-jiăng-huà. 不要講話 . Don't talk. Wŏ-gĕi-nĭ-jiăng-yi-ge-gùshi. 我給你講一個故事 . I'll tell you a story. (3) discuss something which is in dispute or is uncertain. Tāmen-jiănghé-le. 他們講和了 . They have started to negotiate for peace. Nĭ-gēn-ta jiángjiang-jiàqian. 你跟他講講價錢 . (You) bargain with him over the price. (4) pay special attention to, be conscientious about. Tāmen-hĕn-jiăng-jiāoqing. 他們很講交情 . They are very conscientious about friendship. Tā-bu-jiăng-lĭ. 他不講理 . He doesn't pay attention to

reason. (M) lecture (oral or written). Zhè-shi-dìyĭjiăng. 這是第一講 . This is the first lecture.

JIĂNG₃ 獎 (N) prize, reward. Tā-déle-tóujiăng-le. 他得了頭獎了 . He won first prize.

JIĂNG₃ 醬 (N) (1) thick sauce (make from soybeans). (2) edible substances in the form of thick sauce, jam. guŏzijiàng 果子醬 jam. xīhóngshìjiàng 西紅柿醬 ketchup, tomato paste. (TV) pickle or cook in soy sauce. jiàng-ròu 醬肉 cook meat in soy sauce.

JIÀNGDĪ₃ 降低 (TV) lower, reduce. Bă 'jiàqian jiàngdī. 把價錢降低 . Lower the price.

JIĀNGHU₄ 糨糊 or JIÀNGZI 糨子 paste (adhesive).

JIĂNG-JIÀQIAN₃ 講價錢 (VO) bargain over price.

JIĂNGJĪN₄ 獎金 (N) monetary reward, prize. (M: bĭ 筆).

JIĀNGJIU₃ 將就 (TV) tolerate, put up with, make things do. (syn. còuhe 湊合). Nĭ-'jiāngjiu-jiāngjiu-ta-ba. 你將就將就他吧 . Please put up with him. Wŏ-zhīdao zhèige-bùhǎo, nĭ-jiāngjiu-yòng-ba. 我知道這個不好，你將就用吧 . I know it's not good, just try to make it do. (cf: DUÌFU 對付).

JIĂNGJIU₂ 講究 (SV) exquisite, excellent. Tāde-qìchē zhēn-jiăngjiu. 他的汽車真

講究 . His car is really exquisite.

(TV) meticulous about. Tā-zuì-jiăngjiu-chī. 他 最 講 究 吃 . He is particular about food.

(N) particulars, details. 'Năr-yŏu-nènma-xie-jiăngjiu? 那兒 有 那 麼 些 講 究? How can one care so much for particulars?

JIĂNGJÚ₄ 僵 局 (N) a deadlocked situation. 'Zĕnmayàngr cái-néng bă-zhèige-jiāngjú dă-pòle-ne? 怎 麼 樣 兒 才 能 把 這 個 僵 局 打 破 了 呢? How can we break the deadlock in this situation?

JIĀNGJUN₃ 將 軍 (N) general (military rank).

(VO) (1) check (in chess). jiāng-nĭde-jūn 將 你 的 軍 check.
(2) challenge someone. jiāng-ta-yijūn 將 他 一 軍 challenge him.

JIĀNGLÁI₁ 將 來 (TW) future. Jiānglái huì-bĭ-xiànzài-hăo. 將 來 會 比 現 在 好 . The future will be better than the present. Nĭ-jiānglái-zuò-shén-me-ne? 你 將 來 作 甚 麼 呢? What are you going to do in the future?

JIĂNG-LĬ₂ 講 理 (VO) argue logically, appeal to reason. Nĭ-bu-jiăng-lĭ wŏ-'dă-nĭ. 你 不 講 理 我 打 你 . If you do not listen to reason, I'll strike you.

JIĂNGLI₄ 獎 勵 (TV) give

someone a reward or praise for encouragement. Tā-zuò-de-'zèn-ma-hăo, wŏmen-dĕi-'jiăngli-jiăngli-ta. 他 作 的 這 麼 好 . 我 們 得 獎 勵 獎 勵 他 . He has done it so well that we must reward him.

JIÀNGLUOSĂN₄ 降 落 傘 (N) parachute.

JIĂNGPIN₄ 獎 品 (N) prize. dé-jiăngpin 得 獎 品 win a prize.

JIĂNG-QÍNG₄ 講 情 (VO) ask for a favor or forgiveness for someone. Tā-fùqin-yào-dă-ta, ta-mŭ-qin-gĕi-ta-jiăng-qíng. 他 父 親 要 打 他, 他 母 親 給 他 講 情 . His father wants to punish him; his mother speaks for him.

JIĀNGSHENG₅ 韁 繩 (N) reins. (M: tiáo 條).

JIĂNG-SHŪ₃ 講 書 (VO) explain the textbook (for students).

JIĀNGSU₂ 江 蘇 (PW) Kiangsu province.

JIĂNGTÁI₄ 講 臺 (N) speaker's platform or lecture platform.

JIĂNGTÁNG₃ 講 堂 (N) lecture hall.

JIÀNGUÀI₄ 見 怪 (IV) be offended. Nín-bié-jiànguài. 你 別 見 怪 . Don't be offended.

JIĀNGXI₂ 江 西 (PW) Kiangsi province.

JIĂNG-XUÉ₃ 講 學 (VO) give an academic lecture.

JIĂNGXUÉJIN₂ 獎 學 金 (N) scholarship (monetary reward). dé-jiăngxuéjīn 得 獎 學 金 receive a scholarship.

J

JIĂNG-YĂN₂ 講演 or YĂN-
JIĂNG 演講 (VO) give a
speech or lecture. Wǒ-méi-
jiǎngguo-yǎn. 我 沒 講 過
演 . I have never given a
speech.
(N) speech, lecture. (M: cì 次 ,
piān 篇). Tāde-jiǎng-yǎn nǐ-
tīngle-meiyou? 他 的 講演
你 聽 了 沒 有 ? Did you
attend his lecture?
(TV) speak in public. Tā-jīntian-
jiǎng-yǎn-yige-shèhuìxuéde-wèn-
ti. 他 今 天 講演 一 個
社 會 學 的 問 題 . To-
day he is going to talk about a
sociological problem.

JIĀNGYAO₄ 將要 (AV) just
about to. Wǒ-jiāngyao-qu-zhǎo-
ta, ta-jiu-lái-le. 我 將要
去 找 他, 他 就 來 了.
When I was just about to look
for him, he came.

JIĂNGYÌ₃ 講義 (N) lecture
notes.

JIÀNGYÓU₄ 醬油 (N) soy sauce.

JIÀNGZI₄ 糨子 or JIÀNGHU
糨糊 (N) paste (adhesive).

JIĂN-JIÀ₃ 減價 (VO) reduce the
price, on sale.

JIÀNJIĀN(DE)₃ 漸漸(的) (MA)
gradually, little by little. Jiàn-
jiān(de) tiānqi-jiu-muǎnhuo-le.
漸漸(的) 天 氣 就 暖 和
了 . It's getting warmer gradually.

'JIĀNJIĒ₃ 間接 (opp. 'ZHÍJIĒ
直接) (SV) indirect. Wǒmende-guānxi tài-jiānjie-le. 我 們
的 關 係 太 間 接 了 .

Our relationship is very indirect.
(AD) indirectly. Nǐ-zuìhǎo-gēn-
ta-jiānjiēde-jiāoshe. 你 最
好 跟 他 間 接 的 交
涉 . You'd better negotiate
with him through somebody else.

JIÀNJIE₃ 見解 (N) one's view
or understanding of a problem.
Yíge-rén yǒu-yíge-rén-de-jiàn-
jie. 一 個 人 有 一 個 人
的 見 解 . Everyone has his
own view.

JIĀNJUE₄ 堅決 (SV) determined,
firm. Tāde-yìsi hen-jiānjue. 他
的 意 思 很 堅 決 . He
is determined.
(AD) firmly. Wǒ-jiānjue-fǎnduì.
我 堅 決 反 對 . I firmly
oppose it.

JIÀNKANG₃ 健康 (SV) healthy,
in good health. Tāde-shēnti hen
jiànkang. 他 的 身 體 很
健 康 . He is very healthy.
(N) health. Tā-bu-kěn-zuò-nèi-
ge-shìqing, shi-yīnwei-jiàng-
kangde-guānxi. 他 不 肯 作
那 個 事 情, 是 因 為
健 康 的 關 係 . He de-
clined to do the work for reasons
of health.

JIÀNLI₃ 建立 (TV) establish an
organization or something abstract. Wǒmen-děi-bǎ-xuéxiàode-
míngyu jiànli-qilai. 我 們 得
把 學 校 的 名 譽 建
立 起 來 . We have to estab-
lish the reputation of the school.

JIÀN-MIÀN₂ 見面 (VO) meet or
see someone. Wǒ-zuìhao-gēn-ta-
dìng-ge-rìzi jiànjian-miàn. 我

最 好 跟 他 訂 個 日 子 見 見 面 . I better make an appointment to see him. Tā-nèicì-lái, wǒ-gēn-ta jiu-jiànle-yímiàn. 他 那 次 來 , 我 跟 他 就 見 了 一 面 . I saw him only once when he came the other time.

JIĂNMÍNG₅ 簡 明 (SV) (con. jiǎndan 簡 單 and mínglião 明 了). simple and clear.

JIĀNNAN₄ 艱 難 (SV) difficult to manage. Xiànzài shēnghuo-hěn-jiānnan. 現 在 生 活 很 艱 難 . It's difficult to make a living nowadays.

(N) difficulty, hardship. Nián-qīngde bu-zhīdào-shénma-shi-jiānnan. 年 青 的 人 不 知 道 甚 麼 是 艱 難 . Young people don't know what hardship is.

JIÀNNÈI₅ 賤 內 (N) my (humble) wife (polite form).

JIĂNQĪNG₃ 減 輕 (TV) reduce ´burdens). Jīnniande-gōngzuò-jiānqiāng-le. 今 年 的 工 作 減 輕 了 . The work for this year is reduced.

JIĂNSHǍO₃ 減 少 (TV) reduce or decrease the number of some-thing. Zhèr-de-rénkou jiānshǎo-le-yíbàn. 這 兒 的 人 口 減 少 了 一 半 . The pop-ulation here has decreased by half. Wǒmen kéyi-bǎ-xuésheng-de-snumu jiānshǎo-le. 我 們 可 以 把 學 生 的 數 目 減 少 了 . We may re-duce the number of students.

JIÀNSHE₂ 建 設 (TV) build up, develop. jiànshe-xuéxiào 建 設 學 校 build up a school. jiàn-she-guójiā 建 設 國 家 build up a country or reconstruct a country.

(N) (1) development. (2) recon-struction.

JIÁNSHENG₄ 儉 省 (TV) save, conserve. Zhèi-yàngr wǒmen-kéyi-jiānsheng-shíhou. 這 樣 兒 我 們 可 以 儉 省 時 候 . We can save time this way. (SV) thrifty. Tā-hěn-jiānsheng. 他 很 儉 省 . He's quite thrifty.

JIÀNSHI₂ 見 識 (N) experience and knowledge. Tāde-jiànshi hěn-guǎng. 他 的 見 識 很 廣 . His knowledge and expe-rience are very wide.

(TV) experience something. Jiào-tamen-jiànshi-jianshi. 叫 他 們 見 識 見 識 . Let them gain some experience.

JIÁNTAO₃ 檢 討 (TV) review and discuss a matter. Bǎ-wǒ-men-guòqù-zuò-de-shì jiántao-jiantao. 把 我 們 過 去 作 的 事 檢 討 檢 討 . Let us review and discuss what we have done in the past.

JIÀNWÀI₄ 見 外 (VO) regard someone as an outsider. Nín-bié-jiànwài. 您 別 見 外 . (lit. Please do not regard your-self as a stranger.) Please make yourself at home.

JIĀNXI₅ 奸 細 (N) spy (old term). (cf: JIÁNDIÉ 間 諜).

J

JIÀNXIÀO₄ 見笑 (IV) ridicule, laugh at. Ràng-nín-jiànxiào. 讓您見笑. You must have thought it ridiculous. Nín-bié-jiànxiào. 您別見笑. Please do not laugh (at me).

JIÀN-XIÀO₃ 見效 (VO) become or seem to be effective (of medicine or medical treatment). Zhèige-yào bu-jiàn-xiào. 這個藥不見效. This medicine doesn't seem to be effective.

JIÀN-XĪN₃ 見新 (VO) make something new in appearance. Tā-bǎ-fángzi yóule-you, jiàn-jian-xīn. 他把房子油了油, 見見新. He painted the house and made it appear new.

JIĀNYÙ₄ 監獄 (N) jail. (M:suǒ 所). xià-jiānyù 下監獄 go to jail.

JIÀNZHENG₄ 見証 (N) witness. Wǒ-kéyi zuò-jiànzheng. 我可以作見証. I can be the witness.

JIǍNZHÍ(DE)₂ 簡直(的) (AD) simply, just, merely. Wǒ-jiǎn-zh(de)-méi-fázi. 我簡直(的)沒法子. I simply do not know what to do. Tā-jiǎn-zhí(de)-shi-húshuō. 他簡直(的)是胡說. He simply talks nonsense.

JIÀNZHU₃ 建築 (N) (1) architecture (design of buildings, bridges, etc.). Zhèige-jiànzhu zhēn-wěidà. 這個建築真偉大. This architecture is great. Tā-kāi-jiànzhu-gōngsī. 他開建築公司. He runs an architectural firm. (2) or JIÀNZHUXUÉ 建築學 architecture (as a branch of learning). Wǒ-xiǎng-xué-jiànzhu. 我想學建築. I want to learn architecture. (TV) build, make buildings, bridges, roads, etc. Tāmen-zhèng-zai-jiànzhu-yízuò-qiáo. 他們正在建築一座橋. They are building a bridge now.

JIÀNZHUANG₅ 健壯 (SV) strong and healthy. Zhèixie-rénde-shēn-ti fēichang-jiànzhuang. 這些人的身體非常健壯. These people are very healthy and strong.

JIÀNZHUSHĪ₅ 建築師 (N) architect.

JIÀNZHUXUÉ₄ 建築學 see JIÀNZHU 建築 (N) (2).

JIǍNZI₄ 剪子 (N) scissors. (M: bǎ 把). yìbǎ-jiǎnzi 一把剪子 a pair of scissors. Yòng-jiǎnzi jiǎokai. 用剪子鉸開. Use the scissors to cut it.

JIǍNZÌ₂ 簡字 (N) simplified form of Chinese characters.

JIĀO₂ 交 (TV) (1) hand over, deliver. Tā-hái-méi-jiāo-xuéfèi-ne. 他還沒交學費呢. He hasn't paid his tuition yet. Wǒ-bǎ-zhèijian-shìqing jiāogei-ta-le. 我把這件事情交給他了. I passed this matter on to him. Wǒmen-děi-ànzhe-shíhou jiāohuò. 我們得按着時候交貨. We should deliver the merchandise on time. (2) submit something to someone for inspection. Bié-jiāo-bái-juànr. 別交白卷兒. Don't submit a blank examination paper. (3) make friends. Tā-zài-nèr jiāole-hěn-duo-péngyou. 他在那兒交了很多朋友. He made a lot of friends there.

(B) friendship. Tāmen-jué-jiāo-le. 他們絕交了. They broke off their friendship.

JIĀO₁ 教 (TV) teach. Wǒ-jiāo-ni. 我教你. Let me teach you. Tā-jiāo Yīngwén. 他教英文. He teaches English. Wǒ-bǎ-ta-jiāohuì-le. 他把我教會了. I taught him until he mastered it. Zhèige-gēr shi-tā-jiāogei-wo-de. 這個歌兒是他教給我的. It was he who taught me this song.

JIĀO₄ 澆 (TV) pour over, water flowers or plants. Nǐ-jiāo-huār-le-ma? 你澆花兒了嗎? Did you water the flower?

JIÁO₃ 嚼 (TV) chew. Zhèige-ròu-tài-lǎo, jiáobudòng. 這個肉太老, 嚼不動. This meat is too tough, I can't chew it.

JIĀO₂ 脚 (N) foot. (M: zhǐ 隻). Kàn-ta-nèi-liǎngzhi-jiǎo. 看他那兩隻脚. Look at his two feet.

(M) for an instance of kicking.

Wǒ-tīle-ta-yijiao. 我踢了他一脚. I gave him a kick.

JIĀO₄ 鉸 (TV) Peip. cut with scissors. Zhèige-jiǎnzi-bu-kuài, jiāobudòng. 這個剪子不快, 鉸不動. This pair of scissors isn't sharp, it won't cut. (cf: JIĂN 剪).

JIĀO₄ 角 (N) horn (of an animal). (M: zhǐ 隻). niú-jiāo 牛角 horns of a bull or buffalo.

JIĂO₅ 繳 (TV) hand in, hand over. jiǎo-shuì 繳稅 pay duty or tax. jiǎo-xuéfèi 繳學費 pay tuition.

JIÀO₅ 窖 (N) underground storage room or cellar. bīng-jiào 冰窖 ice cellar.

JIÀO₁ 叫 (TV) (1) yell, shout. (syn. hǎn 喊, rǎng 嚷). Tā-dà-shēng-de-jiào. 他大聲的叫. He yelled loudly. (2) call, summon. (syn. hǎn 喊). Nǐ-yi-jiào-wo, wo-jiu-lái-le. 你一叫我, 我就來了. As soon as you called, I came. (3) be called, named. Tā-jiào-shénma-míngzi? 他叫甚麼名子? What (name) is he called? Zhè-jiu-jiào-chōu-xiàng-huàr. 這就叫抽象畫兒. This is called abstract painting. (4) with a direct and indirect object. call, address someone as. Wǒ-jiào-ta-Lǐ-taitai. 我叫他李太太. I address her as Mrs. Li. (5) order something. Nǐ-jiào-cài-le-meiyou? 你叫菜了沒有? Did you order the food (in a restaurant)? (6) blow, whistle. Qìchē-de-lǎba-zhí-jiào. 汽車的喇叭直叫. The horn of the car is blowing. (7) (con. jiào-huan 叫喚).cry or call (of animals, birds, insects,etc.). gǒu-jiào 狗叫 the dog barks. mǎ-jiào 馬叫 the horse neighs. Niǎor-jiàode hěn-hǎotǐng. 鳥兒叫得很好聽. The birds are singing beautifully. (8) dial a telephone or ask the operator to dial the number. Nǐ-yào-dǎ-diànhuàde-shihou, wǒ-gěi-nǐ-jiào. 你要打電話的時候, 我給你叫. When you want to make a phone call, I'll dial for you. (9) tell or ask someone to do something. (syn. ràng讓). Wǒ-jiào-tā-zuò-zhèi-ge, tā-bu-tǐng. 我叫他作這個他不聽. I told him to do this, but he wouldn't listen. (10) make, cause. (syn. ràng讓, shǐ使). Tā-shuō-de-huà jiào-wǒ-hěn-buhǎoyìsi. 他說的話叫我很不好意思. What he said made me very embarrassed. (11) let.(syn. ràng讓). Yàoshi-ta-yídìng-yào-zǒu, jiu-jiào-ta-zǒu-ba. 要是他一定要走, 就叫他走吧. If he insists on leaving, we'd better let him go. Tā-bu-jiào-shuō-huà. 他不叫說話. He won't allow any talking. (CV)by (marking the agent, often accompanied by the adverb gěi

給). (syn. ràng讓, bèi被). Wǒ-de-fángzi-jiào-tāde-qìchē gei-pènghuài-le. 我的房子叫他的汽車給碰壞了. My house was damaged by his car running into it.

(S) guǎn ... jiào ... 管... 叫 ... call someone or something by a specific name. Zhōng-guo-huà (guǎn-)zhèige-jiào-shénma? 中國話(管)這個叫甚麼? What's this called in Chinese? Wǒmen-dou-guǎn-ta-jiào-Lǎo-Lǐ. 我們都管他叫老李. We all call him old Li.

JIĀO'AO$_2$ 驕傲 (SV) proud, haughty. Nǐ-jiùshi-xuéwen-hǎo, yě-bu-yīngdāng-jiāo'ao. 你就是學問好, 也不應當驕傲. You shouldn't be haughty even if you are learned. Wǒmen-dōu-wèi-Zhōngguo-jiāo'ao. 我們都為中國驕傲. We are all proud of China.

(N) pride. Wǎnlichángchéng shì-Zhōngguode-jiāo'ao. 萬里長城是中國的驕傲. The Great Wall is the pride of Chinese people.

JIĀOBĚN$_4$ 教本 (N) textbook.

JIĀOBUR$_4$ 腳步兒 (N) footstep,gait, pace. Tāde-jiāobur hen-qīng. 他的腳步兒很輕. His footsteps are very light. fig. Wǒmen-děi-bǎ-jiāobur zhànwěn-le. 我們得把腳步兒站穩了. We have to take a firm stand.

JIÀOCÁI₃ 教材 (N) teaching materials.

JIĀODAI₃ 交代 (TV) (1) turn over work to someone with instructions. Wǒmen-děi-bǎ-shìqing jiāodai-qīngchu. 我們得把事情交代清楚. We have to turn over things clearly. (2) explain, give a reason for one's action. Wǒ-méifázì duì-shàngsi-jiāodai. 我没法子對上司交代. I have no way of explaining to my boss. Yàoshi-nín-bu-bǎqián-géi wo, wǒ-huíqu-bu-néng-jiāodai. 要是您不把錢給我,我回去不能交代. If you don't give me the money I can't explain it when I go back. (3) explain (for information). Zhèi-yìdiǎn wǒ-zai-gēn-nín-jiāodai-jiaodai. 這一點我再跟您交代交代. As to this point, I have to explain it to you once more. (IV) (1) finished, completed. Nèi-ge-gōngzuo jiu-suàn-jiāodai-le. 那個工作就算交代了. That work can be considered as finished. (2) finished, all gone. Wǒ-nèi-wǔbaikuai-qián jiu-suan-jiāodai-le. 我那五百塊錢就算交代了. That five hundred dollars of mine can be considered as all gone. (N) explanations, excuse. Yǒu-wènti-de-dìfang yídìng-dei-yǒu-

ge-jiāodai. 有問題的地方一定得有個交代. If there is a problem there must be an explanation. (2) transference of work. Tā-zhèng-zai-bàn-jiāodai. 他正在辦交代. He is transferring his work now.

JIĀODĂO₅ 教導 (TV) educate, guide someone in learning. Nín-zhēnhuì-jiàodǎo xuésheng. 您真會教導學生. You really can educate students.

JIĀODĬXIÉ₄ 膠底鞋 (N) sneakers (with rubber sole). (M: shuāng 雙).

JIĂODU₃ 角度 (N) lit or fig. angle. Wǒmen-kéyi-cóng-lìng-wài-yíge-jiǎodu-kàn. 我們可以從另外一個角度看. We may look at it from another angle.

JIÀODUÌ₃ 校對 (TV) proofread. Zhèipiān-wénzhang shì-shéi-jiāoduìde? 這篇文章是誰校對的? Who was the one who proofread this article? (N) proofreader. Tā-zài-bàoguǎn dāng-jiàcduì. 他在報館當校對. He works as a proofreader for a newspaper.

JIÀOGUĀN₄ 教官 (N) military officer who serves as an instructor.

JIĂOHÁNG₄ 脚行 (N) porter, red-cap.

JIĂOHÒUGEN₅ 脚後跟 (N) heel of the foot.

JIĂOHUÁ₃ 狡猾 (SV) sly, cunning.

J

JIĀOHUÀN₄ 交換 (TV) trade, exchange. Shuāngfāng-tóngyì-jiāohuàn-fúluǒ. 雙方同意交換俘虜 . Both sides agreed to exchange prisoners of war. Yàoshi-ni-xǐhuan-wǒde-biǎo, wǒmen-yéyi-jiāohuàn. 要是你喜歡我的表，我們可以交換 . If you like my watch we can trade.

JIÀOHUAN₃ 叫喚 (TV) cry or call (of animals, birds, insects, etc.).

JIÀOHUÌ₂ 教會 (N) church (organization). Tā-zài-jiàohuì-zuò-shì, kěshi-tā-bú-zài-jiàotáng-bàn-gōng. 他在教會作事，可是不在教堂辦公 . He works for the church, but he doesn't work in the church building. (cf: JIÀO-TÁNG 教堂).

JIĀOJÌ₂ 交際 (TV) make social contacts, socialize. Tā-ài-gēn-ren-jiāojì. 他愛跟人交際 . He likes to make social contacts.

(N) social relations, social contact. Tāde-jiāojì hěn-guǎng. 他的交際很廣 . He has broad social relations.

JIĀO-JIÈ₃ 交界 (VO) meet, come together at a border. Měi-guo-gēn-Jiānádà jiāo-jiè.美國跟加拿大交界 . The United States borders Canada.

JIĀO-JIÈ₄ 繳械 see JIĀO-XIÈ 繳械 .

JIĀOJUĂNR₃ 膠捲兒 (N) roll of photographic film.

JIÀOKÈSHŪ₂ 教科書 (N) textbook. (M: běn 本).

JIĀONEN₄ 嬌嫩 (SV) delicate, tender. Zhèi-zhǒng-huār fēi-chang-jiāonen. 這種花兒非常嬌嫩 . This kind of flower is extremely delicate.

JIĀOPÍ₄ 膠皮 (N) rubber.

JIĀOPÍXIÉ₃ 膠皮鞋 (N) rubbers, rubber overshoes. (M: shuāng 雙).

JIĀOQI₅ 腳氣 (N) athlete's foot.

JIĀOQÍNG₃ 交情 (N) friendship. Tāmende-jiāoqing hěn-shēn. 他們的交情很深 . The friendship between them is very profound. Tā-zuò-shì bu-jiǎng-jiāoqing. 他作事不講交情 . Friendship is not considered when he does something.

JIÁOQING₄ 矯情 (SV) unreasonable (of a child). Bié-jiáoqing. 別矯情 . Don't be unreasonable. Zhèi-háizi you-nào-jiáoqing. 這孩子又鬧矯情 . This child is becoming unreasonable again.

JIĂOR₄ 角兒 (N) (1) or JUÉR 角兒 role, part (as in a play). (2) angle. zhíjiǎor直角兒right angle. (3) corner. zhōuzi-jiǎor 桌子角兒 the corner of the table.

JIĀOSHE₃ 交涉 (TV) negotiate. Wǒmen-děi-gēn-ta jiāoshe-jiao-she. 我們得跟他交涉交涉 . We must negotiate with him.

(N) negotiation. Měiguo-gēn-Fàguo-de-jiāoshe-yǐjing-bànwánle. 美國跟法國的交涉已經辦完了. The negotiations between the United States and France have already been completed.

JIÀOSHĪ₃ 教師 (N) teacher, instructor.

JIÀOSHÌ₂ 教室 (N) classroom. (M: jiān 間).

JIÀOSHÒU₂ 教授 (N) professor. (M: wèi 位).

JIĀO-SHŪ₁ 教書 (VO) teach <u>academic subjects.</u>

JIÀOSHUǏR₄ 膠水兒 (N) liquid glue.

·JIĀOTÀCHĒ₃ 脚踏車 (N) bicycle. (<u>syn.</u> zìxíngchē 自行車). (M: liàng 輛). qí-jiǎotàchē 騎脚踏車 ride a bicycle.

JIÀOTÁNG₂ 教堂 (N) church (building). (cf: JIÀOHUÌ 教會).

JIĀOTŌNG₂ 交通 (N) (1) communication, transportation. Jiāotōng-fānbian. 交通方便 . Transportation is very convenient. Méiyou-jiāotōng-gōngjù. 沒有交通工具 . There's no means of transportation. (2) traffic. jiāotōng-jǐngchá 交通警察 traffic policeman.

JIÀOTÚ₄ 教徒 (N) follower, believer (<u>of a religion</u>).

JIĀOWÀI₄ 郊外 (PW) countryside , suburb.

JIĀOWANG₄ 交往 (N) social contact, intercourse. Wǒmen-méi-you-jiāowang. 我們沒有交往 . We don't have any

contact.

JIÀOWÙ₄ 教務 (N) academic affairs (<u>in a school</u>).

JIĀOXIÉ₄ 膠鞋 (N) (1) sneakers. (2) rubbers (<u>worn over shoes</u>). (M: shuāng 雙).

JIĀO-XIÈ₄ 繳械 <u>or</u> JIĂO-JIÈ 繳械 (VO) disarm. Tāmen-bǎ-bàibīng-jiǎole-xiè-le. 他們把敗兵繳了械了 . They disarmed the defeated soldiers.

JIĀO-XĪN₃ 焦心 (VO) worried. Zhèi-jiàn-shì zhēn-jiào-ren-jiāo-xīn. 這件事真教人焦心 . This affair is really making people worry.

JIĂOXÌNG₂ 徼幸 (SV) lucky. Wǒ-zhǎozhao-zěnma-hǎode-shì zhēn-shi-jiǎoxìng-de-hěn. 我找着這麼好的事,真是徼幸得很 . I was really very lucky to get such a good job. (MA) fortunately, by sheer luck. Wǒ-jiǎoxìng kǎoshang-zhèige-xuéxiào-le. 我徼幸考上這個學校了 . I passed this schools's entrance examination by sheer luck.

JIÀOXUÉ₃ 教學 (N) teaching, instruction. yǔ'yán-jiàoxué 語言教學 language teaching. (TV) teach. Tā-zài-xuéxiào-jiāoxué. 他在學校教學 . He teaches school.

JIÀOXUN₂ 教訓 (TV) teach, give <u>someone</u> a lesson. Fùmǔ yīng-dāng-chángchang-jiàoxun-zǐnǚ. 父母應當常常教訓子女 . Parents should

J

teach their children all the time.
Wŏ-děi-hăohăorde-jiàoxun-ta-
yidùn. 我 得 好 好 地 教
訓 他 一 頓 . I'll give him
a good lesson.
(N) lesson, teaching (gained from
an unhappy experience). Zhèi-
shì-yíge-hěn-hăode-jiàoxun. 這
是 一 個 很 好 的 教
訓 . This is a good lesson.
JIÀOYU₁ 教 育 (TV) educate,
train, develop. Wŏ-méi-hăo-
hăorde-jiàoyu-wŏde-érzi. 我
沒 好 好 兒 的 教 育
我 的 兒 子 . I didn't put
much effort into educating my
son.
(N) education. Tā-méi-shòuguo-
shenma-jiàoyu. 他 沒 受 過
甚 麼 教 育 . He didn't
receive much education.
JIÀOYUÁN₁ 教 員 (N) (1) teacher
(in a school). (2) instructor (as
a rank in a college or university).
JIÀOYUBÙ₄ 教 育 部 (N) Min-
istry of Education.
JIĂOZHENG₄ 矯 正 (TV) correct,
rectify mistakes. Nĭ-yīnggāi bă-
bu-hăo-de-xíguan dōu-jiàozheng-
guolai. 你 應 該 把 不 好
的 習 慣 都 矯 正 過
來 . You should correct all
your bad habits.
JIĂOZHÍTOU₅ 脚 指 頭 (N) toe.
JIĂOZI₄ 餃 子 (N) thin piece of
dough filled with chopped meat
and vegetables (usually boiled),
Chinese dumpling. bāo-jiăozi 包
餃 子 make Chinese dumplings
or Chinese dumplings.

JIÀQIAN₁ 價 錢 (N) price.
JIĀQIÁNG₄ 加 強 (TV) strength-
en, reinforce. Wŏmen-yīngdāng
jiāqiáng-wŏmende-jūnduì. 我
們 應 當 加 強 我 們
的 軍 隊 . We should re-
inforce our troops.
JIĀQIĂOR₅ 家 雀 兒 (N) spar-
row. (M: zhī 隻).
JIĀRU₃ 加 入 (TV) join an organization. Nĭ-jiārùguo-shenma-
zhèngdăng-ma? 你 加 入 過
甚 麼 政 黨 嗎 ? Have
you joined any political party?
JIĂRU₃ 假 如 (MA) if, supposing
that. (syn. rúguŏ 如 果 , yàoshi 要 是 , jiăshĭ 假 使).
Jiăru wŏ-shì-ni-fùqin, wŏ-jiu-
bù-xŭ-ni-qù. 假 如 我 是
你 父 親 , 我 就 不 許
你 去 . If I were your father,
I wouldn't let you go.
JIĂSHI₄ 假 使 (MA) if, assuming
that. (syn. yàoshi 要 是 , rúguŏ 如 果 , jiăru 假 如).
Jiăshĭ-míngtian-xià-yŭ wŏ-jiu-
bu-lái-le. 假 使 明 天 下
雨 , 我 就 不 來 了 . I
won't come if it's raining tomorrow.
JIÀSHIYUÁN₄ 駕 駛 員 (N) pilot
(of an airplane).
JIĀSI₅ 家 私 (N) family property.
JIĀTING₂ 家 庭 (N) family.
JIĀXIĀNG₄ 家 鄉 (N) home town,
home country.
JIĀ-XIĂOXIN₃ 加 小 心 (VO)
be more careful. Nĭ-děi-jiā-
dianr-xiăoxin. 你 得 加 點
兒 小 心 . You must be a

little more careful.

JIĀ-YÓU₂ 加 油 (VO) (1) add oil
(for lubrication or fuel). Zhèige-
jīqi gāi-jiā-yóu-le. 這 個 機
器 該 加 油 了. This
machine needs lubrication now.
Wŏde-chē yíge-lǐbài jiā-liǎngcì-
yóu. 我 的 車 一 個 禮
拜 加 兩 次 油. I fill up
my car twice a week. (2) put
more effort into something. Wèi-
le-zǎo-yìdiǎnr-zuòwán, wŏmen-
děi-jiā-yidianr-yóu. 為 了 早
一 點 兒 作 完, 我 們
得 加 一 點 油. In order
to finish it earlier, we have to
put more effort into it.

JIĀZHĂNG₃ 家 長 (N) head of a
family.

JIĀZHI₂ 價 值 (N) value. yŏu-
jiàzhi 有 價 值 valuable.
Zhèige-yŏu-jiàzhi kěshi-bu-zhí-
qián. 這 個 有 價 值 可
是 不 值 錢. This is val-
uable but it has no monetary
value.

JIĀZHUANG₄ 嫁 妝 (N) dowry.
Tā-zhèng-gei-ta-nǚ'ér bàn-jià-
zhuang-ne. 他 正 給 他 女
兒 辦 嫁 妝 呢. He is
providing the dowry for his
daughter.

JIĂZHUĀNGR₃ 假 裝 兒 (TV)
pretend to do something. Wŏ-
jiǎzhuāngr-bu-zhīdào. 我 假
裝 兒 不 知 道. I pre-
tended not to know.

JIĀZI₃ 架 子 (N) (1) stand, scaf-
fold, shelf. shū-jiàzi 書 架 子
book shelf or book case. (2)

haughty behavior. bǎi-jiàzi 擺
架 子 put on airs. Tā-jiàzi
hěn-dà. 他 架 子 很 大.
He is very haughty.

JIĀZÚ₅ 家 族 (N) family clan.

JĪBEN₃ 基 本 (N) foundation,
basis. Yǔyán shi-zuò-xuéwende-
jīben. 語 言 是 作 學 問
的 基 本. Language is the
foundation for research.
(SV) fundamental.

JĪCHĂNG₃ 機 場 (N) airfield,
airport.

JĪCHÉNGCHĒ₃ 計 程 車 (N)
taxi. (M: liàng 輛).

JĪCHU₃ 基 礎 (N) groundwork,
foundation. Wúlun-zuò-'shénma-
shì, bìxū-xiān-bǎ-jīchu dǎhǎo-le.
無 論 作 甚 麼 事 必
須 先 把 基 礎 打 好
了. No matter what you are
doing, you should lay a sound
foundation.

JĪDÀN₂ 鷄 蛋 (N) chicken egg.

JĪDÀNGĀO₃ 鷄 蛋 糕 (N) cake.
(M: kuài 塊).

JÌDE₂ 記 得 (RV) remember.
Nǐ-hái-jìde-wo-ma? 你 還 記
得 我 嗎 ? Do you still re-
member me? Wŏ-jìbude-le. 我
記 不 得 了. I don't re-
member.

JĪDÌ₄ 基 地 (N) base (military).
hǎijūn-jīdì 海 軍 基 地
naval base.

JĪDŪ₂ 基 督 (N) Christ.

JÌDU₃ 嫉 妒 (TV) envy, jealous
of. Bú-yào-jìdu-bieren. 不 要
嫉 妒 別 人. Don't be
jealous of others.

J

(SV) jealous. Tā-hěn-jìdu. 他很嫉妒. He is very jealous.

JÌ-DÚ₃ 忌賭 or JIÈ-DÚ 戒賭 (VO) give up gambling.

JĬDUI₅ 擠兌 (TV) put someone in a difficult position, make difficulties for someone. Nǐ-bié-jǐdui-wo. 你別擠兌我. Don't put me in a difficult position.

JĪDŪJIÀO₂ 基督教 (N) Christianity. (cf: YĒSŪJIÀO 耶穌教)

JĪDŪTÚ₃ 基督徒 (N) Christian (person). Tā-shi-jīdūtú. 他是基督徒. He is a Christian.

JIĒ₁ 街 (N) (1) street. (M: tiáo 條). guò-jiē 過街 cross a street. (2) shopping area (along the street). Wǒ-shàng-jiē-mǎi-dōngxi-qu. 我上街買東西去. I am going shopping.

JIĒ₁ 接 (TV) (1) connect, join. Bǎ-diànxiàn-jiēshang. 把電線接上. Connect the wire. (2) continue, take over. Tā-méi-zuòwán, women-jiēzhe-zuò. 他沒作完, 我們接着作. He didn't finish it, we'll continue. Shéi-jiē-tade-shì? 誰接他的事? Who is taking over his job? (3) catch something thrown through the air. Tā-yòng-shǒu-jiē-qiú. 他用手接球. He catches the ball with his hand. (4) receive guests, mail, a message. Wǒ-jiēzhao-yifēng-xìn. 我接着一封信. I have received a letter.

Qǐng-'Lǐ-xiansheng-jiē-diànhuà. 請李先生接電話. Ask Mr. Li to answer the phone. (5) meet someone, as at a train station. Wǒ-lái-jiē ni. 我來接你. I'll come to meet you there. Tā-dào-fēijīchǎng jiē-péngyou-qu-le. 他到飛機場接朋友去了. He went to the airport to meet a friend.

JIĒ₃ 揭 (TV) (1) lift off a cover. Bǎ-guō-gài jiēkai. 把鍋蓋揭開. Take the cover off the pot. (2) tear off or remove something, such as a sheet of paper, which is attached to something else. jiē-yóupiào 揭郵票 take off a stamp. Shéi-bǎ-bùgào jiēxialai-le? 誰把佈告揭下來了? Who took that bulletin down?

JIĒ₃ 結 (TV) bear fruit (literally only). Shùshang jiēle-hěn-duō-guǒzi. 樹上結了很多果子. This tree bears a lot of fruit.

JIĒ₅ 屆 (M) session, time. dìyī-jiē 第一屆 first session.

JIĒ₅ 解 (TV) (1) untie, unfasten. Bǎ-shéngzi jiēkai. 把繩子解開. Untie that rope. (2) relieve, quench hunger, thirst, etc. Zhèige jiē-kě, bu-jiē-è. 這個解渴, 不解餓. This thing will relieve thirst, but not hunger.

JIÈ₁ 借 (TV) (1) usually with CV gēn 跟, borrow. (2) usually with post verb gěi 給, lend.

Wǒ-gēn-ta-jiè-qián, tā-bu-jiè-gei-wǒ. 我 跟 他 借 錢，他 不 借 給 我. I tried to borrow money from him, but he didn't lend it to me.

JIÈ₃ 界 (-B) circle (social). gèjiè 各 界 various circles. wài-jiāojiè 外 交 界 diplomatic circles. jiàoyujiè 教 育 界 educational field.

JIĒBA₄ 結 巴 (IV) stutter. Tā-shuō-huà jiēba. 他 説 話 結 巴. He stutters when he talks. (N) stutterer. Tā-shì-ge-jiēba. 他 是 個 結 巴. He is a stutterer.

JIÉ-BĪNG₃ 結 冰 (VO) freeze.

JIÈBĬR₅ 隔 壁 兒 (N) next-door neighbor.

JIĒ-DIÀNHUÀ₂ 接 電 話 (VO) answer the telephone.

JIÈ-DŬ₃ 戒 賭 see JÌ-DŬ 忌 賭.

JIĒDUAN₃ 階 段 (N) stage (level of advancement or progress). Wǒmen-dàole-shénma-jiēduan-le? 我 們 到 了 甚 麼 階 段 了? What stage have we reached now?

JIĒFANG₄ 街 坊 (N) neighbor.

JIĔFÀNG₂ 解 放 (TV) liberate. Tāmen -bǎ-Bālí-jiěfàng-le. 他 們 把 巴 黎 解 放 了. They have liberated Paris. (N) liberation. Gòngchǎngdǎngde-bàoshang-shuō: "Jiěfàng-yǐhòu, rénmín-dou-fān-shēn-le." 共 產 黨 的 報 上 説：解 放 以 後，人 民 都 翻 身 了. The communist paper says that people obtained their freedom after liberation.

JIĔFANGJŪN₃ 解 放 軍 (N) people's liberation army.

JIĒ-FĒNG₄ 接 風 (VO) give a welcome party to a newly ar-rived guest from a distant place. Tā-míngtian-qǐng-kè, gei-Lǐ-xiansheng jiē-fēng. 他 明 天 請 客，給 李 先 生 接 風. Tomorrow he will give a welcome party for Mr. Li.

JIĔFU₅ 姐 夫 (N) brother-in-law (husband of older sister).

JIÉGOU₄ 結 構 (N) structure, formation.

JIÈGÙ₄ 藉 故 (AD) use some-thing as a pretext. Tā-jiègù bu-lái. 他 藉 故 不 來. He used a pretext not to come. (cf: JIÈKŎU 藉 口).

JIÈ-GUĀNG₄ 借 光 (VO) Peip. excuse me, please. Jièguāng-jièguāng, ràng-wo-guòqu. 借 光 借 光，讓 我 過 去. Excuse me, may I get by. Jiè-guāng-yóuzhèngjú-zài-nǎr? 借 光 郵 政 局 在 那 兒? Excuse me, where is the post office?

JIÉGUŎ₁ 結 果 (N) result, out-come. Wǒ-gēn-ta-tánle-bàntiān, méi-shénma-jiéguŏ. 我 跟 他 談 了 半 天 没 甚 麼 結 果. I talked with him for a long while, but there was no result. (MA) (1) in the end. Wǒ-qǐngle-ta-sāncì, jiéguŏ ta-háishí-bu-lái. 我 請 了 他 三 次，

J

結果他還是不來.

I invited him three times, and yet he didn't come in the end. (2) as a result. Tā-bu-tīng-wo-de, jiéguǒ-shàng-dàng-le. 他不聽我的, 結果上當了. He didn't listen to me, as a result he was swindled.

JIĒ-HÁNG₅ 隔行 (VO) be in different trades. Wǒ-gēn-ta jiē-zne-háng-ne. 我跟他隔著行呢. He and I are in different trades.

JIĒ-HŪN₁ 結婚 (VO) get married, be married. Tāmen-shi-yǐyue-jiéde-hūn? 他們是幾月結的婚? When did they get married? Wǒmen-jié-hūn sānnián-le. 我們結婚三年了. We have been married for three years. Tā-gēn-shéi jié-hūn-le? 他跟誰結婚了? Whom did he marry?

JIĒJI₃ 階級 (N) (1) class (of society). láodòng-jiēji 勞動階級 labor class. (2) rank (military). shàngwèi-jiēji 上尉階級 rank of captain.

JIĒJIÀN₄ 接見 (TV) meet, receive (usually used in formal situations). Zǒngtǒng jīntian-jiējiàn-Fǎguo-dàshǐ. 總統今天接見法國大使. Today the President will receive the French Ambassador. (See: JIÀN 見).

JIĒJIAN₄ 節儉 (SV) thrifty. Tā-de-tàitai hěn-jiējian. 他的

太太很節儉. His wife is quite thrifty.

JIĒJIE₁ 姐姐 (N) older sister.

JIĒJÌN₃ 接近 (SV) close (in the abstract). Jèi-liǎngge-yìsi hen-jiējìn. 這兩個意思很接近. These two ideas are very close.

(TV) become close to, get mixed up with someone. Tāde-fùmǔ bu-xǔ-ta-he-Lǐ-xiansheng-jiējìn. 他的父母不許他和李先生接近. Her father doesn't allow her to become close with Mr. Li.

JIĒ-JIǓ₃ 戒酒 see JÌ-JIǓ 忌酒.

JIĚJUÉ₂ 解決 (TV) (1) solve a problem, overcome difficulty. Jīntian wǒmen-jiějuéle-hěn-duō-wènti. 今天我們解決了很多問題. Today we solved a lot of problems. (2) do away with, kill. Wǒmen-bǎ-tāmende-yishī-rén dou-jiějué-le. 我們把他們一師人都解決了. We destroyed a whole division of theirs.

JIÈKǑU₄ 藉口 (N) pretext. Tā-shuō-yǒu-shì, bu-shi-zhēnde, nà-buguo-shi-jièkǒu. 他說有事, 不是真的, 那不過是藉口. He said that he had things to do, it's not true, it's only a pretext.

(AD) under pretext of something or using something as a pretext. Tā-jièkǒu-shuō tài-máng. 他藉口說太忙. He uses being too busy as his pretext.(cf:

JIÈGU 藉 故).

JIĒLÌ₄ 接力 (N) relay. pǎo-jiē-lì 跑 接 力 run a relay race. jiēlì-sàipǎo 接 力 賽 跑 relay race.

JIÉLÌ₄ 竭 力 (AD) (lit. exhaust one's strength) do one's utmost. Wǒ-jiélì-gěi-nin-zuò. 我 竭 力 給 您 作 . I'll try my best to do it for you.

JIÉLIÁN₄ 接 連 (AD) consecutively. Tā-jiélián-sāntian-méi-lái. 他 接 連 三 天 没 來 . He didn't come for three days consecutively.

JIÉLÙN₃ 結 論 (N) conclusion. xià-jiélùn 下 結 論 draw a conclusion.

JIĚMEI₂ 姐 妹 or ZǏMEI 姊 妹 (N) sisters. Wǒmen-shì-jiěmei. 我 們 是 姐 妹 . We are sisters.

JIÉMU₂ 節 目 (N) (l) program (performance of what is scheduled). jiému-dānzi 節 目 單 子 program sheet. (2) number, event on a program. (M: xiàng 項). diànshìde-jiému 電 視 的 節 目 television program. (3) planned activity. Nǐ-jīntiān-de-jiému shi-shéma? 你 今 天 的 節 目 是 甚 麼 ? What are your plans for today?

JIÉMU-DĀNZI₃ 節 目 單 子 (VO) printed program (of a show or some event).

JIĚPŌU₄ 解 剖 (TV) dissect (as a cadaver). Wǒ-zuótian-jiěpōule-yìtiáo-gǒu. 我 昨 天 解 剖 了 一 條 狗 . I dissected

a dog yesterday.

ʹJIĒQIÀ₃ 接 洽 (TV) negotiate, make contact. Wǒ-gēn-ta-jiēqia-diǎnr-shìqing. 我 跟 他 接 洽 點 兒 事 情 . I negotiated with him for some business.

JIÈQUAN₁ 解 勸 (TV) (l) mediate a dispute. Tāmen-yòu- dǎ-jià-le. Nǐ-qù-jiěquan-jiequan-ba. 他 們 又 打 架 了 , 你 去 解 勸 解 勸 吧 . They are fighting again, go to settle them down. (2) bring someone around to reason or one's way of thinking. Tā-xiǎngbu-qīngchu, nǐ-jiě-quan-yixiàr-ta-jiu-míngbai-le. 他 想 不 清 楚 , 你 解 勸 一 下 兒 他 就 明 白 了 . He's mixed up, try to bring him around to reason.

JIÈSHAO₁ 介 紹 (TV) introduce, recommend. Wǒ-géi-ni jièshao-yige-péngyou. 我 給 你 介 紹 一 個 朋 友 . I'll introduce a friend to you. Wǒ-bǎ-ta-jièshao-dau-nèige-xuéxiào qù-zuò-shì-qu-le. 我 把 他 介 紹 到 那 個 學 校 去 作 事 去 了 . I recommended him to that school to work.

JIĒSHI₂ 結 實 (SV) (l) solid, strong, durable. Zhèige-fàngzi hěn-jiēshi. 這 個 房 子 很 結 實 . This house is very solid. (2) healthy, strong. Tāde-shēnti hěn-jiēshi. 他 的 身 體 很 結 實 . He is very healthy.

J

JIĚSHI₂ 解釋 (TV) explain. (syn. jiǎng 講). Qǐng-nín-bǎ-zhèige-wènti géi-women-jiěshi-yixiar. 請 您 把 這 個 問 題 給 我 們 解 釋 一 下 兒. Please explain this problem for us. (N) explanation. Tāde-jiěshi wo-bu-mǎnyì. 他 的 解 釋 我 不 滿 意. I'm not satisfied with his explanation.

JIĚSHÒU₃ 接 受 (TV) accept. Nèixie-tiáojian nǐ-dōu-jiēshòu-le-ma? 那 些 條 件 你 都 接 受 了 嗎? Did you accept all those terms?

JIĚ-SHǑUR₄ 解 手 兒 (VO) go to the bathroom. Wǒ-qu-jiě-ge-shǒur. 我 去 解 個 手 兒. I'll go to the washroom. (cf: XǏSHǑU 洗 手).

JIĚSHU₂ 結 束 or JIÉSU (TV) conclude, finish, complete, close out some affair or an organization. Nèijian-shì yǐjing-jiéshu-le. 那 件 事 情 已 經 結 束 了. That matter has already been concluded. (N) closing-out. bàn-jiéshu 辦 結 束 make arrangements for the closing-out.

JIÉSU₂ 結 束 see JIÉSHU 結 束 .

JIĚ-TÓU₃ 接 頭 (VO) make contact with someone. Nǐ-gēn-ta-jiē-tóu-le-ma? 你 跟 他 接 頭 了 嗎? Did you make contact with him? Wǒmen-míng-tian-děi-jiējie-tóu. 我 們 明 天 得 接 接 頭. We have

to contact each other tomorrow.

JIĒ-WĚN₄ 接 吻 (VO) (lit. have mouths touched) kiss. Wǒ-kàn-jian-nǐmen jiē-wěn-le. 我 看 見 你 們 接 吻 了. I saw you kiss.

JIÈXIAN₂ 界 限 (N) boundary, limit, border line. Zhèi-liǎng-ge-dāngzhōngde-jièxian hěn-qīngchu. 這 兩 個 當 中 的 界 限 很 清 楚. The boundary between these two is very clear. Bǎ-jièxian huàzai-shénma-dìfang? 把 界 限 劃 在 甚 麼 地 方? lit. or fig. Where do you draw the line?

JIĒ-YĀN 戒 烟 see JÌ-YĀN 忌 烟 .

JIÈYÁN₄ 戒 嚴 (IV) declare a state of martial law, declare a curfew. Xiànzài jièyán-le. 現 在 戒 嚴 了. Now it's curfew time.

JIÈ-YÌ₃ 介 意 (VO) mind, care about something. Wǒ-shuō-zhèi-ge-huà nín-ke-bié-jiè-yì. 我 說 這 個 話 您 可 別 介 意. Please don't mind what I just said.

JIÉ-ZHANG₃ 結 賬 (VO) (1) draw a balance. Wǒmen-yíge-yuè jié-yicì-zhàng. 我 們 一 個 月 結 一 次 賬. We balance our account once a month. (2) settle an account or debt. Wǒ-men-yǐjing-jiéle-liǎngbǐ-zhàng-le. 我 們 已 經 結 了 兩 筆 賬 了. We have settled two accounts already.

JIĒZHE₂ 接 着 (TV) connect,

follow. yíge-jiēzhe-yigè 一個
接着一個 one follows
another.
(AD) (1) continuously. Tā-jiēzhe-
shuōle-sānge-zhōngtóu. 他接
着説了三個鐘頭.
He talked continuously for three
hours. (2) do something after
something is done. Tā-xiān-
chōule-yizhi-yān, jiēzhe-yòu-
hēle-yibei-jiǔ. 他先抽了
一枝烟,接着又喝
了一杯酒. He smoked
a cigarette first, after that he
drank a glass of wine. Xiàbianr-
wǒ-wàng-le. Nǐ-jiēzhe-shuō-ba.
下邊兒我忘了,你
接着説吧. I forget the
rest. Take it over and tell it.
JIÉZHǏ₄ 截止 (IV) cease, stop
(of a period for doing something).
Míngtian-jiézhǐ. 明天截止.
It will cease tomorrow.
JIÈZHI(R)₃ 戒指兒 ring (on
the finger).
JIÉZI₅ 癤子 (N) boil. Wǒ-shǒushang zhǎngle-yige-jiēzi. 我手
上長了一個癤子.
I have a boil on my hand.
JIÉZI₄ 結子 (N) knot (in string
or rope).
JIĒZI₅ 褯子 (N) diaper. (M:
kuài 塊, tiáo 條).
JIÉZUÒ₃ 傑作 (N) masterpiece.
JÌFÙ₅ 繼父 (N) stepfather.
JÍ-GE₂ 及格 (VO) (lit. reach
the standard) pass an examination. Tā-qu-kǎo-le, kěshi-méi-
jí-gé. 他去考了,可是
没及格. He took the

examination, but didn't pass.
Tā-jíbuliǎo-gé. 他及不了
格. He can't pass.
JĪGUAN₂ 機關 (N) (1) mechanical device. Zhèige-qìchē-li-de-
jīguan hen-duō. 這個汽車
裏的機關很多.There
are a lot of devices in this car.
(2) organization, agency, office.
Nín-zài-něige-jīguan-gōngzuo?
您在那個機關工
作? Which organization are
you working for?
JÍGUAN₄ 籍貫 (N) place of origin of one's family, birthplace.
Bǎ-nǐde-xìngmíng-jíguan-xiě-
xialai. 把你的姓名籍
貫寫下來. Write down
your name and birthplace.
JĪGUĀNQIĀNG₃ 機關鎗 (N)
machine gun. (M: tǐng 挺, jià
架).
JÌHAOR₂ 記號兒 (N) sign,
mark, notation. Qǐng-zài-cuòle-
de-dìfang dǎ-yige-jìhaor. 請
在錯了的地方,打
一個記號兒. Make a
mark where it is wrong. Tāmen-
zài-shùshang zuòle-hen-duōde-
jìhaor. 他們在樹上作
了很多的記號. They
made a lot of marks on the tree.
JÍHÉ₃ 集合 (TV) (1) assemble.
Wǒmen-shénma-shíhou-jíhé? 我
們甚麼時候集合?
When shall we assemble? (2)
used as a military command, fall
in.
'JĪ(JI)HŪ₃ 幾(幾)乎 (MA) (syn.
chà(yi)diānr 差(一)點兒).

J

(1) used with or without an unstressed méi 没 , almost. Wǒ-'jī(ji)hū (mei)-wàng-le. 我 幾 (幾) 乎 (没) 忘 了 . I almost forgot it. (2) used with a stressed méi 没 , the negative meaning of méi 没 remains. Wǒ-'jī(ji)hū 'méi-kànjian-ta. 我 幾 (幾) 乎 没 看 見 他 . I almost didn't see him.

JÌHUA₁ 計 畫 (TV) plan, make plans. Wǒmen-děi-hǎohāorde-jìhua-jihua. 我 們 得 好 好 的 計 畫 計 畫 . We have to plan it carefully. Wǒmen-jì-hua-dào-Xiānggǎng-qu. 我 們 計 畫 到 香 港 去 . We plan to go to Hong Kong. (N) a plan. Zhèige-jìhua-bǐ-nèi-ge-hǎo. 這 個 計 畫 比 那 個 好 . This plan is better than that one.

JĪHUI₁ 機 會 (N) opportunity, chance. Wǒ-chèn-zhèige-jīhui gēn-ta-tántan. 我 趁 這 個 機 會 跟 他 談 談 . I'll take this opportunity to talk with him.

JÌHUI₅ 忌 諱 (TV) avoid doing something (because of superstition). Wǒmen-jìhui-shuō-nèi-zhong-huà. 我 們 忌 諱 說 那 種 話 . We avoid using that kind of language. (N) taboo. Zhèizhong-shì fàn-jì-hui. 這 種 事 犯 忌 諱 . This kind of thing is taboo.

JĪJÍ₃ 積 極 (SV) positive, active, enthusiastic. (opp. xiāojí 消 極). Tā-hěn-jījí. 他 很 積 極 . He is very enthusiastic. (AD) eagerly, enthusiastically. Tāmen-dou-jījí-qiú-jìnbù. 他 們 都 積 極 求 進 步 . They seek eagerly to progress.

JĪJIAO₄ 犄 角 (N) horn (of an animal). (M: zhi 隻 , duì 對).

JÌJIAO₃ 計 較 (TV) dispute with someone about something in detail. Búyào-gēn-ta-jìjiao-nèixie-xiǎo-shì. 不 要 跟 他 計 較 那 些 小 事 . Don't argue with him about trivial things.

JĪJIǍOR₃ 犄 角 兒 (N) corner (as of a table or a room). Yì-zhang-zhuōzi yǒu-sìge-jījiǎor. 一 張 桌 子 有 四 個 犄 角 兒 . A table has four corners. (See: JIǍOR 角 兒).

'JÌJIÈ₃ 機 械 see 'JÌXIE 機 械 .

JÌJIÉ₄ 季 節 (N) season (referring to weather).

JĪJÌN₄ 基 金 (N) reserve fund.

JĪJÌNHUÌ 基 金 會 (N) foundation (which grants money for charitable or educational purposes).

JÌ-JIǓ₄ 忌 酒 or JIÈ-JIǓ 戒 酒 (VO) give up a drinking habit. Tā-bǎ-jiǔ jì-le. 他 把 酒 忌 了 . He gave up drinking.

JÍLE₁ 極 了 (P) used after a SV or AV, extremely. dàjíle 大 極 了 extremely big.

JÍLI₄ 吉 利 (SV) lucky, auspicious. Zhōngguo-ren yǐwei-hóng-yánse-jíli. 中 國 人 以 為 紅 顏 色 吉 利 . Chinese consider red a lucky color.

JĪLIE₂ 激 烈 (SV) (1) radical.

Tāde-sīxiang tài-jīlie. 他的
思想太激烈. His
ideas are very radical. (2) violent. Qiánxiàn-dǎde hěn-jīlie.
前線打得很激烈.
The battle at the front is very
violent.

JÍLÍN₃ 吉林 (PW) Kirin <u>pro-
vince.</u>

JĪLING₄ 機靈 (SV) quick-witted.
Zhèi-háizi zhēn-jīling. 這孩
子真機靈. This child
is very quick-witted.

JĪLÓNG₂ 基隆 (PW) Keelong.

JÌLÙ₂ 記錄 (TV) make a written record of, take minutes. Bǎ-
tade-huà jìlu-xialai. 把他的
話記錄下來. Take
down what he says.
(N) (1) record, minutes. Zhè-
shi-kāi-huì-de-jìlù. 這是開
會的記錄. This is the
record of the meeting. (2) recorder. Qǐng-nín-dāng-jìlù. 請
您當記錄. Will you keep
the record please. (3) record
(as in competitive sports). dǎ-
può-jìlù 打破記錄 break
a record.

JÌLÙ₃ 紀律 (N) discipline (<u>mil-
itary</u>). Tāmende-jūnduì méi-
you-jìlù. 他們的軍隊
沒有紀律. Their troops
have no discipline.

JÍMÁNG₄ 急忙 (AD) hurriedly,
in great haste. Tā-yi-jiào-wo,
wo-jímáng-jiu-qù-le.他一叫
我,我急忙就去了.
As soon as he called me, I hurried over.

JÌMO₂ 寂寞 (SV) lonely. Yíge-
rén hěn-jìmo. 一個人很
寂寞. He is very lonely by
himself.

JÌMǓ₄ 繼母 (N) stepmother.

JĪN₃ 金 (B) (1) gold, golden. jīn-
biǎo 金表 gold watch. jīnpíxié
金皮鞋 gold-colored shoe.
Zhèige shi-jīnde. 這個是
金的. This is made of gold.
(2) money. měijīn 美金 American dollar. xiànjīn 現金 cash.

JĪN₃ 禁 (AV) withstand, endure.
Zhèizhong-xié bu-jīn-chuān. 這
種鞋不禁穿. This
kind of shoes cannot withstand
wear. Hēi-yánse jīn-zāng. 黑
顏色禁髒. Black color
doesn't show dirt easily.

JĪN₃ 斤 (M) <u>a measure for weight,
about 1-1/3 lb.</u>, catty. liǎngjīn-
ròu 兩斤肉 two catties of
meat.

JǏN₁ 緊 (SV) (1) tight, restricting.
(opp. sōng 鬆). Yīshang tài-jǐn.
衣裳太緊. The clothes
are too tight. Tā-zuǐ-jǐn. 他
嘴緊. He is tight-lipped.
Tā-zhèi-jitian qián-jǐn.他這
幾天錢緊. He's short
of money these few days. (2)
strict, stern. (<u>opp</u>. sōng 鬆).
Tā-fùchi guǎnde-jǐn. 他父
親管得緊. His father is
very strict with him. Xuéxiàode-
gōngke hen-jǐn. 學校的功
課很緊. The school is
very strict with schoolwork. <u>or</u>
The schoolwork is on a tight
schedule. (cf: YÁN 嚴). (3)

J

J

(con. jǐnjí 緊急). urgent, critical. Shíhou-tài-jǐn-le, děi-kuài-yidiǎnr-zuò. 時候太緊了,得快一點兒作. Time is urgent, we have to do it quickly. (4) intense, strong, forceful. Yǔ-xiàde hěn-jǐn. 雨下得很緊. It is raining intensely. (5) fast. Tā-zǒude bu-jǐn-bu-màn. 他走得不緊不慢. He walks not too fast and not too slow. (AD) (l) directly, closely. Tā-de-wūzi jǐn-āizhe-wǒde-wūzi. 他的屋子緊挨着我的屋子. His room is directly next to mine. Zhèi-liǎngjian-shì jǐn-jiēzhe. 這兩件事緊接着. These two things are closely connected. (2) continuously. Tā-jǐn-shuō bu-tíng. 他緊說不停. He speaks continuously without stopping. (3) fast, in an intensified manner. Wǒ-jǐn-zǒule-jibu. 我緊走了幾步. I rushed forward a few steps. (TV) tighten. Bǎ-bídài jǐn-yijin. 把皮帶緊一緊. Tighten the belt.

JǏN(JĬN)₃ 僅 (僅)(AD) only, merely. Tā-jǐn(jǐn)-shì-yíge-xuésheng. 他僅 (僅)是一個學生. He is merely a student. Wǒ-jìn(jǐn)-shèngle-wǔkuai-qián-le. 我僅 (僅)剩了五塊錢了. I have only five dollars left.

JĬN₁ 進 (IV) (1) enter, come or go into a place. Huǒchē-jìn-zhàn-

le. 火車進站了. The train is coming into the station. Tā-jìn-dàxué-le. 他進大學了. He entered college. (2) receive, take in money, goods. Tāmen-you-jìnle-bushǎo-de-huò. 他們又進了不少的貨. They took in a lot of merchandise again. Zhèi-ge-yuè wǒ-'méi-jìn-duōshao-qián. 這個月我沒進多少錢. I didn't make much money this month. (B) used after CV such as wàng 往, xiàng 向, etc., in. wàng-jìn-pǎo 往進跑 run in or into.

JĬN₃ 盡 (TV) (1) with limited objects only, exhaust, use up. Wǒ-jìn-suǒyǒude-lìliang bāng-máng. 我盡所有的力量幫忙. I'll do the best I can to help you. (2) fulfill completely one's duty or responsibility. Nǐ-děi-jìn-zéren. 你得盡責任. You should fulfill your duty. (RE) indicates exhausting, finishing. Wǒmen-bǎ-fázi dou-yòngjìn-le. 我們把法子都用盡了. We have exhausted all means. (B) used before a SV, as... as possible. Nǐ-jìn-zǎo-lái. 你盡早來. You come as early as possible.

JĬN₁ 近 (SV) near, close.(opp. yuǎn 遠). Wǒ-jiā lí-xuéxiào-hěn-jìn. 我家離學校很近. My home is very close to the school. Zhèitiao-lù-jìn. 這 條 路 近 . This road is closer. Tāmende-guān-xi hěn-jìn. 他 們 的 關 係 很 近 . They have a very close relationship. (B) recent. Zuìjìn tā-méi-lái. 最 近 他 沒 來 . He hasn't come recently. (c: JÌN-HU 近乎).

JÌNBIAN₃ 近 便 (SV) near and convenient. Zhèr lí-yóuzhèngjú hěn-jìnbian. 這 兒 離 郵 政 局 很 近 便 . It's very near and convenient from here to the post office.

JÌNBIĀO₃ 錦 標 (N) (1) trophy, prize. Tā-déle-yíge-jǐnbiāo. 他 得 了 一 個 錦 標 . He won a trophy. (2) championship.

JÌN-BÙ₂ 進 步 (VO) advance, make progress. Tāmen-yòu-jìn-le-yibù. 他 們 又 進 了 一 步 . They have progressed one more step. (SV) progressive. Tāmende-gōngyè fēichang-jìnbù. 他 們 的 工 業 非 常 進 步 . Their industry is very progressive. (N) progress, improvement. Tā-de-Zhōngwen yǒu-hěn-dàde-jìn-bu. 他 的 中 文 有 很 大 的 進 步 . He showed a great improvement in his Chinese.

JÌNCHÁO₃ 晉 朝 (TW) Chin dynasty.

JÌNDÀI₂ 近 代 (TW) modern times.

JÌNDEZHÙ₃ 禁 得 住 (RV) can endure, can withstand. Zhèige-qiáo jǐndezhù-wǔdūn-zhòng. 這 個 橋 禁 得 住 五 噸 重 . This bridge can hold up to five tons.

JÌNENG₄ 技 能 (N) skill, technical know-how, ability.

JÌNG₄ 井 (N) well. (M: yǎn 眼). yóujǐng 油 井 oil well.

JÌNG₃ 靜 (SV) quiet, peaceful. Zhèige-dìfang hen-jìng. 這 個 地 方 很 靜 . It's very quiet here.

JÌNG₅ 敬 (TV) offer someone something, usually food or drink, with respect. Wǒ-jìng-nín-yibēi-jiǔ. 我 敬 您 一 杯 酒 . May I propose a toast to you. (B) respect, worship. gōngjing 恭 敬 respectful.

JÌNG₃ 竟 (AD) (1) nothing but, only, merely. Tā-jìng-shuō-hǎotīng-de. 他 竟 說 好 聽 的 . He talks about nothing but pleasant things. (2) used after PW, everywhere. Wūzili jìng-shi-tǔ. 屋 子 裏 竟 是 土 . There is dirt everywhere in this room. (3) all the time, keep on doing something. Nǐ-bié-jìng-zhuāng-qióng. 你 別 竟 裝 窮 . Don't keep pretending to be so poor.

JÌNG'ÀI₄ 敬 愛 (TV) respect and love. Wǒmen-yīnggāi jìng'ài-wǒmende-lǎoshi. 我 們 應 該 敬 愛 我 們 的 老 師 . We should pay respect to our teachers.

JĪNGÀNGSHÍ₄ 金 剛 石 (N)

J

diamond. (syn. zhuànshí 鑽石,
jīngāngzuànr 金剛鑽兒).
(M: lì 粒, kē 顆).

JĪNGĀNGZUÀNR₅ 金剛鑽兒
(N) diamond. (syn. jīngangshí
金剛石, zuànshí 鑽石).
(M: lì 粒, kē 顆).

JĪNGCHÁ₂ 警察 (N) policeman.
(syn. xúnjǐng 巡警).

JĪNGCHÁJÚ₂ 警察局 (N)
police department.

JĪNGCHÁNG₃ 經常 (AD) fre-
quently, often. Tā-jīngcháng-
bu-zài-jiā. 他經常不在
家. He's away from home frequently.

JĪNGDONG₃ 驚動 (TV) disturb,
arouse a person. Wǒ-méi-gǎn-
jīngdong-nin. 我沒敢驚
動您. I didn't dare to dis-
turb you.

JĪNGDŪ₃ 京都 (PW) Kyoto.

JĪNGFÈI₃ 經費 (N) operating
funds of an organization. Xué-
xiàode-jīngfèi bu-gòu. 學校
的經費不夠. The funds
of the school are not enough.

JĪNGGAO₃ 警告 (TV) warn,
caution. Nǐ-zuìhǎo jīnggao-ta-
yixiar. 你最好警告他
一下兒. You'd better warn
him.
(N) warning. Wǒ-gei-ni-xià-yi-
ge-jìnggao. 我給你下一
個警告. I am giving you a
warning.

JĪNGGUÒ₂ 經過 (N) develop-
ment of a happening or occurrence from beginning to end.
Bǎ-jīngguode-qíngxing-shuō-yi-

shuo. 把經過的情形
説一説. Tell me the whole
story. Zhèi-shi-nèici-shìqing-
de-jīngguò. 這是那次事
情的經過. This is the
way that matter developed.
(TV) pass by, go through. Wǒ-
men-cóng-xuéxiào jīngguò. 我
們從學校經過. We
passed by the school. Jīngguo-
hěn-duō-niánde-xùnlian cái-
néng-zuòde-zhèiyangr-hǎo. 經
過很多年的訓練
才能作的這樣兒
好. It can't be done as well as
this unless one goes through
many years of training.

JĪNGHUĀNG₄ 驚慌 (SV) a-
larmed, frightened. Bú-yào-
jīnghuāng. 不要驚慌.
Don't be scared.

JĪNGJI₁ 經濟 (N) (1) economics.
Měiguode-jīngji-qíngxing zěn-
ma-yàng? 美國的經濟
情形怎麼樣? What's
the economic situation now in
America? (2) economics (as a
branch of learning). Tā-xué-
jīngji. 他學經濟. He is
studying economics.
(SV) economical. Wǒmen-děi-
jīngji-yidianr. 我們得經
濟一點兒. We have to
be a little economical.

JĪNGJÙ₅ 京劇 (N) Chinese opera
(Peiping style). (M: chū 齣,
tái 台).

JĪNGKUANG₄ 景況 (N) situation,
circumstances. Tāde-jīngkuang-
hěn-kělián. 他的景況很

可憐. His situation is pitiful.

JÌNGKUÀNGR₄ 鏡框兒 (N) picture frame with glass. xiāng-jìngkuàngr 鑲鏡框兒 make a frame (to fit a picture).

JĪNGLĬ₂ 經理 (N) manager (of a commercial enterprise). Tā-shì-jīnglǐ. 他是經理. He is the manager. Zhāng-jīnglǐ 張經理 Manager Chang. (TV) manage, handle a commercial interprise. Tā-zìjǐ jīnglǐ-zhèige-lǚguǎn. 他自己經理這個旅館. He manages this hotel by himself.

JÌNGLĬ₄ 敬禮 (VO) salute. Wǒmen-xiàng-quóqi-jìnglǐ. 我們向國旗敬禮. We salute the national flag. (N) salutation, formal gesture of greeting. xíng-yige-jìnglǐ 行一個敬禮 give a salute.

JĪNGMING₃ 精明 (SV) keen, shrewd. Zhèige-ren yòu-jīng-ming yòu-nénggan. 這個人又精明又能幹. This person is both keen and capable.

JĪNGQIAO₅ 精巧 (SV) skillful, clever, artful. Zhèige-xiǎo-dōngxi zuòde-hen-jīngqiao. 這個小東西作得很精巧. This small thing was skillfully made.

JÌNGSÀI₄ 徑賽 (N) track sports.

JĪNGSHEN₂ 精神 (N) spirit, vitality. hézuò-jīngshen 合作精神 cooperative spirit. Tā-méi-you-jīngshen. 他沒有精神. He has no vitality. (SV) energetic. Nǐ-kàn, 'zhèi-wei-lǎo-xiānsheng duóma-jīng-shen! 你看這位老先生多麼精神! Look at how energetic this old gentlemen is!

JĪNG-SHǑU₃ 經手 (VO)(lit. go through someone's hand) handle something as a middleman. Zhèijiàn-shì méi-jīng-tāde-shǒu. 這件事沒經他的手. He didn't handle this matter.

JÌNGTOU₃ 鏡頭 (N) (1) lens (of a camera, telescope, microscope). Zhèige-zhàoxiàngjī shi-sì-diǎnr-wǔ-de-jìngtóu. 這個照像機是四點兒五的鏡頭. This camera has a 4.5 lens. (2) scene in a motion picture. Diànyingr-li-de nèige-jìngtóu tài-měi-le. 電影兒裏的那個鏡頭太美了. That scene in the movie is really beautiful.

JÌNGUAN₃ 儘管 (MA) (1) to the extent that one wishes. Yǒu-deshì-zhǐ, nǐ-jìnguan-yòng. 有的是紙,你儘管用. There is plenty of paper, you can use as much as you like. (2) do something as one wishes. Tā-jìnguan-bu-zuò, wǒmen-yǒu-rén-zuò. 他儘管不作,我們有人作. Let him not do it if that's what he wants, we have people to do it.

JĪNGYAN₁ 經驗 (N) experience. Tāde-jīngyan hěn-duō. 他的經驗很多. He has a

J

great deal of experience. 'or He
has had many experiences. Wǒ-
méi-you-jiāo-shū-de-jīngyan.
我 没 有 教 書 的 經
驗 . I have no experience in
teaching.
(TV) experience, go through.
Wǒ-jīngyanguo-shībài. 我 經
驗 過 失 敗 . I have expe-
rienced failure.

JÌNGYĂNG₄ 靜 養 (IV) rest and
recuperate (in a quiet situation).
Zhèizhong-bìng fēi-jìngyǎng-bu-
kě. 這 種 病 非 靜 養 不
可 . This kind of illness needs
rest.

JĪNGYING₃ 經 營 (TV) manage
or carry on a business. Tā-hěn-
huì-jīngying. 他 很 會 經
營 . He really knows how to
manage business.

JĪNGYÚ₄ 鯨 魚 (N) whale. (M:
tiáo 條).

JÌNGZHĒNG₃ 競 爭 (TV) com-
pete, be in competition. Méi-
ren-gen-ta-jìngzhēng. 没 人
跟 他 競 爭 . Nobody com-
petes with him.
(N) competition.

JĪNGZHI₃ 精 緻 (SV) fine, delicate. Zhèige-shǒubiāo hěn-jīng-
zhi. 這 個 手 錶 很 精
緻 . This watch is very fine.

JĬNGZHI₄ 景 緻 (N) picturesque
scenery. (cf: FĒNGJĬNG 風
景).

JÌNGZHONG₄ 敬 重 (TV) look
up to someone.

JÌNGZI₃ 鏡 子 (N) mirror. Tā-
ài-jào-jìngzi. 他 愛 照 鏡

子 . He likes to look in the
mirror.

JÌNHU₄ 近 乎 (SV) close (of
personal relationships). Tā-gen-
Lǐ-xiáojie-hen-jìnhu. 他 跟
李 小 姐 很 近 乎 . He's
very close with Miss Li.
(AD) almost, nearly. Nà-jiu-
jìnhu-zhǎo-nǐde-piányi-le. 那
就 近 乎 找 你 的 便
宜 了 . It's almost taking
advantage of you. (cf: JÌN 近).

JÌNIAN₂ 紀 念 (TV) commemo-
rate. Gài-zhèige-lóu wèideshì-
jìnian-ta-fùqin. 蓋 這 個
樓 為 的 是 紀 念 他
父 親 . He built this building
to commemorate his father.
(N) memento. Sòng-nín-zhèige-
biǎo, liú-ge-jìnian. 送 您 這
個 表, 留 個 紀 念 . I'm
giving you this watch as a memento.

JÍNIANG₅ 脊 梁 (N) back (of
human).

JÌNIÀNPĬN₄ 紀 念 品 (N) sou-
venir.

JÌNIÀNRÌ₃ 紀 念 日 (N) anni-
versary.

JǏNJÍ₄ 緊 急 (SV) urgent, critical,
crucial. Zhànshi hěn-jǐnjí. 戰
事 很 緊 急 . The war
situation is critical.(See: JǏN
緊).

JÌN-KŎU₃ 進 口 (VO) (lit. enter
the port) bring something into a
country (of goods). Zhèizhǒng-
huò jìndeliǎo-kǒu ma? 這 種
貨 進 得 了 口 嗎 ? Can
this kind of goods be brought into

J

this country?

(TV) import. Zhōngguo jìnkŏule-hĕn-duō-jīqi. 中國進口了很多機器. China imports a lot of machines.

JÌNKUĂN₃ 進款 (N) (lit. money which comes in) income. (M: bĭ 筆).

JÌNLAI₁ 進來 (RV) come in. Wŏ-jìnbulái. 我進不來. I can't come in. Qĭng-jìnlai. 請進來. Please come in. (RE) in (here).Tāmen bă-ta-qĭngjinlai-le. 他們把他請進來了. They invited him in. Zhuōzi-tài-dà, bānbujin-lái. 桌子太大搬不進來. The table is too big to move in. Zhèige-qìchē kāibu-jin-chēfáng-lai.這個汽車開不進車房來. This car cannot be driven into the garage.

JÌNLÁI₂ 近來 (TW) recently, lately. Jìnlái tā-pàng-le. 近來他胖了. He's getting fatter lately.

JÌN...LÁI₂ 近...來 (S) recent, recently. jìn-jinian-lái 近幾年來 in recent years.

JÌN-LÌ₃ 盡力 (VO) try one's best to do something. Wŏ-jìn-lì-zuò jiu-shì-le. 盡力作就是了. I'll try my best to do it, that's all.

JÌNLIÀNG₃ 儘量 (AD) as much as one can, to the extreme extent. Nĭ-jìnliang-chī. 你儘量吃. You eat as much as you can. Wŏmen-jìnliang-hăo-

hāor-zuò. 我們儘量好好兒作.We'll do the best we can.

JÌNMÌ₅ 緊密 (SV) heavily-guarded, tightly-restricted. Dìxià-zŏngbù-băshŏude-hĕn-jĭnmì. 地下總部把守的很緊密. The underground headquarters is heavily guarded.

JÌNNIAN₁ 今年 (TW) this year. Wŏ-jīnnian-bu-qù. 我今年不去. I won't go this year.

JÌNQIÁN₄ 金錢 (N) (1) gold coin. (2) money.

JÌNQU₁ 進去 (RV) go in. Nĭ-jìnqu-kànkan. 你進去看看. (You) go in and take a look. (RE) (1) in (there). Nĭ-tì-wo-ná-jinqu. 你替我拿進去. Take it in there for me. (2) indicates taking in, absorbing mentally. Wŏ-shuōde-huà ta-tīngbujinqù.我説的話他聽不進去. He can't absorb what I say. Wŏ-shuōbu-jin-huà-qu. 我説不進話去. I can't make him listen.

JÌNR₃ 勁兒 (N) or JÌNTÓUR 勁頭兒 (M: gŭ 股). (1) strength. Nĭ-zài-shĭ-dianr-jìnr. 你再使點兒勁兒. Use more of your strength. Zhèige-jiŭ-méi-jìnr.這個酒沒勁兒. This wine is not strong. (2) manner, attitude, air. Nĭ-kàn ta-nèigŭ-jìnr. 你看他那股勁兒. Look at his manner. (3) vigor. Tā-zuò-shì-

J

de-jìnr hěn-zú. 他作事的 勁兒很足 . He has enough drive to do the work.

(-B) added to TV, the way some-one or something does. Tā-nèi-chàngjìnr méi-rén-ài-tīng. 他 那唱勁兒沒人愛 聽 . Nobody likes the way he sings.

JĬNSHEN₃ 謹慎 (SV) careful, heedful. Yíqiè dōu-yào-jǐnshen. 一切都要謹慎 . Be careful of everything.

JÌNSHIYǍN₃ 進視眼 (N) near-sightedness.

'JĪNSHǓ₄ 金屬 (N) metal.

JĪNTIAN₁ 今天 (TW) today. Jìntian-wǒ-qǐng-kè. 今天我 請客 . I'll treat today.

JĪNTIE₃ 津貼 (N) pension, sub-sidy, financial aid given to sup-plement other sources. (M: bǐ 筆).

(TV) give as supplementary fi-nancial aid. Wǒ-jīntiē-ni-yìbǎi-kuài-qián. 我津貼你一 百塊錢 . I'll give you one hundred dollars extra.

JÌNTÓUR₃ 勁頭兒 or JÌNR 勁兒 (N) strength. Tā-jìn-tóur-bu-xiǎo. 他勁頭兒 不小 . He has a lot of strength.

JÌNXÍNG₂ 進行 (TV) (1) move ahead, progress. Zài-zhèi-zhǒng-qíngxing-zhīxià, shìqing-méi-fázi-jìnxíng. 在這種 情形之下, 事情沒 法子進行 . Under this kind of situation, the work

cannot move ahead. (2) put into operation, carry out, take action on. Jiè-qián-de-shì hái-méi-jìnxíng-ne. 借錢的 事還沒進行呢 . I didn't do anything about the loan. Tā-zhèng-jìnxíng-yíge-jīnglǐ-de-wèizhi. 他正進行一個 經理的位置 . He is now trying to get a manager's position.

'JĪNYÀO₄ 緊要 (SV) important, critical. Dàole-'jǐnyào-guāntóu-le. 到了緊要關頭了 . Now it has reached the critical point. Wǒ-yǒu-'jǐnyào-de-gōng-shì. 我有緊要的公 事 . I have important business to do.

JÌN-YÌWU₃ 盡義務 (VO) (1) fulfill one's duty. (2) do some-thing without getting paid.

JĪNYÚ₃ 金魚 (N) goldfish. (M: tiáo 條).

JĬNZHANG₂ 緊張 (SV) tense. (opp. qīngsōng 輕鬆). Nǐ-bié-zènma-jǐnzhang. 你別這 樣緊張 . Don't be so tense. Nèitian-de-qíngxing hen-jǐn-zhang. 那天的情形很 緊張 . The situation on that day was very tense.

'JÌNZHǏ₃ 禁止 (TV) forbid, prohibit. jìnzhǐ-chōuyān 禁止 抽烟 smoking prohibited. Zhèizhǒng-dōngxi 'jìnzhǐ-chū-kǒu. 這種東西禁止 出口 . This kind of thing is prohibited from being exported.

JĪNZI₁ 金子 (N) gold.

JÍPŬCHĒ₅ 吉普車 (N) jeep. (M: liàng 輛).

JĪQI₁ 機器 (N) machine. (M: jià 架).
(SV) be eccentric (of a person). Zhèige-rén zhēn-jīqi. 這個 人真機器 . He is eccentric.

JÍQI₃ 極其 (AD) used before a SV, extremely. jíqi-zhòngyào 極其重要 extremely important.

JǏR₄ 幾兒 (TW) Peip. what day of the month. Míngtian-shì-jǐr? 明天是幾兒 ? What date is tomorrow?

JÌRÁN₂ 既然 (MA) since, because of. (syn. jìshì 既是). Jìrán-tā-bu-kěn, jiu-suàn-le. 既然他不肯,就算 了 . Since he's not willing, forget it. Jìrán-tā-yuànyì-lái, nǐ-wei-shénma-bu-qǐng-ta-ne? 既然他願意來,你 為甚麼不請他呢? Since he is willing to come, why don't you invite him?

'JÍRÈN₄ 級任 (N) home-room teacher. Tā-shì-'sānniánjí-de- 'jírèn. 他是三年級的 級任 . He is the home-room teacher of the third grade.

'JĪRÒU₅ 肌肉 (N) flesh, muscle.

JÍSHǏ₃ 即使 (MA) followed by a clause with dōu 都 , yě 也 or hái 還 even if (syn. jiùshi 就是). Jíshǐ-tā-yuànyì, wǒ- yě-děi-xiángxiang. 即使他 願意,我也得想想. Even if he agrees, I have to think

it over. (cf: LIÁN 連).

'JǏSHÍ₃ 幾時 (TW) when. Tā- 'jǐshí-lai? 他幾時來 ? When is he coming?

JÌSHÌ₃ 既是 (MA) since, inasmuch as, because of the fact that. (syn. jìrán 既然). Jìshi- ta-bu-kěn, nà-jiu-suàn-le. 即 是他不肯.那就算 了 . Since he isn't willing, forget about it.

JÌSHĪ₄ 技師 (N) technical expert.

JÌSHÙ₃ 技術 (N) technique, skill.

JÌSÌ₄ 祭祀 (TV) bring sacrifices. Zhōngguo-ren jìsi-zǔxiān. 中 國人祭祀祖先 . The Chinese people bring sacrifices to their ancestors.

JÌSUÀN₃ 計算 (TV) compute figure out. Nǐ-jìsuan-jisuan wo- men-xūyao-jǐge-ren? 你計 算計算我們需要 幾個人 ? Please figure out how many people we need? (cf: SUÀNJI 算計).

JÌSUÀNJĪ₃ 計算機 (N)(1) computer.(2) adding machine.

JÍTǏ₄ 集體 (B-) collective. jí- tǐ-huódòng 集體活動 collective action.

JÍTUÁN₃ 集團 (N) bloc, group.

JIǓ₂ 酒 (N) wine, liquor, alcoholic beverage.

JIǓ₁ 九 (NU) nine, ninth. jiǔlóu 九樓 ninth floor.

JIǓ₃ 久 (SV) long (period of time). Hěn-jiu-méi-jiàn. 很久沒 見 . Long time no see. Tā-bù- jiǔ-jiu-dào-le. 他不久就

J

到了 . He will be here before long.

JIÙ₂ 救 (TV) rescue, save. Wǒ-jiùbuliǎo-ta. 我 救 不 了 他 . I can't save him. Jiù-mìng-a! 救命啊 ! Help! help!

JIÙ₁ 舊 (SV) (opp. xīn 新) old, used. Bié-mǎi-jiù-fángzi. 别 買 舊 房 子 . Don't buy old houses. Zhèijian-yī-shang jiù-le. 這 件 衣 裳 舊 了 . These clothes are old. Zhèi-liang-qìchē-bu-jiù, kěshi-yàngzi-hěn-lǎo. 這 輛 汽 車 不 舊 可 是 樣 子 很 老 . This car isn't old, but the shape is old-fashioned. (cf: LǍO 老).

JIÙ₁ 就 (AD) (1) unstressed, after a suppositional clause, in that case, then. Rúguǒ-nǐ-lái, wǒ-jiu-qù. 如 果 你 來, 我 就 去 . If you come, (then) I'll go. (2) unstressed, after a clause of action, with or without yī 一 , as soon as, immediately after. Wǒ-měitian-(yi)-huíle-jiā jiu-shuì. 我 每 天 (一) 回 了 家 就 睡 . I go to bed right after I get home everyday. Tā-men-jiànzhao-jiu-dǎ. 他 們 見 着 就 打 . They fight as soon as they meet. Wǒ-chīle-fàn jiù-chūqu-le. 我 吃 了 飯 就 出 去 了 . As soon as I finished eating I went out. (3) after a stressed TW, as early as a certain time in the past, right at a certain time in

the future. Tā-'zuótian jiu-lái-le. 他 昨 天 就 來 了 .He was here as early as yesterday. Wǒ-xīngqiyī-jiu-géi-ni-chián. 我 星 期 一 就 給 你 錢 . I'll pay you right on Monday. (4) followed by a stressed NU, only, as little as. Wǒ-jiu-qùguo-'yícì-Niǔyuē. 我 就 去 過 一 次 紐 約 . I've been to New York only once. Yìtiān-jiu-xué-'èrshige-zì. 一 天 就 學 二 十 個 字 . Learn only twenty words a day. (5) unstressed, after a phrase in which there is a stressed syllable, and followed by a NU-M, as much as, as many as. Zhǐ-suàn-'lán-xīzhuāng tā-jiu-yǒu-sìshi-tao. 只 算 藍 西 裝 他 就 有 四 十 套 . Blue suits alone, he has as many as forty. 'Yìtiān-jiu-xué-èrshi-ge-zì. 一 天 就 學 二 十 個 字 . Learn as many as twenty words a day. (6) or JIÙ-SHI 就是 stressed, only, merely, nothing else but. Tā-'shénma-dou-bu-chī, 'jiù(shi)-chī-ròu. 他 甚 麼 都 不 吃, 就 (是) 吃 肉 . He eats nothing but meat. (7) or JIÙSHI 就 是 stressed, simply, just. Duó-qíguài, wǒ-'jiù(shi)-bu-zhī-dào. 多 奇 怪 ! 我 就 (是) 不 知 道 . How strange! I just don't know. (8) or JIÙSHI 就 是 stressed, precisely, exactly. Nǐ-shuōde-hěn-duì. Wǒ-'jiù(shi)-xiǎng-nènma-bàn. 我 就 (是)

想 那 麼 辦. What you said was right. That is exactly what I want to do. (9) stressed, at once, immediately. 'Jiù-yào-xià-yǔ-le. 就 要 下 雨 了. It's going to rain right now. Wǒ-'jiù-lái. 我 就 來. I'll come right away. (10) used to emphasize an example given in contradiction to a previous statement. A: Dàjia-dōu-xǐhuan-ta. B: 'Wǒ-jiu-bu-xǐhuan-ta. A: 大 家 都 喜 歡 他. B: 我 就 不 喜 歡 他. A: Everyone likes him. B: I don't.

(TV) go with some food or drink. Tā-yòng-huāshēng-jiù-jiǔ. 他 用 花 生 就 酒. He has peanuts with his drinks.

(CV) take advantage of a situation to do something. Wǒmen-jiù-zhège-jīhui tántan. 我 們 就 這 個 機 會 談 談. We'll take this opportunity to have a talk. Wǒmen-jiù-Zhāng-xiānshengde-dìfang kāihuì-ba. 我 們 就 張 先 生 的 地 方 開 會 吧. Let's take advantage of Mr. Chang's place to hold our meeting.

(S) (1) JIÙ(SHI)...YĚ(DŌU or HÁI)... 就 (是) 也 (都 or 還)... even if... (still)... Nǐ-jiù(shi)-bú-yuànyi-qù, yě-děi-dǎ-ge-diànhuà. 你 就 (是) 不 願 意 去, 也 得 打 個 電 話. Even if you don't want to go, you still have to make a phone call. Jiù(shi)-zènma-pián-

yi tā-hái-bu-mǎi-ne. 就 (是) 這 麼 便 宜 他 還 不 買 呢. Even if it's this cheap, he still won't buy it. (cf: LIÁN 連). (2) BÚ(SHI)...JIÙ(SHI)... 不 (是)... 就 (是)..., if not... then must be..., either... or... Tāmen-míngtian bu(shi) diào-yú, jiu(shi)-yóuyòng. 他 們 明 天 不 (是) 釣 魚 就 是 游 泳. If they are not going fishing tomorrow, then they must be going swimming.

JIŬBĀ₄ 酒 吧 (N) bar, tavern.
JIŬCÀI₅ 韮 菜 (N) a kind of vegetable similar to chives.
JIÙDÌ₃ 就 地 (AD) right on the spot, at that very place. jiùdì-jiějué 就 地 解 決 solve a problem right on the spot.
JIÙFĒN₄ 糾 紛 (N) dispute. Wǒ-jiu-pà yòu-qǐ-jiūfēn. 我 就 怕 又 起 糾 紛. I'm afraid that there will be another dispute.
JIÙFÙ₄ 舅 父 see JIÙJIU 舅 舅.
JIÙJÌ₃ 救 濟 (TV) extend relief to, relieve the distress of. Tāmen-jiùjile-hěn-duō-nàmín. 他 們 救 濟 了 很 多 難 民. They gave relief to a good many refugees.
JIÙJÌN₃ 就 近 (AD) since something is nearby. Nǐ-kéyi-jiùjìn-gēn-ta shāngliang-shāngliang. 你 可 以 就 近 跟 他 商 量 商 量. Since you are nearby, you can discuss it

J

with him.

'JIŪJÌNG₃ 究竟 (MA) (l) finally, after all, anyway. Tā-jiūjìng-shì-nǐ-dìdi. 他究竟是你弟弟. Anyway he is your younger brother. (2) used for pressing for an exact answer, actually, really, indeed. Jiūjìng-shi-zěn-me-yìhui-shì? 究竟是怎麼一回事? What actually is it?

(N) the true fact. Wǒ-yào-zhīdao-ge-jiūjìng. 我要知道個究竟. I want to know the truth. (cf: DÀODǏ 到底).

JIŪJĪNG₃ 酒精 (N) alcohol (ethyl, grain). (syn. huǒjiǔ 火酒).

JIŪJĪNSHĀN₁ 舊金山 (PW) San Francisco.

JIÙJIU₄ 舅舅 (N) uncle (mother's brother).

JIŬLIÀNG₄ 酒量 (N) drinking capacity. Tā-jiǔliàng-hen-dà. 他酒量很大. He can drink a lot.

JIÙMĀ₄ 舅媽 or JIÙMŬ 舅母 (N) aunt (wife of maternal uncle).

JIÙMŬ₄ 舅母 see JIÙMĀ 舅媽.

JIŪR₄ 鬮兒 (N) lot, ticket. Wǒ-men-zhuā-jiūr-ba. 我們抓鬮兒吧. Let's draw lots.

JIÙSHÌ₁ 就是 (MA) followed by a clause with dōu 都, yě 也 or hái 還, even if. (syn. jíshǐ 即使). Nǐ-jiùshi-'bù-shuō ta-yě-zhīdao. 你就是不說他也知道. Even if you didn't say it, he knew it anyway. Jiù-

shi-tā-sònggei-wo wo-dou-bu-yào. 就是他送給我我都不要. Even if he gave it to me, I won't accept it. (cf: LIÁN 連).

(AD) (l) or JIÙ 就 only, merely, nothing else but. Wǒ-jiùshi-bu-xīhuan. 我就是不喜歡. I just don't like it (no other reason). (2) or JIÙ 就 simply, just. Wǒ-jiùshi-bu-gào-song-ni. 我就是不告訴你. I simply don't tell you. (3) or JIÙ 就 precisely, exactly. Tāde-yìsi jiùshi-bu-gěi-qián. 他的意思就是不給錢. What he meant precisely is that he doesn't want to pay.

used to agree with a statement made by someone else, that's right, I agree. A: Zhèige-zhēn-hǎo. B: Jiùshi. A: 這個真好. B: 就是. A: This is really good. B: That's right. (cf: JIÙ 就).

'JIÙSHÌ₃ 舊式 (SV) old-fashioned. Tāde-jiāju-shì-'jiùshìde. 他的傢俱是舊式的. His furniture is old-fashioned.

JIÙSHÌLE₃ 就是了 used at the end of a sentence, that's all. Tā-xiǎng-yào-dianr-qián jiù-shìle. 他想要點兒錢就是了. He wants some money, that's all. Ànzhe-nǐde-yìsi-bàn jiùshìle. 按着你的意思辦就是了. We'll do it your way, that's all.

JIÙSHOUR₃ 就手兒 (AD) at the same time, while (when one is doing something similar). Nǐ-jiùshǒur bǎ-zhèige-yě-xíxi. 你就手兒把這個也洗洗. Please wash this too while you are washing the other things.

JIŬWÉI₃ 久違 (IV) used as a greeting, I haven't seen you for a long time. Jiǔwéi-jiǔwéi! Jìnlai-zhěnma-hǎo? 久違久違! 近來怎麼好? Long time no see, how have you been recently?

JIŬWŌR₅ 酒窩兒 (N) dimples.

JIŬXÍ₃ 酒席 (N) banquet. (M: zhuō 桌). chī-jiǔxí 吃酒席 attend a banquet.

JIŬYÁNG₃ 久仰 used when introduced to someone, (lit. have been looking up to you for a long time) glad to meet you.

JIÙYÀO...LE₂ 就要...了 (S) immediately, very soon. Tā-jiùyào-zǒu-le. 他就要走了. He'll leave very soon.

JIŬYUE₁ 九月 (TW) (lit. ninth month of the year) September.

JIÙ-ZHÍ₃ 就職 (VO) assume a position of responsibility. Zǒng-tǒng míngtian-jiù-zhí. 總統明天就職. The president will assume his duties tomorrow.

JIWĚIJIŬ₃ 鷄尾酒 (N) cock-tail.

JÍXIANG₄ 吉祥 (SV) lucky, auspicious.

'JÌXIÀO₄ 譏笑 (TV) laught at, ridicule, make fun of someone. Tāmen-'jīxiào-wo, wo-shǒubu-

liǎo. 他們譏笑我, 我受不了. I can't bear to have them all laugh at me.

'JÌXIÈ₃ 機械 or 'JĪJIÈ 機械 (N) machinery, mechanical equipment. jīxièhuà 機械化 mechanized. (SV) mechnical. Lǎo-yòng-yí-'yàngde-bànfǎ, nà-búshi-tài-'jí-xiè-le-ma? 老用一樣的辦法, 那不是太機械了嗎? Isn't it too mechanical to use the same method all the time?

JÌXING₂ 記性 (N) memory, ability to recall. Tā-méi-jìxing. 他沒記性: He has a poor memory.

JÍXÌNGZI₄ 急性子 (N) a quick-tempered person.

JÌXU₂ 繼續 (TV) continue to do something. Huìyì you-jìxi-xiaqu-le. 會議又繼續下去了. The meeting is going on again. (AD) continuously. Nǐ-shì-zuò-shì-ne, háishi-jìxu-niàn-shū-ne? 你是作事呢, 還是繼續念書呢? Do you plan to work or continue to study?

JÌ-YĀN₃ 忌烟 or JIÈ-YĀN 戒烟 (VO) give up smoking. Wǒ-jìle-hǎojǐhuí-yān, ye-méi-jì-liǎo. 我忌了好幾回烟, 也忌不了. I tried to give up smoking several times, but failed.

JÌYUÁNHÒU₄ 紀元後 (TW) A. D.

J

JÌYUÁNQIÁN₃ 紀元前 (TW) B.C. jìyuánqián-sānbǎinián 紀 元前三百年 300 B.C.

JÍZÀO₅ 急燥 (SV) irritable, hot-tempered.

JÍZǍOR₄ 及早兒 (AD) when it's early. Wǒmen-jízǎor-qù-ba. 我們及早兒去 吧. Let's go when it's early.

JÌ-ZHÀNG₂ 記賬 (VO) (1) make a notation in an account book. Jīntian-yòng-de-qián, wǒ-hái-méi-jì-zhàng-ne. 今天用 的錢, 我還沒記賬 呢. I still haven't made a notation for the money I spent today. (2) charge to an account for future payment. Wǒde-xiànqián-bú-gòu, kéyi-jì-zhàng-ma? 我 的現錢不够, 可以 記賬嗎? I don't have enough cash, can I charge it?

JÌZHE₂ 記者 (N) reporter.

JÍZHŌNG₃ 集中 (TV) concentrate. Wǒmen-jízhōng-lìliang. 我們集中力量. Let's concentrate our strength. Wǒde-sīxiang bu-néng-jízhōng. 我的 思想不能集中. I can't concentrate (my mind).

JĪZǏR₅ 鷄子兒 (N) Peip. chicken egg.

JÚ₃ 局 (B) bureau, office. yóu-(zhèng)jú 郵 (政) 局 post office.

JŬ₂ 舉 (TV) (1) raise, lift or hold something in the hand up high. Bǎ-jiǔbēi júqilai. 把酒 杯舉起來. Raise your

wine glasses. Shéi-zhīdao? Jǔ-shǒu. 誰知道? 舉手. Who knows, raise your hand. (2) give a reason, example or precedent. Wǒ-géi-ni-jǔ-ge-lì. 我給你舉個例. I'll give you an example. (3) elect, select. Wǒmen-jǔ-tā dāng-zhǔ-xí. 我們舉他當主席. We elected him as chairman.

JÙ₁ 句 (M) sentence of speech, writing,etc. yíju-huà 一句 話 a sentence. yíju-shī 一句 詩 a line of a poem.

JÙ₄ 鋸 (N) saw. (M: bǎ 把). (TV) saw. Ná-bǎ-jù jùxialai. 拿 把鋸鋸下來. Saw it off with a saw.

JÙ 聚 (TV) get together, gather, assemble. Wǒmen-'shénma-shí-hou 'jùju? 我們甚麼時 候聚聚? When shall we get together? Wàitou jùle-hěn-duō-rén. 外頭聚了很 多人. Many people are gathering together outside.

JÙ₃ 據 (CV) according to. jù-wǒ-kàn 據我看 according to the way I look at it. Jù-tā-shuō shì-'zhèiyàngr. 據他說是 這樣兒. According to what he says, it's like this.

JUĀN₂ 捐 (TV) (1) donate, con-tribute. Wǒ-juāngei-tamen-yí-kuài-dì. 我捐給他們 一塊地. I donated a piece of land to them. (2) raise funds, get contributions. Tā-gěi-xué-xiào juān-qián. 他給學校 捐錢. He raises funds for

J

the school. Wǒ-qu-juān-qián-qu. 我 去 捐 錢 去. I'm going to donate some money. or I'm going to collect some contributions.

(N) temporary or special tax. Wǒ-shàngle-wǔkuai-qiánde-juān. 我 上 了 五 塊 錢 的 捐. I paid five dollars, in special taxes.

JUĀN₄ 圈 (TV) confine, imprison, fence in. Bǎ-gǒu.juānqilai. 把 狗 圈 起 來. Don't let the dog out. Tā-zài-jiāli juānbuzhù. 他 在 家 裏 圈 不 住. He can't stay at home.

JUǍN₃ 捲 (TV) roll up. Bǎ-huàr 'juānqǐlai. 把 畫 兒 捲 起 來. Roll up the picture. Tāde-tóufa shì-wǒ-gěi-ta-juǎnde. 他 的 頭 髮 是 我 給 他 捲 的. Her hair was curled by me.

(M) roll, reel. yìjuǎn-piàozi 一 捲 票 子 a roll of paper money.

JUÀN₄ 圈 (N) fenced enclosure for animals. mǎjuàn 馬 圈 stable. jūjuàn 豬 圈 pig sty.

JUÀN₃ 卷 (M) fascicle of a book. Zhèibù-shū yígòng-sìshíjuàn. 這 本 書 一 共 四 十 卷. This book has forty fascicles altogether.

JUǍNCHǏ₅ 捲 尺 (N) measuring tape.

JUĀN-QIÁN₃ 捐 錢 (VO) (1) donate money. (2) raise funds, get contributions.

JUÀNZI₂ 卷 子 (N) examination

paper. Xiānsheng fā-juànzi-le. 先 生 發 卷 子 了. The teacher has started to distribute the examination papers. Tā-zhèng-gǎi-juànzi-ne. 他 正 改 卷 子 呢. He's correcting the examination papers now.

JÙBĚN₄ 劇 本 (N) play or drama written in manuscript or printed in book form. (M: běn 本).

JÙ-CĀN₃ 聚 餐 (VO) eat together (usually go Dutch). Tā-men-měi-lǐbài jù-yici-cān. 他 們 每 禮 拜 聚 一 次 餐. They eat together once each week. Nǐ-bié-qǐng-kè, wǒ-men-jùcān. 你 别 請 客 我 們 聚 餐. You don't have to pay for the meal, we'll each pay.

JǓDÒNG₄ 舉 動 (N) behavior, actions. Nèige-rénde-jǔdòng hěn-tèbié. 那 個 人 的 舉 動 很 特 别. His behavior is very strange.

JŪDUŌ₄ 居 多 (IV) constitute a majority. Yònggōngde-xuésheng jūduō. 用 功 的 學 生 居 多. There are more hard-working students than not.

JUĒ₄ 撅 (TV) stick out and up (as lips, tail of animal, etc.). Tā-juēzhe-zuǐ bu-shuō-huà. 他 撅 着 嘴 不 說 話. He is pursing his lips but isn't saying a word.

JUÉ₃ 撅 (TV) (1) break something long by grasping it at the ends and applying bending pressure.

J

Tā-bǎ-qiānbǐ-jiēduàn-le. 他把 鉛筆 撅斷了. He broke the pencil. (2) embarrass someone in front of other with a question or a blunt statement. Nǐ-bu-néng-dāngzhe-ren juē-wo. 你不能當着人撅我. You can't embarrass me in front of others.

JUÉ₂ 決 (AD) used with negative expressions, definitely. Wǒ-jué-bu-shuō. 我決不説. I definitely won't speak. Tā-jué-mǎibuqǐ. 他決買不起. He definitely cannot affort to buy it.

JUÉDE₁ 覺得 (AV) (1) feel that, think that. Nǐ-juéde duì-bu-dui? 你覺得對不對? Do you think this is right? (2) feel (referring to one's physical or emotional condition). Wǒ-juéde bu-tài-shūfu. 我覺得不太舒服. I don't feel very good.

JUÉDÌNG₂ 決定 (TV) decide. Wǒ-juédìng-bu-qù. 我決定不去. I've decided not to go. (N) decision. zuò-yige-juédìng 作一個決定 reach a decision.

JUÉDUÌ₃ 絕對 (SV) absolute. Méi-yǒu-juéduìde-bànfǎ. 沒有絕對的辦法. There's no absolute method. (AD) absolutely. Wǒ-juéduì-bu-néng-qù. 我絕對不能去. I absolutely can't go.

JUÉR₄ 角兒 see JIǍOR 角兒 (N) (1).

JUÉSÀI₃ 決賽 (IV) hold or participate in the final competition of a series. Shénma-shíhou-juésài? 甚麼時候決賽? When will the final competition be held? (N) final heat, final competition.

JUÉWÙ₃ 覺悟 (TV) become enlightened, realize. Dào-xiànzài ta-hái-méi-juéwù. 到現在他還沒覺悟. He didn't become enlightened until now.

JUÉXĪN₃ 決心 (N) determination. Nǐ-děi-xià-juéxīn bǎ-Zhōngwen-xuéhǎo-le. 你得下決心把中文學好了. You must be determined to learn Chinese successfully. Tā-méi-juéxīn. 他沒決心 He has no determination. (AV) decide to. Wǒ-juéxīn-zhèi yàngr-bàn. 我決心這樣辦. I decided to do it this way.

JUÉYÌ₅ 決議 (N) resolution of an assembly. (TV) decide by a majority vote. Wǒmen-juéyì měi-rén-juān-wǔ-kuài-qián. 我們決議每人捐五塊錢. We decided that each person would donate five dollars.

JŪ-GŌNG₂ 鞠躬 (VO) bow one's head. Nǐ-gěi-kèren jū-ge-gōng. 你給客人鞠個躬. Bow to the guest.

JÚHUĀ(R)₃ 菊花兒 (N) chrysanthemum (flower or plant). (M: duǒ 朵, kē 棵).

JÙHUÌ₃ 聚會 (IV) get together. Wǒmen-yǒu-gōngfude-shihoujùhui-jùhui. 我們有工夫的時候，聚會聚會. Let's get together when we have free time. (N) gathering, get-together. Wǒ-jīntian-yǒu-yíge-jùhui. 我今天有一個聚會. I'm having a get-together today.

'JÙJUÉ₃ 拒絕 (TV) refuse, reject. Tā-bǎ-wǒde-yāoqiu-'jùjué-le. 他把我的要求拒絕了. He rejected my demand.

JÙLEBÙ₃ 俱樂部 (N) club (social).

JǓ-LÌ(ZI)₃ 舉例(子) (VO) give an example. Nǐ-néng-jǔ-yige-lì(zi)-ma? 你能舉一個例(子)嗎? Can you give an example? (cf: LÌZI 例子).

'JÙLÍ₂ 距離 (N) distance between two points. Zhèi-liǎngge-dìfangde-'jùlí hěn-yuǎn. 這兩個地方的距離很遠. The distance between these two places is quite great. Tā-zǒng-gēn-wo-'bǎochí-yige-'jùlí. 他總跟我保持一個距離. She always keeps a distance from me. (CV) from a place. Zhèr-'jùlí-xiéxiào bu-jìn. 這兒距離學校不近. It's not too far from here to the school.

JŪN₃ 軍 (N) army corps consisting of two or more army divisions. (B) military. jūnmào 軍帽 military cap.

JŪNDUÌ₂ 軍隊 (N) troops, armed forces. (M: zhī 支).

JŪNFÁ₄ 軍閥 (N) militarist, warlord.

JŪNFĒN₃ 均分 (TV) divide evenly. Zhèi-diǎnr-qián wǒmen-liǎngge-rén-jūnfēn-le-ba. 這點兒錢我們兩個人均分了吧. Let's split this money equally between us.

JŪNGUĀN₂ 軍官 (N) military officer.

JŪNÌ₄ 拘泥 (SV) restricted, stiff because of concern with petty details. Tāde-yàngzi hěn-jūnì. 他的樣子很拘泥. He looks very stiff.

JŪNJIÀN₃ 軍艦 (N) warship, naval vessel.

JŪNREN₃ 軍人 (N) military man.

JŪNSHÌ₃ 軍事 (B-) military. jūnshi-xuéxiào 軍事學校 military school. jūnshi-jiàoyu 軍事教育 military education.

JŪNSHǓ₅ 軍屬 (N) (con. jūnrén-jiāshǔ 軍人家屬),dependents of military personnel.

JŪNTĀN₄ 均攤 (TV) share expenses equally. Yígòng-yòng-duōshao-qián wǒmen-jūntān. 一共用多少錢我們均攤. Let's share the total expenses.

JŪNXIǍNG₄ 軍餉 (N) military pay.

JŪNYUN₄ 均勻 (SV) even (well-balanced). Nèige-qiáng yóude-

J

hěn-jūnyun. 那 個 牆 油
的 很 均 勻 . That wall
was evenly painted. Tā-fēnde-
bu-tai-jūnyun. 他 分 得 不
太 均 勻 . He didn't divide
them very evenly.

JŪNZHÁNG₄ 軍 長 (N) army
corps commander.

JŪRAN₂ 居 然 (MA) actually
(contrary to expectation), sur-
prisingly. Tā-jūran-gǎn-qù. 他
居 然 敢 去 . He is actually
daring to go.

JÚSHI₃ 局 勢 (N) situation, condition. Kàn-shìjiede-júshi, hé-
píng-háishi-hén-nán. 看 世 界
的 局 勢，和 平 還 是
很 難 . Looking at the world
situation, peace is still difficult
to attain.

JǓ-SHǑU₂ 舉 手 (VO) raise
one's hand.

JÙSHUŌ₁ 據 說 (MA) it's said
that, hear someone say that.
Jùshuō-ta-zhèi-liǎngtian-lái. 據
說 他 這 兩 天 來 . It

is said that he will be here in a
couple of days.

JÙTǏ₂ 具 體 (SV) concrete (not
abstract). (opp. chōuxiàng 抽
象). Shìqing-hái-méi-jùtǐ. 事
情 還 沒 具 體 . Things
are not concrete yet.

JÚXÍNG₂ 舉 行 (TV) hold a ceremony, meeting, etc. Tāmen-
jīntian-jǔxíng-'yíshì. 他 們 今
天 舉 行 儀 式 . They
will have their ceremony today.

JÚZHǍNG₃ 局 長 (N) head of an
office or bureau of which the
last syllable is jú 局 .

JÙZHÙ₄ 居 住 (TV) reside,
dwell. Nèige-dìfang jūzhùde-rén
hěn-duō. 那 個 地 方 居
住 的 人 很 多 . There
are many people living in that
area.

JÚZI₃ 橘 子 (N) orange, tange-
rine.

JÙZI₂ 句 子 (N) sentence.

JÚZISHUǏ₃ 橘 子 水 (N) orange
juice.

J

K

KĀCHĒ₃ 卡車 (N) motor truck. (M: liàng 輛).

KĀFĒI₂ 咖啡 (N) coffee.

KĀFĒIGUĂNR₂ 咖啡館兒 (N) coffee house.

KĀI₁ 開 (TV) (opp. guān 關) (1) open something. kāi-chuānghu 開窗戶 open the window. kāi-suǒ 開鎖 open a lock, unlock. (2) start, begin, open, establish. Zhèige-gōngchǎng shì-'tā-kāide. 這個工廠是他開的 . This factory was started by him. (3) operate, run. kāi-mǎimai 開買賣 run or start a commercial business. kāi-xuéxiào 開學校 run or start a school. (4) operate a motor conveyance. kāi-chē 開車 drive a car. kāi-fēijī 開飛機 fly an airplane. kāi-diàntī 開電梯 operate an elevator. (5) make a list or certain written documents. kāi-yào-fāngr 開藥方兒 write a prescription. kāi-dānzi 開單子 make a list. kāi-zhīpiào 開支票 write a check. (6) serve food. Kāi-fàn! 開飯 ! Start serving dinner! (7) open by digging in the ground. kāi-yóujǐng 開油井 drill an oil well. (8) turn on the electric switch. kāi-dēng 開燈 put on the light. kāi-

diànshì 開電視 turn on the T. V. kāi-diànmén 開電門 turn on the switch. (9) expel, fire (as an employee). Pùzili-kāile-liǎngge-rén. 鋪子裏開了兩個人 . The store fired two persons. (10) perform surgery on, operate on (a part of the body). Dàifu-shuō tāde-yǎn děi-kāi. 大夫說他的眼得開 . The doctor said that his eye has to be operated on. (11) pay (money). kāi-gōngqian 開工錢 pay a wage. (IV) (1) depart. Huǒchē-kāi-le. 火車開了 . The train is leaving. Bādiǎn-zhōng kāi-chuán. 八點鐘開船 . The boat leaves at eight o'clock. (2) boil. Shuǐ-kāi-le. 水開了 . The water is boiling. (3) bloom. Huār-kāi-le. 花兒開了 . The flowers are blooming.

(RE) (1) indicates separation. Tā-líkai-Měiguo-le. 他離開美國了 . He has left America. Nǐ-zǒukai. 你走開 . You go away. Mén kāibukāi. 門開不開 . The door cannot be opened. Dǎkai-shū. 打開書 . Open the book. (2) remove a mental block by thinking. Tā-xiànzài kànkāi-le. 他現在看開了 . Now he has removed his mental block. Nǐ-zěnma-xiǎngbukāi-a? 你怎麼想不開? How come you have a mental block?

KĀICHÚ₃ 開除 (TV) be expelled from school. Tā-jiao-xuéxiào-gei-kāichú-le. 他叫學校給開除了. He was expelled by the school.

KĀI-DĀNZI₃ 開單子 (VO) make out a list.

KĀI-DĀO₃ 開刀 (VO) (1) perform surgery, operate. Tā-kāiguo-yícì-dāo. 他開過一次刀. He was operated on once. (2) start aggressive action with, use someone as the first of a group to be killed or fired. Tā-men-yào-ná-ta-kāi-dāo. 他們要拿他開刀. They want to take care of him first (killed or fired). (See: KĀI 開).

KĀIDAO₄ 開導 (TV) guide or explain to make someone understand something, lead the way (fig.). Děi-yǒu-ren-kāidao cai-néng-mínzhǔ. 要有人開導才能民主. There must be someone who can guide them before they can attain democracy. Tā-xiǎngbukāi wǒmen-bìxu kāidao-kaidao-ta. 他想不開我們必須開導開導他. He has a mental block. We have to talk to him to make him understand.

KĀIDÒNG₄ 開動 (TV) (1) start to do something. (2) start to eat. Wǒmen-yào-kāidòng-le. 我們

要開動了. We are going to start eating.

KĀI-FÀN₂ 開飯 (VO) start to serve dinner.

KĀIFÀNG₃ 開放 (TV) open something private to the public. Jīntian-qǐng-huìyuán-lai-kàn, míngtian-kāifang. 今天請會員來看,明天開放. Today, members are invited to see, tomorrow it will be open to the public.

KĀIFENG₃ 開封 (PW) K'ai-feng (capital of Honan province).

KĀI-GŌNG₃ 開工 (VO) start the work (usually construction work or manual labor).

KĀIGUĀN₄ 開關 (N) (lit. open close) switch (electrical).

KĀIHUÀ₃ 開化 (IV) civilized. Tāmen-shi-yěren, hái-mei-kāi-huà-ne. 他們是野人還沒開化哪. They are savages, they are not yet civilized.

KĀI-HUĀR₂ 開花兒 (VO) the flower opens.

KĀI-HUÌ₁ 開會 (VO) (1) hold a meeting. Wǒmen-děi-kāi-huì-tán-tan. 我們得開會談談. We should hold a meeting to discuss the matter. (2) attend a meeting. Nǐ-qu-kāi-huì-ma? 你去開會嗎? Are you going to the meeting?

KĀI-HUǑR₃ 開火兒 (VO) (1) open fire (with a gun). (2) start to fight.

KĀIKAI₁ 開開 (RV) open up. Zhèige-mén kāibukāi. 這個

門開不開 . This door cannot be opened up. <u>reduplicated verb of</u> kāi 開 , open a little. Kāikai-shìshi. 開 開 試 試.Try to open it a little.

KĀIKĚN₄ 開 墾 (TV) open up virgin land. Pài-rén dào-xīběi-qu-kāikěn. 派 人 到 西 北 去 開 墾 . Send people to the Northwest to open up virgin land.

KĀI-KUÀNG₃ 開 鑛 (VO) mine. kāi-tiěkuàng 開 鐵 鑛 mine iron. kāi-méikuàng 開 煤 鑛 mine coal.

KĀI-LÙ₄ 開 路 (VO) (1) build a road. Zài-zhèr kāi-yitiao-lù. 在 這 兒 開 一 條 路 . Build a road here. (2) lead the way <u>in something new.</u>

KĀI-MÙ₂ 開 幕 (VO) (<u>lit.</u> open the curtain) open, start <u>an ex-hibition, fair, athletic meet, show, etc.</u> Tāde-zhǎnlǎn míng-tian-kāi-mù. 他 的 展 覽 明 天 開 幕. His exhibi-tion opens tomorrow. Wǒmen-xiǎng-zai-kāi-mù-de-shihou qíng-ni-jiǎngyǎn. 我 們 想 在 開 幕 的 時 候 請 你 講 演 . We wish to have you give a speech at the opening.

KĀISHǏ₂ 開 始 (TV) start, begin. kāishǐ-gōngzuò 開 始 工 作 start work. 'Shénma-shíhou-kāishǐ? 甚 麼 時 候 開 始 ? When will it start? (N) the beginning. dì'èrxuéqī de-kāishǐ 第 二 學 期 的

開 始 the beginning of the second semester.

KĀISHUǏ₃ 開 水 (N) boiling water. Yòng-kāishuǐ-qī-chá. 用 開 水 泡 茶 . Use boiling water to make tea. (2) boiled water. Nàlide-shuǐ bu-gānjing, wǒmen-děi-hē-liáng-kāishuǐ. 那 裏 的 水 不 乾 淨 我 們 得 喝 涼 開 水 . The water there is not clean, so we have to drink cooled boiled water.

KĀITONG₃ 開 通 (SV) liberal-minded. Tāde-sīxiang hen-kāi-tong. 他 的 思 想 很 開 通 . His thinking is very liber-al.

KĀI-TÓUR₄ 開 頭 兒 (VO) start. Shì-shéi-kāide-tóur? 是 誰 開 的 頭 兒 ? Who started it?Tāmen-yi-kāi-tóur jiu-méi-zuòhǎo. 他 們 一 開 頭 兒 就 沒 作 好 . They didn't do well right from the beginning.

KĀI-WÁNXIÀO₂ 開 玩 笑 (VO) make a joke, joke. Wǒ-shuō-zhèngjīngde-ne, bié-kāi-wánxiào. 我 說 正 經 的 哪, 別 開 玩 笑 . I'm talking seri-ous business, don't joke. Tā-nà-shi-kāi-nǐde-wánxiào. 他 那 是 開 你 的 玩 笑 . What he is doing is joking with you.

KĀIXIAO₃ 開 銷 (N) operating expenses. (<u>syn.</u> kāizhǐ 開 支). Tāde-kāixiao-tài-dà. 他 的 開 銷 太 大 . His operating expenses are too high.

K

(TV) expend (money). Bǎ-qián-dou-kāixiao-le. 把錢都開銷了 . The money has all been expended.

KĀIXĪN₃ 開心 (SV) pleased, delighted. Kànjian-xiǎoháizi-nènma-gāoxìng, wǒ-zhēn-kāixīn. 看見小孩子那麼高興，我真開心. I am delighted to see the children so happy. Bié-ná-wo-kāixīn. 別拿我開心. Don't use me to please yourself.

KĀI-XUÉ₁ 開學 (VO) begin a school semester. Xià-xuéqī-jiǔyue-kāi-xué. 下學期九月開學 . The next semester will start in September.

KĀIYǍN₃ 開演 (TV) start to perform.

KĀI-YÈCHĒ₃ 開夜車 (VO) work or study late into the night, burn the midnight oil. Míngtian-kǎoshì, jīntian-wǎnshang děi-kāi-yèchē. 明天考試今天晚上得開夜車 . Tomorrow we will have an examination, tonight we must burn the midnight oil.

KĀIZHǍN₄ 開展 (N) development. Tāmende-gōngsī bu-kě-néng yǒu-shénma-dàde-kāizhan. 他們的公司不可能有甚麼大的開展 . Their company cannot have much development.

KĀI-ZHĀNG₃ 開張 (VO) (1) open for business for the first time. Nèige-pùzi kuài-kāi-zhāng-le.那個鋪子快

開張了 That store will open soon. Jīntian kāi-zhāng. 今天開張 . Today is the grand opening. (2) start selling. Jīntian-hái-méi-kāi-zhāng-ne. 今天還沒開張哪· Haven't sold a thing yet today.

KĀIZHĪ₃ 開支 (N) operating expenses. (syn. kāixiao 開銷).

KĀI-ZHĪPIÀO₂ 開支票 (VO) write a check.

KǍLÙLĬ₄ 卡路里 (N) calorie.

KĀN₃ 看 (TV) (1) keep watch, tend, mind. kān-men 看門 watch the door. Tā-gěi-rén-kān-háizi. 他給人看孩子 . She minds children for others. Nǐ-děi-kānzhe-ta. 你得看著他. You have to watch him. (2) put under watch or guard, hold under detention. Bǎ-ta-kānqilai. 把他看起來 . Put him under guard.

KǍN₄ 砍 (TV) (1) cut with a wide swinging motion, as with saber, ax, etc., chop, slash. Tā-bǎ-shù-kǎndǎo-le. 他把樹砍倒了 . He chopped down the tree. Tā-kǎnle-nèige-ren-sān-dāo. 他砍了那個人三刀 . He slashed him three times with a knife. (2) hit by throwing an object. Bié-ná-shí-tou kǎn-rén. 別拿石頭砍人 . Don't throw rocks at people.

KÀN₁ 看 (TV) (1) look at, watch, see. kàn-huàr 看畫兒 look at a painting. kàn-dǎ-qiú 看打球 watch a ball game.

K

Wǒ-ài-kàn-tā-yǎn-xì. 我愛 看他演戲 . I like to see him act in a play. (2) visit, see a person. Wǒ-méi-qu-kàn-ta. 我没去看他 . I didn't visit him. Nǐ-děi-qu-kàn-dàifu. 你得去看大夫 . You must go to see a doctor. (3) examine and treat (a sickness), visit, see (as a doctor or a patient). Nǐde bìng děi-zhǎo-dàifu-kànkan. 你的病得 找大夫看看 . You must call a doctor to treat your illness. Wǒ-qu-kàn-bìng-qu. 我去看病去 . I am going to see a patient about his illness. or I am going to see a doctor about my illness. (4) think that. (syn. xiǎng 想). Wǒ-kàn zhèiyàngr-xíng-le. 我看 這樣兒行了 . I think that this way is all right. Jù-wǒ-kàn méi-wèntí. 據我看没 問題 . According to the way I see it, there is no problem. (5) read silently. kàn-xiǎoshuōr 看小說兒 read novels. Xiànzài wǒ-kàndǒng-le. 現在 我看懂了 . Now I understand it (by reading). (cf: NIÀN 念). (6) it depends on. Nà-děi-kàn tā-gěi-duōshuo-qián. 那得 看他給多少錢 . It depends on how much money he'll pay. Zhèijiàn-shì chéng-bu-chéng, jiu-kàn-tā-kěn-bu-kěn-zuò. 這件事成不成 , 就看他肯不肯作 . Whether this will be successful

or not depends on whether he is willing to do it or not. Kàn-nide-běnshi-le. 看你的本事 了 . It will depend on your ability. (7) (con. kàn-bié.... 看别 ...). try to avoid. Liúshén, kàn (-bié)-shuāi-dǎo-le. 留神看 (别)摔倒了 Be careful try to avoid falling down. (8) for someone's sake. Bié-dǎ-le, kàn-wǒ-le! 别打了 , 看我了! Don't fight anymore for my sake! (See: KÀN...MIÀNZI 看...面 子). (9) used to gain someone's attention, look. Nǐ-kàn, zhè-zěnma-bàn? 你看 , 這怎 麼辦 ? Look, what can be done now? (10) see, find out. Kàn-shéi-xiān-zuòwán. 看誰 先作完 . See who'll finish first. Nǐ-kàn-ni! Zěnma-zènma-húdu-a! 你看你! 怎麼 這麼糊塗啊 ! Look at yourself! How come you are so muddled! (11) used at the end of a sentence which contains a verbal reduplication, and see what happens. shìshi-kan 試試看 try and see. suànsuan-kan 算算 看 compute and see. Wènwen-ta-kan. 問問他看 . Ask him and see.

KÀNBUQĬ₁ 看不起 (RV) (1) look down on. Bié-kànbuqǐ-rén. 别看不起人 . Don't look down on people. (2) cannot afford to see or to look at. Diànyǐngr-tài-guì, wǒ-kànbuqǐ-le. 電影太 貴我看不起了 . Movies are too expensive. I can't afford to see them.

KĀNCÁINÚ₅ 看 財 奴 (N) (lit. watch money slave) a miser.

KÀNCHULAI₁ 看 出 來 (RV) make out what something is by looking. Tā-xiěcuò-le, wǒ-méi-kànchulái. 他 寫 錯 了, 我 沒 看 出 來. He wrote it wrong, but I didn't make it out.

KÀNDAI₄ 看 待 (TV) tend to one's needs, treat. Děi-xiàng-wode-háizi-yiyàng-de-nènma-kàndai-ta. 得 像 我 的 孩 子 一 樣 的 那 麼 看 待 他. I must treat him just as if he were my child.

'KÀNFĀ₁ 看 法 or KÀNFAR (N) viewpoint.

KÀNFAR₁ 看 法 兒 see 'KÀNFĀ 看 法.

KĀNG₅ 糠 (N) chaff, bran, grain husks.

KÁNG₄ 扛 (TV) lift up with one's shoulder or back of neck. Tā-kángzhe-nèige-zhuōzi. 他 扛 着 那 個 桌 子. He is carrying that table on his shoulder.

KÀNG₅ 炕 (N) k'ang (a kind of brick platform built in a room and used for sleeping). Tā-tǎngzai-kàngshang. 他 躺 在 炕 上. He is lying on the k'ang. (TV) heat and dry something over or by a fire. Bǎ-miànbāo zai-lúzishang kàngkang. 把 麵 包 在 爐 子 上 炕 炕. Heat the bread on the stove.

'KĀNGJIÀN₄ 康 健 (SV) healthy. Tā-lǎole, kěshi-hái-'kāngjiàn.

他 老 了 可 是 還 康 健. He is old but he's still healthy.

KĀNGKĂI₄ 慷 慨 (SV) generous, of noble spirit, willing to serve the public.

KÀNGYÌ₄ 抗 議 (TV) protest. Xuésheng-xiàng-zhèngfǔ-kàngyì. 學 生 向 政 府 抗 議. The students are protesting a-gainst the government. (N) protest.

KÀNHU₃ 看 護 (N) nurse (for care of the ill). (syn. hùshi 護 士).

KÀNJIAN₁ 看 見 (RV) see. Wǒ-kànle kěshi-méi-kànjiàn. 我 看 了 可 是 沒 看 見. I looked, but didn't see. Zhèi-zhong-dōngxi wo-méi-kànjianguo. 這 種 東 西 我 沒 看 見 過. I have never seen this kind of thing.

KÀN....MIÀNZI₃ 看 ... 面 子 (S) (lit. for the sake of someone's face) for someone's sake. Kàn-tāde-miànzi, wǒ-bu-néng-bu zhèiyàngr-zuò. 看 他 的 面 子, 我 不 能 不 這 樣 兒 作. For his sake, I cannot but do it this way.

KÀNPÒ₄ 看 破 (RV) see a hidden intention, see through. Tā-xīnli-xiǎngde-shì shénma, wǒ-zǎojiu kànpò-le. 他 心 裏 想 的 是 甚 麼, 我 早 就 看 破 了. I saw long ago what he was thinking about.

KÀNQÍ₂ 看 齊 (RV) dress right to set straight. Xiàng-yòu-kànqí!

向 右 看 齊 ! Dress right, dress! (military drill command). (2) fig. line up in principle with a person or an ideology. Wǒmen děi 'gēn-wǒmende-'lǐngxiu kànqí. 我 們 得 跟 我 們 的 領 袖 看 齊. We have to line up behind our leader.

KÀNQILAI₂ 看 起 來 (RV) start to look at or read. Zhèiyàng-kànqilai, wǒmen-hěn-yǒu-xī-wang. 這 樣 看 起 來, 我 們 很 有 希 望. Looked at in this way, we are very hopeful. Tā-kànqi-shū-lai-le. 他 看 起 書 來 了. He started to read. (cf: KÀNSHANG).

KÀNSHANG₂ 看 上 (RV) (1) or KÀNZHÒNG 看 中 be interested in something or someone which was selected from a group. (2) start to read or look. Tā-kàn-shang-shū-le. 他 看 上 書 了. He started to read.

KÀN-SHŪ₁ 看 書 (VO) read a book silently. (cf: NIÀN-SHŪ 念 書).

KÀNWANG₄ 看 望 (TV) visit, see friends or relatives. Wǒ-lai-kànwang-kànwang-péngyou. 我 來 看 望 看 望 朋 友. I came to visit some friends.

KÀNWU₂ 刊 物 (N) periodical, magazine, publication. Xuéshēng-huì-chūle-yizhǒng-kānwu. 學 生 會 出 了 一 種 刊 物. The student body issued a periodical.

KÀNZHÒNG₄ 看 重 (RV) put emphasis on, pay too much attention to. Bié-tài-kànzhòng-tade-huà. 別 太 看 重 他 的 話. Don't put too much emphasis on what he said.

KÀNZHÒNG₃ 看 中 or KÀN-SHANG 看 上 (RV) be interested in something or someone which was selected from a group. Tā-kànzhòng-Lǐ-xiáojie-le. 他 看 中 李 小 姐 了. He is particularly interested in Miss Li.

KǍO₁ 考 (TV) (1) take or give an examination, examine (for knowledge). Dàxué tā-qù-kǎole, kěshi-méi-kǎoshàng. 大 學 他 去 考 了, 可 是 沒 考 上. He took a college entrance examination but didn't pass. Nǐ-bié-káo-wo. 你 別 考 我. Don't test me. (2) study the historical facts of something. (B) examination. yuèkǎo 月 考 monthly examination. dàkǎo 大 考 final examination.

KǍO₃ 烤 (TV) (1) heat or warm over or by the fire. Hěn-lěng, lái, kǎokǎo-shǒu. 很 冷, 來, 烤 烤 手. It's very cold, come, warm your hands by the fire. (2) bake, toast, roast, broil. Tā-kǎode-ròu hǎochī. 他 烤 的 肉 好 吃. The roast he made is delicious. Qǐng-nǐ-gěi-wǒ kào-yikuài-miànbāo. 請 你 給 我 烤 一 塊 麵 包. Please toast a slice of bread for me. Tā-huì-kǎo-diǎn-xin. 他 會 烤 點 心. He knows how to bake pastries.

K

KÀO₃ 靠 (TV) (1) lean on. Bié-kào-nèige-qiáng. 别 靠 那 個 牆 . Don't lean on that wall. (2) depend on. Zài-jiā kào-fùmǔ, chū-wài kào-péngyou. 在 家 靠 父 母 ， 出 外 靠 朋 友 . At home one depends on one's parents, outside one depends on friends. (3) be located near. Nèige-fángzi tài-kào-xī-le. 那 個 房 子 太 靠 西 了 . That house is too near to the west. Nǐ-kào-'zuǒbianr-zǒu. 你 靠 左 邊 兒 走 . Walk on the left side of the road. Tā-yǐjing-kào-sìshisui-le. 他 已 經 靠 四 十 歲 了 . He is nearly forty years of age. (4) have something touching something else. Chuán hái-méi-kào-àn-ne. 船 還 沒 靠 岸 呢 . The boat has not yet docked. Zhuōzi kào-qiáng-fàng-zhe. 桌 子 靠 牆 放 着 . The table has been put against the wall.

KÀOBUZHÙ₂ 靠 不 住 (RV) cannot depend on. Bié-tīng-tāde, tāde-huà kàobuzhù. 别 聽 他 的 , 他 的 話 靠 不 住 . Don't listen to him. What he said cannot be depended upon. (cf: KĚKÀO 可 靠).

KÀOCHÁ₃ 考 查 (TV) investigate, study by investigation. Zhèngfǔ-pài-ta qu-kǎochá-Fǎguode-nóng-yè-jīngji. 政 府 派 他 去 考 查 法 國 的 農 業 經 濟 . The government sent him to study (investigate)

France's agricultural economy.

KÀO-HUǑ₄ 烤 火 (VO) warm oneself by a stove or a fire. Tā-zuòzai-lúzi-qiánbianr kǎo-huǒ. 他 坐 在 爐 子 前 邊 兒 烤 火 . He is sitting in front of the stove warming himself.

KÀOLǑNG₂ 靠 攏 (RV) (1) get close to or touch (usually of a boat to a dock). Děng-chuán-kào-lǒng-yǐhòu, wǒmen-dōu-xiàqu. 等 船 靠 攏 以 後 我 們 都 下 去 . After the boat docks we will all debark. (2) lean towards, get close to. Tāmen-dou-xiàng-zhōnggòng-kàolǒng-le. 他 們 都 向 中 共 靠 攏 了 . They are all leaning towards the Chinese Communist Government.

KǍOLÜ₂ 考 慮 (TV) give thoughtful consideration weighing all factors. Yīngdāng-zěnma-bàn, nǐ-kǎolǜ-kaolǜ-ba. 應 當 怎 麼 辦 ， 你 考 慮 考 慮 吧 . You'd better give some thought to how this should be done. Zhèizhong-shì, wǒmen-bunéngbu-jiā-kǎolǜ. 這 種 事 我 們 不 能 不 加 考 慮 . In this kind of matter we cannot do without added thoughtful consideration.

KǍOQǓ₃ 考 取 see KǍOSHANG 考 上 .

KǍOSHANG₃ 考 上 or KǍOQǓ 考 取 (RV) pass an examination for school entrance, job, license, etc. Bu-zhīdao ta-kǎodeshang-kǎobushàng. 不知道他考的上考不上. (I) don't know whether he can pass the examination or not.

KǍOSHÌ₁ 考試 (TV) take or give an examination. Wǒmen-jīntian-kǎoshì. 我們今天考試. We'll have an examination today.

(N) examination, test. Tāde-kǎoshì-bu-jígé. 他的考試不及格. He did not pass his examination.

KǍPIÀN₄ 卡片 (N) card (any kind except a playing card). (M: zhāng 張).

KĒ₂ 科 (N) (1) a unit in an organization, section, department. shénma-kē 甚麼科 what section. kuàiji-kē 會計科 accounting department. (2) a branch of learning, subject for study. wén-kē 文科 liberal arts course. lǐ-kē 理科 science course. (3) department or branch of medicine. nèi-kē 內科 internal medicine department. wài-kē 外科 surgery department. yákē-dàifu 牙科大夫 dentist.

(M) section (of an organization). dìsankē 第三科 the third section.

KĒ₃ 棵 (M) for trees or plants. yìkē-dà-shù 一棵大樹 a big tree. yìkē-báicài 一棵白菜 one cabbage.

KĒ₃ 顆 (M) (1) for gems. yìkē-zuànshí 一顆鑽石 a diamond. yìkē-zhūzi 一顆珠

子 a pearl. (2) for bullets. yìkē-zǐdàn 一顆子彈 a bullet. (3) for seed, grain. yìkē-dòuzi 一顆豆子 a bean. (4) for stars. yìkē-xīngxing 一顆星星 a star. (cf: LÌ 粒).

KĒ₄ 磕 (TV) knock against something. Kēke-yāndǒu, bǎ-yānhuī kēchulai. 磕磕烟斗, 把烟灰磕出來. Knock the pipe (smoking) to knock off the ashes. Bǎ-tuǐ kēpò-le. 把腿磕破了. He wounded his leg by knocking it against something.

KĚ₁ 渴 (SV) thirsty. Wǒ-kě-le. 我渴了. I'm thirsty. Qìshuǐ-bu-jiě-kě. 汽水不解渴. Sodas do not quench thirst.

KĚ₁ 可 (AD) (1) (con. kěshi 可是). but, yet. Suīran-hǎo, ke-bu-guì. 雖然好, 可不貴. It's good, but not expensive. (2) indeed, certainly. Nà-ke-hǎo-le! 那可好了! That certainly would be wonderful! Zhè-ke-bu-xíng! 這可不行! This certainly won't do! Yàoshi-nǐ-bu-tīng-huà, wǒ-ke-dǎ-ni. 要是你不聽話我可打你. If you don't obey, I will certainly spank you. (3) unstressed, used in a command or suggestion, absolutely, must. Wàibianr-fàng-qiāng-ne, nǐ-ke-bié-chūqu. 外邊兒放鎗哪, 你可別出去. There is shooting outside, you mustn't go out. Ke-děi-xiǎoxin-a! 可得小心啊! You've got to be careful! (4) stressed, at

K

last (after anxious expectation).
Nǐ-'kě-lái-le! 你可來了!
You came, at last! Zhèi-shì 'kě-
wán-le. 這事可完了.
This affair is ended, at last.

KĚ$_3$ 可 (B-) used before a TV, IV
or AV to form a SV, able. kěhèn
可恨 hateful. Méi-shénma-
kěmǎi-de. 沒甚麼可買
的. There is not much worth
buying.

KĚ$_1$ 課 (N) (1) class (in school).
(M: táng 堂). shàng-kè 上課
go to class or class in session.
Wǒ-xiàwu yǒu-yitáng-kè. 我下
午有一堂課. I have
a class in the afternoon. (2)
course (in school). (M: mén 門).
Wǒ-jīnnian 'yìmén-kè dōu-méi-
jiāo. 我今年一門課
都沒教. This year I am
not teaching even a single course.
(M) lesson (in a textbook). Yíge-
lǐbài niàn-sānkè. 一個禮
拜念三課. Study three
lessons a week.

KĚ$_1$ 刻 (M) quarter (of an hour).
sānkè-zhōng 三刻鐘 three
quarters of an hour. liǎngdiǎn-
yíkè 兩點一刻 two-fifteen
(o'clock).

KĚ$_3$ 刻 (TV) engrave, carve. Tā-
zài-zhuōzishang kèle-xiē-zì. 他
在桌子上刻了些
字. He carved some charac-
ters on the table.
(SV) (con. kèbo 刻薄). mean,
stingy with people. Zhèi-yàngr-
zuò hěn-ke. 這樣兒作很刻.
This is a stingy way to do it.

KĚ(REN)$_1$ 客(人) (N) guest. Jiā-
li yǒu-kè(ren). 家裏有客
(人). There are guests at home.
Lái-kè-le. 來客了. The
guest is here.

KĚ'ÀI$_1$ 可愛 (SV) lovable,
lovely. Zhèi-háizi-kě'ài. 這
孩子可愛. This child is
lovable.

KĚBĚN(R)$_3$ 課本兒 (N) textbook.

KĚBO$_3$ 刻薄 (SV) (1) mean or
stingy with people. Tā-dài-rén
tài-kèbo. 他待人太刻
薄. He treats people in a very
stingy manner.

KĚBUSHÌ(...MA)$_2$ 可不是
(...嗎) (S) it certainly is (used
for agreement with something
stated). A: Tiānqi-zhēn-hǎo. B:
Kěbushì-(ma)! A:天氣真好.
B: 可不是(嗎)! A: The
weather is very good. B: It certainly is! Tā-shuō-shì-Lǐ-xiān-
sheng-lái-le. Wǒ-yi-kàn, kěbu-
shì-tā-(ma)! 他說是李
先生來了,我一看,
可不是他(嗎)! He
said Mr. Lee came. I looked. It
certainly was him. Tā-shuō-wo-
xiěcuò-le. Wǒ-yì-chá-zìdiǎn, kě-
bushi-wo-cuò-le-(ma)! 他說
我寫錯了,我一查
字典,可不是我寫
錯了(嗎)! He said I wrote it
wrong. I looked it up in a dictionary, I certainly was wrong.

KĚCHǏ$_3$ 可恥 (SV) shameful.

KĚFU$_5$ 克服 (TV) overcome
(difficulties). Wǒmen-děi-kèfu-

K

kùnnan. 我們得克服困
難. We must overcome
the difficulty.

KĔGUĀN₄ 可觀 (SV) consider-
able amount, quite a bit. Tā-
mĕi-yuè-yòng-de-qián shùmu-
kĕguān. 他每月用的
錢數目可觀. The a-
mount of money he spends each
month is considerable.

'KÈGUĀN₂ 客觀 (SV) objective.
(opp. zhŭguǎn 主觀). zhàn-
zai-'kèguānde-lìchangshang-lai-
shuō 站在客觀的立
場上來說 speaking from
an objective standpoint. Wŏmen-
kàn-shìqing dĕi-'kèguān. 我們
看事情得客觀. In
looking at things we must be objective.
(AD) objectively. 'Kèguande-
shuō, shì-tā-bu-duì. 客觀的
說,是他不對. Objec-
tively speaking, he is wrong.

KĔKÀO₂ 可靠 (SV) reliable,
dependable, trustworthy. Tāde-
huà bu-kĕkào. 他的話不
可靠. What he said cannot
be relied on. (cf: KÀOBUZHÙ
靠不住).

KÈKOU₅ 尅扣 (TV) deduct un-
lawfully from someone's pay.
Tā-kèkou-gōngren-de-qián. 他
尅扣工人的錢. He
deducted some money from the
workers.

KÈKŬ₃ 刻苦 (SV) be hard on
oneself. kèkŭ-dú-shū 刻苦
讀書 study with hardship. Tā-
néng-kèkŭ. 他能克苦. He

can take hardship.

KĔLIÁN₂ 可憐 (SV) pitiful (for
a person who is miserable or
suffering). Zhèi-háizi fùmŭ-dōu-
sĭle, duóma-kĕlián. 這孩子
父母都死了,多麼
可憐. Both parents of this
child are dead. How pitiful.
(TV) feel sorry for someone.
Méi-rén kĕ-lián-ta. 沒人可
憐他. Nobody feels sorry
for him. (cf: KÈXĪ 可惜).

KĔN₁ 肯 (AV) willing. Tā-zhīdao,
kĕshi-ta-bu-kĕn-shuō. 他知
道,可是他不肯說.
He knows, but he is not willing
to tell.

KĔN₄ 啃 (TV) gnaw, bite off a
piece from something. kĕn-gú-
tou 啃骨頭 gnaw the bone.
kĕ-lăoyùmi 啃老玉米
gnaw the corn (on the cob).

KĔNDÌNG₄ 肯定 (SV) (1) positive. Tāde-dáfu shi-kĕndìngde.
他的答覆是肯定
的. His answer is positive. (2)
definite. Tāde-huà shuōde-hen-
kĕndìng. 他的話說的
很肯定. He said it very
definitely.
(TV) decide something positively.
(opp. fŏudìng 否定). Wŏ-bu-
néng-kĕndìng tā-shì-duìde. 我
不能肯定他是對
的. I cannot decide positively
that he is right.

KĔNÉNG₁ 可能 (SV) possible.
Nà-hĕn-kĕnéng. 那很可能.
That is very possible. Tiānxià
méi-you-bu-kĕ'néngde-shì. 天

K

下 没 有 不 可 能 的
事. There's nothing under the
sky that is impossible.
(MA) possibly. Tā-kĕnéng-bu-
zhĭdào. 他 可 能 不 知
道. Possibly he doesn't know.
(N) possibility. Wŏ-xiăng-yŏu-
zhèizhong-kĕnéng. 我 想 有
這 種 可 能. I think there
is this possibility.

KĒNG₃ 坑 (N) a hole in the ground.
wā-kēng 挖 坑 dig a hole in
the ground. Bié-diàozai-kēngli.
別 掉 在 坑 裹 Don't fall
into the hole.
(TV) defraud, swindle, cheat.
Tā-kĕnéng kēng-biérende-qián.
他 可 能 坑 別 人 的
錢. It is possible that he is
swindling other people's money.
Nĭ-'shuō-nĭ-gĕi-qián kĕshi-nĭ-
bu-gĕi, zhè-búshi-kēng-rén-ma?
你 説 你 給 錢 可 是
你 不 給; 這 不 是 坑
人 嗎? You say you're going
to pay, but you don't, isn't this
cheating?

KĔNQIE₄ 懇 切 (SV) sincere, in
earnest. Tā-hĕn-kĕnqie. 他 很
懇 切. He is very sincere.

KĔPÀ₂ 可 怕 (SV) fearsome,
frightening, terrifying. Zhèige-
rén kĕpà. 這 個 人 可 怕.
That person is fearsome. Hēi-
wūzi yŏu-shénma-kĕpà? 黑 屋
子 有 甚 麼 可 怕?
What's so frightening about a
dark room?

KÈQI₁ 客 氣 (SV) (1) polite, courteous. Tā-kèqijíle. 他 客 氣

極 了. He is extremely po-
lite. Tā-yìdiănr-dou-bu-kèqi, jìn-
lai-jiu-bă-dōngxi názŏu-le. 他
一 點 兒 都 不 客 氣,
進 來 就 把 東 西 拿
走 了. He isn't the least bit
polite, just came in and took the
things away. (2) modest, humble
(in manner). A: Wŏde Zhōngwen-
bu-xíng. B: Nín-tài-kèqi. A: 我
的 中 文 不 行. B: 您
太 客 氣 A: My Chinese is
no good. B: You are too modest.
(cf: XŪXĪN 虛 心). (3) formal,
stand on ceremony. Qĭng-zuò,
bié-kèqi. 請 坐, 別 客 氣
Please sit down, feel at home.
A: Lĭbàiliù, wŏmen-gĕi-nin‹
sòngxíng. B: Bié-kèqi. A: 禮
拜 六, 我 們 給 您 送
行. B: 別 客 氣. A: We are
giving you a farewell party on
Saturday. B: Don't be formal
about it.
(IV) make polite remarks or
polite gestures. Tā-gēn-wo-kè-
qile-liangjiu. 他 跟 我 客
氣 了 兩 句. He make a
couple of polite remarks to me.
A: Xièxie. B: Bié-kèqi. A: 謝
謝. B: 別 客 氣. A: Thank
you. B: (lit. Don't make polite
remarks.) You are welcome.
Yàoshi-ni-bù-gĕi-wŏ-qián, wŏ-
kĕ-yào-gēn-ni-bu-kèqi-le. 要
是 你 不 給 我 錢 我
可 要 跟 你 不 客 氣
了. If you don't give me the
money, I will do something which
you might think is not very polite.

Tāmen-liǎngge-rén zài-mén-kǒur kèqile-bàntiān, shéi-yě-bu-kěn-xiān-jìnqu. 他們兩個人在門口兒客氣了半天, 誰也不肯先進去. They have been making polite gestures at the doorway for a long while, neither one is willing to go in first. (AD) (1) politely. hěn-kèqide-shuō 很客氣的說. say it very politely. (2) beat around the bush (in saying something). Tā-hěn-bu-kèqide-shuō. 他很不客氣的說. He talked in a straightforward manner.

KĚQIǍO₂ 可巧 (MA) coincidentally. Wǒ-zhèngyào-zhǎo-ta, kěqiǎo-pèngjian-ta-le. 我正要找他, 可巧碰見他了 I was about to go look for him, then I bumped into him coincidentally.

KĚQIÚ₄ 苛求 (IV) very particular in requiring something. Bù-néng-kěqiú. 不能苛求. You cannot be too particular.

KĚQǓ₃ 可取 (SV) desirable because of some quality. Tā-zhèiyidiǎn kěqǔ. 他這一點可取. This point of his is desirable.

KÉR₄ 殼兒 (N) shell (outside covering). jīdàn-kér 鷄蛋殼兒 egg shell.

KĚSHI₁ 可是 (MA) (1) used in a clause which follows the first clause with or without suíran

雖然, but. (syn. dànshi 但是, buguò 不過). (Suíran) tā-yào kěshi-wǒ-bu-gěi-ta. (雖然) 他要, 可是我不給他. He wants it, but I won't give it to him. (2) used to inform someone of certain facts or feelings that may not be realized, you know. Yàoshi-zai-wài-bianr-chī-fàn, nǐ-děi-qǐng-kè. Wǒ-kěshi-méi-qián. 要是在外邊兒吃飯, 你得請客, 我可是沒錢. If we eat out you will have to treat, I don't have money, you know. Nǐ-xiǎoxin, tā-kěshi-nǐ-de-shàngsi. 你小心, 他可是你的上司. You must be careful, he's your boss, you know.

KÈSHÌ₂ 課室 or KÈTÁNG 課堂 (N) classroom. (M: jiān 間).

KĚSHUI₅ 瞌睡 (N) involuntary nodding of the head when one falls asleep in a sitting position. dǎ-kēshui 打瞌睡 doze off. (TV) doze off. Tā-chīle-fàn jiu-kēshui. 他吃了飯就瞌睡. After eating he dozes off.

KÉSOU₂ 咳嗽 (IV) cough. Tā-késoule-jǐshēng. 他咳嗽了幾聲. He coughed several times. Wǒ-yǒu-dianr-késou. 我有點兒咳嗽. I have a little cough.

KÈTÁNG₂ 課堂 see KÈSHÌ 課室.

KÈTĪNG₁ 客廳 (N) parlor, living room. (M: jiān 間).

K

KĒ-TÓU₃ 磕頭 (VO) a gesture of respect consisting of kneeling on both knees and knocking the head on the floor, bow, kowtow. Xiànzài méi-rén-kē-tóu-le. 現在沒人磕頭了. Nobody kowtows anymore. (2) used to show appreciation for a favor. Kē-tóu-kē-tóu. 磕頭磕頭. Thank you.

KÈWÀIHUÓDÒNG₃ 課外活動 (N) extra-curricular activities.

KĚWÙ₃ 可惡 (SV) detestable. Zhèige-rén tài-kěwù-le. 這個人太可惡了. This person is detestable. Kěwude-dōngxi. 可惡的東西. Detestable thing (a person).

KĚXĪ₂ 可惜 (SV) be a pity, regrettable (for persons or things which are no longer useful). Zènma-niánqīng jiu-sǐ-le, zhēn-kěxī. 這麼年青就死了. 真可惜. He died so young. It's really a pity. Zhèige-biǎo-huài-le, hěn-kěxī. 這個表壞了, 很可惜. It's a pity that this watch is broken. (MA) what a pity, too bad. Kěxī ta-méi-lái. 可惜他沒來. What a pity he didn't come. (TV) feel pity for losing, wasting or ruining something. Wǒ-bìng-bù-kěxī-nèi-diǎnr-qián. 我並不可惜那點兒錢. I definitely don't feel pity for losing that little money. (cf: KĚLIÁN 可憐).

KĚXIÀO₂ 可笑. (SV)(1)funny. Tā-de-xiàohua bu-kěxiào. 他的笑話不可笑. His joke is not funny. (2) laughable, ridiculous. Yíge-dàxué-jiàoshòu shuō-zhèiyangrde-huà, tài-kě-xiào-le. 一個大學教授說這樣兒的話, 太可笑了. If a professor says something like this, it's really ridiculous.

KĒXUE₁ 科學 (N) science. yán-jiu-kēxue 研究科學 study science. kēxué-fāngfǎ 科學方法 scientific method. (SV) scientific. Tāde-fāngfa bu-kēxué. 他的方法不科學. His method is not scientific.

KĚYǏ₂ 可疑 (SV) doubtful about, suspicious about. Wǒ-kàn-zhèi-ge-rén kěyí. 我看這個人可疑. I am doubtful about this person. Tā-juéde nèi-jian-shì-kěyí. 他覺得那件事可疑. He is suspicious about that matter.

'KĚYǏ₁ 可以 (AV) may. Wǒmen-kěyǐ-zuǒ-le. 我們可以走了. We may go now. Zhǐ-yao-nǐ-yǒu-piào, jiu-kěyǐ-jìnqu. 只要你有票就可以進去. You may go in as long as you have a ticket. Jiāng-lái wǒmen-kěyǐ-zhèiyàngr-bàn. 將來我們可以這樣兒辦. In the future we may do it this way. Cóng-zhèige-mén-jìnqu, kěyǐ-ma? 從這個門進去, 可以嗎? May we

go in from this door?
(SV) (1) acceptable, OK. A: Nèi-ge-xuéxiào zĕnmayàng? B: Hái-'kĕyĭ. A: 那 個 學 校 怎 麼 樣 ? B: 還 可 以 . A: How is that school? B: Acceptable. (2) terrific, (describing something or someone that is out of the ordinary). Tā-men-dăde zhēn-'kĕyĭ. 他 們 打 得 真 可 以 . Their fight was really awful.

KĒZHĂNG₄ 科 長 (N) chief of a unit or section in which the last syllable is kē 科 . jiàoyukē-kēzhăng 教 育 科 科 長 head of the education section.

KĔZHE₃ 可 着 (CV) do something within the limitation of capacity, size or quantity. Kĕ-zhe-zhèixie-qián-măi. 可 着 這 些 錢 買 . Buy what you can with this amount of money. Kĕzhe-zhèige-wūzi pū-yige-dì-tăn. 可 着 這 個 屋 子 鋪 一 個 地 氈 . Lay a rug that is as big as this room.

KÒNG₂ 空 (IV) (1) or KÒNG 空 empty, leave something empty. Nèige-wūzi kōngzhe-ne. 那 個 屋 子 空 着 呢 . That room is empty. Fánzi kōngchu-lai-le. 房 子 空 出 來 了 . The house has been vacated. Wŏ-bu-néng kōngzhe-dùzi hē-jiŭ. 我 不 能 空 着 肚 子 喝 酒 . I cannot drink on an empty stomach. Wŏ-shi-kōngzhe-shŏu-lái-de. 我 是 空 着 手 來 的 . I came empty-handed. (2)

or KÒNG 空 . leave a space empty, skip a word, line, page, etc., in writing. Nèizhang-huàr xià-tou-yŏu-yitiáo-chuán, shàngtou jiu-kōngzhe. 那 張 畫 兒 下 頭 有 一 條 船 , 上 頭 就 空 着 . There is a boat on the bottom of the picture but the top has been left empty. Nĭ-xiĕdao-zhèige-dìfang kōng-yi-háng. 寫 到 這 個 地 方 空 一 行 . Write up to here and skip a line.

(SV) (con. kōngdòng 空 洞). empty, hollow, meaningless. Tā-de-jiăngyăn nèiróng-hĕn-kōng. 他 的 講 演 內 容 : 很 空 . The content of his speech is meaningless. Bié-shuō-kōng-huà. 別 説 空 話 . Don't say empty words.

(AD) without basis. Kōng-shuō méi-yòng. 空 説 没 用 . No use in making empty talk.

KÒNG₃ 空 (TV) turn or hang something upside down. Bié-tóu-chòng-xià-kòngzhe. 別 頭 朝 下 空 着 . Don't let your head hang down. Bă-píngzili-de-yóu kòngchulai. 把 瓶 子 裏 的 油 空 出 來 . Turn the bottle upside down so the oil can come out.

(IV) see KÒNG 空 (IV) (1) (2).
(SV) seem empty (describing a place which gives the appearance of emptiness). Zhèige-dìfang tài-kòng. 這 個 地 方 太 空 . This place seems too empty. Bă-zhuōzi-bānchuqu wūzi-jiu kòng-le.

K

把桌子搬出去屋子就空了. If you take the table out, the room will seem empty.

KÒNGBÁI₃ 空白 (N) blank space. (M: kuài 塊).

KÒNGCHǍNGR₃ 空場兒 see KÒNGCHǍNGR 空場兒.

KÒNGCHǍNGR₃ 空場兒 or KÒNGCHǍNGR 空場兒 (N) open space, vacant lot.

'KŌNGDÒNG₄ 空洞 (SV) empty, hollow, meaningless. Nèibèn-shūli-de-huà hěn-'kōngdòng. 那本書裏的話很空洞. What is said in that book is meaningless.

KÒNGFÁNG₃ 空房 see KÒNG-FÁNG 空房.

KÒNGFÁNG₃ 空房 or KÒNG-FÁNG 空房 (N) empty house, empty room.

KǑNGHUANG₃ 恐慌 (SV) afraid and nervous. Tā-xīnli hěn-kǒng-huang. 他心裏很恐慌. He feels very afraid and nervous.

KŌNGJŪN₃ 空軍 (N) (1) air force. Tā-gei-kōngjun-zuò-shì. 他給空軍作事. He is working for the air force. (2) member of the air force, airman or air force officer. Tā-shi-Měiguo-kōngjūn. 他是美國空軍. He is an American airman.

KǑNGPÀ₁ 恐怕 (TV) afraid. Wǒ-kǒngpà-tā-bu-lái. 我恐怕他不來. I'm afraid he won't come.

(MA) probably. Zhèiběn-shū kǒngpà-shi-tāde. 這本書恐怕是他的. This book is probably his.

KŌNGQÌ₁ 空氣 (N) (1) lit. or fig. air, atmosphere. Kāikai-chuānghu, huànhuan-kōngqì. 開開窗戶, 換換空氣. Open the window to change the air. Wǒmen-chàng-ge-gēr,huàn-huan-kōngqì. 我們唱個歌兒,換換空氣. Let's sing a song to change the atmosphere. Kōngqì hěn-jǐnzhang. 空氣很緊張. The situation is very tense. (2) rumor. Yǒu-rén fàng-zhèizhǒngde-kōngqì. 有人放這種的空氣. There are people who are creating this kind of rumor.

KÒNGR₄ 空兒 (N) (1) spare time. Nǐ-míngtian yǒu-kòngr-ma? 你明天有空兒嗎? Do you have spare time tomorrow? (2) empty space. Liǎngge-zìde-dāng-jiàr liú-ge-kòngr. 兩個字的當間兒留個空兒. Leave an empty space between these two characters.

KŌNG-SHǑUR₄ 空手兒 (VO) (lit. have the hand empty) empty-handed. Wǒ-kōngzhe-shǒur gēn-ta-dǎ. 我空着手兒跟他打. I fought with him bare-handed. Wǒ-buhǎoyìsi kōng-shǒur dàu-ta-jiā-qù. 我不好意思空手兒到他家去. I feel embarrassed to go to his home empty-handed (without a present).

KŌNGTÁN₅ 空 談 (N) empty talk. Zhèi-buguò-shi-kōngtán. 這 不 過 是 空 談. This is only empty talk.

KŌNGTÓUZHĪPIÀO₄ 空 頭 支 票 (N) <u>check written with in-sufficient funds in the bank</u>, rub-ber che k.

'KŌNGXIÁN₅ 空 閒 (N) spare time. Wǒ-yidiǎnr-kōngxiánde-shíhou dou-méi-yǒu. 我 一 點 兒 空 閒 的 時 候 都 沒 有. I don't have any spare time.

KÒNGZHI₃ 控 制 (TV) control. bù-néng-kòngzhi 不 能 控 制 cannot control.

'KŎNG(FU)ZĬ₃ 孔 (夫) 子 (N) Confucius.

KŌU₄ 掘 (TV) (1) pick <u>or</u> dig(<u>out</u>) <u>with the finger</u>. Bié-kōu-bízi. 別 掘 鼻 子. Don't pick your nose. (2) hold on to <u>some-thing with the tip of the finger.</u> Kōuzhù-le, bié-sā-shǒu. 掘 住 了, 別 撒 手. Hold on tight, don't loosen your grip. (SV) be miserly with money. Tā-yàoshi-bu-kōu, zěnma-néng-yǒu-nènma-duō-qián-a? 他 要 是 不 掘, 怎 麼 能 有 那 麼 多 錢 阿? If he were not a miser he couldn't have become as rich as he is.

KŎU₂ 口 (N) mouth. Tā-yi-kāi-kǒu, wǒ-jiu-zhīdao-ta-shi-Pěi-píng-rén. 他 一 開 口 我 就 知 道 他 是 北 平 人. As soon as he opened his mouth I know he was from Peiping. Zhèiyàngrde-huà, ta-shuōbuchu-kǒu-lai. 這 樣 兒 的 話 他 說 不 出 口 來. He is not the type to utter such remarks.

(B) (1) verbal, oral. kǒuxìnr 口 信 兒 verbal message. (2) opening, port, entrance. kǎikǒu 海 口 seaport. chūkǒu 出 口 export <u>or</u> exit. hékǒu 河 口 mouth of a river. (3) mountain pass. Zhāngjiakǒu 張 家 口 Changchiakou pass. (4) edge <u>of</u> <u>a knife.</u> dāokǒu 刀 口 edge of a knife.

(M) (1) mouthful. chīle-liǎngkǒu-fàn 吃 了 兩 口 飯 ate two mouthfuls of rice. Tā-shuō-yikǒu-de-Běipíng-huà. 他 說 一 口 的 北 平 話. He speaks fluent Pekinese. (2) bite (<u>as of</u> <u>dog, insect</u>). Gǒu-yǎole-wo-yikǒu. 狗 咬 了 我 一 口. The dog took a bite out of me. (3) <u>for</u> <u>something spit out.</u> tǔle-yikǒu-xiě 吐 了 一 口 血 spit some blood. (4) <u>for something</u> <u>with a large opening.</u> yìkǒu-zhōng 一 口 鐘 a bell. (5) <u>for a knife.</u> yìkǒu-dāo 一 口 刀 a knife. (cf: KŎUR 口 兒, KŎUZI 口 子).

KÒU₃ 扣 (TV) (1) detain, hold <u>peo-ple or things,</u> arrest. Hǎiguān bǎ-dōngxi-kòu-le. 海 關 把 東 西 扣 了. The customs seized the things. Jǐngchá bǎ-ta-kòuqilai-le. 警 察 把 他 扣 起 來 了. The police put him under arrest. (2) withhold, deduct. Fā-'qián-de-shíhou méi-kòu-shuì.

K

發錢的時候沒扣
稅. When the salary was paid
the taxes were not withheld. (3)
place <u>cups, bowls, etc.</u>, upside
down <u>or</u> cover <u>something with an
inverted cup, bowl, etc.</u> Zhuō-
zishang kòuzhe-yíge-wǎn, wǎn-
dǐxia kòuzhe-yíkuai-diǎnxin. 桌
子上扣着一個碗,
碗底下扣着一塊
點心. On top of the table a
bowl is placed upside down. Under the bowl is a piece of pastry.
(4) button, buckle. kòu-kòuzi 扣
扣子 button the button. (5)
fasten <u>something which has a
latch.</u> Bǎ-mén-kòushang. 把門
扣上. Latch the door.
(M) <u>for the percentage of discount.</u> (<u>syn.</u> zhé 折). dǎ-bákòu
打八扣 (<u>lit.</u> discounted to
eighty per cent of its original
price) twenty per cent discount.
(See: DǍ-ZHÉKOU 打折扣).

KŎUCÁI₃ 口才 (N) ability to
articulate <u>or</u> be eloquent. Tā-
kǒucái-hǎo. 他口才好.
He is very articulate <u>or</u> eloquent.

KŎUCHÉN₅ 口沉 (SV) (<u>lit.</u> heavy
in taste) saltier <u>than usual.</u> (<u>opp.</u>
kǒuqīng 口輕).

KÓUCHI₄ 口齒 (N) diction, enun-
ciation. Tāde-kóuchi bu-qīngchu.
他的口齒不清楚.
His diction is not clear.

KÓUCHĪ₃ 口吃 (SV) stammer.
Tā-kǒuchīde-lìhai. 他口吃
得厲害. He stutters very
much.

KÓUDAI₃ 口袋 (N) bag, sack.
mǐ-kǒudai 米口袋 rice bag
(a sack).

KÓUDÀIR₂ 口袋兒 (N) pock-
ets (<u>to carry things in</u>). Yīshang
yǒu-sìge-kǒudàir. 衣裳有
四個口袋兒. There
are four pockets on the coat.

KÓUFÚ₄ 口福 (N) (<u>lit.</u>the mouth
is blessed) enjoyment derived
from being blessed with good
food. Wǒde-kǒufú bu-cuò. 我
的口福不錯. I am
blessed with having good food.

KÓUGONG₄ 口供 (N) confession,
deposition (<u>of a crime</u>).

KÓUHÀO₃ 口號 (N) slogan
(<u>verbal</u>). hǎn-kǒuhào 喊口號
yell a slogan.

KÓUHÓNG₄ 口紅 (N) (<u>lit.</u> mouth
rouge) lipstick. mǒ-kǒuhóng 抹
口紅 put on lipstick.

KÓUJÌNG₅ 口徑 (N) (<u>lit.</u> mouth
diameter) bore, caliber (<u>of fire-
arms</u>). sānbākǒujìngde-shǒu-
qiāng 三八口徑的手
鎗. 38 caliber pistol.

KÓULÌNG₅ 口令 (N) password.
Jīntian-wǎnshangde-kǒulìng shi-
"zìdiǎn". 今天晚上的
口令是"字典". To-
night's password is "Dictionary."
A: Kǒulìng! B: Zìdiǎn. A: 口
令! B: 字典. A: What's the
password! B: Dictionary.

KÒULIÚ₄ 扣留 (TV) seize, detain (<u>persons or things</u>).

KÓUQI₂ 口氣 (N) tone <u>or</u> meanings <u>implied in speech.</u> Tīng-
tade-kǒuqi ta-kuàiyao-bu-gàn-le.

K

聽 他 的 口 氣 他 快
要 不 幹 了 Listening to
the way he speaks, it seems that
he is quitting soon. Tāde-kǒuqi
hěn-dà. 他 的 口 氣 很
大. It sounds pretty big when he
talks about it. (cf: KǑUWEN 口 吻).

KǑUQÍN₄ 口 琴 (N) harmonica.
chuī-kǒuqín 吹 口 琴 play the
harmonica.

KǑUQĪNG₅ 口 輕 (SV) (lit. light
in taste) less salty than usual.
(opp. kǒuchén 口 況).

KǑUR₃ 口 兒 (N) (1) small cut
(wound or opening). lále-yige-
kǒur 剌 了 一 個 口 兒
made a little cut. (2) small opening. píngzi-kǒur 瓶 子 口 兒
mouth of a bottle or vase. (3)
place where two roads meet.
Dào-kǒurshang-qu-kànkan. 到
口 兒 上 去 看 看. Go
to the corner of the street and
take a look. (4) opening of a
garment. lǐngkǒur 領 口 兒
collar. xiùkǒur 袖 口 兒 cuff.
(M) (1) for number of people in
a family. Nǐmen-jiā 'jǐkǒur-rén?
你 們 家 幾 口 兒 人 ?
How many people are there in
your family? (2) used with liǎng
兩 young husband and wife.
xiǎo-liǎng kǒur 小 兩 口 兒
a young couple. (cf: KǑU 口 ,
KǑUZI 口 子).

KÒUR₄ 扣 兒 (N) knot (of string
or rope). huókòur 活 扣 兒
slip knot. jì-yíge-kòur 繫 一
個 扣 兒 tie a knot.

KǑUSHÌ₃ 口 試 (IV) have or give
an oral test or examination. Wǒmen jīntian-kǒushì. 我 們 今
天 口 試 . We are going to
have an oral examination today.

KǑUTOUYǓR₄ 口 頭 語 兒
(N) habitual utterances.

KǑUWEI₃ 口 味 (N) taste (to the
palate). Cài bu-hé-kǒuwei. 菜
不 合 口 味 . The food does
not have the right taste.

KǑUWEN₄ 口 吻 (N) tone or
meaning implied in speech. (cf:
KǑUQI 口 氣).

KǑUXIĀNGTÁNG₃ 口 香 糖 (N)
(lit. mouth fragrant candy) chewing gum. (M: kuài 塊).

KǑUYIN₂ 口 音 (N) accent (in
speech). Tā-shuō-huà dài-'nán-
fang-kǒuyin. 他 説 話 帶
南 方 口 音 . He speaks
with a southern accent. Tā-kǒu-
yin-hěn-zhòng. 他 口 音 很
重 . He has a heavy accent.

'KǑUYǓ₄ 口 語 (N) spoken language.

KǑUZI₃ 口 子 (N) (1) cut (wound
or opening). Tā-shǒushang lále-
yige-kǒuzi. 他 手 上 剌 了
一 個 口 子 . He made a
big cut on his hand. (2) opening
in a bank or dike of a river. He
kāi-kǒuzi-le. 河 開 口 子
了 . The river broke through
the dike.

(M) used with liǎng 兩 husband
and wife. lǎo-liǎngkǒuzi 老 兩
口 子 the old couple. Tāmen-
liǎngkǒuzi-lái-le. 他 們 兩
口 子 來 了 . They two

K

(husband and wife) have come.
(cf: KŎU 口 , KŎUR 口兒).

KÒUZI₄ 扣子 (N) button. Bǎ-
kòuzi-kòushang. 把扣子
扣上 . Button the button.

KŪ₁ 哭 (IV) cry, weep. Zhèi-hái-
zi-ài-kū. 這孩子愛哭 .
This child cries often. Tā-kū-
qilai-le. 他哭起來了 .
He started to cry.

(TV) cry, weep. Tā-kū-ta-mā-
ne. 他哭他媽呢 . He's
crying for his mother. or He's
weeping in mourning for his
mother.

KŪ₂ 苦 (SV) (opp.tián 甜) (1)
bitter (taste). Zhèi-yào-hǎo-kǔ-
a! 這藥好苦啊 ! How
bitter this medicine is! (2) hard
(referring to work with very
little remuneration). Shìqing tài-
kǔ. 事情太苦 . It's a
hard job with little pay. (3) sor-
rowful, distressing, miserable.
Wǒ-xīnli hěn-kǔ. 我心裏
很苦 I feel very great sorrow
(in my heart). (4) hard, bitter
(of life or an experience). Tāde-
shēnghuo hěn-kǔ. 他的生
活很苦 . His life is hard.
(5) poor (of food or certain things
used in daily life). Tāmen-jiā-
de-fàn hěn-kǔ. 他們家的
飯很苦 . The food in their
house is very poor. (6) make
something short by cutting. Bié-
bǎ-zhǐjia jiǎode tài-kǔ-le. 別
把指甲鉸的太苦
了 . Don't cut your fingernails
too short.

(N) (1) hardship. Tā-bu-néng-
chī-kǔ. 他不能吃苦 .
He can't take hardship. (2) sorrow. Wǒ-xīnlide-kǔ, gēn-shéi-
shuō? 我心裏的苦 , 跟
誰說 ? To whom could I tell
the sorrow in my heart?

KUĀ₃ 誇 (TV) (con. kuājiang 誇
獎). say good things about
something or someone, praise.
Wǒ-kuā-ta zhǎngde-niánqīng, tā-
jiu-gāoxìng-le. 我誇他長
得青年 , 他就高興
了 . I said that she looks young,
that made her happy.

KUĀ₃ 垮 (IV) (1) collapse. Fángzi
kuǎ-le. 房子垮了 . The
house collapsed. (2) fig. collapsed from exhaustion. Yíge-
ren zuò-sānge-rende-shì nà-hái-
bu-kuǎ? 一個人作三
個人的事情 , 那還
不垮 ? One person doing
three person's work, how could
he help from collapsing from
exhaustion? Nèige-pùzi cái-kāile-
'yíge-yuè jiu-kuǎ-le. 那個
鋪子才開了一個
月就垮了 . That store
closed (went bankrupt) after only
one month.

(RE) collapsed. Bǎ-dírén-dǎkuǎle
把敵人打垮了 . The
enemy was beaten (and collapsed
from exhaustion).

KUÀ₄ 跨 (TV) lit. or fig. take a
big step. Tā-wàng-qián kuàle-yíbù
他往前跨了一步 .
He took a big step forward.

KUÀ₄ 跨 (TV) carry something hanging on one side. Tā-kuàzhe-yíge-lánzi. 他 跨 着 一 個 籃 子. He is carrying a basket on his arm. Tā-gēn-ta-nǔ-péngyou kuàzhe-zuǒ. 他 跟 女 朋 友 跨 着 走. He is walking arm in arm with his girl friend. Tā-kuàzhe-yizhe-shǒuqiāng. 他 跨 着 一 枝 手 鎗. He is carrying a pistol.

KUĀDÀ₄ 誇 大 (SV) be exaggerated. Tāde-huà yǒu-yidiǎnr-kuā-dà. 他 的 話 有 一 點 兒 誇 大. What he said is a little exaggerated.

KUĂI₅ 舀 (TV) scoop. kuǎi-shuǐ 舀 水 scoop up water.

KUÀI₁ 快 (SV) (1) fast, quick. (opp. màn 慢). Shíhou-guòde-zhēn-kuài. 時 候 過 得 真 快. Time passes by very quickly. 'Kuàizhe-diǎnr. 快 着 點 兒. Faster. Zhèige-biǎo yì-tiān-kuài-shífēn-zhōng. 這 個 表 一 天 快 十 分 鐘. This watch is ten minutes too fast each day. (2) sharp (edge). Zhèibǎ-dāo bu-kuài. 這 把 刀 不 快. This knife is not sharp.
(AD) (1) fast, quickly. Nǐ-děi-kuài-pǎo. 你 得 快 跑. You must run fast. Tā-yào-kuài-yi-diǎnr-zuòwán. 他 要 快 一 點 兒 作 完. He wants to finish up a little faster. (2) hurry up and... Kuài-bié-shuō-le. 快 別 説 了. Hurry up and

stop talking. Kuài-náqilai-ba. 快 拿 起 來 吧. Hurry up and pick it up. (3) soon, almost, nearly. Bié-chūqu-le. Kuài-chī-fàn-le. 別 出 去 了. 快 吃 飯 了. Don't go out. It will soon be meal time. Tā-kuài-wǔshí-le. 他 快 五 十 了. He is almost fifty years old. Tāde-yǎn-kuài-xiā-le. 他 的 眼 快 瞎 了. He (his eyes) is nearly blind.

KUÀI₁ 塊 (M) (1) piece, hunk of something. yíkuài-táng 一 塊 糖 a piece of candy. yíkuài-dì 一 塊 地 a piece of land. yí-kuài-shítou 一 塊 石 頭 a rock, a stone. (2) dollar. wǔkuài-qián 五 塊 錢 five dollars.

KUÀICHĒ₃ 快 車 (N) express train or bus.

KUÀIHUO₂ 快 活 (SV) happy. Wǒ-xīnli-hen-kuàihuo. 我 心 裏 很 快 活. I am very happy. (cf:'KUÀILÈ 快 樂).

KUÀIJI₂ 會 計 (N) (1) accounting. Tā-xué-kuàiji. 他 學 會 計 He is studying accounting. (2) accountant. Wǒ-děi-gēn-kuàiji-tántan. 我 得 跟 會 計 談 談. I have to talk to the accountant.

'KUÀILÈ₂ 快 樂 (SV) happy. Tā-men-dōu-hěn-'kuàilè. 他 們 都 很 快 樂. They are all very happy.
(N) happiness. Zhè-shì-yizhǒng-'kuàilè. 這 是 一 種 快 樂. This is a kind of happiness. (cf: KUÀIHUO 快 活).

K

KUÀIMÀN₃ 快慢 (N) speed.

KUÀIR₃ 塊兒 (N) size (of objects which take kuài 塊 as a measure). Ròu kuàir-bu-xiǎo. 肉 塊 兒 不 小 . The size of this piece of meat is not small.

KUÀIXÌN₂ 快信 (N) express letter, special delivery. (M: fēng 封). Fā-yìfēng-'kuàixìn-ba. 發 一 封 快 信 吧 . Send a special delivery letter.

KUÀIYÀO₂ 快要 (AD) just about to do something. Nèiben-shū ta-kuàiyao-xiěwán-le. 那 本 書 他 快 要 寫 完 了 . He is just about to finish writing that book.

KUÀIZI₃ 筷子 (N) chopsticks. (M: shuāng 雙 , fu 副).

KUÀJIANG₃ 誇獎 (TV) praise, reward with words (generally from a superior). Wǒ-kuājiangle-ta-liǎngju. 我 誇 獎 了 他 兩 句 . I praised him with a few words.

KUÀ-KǑU₃ 誇口 (VO) boast. Wǒ-bú-shi-xiàng-ni-kuā-kǒu. 我 不 是 向 你 誇 口 . I'm not boasting to you.

KUĀN₁ 寬 (SV) (1) wide. (opp. zhǎi 窄). Zhèitiao-jiē hen-kuān. 這 條 街 很 寬 . This street is very wide. Zhèige-zhuōzi sānchǐ-kuǎn. 這 個 桌 子 三 尺 寬 . This table is three feet wide. (2) unconcerned about minor matters, relaxed. (opp. zhǎi 窄) Tāde-xīn-kuān. 他 的 心 寬 .

He is relaxed (mind). (3) magnanimous. Tā-duì-rén hěn-kuān. 他 對 人 很 寬 . He is very generous towards people. (N) width. Kuān-shi-èrchǐ, cháng-shi-liùchǐ. 寬 是 尺 , 長 是 六 尺 . The width is two feet, the length is six feet. (TV) (1) widen. Zhèige-mén kuānchu-wǔcùn-lai, jiu-hǎo-le. 這 個 門 寬 出 五 寸 來 就 好 了 . It would be good if this door could be widened by five inches. (2) a polite form to ask somebody to take off his coat. Nín-kuānkuan yīshang. 您 寬 寬 衣 裳 . Take off your coat.

KUĂN(ZI)₃ 欵 (子) (N) a sum of money or funds. (syn. kuǎnxiang 欵 項). (M: bǐ 筆).

KUĂNCHANG₄ 寬敞 see KUĂNCHUO 寬綽 (SV) (1).

KUĂNCHUO₄ 寬綽 (SV) (1) or KUĂNCHANG 寬敞 spacious. Dìfang-kuānchuo. 地 方 寬 綽 . The place is spacious. (2) have ample funds. Wǒ-shǒuli ye-bu-kuānchuo. 我 手 裏 也 不 寬 綽 . I don't have much money on hand.

KUĂNDAI₄ 欵待 (TV) treat a guest generously. Tāmen-kuǎn-dai-wo. 他 們 欵 待 我 . They treated me very well.

KUÁNG₃ 狂 (SV) reckless. Tā-tài-kuáng-le. 他 太 狂 了 . He is too reckless.

KUÀNG₃ 礦 (N) mine (minerals)

or mineral deposits. kāi-kuàng 開鑛 (lit. open a mine) mine (minerals) or drill (an oil)well. yóukuàng 油鑛 oil well or oil deposit. jīnkuàng 金鑛 gold mine or gold deposit.

'KUÀNGCHĂN₄ 鑛產 (N) mineral products (raw materials extracted from mines).

KUÀNGGŌNG₅ 鑛工 (N) mine workers, miners.

'KUÁNGHUÀ₄ 狂話 (N) reckless talk.

KUÀNG-KÈ₃ 曠課 (VO) cut class. Wŏ-kuàngde-tài-duò-le. 我曠課曠得太多了. I cut too many classes.

KUÀNGQIE₂ 況且 (MA) moreover. Yòu-hǎo, yòu-piányi, kuàngqie hěn-yǒu-yòng. 又好又便宜, 況且很有用. It's both good and inexpensive, moreover it's very useful.

KUÀNGSHĀN₅ 鑛山 (N) mine or mineral deposits (in the mountains).

KUÀNGWU₃ 鑛物 (N) minerals.

'KUÀNGYÈ₄ 鑛業 (N) mining industry.

KUĀNGZI₃ 筐子 (N) basket (usually without a handle and purely utilitarian). (cf: LÁNZI 籃子).

KUÀNGZI₃ 框子 (N) frame (for a picture or mirror). Zhèi-huàr-xiāngshang-kuàngzi hǎokànduōle. 這畫兒鑛上框子好看多了. After being fitted with a frame, this picture looks much better.

KUĂNSHI₄ 欵式 (SV) be decently arranged. Tāmen-jiéhūn-diǎnlǐ hěn-kuǎnshi. 他們結婚典禮很欵式. Their wedding ceremony was very decently arranged.

KUĂNXIANG₄ 欵項 (N) a sum of money or funds. (syn. kuǎn(zi) 欵(子)). (M: bǐ 筆).

KUĂNZHĂI₃ 寬窄 (N) (lit. wide narrow) width. Zhèige-zhuōzi kuānzhǎi-zhèng-héshì. 這個桌子寬窄正合適. The width of this table is just right.

KUĂ-TÁI₄ 垮台 (VO) (lit. stage is collapsed) collapse (of an organization). Nèige-zhèngfǔ jiù-yao huǎ-tái-le. 那個政府就要垮台了. That government will soon fall (collapse).

KÙCHĂR₅ 褲义兒 (N) short pants, shorts, panties, briefs. (M: tiáo 條).

KŬCHU₃ 苦處 (N) sorrow, hardship.

KÙFÁNG₄ 庫房 (N) storage room.

KŬGÀN₂ 苦幹 (IV) work hard. Tā-zhēn-kěn-kŭgàn. 他真肯苦幹. He is really willing to work hard.

KŬGŌNG₃ 苦工 (N) hard, laborious work. zuò-kŭgōng 作苦工 do laborious work.

KŬHUÓR₃ 苦活兒 (N) hard job which pays very little. Kŭhuór 'shéi-dou-bu-yuànyi-gàn. 苦活兒誰都不願

K

意幹 . Nobody wants to take a hard job that pays very little.

KUĪ₅ 盔 (N) helmet. (M: dǐng 頂). gāngkuī 鋼盔 steel helmet.

KUĪ₃ 虧 (TV) (1) be short of. Tā-nèicì-guǎn-qián, kuīle-yìqiān-duō kuài. 他那次管錢，虧了一千多塊 . The time that he took care of the money, it was over a thousand dollars short. (2) owe. Wǒ-kuī-ta-wǔkuai-qián. 我虧他五塊錢 . I owe him five dollars. (3) betray <u>one's conscience</u>. (See: KUĪ-XĪN 虧心). (4) disappoint <u>someone by not returning a favor or reimbursing fairly</u>. Nǐ-zuò-ba. Wǒ-bu-huì-kuī-ni. 你作吧 . 我不會虧你 . You do it. I won't disappoint you.

(AD) (1) fortunately. Kuǐde-ta-zhènma-xiǎoxin, tā-méi-shòu-shāng. 虧得他這麼小心，他沒受傷 . Fortunately he was so careful that he wasn't injured. Kuīle-ni-méi-lái. 虧了你沒來 . Fortunately you didn't come. (2) that's great, that's something (<u>sarcastic</u>). Zhèiyàngrde-huà kuī-ni-shuōdechu-kǒu-lai. 這樣兒的話虧你說得出口來 . It's great that you could say something like that. (See: CHĪ-KUĪ 吃虧).

KUĪKONG₄ 虧空 (TV) (1) owe (<u>money</u>), be in debt. Tā-zuò-mǎimai kuīkongle-hěn-duō-qián. 他作買賣虧空了

很多錢 . He owes a lot of money from doing business. (N) debt. Zhèige-yuè yòu-lāle-kuīkong-le. 這個月又拉虧空了 . This month we are in debt again.

KUĪLÉI₅ 傀儡 (N) puppet. kuī-lěi-zhèngfǔ 傀儡政府 puppet government.

KUÍWU₅ 魁梧 (SV) excellent physique. Tāde-yàngzi hěn-kuí-wu. 他的樣子很魁梧 . He looks like he has an excellent physique.

KUĪ-XĪN₃ 虧心 (VO) betray <u>one's conscience</u>. Shuō-huà bié-kuī-xīn. 說話別虧心 . When you speak don't betray your conscience.

KǓLÌ₃ 苦力 (N) (1) hard labor. Tā-shi-mài-kǔlì-de. 他是賣苦力的 . (<u>lit.</u> He is the one who sells hard labor.) He is a laborer. (2) laborer, coolie. Tā-shi-yige-kǔlì. 他是一個苦力 . He is a coolie.

KǓLONG₂ 窟窿 (N) (1) hole. wā-yige-kūlong 挖一個窟窿 dig a hole. tǒng-yíge-kūlong 捅一個窟窿 pierce (and make a hole). (2) <u>Peip.</u> debt.

KǓLÓU₅ 骷髏 (N) skeleton.

'KǓMÈN₄ 苦悶 (SV) be distressed, miserable. Wǒ-xīnli-fēichang-'kǔmèn. 我心裏非常苦悶 . I feel very miserable (in my heart).

KǓMÌNG₄ 苦命 (N) fate (<u>which determines that one will have a harsh life</u>).

KŬN₄ 綑 (TV) tie or bind things together with rope or string. Tāmen-yòng-shéngzi bǎ-nèige-rén-kǔnshang-le. 他們用繩子把那個人綑上了. They tied that fellow up with a rope. Shìqing-bǎ-ta-kǔnzhu-le. 事情把他綑住了. The work tied him up. (M) a bundle. yìkǔn-bàozhǐ 一綑報紙 a bundle of news-papers.

KÙN₂ 睏 (SV) sleepy. Wǒ-kùnjíle. 我睏極了. I'm very sleepy.

KÙN₃ 困 (TV) (1) strand, get stuck. Tā-kùnzai-wàiguo-le. 他困在外國了. He was stranded abroad. (2) besieged. Nèixie-bīng zài-chéng-lǐtou kùn-le-sānge-yuè. 那些兵在城裏頭困了三個月. Those soldiers were be-sieged in the city for three months.

'KÙNKŬ₅ 困苦 (SV) harsh or difficult in living.

KÙNNAN₃ 困難 (SV) difficult (referring to a situation or cir-cumstances). shēnghuo-kùnnan 生活困難 difficult to make a living. Xiànzài-tāde-huánjing fēicháng-kùnnan. 現在他的環境非常困難. Now his circum-stances are very difficult. (N) difficulty. Wǒ-yùjian-bu-shǎode-kùnnan. 我遇見不少的困難. I have en-countered many difficulties.

KUÒ₂ 闊 (SV) wealthy, rich. (opp. qióng 窮). Tā-kuò-le. 他闊了. He is rich now. Tāmen-jiā-huòjíle. 他們家闊極了. Their home displays great wealth. Nà-shi-yige-'kuò-dìfang. 那是一個闊地方. This is a wealthy area. (cf: YŎU-QIÁN 有錢).

KUÒCHŌNG₃ 擴充 (TV) expand (make stronger or better, such as facilities). Xuéxiàode-shèbei hái-dei-kuòchōng. 學校的設備還得擴充. The facilities of the school need to be further expanded. (cf: KUÒDÀ 擴大).

KUÒDÀ₃ 擴大 (TV) expand, am-plify, escalate (physically or figuratively). Xuéxiàode-dìfang kuòdà-le. 學校的地方擴大了. The school's area has been expanded. Bǎ-tǎolùnde-fànwei you-kuòdà-le. 把討論的範圍又擴大了. The scope of the discussion has again been expanded. Wǒ-xīwang zhànshì-bié-zai-kuòdà-le. 我希望戰事別再擴大了. I hope that the war will not expand further. (cf: KUÒCHŌNG 擴充).

KUÒQI₄ 闊氣 (SV) (lit. the airs of the wealthy) appear rich. Tā-de-yàngzi hěn-kuòqi. 他的樣子很闊氣 From his ap-pearance, he seems to be very rich.

KUÒYĪNQÌ₄ 擴音器 (N) loud-speaker, amplifier.

K

KŬRÌZI₄ 苦日子 (N) hard day-to-day life. Tā-cóngqián yě-shi-guò-kŭrìzi. 他從前也是過苦日子. Before, he also had a hard day-to-day life.

KŬSHUĬ₄ 苦水 (N) hard water. (opp. tiánshuǐ 甜水).

KŬTÒNG₄ 苦痛 see TÒNGKU 痛苦.

KŬTÓUR₄ 苦頭兒 (N) hardship, trouble. Gěi-ta-diǎnr kŭ-tour-chī. 給他點兒苦頭兒吃. Let him suffer some hardship.

KŬXĪN₃ 苦心 (N) hardship or pains taken in doing something. Wǒ-yòngle-bushǎo-kŭxīn gěi-ta zhǎo-shì, tā-yě-méi-duì-wo-shuō-yìsheng-xièxie. 我用了不少苦心給他找事,他也沒說一聲謝謝. I took great pains to find a job for him, and he didn't even give one word of thanks.

KÙZI₃ 褲子 (N) trousers, pants, slacks. (M: tiáo 條).

K

L

LĀ₁ 拉 (TV) (1) pull, drag. Mǎ-lā-chē. 馬拉車 . The horse pulls the wagon. Tā-lāzhe-wo gēn-ta-qu-mǎi-dōngxi. 她拉着我跟他去買東西 . She dragged me along to go shopping with her. (2) go after someone to bring him into an organization, recruit. Liǎng-ge-xuéxiào dōu-lā-ta, yīnwei-tā-dǎ-qiú dǎde-hǎo. 兩個學校都拉他，因為他打球打得好 . Both of the two schools are after him because he plays ball so well. (3) play a musical instrument by pulling a bow across the strings. lā-tíqín 拉提琴 play the violin.

LĀ₃ 剌 (TV) cut with a knife or anything with a sharp edge. lá-xia-yikuai-ròu-lai 剌下一塊肉來 cut off a piece of meat. Wǒ-shǒushang lále-yige-kǒuzi. 我手上剌了一個口子 . I got a cut on my hand.

LÀ₃ 蠟 (N) (1) wax. shàng-là 上蠟 put on wax. dǎ-là 打蠟 polish with wax. (2) (con. làzhu 蠟燭). candle. (M: zhī 枝). Bǎ-là diǎnshang. 把蠟點上 . Light the candle.

LÀ₃ 落 (TV) (1) leave something behind unintentionally. Wǒ-bǎ-shū làzai-jiāli-le. 我把書落在家裏了 . I left my books at home. (2) leave out something unintentionally. Wǒ-méi-xiǎoxin, làle-yíge-zì. 我沒小心，落了一個字 . I wasn't careful, I left out a character. (3) leave behind (in regard to rate of doing), outdistance. Tā-tài-kuài, bǎ-wǒ-làxiale. 他太快，把我落下了 . He is too fast, he left me behind.

LÀ₃ 辣 (SV) (1) hot (taste), peppery. Zhèizhong-làjiāo bu-là. 這種辣椒不辣 . This kind of pepper is not hot.(2) cruel, harsh. Zhèige-rénde-shǒu-duan hen-là. 這個人的手段很辣 . This man has a cruel manner. (TV) burned by something hot in taste. Làjiāo làle-wo-yixiàzi. 辣椒辣了我一下子 . The pepper burned me.

LĀBA₃ 喇叭 (N) (1) trumpet, bugle, horn. èn-lāba 按喇叭 toot the horn. chuī-lāba 吹喇叭 blow a bugle. (2) loud-speaker.

LĀBAHUĀR₅ 喇叭花兒 (N) morning glory.(syn. qiānniúhuā 牽牛花). (M: kē 棵 , duǒ

朵).

LADĂO₄ 拉倒 (IV) forget about it, never mind. Yàoshi-nǐ-bu-yuànyì, jiu-lādǎo. 要是你不願意，就拉倒. If you don't like it, then forget about it.

LÁI₁ 來 (IV) (1) come. Tā-míng-tian-dào-xuéxiào-lái. 他明天到學校來. He'll come to school tomorrow. Tā-yào-lái-zhèr. 他要來這兒. He wants to come here. Lái-kè-le. 來客了. The guests have come. Nǐ-cóng-nǎr-lái? 你從那兒來? Where have you come from? Wǒde-qián láide-bu-róngyi. 我的錢來得不容易. My money doesn't come to me very easily. Tā-láide-zuì-zǎo. 他來得最早. He was the one who came here earliest. (2) Come on. Lái, hē-yibēi. 來，喝一杯. Come on, let's have a drink. Lái, zuò-yihuǐr. 來，坐一會兒. Come on, sit for a while, (3) send a message toward the speaker. Tā-gāngcái-láile-yige-diànhuà. 他剛才來了一個電話. He called here just a moment ago. Lǐ-xiānsheng lǎo-méi-lái-xìn-le. 李先生老沒來信了. Mr. Li hasn't sent a letter here for a long while. (4) have or take something. Nín-lái-kuai-táng. 您來塊糖. Have a piece of candy. Wǒ-yě-lái-zhang-bào.

我也來張報. I'll take a newspaper too. Zài-lái-yige. 再來一個. Have another one. or Do it once more. (5) do something. Wǒ-zìjǐ-lái, bié-kèqi. 我自己來，別客氣. I'll do it myself, don't bother. Mànmānrde-lái, bié-máng. 慢慢兒的來，別忙. Do it slowly, don't hurry. Nǐ-lái-pái-bu-lai? 你來牌不來? Do you play cards? Tā-zhèiju-huà láide-lìhai. 他這句話來得厲害. The words he said this time were terrific. Wǒ-gěi-ta-lái-yige-mǎn-bu-zàihu. 我給他來一個滿不在乎. I'll take the attitude of not caring about anything at all.

used before and, or after a verb or a VO, come in order to do something. Wǒ-lai-niàn-shū-lai-le. 我來念書來了. I came to study. Wǒ-lai-kāi-mén. 我來開門. I'll (come to) open the door. Kāi-mén-lai. 開門來. Come and open the door.

used between two verbal expressions, in order to. Wǒ-dàibiǎo-xuéxiào lai-shuō-jiju-huà. 我代表學校來説幾句話. I will represent the school to say a few words. Wǒ-men-kěyi-ná-zhèige lai-xiě-zì. 我們可以拿這個來寫字. We can use this to write.

(RE) (1) used with verbs of mo-

L

tion, and with verbs such as
shàng 上 , xià 下 , chū 出 ,
jìn 進 , huí 回 , guò 過 , qǐ
起 , indicates motion toward
the speaker. Note that unlike
other RV, a N or a PW may be
used between the verb and the
RE, come, here. chū-lai 出 來
come out, nálai 拿 來 bring
here. Bǎ-qìchē-kāilai. 把 汽
車 開 來 . Drive the car
here. Wǒ-míngtian huí-bulái.我
明 天 回 不 來 . I cannot
come back tomorrow. Ná-chá-
lai. 拿 茶 來 . Bring some
tea (here). Shàng-lóu-lai. 上
樓 來 Come upstairs. Huí-jiā-
lai. 回 家 來 . Come home.
Tā-yǐjing-dǎ-diànhuà-lai-le.
他 已 經 打 電 話 來 了
He has already called (here).
(2) used in potential RV only,
indicates ability to get along with
someone or something. Wǒmen-
tándelái. 我 們 談 得 來 .
We can get along in talking
about things. Shànghai-huà wǒ-
shuōbulái. 上 海 話 我 說
不 來 . I cannot speak Shanghai dialect.

LÁI₃ 來 (1) used after NU such as
shí 十 , bǎi 百 , qiān 千 , wàn
萬 , or M, approximately, not
more than. shí-lai-ge-rén 十
來 個 人 not more than ten
people. liùchǐ-lai-gāo 六 尺
來 高 not more than six feet
tall. (2) use after a NU-M time
expression, during the past...
zhèi-sānnian-lái 這 三 年

來 during the past three years.
LÁI₃ 賴 (TV) (1) repudiate with
intent of disclaiming responsibility. Bié-lài-zhàng. 別 賴
賬 . Don't deny the debt. (2)
stay somewhere and take advantage of someone's hospitality.
Tā-zài-zhèr-làizhe, bu-zǒu. 他
在 這 兒 賴 著 , 不 走 .
He just stays here living off
others and won't go away. (3)
blame someone else for one's
own mistakes.Tā-yǒu-cuòr bu-
rèn, lǎo-lài-biéren. 他 有
錯 兒 不 認 , 老 賴 別
人 . He won't admit his own
mistakes, he always blames
others.

LÁIBĪN₄ 來 賓 (N) guests (in a
formal occasion).

LÁIBUJÍ₁ 來 不 及 (RV) not
have enough time to do
something, not be able to do
something in time. Zuò-bādiǎn-
bàn-de-huǒchē, xiànzài-láibují-
le. 坐 八 點 半 的 火
車 , 現 在 來 不 及 了 .
Now it is too late to be able to
catch the 8:30 train. Láibují-
mǎi-dōngxi-le. 來 不 及 買
東 西 了 . There's not e-
nough time to buy the things.

LÁIHUÍ₃ 來 回 (IV) go and return. dāngtiān-láihuí 當 天 來
回 go and return in the same
day.
(N) round trip. dāngtiān-dǎ-lái-
huí 當 天 打 來 回 make a
round trip in the same day.
(AD) (1) back and forth. láihuíde-

L

dzǒu 來 回 的 走 walk back and forth. (2) over and over. lái-huíde-shuō 來回的說 say over and over.

LÁILI₄ 來歷 (N) background, past history (of a person). Tā-shi-shénma-láili? 他是甚麼來歷 ? What is his background?

... LÁI... QÙ₁ ... 來 ... 去 (S) (1) back and forth. Tā-zài-wūzi-li zǒu-lái-zǒu-qù. 他在屋子裏走來走去 . He is pacing back and forth in the room. (2) over and over. Tā-shuō-lái-shuō-qù lǎo-shi-nèi-jiju-huà. 他說來說去老是那幾句話 . He says it over and over and it's always the same few sentences.

LÁIWANG₃ 來往 (N) interpersonal or interorganizational relationship, social intercourse. Wǒ-gēn-ta méi-yǒu-láiwang. 我跟他沒有來往 . I have no dealings with him. (IV) have personal or organizational contact. Nǐ-kéyi-gēn-ta-láiwang-laiwang. 你可以跟他來往來往 . You may have personal contact with him.

LÁIYUÁN₃ 來源 (N) source of origin.

LAIZHE₃ 來着 (P) used at the end of affirmative sentences to indicate that an action or state was going on over a period of time in the past, but is probably no longer going on, at one time, during a period of time in the past. Tā-'zài-zhèr-laizhe. 他在這兒來着 . He was here (but isn't any longer). Nǐ-shuō-shénma-laizhe? 你說甚麼來着 ? What were you saying?

LĀJĪ₄ 拉圾 (N) rubbish, garbage.

LÀJIĀO₄ 辣椒 (N) pepper (vegetable). (M: kē 棵).

LĀLĀDUÌ₄ 啦啦隊 (N) cheering team, Rah-Rah Team.

LĀLONG₄ 拉攏 (TV) try to gain someone's favor by social means. Tāmen-xiǎng-lālong-ni. 他們想拉攏你 . They are trying to gain your favor.

LĀMA₅ 喇嘛 (N) lama, Lama priest. Lǎmajiào 喇嘛教 Lamaism.

LÁN₃ 攔 (TV) obstruct, hinder, block the way in order to stop something. Tā-lánzhe-wo, bu-ràng-wo-guòqu. 他攔着我, 不讓我過去 . He blocked the way, wouldn't let me pass. Tā-gāng-yào-shuō, wǒ-bǎ-ta-gei-lánhuiqu-le. 他剛要說, 我把他給攔回去了 . He was just about to tell but I stopped him.

LÁN₁ 藍 (SV) blue (color).

LǍN₂ 懶 (SV) lazy. Nǐ-yuè-bu-zuò-shì yuè-lǎn. 你越不作事越懶 . The less you do the lazier you get.

LÀN₄ 爛 (SV) (1) about to fall apart. Fàn-tài-làn. 飯太爛 . The rice is cooked too soft. Shūlàn-le. 書 爛 了 . The book is ragged (falling apart). (2) be in a state of decay. Guǒzi yǐjing-làn-le. 果子已經爛了 . The fruit is already rotten. Shǒu-làn-le. 手爛了 . The hand is infected.

LǍNDE₂ 懶 得 (AD) not feel like, not in the mood to. Wǒ-lǎnde-zuò-zhèi-zhong-shì. 我懶得作這種事 . I don't feel like doing this kind of thing.

LǍNDUO₅ 懶 惰 (SV) lazy. Zhèi-ge-ren hěn-lǎnduo. 這個人很懶惰 . This person is very lazy.

LÁNG₄ 狼 (N) wolf. (M: zhī 隻).

LÀNG(TOU)₄ 浪 (頭) (N) wave (in any body of water). Làng(tou)-hěn-dà. 浪頭很大 . The waves are very high.

LÀNGFÈI₄ 浪 費 (TV) waste. Bú-yào-làngfèi-jīnqián. 不要浪費金錢 . Don't waste money.

LÁNGZI₄ 廊 子 (N) (1) open porch. (2) a long roofed open corridor.

LÁNHUĀ₄ 蘭花 (N) orchid. (M: duǒ 朵 , kē 棵).

LÁNQIÚ₃ 籃 球 (N) basketball (the ball or the game). (M: chǎng 場). dǎ-yichǎng-lánqiú 打一場籃球 play a game of basketball.

LÁNTÚ₅ 藍 圖 (N) blueprint.

LÁNZHOU₃ 蘭 州 (PW) Lanchow (capital of Kansu province).

LÁNZI₃ 籃 子 (N) basket (usually with a handle curved over the top, may also be used for decorative purposes). (cf: KUĀNGZI 筐 子).

LĀO₄ 撈 (TV) (1) scoop up something from a liquid. lāo-yú 撈魚 fish with a net. Bǎ-miàn lāochulai. 把麵撈出來 . Take the noodles out of the water. (2) get back money which was lost in gambling or investment. Wǒ-děi-bǎ-běnqian lāo-huilai. 我得把本錢撈回來 . I have to get back the money I lost. (3) get money in an easy way. Tā-yòu-lāole-yibǐ. 他又撈了一筆 . He made another killing.

LĀO₁ 老 (SV) (1) old (in age), elderly. (opp. niánqīng 年青). Tāde-fùqin hěn-lǎo. 他的父親很老 . His father is very old. Tā-nènma-lǎo hái-zuò-shì. 他那麼老還作事 . He is so old yet he still works. (2) old (not new). (opp. xīn 新). Zhèi-shi-'lǎo-fángzi. 這是老房子 . This is an old house. Wǒmen-dōu-shi-lǎo-péngyou. 我們都是老朋友 . We are all old friends. (3) tough (of food). (opp.nèn 嫩). Cài-tài-lǎo. 菜太老 . The vegetables are too tough. Niú-ròu-tài-lǎo. 牛肉太老 . The beef is too tough. (4) last-born child (born when the father has reached old age). Tā-shì-lǎo-érzi. 他是老兒子 . He is the youngest son.

L

(AD) always, all the time. Tā-lăo-lái. 他老來. He comes all the time. Wŏ-lăo-méi-gōngfu. 我老沒工夫. I never have time.

usually used after tĭng 挺 and before a SV. very. Tā-nèige-qì-chē tĭng-lăo- dà. 他那個 汽車挺老大. That car is very big. (cf: JIÙ 舊).

LĂO₃ 老 (B-) (1) used before a surname to form an intimate personal name. Lăo-Lĭ 老李 old Li. (2) used before a number to form a noun indicating a person. lăo-èr 老二 the second one.

LÀO₃ 落 or LUÒ 落 (TV) (1) go or come down, drop. Tàiyang-lào-le. 太陽落了. The sun has set. Yèzi dōu-lào-le. 葉子都落了. The leaves have all fallen. Jiàqian méi-lào. 價錢沒落. The price has not dropped. (2) obtain the net result of some activity. Tā-mángle-bàntiān, jiéguŏ-shénma-ye-méi-luòzháo. 他 忙了半天，結果甚 麼也沒落着. He hustled for so long, in the end he got nothing. Tā-nèicì jiu-làole-yibăikuai-qián. 他那 次就落了一百塊 錢. That time he got only one-hundred dollars. Tā-liănshang lào le-yige-bāla. 他臉上 落了一個疤㿔. He has a scar on his face now.

LÀO₄ 烙 (TV) (1) cook a kind of

Chinese flat pastry on a grill. Wŏ-làole-liăngzhang-bĭng. 我 烙了兩張餅. I have grilled a couple of pastries. (2) iron something to make it flat. (syn. yùn 熨). Wŏ-děi-lào-yī-shang. 我得烙衣裳. I have to iron clothes.

LĂOBĂIXÌNG₄ 老百姓 (N) the common people, citizenry.

LĂOBĂN₄ 老板 (N) (1) owner or manager of a business. 'Zhāng-lăobăn 張老板 manager Chang. (2) boss.

LÀO-BĬNG₄ 烙餅 (VO) grill a flat pastry. (N) grilled flat pastry. yizhāng-làobĭng 一張烙餅 one grilled pastry.

LÁODONG₄ 勞動 (TV) (1) do laborious work. Rén-huózhe jiu-bu-néng-bu-láodong. 人活 着就不能不勞動. As long as people are alive they will have to do hard work. (2) cause someone trouble by asking a favor. Wŏ-bu-găn-láodong-nin. 我不敢勞動您. I don't dare to trouble you. (N) laborious work. láodòng-găi-zào 勞動改造 reform through laborious work.

LÁODÒNGJIÉ₄ 勞動節 (N) Labor Day or May Day.

LĂOHU₃ 老虎 see LĂOHŬ 老 虎.

LĂOHŬ₃ 老虎 or LÁOHU 老虎 (N) tiger. (M: zhĭ 隻).

LÁO-JIÀ₃ 勞駕 (VO) (1) used with a request for someone to

L

do something, please. (2) used to express appreciation of something done, thank you, much obliged. Láo-nín-jià. 勞您駕. Please. _or_ Thank you. Láojià, bǎ-yánghuǒ-gei-wo. 勞駕，把洋火給我. Please give me the matches. A: Láojià-láojià. B: Bù-láojià A: 勞駕勞駕. B: 不勞駕. A: Thank you, thank you. B: Not at all.

LĂOJIĀ₃ 老家 (N) old homestead, place of permanent family abode, origin of a person. Wǒde-lǎojiā zài-Shāndong. 我的老家在山東. My home is in Shantung.

LÁOSAO₃ 牢騷 (N) grumbling complaints that are not specific. Bié-fā-láosao. 別發牢騷. Don't complain.

LĂOSHI₃ 老實 (SV) honest. Tā-shi-ge-lǎoshi-ren. 他是個老實人. He is an honest person.

LĂOSHĪ₃ 老師 (N) teacher. (M: wèi 位). Lǐ-lǎoshī 李老師 Teacher Li. (cf: XIĀNSHENG 先生).

LĂOSHǑU(R)₄ 老手兒 (N) old hand (one who is accustomed to doing something).

LĂOSHU₃ 老鼠 (N) mouse, rat. (syn. hàozi 耗子).

LĂOTÀITAI₂ 老太太 (N) old lady. 'Lǐ-lǎotàitai 李老太太 Madame Li (a polite way of referring to an older woman).

LĂOTIĀNYÉ₃ 老天爺 (N) God.

Wǒde-lǎotiānyé! 我的老天爺! My God!

LÀOTIE₄ 烙鐵 (N) iron for ironing clothes or for soldering. (syn. yùndou 熨斗).

LĂOTÓUR₃ 老頭兒 or LĂO-TÓUZI 老頭子 (N) old man.

LĂOTÓUZI₃ 老頭子 or LĂO-TÓUR 老頭兒 (N) old man.

LĂOXIĀNG₃ 老鄉 (N) (1) peasant. Zhèige-lǎoxiāng dàgài-shi-tóuyicì-jìn-chéng. 這個老鄉大概是頭一次進城. This is probably the first time that this peasant has come to the city. (2) people from the same locality. Zánmen-shì-lǎoxiāng, bié-kèqi. 咱們是老鄉,別客氣. We are from the same place, therefore let's dispense with formalities. (3) a friendly address to an unknown person of common status. Lǎoxiāng, huǒchēzhàn-zai-něibianr-ne? 老鄉,火車站在那邊兒呢? Hey partner, where is the railroad station?

LĂOYÙMI₄ 老玉米 or YÙMĬ 玉米 (N) corn.

'LĂOZĂO₃ 老早 (AD) (1) very early. Tā-zènma-lǎozǎo-jiu-qǐ-lai-le. 他這麼老早就起來了. He got up so early. (2) long ago. Wǒ-lǎozǎo jiu-zhí-dao-le. 我老早就知道了. I knew of it long ago.

LĂOZI₄ 老子 (N) father.

'LĂOZĬ₄ 老子 (N) Laotzu (the philosopher).

L

LĀ-QIÀN₄ 拉縴 (VO) (1) pull a boat upstream by a rope tied to the mast. lā-chuánqiàn 拉船縴 pull a boat. (2) act as a go-between. lā-fáng-qiàn 拉房縴 act as a real estate broker.

LĀSĀ₃ 拉薩 (PW) Lhasa (capital of Tibet).

LĀ-SHǏ₄ 拉屎 (VO) defecate.

LĀ-SHǑU₁ 拉手 (VO) (1) hold hands. Tāmen-lāzhe-shǒu-zǒu. 他們拉着手走. They are walking along holding hands. (2) shake hands. Tāmen-jiàn-miàn-de-shihou lāla-shǒu. 他們見面的時候拉拉手, When they saw each other they shook hands. (cf: WÒ-SHǑU 握手).

LÁTA₄ 邋遢 (SV) messy.

LÀYUÈ₄ 臘月 (TW) the twelfth month of a year according to the lunar calendar.

LÀZHU₄ 蠟燭 (N) candle. (M: zhī 枝).

LE₁ 了 (P) when used at the end of a sentence, indicates that the statement used with le 了 is a new situation at a certain time. The time element may be expressed or implied in the sentence. If the time element is expressed, the new situation begins at the time specified by the time element. If the time element is not expressed in the sentence, in most cases it is implied as "now." (1) with SV as a predicate. Xiàn-zài-dōngxi-guì-le. 現在東西貴了. Things are

expensive now. (They were not before). Dōngxi-xiàyue-jiu-guì-le. 東西下月就貴了. Things will be expensive next month. Dōngxi-shàngyue-jiu-guì-le. 東西上月就貴了. Things were expensive last month. (2) with NU-M as a predicate. Bādian-zhōng-le. 八點鐘了. It is eight o'clock (now). (Before now it wasn't). (3) with AV (V-O) as a predicate. Tā-huì-shuō-Zhōngguo-huà-le. 他會說中國話了. He can speak Chinese (now). (Before he couldn't). (4) with shì 是 as a predicate. Tā-shì-Lǐ-tàitai-le. 她是李太太了. She is Mrs. Li(now). (She wasn't before). (5) with TV or IV as a predicate. Tā-zuó-tian-shuō-bu-qù, jīntian-yòu-shuō-qù-le. 他昨天說不去，今天又說去了. Yesterday he said he wasn't going, today he says he is going. (6) used with a predicate which includes kuài 快, yào 要, kuàiyào 快要 or jiùyào 就要 and a verb, soon, immediately. Tā-kuài-hǎo-le. 他快好了. He will be well soon. Kuài-bā-dian-zhōng-le. 快八點鐘了. It will soon be eight o'clock. Wǒ-yào-zǒu-le. 我要走了. I'm leaving. Huǒ-chē-kuàiyào-kāi-le. 火車快要開了. The train will leave soon. Wǒmen-jiùyào-chī-fàn-le. 我們就要吃飯了.

We are eating soon.

When used after a verb, indicates either that the action has started or that the action is completed. (1) used after a verb at the end of a sentence. (Sentence particles such as a 啊, ba 吧, ma 嗎, etc., may follow le 了). Tā-lái-le. 他來了. He has started to come. or He has come. (2) used after a verb and followed by a noun. This is used in rare cases as a complete sentence. Bié-sāle-shǒu. 別撒了手. Don't let go of it (from your hand). Zhèiyang jiu-jiéshule-ta-zài-jiàoyujiè-de-qióngkǔ-shēnghuó. 這樣就結束了他在教育界的窮苦生活. This way, the poor living he has had in the educational field is finished. (3) used after a verb, with or without a noun after it, and followed by another clause. Wǒ-chīle(-fàn) jiu-zǒu. 我吃了(飯)就走. I'll leave right after I finish eating. Wǒ-mǎile jiu-gěi-ta. 我買了就給他. After I buy it, I'll give it to him. (4) used after a verb and followed by a noun with another le 了 at the end of the sentence. (Sentence particles such as a 啊, ba 吧, ma 嗎, etc., may follow le 了). Tā-gěile-qián-le. 他給了錢了. He gave the money. (5) followed by a NU-M (N) without another le 了 at the end of

the sentence. Wǒ-chīle-sānwan-fàn. 我吃了三碗飯. I ate three bowls of rice. Wǒ-xuéle-sānge-yuè(de)-Zhōng-wén. 我學了三個月的中文. I studied Chinese for three months (some time ago). (6) followed by a NU-M (N) with another le 了 at the end of the sentence. (Sentence particles such as a 啊, ba 吧, ma 嗎, etc., may follow le 了). Wǒ-chīle-sānwan-fàn-le. 我吃了三碗飯了. I have been eating three bowls of rice. Wǒ-xuéle-sānge-yuè(-de)-Zhōngwén-le. 我學了三個月的中文了. I have been studying Chinese for three months. Nèizhang-huàr tā-huàle-sāntian-le. 那張畫兒他畫了三天了. He has been painting that picture for three days. or He finished painting that picture three days ago.

used after items which are enumerated. Zhuōzi-le, yǐzi-le, dōu-shi-jiāju. 桌子了，椅子了，都是傢俱. Tables, chairs, they are all furniture. (cf: A 啊).

(S) (1) BU...LE 不...了 not any more (quantity or time). Wǒ-chīde-tài-duō-le bù-chī-le. 我吃得太多了，不吃了. I ate too much, I am not eating any more. Tā-bù-dǎ-ta-tàitai-le. 他不打他太太了. He's not beating

L

his wife any more. (2) MÉI-(N)-LE 没(N)了 have not any more. Wǒ-méi-qián-le. 我没錢了. I have no money any more. Tāde-shū dōu-méi-le. 他的書都没了. All his books are gone. (3) NÙ-M (N)...MÉI-V-LE. have not been <u>doing something for some time</u>. Wǒ-sāntian-méi-chǐ-fàn-le. 我三天没吃飯了. I haven't eaten for three days. (4) SV-LE-QU-LE SV-了去了 very, extremely. Nèige-lǚguǎn dàle-qù-le. 那個旅館大了去了. That hotel is extremely big.

LÈ₄ 樂 (SV) happy. Tā-hěn-lè. 他很樂. He is very happy. (IV) laugh. Wǒ-yi-shuō, tā-jiu-lè-le. 我一説,他就樂了. As soon as I said it he laughed.

LÈGUĀN₃ 樂觀 (<u>opp.</u> bēiguān 悲觀) (SV) optimistic. (N) optimistic attitude. Tā-lǎo-lèguān. 他老樂觀. He is always optimistic.

LÉI₃ 雷 (N) thunder. Dǎ-léi-ne. 打雷呢. It's thundering.

LÉI₅ 鐳 (N) radium.

LÈI₁ 累 (SV) tired, exhausted. Wǒ-lèijíle. 我累極了. I am extremely tired. (IV) make <u>someone</u> tired. Zuò-zhèige-shì, zhēn-lèi-rén. 作這個事真累人. Doing this really makes people tired.

LÈI₂ 類 (M) kind, species, class.

fēn-sānlèi 分三類 divided into three kinds.

LÉIDÁ₃ 雷達 (N) radar.

LÉIZHUI₃ 累贅 (SV) burden, burdensome. Dài-háizi-qu, tài-léizhui-le. 帶孩子去,太累贅了. To take along the children would be too burdensome. (N) burden. Zhèixie-háizi-gen-dōngxi, dōu-shi-wǒde-léizhui. 這些孩子跟東西,都是我的累贅. These children and these things are my burden.

LĚNG₁ 冷 (SV) (1) cold (<u>in temperature</u>). (<u>opp.</u> rè 熱). Wǒ-juéde-hěn-lěng. 我覺得很冷. I feel very cold. Tiānqi-zhēn-lěng. 天氣真冷. The weather is real cold. (2) cold, unfriendly, indifferent. Tā-dài-rén-hěn-lěng. 他待人很冷. He is very cold towards people. (3) rarely used. Zhèige-zì tài-lěng. 這個字太冷. This word is rarely used. (cf: LIÁNG 涼).

LÈNG₂ 楞 (IV) (1) dumfounded. Tā-yí-wèn, dàjiā-dou-lèng-le. 他一問,大家都楞了. When he asked the question everybody was dumfounded. (2) immobile (<u>both physically and mentally</u>). Kuài-zuò-ba, bié-lèngzhe. 快作吧,别楞着. Get to work quickly, don't just stand there.

LÈNG₂ 楞 (SV) brusk, abrupt, blunt. Tā-shuō-huà kě-zhēnlèng. Jiănzhíde shi-ge-lèngxiăo-zi. 他 說 話 可 真 楞. 簡 真 的 是 個 楞 小 子. He speaks really very bluntly. He is a brusk fellow.

(AD) forcefully insist on <u>something without a sound basis</u>. Shì-tā-zìjĭ-náde, tā-lèng shuō-ta-mei-ná. 是 他 自 己 拿 的, 他 楞 說 他 沒 拿. He took it himself, but he insisted that he didn't. Wŏ-gào-song-ta-bu-néng-qù, kĕdshi-ta-lèng-qù. 我 告 訴 他 不 能 去, 可 是 他 楞 去 I told him he couldn't go, but he just went.

(S) LÈNG... YĔ... 楞 ... 也 ... rather. (<u>syn</u>. nìngkĕ... yĕ..., 寧 可 ... 也 ...). Wŏ-lèng-yuànyi-èzhe, yĕ-bu-yuànyì-chī-zhèige. 我 楞 願 意 餓 着, 也 不 願 意 吃 這 個. I would rather be hungry than eat this.

LĔNGBUFÁNG₄ 冷 不 防 (MA) suddenly, without warning. Lĕng-bufáng tā-dăle-wo-yi-xiàzi. 冷 不 防, 他 打 了 我 一 下 子. Suddenly, without warning, he gave me a blow.

(N) a sudden act <u>without warning that would catch one by surprise</u>. Nĭ-lìkè-jiu-qù. Gĕi-ta-yige-lĕngbufáng. 你 立 刻 就 去, 給 他 一 個 冷 不 防. You go at once so as to catch him by surprise.

LĔNGJING₃ 冷 靜 (SV) (1) quiet, desolate. Jiēshang-dàole-yèli jiu-

lĕngjing-le. 街 上 到 了 夜 裏 就 冷 靜 了. At night the streets are quiet. (2) calm, cool-headed, unemotional. Zhèige-rénde-tóunao hĕn-lĕngjing. 這 個 人 的 頭 腦 很 冷 靜. This person is cool-headed.

LÈYÌ₃ 樂 意 (AV) (1) like to, would like to. Tā-lèyì-qù. 他 樂 意 去. He is willing to go. (2) happy. Tā-bu-lèyì-le. 他 不 樂 意 了. He is annoyed.

LÍ₄ 梨 (N) pear (<u>fruit</u>).

LÍ₅ 犁 (N) plow.

LÍ₁ 離 (CV) <u>indicates one point apart from another</u>, from. Xué-xiào-lí-wŏ-jiā yŏu-yìli-lù. 學 校 離 我 家 有 一 里 路. The school is a mile (<u>or</u> li) from my home.

(TV) (1) leave a distance. Nĭ-lí-wo-'yuăn-yidiănr. 你 離 我 遠 一 點 兒. <u>lit. or fig</u>. You keep a little distance from me. Wŏmen-líde-hĕn-jìn. 我 們 離 得 很 近. <u>lit. or fig</u>. We are very close to each other. Tāde-huà lífle-tí-le. 他 的 話 離 了 題 了. What he said has nothing to do with the subject. (2) leave, separate, divorce. Tā-gen-tàitai-lí-le. 他 跟 他 太 太 離 了. He is separated from his wife. Xiăo-háizi lífbukāi-mŭchin 小 孩 子 離 不 開 母 親. Children cannot be separated from their mothers.

L

LǏ₁ 裏 (L) (1) in, inside. Wàng-ιǐ-zǒu. 往 裏 走. Go inside farther. Jiāli-méi-rén. 家 裏 沒 人. There is no one at home. (2) among. Nánrenli-yě-yǒu-hǎode. 男 人 裏 也 有 好 的. There are good people among the males also. used after wàng 望 or wǎng 往 and a SV. Wàng-dàli-xiě. 往 大 裏 寫. Write it bigger. Wǒmen-děi-wàng-chángli-kàn. 我 們 得 往 長 裏 看. We have to look towards the long term interest.

LǏ₂ 里 (M) (1) a unit of measure equal to about one-third of a mile. duō-zǒule-èrlǐ-dì 多 走 了 二 里 地 travelled two li more than necessary. (2) mile.

LǏ₂ 理 (N) principle, reason, rationale for doing something. Nǐ-shuō-nǐ-yǒu-lǐ. Kěshi-nǐde-lǐ zài-nǎr-ne? 你 說 你 有 理, 可 是 你 的 理 在 那 兒 呢? You say you have certain principles, but where are those principles?

LǏ₂ 理 (TV) do something, make a gesture or speak to a person in order to have a relationship. Nǐ-bié-lǐ-ta. 你 别 理 他. Don't bother with him. Nǐ-zěn-ma-bu-lǐ-ta? 你 怎 麼 不 理 他? How come you ignore him?

LǏ₃ 理 (TV) arrange in orderly fashion, put in order. Bǎ-shū-lǐ-yili. 把 書 理 一 理. Put the books in order.

LǏ₂ 禮 (N) (1) (con. lǐwu 禮 物). gift, present. (M: jiàn 件, fēnr 份 兒). sòng-lǐ 送 禮 give a present. shèngdàn-lǐ 聖 誕 禮 Christmas present. shēngri-lǐ 生 日 禮 birthday present. (2) ceremony, ritual. hūn-lǐ 婚 禮 wedding. xíng-lǐ 行 禮 perform a ritual, such as shake hands, salute, curtsy, kaotow, etc., go through a ceremony. huán-lǐ 還 禮 return a salute or give a gift in return.

LǏ₃ 粒 (M) for something small and shaped like grain. yílì-mǐ 一 粒 米 a grain of rice. yílì-zhūzi 一 粒 珠 子 a pearl. yílì-yào 一 粒 藥 a pill (medicine). yílì-shāzi 一 粒 沙 子 a grain of sand. (cf: KĒ 顆).

LǏ₃ 立 (TV) (1) stand something up. Bǎ-shū-lìqilai. 把 書 立 起 來. Stand the book up. Bié-héngzhe-fàng, lìzhe-fàng. 别 橫 着 放, 立 着 放. Don't lay it down, stand it up. (2) establish. Zhè-shi-shéi-lìde-guīju? 這 是 誰 立 的 規 矩? Who established this rule? Tāmen-yao-lì-yige-xuéxiào. 他 們 要 立 一 個 學 校. They want to establish a school.

LIǍ₄ 倆 (NU-M) Peip. (con. liǎng-ge 兩 個). two. Tāmen-liǎ-rén-dōu-qù. 他 們 倆 人 都 去. Both of them are going. Wǒ-mǎile-liǎ. Nǐ-mǎile jǐge? 我 買 了 倆. 你 買 了 幾 個? I bought two. How

L

many did you buy?

LIÁN₂ 連 (TV) connected <u>in a series</u>. Zhèi-tiao-xiàn gēn-nèi-tiao liánzhe. 這 條 線 跟 那 條 連着. This line is connected to that line. Wǒmen-kéyi ba-zhèi-liǎngjian-shì 'lián-qi-lai-kàn. 我們可以把 這 兩 件 事 連起來 看. We can look at these two matters as being connected. Tā-liánzhe-sān-tian méi lai. 他連 着 三 天 没 來. He hasn't come for three days in a row. (CV) <u>used with</u> dōu 都, yě 也, or hái 還, even...(still)... 。 Lián-wǒ dou-zhīdao. 連我都 知道. Even I know. Tā lián-Yīngwen ye-shuōbuhǎo. 他連 英 文 也 説 不 好. He can't even speak English well. Tā-lián-kàn dou-méi-kàn. 他 連看 都 没看. He didn't even look. Tā-lián-bào hái-kàn-budǒng-ne. 他連報還看 不 懂 呢. He cannot even read a newspaper and understand it. (cf: JIÙ 就, JIÙSHI 就是, JÍSHǏ 即使). (S) (1) LIÁN...DÀI... 連...帶 ... including... and. Lián-chī-dài-zhù yíge-yuè bāshikuai-qián. 連吃帶住一個月 八 十 塊 錢 Eighty dollars per month including room and board. (2) LIÁN...YIGÒNG ...連...共...including... total. Lián-wǒ yíyòng-'wǔge-rén. 連我一共五個人. Including me, there is a total of

five people.

LIǍN₂ 臉 (N) (1) face (<u>of people or animals</u>). Tāde-liǎn hóng-le. 他 的 臉 紅 了. His face became red. (2) face (<u>one's reputation, standing or dignity in the opinion of others</u>). (<u>syn.</u> miànzi 面子). diū-liǎn 丢 臉 lose face. Wǒ-méi-lián-jiàn-ta. 我 没 臉 見 他. I'm too embarrassed to see him.

LIÀN₂ 練 (TV) practice. Xué-shuō-huà dei-cháng-liàn. 學 説 話 得 常 練. To learn to speak one must practice often. Wǒ-tiāntian-liàn-zì. 我天天 練字. I practice writing everyday. Tā-liàn-gōng-fu-ne. 他 練 工 夫 呢. He is practing (a certain kind of art which takes time to be success-ful).

LIÀN₄ 煉 (TV) refine, purify (<u>by heating</u>). liàn-gāng 煉 鋼 smelt iron to make steel. liàn-yóu 煉油 refine oil.

LIÀN'ÀI₄ 戀愛 <u>or</u> LUÀN'ÀI 戀 愛 (N) a love affair. Bié-nào-liàn'ài. 別 鬧 戀愛. Don't get involved in love affairs. (TV) have a courtship. Tāmen-méi-liàn'ài jiu-jiéhūn-le. 他們 没 戀 愛 就 結 婚 了. They had no courtship, they just got married.

LIÁNBĀNG₅ 聯 邦 (N) federation of states.

LIÁNDĀO₅ 鐮 刀 (N) sickle.

LIÁNG₃ 量 (TV) measure. Yǒng-chǐ-liángliang. 用 尺 量 量.

L

Measure it with a ruler.

LIÁNG₂ 涼 (SV) cool, cold (of weather or objects). (opp. rè 熱). Tiānqi-liáng-le. 天 氣 涼 了 . The weather has turned cold. Chá-shi-liáng-de 茶 是 涼 的 . The tea is cold.(cf: LĚNG 冷).

LIǍNG₁ 兩 (NU) used before all M except liǎng 兩 (tael); not used before or after shí 十 . (1) two. liǎngge-rén 兩 個 人 two persons. liǎngqiān 兩 千 two thousand. Tā-duō-zhùle-liǎngtian. 他 多 住 了 兩 天 . He stayed two more days. (2) not stressed, a couple, several. zhèi-liangnián 這 兩 年 these several years. duō-zhù-liangtian 多 住 兩 天 stay a couple more days.

(AD) both sides, both parties. liǎng-bu-chīkuī 兩 不 吃 虧 neither side suffers any loss. Liǎng-biàn. 兩 便 . (lit. It's convenient for both parties). Do it separately.

LIǍNG₃ 兩 (M) (1) a unit of weight measure equivalent to approximately 105 grams, tael, one-sixteenth of a catty. èrliang-jīn-zi 二 兩 金 子 two taels of gold. (2) ounce.

LIÀNG₃ 量 (N) (1) quantity. liàng bu-gòu 量 不 够 (the quantity is) not enough. (2) capacity for tolerance or for taking food or drink. Zhèige-ren liàng-dà. 這 個 人 量 大 . This person can tolerate a lot. Tāde-fàn-liang hěn-dà. 他 的 飯 量 很 大 . He can eat a lot.

LIÀNG₃ 晾 (TV) expose something to the air to dry it or to let it cool off. Bǎ-yīshang dāzai-zhéngzishang liàngliang-jiu-gān-le. 把 衣 裳 搭 在 繩 子 上 晾 晾 就 乾 了. Hang the clothes out in the air so that they will dry. Nèi-wǎn-chá-tài-rè, liàng-yihuir jiu-liáng-le. 那 碗 茶 太 熱. 晾 一 會 兒 就 凉 了. That bowl of tea is too hot, let it sit for a while to cool it off.

LIÀNG₂ 亮 (SV) (1) bright, luminous. (opp.àn 暗 , hēi 黑). Wūzili-hěn-liàng. 屋 子 裏 很 亮 . The room is very bright. Tiān-liàng-le. 天 亮 了 . (lit. sky is bright) Dawn is breaking. (2) bright, shiny, highly polished. Zhuōzi-cāde-hen-liàng. 桌 子 擦 得 很 亮 . The table is polished to a high sheen.

LIÀNG₂ 輛 (M) for wheeled vehicles. yīliàng-zìxíngchē 一 輛 自 行 車 a bicycle.

LIÁNGKĚ₃ 兩 可 (IV) could be either of two... Chéng-bu-chéng hái-zai-liǎngkě. 成 不 成 還 在 兩 可 . Whether it will succeed or not, it could go either way.

LIǍNGKǑUZI₄ 兩 口 子 (N) a couple, generally meaning man and wife. Tāmen-liǎngkǒuzi dōu-zuò-shì. 他 們 兩 口 子 都 作 事 . Both he and his

L

wife work.

LIÁNGKUAI₂ 涼快 (opp. nuǎn-huo 暖和) (SV) comfortably cool (of weather, a room or place, or a garment). Zhèr-hěn-liángkuai. 這兒很涼快. It's very comfortably cool here. (IV) become cool (of temperature). Wǒ-chūqu-liángkuai-liangkuai. 我出去涼快涼快. I am going out to cool off.

LIÁNGSHI₄ 糧食 (N) grain, food from grains.

LIǍNGTÓUR₄ 兩頭兒 (PW) (1) both ends. Dàren-zuòzai-dāngjiànr, háizimen-zuòzai-liǎngtóur. 大人坐在當間兒, 孩子們坐在兩頭兒. The grown ups sit in the middle, the children sit at both ends. (2) both parties, both sides. Liǎngtóur dōu-bu-yuànyì. 兩頭兒都不願意. Both sides are unwilling.

LIÁNGXIN₂ 良心 (N) conscience. Píng-liángxin-shuō-huà. 憑良心說話. Speak according to your conscience. Bié-miè-liángxin. 別滅良心. Don't forget your conscience.

LIǍNGYÀNG₃ 兩樣 (SV) different. Tā-gen-biéren liǎngyàng. 他跟別人兩樣. He is different from other people.

LIÁNHÉ₃ 聯合 (TV) join or unite in a league or company. Dàjiā-liánhe-qilai. 大家聯合起來. Everybody join

together.

LIÁNHÉGUÓ₃ 聯合國 (N) The United Nations.

LIÁNLEI₄ 連累 (TV) be adversely affected because of certain connections. Bǎ-ta-lián-lei-shang-le. 把他連累上了. It got him into trouble. (N) adverse effect of certain connections. Tā-yě-shòule-liánlei-le. 他也受了連累了. He was also affected by the trouble.

LIÁNLUO₂ 聯絡 (TV) (1) make or maintain contact or liaison. Nǐ-kéyiyòng-diànhuà gēn-ta-liánluo. 你可以用電話跟他聯絡. You could maintain contact with him by telephone. (2) strengthen the bonds of friendship. liánluo-gǎn-qing 聯絡感情 strengthen the bonds of friendship. (N) contact. (cf: LIÁNXI 聯系).

'LIÁNMÁNG₄ 連忙 (AD) hurriedly.

LIǍNPÉN₄ 臉盆 (N) basin for washing the face.

LIÁNPENG₅ 蓮蓬 (N) lotus pod.

LIǍNPÍ₃ 臉皮 (N) (lit. face skin) ability to withstand embarrassment. liǎnpí-hòu 臉皮厚 thick-skinned. Tā-liǎnpí-báo. 他臉皮薄. He is easily embarrassed.

LIÁNQÌR₅ 連氣兒 (AD) continuously.

LIÁNXI₄ 聯系 (TV) contact someone. Wǒ-méi-gen-ta-liánxi.

L

我 没 跟 他 聯系. I didn't contact him.
(N) contact. (cf: LIÁNLUO 聯絡).

LIÀNXÍ₁ 練習 (TV) practice. Děi-duō-liànxi-lianxi. 得多練習練習. Must practice some more.
(N) exercise problems. Wǒ-zuò-le-liǎngdao-liànxí. 我作了兩道練習. I did two exercises.

LIÁNYÈ₄ 連夜 (AD) do something or work into the night. Wǒmen-liányè-kāi-chē, gǎnhuilai-le. 我們連夜開車,趕回來了. We drove far into the night and rushed back.

LIÁNZI₄ 簾子 (N) curtain.
LIÀNZI₅ 鏈子 (N) chain.

LIĂO₄ 撩 (TV) raise or lift up a part of something which is hanging. Bǎ-liánzi-liǎoqilai. 把簾子撩起來. Raise the curtains.

LIÁO₄ 聊 (TV) chat. Zánmen-děi-liáoliao. 咱們得聊聊. We have to chat.

LIĂO₃ 了 (TV) settle and conclude something. Zhèi-shìqing hái-méi-liǎo-ne. 這事情還没了哪. This matter has not been settled. Zhàng-yě-liǎo-le, wǒde-xīnshi yě-liǎo-le. 賬也了了,我的心事也了了. The debt is settled, and my worry is over.
(RE) used in potential RV only.
(1) indicates success. Méi-běn-shi zuòbuliǎo. 没本事作

不了. If one is not capable, he cannot do it. (2) indicates finishing up something. Cài-tài-duō chībuliǎo. 菜太多,吃不了. Too much food, we cannot finish.

LIĂO₄ 撂 (TV) put something down, lay something down, let drop. Bǎ-liánzi liàoxialai. 把簾子撂下來. Let down the curtain. Tā-bǎ-dōngxi dou-liàozai-dìxia-le. 他把東西都撂在地下了. He put everything down on the floor.

LIÀO₄ 料 (N) (1) fodder. Zhèi-shi-mǎ-chíde-liào. 這是馬吃的料. This is fodder for horses. (2) a kind of opaque colored glassware. Zhèige-píngzi shì-liàode. 這個瓶子是料的. This bottle is made of a kind of glass.
(B) material.

LIÀO₃ 料 (TV) anticipate, either by guess or logical deduction. Wǒ-méi-liàodao 'tā-lái-le. 我没料到他來了. I didn't think that he had come.

'LIĂOBUDÉ₁ 了不得 (RV) (1) extreme, very much. Tā-pàde 'liǎobudé. 他怕得了不得. He is very much afraid.
(2) or LIĂOBUQǏ 了不起 terrific (usually indicates great potential). Méi-shénma-liǎobu-dé-de. 没甚麼了不得的. There is nothing so terrific. Zhèige-ren 'liǎobudé. 這個人了不得. This person

is terrific. Aiyā! ¹liǎobudé-le. 哎呀！了不得了. My goodness, something terrific happened. (cf: BUDÉLIĂO 不得了).

LIĂOBUQĬ₂ 了不起 see ¹LIĂOBUDE 了不得 (RV) (2).

LIÁOCAO₃ 了草 (SV) rough (something done without caring to details). Zì-xiěde-hěn-liáocao. 字寫的很了草. The characters are not neatly written.

LIÁOJIE₂ 了解 (TV) understand. Tā-bu-liáojie-wo. 他不了解我. He doesn't understand me. Wǒ-tīngwán-zhèige-gùshi jiu-liáojie-le. 我聽完這個故事，我就了解了. After I heard this story I understood. Wǒ-hěn-liáojie-nǐde-kùnnan. 我很了解你的困難. I very much understand your difficulty. (N) understanding. Tāmen-bǐcǐ-de-liáojie hěn-shēn. 他們彼此的了解很深. Their mutual understanding is very deep.

LIÁONING₃ 遼寧 (PW) Liaoning province.

LIĂO-SHÌ₃ 了事 (VO) finish up something, settle something. Zhèiyàngr jiu-suàn-liǎole-shì-le-ma? 這樣兒就算了事了嗎 ? Do you consider this done?

LIÁO-TIĀNR₂ 聊天兒 (VO) chat. (syn. tán-tiānr 談天兒). Wǒmen-liǎole-bàntian-tiānr. 我

們聊了半天天兒. We chatted for a long time.

LÍBA₄ 籬笆 (N) fence. (M: dào 道).

LĬBÀI₁ 禮拜 (N) (1) religious service. zuò-lǐbài 作禮拜 attend or hold religious services. (2) or XĪNGQĪ 星期 week. yi-ge-duō-lǐbài 一個多禮拜 more than a week. (TW) or XĪNGQĪ 星期 Sunday. (cf: LĬBÀIRÌ 禮拜日 . LĬ-BÀITIĀN 禮拜天). (SP) see XĪNGQĪ 星期.

LĬBÀI'ÈR₁ 禮拜二 or XĪNG-QĪ'ÈR 星期二 (TW) Tuesday.

LĬBÀIJĬ₁ 禮拜幾 or XĪNGQĬJĬ 星期幾 (TW) which day of the week.

LĬBÀILIÙ₁ 禮拜六 or XĪNG-QĪLIÙ 星期六 (TW) Saturday.

LĬBÀIRÌ₁ 禮拜日 or XĪNGQĪ-RÌ 星期日 (TW) Sunday. (cf: LĬBÀI 禮拜 , LĬBÀITIĀN 禮拜天).

LĬBÀISĀN₁ 禮拜三 or XĪNG-QĪSĀN 星期三 (TW) Wednesday.

LĬBÀISÌ₁ 禮拜四 or XĪNGQĪ-SÌ 星期四 (TW) Thursday.

LĬBÀITIĀN₁ 禮拜天 or XĪNG-QĪTIĀN 星期天 (TW) Sunday. (cf: LĬBÀI 禮拜 , LĬBÀI-RÌ 禮拜日).

LĬBÀIWǓ₁ 禮拜五 or XĪNG-QĪWǓ 星期五 (TW) Friday.

LĬBÀIYĪ₁ 禮拜一 or XĪNGQĪ-YĪ 星期一 (TW) Monday.

L

LĬBIANR₁ 裏邊兒 or LĬTOU
裏頭 or LĬMIAN 裏面 (PW)
inside. Tāmen-dou-zài-lĭbianr-
ne. 他們都在裏邊兒
呢. They are all inside

LÍBIÉ₄ 離別 (TV) separate
from, leave a person or a place.
Tāmen-yào-líbié-le. 他們要
離別了. They are going
to leave each other.

LÌCHĂNG₃ 立場 (N) standpoint.
Nĭ-zhànzai-'shéide-lìchăng-shuō-
huà? 你站在誰的立
場說話? From whose
standpoint are you speaking?

LIÈ₃ 裂 (IV) crack. Mùtou-bănzi
liè-le. 木頭板子裂了.
The board is cracked.
(RE) crack. Dì-dōu-gānlièle. 地
都乾裂了. The earth
was so dry that it cracked.

LIÈ-FÈNGR₃ 裂縫兒 (VO)
develop a crack and separate.
Qiángshang lièle-yidao-fèngr.
牆上裂了一道縫
兒. The wall has cracked.
(N) a crack with space in between.
yídào-lièfèngr 一道裂縫
兒 a crack.(cf: LIÈWÉN 裂
紋).

LIÈSHÌ₃ 烈士 (N) martyr.

LIÈWÉN(R)₄ 裂紋兒 (N) a
line showing a crack. (M: dào
道). Píngzishang-yŏu-yidào-
lièwén. 瓶子上有一道
裂紋. The vase has a crack.
(cf: LIÈ-FÈNGR 裂縫兒).

LĬ-FÀ₂ 理髮 or LĬ-FÀ 理髮
(VO) get or give a haircut. Shéi-
gĕi-ta-lĭ-fà? 誰給他理

髮? Who cut his hair?

LĬ-FÀ₂ 理髮 see LĬ-FÀ 理髮.

LĬFAGUĂN₃ 理髮館 (N) bar-
bershop.

LÌHAI₁ 利害 (SV) (1) severe,
fierce. Tāde-tàitai gen-lăohŭ
yíyangde-lìhai. 他的太太
跟老虎一樣的利
害. His wife is as fierce as
a tiger. (2) terrific (either good
or bad). Tā-shāng-fēng shāng-
de-hĕn-lìhai. 他傷風傷
得很利害. He has a
terrific cold. Tā-zuòshì-de-
jīngshen hĕn-lìhai. 他作事
的精神很利害. His
working spirit is terrific. Yŭ-
xià-de hĕn-lìhai. 雨下'得
很利害. The rain came
down terrifically hard. (3)
strong (of liquor or tobacco).
Zhèizhong-yān tài-lìhai. 這種
煙太利害. This kind of
tobacco is too strong. (4) hard-
hearted. Zhèige-rén-de xīnyănr-
hĕn-lìhai. 這個人的心
眼兒很利害. This
person is very hard-hearted.
(5) stern. Tāde-yàngzi-hĕn-lìhai,
kĕshi-xīnli yidiănr-dōu bu-lìhai.
他的樣子很利害,
可是心裏一點兒
都不利害. His appear-
ance is very stern, but he is not
a bit hard-hearted inside. (cf:
XIONG 兇).

LĬHUÌ₅ 理會 (TV) (1) pay attention to. Bú-yong-lĭhui-ta, 不
用理會他. Don't pay
attention to him. (2) or LŬHUÌ

L

理會 notice something. Wŏ-méi-lĭhuì. 我没理會. I didn't notice.

LÍ-HŪN₂ 離婚 (VO) obtain a divorce, annul a marriage.

LĬJI₅ 痢疾 (N) dysentery.

'LĬJIĔ₄ 理解 (TV) reason and understand. Tā-méi-you-lĭjiede-néngli. 他没有理解的能力. He has no ability to reason. Tāde-bànfa wŏ-bu-néng·lĭjiĕ. 他的辦法我不能理解 I cannot understand his method.

LĬJIĔ₄ 禮節 (N) ceremonial rituals, etiquette, protocol. Zuò-wàijiāo-guān-de bìxū-dŏngde-wàijiāo-lĭjié. 作外交官的必須懂得外交的禮節. A diplomat must understand diplomtic protocol.

LÍKAI₁ 離開 (RV) leave, depart from, separate from. Nĭ-shi-shénma-shíhou lìkaide-Fàguó? 你是甚麼時候離開的法國? When did you leave France? Tā-lìbukāi-zidiăn. 他離不開字典. He cannot be separated from a dictionary.

LÌKÈ₁ 立刻 (AD) immediately. Wŏ-lìkè-jiu-qù. 我立刻就去. I will go immediately.

LÌLIANG₂ 力量 (N) (1) physical strength. Tāde-lìliang-tài-xiăo, bié-jiao-ta-bān-dōngxi. 他的力量太小, 別叫他搬東西. He doesn't have strength. Don't ask him to move things. (2) power, effort. Wŏ-

yídìng jìn-wode-lìliang bāng-máng. 我一定盡我的力量幫忙. I certainly will do everything within my power to help. zhèngfŭde-lìliang 政府的力量 govern-mental power. qìchēde-lìliang 汽車的力量 the power of the car. (cf: LÌQI 力氣).

LÌLÜ₄ 利率 (N) rate of interest.

'LÌLÙN₃ 理論 (N) principle, theory. Bié-kōng-tán-'lĭlùn, bă-shíjide-'qíngxing-shuōshuo. 別空談理論, 把實際的情形説説. Don't just talk about abstract princi-ples, relate the actual situation.

LÌLUO₄ 利落 (SV) (1) neat in doing something. Tā-zuò-shì hĕn-lìluo. 他作事很利落. He does things very quick-ly and neatly.

'LĬMÀO₃ 禮貌 (N) good man-ners, courtesy. Tā-tài-méi-'lĭmào-le. 他太没禮貌了. He is too discourteous. Dào-fēijīchăng-qu-jiē-ta, shì-wŏmende-'lĭmǎo. 到飛機場去接他是我們的禮貌. To go to the air-port to meet him is our courtesy.

LĬMIAN₂ 裏面 see LĬBIANR 裏邊兒.

LÍN₄ 拎 (TV) dial. carry some-thing with the hand. Tā-línzhe-yige-píbāo. 他拎着一個皮包. He is carrying a suit-case.

LÍN₅ 鱗 (N) scale (of fish).

LÍN₃ 臨 (TV) (1) near or next to.

L

Nèijiān-wūzi lín-jiē. 那間屋子臨街. That room is next to the street. Tā-lín'sǐ-yě-méi-míngbai. 他臨死也沒明白. Even when he was near to death, he didn't understand. (2) copy. Zhèizhāng-huàr shì-xiàndàide-ren-lín-de. 這張畫兒是現代的人臨的. This painting is a contemporary copy (of an old work).

LÍN₄ 淋 see LÚN 淋.

LÌN₄ 賃 (TV) rent, lease. lìn-yiliang-chē 賃一輛車 rent a car.

LÍNG₂ 靈 (SV) (1) keen, sharp (in thinking). (opp. bèn 笨).(2) agile, limber. (opp. bèn 笨). Tā-nǎozi hen-líng, dòngzuo yě-hěn-líng. 他腦子很靈, 動作也很靈. His mind is very sharp, also very agile. (3) (con. língyan 靈驗). efficacious, effective (of prayers or medicine). Nèige-miào-líng-jíle. 'Qiú-shénma yǒu-shénma. 那個廟靈極了, 求甚麼有甚麼. That temple is very efficacious, whatever one prays for one gets. Zhèige-yào yi-chī jiu-hǎo, zhēn-líng. 這個藥一吃就好,真靈. This medicine is very effective. Taking it will make one well immediately. (4) all right, O.K., satisfactory. Zhèiyangr-bàn, wǒ-kàn bulíng. 這樣辦,我看不靈. I think doing it this way wil not

be all right. (5) in good working order, sensitive (of a machine). Zhèige-lùyīnjī hěn-líng. 這個錄音機很靈. This tape recorder is very sensitive.

LÍNG₁ 零 (B-) a part, portion or fraction of something, as opposed to a unit of something. língtóur 零頭兒 remnants (textiles). Zhèizhong-zhǐ dōu-shi-yì'běn-yibende, méi-you-língde. 這種紙都是一本一本的,沒有零的. This kind of paper comes in tablets, there are no individual sheets.

(AD) in part, separately. Zhèi-zhong-bǐ-chéng-dá-mài, bu-líng-mài. 這種筆成打賣,不零賣. This kind of pen is sold by the dozen, not individually.

used between NU-M, and, plus. yìchǐ-líng-yidiar 一尺零一點兒 a foot plus something. yinián-líng-sānge-yuè 一年零三個月 a year and three months. yìqiān-líng-èrshí 一千零二十 one thousand and twenty.

(NU) zero (the number). língdù 零度 zero degrees. Er-jiǎn-èr dé-líng. 二減二得零. Two minus two equals zero.

used to read off the digit zero. yī-líng-líng-yī 一零零一 1001.

(N) zero. Kàode-'tài-huài, déle-ge-líng. 考得太壞,得了個零. I failed miserably in the examination; got a zero.

LǏNG₂ 領 (TV) (1) accept <u>or</u> collect <u>something that is issued or given.</u> Zhèibi-qián zai-'nǎr-lǐng? 這筆錢在那兒領? Where does one go to collect this sum of money? Nínde-hǎo-yì wǒ-xīn-lǐngle. 您的好意我心領了. I accept your good intentions gratefully. (2) lead, guide. lǐng-bīng dǎ-zhàng 領兵打仗 lead the soldiers to battle. (B) collar. lǐngzi 領子 collar.

LÌNG₂ 另 (AD) other. Wǒmen-dei-'lìng-xiǎng-bànfa. 我們得另想辦法. We have to think of some other way. (SP) another. Nà-shi-'lìng-yi-huí-shì. 那是另一回事. That's another matter. (cf: LÌNGWÀI 另外).

LÍNGBIAN₄ 靈便 (SV) dexterous (<u>applicable to physical characteristic's only</u>).Tāde-shǒu-jiǎo hěn-língbian. 他的手脚很靈便. He is very dexterous with his hands and feet.

LǏNGDÀI₂ 領帶 (N) necktie. (M: tyáo 條). dǎ-lǐngdài 打領帶 tie the necktie. Bǎ-lǐngdài jiěxialai. 把領帶解下來.Untie <u>or</u> remove the necktie.

LÍNGDANG₅ 鈴鐺 (N) small bell (<u>rung by shaking</u>). (cf: LÍNGR 鈴兒).

'LǏNGDǍO₃ 領導 (TV) guide, lead. Qǐng-nin-'lǐngdǎo. 請您領導. Please guide us.

(N) guidance, leadership. Tóng-shì dōu-kěn-jiēshòu-tāde-'lǐngdǎo. 同事都肯接受他的領導. His co-workers all accept his guidance.

LǏNGHǍI₅ 領海 (N) territorial waters.

LǏNGHUĀR₃ 領花兒 (N) bow-tie. (<u>syn</u>. lǐngjiér 領結兒).

LÍNGHÚN₄ 靈魂 (N) soul.

LÍNGHUO₄ 靈活 (SV) dexterous. Tāde-shǒuduan hen-línghuo. 他的手段很靈活. He handles matters with great dexterity. (AD) with dexterity. línghuo-'yùnyòng 靈活運用 use something with dexterity.

LÍNGJIÀNR₃ 零件兒 (N) part of a machine or mechanism.

LǏNGJIÀO₃ 領教 (<u>lit</u>. receive instruction) (TV) <u>used as a polite request for learning.</u> Wǒ-gēn-nín-'lǐngjiao-lǐngjiao. 我跟您領教領教. I want to ask you for advice.

LǏNGJIÉR₅ 領結兒 (N) bow-tie. (<u>syn</u>. lǐnghuār 領花兒).

LǏNGJĪN₄ 領巾 (N) neck scarf, muffler. (M: tiáo 條).

LǏNGKŌNG₄ 領空 (N) air space <u>above a nation's territory.</u>

LÍNGLI₃ 伶俐 (SV) sprightly. yòu-cōngming yòu-língli 又聰明又伶俐 intelligent and sprightly.

LÍNGMÀI₃ 零賣 (1) sell retail. Tāmen-zhǐ-pīfā, bu-língmài. 他們只批發,不零賣. They do only wholesale, they do

L

not sell retail. (2) sell something in a less than predetermined quantity or part of a unit.
Nǐ-děi-mǎi-yídá, wǒmen-bu-
língmài. 你 得 買 一 打
我 們 不 零 賣. You
must buy a dozen, we won't sell
in lesser quantities.

LÍNGQIÁN₂ 零 錢 (N) small
change (money). Wǒ-yào-huàn-
dianr-língqián. 我 要 換 點
零 錢. I want to exchange
this for some small change.

LÍNGR₃ 鈴 兒 (N) small bell.
diàn-língr 電 鈴 兒 electric
bell. mén-língr 門 鈴 兒 door
bell. èn-língr 摁 鈴 兒 press
the bell. Língr-xiǎng-le. 鈴 兒
響 了. The bell is ringing.
(cf: LÍNGDANG 鈴 鐺).

LÍNGSUÌ₂ 零 碎 (SV) sundry,
miscellaneous. Wǒ-qu-mǎi-
diǎnr-língsui-dōngxi. 我 去
買 點 兒 零 碎 東 西.
I am going to buy some sundries.
Wǒ-hái-you-dianr-língsui-shì-
qing méi-bànwán. 我 還 有
點 兒 零 碎 事 情 沒
辦 完. I still have some miscellaneous items to take care of.

LÍNGTÓUR₄ 零 頭 兒 (N) rem-
nant (textile).

LÍNGTǓ₃ 領 土 (N) territory (of
a nation).

LÍNGWÀI₂ 另 外 (MA) besides,
in addition to. Wǒ-lìngwài gěile-
ta-wǔkuai-qián. 我 另 外 給
了 他 五 塊 錢. I gave
him five dollars besides.
(SP) other. Bùshi-'tā-shuō-de.

Shi-lìngwài-yíge-péngyou-shuō-
de. 不 是 他 說 的,是 另
外 一 個 朋 友 說 的.
It was not he who said it, it was
another friend who said it.

LÍNGXIÙ₃ 領 袖 (N) leader of
men. (M: wèi 位).

LÍNGYAN₄ 靈 驗 (SV) effica-
cious, effective (of prayers or
medicine).

LÍNGYÒNG₃ 零 用 (TV) use
money for miscellaneous items.
Zhèi-wǔkuai-qián nǐ-náqu-líng-
yòng-ba. 這 五 塊 錢 你
拿 去 另 用 吧. Here is
five dollars, take it for pocket
money.

LÍNGZI₄ 領 子 (N) collar.

LÍNJU₂ 隣 居 (N) neighbor.

LÌNSE₄ 吝 嗇 (SV) stingy, miserly.

LÍNSHÍ₂ 臨 時 (TW) at the time
something is needed, at the
time something is expected to
happen. Zhèige-gēr shì-shàng-
tái-yǐqián línshí-xué-de. 這 個
歌 兒 是 上 台 以 前
臨 時 學 的. This song
was learned (at the time) just
before going on stage. Wǒmen-
jiùshi-línshí-bāngbang-máng. 我
們 就 是 臨 時 幫 幫
忙. We just help (at the time)
when we are needed. Zǎo-yidianr-yùbei bié-děngdao-línshí-
zai-zuò. 早 一 點 兒 預
備 別 等 到 臨 時 再
作. Prepare a little earlier,
don't wait until the moment it's
needed to do it.

LÌQI$_2$ 力 氣 (N) physical strength or power. Tā-lìqi-buxiǎo. 他 力 氣 不 小 . He has great strength. Zuò-zhèijian-shì fèile-bu-shǎo-lìqi. 作 這 件 事 費 了 不 少 力 氣 . This matter took a great deal of strength. (cf: LÌLIANG 力 量).

LÌQIAN$_3$ 利 錢 (N) interest (payment for use of money). (syn. lìxi 利 息).

LÌRÚ$_4$ 例 如 used to introduce examples, as an example, for example. Shù-yèzi bu-quán-shi-lüde, lìrú, yǒude-fēngshū yèzi-shi-hóngde. 樹 葉 子 不 全 是 綠 的, 例 如, 有 的 楓 樹 葉 子 是 紅 的. Not all tree leaves are green. For example, the leaves of some maple trees are red.

LÌSHI$_4$ 理 事 (N) member of the board of directors. (M: wèi 位). Xuǎn-'shéi-dāng-lǐshi? 選 誰 當 理 事 ? Whom shall we elect to the board of directors?

LÌSHĬ$_1$ 歷 史 (N) (1) history. (2) history (as a course of study). (M: mén 門).

LÌTÁNG$_2$ 禮 堂 (N) ceremonial hall, auditorium.

LĬTOU$_1$ 裏 頭 see LĬBIANR 裏 邊 兒.

LIŪ$_3$ 溜 (TV) (1) slide. wàng-xià-liū 往 下 溜 slip downward. (2) Peip. slip away, sneak away. Tā-liū-le. 他 溜 了 . He sneaked away.

LIÚ$_2$ 留 (TV) (1) save or keep something for later use. Gěi-ta-liú-dianr-cài. 給 他 留 點 兒 菜 . Save some food for him. Bǎ-qián-liúqilai, yǐhòu-yòng. 把 錢 留 起 來, 以 後 用 . Save the money for use later on. Liúzhe-zhèige yǒu-shénma-yòng? 留 着 這 個 有 甚 麼 用 ? What's the use of keeping this? Tā-liú-húzi-le. 他 留 鬍 子 了 . He grew a beard or mustache. (2) keep or cause someone or something to remain at a certain place. Wǒ-liú-ta-zài-wo-jiā-chī-fàn. 我 留 他 在 我 家 吃 飯. I asked him to remain at my house to eat a meal. Sānkuai-qián, géi-ni-liǎngkuai wǒ-liú-yíkuai. 三 塊 錢 給 你 兩 塊, 我 留 一 塊 . Here are three dollars, I give you two and I keep one. (3) leave something or someone behind. Wǒ-liúle-huà-le. Jiào-ta-yi-huílai jiu-géi-wo-dǎ-diànhuà. 我 留 了 話 了, 叫 他 一 回 來 就 給 我 打 電 話 . I left word for him to telephone me as soon as he gets back. Tā-sǐ-le, liú-xia-sānge-háizi. 他 死 了, 留 下 三 個 孩 子 . He died, leaving three children. Tā-fùqin-sǐ-le, liúgei-ta-yi-suǒ-fángzi. 他 父 親 死 了, 留 給 他 一 所 房 子 . His father died and left him a house. Nǐ-qǐng-ta-liú-ge-dìzhǐ. 你 請 他 留 個 地 址 Ask him to please leave his

L

address. Tā-bǎ-háizi liúzai-jiāli-le. 他把孩子留在家裏了. He left the children at home. (4) remain or stay at a place. Wǒ-bu-néng-lǎo-liúzai-zhèr. 我不能老留在這兒. I can't stay here all the time. (5) reside in a foreign country to study. Tā-shì-liú-'Měi-de-xuésheng. 他是留美的學生. He is a foreign student studying in America.

LIÚ₂ 流 (IV) flow. Shuǐ liúde-hěn-kuài. 水流得很快. The water is flowing very fast. Liú-xiě-le. 流血了. It's bleeding.

LIÙ₁ 六 (NU) six, sixth.

LIÙ₄ 溜 (TV) (1) walk an animal. liù-mǎ 溜馬 walk a horse. (2) go for a walk. Tā-zài-jiē-shang-liùle-liu. 他在街上溜了溜. He took a walk on the street. (M) line, column, row. yīliù-mǎyǐ 一溜螞蟻 a line of ants. (N) current (of a stream). hé-liù 河流 river current.

LIŪ-BĪNG₄ 溜冰 (VO) skate on ice. (syn. huá-bīng 滑冰).

LIŪDA₅ 溜達 (IV) Peip. take a stroll. Wǒmen-chūqu-'liūda-liūda. 我們出去溜達溜達. We'll go out to take a walk.

LIÚDÒNG₅ 流動 (IV) flow.

LIÚHUÁNG₅ 硫磺 (N) sulphur.

LIÚ-JÍ₃ 留級 (VO) remain in the same grade in school without advancement.

LIÚLÌ₃ 流利 (SV) fluent. Zhōngguo-huà ta-néng-shuō, kěshi bu-liúli. 中國話他能說, 可是不流利. He can speak Chinese, but not fluently.

LIÚMÁNG₃ 流氓 (N) hoodlums. Nà-shi-yibāng-liúmáng. 那是一幫流氓. That is a gang of hoodlums.

LIÚ-SHÉN₁ 留神 (VO) be careful. Nǐ-liú-dianr-shén. 你留點兒神. Be a little careful. Wǒmen-děi-liú-tade-shén. 我們得留他的神. We have to be careful with him. (TV) be aware of. Nǐ-liú-shén-zhèige-rén. 你留神這個人. Be aware of this person.

LIÚSHĒNGJĪ₃ 留聲機 (N) phonograph. (M: jià 架). kāi-liúshēngjī 開留聲機 turn on the phonograph.

LIÚSHĒNGPIĀNR₄ 留聲片兒 (N) phonograph record.

LIǓSHÙ₄ 柳樹 (N) willow tree.

LIÙXIÁNQÍN₄ 六弦琴 (N) guitar. tán-liùxiánqín 彈六弦琴 play the guitar.

LIÚXÍNG₃ 流行 (SV) prevalent, popular. Zhèizhǒng-tóufade-yàngzi hěn-liúxíng. 這種頭髮的樣子很流行. This kind of hairdo is very popular. (TV) become prevalent, widespread. Xiànzai-liúxíng-zhèi-zhǒng-yīnyue. 現在流行這種音樂

這種音樂. This kind of music is prevalent now.

LIÚ-XUÉ₂ 留學 (VO) study abroad. Tāde-háizi zài-Fàguo-liú-xué. 他的孩子在法國留學. His children are studying (abroad) in France.

LIÚZI₅ 瘤子 (N) tumor, cyst. zhǎng-liúzi 長瘤子 have a tumor.

LÌWÀI₃ 例外 (N) exception. méi-yǒu-lìwài 沒有例外 no exception. Nèijian-shì lìwài. 那件事例外 That affair is an exception.

LĬWU₂ 禮物 (N) present, gift. (M: fènr 份兒, jiàn 件). Tā-sòngle-yifènr-hěn-zhòngde-lǐwu. 他送了一份兒很重的禮物. He gave a very valuable present.

LÌXI₂ 利息 (N) interest (payment for use of money). Lìxi-hěn-gāo. 利息很高. The interest is very high.(cf: LÌQIAN 利錢).

'LĬXIĂNG₂ 理想 (N) ideal. Zhèiyangr-bàn zuì-hé-'lǐxiǎng. 這樣兒辦最合理想. To do it this way is closest to the ideal. Zhè-shi-tāde-'lǐxiǎng, bú-shi-shìshí. 這是他的理想不是事實. This is his ideal, not the fact.
(SV) idealistic. fēichang-'lǐxiǎng 非常理想 very idealistic.

LÌYI₃ 利益 (N) benefit. Zhèi-yàngr-bàn dàjiā-dōu-yǒu-lìyi.

這樣兒辦大家都有利益. There is benefit for everyone if it's done this way.

LÌYONG₃ 利用 (TV) utilize, take advantage of something or someone for one's benefit. Tā-ràng-ren-lìyong-le. 他讓人利用了. He was taken advantage of by people. Wǒ-lìyong-zuò-huǒchē-de-shíjian kàn-bào. 我利用坐火車的時間看報. I use my time on the train to read the newspaper.

LĬYÓU₂ 理由 (N) reason for certain behavior or for doing something. Méi-you-lǐyóu-'zhèi-yàngr-zuò. 沒有理由這樣兒作. There is no reason to do it this way. Tāde-lǐyóu bu-'chōngzú. 他的理由不充足. He doesn't have sufficient reasons.

LĬYÚ₅ 鯉魚 (N) carp (fish).(M: liáo 條).

LÌZHÈNG₅ 立正 (1) stand at attention.(2) attention (military command).

LÌZHĪ₄ 荔枝 (N) lichee (a kind of fruit).

LĬZI₄ 李子 (N) plum, prune. (M: kē 棵).

LÌZI₅ 栗子 (N) chestnut.

LÌZI₂ 例子 (N) example. Nǐ-gěi-wǒ-jǔ-yíge-lìzi. 你給我舉一個例子. Give me an example. Wǒ-zhèige-ren-tèbié bié-ná-wǒ-dāng-lìzi. 我這個人特別別拿

L

我當例子. I'm a pecul-
iar person. Don't take me as an
exaple. (cf: JǓ-LÌ(ZI) 舉例
(子)).

LÓNG₃ 龍 (N) dragon. (M: tiáo
條).

LÓNG₃ 聾 (SV) deaf. Tā ěrduo-
lóng-le. 他耳朵聾了. He
is deaf.

LǑNG₄ 攏 (TV) get close to. lǒng-
àn 攏岸 get close to the shore.
(RE) get close to. Tāmen-tán-
bulǒng. 他們談不攏.
They talk but never get close to
each other.

LÓNGTÌ₅ 籠屉 (N) steamer
(with multilayered tiers made
of bamboo for Chinese cooking).

LÓNGTONG₃ 籠統 (SV) be over-
generalized. Tā-shuō-de tài-
lóngtong. 他說的太籠
統. His statement is too
general.

LÓNGTÓU₅ 龍頭 (N) faucet,
nozzle of a water hose.

LÓNGXIĀ₃ 龍蝦(N) lobster.
(M: zhǐ 隻).

LÓNGZI₃ 聾子 (N) a deaf person.

LǑNGZǑNG₄ 籠總 (AD) alto-
gether. Lǒngzǒng-budào-shí-
kuai-qián. 攏總不到十
塊錢. Altogether not quite
ten dollars.

LÓU₁ 樓 (N) a multi-storied
building. (M: zuò 座 , céng 層).
wǔlóu 五樓 fifth floor. wǔ-
céng-lóu 五層樓 fifth floor
or five stories. Zhèizuo-lóu
shì-tāde, kěshi-tā-jiu-yòng-yì-

céng. 這座樓是他的,
可是他就用一層.
This building is his, but he
uses only one floor.

LǑU₄ 摟 (TV) embrace, hold in
one's arms. Tā-lǒuzhe-háizi-
shuì. 他摟着孩子睡.
He sleeps with an arm around
the child.
(M) an armload. yìlǒu-cháihuo
摟柴火 an armload of fire-
wood.

LÒU₃ 漏 (IV) leak. Fángzi-lòu-
le. 房子漏了. The house
is leaking. Yóuxiāng-lòu-yóu.
油箱漏油. The gasoline
is leaking from the tank. Zhèi-
ge-xiāoxi shi-zěnma-lòuchuqu-
de? 這個消息是怎
麼漏出去的? How did
this news leak out?
(RE) leak. Tā-bǎ-huà-shuōlòu-
le. 他把話說漏了.
He leaked it out by talking.

LÒU₃ 露 (IV) expose, reveal,
show. Tā-chuānzhe-duǎn-kùzi,
lòuzhe-tuǐ. 他穿着短褲
子,露着腿. He is wear-
ing shorts, exposing his legs.
Tā-méi-zhíjiē-shuō, kěshi-lòule-
yidiǎnr-yìsi. 他沒直接
說,可是露了一點
兒意思. He didn't say it
directly, but revealed some
idea like that. Tā-bu-xiǎng-gào-
song-wo, kěshi-shuōzhe-shuōzhe-
jiu-lòu-le. 他不想告訴
我,可是說着說着
就露了. He didn't plan to

tell me, but by talking he revealed it. Tā-lǎo-xiǎng-'lòu-yi-shǒur. 他 老 想 露 一 手 兒. He always wants to show off.

LÒULIĂN₃ 露 臉 (SV) become known by doing something. Nèi-cì-jiǎngyǎn tā-hen-lòuliǎn. 那 次 講 演 他 很 露 臉. He made himself known when he made that speech.

LÒU-MIÀNR₄ 露 面 兒 (VO) show up. Jīntian tā-yìtiān-méi-lòu-miànr. 今 天 他 一 天 沒 露 面 兒. He didn't show up for a whole day.

LǑUR₄ 簍 兒 see LǑUZI 簍 子.

LÓUTĪ₃ 樓 梯 (N) stairs, staircase, stairway. shàng-lóutī 上 樓 梯 go up by the stairway.

LÓUZI₅ 樓 子 (N) Peip. trouble. chū-lóuzi 出 樓 子 have trouble.

LǑUZI₄ 簍 子 or LǑUR 簍 兒 (N) woven wicker container.

LǙ₃ 驢 (N) donkey. (M: lóu 頭).

LǓ₄ 滷 (TV) cook certain foods in soy sauce and other condiments. lǔ-jīdàn 滷 鷄 蛋 cook eggs in soy sauce, eggs cooked in soy sauce. (N) gravy.

LǙ₄ 旅 (M) brigade. lǚzhǎng 旅 長 brigade commander.

LǓ₄ 理 (TV) (1) straighten out something long and thin by a tugging or pulling action. Yòng-shǒu-lǔ-yiyǔ-húzi. 用 手 理 一 理 鬍 子. Straighten out the beard with the hand.(2)

arrange something in order. Lǔ-lǔ-nǐde-shū. 理 理 你 的 書. Put your books in order.

LǙ₄ 鋁 (N) aluminum.

LÙ₁ 路 (N) (1) road. (M: tiáo 條). yìtiáo-dà-lù 一 條 大 路 a big road. zǒu-lù 走 路 walk (on the road). (2) journey, way. Lù-hěn-yuǎn. 路 很 遠. It's a long way. Wǒ-shízai méi-lù-kězǒu-le. 我 實 在 沒 路 可 走 了. I'm really at a dead-end.

(TV) used before dōng 東 , nán 南 , xī 西 , běi 北 , located on the... side of the street. Tāde-jiā lù-běi. 他 的 家 路 北. His house is on the north side of the street.

(M) kind, type, variety. Zhèilu huò bu-hǎo-mài. 這 路 貨 不 好 賣. This kind of goods is not easy to sell. Tā-men-gēn-wo bu-shi-yìlù-rén. 他 們 跟 我 不 是 一 路 人. They and I are different kinds of people. Zhǐ yǒu-hǎoji-lù. 紙 有 好 幾 路. There are several kinds of paper.

LÙ₃ 鹿 (N) deer. (M: zhī 隻).

LǙ₂ 綠 (SV) green. Yèzi-zhēn-lù, 葉 子 真 綠. The leaves are really green.

LUÀN₁ 亂 (SV) (1) disorderly. Tā-zhuōzi-shang-de-dōngxi tài-luàn. 他 桌 子 上 的 東 西 太 亂. The things on top of his deak are extremely disorderly. Guójia-luàn-le. 國

L

家 亂 了 . The country is in a state of disorder. (2) be confused, mixed up. Wǒ-xīnli hen-huàn. 我 心 裏 很 亂 . My mind is very mixed up. (3) confusing. Tāde-huà-hěn-luàn. 他 的 話 很 亂 . What he said is very confusing. (AD) confusedly. Bié-luàn-shuō. 別 亂 說 . Don't talk nonsense.

LUÀN'ÀI₄ 戀 愛 see LIÀN'ÀI 戀 愛 .

LUANZI₄ 亂 子 (N) accident, trouble. Chūle-luànzi-le. 出 了 亂 子 了 . An accident happened.

LÙDĒNG₅ 路 燈 (N) street lights.

LÙDÌ₃ 陸 地 (N) land (vs. sea).

LǛDOU₅ 綠 豆 (N) a kind of green lentil.

LǛFEI₃ 旅 費 (N) traveling expenses.

LÙFÈI₃ 路 費 (N) traveling expenses.

LǛGUĂN₁ 旅 館 (N) hotel.

LǛHUÌ₃ 理 會 or LǏHUÌ 理 會 (TV) notice something. Tā-láile-ma? Wǒ-méi-lǐhuì. 他 來 了 嗎 ? 我 沒 理 會 . Did he come? I didn't notice.

LÙJŪN₂ 陸 軍 (N) army.

LŪN₄ 掄 (TV) swing something in an arc or a circle. lūnyuán-le 掄 圓 了 swing in a circle.

LÚN₄ 輪 (TV) be someone's turn to do something. Jīntian lúndao-nǐ-zuò-zhǔxí-le. 今 天 輪 到 你 作 主 席 了 . Today it's your turn to be chairman. Zhèimén-kè wǒmen-liǎng-ge-rén lúnzhe-jiāo. 這 門 課 我 們 兩 個 人 輪 着 教 . We take turns in teaching this course. (B) wheel.

LÚN₄ 淋 or LÍN 淋 (IV) hit by water in the form of a spray, such as rain, shower, etc. lún-le-yishēn-shuǐ 淋 了 一 身 水 water was spranyed all over (the body). Tā-ràng-yǔ-lúnshī-le. 他 讓 雨 淋 濕 了 . He got wet from the rain.

LÙN₄ 論 (TV) according to a certain measure, system or principle. Mǐ lùn-'jīn-mài, bú-lùn-bàng. 米 論 斤 賣 . 不 論 磅 . Rice is sold by the catty, not by the pound. Lùn-yuè gěi-gōngqian. 論 月 給 工 錢 . Wages are paid by the month. Lùn-xìngqing, lùn-qùwei, tā-men-liangge-rén méi-you-jié-hūnde-kěnéng. 論 性 情 , 論 趣 味 , 他 們 兩 個 人 沒 有 結 婚 的 可 能 . Judging by these two people's personalities and interest, there is no possibility that they would get married. (See: BÚLÙN 不 論).

LÚNCHUÁN₃ 輪 船 (N) (lit. wheel boat, from old paddle wheel boats) steamship.

LÚNDUN₁ 倫 敦 (PW) London.

LÚNLIÚ₃ 輪 流 (IV) take turns.

L

Wǒmen-lúnliú, hǎo-bu-hao? 我
們 輪 流, 好 不 好 ？
Let's take turns, how about it?
(AD) in turn. Tāmen-lúnliú-qu-
chī-fàn. 他 們 輪 流 去
吃 飯 . They take turns to go
to eat.

LÚNTĀI₃ 輪 胎 (N) tire (of a
wheel).

LÙNWÉN₂ 論 文 (N) written
discourse, thesis, critique,
editorial. (M: piān 篇).

LÚNZI₅ 輪 子 (N) wheel.

LUÓ₄ 鑼 (N) gong. dǎ-luó 打 鑼
beat the gong.

LUÓ₅ 籮 (N) sieve.

LUÒ₄ 摞 (TV) put one on top of
another. Bǎ-zhuān yíkuài-yí-
kuài-de-luòqilai. 把 磚 一
塊 一 塊 的 摞 起 來.
Pile the bricks one on top of the
other.
(M) pile. yí-dà-luò 一 大 摞
a big pile.

LUÒ₃ 落 see LÀO 落 .

LUÓBO₄ 蘿 蔔 (N) root vege-
table of the turnip family. hóng-
luóbo 紅 蘿 蔔 radish. bái-
luóbo 白 蘿 蔔 white turnip.

LUÒHÒU₃ 落 後 (SV) not up to
a certain level, backward, behind. Tāde-sīxiang hěn-luòhòu.
他 的 思 想 很 落 後 .
His thought is very backward.
(IV) lit. or fig. fall behind,
leave behind. Yàoshi-wǒmen-
bu-nǔlì jiu-yao-luòhòu-le. 要
是 我 們 不 努 力 就
要 落 後 了 . If we don't
work hard, we will fall behind.

Shéi-yě-bù-gānxin-luòhòu. 誰
也 不 甘 心 落 後 . No-
body is willing to be left behind.

LUÒHUASHENG₃ 落 花 生 see
HUĀSHENG 花 生 .

LUÓJI₃ 邏 輯 (N) logic. Tāde-
huà bù-hé-luóji. 他 的 話 不
合 邏 輯 . What he said is
illogical.
(SV) logical.

LUÓMǍ₂ 羅 馬 (PW) Rome.

LUÓMǍZI₄ 羅 馬 字 (N) (1)
Roman letters. (2) Romanization
of Chinese characters.

LUÒSHĀNJĪ₂ 落 杉 機 (PW)
Los Angeles.

LUÓSI₃ 螺 絲 (N) (1) animals
with a spiral shell, such as
snails, etc. (2) (con. luósi-
dīngr 螺 絲 釘 兒).screw.
shàng-luósi 上 螺 絲 put in
a screw. qǐ-luósi 起 螺 絲
take out a screw.

LUÓSIDĪNGR₃ 螺 絲 釘 兒
(N) screw, screw bolt.

LUÓSIMǓR₄ 螺 絲 母 兒 (N)
nut (for a screw bolt).

LUÒSUO₄ 囉 唆 (SV) garrulous,
verbose. Tā-shuō-huà hěn-luō-
suo. 他 說 話 很 囉 唆
He is garrulous.
(IV) repeatedly ask for something that has been refused.
Gàosong-ni bu-xǔ-mǎi-táng, nǐ-
zěnma-hái-gen-wo-luōsuo? 告
訴 你 不 許 買 糖, 你
怎 麼 還 跟 我 囉 唆?
I told you we're not going to buy
candy, why do you have to ask
over and over again?

L

LUÒTUO₄ 駱駝 (N) camel. (M: zhī 隻).

LUÒ-WǓ₃ 落伍 (VO) (lit. drop rank) lack of progress, backwards, behind the times. Tā-de-sīxiang luò-wǔ-le. 他的思想落伍了. His thinking is behind the times.

LUÒYÁNG₃ 洛陽 (PW) Lo-yang.

LUÓZI₄ 騾子 (N) mule. (M: zhi 隻).

LÜSHĪ₃ 律師 (N) lawyer.

LÚWĚI₅ 蘆葦 (N) reed.

LÙXIÀN₄ 路線 (N) lit. or' fig. route to reach a certain place.

LǙXÍNG₂ 旅行 (IV) travel. Tā-qu-lǚxíng-qu-le. 他去旅行去了 . He is going travelling.

(N) trip.

LǙXÍNGSHÈ₃ 旅行社 (N) travel agent.

LÙXÙ₃ 陸續 (AD) one after another, in succession. Lùxù-lái-jiàn-ta-de-ren, yìtiān-bu-duàn. 陸續來見他的人, 一天不斷. People come to see him one after the other all day without stopping.

LÙ-YĪN₃ 錄音 (VO) record (sound). Wǒ-qu-lù-yīn-qu. 我去錄音去 . I am going to do some recording.

LÙYĪNJĪ₃ 錄音機 (N) recorder (sound).

LÚZI₃ 爐子 (N) stove, cooking range, heater.

L

M

MA₁ 嗎 (P) (1) <u>used at the end of</u> <u>a sentence on a higher pitch</u> <u>than the beginning of the sen-</u> <u>tence, indicates that the sen-</u> <u>tence is a question.</u> Zhèige-shì-nǐde-ma? 這 個 是 你 的 嗎 ? Is this yours? Nǐ-yào-shuō-shenma-ma? 你 要 說 甚 麼 嗎 ? Do you want to say something? Tā-shì-Yīngguo-rén-ma? 他 是 英 國 人, 嗎 ? Is he English? (2) <u>used at</u> <u>the end of a phrase on a lower</u> <u>pitch than the beginning of the</u> <u>sentence, indicates that what</u> <u>precedes it is an obvious reason</u> <u>for what follows.</u> Zhèige-shì-wǒde-ma, dāngrán-wǒ kéyi-ná-zǒu. 這 個 是 我 的 嗎, 我 當 然 可 以 拿 走. This is mine, of course I can take it away. Tā-shì-Yīngguo-rén-ma, suóyi-Yīngwén-hěn-hǎo. 他 是 英 國 人 嗎, 所 以 英 文 很 好. He is an Englishman, therefore his English is very good. (3) <u>or</u> ME 麼 <u>used to mark a pause</u> <u>after a suppositional phrase or</u> <u>noun.</u> Chī-ma, yě-xíng; bu-chī-ma, yě-xíng. 吃 嗎, 也 行, 不 吃 嗎 也 行. If we eat, O.K., if we don't, that's O.K. too. Wǒ-ma, háishi-bú-qù-hǎo. 我 嗎, 還 是 不 去 好. As for me, I still think I'd better not go. (See: A 啊, BA 吧 <u>and</u> NE 呢).

MA₁ 媽 (N) (1) mamma. hòumā 後 媽 stepmother. Wǒde-mā-ya! 我 的 媽 呀 ! (<u>lit</u>. Oh, my mamma!) Oh, my God! (2) <u>used</u> <u>as a title for a married woman</u> <u>servant;</u> mā 媽 <u>follows the sur-</u> <u>name in direct address.</u> Zhàomā 趙 媽 nanny Chao.

MÁ₄ 麻 (N) hemp. (SV) numb. Wǒ-shuìde bózi-dōu-má-le. 我 睡 的 脖 子 都 麻 了. I slept so long that my neck became numb. Wǒ-shǒu-má-le. 我 手 麻 了. My hand became numb.

MĂ₁ 馬 (N) horse. (M: pǐ 匹 ,pǐ 匹). mǎ'ānzi 馬 鞍 子 sad-dle for a horse. mǎpiào 馬 票 a bet on a horse. sài-mǎ 賽 馬 run in a horserace <u>or</u> horserace.

MĂ₃ 碼 (M) yard (<u>unit of measure-</u> <u>ment</u>). Sānyīngchǐ-shi-yimǎ. 三 英 尺 是 一 碼. Three feet equal one yard.

MÀ₂ 罵 (TV) (1) cuss out, call <u>someone</u> names. mà-ta-yìdùn 罵 他 一 頓 cuss him out, give him a good scolding. āi-yi-dùn-mà 挨 一 頓 罵 get a cussing out <u>or</u> a scolding. Tā-mà-ni-shì-yíge-fēngzi. 他 罵 你 是 一 個 瘋 子. He

M

cussed you out, calling you a nitwit. (2) criticize, tear apart. Nèiben-shū rénren-mà. 那本書人人罵. Everybody tore that book apart.

MǍCHǍNG₃ 馬場 (N) horserace course.

MǍCHĒ₄ 馬車 (N) carriage, horse-drawn cart. (M: liàng 輛).

MǍDÁ₃ 馬達 (N) motor.

MÁDÀI₅ 麻袋 (N) burlap bag. (M: tiáo 條).

MÁFAN₁ 麻煩 (SV) troublesome, annoying. (opp. shēngshì 省事). Zhèige-fázi hěn-máfan. 這個法子很麻煩. This procedure is very troublesome. (TV) bother, cause trouble for, disturb. Nǐ-bié-máfan-rén. 你別麻煩人. Don't bother people (with your petty troubles). (N) trouble. Nèige-háizi lǎo-gěi-ta-mǔqin-zhǎo-máfan. 那個孩子老給他母親找麻煩. That child always makes trouble for his mother. Wǒ-gěi-nín-tiānle-hěn-duō-máfan. 我給你添了很多麻煩. I have put you to a lot of trouble.

MǍHU₁ 馬虎 see MǍHU 馬虎.

MǍHU₁ 馬虎 or MǍHU 馬虎 (SV) (1) careless (not taking care of things in detail). Tā-hěn-mǎhu. 他很馬虎. He's very careless. Zuò-shì bu-néng-mǎhu. 作事不能馬虎. You cannot be careless

when you are doing something. (2) unclear, vague. Shuōqingchu-le, bié-mǎhu. 說清楚了, 別馬虎. Speak clearly, don't be vague.

MÁI₃ 埋 (TV) bury. Dírén-máile-hěn-duō-dìléi. 敵人埋了很多地雷. The enemy planted a lot of land mines. Wǒ-men-bǎ-ta-mái-le. 我們把他埋了. We buried him.

MǍI₁ 買 (TV) (1) buy, purchase. Tā-mǎi-cài-qu-le. 他買菜去了. He went to buy some groceries. Nèiběn-shū xiànzài-mǎibuzháo. 那本書現在買不着. You can't buy that book now. Sānkuai-qián mǎi-liǎngge. 三塊錢買兩個. Three dollars will buy two. (2) buy off someone. Tā-bǎ-jiānyù-li-de-rén dōu-mǎitōng le. 他把監獄裏的人都買通了. He bought off all the personnel of that prison.

MÀI₁ 賣 (TV) (1) sell. Tā-màigei-wǒ-yìzhí-bǐ. 他賣給我一枝筆. He sold me a pen. Zhèizhāng-huàr mài-duōshao-qián? 這張畫兒賣多少錢? What does this picture sell for? Nǐde-huò kéyi-mài-hěn-hǎo-de-jiàqian. 你的貨可以賣很好的價錢. You can sell your merchandise for a good price. (2) sell out, betray. Tā-bǎ-péng-you dōu-mài-le. 他把朋友都賣了. He betrayed all of his friends.

MÀI-BÙ₃ 邁步 (VO) take a
step, walk ahead. Tā-xiàng-
qián-màile-sānbù. 他 向 前
邁 了 三 步. He took
three steps forward.

MÀICHUQU₁ 賣 出 去 (RV)
sell something. Tāde-qìchē
màibuchūqù. 他 的 汽 車
賣 不 出 去. He can't sell
his car.

MÁIFU₄ 埋伏 (TV) lie in am-
bush. Tāmen-zài-qiáo-dǐxia
máifu-le-hěn-duo-rén. 他 們
在 橋 底 下 埋 伏 了
很 多 人. They lay a heavy
ambush under the bridge.
(N) ambush. Wǒmen-zhòngle-
dírende-máifu-le. 我 們 中
了 敵 人 的 埋 伏 了.
We ran into the enemy's ambush.

MÀIKEFĒNG₄ 麥克風 (N)
microphone.

MǍIMAI₁ 買 賣 (N) business,
business establishment, trade.
(syn. shēngyi 生 意). Tā-dào-
chéngli qu-zuò-mǎimai-qu-le.
他 到 城 裏 去 作 買
賣 去 了. He went to the
city on business.

MÁIMO₄ 埋 沒 (TV) suppress
one's real ability. Nǐ-zuò-nèi-
zhong-shì bushi-bǎ-nǐde-cáigan-
dōu-máimo-lema? 你 做 那
種 事 不 是 把 你 的
才 幹 都 埋 沒 了 嗎?
Aren't you wasting your talent
doing that kind of work?

MÀI-QIÁN₂ 賣 錢 (VO) sell for
money. Tāde-wénzhang bu-néng-

mài-qián. 他 的 文 章 不
能 賣 錢. His writing can-
not sell for money.

MÁITÓU₅ 埋 頭 (AD) energeti-
cally, with full strength. Wǒmen-
yīngdāng-máitóu-kǔgàn. 我 們
應 當 埋 頭 苦 幹. We
should work very hard.

MÁIZANG₅ 埋 葬 (TV) bury a
person. Wǒmen-yīngdāng-bǎ-tā
máizang-zài-nǎr? 我 們 應
當 把 他 埋 葬 在 那
兒? Where should we bury
him?

MÀIZI₄ 麥 子 (N) wheat. (M:kē
棵).

MǍKÈSĪ₃ 馬 克 斯 (N) Marx.

MǍLÁIYÀ₂ 馬 來 亞 (PW)
Malaya.

MÁLI₃ 麻 俐 (SV) quick and neat
in doing things. Tā-zuò-fàn hěn-
máli. 他 做 飯 很 麻 俐.
She is quick and neat in preparing
meals.

MǍLI₃ 馬 力 (N) horsepower.
(M: pǐ 匹, pǐ 匹).

MǍLINGSHŪ₅ 馬 鈴 薯 (N) po-
tato.

MǍLÙ₃ 馬 路 (N) avenue. (M:
tiáo 條).

MĀMA₁ 媽 媽 (N) (1) mamma.
(2) used in direct address to an
elderly woman.

MÀMAHŪHŪ₁ 馬 馬 虎 虎 see
MÁMAHŪHŪ 馬 馬 虎 虎.

MÁMAHŪHŪ₁ 馬 馬 虎 虎 or
MÀMAHŪHŪ 馬 馬 虎 虎
(SV) (1) careless (not taking care
of things in detail). Bié-jìng-má-
mahūhū. 別 竟 馬 馬 虎

M

M

虎 . Don't be careless all the
time. (2) vague, unclear. (3)
so-so, not too bad. A: Zěnmayàng? B: Mámahūhū. A: 怎麼
樣 ? B: 馬馬虎虎 . A:
How are things? B: So-so.
(AD) (1) vaguely, unclearly. Tā-
mámahūhūde-shuōle-jijiu. 他
馬馬虎虎 的 說了
幾句 . He said several
words about it vaguely. (2)
carelessly. Tā-mámahūhūde-
zuòle-yidianr. 他 馬馬虎
虎 的 作 了 一 點兒.
He did it a little carelessly.

MÁMU₄ 麻木 (SV) (1) numb,
unfeeling. Wǒde-shǒu cháng-
cháng-mámu. 我 的 手 常
常 麻木 . My hands become
numb from time to time. (2)
slow in thinking. Tāde-nǎozi-
yǒu-yidiǎnr-mámu-le. 他 的
腦子 有 一 點兒 麻
木了 . He is a little slow in
thinking.

MÁN₃ 瞞 (TV) deceive someone
by keeping something from him.
Tāmen-mánzhe-wo, bu-ràng-
wo-zhīdao. 他 們 瞞 著 我,
不讓我知道 . They
deceived me by not letting me
know. Bú-mán-nín-shuō, tā-
zuòde bu-xíng. 不 瞞 您 說
他 作 得 不 行 . Telling
you the truth, what he did isn't
satisfactory.

MÁN₂ 滿 (SV) (1) used before a
noun, whole. Mǎn-wūzi dōu-shì-
shū. 滿 屋子 都 是 書
There are books all over the
whole room. (2) full. Píngzi-li-
de-shuǐ-mǎn-le. 瓶子 裏 的
水 滿了 . The bottle is full
of water.
(TV) complete a period of time.
Tā-hái-méi-mǎn-shísuì. 他 還
沒 滿 十 歲 . He is not ten
years old yet. Qīxiàn yǐjing-mǎn-
le. 期 限 已 經 滿了 .
The deadline has already been
reached.
(AD) (1) used before a negative,
completely. Tā-mǎn-bu-zàihu.
他 滿 不 在 乎 . He's
completely indifferent. (2)
wholeheartedly. Wǒ-mǎn-dǎ-
suan-míngtian-qù, kěshi-qùbu-
liǎo. 我 滿 打 算 明 天
去, 可 是 去 不 了 . I
wholeheartedly planned to go
tomorrow but I can't. (3) quite,
very. Nèige-gēr mǎn-hǎotīng.
那 個 歌兒 滿 好 聽 .
That song is quite pretty.

MÀN₁ 慢 (SV) slow. (opp. kuài
快). Wǒde-biǎo màn-wǔfēn-
zhōng. 我 的 表 慢 五 分
鐘 . My watch is five minutes
slow.
(AD) slowly. Nǐ-màn-yìdianr-
chī. 你 慢 一 點兒 吃 .
Eat a little more slowly. (Used
as a polite expression when one
is finished eating first).

MANCHUR₃ 滿 處 兒 (PW) all
places, everywhere. Tā-mǎn-
chùr-pǎo. 他 滿 處兒 跑 . He
wanders from place to place.
Mǎnchùr-dōu-shì·rén. 滿 處
兒 都 是 人 . There are

M

people everywhere.

MÀNDÀI₃ 慢待 (TV) (1) treat someone coldly or impolitely. (2) used by a host as a polite remark. Guest: Xièxie. Host: Màndài-màndài. Guest: 謝謝. Host: 慢待慢待. Guest: Thank you very much. Host:(lit. I didn't treat you well.) You are welcome.

MÁNG₁ 忙 (SV) busy. Tā-shì-ge-máng-rén, 他是個忙人. He is a busy-body. or He is a busy person.
(TV) (1) be busy with something. Máng-'shénma-ne? 忙甚麼呢? What are you busy with? (2) be in a hurry, rush. A: Wǒ-děi-zǒu-le. B: Máng-shenma? A: 我得走了. B: 忙甚麼? A: I must leave. B: What's the hurry?

MÁNGCÓNG₄ 盲從 (IV) follow blindly. Nǐ-děi-zǐxi-xiángxiang, bunéng-mángcóng. 你得仔細想一想, 不能盲從. You have to think it over carefully, you can't just follow blindly.

MÀNMĀNR₁ 慢慢兒 (AD) slowly. Nǐ-mànmānr-zǒu. 你慢慢兒走. Walk slowly. (SV) slow. Nín-mànmānrde, bié-zhāojí. 您慢慢兒的, 別着急. Take it easy, don't worry.

MĂNSHÌJIE₂ 滿世界 (PW) everywhere (usually used in complaining). Nǐ-kàn, nǐ-nùng-de-mǎnshìjie-dōu-shi-shuǐ. 你

看. 你弄得滿世界都是水. My goodness, you spilled the water everywhere.

MÁNTOU₄ 饅頭 (N) steamed bread roll.

MĂNXĪN₃ 滿心 (AD) from the bottom of one's heart. Wǒ-mǎn-xīn-yuànyì. 我滿心願意 I'm willing from the bottom of my heart.

MÀNXÌNGZI₄ 慢性子 (N) (person with an) easy-going disposition. Tā-shi-yíge-mànxìngzi (de-rén). 他是一個慢性子(的人). He's a person with an easy-going disposition.

MĂNYÌ₁ 滿意 (SV) be content, satisfied. Nǐ-xiànzài yīnggai-mǎnyì-le. 你現在應該滿意了. You should be satisfied now.
(TV) be satisfied with. Wǒ-tài-tai bùmǎnyì-wo. 我太太不滿意我. My wife isn't satisfied with me. (cf: MĂNZÚ 滿足).

MÁNYUAN₃ 埋怨 (TV) blame, hold someone responsible. (syn. bàoyuan 抱怨). Tā-lǎo-ài-mányuan-biéren. 他老愛埋怨別人. He likes to blame other people all the time.

MÀNZŎU₂ 慢走 (IV) used as a polite expression when a friend is leaving after a visit.(lit. walk slowly) watch your step, take it easy.

MĂNZÚ₃ 滿足 (SV) be satisfied, content. Yíge-rén yīngdāng-mǎn-zú. 一個人應當滿足.

M

A man should be content.

(TV) satisfy <u>desires</u>. Wǒ-méi-fázi mǎnzú-tāde-yùwang. 我没法子满足他的慾望. I have no way to satisfy his desire. (cf: MĂNYÌ 滿意).

MĀO₂ 貓 (N) cat. (M: zhī 隻).

MĀO₃ 摸 <u>see</u> MŌ 摸.

MÁO₂ 毛 (N) (1) hair (<u>of animals or on the human body</u>). (2) feather. niǎor-máo 鳥兒毛 bird's feather. (3) wool. máo-bèixīn 毛背心 woolen vest. (4) mold, mildew. Yīshang zhǎng-máo-le. 衣裳長毛了. The clothes became mil-dewed.

(B) coarse, rough. máo-bōli 毛玻璃 frosted glass.

MÁO₄ 毛 (SV) (1) worth less than before (<u>of currency</u>). Qián máo-le. 錢毛了. The money has decreased in value. (2) nervous, flustered. Tā-tīngshuō xiàozhǎng-yào-lái, jiu-máo-le. 他聽說校長要來, 就毛了. He became very nervous when he heard that the principal was coming.

MÁO₁ 毛 (M) <u>a monetary unit</u>, ten cents, dime. liǎngmáo-qián 兩毛錢 twenty cents.

MÀO₄ 冒 (IV) (1) give off <u>smoke, gas, fluids, etc.</u> mào-yān 冒烟 to smoke. mào-hàn 冒汗 to perspire. (2) brave <u>danger or hardship</u>. Bié-mào-xiǎn. 別冒險. Don't take a risk. Tā shi-màozhe-yǔ lái-de. 他是冒着雨來的. He

came braving the rain.

MÁOBǏ₃ 毛筆 (N) (<u>lit</u>. writing instrument made of hair) brush pen (<u>for writing or painting</u>). (M: zhī 枝, guǎn 管).

MÁOBING₁ 毛病 (N) (1) flaw, defect, trouble. Fēijī chūle-máobing-le. 飛機出了毛病了. The airplane has developed some trouble. (2) bad habit. Tā-yǒu-hěn-duō-máobing. 他有很多毛病. He has a lot of bad habits. Tā-de-máobing lǎo-gǎibuliǎo. 他的毛病老改不了. He can't correct his bad habit. (3) sick-ness. Tāde-máobing yòu-fàn-le. 他的毛病又犯了. His sickness has recurred.

MÁODÒU₅ 毛豆 (N) fresh soy beans.

MÁODÙN₃ 矛盾 (SV) contradic-tory. Tā-shuō-de-huà qiánhòu-máodùn-le. 他說的話前後矛盾了. What he said earlier contradicted what he said later.

(N) contradiction, conflict. Tā-xīnli yǒu-yizhong-máodùn. 他心裏有一種矛盾. There's a conflict in his mind.

MÁOFÁNG₅ 茅房 (N) outhouse.

MÁOJĪN₃ 毛巾 (N) terry-cloth towel. (M: tiáo 條).

MÀO-MÍNG₄ 冒名 (VO) falsify a name, use <u>someone</u> else's name. Tā-mào-wǒde-míng qu-lǐng-qián. 他冒我的名去領錢. He used my name to collect the money.

MÀOSHI₃ 冒失 (SV) unthinking, inconsiderate. Wǒ-méi-qǐng-ta, ta-jiu-lái-le, zhēn-yǒu-diǎnr-màoshi. 我 沒 請 他，他 就 來 了，真 有 點 兒 冒 失 I didn't invite him, but he came, it's really inconsiderate.

MÁOXIÀN₃ 毛線 (N) knitting wool.

MÀO-YĀN₃ 冒烟 (VO) emit smoke. Yāntong mào-yān. 烟 筒 冒 烟 . Smoke is coming out of the chimney.

MÁOYI₃ 毛衣 (N) woolen sweater, pullover. (M: jiàn 件).

MÀOYÌ₅ 貿易 (N) trade, exchange of merchandice. guówài-màoyì 國 外 貿 易 foreign trade.

MÀOZI₂ 帽子 (N) hat, cap. (M: dǐng 頂). 戴 上 帽 子 . Put on the hat.

MÁQUÈ₄ 麻雀 (N) sparrow. (M: zhī 隻).

MĀSA₄ 摩挲 (TV) stroke or smooth out something with the hand. Māsa-māsa jiu-píng-le. 摩 挲 摩 挲 就 平 了 . Stroke it a little, it will be flat.

MǍSHÀNG₂ 馬上 (MA) right away, immediately. Wǒ-mǎ-shàng-jiu-qù. 我 馬 上 就 去 . I'll go right away.

MÁSHÉNGR₄ 麻繩兒 (N) hemp rope, hemp towline. (M: tiáo 條).

MǍTǑNG₃ 馬桶 (N) toilet.

MÁYÀO₄ 麻藥 (N) anaesthetic. shàng-máyào 上 麻 藥 apply an anaesthetic.

MÁYI₄ 螞 蟻 see MÁYǏ 螞 蟻 .

MÁYǏ₄ 螞 蟻 or MÁYÌ 螞 蟻 (N) ant.

MÁYÓU₄ 麻油 (N) sesame oil. (syn. xiāngyóu 香·油).

MÀZHA₅ 螞蚱 (N) grasshopper. (M: zhī 隻).

MÁZI₃ 麻子 (N) (1) pock-mark. Tā-liǎnshang-làole-jige-mázi. 他 臉 上 落 了 幾 個 麻 子 . He got a few pock-marks on his face. (2) pock-marked person. Tā-shi-ge-mázi. 他 是 個 麻 子 . He is pock-marked.

MÁZUÌ₅ 麻醉 (TV) anaesthetize, drug, dope.

ME₁ 麽 see MA 嗎 (P) (3).

MÉI₃ 煤 (N) coal. (M: dūn 噸 , jīn 斤).

MÉI₄ 霉 (N) mildew, mold. zhǎng-méi 長 霉 become mildewed.

MÉI₁ 没 (AD) (1) the only negative adverb for yǒu 有 . (See: MÉI-YOU 没 有 , MÉI(YOU) 没 (有) , MÉIYǑU 没 有). (2) used to form the negative equivalent of a verbal expression with le 了 or zhe 着 . When méi 没 is used, le 了 , which indicates the completed action, will not appear, but zhe 着 may appear, have not, did not, is not. A: Nǐ-mǎi-le-ma? B: Méi-mǎi. A: 你 買 了 嗎 ? B: 没 買 . A: Did you buy it? B: I didn't. A: Tā-chuānzhe-dàyī-ne-ma? B: Méi-chuānzhe. A: 他 穿 着 大 衣 呢 嗎 ? B: 没 穿

M

着 . A: Is he wearing an overcoat? B: He is not. (cf: YǑU 有 MÉI(YOU) 没 (有)) (See: MÉI... NE 没 ... 呢). (3) In certain contexts the presence or absence of méi 没 makes no difference in meaning from the English point of view. (See: CHÀ(YI)-DIǍNR 差 一 點 兒 , YǏQIÁN 以 前).

MÉI(YOU)$_1$ 没 (有) (TV) (1) do not have, do not possess. Wǒ-méi-(you)-nǚ-péngyou. 我 没 (有) 女 朋 友 . I don't have a girl friend. (2) there is not. Zhèr méi(you)-rén. 這 兒 没 (有) 人 . There's nobody here. (CV) not as...as. Wǒ-méi(you)-nǐ-gāo. 我 没 (有) 你 高 . I am not as tall as you are. (cf: MÉI 没 , MÉIYOU 没 有 , 'MÉI YǑU 没 有).

MÉI$_3$ 美 (SV) beautiful, fine. Tā-hěn-měi. 她 很 美 . She's beautiful.

(B) America. Měijīn 美 金 American money.

MĚI$_1$ 每 (SP) usually followed by dōu 都 , quán 全 or quándou 全 都 each, every. Měitian dōu-yǒu-rén-lái. 每 天 都 有 人 來 . People come everyday. Měiliǎngge-zhūngtóu yícì. 每 兩 個 鐘 頭 一 次 . Once every two hours.

MÈI$_4$ 昧 (TV) (1) take someone's money or things without letting him know, embezzle. Tā-bǎ-biéren-de-qián mèiqilai-le. 他 把 别 人 的 錢 昧 起

来 了 . He embezzled other people's money. (2) act in violation of one's conscience. Bié-mèizhe-liángxin shuō-huà. 别 昧 着 良 心 説 話 . Don't speak against your own conscience.

MÉI(YOU)-BÀNFA$_1$ 没 (有) 辦 法 see MÉI(YOU)-FǍZI 没 (有) 法 子 .

MÉI(YOU)-DUŌDA$_3$ ... 没 (有) 多 大 ...(S) there isn't much. Tā-qùle-méi(you)-duōda-gōngfu. 他 去 了 没 (有) 多 大 工 夫 . He wasn't gone for long. Wǒ-jiāli méi(you)-duōda-dìfang. 我 家 裏 没 (有) 多 大 地 方 . There isn't much space in my home.

MÉI(YOU)-FǍZI$_1$ 没 (有) 法 子 or MÉI(YOU)-BÀNFA 没 (有) 辦 法 (VO) there is no way out, cannot be helped.

MĚIFÉNG$_3$ 每 逢 or MĚIFÉNG 每 逢 (CV) everytime when, as often as. Měifēng-xīngqiliù tā-yídìng-lái. 每 逢 星 期 六 他 一 定 來 . He'll certainly come whenever it's Saturday.

MÈIFÉNG$_3$ 每 逢 see MĚIFÉNG 每 逢 .

MÉI(YOU)-GUĀNXI$_1$ 没 (有) 關 係 (VO) used for responding to an apology, it doesn't matter, it's nothing. A: Duìbuqǐ. B: Méi-(you)-shénma-guānxi. A: 對 不 起 . B: 没 (有) 甚 麼 關 係 . A: Excuse me. B: It's nothing.

MÉIGUI₄ 玫瑰 (N) rose. (M: duǒ 朵 , kē 棵). méiguihuār 玫瑰花兒 rose flower.

MÉIGUO₁ 美國 (PW) America.

MÉIHUA₄ 梅花 (N) plum blossom. (M: duǒ 朵 , zhī 枝).

MÉILE₁ 没了 (RE) indicates finishing up, using up. màiméile 賣没了 sold out. yòngméile 用没了 used up.(See: MÉI 没).

MÉI...LE₁ 没 ... 了 (S) (1) preceded by a NU-M of time, have not done something for the given length of time. Tā-yíge-yuè méi-xǐzǎo-le. 他一個月没洗澡了 . He hasn't taken a bath for one month. (2) no more. Wǒ-méi(yǒu)-qián-le. 我没有錢了 . I have no more money.

MÉILÌ₃ 美麗 (SV) beautiful.

'MÉIMAN₄ 美滿 (SV) perfect (of a relationship, life). Tā-shìqing bànde-hen-'měimǎn. 他事情辦的很美滿 . He did a perfect job. Tāmende-hūnyin hěn-'měimǎn. 他們的婚姻很美滿 .Their marriage is perfect.

MÉIMAO₄ 眉毛 (N) eyebrow. (M: tiáo 條).

MÉIMEI₂ 妹妹 (N) younger sister.

MÉIMING₅ 没命 (AD) with all one's strength. Tā méimìngde-pǎo. 他没命的跑 . He runs with all his strength.

MÉI...NE₁ 没 ... 呢 (S) have not done something yet. Tā-hái-

méi-lái-ne. 他還没來呢 . He has not come yet.

MĚINIÁN₁ 每年 (TW) every year. Tā-měinián-doū-lái. 他每年都來 . He comes every year.

MÉIQÌ₄ 煤氣 (N) (1) coal gas, natural gas. méiqìlúzi 煤氣爐子 gas stove. Bǎ-méiqì-guānshang. 把煤氣關上 . Turn off the gas. (2) carbon monoxide.

MÉIQIÚR₅ 煤球兒 (N) coal briquettes.

MÉIREN₄ 媒人 (N) marriage broker, match-maker.

MÉI(YOU)-SHENMA₁ 没(有)甚麼 used for responding to an apology, it's nothing. (See: MÉI(YOU)-GUANXI 没(有)關係).

MÉI-SHÌ₁ 没事 (VO) (1) have no job or work. Tā-zhèi-liǎngnián doū-méi-shì. 他這兩年都没事 . He hasn't had a job these past two years. (2) free, not occupied. Wǒ-jīntian-méi-shì. 我今天没事 . I'm free today. (3) all right, be free of trouble. Zuótian-ta-tóu-teng, xiànzài-méi-shì-le. 昨天他頭痛,現在没事了 . He had a headache yesterday, but he's all right today.

MĚISHÙGUǍN₃ 美術館 (N) art gallery or art museum.

MĚITIAN₁ 每天 (TW) everyday. Wǒ-měitian liùdiǎn-zhōng-qǐlai. 我每天六點鐘起

來 . I get up at six o'clock everyday.

MÉIXIǍNGDÀO₁ 没 想 到 (RV) didn't think to a certain aspect or point. Zhèi-yidiǎn, wǒ-méi-xiǎngdào. 這 一 點 ，我 没 想 到 . I didn't think to this point.
(MA) unexpectedly. Méixiǎngdào-tā-lái-le. 没 想 到 他 來 了 . Unexpectedly he came.

MÉI-YǏNGR₄ 没 影 兒 (VO)
(1) disappear. Tā-zěnma-méi-yǐngr-le? 他 怎 麼 没 影 兒 了 ? How come he disappeared? (2) have no evidence. Nà-shi-méi-yǐngr-de-shì. 那 是 没 影 兒 的 事 . There is no such thing. (It's just someone's imagination).

MÉI...YǏQIÁN₁ 没 ... 以 前 (S) before a certain action takes place. wǒ-méi-chī-fàn-yǐqián 我 没 吃 飯 以 前 before I eat. (See: YǏQIÁN 以 前).

MÉI(YǑU)YÌSI₁ 没 (有) 意 思 (SV) not interesting, dull.

MÉIYǑU₁ 没 有 (P) used at the end of a sentence in which le 了 or zhe 着 is added to the main verb, indicates a question. Nǐ-chī-fàn-le-meiyou? 你 吃 飯 了 没 有 ? Have you eaten? Tā-dàizhe-màozi-meiyou? 他 戴 着 帽 子 没 有 ?Is he wearing a hat?
used in answering a question negatively in which le 了 or zhe 着 is added to the main verb, no. A: Nǐ-qù-le-ma? B: Méiyou.

A: 你 去 了 嗎 ? B: 没 有 .
A: Did you go? B: No. (cf: MÉI-(YǑU) 没 (有) , 'MÉIYǑU 没 有).

MÉIYÓU₄ 煤 油 (N) kerosene.

'MÉIYǑU₁ 没 有 (TV) used for a choice type question or for a negative answer, do not have.
A: Nǐ-'yǒu-méiyǒu? B: 'Méiyǒu.
A: 你 有 没 有 ? B: 没 有 .
A: Do you have it? B: No, I don't. (cf: MÉI(YǑU) 没 (有) , MÉIYOU 没 有).

MÉIYÓUDĒNG₅ 煤 油 燈 (N) kerosene lamp. (M: zhǎn 盞).

MĚIYUÁN₄ 美 元 (N) American dollars.

MÉIZĚNMA₃ 没 怎 麼 (AD) didn't do much of something. Tā-méizěnma-niàn-shū. 他 没 怎 麼 念 書 . He didn't study much.

MÉI-ZHÉ₅ 没 轍 (VO) Peip. be at a loss. Wǒ-wánquán-méi-zhé-le. 我 完 全 没 轍 了 . I'm really at a loss!

MĚIZHŌU₂ 美 洲 (PW) American continent.

MEN₁ 們 (-B) used after a personal noun or pronoun to denote an indefinite plural number. wǒ-men 我 們 we, us. zhèiqún-háizi-men 這 群 孩 子 們 this group of children.

MĒN₄ 悶 (SV) (1) stuffy, close. Tiānqi-hěn-men. 天 氣 很 悶 . The weather is very oppressive. Wūzili-tài-mēn, kāikai-chuānghu-ba. 屋 子 裏 太 悶 ，開 開 窗 户 吧 . This

M

room is very stuffy, open the window. (2) muffled (of sound). Tāde-shēngyin hěn-mēn. 他 的 聲 音 很 悶 . His voice is muffled.

(TV) (1) keep <u>oneself</u> alone <u>in an enclosed place</u>. Tā-'yíge-rén mēndzai-jiāli yòng-gōng. 他 一 個 人 悶 在 家 裏 用 功 . He studies at home alone. (2) steep <u>tea</u>. Chá mēn-yihuǐr-zài-hē. 茶 悶 一 會 兒 再 喝 . That tea should steep awhile before you drink it. (3) apply <u>something</u> wet in order to soften <u>or loosen something</u>. Ná-shǐ-shǒujin 'mēn-yimēn. 拿 濕 手 巾 悶 一 悶 . Put a wet towel on it.

MÉN₁ 門 (N) (1) door. (M: shān 扇). (2) doorway, entrance, gateway. (M: dào 道). Wǒ-zhǎo-buzháo-mén-le. 我 找 不 着 門 了 . I couldn't find the doorway.

MÉN(R)₂ 門 (兒) (M) <u>for subject of study or course in school</u>. zhèimén(r)-xuéwen 這 門 兒 學 問 this subject of study. xuǎn-jǐmén(r)-kè 選 幾 門 兒 課 select how many courses.

MÈN₃ 悶 (SV) be bored. Wǒ-xīnli-mèndeheng. 我 心 裏 悶 得 哼 . I'm very bored.

MĒNG₄ 矇 (TV) (1) (<u>con</u>. mēngpiàn 矇 騙). swindle, cheat. Tā-mēngle-wo-wǔkuai-qián. 他 矇 了 我 五 塊 錢 . He swindled me out of five dollars. Bié-mēng-wo. 別 矇 我 . Don't

cheat me. (2) try to hit <u>something</u> by chance, guess wildly. Tā-bu-zhīdào, jìng-xiā-mēng. 他 不 知 道 , 竟 瞎 矇 He doesn't know, but always takes a wild stab. Tā-méngzhao-le. 他 矇 着 了 . He got it right by chance.

MÈNG₂ 夢 (N) dream. Wǒ-zuòle-yige-mèng. 我 作 了 一 個 夢 . I had a dream. Tā-shuō-mèng-huà-ne. 他 說 夢 話 呢 . He is talking in his sleep.

MÉNGGU₃ 蒙 古 (PW) Mongolia.

MĒNGGŪDÌNG₅ 猛 孤 丁 (MA) suddenly, unexpectedly. Huǒchē-mēnggūdǐng-zhànzhù-le. 火 車 猛 孤 丁 站 住 了 . The train stopped unexpectedly.

MÈNGJIAN₁ 夢 見 (RV) dream of, dream about. Zuótian-yèli wǒ-mèngjian-wo-mǔqin-le. 昨 天 夜 裏 我 夢 見 我 母 親 了 . Last night I dreamt about my mother.

'MĚNGLIÈ₄ 猛 烈 (SV) violent, powerful. Dírende-'pàohuǒ hěn-'měngliè. 敵 人 的 炮 火 很 猛 烈 . The enemy's fire is very heavy.

MÈNGPIÀN₄ 矇 騙 (TV) swindle. Nǐ-néng-mēngpiàn-biéren, kěshi-mēngpiàn-buliǎo-wǒ. 你 能 矇 騙 別 人 , 可 是 矇 騙 不 了 我 . You can swindle other people, but not me.

MÈNGXIǍNG₃ 夢 想 (TV) dream, imagine. Tā-mèngxiǎng-fā-cái. 他 夢 想 發 財 . He dreams about being rich.

M

(N) reverie, imagination.

MĚNGZHU₃ 矇住 (RV) be hood-winked. Tā-ràng-ni-gei-měng-zhu-le. 他讓你給矇住了. He was hoodwinked by you.

MĚNGZI₃ 孟子 (N) Mencius (the philosopher or the book).

MÉNKǍNR₅ 門檻兒 (N) threshold.

MÉNKǑUR₂ 門口兒 (N) door-way, gateway, entrance.

MÉNLU₄ 門路 (N) special places which one knows about to get a job done. Bàn-zhèizhong-shì, tā-yǒu-ménlu. 辦這種事, 他有門路. Doing this kind of job, he knows the right places to go.

MÉNPÁI₄ 門牌 (N) house-number. Nǐ-ménpái-duōshao-hào? 你門牌多少號? What is your house-number?

MÉNPIÀO₂ 門票 (N) entrance ticket. (M: zhāng 張).

MÉNRÈ₄ 悶熱 (SV) humid and hot (of weather).

MÉNWÀIHÀN₄ 門外漢 (N) outsider, layman.

MÍ₃ 迷 (TV) (1) lose one's way or direction. Tā-míle-lù-le. 他迷了路了. He got lost. (2) (con. míhuo 迷惑).possess, captivate. Tā-ràng-nèige-nǚren mízhu-le. 他讓那個女人迷住了. He was pos-sessed by that woman. (3) get something in one's eye making it difficult to see. Tǔ-míle-wǒ-yǎn-le. 土迷了我眼了.

I got dirt in my eye. (4) be very fond of, crazy about. Tā-hěn-mí-nèige-chànggērde. 她很迷那個唱歌的. She is crazy about that singer. (-B) person who is captivated by something. qiúmí 球迷 person who is crazy about ball games. páimí 牌迷 person who is crazy about card games.

MǏ₃ 米 (N) rice (uncooked). (M: lì 粒 , kē 顆 , jīn 斤 , dǒu 斗).

MIÀN₃ 面 (M) (1) for a drum. yí-miàn-gǔ 一面鼓 one drum. (2) for a flag. yímiàn-qízi 一面旗子 a flag. (3) for a mirror. yímiàn-jìngzi 一面鏡子 a mirror. (4) page of a book, newspaper, etc. dìsān-miàn 第三面 the third page.

MIÀN₂ 麵 (N) (1) flour. (M: jīn 斤). (2) noodle. (M: gēn 根 , wǎn 碗). (3) dough. (M: kuài 塊).

MIÀNBĀO₂ 麵包 (N) bread. (M: kuài 塊).

MIÁNBÙ₄ 棉布 (N) cotton cloth.

MIÀNBULIǍO₂ 免不了 (RV) cannot avoid. Zuò-nèiyahgrde-shì miǎnbuliǎo-kāi-chē. 作那樣兒的事, 免不了開車. To do that kind of a job, you have to drive.

MIǍNDE₃ 免得 (AD) so that... not, lest. Xiànzài shuōqingchu-le, miǎnde-jiānglái-máfan. 現在說清楚了, 免得將來麻煩. Make it clear now so that we won't have trouble in the future.

MIǍNDIÀN₂ 緬甸 (PW) Burma.

MIÀNDUÌ₄ 面對 (TV) face. Wǒ-men-děi-miànduì-shìshí. 我們 得 面 對 事 實 . We have to face the facts.

MIÀNFĚN₄ 麵 粉 (N) flour.

MIÁNHUA₃ 棉 花 (N) cotton (the plant or the sterilized variety).

MIÀNJI₃ 面 積 (N) (1) surface. (2) area of a surface.

MIÀNLI₂ 勉 勵 (TV) encourage, incite. Nǐ-yīngdāng-miǎnli-ta. 你 應 當 勉 勵 他 . You should encourage him.

MIÀNQIAN₃ 面 前 (PW) in front of someone. Nèiběn-shū jiu-zài-ni-miànqian. 那 本 書 就 在 你 面 前 . That book is right in front of you.

MIÁNQIANG₂ 勉 強 (TV) force or compel someone to do something. Bié-miánqiang-ta. 別 勉 強 他 . Don't force him. (SV) (1) unconvincing, insufficient as a reason or answer. Tāde-lǐyou yǒu-yidiǎnr-miánqiang. 他 的 理 由 有 一 點 兒 勉 強 . His reason seems insufficient. (2) be about par, barely acceptable. Tāde-'Zhōngwén hái-miánqiang. 他 的 中 文 還 勉 強 . His Chinese isn't too bad. (3) reluctant, unwilling. Tā-dāyingde-hěn-miánqiang. 他 答 應 的 很 勉 強 . He was very reluctant to accept. (AD) (1) reluctantly, unwillingly. Wǒ-miánqiang-gěi-ta-zuòwán-le. 我 勉 強 給 他 作 完 了 . I finished it for him

reluctantly. (2) barely, merely. Wǒde-qián miánqiang-gòu-yòng. 我 的 錢 勉 強 夠 用 . I have barely enough money.

MIÀNSHÀN₅ 面 善 (SV) be familiar (of someone's face). Zhèige-rén-miànshàn, kěshi wǒ-xiǎng-buqǐlái tā-shi-shéi. 這 個 人 面 善 , 可 是 我 想 不 起 來 他 是 誰 . This man's face looks familiar, but I can't recall who he is.

MIÁNTIAN₄ 腼 腆 (SV) shy, timid.

MIÀNTIÁOR₄ 麵 條 兒 (N) noodle. (M: gēn 根 , wǎn 碗).

MIÁNYÁNG₄ 綿 羊 (N) sheep. (M: zhī 隻).

MIÀNZI₂ 面 子 (N) (1) face, social standing, prestige. Nǐ-děi-gěi-ta-liú-ge-miànzi. 你 得 給 他 留 個 面 子 . You have to save his face. Tā-bu-jiang-miànzi. 他 不 講 面 子 . He doesn't consider other people's social standing. Jiè-ge-qìchē, zhuāngzhuang-miànzi. 借 個 汽 車 , 裝 裝 面 子 . Borrow a car to give the appearance of prestige. (2) honor or favor gained from someone's action. Kàn-wǒde-miànzi, bié-gào-ta-le. 看 我 的 面 子 , 別 告 他 了 . Do me a favor, don't sue him. Tā-kěn-bāng-máng, zhēn-gòu-miànzi. 他 肯 幫 忙 , 真 夠 面 子 . He is willing to help. It is really a great favor. Nǐ-dé-jiǎng, wǒmen-dōu-yǒu-miànzi. 你 得

M

獎 我 們 都 有 面 子 .
You won a prize, we are all
honored.

MIÀNZI$_4$ 面 子 (N) (1) the right
side of a lined garment. (opp.
lǐzi 裏 子). Yòng-lánbù-zuò-
miànzi. 用 藍 布 作 面
子 . Use blue cloth for the
outside. (2) width of textiles

MIÁO$_4$ 瞄 (TV) aim at something.
Miǎozhǔn-le zài-fàng-qiāng. 瞄
準 了 再 放 鎗 . Aim
accurately and then shoot.

MIǍO$_2$ 秒 (M) second (one-six-
tieth of a minute). yimiǎo-zhōng
一 秒 鐘 one second.

MIÀO$_3$ 廟 (N) temple. (M: zuò
座).

MIÀO$_3$ 妙 (SV) wonderful. Zhèige-
bànfa zhēn-miào. 這 個 辦
法 真 妙 . This method is
really wonderful.

MIÀOHUÌ$_5$ 廟 會 (N) temple festival, fair held at a temple.

MIÁOXIE$_2$ 描 寫 (TV) depict,
describe in detail, realistically.
Wǒ-bu-huì-miáoxie-tāde-xìng-
gé. 我 不 會 描 寫 他
的 性 格 . I can't describe
his personality.

MIE$_3$ 滅 (IV) go out (as lights,
fire). Huǒ-miè-le. 火 滅 了 .
The fire went out.
(TV) (1) extinguish, put out. Bǎ-
dēng miè-le. 把 燈 滅 了 .
Put out that lamp. (2) destroy
completely, annihilate a country.
Dà-guó bà-xiǎo-guó-miè-le. 大
國 把 小 國 滅 了 . That
big country destroyed that small

country.

MǏFÀN$_3$ 米 飯 (N) cooked rice.
(M: wǎn 碗).

MǏFĒNGR$_3$ 蜜 蜂 兒 (N) honey
bee. (M: zhī 隻).

MÍHUO$_3$ 迷 惑 (TV) possess,
captivate. Bié-míhuo-ta-le. 別
迷 惑 他 了 . Don't try to
captivate him.
(SV) confused, fascinated. Wǒ-
xīnli yǒu-diǎnr-míhuo. 我 心
裏 有 點 兒 迷 惑 . I'm
a little bit confused.

MÌJUÉ$_3$ 秘 訣 (N) secret process.
Nǐ-zuò-de-fàn zènme-hǎo, yǒu-
shénme-mìjué? 你 做 的 飯
這 麼 好, 有 甚 麼 秘
訣 . You cook so well, what's
your secret recipe?

MÌMǍR$_3$ 密 碼 兒 (N) cryptical
or special code signal for letters,
words or Chinese characters.
(opp. míngmǎr 明 碼 兒).
(syn. ànmǎr 暗 碼 兒).

MÌMÌ$_2$ 秘 密 (N) secret. bǎoshǒu-
mìmì 保 守 秘 密 keep a
secret.
(SV) secret, confidential. Nèijian-
shì fēichang-mìmì. 那 件 事
非 常 秘 密 . That's an
extremely secret matter.
(AD) secretly, confidentially. Tā-
mìmìde-pǎodao-wàiguo-qu-le.
他 秘 密 的 跑 到 外
國 去 了 . He went abroad
secretly.

MǏN$_5$ 抿 (TV) (1) close the lips or
wings easily. Tā-mǐnzhe-zuǐ-
xiào. 他 抿 著 嘴 笑 . She
smiled with her mouth closed.

(2) drink <u>something with lips</u>
<u>closed.</u> mǐnle-yìkǒu-jiǔ 抿 了
一 口 酒 drink a mouthful of
wine.
MÍNBĪNG₄ 民兵 (N) militia.
MÌNG₂ 命 (N) (1) life. Tā-jiùle-
wǒde-mìng-le. 他 救 了 我
的 命 了 . lit. or fig. He
saved my life. Wǒ-yào-nide-
mìng. 我 要 你 的 命 . I
want to take your life. (2) fate.
Wǒde-mìng-bu-hǎo. 我 的 命
不 好 . My fate is not good.
MÍNGBAI₁ 明 白 (SV) (1) clear,
intelligible. Tāde-huà hěn-míngbai. 他 的 話 很 明 白 .
What he said is very clear. Tā-
xīnli hěn-míngbai. 他 心 裏
很 明 白 . He's very clear
in his mind. (2) perceptive. (opp.
hútu 糊塗) Tā-shi-míngbai-
ren. 他 是 明 白 人 . He
is a perceptive person.
(RE) <u>indicates clearness.</u> Wǒ-
men-yǐjing-shuōmíngbai-le. 我
們 已 經 說 明 白 了 .
We have made it clear.
(TV) understand, comprehend,
be clear about <u>something.</u> Wǒ-
bu-míngbai-tāde-yìsi. 我 不
明 白 他 的 意 思 . I
don't understand what he means.
MÍNGCHAO₂ 明 朝 (TW) Ming
dynasty.
MÍNGCÍ₄ 名 詞 (N) (1) term,
word. xīn-míngcí 新 名 詞
new term. (2) noun.
MÍNGDĀNR₃ 名 單 兒 (N) list
of names, roster. (M: zhāng 張).
MÍNGĒR₄ 民 歌 兒 (N) folk

song. (M: shǒu 首).
MÍNGHÒUTIĀN₃ 明 後 天 (TW)
tomorrow or day after tomorrow.
Mínghòutiān-jiàn. 明 後 天
見 . I'll see you in a couple of
days.
MÍNGLING₂ 命 令 (N) order,
command. (M: dào 道). Tā-
xiàde-mìngling, méi-ren-'fú-
cóng. 他 下 的 命 令 , 沒
人 服 從 . No one obeyed
the order he issued.
MÍNGMǍR₃ 明 碼 兒 (N) plain
clear code signal <u>for letters,</u>
<u>words or Chinese characters.</u>
(opp. ànmǎr 暗 碼 兒 mìmǎr
密 碼 兒).
MÍNGNIAN₁ 明 年 (TW) next
year. Wǒ-míngnian-dào-Zhōng-
gúo-qù. 我 明 年 到 中
國 去 . I'll go to China next
year. Nà-shi-míngniánde-shì.
那 是 明 年 的 事 . That
is a job for next year.
MÍNGPIÀNR₃ 名 片 兒 (N) vis-
iting card, calling card. (M:
zhāng 張).
MÍNGQI₃ 名 氣 (N) name, reputation. Tā-míngqi-hěn-dà. 他
名 氣 很 大 . He's very
famous.
MÍNGQUÈ₅ 明 確 (SV) clear and
definite, precise. Tā-shuōde bu-
gòu-míngquè. 他 說 的 不
夠 明 確 . What he says
isn't precise enough.
MÍNGRÉN₂ 名 人 (N) famous
person.
MÍNGTIAN₁ 明 天 (TW) tomor-
row. Tā-míngtian-qù. 他 明

M

M

天去 . He will go there to-
morrow. Míngtian shì-wǒ-
shēngri. 明天是我生
日 . Tomorrow is my birthday.

MÍNGUÓ₂ 民國 see
ZHŌNGHUÁ-MÍNGUÓ 中華
民國 .

'MÍNGXIǍN₂ 明顯 (SV) obvious.
Lǐyóu-hěn-'míngxiǎn. 理由
很 明 顯 . The reason is
obvious.

MÍNGXĪNG₃ 明星 (N) (1) bright
star. (2) star (of movies, sports,
stage, etc.).

MÍNGXÌNPIÀNR₃ 明信片兒
(N) post card. (M: zhāng 張).

MÍNGYI₃ 名義 (N) title (of one's
position). Míngyi-hěn-hǎoting.
名義很好聽 . The title
is very high-sounding.

MÍNGYU₃ 名譽 (N) reputation,
name. Tāde-míngyu hěn-huài.
他的名譽很壞 . He
has a bad reputation.

MÌNGYUN₄ 命運 (N) fate, des-
tiny.

MÍNGZI₁ 名子 (N) given name.
qǐ-míngzi 起名子 give a
name. Tā-jiào-shénma-mingzi?
他叫甚麼名子 ?
What is his name?

'MǏNJIÉ₅ 敏捷 (SV) quick, fast
in thought or action. Tāde-sī-
xiǎng hěn-'mǐnjié. 他的思
想 很 敏捷 . He is quick-
witted.

MÍNQUÁN₃ 民權 (N) people's
rights (one of the Three People's
Principles of Dr. Sun Yat-sen).

MÍNSHĒNG₃ 民生 (N) people's

livelihood (one of the Three People's Principles of Dr. Sun Yat-
sen).

MÍNZHǓ₁ 民主 (N) democracy.
(SV) democratic. Wǒmende-xué-
xiào bu-mínzhǔ. 我們的學
校不民主 . Our school is
not a bit democratic.

MÍNZHǓGUÓJIĀ₂ 民主國家
(N) democratic country.

MÍNZHǓZHǓYÌ₂ 民主主義
(N) democratic principles.

MÍNZÚ₂ 民族 (N) race, ethnic
group, people's nationalism (one
of the Three People's Principles
of Dr. Sun Yat-sen). shǎoshù-
mínzú 少數民族 national
minority.

MÌQIE₂ 密切 (SV) close (of a
relationship). Tāmende-guānxi
hěn-mìqie. 他們的關係
很密切 . They have a close
relationship.

MÌSHŪ₃ 秘書 (N) secretary (in
an office).
used after a surname to form a
title. Lǐ-mìshu 李秘書
Secretary Li.

MÍXÌN₂ 迷信 (N) superstition.
(SV) superstitious. Nèige-lǎo-
tàitai hěn-míxìn. 那個老太
太很迷信 . That old lady
is very superstitious.

MÍYǓ₃ 謎語 (N) riddle, conun-
drum. cāi-míyǔ 猜謎語
guess a riddle.

MŌ₃ 摸 or MĀO 摸 (TV) (1) feel
or touch with the hand. Nǐ-mōmo-
zhèige-zhǐ, gòu-báo-bugou? 你
摸摸這個紙, 夠薄

M

不夠? Feel this paper and tell me if it's thin enough? Bié-mō-nèige-dēng, hěn-rè. 別摸那個燈, 很熱. Don't touch that lamp, it's very hot. (2) lit. or fig. grope for. Tā-bì-zhe-yǎn, xiā-mō. 他閉着眼瞎摸. He is groping with his eyes closed. Wǒ-mōbu-qīng tā-yào-zuò-shénma. 我摸不清他要作甚麼 I cannot grasp what he wants. Wūzili-tài-hēi, wǒ-mō-diànmén ye-mōbuzháo. 屋子裏太黑, 我摸電門也摸不着. This room is too dark, I can't find the light switch. Nǐ-mōmo nǐ-kǒudàirli hái-yǒu-qián-ma? 你摸摸你口袋兒裏還有錢嗎? Will you reach into your pocket and see if you have any money left? (cf: GǍNJUÉ 感覺).

MÓ₃ 磨 (TV) (1) grind, rub, sharpen. mó-shítou 磨石頭 grind a stone. mó-dāo 磨刀 sharpen a knife. (2) dawdle. mó-shíhou 磨時候 dawdle, waste time. (3) pester. (syn. mógu 蘑菇). Zhèi-háizi jìng-mó-wo. 這孩子竟磨我. This child is always pestering me. (cf: MÒFAN 磨煩).

MÒ₃ 抹 (TV) (1) smear on, apply. Wàng-liǎnshang-mǒ-diǎnr-fěn. 往臉上抹點兒粉. Put some powder on your face. Mǒ-yidiǎnr-kǒuhóng. 抹一點兒口紅. Put on some lipstick. (2) wipe off. mǒ-yǎnlèi

抹眼淚 wipe away the tears. Bǎ-zhèige-zì mǒle-qu. 把這個字抹去了. Erase this word.

MÒ₃ 墨 (N) (1) inkstick. (M: kuài 塊). (2) ink (Chinese ink in liquid form). mó-diǎnr-mò 磨點兒墨 prepare some ink (by rubbing an inkstick on an inkstone). (cf: MÒSHUǏR 墨水兒).

MÒ₅ 磨 (N) grinder, mill. (M: pán 盤). tuī-mò 推磨 turn a grinder.

MÒBUSHI...(MA)₄ 莫不是... (嗎) (MA) is it possible that, could it be that. (syn. mòfēi...(ma) 莫非...(嗎) nándao-(shuō)...(ma) 難道(説)...(嗎)) Mòbushi-ta-bu-zhīdào (ma)? 莫不是他不知道(嗎)? Is it possible that he doesn't know?

MÓCǍ₃ 磨擦 (TV) rub. Mócǎ-shēng-rè. 磨擦生熱. Rubbing produces heat. (N) lit. or fig. friction. Tāmen-dāngshōng méi-yǒu-mócǎ. 他們當中沒有磨擦. There is no friction among them.

MÓCENG₄ 磨蹭 (TV) dawdle, waste time. (syn. mòfan 磨煩, mógu 蘑菇). Nǐ-móceng-shénma-ne? 你磨蹭甚麼呢? What are you doing there (keeping you from doing other things)?

MÒDA₅ 莫大 (B-) a great deal. mòdàde-sǔnshi 莫大的損失 a great deal of damage.

M

MÓDĒNG₂ 摩登 (SV) modern, fashionable. Tā-chwānde lǎo-shi-hěn-módēng. 她穿的老是很摩登. What she wears is always in fashion.

MÓFÀN₁ 模範 (N) model, example of what is good. láodòng-mófàn 勞動模範 model wórker. Ná-tā-dāng-mófàn. 拿他當模範. Take him as a model.

MÒFAN₃ 磨煩 (TV) (1) dawdle, waste time. (syn. móceng 磨蹭, mógu 蘑菇). Kuài-diǎnr-ba, bié-mòfan-le. 快點兒吧,別磨煩了. Hurry up, don't waste any more time. (2) pester about something, nag. Tā-gēn-wo-mòfanle bàntiān. 他跟我磨煩了半天. He pestered me for a long time.(cf: MÓ 磨).

MÓFǍNG₄ 模仿 (TV) imitate. Hóuzi mófǎng-rénde-dòngzuo. 猴子模仿人的動作. Monkeys imitate what people are doing.

MÒFĒI、(MA)₃ 莫非…(嗎) (MA) Is it possible that, could it be that. (syn. mòbushi...(ma) 莫不是…(嗎), nádào (shuō)...(ma) 難道(説)…(ma)). Tā-mòfēi-yào-líkai(-ma)? 他莫非要離開(嗎)? Could it be that he wants to leave?

MÓGU₄ 蘑菇 (N) mushroom. pào-mógu 泡蘑菇 soak dried mushrooms in water in order to make them soft. or fig.

pester.

(TV) dawdle, waste time. (syn. mòfan 磨煩, móceng 磨蹭). Kuàizhe-ba. Bié-mógu-le. 快着吧,別蘑菇了. Hurry up, don't waste any more time. (2) pester. (syn. mó 磨). Zhèi-háizi lǎo-gēn-ren-mógu. 這孩子老跟人蘑菇. This child is always pestering people.

(SV) troublesome. (syn. máfan 麻煩). Zhèi-shìqing, zěnma-nèn ma-mógu? 這事情怎麼那麼蘑菇? How come this thing is so troublesome?

MÓHU₃ 糢糊 (SV) unclear, confused, indistinct. (opp. qīngchu 清楚). Zhèizhāng-xiàng-piānr hěn-móhu. 這張相片兒很糢糊. This photo isn't clear at all.

MÒLI₅ 茉莉 (N) jasmine. (M: duǒ 朵, kē 棵).

MÒ(MO)LIAOR₄ 末(末)了兒 (W) (1) the very last, the very end. Dàole-mò(mo)liǎor, háishi-bu-xíng. 到了末(末)了兒,還是不行. It won't do until the very end. (2) at last, in the end. Mòliǎor tā-yòu-qùle. 末了兒他又去了. He was going at last.

(SP) last of a series. mòliǎor-sānge 末了兒三個 the last three.

MÒR₅ 末兒 (N) substance in the form of powder. yáncheng-mòr 研成末兒 grind into powder.

M

MÒSHUǏR₃ 墨 水 兒 (N) ink (Chinese or Western in liquid form). (M: píng 瓶). (cf: MÒ 墨).

MÒSIKĒ₂ 莫 斯 科 (PW) Moscow.

MÓTUOCHĒ₄ 摩 托 車 (N) motor car, motorcycle, motorbike.

MǑU₂ 某 (B) (1) a certain person or thing. mǒurén 某 人 a certain person. mǒuwèi 某 位 a certain person. mǒuchu 某 處 a certain place. (2) used after a surname, a certain Mr. ... Zhāng-mǒu 張 某 a certain Mr. Chang. (3) so and so. Tā-lǎo-shuō mǒu-mǒu-mǒu shì-ta-de-péngyou. 他 老 説 某 某 某 是 他 的 朋 友 He always says that so and so are his friends.

MǑU(MǑU)RÉN₃ 某 (某) 人 (N) a certain person.

MÓU-SHÌ₃ 謀 事 (VO) find a job. Nǐ-xiǎng-móu-shénma-shì? 你 想 謀 甚 麼 事 ? What kind of job are you looking for?

MÒXIĚ₂ 默 寫 (TV) write from memory or from dictation. Nǐ-néng-mòxiě-zhèiyíduàn-ma? 你 能 默 寫 這 一 段 嗎 ? Can you write down this paragraph from memory? (N) dictation.

MÒXĪGĒ₃ 墨 西 哥 (PW) Mexico.

MÓXÍNG₃ 模 型 (N) scale model.

MǓ₄ 母 (B) (1) female (for animals only). (opp. gōng 公). mǔjī 母 鷄 hen. (2) mother. zǔmǔ 祖 母 grandmother.

MǓ₄ 畝 (M) Chinese acre (about 1/6 acre). shímǔ-dì 十 畝 地 ten Chinese acres of land. yīn-mǔ 英 畝 acre.

MÙBIĀO₂ 目 標 (N) goal, target. dìng-mùbiāo 定 目 標 set a goal.

MǓDĀN₄ 牡 丹 (N) peony. (M: duǒ 朵 , kē 棵).

'MÙDÌ₂ 目 的 (N) purpose, aim, objective. dádao-'mùdì 達 到 目 的 reach the destination, achieve the goal. Nǐ-yǒu-shén-me-'mùdì? 你 有 甚 麼 目 的 ? What's your purpose?

MÙGŌNG₄ 木 工 (N) (1) woodwork. (M: jiàn 件). (2) carpenter.

MǓJĪ₃ 母 鷄 (N) hen. (M: zhī 隻).

MÙJIANG₃ 木 匠 (N) carpenter.

MÙLIÀO₃ 木 料 (N) lumber.

MÙLÙ₃ 目 錄 (N) (1) table of contents. (M: piān 篇). (2) bibliography, catalogue, etc.

MǓNIÚ₄ 母 牛 (N) cow. (M: tiáo 條).

MÙQIÁN₂ 目 前 (TW) présent. Mùqián chíngxing-hái-hǎo. 目 前 情 形 還 好 . The situation is all right at present. Mùqián shi-zuì-hǎo-de-shíhou. 目 前 是 最 好 的 時 候 . The present is the best time.

MǓQIN₁ 母 親 (N) mother.

MÙSHI₂ 牧 師 (N) pastor, minister, preacher (Christian). Wáng-Mùshi 王 牧 師 Rev. Wang, the minister.

M

MÙTÀN₄ 木炭 (N) charcoal.

MÙTOU₃ 木頭 (N) wood. (M: kuài 塊).

MÚYANGR₄ 模樣兒 (N) Peip. facial appearance. Tāde-mú-yangr zēn-bu-cuò. 他的模樣兒真不錯. She has a beautiful face.

N

NÁ₁ 拿 (TV) (1) hold, grasp <u>in the</u> <u>hand</u>. Tā-názhe-yiběn-shū. 他 拿 着 一 本 書. He is holding a book in his hand. Wǒ-nábudòng-le. 我 拿 不 動 了. I can't hold it any longer. (2) fetch, get, take, bring. Wǒ-huíjiā-ná-qián-qu. 我 回 家 拿 錢 去. I'm going back home to get the money. Tā-bǎ-dōngxi názǒu-le. 他 把 東 西 拿 走 了. He took the things away. Gěi-wǒ-ná-jizhang-zhǐ-lai. 給 我 拿 幾 張 紙 來. Please bring me a few pieces of paper.(3) give out (<u>money</u>). Yàoshi-nǐ-kěn-ná-qián, yídìng-yǒu-ren-kěn-zuò. 要 是 你 肯 拿 錢 一 定 有 人 肯 作. If you are willing to pay the money, certainly some people will do it. Gài-nèige-jiàotáng shi-ta-yíge-ren-náde-qián. 蓋 那 個 教 堂 是 他 一 個 人 拿 的 錢. He alone donated the money to build that church. (4) earn <u>money</u>. Wǒ-yíge-yuè ná-èrbǎi-duokuai-qiánde-gōngqian. 我 一 個 月 拿 二 百 多 塊 錢 的 工 錢. I earn two hundred somè dollars per month (as my wage). (5) make <u>a decision</u>, make up <u>one's</u> mind. Nǐ-děi-zìjǐ-ná-zhúyi. 你 得 自 己 拿 主 意. You have to make your own decision. Nábudìng-zhúyi bànbuliǎo-shì. 拿 不 定 主 意 辨 不 了 事. If you can't make up your mind, nothing can be done. (6) catch, capture, seize. Jǐng-chá-ná-zéi méi-názháo. 警 察 拿 賊 沒 拿 着. The police tried to catch the thief but failed. (7) obtain, receive, get. Qián, wǒ-yǐjing-gěi-le, kěshi-dōngxi méi-nádào. 錢, 我 已 經 給 了, 可 是 東 西 沒 拿 到. I've already paid the money, yet I didn't get the things. (8) accept, take. Tā-géi-wo-qián, wǒ-méi-ná. 他 給 我 錢 我 沒 拿. He tried to give me the money, but I didn't take it. (9) make things difficult <u>by</u> <u>refusing an offer</u>. Tā-ná-wo-yi-bǎr. 他 拿 我 一 把 兒. He made things difficult for me. (10) pick <u>the right moment</u>. Nǐ-zhēn-huì-ná-shíhou. 你 真 會 拿 時 候. You really know how to pick the right time. (CV) with, use.(<u>syn</u>. yòng 用). Tā-ná-'máobǐ-xiě-zì. 他 拿 毛 筆 寫 字. He writes with a brush. Bié-ná-háizi-chū-qì. 別 拿 孩 子 出 氣.

N

Don't vent your spleen upon children. Ná-nǐ gēn-tā-'bǐ-yi-bǐ. 拿 你 跟 他 比 一 比. Compare him with yourself. Wǒ-ná-ta-méi-bànfa. 我 拿 他 没 辦 法. I have no way to deal with him.

NĂ₁ 哪 (SP) which. Nǎ-sānzhāng-zhuōzi? 那 三 張 桌 子? Which three tables?

(N) used as subject only, which. Nǎ-shi-nǐde? 那 是 你 的. Which one is yours? (cf: NĔI 那).

NÀ₁ 那 (SP) or NÈI 那 that, those. nà-liǎngnián 那 兩 年 those two years.

(N) or NÈI 那 used as subject only, that (referring to persons, things, events, etc.). Nǐ-zhǐdao-nà-shi-shéi-ma? 你 知 道 那 是 誰 嗎? Do you know who that person is? Cóng-nà-yǐhòu, tā-jiu-bù-lái-le. 從 那 以 後, 他 就 不 來 了. He never came again after that. Nà-shì-'wǒ-shuō-de. 那 是 我 說 的. That is what I said. Nà-bù-xíng. 那 不 行. That won't do. Nà-bu-yàojǐn. 那 不 要 緊. That doesn't matter.

(AD) (1) in that case, if so, then. (syn. nènma 那 麼). Nà-wǒ-men-míngtian-zai-qù. 那 我 們 明 天 再 去. If so, we will go tomorrow. Nà-zěnma-bàn? 那 怎 麼 辦? Then what can be done? (2) used before

SV, IV or TV, how (exclamatory). Tā-nà-gāoxìng-a! 他 那 高 興 啊! How happy he is! Tā-nà-suì-a! 他 那 睡 啊! How he slept! (cf: ZHE 這, NÈI 那).

NÁ...DÀNG(ZUO)...₁ 拿 ... 當 (作)... (S) take...as... Wǒ-ná-tā dàng(zuo)-hǎo-rén-le. 我 那 他 當 (作) 好 人 了. I took him to be a good person.

NÀGE₃ 那 個 (SV) used for substituting an exact word to indicate something is not right, awkward, not very good. Yàoshi-nènma-bàn hǎoxiàng-yǒu-yidianr-nàge. 要 是 那 麼 辦 好 像 有 一 點 兒 那 個. If we do it that way, it seems a little awkward or something. (See: NÀ 那).

NĂI₃ 奶 (N) milk. yáng-nǎi 羊 奶 goat milk. chī-nǎi 吃 奶 drink milk.

NÀIJIŬ₄ 耐 久 (SV) durable. Zhèige-liàozi hěn-nàijiǔ. 這 個 料 子 很 耐 久. This material is quite durable.

NĂINAI₄ 奶 奶 (N) grandmother (paternal). (syn. zǔmǔ 祖 母).

NÀIXĪN₃ 耐 心 (N) patience. (syn. nàixìngr 耐 性 兒).
(SV) patient. Tā-hěn-nàixīn. 他 很 耐 心. He is very patient.

NÀIXÌNGR₄ 耐 性 兒 (N) patience. (syn. nàixīn 耐 心). Wǒ-méiyou-nàixìngr. 我 没 有 耐 性 兒. I don't have patience.

NĂIYÓU₂ 奶油 (N) (l) butter.
(2) cream, whipped cream.

NÁLI₁ 哪裏 (PW) where. (syn.
năr 哪兒). Nǐ-dào-náli-qù?
你到那裏去 ? Where
are you going?

used to answer a compliment in
a polite way, that's not true,
you flatter me. (syn. nărde-huà
那兒的話). A: Nín-
chàngde-zhēn-hǎo. B:'Náli-náli.
A: 您唱的真好 . B:哪
裏哪裏 . A: You sing very
well. B: You flatter me.

NÀLI₂ 那裏 (PW) there, that
place. (syn. nèr 那兒).

NĂMA₃ 那麼 see NĚNMA 那
麼.

NÀ-MÉR₃ 納悶兒 (VO) try to
figure out the reason why, wonder. Nǐ-nà-shénme-mèr-ne?
你納甚麼悶兒呢 ?
What are you thinking about?

NÁN₁ 南 (L) south, south side,
south part of. nánbànqiú 南半
球 southern hemisphere. Nèige-fángzi cháo-nán. 那個房
子朝南 . That house faces
the south.

NÁN₂ 男 (B-) male. nánde 男的
male person.

NÁN₁ 難 (SV) (l) difficult, hard.
Déwen-nán-bunan? 德文難
不難 ? Is German difficult?
(2) unreasonable, unacceptable,
far-out, hard to take. Tā-lián-
yī-èr-sān dōu-wàng-le, zhēn-
tài-nán-le. 他連一二三
都忘了真太難了 .
He even forgot one, two, three,

that's really too much. Nà nǐ-
tài-nán-le. 那你太難了 .
If so, you are too unreasonable.
(TV) present someone with a
problem, ask someone something
too difficult. Nán-ta-yíxiàzi. 難
他一下子 . Try to stump
him.
(B-) used before a TV or IV to
form a SV, (l) difficult to, hard
to. Zhēn-nán-bàn. 真難辨
It's very difficult to do. Nà-hěn-
nán-shuō. 那很難說 .
That's hard to say. (2) unpleasant
to. nán-kàn 難看 ugly. nán-
shòu 難受 sad, unhappy.

NÁNBIANR₂ 南邊兒 (PW)
south side, southern part, south
of. chéng-nánbianr 城南邊
兒 south of the city or southern
part of the city. Wǒde-jiā-zài-
pùzi-nánbianr. 我的家在
鋪子南邊兒 . My house
is south of the store.

NÁNBĪNGYÁNG₄ 南氷洋 (PW)
Antarctic Ocean.

NÁNCHU₃ 難處 (N) difficulty.
Nǐ-bu-zhīdào-wǒde-nánchu. 你
不知道我的難處 .
You don't know my difficulty.

NÁNDAO(SHUŌ)...(MA)₂ 難
道 (說)...(嗎) (MA) is it possible
that, could it be that. (syn. mòfēi...(ma) 莫非 ··· (嗎),
mòbushì...(ma) 莫不是 ···
(嗎)). Nándao-tā-shi-nǐ-tàitai?
難道他是你太太 ?
Could it be that she is your wife?
Nǐ-nándao(shuō)-bù-rènshi-ta(ma)?
你難道說不認識

N

他 (嗎)? Is it possible that you don't know him?

NÁNFĀNG₃ 南方 (PW) south, south side.

NÁNGUA₅ 南瓜 (N) pumpkin (the plant or the fruit).(M: kē 棵).

NÁNGUÀI₂ 難怪 (TV) difficult to blame, cannot blame. Suírán-ta-méi-zuòwán, kěshi-nà-ye-nánguài. 雖然他沒作完,可是那也難怪. It's hard to blame him even though he didn't finish it. (MA) no wonder... Nánguai-ta-bu-xǐhuan-ni. 難怪他不喜歡你 . No wonder he doesn't like you.

NÁNGUÒ₂ 難過 (SV) sad, unhappy, sorry. Wǒ-tīngshuo tā-sǐ-le, xīnli-hěn-nánguò. 我聽說他死了,心裏很難過 . I'm very sorry to hear that he is dead. (cf: NÁN-SHÒU 難受).

NÁNHÁIR₂ 男孩兒 See NÁN-HÁIZI 男孩子 .

NÁNHÁIZI₂ 男孩子 or NÁN-HÁIR 男孩兒 (N) boy child.

NÁNJÍ₄ 南極 (PW) South Pole.

NÁNJĪNG₂ 南京 (PW) Nanking.

NÁNJÍZHŌU₄ 南極洲 (PW) Antarctica.

NÁNKÀN₁ 難看 (SV) (1) hard to look at or read. (2) ugly, repulsive. (3) be embarrassed. Ràng-ta-hěn-nákàn. 讓他很難看 . It made him feel very embarrassed.

NÁNMĚIZHŌU₂ 南美洲 (PW) South America.

NÀNMÍN₃ 難民 (N) refugee.

NÁNNǙ₃ 男女 (N) men and women. Nánnǚ-dōu-kéyi-xué. 男女都可以學 . Both men and women can learn.

NÁNQĪNGNIÁNHUÌ₃ 男青年會 (N) YMCA.

NÁNREN₁ 男人 (N) (1) man. (2) husband.

NÁNSHĒNG₂ 男生 (N) male student.

NÁNSHÒU₂ 難受 (SV) (lit. hard to endure) feel bad (physically or mentally). Wǒ-dùzi hěn-nán-shòu. 我肚子很難受 . My stomach feels very uncomfortable. Tā-xīn-li hěn-nánshòu. 他心裏很難受 . He is very unhappy.(cf: NÁNGUÒ 難過).

NÁNTĪNG₂ 難聽 (SV) (1) hard to hear, hard to listen to. (2) unpleasant to hear. Tāde-huà-hen-nántīng. 他的話很難聽 . What he said wasn't very good to hear.

NÁNWEI₂ 難為 (TV) (1) or WÉI-NAN 為難 give someone a hard time, put someone in a difficult position. Nánwei-ta-yi-xiàzi. 難為他一下子 . Give him a difficult problem.(2) be not easy for someone to do something. Zènma-xiǎo-de-zì, nánwei-ta-xiě. 這麼小的字,難為他寫 . It's not easy for him to write such small characters. Guài-nánwei-ta-de. 怪難為他的 . It's not easy for him (to do this).

NÁNWÉIQÍNG₃ 難 為 情 (SV)
be embarrassed.

NÁNWÉN₃ 難 聞 (SV)
(1) hard to smell. (2) unpleasant
to smell.

'NÁNZĬ₃ 男 子 (N) man.

NÁO₄ 撓 (TV) scratch. náo-tóu
撓 頭 scratch one's head.
náo-yǎngyang 撓 痒 痒 scratch
where it itches. (cf: ZHUA 抓).

NǍO₃ 惱 (TV) be mad at, annoyed
with someone. Tā-nǎole-wo-le.
他 惱 了 我 了 . He's
mad at me.

(SV) mad, angry, annoyed. Tā-
yòu-nǎo-le. 他 又 惱 了 .
He's angry again.

NÀO₁ 鬧 (SV) (1) distrubingly
noisy. Zhèige-dìfang tài-nào.
這 個 地 方 太 鬧 . It's
very noisy here. (2) be naughty.
Zhèixie-háizi tài-nào. 這 些
孩 子 太 鬧 . These kids
are very naughty.

(IV) (1) make noise, make a fuss.
Tā-gēn-wo-nàole-yizhèn. 他
跟 我 鬧 了 一 陣 . He
made a big fuss with me for
awhile. Tā-yi-shēngqì yòu-kū-
yòu-nào. 他 一 生 氣 又
哭 又 鬧 . Everytime he
gets angry, he cries and shouts.
Tā-nàozhe-yào-mǎi-dàyī. 他
鬧 着 要 買 大 衣 . She
made a big fuss because she
wanted to buy a coat. (2) be
disturbed by, suffer from something. nào-qíngxu 鬧 情 緒
be emotionally disturbed. Yòu-

nào-bà-gōng-ne. 又 鬧 罷
工 呢 . There is a strike
again. Bié-nào-liàn'ài. 別 鬧
戀 愛 . Don't get messed up
in a love affair. Zhèi-liǎngtian
nào-tiānr. 這 兩 天 鬧 天
兒 . The weather has been very
bad these couple of days. Nàole-
bàntiān shì-'zěnma-huì-shì. 鬧
了 半 天 是 這 麼 回
事 . This is what it's like after
all these distrubances. Tā-nào-
dùzi. 他 鬧 肚 子 . He has
diarrhea.

(TV) (1) cause trouble, dispute.
Tā-jìng-nào-luànzi. 他 竟 鬧
亂 子 . He always causes
trouble. Nǐ-kàn qìchē-huài-le.
dōushi-nǐ-nàode. 你 看 汽
車 壞 了 , 都 是 你 鬧
的 . See, the car is damaged,
all because you caused the trouble. (2) Peip. get something.
Wǒ-děi-nào-yítào-xīn-yīshang-
le. 我 得 鬧 一 套 新 衣
裳 了 . I have to get a new
suit no matter what. (3) end up
with. Tā-nàole-ge-zìshā. 他
鬧 了 個 自 殺 . He ended
up with committing suicide.

NǍODAI₅ 腦 袋 (N) head (on the
body).

NÀOHONG₄ 鬧 哄 (IV) make
noise. Nǐmen-bié-nàohong-le.
你 們 別 鬧 哄 了 .
Would you cut out the noise?

NǍOJĪN₃ 腦 筋 (N) mind, brains.
dòng-nǎojīn 動 腦 筋 do
mental work, shāng-nǎojīn 傷
腦 筋 be troublesome. Tā-

nǎojīn-hǎo. 他 腦 筋 好. He has a good brain.

NÀOZHEWÁNR₃ 鬧 着 玩 (IV) tease, make fun. Wǒ-gēn-ni-nàozhewánr-ne. 我 跟 你 鬧 着 玩 呢. I was just teasing you.

NǍOZI₃ 腦 子 (N) (1) brain. (2) memory. Tā-méi-nǎozi. 他 没 腦 子. He has no memory.

NǍPA₃ 哪 怕 (MA) even if, though. Nǎpa-nǐ-gěi-ta-'yíkuai-qián-ne, yě-suànshi-gěi-le. 哪 怕 你 給 他 一 塊 錢 呢，也 算 是 賠 了. Even if you give him one dollar, it will be considered paid.

NAR₁ 哪 兒 (PW) (syn. náli 哪 裏) (1) stressed, where. Nǐ-qù-nǎr? 你 去 哪 兒? Where are you going? Wǒ-bu-zhīdào tā-zài-nǎr-ne. 我 不 知 道 他 在 哪 兒 呢. I don't know where he is. (2) used after a stressed negative expression, anywhere. Wǒ-'bú-dào-nar-qù. 我 不 到 哪 兒 去. I don't go anywhere. (3) unstressed, used after a verb, somewhere. Nǐ-yào-dao-nar-qù-ma? 你 要 到 哪 兒 去 嗎? Are you going somewhere? (4) stressed, may be repeated and followed by a phrase with dōu 都 everywhere, anywhere. 'Nǎr-dōu-méi-yǒu. 哪 兒 都 没 有. There's none anywhere. Zài-'nǎr-mǎi dou-xíng. 在 那 兒 買 都 行. You may buy it anywhere.

Wūzili 'nǎr-nǎr-dōu-shi-tǔ. 屋 子 裏 哪 兒 哪 兒 都 是 土. There's dust everywhere in the room. (5) repeated in two phrases, wherever. Nǐ-jiào-wo-'zuòzai-nǎr wǒ-jiu-'zuòzai-nǎr. 你 叫 我 坐 在 哪 兒 我 就 坐 在 哪 兒. I'll sit wherever you want me to sit. (6) used repeatedly, such and such a place, certain place. Tā-cháng-shuō nǎr-nǎr-nǎr fēngjing-hǎo. 他 常 説 哪 兒 哪 兒 哪 兒 風 景 好. He often says that the scenery at such and such a place is beautiful.

(AD) how, in which way. (syn. zěnma 怎 麼). Nǎr-néng-nèn-ma-shuō? 哪 能 那 麼 説 呢? How can you say it that way? 'Wǒ-nǎr-yǒu-qián? 我 哪 兒 有 錢? How do I have money? 'Tā-nǎr-zhīdào? 他 哪 兒 知 道? How does he know?

NÀR₁ 那 兒 see NÈR 那 兒.

NǍRDE-HUÀ₃ 哪 兒 的 話 (VO) used to answer a compliment in a polite way, that's not true, you flatter me. (syn. náli 哪 裏). A: Nǐde-xīn-yīshang zhēn-hǎo-kàn. B: Nǎrde-huà. A: 你 的 新 衣 裳 真 好 看. B: 哪 兒 的 話. A: Your dress is really beautiful. B: Oh, come now.

NÁSHOU₂ 拿 手 (N) specialty, excellent ability, skill one has perfect control of. náshou-xì 拿

手戲 the play <u>one</u> does
best <u>or</u> one's forte. Yóuyǒng
shì-tā-de-náshou! 游泳是
他的拿手. Swimming is
his forte.

NÁ...(LAI) SHUŌ₁ 拿...(來)
説 (S) take...as an example,
take...for instance. Jiù-ná-
'zhèijian-shi-shuō-ba. 就拿
這件事説吧. Let's
take this case as an example.
(cf: NÁ...ZUÒ-BǏFANG 拿...
作 比方).

'NÀYÀNGR₁ 那 樣兒 <u>see</u>
'NÈIYÀNGR 那 樣兒.

NÁ...ZUÒ-BǏFANG₁ 拿...作
比 方 (S) take...as an example, take...for instance. Wǒ-
men-ná-tā-zuò-ge-bǐfang-ba.
我們拿他作個比
方吧. Let's take him as an
example. (cf: NÁ...(LAI)-SHUŌ
拿...(來)説).

NE₁ 呢 (P) (1) <u>used at the end of</u>
<u>a question formed by an inter-</u>
<u>rogative word, indicates a ques-</u>
<u>tion for which a definite answer</u>
<u>is expected.</u> Nǐ-wèi-shénma-gěi-
ta-ne? 你為甚麼給他
呢 ? Why did you give it to
him? Nà-zěnma-bàn-ne? 那怎
麼辦呢 ? In that case what
can be done? (2) <u>used in a choice-</u>
<u>type question at the end of one</u>
<u>or both clauses, with or without</u>
(hái)shi (還) 是 . Shì-nǐ-qù-
ne, háishi-wǒ-qù-ne? 是你
去呢,還是我去呢 ?
Are you going or am I going?
Tā-xǐhuan-wo-ne, háishi-'bù-xǐ-
huan. 他喜歡我呢還

是不喜歡 ? Does he
like me or not? Wǒ-mǎi-bu-
mai-ne? 我買不買呢 ?
Am I going to buy it or not? (3)
<u>used after a noun in a contrast</u>
<u>situation,</u> how about. Wǒ-bu-yào,
nǐ-ne? 我不要,你 呢 ?
I don't want it, how about you?
Xiànzài-méi-wèntí, yǐhòu-ne?
現在沒問題,以後
呢 ? Now there are no questions,
how about later? (4) <u>used after</u>
<u>a noun in a situation of looking</u>
<u>for someone or something,</u> where
is, where are. Lǐ-xiānsheng-ne?
李先生 呢 ? Where is
Mr. Li? <u>or</u> How about Mr. Li?
Wǒ-nèixie-shū-ne? 我那些
書 呢 ? Where are my books?
<u>or</u> How about my books? (5) <u>used</u>
<u>to mark a pause after a noun, as</u>
<u>far as... is concerned.</u> Wǒ-ne,
háishi-bu-qù-hǎo. 我 呢 ,還
是不去好 . As far as I
am concerned, I'd better not go.
(6) <u>used after a suppositional</u>
<u>phrase, indicates an alternative</u>
<u>situation.</u> Yàoshi-bú-xià-yǔ-ne,
wǒmen-qù. Xià-yǔ-ne, jiu-bú-qu.
要是不下雨 呢 ,我
們去 . 下雨 呢 ,就不
去 . If it doesn't rain we will
go. If it does rain, then we won't
go. (7) <u>used at the end of a sen-</u>
<u>tence, indicates the action of the</u>
<u>verb is going on or that the state</u>
<u>of the verb is continuing at a</u>
<u>certain time.</u> Tā-chī(zhe)-fàn-
ne. 他吃 (着) 飯 呢 . He
is eating. Nèige-shihou, xià-yǔ-

N

N

ne. 那個時候下雨呢. It was raining at that time. Tā-zài-jiā-ne. 他在家呢. He is at home. Nèige-shíhou, tā-dāng-xiàozhǎng-ne. 那個時候,他當校長呢. At that time, he was a principal. (8) used at the end of a sentence with cái 才 which indicates the contradiction of a previous statement. Wǒ-cai-bu-mǎi-ne. 我才不買呢. I don't want to buy it. (Who said I do?) (9) used after a NU-M structure, indicates the number is more than usual, as much as. Nèisuo-fángzi liùwankuai-qián-ne. 那所房子六萬塊錢呢. That house is as much as sixty thousand dollars. (10) used after a negative with or without a verb, (not) yet. méi-ne 沒呢 didn't do it yet. méi-qù-ne 沒去呢 didn't go yet. Bié-chī-ne. 別吃呢. Don't eat yet. (cf: A 啊, MA 嗎) (See: HÁI...NE 還...呢, MÉI...NE 沒...呢.).

NĚI₁ 哪 (SP) (1) which, what. Nǐ-yào-něige? 你要哪個? Which one do you want? (2) stressed and followed by a phrase with dōu 都 or yě 也, any. 'Něitian-'dou-xíng. 哪天都行. Any day will do. (3) repeated in two phrases, whichever. Něige-hǎo wǒ-yào-něige. 哪個好我要哪個. I want whichever is good. (4) used repeatedly, such and such.

Tā-lǎo-shuō něige-něige-fànguǎnr-hǎo. 他老説哪個哪個飯館兒好. He always says such and such restaurants are good. (cf: NǍ 哪).

NÈI₁ 那 or NÀ 那 (SP) that, those. Nèi-liǎngge dōu-bu-xíng. 那兩個都不行. Those two are both no good. (N) used before a verb, that, those. Nèi-shi-shéide? 那是誰的? Whose is that? (cf: ZHÈI 這).

'NÈIBÙ₄ 内部 (N) the inside, the interior, inner part. Zhè-shi-wǒmen-'nèibùde-shì, búbi-gen-'wàiren-shuō. 這是我們内部的事,不必跟外人説. This is our internal affair, don't tell the outsiders.

NÈIDÌ₄ 内地 (PW) inland.

NÈIGE₄ 内閣 (N) cabinet, council of ministers.

NÈIHÁNG₃ 内行 (opp. wàihang 外行) (N) professional person.
(SV) professional. Tā-xiūli-qì-chē hěn-nèiháng. 他修理汽車很内行. He is very professional in repairing cars.

NÈIKĒ₃ 内科 (N) medical department or clinic (in a hospital for general treatment of disease or injuries). (opp. wàikē 外科).

NÈIREN₃ 内人 (N) (lit. the person inside) my wife.

NÈIRÓNG₃ 内容 (N) content,

substance of something. Tāde-yǎnjiǎng méiyou-nèiróng. 他 的 演 講 沒 有 內 容 . His speech has no substance.

'NÈIYÀNGR₁ 那 樣 兒 or 'NÀYÀNGR 那 樣 兒 (IV) (1) do something that way. Jiù-nèi-yàngr-bà. 就 那 樣 兒 吧 . Do it that way. or Leave it that way. (2) be like that. Tā-jiù-nà-yàngr-le. 他 就 那 樣 兒 了 . He will be like that all the time.

(AD) (1) in that way, in that manner, like that. Nèiyàngr-bàn yě-xíng. 那 樣 兒 辦 也 行 . It'll also be all right if we do it that way. (See: NÈI 那 , YÀNGR 樣 兒). (2) used before SV, to such an extent, so, that. Nǐ-méiyou-tā-nàyang-máng. 你 沒 有 他 那 樣 兒 忙 . You are not as busy as he.

NÈIZHÈNG₄ 內 政 (N) interior affairs of a country. guójia-de nèizhèng 國 家 的 內 政 a nation's interior affair.

NÈIZHÈNG-BÙ₄ 內 政 部 (VO) Department of Interior Affairs.

NÈN₃ 嫩 or NÙN 嫩 (SV) (1) tender, delicate. Xiǎoháir-de-pífu hěn-nèn. 小 孩 兒 的 皮 膚 很 嫩 . Baby's skin is so delicate. (2) light (of color). Yán-se tài-nèn-le. 顏 色 太 嫩 了 . The color is too light. (3) inexperienced. Tā-dāng-shěng-zhǎng hái-nèn-yìdianr. 他 當 省 長 還 嫩 一 點 兒 . He is too inexperienced to be a governor.

NÈNG₅ 膿 see NÓNG 膿 .

NÉNG₁ 能 (AV) or NÉNGGOU 能 夠 (1) can, be able to. Wǒde-yǎnjing-téng, bu-néng-kàn-shū. 我 的 眼 睛 疼 , 不 能 看 書 . My eyes hurt, I can't read. Tā-zhēn-néng-shuō. 他 真 能 說 . He really can talk. Tā-yi-shēngqì, néng-yíge-lǐbài-bu-shuō-huà. 他 一 生 氣 , 能 一 個 禮 拜 不 說 話 . He can shut his mouth for one week when he gets angry. (2) may, be permitted to. Shàng-kè-de-shihou bu-néng-shuō-huà. 上 課 的 時 候 不 能 說 話 . You can't speak in class. (3) could be possible to. Zhèr-shíyíyuè-jiu-néng-xià-xuě. 這 兒 十 一 月 就 能 下 雪 . It's possible to have snow here in November. Tā-lái wǒ-néng-bu-zhídào-ma? 他 來 我 能 不 知 道 嗎 ? How could it be that he's coming without my knowing it? Nà-zěnma-néng-ne? 那 怎 麼 能 呢 ? How could it be possible?

(SV) capable. Zhèige-rén zhēn-néng, nánguài-rén-shuō tā-shì-ge-'néngrén. 這 個 人 真 能 , 難 怪 人 說 他 是 個 能 人 . He's very capable, no wonder people think he is an efficient person.

NÈNG₁ 弄 see NÒNG 弄 .

NÉNGGAN₁ 能 幹 (SV) capable. Tā-zhēn-nénggan. 他 真 能 幹 . He's very capable.

N

N

NÉNGGOU₂ 能够 see NÉNG 能
(AV)

NÉNG...JIU...₂ 能 ... 就 ...
(S) if possible... then... Nǐ-
néng-lái jiu-lái-ba. 你 能 來
就 來 吧. Come if you can.

NÉNGLI₂ 能力 (N) ability,
strength. Tā-néngli-bu-gòu. 他
能 力 不 夠. He doesn't
have enough ability. Wǒde-néng-
li-yǒuxiàn. 我 的 能 力 有
限. My ability is limited.

NÉNGNAI₄ 能耐 (N) ability,
talent. méi-néngnai 沒 能 耐
incapable.

NÈNMA₁ 那麼 (MA) in that
case, then, if so. (syn. nà 那).
Nènma, wǒ-jiu-màigei-ni. 那
麼 我 就 賣 給 你. In
that case, I'll sell it to you.
(AD) like that. nènma-dà-de-
zhuōzi 那 麼 大 的 桌子
a table as big as that. Bié-nèn-
ma-shuō. 别 那 麼 説.
Don't talk like that.

'NÈNMAYÀNGR₁ 那麼樣兒
(IV) do something that way. Nǐ-
bù-yīngdāng-nènmayàngr. 你
不 應 該 那 麼 樣兒.
You shouldn't do it that way.
(AD) in that way, in that manner.
Nǐ-nènmayàngr-kàn, kànbujiàn.
你 那 麼 樣兒 看, 看
不 見. You cannot see it if
you look at it that way.

NÈR₁ 那兒 or NÀR 那兒 (PW)
(1) that place, there. (syn. nàli
那裏). Nèr-méi-rén. 那兒
沒 人. Nobody's there. Dào-
wǒ-ner-qu-zuòzuo. 到 我 那

兒 去 坐 坐. Come to my
place and sit for awhile. (2) that
time, that instance. Cóng-nèr-
qǐ, ta-jiu-hèn-wo. 從 那 兒
起, 他 就 恨 我. He began
to hate me since that time.

NÍ₃ 泥 (N) (1) mud, clay. ní-qiáng
泥牆 wall of mud. Zhèige-
cháhú shì-níde. 這 個 茶 壺
是 泥 的. This teapot is
made of clay. (2) something in
the form of mud. bócàiní 菠
菜 泥 mashed spinach.

NǏ₁ 你 (PR) (1) you (singular). (2)
used before a noun,your (singular). nǐ-tàitai 你 太 太 your
wife.
(S) nǐ...wǒ, wǒ...nǐ. 你 ...
我, 我 ... 你 each other.
Cóng-you-lìshǐ-yǐlái, rén-lǎo-
shi-zhèiyangr nǐ-dǎ-wǒ wǒ-dǎ-
nǐ. 從 有 歷 史 以 來, 人
老 是 這 樣 你 打 我
我 打 你. Since history
began, people have been fighting
each other all the time.

NÌ₄ 膩 (SV) (1) greasy, oily (of
food). Féi-ròu tài-nì. 肥 肉
太 膩. Fat meat is awfully
greasy. (2) bored, tired of
something. Diànyǐngr-tài-cháng,
wǒ-juéde-hěn-nì. 電 影 兒
太 長, 我 覺 得 很 膩.
The movie is too long, I feel
very board. Lǎo-děi-xǐ-pánzi,
zhēn-nì. 老 得 洗 盤 子,
真 膩. One has to wash
dishes all the time, it's really
boring.

NIÁN₄ 蔫 (SV) (1) shrivel (of

plants). Huār-niān-le. 花兒蔫
了 . The flower has shrivelled
up. (2) be slow-moving (of a
person). Zhèige-rén hěn-niān
這 個 人 很 蔫 . This
person is very slow-moving.

NIÁN₁ 年 (M) year. sānnián 三
年 three years. yījiǔliùliù-nián
一 九 六 六 年 1966.
(N) (1) new year. Wǒ-zài-zhèr
guòle-sānge-nián-le. 我 在
這 兒 過 了 三 個 年
了 . I spent three New Year's
here. (2) year. Jīnnian-shi-mǎ-
nián. 今 年 是 馬 年 .
This year is the year of horse.

NIÁN₃ 黏 (SV) sticky. Fàn-hěn-
nián. 飯 很 黏 . The rice
(cooked) is very sticky. fig. Tā-
shǒu-nián. 他 手 黏 . He has
sticky fingers.

NIǍN₄ 攆 (TV) (1) chase away,
drive away. Wǒ bǎ-ta-niǎnzǒu-
le. 我 把 他 攆 走 了 . I
chased him away. (2) dial. try
to catch up, catch someone. Wǒ-
niǎnbushàng-ta. 我 攆 不 上
他 . I cannot catch up with him.

NIǍN₄ 碾 (TV) grind, mill. Bǎ-
yào-niǎncheng-fěn. 把 藥 碾
成 粉 . Grind the medicine
into powder form.

NIÀN₁ 念 (TV) (1) read aloud. Nǐ-
niànnian wǒ-tīngting. 你 念
念, 我 聽 聽 . Please read
it to me. (cf: KÀN 看). (2)
study. Nǐ-zài-něige-xuéxiào-
niàn-shū? 你 在 哪 個 學
校 念 書 ? In which school
do you study? Tā-niàn-dàxué-le.

他 念 大 學 了 . He goes
to college now (to study). Tā-
niàn-lìshǐ. 他 念 歷 史 . He
studies history. Nǐ-dǎsuan-niàn-
bóshi-ma? 你 打 算 念 博
士 嗎 ? Do you plan to study
for a doctor's degree?

NIÀN-DÀXUÉ₂ 念 大 學 (VO)
study in a college.

NIÁNDǏ₃ 年 底 (TW) the end of
the year. Wǒ-niándǐ-qù. 我 年
底 去 . I'll go at the end of
the year.

NIÁNG₄ 娘 (N) mother.

NIÀNG₅ 釀 (VT) brew, germinate,
ferment. niàng-jiǔ 釀 酒 ferment wine.

NIÁNGJIA₅ 娘 家 (N) a wife's
family.

NIÁNJI₂ 年 紀 (N) age (of people).
(syn. suìshu 歲 數). Tā-nián-
ji-bu-xiǎo-le. 他 年 紀 不
小 了 . He's not young any-
more.

NIÁNJÍ₁ 年 級 (M) grade in
school, year in high school, college. èrniánjí 二 年 級 sec-
ond grade or sophomore year.

NIÁNKĀN₄ 年 刊 (N) yearbook,
yearly.

'NIÁNLÍNG₄ 年 齡 (N) age (of
a person).

NIÁNNIAN₁ 年 年 (TW) every
year.

NIÁNQĪNG₂ 年 青 (SV) be young
(of a person). Tā-hái-hěn-nián-
qīng. 他 還 很 年 青 . He
is still quite young.

NIÀN-SHŪ₁ 念 書 (VO) (1) study.
zài-xuéxiào-niàn-shū 在 學

N

校念書 study in the school.
(2) read books aloud. Nǐ-niàn-
shūde-shēngyin tài-xiǎo. 你念
書 的 聲 音 太 小 . The
sound of your reading is not loud
enough. (cf: DÚ-SHŪ 讀書,
KÀN-SHŪ 看書).

NIÀNTOU₄ 念頭 (N) idea,
thought (for future action). Tā-
yǒu-zhèiyangr-yíge-niàntou. 他
有 這 樣 一 個 念 頭 .
He has an idea like this.

NIÁNTÓUR₄ 年頭兒(N) (1) time,
era, days. Bú-shi-cóngqián-de-
niántóur-le. 不 是 從 前 的
年 頭 兒 了 . It's not the
old days any longer. (2) production in agriculture or business
in a year. Niántóur-zěnmayàng?
年 頭 兒 怎 麼 樣? How are
the crops this year?

NIǍNZI₅ 碾子 (N) stone-roller,
roller for smoothening the
ground or grinding grain.

NIÀO₃ 尿 (N) or SUĪ 尿 urine.
sā-niào 撒尿 urinate.
(TV) urinate. niào-niào 尿尿
urinate. niào-kàng 尿炕 wet
the bed.

NIǍOR₁ 鳥兒 (N) bird. (M: zhī
隻).

NIĒ₃ 捏 (TV) (1) hold tightly between the thumb and other fingers. Yòng-shǒu-zhítou-nièzhe.
用 手 指 頭 捏 着 . Hold
it with your fingers. (2) pinch.
Nǐ-niē-wo gàn-má? 你 捏 我
幹 麼 ? Why did you pinch
me? (3) mold, shape with fingers.
Tā-yòng-ní-niē-le-yíge-mǎ. 他

用 泥 捏 了 一 個 馬 . He
molded a horse out of clay.

NIĒ₅ 鎳 (N) nickel (metal).

NIĒZI₄ 攝子 (N) small tongs or
pincers.(M: bǎ 把).

NIHÓNGDĒNG₃ 霓紅燈(N)
neon light.

NÍLÓNG₄ 尼龍 (N) nylon.

NǏMEN₁ 你們 (PR) (1) you
(plural). (2) used before a noun,
your (plural). nǐmen-xiàozhǎng
你 們 校 長 your principal.

NÍN₁ 您 (PR) (1) you (singular)
(honorific term). Nín-zǎo! 您
早 ! Good morning, sir! (2)
used before a noun, your(singular). Nín-péngyou-láile-ma?
您 朋 友 來 了 嗎? Has
your friend come?

NÍNG₃ 擰 (TV) grab and twist
something with fingers or hands.
níng-ěrduo 擰耳朵 twist the
ear. níng-shǒujin 擰手巾
wring out the towel. (cf: NǏNG
擰).

NǏNG₃ 擰 (TV) (1) screw in or
unscrew. nǐng-luósi 擰螺絲
screw in or unscrew a screw.
(2) grab and twist something with
the hand. Bié-nǐng-wǒ-gēbē. 別
擰 我 胳 臂 . Don't twist
my arm.
(SV) (1) go wrong. Tā-yìzǒu,
'shénme-dōu-nǐng-le. 他 一
走, 甚 麼 都 擰 了.
Everything has gone wrong since
he left. (2) at odds, incompati-
ble. Zuìjìn tāmen-nǐng-le. 最
近 他 們 擰 了 . They
have been at odds lately.(cf:

NÍNG 撐).

NÌNGKĚ₂ 寧可 (MA) would rather, prefer to. Yàoshi-yídìng-děi-zuò-fēijī, nà-wo-nìngkě-bu-qù. 要是一定得坐飛機,那我寧可不去. If we must go there by airplane, I would rather not go.

(S) NÌNGKĚ...YĚ... 寧可...也...(syn. lèng...yě... 楞...也...) would rather... than... Tā-nìngkě-bú-shuì-jiào, yě-yào-bǎ-shìqing-zuòwán. 他寧可不睡覺,也要把事情作完. He would rather finish his work than go to bed.

NÍNGXIÀ₄ 寧夏 (PW) (1) Ningsia province. (2) Ningsia (capital of Ningsia province).

NÍSHUǏJIÀNG₅ 泥水匠 (N) mason, bricklayer.

NIÚ₁ 牛 (N) cow, bull, ox. (M: tóu 頭).

NIǓ₃ 扭 (TV) (1) turn or twist the head or body around. Tā-bǎ-tóu niǔguoqu-le. 他把頭扭過去了. He turned his head away. (2) twist, wrench. Wǒ-bǎ-tuǐ-niǔ-le. 我把腿扭了. I twisted my leg. (3) swing one's hips, sway in walking. Tā-zuǒ-dàor ài-niǔ. 她走道兒愛扭. She likes to sway while she's walking.

NIǓKÒUR₄ 紐扣兒 (N) button (on clothing).

NIÚNǍI₁ 牛奶 (N) cow's milk. jǐ-niúnǎi 擠牛奶 milk a cow.

NIÚPÁI₄ 牛排 (N) beef steak. (M: kuài 塊).

NIŪR₄ 妞兒 (N) an idiomatic or affectionate way of referring to a girl in northern China, young girl.

NIÚRÒU₁ 牛肉 (N) beef. (M:jīn 斤).

NIÚYÓU₃ 牛油 (N) (1) butter. (2) fat of beef.

NIǓYUĒ₁ 紐約 (PW) New York.

NÍZI₃ 呢子 (N) woolen material.

NÓNG 膿 or NÉNG 膿 (N) pus. liú-nóng 流膿 suppurating.

NÒNG₁ 弄 or NENG 弄 (TV) (1) do something or work on something in a casual way, straighten out, fix, repair, tinker with. Wǒ-zìjǐ-nòng-ba. 我自己弄吧. Let me do it myself. Qǐng-ni-bà-zhèige-biǎo nòngnong. 請你把這個表弄弄. Will you please fix this watch. Wǒ-bu-huì-nòng-cài. 我不會弄菜. I don't know how to cook. (2) fool with, play with. Bié-ná-shǒu nòng-nèikuài-miàn. 別拿手弄那塊麵. Don't fool with that dough. (3) do something and get something. Tā-nòngle-bù-shǎo-qián. 他弄了不少錢. He got a lot of money (by doing something). Gěi-wǒ-nòng-dianr-chá-lai. 給我弄點兒茶來. Please get me some tea. Wǒ-nòngle-liángshou-tǔ. 我弄了兩手土. I got mud smeared on my hands. (4) do something and make or cause someone to

N

be in a certain state. Tā-nòngde-wo-hěn-buhǎoyìsi. 他 弄 得 我 很 不 好 意 思. He made me feel embarrassed.

NÓNGCHǍNG₃ 農場 (N) farm.

NÓNGCŪN₃ 農村 (N) farm village.

NÓNGFU₃ 農夫 (N) farmer.

NÓNGJÙ₄ 農具 (N) farm tool, farm implement.

NÓNGMÍN₃ 農民 (N) peasant, farmer.

NÓNGREN₂ 農人 (N) farmer, peasant.

NÓNGYÈ₂ 農業 (N) agriculture.

NǓ₁ 女 (B-) female. nǚde 女的 female person.

NUǍN₃ 暖 (SV) warm (of weather). Tiānqì-hen-nuǎn. 天氣很暖. The weather is very warm.

NUǍNHUO₂ 暖和(opp. liángkuai 涼快) (IV) become warm (of temperature). Qǐng-jìnlai nuǎnhuo-nuanhuo. 請進來暖和暖和. Please come in to warm yourself.

(SV) comfortably warm (of weather, a room or place, or a garment). Jīntian-hěn-nuǎnhuo, kě-shi-bu-rè. 今天很暖和, 可是不熱. Today is very warm, but not hot.

NUǍNQIGUǍNZI₃ 暖氣管子 (N) heating pipe.

NUǍNSHUǏPÍNG₄ 暖水瓶(N) thermos bottle.

NǓ'ÉR₂ 女兒 (N) daughter.

NǙGŌNG₄ 女工 (N) female worker.

NǙHÁIR₂ 女孩兒 see NǙHÁIZI

女孩子.

NǙHÁIZI₂女孩子 or NǙHÁIR 女孩兒 (N) (l) girl child.

NÚLI₃ 奴隸(N) slave. Wǒ bu-néng-géi-nimen-dāng núli. 我不能給你們當奴隸. I cannot be a slave for you.

NǓLÌ₂ 努力 (VO) do one's best, work hard. Nǐ-dei-nǔlì. 你得努力. You must work hard. Tā-nǔle-bàntiān-lì, háishi-bu-xíng. 他努了半天力, 還是不行. He failed although he worked very hard. (SV) be diligent, industrious. Tā-zuòshì hěn-nǔlì. 他做事很努力. He works diligently. (AD) with great effort. Tāmen-dou-mǔlì-gōngzuò. 他們都努力工作. They all work very hard. (N) effort, hard work. Tāde-nǔ-lì dōu-báifèi-le. 他的努力都白費了. All of his effort has been wasted.

NÙN₃ 嫩 see NÈN 嫩.

NUÓ₃ 挪 (TV) shift, move. Bǎ-chì-chē nuó-nuo. 把汽車挪挪. Would you move the car a little bit. Nǐ-bǎ-wǒde-shū-zhuōr nuódao-nǎr-qu-le? 你把我的書桌兒挪到那兒去了? Where did you move my desk to?

NUORUÒ₅ 懦弱 (SV) be weak, cowardly.

NUÓWĒI₄ 挪威 (PW) Norway.

NǙQĪNGNIÁNHUÌ₃女青年會 (N) YWCA.

NǓREN₂ 女人 (N) (1) woman.
(2) wife (not polite). Tāde-nǚren-
huàijíle. 他的女人壞
極了. His wife is very bad.

NǓSHĒNG₂ 女生 (N) female
student.

'NǓSHÌ₂ 女士 (N) lady (married
or unmarried).

used after surnames, Miss,
Mrs. Zhāng-'nǚshì 張女士
Madame Chang.

NǙXU₄ 女婿 (N) son-in-law.

NǙZHĀODÀI₄ 女招待 (N)
waitress.

'NǙZǏ₃ 女子 (N) woman.

N

O

OU₂ 喔 (P) used at the end of a sentence. (1) to make the statement open to everyone who can hear it. Jiù-mìng-ou! 救命喔! Save! (I am speaking to everyone). Zháo-huǒ-le-ou. 着火了喔. Fire! Zhè-ke-zěnma-hǎo-ou! 這可怎麼好喔! Everybody listen! What can be done? Chī-fàn-le-ou! 吃飯了喔! Everybody! It's time to eat now! (2) to give a warning. Wǒ-yao-zǒu-le-ou. 我要走了喔. I am leaving (I warn you). Bié-shuō-ou. 別說喔. Don't say it (I warn you).

The sound ou may be changed according to the final sound of the syllable which immediately precedes it. ou may be changed into you, when after e, i, ü, ua or uo; into wou, when after u or ao; into nou, when after n; into ngou, when after ng; and into rou when after zhi, chi, shi or ri. However, if a final e in the preceding syllable is in the neutral tone, it often links with the initial of the preceding syllable, such as le-ou becomes lou, de-ou becomes dou, zhe-ou becomes zhou, etc.

ŌU₂ 喔 see ÒU 喔.

ÓU₃ 喔 or ŌU 喔 (I) indicates surprise, What! How strange! Óu! Tā-gǎn-zhèyangr! 喔! 他敢這樣兒! What! He dares to do this!

ǑU₃ 喔 see ÓU 喔.

ǑU₅ 藕 (N) lotus root (used as a fruit or vegetable). (M: gēn 根).

ÒU₂ 喔 or ŌU 喔 (I) used to show that something has just come to light, Oh, I see. Òu, Wǒ-dǒng-le. 喔, 我懂了. Oh, I understand it now. Òu, shì-nǐ! 喔, 是你! Oh, it is you!

ŎU'ĚR₂ 偶爾 see ŎURÁN 偶然 (MA) (1).

ŌUHUÀ₃ 歐化 (TV) assume or take on European ways. (N) Europeanization.

ÒU-QÌ₄ 慪氣 (VO) build up anger.

ŎURÁN₂ 偶然 (MA) (1) or ŎU'ĚR 偶爾 occasionally, once in a while. Wǒmen ǒurán-chī-yicì-Fàguo-fàn. 我們偶然吃一次法國飯. We have French food once in a while. (2) accidentally, by chance. Zuó-tian-wǒ-ǒurán-pèngjian-ta-le. 昨天我偶然碰見他了. Yesterday I accidentally ran into him.

ŌUZHOU₂ 歐洲 (PW) Europe.

P

PĀ₄ 趴 (TV)(1) lie on one's stomach. Gǒu-zai-yuànzili pāzhe. 狗 在 院 子 裏 趴 着 . The dog is lying in the yard. (2) lean both arms on with the head down. Tā-pāzai-zhuōzishang shuìzháo-le. 他 趴 在 桌 子 上 睡 着 了 . He leaned on the table and went to sleep.

PÁ₃ 爬 (TV) (1) crawl, creep. Chóngzi zài-dìxia-pá. 蟲 子 在 地 下 爬 . The worm is crawling on the ground. (2) climb. Māo páshang-shù-qu-le. 貓 爬 上 樹 去 了 . The cat climbed up on the tree. Tā-ài-pá-shān. 他 愛 爬 山 . He likes to climb the mountains. (3) climb the ladder of success. Tā-páde-hěn-kuài, bú-dao-yì-nián, yǐjing-pádao-júzhǎng-le. 他 爬 得 很 快, 不 到 一 年 已 經 爬 到 局 長 了 . He climbed very fast, he has become the head of the bureau in less than one year.

PÀ₁ 怕 (TV) (1) be afraid (of), fear to. Tā-pà-tàitai. 他 怕 太 太 . He is afraid of his wife. Tā-pà-zuò-fēijī. 他 怕 坐 飛 機 . He's afraid to travel by airplane. (2) worry about, fear that. Wǒ-pà-ta-bu-lái. 我 怕 他 不 來 . I fear that

he's not coming. Nǐ-yǒu-qián, hái-pà-mǎibuzháo-ma? 你 有 錢 還 怕 買 不 着 嗎 ? Since you have the money, why should you worry about not being able to buy it? (3) can be damaged by something. Zhèige-biǎo bú-pà-shuǐ. 這 個 表 不 怕 水 . This watch is waterproof.

(SV) be scared, frightened. Nǐ-yíge-rén-zài-jiā pà-bu-pa? 你 一 個 人 在 家 怕 不 怕 ? Are you scared that you are home all by yourself? (AD)(con. kǒngpà 恐 怕). probably, perhaps. Míngtian pà-yao-yīntiān. 明 天 怕 要 陰 天 . Tomorrow will probably be cloudy.

PĀI₂ 拍 (TV) (1) pat. Nǐ-pāipai-ta, ta-jiu shuìzháo-le. 你 拍 拍 他, 他 就 睡 着 了 . You pat him a little while, he'll fall asleep. (2) slap, strike something with the hand open. Tā-gēn-wo-pāi-zhuōzi. 他 跟 我 拍 桌 子 . He slapped the table in front of me. (3) bounce. Pāi-píqiú-war. 拍 皮 球 玩 兒 . Play by bouncing a ball. (4) clap. pāi-shǒu 拍 手 clap hands, applaud. (5) take a picture. pāi-diànyǐngr 拍 電

P

影兒 take moving pictures.
(6) send a telegram. pāi-diàn-
bào 拍電報 to telegraph.
(7) fawn on. Tā-xǐhuan-pāi-yǒu-
qián-de-ren. 他喜歡拍
有錢的人. He likes to
fawn on rich people. (8) beat
time to music. pāi-pāizi 拍拍
子 beat time.
(M) beat in a measure of music.
èrfēnzhiyī-pāi 二分之一
拍 one half of a beat.
PÁI₂ 排 (TV) (1) arrange in a row
or column, line up. pái-duì 排
隊 line up. pái-gōngkebiǎo 排
功課表 arrange schedule
of classes. (2) be numbered as
(among brothers and/or sisters).
Nǐ-páijǐ? 你排幾 ? Which
number are you (among your
brothers and sisters)? (3) exe-
cute (by firing squad). Bǎ-ta-
lāchuqu-pái-le. 把他拉出
去排了. Take him out and
shoot him. (4) rehearse. Tāmen-
yào-pái-yichu-xīnxì. 他們要
排一齣新戲. They
want to rehearse a new play.
Míngtiande-biǎoyǎn, páile-mei-
you? 明天的表演,排
了沒有? Have you re-
hearsed for tomorrow's performance?
(M) (1) row. dìsìpái 第四排
the fourth row. (2) platoon. Jǐ-
ge-bǐng shi-yìpái? 幾個兵
是一排? How many sol-
diers does one platoon have?
(cf: HÁNG 行).
PÁI₃ 牌 (N) playing cards. (M: fù

副, zhāng 張). pūke-pái 撲
克牌 poker cards. májiàng-
pái 麻將牌 mah-jong cards.
PÀI₂ 派 (TV) assign something,
appoint someone, send someone.
Pài-yíge-rén-lai. 派一個
人來. Send one man here.
Pài-qìchē-qu-jié-ta-qu. 派汽
車去接他去. Send a
car to bring him here. Bié-bǎ-
bīng pàidao-wàiguo-qu. 別把
兵派到外國去.
Don't send troops abroad. Tā-
méi-pàigei-wo-shì-zuò. 他沒
派給我事作. He didn't
assign anything to me.
(M) (1) school of thought, art,
etc. Tā-shi-lìngwài-yípài. 他
是另外一派. He be-
longs to another school. (2)
clique, party, group. Tāmen-
fēn-liǎngpài. 他們分兩
派. They divided into two
groups.
PÀIBIE₄ 派別 (N) groups of
people divided by different opinions. Pàibie-hěn-duō. 派別
很多. There are many fac-
tions.
PÁICHANG₄ 排場 (N) arrange-
ment of items to give an occasion a lavish appearance. jiǎng-
páichang 講排場 pay atten-
tion to elaborate arrangement.
Hǎo-dàde-páichang! 好大的
排場! How very lavish!
PÁI-DUÌ₃ 排隊 (VO) (1) form a
line (military formation). Tā-
men-páizhe-duì-zǒu. 他們
排着隊走. They are

marching in line. (2) line up (one person behind another). Măi-dōngxi dĕi-pái-duì. 買東西 得 排隊. To buy something it is necessary to get in line.

PÁIHAOR₅ 牌 號 兒 (N) brand, trade-mark.

PÁILOU₅ 牌 樓 (N) an arch, portal, honor gate. (M: zuò 座).

PĀIMÀI₃ 拍 賣 (N) auction. (TV) auction. Zhèizhang-huàr pāimàile-yíwànkuai-qián. 這 張 畫 兒 拍 賣 了 一 萬 塊 錢. This painting was auctioned off for ten thousand dollars.

PÁIQIÚ₃ 排 球 (N) volley ball (the game or the ball). (M: chăng 場).

PÁIR₃ 牌 兒 see PÁIZI 牌 子.

PĀI-SHŎU₂ 拍 手 (VO) clap one's hands, applaud. Tīngzhòng-pāile-wŭfēn-zhōng-shŏu. 聽 眾 拍 了 五 分 鐘 手. The audience applauded for five minutes.

PÀITÓUR₄ 派 頭 兒 (N) manner, style, air. (syn. qìpai 氣 派). Tā-pàitóur-bù-xiăo. 他 派 頭 兒 不 小. He has a spectacular manner. Tā-shi-xuézhĕde-pàitóur. 他 是 學 者 的 派 頭 兒. He has the air of a scholar.

PĀI-ZHÀO₄ 拍 照 (VO) dial. take a picture, have a picture taken. Wŏmen-qu-pāi-yíge-zhào-ba. 我 們 去 拍 一 個 照 吧. Let's go to take a picture. or Let's go to have a

picture taken. (cf: ZHÀO-XIÀNG 照 像).

PAIZHÀO₄ 牌 照 (N) license, certificate.

PĀIZI₃ 拍 子 (N) (1) racket, paddle (for tennis, table-tennis or similar games). (2) beat (of music).

PÁIZI₃ 牌 子 or PÁIR 牌 兒 (N) (1) tag, sign. Tāde-ménshang guàzhe-yíge-páizi. 他 的 門 上 掛 着 一 個 牌 子. There is a sign hanging on his door. (2) brand, make. Nĭde-qì-chē shi-shénma-páizi? 你 的 汽 車 是 甚 麼 牌 子? What make is your car?

PÁN₄ 盤 (TV) coil up. pán-biànzi 盤 辮 子 coil up a pigtail on one's head.

(M) (1) dish of, plate of. zuò-yì-pán-cài 作 一 盤 菜 prepare a dish (of food). (2) game of checkers, chess, go, etc. xià-yìpan-qí 下 一 盤 棋 play a game of chess.

PÁNCHAN₅ 盤 纏 (N) travel expenditure. (M: bĭ 筆). pán-chan-qián 盤 纏 錢 travel money.

PÀNDUAN₃ 判 斷 (TV) judge, evaluate, ascertain. Wŏ-méi-fázi pànduan-zhèibĕn-shū-de-hăohuài. 我 沒 法 子 判 斷 這 本 書 的 好 壞. I have no way to judge this book. (N) judgment, evaluation. xià-pànduan 下 判 斷 make a judgment.

PĂNG₅ 耪 (TV) plow. păng-dì

P

P

耕 地 plow the land.

PÀNG₂ 胖 (SV) fat (of a person). Nǐ-yòu-pàng-le. 你 又 胖 了 . You are getting fat again. (cf: FÉI 肥).

PÁNGBIĀNR₁ 旁 邊 兒 (PW) (by) the side of, (the area) near. Xiāngzi-de-pángbiānr-huài-le. 箱 子 的 旁 邊 兒 壞 了 . The side of the trunk is broken. Lù-pángbiānr-yǒu-bù-shǎo-qìchē. 路 旁 邊 兒 有 不 少 汽 車 . There are a lot of cars by the side of the road.

PÁNGCHU₄ 旁 處 (PW) another place. (See: BIÉCHU 別 處).

PÁNGDE₃ 旁 的 (N) other things. Pángde-wǒ-bu-guǎn. 旁 的 我 不 管 . I don't take care of the other things. (See: BIÉDE 別 的).

PÁNGREN₃ 旁 人 (N) other people. Nà-shi-pángrende-shì. 那 是 旁 人 的 事 . That is other people's business. (See: BIÉREN 別 人).

PÁNGTĪNG₂ 旁 聽 (TV) audit (a course in school). Wǒ-pángtīng-yimen-kè. 我 旁 聽 一 門 課 . I audit one course.

PÁNGXIE₄ 螃 蟹 (N) crab. (M: zhǐ 隻).

PÀNGZI₄ 胖 子 (N) fat person.

PÁNNIXILIN₃ 盤 尼 西 林 (N) penicillin. dǎ-yizhen-pán-nixilín 打 一 針 盤 尼 西 林 . inject penicillin.

PÁNSUAN₄ 盤 算 (TV) estimate, figure out. Méi-mǎi-yǐqián ni-zuìhǎo-xiān-pánsuan-pansuan. 沒 買 以 前 你 最 好 先 盤 算 盤 算 . You'd better figure it out before you buy it.

PÀNWANG₂ 盼 望 (TV) (1) wish, hope, expect. Wǒ-pànwang-hái-zi-gǎnkuai-zhǎngdà-le. 我 盼 望 孩 子 趕 快 長 大 了 . I wish that my children would grow up sooner. (2) long for. Tā-hěn-pànwang-ni. 他 很 盼 望 你 . He longs for you very much. (N) hope. Hái-yǒu-pànwang-ma? 還 有 盼 望 嗎 ? Is there still hope? (cf: XĪWANG 希 望 , ZHĪWANG 指 望)

PÁNZI₂ 盤 子 (N) plate, dish, platter, tray.

PĀO₅ 泡 (M) for bowel movements, urination. sā-yìpāo-niào 撒 一 泡 尿 urinate once. lā-yìpāo-shǐ 拉 一 泡 屎 move the bowels once.

PÁO₄ 刨 (TV) (1) dig. Gǒu-páole-yíge-kēng. 狗 刨 了 一 個 坑 . That dog dug a hole in the ground. Bǎ-dìli-de-shítou páo-chulai. 把 地 裏 的 石 頭 刨 出 來 . Dig out the stones in the ground. (2) exclude, subtract. Bǎ-kāixiao-páochuqu, jiu-shèng-shíkuai-qian-le. 把 開 銷 刨 出 去 就 剩 十 塊 錢 了 . There's only ten dollars left, excluding the expense money.

PĂO₁ 跑 (IV) (1) run. Háizi-lái-huíde-pǎo. 孩 子 來 回 的

跑 . The children are running back and forth. Wǒ-pǎobu-guò-ta. 我 跑 不 過 他 . I cannot beat him in running. (2) go, leave. Tā-ná-qi-màozi jiu-pǎo-le. 他 拿 起 帽子 就 跑了 . He took his hat and left. Tā-xiàle·bān jiu-wàng-jiā-pǎo. 他 下 了 班 就 往 家 跑 . He leaves for home right after office hours. Wǒde-bǐ zěnma-pǎodao-nǐ-ner-qu-le? 我 的 筆 怎麼 跑 到 你 那 兒 去 了 ? How come my pen is in your place? Tā-cháng-pǎo-Shànghai. 他 常 跑 上 海 . He goes to Shanghai very often. (3) engage in business as a broker. Jīntian wǒ-pǎochéng-le-liǎngdàngzi-mǎimai. 今 天 我 跑 成 了 兩 檔 子 買 賣 . I made two deals to-day. (4) run away, escape. Jǐng-chá-dǎizhao-sānge-zéi, pǎole-liǎngge. 警 察 逮 着 三 個 賊 跑 了 兩 個 . The police caught three thieves and two escaped. Tā-tàitai-gen-ren-pǎo-le. 他 太 太 跟 人 跑 了 . His wife ran away with someone else.

PÀO₃ 炮 (N) cannon, artillery. (M: mén 門 , shēng 聲). fàng-le-sānshēng-pào 放 了 三 聲 炮 have fired three cannon shots.

PÀO₃ 泡 (TV) (1) steep, soak. pào-chá 泡 茶 make tea. Fàng-zai-shuǐli pào-yihuir. 放 在

水 裏 泡 一 會 兒 . Soak it in the water for awhile. (2) Peip. pester. Nǐ-bùdāying wǒ-jiu-gēn-nǐ-pào-le. 你 不 答 應 我 就 跟 你 泡 了 . I'll keep pestering you until you promise me. (3) Peip. fool around. Tā-bu-niàn-shū, jìng-pào. 他 不 念 書, 竟 泡 . He doesn't study, he's always fooling around.

PÀODÀN₄ 砲 彈 (N) artillery shell.(M: fā 發).

PǍO-MǍ₃ 跑 馬 (VO) have a horserace.

PǍOMǍCHǍNG₄ 跑 馬 場 (N) race course.

PÀO-MÁO₃ 拋 錨 (VO)(1) drop an anchor. Wǒmen-zài shénme-dì-fang pāo-máo? 我 們 在 甚 麼 地 方 拋 錨 ? Where should we drop the anchor? (2) break down (as a car). Tāde-chē zài-lùshang-pāo-máole. 他 的 車 在 路 上 拋 錨 了 . His car broke down on the road.

PÀOQI₅ 拋 棄 (TV)(lit. throw away) abandon, desert. Tā-pāo-qi-le-tā-tàitai yǒu-sānnián-le. 他 拋 棄 了 他 太 太 有 三 年 了 . It has been three years since he deserted his wife.

PÀOR₄ 泡 兒 (N) (1) bubble. (2) bulb (electric). diàndēng-pàor 電 燈 泡 兒 electric bulb.

PÀOZHANG₃ 砲 仗 or PÀOZHU 砲 竹 (N) firecracker. fàn-pàozhang 放 砲 仗 light a firecracker.

P

P

PÀOZHU₃ 炮竹 see PÀOZHANG
炮仗.

PÁQILAI₃ 爬起來 (RV) get up
from a prone position. Tā-
shuāidǎo-le, pábuqilái-le. 他
摔倒了，爬不起來
了. He fell down and couldn't
get up.

PÀXIA₄ 趴下 (RC) (1) lie down
on one's stomach. Tā-tīngjian-
fàngqiāng jiu-pāxia-le. 他聽
見放鎗就趴下了.
He lay down as soon as he heard
the firing. (2) fall down. Wǒ-
tuī-ta-yixiar, tā-jiu-pāxia-le.
我推他一下他就
趴下了. I just pushed him
once, and he fell down.
(RE) indicates falling face down.
shuāipāxia 摔趴下 trip and
fall flat. lèipāxia 累趴下
fall down with exhaustion.

PĒI₄ 披 (TV) throw on clothing
on one's shoulders. Tā-pēizhe-
yīshang-chūqu-le. 他披着
衣裳出去了. He threw
on his clothes and went out.

PĒI₃ 呸 (I) used to indicate contempt for someone. Pēi, duǒ-
kai-wo. 呸，躲開我. You,
ugh, get out of my sight.

PÉI₃ 陪 (TV) keep someone company. péi-kè 陪客 entertain
a guest. péike 陪客 guest
who keeps the honored guest
company. Wǒ-bu-péi-le. 我不
陪了. (lit. I can't keep you
company any longer.) Excuse
me. Wǒ-péi-ta-qu. 我陪他
去. I'll go with him (to keep

him company).

PÉI₂ 賠 (TV) (1) pay damages,
pay for something spoiled or
broken. Yàoshi-wǒ-bǎ-tade-dōng-
xi nònghuài-le, wǒ-děi-péi-ta.
要是我把他的東
西弄壞了，我得賠
他. If I ruined anything of his,
I have to pay for it. (2) lose
money (in business). (opp. zhuàn
賺). Nèige-pùzi péi-qián. 那
個鋪子賠錢. That
store is losing money.
(cf: DIŪ 丟, SHŪ 輸).

PÉI₃ 配 (TV) (1) find something
to match or fit something else.
Yòng-hóngde-pèi-lǜde. 用紅
的配綠的. Use red to
match green. pèi-yàoshi 配
鑰匙 fit a key. pèi-yǎnjìngr
配眼鏡兒 have specta-
cles made (according to a prescription). (2) mate (except human beings). Zhèizhong-jī shi-
zhèi-liǎngzhong-jī pèichulai-de.
這種鷄是這兩種
鷄配出來的. This
kind of chicken is produced when
these two kinds are mated.
(SV) be a good match. Tā-nǔer
gēn-nǐ-érzi-hěn-pèi. 他女兒
跟你兒子很配. His
daughter and your son will be a
very good match.
(AV) be qualified to, fit to, deserve to. Xiǎng-dāng-xiàozhǎng,
tā-pèi-ma? 想當校長，
他配嗎? He wants to be a
principal, is he qualified?

PÉI-BĚNR₃ 賠本兒 (VO) lose

capital, have losses. Tā-zhèi-huí-yòu-péile-běnr-le. 他這回又賠了本兒了. This time he lost money again.

PÉI-BÚSHI₂ 賠不是 (VO) ask for pardon, apologize. (syn. péi-lǐ 賠禮, péi-zuì 賠罪). Nǐ-gěi-ta-péi-ge-búshi-ba. 你給他賠個不是吧. Apologize to him.

PÉICHANG₃ 賠償 (TV) make up a loss, make restitution. Nǐ-děi-péichang-wǒde-sǔnshī. 你得賠償我的損失. You must make up my losses. (N) indemnity, reparation.

PÈIFU₁ 佩服 (TV) admire and respect. Wǒ-hěn-pèifu-tāde-tiāncai. 我很佩服他的天才. I admire and respect his talent.

PÈIJǏ₃ 配給 (TV) allot, ration. Zhèngfǔ-pèijǐ-měi-rén-liǎng-tào-zhìfú. 政府配給每人兩套制服. The government allotted two uniforms to eacn person. (N) ration.

PÉI-LǏ₃ 賠禮 (VO) ask for pardon, apologize. (syn. péi-búshi 賠不是, péi-zuì 賠罪).

PÉIYANG₃ 培養 (TV) cultivate, nourish. péiyang-réncai 培養人才 develop talented people. péiyang-xìngqu 培養興趣 cultivate one's interest.

PÈI-YÀO₃ 配藥 (VO) fill a prescription, compound medicine.

PÉI-ZUÌ₄ 賠罪 (VO) ask for pardon, apologize. (syn. péi-búshi 賠不是, péi-lǐ 賠禮).

PĒN₁ 噴 (TV) (1) spurt, puff. Tā-yi-xiào bǎ-zuǐli-de-shuǐ dōu-pēn-chulai-le. 他一笑把嘴裏的水都噴出來了. He spit the water from his mouth as he burst into laughter. Huǒshān pēn-huǒ. 火山噴火. The volcano spurts lava. (2) spray. Tā-pēnle-hěn-duō-xiāngshuǐr. 她噴了很多香水. She sprayed a lot of perfume.

PÉN₃ 盆 (N) basin, bowl, tub, pot. zǎopén 澡盆 bathtub.

PÉNG₄ 棚 (N) tent, shed, awning. dā-péng 搭棚 set up a tent.

PĚNG₃ 捧 (1) hold something out or up in both hands. Tā-pěngzhe-yíge-dà-wǎn. 他捧着一個大碗. He is holding a big bowl with both hands. (2) flatter, praise, fawn on. Nǐ-yi-pěng-ta, ta-jiu-gāoxìng. 你一捧他，他就高興. He gets very happy as soon as you start to flatter him. (3) be the patron of (a performer, actor, artist, etc.). pěng-chàng-xì-de 捧唱戲的 be a patron of an opera singer. (M) for amounts of something one can carry with the hands cupped together. Tā-pěngzhe-yipěng-tǔ. 他捧着一捧土. He is carrying a double handful of dirt.

PÈNG₁ 碰 (TV) (1) bump, knock,

P

run into <u>something</u> accidentally. Qìchē-pèngzai-shùshang-le. 汽車碰在樹上了. A car bumped into a tree. (2) run into a <u>situation</u> accidentally. pèng-jīhui 碰機會 (<u>lit.</u> run into chance) try one's luck. Nà-jiu-pèng-nǐde-yùnqi-le. 那就碰你的運氣了. In that case, it all depends on your luck. Pèngshang-shenma mǎi-shenma. 碰上甚麼買甚麼. I'll buy whatever I find. (3) touch, touch against. Nǐ-bié-pèng-zhèige-zhuōzi. 你別碰這個桌子. Don't touch against this table. Nèi-zhong-shì wǒ-bu-gǎn-pèng. 那種事我不敢碰. I don't dare to touch that kind of thing.

PÈNG-DĪNGZI₂ 碰釘子 (VO) (<u>lit.</u> bump into a nail) run into difficulties <u>or</u> resistance, be rebuffed. Wǒ-pèngle-dīngzi-le. 我碰了釘子了. I was rebuffed. Tā-gěi-wǒ-yíge-ruǎn-dīngzi pèng. 他給我一個軟釘子碰. I was gently rebuffed.

PÈNGJIAN₁ 碰見 (RV) run into accidentally, meet by chance. (<u>syn.</u> yùjyan 遇見). Wǒ-pèngjian-tā-le. 我碰見他了. I met him accidentally.

PÉNGYOU₁ 朋友 (N) friend. Tā-zuì-ài-jiāo-péngyou. 他最愛交朋友. He likes to make friends.

PĒNSHÈJI₁ 噴射機 (N) jet plane. (M: jià 架). PĒNSHUǏCHÍ₅ 噴水池 (N) water fountain (<u>for display</u>). PĪ₃ 批 (M) (1) batch. dìngle-yipī-huò 定了一批貨 ordered a batch of merchandise. (2) group <u>of people</u>. yìpī-jiàoyuán 一批教員 a group of teachers. PĪ₄ 批 (TV) write down <u>one's</u> opinion, comment on a document. Wǒ-yǐjing-bǎ-gōngshì-pīhǎo-le. 我已經把公事批好了. I've already written my opinion concerning that document. Xiānsheng-pī-juànzi. 先生批卷子. The teacher commented on his paper.

PĪ₃ 匹 <u>see</u> PĬ 匹 .

PÍ₁ 皮 (N) skin, hide, peel, bark. (M: zhāng 張 , kuài 塊). shǒu shangde-pí 手上的皮 skin on the hand. yáng-pí 羊皮 sheepskin. shù-pí 樹皮 bark of a tree. júzi-pí 橘子皮 orange peel. huāsheng-pí 花生皮 shell of a peanut.

(SV) (1) not crisp, stale. Huā-shēng-dōu-pí-le. 花生都皮了. The peanuts are not crisp anymore. (2) naughty, un-mindful of scolding. Tàde-xiǎo-dìdi-pí jíle. 他的小弟弟皮極了. His younger brother is very naughty.

PǏ₃ 匹 <u>or</u> PĪ 匹 (M) (1) bolt <u>of cloth.</u> yìpǐ-bù 一匹布 a bolt of cloth. (2) <u>for horses.</u> yì-pǐ-mǎ 一匹馬 a horse. (3) <u>for horsepower.</u> wǔbǎipǐ-mǎli

五百匹馬力 five hundred horsepower.

PÌ₅ 屁 (N) gas (in the stomach). fàng-pì 放屁 give off gas (from the rectum) or nonsense (vulgar expression).

PIĀN₂ 篇 (M) (1) for formal writings. xiě-yipiān-wénzhang 寫一篇文章 write an article. (2) section of a book. dì-sānpiān 第三篇 section three.

PIĀN₃ 偏 (SV) be inclined to one side, leaning. (opp. zhèng 正). Nèi-zhāng-huàr méi-guàzhèng, piānzhene. 那張畫兒沒掛正，偏着呢. That picture isn't hanging straight, it's leaning to one side. Tāde-kànfa yǒu-yidiǎnr-piān. 他的看法有一點兒偏. His view leans slightly to one side.

(AD) perversely, stubbornly maintain an opposite position. Tā-jiào-'wǒ-qù, wǒ-'piān-bu-qù. 他叫我去我偏不去. He asked me to go, but I'm not going on purpose.

PIÀN₁ 騙 (TV) (1) fool, joke with. Nǐ-piàn-wo, shì-bu-shì? 你騙我，是不是？ You are joking with me, aren't you? (2) swindle, cheat. Tā-piànle-wǒ-yibǎikuai-qián-qu. 他騙了我一百塊錢去. He cheated me out of one hundred dollars.

PIÀN₃ 片 (M) (1) or PIÀNR 片兒 tablet of medicine. yípiàn-yào 一片藥 a tablet of medicine.

(2) or PIÀNR 片兒 slice, thin piece. yípiàn-miànbāo 一片麵包 a slice of bread. (3) expanse. yípiàn-dàhǎi 一片大海 a broad expanse of ocean.

(TV) slice something with a knife.

(B) or PIANR 片兒 something thin and flat, such as card, record, disc, film, etc.

PIĀNJIÀN₃ 偏見 (N) prejudice. Tā-yǒu-piānjiàn. 他有偏見. He is prejudiced.

PIĀNPIAN₃ 偏偏 (MA) (1) insistently, persistently. Tā-piānpian-yào-zhèiyangr. 他偏偏要這樣兒. He insists on doing it this way. (2) contrary to expectations. Nèige-shihou piānpian-ta-méi-zài-zher. 那個時候偏偏他沒在這兒. That time, contrary to what was expected, he wasn't here.

PIÀNR₄ 片兒 see PIÀN 片 (B).

PIĀNR₃ 篇兒 (N) leaf of a book. Zhèibén-shū diàole-sānpiānr. 這本書掉了三篇兒. Three leaves are missing in this book.

PIÀNR₃ 片兒 (M) see PIÀN 片 (M) (1) (2).

(N) (1) something thin and flat, such as slice, tablet, blade, etc. ròu-piànr 肉片兒 a slice of meat. yào-piànr 藥片兒 medicine tablet. dāo-piànr 刀片兒 razor blade. (2) or

P

P

PIÀNZI 片子 calling card.
(3) size (of objects which take
piàn 片 as a measure).

PIÁNYI₁ 便宜 (SV) inexpensive,
cheap, reasonable in price.
Zhèisuǒ-fángzi hěn-piányi. 這
所房子很便宜. This
house is inexpensive.
(N) advantage. zhàn-piányi 佔
便宜 take advantage.
(TV) let someone off easy. Zhèi-
huí-piányi-ni. 這回便宜
你. I'll let you off easy this
time.

PIÁNZI₃ 片子 or PIÀNZI 片
子 (N) something thin and flat,
such as card, record, disc,
film, etc. (M: zhāng 張). diàn-
yǐngr-piānzi 電影兒片子
movie film.

PIÀNZI₃ 片子 (N) (1) or PIÀNR
片兒 calling card. (M:zhāng
張).(2) see PIÀNZI 片子.

PIÀNZI₃ 騙子 (N) swindler.

PIĀO₃ 漂 (IV) float on water. Yí-
kuài-mùtou zài-shuǐshang-piāo-
zhe. 一塊木頭在水
上漂着. A piece of wood
is floating on the water.

PIĀO₃ 飄 (IV) float in the air.
Yèzi zai-kōngzhōng-piāolaipiāo-
qu. 葉子在空中飄
來飄去. Leaves are float-
ing back and forth in the air.

PIĀO₄ 漂 (TV) bleach. piāobái 漂
白 bleach white. Zhèige-zhěn-
toutàor-děi-piāo-yipiao-le. 這
個枕頭套兒得漂
一漂了. This pillow case
needs to be bleached.

PIÀO₂ 票 (N) (1). ticket. (M:zhāng
張). xì-piào 戲票 theater
ticket. fēijī-piào 飛機票
airplane ticket. yóupiào 郵票
postage stamp. (2) ballot. (M:
zhāng 張). tóupiào投票 vote.

PIÀOFÁNGR₃ 票房兒 (N) (1)
ticket office. (2) an organization
of amateur opera singers.

PIÀOLIANG₁ 漂亮 (SV) (1) handsome, pretty, attractive. Yán-
shair-piàoliang. 顏色兒
漂亮. The color is attrac-
tive. Zhèiwei-xiáojie piàoliang.
這位小姐漂亮. This
young lady is very pretty. (2)
smartly done and meeting all
needs. Tā-zuò-shi zuòde-piào-
liang. 他作事作得漂
亮. He handled this matter
very well and met all needs.

PÍBÃO₁ 皮包 (N) leather case
or bag, including suitcase,
briefcase, handbag, etc. gōng-
shi-píbāo 公事皮包 brief-
case. Nǔrende-píbāoli shénma-
dōu-yǒu. 女人的皮包
裏甚麼都有. In a
woman's handbag, there is
everything.

PÍDÀI₂ 皮帶 (N) (1) leather belt.
(M: gēn 根, tiáo 條). jì-pídài
繫皮帶 fasten a leather
belt. (2) rubber tire.(M: tiáo
條). qìchē-de-pídài 汽車
的皮帶 automobile tire.

PIĔ₄ 撇 (TV) throw, throw away.
(syn. rēng 扔). Tā-bǎ-qiú-piě-
de-hěn-yuǎn. 他把球撇
的很遠. He threw the ball

quite far. Bǎ-dōngxi-dou-piě-le.
把 東 西 都 撇 了 .
Throw away all these things.
PIĔ-ZUĬ₅ 撇 嘴 (VO) turn the
corners of one's mouth down to
show contempt for someone. Nǐ-
wèishénma-jiànzhao-wo-jiu-piě-
zuǐ? 你 為 甚 麼 見 着
我 就 撇 嘴 ? Why do you
always give me that dirty look
as soon as you see me?
PÍFA₃ 批 發 (TV) sell wholesale.
Tāmen-jiu-pīfā, bu-líng-mài.
他 們 就 批 發, 不 零
賣 . They only sell wholesale
not retail.
(N) wholesale.
PÍFA₃ 疲 乏 (SV) tired, fatigued.
Nǐ-juéde-pífá-ma? 你 覺 得
疲 乏 嗎 ? Do you feel tired?
PÍFU₃ 皮 膚 (N) skin (of a person). Tā-pífu hen-xì.他 皮 膚
很 細 . Her skin is very fine.
(cf: PÍ 皮 , PÍZI 皮 子).
PÌGU₄ 屁 股 (N) (1) buttocks. Dǎ-
tade-pìgu. 打 他 的 屁 股 ·
Spank him. (2) rear end of something. yānpìgu 煙 屁 股 cig-
arette butt.
PÍJIǓ₃ 啤 酒 (N) beer. (M: píng
瓶).
PÌN₄ 拼 (TV) (con. pīn-mìng 拼
命). fight to the point of even
giving up one's life. Wǒ-gēn-ni-
pīn-le. 我 跟 你 拼 了 ·
I'll fight you with all I've got.
PÍN₃ 拼 (TV) (1) piece or put
something together. Qǐng-nǐ-bǎ-
zhuōzi pīnzai-yíkuàir. 請 你
把 桌 子 拼 在 一 塊

兒 . Please put those tables together. (2) spell a word. Wǒ-
búhuì-pīn-nǐde-míngzi. 我 不
會 拼 你 的 名 字 . I
don't know how to spell your
name.
PÌN₄ 聘 (TV) (1) (con. pìn-qǐng
聘 請). employ, offer em-
ployment. Xuéxiào-pìnle-sān-
wei-xīn-jiàoyuán. 學 校 聘
了 三 位 新 教 員 .The
school appointed three new
teachers. (2) marry a daughter
to someone. Tā-bǎ-mǔ'er-pìn-le.
他 把 女 兒, 聘 了 . She
married off her daughter.
PÍNG₂ 憑 (TV) depend on, according to. Wǒmende-gōngzuo chuán-
píng-nǐ-le. 我 們 工 作 全
憑 你 了 . Our work totally
depends on you. Wǒmen-píng-
běnshi-zhèng-qián. 我 們 憑
本 事 掙 錢 . We make
our living based on our abilities.
Nǐ-píng-shénma dǎ-ren?你 憑
甚 麼 打 人 ? What right
do you have to beat people?
Píng-liángxin-ba. 憑 良 心
吧 . All right, do it according
to your conscience.
PÍNG₁ 平 (SV) (1) level, flat,
smooth. Dì-bu-píng, liú-diǎnr-
shén. 地 不 平, 留 點 兒
神 . Watch out, the ground is
not level. (2) be a draw (in a
match). Sān-bi-sān, píng. 三
比 三, 平 . It's a draw, three
to three.
(IV) have one's anger subside.
Tā-tīngle-zhèi-xie-huà, qì-jiu-

P

P

píng-le. 他聽了這些
話, 氣就平了 . After
he heard that, he cooled off.

(TV) tranquilize, pacify a country, an uprising, etc. Tā-bǎ-
tiānxìa-píng-le. 他把天下
平了 . He tranquilized the
whole world.

(AD) equally. Zhèi-shíkuai-qián
nimen-liǎngge-ren píng-fēn. 這
十塊錢你們兩個
人平分 . You two may
share this ten dollars equally.

PÍNG₃ 瓶 (M) bottle. yì-píng-jiǔ
一瓶酒 a bottle of wine.
(B) bottle, vase. dǎn-píng 膽
瓶 bladder-shaped vase.

PÍNG'AN₁ 平安 (SV) (1) safe,
secure. yílù-píng'ān 一路平
安 have a safe journey. Yìjia-
dàxiǎo dōu-hěn-píng'ān. 一家
大小都很平安. The
whole family is fine. (2) be
peaceful. Wǒ-zhèiyangr-zuò
xīnli-hěn-píng'ān. 我這樣
做心裏很平安 . By
doing this, I feel peaceful in my
mind.

PÍNGCHÁNG₁ 平常 (SV) (syn.
xúncháng 尋常) (opp. tèbié
特別) common, usual, ordi-
nary.
(MA) normally, most of the time.
Wǒ-píngcháng-bu-hē-jiǔ. 我平
常不喝酒 . I don't nor-
mally drink.

PÍNGDĚNG₁ 平等 (SV) equal
(of people). nán-nǚ-píngděng 男
女平等 men and women
are equal.

(N) equality. Méiyou-zhēnzhèng-
de-píngděng. 沒有真正
的平等 . There isn't real
equality.

PÍNGGUO₂ 蘋果 see PÍNGGUǑ
蘋果.
PÍNGGUǑ₂ 蘋果 or PÍNGGUO
蘋果 (N) apple. (M: zhī 隻).

PÍNGJING₃ 平靜 (SV) peaceful
and quiet. Hǎibiānrshang-hěn-
píngjing. 海邊兒上很
平靜 . It's very peaceful and
quiet along the seashore.

PÍNGJU₃ 憑據 (N) (1) proof, evidence. (2) documentation of
proof.

PÍNGJÚN₃ 平均 (SV) equal. Tā-
fēnde bu-píngjūn. 他分得
不平均 . He divided it un-
equally.
(MA) (1) on the average. Píngjūn
yíge-rén-wǔkuai-qián. 平均
一個人五塊錢 . On
the average, five dollars a
person. (2) equally. Qǐng-nǐ-
píngjūn-fèn-yifen. 請你平
均分一分 . Please di-
vide it equally.
(TV) average up. Wǒ-búhuì-píng-
jūn-zhèige-shùr. 我不會
平均這個數兒 . I
don't know how to average this
figure up.

PÍNG-LǏ₃ 評理 (VO) judge, be
an umpire of an argument. Qǐng-
nín-pingping-lǐ. 請您評評
理 . You judge which side is
right.

PÍNGLUN₃ 評論 (TV) discuss
critically. Tāmen-xǐhuan-píng-

lun-zhèngzhi. 他們喜歡
評論政治. They like to
discuss politics.
(N) editorial, commentator's or
critic's piece in a publication.
Wǒ-bu-guǎn bàoshang-de-píng-
lun-zěnmayàng. 我不管報
上的評論怎麼樣
I don't care what criticism ap-
pears in the newspaper.
PÍNGMÍN₃ 平民 (N) common
people.
PÍNGPÀN₃ 評判 (TV) judge,
decide (in a contest or a game).
Xiānsheng-píngpàn-wǒ-yíng-le.
先生評判我贏了.
The teacher decided that I won.
(N) (1) judge, referee (of a contest or game). (2) judgment.
PÍNGPĀNGQIÚ₃ 乒乓球 (N)
ping-pong (the ball or the game).
(M: pán 盤).
PÍNGXÌN₄ 平信 (N) ordinary
letter.(M: fēng 封).
PÍNGYÚAN₄ 平原 (N) plain. (M:
piàn 片).
PÍNGZI₃ 瓶子 (N) bottle, vase.
PÌNLǏ₅ 聘禮 (N) presents sent
at the betrothal.
PÌN-MÌNG₃ 拼命 (VO) fight to
the point of even giving up one's
life. Nǐ-búràng-wo-qù, wǒ-gēn-
ni-pīn-mìng. 你不讓我
去，我跟你拼命. If
you don't let me go, I'll fight
you with all I've got.
(AD) with all strength, desperately. Tā-pīn-mìng-pǎo. 他拼
命跑. He runs desperately.
PÍNQIÓNG₅ 貧窮 (N) poverty.

fǎn-pínqióng-jìhuà 反貧窮
計劃 anti-poverty plan.
PÌNSHŪ₃ 聘書 (N) letter of
appointment from the employer.
PĪNYĪN₂ 拼音 (N) (1) phonetic
spelling. pīnyīn-wénzì 拼音
文字 words written in phonetic system. (2) the official romanization system used in Mainland China.
ᵗPĪNZHÌ₅ 品質 (N) quality (of
a thing or person).
PĪPÀN₄ 批判 (TV) criticize.
Tā-bǎ-nèiběn-shū pīpànde-hěn-
lìhai. 他把那本書批
判得很厲害. He crit-
icized that book strongly.
(N) critique. (cf: PĪPING 批
評).
PĪPING₁ 批評 (TV) criticize.
Bíe-lǎo-pīping-ta. 別老批
評他. Don't always criticize
him.
(N) criticism. jiēshòu-pīping
接受批評 accept criti-
cism. (cf: PĪPÀN 批判).
PÍQI₁ 脾氣 (N) (1) temper. yǒu-
píqi 有脾氣 have a bad tem-
per. Tā-píqi hěn-dà. 他脾
氣很大. He's quick-tem-
pered. Bié-fā-píqi. 別發脾
氣. Control your temper.
Xiǎo-háizi nào-píqi. 小孩子
鬧脾氣. The small child
showed his temper. (2) temperament, disposition. Gèren-yǒu-
gèrende-píqi. 各人有各
人的脾氣. Each person
has his own temperament. (cf:
XÌNGQING 性情).

PÍQIÚ₃ 皮球 (N) ball (rubber or leather).

PĪZHǓN₃ 批准 (RV) approve, sanction, ratify. Nǐ-xiǎng wǒde-shēnqǐng néng-pīzhǔn-ma? 你想我的申請能批准嗎? Do you think my application can be approved?

PŌ₃ 潑 (TV) toss, throw liquid out of a container. Tā-bǎ-shuǐ pōzai-wǒ-shēngshang-le. 他把水潑在我身上了. He threw the water onto me (accidentally or purposely). (SV) shrewish. Tā-tàitai pō-jíle. 他太太潑極了. His wife is really shrewish. (N) shrewishness. sā-pō 撒潑 display shrewishness.

PÒ₁ 破 (IV) be damaged, broken, worn out, torn. Yīshang-pò-le. 衣裳破了. The clothes are torn. Bōli-pò-le. 玻璃破了. The glass is broken. (TV) (1) solve a case. Nèige-àn-zi 'yìtian-jiu-pò-le. 那個案子一天就破了. That case was solved within one day. (2) spend, use. Wǒ-dǎsuan pò-yìniánde-gōngfu xiě-zhèiben-shū. 我打算破一年的工夫寫這本書. I plan to spend a whole year to write this book. (3) break a large bill. Wǔkuai-qiánde-piào-zi nǐ-pòdekāi-pòbukāi? 五塊錢的票子你破得開破不開? Can you break this five dollar bill? (SV) bad, lousy. Tāde-qìchē

zhēn-pò. 他的汽車真破. This car is really a jalopy. Zhèisuo-pò-fángzi hái-yào-mài-yi'wànkuai-qián. 這所破房子還要賣一萬塊錢. This lousy house still sells for ten thousand dollars.

PÒFEI₃ 破費 (TV) spend money. Ràng-nin-pòfei. 讓您破費. You really shouldn't have spént all this money (as when one receives a gift or a treat from a friend).

PÒHUAI₃ 破壞 (TV) (1) spoil, ruin, destroy. Tā-'lǎo-xiǎng pòhuai-wǒde shìqing. 他老想破壞我的事情 He always tries to spoil my plans. Tā-zài-wo shàngsi-miàn-qián pòhuai-wo. 他在我上司面前破壞我. He tried to ruin me in front of my boss. (2) violate a rule, regulation, agreement, etc. Tā-cháng-pòhuai-guīju. 他常破壞規矩. He often violates the regulations.

PÒLÁN₂ 波蘭 (PW) Poland.

PÒLANG₄ 波浪 see BŌLANG 波浪

PÓPO₄ 婆婆 (N) (1) mother-in-law (husband's mother). (2) grandmother.

PŌR₃ 坡兒 (N) slope. shàng-pōr 上坡兒 go up the hill.

PŪ₃ 鋪 (TV) (1) spread out or over. pū-zhuōbù 鋪桌布 put a tablecloth on a table. (2) pave. pū-lù 鋪路 pave a road.

PŪ₄ 撲 (TV) (1) spring, pounce at,

throw <u>oneself on</u>. Māo-pū-niǎor
méi-pū-zháo. 貓 撲 鳥 兒．
沒 撲 着．The cat sprang
at the bird but missed. (2) apply
<u>powder with a powder puff</u>. pū-
fěn 撲 粉 put on powder.

'PŪBIÀN₂ 普 遍 (SV) prevailing,
widespread. Tiào-wǔ zài-Zhōngguo bútai-pǔbiàn. 跳 舞 在
中 國 不 太 普 遍．
Dancing isn't very widespread
in China.

PŪBÙ₃ 瀑 布 (N) waterfall.

PŪ-CHUÁNG₃ 鋪 床 (VO) make
a bed.

PŪKE₄ 撲 克 (N) (1) playing
card. (M: fù 副 , zhāng 張).
(2) poker (<u>the game</u>). (M: chǎng
場). dǎ-pūke 打 撲 克 play
poker.

PÚSA₅ 菩 薩 (N) (1) bodhisattva.
(M: wèi 位). (2) statue
of bodhisattva. (M: zūn 尊).

PÚTAO₂ 葡 萄 (N) grape.

PÚTAOJIǓ₃ 葡 萄 酒 (N) wine.
(<u>made of grapes</u>). (M: píng 瓶 ,
bēi 杯).

PÚTÁOYÁ₂ 葡 萄 牙 (PW) Por-
tugal.

PŪTŌNG₂ 撲 通 (ONO) (1) <u>sound
of something splashing in the</u>

<u>water</u>. Pūtōng, diàozai-shuǐli-
le. 撲 通 , 掉 在 水 裏 了．
Splash, it dropped into the water.
(2) <u>sound of something heavy</u>
<u>hitting the ground</u>. Pūtōng, diào-
zai-dìxia-le. 撲 通 , 掉 在
地 下 了．Crash, it hit the
floor.

PŪTONG₁ 普 通 (SV) common,
oridinary. Zhèizhong-fángzi
hěn-pǔtōng. 這 種 房 子 很
普 通．This kind of house is
very common.

(MA) usually, commonly. Zhèijiu-huà pǔtōng-bu-zènma-shuō.
這 句 話 普 通 不 這
麼 說．This sentence isn't
usually said this way.

PŪTŌNGHUÀ₁ 普 通 話 (N)
mandarin language <u>in ordinary</u>
<u>use and incorporating dialectical</u>
<u>peculiarities</u>.

PŪZHANG₃ 鋪 張 (IV) do something to make a big impression.
Nǐmende-hūnlǐ bùyīngdāng-nèn-
ma-pūzhang. 你 們 的 婚
禮 不 應 當 那 麼 鋪
張．Your wedding shouldn't be
so overdone.

PÙZI₁ 鋪 子 (N) store, shop. (M:
jiā 家).

P

Q

QĪ₄ 漆 (TV) paint, varnish. Bǎ-zhuōzi-qīqi. 把桌子漆漆. Paint the table. (N) (1) lacquer. (2) paint. shàng-qī 上漆 put on paint or lacquer. (cf: YÓUQĪ 油漆, YÓU 油).

QĪ₄ 沏 (TV) pour boiling water over something to make something for drinking. Qī-dianr-kā-fēi-hē. 沏點兒咖啡喝. Make some instant coffee to drink.

QĪ₃ 期 (M) (1) issue of a magazine. (2) period, stage.

QĪ₁ 七 (NU) seven, seventh. The tone may be changed into rising tone when it precedes a syllable with a falling tone. qītiān 七天 seven days. qí-liàng 七輛 seven cars.

QÍ₁ 七 see QĪ 七.

QÍ₂ 棋 (N) chess, checkers (and similar games). (M: pán 盤, bù 步). xià-yìpán-qí 下一盤棋 play a game of chess. Zhèibu-qí zǒucuò-le. 這步棋走錯了. lit. or fig. This was a wrong move.

QÍ₃ 騎 (TV) ride, straddle. qí-chē 騎車 ride a bicycle. qí-qiáng 騎牆 lit. or fig. sit astride a wall.

QĬ₁ 起 (IV) (1) go or come up, arise, get up. zǎo-zhuì-zǎo-qǐ 早睡早起 early to bed early to rise. Píqiú bù-qǐ-le. 皮球不起了. The rubber ball doesn't bounce. qǐ-yìsuo-fángzi 起一所房子 build a house. (2) develop, go on. qǐ-yíxīn 起疑心 develop suspicions. qǐ-zuòyong 起作用 the function is going on. qǐ-biànhua 起變化 the change is occurring. (3) develop, grow (of skin diseases). Liǎnshang-qǐle-hǎoxiē-hóng-diǎnr. 臉上起了好些紅點兒. Some red spots have developed on the face. (TV) (1) lift and remove something which is fastened. qǐ-dīngzi 起釘子 remove a nail. (2) start, begin. qǐ-gǎor 起稿兒 start a draft. qǐ-tóur 起頭兒 start off, in the beginning. (3) give a name to someone or something. Nǐde-míngzi shí-shéi-qǐ-de? 你的名子是誰起的? Who gave you your name? used after CV such as wàng 往, xiàng 向, etc., up. wàng-qǐ-tái 往起抬 lift up. (CV) Peip. from (a time, a place or a point of view). qǐ-jīntian-suàn 起今天算 start counting from today.

(RE) (1) (<u>con</u>. qǐlai 起來).
upward, up. Tā-náqi-jiǔ-jiu-hē.
他拿起酒就喝 . He
picked up the wine and drank.
(2) <u>in potential RV only</u> afford
to do <u>something</u>. mǎibuqǐ 買
不起 cannot afford to buy.
Wǒ-kànbuqǐ-diànyǐngr. 我看
不起電影兒 . I cannot
afford to see a movie. (3) <u>in
potential RV only</u>, up to <u>a certain standard</u>. Wǒ-kànbuqǐ-ta.
我看不起他 . I look
down on him.
(S) cóng...qǐ 從...起 from...
on. cóng-xiànzài-qǐ 從現在
起 from now on. cóng-zhèitiáo-
xiàn-qǐ 從這條線起
from this line on. (See: CÓNG
從).

QÌ₁ 氣 (N) (1) breath. (M: kǒu
口). Tā-chuǎnle-yikǒu-qì. 他
喘了一口氣 . He took
a breath. (2) air. Qiúli-de-qì
bu-gòu. 球裏的氣不
夠 . There is not enough air
in the ball. (3) anger. xīnli-yǒu-
qì 心裏有氣 build up anger
inside. Wǒ-bu-néng-shòu-zhèi-
yàngrde-qì. 我不能受
這樣兒的氣 . I can't
stand this kind of attitude (which
makes me angry).
(SV) angry. Tā-hěn-qì. 他很
氣 . He is very angry.
(TV) make <u>someone</u> angry. Bié-
qì-wo-le. 別氣我了 .
Don't make me angry.
(B) attitude, spirit. háiziqi 孩

子氣 childish attitude.

QÌ₄ 砌 (TV) build <u>with bricks or
rocks</u>. qì-qiáng 砌牆 · build a
wall.

QIĀ₃ 掐 (TV) (1) pinch. Tā-qiāle-
wo-yixia. 他掐了我一
下 . He pinched me. (2) stran-
gle <u>with one's fingers</u>. Nèige-
nǚren shi-qiāsi-de. 那個女
人是掐死的 . That
girl was strangled to death. (3)
break off, cut off. Bǎ-tāmende-
diànhuà qiā-le. 把他們的
電話掐了 . Their tele-
phone service was cut off. Tā-
qiāle-yiduor-huār. 他掐了
一朵花兒 . He picked a
flower.

QIÁ₄ 卡 <u>see</u> QIǍ 卡 .

QIǍ₄ 卡 <u>or</u> QIÁ 卡 (TV) get
caught (<u>as when an obstruction
catches a moving object</u>). Chuāng-
hu-qiǎzhu-le, kāibukāi-le. 窗
戶卡住了, 開不開
了 . The window is stuck, it
can't be opened. Gútou-qiǎle-
sǎnzi-le. 骨頭卡了嗓
子了 . A bone got caught in
his throat.

QIÀHǍO₄ 恰好 (MA) opportunely,
fortunately. (<u>syn</u>. qiàqiǎo 恰
巧). Qiàhǎo-ta-lái-le. 恰好
他來了 . Fortunately he
came.

QIÁN₃ 鉛 (N) (1) lead (<u>the metal</u>).
(2) pencil lead. Wǒde-bǐli-méi-
qiān-le. 我筆裏没鉛
了 . There isn't any lead in my
pencil.

QIÁN₃ 牽 (TV) (1) lead <u>or</u> pull

Q

along <u>on a rope</u>. Bǎ-niú-qiānlai. 把牛牽來. Lead the cow here. (2) hold onto <u>a person's hand or clothes</u>. Háizi qiānzhe-ta-mǔqinde-yīshang. 孩子牽著他母親的衣裳. The child is holding on to his mother's clothes.

QIĀN₁ 千 (NU) thousand.

QIÁN₁ 錢 (N) (1) money. (M: bǐ 筆, kuài 塊, máo 毛, fēn 分). Tā-yǒu-qián. 他有錢. He is rich. <u>or</u> He has money. (2) coin. Zhèige-qián bú-shi-tóng-zuò-de. 這個錢不是銅作的. This coin is not made of copper.

QIÁN₁ 前 (L) (1) front, ahead. qiánménr 前門兒 front door. wàng-qián-kàn 往前看 look ahead. (2) ago. liǎngnian-qián 兩年前 two years ago. (3) before. chī-fàn-qián 吃飯前 before eating. (4) former, previous. qiánrèn 前任 predecessor. (SP) (1) past (<u>time immediately preceding the present</u>). qián-liangnian 前兩年 the past two years. (2) first <u>part of something</u>. qián-sānge-lǐbài 前三個禮拜 the first three weeks. qiánbànběn 前半本 first half of the book.

QIÁN₁ 淺 (SV) (<u>opp</u>. shēn 深). (1) shallow, superficial. Shuǐ hěn-qiǎn 水很淺. The water is shallow. Zhèiben-shū hěn-qiǎn 這本書很淺. This book isn't very deep. Tāde-

xuéwen-hěn-qiǎn. 他的學問很淺. His knowledge is superficial. (2) short (<u>in duration or view</u>). Wǒ-zài-zhèr-gōng-zuò-de shíjian hěn-qiǎn. 我在這兒工作的時間很淺. I didn't work here very long. Tāde yǎnguāng-tài-qiǎn. 他的眼光太淺. He is too short-sighted. (3) light (<u>in color</u>). qiǎn-lán 淺藍 light blue. Yánse tài-qiǎn. 顏色太淺. The color is too light.

QIÀN₂ 欠 (TV) (1) owe. (<u>syn</u>. gāi 該, duǎn 短). Wǒ-qiàn-ta-qián. 我欠他錢. I owe him money. Tā-qiànle-hěn-duō-zhàng. 他欠了很多賬. He has a lot of debts. (2) lack, short of. (<u>syn</u>. quē 缺). Zhèi-zhāng-huàr qiàn-dianr-hóng-yán-se. 這張畫兒欠點兒紅顏色. This picture lacks a little red. (3) deserve <u>punishment</u>. Zhèi-háizi qiàn-dǎ. 這孩子欠打. This child deserves a spanking.

QIÁNBANTIANR₃ 前半天兒 (TW) morning, forenoon.

QIÁNBÈI₄ 前輩 (N) (1) older generation. (2) person of the older generation. Tā-shi-lǎo-qiánbèi. 他是老前輩 He is of the older generation. (<u>complimentary statement made about an older person</u>).

QIÁNBǏ₁ 鉛筆 (N) pencil. (M: zhī 枝).

QIÁNBIANR₁ 前邊兒 <u>or</u> QIÁN-TOU 前頭 <u>or</u> QIÁNMIAN 前

面 (PW) front or front part of something. fángzi-qiánbianr 房子 前 邊 兒 in front of the house or the front part of the house.

QIĀN-DÀO₄ 簽 到 (VO) sign in to work.

QIÁNFĀNG₃ 前 方 (PW) front (military).

QIĀNG₁ 鎗 (N) (1) spear, lance. (2) rifle, pistol. (M: zhī 枝, gǎn 桿). fàng-qiān 放 鎗 shoot a gun.

QIÁNG₁ 牆 (N) wall. (M: dào 道, dǔ 堵).

QIÁNG₄ 強 (SV) (1) strong, powerful. (opp. ruǎn 軟, ruò 弱). Tāmen-de-lìliang hěn-qiáng. 他 們 的 力 量 很 強. They are very powerful. (2) superior, better. Tā-bǐ-wǒ-qiáng. 他 比 我 強. He is better than I.

QIĂNG₃ 搶 (1) rob. qiǎng-yínháng 搶 銀 行 rob a bank. (2) snatch. Tā-qiǎng-wǒde-qián. 他 搶 我 的 錢. He snatched my money. (3) make an attempt to get ahead of someone else, beat out. Ràng-tāmen-xiān-zǒu, bié-qiǎng. 讓 他 們 先 走, 別 搶. Let them go first, don't try to beat them out.

QIĀNGBÌ₂ 鎗 斃 (TV) shoot to death.

QIĂNGBIÀN₄ 強 辯 (IV) argue stubbornly or obstinately.

QIÁNGDÀ₅ 強 大 (SV) strong and great (of an organization).

QIÁNGDAO₁ 強 盜 (N) robber.

QIÁNGDIÀO₄ 強 調 (TV) emphasize, stress a point.

QIÁNGDIÀOR₄ 腔 調 兒 (N) (1) tune, melody. (2) tone of speech.

QIÁNGPO₃ 強 迫 (TV) force, compel someone to do something. Bié-qiǎngpo-ta-zuò. 別 強 迫 他 作. Don't force him to do it.

QIÁNHÒU₃ 前 後 (PW) front and back. Xuéxiào qiánhòu-dōu-yǒu-fànguǎnr. 學 校 前 後 都 有 飯 館 兒. There are restaurants in front and back of the school.

(AD) altogether from the beginning to the end. Tā-qiánhòu jiè-gei-wo-yibǎikuai-qián. 他 前 後 借 給 我 一 百 塊 錢. He lent me one hundred dollars altogether.

QIÁNJÌN₂ 前 進 (SV) progressive. Tāde-sīxiang hen-qiánjìn. 他 的 思 想 很 前 進. His ideas are progressive. (IV) go forward, progress.

QIÁNMIAN₁ 前 面 see QIÁN-BIANR 前 邊 兒.

QIĀN-MÍNG₂ 簽 名 (VO) sign one's name.

QIÁNNIAN₁ 前 年 (TW) year before last year.

QIĀNNIÚHUĀ₃ 牽 牛 花 (N) morning glory. (syn. lǎbahuār 喇 叭 花 兒). (M: kē 棵, duǒ 朵).

QIÁNPAI₃ 前 排 (N) the front row.

QIÁNPIÀOZI₁ 錢 票 子 (N) bank note. (M: zhāng 張).

Q

Q

QIÁNSHUǏTǏNG₃ 潜水艇 (N) submarine.

QIÁNTIAN₁ 前天 (TW) day before yesterday.

QIÁNTOU₁ 前頭 see QIÁN-BIANR 前邊兒.

QIÁNTU₃ 前途 (N) future. Wǒ-méi-you-qiántu. 我没有前途. I have no future.

QIĀNWÀN₂ 千萬 (MA) by all means, be sure. Nǐ-qiānwàn-bié-zǒu. 你千萬別走. Be sure not to leave.

QIÁNXIÀN₃ 前綫 (N) front line (in a war).

QIĀNXU₄ 謙虛 (SV) modest (in feeling and/or manner). Zhèi-ge-rén qiānxu-jíle. 這個人謙虛極了. This person is extremely modest. (cf: XŪ-XĪN 虛心).

QIÀN-ZHÀI₃ 欠債 (VO) owe money, have debts. Tā-qiànle-bushǎode-zhài. 他欠了不少的債. He has quite a few debts.

QIĀN-ZÌ₂ 簽字 (VO) sign one's name. Tā-bù-qiān-zì wǒmen-bù-néng-lǐng-qián. 他不簽字我們不能領錢. If he doesn't sign, we cannot get the money.

QIÁNZI₅ 箝子 (N) pliers. (M: bǎ 把).

QIĀO₃ 敲 (TV) (1) beat or strike something. qiāo-ló 敲鑼 beat a gong. qiāo-mén 敲門 knock on a door. (2) (con. qiāo-zhú-gàng 敲竹槓). gyp someone. Tā-ràng-ren-qiāole-yibi. 他讓人敲了一筆.

He was gypped out of a sum of money by somebody.

QIÁO₂ 橋 (N) (1) bridge. (M: zuò 座). (2) (con. qiáopái 橋牌). bridge (card game). (M: chǎng 場). dǎ-qiáo 打橋 play bridge.

QIÁO₄ 瞧 (TV) Peip. look, see. (cf: KÀN 看).

QIǍO₃ 巧 (SV) (1) skilful, ingenious. Tāde-shǒu-hen-qiǎo. 他的手很巧. She is very skilful with her hand. (2) coincident, timely, opportune. Zhēn-qiǎo, wǒ-yi-chūqu jiu-pèngjian-ta-le. 真巧, 我一出去就碰見他了. What a coincidence, as soon as I went out I ran into him.

QIǍOKELÌ₄ 巧克力 (N) chocolate.

QIǍOMIÀO₃ 巧妙 (SV) clever, ingenious (of method, way of thinking). Zhèige-fázi hěn-qiǎo-miao. 這個法子很巧妙. This method is very clever.

QIÁOMÍN₄ 僑民 (N) people overseas.

QIÁOPÁI₄ 橋牌 (N) bridge (card game). dǎ-qiáopái 打橋牌 play bridge.

QIÀOPI₄ 俏皮 (SV) cute, clever. Tāde-yàngzi hěn-qiàopi. 他的樣子很俏皮. Her appearance is very cute. Tā-shuōde-huà hěn-qiàopi. 他説的話很俏皮. What he said is very clever.

QIÀOPIHUÀR₄ 俏皮話兒 (N) witty remark.

QIĀOQIĀORDE₅ 俏俏兒的

(AD) quietly.

QIĀOZHÀ₅ 敲詐 (TV) blackmail.

QIÀQIĂO₃ 恰巧 (MA) by a happy coincidence. (syn. qiàhǎo 恰好).

QĬBUSHI₃ 豈不是 used for a negative rhetorical question, isn't it that. Nà-qǐbushi-máfan? 那豈不是麻煩？Isn't it troublesome?

QĪ-CHÁ₃ 沏茶 (VO) make tea.

QÌCHĒ₁ 汽車 (N) automobile. (M: liàng 輛). kāi-qìchē 開汽車 drive an automobile.

QǏCHŪ₃ 起初 (MA) at first. Qǐchū ta-bu-kěn. 起初他不肯. He was not willing at first.

QÍCÌ₃ 其次 (PW) second, next. Dìyī-shi-xué-shuō-huà, qícì-shi-niàn-shū, zài-qícì-cái-shi-xiě-zì. 第一是學説話,其次是念書,再其次才是寫字. The first thing is to learn to speak, second is reading and next is writing. Yàojǐn-shi-wǒmen-tántan, chī-fàn dào-zài-qícì. 要緊是我們談談,吃飯倒在其次. The important thing is that we can have a chat, eating is secondary.

QÍDĂO₃ 祈禱 (TV) pray.

QIĒ₃ 切 (TV) cut downward with a knife, slice, carve. qiē-dàngāo 切蛋糕 cut the cake. qiē-ròu 切肉 cut the meat.

QIÈ₄ 怯 (SV) (1) fearful, hesitant. Tā-dìyícì-jiǎngyǎn, xīnli-yǒu-diǎnr-qiè. 他第一次講演心裏有點兒怯. The first time he gave a speech, he was a little fearful. (2) used to describe a rural person's action or speech, local, rustic. Xiāng-xia-rén hěn-qiè. 鄉下人很怯. Country people are very provincial. Tāde-kǒuyin qiè. 他的口音怯. His accent is rustic.

QIESHI₄ 切實 (SV) accurate and thorough. Tā-zuò-shì hěn-qiè-shi. 他作事很切實. When he does some work, it is very accurate and thorough. (AD) accurately and thoroughly. Děi-qìshi-yánjiu-yixia. 得切實研究一下. We must study it accurately and thoroughly.

QIEZI₅ 茄子 (N) eggplant.

QǏFĀ₄ 啟發 (TV) enlighten, make someone think and understand. (N) enlightenment.

QǏFĒI₂ 起飛 (IV) take off (for an airplane).

QĪFU₁ 欺負 (TV) take advantage of someone. Bié-qīfu-háizi. 別欺負孩子. Don't take advantage of children.

QǏGĂN₃ 豈敢 (IV) used to answer a compliment, (lit. how could I dare to assume such an honor?) you flatter me. A: Nín-shì-wǒde-lǎoshī. B: 'Qǐgǎn-qǐ-gǎn. A: 您是我的老師. B: 豈敢豈敢. A: You are my teacher. B: That is not right. (cf: BÙGĂNDĀNG 不.

敢當).

QÍGUAI₁ 奇怪 (SV) strange.
Zhèige-hěn-qíguai. 這個很
奇怪. This is very strange.
(TV) wonder about. Wǒ-qíguai-
ta-wèi-shénma-gěi-qián. 我
奇怪他為甚麼給
錢. I wonder why he paid.

QÌHOU₃ 氣候 (N) climate.

QĪJIĀN₃ 期間 (N) period (of
time). zài-nèige-qījiān 在那
個期間 in that period.

QǏJÌNR₃ 起勁兒 (SV) eager,
enthusiastic. Tā-zuòde-hěn-qǐ-
jìnr. 他作得很起勁
兒. He worked very enthusiastically. (cf: SHÀNGJÌNR 上
勁兒).

QǏLAI₁ 起來 (RV) (1) rise, get
up. Tā-gāng-qǐlai. 他剛起
來. He just got up. (2) start.
Gémìng-qǐbulái. 革命起不
來. The revolution cannot
start.

(RE) (1) upward, up. náqilai 拿
起來 pick up. zuòqilai 坐
起來 sit up. (2) up (indi-
cates finishing or completing an
action). jiāqilai 加起來 add
up. suóqilai 鎖起來 lock up.
(3) start, begin. kūqilai-le 哭
起來了 started crying. Tā-
yòu-niànqi-shū-lai-le. 他又
念起書來了. He
started to study again.

QÍLIANG₅ 淒涼 (SV) (1) sad,
lonely. (2) deserted.

QǏMǍ₂ 起碼 (IV) start from a
certain number. shíkuai-qián-
qǐmǎ 十塊錢起碼

ten dollars and up.
(MA) at least. Nǐ-qǐmǎ děi-dà-
xué-bìyè. 你起碼得大
學畢業. You must at least
be graduated from college.

QǏ-MÍNGZI₂ 起名子 (VO)
give a name. Shéi-géi-ni-qǐde-
míngzi? 誰給你起的
名子 ? Who gave you your
name?

QĪN₄ 親 (TV) kiss, caress. Nǐ-
qīnqin-māmade-liǎn. 你親
親媽媽的臉. Give
your mother a kiss (on her face).

QÍN₄ 琴 (N) (1) string instrument.
(2) a certain type of Chinese
instrument with seven strings,
Chinese lute. (M: zhāng 張).

QĪN'ÀIDE₂ 親愛的 (N) be-
loved, dear.

QĪNBǏ₄ 親筆 (N) one's own
handwriting.

QÍNCÀI₄ 芹菜 (N) celery. (M:
bǎr 把兒).

QÍNCHAO₃ 秦朝 (TW) Ch'in
dynasty.

QĪNG₃ 青 (SV) (1) green (of grass,
plants, mountain, etc.). qīng-cǎo
青草 green grass. (2) blue
(of sky, granite, etc.). qīng-tiān
青天 blue sky. (3) black (of
cloth, hair, a bruise). qīng-bù-
xié 青布鞋 black cloth shoes.
(4) young (of a person). Tā-niánji-
hěn-qīng. 他年紀很青.
He is very young (in age).

QĪNG₁ 輕 (SV) (opp. zhòng 重)
(1) light (in weight). (opp. chén
沉). Zhèige-xiāngzi hěn-qīng.
這個箱子很輕. This

trunk is very light. (2) slight (not serious).

Tāde-bìng bu-qīng. 他 的 病 不 輕. His illness is rather serious. (3) light, not much.

Wǒ-zhèi-xuéqīde-kè hěn-qīng. 我 這 學 期 的 課 很 輕. My course load is very light this semester.

(AD) (l) lightly, without much regard. Nǐ-bié-qīng-kàn-zhèige-shì. 你 別 輕 看 這 個 事. Don't look at this thing lightly. (2) lightly, softly. Qīng-qīngde-dǎ-ta-yixia. 輕 輕 的 打 他 一 下. Hit him once softly.

QĪNG₂ 清 (SV) clear. Shuǐ-hěn-qīng. 水 很 清. Water is clear.

(TV) clear up an account. qīng-zhàng 清 賬 clear up an account.

(RE) (con. qīngchu 清 楚). clear. zhuōbuqīng 説 不 清 cannot say clearly. Xīngxing shǔbuqīng. 星 星 數 不 清. The stars cannot be counted clearly. Tāde-zhàng-hái-méi-huánqīng-ne. 他 的 賬 還 沒 還 清 呢. His account has not been cleared up yet.

QĪNG₃ 晴 (IV) clear (of the sky or weather).

QĪNG₁ 請 (TV) (l) ask, invite. Shéi-qīng-kè? 誰 請 客? Who is inviting guests? Tā-bu-qīng-wo, wǒ-bu-qù. 他 不 請 我, 我 不 去. If he doesn't invite me, I won't go. Bǎ-ta-

qīngjinlai. 把 他 請 進 來. Ask him to come in. (2) treat someone. Wǒmen děi-qǐngqing-ta. 我 們 得 請 請 他. We have to treat him. (3) engage the services of someone, hire professional personnel or white-collar workers. Xuéxiào-yòu-qǐngle-yiwèi-xīn-jiàoyuán. 學 校 又 請 了 一 位 新 教 員. The school has hired a new teacher. (cf: GÙ 雇). (4) apply for. qǐng-jiǎngxuéjīn 請 獎 學 金 apply for a scholarship.

(AV) (l) please do. Nín-qǐng. 您 請. Please help yourself. or Please go ahead. (2) please. Qǐngjìnlai. 請 進 來. Please come in.

QĪNGBAI₄ 清 白 (SV) unsullied (of family origin or one's be-havior).

QĪNGBIAN₄ 輕 便 (SV) light and easy to handle.

QĪNGBO₄ 輕 薄 (SV) frivolous (of a man in a love affair).

QĪNGCÀI₂ 青 菜 (N) green veg-etable. (M: kē 棵).

QĪNGCHAO₃ 清 朝 (TW) Ch'ing dynasty.

QĪNGCHU₁ 清 楚 (SV) (l) clear, intelligible. Tā-shuō-huà měi-yíge-zì dōu-shuōde-hěn-qīngchu. 他 説 話 每 一 個 字 都 説 得 很 清 楚. Every word he says is very clear. Zhèizhang-xiàngpiānr hěn-qīngchu. 這 張 像 片 兒 很 清 楚. This

Q

Q

photograph is very clear. Tāde-zhàng hěn-qīngchu. 他 的 賬 很 清 楚 . His account is kept very clearly. (2) well organized. Tāde-shū bǎide-hěn-qīngchu. 他 的 書 擺 得 很 清 楚 . He arranged his books in good order.

QĪNGDAN₄ 清 淡 (SV) (1) light (of food). Chī-yidianr-qīngdan-de. 吃 一 點 兒 清 淡 的. Eat some light food. (2) slow (of business). Shēngyi hen-qīngdan. 生 意 很 清 淡 . Business is very slow.

QĪNGDÀN₄ 氫 彈 (N) hydrogen bomb.

QĪNGDĀNR₄ 清 單 兒 (N) clearly itemized list. kāi-qīngdānr 開 清 單 兒 make a clearly itemized list.

QĪNGDǍO₃ 青 島 (PW) Ch'ingtao.

'QÍNGGǍN₂ 情 感 (N) friendly feeling, friendship. (syn. 'gān-qíng 感 情).

QĪNGGŌNGYE₃ 輕 工 業 (N) light industry.

QĪNGHǍI₄ 青 海 (PW) (1) Tsinghai province. (2) Ching Hai Lake.

QÌNGHE₃ 慶 賀 (TV) celebrate. (syn. qìngzhu 慶 祝). qìnghe-xīnnián 慶 賀 新 年 celebrate New Year. Tā-dé-jiǎng-le. Wǒmen-yīngdāng-gěi-ta qìnghe-qinghe. 他 得 獎 了, 我 們 應 當 給 他 慶 賀 慶 賀 . He got a reward. We should celebrate.

QĪNGHUÍ₃ 請 回 used by a guest when the host accompanies him

to the door, don't accompany me any farther.

QĪNG-JIÀ₂ 請 假 (VO) request leave, ask for time off. Tā-yào-qǐng-yitian-jià. 他 要 請 一 天 假 . He wants to ask for one day's leave.

QĪNGJIÀO₃ 請 教 (TV) a polite form to ask someone's advice. Wǒ-gēn-nín-'qǐngjiao-qǐngjiao. 我 跟 您 請 教 請 教 . I would like to ask your advice about something. Wǒ-qǐngjiao-nin-yíjian-shì. 我 請 教 您 一 件 事 . I have something I would like advice about from you. Zhèizhong-shi nǐ-zuìhǎo-qǐngjiao-tā. 這 種 事 你 最 好 請 教 他 . You'd better ask his advice about this kind of thing. Qǐngjiào, zhèige-zì niàn-shénma? 請 教, 這 個 字 念 甚 麼 ? May I ask how this word is pronounced?

QĪNGJIÉ₅ 清 潔 (SV) clean.

QĪNGJING₁ 清 靜 (SV) quiet. Zhèr-zhen-qīngjing. 這 兒 真 清 靜 . It's very quiet here.

QĬNG-KÈ₁ 請 客 (VO) (1) invite guests, have a party. Tā-qǐngle-hěn-duō-kè. 他 請 了 很 多 客 . He has invited many guests. (2) treat some one to a meal, a party, etc. Wǒmen-kàn-diànyǐngr-qu, wǒ-qǐng-kè. 我 們 看 電 影 兒 去 我 請 客 . Let's go to a movie, I'll treat.

QÍNGKUANG₄ 情 況 (N) situation, circumstances. (cf: JĪNGKUANG

景況 ZHUÀNGKUANG 狀況).

QĪNGLI₃ 清理 (TV) lit. or fig. take care of and clear up something. Bǎ-zhèi-jitian-lái-de-xìn qīngli-yixia. 把這幾天來的信清理一下. Clear up the letters which have arrived these past few days.

QĪNGMIAN₅ 情面 (N) friendly feeling. Tā-bu-jiǎng-qíngmian. 他不講情面. He doesn't pay attention to friendly feelings.

QĪNGNIAN₂ 青年 (N) youth (a person or a period of time). Nèishihou wǒ hái-shi-qīngniàn. 那時候我還是青年. At that time I was still a youth.

QĪNGNIANHUÌ₃ 青年會 (N) YMCA or YWCA. Wǒ-zhùzaiqīngnianhuì. 我住在青年會. I stayed at the Y.

QĪNGQÌ₄ 輕氣 (N) hydrogen.

QĪNGQĪNGRDE₄ 輕輕兒的 (AD) lightly, slightly.

QĪNGQÌQIÚ₄ 輕氣球 (N) balloon. (syn. qìqiú 氣球).

'QĪNGQIÚ₂ 請求 (TV) request, petition. (N) request, petition. Wǒ-yǒuyige-'qīngqiú. 我有一個請求. I have a request.

QĪNGR₄ 清兒 (N) white of the egg. (opp. huángr 黃兒).

QĪNGREN₃ 情人 (N) lover.

QĪNGSHÌ₄ 輕視 (TV) (1) look down on. Tā-qīngshì-wo. 他輕視我. He looks down on me. (2) underestimate. Wǒmen-bunéng-qīngshi-dírende-lìliang. 我們不能輕視敵人的力量. We must not underestimate the enemy's strength.

'QĪNGSHÌ₃ 請示 (TV) ask for instructions from a higher authority. Wǒmen-dei-gēn-ta 'qīngshi. 我們得跟他請示. We must ask instructions from him.

QĪNGSHŪ₃ 情書 (N) love letter. (M: fēng 封).

QĪNGSŌNG₃ 輕鬆 (SV) carefree, relaxed. (opp. jǐnzhang 緊張). Tā-hǎoxiang hen-qīngsōngdeyàngzi. 他好像很輕鬆的樣子. He has a very relaxed appearance.

QĪNGSUÀN₃ 清算 (TV) (lit. settle accounts clearly) purge. Bǎ-ta-qīngsuàn-le. 把他清算了. He was purged.

QĪNGTĀI₅ 青苔 (N) moss.

QÍNG-TIĀN₂ 晴天 (VO) clear (of the sky). (opp. yīn-tiān 陰天). Tiān-qíng-le. 天晴了. The sky is clear. (N) clear day. Jīntiān shi-qíngtiān. 今天是晴天. It's clear today.

QĪNGTIĚ₃ 請帖 (N) written invitation. (M: zhāng 張, fènr 份兒). xià-qīngtiě 下請帖 or fā-qǐngtiě 發請帖 send out invitations.

QĪNGTÍNG₅ 蜻蜓 (N) dragonfly. (M: zhī 隻).

QĪNGWĀ₅ 青蛙 (N) frog. (M: zhī 隻).

Q

Q

QĬNGWÈN$_2$ 請問 used to introduce a question, may I ask you.
Qǐngwèn, huǒzhēzhàn-zài-nǎr?
請問,火車站在那
兒? Could you please tell me
where the railroad station is?

'QĪNGXĬNG$_5$ 清醒 (SV) clear-
headed, sober.

QÍNGXING$_1$ 情形 (N) situation,
condition, circumstances. Tāde-
qíngxing zěnmayàng? 他的情
形怎麼樣? How is his
situation?

QÍNGXU$_3$ 情緒 (N) mood, emotion. nào-qíngxu 鬧情緒
disturbed by emotion. Tā-zhèi-
liangtian-'qíngxu-bu-hǎo. 他這
兩天情緒不好. He
has not been in a good mood
these couple of days.

QĪNGYÌ$_4$ 輕易 (AD) often used
with negative. (1) often. Tā-qǐng-
yi-bu-dǎ-qiú. 他輕易不
打球. He doesn't play ball
often. (2) casually. Tā-bu-qing-
yi-qiú-rén. 他不輕易求
人. He doesn't ask favors
from others casually.

QÍNGYUAN$_3$ 情願 (AV) (1) prefer to, would rather. Wǒ-qíng-
yuan-bu-yào-qián. 我情願
不要錢. I prefer not to
take the money. (2) be willing to.
Nèiyangr-bàn, wǒ-bu-qíngyuan.
那樣兒辦,我不情
願. I am not willing to do it
that way.

QĪNGZǍOR$_4$ 清早兒 (TW)
early morning.

QĪNGZHÒNG$_3$ 輕重 (N) weight.

Zhèige-píbāode-qīngzhòng zěnmayang? 這個皮包的
輕重怎麼樣? What is
the weight of this suitcase? Tā-
shuō-huà bu-zhīdao-qīngzhòng.
他說話不知道輕
重. He doesn't understand the
weight of what he says.

QÌNGZHU$_3$ 慶祝 (TV) celebrate.
(syn. qìnghe 慶賀).

QĬNGZUÒ$_2$ 請坐 (IV) please
sit down.

QÍNJIN$_4$ 勤謹 (SV) diligent,
industrious.

QĪNLUÈ 侵略 (TV) invade.
Riběn-qīnlüè-Zhōngguo. 日本
侵略中國. Japan in-
vaded China.
(N) invasion.

QĪNMI$_4$ 親密 (SV) intimate,
close (of personal relationship).

QĪNPÈI$_4$ 欽佩 (TV) admire
someone. Wǒ-fēichang-qīnpèi-
ta. 我非常欽佩他. I
admire him very much.

QĪNQI$_3$ 親戚 (N) relative (excluding members of his own
family). Tāmen-shi-qīnqi. 他
們是親戚. They are
relatives.

QĪNRE$_3$ 親熱 (SV) warm, close
(of emotional feeling toward people). Tāmen-háojinián-méi-jiàn-
le, jiànzhao-hěn-qīnre. 他們
好幾年沒見了,見
着很親熱. They hadn't
seen each other for several
years, when they met, they felt
very close.

'QĪNZÌ$_2$ 親自 (AD) personally,

by oneself. Qián, shi-wǒ-qīnzì-jiāogei-ta-de. 錢, 是 我 親 自 交 給 他 的. I handed over the money myself.

QIÓNG₂ 窮 (SV) poor (not rich). (opp. kuò 潤). 'qióng-rén 窮 人 poor people. (AD) aimlessly, pointlessly. qióng-shuō 窮 說 talk aimlessly.

QIÓNGKǓ₅ 窮 苦 (SV) poor and suffer hardship.

QIÓNGMÁNG₄ 窮 忙 (SV) pointlessly busy. Wǒ-zhěngtiān-qióngmáng. 我 整 天 窮 忙. I am busy aimlessly all the time.

QÌPAI₃ 氣 派 (N) manner, style, air. (syn. pàitóur 派 頭 兒). Tāde-qìpai-hěn-dà. 他 的 氣 派 很 大. His style is very grand.

QÍPÁOR₃ 旗 袍 (N) a long Chinese dress for women. (M: jiàn 件).

'QÍPIÀN₃ 欺 騙 (TV) cheat. 'Qī-piàn-'rén-de-rén yě-shòu-ren-'qīpiàn. 欺 騙 人 的 人 也 受 人 欺 騙. The one who cheats people is also cheated by others.

QÍ-QIÁNG₄ 騎 牆 (VO) lit. or fig. straddle a wall.

QÌQIĀNG₅ 氣 鎗 (N) air gun.

QÌQIÚ₃ 氣 球 (N) balloon. (syn. qīngqìqiú 輕 氣 球).

QÍQUAN₃ 齊 全 (SV) complete. Zhèitao-pánzi-wǎn bù-qíquan-le. 這 套 盤 子 盌 不 齊 全 了. This set of dishes is not complete anymore.

QÌ-QUÁN₄ 棄 權 (VO) give up one's rights.

QÌSHĒN₃ 起 身 (VO) start a trip, take off. Nǐ-shi-něitian-qǐde-shēn? 你 是 那 天 起 的 身? Which day did you start your trip?

QÍSHÍ₃ 其 實 (MA) as a matter of fact, in fact, actually. Wǒ-yǐwei ta-zhīdào, qíshí tā-bù-zhīdào. 我 以 為 他 知 道, 其 實 他 不 知 道 I thought he knew, actually he didn't.

QÍSHÌ₃ 歧 視 (TV) have prejudice against. bù-qíshì-wàiguo-ren 不 歧 視 外 國 人 have no prejudice against foreigners. (N) prejudice. zhǒngzú-qíshì 種 族 歧 視 racial prejudice.

QǏ-SHÌ₃ 起 誓 (VO) swear, make a solemn statement. Wǒ-méi-shuō, wǒ-kéyi-qǐ-shì. 我 没 説, 我 可 以 起 誓. I didn't say it, I can swear.

QÌSHUǏ₂ 汽 水 (N) seltzer water, soda. (M: píng 瓶).

QÍTĀ₂ 其 他 (N) the others. Zhèige-hǎo, qítā-dou-tài-dà. 這 個 好, 其 他 都 太 大. This one is good, all the others are too big. (cf: QÍYÚ 其 餘).

QǏ-TÓUR₃ 起 頭 兒 (VO) start something. Wǒ-gěi-nǐ-qǐ-ge-tóur-ba. 我 給 你 起 個 頭 兒 吧. Let me start it for you.

Q

(MA) at first, in the beginning. Qǐ-tóur wǒ-bu-zhīdào. 起頭 我 不 知道 . At first I didn't know.

QǏTÚ₄ 企圖 (TV) intend, plan. (N) intention, plan. Tā-méiyou-nèizhong-qǐtú. 他 没有 那 種 企圖 . He doesn't have that kind of intention.

QIÚ₁ 球 (N) (1) ball. dǎ-qiú 打 球 play ball. jiē-qiú 接 球 catch a ball. tī-qiú 踢 球 kick a ball. (2) sphere, ball-like object. tiě-qiú 鐵 球 shot put. dì-qiú 地球 earth, globe or bowling.

QIÚ₂ 求 (TV) (1) beg, implore. Tā-guìxia-qiú-wo. 他 跪 下 求 我 . He knelt down and begged me. (2) ask someone for a favor. Wǒ-qiú-nín-dianr-shì. 我 求 您 點 兒 事 . I'll ask you for a favor. Wǒ-qiú-ta-tì-wo mǎi-dianr-dōngxi. 我 求 他 替 我 買 點 兒 東 西 . I asked him to buy a little something for me. (3) seek for. qiú-jìnbù 求 進步 seek for progress.

QIÚCHǍNG₃ 球場 (N) ball field.

QIÚFÀN₄ 囚犯 (N) prisoner, prison inmate.

QIŪQIAN₄ 秋千 (N) swing. dǎ-qiūqian 打 秋 千 play on a swing.

QIŪTIAN₁ 秋天 (TW) autumn.

QIÚ-XUÉ₃ 求學 (VO) (lit. seek for learning) devote oneself to study. Wǒ-shi-dào-zhèr-lai-qiú-xué-lai-de. 我 是 到 這 兒

來 求 學 來 的 . I came here for the sole purpose of studying.

QÌWEI₃ 氣味 (N) smell. Zhèige-qìwei hěn-nánwén. 這 個 氣 味 很 難 聞 . This smell is very bad.

QĪXIAN₄ 期限 (N) deadline. Qīxiàn-hěn-jìn-le. 期 限 很 近 了 . The deadline is near.

QǏXIĀN₃ 起先 (TW) before, previously, earlier. Tā-qǐxiān-shì-zènma-shuō-de. 他 起 先 是 這 麼 說 的 . He said it this way before.

QÌXIÀNG₅ 氣象 (N) meteorological phenomena.

QÍ-XĪN₃ 齊心 (VO) (lit. unify the intentions) unite, be all of one mind. Tāmen-dàjiā-qíle-xīn-le. 他 們 大 家 齊 了 心 了 . All of them are of one mind.

QǏYÈ₄ 企業 (N) business enterprise.

QǏ-YÌ₄ 起義 (VO) do something against improper government authority, revolt.

QÌYÓU₂ 汽油 (N) benzene, gasoline.

QÍYÚ₂ 其餘 (N) remainder, the remaining ones. Qíyúde wǒ-dōu-bu-yào-le. 其 餘 的 我 都 不 要 了 . I want none of the rest. (cf: QÍTĀ 其他).

QĪYUE₁ 七月 see QÍYUE 七月 .

QÍYUE₁ 七月 or QĪYUE 七月 (TW) (lit. the seventh month of the year) July.

QÍZHENG₄ 齊整 see ZHĚNGQÍ

5

整齊

QÍZHŌNG₃ 其中 (PW) inside. Tāde-huà qízhōng-hái-yǒu-qí-tāde-yìsi. 他的話其中還有其他的意思. Within what he said there is some other meaning.

¹QÍZĬ₄ 妻子 (N) wife.

QÍZI₃ 旗子 (N) flag. (M: miàn 面). dǎ-qízi 打旗子 hold up a flag. guà-qízi 掛旗子 fly a flag.

QŪ₃ 區 (M) region. dìyīqū 第一區 the first region. fēn-sānqū 分三區 divide into three regions.

QŪ₅ 蛆 (N) maggots.

QŬ₂ 取 (TV) (1) go somewhere to get something, fetch. Wǒ-huíjiā qu-qǔ-qu. 我回家去取去. I'll go home to get it. (2) take or accept someone from a selection. Yǒu-'wǔbǎi-duō-rén-shēnqǐng, jiù-qǔle-shíge. 有五百多人申請就取了十個. There were more than five hundred people who applied, but only ten were selected. (RE) be selected. Tā-méi-kǎoqǔ. 他沒考取. He didn't pass the entrance examination.

QŬ₃ 娶 (TV) marry (as a husband). qǔ-tàitai 娶太太 take a wife.

QÙ₁ 去 (IV) (1) go, leave. Wǒ-qù. 我去. I'll go. Tā-dào-nǎr-qu? 他到那兒去? Where is he going? Tā-qù-xué-xiào-le. 他去學校了. He went to school. Qù-nǐde-ba.

Q

去你的吧. lit. or fig. Go your way. or Go away. Tā-lái-nále-yīkuài-qián-qu. 他來拿了一塊錢去. He came, took a dollar and left. (2) send something away from the speaker. Nǐ-gěi-ta-qù-xìn-le-ma? 你給他去信了嗎? Did you send him a letter? (3) remove, do away with. Zhèige-yīngdāng-qù-yícùn. 這個應當去一寸. This ought to be shortened one inch. Bǎ-zhèiju-huà-qù-le. 把這句話去了. Delete this sentence. used before and/or after a verb or a VO, go in order to do something. Tā-chī-fàn-qu-le. 他吃飯去了. He went to eat. Shéi-yao-qu-kàn-diànyǐngr? 誰要去看電影兒? Who wants to go to see a movie? (RE) used with verbs of motion, and with verbs such as shàng 上, xià 下, chū 出, jìn 進, huí 回, guò 過, indicates motion away from the speaker, go, there. Nèige-bǐ-ràng-tā-mǎiqu-le. 那個筆讓他買去了. That pen was bought by him (and taken away). Shān-tài-gāo shàngbuqù. 山太高上不去. The mountain is too high, it can't be climbed. (S) SVle-qùle SV 了-去了 very, extremly. Tāde-jiā yuǎnle-qùle. 他家遠了去了. His home is far far away. (cf: LÁI 來).

QÙAN₄ 圈 (TV) (1) encircle,

surround. (2) draw a circle.
guān-yíge-guānr 圈一個
圈兒 make a circle.

QUÁN₃ 全 (SV) complete. Zhèitao-pánzi-wǎn buquán-le. 這
套盤子盌不全了.
This set of dishes is not complete.

(AD) completely, all. Nèijian-shì ta-quán-zhīdao. 那件
事他全知道. He
knows that affair completely.

(RE) completely. Tā-huì-yi-
dianr, kěshi huìbuquán. 他會
一點兒,可是會不
全. He knows how to do a
little bit, but not completely.

QUÀN₃ 勸 (TV) advise, persuade,
exhort. Wǒ-quàn-ta-shàng-dà-
xué. 我勸他上大學.
I have tried to persuade him to
go to college. Wǒ-bǎ-ta-quàn-
huilai-le. 我把他勸回來
了. I persuaded him to come
back.

QUÁNBÙ₃ 全部 (N) the whole
group (of something), the whole
thing.

QUÁNDOU₂ 全都 (AD) all,
completely. Wǒ-quándou-wàng-
le. 我全都忘了. I
forgot them completely.

QUÁNGUÓ₃ 全國 (N) entire
country.

QUÁNJÍ₃ 全集 (N) complete
works (of a writer).

QUÁNJIĀ₃ 全家 (N) whole family.

QUÀN-JIÀ₃ 勸架 (VO) advise
someone to stop fighting. Tāmen-

dǎ-jià méi-rén-qiàn. 他們
打架沒人勸. They
are fighting but no one is ad-
vising them to stop.

QUÁNLÌ₃ 權力 (N) right, power, authority (given by law or
tradition). Tāde-quánli hěn-dà.
他的權力很大. His
power is very great.

QUÁNLÌ₃ 權利 (N) right. Zhèi-
shi-wǒmende-quánli. 這是
我們的權利. This is
our right. Wǒ-jìrán-jìn-yìwu,
jiu-yào xiǎngshou-quánli. 我
既然盡義務就要
享受權利. Since I have
fulfilled my duties, I want to
enjoy my rights.

QUÁNLÌ₄ 全力 (N) all of one's
energy. Wǒ-yòng-quánlì-zhīchi-
ta. 我用全力支持他.
I'll support him with all my
energy.

QUÁNMIÀN₃ 全面 (SV) whole,
complete.

(AD) from all sides, totally.

QUĀNR₃ 圈兒 or QUĀNZI 圈
子 (N) (1) circle. huà-quānr
畫圈兒 draw a circle.
zhuàn-quānr 轉圈兒 go
around in a circle. (2) scope (as
of a topic). chūle-quānr-le 出
了圈兒了 beyond the
scope.

QUÁNSHĒN₄ 全身 (N) entire
body. quánshēnde-lìliang 全身
的力量 strength of the en-
tire body.

QUÁNSHÌJIÈ₂ 全世界 (N)
whole world.

QUĀNTÀOR₄ 圈套兒 (N) trap.
Bié-shàngle-tade-quāntàor. 別
上 了 他 的 圈套兒.
Don't fall into his trap.

QUÁNTǏ₃ 全體 (N) whole group
(of people). Wǒmen-quántǐ-fǎn-
diù. 我們 全體 反對.
The whole group of us opposed.

QUÁNTOU₄ 拳頭 (N) fist. zuàn-
quántou 攥拳頭 make a fist.

QUÁNWĒI₄ 權威 (N) authority,
expert. Tā-shi-zhèi-yijiède-
quánwēi. 他是這一界
的 權威. He is the author-
ity in this field.

QUÁNYUAN₄ 泉源 (N) spring
(of water).

QŪBIÉ₃ 區別 (N) difference.
(syn. fēnbie 分別).

QŬDÉ₄ 取得 (TV) obtain. qǔde-
tāde-tóngyì 取得 他 的 同
意 obtain his agreement. Wǒ-
děi-gēn-ta-qǔdé-liánluo. 我 得
跟 他 取 得 聯絡 I
have to contact him.

QUĒ₂ 缺 (TV) (1) lack, short of.
(syn. duǎn 短 , qiàn 欠). Zhèr-
jīnnian-quē-yǔ. 這兒今年
缺雨 . Rain was insufficient
here this year. Zhèiben-shū-
quē-yiyè. 這本書缺一
頁 . A leaf is missing from the
book. Wǒmen-quē-rén-bāng-
máng. 我們缺人幫忙.
We lack people to help. (2) (con.
quē-dé 缺 德). (lit. lack of
good character) bad (of a person).
Nǐ-zhēn-quē. 你 真 缺 . You
are really bad.
(N) vacant post, vacancy. Zhèr-

chūle-yige-quē. 這兒出了
一 個 缺 . There is a
vacancy here.

QUĒ₄ 瘸 (IV) be lame. Tā-tuǐ-
qué-le. 他腿瘸了. He
is lame.

QUĒBĀN₅ 雀斑 (N) freckles.

QUĒ-DÉ₄ 缺德 (VO) (lit. lack
of good character) bad (of a
person).

QUĒDIĂN₃ 缺點 (N) short-
coming, defect. Bú-huì-shuō-
wàiguo-huà, shi-yíge-quēdiǎn.
不會說外國話是
一 個 缺點. It is a short-
coming not to know a foreign
language.

QUÈDÌNG₃ 確定 (TV) decide,
settle. Jìhua hái-méi-quèdìng.
計劃還沒確定. The
plan still hasn't been decided
upon.
(SV) certain, definite. quèdìng-
de-bànfa 確定的辦法
definite method.

QUĒFÁ₃ 缺乏 (TV) lack, be
short of, need. Zhèr-zuì-quē-
fa-zhèiyàngrde-rén. 這兒最
缺乏這樣兒的人.
Here we need this kind of person the most.

QUÈHU₂ 確乎 (AD) really.
(syn. quèshi 確實). Wǒ-què-
hu-juéde-duìbuqǐ-ta. 我 確
乎覺得對不起他.
I really feel that I owe him an
apology.

QUĒSHĂO₃ 缺少 (TV) lack, be
short of.

QUÈSHI₃ 確實 (SV) accurate.

Q

Tāde-xiāoxi-bu-quèshi. 他的消息不確實. His information is not accurate.

(AD) really. (syn. quèhu 確乎).

Wǒ-quèshi-bu-zhidào. 我確實不知道. I really don't know.

QUĒ-XÍ₄ 缺席 (VO) absent <u>from a meeting.</u> (opp. chū-xí 出席).

QUÉZI₄ 瘸子 (N) lame person.

QŪJIĚ₄ 曲解 (TV) distort, misinterpret <u>what someone means.</u> (N) distorted explanation.

QÚN₂ 群 (M) crowd, group, herd, flock. yìqún-rén 一群人 a group of people. yìqún-yáng 一群羊 a herd of sheep.

QÚNDǍO₅ 群島 (N) group of islands, archipelago.

QÙNIÁN₁ 去年 (TW) last year.

QÚNZHÒNG₃ 群眾 (N) the people, the masses.

QÚNZI₄ 裙子 (N) skirt. (M:

tiáo 條).

QŪQUR₅ 蛐蛐兒 (N) cricket (insect).

QÙ-SHÌ₃ 去世 (VO) pass away, die.

QÙWEI₃ 趣味 (N) interest. Zhèiben-shū méi-shenma-qùwei. 這本書沒甚麼趣味. This book is of little interest.

QŪXIÀN₄ 曲線 (N) curve.

QŪXIĀO₃ 取消 (TV) (1) cancel. Nèige-jìhua qǔxiāo-le. 那個計劃取消了. That plan is cancelled. (2) delete. Bǎ-nèige-zì qùxiāo. 把那個字取消. Delete that character.

QŪYÙ₄ 區域 (N) district, region.

QŬZI₄ 曲子 (N) (1) piece of music. (2) song.

R

R₁ 兒 (-B) (1) added to certain B to form a N, with or without diminutive sense. yìzhi-dà-niǎor, yìzhi-xiǎo-niǎor 一隻大鳥兒, 一隻小鳥兒 a big bird, a small bird. Tā-huàle-yige-dà-quánr. 他畫了一個大圈兒. He drew a big circle. (2) added to certain N to form another N with a different meaning. huā 花 as a N fireworks but huār 花兒 flower. tóu 頭 as a N head but tóur 頭兒 boss. (3) added to certain M to form a noun, indicates the size, shape or quality of individual physical objects. Gèr-hèn-dà. 個兒很大. The size is very big. Piànr-tài-báo. 片兒太薄. The thickness of the slice is too thin. Kuàir-shi-fāngde. 塊兒是方的. The shape is square. (4) added to a N, NU or M to indicate diminutive. yìběnr-xiǎo-shūr 一本兒小書兒 a small (volume of a) book. (5) Peip. added to certain elements to form TW. jīnr 今兒 today. zuór 昨兒 yesterday. (6) Peip. added to SP to form PW. jèr 這兒 here. nèr 那兒 there. nǎr 那兒 where. (7) Peip. added to a certain few elements to form

Verbs. Tā-zhēn-huǒr-le. 他真火兒了. He really got angry. (8) added to certain redupli-cated SVs or Ms. mànmānrde-zǒu 慢慢兒的走 walk slowly. Tā-tiāntiānr-lái. 他天天兒來. He comes every-day. (cf: ZI 子).

RǍN₃ 染 (TV) (1) dye. Zhèijian-yīshang nǐ-yào-rǎn-shénma-yán-se? 這件衣裳你要染甚麽顏色? What color do you want to dye this dress? (2) acquire a bad habit. Tā-rǎnshang-zhèizhong-xíguan-le. 他染上這種習慣了. He acquired this kind of habit.

RÁN'ER₃ 然而 (MA) nevertheless, but, yet. Zhèiyàngr-bàn gùrán-kéyi, rán'er-wènti-hěn-duō. 這樣辦固然可以然而問題很多. Of course, it is all right to do it this way, but there are many problems.

RǍNG₂ 嚷 (TV) shout, call out. (syn. jiào 叫, hǎn 喊). Bié-rǎng. 别嚷. Don't shout. (cf: RǍNGRANG 嚷嚷).

RÀNG₂ 讓 (TV) (1) yield to, give in to. Shéi-yě-bu-ràng-shéi. 誰也不讓誰. Nobody gave in to anybody else. Gēn-ta-wár,

nǐ-ràngzhe-ta-dianr. 跟 他 玩
兒 你 讓 着 他 點 兒.
Give in to him a little when you
play with him. (2) reduce <u>or</u>
lower <u>a price as a courtesy</u>. Nǐ-
'néng-bu-néng-ràng-dianr-jià-
qian? 你 能 不 能 讓 點
兒 價 錢 ? Can you lower
the price a little ?(3) let <u>some-
one</u> have <u>something</u>. Bǎ-wǒde-
wūzi ràanggei-tā-zhù. 把 我 的
屋 子 讓 給 他 住. I
let him have my room to stay in.
(4) offer <u>food, drink, cigarette,
etc.</u> Nǐ-ràngrang-ta, kàn-ta-
'chī-bu-chī. 你 讓 讓 他,
看 他 吃 不 吃. Offer it
to him and see if he eats it or
not. (5) usher <u>or</u> bring <u>someone</u>
in <u>or</u> out. Jiāli-tài-zāng, wǒ-
buhǎoyìsi-bǎ-ta-ràngjinlai. 家
裏 太 髒, 我 不 好 意
思 把 他 讓 進 來. The
house is too dirty, I'm embarrassed to bring him in. (6) let,
allow. (syn. jiào 叫). Yàoshi-
ta-yídìng-yao-zǒu, jiu-ràng-ta-
zǒu-ba. 要 是 他 一 定 要
走, 就 讓 他 走 吧.
If he insists on leaving, then let
him leave. Ràng-ta-'xiūxi-xiū-
xi. 讓 他 休 息 休 息.
Let him rest. (7) ask <u>or</u> make
<u>someone</u> do <u>something</u>. (syn.
jiào 叫, shǐ 使). Shì-wǒ-
'ràng-ta-qù-de. Tā-méi-yào-qù.
是 我 讓 他 去 的. 他
沒 要 去. I made him go.
He didn't want to go.
(CV) by (<u>marking the agent</u>).

(syn. jiào 叫). Tā-ràng-ren-
dǎ-le. 他 讓 人 打 了. He
was hit by somebody.
RÀNG-BÙ₃ 讓 步 (VO) concede,
yield. Nǐ-děi-ràng-dianr-bù.
你 得 讓 點 兒 步. You
have to give in a little.
RĀNGRANG₄ 嚷 嚷 (TV) (1)
shout. Shéi-zài-wàitou-rāngrang-
ne? 誰 在 外 頭 嚷 嚷
呢 ? Who is shouting outside?
(2) blab, blurt out a secret, publicize. Wǒ-gěi-ta-rāngrang-rang-
rang. 我 給 他 嚷 嚷 嚷
嚷. I will give him publicity.
(cf: RĀNG 嚷).
RÁNHÒU₂ 然 後 (MA) afterward,
subsequently, then. Wǒmen-chī-
le-fàn ránhòu-zai-chūqu. 我 們
吃 了 飯 然 後 再 出
去. We will eat and then we
will go out.
RÁNLIÀO₄ 燃 料 (N) fuel.
RǍNLIÀO₅ 染 料 (N) dye materials.
RÁNSHĀODÀN₅ 燃 燒 彈 (N)
incendiary bomb.
RÁO₃ 饒 (TV) (1) let <u>someone</u> get
away with <u>something for which
he should be punished,</u> spare.
ráo-mìng 饒 命 spare one's
life. Zhèihui-ráole-ta-ba, xià-
hui-zai-fá. 這 回 饒 了 他
吧, 下 回 再 罰. We'll let
him go this time, but next time
he'll be punished. (2) give <u>some-
thing free in addition to what has
been bought.</u> Mǎi-yíge, ráo-yige.
買 一 個 饒 一 個. Buy
one and get one free.

R

RÀO₃ 繞 (TV) (1) wind <u>something</u> around <u>something</u>. Bǎ-xiàn-rào-zai-shǒushang. 把線繞在手上 . Wind the wire around the hand. (2) go around (<u>move in a circle around something</u>). rào-yiquānr 繞一圈兒 circle around once. (3) detour. Zhèi-tiao-xīn-lù, hái-méi-xiūhǎo, wǒmen-děi-ràozhe-zǒu. 這條新路,還沒修好,我們得繞着走 . This new road isn't completed yet, we have to detour around it.

RÀOKǑULÌNGR₅ 繞口令兒 (N) tongue-twister.

RÀOLUÀN₅ 擾亂 (TV) make a disturbance.

RÀO-WĀNR₃ 繞灣兒 (VO) (1) go around. Wǒmen-ràole-yige-dà-wānr. 我們繞了一個大灣兒 . We went around a big circle. (2) <u>talk in circles</u>. Tā-shuō-huà, ài-rào-wānr. 他說話愛繞灣 . He loves to talk in circles.

RÀO-YUǍNR₂ 繞遠兒 (VO) take the long way around. (<u>opp.</u> chāo-jìnr 抄近兒). Zǒu-zhèitiao-lù rào-yuǎnr. 走這條路繞遠兒 . Going by this road is taking the long way.

RĚ₃ 惹 (TV) stir up, provoke. Bié-rě-ta. 別惹他 . Don't provoke him. Tā-yòu-rě-huò-le. 他又惹禍了 . He caused a disaster again. Tāde-màozi rě-ren-zhù-yì. 他的帽子惹人注意 .His

hat makes people pay attention.

RÈ₁ 熱 (SV) hot. (<u>opp.</u> lěng 冷 , liáng 涼). Tiānqi-tài-rè. 天氣太熱 . The weather is too hot.

(TV) heat, warm. Bǎ-cài-rère. 把菜熱熱 . Heat the food. (N) (1) heat. Tā-shòule-rè-le. 他受了熱了 . He was felled by the heat. (2) fever. Tā-yǒu-méi-you-rè? 他有沒有熱 ? Does he have a fever?

RÈÀI₃ 熱愛 (TV) love <u>ardently</u>. Tā-rè'ài-zǔguo-wénhuà. 他熱愛祖國文化 . He loves his country's culture.

RÈDÀI₄ 熱帶 (N) tropical zone.

RÈDÙ₃ 熱度 (N) temperature. Rèdù-hěn-gāo. 熱度很高 The temperature is very high.

'RÈLIÈ₃ 熱烈 (SV) exuberant, fervent. Dàjiāde-qíngxu hěn-'rè-liè. 大家的情緒很熱烈 . Everybody is very fervent.

(AD) exuberantly, fervently. rè-liè-huānyíng 熱烈歡迎 welcome exuberantly.

RÉN₁ 人 (N) (1) person, human being. (M: kǒu 口). Tā-jiā yǒu-'jǐkǒur-rén? 他家有幾口兒人 ? How many people are there in his family? (2) bodily health (<u>of a person</u>). Wǒ-'rén-bu-shūfu. 我人不舒服 . I don't feel well. (3) character (<u>of a person</u>). Tā-rén shi-hǎo-rén. 他人是好人 . He has a fine character. (4) someone. Zhēn-jiào-ren-zhāo-jí. 真叫

R

人着急 . It really made someone worry. Néng-bǎ-ren-qìsi. 能把人氣死 . It can make someone extremely angry.

RĔN₃ 忍 (TV) (1) have patience. Rĕnzhe-ba. 忍着吧 . Put up with it. (2) endure, tolerate, stand. Wǒ-zhēn-rĕnbuzhù-le. 我真忍不住了 . I really cannot endure it any longer.

RÈN₂ 認 (TV) (1) admit. Tā-cuò-le, tā-bu-rèn. 他錯了, 他不認 . He was wrong, but he didn't admit it. (2) learn to recognize Chinese characters. Tā-rènle-bùshǎo-zìle. 他認了不少字了 . He has learned to recognize quite a few characters. (3) identify. Něige-shi-nǐde? Wǒ-rènbuchulái. 那個是你的? 我認不出來 . Which one is yours, I cannot identify it. (4) resigned to the fact. Wǒ-chī-kuī, wǒ-rèn-le. 我吃虧, 我認了. I'm resigned to the fact that I lost. (5) make someone an honorary relative. Tā-rènle-yige-gānmā. 他認了一個乾媽 . He has taken someone as his adopted mother.

REN'ÀI₅ 仁愛 (N) benevolent.

RÈNAO₁ 熱鬧 (SV) lively, bustling with noise and excitement. (opp. ānjing 安靜). Zhèr-zhēn-rènao. 這兒真熱鬧 : It's really lively here. (N) noise and excitement. kàn-

rènao 看熱鬧 look at the excitement.

RÉNCAI₃ 人才 (N) talented person. Zhèiyàngrde-réncai hĕn-nándé. 這樣兒的人才很難得 . This kind of talented person is difficult to get. Nà-shì-yíge-réncai. 那是一個人才 . That is a talented person.

RÉNDÀO₄ 人道 (N) human welfare. jiǎng-réndào 講人道 concerned about human welfare. (SV) humanitarian. Tài-bu-rén-dào-le. 太不人道了 . It's too inhuman.

RÈNDE₂ 認得 (TV) recognize, know. (syn. rènshi 認識). Nǐ-hái-rènde-wo-ma? 你還認得我嗎 ? Do you still recognize me?

RĒNG₂ 扔 (TV) throw. rēng-qiú 扔球 throw a ball. Nǐ-rēng, wǒ-jiē. 你扔, 我接 . You throw it and I'll catch. Bǎ-shū-rēngzai-yibiānr-le. 把書扔在一邊兒了 . Throw the book. or fig. Put the book aside. Nǐ-bu-yào jiu-rēng-le. 你不要就扔了. If you don't want it, then throw it away.

RÉNGÉR₃ 人格兒 (N) character (of a person).

RÉNGJIÙ₃ 仍舊 (IV) go on or be the same as before, go on as usual. Yíqiè-réngjiù. 一切仍舊 . Everything is the same as before. (AD) or RÉNGRÁN 仍然

still, as before, as usual. (syn. háishi 還是). Tā-réngjiù- bu-zhīdào. 他仍舊不知道 . He still doesn't know it.

RÉNGŌNG₂ 人工 (N) (1) labor. Xiànzài-réngōng-hěn-guì. 現在人工很貴 . Labor is very expensive now. (2) man- made, artificial. Shì-tiānránde, bu-shì-réngong-zuòde. 是天然的，不是人工作的 . It's natural, not man- made.

RÉNGRAN₃ 仍然 or RÉNGJIÙ 仍舊 (AD) still, as before, as usual. (syn. háishi 還是). Tā-réngran-shi-nàyàngr. 他仍然是那樣 . He is still like that.

RÈNHÉ₃ 任何 (SP) any. 'Rèn- hé-rén dou-kéyi-qù. 任何人都可以去 . Anyone can go. Wǒ-bu-xiǎng-mǎi-rènhéde- dōngxi. 我不想買任何的東西 . I don't want to buy anything.

RÉNJIA₂ 人家 (N) (1) others, other people. Wǒ-'zěnma-gen- rénjia-shuō? 我怎麼跟人家説 ? How do I explain it to the others? Bié-jiao-rén- jia-xiào-ni. 別叫人家笑你 . Don't let the others laugh at you. (2) that or those respectable or esteemed. Rén- jia-Lǐ-xiaojie, shéi-bǐdeliǎo? 人家李小姐,誰比得了 ? Who can compare with the esteemed Miss Li?

RENJIĀR₄ 人家兒 (N) (1)

household, family. Nèitiáo- lushang méi-you-rénjiār. 那條路上沒有人家兒 . There is no house on that road. (2) family of a girl's fiancé. Tā- de-xiǎojie yǒu-rénjiār-le-ma? 他的小姐有人家兒了嗎 ? Is his daughter engaged?

RÉNKǑU₃ 人口 (N) population. Zhèige-chéng yǒu-duōshao-rén- kǒu? 這個城有多少人口 ? What is the popula- tion of this city?

RÉNLÈI₄ 人類 (N) mankind.

RÉNMÍN₂ 人民 (N) (1) people (of a country). (2) citizen of a nation (used in Mainland China). (cf: GUÓMÍN 國民).

RÉNMÍNBÌ₄ 人民幣 (N) cur- rency issued by the People's Bank of China.

RÈN-MÌNG₅ 認命 (VO) resigned to one's fate.

RÉNMÍN-GÒNGHÉGUÓ₃ 人民共和國 (VO) people's re- public.

RÉNMÍN-JIĚFÀNGJŪN₅ 人民解放軍 (VO) people's lib- eration army.

RĚNNÀI₃ 忍耐 (TV) have pa- tience. Xiànzài wǒmen-bìxū- rěnnài. 現在我們必須忍耐 . Now, we must have patience. (N) patience. (cf: RĚNSHÒU 忍受).

RÈNPÍNG₄ 任憑 (MA) no matter, regardless. Rènpíng-shì-shéi, yě-dei-mǎi-piào. 任憑是

R

誰, 也 得 買 票 . No matter who it is, he has to buy a ticket.

RÉNQÍNG₃ 人 情 (N) (1) human friendship. tuō-rénqíng 托 人 情 ask a favor out of friendship. (2) human feelings. Tā-tài-bu-jiǎng-rénqíng-le. 他 太 不 講 人 情 了 . He has no concern for human feelings. (3) human relations. Tā-bu-tōng-rénqíng. 他 不 通 人 情 . He doesn't understand human relations.

RÉNQUÁN₅ 人 權 (N) human rights.

RÈNR₄ 刃 兒 (N) sharpness of a cutting edge. Zhèige-dāo-méi-rènr-le. 這 個 刀 沒 刃 兒 了 . This knife isn't sharp.

RÉNREN₁ 人 人 (N) used before the main verb of a sentence, usually followed by dōu 都 , quán 全 ,quándōu 全 都 , etc., everybody. Rénren-dou-qù. 人 人 都 去. Everybody will go.

RÉNSHEN₅ 人 參 (N) a kind of medicinal herb, ginseng.

RÉNSHĒNG₄ 人 生 (N) human life.

RÉNSHÌ₅ 人 士 (N) person. gè-jiè-rénshi 各 界 人 士 people in all walks of life.

RÈNSHÌ₁ 認 識 (TV) recognize, know. (syn. rènde 認 得).Wǒ-bu-rènshi-ta. 我 不 認 識 他 . I don't know him. Nǐ-rèn-shi-duōshao-zì? 你 認 識 多 少 字 ?. How many characters do you know? Tā-bu-

rènshi-lù. 他 不 認 識 路 He doesn't know the way. Wǒ-shi-qùnián-gēn-ta-rènshide. 我 是 去 年 跟 他 認 識 的 . It was last year that I knew him.

(N) understanding. Tā-duì-Zhōngguo-wénhuà-de-rènshi hěn-shēn. 他 對 中 國 文 化 的 認 識 很 深 . He has a very deep understanding of Chinese culture.

RÉNSHOU₃ 人 手 (N) worker, helping hand. Rénshou-bu-gòu. 人 手 不 夠 . There are not enough workers.

'RÈNSHÒU₂ 忍 受 (TV) endure, tolerate, stand. Tā-shuō-de-huà, wǒ-bu-néng-'rěnshòu. 他 說 的 話 , 我 不 能 忍 受 . I cannot stand what he said. (cf: RĚNNÀI 忍 耐).

RÈNWÉI₃ 認 為 (TV) according to one's opinion, think, feel. (syn. yǐwéi 以 為). Wǒ-rènwéi ta-shuō-de-bu-duì. 我 認 為 他 說 的 不 對 . I think that what he said is not right.

RÉNWÙ₃ 人 物 (N) (1) prominent individual. dà-rénwu 大 人 物 VIP. (2) paintings (of people) a kind of Chinese painting with figures as the main subject matter.

RÈNWÙ₄ 任 務 (N) mission, assignment.

RÈN-XÌNG₃ 任 性 (VO) have no desire to limit oneself, do something according to one's own desire. Tā-tài-rènxìng, 'xiǎng-

yào-shénma,. jiu-'mǎi-shénma.
他 太 任 性, 想 要 甚 麼, 就 買 甚 麼. She has no desire to limit herself. She buys whatever she wants.

RÉNXÍNGDÀO₅ 人 行 道 (N) sidewalk.

RÉNYUÁNR₃ 人 緣 兒 (N) popularity. Tā-zhēn-yǒu-rényuánr. 他 真 有 人 緣 兒. He is really popular.

RÉNZÀO₃ 人 造 (b-) artificial, man-made. rénzàosī 人 造 絲 synthetic silk.

RÉNZÀOWÈIXÍNG₄ 人 造 衛 星 (N) sputnik, artificial satellite.

RÈN-ZHĒN₂ 認 真 (SV) conscientious, serious. Tā-niàn-shū hěn-rèn-zhēn. 他 念 書 很 認 真. He is very conscientious in studying.

(AD) seriously, conscientiously. Tā-rèn-zhēn-zuò-shì. 他 認 真 作 事. He works very conscientiously.

RÉNZHǑNG₅ 人 種 (N) human race.

RÈN-ZÌ₃ 認 字 (VO) learn to recognize characters for the purpose of reading. (cf: SHÍ-ZÌ 識 字).

RÈQÍNG₄ 熱 情 (SV) warm, passionate. Tā-duì-péngyou hěn-rèqíng. 他 對 朋 友 很 熱 情. He is very passionate about his friends.

RĚ-SHÌ₄ 惹 事 (VO) cause trouble. Bié-chūqu-rě-shì. 別 出 去 惹 事. Don't go out to make trouble.

RÈSHUǏPÍNG₄ 熱 水 瓶 (N) thermos bottle.

RÈXĪN₂ 熱 心 (SV) (1) enthusiastic, earnest. Tā-duì-jiàohuì hěn-rexīn. 他 對 教 會 很 熱 心. He is very enthusiastic about the church. (2) warm-blooded, cordial. Tā-duì-péng-you-hěn-rèxīn. 他 對 朋 友 很 熱 心. He is very cordial with his friends.

(AD) enthusiastically. Tā-rèxīn-bāngmáng. 他 熱 心 幫 忙. He helps enthusiastically.

(N) enthusiasm.

RÌBĚN₁ 日 本 (PW) Japan.

RÌCHÁNG₃ 日 常 (AD) daily. Zhè-dou-shì-rìcháng-bìxū-'yòngde-dōngxi. 這 都 是 日 常 必 須 用 的 東 西. These are all the things for daily use. Zhè-shi-wǒ-rìcháng-zuò-de-shìqing. 這 是 我 日 常 作 的 事 情. This is the kind of thing I do daily.

RÌGUĀNG₄ 日 光 (N) sunlight.

RÌGUĀNGDĒNG₄ 日 光 燈 (N) sun-lamp.

RÌJÌ₂ 日 記 (N) (1) diary. jì-rìjì 記 日 記 keep a diary. (2) or RÌJÌBĚNR 日 記 本 兒 book (for keeping a diary). (M: běn 本).

RÌJÌBĚNR₃ 日 記 本 兒 see RÌJÌ 日 記 (N) (2).

RÌLÌ₃ 日 曆 (N) calendar. (syn. yuèfenpái(r) 月 份 牌 (兒)).

RÌNÈIWǍ₃ 日 內 瓦 (PW) Geneva.

RÌSHÍ₄ 日 蝕 (N) solar eclipse.

R

Jīntian-rìshí. 今 天 日 餃 .
There will be a solar eclipse
today.

RÌTOU₄ 日 頭 (N) sun. (syn. tàiyang 太 陽).

RÌYÒNG₄ 日 用 (AD) in daily
use. Zhè-dou-shì-rìyòng-bìxūde-
dōngxi. 這 都 是 日 用
必 須 的 東 西 . These are
all the things which are needed
in daily use.

RÌZI₂ 日 子 (N) (1) day, date.
dìng-yige-rìzi 定 一 個 日
子 set a date. Rìzi-guò-de-
zhēn-kuài. 日 子 過 得 真
快 . The days pass very quickly. (2) special day. Jiēshang-
zěnma-zènma-duō-rén? Jīntian-
shi-shénma-rìzi? 街 上 怎
麼 這 麼 多 人? 今 天
是 甚 麼 日 子 ? Why
are there so many people on the
street? What kind of a special
day is today?

RÓNGYI₁ 容 易 (SV) easy. (opp.
nán 難).

(AD) easily. Zhōngguo-shū bu-
róngyi-dǒng. 中 國 書 不
容 易 懂 . Chinese books
cannot be easily understood.

RÓU₄ 揉 (TV) rub, massage,
knead. róu-yǎnjing 揉 眼 睛
rub the eyes. róucheng-yíge-qiú
揉 成 一 個 球 make a
ball with the palms. Yòng-shǒu-
róurou. 用 手 揉 揉 . Mas-
sage it with the hands.

RÒU₁ 肉 (N) (1) meat, flesh. (M:
kuài 塊). niú-ròu 牛 肉 beef.
(2) pulp (of fruit).

(SV) Peip. slow in movement,
sluggish. Tā-tài-ròu. 他 太
肉 . He is too slow.

RÓUHE₃ 柔 和 (SV) (1) soft (of
light, color or sound). Tāde-
shēngyin hěn-róuhe. 他 的 聲
音 很 柔 和 . Her voice is
very soft. (2) gentle, mild (of a
person or one's temperament).
Tāde-xìngqing hěn-róuhe. 他
的 性 情 很 柔 和 . He
has a very mild disposition.

RÒUMÁ₃ 肉 麻 (SV) have goose-
flesh, get goose-bumps. Zhèi-
zhǒng-huà tīngzhe zhēn-ròumá.
這 種 話 聽 着 真 肉
麻 . People get goose-bumps
when they hear this kind of talk.

RÓURUAN₄ 柔 軟 (SV) soft (of
something concrete). Zhèizhǒng-
pízi hěn-róuruan. 這 種 皮
子 很 柔 軟 . This kind of
leather is very soft.

RÒUWÁNZI₄ 肉 丸 子 (N) meat-
ball.

RUĂN₂ 軟 (SV) (1) lit. or fig.
soft, yielding to the touch. (opp.
yìng 硬). Zhèizhǒng-dōngxi
tiān-yí-rè jiu-ruǎn-le. 這 種
東 西 天 一 熱 就 軟
了 . This kind of thing becomes
soft when the weather gets hot.
Tāde-xīn-ruǎn. 他 的 心 軟 .
He is soft-hearted. (2) weak, of
inferior quality. (opp. qiáng 強).
Zhèige-xuéxiào Yīngwenxì-hěn-
qiáng, Jūngwenxì-ruǎn-yidianr.
這 個 學 校 英 文 系
很 強, 中 文 系 軟 一
點 兒 . This schools's English

department is strong but the
Chinese department is weak.

RUǍNHUO₂ 軟和 (SV) nice and
soft, comfortably soft. (opp.
yìng 硬).

RUǍNRUO₃ 軟弱 (SV) weak (of
a human body or a statement).
Tāde-shēnti hěn-ruǎnruo. 他
的 身 體 很 軟 弱 . He
is very weak.

RÙCHǍNGQUÀN₄ 入 場 券 (N)
entrance ticket. (M: zhāng 張).

RÚGUO₂ 如 果 (MA) if, in case.
(syn. yàoshi 要 是). Wǒ-rú-
guo-yǒu-qián, wǒ-yě-mǎi. 我
如 果 有 錢 , 我 也 買 .
If I have money, I'll also buy it.

RÙ-HUI₄ 入 會 (VO) join an
organization.

RÙ-HUǑ₅ 入 夥 (VO) join a
group.

RUIDIǍN₃ 瑞 典 (PW) Sweden.

RUISHÌ₃ 瑞 士 (PW) Switzerland.

RÙ-MÉN₃ 入 門 (VO) (lit. go in
the door) have a good start in
learning something. Tā-hái-méi-
rù-mén-ne. 他 還 沒 入
門 呢 . He hasn't learned
much yet.

(N) used in the title of a book,
primer. Guóyǔ-rùmén 國 語

入 門 Mandarin primer.

RÙNNIÁN₃ 閏 年 (N) leap year.

RUÒ₃ 弱 (SV) (1) weak (of a human
body). (opp. zhuàng 壯). Tā-
shēnti-hěn-ruò. 他 身 體 很
弱 . He is very weak. (2) weak
(of a country). (opp. qiáng 強).
Guójiā-hěn-ruò. 國 家 很
弱 . The country is very weak.

RUÒGĀN₄ 若 干 (N) (1) how
many, how much. (2) certain
amount.

RÙSHÉN₃ 入 神 (SV) become
absorbed in something. Tā-tīng-
chàng-gēr-de-shíhou, tīngde
hen-rùshén. 他 聽 唱 歌 兒
的 時 候 , 聽 得 很 入
神 . When he listens to singing
he becomes absorbed in it.

RÚSHÙ₄ 如 數 (AD) in the right
amount. Tāde-qián wǒ-dou-rú-
shù-gěi-ta-le. 他 的 錢 我
都 如 數 給 他 了 . I
gave him the right amount of his
money.

RÙ-XUÉ₄ 入 學 (VO) enter
school.

RÙ-YUÀN₃ 入 院 (VO) be hospi-
talized.

RÙZI₅ 褥 子 (N) mattress, bedding. (M: chuáng 牀).

R

S

SĀ₃ 撒 (TV) (1) let go, release (from the hand, mouth, etc.). Bié-sā-shŏu. 別撒手 . Don't let it go (from your hand). Tā-bă-niăor sā-le. 他把鳥兒撒了 . He let go of the bird. (2) let something bad go out. sā-jiŭfēngr 撒酒瘋兒 release inhibitions after drinking. sā-niào 撒尿 urinate. (3) pass out, distribute. sā-chuándān 撒傳單 pass out handbills.

SĀ₄ 仨 (NU-M) (con. sānge 三個). three items.

SĂ₃ 灑 (TV) (1) sprinkle liquid. să-shuĭ 灑水 sprinkle water. (2) spill liquid. Chá dōu săzai zhuōzishang-le. 茶都灑在桌子上了 . The tea has spilled on the table.

SĂ₃ 撒 (TV) (1) scatter, sprinkle. să-zhŏngzi 撒種子 sow seeds. Zài-ròushang să-yidianr-yán. 在肉上撒一點兒鹽 . Sprinkle a little salt on the meat. (2) spill. Tāng-dōu-sā-le. 糖都撒了 . The sugar was spilled.

SĀ-HUĂNG₃ 撒謊 (VO) tell a lie.

SĀI₂ 塞 (TV) (1) block, stop up. Shuĭ-guănzi sāizhu-le. 水管子塞住了 . The water pipe is blocked. Bă-sāizi sāi-shang. 把塞子塞上 . Put the stopper on. (2) stuff something forcibly into a small opening. Bă-wăn zhuāngzai-hé-zili, pángbiānr-yòng-bàozhĭ-sāi-yisai. 把碗裝在盒子裏,旁邊兒用報紙塞一塞 . Put the bowls in the box and stuff papers around them. Tā-bă-qián dōu-sāizai-kŏudàirli-le. 他把幾都塞在口袋兒裏了 . All of his money is stuffed into his pockets. Wŏ-sāile-yá-le. 我塞了牙了 . I have food stuck in between my teeth.

SÀI₂ 賽 (TV) compete. Tā-yào-gēn-wo-sài, kěshi-wŏ-pà-sàibu-guò-ta. 他要跟我賽,可是我怕賽不過他 . He wants to compete with me, but I am afraid I cannot win. (2) be as...as. Shuĭ-liángde sài-bīng. 水涼得賽冰 . The water is as cold as ice.

SÀI-MĂ₂ 賽馬 (VO) (1) race horses, hold a horse race. (2) gamble on horses. Tā-tiāntiān-dōu-qù-sàimă. 他天天都去賽馬 . He goes to play the horses everyday. or He goes to race horses everyday. (N) (1) horserace. (M: chăng 場). (2) horseracing.

SÀI-PǍO₂ 賽跑 (VO) run a foot-race. Tā-yào-gen-wo-sài-pǎo. 他要跟我賽跑. He wants to race against me. (N) running footrace.

SÀI-QIÚ₁ 賽球 (VO) compete in or have a ball game. Nǐmen-měitiān sài-'jǐchǎng-qiú? 你們每天賽幾場球? How many ball games do you have everyday? (N) ball game. (M: chǎng 場). Wǒmen-qù-kàn-sài-qiú-qu. 我們去看賽球去. Let's go to see the ball game.

SĀIZI₄ 塞子 (N) cork, stopper.

SĀN₁ 三 (NU) three, third. sān-lóu 三樓 third floor.

SǍN₂ 傘 (N) umbrella, parasol, parachute. (M: bǎ 把). dǎ-sǎn 打傘 hold up the umbrella. tiào-sǎn 跳傘 bail out (from an aircraft).

SÀN₂ 散 (IV) (1) fall to pieces, come apart. Nèige-zhuōzi-sàn-le. 那個桌子散了. That desk fell apart. (2) break up (of a group). Nèige-zúqiúduì sàn-le. 那個足球隊散了. That football team broke up. (B) medicinal powder. tóuténg-sǎn 頭痛散 headache pow-der. (TV) dispel worries. Nǐ-chūqu-sànsǎn-xīn-qu. 你出去散散心去. Go out, have some fun and forget your prob-lems.

SÀN₂ 散 (TV) (1) distribute, pass out. sàn-chuándān 散傳單 distribute handbills. (2) dismiss, fire a servant or an employee. Wǒ-bǎ-sānge-yòngren dōu-sàn-le. 我把三個用人都散了. I fired all three of my servants. (IV) dismiss, break up (as a meeting). Nǐmen-zuótian shén-ma-shíhou-sànde? 你們昨天甚麼時候散的? What time did you break up last night?

SÀN-BÙ₂ 散步 (VO) stroll, go for a walk. Wǒ-sànle-yíge-xià-wǔ-de-bù. 我散了一個下午的步. I've strolled for a whole afternoon. Wǒ-chūqu-sànsan-bù. 我出去散散步. I'll go out to take a walk.

SĀNFĀNSHÌ₃ 三藩市 (PW) San Francisco.(syn. Jiùjǐnshān 舊金山).

SÀNGQI₁ 喪氣 (SV) be down on one's luck. Zhēn-sàngqi bǎ-biǎo yě-diū-le. 真喪氣把表也丟了. It's really bad luck, I lost my watch too.

SǍNGZI₃ 嗓子 (N) (1) throat. (2) voice. (M: tiáo 條).

SĀNHÉTǓ₅ 三合土 (N) mor-tar (mixture of lime and sand with water).

SÀN-HUÌ₂ 散會 (VO) adjourn a meeting. Xiànzài sànhuì. 現在散會. The meeting is now adjourned. Huì bādian-zhōng sàndeliǎo-ma? 會三點鐘散得了嗎? Will the meeting be over by eight o'clock?

S

SĀ-NIÀO₄ 撒尿 (VO) urinate.

SĀNJIǍOJIÀ₅ 三腳架 (N) tripod.

SĀNJIǍOXÍNG₄ 三角形 (N) triangle.

SĀNJINGBÀNYÈ₄ 三更半夜 (TW) in the middle of the night. Sānjingbànyè nǐ-shàng-nǎr? 三更半夜你上那兒? Where are you going in the middle of the night? Tāmen yìzhí-wánrdao-sānjingbànyè. 他們一直玩兒到三更半夜. They played straight to the middle of the night.

SĀNLÚNCHĒ₄ 三輪車 (N) pedicab. (M: liàng 輛). dēng-sānlúnchē 蹬三輪車 pedal the pedicab.

SĀNMÍNZHǓYÌ₂ 三民主義 (N) Three People's Principles (of Dr. Sun Yat-sen).

SĂNWÉN₃ 散文 (N) prose. (M: piān 篇).

SĀNYUÈ₁ 三月 (TW) (lit. the third month of the year) March.

SĀO₄ 臊 (SV) odor (of urine or underarm perspiration).

SĂO₃ 掃 (TV) (1) sweep, brush away. Suǒyǒude-wūzi nǐ-dou-sǎo-le-ma? 所有的屋子你都掃了嗎? Did you sweep all the rooms? (2) fig. sweep, rake. yòng-yǎnjing-yì-sǎo 用眼睛一掃 give a sweeping glance. ná-jīguān-qiāng-suǒ 拿機關槍掃 rake a target with machine-guns.

SĂO-DÌ₃ 掃地 (VO) sweep the floor or ground. Tā-yìtian sǎo-sānhui-dì. 他一天掃三回地. He sweeps the floor three times a day.

SĂO-XÌNG₃ 掃興 (VO) dampen enthusiasm, spoil someone's fun. Bié-sǎo-wode-xìng. 別掃我的興. Don't spoil my fun. (SV) disconcerted. Xiànzai-dà-jiā-dōu-hěn-sǎo-xìng. 現在大家都很掃興. Everybody is disconcerted now.

SĂOZI₄ 嫂子 (N) sister-in-law (older brother's wife).

SĀ-YĚ₄ 撒野 (VO) act crudely. Nǐ-bú-yào-zài-zhèr-sā-yě. 你不要在這兒撒野. Don't behave so crudely here.

SE₃ 澀 (SV) (1) astringent, mouth-puckering. Zhèige-shíliu sè-bu-se? 這個石榴澀不澀? Is this pomergranate astringent? (2) frictional, fricative (opposite of slippery). Dìbǎn tài-sè. 地板太澀. The floor isn't slippery at all (not suitable for dancing).

SÈ₄ 四 (NU-M) (con. sìge 四個). four items.

SĒNLÍN₂ 森林 (N) forest.

SHĀ₄ 紗 (N) guaze, sheer cloth, veil.

SHĀ₁ 殺 (TV) kill, murder. shā-rén 殺人 kill people.

SHĂ₁ 傻 (SV) silly, foolish, dumb. Tā-hěn-shǎ. 他很傻. He's very foolish. (AD) stupidly, senselessly. Tā-zài-nèr-shǎ-zhànzhe. 他在那兒傻站着. He is standing there senselessly.

SHĀDÀI₅ 沙袋 (N) sandbag.

SHĀDĪNGYÚ₅ 沙丁魚 (N) sardine. (M: tiáo 條).

SHĀFĀ₂ 沙發 (N) sofa. (M: tào 套). yíge-shāfā 一個沙發 one sofa. yítào-shāfā 一套沙發 a sofa set (generally a sofa and two matching upholstered chairs).

SHĀGUŌ₅ 沙鍋 (N) rough earthenware pot.

SHĀI₄ 篩 (TV) sift. shāi-miàn 篩麵 sift flour.

SHÀI₃ 晒 (TV) sun something. shài-yīshang 晒衣裳 dry clothes in the sun. shài-tàiyang 晒太陽 take a sunbath. (SV) be exposed to the sun, sunny and hot. Zhèige-wūdǐng tài-shài. 這個屋頂太晒. There is too much sun on this roof.

SHÀITÁI₅ 晒台 (N) (1) sun porch or terrace. (2) a place for sunning.

SHĀIZI₅ 篩子 (N) sieve.

SHǍIZI₄ 骰子 (N) dice. (M: fù 副).

SHĀMÒ₃ 沙漠 (N) desert.

SHĀN₁ 山 (N) mountain, hill, (M: zuò 座).

SHĀN₄ 衫 (B) (1) garment for upper part of the body, shirt, undershirt. yángmáoshān 羊毛衫 woolen undershirt. (2) robe, gown. chángshān 長衫 long gown.

SHĀN₃ 搧 (TV) fan. shān-shànzi 搧扇子 fan with a fan. Nǐ-gěi-wǒ-shānshan. 你給我搧 搧 . Fan me. or Fan for me.

SHĀN₂ 刪 (TV) delete written material. Wǒ-shānle-liangju. 我刪了兩句 . I've deleted two sentences. Bǎ-nèiduan-shānqu. 把那段刪去 . Delete that paragraph.

SHĀN₃ 閃 (IV) (1) flash. Dēng-yì-shān jiù-miè-le. 燈一閃 就滅了 . That light flashed and then went out. (2) dodge, evade (implies rapid motion). Wǒ-dǎ-ta, tā-yi-shān, wǒ-méi-dǎ-zháo. 我打他, 他一閃 我沒打着 . I wanted to hit him, but he dodged and I missed. Wǒ-zhǎo-ta, tā-lǎo-shānzhe. 我找他, 他老 閃着 . He is always dodging away when I'm looking for him. (N) lightning. bǐ-shǎn-hái-kuài 比閃還快 faster than lightning.

SHĀNDÌ₄ 山地 (N) mountain region, mountain land.

SHǍNDIÀN₅ 閃電 (N) lightning flash.

SHĀNDǏNG₃ 山頂 (PW) (at the) mountain peak, hilltop. Shān-dǐng yǒu-hěn-duō-shù. 山頂 有很多樹 . There are a lot of trees at the mountain peak. Yìhuǐr jiu-dào-shāndǐng-le. 一會 兒就到山頂了 . Before long we will arrive at the peak.

SHĀNDONG₅ 搧動 (TV) stir up, incite, instigate. Tā-xiǎng shān-dong-gōngren-bàgong. 他想 搧動工人罷工 . He

S

plans to stir up the workers to go on strike.

SHĀNDŌNG₂ 山東 (PW) Shantung province.

SHĀNDÒNG₃ 山洞 (N) cave. zhù-shāngdòng 住山洞 live in a cave. (2) tunnel (through a mountain). chuāng-shāngdòng 穿山洞 go through a tunnel.

SHĀNG₂ 傷 (TV) hurt, injure. Nèicì-zháo-huǒ shāngle-hěn-duō-rén. 那次着火傷了很多人. That fire injured many people. shāng-gǎnqíng 傷感情 hurt (someone's) feelings.

(SV) revulsion toward someone or something. Wǒ-duì-biān-zìdiǎn dōu-shāng-le. 我對編字典都傷了. I'm already sick of compiling dictionaries.

SHĂNG₃ 賞 (TV) award or reward a person of lower rank. Zǒng-sīlìng-shánggei-tā-yíge-qízi. 總司令賞給他一個旗子. The commander-in-chief awarded him a banner.

SHÀNG₁ 上 (TV) (1) come or go up. shàng-lóu 上樓 go upstairs. (2) go somewhere. shàng-kè 上課 go to class. Nǐ-shàng-nǎr? 你上那兒? Where are you going? (3) get on a conveyance, board. shàng-huǒchē 上火車 get on a train. (4) serve. shàng-tāng 上湯 serve the soup. (5) apply to a surface. shàng-yào 上藥 apply medicine. (6) pay taxes.

shàng-shuì 上稅 pay taxes. (7) tighten a spring, wind. shàng-zhōng 上鐘 wind a clock. (8) post in a record book. shàng-zhàng 上賬 post an account. (9) submit something to a superior or a government branch. Tā-gěi-zǒngtǒng shàngle-yíge-gōngshì. 他給總統上了一個公事. He submitted a document to the president. (10) secure. shàng-mén 上門 secure (bolt) the door. shàng-suǒ 上鎖 lock. (11) put in or attach. shàng-yige-lósi 上一個螺絲 put in a screw.

(SP) (1) higher, upper. shàng-děng 上等 high class. (2) past, last. shàng (ge)-yuè 上(個)月 last month. shàng-sānge-libài 上三個禮拜 the past three weeks.

used before the numbers bǎi 百, qiān 千, wàn 萬 etc., up to hundred, thousand, ten thousand. shàngwàn 上萬 up to ten thousand.

(L) (1) up, above. xiàng-shàng-kàn 向上看 look up. (2) on. qiáng-shang 牆上 on the wall. (3) in (based upon). lǐlùn-shang 理論上 in theory.

(RE) (1) up, upon. Tā-pǎoshang-lóu jiu-shuì-le. 他跑上樓就睡了. He went to bed as soon as he ran upstairs. (2) indicates that an activity is already going on. Tāmen-dǎshang-pái-le. 他們打上牌了. They have already started to play

cards. (3) <u>indicates joining
tightly.</u> guānshang 關 上 close
up. (4) <u>indicates attainment of
an objective.</u> Wǒ-zhuībushàng-
ta. 我 追 不 上 他 . I
cannot catch up with him. Tā-
mǎishang-qìchē-le. 他 買 上
汽 車 了 . He has attained
his objective of buying a car.

SHÀNG-BĂI₃ 上 百 (VO) up to
a hundred.

SHÀNG-BĀN₁ 上 班 (VO) go to
work, go to class. Wǒ-yìtiān
jiù-shàng-wǔge-zhōngtóu-de-
bān. 我 一 天 就 上 五
個 鐘 頭 的 班 . I work
only five hours a day.

'SHÀNGBÀNTIĀNR₃ 上 半 天
兒 (TW) the forenoon.

'SHÀNGBÀNYUÈ₃ 上 半 月
(TW) the first half of the month.

SHÀNGBIANR₁ 上 邊 兒 <u>or</u>
SHÀNGTOU 上 頭 <u>or</u> SHÀNG-
MIAN 上 面 (PW) (1) the top,
upper surface. Zhuōzi-shàng-
bianr yǒu-yige-diànhuà. 桌 子
上 邊 兒 有 一 個 電
話 . There's a telephone on
top of the table. (2) a place up <u>or</u>
above. Wǒ-gēge zài-shàngbianr-
ne. 我 哥 哥 在 上 邊 兒 呢 .
My brother is up there. Wǒ-
shàngbianr hái-yǒu-fùjīnglǐ-ne.
我 上 邊 兒 還 有 副
經 理 呢 . There's still a
vice-president above me. (3)
upper part <u>or</u> area <u>of something.</u>
Zhèizhang-huàr, shàngbianr-bu-
cuò, xiàbianr-yánse-bu-hǎo. 這
張 畫 兒 , 上 邊 兒 不

錯 , 下 邊 兒 顏 色 不 好 .
The upper part of this picture is
not bad, but the color of the
lower part is not good.
(N) higher-ups. Shàngbianr-bù-
gěi-jiāxīn. 上 邊 兒 不 給
加 薪 . The higher ups won't
give me a raise.

SHÀNGBIĀO₄ 商 標 (N) trade
mark.

SHÀNGBULÁI₄ 上 不 來 (RV)
cannot get along. Tāmen-liǎngge-ren shàngbulái. 他 們 兩
個 人 上 不 來 . They
two cannot get along. (See:
SHÀNGLAI 上 來).

SHĀNGCHǍNG₄ 商 場 (N) mer-
chandise mart, bazaar, empo-
rium. (M: zuò 座).

SHĀNGCHAO₄ 商 朝 (TW) Shang
dynasty.

SHĀNGCHUÁN₄ 商 船 (N) mer-
chant ship.

SHÀNGCI₂ 上 次 (TW) the previous time. (<u>syn.</u> shànghui
上 回).

SHÀNG-DÀNG₂ 上 當 (VO) be
swindled, be taken in. Wǒ-
shàngle-ta-háujicì-dàng-le. 我
上 了 他 好 幾 次 當
了 . I have been swindled by
him several times.
(RE) be swindled, be taken in.
Zhèige wǒ-mǎishàngdàng-le. 這
個 我 買 上 當 了 . I
was taken in when I bought this.

SHÀNGDĚNG₃ 上 等 (B) high
class, high quality. shàngděng-
chá 上 等 茶 high quality tea.

SHÀNGDÌ₂ 上 帝 (N) God.

S

SHĀNGDIÀN₃ 商店 (N) shop, store (<u>retail</u>). (M: jiā 家).

SHÀNGDÒNG₄ 上凍 (VO) begin to freeze over (<u>as rivers and lakes</u>). Xiànzài-cái-shíyue, yǐjing-shàngdòng-le. 現在才十月，已經上凍了. Now it's only October, it has already begun to freeze.

'SHÀNGFÁNG₅ 上房 (N) main rooms <u>of a Chinese house, usually larger than the other rooms and facing south.</u>

SHĀNG-FĒNG₂ 傷風 (VO) catch a cold, have a cold. Wǒ-shāng-le-sāntian-fēng. 我傷了三天風. I've had a cold for three days.
(N) the common cold. Nǐde-shāng-fēng hǎole-méiyou? 你的傷風好了沒有? Have you gotten over your cold? (cf: ZHÁO-LIÁNG 着凉).

SHĀNGGĂNG₄ 商港 (N) commercial port.

SHĀNGHAI₄ 傷害 (TV) injure, hurt, wound. Bié-shānghai-xiǎo-dòngwu. 別傷害小動物. Don't hurt small animals.
(N) damage.

SHÀNGHAI₁ 上海 (PW) Shanghai.

SHĀNGHÁN₄ 傷寒 (N) typhoid fever.

SHÀNGHUI₂ 上回 (TW) the preceding time.(<u>syn.</u> shàngci 上次).

SHÀNGHUO₄ 晌午 (TW) noon. Tā-shǎnghuo-qù. 他晌午去. He will go at noon.

SHÀNG-HUǑ₃ 上火 (VO) get indigestion, sore throat, headache <u>or some other discomfort from spicy and very rich food.</u> (<u>opp.</u> bài-huǒ 敗火). Chī-là-de shàng-huǒ. 吃辣的上火. Eating hot things causes discomfort.

SHÀNGJÍ₃ 上級 (N) superior (<u>someone in a high position</u>).

SHĀNGJIÀO₄ 晌覺 (N) (<u>lit.</u> noontime sleep) nap. shuì-shǎngjiào 睡晌覺 take a nap.

SHÀNG-JIĒ₁ 上街 (VO) (1) go out to the street. (2) go to the shopping area.

SHÀNG-JÌNR₄ 上勁兒 (VO) put effort into <u>something</u>. (SV) enthusiastic. Tā-zuò-shì zuòde-hěn-shàng-jìnr. 他作事作的很上勁兒. He works very enthusiastically. (cf: QĬ-JÌNR 起勁兒).

SHÀNG-KÈ₁ 上課 (VO) (1) go to class, attend <u>or</u> hold class. Nǐ-wèishenma hái-bú-qù-shàng-kè? 你為甚麼還不去上課? Why haven't you gone to class yet? (2) start (<u>of a class</u>). 'Bādiǎnzhong shàng-kè. 八點鐘上課. The class starts at eight o'clock.

SHÀNGLAI₁ 上來 (RV) come up. Tāmen-dōu-shànglai-le. 他們都上來了. They are all coming up.
(RE) (1) up (<u>here</u>). Zhuōzi-tài-dà, bānbúshanglai. 桌子太大，搬不上來. The table is too big, it cannot be moved up

here. (2) <u>indicates reproduction from memory</u>. Nèige-zi wǒ-xiěbu-shànglái-le. 那個字我寫不上來了. I cannot remember how to write that character. (3) <u>indicates ability to do something</u>. Wǒ-shuōbushanglái nà-shi-wèi-shénma. 我說不上來那是為甚麼. I cannot say why.

SHĀNGLIANG₂ 商量 (TV) discuss, talk over, consult. Wǒ yǒu-yijian-shìqing gēn-ni-shāngliang. 我有一件事情跟你商量. I have something to discuss with you. (cf: ʼSHĀNGTĀO 商討).

SHÀNG(GE)LǏBÀI₁ 上(個)禮拜 or SHÀNG(GE)XĪNGQĪ 上(個)星期 (TW) preceding week.

SHÀNGMIAN₂ 上面 (PW) see SHÀNGBIANR 上邊兒.

SHĀNGPǏN₅ 商品 (N) merchandise, goods.

SHĀNGPÙ₅ 商埠 (N) commercial city, trading port.

SHĂNGQIAN₄ 賞錢 (N) gratuity, monetary rewards (<u>given to persons of lower rank for services performed</u>).

SHÀNG-QIĀN₃ 上千 (VO) up to a thousand. Zuótian lái-de-rén shàng-qiān. 昨天來的人上千. Yesterday up to a thousand people came.

SHÀNGQIÁN₃ 上前 (IV) go forward, go ahead. Tā-bù-gǎn shàngqián-shuō-huà. 他不敢上前說話. He's

afraid to go forward to speak.

SHÀNGQU₁ 上去 (RV) go up. Shàngdeqù-ma? 上得去嗎? Can it go up? (RE) up (<u>there</u>). bānshangqu 搬上去 move it up (there). ná-shang-lóu-qu 拿上樓去 take it upstairs (there).

SHĀNGREN₂ 商人 (N) merchant, businessman.

SHÀNGSHANG₃ 上上 (SP) <u>the month or week</u> before the last. shàngshang-lǐbài 上上禮拜 the week before last week.

SHÀNGSI₃ 上司 (N) boss, superior.

SHĀNGTĀO₄ 商討 (TV) discuss, talk over, consult. Zhèige-tíyì wǒmen-zhànshí-bubi-shāngtāo. 這個提議我們暫時不必商討. Temporarily we don't have to discuss this motion. (cf: SHĀNGLIANG 商量).

SHÀNGTOU₁ 上頭 see SHÀNGBIANR 上邊兒.

SHÀNG-WÀN₃ 上萬 (VO) up to ten thousand. Tāde-xīnshui yǐ-jing-shàngle-wàn-le. 他的薪水已經上了萬了. His salary has gone up to ten thousand already.

SHÀNGWU₁ 上午 (TW) the morning, forenoon. Shàngwu-bǐ-xiàwu-hǎo. 上午比下午好. The morning is better than the afternoon. Wǒ-shàngwu-bu-zuò-shì. 我上午不作事. I don't work in the morning.

S

SHÀNGXIÀ$_2$ 上下 (B) used after NU-M, around, about the given figure. (syn. zuǒyou 左右). sānshikuài-qían-shàngxià 三十塊錢上下 around thirty dollars.

(PW) (con. shàngtou-xiàtou 上頭下頭). (1) upper and lower ranks. Shàngxià dōu-zànchéng. 上下都贊成. Everybody from the top level to the bottom level approves. (2) top and bottom. Dāngzhōng-hai-hǎo, shàngxià-dōu-huài-le. 當中還好，上下都壞了. The middle part is all right, but the top and bottom are broken. (3) from top to bottom. Zhèige-lǚguǎn shàngxià-dōu mǎn-le. 這個旅館上下都滿了. This hotel is full from top to bottom.

SHÀNGXIÀWÉN(R)$_3$ 上下文(兒) (N) context.

SHĀNGXĪN$_2$ 傷心 (SV) feel grief, heart-broken. Zhēn-rang-wo-shāngxīn-tòule. 真讓我傷心透了. It made me feel extremely heart-broken.

SHÀNG(GE)XĪNGQĪ$_1$ 上(個)星期 see SHÀNG(GE)LIBÀI 上(個)禮拜.

SHÀNG-XUÉ$_1$ 上學 (VO) (1) go to school. Wǒ-bādian-zhōng shàng-xué. 我八點鐘上學. I go to school at eight o'clock. (2) attend school. Wǒ-zài-Měiguo-shàng-xué. 我在美國上學. I am attending school in America.

S

SHÀNGYǍN$_2$ 上演 (IV) start (a show, play, movie, etc.). Zhèng-piānzi hái méi-shàngyǎn-ne. 正片子還沒上演呢. The main feature is not on yet.

SHĀNGYÈ$_2$ 商業 (N) commerce.

SHÀNGYĪ$_4$ 上衣 (N) a garment covering the upper part of the body, jacket. (M: jiàn 件).

SHÀNG-YǏN$_3$ 上癮 (VO) be addicted to. Bié-chī-nèige-yào, nèige-yào néng-shàng-yǐn. 別吃那個藥，那個藥能上癮. Don't take that medicine, you may become addicted to it.

SHÀNGYUE$_1$ 上月 (TW) the preceding month.

SHĀNMÀI$_4$ 山脈 (N) mountain range. (M: tíao 條).

SHĀNPŌR$_3$ 山坡兒 (N) mountain slope.

SHĀNXI$_2$ 山西 (PW) Shansi province.

SHǍNXI$_2$ 陝西 (PW) Shensi province.

SHĀNYÁNG$_3$ 山羊 (N) mountain goat, goat. (M: zhī 隻).

SHĀNYAO$_5$ 山藥 (N) an edible root of certain peony plants.

SHĀNYĀO$_5$ 山腰 (N) halfway up a mountain.

SHÀNZI$_3$ 扇子 (N) fan (hand variety). (M: bǎ 把). Yòng-shànzi-shān-huǒ. 用扇子搧火. Use a fan to fan the fire.

SHĀO$_1$ 燒 (TV) (1) burn. shāo-lājī 燒垃圾 burn trash. shāo-huǒ 燒火 burn. (2) cook.

shāo-fàn 燒飯 cook a meal. shāo-kāishuǐ 燒開水 boil water.

(IV) (1) have a fever. Tā-hái-shāo-ne. 他還燒呢. He still has a fever. (2) do unusual things because of having too much money. Tā-shì-qián-shāo-de. 他是錢燒的. The money made him lose his head. (N) fever. Shāo tuìle-méiyou? 燒退了沒有? Has the fever gone?

SHĀO₄ 捎 (TV) bring along, take along. Qǐng-nǐ bǎ-zhèifēng-xìn-shāoqu. 請你把這封信捎去. Please take this letter along.

SHĂO₁ 少 (opp. duō 多). (SV) few, scarce. Zhèr Zhōngguo-rén-hěn-shǎo. 這兒中國人很少. There are few Chinese here.

(TV) lack, be missing. Xiànzài hái-shǎo-liǎngge-rén. 現在還少兩個人. Now we are still short two people.

(AD) (1) less, not so much. Shǎo-chī-ròu. 少吃肉. Eat meat less. (2) seldom, rarely. Tā-hěn-shǎo-chàng. 他很少唱. He rarely sings.

SHÀO₄ 捎 (IV) have slanting rain come into an area protected by a roof. Yǔ wàng-wūzili-shào. 雨往屋子裏捎. The slanting rain is coming into the room.

SHĀOBING₄ 燒餅 (N) a salted baked pastry with sesame seeds

on top.

SHĂOJIÀN₂ 少見 (SV) (1) be rarely seen. Zhèizhǒng-dòngwu hěn-shǎojiàn. 這種動物很少見. This kind of animal is rarely seen. (2) used for greetings. Shǎojiàn-shǎojiàn. 少見少見. It's been a long time since I've seen you.

SHĀOJIǓ₂ 燒酒 (N) distilled alcoholic beverage, hard liquor.

SHÀONIÁN₂ 少年 (N) (1) youth, young person, (2) period of youth, one's youth. Shéi-dou-jīngguo-shàoniande-shíhou. 誰都經過少年的時候. Everybody has gone through a period of youthfulness.

SHĂOPÉI₄ 少陪 (IV) excuse me (a polite expression said to other guests at a party when one is leaving the party).

SHĀOR₄ 梢兒 (N) tip of a branch, a whip, or similar long and thin objects. shù-shāor 樹梢兒 tip of the branch.

SHÁOR₂ 勺兒 or SHÁOZI 勺子 (N) spoon, ladle. (M: bǎ 把). (cf: TIÁOGĒNG 調羹).

SHÀOR₃ 哨兒 (N) whistle. chuī-shàor 吹哨兒 blow a whistle or whistle.

SHÀOSHǍI₄ 捎色 (VO) fade (as colors). Nèige-liánzi shàole-shǎi-le. 那個簾子捎了色了. The color of that curtain has faded.

SHĂOSHÙ₂ 少數 (N) minority. zhàn-shǎoshù 佔少數 be in the minority.

S

SHĀOWEI₃ 稍微 (AD) followed by yidiǎnr 一點兒, slightly, just a little. Nǐ-shāowēi chī-yidiǎnr. 你稍微吃一點兒. Eat just a little. Shāowēi-dà-yidianr-gèng-hǎo. 稍微大一點兒更好. Slightly larger would be even better. Wǒ-shāowēi yǒu-yidiǎnr-shāo. 我稍微有點兒燒. I have a slight fever. (cf: DUŌSHǍO 多少).

SHÁOYAO₅ 芍藥 (N) herbacious peony. (M: duǒ 朵, kē 棵).

SHǍOYǑU₃ 少有 (SV) rare. Zhèiyàngr-ren shǎoyǒu. 這樣人少有. This kind of person is rare.

SHÁOZI₂ 勺子 see SHAOR 勺兒.

SHĀTÁNG₄ 砂糖 (N) granulated sugar.

SHĀYǍN₅ 沙眼 (N) trachoma.

SHĀYÚ₄ 沙魚 (N) shark. (M: tiáo 條).

SHĀ-ZHÀNG₄ 殺賬 (VO) summarize accounts (done periodically to check balance of running accounts for collecting purposes, and to make disposition of certain inequities). Nǐ-shāle-zhàng-le-ma? 你殺了賬了嗎? Did you summarize the accounts?

SHĀZHǏ₃ 砂紙 (N) sandpaper. (M: zhāng 張). Yòng-shāzhǐ-dǎmo-yixia. 用砂紙打磨一下. Use sandpaper to smooth it off.

SHĀZI₃ 沙子 (N) sand.

SHǍZI₃ 傻子 (N) fool, idiot.

SHĒ₄ 賒 (TV) buy or sell on credit. Nǐ-qu-shē-liǎngpíngr-jiǔ-lai. 你去賒兩瓶兒酒來. Go to buy two bottles of wine on credit. Tāmen-bushē-gei wo. 他們不賒給我. They won't sell it to me on credit.

SHÉ₂ 蛇 (N) snake. (M: tiáo 條).

SHÉ₃ 折 (IV) (1) be broken (long objects). qiānbǐ shé-le 鉛筆折了 the pencil is broken. (2) lose money in business. shé-bēnqian 折本錢 lose part or all of an investment. Tā-shéle-wǔwànkuai-qián. 他折了五萬塊錢. He lost fifty thousand dollars in business.

SHÈ₄ 射 (TV) shoot. shè-jiàn 射箭 shoot an arrow.

SHÈBÈI₂ 設備 (N) facilities, equipment, furnishings.

SHĚBUDE₂ 捨不得 (RV) (1) reluctant or hate to part with. Wǒ-shěbude-ni. 我捨不得你. I hate to leave you. (2) reluctant to do something because of reluctance to part with something or someone. Tā-shěbude-chuān. 他捨不得穿. He is reluctant to wear it (so that he won't wear it out). Tā-shěbude-mǎi, yīnwei-ta-shěbude-qián. 他捨不得買,因為他捨不得錢. He is reluctant to buy because he is reluctant to part with money.

SHĒCHI₃ 奢侈 (SV) (1) extravagant, indulgent in luxuries. (2)

excessively lavish.

SHÈDÌ₄ 舍弟 (N) my younger brother (polite form).

SHÈFĂ₃ 設法 (AD) (lit. devise a way) try to. Nǐ-shèfǎ-lái-yicì. 你設法來一次. Try to come once. (cf: XIĂNG-FÁZI 想法子).

SHÈHUÌ₁ 社會 (N) society, community. shèhuì-zhǔyì 社會主義 socialism. shèhuì-wèntí 社會問題 social problems.

SHÈHUÌZHǓYÌ₃ 社會主義 (N) socialism.

SHÉI₁ 誰 or SHUÉI 誰 (PR) (1) who, whom. Shéi-qù? 誰去? Who is going? Nǐ-qǐng-shéi-le? 你請誰了? Whom did you invite? (2) preceded by a stressed negative expression, anybody. Wǒ-'bù-zhǎo-shei. 我不找誰. I'm not looking for anybody. (3) unstressed, used after a TV, somebody. Nǐ-yào-zhǎo-shei-ma? 你要找誰嗎? Are you looking for someone? (4) when vocally stressed and followed by a phrase with yě 也 or dōu 都, anybody, everybody. 'Shéi-dōu-lái. 誰都來. Everyone comes. Shéi-yě-buyào. 誰也不要. Nobody wants it. (5) repeated in two phrases, whoever. Shéi-xiān-dào, shéi-xiān-chī. 誰先到,誰先吃. Whoever arrives first will eat first. (6) used repeatedly, somebody, such and such a person.

Tā-lǎo-ài-shuō-shéi-shéi-shéi-yǒu-qián. 他老愛説誰誰誰有錢. He always likes to say that such and such has money. (7) used both before and after a TV, one does something to the other. Shéi-ye-kàn-buqǐ-shéi. 誰也看不起誰. Nobody has any respect for the other. Shéi-xiān-dào shéi-děng-shéi. 誰先到誰等誰. Whoever arrives first should wait for the other. (8) used both before and after shì 是, who. Wǒ-bu-zhīdào shéi-shi-shéi. 我不知道誰是誰. I don't know who is who.

SHÈJÍ₄ 射擊 (TV) shoot with a gun. Tāmen-duìzhǔn-mùbiāo-shèjī. 他們對準目標射擊. They aimed at the target (accurately) and shot.

SHÈJÌ₄ 設計 (TV) design. Zhèi-zuò-qiáo shì-tā-shèjìde. 這座橋是他設計的. This bridge was designed by him. (N) design.

SHÈLÙN₃ 社論 (N) editorial. (M: piān 篇).

SHĒN₃ 伸 (TV) stretch out a part of the body. shēn-shǒu 伸手 stretch out the hand. shēn-shé-tou 伸舌頭 stick out the tongue.

SHĒN₂ 深 (SV) (1) lit. or fig. deep. Zhèige-hú hěn-shēn. 這個湖很深. This lake is very deep. Zhèige-shū hěn-shēn. 這個書很深. This book is

S

S

too deep. (2) deep <u>or</u> dark (<u>of a color</u>). Zhèige-hóng-yánse tài-shēn-le. 這個紅顏色太深了. This red color is too dark.

SHÉN₂ 神 (N) (1) deity, god, goddess. (M: wèi 位). (2) expression, spirit. Tāde-yǎnjing yǒu-shén. 他的眼睛有神. His eyes are expressive. (SV) <u>Peip.</u> fantastic. Tā-shuō-de-nèige-gùshi shénle, 他說的那個故事神了. The story he told is fantastic.

SHÈN₄ 滲 (IV) seep (through). Xiě cóng-bēngdàili shènchulai-le. 血從繃帶裏滲出來了. The blood is seeping through the bandage. Shuǐ dōu-shènxiaqu-le. 水都滲下去了. The water is seeping down.

'SHÉNCHÁ₃ 審查 (TV) examine, investigate (<u>with judgment resulting</u>). Zhèijiàn-ànzi guǐ-'shéi-'shénchá? 這個案子歸誰審查? Who will examine this case?

SHÉNFEN₃ 身分 (N) status (<u>of a person</u>).

SHÉNFU₃ 神父 (N) Catholic priest.

SHĒNG₁ 生 (TV) (1) give birth. shēng-érzi 生兒子 give birth to a son. (2) be born. Nǐ-shēngzai-nǎr? 你生在那兒? Where were you born? (3) have <u>a baby</u>. Zhāng-xiansheng shēngle-yige-nǚ'er. 張先生生了一個女兒. Mr.

Chang had a baby girl. (SV) (1) raw, unripe, insufficiently cooked. Zhèige-lí hěn-shēng. 這個梨很生. This pear is not ripe. Ròu hái-tài-shēng. 肉還太生. The meat is still too rare. (2) be unfamiliar, strange. Wǒ-gēn-tā hěn-shēng. 我跟他很生. I'm notfamiliar with him. (3) <u>or</u> ZHǍNG 長 grow, develop. Wǒ-shǒushang shēng-yige-chuāng. 我手上生了一個瘡. A boil developed on my hand. (4) produce, put forth. Bǎ-qián-fàngchuqu kéyi-shēng-yi-dianr-lì. 把錢放出去可以生一點兒利. Lending money out can produce a little interest. (5) create <u>or</u> make trouble. Bié-shēng-shì. 別生事. Don't create any trouble. Tā-láile-yǐhòu shēngle bu-shǎo-de-máfan. 他來了以後生了不少的麻煩. After he came he made a lot of trouble. (B) (1) life. shēnghuo 生活 living. (2) student, disciple. nán-shēng 男生 male student.

SHĒNG₃ 聲 (M) for sound. Diàn-língr xiǎngle-liǎngsheng. 電鈴兒響了兩聲. The bell rang two times. (cf: SHĒNGR 聲兒).

SHĒNG₄ 升 (TV) raise, hoist. shēng-qí 升旗 hoist a flag. (IV) (1) promote. Tā-shēngle-guān-le. 他升了官了. He has been promoted (to a higher official rank). (2) ascend, rise. Tàiyang-shēngqilai-le. 太陽升起來了. The sun rose.

SHĒNG₄ 升 (M) a Chinese form of measurement for quantity equal to one-tenth of dǒu 斗. wǔshēng-dàdòu 五升大豆 five shēng of beans.

(N) the container which holds one shēng. (See: DǑU 斗).

SHĚNG₃ 省 (N) province, state. Máshěng 麻省 Massachusetts. Guǎngdongshěng 廣東省 Kwangtung province.

(M) province, state.

SHĚNG₂ 省 (SV) frugal, sparing. Quánjiā-dōu-hěn-shěng. 全家都很省. The entire family is very thrifty.

(TV) save, economize on. Zuò-gōnggòng-qìchē-shěng-qián. 坐公共汽車省錢. It will save money to go by bus.

SHÈNG₃ 剩 (IV) be left, have left. shèng-fàn 剩飯 leave food or left-over food. Wǒ-jiu-shèngle-liǎngkuài-qián-le. 我就剩了兩塊錢了. I have only two dollars left.

SHĒNG 勝 (IV) win a battle, war, game, etc.

(RE) indicates victory. dǎshèng-le 打勝了 win by fighting.

SHĒNG-BĀN₂ 升班 (VO) enter or get promoted to a higher class.

SHĒNG-BÌNG₃ 生病 (VO) get sick, become ill. Tā-qùnian shēngle-yichang-dà-bìng. 他

去年生了一場大病. Last year he was very seriously ill.

SHĒNGCÀI₃ 生菜 (N) raw vegetable. (2) salad. bàn-shēngcài 拌生菜 mix a salad.

SHĒNGCHǍN₃ 生產 (IV) have a baby. Zhāng-tàitai zuótian-yǐ-jing-shēngchǎn-le. 張太太昨天已經生產了. Mrs. Chang had a baby yesterday.

(TV) produce. Wǒmen-xiànzài bushēngchan-zhèzhǒng-qìchē-le. 我們現在不生產這種汽車了. We no longer produce this type of car.

(N) (1) production. (2) childbirth.

SHÈNGDÀ₅ 盛大 (AD) great, magnificent. shèngdà-huānyíng 盛大歡迎 big welcome.

SHĒNGDÀNJIÉ₁ 聖誕節 (TW) Christmas.

SHĒNGDÀNLǍORÉN₂ 聖誕老人 (N) Santa Claus.

SHĚNGDE₂ 省得 (MA) so that ... not, lest. Jiè-yige-suànle, shěngde-wǒmen-mǎi-le. 借一個算了, 省得我們買了. Try to borrow one so that we won't have to buy one.

SHĒNGDIAO₄ 聲調 (N) (1) tone (of Chinese syllables). (2) voice (in talking). Tā-shuō-huà-de-shēngdiao hěn-hǎotīng. 他說話的聲調很好聽. When he speaks he has a melodious voice which is good to listen to.

SHĒNGDÒNG₃ 生動 (SV) lively.

S

Tā-miáoxiede hěn-shēngdòng. 他 描 寫 的 很 生 動. His description is very lively.

SHĚNGHUÌ₄ 省 會 (N) provincial or state capital.

SHÈNGHUÌ₅ 盛 會 (N) great gathering.

SHĒNGHUÓ₁ 生 活 (IV) live. Tā-gēn-tā-fùmǔ zài-yíkuàir-shēnghuo. 他 跟 他 父 母 在 一 塊 兒 生 活. He lives together with his parents. (N) (1) life. shēnghuo-fāngshì 生 活 方 式 way of life. (2) livelihood, living. móu-shēnghuo 謀 生 活 make a living.

SHÈNGHUÒ₄ 剩 貨 (N) surplus goods, left-over goods. Zhè-dōu-shi-màibuchūqù-de-shèng-huò. 這 都 是 賣 不 出 去 的 剩 貨. These are all the left-over goods which cannot be sold.

SHĒNGJIÀNGJĪ₄ 升 降 機(N) elevator. (syn. diàntī 電 梯). zuò-shēngjiàngjī 坐 升 降 機 ride in an elevator.

SHÈNGJĪNG₂ 聖 經 (N) Holy Bible.(M: běn 本).

SHĒNGKOU₃ 牲 口 (N) livestock. (M: tóu 頭, pǐ 匹, zhī 隻).

SHÈNGLÌ₃ 勝 利 (IV) win, be victorious. Zuìhòu wǒmen-shènglì-le. 最 後 我 們 勝 利 了. At last, we won. (N) victory. dédao-shènglì 得 到 勝 利 gain victory.

'SHĚNGLUÈ₃ 省 略 (TV) leave out, omit. Nèige-yǎnjiǎng wǒ-

'shěngluèle-yíduàn. 那 個 演 講 我 省 略 了 一 段. I omitted one paragraph in that speech.

SHĒNGMÍNG₂ 聲 明 (TV) declare, announce. Tā-shēngmíng tā-tuì-chu-nèige-zǔzhi-le. 他 聲 明 他 退 出 那 個 組 織 了. He announced that he had withdrawn from that organiza-tion. (N) announcement. fābiǎo-shēng-míng 發 表 聲 明 make an announcement.

SHĒNGMÌNG₃ 生 命 (N) life (opposed to death). Huǒxīng-shang yǒu-méiyou-shēngmìng? 火 星 上 有 沒 有 生 命? Is there life on Mars? Tā-yǒu-shēngmìngde-wēixian. 他 有 生 命 的 危 險. His life is in danger.

SHĒNGQÌ₃ 生 氣 (N) spirit, vitality. Zhèi-ge-xuéxiào méi-you-shēngqi. 這 個 學 校 沒 有 生 氣. This school has no spirit.

SHĒNG-QÌ₁ 生 氣 (VO) get an-gry. Nǐ-hái-shēng-wǒde-qì-ma? 你 還 生 我 的 氣 嗎? Are you still angry with me? Tā-hěn-shēng-qì. 他 很 生 氣. He is very angry.

SHĒNGR₃ 聲 兒 or SHĒNGYIN 聲 音 (N) sound, voice. Bié-chū-shēngr. 別 出 聲 兒. Don't make a sound. Dà-dianr-shēngr-shuō. 大 點 兒 聲 兒 說. Speak a little louder.

'SHĒNGRÉN₂ 生 人 (N) stranger.

SHĒNG-RÉN₄ 生人 (VO) be born.
Nǐ-shi-něinian-shēng-rén? 你
是那年生人 ? In which
year were you born?

SHÈNGREN₃ 聖人 (N) (1) sage.
(M: wèi 位). (2) saint. (M: wèi
位).

SHĒNGRI₁ 生日 (N) birthday.
guò-shēngri 過生日 cele-
brate a birthday.

SHĒNG-SHÌ₂ 省事 (VO) save
trouble and work. Zhèyàngr
shěngle-wo-bushǎo-shì. 這樣
兒省了我不少事.
I save a lot of trouble this way.

SHĒNGSHǑUR₄ 生手兒 (N)
new hand (person without experience in certain fields).

SHĒNGWÙXUÉ₄ 生物學 (N)
biology.

SHÈNGXIA₃ 剩下 (RV) leave
over. Chàbuduō-dōu-mài-le,
méi-shèngxia-shenma. 差不
多都賣了, 沒剩下
甚麼. Almost everything
was sold, there wasn't much
left.
(RE) leave over. Zhè-shi-ta-
men-tiāoshèngxia-de. 這是
他們挑剩下的. This
is what was left over after their
selection.

SHĒNG-XUÉ₂ 升學 (VO) enter
or get promoted to a higher
school. Tā-bu-xiǎng-shēng-xué-
le. 他不想升學了.
He doesn't want to go any further
in school.

SHĒNGYI₂ 生意 (N) (commer-
cial) business. (syn. mǎimai

買賣). zuò-shēngyi 作生
意 do business. Shēngyi zěnme-
yàng? 生意怎麼樣?
How's business?

SHĒNGYIN₂ 聲音 or SHĒNGR
聲兒 (N) sound, voice. Shēngyin-hěn-dà. 聲音很大.
The sound is very loud. Diànhuà-
de-shēngyin bu-qīngchu. 電話
的聲音不清楚. The
voice on the telephone is not
clear.

SHĒNGZHǍNG₃ 生長 (IV) (1)
live and grow. Zhèizhǒng-shù
zài-rèdài-bùnéng-shēngzhǎng.
這種樹在熱帶不
能生長. This kind of tree
can't grow in the tropics. (2) be
born and raised. Tā shi-zai-Měi-
guo-shēngzhǎng-de. 他是在
美國生長的. He was
born and raised in America.

SHÉNGZI₄ 繩子 (N) rope, string.
(M: gēn 根, tiáo 條).

SHĒNGZÌ₂ 生字 (N) new words.
Zhèiben-shūli wo-shēngzì-tài-
duō. 這本書裏我生
字太多. There are too
many new words for me in this
book.

SHÉNHUÀ₃ 神話 (N) myth, le-
gend, mythology.

SHÉNJĪNG₂ 神經 (SV) lit. or
fig. insane, crazy. Tā-gēge
shénjǐng-le. 他哥哥神
經了. His brother went in-
sane. Nǐ-kàn tā-dwó-shénjǐng!
你看他多神經!
See how crazy he is!
(N) (1) nerve. (M: gēn 根) (2)

S

insanity.

SHÉNJÍNGBÌNG₂ 神經病 (N)
(1) neural sickness. (2) insanity.
(SV) lit. or fig. insane, crazy.
'SHĒNKÈ₃ 深刻 (SV) deep, profound. Tā-shuō-de-huà bu-gòu-
'shēnkè. 他說的話不
很深刻. What he said is
not very deep. Tā-hén-'shēnkè.
他很深刻. He is very
pensive.
SHĒNLIANGR₅ 身量兒 (N)
Peip. height of a person. Tā-
shēnliangr bu-gāo. 他身量
不高. He is not tall.
SHÉNMA₁ 甚麼 (QW) (1) what.
Nèige-shì-shénma? 那個是
甚麼? What's that? Nèige-
jiào-shénma-laizhe? 那個
叫甚麼來着? What
is that called? (2) used after a
stressed negative expression,
anything. Tā-'bùmǎi-shenma.
他不買甚麼. He
doesn't want to buy anything.
Nà-'búshi-shenma-yàojǐn-de-
shì. 那不是甚麼要
緊的事. That is not any-
thing important. (3) unstressed,
used after an affirmative verb,
usually with yidiǎnr 一點兒,
something. Wǒ-yào-chī-yidiǎnr-
shenma. 我要吃一點
兒甚麼. I want to eat a
little something. (4) unstressed,
used between a VO, what for,
for what reason. Yǔ-bu-xià-le,
nǐ-hái-dǎ-shenma-sǎn-a? 雨
不下了,你還打甚
麼傘呢? The rain has

stopped, why are you still holding up your umbrella? (5) (con.
xiàng-shénma 像甚麼).
used before a series of items,
such as, things like. Shénme-
Déwén-a, Fàwén-a, tā-dōu-huì-
shuō. 甚麼德文呢,法
文呢,他都會說. He
can speak many languages, such
as German and French. (6) when
vocally stressed and followed by
a phrase with dōu 都 or yě 也,
every, any. Tā-'shénme-dōng-
xi-dōu-yào. 他甚麼東
西都要. He wants every-
thing. Tā-'shénme-yě-méishuō.
他甚麼也沒說. He
didn't say anything. (7) repeated
in two phrases, whatever. Nǐ-
zuò-shenme, wǒ-chī-shenme.
你做甚麼,我吃甚
麼. I'll eat whatever you
cooked. (8) used repeatedly,
something. Nèi-sānge-zì wǒ-
jiù-rènshi zuì-hòu-liǎngge.
Shénma-shénma-"xuéxiào". 那
四個字我就認識
最後兩個.甚麼甚
麼"學校". I only know the
last two of those four characters.
They are something something
"school". (9) what would you
call it. Zhèiyàngr-bàn you-
diǎnr na-shénma. 這樣兒
辦有點兒那甚麼.
To do it this way, it is a little
what would you call it. (10)
stressed, used at the beginning
of a sentence to show disappro-
al or disbelief, how can it be.

S

A: Tā-shuō ta-bu-zhīdào. B: Shénma-bu-zhīdào! A: 他說他不知道．B: 甚麼不知道！A: He said he didn't know. B: How can it be that he didn't know! (See: MEI-SHÉNMA 沒甚麼).

SHÉNMADE₄ 甚麼的 (N) used after a series of items, and so on, and the like. Zhuō-zi-yǐzi-shenmade dōu-dei-mǎi. 桌子椅子甚麼的都得買．Tables, chairs, and the like, we have to buy them all.

SHÉNPÀN₄ 審判 (TV) try a person or case at law. Něige-fǎguān shěnpàn-jèijiàn-ànzi? 那個法官審判這件案子？Which judge will try this case? (N) trial, judgment.

SHÉNQI₃ 神氣 (N) appearance, bearing, air, carriage. Zhèige-háizi-de-shénqi hěn-xiàng-ta-fùchin. 這個孩子的神氣很像他父親．This child's appearance is very much like his father's. (SV) successful and content. Tā-xiànzài hěn-shénqi-le. 他現在很神氣了．He is well-off now.

SHÉNQING₃ 申請 (TV) apply for. Nǐ-shēnqing hùzhào-le-ma? 你申請護照了嗎？Did you apply for the passport? (N) application.

SHÉNR₄ 身兒 (M) for suits, outfits (of clothing).yishēnr-xīn-yīshang 一身兒新衣裳 a new suit.

SHÉNR₄ 嬸兒 or SHÉNZI 嬸子 (N) aunt (father's younger brother's wife).

SHÉNRÙ₄ 深入 (SV) penetrating, thorough. Tā-duì-lìshǐ-de-yánjiu hái-bu-gòu-shēnrù. 他對歷史的研究還不夠深入．His study of history is not thorough enough.

SHÉNSHANG₄ 身上 (PW) on the body, on one's person. Tā-shēn-shang yǒu-hěn-duō-máo. 他身上有很多毛．He has hair all over his body. Wǒ-shēn-shang-méi-qián. 我身上沒錢．I don't have any money on me. Bié-bǎ-cuòr dōu-tuīdao-wǒde-shēnshang. 別把錯兒都推到我的身上．Don't shift the mistakes onto me.

SHÉNTI₃ 身體 (N) (1) body. (2) health. Tāde-shēnti bu-tài-hǎo. 他的身體不太好．His health isn't very good.

SHÉNXIAN₅ 神仙 (N) fairy, gods.

SHÉNYÁNG₃ 瀋陽 (PW) Shen-yang (capital of Liaoning province).

SHÈNZÀNG₅ 腎臟 (N) kidney.

SHÈNZHIYU₃ 甚至於 (MA) even to the extent that, even so far as, so...that... Tā-lèide shènzhiyu-shǒu dou táibuqǐlái-le. 他累的甚至於手都抬不起來了．He was so tired that he couldn't even raise his hand.

S

S

SHĒNZI₄ 身子 (N) (1) body. (2) health. (3) pregnancy. Tā-yǒu-shēnzi-le. 他有身子了. She's pregnant.

SHĒNZI₄ 矯子 see SHĒNR 矯兒.

SHÉTOU₅ 舌頭 (N) tongue. (M: tiáo 條).

SHÈYǏNG₅ 攝影 (VO) take a photograph. Wǒmen-yíkuàɪr-shè-yíge-yǐng-ba. 我們一塊兒攝一個影吧 Let's have a photo taken together.

SHĪ₂ 詩 (N) peom, poetry. (M: shǒu 首). zuò-shī 作詩 write poems.

SHĪ₄ 師 (N) division (military). (M) division. dìsānshī 第三師 Third Division. (B) (1) teacher. lǎoshī 老師 teacher. (2) specialist. yīshī 醫師 physician.

SHĪ₄ 失 (B) (1) lose. yíshī 遺失 lose. shīwàng 失望 disappointed. (2) miss, lose control. shīsuàn 失算 miscalculate.

SHĪ₃ 濕 (SV) damp, wet, humid. (opp. gān 乾). Wǒde-yīshang quán-shī-le. 我的衣裳全濕了. My clothes are all wet. Zhèrde-tiānqi zhēn-shī. 這兒的天氣真濕. The weather is really humid here.

SHÍ₃ 拾 (TV) (syn. jiǎn 撿) (1) find something accidentally. Wǒ-shíle-yizhī-gāngbǐ. 我拾了一枝鋼筆. I found a pen. (2) pick something up (as from the floor). Bǎ-dìshang-nèimáo-qián-shíqilai. 把地

上那毛錢拾起來. Pick up that dime on the floor.

SHÍ₁ 十 (NU) ten, tenth. shípǐmǎ 十匹馬 ten horses. shímǎlù 十馬路 Tenth Avenue. (M) used after the numbers one through nine to form ten through ninety, ten. yìshí 一十 ten. sānshi 三十 thirty. used before the numbers one through nine to form the numbers eleven through nineteen, ten plus. shíyī 十一 eleven. shí'èr 十二 twelve. shísān 十三 thirteen. used before wàn 萬, shíwan 十萬 one hundred thousand.

SHǏ₄ 屎 (N) excrement, dung. (M: pāo 泡). lā-shǐ 拉屎 defecate, move the bowels. (B) secretion. yǎnshǐ 眼屎 secretion from the eyes.

SHǏ₂ 使 (TV) (1) use. (syn. yòng 用). Nǐ-kéyi-shǐ-wǒde-zhàoxiàngjī. 你可以使我的照像機. You may use my camera. (2) make, cause. (syn. ràng 讓; jiào 叫). Zhèijiàn-shìqing-shǐ-wǒ-hěn-nánguò. 這件事情使我很難過. This matter makes me very sad. (CV) with, using. (syn. yòng 用). Shǐ-kuàizi-chī-fàn. 使筷子吃飯. Eat with chopsticks. (B) envoy. dàshǐ 大使 ambassador.

SHÌ₃ 市 (N) (1) city, municipality. Niǔyue-shì 紐約市 New York City. (2) market (place or action of buying or selling).

hēishì 黑市 black market.

shìjià 市價 market price.

Shìshang méi-huò. 市 上 沒 貨. There is no merchandise in the market.

SHÌ₁ 試 (TV) try, try out, try on.

shìshikan 試 試看 try and see. Wǒ-buxiǎng-shì. 我 不 想 試. I don't want to try.

Nǐ-shìshi nèijian-yīshang. 你 試 試 那件 衣裳. Try that dress on. Dàidai-zhèige-màozi shìshi. 戴 戴 這 個 帽子 試 試. Put on this hat and try it.

(B) examine, test. bǐshì 筆 試 written test.

SHÌ₁ 是 (TV) (1) used between two nominal elements, be (is, are, etc.), (negated with bú 不 only, never méi 沒). Tā-shì-wǒ-gēge. 他 是 我 哥哥. He is my brother. (2) used before an element of a sentence to emphasize it. Tā-shì-shànglǐbài-qù-de. 他 是 上 禮 拜 去 的. It was last week that he went. Wǒ-shi-wǒ nǐ-shi-nǐ, zánmen-méi-guānxi. 我 是 我 你 是 你, 咱 們 沒 關 係. I am myself and you are yourself, there is no relation between us. Yìbǎikuai-qián shì-yìbǎikuai-qián, bié-bu-yào. 一 百 塊 錢 是 一 百 塊 錢, 別 不 要. Don't refuse. One hundred dollars is one hundred dollars. Shì-wo-mǔqin gěi-wǒ-mǎi-de. 是 我 母 親 給

我 買 的. It was my mother who bought it for me. Wǒmen-chī-de shi-Fàguo-fàn. 我 們 吃 的 是 法 國 飯. It was French food that we ate.

(3) stressed, used before a predicate of a sentence, it is true that. Tā-'shì-méi-qián. 他 是 沒 錢. It is true that he doesn't have any money. Zhōngguo-huà 'shì-róngyi. 中 國 話 是 容 易. It is true that Chinese language is easy. Wǒ-'shì-gěile-qián-le. 我 是 給 了 錢 了. It is true that I paid. (4) used after PW as a predicate, there is, there are. Zhōngguo-fànguǎnr dàochu-dou-shì. 中 國 飯 館 到 處 都 是. There are Chinese restaurants everywhere. (5) be the right place, time, flavor, etc. Tā-lái-de shì-shíhou. 他 來 得 是 時 候. He came at the right time. Zhèige-cài bú-shi-wèir. 這 個 菜 不 是 味 兒. This food does not have the right flavor. (6) indicates that the element following it contrasts with a previous element in the sentence. Tā-ài-hē-báilándì, wǒ-shi-píjiǔ. 他 愛 喝 白 蘭 地, 我 是 啤 酒. He likes to drink brandy, I like beer. (7) (con. fánshi 凡 是). stressed, only if it is. Shì-dāo jiu-xíng. 是 刀 就 行. Only if it is a knife will it do. (8) used for an affirmative response.

S

yes. A: Nǐ-mǎi-xīnchē-le-ba.
B: Shì. A: 你買新車了
吧. B: 是. A: You bought a
new car, I suppose. B: Yes. (9)
used with de 的 at the end of
the sentence, that'swhat it is.
Wǒ-shi-bu-néng-gàosong-ni-de.
我是不能告訴你
的. I cannot tell you, that's
the way it is.
(B) added to adverbs without
changing their function or meaning. Tā-búdànshi-cōngming,
érqiě-piàoliang.她不但是
聰明,而且漂亮.She's
not only smart but also pretty.
(S) (1) ... SHÌ 是 ... KĚSHI 可
是 ... (or BÚGUO 不過...).
...all right (or sure it is...)
but.... Piányi-shì-piányi, kěshi wǒ-méi-qián. 便宜是
便宜可是我沒錢.
It's cheap all right, but I don't
have the money. Hǎo-shi-bu-hǎo
kěshì-piányi. 好是不好
可是便宜. It isn't that
it's good, but it's reasonable.
(2) SHÌ...(HÁI) SHÌ... 是...
(還) 是... see HÁISHI...
(HAI)SHI... 還是...（還)
是....
SHÌ(QING)₁ 事（情）(N) (1) matter, affair, business, thing.(M:
jiàn 件 dàngzi 當子). Méi-
nǐde-shì(qing). 沒你的事
（情）. It's not your business.or
Nothing here concerns you.
Zhè-shi-zěnma-hui-shì(qing) ?
這是怎麼回事(情)?
What is this all about? (2) work,

job. Tā-xiànzài méi-shì(qing)-
le. 他現在沒事（情）
了. He lost his job. (3) trouble. shēng-shì(qing) 生事
（情）make trouble. Nèige-
gōngsī chūle-shì(qing)-le. 那
個公司出了事情
了. That company is in trouble.
SHÌBÀI₂ 失敗 (IV) fail. Tā-
zuò-mǎimai shìbài-le. 他做
買賣失敗了. He failed
in doing business.
(N) failure. (M: cì 次).
SHÍBǍN₄ 石板 (N) flagstone,
slate. (M: kuài 塊).
SHÌBĪNG₅ 士兵 (N) enlisted
man, soldier.
SHÍCHÁNG₂ 時常 (AD) often.
Wǒmen-shícháng-dǎ-pái. 我
們時常打牌. We often
play cards.
SHÌCHǍNG₃ 市場 (N) (1) market-
place. Dào-shìchǎng-qu-mǎi-qu.
到市場去買去. Go
to the market to buy it. (2) market (demand for commodities).
Zhèizhong-huò xiànzài-méi-you-
shìchǎng. 這種貨現在
沒有市場. Now there
is no market for this kind of
goods.
SHÍDÀI₂ 時代 (N) age, era,
period. shíqi-shídai 石器時
代 stone age. Wǒ-gēnbushàng-
shídài. 我跟不上時
代. I cannot keep up with the
times.
SHǏDE₄ 使得 (RV) (1) can use.
Zhèige-dǎzìjī shǐde-ma? 這

個 打 字 機 使 得 嗎?
Can this typewriter be used?
(2) all right. Nĭ-juéde zhèige-
bànfa-hái-shĭde-ma? 你 覺 得
這 個 辦 法 還 使 得
嗎? Do you feel that this plan
is all right?
(CV) make or cause someone or
something to be in a certain
state. Tiānqi-shĭde-wo-hen-lei.
天 氣 使 得 我 很 累.
The weather made me very tired.

SHĬDE₂ 似 的 (P) (1) used after
verbal expressions with or without xiàng 像, hǎoxiàng 好 像,
fǎnfu 彷 彿, sìhu 似 乎 or
gēn 跟, as if. Tā(-hǎoxiàng-)
hěn-nánguò-shìde. 他 (好 像)
很 難 過 似 的. He looks
as if he's suffering. Wǒ(-sìhu-)
láiguo-zhèr-shìde. 我 (似 乎)
來 過 這 兒 似 的. It
seems as if I've been here before. (2) used after nominal expressions with or without xiàng
像, hǎoxiàng 好 像, fǎngfu
彷 彿 or gēn 跟, be the same
as, be like. Tāde-yǎnjing (xiàng-)
sǐ-yú-shìde. 他 的 眼 睛
(像) 死 魚 似 的, His eyes are
like the eyes of a dead fish. Tā-
pàngde (hǎoxiàng-)zhū-shide.
他 胖 的 (好 像) 豬 似
的. He's as fat as a pig.

SHĬDE₂ 是 的 used for an affirmative response, yes, right.

SHÍDUO₄ 拾 掇 (TV) (syn. shōu-
shi 收 拾) (1) repair, fix.
shíduo-yǔsǎn 拾 掇 雨 傘
repair an umbrella. (2) straighten

out, put in order. shíduo-wūzi
拾 掇 屋 子 straighten
out a room. (3) fix someone for
what he has done. Ràng-wo-shí-
duo-ta. 讓 我 拾 掇 他.
Let me fix him.

SHÍ'ÈRYUE₁ 十 二 月 (TW)
(lit. the twelfth month of the
year) December.

SHĪFÀN₃ 師 範 (B-) normal
(referring to a school which
trains teachers). shīfàn-dàxué
師 範 大 學 teacher's col-
lege. shīfàn-xuéxiào 師 範
學 校 normal school.

SHÌFÀNG₅ 釋 放 (TV) release a
prisoner. Wǒmen-míngtian jiù-
yao-bǎ-ta shìfàng-le. 我 們
明 天 就 要 把 他 釋
放 了. We'll release him
tomorrow.

SHÌFEI₃ 是 非 (N) (lit. right and
wrong) (1) gossip (which may
cause trouble). shuō-shìfei 說
是 非 to gossip. Wǒ-bu-yuàn-
yi-tīng-shìfei. 我 不 願 意
聽 是 非. I don't like to
listen to gossip. (2) trouble
caused by gossip. (M: chǎng 場).
rě-shìfei 惹 是 非 cause
trouble. nào-yichang-shìfei 鬧
一 場 是 非 have a dis-
turbance caused by gossip.

SHÍFEN₂ 十 分 (AD) (lit. one
hundred percent) completely,
very. shífen-fāngbian 十 分 方
便 very convenient. Zuìjìn
shēngyi-shífen-hǎo. 最 近 生
意 十 分 好. Business has
been very good lately.

S

SHĪFU₄ 師傅 (N) (1) teacher
(old-fashioned term). (2) specialist (referring to people in
certain trades, such as a barber, carpenter, tailor, cook,
etc.). (3) used politely after
surnames of people in certain
trades mentioned above.

SHĪGE₅ 詩歌 (N) poems and
songs.

SHĪGUǍN₃ 使館 (N) legation,
embassy.

SHĪHAO₃ 嗜好 (N) (1) addiction.
Tā-yǒu-shìhao. 他有嗜
好. He's an addict. (2) hobby.
Sōuji-yóupiào shi-tade-shìhao.
蒐集郵票是他的
嗜好. Collecting stamps is
his hobby.

SHĪHOU(R)₁ 時候(兒)(N) (syn.
shíjian 時間) (1) time (at a
certain point). Xiānzài shénmá-
shìhou(r)-le? 現在甚麼
時候(兒)了? What's the
time now? (2) time, period of
time. Wǒ-méiyou-shíhou(r) zuò-
gōngke. 我沒有時候
(兒)做功課. I don't have
time to do my homework.

SHĪHUÀ₃ 實話 (N) truth, true
words. (M: jù 句). Nǐ-fēi-shuō-
shíhuà-bùkě. 你非説實
話不可. You have to tell
the truth. Tā-yíjiu-shíhua dou-
méiyǒu. 他一句實話
都沒有. There isn't one
true word in what he said.

SHĪHUAN₅ 使喚 (TV) (1) use,
manage servants. Xiānzài wǒ-
men-shǐhuan-liǎngge-rén. 現

在我們使喚兩個
人. We use two servants now.
(2) boss someone around. Tā-
xǐhuan-shǐhuan-rén. 他喜歡
使喚人. He like to boss
people around.

SHĪHUI₅ 石灰 (N) lime (chemical).

SHĪ-HUǑ₄ 失火 (VO) catch on
fire. Zuótian tā-jiā-shīle-huǒ-
le. 昨天他家失了火
了. His house caught on fire
yesterday.

'SHÍJÌ₂ 實際 (SV) (1) practical.
Nǐde-jìhuà-bu-shíjì. 你的計
劃不實際. Your plan is
not practical. (2) actual. Qǐng-
nín-bǎ-shíjide-qíngxing gàosòng-
wo. 請您把實際的
情形告訴我. Please
tell me what the actual situation
is.
(AD) actually. Tā-zhǎngde shíji-
bìng-bù-nánkàn. 她長的實
際並不難看. Actually
she isn't bad-looking.
(N) reality. bu-hé-shíjì 不合
實際 doesn't fit reality. zài-
shíji-shang 在實際上
actually.

SHÌJÌ₂ 世紀 (M) century, era.
gōngyuánqián-sānshìjì 公元
前三世紀 third century
B.C. èrshi-shìjì 二十世紀
twentieth century.

SHÌJIÀ₃ 市價 (N) market price.

SHÍJIAN₄ 時間 (N) (syn. shí-
hou(r) 時候(兒)) (1) time
(at a certain point). Shíjian-dào-
le, wǒmen-zǒu-ba. 時間到

了，我們走吧. It's time now, let's go. (2) time, period of time. Wŏmen-yŏu-shí-jian-tăolun-ma? 我們有時間討論嗎? Do we have any time to discuss this?

SHÌJIÀN₅ 事件 (N) incident, event, occurrence. Bólín-shì-jiàn 柏林事件 Berlin incident.

SHÍJIANBIĂO₃ 時間表 (N) timetable, schedule.

SHÍJIANG₅ 石匠 (N) stone cutter (person).

SHÌJIE₁ 世界 (N) the world. Shìjieshang-de-shìqing dōu-hen-yŏu-yìsi. 世界上的事情都很有意思. All the things in the world are very interesting.

SHÌJIEDÀZHÀN₂ 世界大戰 (N) World War. (M: ci 次).

SHÌJIÈ-YÙNDONGHUÌ₃ 世界運動會 (VO) Olympic games.

SHĬ-JÌN₃ 使勁 (VO) use strength. Zài-shĭ-yìdiănr-jìn. 再使一點兒勁. Use more strength.

(AD) with all one's strength, hard. Nĭ-shĭ-jìn-lāzhe-shéngzi. 你使勁拉着繩子. Pull the rope hard.

SHĪ-LĬ₄ 失禮 (VO) make an error in etiquette. Wŏ-mei-shí-shenme-lĭ-ba. 我没失甚麼禮吧. I didn't do anything impolite, did I? used as a polite expression after committing a breach of etiquette.

Wŏ-méi-dào-fēijichang-qu-jiē-nín, shĭ-lĭ-shĭ-lĭ. 我没到飛機場去接您, 失禮失禮. I didn't go to the airport to meet you, please excuse me.

(SV) impolite. Tā-bùlái hěn-shĭ-lĭ. 他不來很失禮. He's very impolite for not coming.

SHÍLÌ₄ 實力 (N) strength, power. Tāmende-shílì-hěn-qiáng. 他們的實力很強. Their power is very strong.

SHÌLI₂ 勢力 (N) power, influence. yŏu-shìli 有勢力 influential. Tā-zai-yínhángjie hěn-yŏu-shìli. 他在銀行界很有勢力. He has a lot of influence among bankers.

SHÌLI₃ 勢利 (SV) flattering or catering only to those who have power or money. Tā-tài-shìli. 他太勢利. He is a person who flatters those with power or money.

SHÌLÌ₃ 市立 (B) municipal. shìlì-yīyuàn 市立醫院 municipal hospital.

'SHÌLÌ₄ 視力 (N) eyesight.

SHÍLING₄ 時令 (N) seasonable weather. Zhèixie-rìzi shíling-bu-zhèng. 這些日子時令不正. These few days have been unseasonable.

SHÍLIU₅ 石榴 (N) pomegranate.

SHÍMÁO₃ 時髦 (SV) stylish, fashionable. Tā-hěn-shímáo. 她很時髦. She is very stylish.

S

(N) thing which is in fashion. Tā-xǐhuan-shímáo. 她喜歡時髦. She likes anything in fashion.

SHĪ-MIÁN₃ 失眠 (VO) suffer from insomnia. Zuótian-yèli wǒ-shī-mián-le. 昨天夜裏我失眠了. I couldn't sleep last night.

SHÌMÍN₅ 市民 (N) citizen(of a city), city people, city dweller.

SHĪPÉI₃ 失陪 used as a polite expression when leavning a party before it is over, excuse me, I have to leave.

SHÍPĬN₅ 食品 (N) foodstuffs. shípin-gōngsī 食品公司 food company.

SHÍQĪ₂ 時期 (N) period of time. èrcìdàzhàn-shíqī 二次大戰時期 the World War II period. Zhèiduàn-lìshǐ fēn-sān-ge-shíqī. 這一段歷史分三個時期. This section of history is divided into three periods.

SHÌQÍNG₁ 事情 see SHÌ(QÍNG) 事情.

SHÍQUÁN₄ 十全 (B-) perfect in every detail. Méi-you-shíquán-de-shìqing. 沒有十全的事情. There's nothing that is completely perfect.

SHĪRÉN₄ 詩人 (N) poet. (M: wèi 位).

SHÌ(JIE)SHANG₃ 世(界)上 (PW) in the world, on earth. Shì(jie)shang yǒu-hěn-duō-bu-gōngping-de-shì. 世(界)上有很多不公平的

事. There are a lot of unfair things on earth.

SHÍSHÌ₄ 實事 (N) (1) actual occurrence, fact. Wǒ-shuō-de-shì-yijian-shíshì. 我說的是一件實事. What I talked about is something that really happened. (2) actual work. bàn-shíshì 辦實事 do the actual work.

SHÍSHÌ₄ 時事 (N) current affairs.

SHÌSHÍ₂ 事實 (N) fact, truth. Bǎ-shìshí gàosong-wo. 把事實告訴我. Tell me the facts. Tā-shì-nènma-shuō-de, kěshi shìshí shéi-zhīdao? 他是那麼說的,可是事實誰知道? That's what he said, but who knows the facts?

SHĪ-SHǑU₄ 失手 (VO) cause an accident by losing control of the hand. Tā-cónglái-méi-shī-guo=shǒu. 他從來沒失過手. He has never caused any accidents. Tā-yi-shī-shǒu bǎ-huāpíng-dǎ-le. 他一失手把花瓶打了. He broke the vase accidentally (by losing control of his hand).

SHÍSHUŌ₂ 實說 (IV) tell the truth. Nǐ-wèi-shénme bù-shí-shuō-ne? 你為甚麼不實說呢? Why don't you tell the truth?

SHÍTÁNG₄ 食堂 (N) (1) dining hall. (M: jiān 間). (2) restaurant. (M: jiā 家).

SHÍTOU₃ 石頭 (N) stone, rock.

(M: kuài 塊).

SHĪ-WÀNG₂ 失望 (VO) be disappointed. Shìqing hái-bù-yí-dìng-ne, nǐ-shī-shenme-wàng-ne? 事情還不一定呢，你失甚麼望呢? Things are still uncertain, what are you disappointed for? Tā-zhen-ràng-wo-shī-wàng. 他真讓我失望. He really disappointed me.

SHÌWĒI₃ 示威 (VO) stage a demonstration, demonstrate. Hěn-duō-rén zài-jiēshang-shì-wēi-ne. 很多人在街上示威呢. There are many people demonstrating down the street.

(N) demonstration. shìwēi-yóu-xíng 示威遊行 demonstration march.

SHÌ-WĒNDÙ₃ 試溫度 (VO) take one's temperature.

SHÍWÙ₅ 食物 (N) provisions, foodstuffs.

SHÌWÙ₅ 事務 (N) business, affair.

SHÍXIÀN₃ 實現 (IV) come true, materialize. Wǒmende-jìhua dōu-shíxiàn-le. 我們的計劃都實現了. All our plans came true.

SHÌXIÀN₅ 視線 (N) line of vision, view.

SHĪ-XÌN₃ 失信 (VO) break one's word. Tā-yǐjing shíguo-liǎngcì-xìn-le. 他已經失過兩次信了. He has already broken his word twice.

SHĪXÍNG₄ 施行 (TV) put rules

or regulations into effect. Nèi-ge-fǎlǜ hai-méi-shīxíng-ne. 那個法律還沒施行呢. That law has not been put into effect yet.

SHÍXÍNG₄ 時興 (TV) be in fashion. Cháng-tóufa xiànzài-bu-shíxíng-le. 長頭髮現在不時興了. Long hair is not in fashion now.

SHÍXÍNG₃ 實行 (TV) put a plan or idea into effect. Nǐde-jìhua hěn-líxiang, kěshi bù-néng-shí-xíng. 你的計劃很理想，可是不能實行.

Your plan is quite idealistic but I don't think you can put it into effect.

SHÍYÀN₃ 實驗 (TV) make an experiment. Wǒmen-yào-shíyàn-zhèige-lǐlun. 我們要實驗這個理論. We want to make an experiment with this theory.

(N) experiment, test. huàxué-shíyàn 化學實驗 chemistry experiment. zuò-shíyàn 作實驗 conduct an experiment. (cf: SHÌYAN 試驗).

SHÌYAN₂ 試驗 (TV) test, try out. Wǒ-xiǎng-shìyan-shiyan. 我想試驗試驗. I want to try it out. Tāmen-zhèng-zai-shìyan-yìzhong-xīn-yào. 他們正在試驗一種新藥. They are testing a new medicine.

(N) experiment, test. zuò-shì-yan 作試驗 do something as

S

an experiment. (cf: SHÍYÀN 實
驗).

SHÍYÀNSHÌ₃ 實驗室 or SHÌ-
YÀNSHÌ 試驗室 (N) labo-
ratory.

SHÌYÀNSHÌ₃ 試驗室 or SHÍ-
YÀNSHÌ 實驗室 (N) labo-
ratory.

SHĪ-YÈ₃ 失業 (VO) lose one's
job, unemployed. Tā-shī-yè-le.
他失業了. He is un-
employed. Jìnlái shī-yì-de-ren
hěn-duō. 近來失業的
人很多. Many people have
lost their jobs recently.

SHÌYÈ₃ 事業 (N) (1) enterprise,
undertaking, task. Tāmen-gōng-
sīde-shìyè bu-xiǎo. 他們公
司的事業不小. Their
company's enterprises are not
small. (2) career. Jiāo-shū-jiù-
shi-tāde-shìye. 教書就是
他的事業. Teaching is
his career.

SHÌYÌ₅ 示意 (TV) give someone
a hint, hint. Tā-duì-wo-shìyì,
jiào-wo-bié-shuō. 他對我
示意,叫我別說. He
hinted that I should not say it.

SHĪYÍNG₄ 失迎 (SV) used to
apologize for not being able to
meet or receive someone who
came to see the speaker, sorry
to have missed you. Zuótiān
zhēn-shi-shīyíng-dehěn. 昨天
真是失迎得很. I
am really sorry to have missed
you yesterday.

SHÍYĪYUE₁ 十一月 (TW) (lit.
the eleventh month of the year)

November.

SHÍYÒNG₂ 實用 (SV) useful,
practical. Hǎokàn-dàoshi-hǎo-
kàn, kěshi-bù-shíyòng. 好看
倒是好看,可是不
實用. It's pretty all right,
but it's not practical. Tāde-
xuéwen méi-you-shíyòngde-jià-
zhi. 他的學問沒有
實用的價值. There
is not any practical value in his
learning.

SHÍYÒNG₄ 使用 (TV) use,
make use of. Wǒmen-yīnggāi-
shíyòng-shénme-fāngfa? 我們
應該使用甚麼方
法? What kind of method
should we use?

SHÍYÓU₅ 石油 (N) petroleum,
kerosene.

SHĪ-YUĒ₄ 失約 (VO) fail to keep
an appointment. Zuótian tā-yòu-
shī-yuē-le. 昨天他又失
約了. He failed to keep his
appointment again yesterday.

SHÍYUE₁ 十月 (TW) (lit. the
tenth month of the year) October.

SHÍZAI₂ 實在 (SV) (1) honest.
Tā-hěn-shízai. 他很實在.
He is very honet. (2) true, real.
Shuō-shízai-de. 說實在的
Tell the truth. Nèige-xiāoxi
kǒngpa-bushízai. 那個消
息恐怕不實在. I'm
afraid that news is not true.
(MA) really, actually. Wǒ-shí-
zai-bu-zhīdào. 我實在不
知道. I really don't know.

SHĬZHŌNG₃ 始終 (MA) all the
time, from beginning to end.

Tā-shǐzhōng shuō-nèi-yíju-huà.
他 始 終 説 那 一 句
話. He says that sentence all
the time. Wǒ-shǐzhōng-budǒng.
我 始 終 不 懂. I don't
understand at all.

SHĪZI₅ 獅子 (N) lion. (M: zhī
隻, tóu 頭).

SHĪZI₅ 蝨子 (N) louse (insect).
(M: zhī 隻).

SHÍ-ZÌ₃ 識字 (VO) (lit. recognize characters) learn the form
of characters as a first step in
learning how to read. Tā-yǐjing-
kāishǐ-shí-zì-le. 他 已 經
開 始 識 字 了. He has
already started to learn how to
read. Tāmen-bu-shí-zì. 他們
不 識 字. They are illiter-
ate. (cf: RÈN-ZÌ 認字).

'SHÍZÌ₄ 十字 (N) (1) cross (in
the form of the character 十
shí). 'shízì-lùkǒur 十字 路口
兒 intersection. (2) check mark
(in the form of a cross). huà-yi-
ge-'shízì 畫 一 個 十字
make a check mark.

SHÌZI₅ 柿子 (N) persimmon.

SHÍZÌJIA₄ 十字架 (N) cross
(for crucifixion).

SHÍZÌLÙKǑUR₄ 十字 路口
兒 (N) street intersection.

SHÍZÚ₃ 十足 (SV) full of something. Tāde-jīnglì-shízú. 他 的
精 力 十 足. He's full of
strength.

(AD) completely (having all the
attributes of). Tā-shízú-shì-
yige-Déguo-ren. 他 十 足 是
一 個 德 國 人. or Tā-

shì-yíge-shízúde- Déguo-ren.
他 是 一 個 十 足 的
德 國 人. He is completely
a German.

SHŌU₂ 收 (TV) (1) receive. shōu-
xìn 收信 receive a letter.
Pùzi-sònglaide-dōngxi yǐjing-
shōudào-le. 鋪 子 送 來
的 東 西 已 經 收 到
了. The things which the
store sent have already been
received. (2) accept a gift. Tā-
sòng-wo-yíge-biǎo, wǒ-méi-
shōu. 他 送 我 一 個 表.
我 没 收. He tried to give
me a watch, I didn't accept.
Tā-géi-ni-de-dōngxi, nǐ-kéyi-
shōuxia. 他 給 你 的 東
西, 你 可 以 收 下. You
may accept the things he gave
you. (3) collect, gather. shōu-
zū 收租 collect rent. (4) put
away, keep. Kuài-shōuqilai-ba,
bié-ràng-ta-kànjian. 快 收 起
來 吧, 别 讓 他 看 見
Hurry up and put it away, don't
let him see it. Wǒ-bǎ-yàoshr
shōuzai-xiāngzili-le. 我 把
鑰 匙 收 在 箱 子 裏
了. I kept the key in the trunk.

SHÓU₂ 熟 see SHÚ 熟.

SHǑU₁ 手 (N) hand. (M: zhī 隻).
(2) good hand, expert. (M: bǎ
把). Zuò-fàn tā-zhēn-shì-yì-
bǎ-shǒu. 做 飯 他 真 是
一 把 手. He's really a
good hand at cooking. (3) par-
ticipant (in work or a game).
(M: bǎ 把). Wǒmen-hái-shǎo-
yìbǎ-shǒu. 我 們 還 少 一

S

S-

把手. We're still short one player.

(M) hand (in playing cards). Tā-zhèishǒu-pái bucuò. 他這手牌不錯. He has a strong hand.

(-B) person who does something, -er, -man. gēshǒu 歌手 singer. xiōngshǒu 兇手 murderer. shuǐshǒu 水手 seaman, sailor.

SHǑU₃ 守 (TV) (1) defend, guard. Wǒmen-yídìng-děi-shǒu-zhèige-dìfang. 我們一定得守這個地方. We must defend this place. (2) keep a secret or a promise. shǒu-mì-mi 守秘密 keep a secret. shǒu-xìngyong 守信用 keep a promise. (3) observe a law, rule, principle, etc. Nǐ-wèi-shénma-bushǒu-guīju? 你為甚麼不守規矩? Why don't you observe the rules?

SHǑU₄ 首 (M) for poems. sān-shǒu-shī 三首詩 three poems.

SHÒU₁ 瘦 (SV) (1) thin (of people or animals). Tā-busuàn-shòu. 他不算瘦. He can't be considered thin. (2) lean (of meat). shòu-zhū-ròu 瘦豬肉 lean pork. (3) tight (of clothing). Zhèijiàn-yīshang tài-shòu. 這件衣裳太瘦. This dress is too tight.

SHÒU₂ 受 (TV) (1) receive, get. shòu-jiàoyu 受教育 receive education. shòu-yíngxiang 受影響 be influenced. (2) endure,

accept. shòu-kǔ 受苦 endure hardship. Wǒ-néng-shòu-lèi, kěshi-bu-néng-shòu-qì. 我能受累, 可是不能受氣. I can accept being tired, but I cannot endure anger.

(B) used before a verb to form SV, good to, nice to. Tāde-huà-bu-shòu-tīng. 他的話不受聽. His words are not good to listen to.

SHǑUBIǍO₂ 手錶 (N) wrist-watch.

SHÒUBULIǍO₃ 受不了 (RV) cannot endure, cannot stand.

SHǑUCÈ₄ 手冊 (N) handbook. (M: běn 本).

SHŌUCHENG₃ 收成 (N) harvest. Jīnniande-shōucheng-bu-hǎo. 今年的收成不好. This year's harvest wasn't good.

SHÒU-CÌJI₃ 受刺激 (VO) receive a mental shock.

SHŌUDÀO₃ 收到 (RV) receive. Tāde-xìn wǒ-méi-shōudào. 他的信我沒收到. I didn't receive his letter.

SHÓUDÀOR₄ 熟道兒 see SHÚDÀOR 熟道兒.

SHǑUDIÀNDĒNG₃ 手電燈 or SHǑUDIÀNTǑNG 手電筒 (N) flashlight.

SHǑUDIÀNTǑNG₄ 手電筒 see SHǑUDIÀNDĒNG 手電燈.

SHǑUDŪ₃ 首都 (N) capital of a country.

SHǑUDUAN₃ 手段 (N) (1) meth-od, means, steps to be taken.

Wǒmen-yīngdāng-yòng-'shénme shǒuduan? 我們應當用甚麼手段? What kind of steps should we take? (2) indirect method. Tā-lǎo-yòng-shǒuduan. 他老用手段. He always uses indirect methods to do things.

SHÒU-FÁ₃ 受罰 (VO) receive punishment or fine.

SHÒU-FĒNG₄ 受風 (VO) be in a draft.

SHŌUFĒNGQÍN₅ 手風琴 (N) accordion.

SHŌUGĒ₅ 收割 (TV) reap. Mài-zi hái-méi-shōugē-ne. 麥子還沒收割呢. The wheat hasn't been reaped yet.

SHŎUGŌNGYÈ₃ 手工業 (N) handicraft industry.

SHŎU-GUǍ₄ 守寡 (VO) be a widow. Tā yǐjìng-shǒule-sān-nián-guǎ-le. 她已經守了三年寡了. She has been a widow for three years.

'SHŌUHUÒ₃ 收穫 (TV)(1) harvest. Dàozi yǐjìng-'shōuhuò-le. 稻子已經收穫了. The rice has been harvested. (2) gain, obtain from doing something. Zhèicì-cānguān wǒ- shōuhuòle hěn-duō- zhīshi. 這次參觀我收穫了很多知識. I gained a lot of knowledge from this visit. (N) (1) crops. jīnniande-'shōuhuo 今年的收穫 this year's crops. (2) results or informa-tion obtained from doing some-thing. Wǒ-jīntian-tīng-jiǎngyǎn-

de-'shōuhuò hěn-duō. 我今天聽講演的收穫很多. I gained a lot from the speech today.

SHŌUJÍ₄ 收集 (TV) collect and keep (as a hobby or for future use). (cf: SŌUJÍ 蒐集).

SHÒU-JIÀOYU₃ 受教育 (VO) receive education.

SHŎUJIN₃ 手巾 (N) (1) towel. (2) handkerchief.(M: kuài 塊, tiáo 條).

SHÒU-JĪNG₅ 受驚 (VO) be startled.

SHŌUJÙ₂ 收據 (N) receipt. (syn. shōutiáor 收條兒). (M: zhāng 張).

SHŌUJUÀNR₄ 手絹兒 (N) Peip. handkerchief. (M: kuài 塊, tiáo 條).

SHÒU-LÈI₃ 受累 (VO) (1) (lit. accept being tired from working hard) do tiresome work. Wǒ-men-jié-hūn-de-shíhou, tā-shòule-bu-shǎo-de-lèi. 我們結婚的時候,他受了不少的累. When we were married, he did a lot of the hard work. (2) used as a polite term before or after a favor, be troubled, bothered. Zhēn-buhǎoyìsi, yòu-jiào-nín-shòu-lèi-le. 真不好意思,又叫您受累了. I'm really embarrassed to have put you through the trouble a-gain.

SHÓULIÀN₃ 熟練 see SHÚLIÀN 熟練.

SHÒU-LIÁNG₃ 受涼 (VO) catch

S

cold.

SHǑULIÚDÀN₄ 手榴彈 (N) hand grenade.

SHÒUMÍNG₄ 壽命 (N) lifespan.

SHǑUNǍO₅ 首腦 (N) head, leader. Wǒ-hái-buzhīdào, tā-mende-shǒunǎo-shì-shéi. 我還不知道他們的首腦是誰. I still don't know who their leader is.

SHŌU-PIÀO₄ 收票 (VO) check and take one's ticket.

SHŌUPIÀOCHÙ₅ 售票處 (N) ticket office, box office.

SHÒU-PĪPÍNG₃ 受批評 (VO) be criticized.

SHÒU-QÌ₂ 受氣 (VO) be the object of someone's anger, take guff. Wǒ-lǎo-shòu-tāde-qì. 我老受他的氣. I'm always the object of his anger. Wǒ-bu-pà-shòu-lèi, kěshì wǒ-bu-yuànyi-shòu-qì. 我不怕受累,可是我不願意受氣. I don't mind doing tiresome work, but I'm not willing to take any guff.

SHǑUQIĀNG₃ 手鎗 (N) pistol, revolver. (M: zhī 枝, bǎ 把).

SHÒU-QĪFU₃ 受欺負 (VO) be taken advantage of.

SHÒU-(WĚI)QŪ₄ 受(委)屈 (VO) suffer injustice.

SHÒU-RÈ₃ 受熱 (VO) suffer from heat.

SHÓUREN₂ 熟人 see SHÚREN 熟人.

SHŌURÙ₃ 收入 (TV) have an income. Tā-yìnián shōurù-liǎngwànkuài-qián. 他一年

收入兩萬塊錢. He has an income of twenty thousand dollars a year.

(N) income. Wǒde-shōurù bu-gòu. 我的收入不够. My income is not enough.

SHÒU-SHĀNG₃ 受傷 (VO) receive a wound.

SHŌUSHI₂ 收拾 (TV) (syn. shí-duo 拾掇) (1) straighten up, put in order. shōushi-xíngli 收拾行李 straighten up the baggage, pack. Nǐ-bǎ-zhuōzi-shang-de-dōngxi shōushi-yixia. 你把桌子上的東西收拾一下. Straighten out the things on the table. (2) repair, fix. shōushi-biǎo 收拾錶 repair a watch. (3) fix someone for what he has done. Bié-máng, wǒ-zǎowǎn-huì-shōushi-ta-de. 別忙,我早晚會收拾他的. Don't hurry, I'll fix him sooner or later.

SHǑUSHI₃ 首飾 (N) jewelry, piece of jewelry. (M: jiàn 件). dài-shǒushi 帶首飾 wear jewelry. dǎ-shǒushi 打首飾 have jewelry made or make jewelry.

SHǑUSHÌ₄ 手勢 (N) hand gesture (as a means of expression). dǎ-shǒushì 打手勢 make a gesture with the hands.

SHÓUSHÒUR₃ 熟手兒 see SHÚSHÒUR 熟手兒.

SHǑUSHU₃ 手術 (N) operation (surgical). (M: cì 次). dòng-shǒushu 動手術 perform an operation <u>or</u> have an operation.

SHÒU-SHǓ₃ 受暑 (VO) suffer from heat-stroke.

SHǑUTÀOR₃ 手套兒 (N) glove, mitten. (M: zhǐ 隻 , fù 付).

SHŌUTIÁOR₂ 收條兒 (N) receipt. (<u>syn</u>. shōujù 收據). (M: zhāng 張). kāi-shōutiáor 開 收條兒 write a receipt.

SHǑUTÍBĀO₄ 手提包 (N) (1) suitcase. (2) brief case.

SHŌUTĪNG₅ 收聽 (TV) listen to a radio broadcast. Yǒu-shénma-hǎo-jiému kéyi-shōutīng-ma? 有甚麼好節目可以收聽嗎? Are there any good programs to listen to?

SHǑUTÍXIĀNG₄ 手提箱 (N) suitcase.

SHǑUWÀNR₃ 手腕兒 (N) (1) <u>or</u> SHǑUWÀNZI 手腕子 wrist. (2) craftiness. yǒu-shǒuwànr 有 手腕兒 have many ways of doing things. Tā-xǐhuan-shuǎ-shǒuwànr. 他很會耍手腕兒. He likes to do things in a crafty way. Tā-shǒuwànr hěn-gāo. 他手腕兒很高. He is quite crafty.

SHǑUWÀNZI₃ 手腕子 <u>see</u> SHǑUWÀNR 手腕兒 (N) (1).

SHÓUXÍ₃ 熟習 <u>see</u> SHÚXI 熟習

SHǑUXÍ₅ 首席 (N) place of honor. (B-) chief. shǒuxí-dàibiǎo 首席代表 chief delegate.

SHǑU(DÌ)XIA₄ 手(底)下 (PW) under <u>someone's</u> supervision.

Wǒ-shǒu(dǐ)xia yǒu-liùge-rén. 我手(底)下有六個人. There are six people under my supervision.

SHǑUXIĀN₃ 首先 (MA) first, at first. Shǒuxiān wǒmen-děi-jìhuà. 首先我們得計劃. We must plan first.

SHǑUXIÀNG₃ 首相 (N) premier, prime minister <u>of a cabinet.</u>

SHǑUXĪN₅ 手心 (N) palm (<u>of the hand</u>).

SHǑUXU₃ 手續 (N) process, procedure. bàn-chū-guó-de-shǒuxu 辦出國的手續 go through the procedures to go abroad. Shǒuxu hěn-jiǎndan. 手續很簡單. The procedure is very simple.

SHÒU-XÙN(LIAN)₃ 受訓(練) (VO) receive training.

SHǑUYI₃ 手藝 (N) skill <u>in a craft, such as carpentry, masonry, tailoring, cooking, etc.</u> Nèige-cáifengde-shǒuyi hěn-hǎo. 那個裁縫的手藝很好. That tailor has quite a bit of skill.

SHÒU-YÍNGXIANG₂ 受影響 (VO) be influenced.

SHǑUYĪNJĪ₃ 收音機 (N) receiving set (<u>radio</u>). (M: jià 架).

SHǑUZHÍTOU₃ 手指頭 (N) finger.

SHÒUZI₄ 瘦子 (N) (1) thin person. (2) skinny (<u>nickname</u>).

SHÒU-ZUÌ₂ 受罪 (VO) suffer, endure suffering. Wǒ-shòubu-liǎo-zhèige-zuì. 我受不了這個罪. I cannot stand

S

this kind of suffering.

SHŪ₁ 書 (N) book. (M: běn 本, cè 冊, tào 套, bù 部).
(B) (1) letter. jiāshū 家書 letter from home. (2) statement. zhèngmíngshū 証明書 certificate. (3) calligraphy. xíngshū 行書 running style of handwriting.

SHŪ₃ 輸 (TV) lose <u>a game, money in gambling</u>. Wǒ-shūle-yì-pán-qí. 我輸了一盤棋. I lost a game of chess. Tā-shū--le-shíkuài-qián. 他輸了十塊錢. He lost ten dollars (in gambling). (cf: DIŪ 丟, PÉI 賠).

SHŪ₄ 梳 (TV) comb. shū-tóufa 梳頭髮 comb the hair.

SHÚ₂熟 or SHÓU 熟 (SV) (1) ripe. Guǒzi-dōu-shú-le. 果子都熟了. All the fruit is ripe. (2) be done, cooked. Jī-hái-méi-shú-ne. 雞還沒熟呢. The chicken isn't done yet. (3) familiar with. Wǒ-gēn-tā-bu-shú. 我跟他不熟. I'm not familiar with him.

SHÚ₃ 贖 (TV) (1) redeem <u>something which was pawned or used as collateral</u>. shú-dàng 贖當 redeem something which was pawned. Wǒ-méi-qián-shù-wǒ-dàyī. 我沒錢贖我的大衣. I don't have the money to redeem my overcoat. (2) ransom. shú-piàor 贖票兒 ransom a person. Wǒmen yòng-wǔ-wànkuai-qián bǎ-ta-shúhuilai-le. 我們用五萬塊錢

把他贖回來了. We ransomed him with fifty thousand dollars.

SHŬ₃ 數 (TV) count. Nǐ-shǔ-yi-shǔ-qián. 你數一數錢. Please count the money. (2) be considered <u>as the most in a group</u>. Wǒmen-zhèixie-rén-li, jiù-shǔ-nǐ-niánqīng-le. 我們這些人裏就數你年輕了. You can be considered the youngest in our group.

SHǓ₃ 屬 (TV) belong to, be a part of, be under control of. Zhèige-dǎo-shǔ-Měiguo. 這個島屬美國. This island belongs to the United States. (S) SHǓ...GUǍN 屬...管 be under the control of. Zhèi-zhong-shìqing bu-shǔ-wǒ-guǎn. 這種事情不屬我管. This type of affair is not under my control. Zhèige-xué-xiào yě-shǔ-zhèngfǔ-guǎn-ma? 這個學校也屬政府管嗎? Is this school also under the control of the government?

SHÙ₂ 樹 (N) tree. (M: kē 棵).

SHÙ₃ 豎 (IV) place <u>something</u> lengthwise <u>or</u> vertically (<u>across the short or horizontal axis</u>). (opp. héng 橫). shùzhe-fàng 豎着放 put it lengthwise. Bǎ-gùnzi shùqilai. 把棍子豎起來. Put the stick vertically.
(TV) set up <u>vertically</u>, erect. Tāmen-zài-lùkǒur shùle-yíge.

páizi. 他們在路口兒豎了一個牌子. They set up a sign at the intersection.

SHUĀ₂ 刷 (TV) (1) brush (with a brush). shuā-xié 刷鞋 brush shoes. (2) whitewash. shuā-qiáng 刷牆 whitewash a wall. (3) cut a class. Zuótian wǒ-shuāle-yìtáng-huàxué. 昨天我刷了一堂化學. I cut chemistry class yesterday. (4) give someone the brush-off. Tāde-nǚpéngyou bǎ-tā-shuā-le. 他的女朋友把他刷了. His girl friend gave him the brush-off.

;HUĀ₃ 耍 (TV) (1) twirl something. shuǎ-gùnr 耍棍兒 twirl a stick. (2) gamble. shuǎ-qián 耍錢 gamble. (3) make a fool out of someone. Bié-shuá-wo-a! 別耍我了! Don't make a fool out of me!

SHUĀI₃ 摔 (TV) (1) throw hard. Bié-shuāi-mén. 別摔門. Don't slam the door. Tā-bǎ-huāpíngr wàng-dìxia-yì-shuāi. 他把花瓶往地下一摔. He threw the vase down on the ground. (2) drop and break something heavy. Tā-shuāile-yíge-jìngzi. 他摔了一個鏡子. He dropped a mirror and it broke. (IV) fall (of persons, animals). shuāi-gēntou 摔跟頭 fall down. Tā-yí-xià-chē jiu shuāi-le-yíxia. 他一下車就摔了一下. He fell down when he got out the car.

SHUĀI₃ 甩 (TV) (1) shake something at one's side with a jerking motion. Bié-zài-zhèr-shuāi-bǐ. 別在這兒甩筆. Don't shake the brush here. (2) jilt. Tā-bǎ-nèige-nǚde-shuāi-le. 他把那個女的甩了. He jilted that girl.

SHUĀI-JIĀO₄ 摔跤 (VO) (1) wrestle. Tā-yào-gēn-wo-shuāi-jiāo. 他要跟我摔跤. He wanted to wrestle with me. (2) fall. Tā-shuāile-yìjiāo. 他摔了一跤. He fell.

SHUĀILĂO₅ 衰老 (SV) feeble (because of old age). Tā-nián-ji-bu-dà, kěshi-yǐjing-hěn-shuāilǎo-le. 他年紀不大,可是已經很衰老了. Although he isn't very old, he's already quite feeble.

'SHUÀILǏNG₅ 率領 (TV) lit. or fig. lead, guide. Shéi-shuàiling-women? 誰率領我們? Who's going to lead us?

'SHUĀIRUÒ₃ 衰弱 (SV) poor (of health), weak (physically). Tā-de-xīnzàng hěn-shuāiruò. 他的心臟很衰弱. His heart is very weak.

SHUĀN₄ 閂 (N) door bolt. mén-shuān 門閂 door bolt.

SHUĀN₃ 拴 (TV) tie something to something else. Tā-bǎ-mǎ shuānzai-shùshang-le. 他把馬拴在樹上了. He tied the horse to a tree. fig. Tā-ràng-shìqing-shuānzhu-le. Nǎr-dou-bu-néng-qù. 他讓

S

事 情 拴 住 了. 那 兒
都 不 能 去. He was tied
up with business and couldn't go
anywhere.

SHUÀN₄ 涮 (TV) rinse. shuàn-
cháhú 涮 茶 壺 rinse the
teapot. Bǎ-nǐde-shǒu zài-shuǐ-
shuàn-yishuan. 把 你 的 手
在 水 裏 涮 一 涮.
Rinse your hands in the water.

SHUĀNG₃ 霜 (N) frost. (M: chǎng
場, céng 層). xià-shuāng 下
霜 have a frost.

SHUĀNG₁ 雙 (M) for shoes,
socks, stockings, chopsticks,
etc., pair. Zhèi-liǎngzhi-wàzi
bú-shi-yishuāng. 這 兩 隻
襪 子 不 是 一 雙.These
two socks are not a pair. (cf:
DUÌ 對).
(B) two, double. shuāngfāng 雙
方 both sides. shuāngshùr 雙
數 兒 even number.

SHUĂNGKUAI₃ 爽 快 (SV) (1) dry
and cool (of weather). (2)
straightforward. Tā rén-hěn-
shuǎngkuai. 他 人 很 爽
快. He is very straight-
forward.

SHUĀNGSHENG₃ 雙 生 (N) twins.
(M: duì 對).

SHUĀNGSHIJIÉ₃ 雙 十 節 (N)
double tenth celebration (celebration of the Chinese independence day which falls on October
10).

SHUĀNGSHǑU₅ 雙 手 (N) two
hands.

SHUĀNGSHÙR₃ 雙 數 兒 (N)
even number.

SHUĂNGXING₃ 爽 性 see SUǑ-
XING 索 性.

SHUĂ-QIÁN₃ 耍 錢 (VO) gam-
ble with money. Tāmen-yìzhí
shuǎle-sāntiān-qián. 他 們
一 直 耍 了 三 天 錢.
They gambled continuously for
three days.

SHUĂZI₃ 刷 子 (N) brush. (M:
bǎ 把).

SHŪBAO₃ 書 包 (N) school bag,
briefcase for books.

SHŪCHŪ₅ 輸 出 (TV) export.
Nǐmen-xiànzài shūchū-shénme?
你 們 現 在 輸 出 甚
麼? What do you export now?

SHŪDAÒR₄ 熟 道 兒 or
SHOÙDAOR 熟 道 兒 (N)
familiar route.

SHŪDIÀN₂ 書 店 (N) bookstore.
(syn. shūpù 書 鋪). (M: jiā
家).

SHŪFÁNG₂ 書 房 (N) study,
den. (M: jiān 間).

SHŪFU₁ 舒 服 (SV) comforta-
ble. Tā-xiànzài-shūfu-diǎnr-le.
他 現 在 舒 服 點 兒
了. He's a little more comfortable now. Zhèige-chuáng
hen-shūfu. 這 個 床 很 舒
服. This bed is very comfortable. (See: BUSHŪFU 不 舒
服).

SHŪFÙ₄ 叔 父 (N) uncle (fa-
ther's younger brother).

SHŪGUI₃ 書 櫃 (N) bookcase.

SHŪHU₃ 疏 忽 or SŪHU 疏 忽
(SV) careless,negligent. Tā-
hěn-shūhu. 他 很 疏 忽.
He's very careless.

(TV) neglect. Wǒ-bǎ-nèijian-shì gěi-shūhu-le. 我 把 那 件 事 給 疏 忽 了. I neglected that matter.

SHUÍ₁ 誰 see SHEÍ 誰.

SHUǏ₁ 水 (N) water. hē-shuǐ 喝 水 drink water.

(M) washing of a garment. Zhèi-tiao-kùzi xǐguo-liǎngshuǐ-le. 這 條 褲 子 洗 過 兩 水 了. This pair of trousers has gone through two washings.

SHUÌ₂ 稅 (N) tax, duty, impost, customs. (M: dào 道). shàng-shuì 上 稅 pay a tax. Shuì-hěn zhòng. 稅 甚 重. Taxes are very heavy.

SHUÌ₁ 睡 (IV) (1) sleep. Wǒ-shuì-le-liǎngtiān-liǎngyè. 我 睡 了 兩 天 兩 夜. I slept for two days and two nights. Tā-shuì-de-hěn-xiāng. 他 睡 得 很 香. He slept very soundly. (2) sleep on something. Nǐ-shuì-shāfā, wǒ-shuì-dìbǎn. 你 睡 沙 發, 我 睡 地 板. You sleep on the sofa, I'll sleep on the floor.

SHUǏCǍIHUÀR₄ 水 彩 畫 兒 (N) water-color picture. (M: zhāng 張).

SHUǏCHĒ₅ 水 車 (N) (1) water wheel for irrigation. (2) water cart. (M: liàng 輛).

SHUǏGUǍNZI₄ 水 管 子 (N) water pipe, drain pipe.

SHUǏGUǑ₃ 水 果 (N) fruit.

SHUÌ-JIÀO₁ 睡 覺 (VO) sleep. Wǒ-měitian jiu-shuì-liùge-zhōngtóu-de-jiào. 我 每 天 就 睡 六 個 鐘 頭 的 覺. I sleep only six hours everyday. Wǒ-zuótian-yíyè méi-shuìzháo-jiào. 我 昨 天 一 夜 没 睡 着 覺. I didn't sleep at all last night.

SHUǏJĪNG₄ 水 晶 (N) rock crystal.

SHUǏKÙ₅ 水 庫 (N) reservoir.

SHUÌKUĂN₅ 稅 欵 (N) money for or from tax, duty. (M: bǐ 筆).

SHUǏLÌ₄ 水 利 (N) water conservation, water utilization.

SHUǏLÓNG₃ 水 龍 (N) (lit. water dragon) water hose.

SHUǏNÍ₃ 水 泥 (N) cement.

SHUǏPÍNG₃ 水 平 (N) (1) level (instrument). (2) standard, average. shuǐpíng-yǐxià 水 平 以 下 below average. shuǐ-píng-hěn-dī 水 平 很 底 standard is very low.

SHUǏSHǑU₃ 水 手 (N) sailor, seaman.

SHUǏTǍ₄ 水 塔 (N) water tower. (M: zuò 座).

SHUǏTIÁN₅ 水 田 (N) rice field.

SHUǏZĀI₃ 水 災 (N) flood catastrophe, flood disaster. nào-shuǐzāi 鬧 水 災 have a flood.

SHŪJI₃ 書 籍 (N) books.

SHŪJI₃ 書 記 (N) clerk (in an office), secretary.

SHŪJIÀ₂ 暑 假 (N) summer vacation. fàng-shǔjià 放 暑 假 have summer vacation.

SHŪJIÀZI₃ 書 架 子 (N) bookshelf, bookcase.

SHÙ-KǑU₃ 漱 口 (VO) rinse one's mouth. Wǒ-yìtiān-shù-

S

S

háojihuí-kǒu. 我 一 天 漱 好 幾 回 口 . I rinse my mouth several times a day.

'SHÚLIÀN₃ 熟 練 or SHÓULIÀN 熟 練 (SV) skilful. Tāde-dòng-zuò hěn-'shúliàn. 他 的 勁 作 很 熟 練. His action is very skilful.

SHÙLIÀNG₃ 數 量 (N) quantity, amount. Shùliàng-duō-bu-duo? 數 量 多 不 多 ? Is the quantity great or not?

SHÙLÍNZI₂ 樹 林 子 (N) forest, woods. (M: piàn 片).

SHŪMŪ₄ 叔 母 (N) aunt (wife of father's younger brother).

SHÙMÙ(LU)₃ 書 目 (錄) (N) catalogue of books.

SHÙMU₅ 樹 木 (N) tree (in general).

SHÙMU₂ 數 目 (N) number, amount. Shùmu-hěn-dà. 數 目 很 大 . The number is very high.or The amount is very large. Wǒmen-děi-còu-yíge xiāngdāngde-shùmu. 我 們 得 湊 一 個 相 當 的 數 目 . We have to pitch in to get a suitable amount.

SHÙN₃ 順 (TV) (1) go along with, agree with. Nǐ-děi-shùnzhe-ta. 你 得 順 着 他 . You should go along with him. Tā-lǎo-shùnzhe-wǒde-yìsi-zuò. 他 老 順 着 我 的 意 恩 作 . He always goes along with me and does it according to my idea. (2) put in order. Qǐng-nǐ-bǎ-zhèi-xie-shū shùn-yishun. 請 你 把 這 些 書 順 一

順 . Please put these books in order.

(SV) (1) (con. tōngshùn 通 順). smooth, fluent (of speaking or writing). Zhèi-duan-wénzhang bu-tài-shùn. 這 段 文 章 不 太 順 . This paragraph isn't very smooth. (2) (con. shùndang 順 當). lucky, in favorable circumstances. Tā-dǔ-qián shǒuqi-hěn-shùn. 他 睹 錢 手 氣 很 順. He's quite lucky in gambling.

(CV) (1) by way of a road or a river. Nǐ-děi-shùn-gōnglù-zǒu. 你 得 順 公 路 走. You should take the highway. (2) along. Tāmen-shùnzhe-nèitiao-hé sàn-bù. 他 們 順 着 那 條 河 散 步. They are taking a stroll along the river.

SHÙNBIÀN₃ 順 便 (AD) do something in addition to what one is already doing, without much extra effort, while one is at it. Wǒ-dào-Niǔyue-qu-wánr-qu, shùnbiàn-qu-kànkan-ta. 我 到 紐 約 去 玩 兒 去, 順 便 去 看 看 他. I'm going to New York to have some fun; I'll visit him while I am there. (cf: SHUN-SHǑU 順 手 , SUISHǑU 隨 手).

SHÙNDANG₃ 順 當 (SV) lucky, in favorable circumstances. (opp. bièniu 彆 扭). Zhèi-liǎngnián tāde-shìqing hěn-shùn-dang. 這 兩 年 他 的 事 情 很 順 當. Things have been favorable for him these couple of years.

SHÙN'ĚR₃ 順耳 (SV) appealing <u>or</u> pleasant to the ear. Tā-shuō-de-huà hěn-shùn'ěr. 他說的話很順耳. What he said is very pleasant. Zhèizhong-yīnyue wǒ-tingzhe bu-shùn'ěr. 這種音樂我聽着不順耳. This kind of music isn't very pleasant for me to listen to.

SHÙNKǑU₄ 順口 (SV) (1) easy to pronounce. Zhèijiù-huà shuō-zhe bu-shùnkǒu. 這句話說着不順口. This sentence is not easy to say. (2) appealing <u>or</u> pleasant to the mouth. Jīntiande-cài tā-chǐzhe bu-shùn-kǒu. 今天的菜他吃着不順口. Today's food is not appealing to him. (AD) <u>talk</u> without thinking. Tā-shùnkǒu jiu-shūlòu-le. 他順口就說漏了. He revealed it without thinking.

SHÙNLI₂ 順利 (SV) go well, without difficulty. Zuìjìn-hěn-shùnli-ba. 最近很順利吧. Everything has been going well recently, I suppose. Zuó-tian-wǒmen-qu-bàn-shì, yíqiè-dou-hěn-shùnli. 昨天我們去辦事, 一切都很順利. Yesterday we went on business and everything went very well. (AD) without difficulty, smoothly. Nèige-yì'àn shùnli-tōngguò-le. 那個議案順利通

過了. That bill was passed without difficulty.

SHÙN-LÙ₃ 順路 (VO) be on one's way. Bié-sòng-wo-dao-chēzhàn-qu. Nín-huí-jiā bu-shùn-lù. 別送我到車站去. 您回家不順路. Don't take me to the station, it's not on your way home. (AD) while on the way, on one's way. Nǐ-wèi-shénma bu-shùnlù qu-kànkan-ta. 你為甚麼不順路去看看他. Why don't you visit him while you're going that way.

SHÙNSHǑU₃ 順手 (AD) <u>do something with the hand in addition to what one is already doing, without much extra effort, while one is at it.</u> (<u>syn.</u> suíshōu 隨手). Qǐng-nǐ-chūqu-de-shihou, shùnshǒu-bǎ-zhèifēng-xìn-fā-le. 請你出去的時候, 順手把這封信發了. Would you please mail this letter on your way out? (cf: SHÙNBIÀN 順便). (SV) easy to reach (<u>with the hand</u>). Shìqing-bu-shùn-shǒu. 事情不順手. Things are difficult to handle.

SHÙNYǍN₃ 順眼 (SV) appealing <u>or</u> pleasant to the eye.

SHÙN-ZUǏR₄ 順嘴兒 (SV) smooth-flowing (<u>of phrases or sentences</u>).

SHUŌ₁ 說 (TV) (1) say, speak, talk. (<u>syn.</u> jiǎng 講). shuō-gù-shi 說故事 tell a story.

S

shuō-xiàohua 説笑話 tell a joke. Nǐ-huì-shuō-Fàwén-ma? 你會說法文嗎? Can you speak French? Lái, wǒ-gēn-ni-shuō-ju-huà. 來，我跟你説句話. Come here, I would like to speak with you. Wǒmen-bu-yào-zài-shuō-tā-le. 我們不要再說他了. Let's not talk about him anymore. Tā-shuō-huà-bu-suàn-huà. 他説話不算話. He says it but he won't do it. Wǒ-men-zhèng-shuō-ni, nǐ-jiu-lái-le. 我們正説你，你就來了. We were just talking about you and in you came. Wǒ-men-shuōzhe-shuōzhe jiu-dào-le. 我們説着説着就到了. While we were chatting we arrived. (2) scold. Wǒ-mǔ-qin-lǎo-shuō-wo. 我母親老説我. My mother scolds me all the time. (3) used after wǒ 我 to gain the attention of the person spoken to, say. Wǒ-shuō Lǐ-xiansheng-a, nín-qù-ma? 我説李先生啊，您去嗎? Say, Mr. Li, are you going?

SHUŌBULAI₂ 説不來 (RV) (1) cannot speak. Wǒ-shuōbulái-Shànghǎi-huà. 我説不來上海話. I can't speak Shanghai dialect. (2) cannot get along with someone. Wǒ-gēn-ta-shuōbulái. 我跟他説不來. I can't get along with him.

SHUŌBUSHANG₃ 説不上 (RV)(1) cannot make someone in a higher position listen. Wǒ-shuōbushang-huà-qu. 我説不上話去. I cannot make him listen. (2) it cannot be said that. Tā-shuōbushang-yǒu-xuéwen. 他説不上有學問. It cannot be said that he is learned.

SHUŌBUSHÀNGLÁI₂ 説不上來 (RV) cannot say something from memory. Wǒ-xiànzài-shuōbushànglái-le. 我現在説不上來了. I cannot repeat it now. (2) cannot get along with someone. Tāmen-liǎngge-ren shuōbushànglái. 他們兩個人説不上來. Those two cannot get along with each other.

'SHUŌFÁ₂ 説法 or SHUŌFAR 説法兒 (N) way of expression.

SHUŌFAR₂ 説法兒 see 'SHUŌFÁ 説法.

SHUŌFÚ₃ 説服 (RV) convince by persuasion. Nǐ-shuōdefú-ta-ma? 你説的服他嗎? Can you convince him?

'SHUŌHE₃ 説和 (TV) act as a mediator, mediate. Nǐ-gěi-liǎngbiānr shuōhe-shuohe-ba. 你給兩邊兒説和説和吧. You'd better reconcile both parties.

SHUŌ-HUǍNG₂ 説謊 (VO) tell a lie, lie. Wǒ-cónglái-méi-shuōguo-huǎng. 我從來沒説過謊. I have never told a lie.

SHUŌ-MÉI₄ 説媒 (VO) act as a matchmaker. Xiànzài jìsuànjīkěyǐ-shuōméi. 現在計算機可以說媒. Computers can act as matchmakers now.

SHUŌ-MÈNGHUÀ₂ 説夢話 (VO) talk in one's sleep. fig. Bié-shuō-mènghuà-le. 別説夢話了. Don't talk nonsense.

SHUŌMÍNG₁ 説明 (TV) explain, illustrate. Qǐng-nǐ-shuōmíng zhè-shi-shénme-dàoli. 請你説明這是甚麼道理. Please explain what the reason is for this. (N) (1) explanation. (2) explanatory writings, such as a caption, synopsis, directions, technical manual, etc.

SHUŌMÍNGSHŪ₃ 説明書 (N) (1) book of directions, technical manual (such as one accompanying a machine or apparatus). (2) playbill, program (of a play or movie, including a synopsis). (M: zhāng 張, běn 本, fènr 份兒).

SHUŌQI(...)LAI₁ 説起(...)來 (RV) start to talk about, speak of. Shuōqilai zhēn-qíguài. 説起來真奇怪. Come to talk about it, it's very strange. Yì-shuōqi-tā-lai wǒ-jiu-shēng-qì. 一説起他來我就生氣. As soon as we started to speak of him, I became angry.

SHUŌ-QÍNG₃ 説情 (VO) ask someone for a favor on someone else's behalf. Xuéxiào yào-kāi-chú-wo-dìdi, wǒ-qu-gěi-tā-shuō-

qíng-qu. 學校要開除我弟弟,我去給他説情去. The school wants to dismiss my younger brother, I'm going to ask a favor on his behalf.

SHŪPÙ₂ 書鋪 (N) bookstore. (syn. shūdiàn 書店). (M: jiā 家).

SHŬQĪ₃ 暑期 (TW) summertime. shǔqī-xuéxiào 暑期學校 summer school.

SHÙR₂ 數兒 (N) (1) number, figure. shǔ-shùr 數數兒 count numbers. méi-shùr 沒數兒 no definite number or countless. còu-zhěng-shùr 湊整數兒 make a round number. (2) definite plan. Tā-xīnli-yǒu-shùr. 他心裏有數兒. He has a definite plan in his mind.

SHÚREN₃ 熟人 or SHÓUREN 熟人 (N) familiar person, acquaintance, friend.

SHŪRÙ₅ 輸入 (TV) import. Zhèizhǒng-jiǔ shi-cóng-Yīngguo-shūrùde. 這種酒是從英國輸入的. This kind of wine is imported from England.

SHÚSHǑUR₃ 熟手兒 or SHÓUSHǑUR 熟手兒 (N) experienced person, old hand.

SHŪSHU₄ 叔叔 (N) (1) uncle (father's younger brother). (2) brother-in-law (husband's younger brother).

SHÚXÍ₃ 熟習 or SHÓUXÍ 熟習 (TV) familiarize oneself with.

S

Nǐ-zuìhǎo bǎ-jèr-de-qíngxing shúxi-shuxi. 你 最 好 把 這 兒 的 情 形 熟 習 熟 習 . You'd better familiarize yourself with the situation here.
(SV) be familiar with a process, a matter, etc. Duì-shǒuxu wǒ-hěn-shúxi. 對 手 續 我 很 熟 習 . I'm very familiar with the procedures.

SHÙXUÉ₃ 數 學 (N) mathematics. (M: mén 門). (cf: SUÀNXUÉ 算 學).

SHÙYÍNG₃ 輸 贏 (N) outcome of a competition. Shūyíng wǒ-bu-zàihu. 輸 贏 我 不 在 乎 . I don't care about the outcome.

SHǓYU₄ 屬 於 (TV) belong to. Yuènán cóngqián-shǔyu-Fǎguó. 越 南 從 前 屬 於 法 國 . Viet Nam formerly belonged to France. Wǒmen-dōu-shǔyu-gōngren-jiēji. 我 們 都 屬 於 工 人 階 級 . We all belong to the laboring class.

SHŪYUAN₃ 疏 遠 or SŪYUAN 疏 遠 (SV) estranged. Wǒmen-zuì-jìn hěn-shūyuan. 我 們 最 近 很 疏 遠 . Recently we have become quite estranged.

SHÙZHĪR₅ 樹 枝 兒 see SHÙ-ZHĪZI 樹 枝 子 .

SHÙZHĪZI₅ 樹 枝 子 or SHÙ-ZHĪR 樹 枝 兒 (N) twig, branch of a tree.

SHŪZHUŌR₂ 書 桌 兒 (N) desk. (M: zhāng 張).

SHŪZI₄ 梳 子 (N) comb. (M: bǎ 把).

SHÙ(MU)ZÌ₃ 數 (目) 字 (N) figure, numerals. Shù(mu)zì-hěn-dà. 數 (目) 字 很 大 . The figure is very large.

SĪ₄ 絲 (N) silk (before weaving). Zhèige-cáiliao shì-sī-zuò-de. 這 個 材 料 是 絲 作 的 . This material is made of silk.

SĪ(R)₃ 絲 兒 (N) thread shaped object. ròu-sī(r) 肉 絲 (兒) meat cut into slivers. tiě-sī(r) 鐵 絲 (兒) wire made of iron.

SĪ₃ 撕 (TV) tear, rip. Bié-sī-nèifēng-xìn. 別 撕 那 封 信 . Don't tear that letter up.

SĬ₁ 死 (IV) die. (opp. huó 活). Qiántian tā-zǔmǔ-sǐ-le. 前 天 他 祖 母 死 了 . His grandmother died the day before yesterday.
(SV) (opp. huó 活) (1) (con. sí-ban 死 板). stiff, not lively. Zhèizhang-huàr-shang-de-niǎor huàde-hen-sǐ. 這 張 畫 兒 上 的 鳥 兒 畫 的 很 死 . The bird in that painting looks stiff. (2) fixed, fastened. Zhèige-shūjiàshang-de-bǎnzi shì-sǐ-de, bu-néng-náxialai. 這 個 書 架 上 的 板 子 是 死 的 , 不 能 拿 下 來 . The board in this book-case is fixed, it can't be taken down. (3) (con. sǐban 死 板). inflexible, unbending. sǐ-fázi 死 法 子 inflexible method. (AD) usually used before a negative verb, stubbornly. Tā-sǐ-

S

bu-chéngrèn. 他死不承
認 . He denied stubbornly.
(N) death. Yǒu-shēng jiu-yǒu-sǐ.
有生就有死. If there
is birth, there is death.
(RE) (1) indicates fixed, fastened.
Bǎ-mén-dīngsǐ-le. 把門釘
死了 . Nail the door tight
shut. (2) indicates dying. diàosǐ
吊死 hang to death. Tā-zìshā
méi-shāsǐ. 他自殺沒殺
死 . He tried to commit suicide but didn't die. (cf: SǏLE 死了).
SÌ₁ 四 (NU) four, fourth. sìpǐ-mǎ
四匹馬 four horses. sìmǎ-
lù 四馬路 Fourth Ave.
SǏBAN₃ 死板 (SV) (1) stiff, not
lively (of a person). Tāde-dòngzuo
hěn-sǐban. 他的動作很
死板. His movements are
very stiff. (2) inflexible, unbending. Tāde-sīxiang hěn-sǐban.
他的思想很死板.
His thought is very inflexible.
SÌBIĀNXÍNG₅ 四邊形 (N) rec-
tangular shape.
SÌCHUĀN₃ 四川 (PW) Szechwan
province.
SĪGUA₅ 絲瓜 (N) loofa gourd,
sponge gourd (a variety of gourd
eaten as a vegetable).
SÌHU(...SHIDE)₂ 似乎 (...似
的) (MA) seemingly. Tā-sìhu
bu-tài-gāoxìng(shide). 他似
乎不太高興(似的).
She doesn't seem very happy.
SǏHUÓ₃ 死活 (N) (lit. death or
life) living conditions. Tā-bu-
guǎn-biérende-sǐhuó. 他不管
別人的死活. He

doesn't care about other's living
conditions.
SǏHÚTÒNGR₅ 死胡同兒
(N) dead-end alley or street.
(M: tiáo 條).
SĪJĪ₃ 司機 (N) operator of a
vehicle, driver, chauffeur.
SǏJÌ₄ 死記 (TV) remember
mechanically (without understanding). Nǐ-buyīngdāng sǐjì-
shēngzì. 你不應當死
記生字. You should not
remember the new words mechanically.
SÌJÌ₃ 四季 (N) the four seasons.
SǏLE₂ 死了 (P) used after a
SV, indicates an extreme condition. Wǒ-èsile. 我餓死
了. I am starved. Tā-gāoxìng-
sile. 他高興死了. He
is tickled to death. (cf: SǏ 死).
SĪLÌ₂ 私立 (B-) private (as a
hospital, school, and other
organizations which serve the
public). (opp. gōnglì 公立).
sīlìyīyuàn 私立醫院
private hospital.
SĪMIÁN₅ 絲棉 (N) silk (in a
form similar to that of raw cotton), floss-silk.
SÌMIÀNR₃ 四面兒 (PW) four
sides, all sides. Sìmiànr-dōu-
shì-rén. 四面兒都是
人. There are people all
around.
SĪRÉN₃ 私人 (B-) private, personal. sīrén-cáichǎn 私人
財產 private property. Zhè-
shi-wo-sīrénde-shìqing. 這是
我私人的事情. This

S

is my private affair.
(N) staff selected on the basis
of favoritism or friendship. Tā-
bu-yòng-sīrén. 他 不 用 私
人 . He doesn't choose his
staff on a basis of favoritism.
SĪSHĒNG₄ 四 聲 (N) four tones
(of Chinese language). Tāde-sì-
shēng-bu-zhǔn. 他 的 四 聲
不 準 . His tones are not
accurate.
SĪSHÌ₃ 私 事 (N) private or personal affair. (M: jiàn 件). Wǒ-
qu-bàn-yidiǎnr-sīshì. 我 去
辦 一 點 兒 私 事 . I
am going to attend to a small
personal matter.
SĪWÁNG₄ 死 亡 (IV) die. Nèicì-
zháo-huǒ sǐwáng-le-bushǎo-rén.
那 次 着 火 死 亡 了
不 少 人 . A lot of people
lost their lives in that fire.
(N) death.
SĪWÀZI₅ 絲 襪 子 (N) silk
stocking. (M: zhǐ 隻 , shuāng 雙).
SĪWEN₃ 斯 文 (SV) genteel, refined. Zhèige-rén hěn-sīwen. 這
個 人 很 斯 文 . This
person is very refined.
SĪXIALI₃ 私 下 裏 (MA) in
secret, privately. Tāmen-sīxia-
li-jiāoshè. 他 們 私 下 裏
交 涉 . They negotiated se-
cretly. Tā-sīxiali-gēn-wo-shuō.
他 私 下 裏 跟 我 説
He talked to me privately.
SĪXIALI₄ 四 下 裏 (MA) everywhere, on all sides. Wǒ-sìxiali
zhǎo-nǐ. 我 四 下 裏 找
你 . I have tried to find you

everywhere.
SĪXIÀN₅ 絲 線 (N) silk thread.
'SĪXIǍNG₁ 思 想 (N) thought,
way of thinking. Tāde-'sīxiǎng
hái-méi-gǎotōng. 他 的 思
想 還 沒 搞 通 . The
mental block still hasn't been
removed from his thought. or
His thought still hasn't been
reformed. Tāde-sixiang hěn-
zuǒ. 他 的 思 想 很 左 .
His thought is very far left.
SǏ-XĪN₃ 死 心 (VO) give up
hope. Nǐ-jiu-sǐle-zhèitiao-xīnba.
你 就 死 了 這 條
心 吧 . You'd better give up
this hope.
SǏXĪNYǍNR₃ 死 心 眼 兒
(SV) have a one-track mind.
SĪYÍ₅ 司 儀 (N) master of cer-
emonies.
SĪYǑU₅ 私 有 (B-) privately
owned. sīyǒu-cáichǎn 私 有
財 產 private property.
SÌYUE₁ 四 月 (TW) (lit. the
fourth month of the year) April.
SĪZHĪPǏN₅ 絲 織 品 (N) silk
goods.
SŌNG₁ 鬆 (SV) (opp. jǐn 緊) (1)
loose, not tight. Nèige-jiézi
sōng-le. 那 個 結 子 鬆
了 . That knot is loose. (2)
easy-going, not strict. Wǒmen-
de-lǎoshī hěn-sōng. 我 們 的
老 師 很 鬆 . Our teacher
is not strict at all. (3) not firm
(of texture). Zhèige-dàngāo hěn-
sōng. 這 個 蛋 糕 很 鬆 .
This cake is very fluffy.
(TV) (1) loosen. Nǐ-bǎ-lǐngdài

sŏng-yisong. 你把領帶鬆一鬆. Loosen your tie a bit. Bié-sŏng-shŏu. 別鬆手. Don't loosen your grip. (2) relax one's demand. Tāde-kŏuqi sŏng-le. 他的口氣鬆了. His tone of voice is less demanding. (3) loosen or relax one's tension. Zuòwán-le, wŏ-kéyi-sŏng-yikou-qì. 作完了,我可以鬆一口氣. After I finish, I can relax a bit.

SÒNG₁ 送 (TV) (1) give something to someone as a present. Tā-sònggei-wo-yíge-biăo. 他送給我一個表. He gave me a watch. (2) send, deliver. sòng-huò 送貨 deliver goods. Wŏ-gĕi-ta sòng-niúnăi. 我給他送牛奶. I deliver milk to him. (3) see someone off. Wŏ-míngtian dĕi-qù-sòng-ta. 我明天得去送他. I have to see him off tomorrow. (4) escort. Tā-sòng-ta-huí-jiā-le. 他送她回家了. He escorted her home.

SÒNGCHAO₄ 宋朝 (TW) Sung dynasty.

SÒNG-LĬ₂ 送禮 (VO) give someone a present. sòng-shēngr-lĭ 送生日禮 give a birthday gift.

SŌNGSHÙ₄ 松樹 (N) pine tree, spruce.

SÒNGXÍNG₃ 送行 (IV) (1) see someone off. Wŏ-dao-chēzhàn-qu gĕi-ren-sòngxíng. 我到車站去給人送行. I am going to the station to see someone off. (2) give a farewell party. Míngtian-wŏmen-qĭng-kè, gĕi-Lĭ-xiansheng-sòngxíng. 明天我們請客,給李先生送行. Tomorrow we are going to give a farewell party for Mr. Li.

SŌU₄ 餿 (IV) smell bad (of food or something wet because of dampness and heat). Niúnăi-sōu-le. 牛奶餿了. The milk has gone sour.

SŌUJI₃ 搜集 (TV) (lit. search and assemble) collect (as a hobby or by research). Tā-sōu-ji-yóupiào. 他搜集郵票. He collects stamps. Tā-sōujile-hĕn-duōde-zhèngju. 他搜集了很多的証據. He has collected a lot of evidence. (cf: ZĂN 攢, SHŌU-JÍ 收集).

SS₃ 嘶 voiceless dental fricative, with air sucked in. (1) used to indicate discomfort from cold weather. Ss! Hăo-lĕng! 嘶! 好冷! Brr! It's cold! (2) used to indicate a sudden pain, ouch! Ss! Hăo-téng. 嘶! 好痛! Ouch! What a pain! (3) used to indicate that the speaker is in the process of thinking, let me think. Ss! Zhè-zĕnma-bàn! 嘶! 這怎麼辦! Let me think! What can be done!

SÚ₃ 俗 (SV) vulgar. Zhèige-rén-zhēn-sú. 這個人真俗. This person is really vulgar.

SÙ₄ 塑 (TV) form, model,

S

something in clay, wax, etc.
(See: SÙ-XIÀNG 塑像).

SUĀN₂ 酸 (SV) (1) sour tasting.
Zhèige-píngguo shì-suānde. 這
個 蘋 果 是 酸 的 . This
apple is a sour one. (2) muscu-
lar discomfort, tired. Wǒde-tuǐ
hěn-suān. 我 的 腿 很 酸 .
My legs are very tired. (3) be
sour (figuratively). Nǐ-wèishén-
me-zhènme-suān-ne? 你 為
甚 麼 這 麼 酸 呢? What
are you so sour about? (4) be
pedantic. Wǒmende-xiàozhǎng
hěn-suān. 我 們 的 校 長
很 酸 . Our principal is quite
pedantic.
(N) acid.

SUÀN₃ 蒜 (N) garlic. (M: tóu 頭,
kē 棵).

SUÀN₂ 算 (TV) (1) calculate,
compute, figure out. Wǒ-bu-
huì-suàn-zhèixie-shùr. 我 不
會 算 這 些 數 兒 . I
can't calculate these figures.
Yígòng-duōshao-qián nǐ-suàn-
chulai-le-ma? 一 共 多 少
錢 你 算 出 來 了 嗎?
Have you figured out how much
it is altogether? (2) include,
count in. Nǐ-suànshang-tā-le-
ma? 你 算 上 他 了 嗎?
Did you include him? Yàoshi-
nǐmen-dǎ-pái suàn-wǒ-yige. 要
是 你 們 打 牌 算 我
一 個 . If you are going to play
cards, count me in as one of
the players. (3) count (add up).
Gàn-yitiān suàn-yitiān. 幹 一
天, 算 一 天 Work for a

day, we will count it as a day.
Cóng-jīntiān-suàn, yígòng-shí-
tiān. 從 今 天 算, 一 共
十 天 . Counting from today,
there are ten days altogether.
Tā-shuō-de bu-suàn. 他 說
的 不 算 . What he said
doesn't count. (4) count on.
Wǒ-shuōle jiu-suàn. 我 說
了 就 算 . Whatever I say
can be counted on. (5) (often
followed by shì 是) be regarded as. Zhèibǐ-qián xiànzài-
suàn(shi)-wǒde-le. 這 筆 錢
現 在 算 (是) 我 的 了 .
This sum is regarded as mine
now. Zhèige-busuàn-tài-guì.
這 個 不 算 太 貴 . This
isn't considered too expensive.
Hái-suàn-bu-cuò. 還 算 不
錯 . It's still considered not
bad. Tā-suàn-gàn-shénma-de-
ne? 他 算 幹 甚 麼 的
呢 ? What is he supposed to
do? Nǐ-suàn-shi-shéi? 你 算
是 誰 ? Whom are you sup-
posed to be? (6) (con. suàn-wán
算完). that will be the end
of it. Zhǎowan-bǎ-qián huāwán-
le-suàn. 早 晚 把 錢 花
完 了 算 . Sooner or later
he'll use up the money and that
will be that. (cf: BÚSUÀN 不
算). (See: SUÀNLE 算 了).

SUÀNJI₃ 算 計 (TV) (1) calculate,
figure out. Ràng-wǒ 'suànji-
suànji, kànkan-gòu-bu-gou. 讓
我 算 計 算 計, 看 看
夠 不 夠 . Let me figure it
out and see whether it will be

enough or not. (2) plan. Zhèi-jian-shi wǒmen hái-dei-suànji-yixia. 這件事我們還得算計一下. We still have to make further plans for this affair. (3) size up someone else's position to take advantage of it. Tā·lǎo-ài-suànji-rén. 他老愛算計人. He always likes to size people up (to see what he can get from it). (N) plan. Tā-xīnli-you-ge-suànji. 他心裏有個算計. He has a plan in mind. (cf: JÌ-SUAN 計算).

SUĀNLĂN₅ 痠懶 (SV) tired and lazy. Wǒ-quánshēn-suānlǎn. 我全身痠懶. I feel tired and lazy.

SUÀNLE₂ 算了 (1) call it quits, call it off, forget it. (syn. bàle 罷了). Nǐ-buyuànyì jiu-suàn-le. 你不願意就算了. If you are not willing, let's call it off. (2) get it over with. Suí-biàn-chī-yidianr-suànle. 隨便吃一點兒算了. Let's eat a little something and get it over with. (3) stop. Nǐ-suànle-ba. 你算了吧. You better stop it. Suànle-suànle, bié-shuō-le. 算了算了, 別說了. All right, all right, don't say anything else.

SUÀN-MÌNG₄ 算命 (VO) tell fortunes. Tā-gei-wo-suànle-yige-mìng. 他給我算了一個命. He told my fortune once.

SUÀNPAN₃ 算盤 (N) abacus.

dǎ-suànpan 打算盤 calculate on an abacus or fig. be careful with money.

SUÀNSHÙ₂ 算術 (N) arithmetic. suàn-suànshù 算算術 do arithmetic problems. (cf: SUÀNXUÉ 算學).

SUÀNXUÉ₂ 算學 (N) (1) arithmetic. (2) mathematics. (M: mén 門). Tā-xué-suànxué. 他學算學. He is studying mathematics. (cf: SUÀNSHÙ 算術, SHUXUÉ 數學).

SUÀN-ZHÀNG₃ 算賬 (VO) (1) figure out accounts. Nǐ-suàn-shénme-zhàng-ne? 你算甚麼賬呢? What account are you figuring out? Wǒ-yí-gòng-qiàn-ni- duōshao-qián? Wǒmen-děi-suànsuan-zhàng. 我一共欠你多少錢? 我們得算算賬. How much money do I owe you altogether? We have to figure it out. (2) set things straight with someone. Wǒ-míngtian-zai-gēn-ta-suàn-zhàng. 我明天再跟他算賬. I'll set things straight with him tomorrow.

SÙCHÁNG 素常 (MA) ordinarily. Tā-sùcháng-liú-píngtóu. 他素常留平頭. Ordinarily he has a crew-cut.

SÙDÙ₂ 速度 see SÙDÙ 速度. SÙDÙ₂ 速度 or SÙDÙ 速度 (N) speed. Sùdù tài-kuài. 速度太快. The speed is too fast.

SÙ'È₂ 蘇俄 (PW) Soviet Russia.

S

SŪHU₃ 疏忽 see SHŪHU 疏忽.

SÚHUÀ₄ 俗話 (N) (1) vulgar speech. (M: jiù 句). Tā-méi-niànguo-shū shuō-de-dōu-shi-súhuà. 他没念過書説的都是俗話. He has never been educated, everything he says is vulgar. (2) or SÚYÙR 俗語兒 set sayings in colloquial speech. (M: jiù 句). Yǒu-zènma-yijiu-súhuà, "Bú-pà-màn, jiu-pà-zhàn". 有這麼一句俗話，"不怕慢，就怕站". There is a set saying, "It doesn't matter if you are slow, only if you stop."

SUĪ₄ 尿 or NIÀO 尿 (N) urine.

SUÍ₃ 隨 (TV) (1) let something be. Nǐ-bié-guǎn-le, suí-tāmen-qù-ba. 你别管了，隨他們去吧. Don't bother. Let them go their way. (2) be up to someone. Yào-bu-yào suí-nǐ. 要不要隨你. Whether you want it or not is up to you. Suí-tā-bàn, béng-wèn-wǒ. 隨他辦甭問我. It's up to him how he handles it, don't ask me. (3) with, along with, follow. Tā-lǎo-suí-biéren-shuō. 他老隨别人説. He always talks with other people's ideas. Wǒmen-děi-suízhe-shí-dài. 我們得隨着時代. We have to follow the time. (S) (1) SUÍ...SUÍ... 隨...隨... do one thing continuously right after another. suí-zuò-suí-chī 隨做隨吃 eat

right after it is cooked. suí-zhèng-suí-huā 隨掙隨花 spend right after earning. suí-mǎi-suí-mài 隨買隨賣 sell right after buying. (2) SUÍ ... YĚ... 隨...也... or SUÍ... DŌU...隨...都... no matter. Suí-ni-gěi-'duōshao-qián dōu-chéng. 隨你給多少錢都成. No matter how much money you give, it will do.

SUÌ₃ 碎 (IV) be in bits, break into bits. Wǒde-yǎnjìngr suì-le. 我的眼鏡兒碎了. My eyeglasses are broken into bits. Tāde-xīn-suì-le. 他的心碎了. His heart is broken. (SV) (con. suǒsui 瑣碎). minutely detailed and annoying. Biān-zìdiǎn shìqing-tài-suì. 編字典事情太碎. The work of compiling a dictionary is too detailed. (RE) be in bits, break into bits. Tā-bǎ-bōli-bēi suāisuì-le. 他把玻璃杯摔碎了. He smashed the glass into bits.

SUÌ₁ 歲 (M) year of age, year old. Tā-sānsuì-le. 他三歲了. He is three years old.

SUÍBIÀN₁ 隨便 (SV) (1) informal. Wǒmen-kāihuì hěn-suíbiàn. 我們開會很隨便. Our meeting is very informal. (2) loose, improper (of behavior). Nèige-nǚde tài-suíbiàn. 那個女的太隨便. That girl's behavior is very loose.

(AD) as <u>one</u> pleases. Nǐ-suíbiàn-mǎi-ba. 你 隨 便 買 吧 .
Buy what you want. Suíbiàn-zuò. 隨 便 坐 Sit wherever you want.

(VO) do whatever <u>one</u> wishes. Wǒ-suí-nǐde-biàn. 我 隨 你 的 便 . I'll do whatever you like.

followed by a question word or a choice type interrogative expression and dōu 都 <u>or</u> yě 也 , no matter <u>what</u>, <u>how</u>, <u>where</u>, etc. Suíbiàn-nǐ-ná-'něige dōu-kéyi. 隨 便 你 拿 那 個 都 可 以 . It will be all right no matter which one you take.

SUÍCHAO₄ 隋 朝 (TW) Sui dynasty.

SUÍDÀO₅ 隧 道 (N) tunnel. (M: tiáo 條).

SUÍHE₃ 隨 和 (SV) agreeable (<u>of</u> personality). Tā-hěn-suíhe. 他 很 隨 和 . He's very agreeable.

SUIR₅ 穗 兒 <u>see</u> SUIZI 穗 子 .

SUÍRÁN₁ 雖 然 (MA) although, even though (followed·by a clause introduced by adverbs like kěshì 可 是 , dànshì 但 是 , búguo 不 過 , etc. Suírán tā-bu-gěi-wǒ-qián, kěshì wǒhái-gàn. 雖 然 他 不 給 我 錢 , 可 是 我 還 幹 . Even though he doesn't pay me, I still do it.

SUÍSHÍ₂ 隨 時 (MA) any time. Suíshí-dōu-neng-mǎi. 隨 時 都 能 買 . You can buy it at any time. Qǐng-suíshí-lái. 請 隨 時 來 . Please come any time.

SUÍSHǑU₃ 隨 手 (AD) <u>do some</u>-<u>thing with the hand in addition</u> <u>to what one is already doing</u>, <u>without much extra effort</u>, while <u>one is at it</u>. (<u>syn.</u> shùnshǒu 順 手). Qǐng-ni-suíshǒu-guān-mén. 請 你 隨 手 關 門 . Shut the door while you are passing.

SUÌSHU(R)₂ 歲 數 (兒) (N) age (<u>not used when referring to</u> <u>children</u>). Tā-duó-da-suìshu(r)-le? 他 多 大 歲·數 (兒) 了 ? How old is he? Tā-shàngle-suì-shu(r)-le. 他 上 了 歲 數 (兒) 了 . He is getting old. Tā-suìshu(r) tài-dà-le. 他 歲 數 太 大 了 . He is too old.

SUÍSHUŌ₄ 雖 説 (MA) although it is said that, although one says (followed by a clause introduced by adverbs like kěshì 可 是 , dànshì 但 是 , bú-guo 不 過 , etc. Suíshuō-jīn-tian-liùshidù, kěshi-wǒ-juéde-hěn-liáng. 雖 説 今 天 六 十 度 , 可 是 我 覺 得 很 涼 . Although it is said that it's sixty degrees today, I feel quite chilly.

SUIZI₅ 穗 子 <u>or</u> SUIR 穗 兒 (N) (1) ear of grain. (2) tassel.

SÙJÌ₄ 速 記 <u>see</u> SÙJÌ 速 記 .

SÙJÌ₄ 速 記 <u>or</u> SÙJÌ 速 記 (IV) write in shorthand. Tā-huì-

S

sùjì. 她會速記 . She can take shorthand. (N) shorthand.

SÙJIÃO₄ 塑膠 (N) plastic, bakelite.

SÙJÌNG₄ 素淨 (SV) simple and undecorated. Tā-chuānde hěn-sùjìng. 她穿的很素淨 . The way she dresses is very simple.

'SÙJÌNG₅ 肅靜 (SV) solemn, quiet. Huìchǎngli-hěn-'sùjìng. 會場裏很肅靜 . It's very solemn in the meeting place.

SÙ-KŬ₃ 訴苦 (VO) complain about something, state one's grievance. Tā-yòu-sù-shénme-kǔ-ne? 他又訴甚麼苦呢 ? What is he complaining about this time?

SÙLIÁN₁ 蘇聯 (PW) The Soviet Union.

SÙMIÁO₅ 素描 (N) sketch.

SŬN₅ 筍 (N) bamboo shoot (eaten as a vegetable). (M: kē 棵).

'SŬNHÀI₃ 損害 (TV) damage, harm. Tā-sǔnhài-wode-míngyu. 他損害我的名譽 . My reputation was damaged by him. (N) damage, harm.

SŪNNǓR₄ 孫女兒 (N) granddaughter.

SŬNSHI₂ 損失 (TV) lose, suffer loss of. Wǒ-sǔnshile-hěnduō-cáichǎn. 我損失了很多財產 . I lost a lot of property. (N) loss. Wǒ-méi-shòu-shénma-sǔnshi. 我沒受甚麼

損失 . I didn't suffer any loss.

SŪNZI₃ 孫子 (N) grandson.

SUŌ₃ 縮 (IV) (1) shrink. Zhèige-liàozi 'xǐ-yìhuí-suō-yìhuí. 這個料子洗一回, 縮一回 . This material shrinks after each washing. (2) draw back, withdraw. Nèige-chóngzi yòu-suōhuiqu-le. 那個虫子又縮回去了 . That worm drew back.

SUŎ₂ 鎖 (TV) lock. shuōshang 鎖上 lock up. Bié-wàngle-suǒ-mén. 別忘了鎖門 . Don't forget to lock the door. Tā-bǎ-ta-zìjǐ suǒzai-wàitou-le. 他把他自己鎖在外頭了 . He locked himself out. (N) lock. (M: bǎ 把). yìba-suǒ 一把鎖 one lock. Bǎ-suǒ-kāikai. 把鎖開開 . Open the lock.

SUŎ(R)₃ 所 (兒) (M) for houses. liǎngsuǒ(r)-fángzi 兩所(兒)房子 two houses.

SUŎLIÀNR₅ 鎖鏈兒 or SUŎLIÀNZI 鎖鏈子 (N) chain, fetter. (M: tiáo 條).

SUŎLIÀNZI₅ 鎖鏈子 see SUŎLIÀNR 鎖鏈兒

SUŎSUÌ₃ 瑣碎 (SV) minutely detailed and annoying. Wǒ-zuò-de-shìqing hěn-suǒsui. 我做的事情很瑣碎 . What I'm doing is very minutely detailed.

SUŎWÈI(DE)₂ 所謂(的) (B-) the so-called. suǒwèi(de)-kēxuéjiā 所謂（的）科學家 the so-called scientists.

SUÓXING₃ 索性 or SUÓXING 索性 or SHUÁNGXING 爽性 (MA) just simply, might as well. Wǒmen-suóxing-bié-qù-le. 我們索性別去了. Why don't we just simply not go. Zūfáng-tài-máfan, nǐ-suóxing-zhù-lǚguǎn-suànle. 租房太麻煩,你索性住旅館算了. Since it's too much trouble to rent a house, why don't you simply stay in a hotel.

SUÓXING₃ 索性 see SUÓXING 索性.

'SUÓYI₁ 所以 (MA) (1) therefore, so. Tiān-tài-lěng, suóyi-wǒ-bu-qù. 天太冷,所以我不去. The weather is too cold, so I'm not going. (2) the reason why... (usually followed by another claus introduced by yīnwei 因為). Wǒ-suóyǐ-bú-mǎi, yīnwei-wo-méi-qián. 我所以不買,因為我沒錢. The reason why I didn't buy it was because I didn't have the money. (3) used to reaffirm one's original reason for doing or saying something, that's why I said it, that's why I did it. A: Jīntian-xià-yǔ, bú-yong-qù-le. B: Lù-bu-hǎo-zǒu. A: Suóyi-a. A: 今天下雨,不用去了. B: 路不好走. A: 所以啊. A: It's raining, we better not go. B: The road is not good for

travelling. A: That's why I said it. (cf: ZHĪ-SUÓYǏ 之所以人).

SUÓYǏN₄ 索引 (N) index.

SUÓYǑUDE₁ 所有的 (N) all. suóyǒude-xuésheng 所有的學生 all the students. Suǒ-yǒude wǒ-dōu-yào. 所有的我都要. I want all of them.

SUÓZHǍNG₃ 所長 (N) head of an office (used only when the last syllable in the office referred to is suǒ 所).

SÚQI₃ 俗氣 (SV) vulgar, unrefined, in poor taste. Tā-hěn-piàoliang, kěshi-súqi. 她很漂亮,可是俗氣. She is beautiful all right, but unrefined.

SÙSHÈ₂ 宿舍 (N) dormitory. zhù-sùshè 住宿舍 live in the dormitory.

SÚYǓR₄ 俗語兒 see SÚHUÀ 俗話.

SÙ-XIÀNG₄ 塑像 (VO) make a statue of clay, wax, etc. Tā-sùle-yíge-Yēsū-xiàng. 他塑了一個耶穌像. He made a statue of Jesus. (N) statue. (M: zuò 座).

SÚXIĚ₄ 速寫 see SÙXIĚ 速寫.

SÙXIĚ₄ 速寫 or SÚXIĚ 速寫 (TV) sketch (a picture or portrait). (N) sketch.

SÙYUAN₃ 疏遠 see SHÙYUAN 疏遠.

SŪZHOU₂ 蘇州 (PW) Soochow

S

(city in Kiangsu province).

SÙZHUR₅ 數珠兒 (N) rosary.

(M: chuàn 串 , guà 掛).

S

T

TĀ₁ 他 (PR) (1) he, she, him, her. Tā-bu rènshi-wo. 他不認識我. He (or she) doesn't know me. Shéi-gěi-ta? 誰給他 ? Who'll give it to him (or her)?.(2) used before N, his, her. tā-mǔqin 他母親 his (or her) mother. (3) it often used as an object. Bǎ-ta-bānguoqu. 把他搬過去. Move it over there. Nǐ-dǐng-ta-liǎngxiazi. 你釘他兩下子. Pound it a couple of times. Zhèige-táng-bu-cuò, nǐ-ye-chǐ-ta-yikuài. 這個糖不錯,你也吃他一塊. This candy is not bad, you have one, also.

TĀ₃ 塌 (IV) (1) collapse, fall to pieces. Nèige-lóu-yào-tā-le. 那個樓要塌了. That building is about to collapse.

TĀ₅ 塔 (N) (1) pagoda. (M: zuò 座 , céng 層). (2) tower-like structure. (zuò 座). shuǐ-tǎ 水塔 water tower. dēng-tǎ 燈塔 lighthouse.

TÁI₃ 抬 (TV) (1) lift, carry (by two or more people). Wǒmen-liǎngge-rén-tái-ba! 我們兩個人抬吧! Let's two of us carry it ! (2) raise a price. tái-jiàqian 抬價錢 raise a price.

TÀI₁ 太 (AD) excessively, too, too much. Zhèige-xiāngzi tài-zhòng, wǒ-nábudòng.這個箱子太重我拿不動 This suitcase is too heavy, I can't lift it up. Tā-tàitai tài-ài-shuō-huà. 他太太太愛說話. His wife loves to talk too much.

TÁIBĚI₁ 台北 (PW) Taipei.

TÀIDU₂ 態度 (N) (1) gestures, actions. Tā-shuō-huà-de-shihou tàidu-hěn-huópo. 他說話的時候態度很活潑. When he speaks, his gestures are very lively. (2) attitude (of people). Zhèizǒng-zuò-shì-de tàidu wǒ-bu-xǐhuan. 這種作事的態度我不喜歡. I don't like this kind of attitude in working. Bié-cǎiqǔ zhèizhong-tàidu.別採取這種態度. Don't take this kind of attitude.

TÁIFĒNG₃ 颱風 (N) typhoon. (M: cì 次). guā-táifēng 颳颱風 have a typhoon.

TÀIGUO₃ 泰國 (PW) Thailand.

TÁIJIĚR₅ 臺階兒 (N) outside stairs or steps. (M: céng 層). shàng-táijiēr 上臺階兒 go up the stairs.

TÀIPÍNGYÁNG₂ 太平洋 (N) Pacific Ocean.

TÀITAI₁ 太太 (N) (1) married
woman. (M: wèi 位). lǎo-tài-
tai 老太太 old lady. (2)
wife. wǒ-tàitai 我太太 my
wife. sānwèi-tàitai 三位太
太 three married ladies or
three wives.

used before a surname, Mrs.
Wáng-tàitai 王太太 Mrs.
Wang. (cf: XÍFU 媳婦).

TÁI-TÓU₃ 抬頭 (VO) raise
one's head. (opp. dǐ-tóu 低頭).
Nǐ-táiqi-tóu-lai. 你抬起
頭來 . Lift your head.

TÁIWĀN₁ 台灣 (PW) Taiwan,
Formosa.

TÀIYANG₂ 太陽 (N) the sun.
Tàiyang hái-méi-chūlai-ne. 太
陽還沒出來呢. The
sun isn't out yet.

TĀMEN₁ 他們 (PR) (1) they,
them. Tāmen-bu-lái. 他們
不來 . They won't come. (2)
used before a noun, their. Tā-
men-xiānsheng 他們先生
their teacher. Tāmen-háizi-yě-
lái-le. 他們孩子
也來了 . Their children
have come also. or The children, they have come also.

TĀN₄ 灘 (N) (1) sandy shore. hǎi-
tān 海灘 seashore. (2) rapids.
(M) a pool or a blob of. yìtān-ní
一灘泥 a blob of mud.

TĀN₄ 攤 (TV) (1) spread things
out (as for a display). Tā-bǎ-
dōngxi dōu-tānzai-dìxia-le. 他
把東西都攤在地
下了 . He spread the things
out on the floor. (2) share a

financial burden. Bié-yíge-rén-
gěi. Dàjiā-tān. 別一個人
給‧大家攤 . Let's not
have just one person pay. Let's
all chip in.

TĀN₃ 貪 (SV) covetous, greedy,
insatiably desirous. Nǐ-tài-tān-
le. 你太貪了 . You are
too greedy.
(TV) desire, covet. Tā-lǎo-ài-
tān-piányi. 他老愛貪便
宜 . He always desires to get
things for his own benefit.

TÁN₅ 痰 (N) spittle, phlegm. (M:
kǒu 口). tǔ-tán 吐痰 spit
(phlegm).

TÁN₂ 談 (TV) talk, talk about,
discuss, chat. tán-tiānr 談天
兒 chat. Wǒ-néng-bunéng gēn-
ni-tān-wǔfēn-zhōng? 我能不
能跟你談五分鐘?
May I talk with you for five minutes? Nǐmen-tán-shénma-ne?
你們談甚麼呢? What
are you talking about?

TÁN₃ 彈 (TV) (1) pluck a stringed
instrument, play the piano or
organ. tán-liùxiánqín 彈六
弦琴 play a guitar. tán-gāngqín 彈鋼琴 play a piano. (2)
flick. Nǐ-bǎ-yānhuī tān-yitan.
你把煙灰彈一彈‧
You should flick the ashes off
your cigarette. (3) rebound. Qiú
tánde-hěn-gāo. 球彈的很
高 . The ball rebounded very
high.

TÁN₅ 炭 (N) charcoal.

TÀN₄ 歎 (TV) sigh. tàn-qì 歎氣
sigh.

TÀN₃ 探 (TV) search out, reconnoiter. Wŏmen-xiān-qu-tàntan-lù. 我們先去探探路. Let's explore the way first.

(IV) lean out, lean toward. Bié-bă-shēnzi tàndao-chuānghu-wàitou-qu. 別把身子探到窗戶外頭去. Don't lean (your body) out of the window.

TĂNBAI₂ 坦白 (SV) frank, straightforward, open.

(TV) confess to the public (used in Mainland China). Nĭ-dĕi-bă-ni-guòqù-de-shìqing tănbai-chu-lai. 你得把你過去的事情坦白出來. You have to confess your past affairs.

(AD) frankly. Wŏ-tănbaide-gào-song-ni. 我坦白的告訴你. I am telling you frankly.

TĀNG₁ 湯 (N) soup. (M: wăn 盌).

TĀNG₅ 蹚 (TV) wade through water. Xiăoháizi dōu-ài-tāng-shuĭ. 小孩都愛蹚水. All children like to wade through water.

TÁNG₁ 糖 (N) (1) sugar. (2) candy. (M: kuài 塊).

TÁNG₃ 搪 (TV) parry, put someone off. yòng-gēbei-táng 用胳臂搪 parry with the arm. Qĭng-ni-tì-wo-táng-ta-jĭtiān. 請你替我搪他幾天. Please put him off a few days for me.

TÁNG₃ 堂 (M) class (as a period of time). yìtáng-lìshĭ 一堂歷史 a history class. shàng-yi-táng-kè 上一堂課 attend or hold a class.

TĂNG₂ 躺 (IV) lie down. Tā-tăng-zai-căodìshang xiūxi. 他躺在草地上休息. He is lying down on the grass resting. Tā-zai-chuángshang-tăngzhe-ne. 他在床上躺着呢. He is lying in bed. Dàifu jiào-wo-tăngxia. 大夫叫我躺下. The doctor told me to lie down.

TÀNG₃ 燙 (TV) (1) iron. tàng-yī-shang 燙衣裳 iron clothes. (2) get a permanent. Nĭde-tóufa yòu-gāi-tàng-le. 你的頭髮又該燙了. Your hair needs a permanent again. (3) scald something or oneself. Wŏ-bă-jiăo tàng-le. 我把我的腳燙了. I scalded my foot. (4) warm something. tàng-jiŭ 燙酒 warm the wine. (SV) scalding hot, burning hot. Tāng-hĕn-tàng. 湯很燙. The soup is very hot.

TÀNG₃ 趟 (M) (1) time of trips to a place. Wŏ-dào-Niŭyue qùguo-sāntàng. 我到紐約去過三趟. I have been to New York three times. (2) column, row. Yĭzi páicheng-sāntàng. 椅子排成三趟. The chairs are arranged into three rows.

TÁNGCHAO₂ 唐朝 (TW) T'ang dynasty.

TĂNGHUO₄ 倘或 (MA) if, supposing. Tănghuo nĭ-yuànyi-qù,

T

wǒ-jiu-gàosong-ta. 倘或你
願意去, 我就告訴
他. I'll inform him if you
want to go.

TÁNGJIĚMÈI₅ 堂姐妹 or
TÁNGZǏMÈI 堂姊妹 (N)
female cousins (daughters of
father's brother). (cf: BIǍOJIĚ-
MÈI 表姐妹).

TÁNGXIŌNGDÌ₅ 堂兄弟 (N)
male cousins (sons of father's
brother). (cf: BIǍOXIŌNGDÌ 表
兄弟).

TÁNGZǏMÈI₅ 堂姊妹 see
TÁNGJIĚMÈI 堂姐妹.

TÁNHUÁNG₃ 彈簧 (N) coiled
spring. (M: gēn 根).

TǍNKECHĒ₃ 坦克車 (N) tank
(military vehicle). (M: liàng
輛).

TÁNPÀN₄ 談判 (IV) confer and
negotiate. Tāmen-míngtian cái-
kāishǐ-tánpàn-ne. 他們明
天才開始談判呢.
They won't start to negotiate
until tomorrow.
(N) negotiation. kāi-tánpàn 開
談判 open negotiations.

TÀN-QÌ₃ 嘆氣 (VO) breathe a
sigh.

TĀNR₄ 攤兒 or TĀNZI 攤子
(N) stand or place on the ground
(for vending). bǎi-tānr 擺攤
兒 set up a display on a stand
or on the ground for vending.

TÁN-TIĀNR₂ 談天兒 (VO)
chat, converse. (syn. liáo-tiānr
聊天兒). Wǒmen-tánle-sānge-
zhōngtóu-tiānr. 我們談了
三個鐘頭天兒. We

chatted for three hours.

TÀNTING₃ 探聽 (TV) find out,
seek out news, information. tàn-
ting-xiāoxi 探聽消息 seek
out news. Wǒ-shénme yě-méi-
tàntíng-chulái. 我甚麼也
沒探聽出來. I didn't
find out any information.

TÀNXI₄ 歎息 (IV) sigh. Tā-tàn-
xile-yìshēng. 他歎息了
一聲 . He sighed once.

TÁNXIANGSHĀN₂ 檀香山
(PW) Hawaii.

TÁN-XĪN₃ 談心 (VO) have a
heart-to-heart talk. Tāmen-
liǎngge-rén zhèng-tánxīn-ne. 他
們兩個人正談心
呢. They are having a heart-
to-heart talk now.

TĀNZI₄ 攤子 see TĀNR 攤兒.

TÁNZI₅ 壜子 (N) earthenware
jar or jug.

TǍNZI₃ 毯子 (N) blanket. (M:
tiáo 條 , zhāng 張).

TĀO₄ 掏 (TV) take something out
of something with a small opening. tāo-ěrduo 掏耳朵 re-
move wax from the ear. Tā-
cóng-kǒudàirli bǎ-qián-tāochu-
lai-le. 他從口袋兒裏
把錢掏出來了 . He
took the money out of his pocket.

TÁO₃ 逃 (IV) escape, flee. Méi-
fázi-táo. 沒法子逃 .
There is no way to escape.

TÁO₅ 淘 (TV) (1) wash something
by swirling it around in water.
táo-mǐ 淘米 wash rice. (2)dredge.
táo-jǐng 淘井 clean a well.

TǍO₄ 討 (TV) (1) ask for, beg for.

tǎo-zhài 討債 ask for payment of a debt. Wǒ-qiàn-ta-qián, tā-lǎo-bù-lái-tǎo. 我欠他錢，他老不來討. I owed him money, but he never came to ask for it. (2) marry a woman. Tā-hái-méi-tǎo-tài-tai-ne. 他還沒討太太呢. He hasn't married yet. (3) gain affection or cause annoyance. Zhèi-háizi zhēn-tǎo-ren-xǐhuan. 這孩子真討人喜歡. This child really makes people like him.

TÀO₃ 套 (TV) (1) put something on as a cover, slip on. Bǎ-yǐ-zi-tào tàoshang. 把椅子套套上. Put the slip-cover on. (2) hitch an animal to a cart. tào-chē 套車 hitch up a cart. (3) follow a pattern to write articles or to make sentences. Tāde-huà-dōu-shi-tàode-shūshangde. 他的話都是套的書上的. His sentences are all made up according to the patterns of the sentences in the book. (4) use certain speech to trick a person into telling the truth. Wǒ-yòng-huà-yítào-ta, tā-jiu-dōu-shuō-le. 我用話一套他，他就都説了. As soon as I got around him he told me everything. (5) print in colors. Yìn-zhèizhang-huàr děi-tào-sāncì. 印這張畫兒得套三次. This picture has to be printed three times (to bring out the colors). (6)

inter-connect, intertwined. Nèi-liǎngge-quānr tàozai-yíkuàir-le. 那兩個圈兒套在一塊兒了. Those two circles are inter-connected.

(N) covering, wrapper. zhěntou-tào 枕頭套 pillow case. (M) set, suit. yítào-jiāju 一套傢俱 a set of furniture. yí-tào-yīshang 一套衣裳 a suit of clothing.

TÀO-FÀN₄ 討飯 (VO) (lit. beg for food) beg (to maintain one's existence). (syn. yào-fàn 要飯).

TÁOHUĀ(R)₄ 桃花兒 (N) peach blossom. (M: duǒ 朵 , zhī 枝).

TǍOLUN₂ 討論 (TV) discuss. Wǒmen-míngtian zai-tǎolun-zhèi-jiàn-shì-ba. 我們明天再討論這件事吧. Let's discuss this matter tomorrow.

(N) discussion. Zhèicìde-tǎolun hěn-yǒu-jiàzhi. 這次的討論很有價值. The discussion this time was very valuable.

TÁO-MÌNG₅ 逃命 (VO) flee, run away in order to save one's life. Tǔfěi-jiù-yao-lái-le, nǐ-hái-bu-táo-mìng-ma? 土匪就要來了，你還不逃命嗎? The bandits are coming, why don't you flee?

TÁOPǍO₃ 逃跑 see TÁOZǑU 逃走.

TÁOQÌ₃ 淘氣 (SV) naughty. Nèi-háizi hěn-táoqì. 那孩子很淘氣. That child is really

T

naughty.

TÁOR₃ 桃兒 or **TÁOZI** 桃子 (N) peach.

TÁO-XUÉ₃ 逃學 (VO) (lit. escape from school) play hooky. Tā-yòu-táo-xué-le. 他又逃學了. He played hooky again.

TĂOYÀN₂ 討厭 (TV) feel disgusted or annoyed by someone or something. Tā tǎoyan-tā-yuèmǔ. 他討厭他岳母. He is annoyed by his mother-in-law.

(SV) disgusting, annoying. Tā-de-érzi hěn-tǎoyàn. 他的兒子很討厭. His son is very annoying.

TÁOZI₃ 桃子 see TÁOR 桃兒.

TÁOZŎU₃ 逃走 or **TÁOPĂO** 逃跑 (IV) flee, run away, escape. Liǎngge-fànren táozǒu-le. 兩個犯人逃走了. Two prisoners escaped.

TĀSHI₄ 塌實 (SV) peaceful, calm (of a person). Wǒ-xīnli hěn-tāshi. 我心裏很塌實. I feel very calm.

TÈBIÉ₁ 特別 (SV) special, distinctive, uncommon. (opp. píng-cháng 平常). Lùtóufa tài-tèbié-le. 綠頭髮太特別了. Green hair is really uncommon. Zhèige-bu-zěnma-tèbié. 這個不怎麼特別. This is nothing special.

(AD) especially, particularly. Wǒ-shi-tèbié-gěi-'nǐ-mǎi-de. 我是特別給你買的. I bought it especially for you.

TÈCHÁNG₃ 特長 (N) special capacity, particular excellence. (M: zhǒng 種). Tā-yǒu-hěn-duō-tècháng. 他有很多特長. He has a lot of specialties.

TÈDIĂN₃ 特點 (N) special characteristic or feature. Zhèi-shi-zhèiben-shū-de-yige-tèdiǎn. 這是這本書的一個特點. This is a special characteristic of this book.(cf: TÈSÈ 特色).

TÉNG₄ 謄 (TV) copy, rewrite, make a clear copy. Qíng-ni-bǎ-zhèifēng-xìn-téngxialai. 請你把這封信謄下來. Please make a clear copy of this letter.

TÉNG₃ 騰 (TV) (1) move things out to make room. Nǐ-gěi-wǒ-téng-yijian-wūzi-ba. 你給我騰一間屋子吧. Will you clear out a room for me. (2) make time for. Wǒ-zìjǐ-téngbuchu-gōngfu-lai. 我自己騰不出工夫來. I can't make any time for myself.

TÉNG₂ 疼 (TV) love children. Tā-hen-téng-tade-háizi. 她很疼她的孩子. She dotes on her children.

(SV) painful, sore. Wǒde-tóu bu-téng-le. 我的頭不疼了. My headache went away. Wǒ-yá téngde-hen-lìhai. 我牙疼得很利害. My tooth aches very much.

TÉNGLUO₅ 藤蘿 (N) wisteria.
(M: kē 棵).

TÉNGZI₅ 藤子 (N) rattan.

TÈSÈ₃ 特色 (N) properties,
special characteristic. (cf:
TÈDIĂN 特點).

TÈSHŪ₃ 特殊 (SV) special, exceptional. Nǐde-qíngxing bìng-
bu-tèshū. 你 的 情 形 並
不 特 殊 . Your case isn't
exceptional at all.

TÈWÙ₃ 特務 (N) secret agent,
spy.

TÈYÌ₃ 特意 (AD) intentionally,
purposely. Wǒ-tèyì-méi-gěi-
qián. 我 特 意 沒 給 錢 .
I purposely didn't pay.

TĪ₂ 踢 (TV) lit.or fig. kick. tī-qiú
踢球 kick the ball. Mǎ-bǎ-
xiǎoháir tī-le. 馬 把 小 孩
兒 踢 了 . The horse kicked
the child. Wǒmen-bǎ-ta tīchuqu-
le. 我 們 把 他 踢 出
去 了 . We kicked him out.
Tā-tīle-wo-yijiǎo. 他 踢 了
我 一 腳 . He gave me a
kick.

TĪ₄ 剔 (TV) (1) scrape off. tī-gú-
tou 剔 骨 頭 scrape the
meat off the bone. (2) pick out
the undesirable things. Bǎ-làn-
píngguo dōu-tīchu-lai. 把 爛
蘋 果 都 剔 出 來 . Pick
out the rotten apples and throw
them away.

TÍ₂ 提 (TV) (1) carry, lift with
the hand under shoulder level.
Tā-tízhe-yíge-lánzi. 她 提
著 一 個 籃 子 . She is
carrying a basket. (2) bring up,

mention. Xiànzài hái-tí-ta-gàn-
má? 現 在 還 提 它 幹
麼 ? What's the use of bringing
it up now? Bié-tí-le. 別 提 了 .
Don t bring that up anymore. (3)
(con. tíxǐng 提醒). remind.
Bié-wàngle-tí-wo. 別 忘 了
提 我 . Don't forget to remind
me. (4) express an opinion, suggest. tí-yìjian 提意見 make
a suggestion. (5) draw out, take
out. tí-qián 提錢 draw out
money.

TÍ₃ 題 (N) (con. tímu 題目).
topic for exercise, problem. (M:
dào 道).

TÌ₁ 替 (TV) take the place of,
substitute for someone. Míngtiān
wǒ-tì-ni. 明 天 我 替 你 .
I'll take your place tomorrow.
(CV) for, in the place of someone. Nǐ-tì-wo-mǎi-piào-ba! 你
替 我 買 票 吧 ! Buy the
ticket for me, will you?

TÌ₃ 剃 (TV) shave. Wǒ-sāntiān
méi-tì-húzi-le. 我 三 天 沒
剃 鬍 子 了 . I didn't shave
for three days.

TÍ'ÀN₅ 提案 (N) motion, proposal.
(M: jiàn 件). Jīntian-kāi-kuì
tí'àn-bu-duō. 今 天 開 會
提 案 不 多 . There were
not many proposals at today's
meeting.

TIĀN₁ 天 (M) day. wǔtiān 五天
five days. yǒu-yitiān 有 一 天
there was a time. Wǒ-yìtiān méi-
chuqu. 我 一 天 沒 出 去 .
I haven't been out for a whole day.
(N) (1) sky. Tiānshang méi-you

T

yúncai. 天 上 沒 有 雲 彩. There are no clouds in the sky. (2) Heaven. Tiān-zhĭdao! 天 知 道 ! Heaven knows. Wŏde-tiān! 我 的 天 ! My Heavens! (3) daytime, daylight. Tiān-duăn-le. 天 短 了. The days are short now. Tiān-hēi-le. 天 黑 了. It's getting dark. Tiān-hái-méi-liàng-ne. 天 還 沒 亮 呢. It's still not light yet.

TIĀN(R)₁ 天 (兒) (N) weather. (syn. tiān-qi 天 氣). Shàng-wu-tiān(r)-bu-cuò, xiàwu-jiu-biàn-le. 上 午 天 (兒) 不 錯, 下 午 就 變 了. The weather was not bad in the morning but it changed in the afternoon. (See: TÁN-TIĀNR 談 天 兒).

TIĀN₂ 添 (IV) add, obtain additional personnel, money, materials, etc. tiān-xiăoháir 添 小 孩 兒 have a baby. Nèige-gōngsī yòu-tiān-rén-le. 那 個 公 司 又 添 人 了. That company added more employees again. Wŏ-zai-gĕi-nin-tiān-dianr-fàn. 我 再 給 您 添 點 兒 飯. I'll add a little more rice for you. Nĭ-dĕi-tiān-yíjian-máoyī. 你 得 添 一 件 毛 衣. You should put on another sweater.

TIÁN₃ 田 (N) farmland. (M: mŭ 畝). zhòng-tián 種 田 to farm.

TIÁN₃ 填 (TV) fill, stuff. tián-biăo 填 表 fill out a form. Nĭ-

yòng-shénme tián-nèige-dòng? 你 用 甚 麼 填 那 個 洞? What do you use to fill that hole?

TIÁN₂ 甜 (SV) sweet. Zhèige-dàn-gāo tài-tián-le. 這 個 蛋 糕 太 甜 了. This cake is too sweet.

TIĂN₄ 舔 (TV) lick, lap. Bié-tiăn-nĭde-pánzi. 別 舔 你 的 盤 子. Don't lick your plate.

TIĀN'ĀNMÉN₄ 天 安 門 (PW) (1) front gate of the Forbidden City in Peking. (2) Tien An Men Square.

TIÁN-BIĂO₃ 填 表 (VO) fill in a schedule.

TIĀNCAI₃ 天 才 (N) (1) genius. Tā-shi-ge-tiāncai. 他 是 個 天 才. He is a genius. (2) talent. Tā-yŏu-tiāncai. 他 有 天 才. He has talent.

TIÁNDÌ₄ 田 地 (N) (1) arable land, fields.(M: kuài 塊). (2) difficult straits. (M: bù 步). Wŏ-wàn-méi-xiăngdào wŏ-huì-dàole-zhèibu-tiándì. 我 萬 沒 想 到 我 會 到 了 這 步 田 地. I never thought I could get into a mess like this.

TIĀNFEN₃ 天 分 (N) natural aptitude, talent. Tāde-tiānfen hĕn-gāo. 他 的 天 分 很 高. His aptitude is very high.

TIÁNGUA₄ 甜 瓜 see XIĀNG-GUĀR 香 瓜 兒.

TIĀNHUĀBĂN₅ 天 花 板 (N) ceiling (of a room).

TIĀNHUĀR₄ 天 花 兒 (N) small-pox. chū-tiānhuār 出 天 花

兒 break out with smallpox.

TIĀNJIN₃ 天津 see TIĀNJING
天津.

TIĀNJING₂ 天津 or TIĀNJIN 天
津 (PW) Tientsin.

TIÁNJÌNGSÀI₃ 田徑賽 (N)
track and field meet.

TIĀNKŌNG₄ 天空 (PW) sky.
Tiānkōng yǒu-shénme? 天空
有甚麼? What's in the sky?

TIĀNQI₁ 天氣 (N) weather. (syn.
tiān(r) 天(兒)). Jīntian-tiānqi-
hen-hǎo. 今天天氣很
好. The weather today is very
good.

TIĀNRÁN₄ 天然 (B) natural, not
artificial. tiānrán-cǎisè 天然
彩色 natural color. Zhèige-
shi-tiánránde, bu-shi-rénzàode.
這個是天然的, 不
是人造的. This is nat-
ural, it's not man-made.

TIÁNSÀI₃ 田賽 (N) track meet.

TIÁNSHUǏ₄ 甜水 (N) soft water.
(opp. kǔshuǐ 苦水).

TIĀNTÁNG₂ 天堂 (N) Heaven,
paradise. shàng-tiāntáng 上
天堂 go up to Heaven.

TIĀNTIĀN₁ 天天 (MA) daily,
day by day, everyday. Tā-tiān-
tiān qǐdiǎn-zhōng-qǐ. 他天天
七點鐘起. He gets up at
seven o'clock everyday.

TIĀNWÉNXUÉ₅ 天文學 (N)
astronomy.

TIĀNXIÀ₄ 天下 (N) the entire
world. tiānxià-dà-luàn 天下
大亂 a big mess in the world.

TIÁNXIĚ₅ 填寫 (TV) fill out a
form or blank. Qǐng-nǐmeń yòng-

gāngbǐ-tiánxiě. 請你們用
銅筆填寫. Please fill
out the form with a pen.

TIĀNXÌNG₃ 天性 (N) nature (of
a person). Tāde-tiānxìng jiu-shi-
zhè-yàngr. 他的天性就
是這樣兒. His nature is
just this way.

TIĀNZĀI₃ 天災 (N) natural disaster, catastrophe. nào-tiānzāi
鬧天災 have a natural dis-
aster.

TIĀNZHĒN₂ 天真 (SV) innocent,
natural, unaffected (of a person
or his behavior). Zhèige-nǚháizi
hen-tiānzhēn. 這個女孩
子很天真. This young
girl is very innocent. (2) naive.
tiānzhēnde-'xiǎngfǎ 天真的
想法 naive way of thinking.

TIĀNZHǓJIÀO₂ 天主教 (N)
Catholic.

TIĀO₃ 挑 (TV) (1) carry on the
shoulder with a pole. Nǐ-tiāode-
dòng-zhèige-dànzi ma? 你挑
得動這個担子嗎?
Can you carry this load? (2) pick
out, select. (syn. jiǎn 撿, xuǎn
選). Nǐ-tì-wo tiāo-yíge-hǎode-
ba! 你替我挑一個
好的吧! Will you select a
good one for me?
(M) for a load carried with a pole.
yìtiāo-shuǐ 一挑水 load of
water.

TIÁO₁ 條 (M) (1) for long narrow
things. yìtiáo-shéngzi 一條
繩子 a rope. yìtiáo-shé 一
條蛇 a snake. yìtiáo-jiē 一
條街 a street. yítiáo-he 一

T

條河 a river. yìtiáo-yán 一
條煙 a carton of cigarettes.
(2) article in a newspaper, magazine, or document. yìtiáo-
xīnwén 一條新聞 a news
article. dìsānzhāng-dì'èrtiáo第
三章第二條 Chapter
3, Article 2. (3) for fish or
certain animals. yìtiáo-niú 一
條牛 a cow. yìtiáo-yú 一
條魚 a fish. (4) for the mind.
Qíwànwan-rén yìtiáo-xīn. 七
萬萬人一條心.
Seven hundred million people
with one mind.

TIĂO₄ 挑 (TV) (1) insert a long
thin object under something to
pick it up. tiāo-cì 挑刺 dig
out a splinter. tiāo-huǒ 挑火
poke a fire. (2) (con. tiāobo 挑
撥). provoke, stir up bad relations between people, agitate
a dispute. Nǐ-bié-gěi-tamen-
tiāo-le. 你別給他們
挑了. Don't provoke bad
relations between them any
more.

TIÀO₁ 跳 (IV) (1) jump, leap, hop.
Nǐ-néng-tiào-duóme-gāo? 你
能跳多麼高? How
high can you jump? (2) pulsate,
beat. Wǒ-xīn xiànzài tiàode-
hěn-kuài. 我心現在跳
得很快. My heart is beat-
ing very fast now. (3) skip a line,
row, column. Zài-tiào-yìháng.
再跳一行. Skip one
more line.

TIÀOBO₃ 挑撥 (TV) provoke
bad relations between people,

agitate a dispute. Nǐ-wèi-shénme lǎo-tiāobo-tamen? 你為
甚麼老挑撥他們?
Why do you always provoke dis-
putes between them?

TIÀO-GĀOR₃ 跳高兒 (VO) do
the high-jump. Tā-tiào-gāor
tiàode-hěn-hǎo. 他跳高兒
跳得很好. He does the
high-jump very well.
(N) high-jump. Wǒ-méi-cānjiā-
tiàogāor. 我沒參加跳
高兒. I didn't participate in
the high-jump.

TIÁOGĒNG₃ 調羹 (N) soup
spoon. (M: bǎ 把). (cf: SHÁOR
勺兒).

TIÁOHE₄ 調和 (TV) (1) mediate.
Nǐ-gěi-tamen tiáohe-tiaohe ba!
你給他們調和調
和吧! Why don't you mediate
between them? (2) make something harmonious. Jiā-yidianr-
hóng-yánse, tiáohe-yixia. 加
一點兒紅顏色調
和一下. Add a little more
red to balance it off.
(SV) harmonious. Xīnshi-fángzi-
li guà-Zhōngguo-huàr yě-hěn-
tiáohe. 新式房子裏掛
中國畫兒也很調
和. It's still very harmonious
to hang Chinese paintings in a
modern house.

TIÁOJI₃ 調劑 (TV) balance by
doing something different, add
variety to. Nǐ-yīnggāi tiáoji-
tiaoji-nǐde-shēnghuo. 你應
當調劑調劑你的
生活. You should add variety

to your life.

TIÁOJIÀN₁ 條件 (N) conditions, terms. Yǒu-mei-you fùdàide-tiáojian? 有沒有附帶的條件? Are there any additional conditions?

TIÁOR₄ 挑兒 see TIÁOZI 挑子.

TIÁOR₃ 條兒 or TIÁOZI 條子 (N) (1) stripe, band. Zhèige-bù-shang yǒu-hěn-duō-tiáor. 這個布上有很多條兒. This pattern has many stripes. (2) slip (something narrow and long).zhǐtiáor 紙條兒 paper slip. (3) note or short message on a slip of paper. xiě-ge-tiáor 寫個條兒 write a note. liú-ge-tiáor 留個條兒 leave a message.

TIÁOSUO₅ 調唆 (TV) incite, agitate someone to do something. Búshi-wǒ-tiáosuo-ta-gào-nǐ-de. 不是我調唆他告你的. I didn't incite him to sue you.

TIÁOTING₃ 調停 (TV) mediate, act as an intermediary in the settlement of difficulties. Wǒ-gěi-tamen tiáotingguo, kěshi-tāmen-bu-tīng. 我給他們調停過,可是他們不聽. I have mediated be-tween them, but they wouldn't listen.

TIÀO-WǓ₂ 跳舞 (VO) dance. Tāmen-tiàole-sānge-zhōngtóu-wǔ. 他們跳了三個鐘頭舞. They danced for three hours. Nǐ-huì-tiào-něi-

zhǒng-wǔ? 你會跳那種舞? What kind of dances can you do?

TIÀOXÌN₅ 挑釁 (IV) provoke, challenge. Tā-xiān-xiàng-wǒ-tiǎo-xìn-de. 他先向我挑釁的. He challenged me first.

TIǍO-YǍN₃ 挑眼 (VO) (1) pick on others. Tā-lǎo-tiǎo-yǎn. 他老挑眼. He always picks. (2) feel offended. Tā-yòu-tiǎo-yǎn-le. 他又挑眼了. He felt he was offended again.

TIÀO-YUǍNR₃ 跳遠兒 (VO) do the broad-jump. Wǒ-xiànzài-tiào-yuǎnr tiàobuliǎo-le. 我現在跳遠兒跳不了了. I can't do the broad-jump anymore.

(N) broad-jump.

TIÁOYUĒ₂ 條約 (N) treaty. dìng-tiáoyuē 訂條約 or lì-tiáoyuē 立條約 draw up a treaty.

TIÀOZAO₅ 跳蚤 (N) flea. (M: zhǐ 隻).

TIǍO-ZHÀN₄ 挑戰 (VO) chal-lenge to battle, provoke a fight. Nǐ-wèi-shénme xiàng-ta-tiǎo-zhàn? 你為甚麼向他挑戰? Why do you challenge him?

(N) challenge. Shéide-tiǎozhàn wǒ-dōu-jiēshòu. 誰的挑戰我都接受. I'll accept anybody's challenge.

TIÁOZHOU₄ 笤帚 (N) broom. (M: bǎ 把).

TIǍOZI₄ 挑子 or TIÁOR 挑

T

兒 (N) carrying pole <u>with bas-</u>
<u>kets or buckets on each end.</u>
Tā-tiāozhe-yige-tiāozi. 他 挑
着 一 個 挑 子. He is
carrying something with a pole.
(cf: DÀNZI 担子).

TIÁOZI₃ 條 子 <u>see</u> TIÁOR 條
兒 .

TÍBĀO₃ 提包 (N) suitcase. Tā-
tízhe-yíge-tíbāo. 他 提 着
一 個 提 包 . He is car-
rying a suitcase.

TĬ-CĀO₄ 體 操 (N) calisthenics,
physical exercise, drill.
(VO) do physical exercise. tǐle-
yitang-cāo 體 了 一 堂 操
have a class of physical exer-
cise.

TÍCHÀNG₃ 提 倡 (TV) promote.
Tā-tíchang yánjiu-dōngfangde-
wénhuà. 他 提 倡 研 究
東 方 的 文 化. He pro-
motes the study of Oriental civ-
ilization.

TÍCHŪ₃ 提 出 (RV) bring up,
set forth. Tā-tíchule-yíge-hěn-
hǎo-de-bànfa. 他 提 出 了
一 個 很 好 的 辦 法.
He brought up a very good reso-
lution.

TIĒ₃ 貼 (TV) (1) stick <u>something</u>
to, paste <u>something</u> onto. Bǎ-
zhèizhang-guǎnggào tiēzai-
qiángshang-ba. 把 這 張 廣
告 貼 在 牆 上 吧！
Let's paste this bill on the wall.
(2) pay <u>a part of the expense,</u>
make up <u>a shortage.</u> Zhèihuí-
wǒ-dàibiǎo-xuéxiào-qu-kāi-huì
wǒ-tiēle-wǔshikuài-qián. 這

回 我 代 表 學 校 去
開 會，我 貼 了 五 十
塊 錢. When I represented
the school at the meeting this
time, I paid fifty dollars out of
my own pocket (in addition to
what the school gave me). Zhèi-
huì-wǒ-chūqu-kāi-huì, xuéxiào
tiēgei-wo-wǔshikuai-qián. 這
回 我 出 去 開 會，學
校 貼 給 我 五 十 塊
錢. When I attended the meet-
ing this time, the school gave me
fifty dollars (to help cover the
expense).

TIĚ₃ 鐵 (N) iron (<u>metal</u>).

TIĚBǏNG₃ 鐵 餅 (N) discus.
rēng-tiěbǐng 扔 鐵 餅 throw
the discus.

TIĚJIǍCHĒ₅ 鐵 甲 車 (N) ar-
mored car. (M: liàng 輛).

TIĚJIANG₅ 鐵 匠 (N) blacksmith.

TIĚLÙ₂ 鐵 路 (N) railroad. (M:
tiáo 條).

TIĚQIĀO₅ 鐵 鍬 (N) shovel,
spade. (M: bǎ 把).

TIĚQIÚ₃ 鐵 球 (N) shot-put. rēn-
tiěqiú 扔 鐵 球 put the shot.

TIĚZI₄ 帖 子 (N) written invita-
tion. (M: zhāng 張). (<u>syn.</u> qǐng-
tiě 請 帖). fā-tiězi 發 請
帖 <u>or</u> xià-tiězi 下 帖 兒 send
out invitations.

TÌFEN₄ 嚏 噴 (N) sneeze. dǎ-
tìfen 打 嚏 噴 to sneeze.

TÍGĀO₃ 提 高 (RV) raise (<u>a</u>
<u>standard, salary, etc.</u>). Tāmen-
de-shēnghuo-shuǐzhǔn yǐjing-tí-
gāo-le. 他 們 的 生 活 水
準 已 經 提 高 了. Their

T

standard of living has already been raised.

TÌHUAN₄ 替換 (TV) replace, substitute for. Nǐ-bǎ-ta-tìhuan-xialai-ba! 你把他替換下來吧! You'd better replace him now!

TǏHUÌ₃ 體會 (TV) comprehend, understand by feeling. Wǒ-bu-néng-tǐhuì-zhèibèn-shū-de-yìsi. 我不能體會這本書的意思. I don't comprehend the meaning of this book.

TǏMIAN₃ 體面 (SV) decent. Tā-zhǎngde hěn-tǐmian. 他長的很體面. She looks very decent. Tāmende-bìyè-diǎnlǐ hěn-tǐmian. 他們的畢業典禮很體面. The graduation ceremony was very decent. Nǐde-lǐwu yǒu-diǎnr-bu-tǐmian. 你的禮物有點兒不體面.Your gift is somewhat indecent.

TÍMU₁ 題目 (N) (1) title, heading, subject, topic. Míngtian nǐ-jiǎng-shénme-tímu? 明天你講甚麼題目? What will be the subject of your speech tomorrow? Nǐ-géi-wo xiǎng-yige-tímu. 你給我想一個題目. Think of a topic for me. (2) problem, exercise.(M: dào 道). shùxué-tí-mu 數學題目 mathematics problems. Míngtian-kǎoshì wǒ-děi-gei-xuésheng-chū-tímu. 明天考試我得給學生出題目. Tomorrow is a test, I have to make up

questions for the students.

TÌNG₁ 聽 (TV) (1) listen to. Nǐ-bié-tǐng-tā-de. 你別聽他的.(lit. Don't listen to his (words).) Don't listen to him. Wǒ-gàosong-ta, ta-bu-tǐng. 我告訴他,他不聽. I told him, but he won't listen. (2) hear. Nǐ-shi-nǎr-tǐnglai-de? 你是那兒聽來的? Where did you hear this? Wǒ-shì-tǐng-'tā-shūo-de. 我是聽他說的. I heard it from him.

TÌNG₂ 停 (IV) (1) stop, cease. Yǔ yǐjing-tíng-le. 雨已經停了. The rain has stopped. (2) stay, stop over. Wǒ-yào-zai-Niǔyuē-tíng-sāntiān. 我要在紐約停三天.I'll stay in New York for three days. (TV) park a vehicle, dock a ship. Zhèir bu-xǔ-tíng-chē. 這兒不許停車 No parking here.

TǏNG₃ 挺 (TV) (1) straighten up (physically). tǐng-xiōng 挺胸 throw out one's chest. (2) hold on, endure. Wǒ-hái-kéyi-tǐng-yíge-zhōngtóu. 我還可以挺一個鐘頭. I can hold on for another hour. (SV) straight and still. Tā-zhàn-de duó-tǐng-a! 他站得多挺啊! See how upright he stands.

TǏNG₂ 挺 (AD) before SV, fairly, pretty. Zhèige-búshi-tǐng-hǎo-ma? 這個不是挺好嗎? Isn't this one pretty good?

TǏNG₄ 挺 (M) for a machine gun.

T

yìtǐng qīng-jǐguānqiāng 一挺
輕機關鎗 a light machine
gun.

TÍNG-CHÉ₃ 停車 (VO) park
a car.

TÍNGCHĒCHǍNG₃ 停車場 (N)
parking lot.

TÍNGDUN₃ 停頓 (IV) be stopped
for the time being. Nèige-gōng-
cheng yǐjing-tíngdun-le. 那個
工程已經停頓了.
The construction work has been
stopped for the time being.

TÍNG-HUÀ₂ 聽話 (VO) listen to
what someone says, obey someone's orders. Tā-bu-tīng-wǒde-
huà. 他不聽我的話.
He won't obey me.
(SV) obedient. Zhèige-háizi hěn-
tīng-huà. 這個孩子很
聽話 . This child is very
obedient.

TÍNGJIAN₁ 聽見 (RV) hear. Tā-
shuōde-huà wǒ-tīngbujiàn. 他
說的話我聽不見.
I can't hear what he says. Wǒ-
méi-tīngjianguo. 我沒聽
見過 . I have never heard
of it.

TÍNGSHUŌ₁ 聽說 (TV) hear
that. Wǒ-tīngshuō tā-yǐjing-zǒu-
le. 我聽說他已經
走了 . I heard that he has
already left. Shànghai tīngshuō-
budòng-bīng. 上海聽說
不凍冰 . I've heard that
it doesn't freeze in Shanghai.

TÍNG-XÌ₃ 聽戲 (VO) listen to
opera.

TÍNG-ZHÀN₄ 停戰 (VO) stop

fighting, cease fire, arrange an
armistice. Tāmen yǐjing-tíng-
zhàn-le. 他們已經停
戰了 . They have already
stopped fighting.

TÍNGZHǏ₃ 停止 (TV) stop doing
something. tíngzhǐ-bàngōng 停
止辦公 stop working. Tā-
fùqin tíngzhǐ-gěi-ta-qián-le. 他
父親停止給他錢
了 . His father stopped giving
him money.

TÍNGZHÒNG₃ 聽眾 (N) audience
(at a musical performance or
speech), listeners.

TÍQIÁN₂ 提前 (IV) move the
time ahead. tíqián-liǎngtian 提
前兩天 move the time two
days ahead.

TÍQÍN₃ 提琴 (N) western stringed
musical instrument (played with
a bow), violin, viola, cello, etc.

TÍ-QIÚ₃ 踢球 (VO) kick a ball.

TǏTIE₃ 體貼 (TV) think or act
considerately or solicitously.
Tāde-tàitai hen-tǐtie-ta. 他的
太太很體貼他 . His
wife is very considerate of him.

TǏXÌ₄ 體系 (N) system (of a
theory or organization). jiàoyù-
tǐxì 教育體系 educational
system. Tāde-lǐlùn bu-chéng-tǐ-
xì. 他的理論不成
體系 . His theory doesn't
form a system.

TÍXÍNG₂ 提醒 (TV) remind
someone. Nǐ-bié-wàngle tíxíng-
ta. 你別忘了提醒
他 . Don't forget to remind him.

TÍYÌ₂ 提議 (VO) (1) make a

motion <u>or</u> proposal <u>at a meeting.</u>
Jīntian méiyou-rén-tí-shénme-yì. 今天沒有人提甚麼議 . No one made any proposals today. (2) suggest. Wǒ-tíyì wǒmen-dōu-qu-kàn-diànyǐngr. 我提議我們都去看電影兒 . I suggest that we all go to see a movie.

TǏYU₂ 體育 (N) (1) physical training, physical education. Tā-xué-tǐyu. 他學體育 . He is studying physical education. (2) athletic sports.

TǏYUCHǍNG₃ 體育場 (N) athletic field.

TǏYUGUǍN₃ 體育館 (N) gymnasium.

TǏZHÒNG₄ 體重 (N) body weight.

TǏZI₄ 梯子 (N) ladder. shàng-tīzi 上梯子 go up a ladder.

TÍZI₅ 蹄子 (N) hoof. (M: zhī 隻).

TŌNG₂ 通 (IV) (1) open <u>to traffic,</u> free <u>of traffic or obstructions.</u> Xīn-xiū-de-lù yǐjing-tōng-le. 新修的路已經通了 . The new road is already open. Zhèitiáo-gōu bu-tōng-le. 這條溝不通了 . This ditch is blocked. Wǒde-bízi bu-tōng. 我的鼻子不通 . My nose is stuffed up. Nèige-dìfang bu-tōng-huǒchē. 那個地方不通火車 . That place cannot be reached by train. (2) lead to <u>some place</u> (such as a road). Zhèitiáo-lù tōngdao-wo-jiā. 這條路通到我

家 . This road leads to my house. (3) have a thorough knowledge of. Tā-tōng-Rìwén. 他通日文 . He has a thorough knowledge of Japanese.

(TV) (1) unblock <u>something</u> by removing the obstruction. Yòng-tiěsī tōngtong-yāndǒu. 用鐵絲通通烟斗 . Use a wire to clean out the pipe. (2) communicate <u>with someone by</u> <u>telephone or letter.</u> Wǒ-gen-ta tōng-ge-diànhuà. 我跟他通個電話 . I'll call him on the phone. Wǒmen bu-tōng-xìn. 我們不通信 . We don't correspond.

(SV) logical. Nǐ-jiǎnzhí-butōng. 你簡直不通 . You are simply illogical.

(RE) <u>indicates penetrating or</u> <u>getting through to without being</u> <u>blocked.</u> xiǎngbutōng 想不通 have a mental block.

(-B) <u>used after the name of a</u> <u>country or place, indicates a</u> <u>person who knows a great deal</u> <u>about that country or place,</u> expert. Zhōngguo-tūng 中國通 China expert.

TÓNG₃ 銅 (N) copper, brass, bronze.

TÓNG₃ 同 (SV) be the same. yīn-tóng zì-bùtóng 音同字不同 the same sound but different characters.

(CV) with, accompanying. Shéi-tóng-wo-qù? 誰同我去 ? Who is going with me? (TV) be in the same <u>group,</u>

organization or category. Wŏ-
gēn-ta tóngle-liăngnian-shì. 我
跟 他 同 了 兩 年 事.
I have been a colleague of his
for two years.

TŎNG₄ 捅 (N) bucket, keg, cask.

TŎNG₄ 捅 (TV) (1) poke. tŏngle-
yíge-kūlung 捅 了 一 個
窟 窿 poke a hole. (2) reveal
a secret.

TÓNGBĀN₂ 同 班 (N) classmate.
Tā-shi-wŏde-tóngbān. 他 是
我 的 同 班. He is my
classmate.
(VO) be in the same class. Wŏ-
gēn-ta tóng-bān. 我 跟 他
同 班. He and I are in the
same class.

TŎNGGÒNG₄ 統 共 (AD) alto-
gether. Wŏmen-tŏnggòng-yòng-
le-liùshikuài-qián. 我 們 統
共 用 了 六 十 塊 錢.
We spent sixty dollars altogether.

TŌNGGUÒ₃ 通 過 (TV) (1) go
through, pass through. Zhèi-
tiáo-hé tōngguò-sānshěng. 這
條 河 通 過 三 省. This
river passes through three provinces. (2) be passed as a proposal. Wŏde-yì'àn tōngguò-le.
我 的 議 案 通 過 了
My bill has been passed.

TÓNGHÁNG₂ 同 行 (IV) be of
the same occupation or trade.
Wŏmen-tóngh2áng. 我 們 同
行. We are of the same trade.
(N) people of the same occupation or trade. Tā-shì-wŏde-tóng-
háng. 他 是 我 的 同 行.
(lit. He is a person who is in the

same trade as I am). He has the
same trade as I do.

TÓNGHUÀ₄ 童 話 (N) children's
story, fairy tale.

TÓNGJIANG₅ 銅 匠 (N) person
who works with copper, bronze,
brass, coppersmith, brass-
founder.

TÓNGJŪ₃ 同 居 (IV) live together.

TÒNGKU₂ 痛 苦 or KUTONG 苦
痛 (SV) suffering, painful, miserable, bitter (of experience).
Wŏ-xiànzài tòngku-jíle. 我 現
在 痛 苦 極 了. I'm ex-
tremely miserable now.
(N) sorrow, pain, bitterness,
suffering. Zhèi-shi-wŏde-tŏngku.
這 是 我 的 痛 苦. This
is my sorrow.

TÒNGKUAI₁ 痛 快 (SV) (1) (opp.
biēmen 憋 悶). happy, satisfied.
Jīntiān-wŏ-xīnli tèbie-tòngkuai.
今 天 我 心 裏 特 別
痛 快. I feel very happy today.
(2) (opp. bièniu 彆 扭). un-
reserved, straightforward, frank.
Tā-zuò-shì hěn-tòngkuai. 他 做
事 很 痛 快. He is very
straightforward in doing things.
(3) unblocked, free of traffic or
obstructions. Wŏde-bízi bu-tòng-
kuai. 我 的 鼻 子 不 痛
快. My nose is congested. Zŏu-
dà-lù-ba, tòngkuai. 走 大 路
吧, 痛 快. Let's take the
highway, it's free of congestion.
Dìfang-dà hěn-tòngkuai. 地 方
大 很 痛 快. A large place
makes us feel free.

TÓNGQÍNG₂ 同情 (TV) sympathize with, show sympathy for. Tā-bu-tóngqíng-wo. 他 不 同 情 我 . He doesn't sympathize with me. (SV) sympathetic. Wǒ-duì-nǐde-huánjing hěn-tóngqíng. 我 對 你 的 環 境 很 同 情 . I'm very sympathetic about your situation.

TÓNGQÍNG(XĪN)₂ 同 情 (心) (N) sympathy. Tā-duì-wo yìdiǎnr-tóngqíng(xīn) dōu-méi-yǒu. 他 對 我 一 點 兒 同 情 (心) 都 沒 有 . He doesn't have the least bit of sympathy toward me.

TǑNGR₄ 筒 兒 or TǑNGZI 筒 子 . (N) hollow cylinder.

TŌNGRONG₄ 通 融 (IV) (1) make a temporary and compromised arrangement, make something an exceptional case. Tā-yìdiǎnr dōu-bu-tōngrong. 他 一 點 都 不 通 融 . He doesn't compromise even a little bit. (2) borrow money. Wǒ-děi-gen-nin tōngrong-wǔbǎikuai-qián. 我 得 跟 您 通 融 五 百 塊 錢 . I have to borrow five hundred dollars from you.

TÓNGSHÍ₂ 同 時 (MA) (1) at the same time. Tāmen-tóngshí-bì-yè de. 他 們 同 時 畢 業 的 . They graduated at the same time. (2) and, also, as well as. Tā-hěn-cōngming tóng-shí-yě-piàoliang. 他 聰 明 同 時 也 漂 亮 . She is very clever as well as beautiful.

(IV) be contemporaries, be contemporaneous. Wǒ-gen-ta tóngshí. 我 跟 他 同 時 . He and I are contemporaries.

TÓNGSHÌ₂ 同 事 (N) fellow worker, colleague. (VO) be a colleague of someone. Wǒmen-cónglái méi-tóngguo-shì. 我 們 從 來 沒 同 過 事 . We have never been colleagues.

TŌNGSÚ₄ 通 俗 (SV) popular or understandable to common people. Tā-xiě-de-wénzhang tōngsú. 他 寫 的 文 章 通 俗 . The articles he wrote are popular.

TÓNGSUÌ₃ 同 歲 (IV) be the same age.

TŌNGTŌNG₃ 通 通 (AD) thoroughly, completely. Wǒ-tōng-tōng-zhīdao. 我 通 通 知 道 . I know everything about it.

TÓNG-WŪ₂ 同 屋 (VO) live in the same room. (N) roommate.

TÓNGXIĀNG₃ 同 鄉 (N) fellow-countryman. Tā-shi-wǒde-tóng-xiāng. 他 是 我 的 同 鄉 . He is my fellow-countryman. (IV) be from the same place. Wǒ-men-tóngxiāng. 我 們 同 鄉 . We are from the same place.

TŌNG-XÌN₂ 通 信 (VO) communicate by letter, correspond. Wǒ-men-'měige-yuè dōu-tōng-yicì-xìn. 我 們 每 個 月 都 通 一 次 信 . We write each other once every month. (N) (1) news dispatch. (M: piān 篇). (2) letter to the editor (信

the newspaper). dúzhě-toñgxìn 讀者通信 letter-to-the-editor column.

TŌNGXÌNCHÙ₃ 通信處 see TŌNGXÙNCHÙ 通訊處.

TÓNGXÌNG₃ 同姓 (IV) have the same surname.

TÓNGXUÉ₂ 同學 (N) schoolmate, fellow-student. zhūwei-tóngxué 諸位同學 fellow students (used in opening an address). Zhèiwei-tóngxué guìxìng? 這位同學貴姓? What is your surname (asked of a fellow student)?

(VO) be a school-mate of. Tā-gēn-wo tóngle-liùnián-xué. 他跟我同了六年學. He was in the same school with me for six years.

TÓNGXUÉHUÌ₃ 同學會 (N) student body.

TŌNGXÙNCHÙ₃ 通訊處 or TŌNGXÌNCHÙ 通信處 (N) mailing address.

TŌNGXÙNSHÈ₄ 通訊社 (N) news agency. (M: jiā 家).

TÓNGYÌ₂ 同意 (TV) consent, agree with. Wǒ-tóngyì-nǐde-'kànfǎ. 我同意你的看法. I agree with your view. (AV) agree to, consent to. Tā-tongyì-lái le. 他同意來了. He agreed to come. (N) agreement, consent. zhēng-qiú-tóngyì 徵求同意 seek agreement. Wǒ-débudào-tāde-tóngyì. 我得不到他的同意. I can't get his consent.

TÓNGYÌ₃ 統一 (TV) unify. Shéi-

bǎ-Yìdàlì tǒngyī-le? 誰把意大利統一了? Who unified Italy?

(SV) be in accord with, be the same as a given standard. Wǒ-mende-bànfa bu-tǒngyī. 我們的辦法不統一. Our way of doing things is not in accord.

(N) unity.

TŌNGZHĪ₂ 通知 (TV) inform, notify. Nǐ-bānjiā wèi-shénme-butōngshī-wo? 他搬家為甚麼不通知我? Why didn't you inform me that you had moved?

(N) notice, information. (M: fènr 份兒). Wǒ-fāle-sānshí fenr-tōngzhī. 我發了三十份兒通知. I sent out thirty notices.

TÓNGZHÌ₃ 同志 (N) comrade. Zhāng-tóngzhì 張同志 Comrade Chang.

TǑNGZHÌ₄ 統治 (TV) control, dominate, rule. Yīngguo tǒngzhì-le-Yìndū-hěn-duō-nián. 英國統治了印度很多年. The British ruled India for many many years.

(N) rule, domination, control.

TǑNGZI₄ 筒子 see TŌNGR 筒兒.

TOU₁ 頭 (-B) (1) used after certain L to form PW. qiántou 前頭 front. wàitou 外頭 outside. (2) used as a nominal suffix. xiǎngtou 想頭 thinking, desire. mùtou 木頭 wood.

TŌU₁ 偷 (TV) (1) steal. Wǒde-dàyǐ jiào-ren-tōu-le. 我 的 大 衣 叫 人 偷 了. My overcoat was stolen. (2) make <u>time from a busy schedule</u>. tōuchu-yidianr-gōngfu-lai 偷 出 一 點 兒 工 夫 來 make a little time. (3) have a secret love affair with a man. tōu-rén 偷 人 have a secret love affair.

(AD) secretly, stealthily. Bié-tōu-kàn biérende-xìn. 別 偷 看 别 人 的 信. Don't read other's letters on the sly.

TÓU₁ 頭 (N) (1) head (<u>of a body</u>). Wǒ-tóu-teng. 我 頭 疼 My head hurts. (2) hair, hair-do. shū-tóu 梳 頭 comb the hair. tóu-yóu 頭 油 hair oil.

(M) (1) head (<u>of a body</u>). Tā-bǐ-wǒ gāo-yitóu. 他 比 我 高 一 頭. He is one head taller than I am. (2) head (<u>for some domestic animals</u>) yìtóu-niú 一 頭 牛 a head of cattle. (3) <u>for some vegetables</u>. yìtóu-báicài 一 頭 白 菜 a head of cabbage.

(SP) (1) first. tóu-yitiān 頭 一 天 the first day. Tóu-liǎngcì wǒ-dou-méi-zuòduì. 頭 兩 次 我 都 沒 作 對. I didn't do it right either of the first two times. (2) <u>with NU-M of time,</u> ago, before. Tā-shi-tóu-liǎng-tian-lái-de. 他 是 頭 兩 天 來 的. It was a couple of days ago that he came.

TÓUDĚNG₃ 頭 等 (N) first class, best quality. tóuděngchē 頭 等

車 first class coach. Wǒ-zuò-tóuděng. 我 坐 頭 等. I go first class. Zhè-shì-tóuděngde-huò. 這 是 頭 等 的 貨. This is first class merchandise.

TÓUFA₃ 頭 髮 (N) hair (<u>on the top of the human head</u>). (M: gēn 根).

TÓUJĪ₃ 投 機 (VO) (1) take a chance. Zuò-'shénme-shì tā-dōu-tóujī. 做 甚 麼 事 他 都 投 機. No matter what he does he always takes chances. (2) speculate (<u>financially</u>). Gǔ-piào-zhǎng-de-shihou, tā tóule-yici-jī. 股 票 漲 的 時 候, 他 投 了 一 次 機. He speculated once when stock prices were high.

TÓUKǍO₄ 投 考 (TV) take the entrance examination. Nǐ-tóukǎo něige-dàxué? 你 投 考 那 個 大 學 ? Which college are you going to take the entrance examination for?

TÒULE₃ 透 了 (P) <u>used after SV</u>, utterly, extremely. máfan-tòule 麻 煩 透 了 extremely troublesome. kěwù-tòule 可 惡 透 了 extremely hateful.

TÒULIÀNGR₃ 透 亮 兒 (SV) transparent. (<u>syn</u>. tòumíng 透 明). Bōli-tài-zāng-le, bu-tòu-liàng-le. 玻 璃 太 髒 了, 不 透 亮 兒 了. The glass is too dirty, the light cannot come through.

(VO) have light leak in. Bǎ-liáng-zi-lāxialai, wūzili jiu-bu-tòu-liàngr-le. 把 簾 子 拉 下

T

來,屋子裏就不透亮兒了. Pull down the curtain so that no light leaks into the room.

TÒUMÍNG₃ 透明 (SV) transparent. (syn. tòuliàngr 透亮兒). Zhèizhŏng-zhǐ tòumíng. 這種紙透明. This kind of paper is transparent.

TÓU-PIÀO₃ 投票 (VO) cast a vote, vote. Búshi-huìyuán bunéng-tóu-piào. 不是會員不能投票. Non-members cannot vote. Wŏ-kéyi-tóu-ni-yipiào. 我可以投你一票. I can cast a vote for you.

TÓUR₁ 頭兒 (N) (1) boss. Tā-shi-tóur. 他是頭兒. He is the boss. Zhāngtour 張頭兒 Mr. Chang, the boss. (2) beginning or ending point. Wŏ-gĕi-ta qĭle-ge-tóur. 我給他起了個頭兒. I started it for him. Shìqing méi-tóur-le. 事情沒頭兒. There is no end to this. (3) end of something long. dōng-tóur 東頭 east end (of a street). (4) remnant. bù-tóur 布頭兒 remnant of cloth. xiàn-tóur 線頭兒 remnant of thread. (M) end, side. zhèi-tóur 這頭兒 this end or this side. Liăng-tóur dōu-bu-yuànyì. 兩頭都不願意. Both sides are not willing.

used after a verb to form a N, interest or enjoyment of doing something. Méi-shuōtour. 沒說頭兒. There is no fun in talking about it.

TÓUTENG₁ 頭疼 (SV) lit. or fig. headache. Wŏ-hĕn-tóuteng. 我很頭疼. I have a terrible headache. Tóutengde-shìqing tài-duō. 頭疼的事情太多. There are a lot of headaches.

TŌUTŌUR(DE)₄ 偷偷兒(的) (AD) stealthily, secretly. Tā-tōutōur(de) chūqu-le. 他偷偷兒(的) 出去了. He sneaked out.

TÓUXIÁNG₃ 投降 (TV) surrender. Dírén yĭjing-tóuxiáng-le. 敵人已經投降了. The enemy has already surrendered.

TÓUZI₅ 頭子 (N)head man(usually refers to the leader of a group of outlaws).

TÓU-ZĪ₃ 投資 (VO) invest, invest capital. Tā-tóule-wŭwàn-kuài-qián-zī. 他投了五萬塊錢資. He invested fifty thousand dollars. (N) investment. Tāde-tóuzī dōu-sŭnshi-le. 他的投資都損失了. He lost his whole investment.

TSK₃ 嘖 (I) with air sucked in. (1) once or repeated, indicates admiration for something which looks good. Tsk, zhēn-hăo. 嘖, 真好. Gee, really good. (2) repeated, indicates that something has gone wrong, How

awful! Tsk, tsk! Tsk, tsk! zhè-
zěnma-bàn? 嘖 嘖 ! 這 怎
麼 辦 ? Tsk, tsk! What can
be done?

TŪ₄ 秃 (SV) (1) bald. (2) blunt,
worn out (of a writing instrument).

TÚ₃ 圖 (N) diagram, chart, il-
lustration. (M: zhāng 張).
(TV) wish to get. Wǒ-tú-ni-
shénma? 我 圖 你 甚 麼 ?
What do I wish to get from you?

TŬ₂ 土 (N) (1) earth, soil. Xī-
hóngshì bunéng-zhòngzai-zhèi-
zhong-túli. 西 紅 柿 不
能 種 在 這 種 土 裏
Tomatoes cannot be planted in
this soil.(2) dirt, dust. Wūzili
nǎr-dōu-shì-tǔ. 屋 子 裏
那 兒 都 是 土 . There is
dust everywhere in the room.
(SV) (1) uncouth or unrefined
because of a rustic existence.
Tā-tǔ-dehěn. 他 土 得 很 .
His manner is very uncouth. (2)
local. tǔchǎn 土 產 local products. Tāde-huà tài-tǔ. 他 的
話 太 土 . His language is
too local.

TŬ₃ 吐 or TÙ 吐 (TV) spew forth,
spit out. Bié-bǎ-tán tǔzai-dì-
shang. 別 把 痰 吐 在 地
上 . Don't spit on the floor.

TŬ₃ 吐 (TV) (1) or TÙ 吐 spew
forth, spit out. tù-tán 吐 痰
spit. (2) vomit, throw up. Tā-
tù-le. 他 吐 了 . He threw
up. Tā-hēle-jiǔ jiu-tù. 他 喝
了 酒 就 吐 . After he
drinks he throws up. (3) give

back (willingly or unwillingly).
Tā-bǎ-yíng-de-qián dōu-tùchu-
lai-le. 他 把 贏 的 錢 都
吐 出 來 了 . He lost all
the money that he had won.

TUÁN₄ 團 (TV) crumple up. Tā-
bǎ-nèifēng-xìn tuán-le. 他 把
那 封 信 團 了 . He
crumpled that letter.
(N) regiment.
(M) (1) ball of yarn, string, etc.
yìtuán-xiàn 一 團 線 a ball
of thread. (2) hunk of clay, mud
etc. yìtuán-ní 一 團 泥 a
hunk of mud.

TUÁNJIE₃ 團 結 (TV) unite. Wǒ-
men-yīngdāng-bǎ-lìliang tuánjie-
qilai. 我 們 應 當 把 力
量 團 結 起 來 . We
should unite everybody's power
together. Tuánjie jiu-shi-lìliang.
團 結 就 是 力 量 . To
unite is to produce strength.
(SV) be unified. Tāmen-hěn-
tuánjie. 他 們 很 團 結 .
They are very unified.

TUÁNTǏ₃ 團 體 (N) group, organization.

TUÁNYUÁN₄ 團 員 (N) member
of a group or organization in
which the last syllable is tuán
團 .

TUÁNZHǍNG₄ 團 長 (N) (1) reg-
imental commander. (2) head or
chief of an organization in which
the last syllable is tuán 團 .

TÚDI₄ 徒 弟 (N) apprentice.
TŬDÌ₃ 土 地 (N) land.
TÚDĪNGR₄ 圖 釘 兒 (N) thumb-
tack. (M: kē 顆).

T

TŬDÒUR₄ 土豆兒 (N) potato.

TŬ'ĒRQÍ₃ 土耳其 (PW) Turkey.

TŬFĒNGWŬ₅ 土風舞 (N) folk dance. tiào-tŭfēngwŭ 跳土風舞 do a folk dance.

TŬGĂI₃ 土改 (N) (con. tŭdìgăigé 土地改革). land reform.

TÚHUÀ₂ 圖畫 (N) picture, drawing, painting.

TŬHUÀ₃ 土話 (N) local dialect, local idiom.

TUĪ₂ 推 (TV) (1) push. Tā-bă-mén tuīkai-le. 他把門推開了. He pushed the door open. (2) elect, select. Wŏmen-tuī-ta dāng-wŏmende-lǐngxiu. 我們推他當我們的領袖. We elected him as our leader. (3) make excuses for not doing something. Nèige-yuēhui wŏ-tuī-le. 那個約會我推了. I made excuses and declined that appointment. (4) postpone a date. Tā-men-jiéhūn-de-r̀zi tuīdao-xià-lǐbàitiān-le. 他們結婚的日子推到下禮拜天了. Their wedding has been postponed until next Sunday. (5) shift on to somebody else. tuī-zéren 推責任 shift responsibility on to others. Tā-lăo-bă-shìqing wàng-biéren-shēnshang-tuī. 他老把事情往別人身上推. He always passes matters on to somebody else.

TUĬ₃ 腿 (N) leg. (M: tiáo 條).

dàtuǐ 大腿 thigh.

TUÌ₃ 退 (TV) (1) withdraw, retreat, move back. tuì-cháo 退潮 the tide has receded. Díren yǐjing-tuì-le. 敵人已經退了. The enemy has already retreated. Wŏ-wàng-hòu tuìle-yibu. 我往後退了一步. I took one step backward. (2) fade (of color). Huàr-shangde-yánsè dōu-tuì-le. 畫兒上的顏色都退了. The color of this painting is all faded. (3) go down (of a fever). Tā-yǐjing-tuì-shāo-le. 他已經退燒了. His fever has gone down. (4) return money, merchandise, gifts, cancel an order or reservation. Wŏ-bă-gāng-măide-chē tuì-le. 我把剛買的車退了. I returned the car I just bought to the dealer. Wŏ-tuìgei-ta yīkuai-qián. 我退給他一塊錢. I gave him one dollar back. Tā-kéyi-tuì-xué, kěshi-bu-néng-tuì-xuéfèi. 他可以退學,可是不能退學費. He can withdraw from school but he can't get his tuition back.

TUĪCE₄ 推測 (TV) predict. Wŏ-tuīce tā-yídìng-bugăn-qù. 我推測他一定不敢去. I predict that he certainly will not dare to go. (N) prediction. Zhèi-shi-wŏde-tuīce. 這是我的推測. This is my prediction.

TUĪCI₃ 推辭 (TV) decline, refuse an offer. Zhèige-lǐwu nín-shōu-

xia-ba, bié-tuīci-le. 這個
禮物您收下吧,别
推辭了. You better ac-
cept this gift, don't refuse it.
Wǒ-qǐng-ta-zuò-zhǔxí, tā-méi-
tuīci. 我請他作主席
他没推辭. I asked him
to be the chairman, he didn't
decline.

TUĪFĀN₃ 推翻 (RV) (1) push
over. Tā-bǎ-yǐzi tuīfān-le. 他
把椅子推翻了. He
pushed the chair over. (2) overthrow. Gémìngdǎng-bǎ-zhèngfǔ-
tuīfān-le. 革命黨把政
府推翻了. The revolu-
tionarier overthrew the government. (3) disprove a theory or
idea. Tāmen-bǎ-wǒde-lǐlun tuīfān-le. 他們把我的理
論推翻了. They dis-
proved my theory.

TUĪGUǍNG₄ 推廣 (TV) broad-
en, promote, expand, popularize.
Wǒmen-zhèng-tuīguǎng-jièyān-
yùndòng. 我們正推廣
戒煙運動. We are now
promoting the movement of giving up smoking. Zhèizhǒng-huò-
bu-róngyi-tuīguǎng. 這種貨
不容易推廣. This
kind of goods is not easy to promote.

TUĪXIǍNG₄ 推想 (TV) deduce,
infer that. Wǒ-tuīxiǎng tā-yí-
dìng-shì yíge-jiāndié. 我推
想他一定是一個
間諜. I deduced that he
must be a spy.

TUĪXÍNG₃ 推行 (TV) put into

action, promote. Tāmen-yào-
tuīxíng-yíge-xīn-jìhua. 他們
要推行一個新計
劃. They want to put a new
plan into action.

TUĪZI₅ 推子 (N) barber's clip-
pers. (M: bǎ 把).

TŪN₃ 吞 (TV) (1) swallow without
chewing. Nǐ-bǎ-zhèilì-yào tūn-le.
你把這粒藥吞了.
Swallow this pill. (2) appropriate
illicitly. Tā-bǎ-gōngkuǎn tūn-le.
他把公欵吞了. He
embezzled public funds.

TÚN₅ 囤 (TV) store up grain. Mài-
zi yǐjìng-tún-qilai-le. 麥子
已經囤起來了. The
wheat has already been stored
up.

TŪNTŪNTŪTŪ₅ 吞吞吐吐
(AD) hesitatingly in speaking. Tā-
tūntūntūtūde-shuōle-bàntiān. 他
吞吞吐吐的說了
半天. He spoke hesitatingly
for a long while.

TUŌ₃ 拖 (TV) (1) drag. Nǐ-bié-bǎ-
wǒ-tuōjinqu. 你别把我
拖進去. lit. or fig. Don't
drag me into that. (2) mop. tuō-
dìbǎn 拖地板 mop the floor.
(IV) (1) drag along (on the ground).
Tāde-dàizi tài-cháng, tuōzai-dì-
shang-le. 她的帶子太
長,拖在地上了. Her
belt is too long, it is being
dragged along on the floor. (2)
put off, delay. Bié-zài-tuō-le.
别再拖了. Don't delay
any longer.

TUŌ₂ 託 (TV) entrust, ask someone

T

to take care of <u>something for
one as a favor</u>. Bú-yong-tuō-
rén, zìjǐ-bàn. 不 用 託 人
自 己 辦. There is no need
to ask people, do it yourself.
TUŌ₃ 托 (TV) (1) carry <u>or</u> support
<u>on the palm.</u> Yòng-shǒu-tuōzhe-
yíge-pánzi. 用 手 托 着 一
個 盤 子. Carry a tray
on the palm.   (2) place <u>a</u>
<u>sheet of something</u> underneath
<u>something.</u> Zài-zhèizhāng-zhǐ-
dǐxia tuō-yizhang-hóngde. 在
這 張 紙 底 下 托 一
張 紅 的. Put a red one
underneath this sheet of paper.
TUŌ₁ 脫 (TV) (1) take off <u>clothes,</u>
<u>footgear.</u> (<u>opp.</u> chuān 穿).
Qǐng-bǎ-yǔyī tuō-le-ba. 請 把
雨 衣 脫 了 吧. Please
take off your raincoat. (cf:
ZHāI 摘). (2) peel (<u>of human</u>
<u>skin</u>). Tāde-shǒu-tuō-pí. 他
的 手 脫 皮. The skin on
his hand is peeling. (3) lose
<u>one's hair.</u> tuō-tóufa 脫 頭
髮 lose hair. (4) shed, cast off,
molt. Shé-tuō-pí-le. 蛇 脫 皮
了. The snake shedded. Gǒu-
tuō-máo-le. 狗 脫 毛 了.
The dog shedded. (5) omit, miss,
leave out <u>words unintentionally.</u>
Wǒmen tuōle-yìháng. 我 們
脫 了 一 行. We missed
one line.
TUŌ₃ 妥 (SV) (<u>con.</u> tuōdang 妥
當). (1) safe, secure. Zhèiyangr-bàn bu-tuō. 這 樣 兒
辦 不 妥. It's not safe to
do it this way. (2) reliable.

(RE) indicates settlement of
something. Nèige-shì yǐjing-bàn-
tuō-le. 那 個 事 已 經 辦
妥 了. That affair has al-
ready been settled.
TUŌDANG₂ 妥 當 (SV) (1) safe
(<u>taking all possible develop-</u>
<u>ments into consideration</u>). Wǒ-
men xiǎng-yige-tuǒdangde-bàn-
fa. 我 們 想 一 個 妥 當
的 辦 法. We'll think of a
safe way. Tā-bàn-shì hěn-tuǒdang. 他 辦 事 很 妥 當.
He is very safe when he does
things. (2) reliable. Nèige-gōngsī hěn-tuǒdang. 那 個 公 司
很 妥 當. That company is
very reliable.

(RE) indicates settlement of
something. Wǒmen-shuō-tuǒ-
dang-le. 我 們 說 妥 當
了. We have talked it over and
settled it.
TUŌ'ERSUǑ₄ 托 兒 所 (N)
nursery (<u>for small children</u>).
(M: jiā 家).
TUŌ-FÚ₃ 託 福 (VO) <u>very polite</u>
<u>answer to a greeting, implying</u>
<u>that one is well because of the be-</u>
<u>nign influence of the person</u>
<u>spoken to.</u> A: Nín-hǎo-a? B:
Tuō-fú-tuō-fú. A: 您 好 啊 ?
B: 託 福 託 福. A: How are
you? B: I'm very well, thank you.
TUŌJIÉ₃ 脫 節 (VO) lose contact
<u>or</u> connection. Wǒ-gēn-zhèngzhì
yǐjing-tuōjié-le. 我 跟 政 治
已 經 脫 節 了. I have
already lost contact with politics.
TUŌLĀJĪ₅ 拖 拉 機 (N) tractor.

(M: liàng 輛).

TUŌLÍ₃ 脫離 (TV) break off,
cease a relationship. Tā-yǐjing-
tuōlí-nèige-tuántǐ-le. 他已
經 脫 離 那 個 團 體
了 . He has already broken off
with that organization.

TUÓLUO₅ 陀螺 (N) top (toy).

TUÒMO₅ 唾沫 (N) saliva. (M:
kǒu ㄩ). tǔ-tuòmo or tù-tuòmo
吐 唾 沫 spit (saliva).

TUŌXIÉ₄ 拖鞋 (N) slipper. (M:
zhī 隻 , shuāng 雙).

TÚRAN₃ 突然 (SV) sudden. Wǒ-
xiànzài-qu yǒu-yidiǎnr-túran.
我 現 在 去 有 一 點
兒 突 然 . It is a little sudden
if I go there now.

(MA) suddenly. Tā-túran-huíqu-
le. 他 突 然 回 去 了 ·
He went back suddenly.

TÚSHŪGUǍN₂ 圖書館 (N)
library.

TÚZHANG₃ 圖章 (N) (1) stamp,
seal (for making an imprint).
(M: kē 顆). gàn-túzhang 蓋圖
章 or dǎ-túzhang 打圖章
make an imprint with a seal. (2)
imprint made from a stamp,
similar to a signature and used
mostly for the purpose of identification of an organization or a
person, also used for decoration
on paintings and other art objects.

TÙZI₅ 禿子 (N) baldheaded
person.

TÙZI₄ 兔子 (N) hare, rabbit.
(M: zhī 隻).

T

W

WA₁ 哇 (P) <u>used in place of a</u>
啊 , <u>when the preceding syllable ends in the sound</u> u <u>or</u> ao.
Nǐ-zěnma-hái-bu-zǒu-wa? 你
怎麼還不走哇?
Why don't you leave now? (See:
A 啊).

WĀ₃ 挖 (TV) (1) dig. wā-kēng 挖
坑 dig a hole in the ground (2)
scoop out, dig out. Tā-wāle-
hěn-duō-tǔdòur. 他挖了
很多土豆兒. He dug a
lot of potatoes out of the field.
(3) take, snatch <u>personnel away</u>
<u>from a firm or institution.</u> Nèi-
ge-fànguǎnr bǎ-wǒmende-chúzi
wāqu-le. 那個飯館兒
把我們的廚子挖
去了. That restaurant took
our cook away. (cf: PÁO 刨).

WǍ₄ 瓦 (N) roof tile. (M: kuài
塊 , piàn 片).
(B-) earthenware, clay. wǎ-
guàn 瓦罐 earthenware jar.

WĀI₂ 歪 (SV) (opp. zhèng 正).
crooked, askew, tilted. Nèike-
shù wāi-le. 那棵樹歪了.
That tree is tilted.
(IV) lean to <u>one side,</u> tip. Qǐng-
nǐ wàng-yòu wāi-yiwai. 請你
往右歪一歪. Please
lean to the right a little bit.
(AD) at an angle. Tā-wāi-dàizhe-
màozi. 他歪帶着帽子.

He wears his hat at an angle.
(B-) wicked. wāi-zhúyi 歪主
意 crooked idea.

WÀI₁ 外 (L) outside. chéngwài
城外 outside the city. Bié-
wàng-wài-pǎo. 别往外跑.
Don't run outside.

WÀI₂ 外 (I)hello (<u>used in telephone</u>
<u>conversations</u>).

WÀIBIANR₁ 外邊兒 or WÀI-
TOU 外頭 or WÀIMIAN (PW)
(1) outer surface <u>of something.</u>
Zhèige-xiāngzi-de-wàibianr hěn-
zāng. 這個箱子的外
邊兒很髒. The outside
of this suitcase is very dirty.
(2) area <u>outside something.</u> xué-
xiào-wàibianr 學校外邊
兒 the area outside the school.
(3) outside. Wàibiānr-yǒu-hěn-
duō-shù. 外邊兒有很
多樹. There are a lot of
trees outside.

WÀIBIǍO₃ 外表 (N) outer ap-
pearance. Nǐ-bu-néng-jiu-kàn-
wàibiǎo. 你不能就看
外表. You cannot just look
at the appearance.

WÀIBĪN₅ 外賓 (N) foreign guest.

WÀIGŌNG₅ 外公 or WÀIZǓFÙ
外祖父 (N) grandfather
(<u>mother's father</u>).

WÀIGUÓ₁ 外國 (N) foreign
country.

WÀIHÁNG₃ 外行 (opp. nèi-háng 内行) (N) layman (person who lacks knowledge of a certain subject). Wǒ-shi-wàiháng. 我 是 外 行. I am a layman. (SV) ignorant about a particular profession or subject. Wǒ-duì-gǔpiào hěn-wàiháng. 我 對 股 票 很 外 行. I'm quite ignorant about stocks.

WÀIHÀOR₄ 外 號 兒 (N) nickname. qǐ-wàihàor 起 外 號 兒 give a nickname.

WÀIHUÌ₃ 外 匯 (N) foreign exchange.

WÀIJIĀO₃ 外 交 (N) diplomacy. wàijiāo-guānxi 外 交 關 係 diplomatic relations. (SV) diplomatic. Tā shuōhuà hěn-wàijiāo. 他 說 話 很 外 交. His way of talking is very diplomatic.

WÀIKĒ₃ 外 科 (N) (1) surgery. (2) surgical department.

WÀIMIAN₁ 外 面 see WÀI-BIANR 外 邊 兒

WÀIPÓ₅ 外 婆 or WÀIZǓMǓ 外 祖 母 (N) grandmother (mother's mother).

WÀIREN₃ 外 人 (N) outsider, stranger. Wǒmen dōu-bu-shi-wàiren. 我 們 都 不 是 外 人. None of us is an outsider.

WÀISHENG₄ 外 省 (N) other province. wàisheng-rén 外 省 人 person from another province.

WÀISHENG₅ 外 甥 (N) nephew (sister's son).

WÀISHENGNǓR₅ 外 甥 女 兒 (N) niece (sister's daughter).

WÀISŪN(ZI)₅ 外 孫 (子) (N) grandson (daughter's son).

WÀISŪNNǓR₅ 外 孫 女 兒 (N) granddaughter (daughter's daughter).

WÀITÀOR₃ 外 套 兒 (N) coat, outer garment. (M: jiàn 件).

WÀITOU₁ 外 頭 see WÀIBIANR 外 邊 兒

WÀIZǓFÙ₅ 外 祖 父 or WÀI-GŌNG 外 公 (N) grandfather (mother's father).

WÀIZǓMǓ₅ 外 祖 母 or WÀI-PÓ 外 婆 (N) grandmother (mother's mother).

WǍJIANG₄ 瓦 匠 (N) mason.

WĀKU₄ 挖 苦 (TV) ridicule someone sarcastically. Nǐ-bié-wāku-wǒ-le. 你 别 挖 苦 我 了. Don't ridicule me.

WĀN₃ 彎 (TV) bend. wān-yāo 彎 腰 bend the back. (SV) bent, curved, curly (of hair). Nèi-bǎ-dāo-wān-le. 那 把 刀 彎 了. That knife is bent.

WÁN₁ 完 (IV) finish, complete. Wǒde-gōngke hái-mei-wán-ne. 我 的 功 課 還 没 完 呢. I haven't finished my homework yet. Tā-wán-le. 他 完 了. He's finished. Děng-wánle-shì zai-shuō. 等 完 了 事 再 說. We'll talk about it when I'm finished. (RE) indicates completion, finishing. Tāde-qián yòngbuwán.

W

他的錢用不完. He
cannot use up his money.
(N) end. Tā-lǎo-shuō méi-ge-
wán. 他老說沒個完.
He always talks, there is no end
of it. Zhèi-cái-suàn-wán. 這
才算完. Only then can it
be considered at an end.

WǍN₂ 碗 (N) bowl, cup. (M: zhī
隻).

WǍN₁ 晚 (TW) evening, night.
wǎnbān 晚班 evening class
or night shift. cóng-zǎo-dào-
wǎn 從早到晚 from
morning to evening. yìtian-
mángdao-wǎn 一天忙到
晚 busy all day until the night.
(SV) late. Míngtian-ke-bié-wǎn-
le. 明天可別晚了.
Don't be late tomorrow. Tā-bǐ-
wǒ wǎn-yinián. 他比我晚
一年. He is one year behind
me.
(RE) late. Wǒ-láiwǎn-le. 我來
晚了. I came late.
(AD) late. Tā-bǐ-wǒ-ʼwǎn-lái-
yíge-zhōngtóu. 他比我晚
來一個鐘頭. He came
one hour later than I. Tā-wǎn-
lái-wǎn-zǒu. 他晚來晚
走. He comes late and leaves
late.

WÀN₁ 萬 (NU) ten thousand.
liǎngwàn-xuésheng 兩萬學
生 twenty thousand students.
(AD) used before a negative expression, absolutely. Nǐ-wàn-
bunéng-chī-zhèige. 你萬不
能吃這個. You abso-
lutely should not eat this.

(B) indicates a numerous amount.
Wànli-chángchéng 萬里長
城 Great Wall.

ʼWÀNBÀNTIANR₃ 晚半天兒
(TW) afternoon.

WǍNBÀO₂ 晚報 (N) evening
newspaper.

WÁNBEI₄ 完備 (SV) complete,
well-prepared.

WǍNBÈI₄ 晚輩 (N) younger
generation.

WÁNBÌ₄ 完畢 (IV) be finished,
completed. Jié-hūn-diǎnlǐ yǐ-
jing-wánbì-le. 結婚典禮
已經完畢了. The wed-
ding ceremony has already been
completed.

WÁNCHÉNG₂ 完成 (TV) finish,
complete (some work). Nèitiáo-
tiělù hái-méi-wánchéng-ne. 那
條鐵路還沒完成
呢. That railroad is not completed yet.

WĀNDÒU₅ 豌豆 (N) pea. (M:
kē 顆, lì 粒).

WǍNFÀN₁ 晚飯 (N) supper.
(M: dùn 頓).

WÀNFĒN₃ 萬分 (AD) extremely,
to the highest degree. Tā-wànfēn-
nánguò. 他萬分難過.
He is extremely sad.

WǍNG₄ 網 (N) net, web. tōngxùn-
wǎng 通訊網 communication
network. yúwǎng 魚網 fish net.
zhīzhuwǎng 蜘蛛網 spider
web.

WǍNG₁ 往 or WÀNG 望 (CV) toward, in the direction of. wǎng-
dōng-qù 往東去 go to the
east. Wǎng-hǎochu-xiǎng. 往好

處 想 . Think about the good side of it. Wǎng-chánglixiǎng. 往 長 裏 想 . Think about the long run. wǎng-huízǒu 往 回 走 go back.

WÀNG₁ 忘 (TV) forget. (syn. wàngji 忘 記). Bié-bǎ-wǒwàng-le. 別 把 我 忘 了 . Don't forget me. Wǒ-wànglegàosong-ta-le. 我 忘 了 告 訴 他 了 . I forgot to tell him. Jìzhe, bié-wàng-le. 記 着 別 忘 了 . Remember, don't forget.

WÀNG₁ 望 or WǍNG 往 (CV) toward, in the direction of. wàngnán-kàn 望 南 看 look southward.

(TV) look toward something in the distance. Wǒ-shàng-lóu-qu wàngwang. 我 上 樓 去 望 望 . I am going upstairs to look.

WǍNGHÒU₃ 往 後 (TW) from now on, in the future. Wǒ-wǎnghòu bu-chōu-yān-le. 我 往 後 不 抽 煙 了 . I'll give up smoking from now on.

WÀNGJI₃ 忘 記 (TV) forget. (syn. wàng 忘). Wǒ-wàngji-gǎita-qián-le. 我 忘 記 給 他 錢 了 . I forgot to give him the money. Wǒ-bǎ-tade-míngzi wàngji-le. 我 把 他 的 名 字 忘 記 了 . I forgot his name.

WǍNGNIAN₄ 往 年 (TW) the years gone by, in the past. Jīnnian bǐ-wǎngnián-hǎo. 今 年 比 往 年 好 . This year is much better than the years past.

Wǎngnian tā-lǎo-gēn-women yíkuàir-guò-shēngdànjié. 往 年 他 老 跟 我 們 一 塊 過 聖 誕 節 . He used to celebrate every Christmas with us in the past.

WÁN-GŌNG₄ 完 工 (VO) finish, complete a job. Háiyou-sāntian jiu-wán-gōng-le. 還 有 三 天 就 完 工 了 . The work will be completed in three more days.

WǍNGQIÚ₃ 網 球 (N) tennis (ball or game). (M: chǎng 場). mǎi-liǎngge-wǎngqiú 買 兩 個 網 球 buy a couple of tennis balls. dǎ-yīchang-wǎngqiú 打 一 場 網 球 play a game of tennis.

WÁNGU₃ 頑 固 (SV) obstinate, stubborn.

WǍNGWǍNG₃ 往 往 (MA) sometimes. Tā-wǎngwǎng-jiào-woshēng-qì. 他 往 往 叫 我 生 氣 . He sometimes makes me mad.

WÀNGYUǍNJÌNG₄ 望 遠 鏡 (N) telescope, fieldglasses.(M: fù 付 , jià 架).

WǍNHUÍ₃ 挽 回 (TV) return a situation to its original condition. Wǒ-kàn méi-fázi-wǎnhuí-nèigejúshi-le. 我 看 沒 法 子 挽 回 那 個 局 勢 了 . I think there's no way to return the situation to its original condition.

WǍNHUÌ₃ 晚 會 (N) evening gathering, party. tiàowǔ-wǎnhuì 跳 舞 晚 會 evening dancing

W

party.

WÁNJÙ₄ 玩具 (N) toy. (syn.
wányìr 玩意兒).

WÁNLIÁO₄ 完了 used at the
end of a speech, that's all.

WÀNLICHÁNGCHÉNG₄ 萬里
長城 (N) The Great Wall.

WÁNLIÚ₃ 挽留 (TV) prevent a
desirable person from leaving,
detain a friend. Tā-yào-cízhí,
jīnglǐ-zhèng-wǎnliú-ta-ne. 他
要辭職，經理正挽
留他呢. He wants to re-
sign, and the manager is trying
to stop him.

WÀNNÉNG₄ 萬能 (IV) able to
do everything. wànnéng-bóshi
萬能博士 jack-of-all-
trades. Zhèige-rén zhēn-shi-
wànnéng. 這個人真是
萬能. This person can
really do everything.

WÁNNÒNG₄ 玩弄 (TV) play
with, toy with. Tā-zǒngshi-
xiǎng-wánnong-biéren. 他總
是想玩弄別人. He
always wants to toy with other
people. wánnòng-zhèngzhì 玩
弄政治 play politics.

WÁNPI₂ 頑皮 (SV) naughty,
mischievous. Tā-tài-wánpi. 他
太頑皮. He's really
naughty.

WÁNQUÁN₂ 完全 (SV) complete.
Zhèige bu-wánquan, kěshi-gòu-
le. 這個不完全，可是
够了. This is not complete
but it is enough.
(AD) perfectly, entirely, completely. Tā-wánquán-míngbai.

他完全明白. He
understands perfectly. Nǐ-shuō-
de wánquán-bu-duì. 你說的
完全不對. What you
said is completely wrong.

WĀNR₃ 彎兒 (N) curl, bend,
curve. Tā-tóufa-shang-de-wānr
dou-zhí-le. 他頭髮上的
彎兒都直了. The curl
in her hair went straight. Guǎi-
guo-wānr-qu jiu-dào. 拐過
彎兒去就到. Make a
turn and then you'll be there.

WÁNR₁ 玩兒 (TV) (1) play, have
a good time. wánr-qiú 玩兒
球 play ball. Lái-wánr-a. 來
玩兒啊. Come over to
have a good time. (2) amuse oneself with something as a hobby.
Tā-wánr-yóupiào. 他玩
兒郵票. He collects
stamps (as a hobby). (cf: YÓUXI
遊戲).

WǍNSHANG₁ 晚上 (TW) the
evening. Wǒ-wǎnshang-shàng-
xué. 我晚上上學. I go
to school in the evening. Wǎn-
shang zuì-hǎo. 晚上最好.
Evening is the perfect time.

WÁNSHUǍ₄ 玩耍 (IV) play. Tā-
men-dōu-zài-yuànzi-li wánshuǎ.
他們都在院子裏
玩耍. They are all playing in
the courtyard.

WÀNSUÌ₃ 萬歲 used after the
title of a leader of a country, a
political party or a country as a
shout of approval, long live. Nǚ-
huáng-wànsuì! 女皇萬歲！
Long live the queen! Zhōnghua-

W

mínguó-wànsuì! 中華民
國萬歲! Long live China!

WÀNWÀN₂ 萬萬 (M) hundred
million. yíwànwàn 一萬萬
one hundred million. (cf: YÌ
億).

(AD) used before a negative expression, absolutely, by all
means (more emphatic than wàn
萬). Nǐ-wanwan bu-néng-qù.
你萬萬不能去.You
absolutely cannot go.

WÁNXIÀO₂ 玩笑 (N) prank,
joke. kāi-wánxiào 開玩笑
play a joke.

(IV) play a prank on, joke with
someone. Tā-ài-jí, bié-gēn-ta-
wánxiào. 他愛急,別跟
他玩笑. He gets mad
easily, don't joke with him.

WÁNYÀO₃ 丸樂 (N) medicine
in pill form, pill. (M: lì 粒).

WÀNYĪ₂ 萬一 (MA) in case, if
by any chance. Wànyī-tā-bu-
néng-lái, wǒ-jiu-tì-ta. 萬一
他不能來, 我就替
他. I'll substitute for him in
case he can't come.

WÁNYÌR₂ 玩意兒 (N) (1) toy.
(syn. wánju 玩具). (2) skill,
talent of a performer on the
stage. Tāde-wányìr bu-cuò. 他
的玩意兒不錯. He
has talent. (3) thing, stuff. Hái-
shi-nèige-wánjìr. 還是那
個玩意兒 . (lit. It's still
that old stuff). Nothing new. (4)
jerk (the person). Tā-suàn-shén-
ma-wányìr? 他算甚麼玩
意兒 ? What kind of a jerk

is he?

WÁWA₄ 娃娃 (N) (1) baby. (2)
doll.

WÀZI₃ 襪子 (N) sock, stocking.
(M: zhǐ 隻 , shuāng 雙). chuān-
wàzi 穿襪子 wear socks.

WEI₄ 煨 (TV) cook something on
a slow fire. Zhèige-jī děi-yǒng-
huǒ-wēizhe. 這個鷄得
用火煨着. You have to
cook this chicken with a slow
fire.

WÈI₃ 餧 (TV) (1) feed (an animal).
wèi-gǒu 餧狗 feed a dog. (2)
feed food to someone unable to
feed himself. wèi-xiǎoháir 餧
小孩兒 feed a baby. Hùshi-wèi-
bìngrén-chī-fàn. 護士餧病
人吃飯 . The nurse fed the
food to the patients.

WÈI₁ 位 (M) (1) for persons (polite form). liǎngwèi-jūnguān 兩
位軍官 two officers. (2)
for digits in a number. sìwèi-
shùr 四位數兒 figure with
four digits.

WÈI₂ 為 (CV) for the benefit of,
for the purpose of, for the sake
of. Wǒ-wèi-nǐmen cai-zùo-de.
我為你們才做的.
I only did it for your benefit.
(TV) do something for the sake
of. Nǐ-zhè-shi-wèi-shéi? 你這
是為誰 ? For whom did you
do it? Tā-wèide shi-qián, nǐ-
wèi-shénma? 他為的是
錢, 你為甚麼 ? He does
it for money, what do you do it
for? (cf: WÈILE 為了).

WÈI₄ 喂 (I) hello, hi. Wèi! Nǐ-

W

zhǎo-wǒ-ma? 喂! 你找我
嗎 ? Hi, are you looking for
me?

WĔIBA₃ 尾巴 <u>see</u> YĬBA 尾巴 .

WÈIBÌ₂ 未必 (AD) not neces-
sarily. Tā-wèibì-jiēshòu. 他
未必接受. He may not
necessarily accept.

<u>used to express a different</u>
<u>opinion mildly.</u> A: Míngtian-
yídìng-xià-yǔ. B: Wèibì-ba. A:
明天一定下雨. B:
未必吧. A: Tomorrow it
will certainly rain. B: Not necessarily.

WÈIBÌNG₄ 胃病 (N) stomach
trouble (<u>usually chronical</u>).

WÉIBÓR₅ 圍脖兒 (N) scarf,
muffler, shawl. (M: tiáo 條).

WÉICHI₂ 維持 (TV) (1) maintain,
keep up, hold together. Wǒmen-
yīnggāi wéichi-yídìngde-biāo-
zhun. 我們應該維持
一定的標準. We should
maintain a certain standard. (2)
give support. Nǐ néng-bu-neng
wéichi-weichi-ta? 你能不
能維持維持他? Can
you give him some support?

WĔIDA₃ 偉大 (SV) great. Tāde-
chéngjiù zhēn-wěidà. 他的
成就真偉大. His
achievement is really great.

WÈIDAO₃ 味道 (N) (1) taste,
flavor. Jiā-dianr-táng, wèidao-
jiu-hǎo-le. 加點兒糖 ,
味道就好了. Add a
little sugar, it will taste better.
(2) smell, odor. (M: gǔ 股).
Zhèige-wèidao hěn-nánwén. 這

個味道很難聞 .
This smell is very bad. (cf:
WÈIR 味兒).

WÈIDESHI₂ 為得是 (MA) in
order to. Tā-qù-Fàguo wèide-
shi-xué-Fàwén. 他去法
國為得是學法文.
He is going to France in order
to study French.

WĒIFÊNG₄ 威風 (SV) impres-
sive, awe-inspiring. Nèige-
jiāngjun-zhēn-wēifeng. 那個
將軍真威風. That
general is really impressive.
(N) awe-inspiring appearance
(<u>of a person</u>). Tāde-wēifeng hěn-
dà. 他的威風很大.
His appearance is very awe-
inspiring.

WÉIHÙ₄ 維護 (TV) preserve,
protect, support. Zhèngfǔ-yīng-
dāng-wéihù-rénmínde-lìyi. 政
府應當維護僑民
的利益. Government
should protect the profits of people overseas.

WÉIJI₄ 危機 (N) crisis.

WÈIKOU₃ 胃口 (N) lit or fig.
appetite, taste. Jīntian-wǒde-
wèikou bu-cuò. 今天我的
胃口不錯 . I have a good
appetite today. Zhèchū-xì bu-duì-
tāde-wèikou. 這齣戲不
對他的胃口 . This play
isn't to his taste.

WÈILÁI₃ 未來 (N) future. Nǐ-
bunéng-yùcè-wèilái. 你不能
預測未來 .. You can't
predict the future.

WÈILAO₄ 慰勞 (TV) comfort

(usually of troops). Wǒmen-qu-
wèilao-qiánxiàn-de-quānbǐng.
我 們 去 慰 勞 前 線
的 官 兵 ． We are going to
comfort the officers and soldiers
at the front line.

WÈILE₂ 為 了 or WÈIZHE 為
着 (CV) for the sake of, for the
purpose of, for the benefit of.
Wèile-niàn-shū, wǒ-yíyè-méi-
shuì-jiào. 為 了 念 書, 我
一 夜 沒 睡 覺 . I stayed
awake a whole night to study.
(TV) do something for the sake
of. Wǒ-zhèiyangr-zuò shì-wèile-
nǐ. 我 這 樣 作 是 為 了
你 ． I did this for your sake.
(cf: WÈI 為).

WÈIMIǍN₂ 未 免 (AD) rather,
more or less. Tā-hěn-piàoliang,
kěshi wèimiǎn-gāo-yìdyanr. 他
很 漂 亮, 可 是 未 免
高 一 點 兒 ． She's quite
beautiful, but rather tall.

WÈIMIÀO₃ 微 妙 (SV) subtle.
Tāmende-quānxi hěn-wēimiào.
他 們 的 關 係 很 微
妙 . The relationship between
those two is very subtle.

WÉINAN₃ 為 難 or NÁNWEI 難
為 (TV) put someone in a difficult position. Bié-wéinan-ta.
別 為 難 他 ． Don't put him
in a difficult position.

WÉI-NÁN₂ 為 難 (VO) be in a
difficult position. Zhèijiàn-shì
jiào-wǒ-wéile hěn-duō-nán.
這 件 事 叫 我 為 了
很 多 難 ． I was really in a
difficult position about this

matter. Nín-bié-wéi-nán. 您
別 為 難 ． Don't put yourself
in a difficult position.

WÉIQÍ₅ 圍 棋 (N) game of go.
(M: pán 盤). xià-yipán-wéiqí
下 一 盤 圍 棋 play a
game of go.

WĚIQU₃ 委 屈 (SV) feel wronged,
feel grievances. Tā-hěn-wěiqu.
他 很 委 屈 ． He feels that
he's been wronged.
(TV) wrong someone, treat someone unjustly. Wǒmen-bunéng-
wěiqu-ta. 我 們 不 能 委
屈 他 ． We can't treat him
unjustly.
(N) raw deal, grievance. Bié-shòu
wěiqu. 別 受 委 屈 ． Don't
accept any injustices.

WÉIQUN₄ 圍 裙 (N) apron. (M:
tiáo 條).

WÈIR₂ 味 兒 (N) (1) taste, flavor.
tiánwèir 甜 味 兒 sweet taste.
Cài-bú-shi-wèir. 菜 不 是
味 兒 ． The taste of the food
isn't right. Tā-shuō-de-huà méi-
wèir. 他 說 的 話 沒 味
兒 ． What he said has no spice
in it. Tā-shuō-de-Yīngwén yǒu-
Yīngguo-wèir. 他 說 的 英
文 有 英 國 味 兒 ． His
English has a British flavor about
it. (2) smell, odor.(M: gǔ 股).
xiāng-wèir 香 味 兒 fragrant.
Wèir-hǎowén. 味 兒 好 聞 ．
It smells good. (3) air, atmosphere. Tāde-fángzi yǒu-yidianr
Rìběnwèir. 他 的 房 子 有
一 點 兒 日 本 味 兒 ．
His house has a slight Japanese

W

atmosphere. (4) feeling. Wǒ-
yuè-xiǎng-yuè-bu-shì-wèir. 我
越 想 越 不 是 味 兒.
The more I think about it, the
more I have the feeling that it's
not right. (cf: WĒIDAO 味 道).
WÉIRÉN₃ 為 人 (N) behavior.
Tāde-wéirén butài-hǎo. 他 的
為 人 不 太 好. His
behavior is not very good.
(IV) behavior. Nǐ-yǐhòu bunéng-
zài-zhènma-wéirén-le. 你 以
後 不 能 再 這 麼 為
人 了. From now on you
can't behave like this (any
longer). Yǐhòu wǒ-zěnma-wéi-
rén-ne? 以 後 我 怎 麼
為 人 呢 ? How should I
behave later on?
WÈISHĒNG₂ 衛 生 (SV) hygienic,
sanitary.
(N) hygiene, sanitation. zhùyì-
wèishēng 注 意 衛 生 pay
attention to hygiene.
WÈISHÉNMA₁ 為 甚 麼 (MA)
why, for what.
WĒISHÌJÌ₅ 威 士 忌 (N) whisky.
WÉITĀMÌNG₄ 維 他 命 (N)
vitamin. chī-wéitāmìng 吃 維
他 命 take vitamin pills.
WĚITUŌ₄ 委 託 (TV) entrust
someone to do something or
something to someone. Wǒmen-
wěituō-lùshǐ-bàn-hǎo-le. 我 們
委 託 律 師 辦 好 了.
Let's entrust a lawyer to do it.
Tā-bǎ-tāde-dìchǎn dōu-wěituō-
wǒ-le. 他 把 他 的 地 產
都 委 託 我 了. He en-
trusted all his real estate to me.

WÈIWÈN₄ 慰 問 (TV) comfort,
console.
WÉIWÙLÙN₅ 唯 物 論 (N) ma-
terialism.
WĒIXIĀN₂ 危 險 or WĒIXIAN 危
險 (SV) dangerous, critical.
(opp. ānquán 安 全). Nèige-
qiáo hěn-wēixian. 那 個 橋
很 危 險. That bridge is
very dangerous.
(N) danger. Zhèiyàngr-zuò yǒu-
hěn-dà-de-wēixian. 這 樣 兒
作 有 很 大 的 危 險.
There is great danger in doing
it this way.
WĒIXIAN₂ 危 險 see WĒIXIĀN
危 險.
WĒIXIE₄ 威 脅 (TV) intimidate,
threaten. Nǐ-wēixie-wo yě-méi-
yòng. 你 威 脅 我 也 没
用. It's no use for you to
threaten me.
(N) threat, intimidation. jīng-
shen-wēixie 精 神 威 脅
mental threat. shòu-wēixie 受
威 脅 be threatened.
WÈIXĪNG₄ 衛 星 (N) satellite.
rénzào-wèixīng 人 造 衛 星
artificial satellite.
WÉIXĪNLÙN₅ 唯 心 論 (N)
idealism.
WÉIYĚNÀ₃ 維 也 納 (PW)
Vienna.
WÉIYĪ₃ 唯 一 (B-) only, sole.
Zhè-shì-wǒ-wéiyīde-yítào-yī-
shang. 這 是 我 唯 一 的
一 套 衣 裳. This is the
only suit I have.
WĚIYUAN₃ 委 員 (N) (1) member
of a committee. (2) commissioner.

WĚIYUÁNHUÌ₃ 委員會 (N) committee.

WĚIZÀO₄ 偽造 (TV) falsify, counterfeit. Tāmen-wěizàole-hěn-duō-'zhèngjiàn. 他們偽造了很多証件. They falsified many certificates.

WÈIZHE₄ 為着 see WÈILE 為了.

WÈIZHI₃ 位置 (N) position. Zhèi-shi-yige-hěn-hǎo-de-wèi-zhi. 這是一個很好的位置. This is a very good position. (TV) put someone in a position in an organization. Tā-zài-jī-guanli wèizhile-jige-péngyou. 他在機關裏位置了幾個朋友. He gave jobs to several of his friends.

WÈIZI₃ 位子 (N) seat, position. zhànwèizi 佔位子 occupy a seat or position.

WĒN₄ 溫 (TV) (1) warm or heat food. Bǎ-cài-wēnwen. 把菜溫溫. Warm up the food. (2) (con. wēnxi 溫習). review (of studies).

WÉN₁ 聞 (TV) smell, sniff. Wǒ-'shénme-dōu-wénbujiàn. 我甚麼都聞不見. I can't smell anything.

WĚN(DANG)₃ 穩(當) (SV) steady, stable. Zhèiyàng-bàn hěn-wěn-(dang). 這樣辦很穩(當). Doing it this way will be very safe. Xiànzài-jīngji-qíng-xing buda-wěn(dang). 現在經濟情形不大穩

(當). Now the economic situation is not stable. Zhèige-rén hěn-wěn(dang). 這個人很穩(當). This person is very steady. Zhuōzi bù-wěn(dang). 桌子不穩(當). The table isn't steady.

WÈN₁ 問 (TV) ask, interrogate. Bié-wèn-wǒ, wǒ-yě-bùzhīdào. 別問我, 我也不知道. Don't ask me, I don't know either. Wǒ-wèn-ni-yijian-shì. 我問你一件事. I'll ask you something.

WĒNDÙ₂ 溫度 (N) temperature. shì-wēndù 試溫度 take a temperature. Wēndu hěn -gāo. 溫度很高. The tempera-ture is very high.

WĒNDÙBIĂO₄ 溫度表 (N) thermometer. shì-wēndùbiǎo 試溫度表 take a temper-ature.

WÉNFǍ₃ 文法 (N) grammar. (syn. yǔfǎ 語法).

WÈN-HǍO₁ 問好 (VO) give re-gards to. Qǐng-nǐ-tì-wo wèn-nǐ-tàitai-hǎo. 請你替我問你太太好. Please give my regards to your wife.

WÉNHUÀ₃ 文化 (N) culture..

WÉNHUÀGUǍN₄ 文化館 (N) museum of culture.

WĒNHUO₄ 溫和 (SV) lukewarm, tepid, warm. Shuǐ shi-wēnhuo-de. 水是溫和的. The water is warm.

WÉNJIAN₂ 聞見 (RV) smell, get a whiff of. Zài ménkǒur wǒ-jiu wénjian-ni-zuò-fàn-de

W

wèir-le. 在門口兒我
就聞見你做飯的
味兒了. I can smell your
cooking at the door.

WÉNJIÀN₃ 文件 (N) documents,
papers. (M: jiàn 件).

WÉNJÙ₃ 文具 (N) writing
equipment.

WÉNMÁNG₅ 文盲 (N) illiterate.

WÉNMÍNG₃ 文明 (SV) be civi-
lized. Xiànzài tā-wénmíngduō-
le. 現在他文明多了.
He's much more civilized now.
(N) civilization.

WĒNNUĂN₄ 溫暖 (SV) warm
(of weather or friendship).

WÉNPÍNG₄ 文憑 (N) diploma,
certificate. (M: zhāng 張). dé-
wénpíng 得文憑 receive a
diploma.

WĒNQUÁN₄ 溫泉 (N) hot spring.

WĒNROU₃ 溫柔 (SV) gentle,
softhearted. Tā-tàitai-de-xìng-
qing hen-wēnrou. 他太太
的性情很溫柔. His
wife has a gentle disposition.

WÈNTÍ₁ 問題 (N) (1) problem.
Wǒmen-de-wèntí-hái-méi-jiě-
jué-ne. 我們的問題
還沒解決呢. Our
problems haven't been solved
yet. Zhèige-wèntí hěn-dà. 這
個問題很大. This is
a very big problem. (2) question.
Bié-huídá-tāde-wèntí. 別回
答他的問題. Don't
answer his question.

WĒNXÍ₂ 溫習 (TV) review (of
studies). Wǒ-bǎ-lìshǐ dōu-wàng-
le, wǒ-děi-wēnxi-yixia. 我把

歷史都忘了,我得
溫習一下. I forget all my
history, I have to review it a
little bit.

WÉNXUÉ₃ 文學 (N) literature.

'WÉNYĂ₃ 文雅 (SV) refined,
genteel, elegant (of a person).
(opp. cūbào 粗暴). Tā-shuō-
huà hen-'wényă. 他說話很
文雅. When he talks he is
very elegant.

WÉNYÁN₃ 文言 (N) classical
or literary style (of Chinese
writings).

WÉNYANWÉN₂ 文言文 (N)
Chinese writings (done in classical or literary style).

WÉNYÌ₃ 文藝 (N) literature and
fine arts.

WÉNZHANG₃ 文章 (N) (1) article, essay. (M: piān 篇). xiě-
wénzhang 寫文章 write ar-
ticles. fābiǎo-wénzhang 發表
文章 publish articles. (2)
implication. Lǐbianr-yídìng-yǒu-
wénzhang. 裏邊兒一定
有文章. There must be
some implication in it.

WÉNZHÀNG₅ 蚊帳 (N) mosquito
net. (M: dǐng 頂).

WĚNZHONG₄ 穩重 (SV) calm,
steady. Tāde-tàidu hěn-wěnzhong.
他的態度很穩重.
His attitude is very calm.

WÉNZI₄ 蚊子 (N) mosquito.
(M: zhī 隻).

WÉNZÌ₂ 文字 (N) (1) writing
system (of a language), Chinese
characters. gǔdàide-wénzì 古
代的文字 ancient writing

system. Yǒude-yǔyán méi-you wénzì. 有的語言沒有文字. Some languages have no writing system. (2) phraseology. Wénzì-hěn-hǎo, kěshi-nèiróng-bu-xíng. 文字很好，可是內容不行. The phraseology is quite good, but the content is poor.

WŌ₃ 窩 (N) nest, burrow, hive, or other home of animals, birds, or insects. fēngwō 蜂窩 bee-hive. Niǎor dā-wō-ne. 鳥兒搭窩呢. The bird is building a nest.

(TV) (1) bend, twist something. Bié-wǒ-nèige-zhǐbǎnr. 別窩那個紙板兒. Don't bend that cardboard. (2) shelter, har-bor a criminal. Tā-jiā wōzhe-yige-tǔfěi. 他家窩着一個土匪. He harbored a robber in his house.

WŎ₁ 我 (PR) (1) I, me. Géi-wo. 給我. Give it to me. (2) used before a noun, my. wǒ-jiějie 我姐姐 my sister.

WŎCHĒ₄ 卧車 (N) sleeping car, pullman. (M: liàng 輛).

WŎFÁNG₃ 卧房 (N) bedroom. (M: jiān 間).

WŎMEN₁ 我們 (PR) (1) we, us (may or may not include the per-son or persons spoken to). Wǒ-men-chīle-fàn-le, nǐmen-ne? 我們吃了飯了，你們呢? We have eaten, how about you? Wǒmen-yíkuàir-qù-be. 我們一塊兒去吧. Let's go together. (2)

used before a noun, our. wǒmen-mǔqin 我們母親 our moth-er. (cf: ZÁNMEN 咱們).

WÒ-SHǑU₄ 握手 (VO) shake hands. Wǒ-qu-gēn-ta-wòwo-shǒu. 我去跟他握握手. I will go to shake hands with him. (cf: LĀ-SHǑU 拉手).

WŬ₄ 搗 (TV) cover, conceal (es-pecially with the hand). Tā-yòng-shǒu wǔzhe-zuǐ. 他用手搗着嘴. He put his hand over his mouth.

WŬ₄ 舞 (N) dancing. tǔfēngwǔ 土風舞 folk dance. (TV) dance with movement of the hands, with or without something in them. wǔ-jiàn 舞劍 do a sword dance.

WŬ₁ 五 (NU) five, fifth. wǔpǐ-mǎ 五匹馬 five horses. wǔlóu 五樓 fifth floor.

WÙ₄ 霧 (N) fog, mist, vapor. xià-wù 下霧 have fog.

WÙ₃ 誤 (TV) let an opportunity go by, cause something to be missed by delaying. Tā-láiwǎn-le, wù-le. 他來晚了，誤了. He came late and missed it. Hē-jiǔ róngyi-wù-shì. 喝酒容易誤事. In drinking, it's easy to let responsibilities slip by. (See: DĀNWU 耽誤).

WÙBÌ₃ 務必 (AD) without fail, of necessity. Qǐng-nín míngtian-wùbì-lái. 請您明天務必來. Please do come to-morrow without fail.

WŬCHĀNG₃ 武昌 (PW) Wu-ch'ang (capital of Hupeh province).

W

WŬCHĂNG₄ 舞場 (N) dance hall, night club where dance music is provided. (M: jiā 家).

WŬCHĂNJIÉJI₄ 無產階級 (N) proletarian class.

WŬDĂO₅ 舞蹈 (N) (1) the dance (as an art form). (2) dancing.

WÙ-DIĂN₃ 誤點 (VO) behind schedule, late (of train, bus, airplane, etc.).

WŬDĬNG₄ 屋頂 (N) roof.

WŬFÀN₁ 午飯 (N) lunch. (M: dùn 頓).

WÚFÁNG₃ 無妨 (TV) wouldn't be any harm. Nǐ-wúfáng-shì-yishi. 你無妨試一試. There wouldn't be any harm in trying it. Qù-ye-wúfáng. 去也無妨. There's no harm in going.

WÚFĒI₃ 無非 (AD) no more than, merely. Tā-wúfēi-shì-yí-ge-bīng. 他無非是一個兵. He is no more than a private. Wŏ-wúfei-dĕi-qù-yi-tàng. 我無非得去一趙. I merely have to go there once.

WÚGÙ₃ 無故 (AD) without a cause or reason. Tā-wúgù jiu-cí-zhí-le. 他無故就辭職了. He resigned without any reason.

WÚGUAI₄ 無怪 (MA) no wonder. (syn. nánguai 難怪). Wúguài-ni-bă-ta-jùjué-le. 無怪你把他拒絕了. No wonder you refused him.

WŪGUĪ₄ 烏龜 (N) (1) black tortoise. (2) cuckold (husband of an adultress).

WŬHÒU₃ 午後 (TW) the afternoon. Wŭhòu-bĭ-wŭqián-hăo. 午後比午前好. The afternoon is better than the morning. Wŏmen-wŭhòu-zai-qù-ba! 我們午後再去吧! Let's not go until the afternoon!

WŬHUĀGUŎ₄ 無花果 (N) fig.

WÙHUI₂ 誤會 (TV) misunderstand. Qĭng-nĭ-buyào-wùhui-wŏ-de-yìsi. 請你不要誤會我的意思. Please don't misunderstand what I mean. (N) misunderstanding. Tā-gēn-wo-fāshēngle-hĕn-dà-de-wùhui. 他跟我發生了很大的誤會. A great misunderstanding developed between him and me.

WÙJIÀ₄ 物價 (N) price of things. Wùjià yuè-lai-yuè-gāo. 物價越來越高. The price of things goes higher and higher.

WŬJĬN₅ 五金 (N) (lit. the five kinds of metal, referring to jīn 金 gold, yín 銀 silver, tóng 銅 copper, tiĕ 鐵 iron and xī 錫 tin) metal. wŭjīnháng 五金行 hardware store.

WÚJĬNGDĂCĂI₄ 無精打彩 (SV) be depressed, in low spirit. Zhèi-liăngtiān tā-lăo-wújīngdă-căi. 這兩天他老無精打彩. He has been very depressed these past few days.

WŪLÀI₃ 誣賴 (TV) implicate or accuse falsely. Nǐ-bunéng-wūlài-

-wo. 你 不 能 誣 賴 我 . You can't accuse me without any proof.

WŬLÌ₄ 武 力 (N) force of arms, force.

WÙLÌ₃ 物 理 (N) physics. (M: mén 門). xué-wùlǐ 學 物 理 study physics.

WÚLIÁO₃ 無 聊 (SV) (1) bored, uninterested. Zuìjìn wǒ-juéde-hěn-wúliáo. 最 近 我 覺 得 很 無 聊 . I feel really bored recently. (2) be boring. Nǐ-tài-wúliáo-le. 你 太 無 聊 了 . You're really boring.

WÚLÙN₂ 無 論 (AD) regardless of, no matter (whether), it doesn't matter (whether). (syn. bùguǎn 不 管 , búlùn 不 論). Wúlùn-shì-zhōng-shì-biǎo wǒ-dōu-yào. 無 論 是 鐘 是 錶 我 都 要 . It doesn't matter whether it's a clock or a watch, I still want it.

WŬNÜ₃ 舞 女 (N) dance-hall girl.

WŬQÌ₄ 武 器 (N) weapon, arms. (M: jiàn 件).

WŬQIÁN₃ 午 前 (TW) the morning, forenoon. Wǔqián-bǐ-wǔhòu duǎn-yidianr. 午 前 比 午 後 短 一 點 兒 . The morning is shorter than the afternoon. Wǔqián kōngqì-bǐjiáo-xīnxian. 午 前 空 氣 比 較 新 鮮 . The air is fresher in the morning.

WŬRU₃ 侮 辱 (TV) insult. Nǐ-wèi-shénme wǔru-ta? 你 為 甚 麼 侮 辱 他 ? Why do

you insult him? (N) insult. Wǒ-bu-néng-shòu-zhèizhongde-wǔru. 我 不 能 受 這 種 的 侮 辱 . I can't take this kind of insult.

WÚSHÙ₄ 無 數 (B-) countless, numerous. wúshùcì 無 數 次 many many times.

WÚSUǑWÈI₂ 無 所 謂 (SV) make no difference, of no importance. Tiānqi-rè-yidianr ye-wúsuǒwèi. 天 氣 熱 一 點 兒 也 無 所 謂 . The weather's a little hot, it doesn't matter. A: Zhèibe-shū-hǎo-ma? B: Wúsuǒwèi. A: 這 本 書 好 嗎 ? B: 無 所 謂 . A: Is this book good? B: Not much. Zhèizhong-dōngxi wúsuǒwèi-hǎo-bu-hǎo. 這 種 東 西 無 所 謂 好 不 好 . It doesn't make any difference whether this kind of thing is good or not.

WÚTONG₅ 梧 桐 (N) sterculia platanifolia.(M: kē 棵).

WÚXIÀN₄ 無 限 (SV) endless, boundless, unlimited. Tāde-qián tú wúxiàn. 他 的 前 途 無 限 . His future is unlimited.

WÚXIÀNDÌAN₃ 無 線 電 (N) radio. (M: jià 架). kāi-wúxiàn-diàn 開 無 線 電 turn on the radio.

WŪYĀ₅ 烏 鴉 (N) crow. (M: zhī 隻).

WÚYÌ₄ 無 意 (AD) without any intention, not on purpose. Wǒ-wúyì bǎ-ta-déizuì-le. 我 無 意 把 他 得 罪 了 . I offended him without knowing it.

W

WŬYÌ₄ 武藝 (N) art or technique of fighting.

WŬYUE₁ 五月 (TW) (lit. the fifth month of the year) May.

WÙZHÌ₄ 物質 (N) material (vs. spiritual), substance.

WŬZHUĀNG₄ 武裝 (TV) take up arms, arm. Xuésheng dōu-wǔzhuāngqilai-le. 學生都武裝起來了. The students all took up arms.

(N) arms. quánfù-wǔzhuāng 全付武裝 fully armed.

WŪZI₁ 屋子 (N) room. (M:jiān 間).

X

XĪ₁ 西 (L) west. chéngxī 城西 (the area) west of the city. xībù 西部 western part. wàng-xī-kàn 往西看 look towards the west.

(B) western (countries). xīfang-rén 西方人 Occidentals, westerners.

XĪ₃ 吸 (TV) (1) inhale. Gǎnkuài-xī-yìdiǎnr-yǎngqì-ba. 趕快吸一點兒氧氣吧. Quick, breathe in some oxygen. (2) smoke. Xī-yizhi-yān. 吸一枝煙. Smoke a cigarette. (3) absorb, soak up. Miánhua-néng-xī-hěn-duō-shuǐ. 棉花能吸很多水. Cotton can absorb a lot of water.

XĪ₃ 稀 (SV) (1) thin, watery. Zhōu tài-xī. 粥太稀. The porridge is too watery. (2) thin, sparse. Tā-tóufa xī-le. 他頭髮稀了. His hair is thin. rénkou hěn-xī 人口很稀 sparsely populated.

XĪ₅ 錫 see XÍLA 錫鑞.

XĪ₄ 席 (N) (1) woven mat made of bamboo or reed. (M: zhāng 張). (2) banquet, feast. (M: zhuō 桌). jiǔxí 酒席 banquet.

XĪ₁ 洗 (TV) (1) wash. xǐ-yīshang 洗衣裳 wash clothes. (2) shuffle cards. xǐ-pái 洗牌 shuffle cards. (3) develop photographs. Tā-zìjǐ xǐ-xiàng-piānr. 他自己洗像片兒. He develops film by himself.

XÌ₂ 戲 (N) play, opera. (M: chū 齣, mù 幕, tái 臺). yǎn-xì 演戲 act in a play or put on a play. chàng-xì 唱戲 sing opera.

XÌ₃ 系 (N) department (in a university or college). shénma-xì 甚麼系 what department. wùlǐ-xì 物理系 department of physics.

(M) department. sānxì 三系 three departments.

XÌ₂ 細 (SV) (opp. cū 粗). (1) fine, delicate. Tāde-pífu hěn-xì. 他的皮膚很細. Her skin is very delicate. (2) thin (in dimension), slender. Zhèige tiěsī tài-xì. 這個鐵絲太細. This iron wire is too thin. (3) fine and detailed. Tā-huàde hěn-xì. 他畫的很細. He painted it in detail. (4) careful in thinking. Tā-zhèige-rén hěn-xì. 他這個人很細. He has a careful mind. (AD) minutely, in detail, carefully. Nǐ-zai xì-xiǎng-yixiang. 你再細想一想. You'd better think it over more carefully.

XIĀ₃ 蝦 (N) shrimp, prawn. (M: zhǐ 隻).

XIĀ₂ 瞎 (IV) blind, go blind. Tā-liǎngzhi-yǎnjing dōu-xiāle. 他兩隻眼睛都瞎了. He is blind in both eyes. (AD) blindly, aimlessly. (syn. hú 胡). xiāshuō 瞎說 talk nonsensically. xiāpǎo 瞎跑 wander around aimlessly. (SV) tangled. Xiàn-xiā-le. 線瞎了 . The thread is tangled.

XIÀ₁ 下 (IV) (1) descend from a higher place. xià-shān 下山 descend from the mountain. xià-lóu 下樓 descend from an upper story of a building. (2) get off a conveyance, dismount, disembark. xià-chē 下車 get off a car or train. xià-mǎ 下馬 dismount from a horse. Wǒ-yí-xià-diàntī, jiu-kànjian-ta-le. 我一下電梯就看見他了 . As soon as I got off the elevator I saw him. (3) lit or fig. descend to a lower place. xià-shuǐ 下水 get into the water. xià-dìyu 下地獄 go down to hell. xià-chúfáng 下廚房 go to the kitchen to work. xià-fànguǎnr 下飯館兒 go to a restaurant to eat. (4) go from north to south or to a less developed area. xià-xiāng 下鄉 go to the country. (5) get out of class, school, office, work. xià-kè 下課 get out of class. xià-bān 下班 get out of class or work. (6) come down from the sky, such as rain, snow, hail, etc. xià-báozi 下電子 hail. xià-shuāng 下霜 have frost.(7) lay eggs, drop a litter. xià-dàn 下蛋 lay eggs. xià-xiǎo-māor 下小貓兒 drop a litter of kittens. (8) put in or down, ingredients of food, fertilizer, medicine, poison, down payment or deposit, color, capital, effort, etc. xià-miàn 下麵 put noodles in (the pot) to cook. xià-fèiliào 下肥料 put in fertilizer. Zhèibēi-jiǔ xiàle-dúyào-le. 這杯酒下了毒藥了 This drink (alcoholic) has been poisoned. xià-dìngyì 下定義 give a definition. xià-pīping 下批評 criticize. xià-jiélùn 下結論 give a conclusion. xià-dìngqian 下定錢 put down a deposit. xià-gōngfu 下工夫 put in time and effort. (9) issue an order or summons, send out invitations. xià-mìngling 下命令 issue an order. xià-chuán-piào 下傳票 issue a summons. xià-tiězi 下帖子 send invitations. (10) lower a flag. xià-qí 下旗 lower the flag. xià-bànqí 下半旗 fly the flag at half-mast. (11) play or make a move in chess, checkers, go or similar games. xià-yipan-qí. 下一盤棋 play a game of chess. Gāi-ni-xià-le. 該你下了 Your turn to move.or Your turn to play. (12) get food or drink down by taking a small amount of something tasty along with it. xià-fàn 下飯 get the rice down. Yòng-shénma-xià-jiǔ? 用甚麼下酒 ? What shall we have with the wine? (RE) (1) down. zuòxia 坐下 sit down. guìxia 跪下 kneel down. (2) indicates the capacity for holding or containing. fàng-buxià 放不下 cannot hold (a certain of something). zuòde-xia 坐得下 can seat (a certain number of people). (3) indicates that an action is settled. Tā-méi-liúxia-qián. 他没留下錢. He didn't leave money behind. Nín-shōuxia-ba. 您收下吧 You better accept it. IÀ₁ 下 (L) below, down. lóuxià 樓下 downstairs. yǐxià 以下 from this point on. wàng-xià-kàn 往下看 look downward. zài-zhèizong-qíngxing-xià 在這種情形下 under this kind of circumstances. (SP) next. xiàyicì 下一次 next time. xiàcè 下冊 second volume. xià(ge)yuè 下(個)月 next month. xià(ge)lǐbài 下個禮拜 next week. (B) lower. xiàděng 下等 lower class. xiàjí 下級 lower rank. Zhèibu-shū yǒu-shàng-zhōng-xià sānběn. 這部書有上中下三本. This set of books has three volumes, first, second and last.

IÀ₃ 嚇 (TV) scare. Wǒ-děi-xià-ta-yixiàzi. 我得嚇他下子. I have to scare him (once). Bǎ-wǒ-xiàzháo-le. 把

我嚇着了 It scared me. Zhēn-xià-rén. 真嚇人. It's really frightening. (See: XIÀ-YITIÀO 嚇一跳, XIÀHU 嚇唬).

XIÀBA(KĒR)₄ 下巴(頦兒) (N) chin.

XIÀ-BAN₂ 下班 (VO) get out of work, go off duty, get out of class. Nǐmen-xiàle-bān gàn-shénma? 他們下了班幹甚麼 ? What are you doing after you're off duty?

'XIÀBÀNTIANR₄ 下半天兒 (TW) afternoon.

XIÀ-BÁOZI₄ 下雹子 (VO) hail.

'XIÀBÈIZI₄ 下輩子 (TW) next life-time, next reincarnation (Buddhist belief).

XIÀBIANR₁ 下邊兒 or XIA-TOU 下頭 or XIÀMIAN 下面 (PW) (1) bottom, lower surface. Wǎn-xiàbianr-yǒu-zì. 碗下邊兒有字. There are characters on the lower surface of the bowl. (2) lower part or area of something. Nèizhang-huàr shàngbianr-shi-yúncai, xià-bianr-shi-hǎi. 那張畫兒上邊兒是雲彩下邊兒是海. The higher part of the painting is clouds and the lower part is the sea. (3) lit. or fig. under, below. Bào-zai-shū-xià-bianr-ne. 報在書下邊兒呢. The newspaper is under the books. Shàngbianrde-mìnglìng, xiàbianr-dei-fúcóng. 上邊兒的命令, 下

X

邊兒得服從. The
orders are from above, those
below must obey. (4) latter part
of a speech, book or event. Tā-
jiu-shuōdao-zhèr, xiàbianr-méi-
shuō. 他就説到這兒，
下邊兒沒説. He
talked only up to this point and
didn't say anything about the
latter part.

XIÀCHAO₃ 夏朝 (TW) Hsia dy-
nasty.

'XIÀCÌ₂ 下次 (TW) next time.
(syn. xiàhuí 下回).

XIÀ-DÌ₄ 下地 (VO) (1) get out
of bed (as a patient after a long
illness). Nǐ-hái-bùnéng-xiàdì-
ne. 你還不能下地
呢. You can't get out of bed
yet. (2) go to the field to work.
Tā-xià-dì-zuò-huó-qu-le. 他
下地作活去了. He
went to the field to work.

XIÀHU₄ 嚇唬 (TV) Peip. scare
someone on purpose. Nǐ-bié-
xiàhu-nǐ-xiǎodìdi. 你別嚇
唬你小弟弟. Don't
scare your little brother.

XIÀHUÀ₃ 瞎話 (N) lie, untruth.
(syn. huǎnghuà 謊話). shuō-
xiāhuà 説瞎話 tell a lie.
biān-xiāhuà 編瞎話 fabricate
a lie. (See: HUǍNG 謊).

XIÀHUÍ₁ 下回 (TW) next time.
(syn. xiàcì 下次).

XIÀJÍ₄ 下級 (N) lower ranks,
subordinates.

XIÀJIÀNG₄ 下降 (IV) descend,
come down. Xiàjiàng-dao-'wǔ-
qiān-chǐ. 下降到五千

尺. Descend to five thousand
feet.

XIÀ-KÈ₁ 下課 (VO) get out of
class.

XIÀLAI₁ 下來 (RV) (1) come
down. Cóng-shùshang xiàlai-yi-
zhī-niǎor. 從樹上下來
一隻鳥兒. A bird came
down from the tree. (2) enough
to cover the expense. Háizi-
niàn-shū, yíge-yuè-yǒu-wǔshi-
kuai-qián jiu-xiàlai-le. 孩子
念書一個月有五
十塊錢就下來了.
Fifty dollars a month will be
enough to cover expenses for the
child to study.
(RE) (1) down (here). náxialai
拿下來 take it down (here).
qiēxialai 切下來 cut it down.
(2) indicates finalizing the action,
up. cúnxialai 存下來 save
up. (3) get approval from a superior or authority. Nèijian-shì
tā-méi-bànxialái. 那件事
他沒辦下來. He didn't
get approval for that matter. (4)
enough to cover the expense. Zhèige-biǎo wǒ-kan-yibǎikuai-qián
mǎibuxiàlái. 這個表我
看一百塊錢買不
下來. I don't think one
hundred dollars is enough to buy
this watch.

XIÀ(GE)LǏBÀI₁ 下(個)禮拜
see XIÀ(GE)XĪNGQĪ 下(個)星
期.

XIÀLIÚ₃ 下流 (SV) mean, vulgar.

XIÀLIÚ₃ 下 流 (N) lower part of a river.

XIÀ-LÙSHUI₄ 下 露 水 (VO) have dew.

XIĀMI₅ 蝦 米 (N) (1) small shrimp. (2) dried shrimp.

XIÀMIAN₃ 下 面 see XIÀBIANR 下 邊 兒.

XI'ĀN₂ 西 安 (PW) Sian (capital of Shensi province).

XIĀN₄ 掀 (TV) lift up, pick up a cover. Bǎ-tǎnzi-xiānqilai.. 把 毯 子 掀 起 來. Lift up the blanket. xiān-liánzi 掀 簾 子 lift up the curtain.

XIĀN₁ 先 (AD) beforehand, first, earlier. (opp. hòu 後). Wǒmen-xiān-chī-zài-qù. 我 們 先 吃 再 去. Let's eat first before we go. Nín-xiān-qǐng.您 先 請. You go first. or After you.

(B) preceding. xiānlì 先 例 precedent.

(B-) my late (referring to deceased family members who are older than oneself). xiānfū 先 夫 my late husband.

XIĀN₃ 鮮 (SV) fresh (in taste). Zhèige-tāng-zhēn-xiān. 這 個 湯 真 鮮. This soup is really fresh tasting.

(B) fresh (in the original state). xiānyú 鮮 魚 fresh fish. (cf: XĪNXIAN 新 鮮).

XIÁN₃ 嫌 (TV) (1) dislike. Nǐ-xián-zhèige-yánse-ba! 你 嫌 這 個 顏 色 吧! You don't like this color, I suppose.

(2) find something or someone unsatisfactory because... Wǒ-xián-ta-bu-yònggōng. 我 嫌 他 不 用 功. I found him unsatisfactory because he doesn't work hard. Tā-xián-zhèr-tài-lěng.他 嫌 這 兒 太 冷. He finds it too cold here.

XIÁN₃ 鹹 (SV) salty. xiányú 鹹 魚 salted fish.

XIÁN₄ 閒 (SV) have free time, be unoccupied, idle. Tā-xiànzài-hěn-xián. 他 現 在 很 閒. He has free time now.

(N) free or leisure time. Wǒ-lǐbàitiān-dou-bu-dé-xián. 我 禮 拜 天 都 不 得 閒. I don't have any free time even on Sunday.

(AD) idly, leisurely. xiánguàng 閒 逛 wandering around liesurely.

XIĂN₃ 顯 (SV) noticeable, be easily seen. Zāngde-nèikuài hěn-xiǎn.髒 的 那 塊 很 顯. That spot of dirt is very noticeable.

XIÀN₃ 線 (N) (1) thread, string, yarn. (M: tiáo 條, gēn 根). sī-xiàn 絲 線 silk thread. máo-xiàn 毛 線 yarn. (2) wire. (M: tiáo 條, gēn 根). diànhuà-xiàn 電 話 線 telephone wire. (3) line. (M: dào 道). huà-yidao-xiàn 畫 一 道 線 draw a line.

XIÀN₄ 縣 (N) hsien (a subdivision of a Chinese province, similar to a county). xiànzhǎng 縣 長 magistrate of a hsien.

XIÀN₃ 現 or XUÀN 現 (AD) take or start action at the time when

X

the action is needed. Zhèi-shi-yàngzi. Nǐ-yào-mǎi, wǒ-děi-gěi-nǐ-xiàn-zuò. 這是樣子，你要買，我得給你現作 . This is a sample. If you want to buy we will have to have them made for you. Zǎo-yidianr-yùbei, dào-shíhou xiàn-zuò jiu-tài-wǎn-le. 早一點兒預備，到時候現作就太晚了 . Prepare it a little earlier, if you do it when the time comes, it will be too late.

(S) xiàn...xiàn... 現 ... 現 ... do the first action only when one also wants to do the second. Tā-bù-cún-huò, zhǒng-shi xiàn-mǎi-xiàn-mài. 他不存貨總是現買現賣 . He doesn't hoard merchandise, he buys it only when it can be sold.

XIÀNCHÉNG(R)₃ 現成(兒) (SV) ready and available. xiànchéngr-de 現成兒的 what is already prepared and available. Hěn-róngyi-zuò, cáiliao-dou-xiànchéng(r). 容易作，材料都現成(兒) . It's easy to make. The materials are ready and available. Yǒu-xiàn-chéngrde-wǒ-jiu-mǎi, dìng-zuò láibují-le. 有現成兒的我就買，定作來不及了 . If you have one ready made I'll buy it. I don't have the time to have it made to order.

XIÀNDÀI₂ 現代 (B-) modern, contemporary. xiàndài-lìshǐ 現代歷史 modern history.

XIÀNFǍ₄ 憲法 (N) constitution (of a government). (M: bù 部 , tiáo 條).

XIĀNFÙ₅ 先父 (N) my late father.

XIĀNG₁ 香 (SV) (1) fragrant, aromatic, good-smelling. (opp. chòu 臭). Zhèi-huār hěn-xiāng. 這花兒很香 . This flower is very fragrant. Nǐ-zuò-shénma-cài-ne? Zhēn-xiāng. 你作甚麼菜呢? 真香 . What are you cooking? It smells so good. (2) with relish (of eating). Tā-chīle-sānwan-fàn, chǐde-zhēn-xiāng. 他吃了三碗飯，吃的真香 . He ate three bowls of rice with real relish. (3) sound (of sleep). Tā-shuì-de hěn-xiāng. 他睡的很香 . He is sound asleep. (4) popular (of commodities). Xiànzài Zhōngguohuò zài-Měiguo-hěn-xiāng. 現在中國貨在美國很香 . Chinese merchandise is very popular in America now. (N) incense. shāo-xiāng 燒香 burn incense.

XIĀNG₃ 鑲 (TV) (1) set, mount jewels and the like. xiāng-yá 鑲牙 mount false teeth. yòng-zuànshí xiāng-jièzhi 用鑽石鑲戒指 set a diamond in the ring. (2) put on trim. xiāng-biānr 鑲邊兒 put trim on the edge. xiāng-jìngkuàngr 鑲鏡框兒 make a frame (for a picture).

X

XIĂNG₁ 想 (TV) (1) think (opinion). (syn. kàn 看). Wǒ-xiǎng zhèi-ge-buduì. 我 想 這 個 不 對. I don't think this is right. Wǒ-xiǎng-kuài-xià-yǔ-le. 我 想 快 下 雨 了. I think it's going to rain. (2) think, ponder. Nǐ-wèi-shénma-bu-xiǎng-xiang? 你 為 甚 麼 不 想 想? Why don't you think about it. (3) (con. xiǎngnian 想 念). long for, miss, think of. Wǒ-bùxiǎng-ta. 我 不 想 他. I don't miss him. (AV) wish to, want to. Wǒ-xiǎng-hē-shuǐ. 我 想 喝 水. I want to drink some water. Wǒ-bu-xiǎng-qù. 我 不 想 去. I don't want to go. (cf: XĪN-XIĂNG 心 想).

XIĂNG₂ 響 (IV) (1) sound, ring. Diànhuà-xiǎng-le. 電 話 響 了. The telephone is ringing. (2) dial. make a sound, say a word. Tā-yìshēng yě-buxiǎng. 他 一 聲 也 不 響. He doesn't say a word. (SV) (1) make noise. Guān-mén bu-neng-bu-xiǎng. 關 門 不 能 不 響. In closing a door one can't help but make a noise. (2) loud. Wúxiàndiàn-tài-xiǎng-le. 無 線 電 太 響 了. The radio is too loud.

XIÀNG₄ 象 (N) (1) elephant. (M: zhī 隻). wèi-xiàng 餵 象 feed the elephant.

XIÀNG₁ 像 (TV) (1) resemble, look like. Tā-xiàng-ta-fùqin. 他 像 他 父 親. He resembles

his father. (2) (con. hǎoxiàng 好 像). may be followed by shide 似 的 , it seems that, appears to be. (syn. gēn... shide 跟 ... 似 的). Tā-xiàng-méi-chī-fàn-(shide). 他 像 沒 吃 飯 (似 的). It seems that he didn't eat. (3) followed by examples ending in shénmade 甚 麼 的 or děngděng 等 等 , such as... etc. xiàng-zhuōzi-yǐzi-shénmade 像 桌 子 椅 子 甚 麼 的 such as tables, chairs, etc. (SV) alike. Zhèi-liǎngge-ren hěn-xiàng. 這 兩 個 人 很 像. These two persons are very much alike. (N) (1) portrait, picture. (M: zhāng 張). huà-yizhāng-xiàng 畫 一 張 像 paint a portrait. Wǒ-zhàole-yizhang-xiàng. 我 照 了 一 張 像. I took a photograph. (2) statue (of a person). shíxiàng 石 像 stone statue (of a person).

XIÀNG₄ 項 (M) (1) article (of formal documents). dì-èrjié dì-wǔxiàng 第 二 節 第 五 項 section two, article five. (2) item (of business), entry (of accounting). yíxiàng-shìqing 一 項 事 情 an item of business. yíxiàng-jìnkuǎn 一 項 進 欸 one item of income.

XIÀNG₂ 向 (TV) (1) face. Nèige-fángzi xiàng-běi. 那 個 房 子 向 北. That house faces north. (2) show partiality toward, take someone's side. Nǐ-wèi-

X

shemma-búxiàngzhe-wǒ? 你
為 甚 麼 不 向 着 我 ?
Why don't you take my side?
(CV) toward. Wǒmen-xiàng-nán-
zǒu. 我 們 向 南 走 . Let's
go toward the south. (cf: CHÒNG
衝 , CHÁO 朝).

XIÀNG-BÀNFA₁ 想 辦 法
see XIǍNG-FǍZI 想 法 子.

XIĀNGBĪNJIǓ₄ 香 檳 酒 (N)
champagne. (M: píng 瓶).

XIǍNGBUKĀI₃ 想 不 開 (RV)
cannot remove the mental block.
Nǐ-zěnma-lǎo-xiǎngbukāi? 你
怎 麼 老 想 不 開 ?
How come you can never get rid
of your mental block?

XIĀNGCHÁNGR₄ 香 腸 兒 (N)
a kind of Chinese sausage.

XIĀNGCŪN₄ 鄉 村 (N) village,
rural area.

XIĀNGDĀNG₂ 相 當 (SV) suit-
able, proper. Tā-zuò-zhèige-
shì bu-xiāngdāng. 他 作 這
個 事 不 相 當 . It is not
suitable for him to do this job.
(AD) quite, considerably. Tā-
mèimei xiāngdāng-piàoliang. 他
妹 妹 相 當 漂 亮 . His
younger sister is quite pretty.

'XIǍNGFǍ₁ 想 法 or XIÁNGFAR
想 法 (N) way of thinking.

XIĀNGFǍN₂ 相 反 (IV) opposite
of, contrary to. Tāde-yìsi-gen-
wo-xiāngfǎn. 他 的 意 思
跟 我 相 反 . His opinion
and mine are opposite.

XIÁNGFAR₁ 想 法 兒 see
'XIǍNGFǍ 想 法 .

XIǍNG-FǍR₁ 想 法 兒 see
XIǍNG-FǍZI 想 法 子 .

XIǍNG-FǍZI₁ 想 法 子 or XIǍNG-
BÀNFA 想 辦 法 or XIǍNG-
FǍR 想 法 兒 (VO) think of
a way. Wúlùnrúhé nǐ-dei-xiǎng-
ge-fǎzi. 無 論 如 何 你
得 想 個 法 子 . No mat-
ter how, you have to think of a
way.
(AD) try to. Wǒmen-xiǎng-fǎzi
mǎi-yige. 我 們 想 法 子
買 一 個 . Let's try to buy
one.(cf: SHÈFǍ 設 法).

XIǍNG-FÚ₃ 享 福 (VO) (lit.
enjoy blessings) have a happy
life. Wǒ-méi-xiǎngguo-fú.. 我
沒 享 過 福 . I have never
had an easy life.

XIĀNGGĀN₃ 相 干 (N) concern,
connection, relation. Nèijiàn-
shìqing gēn-wo-méi-shenma-
xiānggān. 那 件 事 情 跟
我 沒 甚 麼 相 干 · I
don't have much concern with
that matter.
(IV) have a connection, concern.
Tài-buxiānggān-le. 太 不 相
干 了 . There's no connection
at all. Nèijian-shì gēn-wo-bu-
xiānggān. 那 件 事 跟 我
不 相 干 . That matter does
not concern me.

XIĀNGGǍNG₂ 香 港 (PW) Hong
Kong.

XIĀNGGUAR₅ 香 瓜 兒 or
TIÁNGUA 甜 瓜 (N) general
term for muskmelons.

XIǍNG-JIĀ₂ 想 家 (VO) home-
sick.

XIĀNGJIĀO₃ 香蕉 (N) banana (fruit). (M: tiáo 條 , gēn 根). (cf: BĀJIĀO 芭蕉).

XIǍNGKĀI₃ 想開 (RV) remove a mental block. Tā-xiànzài-xiǎngkāi-le. 他現在想開了. He is freer in his thinking now.

XIÀNGLÁI₂ 向來 (MA) always (up until now). Wǒ-xiànglái buài-hē-jiu. 我向來不愛喝酒 . I have never liked to drink. Tā-xiànglái-jiu-zhèyàngr. 他向來就這樣兒. He has been like this all the time.

XIǍNGLIANG₅ 響亮 (SV) loud and clear. Tā-shuōhuà hěn-xiǎngliang. 他說話很響亮. His voice is loud and clear.

XIĀNGLIÀO₄ 香料 (N) aromatic ingredients, spices.

XIÀNGMAO₃ 相貌 (N) looks (of a person).

XIÀNG-MIÀN₄ 相面 (VO) practice physiognomy. Xiàng-miàn-de gěi-wo-xiàngle-yíge-miàn. 相面的給我相了一個面 . The physiognomist studied my face once.

XIÀNGMU₄ 項目 (N) list of items.

XIǍNGNIAN₂ 想念 (TV) long for, think of, miss. Wǒ-hěn-xiǎngnian-ta. 我很想念他 . I missed him a lot.

XIÁNGŌNGFU(R)₄ 閒工夫(兒) (N) free or leisure time.

XIÀNGPÍ₃ 橡皮 (N) (1) rubber. xiàngpí-zuò-de 橡皮作的 made of rubber. (2) eraser. (M: kuài 塊).

XIÁNGPIÀN₅ 香片 (N) jasmine tea.

XIÀNGPIÀNR₂ 相片兒 (N) photograph. (M: zhāng 張). zhào-xiàngpiānr 照相片兒 take a photograph. xǐ-xiàngpiānr 洗相片兒 develop photographs. (cf: ZHÀOPIÀN 照片).

XIÀNGPÍGĀO₄ 橡皮膏 (N) adhesive tape. (M: kuài 塊).

XIÀNGQÍ₃ 象棋 (N) a Chinese board game similar to chess. (M: fù 副 , pán 盤). xià-yipán-xiàngqí 下一盤象棋 play a game of Chinese chess. Wǒ-nèifu-xiàngqí diū-le. 我那副象棋丟了 . My set of Chinese chess was lost.

XIÁNGQILAI₁ 想起來 (RV) recall, remember. Wǒ-xiǎngbu-qilái-le. 我想不起來了 . I cannot recall it.

XIÀNGQÌR₄ 香氣兒 see XIÀNGWÈIR 香味兒 .

XIÀNGRÌKUÍ₅ 向日葵 (N) sunflower. (M: kē 棵).

XIÀNGSHENGR₄ 相聲兒 (N) comic dialogue. (M: tiáo 套).

XIÀNGSHÌ₅ 相識 (IV) know each other. Wǒ-gēn-ta-bùxiāngshì. 我跟他不相識. We don't know each other.

XIǍNGSHOU₂ 享受 (TV) (1) enjoy the pleasures of life. Chèn-niánqīngde-shíhou 'xiǎngshou-xiǎngshou-ba. 趁年青的時候享受享受吧 . Enjoy yourself when you are young. (2) enjoy a privilege or right. Wǒ-cónglái méi-xiǎngshouguo-

X

huìyuánde-quánli. 我從來沒享受過會員的權利 . I've never enjoyed the privileges of a member. (N) enjoyment, pleasure.

XIĀNGSHUǏ(R)₃ 香水 (兒) (N) perfume, cologne.

XIĀNGSÌ₃ 相似 (IV) alike, similar. Zhèiliǎngge-xiāngzi hěn-xiāngsì. 這兩個箱子很相似 . These two trunks are about the same.

XIĀNGTÓNG₂ 相同 (IV) the same, identical. Tāde-qìchē-gen-wǒde wánquán-xiāngtóng. 他的汽車跟我的完全相同 . His car and mine are exactly the same.

XIĀNGTOU₄ 想頭 (N) hope, expectations. Wǒ-gēnben-méi-nèizhong-xiǎngtou. 我根本沒那種想頭 . I've never had such expectations.

XIĀNGUǑZI₃ 鮮菓子 (N) fresh fruit.

XIĀNGWÈIR₃ 香味兒 or XIĀNGQÌR 香氣兒 (N) aroma, fragrance. (M: gǔ 股).

XIÁNGXI₁ 詳細 (SV) clearly and carefully detailed. Tāde-jiěshì hěn-xiángxi. 他的解釋很詳細 . His explanations are very detailed. (AD) in detail. Qǐng-nin-xiángxi-gěi-wǒmen-shuō-yishuo. 請您詳細給我們說一說 . Please tell us in detail.

XIĀNGXIA₁ 鄉下 (PW) countryside.

'XIǍNGXIÀNG₂ 想像 (TV) imagine. Wǒ-xiǎngxiàng tā-yídìng-hěn-shēngqì. 我想像他一定很生氣 . I imagine that he must be very angry. (N) imagination. Nà-buguo-shì-nǐde-xiǎngxiàng. 那不過是你的想像 . That is only your imagination.

XIĀNGXÌN₂ 相信 (TV) believe, trust. Wǒ-xiāngxìn nǐ-shuōde-shì-zhēnde. 我相信你說的是真的 . I believe that what you said is true. Wǒmen-bǐcǐ-xiāngxìn. 我們彼此相信 . We trust each other.

XIÀNGYÁ₄ 象牙 (N) ivory, elephant tusk.

XIĀNGYĀN₂ 香烟 (N) cigarette. (syn. yānjuǎnr 烟捲兒 , zhǐ-yān 紙烟). (M: zhī 枝 , bāo 包 , tiáo 條).

XIÀNG-YÀNGR₂ 像樣兒 or XIÀNGYÀNGZI 像樣子 (VO) look good, presentable. Tāde-Yīngwén hěn-xiàng-yàngr. 他的英文很像樣兒 . His English is presentable. Tā-zhǎngde-hěn-xiàngyàngr. 他長的很像樣兒 . His appearance is quite presentable. Zhèige-fángzi bu-xiàng-yàngr. 這個房子不像樣兒 . This house doesn't look good.

XIÀNGYÀNGZI₂ 像樣子 see XIÀNG-YÀNGR 像樣兒 .

XIĂNGYÌNG₄ 響應 (TV) respond. Méi-rén-xiǎngyìng-wǒde-jiànyì. 沒人響應我的建

X

議. Nobody responds to my suggestion.

XIĀNGYÓU₅ 香油 or MÁYÓU 麻油 (N) sesame oil.

XIÀNGZHĒNG₃ 象徵 (TV) be a manifestation of, symbolize, represent. Zài-Zhōngguo hóng-sè-xiàngzhēng-xǐshì. 在中國紅色象徵喜事. In China, red symbolizes happy occasions.

(N) symbol, manifestation.

XIĂNG-ZHÚYI₁ 想主意 (VO) think up a plan.

XIĀNGZI₂ 箱子 (N) box, suitcase, trunk. (M: zhǐ 隻).

XIÀNHAI₅ 陷害 (TV) set a trap for someone, involve someone in trouble. Tā-lǎo-xiànhai-biéren. 他老陷害別人. He always tries to get other people into trouble.

(N) plot, involvement. Wǒ-shòu-le-ta-de-xiànhai-le. 我受了他的陷害了. I fell into his snare.

XIÁNHUÀ₄ 閒話 (N) (1) gossip. (2) idle talk.

XIĀNHUĀR₃ 鮮花兒 (N) fresh flower. (M: duǒ 朵).

XIÀNKUĂN₃ 現款 (N) cash. Zhīpiào jiu-suàn-xiànkuǎn. 支票就算現款. A check is considered cash.

XIĀNMÍNG₄ 鮮明 (SV) (1) bright and fresh. yánse-xiānmíng 顏色鮮明 bright and fresh in color. (2) clear and distinct, obvious. xiānmíngde-kǒuhào 鮮明的口號 a clear slogan.

XIĀNMǓ₅ 先母 (N) my late mother.

XIÀNMU₃ 羨慕 (TV) admire someone and be desirous of what he possesses. Tāde-xuéwen-hǎo, wǒ-hěn-xiànmu-ta. 他的學問好, 我很羨慕他. His learning is great. I admire him (and would like to possess his learning).

XIĀNQIÁN₂ 先前 (TW) previously, former times, the old days, before. Xiānqián tā-buhē-jiǔ. 先前他不喝酒. He didn't drink before. Xiānqián hái-bùrú-xiànzài-ne. 先前還不如現在呢. The old days were not as good as now.

XIÁNQIÁN₄ 閒錢 (N) idle money.

XIÀNQIÁN₂ 現錢 (N) cash. Wǒ-yào-xiànqián, bié-géi-wo-zhī-piào. 我要現錢別給我支票. I want hard cash, don't give me a check.

XIÀNR₅ 餡兒 (N) stuffing, filling (in cooking).

XIÁNRÉN₄ 閒人 (N) idler, gad-about.

XIĀNSHENG₁ 先生 (N) (1) sir (in direct address). Xiānsheng, jídian-le? 先生, 幾點了? Sir, what time is it? (2) teacher. (3) husband. (4) gentleman. zhèi-wèi-xiānsheng 這位先生 this gentleman.

used after surnames, Mr. Zhāng xiānsheng 張先生 Mr. Chang. (cf: LǍOSHĪ 老師, ZHÀNGFU 丈夫).

XIÁNSHÌ₃ 閒事 (N) another

X

person's affair, matters that one gets into only when one is an idler. Nǐ-bú-yao-guǎn-rén-jiade-xiánshì. 你 不 要 管 人 家 的 閒 事 . Don't bother with other people's business.

XIÀNSHÍ₃ 現 實 (SV) realistic, practical. Tā-hěn-xiànshí. 他 很 現 實 . He's very practical.

(N) fact, reality. Xiànshí zuì-yàojǐn. 現 實 最 要 緊 . Reality is most important.

XIĀNTIĀN₄ 先 天 (AT) innate, prenatal. xiāntiānde-máobing 先 天 的 毛 病 prenatal defect.

XIĀNWÉI₅ 纖 維 (N) fiber.

XIǍNWÉIJÌNG₄ 顯 微 鏡 (N) microscope. (M: jià 架).

XIÀNXIÀNG₃ 現 象 (N) phenomenon, immediate appearance (of a situation). zìran-xiànxiàng 自 然 現 象 natural phenomenon. Zhèi-shi-cháng-yǒu-de-xiànxiàng. 這 是 常 有 的 現 象 . This is a frequent phenomenon.

XIÁNYÍ₃ 嫌 疑 (N) suspicion. Tā-yǒu-tōu-chē-de-xiányi. 他 有 偷 車 的 嫌 疑 . He is under suspicion of stealing the car. Nǐde-xiányi zuìdà. 你 的 嫌 疑 最 大 . You are most suspicious.

XIÀNZÀI₁ 現 在 (TW) the present time, now. Xiànzài tā-bu-máng-le. 現 在 他 不 忙 了 . He's not busy now. Xiàn

zài bǐ-cóngqián-hǎo. 現 在 比 從 前 好 . Present times are better than the past.

XIÀNZHÌ₂ 限 制 (TV) set a limit, limit someone to. Tā-xiànzhi-wo měige-yuè yòng-sānbǎikuài-qián. 他 限 制 我 每 個 月 用 三 百 塊 錢 . She limited me to three hundred dollars each month.

(N) limit, restriction. méi-you-xiànzhi 沒 有 限 制 no limit. Xiàn-zhi-hěn-yán. 限 制 很 嚴 . The restrictions are very strict.

XIÁNZI₅ 弦 子 (N) a banjo-like Chinese instrument of three strings, Chinese banjo. (M: bǎ 把). tán-xiánzi 彈 弦 子 play the Chinese banjo.

XIĀO₃ 削 or XIŪ 修 (TV) shave off, peel with a knife. Nǐ-gěi-wǒ-xiāo-yíge-lí-ba. 你 給 我 削 一 個 梨 吧 . Please peel a pear for me. xiāo-qiānbǐ 削 鉛 筆 sharpen the pencil.

XIĀO₅ 硝 (N) a kind of nitric compound, saltpeter.

XIÁO₁ 學 see XUÉ 學 .

XIǍO₁ 小 (SV) (opp. dà 大). (1) small, little (size, capacity). xiǎo-yú 小 魚 small fish. Nǐ-de-shēngyi-tài-xiǎo. 你 的 聲 音 太 小 . Your voice is too soft. Zhèige-ren tài-xiǎo-le. 這 個 人 太 小 了 . lit. or fig. This person is too small. (2) young. Nǐ-yě-buxiǎo-le. 你 也 不 小 了 . You're not young any more. (3) trivial, insignificant.

xiǎo-zhì 小事 unimportant matter.

(B-) my, our (<u>polite form referring to offspring</u>). xiǎo'ér 小兒 my son. xiǎonǚ 小女 my daughter.

XIÀO₁ 笑 (IV) (1) smile, laugh. Tā-zuì-ài-xiào. 他最愛笑. He smiles very often. (TV) laugh at. (<u>syn</u>. xiàohua 笑話). Nǐ-bu-yào-xiào-wo. 你不要笑我. Don't laugh at me.

XIǍOBIÀN₃ 小便 (IV) urinate. Tā-yìtiān-xiǎobiàn-haǒjicì. 他一天小便好幾次. He urinates several times a day. (N) (1) urine. (2) penis.

XIǍOBIÀNR₄ 小辮兒 (N) small plait of hair, pigtail. (M: tiáo 條). shū-xiǎobiànr 梳小辮兒 <u>or</u> biān-xiǎobiànr 編小辮兒 plait hair into a pigtail. (cf: BIÀNZI 辮子).

XIǍODE₂ 曉得 (TV) know, know of. Wǒ-buxiǎode-zěnma-bàn. 我不曉得怎麼辦. I don't know how to do it. (cf: ZHĪDAO 知道).

XIĀO-DÚ₃ 消毒 (VO) disinfect. Zhèige-zhēn yǐjing-xiāoguo-dúle. 這個針已經消過毒了. This needle has already been disinfected.

XIǍO'ÉRKĒ₄ 小兒科 (N) pediatrics. xiǎo'érkē-dàifu 小兒科大夫 pediatrician.

XIǍOFÀN₄ 小販 (N) huckster, hawker.

XIĀOFÈI₄ 消費 (TV) consume, use. Zhèige-gōngchǎng yìtian-xiāofèi-duōshao-méi? 這個工廠一天消費多少煤? How much coal does this factory consume each day? (N) consumption.

XIĀOFÈI₂ 小費 (N) tip (<u>money</u>).

XIÀOFĒNG₄ 校風 (N) tradition of a school.

XIÀOGŌNG₄ 校工 (N) laborer <u>in a school</u>.

XIÀOGUO₃ 效果 (N) result, effect <u>of any cause</u>. méi-you-xiàoguo 沒有效果 no effect.

XIǍOHÁIR₁ 小孩兒 <u>or</u> XIǍOHÁIZI 小孩子 (N) child.

XIǍOHÁIZI₁ 小孩子 <u>see</u> XIǍOHÁIR 小孩兒.

XIĀOHAO₄ 消耗 (TV) use, consume. Nèijiàn-shì fēicháng-xiāohao-shíjiān. 那件事非常消耗時間. That matter is really time-consuming. (N) consumption.

XIĀOHUA₂ 消化 (TV) digest. Wǒ-bunéng-xiāohua-féide-dōngxi. 我不能消化肥的東西. I can't digest fatty things. Xuéde tài-duō méi-fázi-xiāohua. 學的太多沒法子消化. I have learned too much, there's no way to digest it all. (N) digestion. Wǒde-xiāohua-bu-hǎo. 我的消化不好. My digestion is not good.

XIÀOHUA₁ 笑話 (TV) laugh at, ridicule. (<u>syn</u>. xiào 笑). Tā-

X

ài-xiàohua-rén. 他愛笑話人. He likes to laugh at people.

(SV) ridiculous. Tài-xiàohua-le. 太笑話了. It's ridiculous.

XIÀOHUA(R)$_1$ 笑話(兒)(N) (1) joke. shuō-xiàohua(r) 説笑話(兒) tell a joke. (2) ridiculous situation, a laugh. Nà-chéngle-xiàohua(r)-le. 那成了笑話(兒)了. That became a joke. Nǐ-shuō-huà-xiǎoxin. Bié-chū-xiàohua(r). 你説話小心, 別出笑話(兒). Speak carefully, don't make yourself a laughingstock.

XIĂOHUŎR$_4$ 小彩兒 see XIĂO-HUŎZI 小彩子.

XIĂOHUŎZI$_3$ 彩子 or XIĂO-HUŎR 小彩兒 (N) young man.

'XIĂOJÍ$_3$ 消極 (SV) have a negative attitude. (opp. jījí 積極). Zuìjìn tā-hěn-'xiǎojí. 最近他很消極. He has had a negative attitude recently.

XIÁOJIE$_1$ 小姐 (N) (1) young lady, Miss. (2) daughter (referring to the daughter of a person spoken to or about). Tā-yǒu-sānwei-xiáojie. 他有三位小姐. He has three daughters.

used after surnames, Miss. Zhāng-xiáojie 張小姐 Miss Chang.

XIĂOKÀN$_2$ 小看 (TV) look down on, belittle, underestimate. Nǐ-bié-xiǎokàn-ta. 你別小看

他. Don't look down on him.

XIÀOLI$_3$ 效力 (N) effect. Zhèi-ge-yào méi-fāsheng-xiàoli. 這個藥沒發生效力. This medicine produced no effect.

XIÀO-LÌ$_4$ 效力 (VO) devote one's effort to a country or superior. Děi-gěi-guójiā-xiào-lì. 得給國家効力. (You) must devote your effort to the country.

XIÀOLU$_3$ 銷路 (N) market or demand for some product. Xiāo-lu-hěn-guǎng. 銷路很廣. The market is very broad.

XIÀOLŪ$_3$ 效率 (N) efficiency. Tā-zuò-shì-de-xiàolū hen-gāo. 他作事的效率很高. The efficiency of his work is very high.

XIĂOMÀI$_4$ 小麥 (N) wheat. (M: lì 粒, kē 棵).

XIĂOMIE$_3$ 消滅 (TV) annihilate. Wǒmen-bǎ-tǔfěi dōu-xiāomie-le. 我們把土匪都消滅了. We have annihilated the bandits.

XIĂOMÍNGR$_4$ 小名兒 (N) child's pet name.

XIĂOMǏR$_5$ 小米兒 (N) yellow millet. (M: lì 粒).

XIĂONIŬR$_5$ 小妞兒 (N) young girl, girlie.

XIĂOQI$_3$ 小氣 (SV) (opp. dàfang 大方). (1) stingy. Yàoshi-nǐ-gěi-de xiǎofèi-tài-shǎo, tāmen-shuō-ni-xiǎoqi. 要是你給的小費太少, 他們説你小氣. If the tip you give is too small, they will say you are stingy. (2) petty, small, narrow-minded. Nǐ-rúguǒ-bùlǐ-ta, nà-jiù-xiǎnde-xiǎoqi-le. 你 如 果 不 理 他, 那 就 顯 得 小 氣 了. If you don't talk to him, it would be petty of you. (3) unstylish, gaudy. Tāde-jiāju hěn-xiǎoqi. 他 的 傢 俱 很 小 氣. His furniture doesn't have any style at all. (4) undignified, not poised. Tā-jiǎngyǎn-de-shihou, yàngzi bu-xiǎoqi. 他 講 演 的 時 候 樣 子 不 小 氣. When he gives a speech, he is poised in manner.

XIĀOQIAN₄ 消 遣 (IV) amuse oneself, have fun. Zuǒ! zánmen-qù-'xiāoqian-xiāoqian-qu. 走 ! 咱 們 去 消 遣 消 遣 去. Let's go to have some fun. Nín-cháng-zuò-shénma-xiāo-qian? 您 常 作 甚 麼 消 遣 ? What do you do to amuse yourself?

(N) amusement. Zhèi-shì-wǒde-xiāoqian. 這 是 我 的 消 遣. This is my way of having fun.

XIĀORÉNRSHŪ₄ 小 人 兒 書 (N) comics, children's picture book. (M: běn 本).

XIĀOSHÈ₃ 校 舍 (N) school building.

XIĀOSHÍ₂ 小 時 (N) hour. (syn. zhōngtóu 鐘 頭 , zhōngdiǎnr 鐘 點 兒).yígebàn-xiāoshí 一 個 半 小 時 an hour and a half.

(M) hour. yìxiāoshibàn 一 小

時 半 an hour and a half.

XIĀOSHÒU₅ 銷 售 (TU) sell (in quantity). Zhèizhǒng-huò-bu-róngyi-xiāoshòu. 這 種 貨 不 容 易 銷 售. This type of goods is not easy to sell.

XIĀOSHUŌR₂ 小 說 兒 (N) novel, fiction. (M: běn 本 , bù 部). duǎn-piān xiǎshuǒr 短 篇 小 說 兒 short stories. xiě-xiǎoshuōr 寫 小 說 兒 write a novel.

XIĀOTIAO₄ 蕭 條 (SV) feeble, inactive, not lively. Zuìjìn-shì-chǎng-hen-xiāotiao. 最 近 市 場 很 蕭 條. The market has been at its low recently.

XIĀOTŌUR₄ 小 偷 兒 (N) sneak thief.

XIĀOXI₂ 消 息 (N) information, news. Yǒu-shénma-hǎo-xiāoxi? 有 甚 麼 好 消 息 ? What is the good news?

XIĀOXIN₁ 小 心 (TV) beware of, be careful of. xiǎoxin-huǒchē 小 心 火 車 beware of trains. (SV) careful. Tā-hěn-xiǎoxin. 他 很 小 心. He's quite careful.

(AD) carefully, with care. Nǐ-děi-xiǎoxin-guò-jiē. 你 得 小 心 過 街. You must cross the streets with care. (cf: LIÚ-SHÉN 留 神).

XIĀOXĪNYǍNR₃ 小 心 眼 兒 (SV) narrow-minded. Tā-xiǎoxīn-yǎnr, ni-shuō-ta bu-duì, ta-jiu-shēngqì. 他 小 心 眼 兒, 你 說 他 不 對 他 就 生 氣. He is narrow-minded. If you tell him he is wrong, he

X

becomes angry.

XIĂOXUÉ₁ 小學 (N) elementary school.

XIĀOYÈ₄ 消夜 (N) snack at night. (syn. yèxiāor 夜宵兒). chī-xiāoyè 吃消夜 have a midnight snack.

XIĂOYISI₂ 小意思 (N) a polite way of saying that one's help or gift is a trifle, token. Zhèi-shi-wŏde-yidianr-xiăoyisi. 這是我的一點兒小意思. This is only a token of my esteem.

XIÀOYUÁN₃ 校園 (N) campus.

XIÀOZHĂNG₂ 校長 (N) principal, president (of a school).

XIĂOZŬ₄ 小組 (N) group in an organization with a special assignment. yùnshū-xiăozŭ 運輸小組 transportation group.

XIÀ-PŌR₃ 下坡兒 (VO) go downhill. zŏu-xià-pōr-lù 走下坡兒路 lit. or fig. go downhill.

XIÀQU₁ 下去 (RV) (1) go down. Nǐ-xiàqu-kànkan. 你下去看看. You go down and take a look. (2) continue, go on. Zhào-zhèiyangr-xiàqu, hăobu-liăo. 照這樣下去, 好不了. If it goes on like this, it cannot be good. Wŏ-kàn tā-jiu-zhèiyangr-xiàqu-le. 我看他就這樣兒下去了. I think he'll go on like this.

(RE) (1) down (there). náxiaqu 拿下去 take it down there.

rēngxiaqu 扔下去 throw it down there. (2) continue, go on. Nǐ-kànxiaqu-jiu-míngbai-le. 你看下去就明白了. If you read on, you'll understand it. Huà-shuōdao-zhèr, tā-jiu-shuōbuxiàqù-le. 話說到這兒, 他就說不下去了. When he spoke up to this point, he couldn't go on.

XIÀR₂ 下兒 or **XIÀZI** 下子 (M) time, instance of movement. Tā-dăle-wo-liăngxiàr. 他打了我兩下兒 He gave me a couple blows. (See: YÍXIÀR 一下兒).

XIÀ-SHŎU₃ 下手 (VO) take action, make a move. Bié-zhāo-jí, děng-ta-jìnqule zai-xià-shŏu. 別着急. 等他進去了再下手. Don't be impatient, wait until he goes in and then we'll get him. (cf: DÒNG-SHŎU 動手).

XIÀ-SHUĀNG₄ 下霜 (VO) have frost.

XIĀSHUŌ₂ 瞎說 (IV) talk nonsense, say something without foundation. (syn. húshuō 胡說). Tā-lăo-ài-xiāshuō. 他老愛瞎說. He likes to talk nonsense all the time.

XIÀ-TÁI₃ 下台 (VO) (1) get off or down from the stage or platform. Tā-chàng-de bu-hăo xià-tái-jiu-kū. 她唱的不好, 下台就苦. She sang badly, she cried when she came off the stage. (2) step down from official or public life. (syn. xià-yě 下

野). Tā-shòule-huìluo, rén-jia-bīzhe-ta-xià-tái. 他受了賄賂, 人家逼着他下台. He took bribes, people forced him to step down from public life. (3) get out of an embarrassing situation. Bié-ràng-ta-tài-buhǎoyìsi, děi-xiǎng-fázi ràng-ta-xià-tái. 別讓他太不好意思 得想法子讓他下台. Don't embarrass him too much. We have to find a way for him to get out.

XIÀTIAN₁ 夏天 (TW) the summer. Wǒ-lǎo-wàngbuliǎo-qùnian-de-xìatian. 我老忘不了 去年的夏天. I can never forget last summer. Xià-tian-hǎibiānr-rén-hěn-duō. 夏天海邊兒人很多. There are a lot of people on the beach in the summer.

XIÀTOU₁ 下頭 see XIÀBIANR 下邊兒.

XIÀWEIYÍ₃ 夏威夷 (PW) Hawaii.

XIÀWU₁ 下午 (TW) afternoon. Xiàwu-bǐ-shàngwu-cháng. 下 午比上午長. The afternoon is longer than the morning. Wǒmen-xiàwu-qù-ba! 我們下午去吧! Let's go in the afternoon!

XIÀ-WÙ₄ 下霧 (VO) be foggy.

XIÀXIÀ₃ 下下 (SP) the month or week after next. xiàxiàyuè 下下月 the month after next month.

XIÀ-XIÀNG₂ 下鄉 (VO) go to the country. Tā-yòu-xià-xiāng-qu-le. 他又下鄉去了 He went to the country again.

XIÀ(GE)XĪNGQĪ₁ 下(個)星期 or XIÀ(GE)LĪBÀI 下(個)禮 拜 (TW) next week. Wǒmen-xiàxīngqī-qù. 我們下星 期去. We'll go next week.

XIÀ-XUÉ₁ 下學 (VO) get out of class.

XIÀ-XUĚ₂ 下雪 (VO) snow.

XIÀ(GE)XUÉQĪ₁ 下(個)學期 (N) next semester, next term.

XIÀ-YĚ₄ 下野 (lit. go down to wilderness) step down from official or public life. (syn. xià-tái 下台). Xīn-zhèngdǎng yí-shàng-tái, ta-jiu-xià-yě-le. 新 政黨上台他就下 野了. As soon as the new party(political) came into power, he stepped down.

XIÀ-YITIÀO₂ 嚇一跳 (VO) (lit. scared to a jump) startled. Tā-xiàle-wo-yitiào. 他嚇了 我一跳. He scared me. Wǒ-xiàle-yitiào. 我嚇了 一跳. I was startled.

XIÀ-YǓ₁ 下雨 (VO) rain.

XIÀ(GE)YUE₁ 下(個)月 (TW) next month. Xiàyuè-shì-sìyuè. 下月是四月. Next month is April. Tā-xiàyue-lái. 他下月來. He is coming next month.

XIÀ-ZÀNG₅ 下葬 (VO) be buried. Tā-hái-méi-xià-zàng-ne. 他 還没下葬呢. He has not been buried yet.

X

XIÀ-ZHǑNGZI₃ 下種子 (VO) seed, plant seeds. Xiàle-zhǒng-zi jǐ'tiān-jiu-zhǎngchulai. 下了種子幾天就長出來. Shoots will come out a few days after seeding.

XIĀZI₃ 瞎子 (N) blind person.

XIÁZI₄ 匣子 (N) small box.

XIÀZI₂ 下子 see XIÀR 下兒.

XĪBANYA₂ 西班牙 (PW) Spain.

XĪBĚI₂ 西北 (L) northwest. Zhōngguó-xīběi 中國西北 northwest of China.

XĪBIANR₁ 西邊兒 (PW) west, west side, west part of. Jiùjin-shān zài-Měiguode-xībianr. 舊金山在美國的西邊兒. San Francisco is in the western part of America. Nèige-pùzi zài-xībianr. 那個鋪子在西邊兒. That store is west (of here).

'XĪBÓ₅ 稀薄 (SV) be thin (of air). Kōngqì-'xībó. 空氣稀薄 The air is thin.

XĪCĀN₃ 西餐 (N) western style meal. (M: dùn 頓).

XĪDÉ₂ 西德 (PW) West Germany.

XIĒ₁ 些 (NU) used with or without a M before a N, several, some. zhèi-xie(zhāng)-zhǐ 這些張紙 these sheets of paper. Jiā-li láile-xie(wei)-kèren. 家裏來了'些 (位) 客人. Some guests came to my home. Guò-xie(ge)-rìzi zai-shuō-ba. 過些 (個) 日子再說吧. We'll talk about it after several days.

(M) usually the number which precedes it is yī 一. (1) used after a SV, a little. (syn. diǎnr 點兒). Wǒ-jīntian juéde-hǎo-(yi)xie. 我今天覺得好 (一) 些. I feel a little better today. Zhèige-dà-(yi)xie. 這個大 (一) 些. This is little bigger. (2) indicates an indefinite amount. Tā-shuōle-yi-dà-xiē. 他說了一大些. He said quite a lot. used between a S P (yi) and a M, many, much. Zhèi(yi) xiē(-ge)-péngyou dōu-yào-bāng-máng. 這 (一) 些 (個) 朋友都要幫忙. All these friends want to help. Zènma-xiē(-ge) jiu-gòu-le. 這麼些 (個) 就够了. This much will be enough. Tā-zěnma-yǒu-nènma-xiē(-ge)-qián? 他怎麼有那麼些 (個) 錢? How come he has that much money?

XIĒ₂ 歇 (IV) rest. Ràng-wǒ-xiē-yihuir-ba! 讓我歇一會吧! Let me rest for a while!

XIÉ₃ 斜 (SV) slanted, tilted. (opp. zhèng 正). Zhèige-fángzi xié-le. 這個房子斜了. This house is tilted. Tāde-zhuōzi xié-zhe-fàngzhe. 他的桌子斜着放着. His desk has been placed on an angle. (RE) slanted. Wǒ-bǎ-xiàn-huà-xié-le. 我把線畫斜了. I made a slanted line.

XIÉ₂ 鞋 (N) shoe. (M: zhǐ 隻, shuāng 雙).

X

XIĚ₁ 血 _or_ XUĚ 血 (N) blood. liú-xiě 流血 bleed.

XIĚ₁ 寫 (TV) write, describe _in_ writing. xiě-zì 寫字 write (characters _or_ words). xiě-shū 寫書 write a book. Tā-lián-tāde-míngzi dōu-bu-huì-xiě. 他連他的名子都不會寫. He doesn't even know how to write his name.

XIÈ₁ 謝 (TV) thank. Wǒ-méi-bāng-shenme-máng, bié-xiè-wǒ. 我沒幫甚麼忙,別謝我. I didn't help you much, don't thank me for it.

(IV) fade, wither. Huār-yǐjing-xiè-le. 花兒已經謝了. The flowers have already withered.

XIÈ₃ 卸 (TV) (1) unload. xiè-huò 卸貨 unload the goods. (2) unhitch _an animal from a cart._ xiè-chē 卸車 unhitch the animal from the cart _or_ unload the cart. (3) get rid of, throw off. xiè-zérèn 卸責任 avoid responsibility. (4) dismantle. Děi-bǎ-lúnzi zièxialai. 得把輪子卸下來. We have to take off the wheel.

XIÈDAI₄ 懈怠 (SV) listless, lazy. Tā-lǎo-nènme-xièdai. 他老那麼懈怠. He's always listless like that.

XIÉDÌNG₅ 協定 (N) agreement. jūnzǐ-xiédìng 君子協定 gentlemen's agreement.

XIÉLÌ₅ 協力 (AD) do something together, jointly, in joint effort. Wǒmen-xiélì-bǎ-nèijian-shì-

zuòhǎo. 我們協力把那件事做好. Let's work together and do it well.

XIÉPŌR₄ 斜坡兒 (N) slope.

XIÈ-QÌ₃ 洩氣 (VO) lose one's spirit _or_ drive. Tāmen-yòu-xiè-le-qì-le. 他們又洩了氣了. They lost their drive again.

(SV) fail to live up to expectations, resulting in disappointment, disappointing.

XIÉSHĀNG₅ 協商 (TV) discuss something together _in a formal way._ Tāmen-zhèng-xiéshāng-juān-qián-de-shì-ne. 他們正協商捐錢的事呢. They are discussing the matter of raising money.

(N) mutual agreement.

XIĚ-SHĒNG₃ 寫生 (VO) draw, sketch living objects.

XIĚSHÍ₄ 寫實 (SV) realistic (_of_ writing). Nèiběn-xiǎoshuōr hěn-xiěshí. 那本小說很寫實. That novel is realistic.

XIÈXIE₁ 謝謝 (TV) thank. Nǐ-děi-xièxie-wo. 你得謝謝我. You should thank me. Xièxie-xiexie. 謝謝謝謝. Thanks a million.

XIĒ-YÈ₃ 歇業 (VO) go out of business. Nèige-pùzi-xiē-yè-le. 那個鋪子歇業了. That store went out of business.

XIĚYÌ₄ 寫意 (VO) portray the idea leaving the details out (a type of Chinese painting). Tā-huà-de-huàr shi-xiěyì. 他畫的畫兒是寫意. The

X

X

picture he painted is the type that leaves out the details.
(SV) pleasant, fun. Kāi-chǎng-péngr-qìchē hen-xiěyì. 開敞蓬兒汽車很寫意. It's fun to drive a convertible.

XIĒZI₄ 蝎子 (N) scorpion. (M: zhī 隻).

XĪFÀN₄ 稀飯 (N) porridge. (syn. zhōu 粥). chī-xīfàn 吃稀飯 eat porridge.

XĪFĀNG₃ 西方 (N) the West, western world.

XÌFĂR₃ 戲法兒 (N) magician's trick. biàn-xìfăr 變戲法兒 perform a trick. Tāde-xì-făr biànlòu-le. 他戲法兒變漏了. lit. or fig. His trick was seen through.

XĪFÚ₁ 西服 (N) western style clothing. (syn. yángfú 洋服). (M: jiàn 件, tào 套).

XÍFU₃ 媳婦 (N) (1) daughter-in-law. (2) wife (old term). qǔ-xífu 娶媳婦 take a wife or have a son marry. (3) young married woman. (cf: TÀITAI 太太).

XĪGUA₃ 西瓜 (N) watermelon.

XÍGUAN₁ 習慣 (SV) be accustomed to, be used to. Zhèi-zhong-de-shēnghuo wǒ-yǐjing-xíguan-le. 這種的生活我已經習慣了. I'm already used to this kind of life. (N) habit. yǎngcheng-xíguan 養成習慣 develop a habit.

XĪHAN₄ 希罕 (lit. rare and scare) (SV) rare, uncommon. Zhèizhong-shítou búshi-shénma-xīhande-dōngxi. 這種石頭不是甚麼希罕的東西. This kind of stone is not a very rare thing. (TV) care about something which may be considered a rare item. Wǒ-bu-xīhan-tāde-lǐwù. 我不希罕他的禮物. I don't care about his gift.

XĪHÓNGSHÌ₃ 西紅柿 (N) tomato.

XĪHÚ₃ 西湖 (PW) West Lake.

XĪHUAN₁ 喜歡 or HUĀNXI 歡喜 (TV) like. Wǒ-xǐhuan-ni. 我喜歡你. I like you. (AV) like to. Tā-xǐhuan-chàng-gēr. 他喜歡唱歌兒. He likes to sing. (SV) glad, happy. Tā-xīnli-hěn-xǐhuan. 他心裏很喜歡. He is very happy (in his heart).

XÌJÙ₃ 戲劇 (N) play, drama, musical, opera.

XĪKĀNG₃ 西康 (PW) Sikang province.

XĪLA₅ 錫鑞 or XĪ 錫 (N) (1) tin. (2) pewter. (3) solder.

XĪLÀ₃ 希臘 (PW) Greece.

XĪLÌ₃ 吸力 (N) force of attraction (of a magnet, interest or someone's personality).

XĪN₁ 心 (N) (1) heart. (M: kē 顆). Tā-xīn-tiào-de-hěn-kuài. 他心跳得很快. His heart is beating very fast. Tāde-xīn-huài-le. 他的心壞了. lit. or fig. He has a bad heart. (2) mind. (M: tiáo 條). Wǒmen-liǎngge-ren shì-yìtiáo-xīn. 我們兩

個人是一條心. We two are of the same mind. Nǐ-xīnli yǒu-shénme-shì? 你心裏有甚麼事? What's on your mind? Wǒ-méi-bǎ-ta-fàngzai-xīnshang. 我没把他放在心上. She's not on my mind. or I don't think of her. Wǒ-xīnli-xiǎng. 我心裏想 I think (in my mind). Nèige-rén-méi-xīn. 那個人没心. He doesn't think much (in his mind). (3) intention. Tā-méi-xīn-zuò-shì. 他没心作事. He has no intention of working.

XĪN₁ 新 (SV) new, not used. (opp. jiù 舊, lǎo 老). Wǒ-zhèitào-yīshang-hen-xīn. 我這套衣裳很新. These clothes of mine are quite new. (AD) newly, recently. Tāde-màozi-shì-xīn-mǎi-de. 他的帽子是新買的. He bought his hat recently.

XÌN₁ 信 (TV) (1) believe, trust. Wǒ-buxìn-nèige-xiāoxi. 我不信那個消息. I don't believe that news. (2) believe in. Nǐ-xìn-shénme-jiào? 你信甚麼教? What religion do you you believe in?

XÌN₁ 信 (N) letter. (M: fēng 封). jì-xìn 寄信 mail a letter.

XĪNÁN₂ 西南 (L) southwest.

XĪNBÌNG₃ 心病 (N) worry, problem (in one's mind). (M: kuài 塊). Tāde-háizi shì-tāde-xīnbìng. 他的孩子是他的心病. His child is

his worry.

XĪNCHÁNG₃ 心腸 (N) heart, inner feelings. Tāde-'xīncháng hěn-ruǎn. 他的心腸很軟. He is soft-hearted.

XÌNFĒNGR₁ 信封兒 (N) envelope.

XÌN-FÓ₄ 信佛 (VO) believe in Buddha.

XĪNG₃ 腥 (SV) smell of fish or raw meat. Zhèitiáo-yú yìdiǎnr-dou-buxīng. 這條魚一點都不腥. This fish doesn't smell at all.

XÍNG₁ 行 (SV) (1) O.K., all right, satisfactory. (syn. chéng 成). Néng-xíng. 能行. It can be all right. Zhèiyangr-bàn xíngbuxíng? 這樣兒辦行不行? Is it all right to do it this way? (2) capable. Nǐ-dìdi zhēn-xíng. 你弟弟真行. Your younger brother is really capable. (3) ready. Chá-xíng-le. 茶行了. The tea is ready.

XǏNG₂ 醒 (IV) (1) wake up. Wǒ-tiāntian-qīdianzhong-xǐng. 我天天七點鐘醒. I wake up at seven o'clock everyday. (2) become sober, sober up. Gāngcái-tā-zuìle, xiànzài-xǐngle. 剛才他醉了, 現在醒了. He was drunk a moment ago, now he is sober. (RE) wake someone up by the action indicated by the preceding verb. Tā-qīdian-zhong jiu-bǎ-wǒ-jiàoxǐng-le. 他七點鐘就把我叫醒了. He woke me up as early as seven o'clock.

X

Tāmen-chàng-gēr bǎ-wǒ-chàng-
xǐng-le. 他們唱歌兒
把我唱醒了. They
woke me up by singing.

XÌNG₁ 姓 (TV) be surnamed. Tā-
xìng-Wáng. 他姓王. His
surname is Wang.

(N) surname. Nǚren jié-le-hūn
xìng-jiu-gǎi-le. 女人結了
婚姓就改了. When a
girl gets married her surname
will be changed.

XÌNG₂ 性 used as a suffix to form
a noun. (1) nature of. zhèngzhi-
xìng 政治性 in the nature of
politics. (2) capacity, power.
kěnéngxìng 可能性 possibil-
ity.

(B) (1) nature, innate quality,
temperament (of people). gèxìng
個性 individual character.(2)
sex. xìng-jiàoyu 性教育
sex education.

XÌNGDONG₃ 行動 (N) action,
move, movement. Tāde-xíng-
dong-bu-zìyóu. 他的行動
不自由. His actions are
not free.

XÌNG'ÉR₂ 幸而 (MA) fortu-
nately. (syn. xìngkuī 幸虧).
Xìng'ér-tā-méi-lái. 幸而他
沒來. Fortunately he didn't
come.

'XÍNGFÁ₄ 刑罰 (N) punishment,
torture. (M: zhǒng 種). shòu-
xíngfá 受刑罰 receive pun-
ishment or be tortured.

XĪNGFÈN₂ 興奮 (SV) be excited.
Nǐ-bié-tài-xīngfèn-le. 你別
太興奮了. Don't be too

excited.

XÌNGFU₂ 幸福 happy (of life
because of good fortune). Nǐde-
jiāting-shēnghuo bǐ-wǒ xìngfu-
duōle. 你的家庭生活
比我幸福多了. Your
family life is much happier than
mine.

XÌNGGÉ₅ 性格 (N) character of
a person.

XÌNGJÍ₂ 性急 (SV) hasty in nature, fast-moving. Tā-yi-tīng-
shuō, jiu-yào-qù. Zhēn-xìngjí.
他一聽說,就要去.
真性急. As soon as he
heard it, he wanted to go. He is
really fast-moving.

XÌNGKUĪ₂ 幸虧 (MA) fortunately.
(syn. xìng'ér 幸而). Xìngkuī-
wǒ-mǎi-le. 幸虧我買了.
Fortunately I bought it.

XÍNGLI₂ 行李 (N) luggage, baggage. (M: jiàn 件).

XÍNG-LǏ₂ 行禮 (VO) (1) perform
a courtesy, salute. Nèige-jǐng-
chá duì-wǒ-xínglè-yíge-lǐ. 那
個警察對我行了
一個禮. That policeman
saluted me. (2) hold a ceremony.
Nǐmen-shénme-shíhou-xíng-bì-
yè-lǐ? 你們甚麼時候
行畢業禮? What time is
your commencement being held?

XÌNGMING₃ 性命 (N) life. Wǒ-
jiùshi-bǎ-xìngming-xīshēngle, yě-
bu-hòuhuǐ. 我就是把性
命犧牲了,也不後
悔. Even if I have to sacrifice
my life, I won't regret it.

XÌNGMÍNG₃ 姓名 (N) full name.

X

XĪNGQĪ₁ 星期 or LĬBÀI 禮拜 (N) week. xiàliǎngge-xīngqī 下兩個星期 next two weeks. (TW) Sunday. Jīntian-xīngqī. 今天星期 . Today is Sunday. (cf: XĪNGQĪTIĀN 星期天 , XĪNGQĪRÌ 星期日). (SP) <u>used with numbers one to six, indicates the sequence of days in a week.</u> xīngqīyī 星期一 (lit. first day of a week) Monday.

XĪNGQĪ'ÈR₁ 星期二 or LĬBÀI'ÈR 禮拜二 (TW) Tuesday.

XĪNGQĪJĬ₁ 星期幾 or LĬBÀI-JĬ 禮拜幾 (TW) which day of the week. Jīntian-xīngqījǐ? 今天星期幾 ? Which day of the week is today?

XĪNGQĪLIÙ₁ 星期六 or LĬ-BÀILIÙ 禮拜六 (TW) Saturday.

XÌNGQÍNG₂ 性情 (N) temperament, disposition. (cf: PÍQI 脾氣).

XĪNGQĪRÌ₁ 星期日 or LĬBÀI-RÌ 禮拜日 (TW) Sunday. Xīngqīrì-méiyǒu-xīngqīliù-hǎo. 星期日沒有星期六好 . Sunday is not as good as Saturday. Tā-zhèige-xīngqī-rì-lái. 他這個星期日來 . He will come this Sunday. (cf: XĪNGQĪ 星期 , XĪNGQĪ-TIĀN 星期天).

XĪNGQĪSĀN₁ 星期三 or LĬ-BÀISĀN 禮拜三 (TW) Wednesday.

XĪNGQĪSÌ₁ 星期四 or LĬBÀI-SÌ 禮拜四 (TW) Thursday.

XĪNGQĪTIĀN₁ 星期天 or LĬ-BÀITIĀN 禮拜天 (TW) Sunday. (cf: XĪNGQĪ 星期 , XĪNG-QĪRÌ 星期日).

XĪNGQĪWǓ₁ 星期五 or LĬ-BÀIWǓ 禮拜五 (TW) Friday.

XĪNGQĪYĪ₁ 星期一 or LĬBÀI-YĪ 禮拜一 (TW) Monday.

XÌNGQU₁ 興趣 (N) interest. Tā-duì-shénme dou-méiyou-xìngqu. 他對甚麼都沒有興趣 . He has no interest in anything.

XÌNGR₄ 杏兒 (N) apricot.

XÍNGRONG₃ 形容 (TV) describe. Nǐ-xíngrong-xíngrong tā-zhǎng-de-shénme-yàngr. 你形容形容他長的甚麼樣兒 . Please describe what he looks like. Wǒ-xíngrong-bu-chulái. 我形容不出來 . I cannot describe it.

XÍNGSHÌ₂ 形式 (N) (1) external form. Xíngshì-hen-hǎokàn. 形式很好看 . The form is very pretty. (2) formality. Nà-buguò-shi-yizhong-xíngshi. 那不過是一種形式 . That is only a kind of formality.

XÍNGTÀI₅ 形態 (N) shape, form (abstract).

XĪNGWÀNG₃ 興旺 (SV) prosperous and flourishing. Zhèige-dì-fangde-'shāngyè jìnlái-hěn-xīng-wang. 這個地方的商業近來很興旺 . The commerce here has been very prosperous recently.

X

XÍNGWEI₃ 行為 (N) conduct, behavior. Tāde-xíngwei bu-zhèngdang. 他的行為不正當. His behavior is not what it should be.

XĬNGWU₃ 省悟 (IV) find one's own error, realize something done by oneself is wrong. Tā-yǐjing-xǐngwu-le. 他已經省悟了. He realized he was wrong in the past.

XĪNGXING₂ 星星 (N) star. (M: kē 顆).

XÍNGZHÈNG₃ 行政 (N) administration. xíngzhèng-rényuán 行政人員 administrative personnel.

XÌNGZHI₁ 性質 (N) nature, property of something. Nǐde-gōng-zuo shì-shénme-xìngzhi? 你的工作是甚麼性質? What's the nature of your work?

'XÍNGZHUÀNG₄ 形狀 (N) shape, appearance, form.

XÌNGZI₂ 性子 (N) nature of a person. Tāde-xìngzi-hěn-jí. 他的性子很急. He has a very fast-moving nature.

XÌNHAO₃ 信號 (N) signal. dǎ-xìnhao 打信號 send a signal.

XĪNHĚN₃ 心狠 (SV) be hard-hearted, merciless. Zhèige-rén-xīnhěn, jiàn-sǐ-bu-jiù. 這個人心狠,見死不救. This person is hard-hearted, he sees somebody about to die but won't save him.

XĪNHUĀNG₃ 心慌 (SV) nervous, restless, uneasy. Jǐngchá-lái-de-shíhou wǒ-hěn-xīnhuāng. 警察來的時候我很心慌. I was very uneasy when the police came.

XĪNJÍ₂ 心急 (SV) impatient, excited. Bié-xīnjí, jiu-lúndao-nǐ-le. 別心急,就輪到你了. Be patient, it will be your turn soon.

XĪNJIĀNG₃ 新疆 (PW) Sinkiang province.

XÌN-JIÀO₂ 信教 (VO) believe in a religion. Nǐ-xìn-jiào-ma? 你信教嗎? Do you believe in any religion?

XĪNJIĀPŌ₂ 新加坡 (PW) Singapore.

XĪNJÌLÙ₅ 新紀錄 (N) new record (of accomplishment). zào-xīnjìlù 造新紀錄 set a new record.

XĪNKU₂ 辛苦 (SV) toilsome, tiring. Tā-zhèijinian, zuòle-zèn-ma-duōde-shì, hěn-xīnku. 他這幾年,作了這麼多的事,很辛苦. He's done so much work these past few years, it's been very tiring for him.

(N) hardship, toil. Tā-bùzhīdào-xīnku. 他不知道辛苦. He doesn't know what toil is.

(IV) (1) a friendly remark to a person who has just done some kind of work. Xīnku-xīnku. 辛苦辛苦. You must be tired. (2) take the trouble to go somewhere. Nín-xīnku-yitàng-ba. 您辛苦一趟吧. Please (take the trouble to) go there once.

ĪNLÁNG₂ 新郎 (N) bridegroom. (M: wèi 位).

ĪNLĬ₂ 心理 (N) (1) psychology. xīnlixuéjiā 心理學家 psychologist.(2) intention, way of thinking. Shéi-yě-bu-míngbai-tā-de-xīnlĭ. 誰也不明白他的心理. No one understands his intention.

ĪNNIÁN₁ 新年 (TW) New Year's Day. Jīntian-shi-xīnnián. 今天是新年. Today is New Year's Day. (N) new year. yíngjiē-xīnnián 迎接新年 welcome a new year. guò-xīnnián 過新年 celebrate the new year.

ĪNNIÁNG(ZI)₂ 新娘(子)(N) bride. (M: wèi 位).

ĪNQÍNG₃ 心情 (N) feeling, mood. Wǒ-xīnqing-butài-hǎo. 我心情不太好. My mood is not too good. Wǒ-méi-you-nèige-xīnqing. 我沒有那個心情 I am not in the mood.

XÌNR₃ 信兒 (N) message, news. Bié-wàngle-tì-wǒ-dài-yíge-xìnr-qu. 別忘了替我帶一個信兒去. Don't forget to take along a message for me.

XÌNREN₂ 信任 (TV) trust. Wǒ-xìnren-ta. 我信任他. I trust him. (N) trust. Wǒ-débuzháo tāde-xìnren. 我得不着他的信任. I cannot gain his trust.

'XĪNSHÌ₂ 新式 (SV) fashionable, modern. Tāmende-fāngfǎ hěn-xīnshì. 他們的方法很新式. Their method is very modern.

'XĪNSHÌ₃ 心事 (N) matters in one's heart, what one cares about. Tā-yǒu-hěn-duō-'xīnshì. 他有很多心事. There are a lot of things on his mind. Tā-xiǎng-'xīnshì-ne. 他想心事呢. He is thinking about his cares.

XĪNSHǑUR₄ 新手兒 (N) (lit. new hand) inexperienced worker.

XĪNSHUI₃ 薪水 (N) salary. jiā-xīnshui 加薪水 increase the salary.

XĪNSI₄ 心思 (N) mind, manner of thought. Tāde-xīnsi hěn-xì. 他的心思很細. She has a keen mind.

XÍN-SĬ₄ 尋死 (VO) attempt or commit suicide. Tā-lǎo-xiǎng-xín-sĭ. 他老想尋死. He's always thinking of committing suicide.

XĪNTÉNG₃ 心疼 (TV) be deeply distressed about a loved one. Wǒ-hěn-xīnteng-ta. 我很心疼他. I feel distressed about him.

XĪNTÉNG₃ 心疼 (SV) painful, distressed. Jiāo-shuì tā-jiu-xīnténg. 交稅他就心疼. It pains him to pay taxes.

XÌNTǑNGZI₄ 信筒子 (N) mailbox (in the form of a cylinder).

XĪNWÉN₁ 新聞 (N) news. (M: piān 篇, duàn 段).

XĪNXĬ₂ 新禧 used for New Year

X

greetings, Happy New Year.

XĪNXIAN₁ 新鮮 (SV) (1) fresh
(of air, fruits, flowers, meat,
etc.). (2) refreshingly new (in
style). (3) strange, odd. Tā-
dāngle shìzhǎng le, nǐ shuō
xīnxian-buxīnxian. 他當了
市長了，你說新鮮
不新鮮 Don't you think
it's strange, he is the mayor
now. (cf: XIĀN 鮮).

XĪNXIǍNG₃ 心想 (TV) think,
consider. Tā-xīnxiǎng jèiyàngr-
jiù-hǎo-le. 他心想這
樣兒就好了. He
thought that it would be better
this way. (cf: XIǍNG 想).

XÌNXIĀNG₃ 信箱 (N) mailbox.

XÌNXĪN₃ 信心 (N) faith, confidence.

XĪNXŪ₃ 心虛 (SV) uneasy about
something being found out. Yīn-
wei-jǐngchá-láile, suóyi tā-hěn-
xīnxū. 因為警察來了，
所以他很心虛. He's
very uneasy because the policemen came.

'XÌNYǍNG₃ 信仰 (TV) believe,
have faith in a religion, principle. Tā-'xìnyǎng-yìzhong-hěn-
qíguàide-zōngjiào. 他信仰
一種很奇怪的宗
教. He believes in a very
strange religion.
(N) faith, belief. Tāde-xìnyǎng-
hěn-shēn. 他的信仰很
深. His faith is very deep.

XĪNYǍNR₃ 心眼兒 (N) (1)
mind (able to work in several
different directions). Tā-xīn-

yǎnr-hen-duō. 他心眼兒
很多. His mind has many
facets. (2) intentions. Tā-méi-
ānzhe-hǎo-xīnyǎnr. 他沒安
着好心眼兒. He didn't
have good intentions. (3) intelli-
gence, power of comprehension.
Tā-méi-xīnyǎnr. 他沒心
眼兒. He isn't intelligent.

XÌNYONG₂ 信用 (N) credit,
trustworthiness. Tāde-'xìnyong-
buhǎo. 他的信用不好.
His credit is not good. Zhèige-
ren-méi-xìnyong. 這個人
沒信用. This man is not
trustworthy.

XÌNYUÀN₄ 心願 (N) wish, de-
sire. Zhè-suànshi-huánle-wǒde-
xīnyuan-le. 這算是還了
我的心願了. This can
be considered a fulfillment of my
desire.

XĪNZÀNG₄ 心臟 (N) heart (the
organ). (M: kē 顆). xīnzàng-
bìng 心臟病 heart disease.

XÌNZHǏ₁ 信紙 (N) letter-writing
paper, stationery. (M: zhāng
張).

XIÓNG₃ 兇 (SV) (1) severe, fierce.
Nǐ-buyào-duì-wǒ-zhènme-xiōng.
你不要對我這麽
兇. Don't you be so severe
with me. Lǎohǔ hěn-xiōng. 老
虎很兇. Tigers are very
fierce. Tāmen yuè-chǎo-yuè-
xiōng. 他們越吵越兇
The more they argue the more
severe it gets. (2) stern. Tāde-
yàngzi hěn-xiōng, kěshi-xīnli
bìng-bú-lìhai. 他的樣子

很凶,可是心裏並不利害. His appearance is very stern, but he is not hard-hearted inside. (3) strong (of liquor or tobacco). Zhèige-jiǔ hěn-xiōng. 這個酒很凶. This wine is very strong. (cf: LÌHAI 利害).

XIÓNG₄ 熊 (N) bear. (M: zhǐ 隻).

XIŌNGDÌ₃ 兄弟 (N) (1) younger brother. (2) a polite form used by a male to refer to himself, usually in a public speech, I, me.

XIŌNG'È₅ 凶惡 (SV) cruel, brutal, evil.

XIŌNGFÀN₅ 凶犯 (N) criminal.

XIŌNGHĚN₅ 凶狠 (SV) evil and cruel.

XIŌNGKǑU₅ 胸口 (N) center part of the chest.

XIŌNGPÚR₅ 胸脯兒 (N) breast, chest.

XIŌNGSHǑU₃ 凶手 (N) murderer.

XIŌNGYALÌ₃ 匈牙利 (PW) Hungary.

XIÓNGZHUÀNG₅ 雄壯 (SV) (1) strong, robust (of people). (2) lusty, spirited (of songs, poems, speeches).

XĪQÍ₃ 希奇 (SV) rare, strange, uncommon.

XÍQÌ₃ 習氣 (N) habit considered bad by another society. Tā-yǒu-hen-duō-xíqì. 他有很多習氣. He has a lot of bad habits.

XĪQIAO₄ 喜鵲 (N) magpie. (M: zhǐ 隻).

'XĪSHǍO₄ 稀少 (SV) scarce, sparse. Zhèrde-shù hěn-'xīshǎo. 這兒的樹很稀少. Trees are very sparse in this area.

XĪSHĒNG₂ 犧牲 (TV) sacrifice. Wǒ-jué-bùhuì-xīshēng-wǒmende-yuánzé-de. 我決不會犧牲我們的原則的. I will never sacrifice our principles.

(N) sacrifice. Zuò-zhèiyàngrde-shì shì-yizhǒng-xīshēng. 作這樣兒的事是一種犧牲. To do this kind of thing is a kind of sacrifice.

XĪSHÌ₂ 喜事 (N) happy occasion (wedding, birth of a child, etc.). (M: jiàn 件).

XĪSHǑU₃ 吸收 (TV) (1) lit.or fig. absorb. Tāmen-néng-xīshōu zènme-duō-gōngke-ma? 他們能吸收這麼多功課嗎? Can they absorb so many lessons? (2) take members into an organization. Tāmen-zhèng-xīshōu-xīnhuìyuán-ne. 他們正吸收新會員呢. They are now taking in new members.

XĪ-SHǑU₂ 洗手 (VO) (1) wash one's hands. Wǒ-qu-xíxi-shǒu. 我去洗洗手. lit. or fig. I'll go to wash my hands. (2) quit, wash one's hands of a criminal profession. Cóngqián-tā-zǒusī, xiànzài-xǐ-shǒu-búgàn-le. 從前他走私,現在洗手不幹了. Formerly he was a smuggler, but he has

X

nothing to do with it now. (cf:
JIĔ-SHŎUR 解手兒).

XÌTÁI₃ 戲台 (N) stage (for a
theatrical performance). (M:
zuò 座).

XÍTÍ₃ 習題 (N) exercise problem (in a textbook). (M: dào 道).
Tā-zuòle-wŭdao-xítí. 他作
了五道習題 . He did
five problems.

XÍTIĔSHÍ₄ 吸鐵石 (N) magnet.
(M: kuài 塊).

XÌTONG₂ 系統 (N) system, co-
herence, organization. xiāohua-
xìtong 消化系統 digestive
system. Tāde-sīxiang méi-you-
xìtong. 他的思想没有
系統 . There is no system
to his thought.(cf: ZHÌDU 制度).

XIŪ₂ 修 (TV) (l) build, erect.
Zhèngfŭ-zuìjìn-xiūle-yízuò-dà-
qiáo. 政府最近修了
一座大橋 . The govern-
ment built a big bridge recently.
(2) (con. xiūli 修理). repair.
xiū-biāo 修表 repair a watch.
xiū-fángzi 修房子 repair a
house or build a house.

XIŪ₃ 修 see XIĀO 削 .

XIŪ₄ 宿 (M) Peip. night. sāntian-
liăngxiŭ 三天兩宿 three
days and two nights.

XIÙ₄ 繡 (TV) embroider. Tā-xiù-
le-yige-zhĕntou. 她繡了
一個枕頭 . She embroi-
dered a pillow. Tā-xiùle-yìtiáo-
yú. 她繡了一條魚 .
She embroidered a pattern of a
fish. (cf: ZHĀ 札).

XIÙ₄ 銹 (SV) rusty, corroded.

Suŏ-xiù-le. 鎖銹了 . The
lock is rusty.
(N) rust. (M: céng 層). zhăng-
le-yicéng-xiù 長了一層
銹 (lit. grow a layer of rust)
become rusty.

XIŪBŬ₃ 修補 (TV) fix, repair
by darning or patching. Zhèijiàn-yīshang néng-xiūbŭ-ma?
這件衣服能修補
嗎 ? Can this dress be fixed?
xiūbŭ-pídài 修補皮帶
repair tires.

XIŪCHI₃ 羞恥 (N) shame. Tā-
buzhĭdao-xiūchi. 他不知
道羞恥 . He doesn't know
what shame is.

XIŪGĂI₃ 修改 (TV) alter, revise..
Zhèitào-yīshang shì-cáifeng-xiū-
găide. 這套衣裳是裁
縫修改的 . These clothes
were altered by a tailor. Nèi-
pian-wénzhang ta-xiūgăile-sāncì.
那篇文章他修改
了三次 . He revised that
article three times.

XIÙ-HUĀR₄ 繡花兒 (VO)
embroider with (flower) patterns.
Tā-zài-zhuōbushang-xiù-huār.
他在桌布上繡花
兒 . She embroidered the table
cloth with flower patterns.

XIŪLI₂ 修理 (TV) repair, fix.
Nĭ-huì-xiūli-qìchē-ma? 你會
修理汽車嗎 ? Can you
repair automobiles?

XIÙQI₄ 秀氣 (SV) refined, delicate (in looks). Tā-mèimei-
hĕn-xiùqi. 他妹妹很秀
氣 . His younger sister is very

refined.

XIŪXI₁ 休息 (IV) rest. Nǐ-xiū-xi-yìhuǐr-ba. 你 休息 一 會兒吧. You'd better rest for a while.
(N) rest. Wǒ-yíge-yuè méi-dé-xiūxi. 我 一 個 月 没 得 休息. I have not had any rest in a month.

XIŪYANG₃ 修養 (N) (1) cultivated quality of a person in dealing with difficult situations without becoming emotional. Mà-ta tā-ye-bu-shēng-qì. Tā-zhēn-yǒu-xiūyang. 罵 他 他 也 不 生氣, 他 真 有 修養. Even when he is cursed at he doesn't get angry, he really has cultivated control of his emotions. (2) cultivation in certain areas of learning. yìshu-xiūyang 藝術修養 cultivation in art.

'XIŪYǍNG₃ 休養 (IV) recuperate. Yīsheng-shuō tā-hái-děi-'xiūyǎng-sānge-yuè. 醫生説 他 還 得 休養 三 個 月. The doctor said that he needed three more months to recuperate.

XIŪZHÈNG₄ 修正 (TV) revise, edit, correct. Zhèipiān-wén-zhang qǐng-nin gěi-wǒ-'xiūzheng-xiūzheng. 這 篇 文章 請 您 給 我 修正 修正. Please revise this article for me.

XIÙZI₃ 袖子 (N) sleeve. (M: zhǐ 隻, duì 對).

XĪWANG₁ 希望 (TV) hope. Wǒ-

xīwang-dàjiā-dōu-qù. 我 希 望 大家 都 去. I hope everybody can go.
(AV) wish to, hope to. Wǒ-hěn-xīwang-qù. 我 很 希望 去. I'm really hoping to go.
(N) hope, wish. Tā-méi-you-xīwang-le. 他 没 有 希望 了. He is hopeless. or He has no hope anymore.

XÌXIN₂ 細心 (SV) careful, meticulous. 'Shéi-dou-bǐ-nǐ-xìxīn. 誰 都 比 你 細心. Everyone is more careful than you are.

'XĪYÁNG₂ 西洋 (B) European, Occidental. Xíyángrén 西洋 人 European (people).

XÌYUÁNZI₃ 戲園子 (N) theater. (M: jiā 家).

XĪZÀNG₃ 西藏 (PW) Tibet.

XĪ-ZǍO₁ 洗澡 (VO) take a bath. Tā-yíge-yuè cái-xǐ-yìhuí-zǎo. 他 一 個 月 才 洗 一 回 澡. He takes a bath only once a month.

XÌZHI₂ 細緻 (SV) refined, detailed (in workmanship). Zhèige-cháhú-hěn-xìzhi. 這 個 茶 壺 很 細緻. This teapot is very detailed. Tā-zuò-shì hěn-xìzhi. 他 作 事 很 細 緻. He goes into great detail in his work.

XŬ₂ 許 (TV) (1) permit, allow. bù-xǔ-chōu-yān 不 許 抽 烟 smoking is not allowed. Wǒ-yào-jiéhūn kěshi-jūnduì-bù-'xǔ-wǒ. 我 要 結婚, 可 是 軍 隊 不 許 我. I want to get

X

married, but the army doesn't allow me. Nǐ-bu-xǔ-chūqu. 你不許出去. You are not allowed to go out. (2) promise someone someone something. Wǒ-xǔle-wǒ-dìdi yíge-xīn-shǒubiǎo. 我許了我弟弟一個新手錶. I promised my kid brother a new wristwatch. (AD) (con. yěxǔ 也許). perhaps, probably. Tā-xǔ-zǒu-le. 他許走了. He probably has gone.

XÙ₄ 續 (TV) add to increase the amount. Zài-cháhúli xù-dianr-shuǐ. 在茶壺裏續點兒水. Add some more water to the teapot. Tā-shuōwánle, wǒ-you-xùle-jiju. 他說完了我又續了幾句. After he finished talking, I added a few remarks.

XÙ₄ 序 (N) introduction of a book. Wǒ-gěi-tade-shū xiě-yipian-xù. 我給他的書寫一篇序. I wrote an introduction for his book.

XUÁN₃ 懸 (IV) (1) hang, s spend. Nèige-diàndēng zài-kōngzhōng-xuánzhe-ne. 那個電燈在空中懸着呢. That light is suspended in mid-air. (2) undecided, unresolved. xuán'àn 懸案 undecided case. Nèijiàn-shì méi-juédìng, hái-xuánzhe-ne. 那件事沒決定, 還懸着呢. That matter hasn't been decided, it's still unresolved.

XUÁN₄ 險 (SV) dangerous. zhēn-

xuán 真險 really dangerous.

XUÁN₅ 玄 (SV) beyond the power of understanding, above reasoning, mysterious. Ràng-tā-yi-shuō, nà-kě-xuán-le. 讓他一說,那可玄了. When he said it, it was beyond everybody's comprehension.

XUǍN₂ 選 (TV) (1) (con. xuǎnzé 選擇). select, choose. (syn. tiāo 挑, jiǎn 撿). Nǐ-kéyi-suíbiàn-xuǎn-yige. 你可以隨便選一個. You can choose any one you want. Zhè-dōu-shi-biéren-xiǎnshèngxia-de. 這都是別人選剩下的. These are what were left over after the other people had selected. (2) (con. xuǎnjǔ 選舉). elect, vote for.

XUÀN₃ 現 see XIÀN 現.

XUĀNBÙ₃ 宣布 (TV) announce formally. Tāmen-xuānbù tāmen-shànglǐbài-yǐjìng-jié-hūn-le. 他們宣布他們上禮拜已經結婚了. They announced that they got married last week.

XUĀNCHUÁN₂ 宣傳 (TV) propagate, advertise, publicize. Diànshì-shang tiāntian-xuān-chuán-nèizhǒng-féizào. 電視上天天宣傳那種肥皂. That brand of soap is advertised on television every-day. Bié-xuānchuan-le. 別宣傳了. lit. or fig. Don't advertise it anymore. (N) propaganda, publicity. Nà-shi-xuānchuan, bié-xìn. 那是

X

宣傳，別信. That is prop-
aganda, don't believe it. Děi-
zuò-xuānchuan. 得作宣傳.
We have to work on publicity.
XUÀNFENG₄ 旋風 (N) whirl-
wind, tornado. (M: zhèn 陣).
XUǍNJǓ₂ 選舉 (TV) elect, select. Wǒmen-xuǎnjǔ-ta dāng-
zhǔxí. 我們選舉他當
主席. We'll elect him to
serve as chairman.
(N) election.
XUÁNMIÀO₅ 玄妙 (SV) myste-
riously wonderful.
XUǍNSHǑU₃ 選手 (N) athlete
selected to represent a group.
Tā-shì-wǒmen-xuéxiàode-xuǎn-
shǒu. 他是我們學校
的選手. He represents
our school.
XUÁNXU₅ 玄虛 (SV) unimagi-
nable. Nèijiàn-shì tài-xuánxu-le.
那件事太玄虛了.
That matter is beyond everybody's imagination.
XUĀNYÁN₃ 宣言 (N) declara-
tion. fā-xuānyán 發宣言
issue a declaration.
'XUǍNZÉ₂ 選擇 (TV) choose,
select. Nǐ-zìjǐ-'xuǎnzé-ba! 你
自己選擇吧! You'd
better choose by yourself!
(N) choice, selection. Zhè-shì-
wǒde-'xuǎnzé. 這是我的
選擇. This is my selection.
XǓDUŌ₂ 許多 (NU) used with
or without a M, many, much.
xǔduō(ge)-rén 許多(個)人
many people.
(N) much, many (things). Shéi-

zhīdao-nènma-xǔduō. 誰知
道那麼許多. Who
knows so many things? Wǒ-chi-
buliǎo-xǔduō. 我吃不了
許多. I cannot eat much.
XUÉ₁ 學 or XIÁO 學 (TV) (1)
learn, study. Tā-xué-wùlǐ. 他
學物理. He is studying
physics. Nǐ-gēn-shéi-xué-de-
zhèige?你跟誰學的這
個? From whom did you learn
this? Tā-méi-xuéhuì. 他沒
學會. He didn't master it.
(2) imitate. Tā-huì-xué-'gǒu-
jiào. 他會學狗叫. He
can imitate a dog's barking. (3)
mock. Tā-lǎo-xué-ta-tàitai. 他
老學他太太. He al-
ways mocks his wife.
(-B) branch of learning. dòng-
wùxué 動物學 zoology.
XUĚ₂ 雪 (N) snow. (M: chǎng 場).
xià-xuě 下雪 snowfall.
XUĚ₂ 血 see XIĚ 血.
XUĚBÁI₃ 雪白 (N) snow-white.
XUÉFÈI₂ 學費 (N) tuition,
school fees. (M: bǐ 筆). jiāo-
xuéfèi 交學費 pay tuition.
XUĚGUǍN(ZI)₄ 血管(子) (N)
blood vessels, arteries, veins.
XUĚHUĀR₃ 雪花兒 (N) snow-
flake. (M: piàn 片).
XUÉHUÌ₁ 學會 (RV) learn,
master. Tā-xuéhuìle-kāi-chē-le.
他學會了開車了.
He learned how to drive.
XUÉHUÌ₄ 學會 (N) academic
society.
XUĚJIĀ₄ 雪茄 (N) cigar. (M:
gēn 根, zhī 隻).

X

XUEKE₄ 學科 (N) course of
study

XUENIAN₃ 學年 (N) academic
year. yí(ge)-xuénián 一(個)
學年 one academic year.

XUEQI₁ 學期 (N) semester,
term. xià(ge)xuéqī 下(個)學
期 next semester.

XUEQINGR₅ 血清兒 (N) blood
serum.

XUEQIU₄ 血球 (N) blood cell.

XUESHENG₁ 學生 (N) student.

'XUESHU₃ 學術 (N) academic
study. xuéshù-jījuān 學術
機關 academic organization.
xuéshù-lùnwén 學術論文
academic thesis.

XUETU₄ 學徒 (N) pupil who
learns a trade.

XUEWEN₂ 學問 (N) learning,
knowledge. Tā-yǒu-xuéwen. 他
有學問. He is a learned
person. zuò-xuéwen 作學問
do research.

XUEXI₁ 學習 (TV) study, learn.
xiàng-shībài-xuéxi 向失敗
學習 learn from failure.
Xiànzài-tā-xuéxi-Fànwén-ne.
現在他學習法文
呢. He's studying French now.

XUEXIAO₁ 學校 (N) school. (M:
suǒ 所, jiā 家).

XUEXING₅ 血型 (N) blood types.
(M: zhǒng 種).

XUEYA₄ 血壓 (N) blood pres-
sure.

XUEYE₅ 血液 (N) blood.

XUEYUAN₂ 學院 (N) (1) college
or school within a university.
Nèige-dàxué you-sānge-xuéyuàn.

那個大學有三個
學院. That university has
three schools. (2) institute, acad-
my. Yuǎndōng-xuéyuàn 遠東
學院 Institute of Far Eastern
Studies.

XUEZHE₂ 學者 (N) scholar.
(M: wèi 位).

XUEZI₄ 靴子 (N) boot. (M: zhī
隻, shuāng 雙).

XUKE₃ 許可 (TV) permit, allow.
Tāmen-bùxǔkě-wo-líkai. 他們
不許可我離開.They
don't allow me to leave.
(N) permission. Méi-yǒu-tāde-
xǔkě, wǒ-bu-néng-géi-ni. 沒
有他的許可,我不
能給你. I cannot give it
to you without his permission.

XUNCHANG₅ 尋常 (SV) usual,
common. (syn. píngcháng 平
常). Zhèizhǒng-shìqing hěn-
xúncháng. 這種事情很
尋常. This kind of thing is
very common.

XUNHUAN₅ 循環 (IV) circulate,
move in an orbit. Xuěyè-zài-wǒ-
men-shēntǐli-xúnhuán. 血液
在我們身體裏循
環. Blood circulates in our
bodies.

XUNJING₃ 巡警 (N) policeman,
patrolman. (syn. jǐngchá 警
察).

XUNLIAN₁ 訓練 (TV) train,
drill. Tāmen-xùnlian-xīnbīng-ne.
他們訓練新兵呢.
They are training the recruits.
(N) training. Wǒ-méi-shòuguo-
zhèizhong-xùnlian. 我沒受

X

過這種訓練 . I have never received this kind of training.

XÙNSU₅ 迅速 (SV) fast, prompt. (opp. 'chíhuǎn 遲緩). Tāmende-dòngzuo hěn-xùnsu. 他們的動作很迅速. Their action is very prompt. (AD) promptly. Wǒmen-děi-xùnsu-jiějué-zhèijian-shì. 我們得迅速解決這件事 . We have to resolve this matter promptly.

XŪNZHĀNG₄ 勳章 (N) medal, decoration for any kind of merit.

XŪRÓNGXĪN₃ 虛榮心 (N) vanity. Tāde-xūróngxīn tài-dà. 他的虛榮心太大 . He has a great deal of vanity.

'XŪWĚI₄ 虛偽 (SV) false, hypocritical. Tā-hěn-'xūwěi. 他很虛偽 . He is an hypocritical man.

XÙ-XIÁN₄ 續弦 (VO) remarry (of a man).

XŪXĪN₂ 虛心 (SV) humble, modest (in feeling). Tā-duì-'shénme-shì dōu-hěn-xūxīn. 他對甚麼事都很虛心. He is very modest about everything. Nǐ-děi-xūxīn. 你得虛心 . You have to be humble.

(AD) with an open mind. Wǒmenyīnggāi xūxīn-tǎolun. 我們應該虛心討論 . We should discuss it with open minds. (cf:KÈQI 客氣 , QIĀN-XU 謙虛).

XŪYÀO₂ 須要 (AV) must. Wǒmen-xūyào lǐbàiyī-yǐqián zuòhǎo. 我們須要禮拜一以前作好 . We must finish it before Monday.

XŪYÀO₂ 需要 (TV) need, need to. Tāmen-hái-xūyào-sānge-rén. 他們還需要三個人 . They need three more people. Wǒ-xūyào-zhǎo-yíge-bǎoren. 我需要找一個保人 . I need to find a guarantor. (N) need, necessity. Méiyou-zhèzhong-xūyào. 沒有這種需要 . There is not this kind of need. (SV) necessary. Nèizhǒng-wǔqì hái-hěn-xūyào. 那種武器還很需要 . That kind of weapon is still necessary.

XŬ-YUÀN₄ 許願 (VO) make a vow. . Nǐ-xǔ-de-yuàn-tài-duō-le. 你許的願太多了 . You made too many vows. Tā-xǔle-yuàn bu-huán. 他許了願不還 . He made a vow but won't fulfill it.

X

Y

YA₁ 呀 (P) <u>used in place of</u> a when the preceding word ends in the sounds e, i, ū ,ua <u>or</u> uo. Shéi-ya? 誰 呀 ? Who is it? (I) <u>indicates surprise</u>, my goodness! Ya! wǒ-pǐbāo-diū-le. 呀! 我 皮 包 丢 了. My goodness! I lost my purse.

YĀ₄ 押 (TV) (1) borrow money on something, mortgage. Tā-bǎ-qìchē yāchuqu-le. 他 把 汽 車 押 出 去 了. He mortgaged his car. (2) hold <u>in custo-dy</u>. Jǐngchájú-yāle-ta-liǎngtiān. 警察局 押 了 他 兩 天 . The police held him for two days. (3) bet <u>in a number game similar to roulette</u>. Wǒ-yā-shuāngshur. 我 押 雙 數 兒 . I bet on even numbers.

YĀ₂ 壓 (TV) (1) place <u>something on top of something else in order to</u> weigh it down,press down. Ná-shū bǎ-zhèixie-zhǐ yāshang, shěngde-ràng-fēng guāpǎo-le. 拿 書 把 這 些 紙 壓 上 , 省 得 讓 風 颰 跑 了 . Put a book on top of these papers so that the wind won't blow them away. Zhèige-hézi-li shì-bōlibēi, bié-yā. 這 盒 子 裏 是 玻 璃 杯 , 別 壓 . There are glasses in this box. Don't press down on it.

Tǎnzi-tài-zhòng, yādeheng. 毯 子 太 重 壓 得 哼 . The blanket is too heavy. Its weight on me makes me uncomfortable. (2) place <u>something</u> directly atop of <u>something</u>. Jīntiande-bào yā-zhe-zuótiande-bào. 今 天 的 報 壓 着 昨 天 的 報 . Today's paper is on top of yesterday's paper. Nèi-fēng-xìn yāzai-shū-dǐxia-le. 那 封 信 壓 在 書 底 下 了 .That letter was underneath the books. (3) oppress. Tāmen ná-shìli-yā-ta, yě-méi-bǎ-ta-yāfú-le. 他 們 拿 勢 力 壓 他 , 也 沒 把 他 壓 服 了 . They oppressed him with power, but did not subjugate him. (4) hold <u>a business matter not taking any action on it</u>. Tā-yāzhe-gōngshì-bu-bàn. 他 壓 着 公 事 不 辦 . He is holding the matter not taking any action. (5) hold down, suppress <u>an emotion</u>. Wǒ-bǎ-xīnli-de-huǒr yāxiaqu-le. 把 心 裏 的 火 兒 壓 下 去 了 . I suppressed my anger. (6) hold <u>or</u> detain <u>a person</u>, put under guard, arrest. Bǎ-ta-yā-qilai. 把 他 壓 起 來 Put him under guard.

(B) pressure. xuěyā 血 壓 blood pressure. qìyā 氣 壓

atmospheric or barometric pressure. diànyā 電壓 voltage.

YÁ₁ 牙 (N) tooth. (M: kē 顆). shuā-yá 刷牙 brush teeth.

YĂ₄ 啞 (SV) hoarse. Tāde-shēng-yin hěn-yă. 他的聲音很啞. His voice is very hoarse.

YĂ₄ 雅 (SV) elegant.

YÀ₃ 軋 (TV) roll over something with great downward pressure. Chē-bă-gǒu yà-le. 車把狗軋了. The car has run over a dog. Tāmen-bă-dì-yàpíng-le. 他們把地軋平了. They have smoothed down the ground with a roller.

YĂBA₃ 啞巴 (N) mute person.

YÁCHEN₅ 牙磣 (SV) gritty (of food).

YÁCHI₄ 牙齒 (N) tooth. (M: kē 顆).

YĀDÀN₄ 鴨蛋 (N) duck egg.

YÁFĚN₄ 牙粉 (N) tooth powder. (M: hér 盒兒).

YÁGÀO₃ 牙膏 (N) tooth-paste. (M: tǒngr 筒兒).

YÀGĒNR₃ 壓根兒 (AD) from the very beginning. Tā-yàgēnr jiu-méi-xiăng. 他壓根兒就沒想. From the very beginning he didn't think.

YĀLI₂ 壓力 (N) lit. or fig. pressure. Yāli-tài-dà. 壓力太大. The pressure is too great.

YĀN₅ 醃 (TV) salt, pickle, corn (as corned beef) yān-xiáncài 醃鹹菜 make salted vegetables.

yānròu 醃肉 salt meat or salted meat.

YĀN₁ 煙 (N) (1) smoke. (M: gŭ 股). mào-yān 冒煙 emit smoke. (2) tobacco, cigarette. (M: zhī 枝, bāo 包, tiáo 條). xī-yān 吸煙 (lit. inhale smoke) smoke. Wǒ-yìtiān chōu-yìbāo-yān. 我一天抽一包煙. I smoke a pack of cigarettes a day.

YĀN₃ 淹 (TV) inundate, flood. Shuǐ-bă-wǒmende-fángzi yān-le. 水把我們的房子淹了. The water inundated our house.

YÁN₄ 嚴 (SV) strict, stern. Tāde-fùqin-guăn-ta guănde-tài-yán-le. 他的父親管他管的太嚴了. His father disciplined him too rigorously. Lăoshī duì-women-hen-yán. 老師對我們太嚴. Our teacher is quite strict with us. (cf: JĬN 緊).

YÁN₃ 鹽 (N) salt. să-yidianr-yán 撒一點兒鹽 sprinkle on a little salt.

YÁN₄ 沿 (TV) edge, trim a dress. yán-huābiānr 沿花邊兒 trim a dress with lace. (CV) extending along, bordering. yán-hăi-zǒu 沿海走 go along the seashore.

YĂN₁ 眼 (N) (1) or YANJING 眼睛 eye. (M: zhī 隻) zhēng-yăn 睜眼 open the eyes. hé-yăn 合眼 or bì-yăn 閉眼 close the eyes. dèng-yăn 瞪眼 open the eyes wide, stare at something,

Y

be angry. Tāde-yǎn yǒu-shén. 他 的 眼 有 神 . He has a gleam in his eye. (2) or YĂN-JING 眼 睛 vision. Tāde-yǎn zhēn-jiān. 他 的 眼 真 尖 . His eyes are really sharp. (3) hole. Zài-tiěbǎn-shang dǎle liǎngge-yǎn. 在 鐵 板 上 打 了 兩 個 眼 . Two holes were made in the sheet iron. (cf: YĂNR 眼 兒). (M) (1) for an instance of looking at something. Wǒ-kànle-ta yìyǎn. 我 看 了 他 一 眼 . I gave him a look. (2) for a well. yìyan-jǐng 一 眼 井 a well.

YĂN₃ 演 (TV) (1) act, perform in the performing arts. yǎn-xì 演 戲 perform in an opera or play. Yǎn-diànyǐngr děi-yǒu-tiāncai. 演 電 影 兒 得 有 天 才 . To act in motion pictures one has to have talent. (2) put on a show. Zhèijia-diànyǐngryuàn yǎn-shénma-diànyǐngr-ne? 這 家 電 影 兒 院 演 甚 麼 電 影 兒 呢 ?What movie is this theater showing?

YÀN₃ 嚥 (TV) swallow. Zhèkuài-táng-tài-dà, yàn-buxiàqù. 這 塊 糖 太 大 , 嚥 不 下 去 . This piece of candy is too big to swallow.

YÀN₅ 釅 (SV) concentrated, strong (of a solution, especially tea).

YÁNCHÁNG₃ 延 長 (TV) prolong. Wǒmende-jiàqī yánchángle-yíge-lǐbài. 我 們 的 假 期 延 長 了 一 個 禮 拜 . Our

vacation has been extended for another week.

YÁN-DÀOR₅ 沿 道 兒 (VO) along the road. Yán-dàor yǒu-hěn-duō-shù. 沿 道 兒 有 很 多 樹 . There are many trees along the road.

YĀNDǑU₃ 烟 斗 (N) smoking pipe. chōu-yāndǒu 抽 烟 斗 smoke a pipe.

YĂNFÚ₄ 眼 福 (N) the good fortune of seeing something beautiful or delightful. Jīntian kànjian-zènma-duō-hǎo-dōngxi, zhēn-yǒu-yǎnfú. 今 天 看 見 這 麼 多 好 東 西 , 真 有 眼 福 . Today I saw so many good things, I was really fortunate.

YÁNG₃ 羊 (N) sheep, goat. (M:zhī 隻 , qún 羣). (See: SHĀNYÁNG 山 羊 , MIÁNYÁNG 綿 羊).

YÁNG₃ 洋 (N) ocean. hǎiyáng 海 洋 ocean.
(B-) foreign, imported, western. yángrén 洋 人 a Westerner. yánghuò 洋 貨 imported goods.

YĂNG₄ 仰 (TV) lift the head to face upward. Tā-yǎngzhe-tóu kàn-tiān. 他 仰 着 頭 看 天 . He is lifting his head to look at the sky.

YĂNG₄ 氧 (B) oxygen. yǎnghuà 氧 化 oxidize, oxidation.

YĂNG₃ 養 (TV) (1) give birth to a child. Tā-lǐbàitiān yǎngle-yí-ge-érzi. 他 禮 拜 天 養 了 一 個 兒 子 . She gave birth to a son on Sunday. (2) raise children, flowers,

domestic animals, etc. Nǐ-hái-
yǎng-yāzi-ma? 你還養鴨
子嗎？ Do you still raise
ducks? (3) support a family or
a member of a family. Wǒ-děi-
yǎng-wǒ-fùqin. 我得養我
父親. I have to support my
father. (4) nourish, rest and
care for. yǎng-bìng 養病
convalesce. yǎng-shāng 養傷
recuperate from a wound. yǎng-
shén 養神 rest the mind.

YĂNG₄ 癢 (SV) lit. or fig. itchy.
shǒu-yǎng 手癢 the hand
itches or itchy fingers. shēn-
shang fā-yǎng 身上發癢
feel itchy all over the body. (cf:
YĂNGYANG 癢癢).

YÀNG₄ 樣 (M) kind, sort. liǎng-
yàng-dōngxi 兩樣東西
two kinds of things.
(B) (1) appearance, shape. shì-
yàng 式樣 model, pattern. (2)
sample. yàngpǐn 樣品 sample,
specimen. (See: YÀNGR 樣兒.
YÀNGZI 樣子).

YÁNGCHĒ₄ 洋車 (N) rickshaw.
(M: liàng 輛). lā-yángchē 拉
洋車 pull a rickshaw.

YÁNGÉ₃ 嚴格 (SV) strict, rig-
orous.
(AD) strictly. yángéde-shuō 嚴
格的說 strictly speaking.

YÁNGFÚ₃ 洋服 (N) western
style clothes. (syn. xīfú 西服).
(M: jiàn 件, tào 套).

YÁNGGĒ₂ 秧歌 (N) songs sung
when transplanting rice seedlings
which have developed into a kind
of dance popular now in mainland
China. niǔ-yānggē 扭秧歌
do the yānggē dance.

YÁNGGUĀNG₄ 陽光 (N) sun-
light.

YÁNGGUĬZI₃ 洋鬼子 (N) (lit.
foreign wise guy) derogatory
term for non-Chinese.

YÁNGHUĪ₃ 洋灰 (N) cement.

YĂNGHUO₄ 養活 (TV) support
a family or a member of a family. Xiànzài tā-érzi-yǎnghuo-
tā-le. 現在他兒子養
活他了. Now his son is
supporting him.

YÁNGHUǑ₂ 洋火 (N) match.
(syn. huǒchái 火柴). (M: gēn
根, hér 盒兒, bāo 包).

YÁNGLÌ₃ 陽曆 (N) solar calendar.

YĂNGLIÀO₄ 養料 (N) nutriment.

YÁNGLIǓ₄ 楊柳 (N) willow. (M:
kē 棵).

YÁNGMÁO₃ 羊毛 (N) wool.

YĂNGQÌ₃ 氧氣 (N) oxygen.

YÀNGR₁ 樣兒 (N) (1) or YÀNG-
ZI 樣子 appearance. Tāde-
mèimei shénma-yàngr? 他的
妹妹甚麼樣兒? What
does his younger sister look
like? Zhèige-fángzi bú-shì-
yàngr. 這個房子不是
樣兒. This house doesn't
look right. (2) or YÀNGZI 樣
子 model, pattern. xié-yàngr
鞋樣兒 shoe patterns. (3)
or YÀNGZI 樣子 shape, form.
zǒu-yàngr 走樣兒 lose the
original shape. Zhèige-píngzi
yàngr-hǎo. 這個瓶子樣
兒好. The shape of this vase

Y

is very good. (4) kind, sort.
Yàngr-bu-shǎo. 樣兒不少.
There are many kinds.
(M) kind, sort. sìyàngr-cài 四
樣兒菜 four kinds of food.
sòng-liǎngyàngr-lǐ 送兩樣
兒禮 give two kinds of gifts.
used after SP, manner, way.
Bié-zhèiyangr-shuō.別這樣
兒說. Don't say it this way.
(cf: ZHÈIYANGR 這樣兒,
NÈIYANGR 那樣兒).

YÁNGRÉN₃ 洋人 (N) foreigner.

YÁNGRÒU₃ 羊肉 (N)mutton,
lamb (meat).

YÁNGSHI₂ 洋式 (N) foreign
style. yángshi-jiāju 洋式傢
俱 western style furniture.

YǍNGUĀNG₄ 眼光 (N) insight,
outlook. Tāde-yǎnguang tài-qiǎn.
他的眼光太淺. His
outlook is very shallow. Tā-hěn-
yǒu-yǎnguāng, shìjie-dàshì kàn-
de-hěn-qīngchu. 他很有
眼光,世界大事看
得很清楚. He has great
insight, he sees world affairs
very clearly.

YǍNGYANG₃ 痒痒 (SV) lit. or
fig. itchy.
(N) an itch. zhuā-yǎngyang 抓
痒痒 scratch an itch. (cf:
YǍNG 痒).

YǍNGZHANG₅ 仰仗 (TV) rely
on someone who is capable or a
superior. Wǒ-quán-yǎngzhang-
nǐ-le. 我全仰仗你了.
I'm relying completely on you.

YÀNGZI₁ 樣子 (N) (1) or YÀNGR
樣兒 appearance. Tā-de-

yàngzi-xiàng-yíge-xuésheng.
他的樣子像一個
學生. His appearance looks
like that of a student. (2) or
YÀNGR 樣兒 model, pattern.
yīshang-yàngzi 衣裳樣子
clothes pattern. (3) or YÀNGR
樣兒 shape, form. Tā-yǎn-
jìngrde-yàngzi bu-hǎokàn. 他
眼鏡兒的樣子不
好看. The shape of her
eyeglasses is not good-looking.
(4) sample. Zhèige bu-guò-shì-
yíge-yàngzi. 這個不過
是一個樣子. This is
only a sample.

YÁNGZǏJIĀNG₃ 揚子江 (N)
Yangtze River.

YÁN-HǍI₃ 沿海 (VO) along
the seashore or seacoast. Yán-
hǎi yóu-hěn-duō-chuán. 沿海
有很多船. There are
many ships along the coast.
Wǒmen-yánzhe-hái-zǒu.我們
沿着海走. We go along
the seashore. Tā-zhùzai-yán-
hǎi-yídài.他住在沿海
一帶. He lives in the area
along the seasnore.

YǍNHÓNG₃ 眼紅 (SV) envious
to the point of anger. Rénjia-
jiā-xīn, tā-jiu-yǎnhóng.人家
加薪他就眼紅.When
others get a raise he gets mad
with envy.

YÁNHUĪ₃ 烟灰 (N) cigarette
or tobacco ashes.

YÀNHUÌ₄ 宴會 (N) feast, banquet.

YÀNHUO₃ 烟火 (N) fireworks.

Y

fàng-yānhuo 放烟火 display fireworks.

YĂN-JIĂNG₂ 演講 or JIĂNG-YĂN 講演 (VO)make a speech. Tā-méi-yǎnguo-jiǎng. 他没演過講. He has never made a speech. (TV) speak about in public. Nǐ-yǎnjiang shénma-tímu? 你演講甚麼題目? What subject are you going to speak about? (N) speech.

YĂNJIÈ₄ 眼界 (N) visual experiences that broaden one's outlook. kāikai-yǎnjiè 開開眼界 broaden one's outlook.

YĂNJING₁ 眼睛 (N) (1) eye. (M: zhī 隻). (2) vision. (See: YĂN 眼).

YĂNJÌNGR₂ 眼鏡兒 (N) spectacles, eyeglasses. (M: fù 副). dài-yǎnjìngr 戴眼鏡兒 wear glasses. zhāi-yǎnjìngr 摘眼鏡兒 take off the eyeglasses.

YÁNJIU₁ 研究 (TV) do research, study. Tā-yánjiu-Měiguo-gìhou. 他研究美國氣候 He's doing research on American climate. (N) (1) study, research. zuò-yánjiu 作研究 do research.(2) knowledge. hěn-yǒu-yánjiu 很有研究 have a profound knowledge.

YĂNJUĂNR₄ 烟捲兒 (N) cigarette.(syn. xiāngyān 香烟, zhǐyān 紙烟). (M: zhī 枝 , bāo 包 , tiáo 條). chōu-

yānjuǎnr 抽烟捲兒 smoke cigarettes.

YĂNKÀNZHE₃ 眼看着 (AD) (lit. while watching with eyes) (1) in front of someone. Wǒ-yǎnkànzhe-nèi-liǎngge-qìchē-zhuàngshang-le. 我眼看着那兩個汽車撞上了. Those two cars collided right in front of me. (2) in the immediate future, right away. Yǎnkànzhe-jiu-guò-nián-le. 眼看着就過年了. It will be new year right away. (cf: YĂNQIÁN 眼前).

YĂNKĒ₃ 眼科 (N) ophthalmology.

YĂNLÈI₂ 眼淚 (N) teardrops. (M: dī 滴). liú-yǎnlèi 流眼淚 tears are rolling (down the cheek).

YÁNLÌ₅ 嚴厲 (SV) strict, stern. Laǒshī-duìwomen-hěn-yánlì. 老師對我們很嚴厲. Our teacher is quite strict with us.

YÁNLIÀO₄ 顏料 (N) color pigments, dyes.

YAN(ZHI)MÁO₄ 眼(睫)毛 (N) eyelash.

YÁN-MÒ₅ 研墨 (VO) make liquid ink by grinding an inkstick with water on an ink-stone.

YĂNPÍR₄ 眼皮兒 (N) eyelid.

YÁN-QĪ₃ 延期 (VO) postpone a date. Nèige-huì yòu-yánle-sān-tiān-qī. 那個會又延了三天期. That meeting was again postponed for three days. Wǒmen-bu-néng-zài-yán-

Y

qī-le. 我們不能再延
期了. We cannot postpone it
any longer.

YĂNQIÁN₄ 眼前 (PW) in front of
someone. Jiu-zài-ni-yănqián,
nĭ-zĕnma-kànbujiàn? 就在
你眼前,你怎麼看
不見? It is right in front of
you, why can't you see it?
(TW) right now, imminent. Shòu-
zuì jiu-zài-yănqián. 受罪就
在眼前. The suffering is
imminent. (cf: YĂNKÀNZHE 眼
看着).

YĂNQUĀNR₅ 眼圈兒 (N) eye
socket or the facial area around
the eyes. Tā-yănlèi-wéizhe-yăn-
quānr-zhuàn. 他眼淚圍
着眼圈兒轉. Her tears
are rolling around the corners of
her eyes.

YĂNR₃ 眼兒 (N) small hole. kū-
long-yănr 窟窿眼兒 a
small hole. zhēn-yănr 針眼
兒 the eye of a needle. zhā-yi-
ge-yănr 扎一個眼兒
pierce something to make a hole.
Zài-zhĭshang dă-sānge-yănr. 在
紙上打三個眼兒.
Make three holes in the paper.
(cf: YĂN 眼).

YÀNR₅ 燕兒 see YÀNZI 燕子.
YÁNSE₂ 顏色 or YÁNSHAIR 顏
色兒 (N) color.
YĂNSE₄ 眼色 (N) hint by eye or
facial expression. Tā-yi-shř-
yănse, wŏ-jiu-míngbai-le. 他
一使眼色,我就明
白了. As soon as he hinted
to me by the way he looked at me,

I understood. Wúlùn-zuò-shén-
ma wŏmen-dōu-dei-kàn-tade-
yănse. 無論作甚麼
我們都得看他的
眼色. It doesn't matter
what we are going to do, we
have to watch his expression.

YÁNSHAIR₂ 顏色兒 see
YÁNSE 顏色.

YĂNSHÉN₃ 眼神 (N) (1)
gleam of the eye. Tāde-yăn-
shén-hĕn-zú. 他的眼神
很足. He has a bright
gleam in his eyes. (2) thoughts
or emotions revealed through
one's eyes. Wŏ-kàn tāde-yăn-
shén-bu-duì, yuánlái-ta-shi-
ge-zéi. 我看他的眼
神不對,原來他
是個賊. I saw that there
was something wrong in the
way he looked. Later I found
out that he is a thief.

'YÁNSÙ₄ 嚴肅 (SV) serious,
solemn. Dàjiāde-tàidu dōu-hen-
'yánsù. 大家的態度
都很嚴肅. The attitude
of the whole group is very solemn.

YĂNTÁI₄ 烟台 (PW) Chefoo
(city in Shantung province).

YÀNTAI₅ 硯台 (N) ink-stone.
(M: kuài 塊). Yòng-zhèikuai-
yàntai yán-mò. 用這塊
硯台研墨. Use this
ink-stone to make ink.

YĂNTONG₄ 烟筒 (N) chimney,
flue, stovepipe.

YĂN-XÌ₂ 演戲 (VO) (1) per-
form in an opera or a play.

Y

Jīnnian wǒ-yǎnle-sāncì-xì. 今
年 我 演 了 三 次 戲 .
I have acted three times this
year. (2) put on an opera or a
play. Wǒmen yǎn-xì-juān-qián.
我 們 演 戲 捐 錢 .We
put on a play to raise money.
YÁNYU4 言語 (IV) make re-
marks, say something. Tā-yì-
shēngr méi-yányu jiu-zǒu-le.他
一 聲 兒 沒 言 語 就
走 了 . He left without saying
a word.
'YÁNYǓ5 言語 (N) language,
speech. Wǒmen-yányǔ-bù-tōng.
我 們 言 語 不 通 . We
don't understand the same language. (cf: YÚYÁN 語言).
YǍNYUÁN3 演員 (N) actor,
actress.
YĀNZHI4 胭脂 (N) rouge, make-
up. (M: hér 盒兒).
YÁNZHONG2 嚴重 (SV) serious.
Tāde-bìng hěn-yánzhong.他 的
病 很 嚴 重 . His illness is
quite serious. Zhèige-qíngxing
xiāngdāngde-yánzhong. 這 個
情 形 相 當 的 嚴 重 .
This situation is rather serious.
YǍNZHŪR5 眼珠兒 or YǍN-
ZHŪZI 眼 珠 子 (N) pupil,
eyeball.
YǍNZHŪZI5 眼珠子 see
YǍNZHŪR 眼珠兒 .
YÀNZI5 燕子 or YÀNR 燕兒
(N) swallow (bird). (M: zhī 隻).
YĀO3 腰 (N) (1) waist. Tāde-yao
hěn-xì. 他 的 腰 很 細 .
Her waist is very thin. (2) the
small of one's back. Wǒ-yāo-téng.

我 腰 疼 . I have a pain at
the small of my back.
(B) (1) mid-section of something.
shān-yāo 山 腰 half-way up
a mountain. (2) kidney. niúyāo
牛 腰 ox's kidney.
YĀO3 邀 (TV) invite. Wǒ-méi-
yāo-ta. 我 沒 邀 他 . I
didn't invite him. (cf: YUĒ 約).
YĀO4 幺 (NU) one, ace (in a card
game or in dice).
YÁO4 窰 (N) (1) kiln. (M: zuò 座).
(2) mine (of coal). méiyáo 煤
窰 coal mine.
YÁO3 搖 (TV) (1) shake, rock,
swing to and fro. yáo-tóu 搖
頭 shake the head. Bǎ-píngzi-
yáoyao. 把 瓶 子 搖 搖 .
Shake the bottle. (2) row a boat.
yáo-chuán 搖 船 row a boat.
(See: HUÀNG(YAO) 晃(搖)).
YǍO3 咬 (TV) (1) bite. Wǒ-yǎole-
wǒde-shétou-le. 我 咬 了
我 的 舌 頭 了 . I bit my
tongue. (2) pronounce. Tā-yǎo-
zìr-yǎode hěn-qīngchu.他 咬
字 兒 咬 得 很 清 楚 .
He pronounces his syllables
very clearly. (3) incriminate
an innocent person by giving
false testimony. Nǐ-bié-yǎo-
hǎo-rén. 你 別 咬 好 人 .
Don't implicate the innocent. (4)
bark (of a dog). Wǒ-tīngjian-
gǒu-yǎo. 我 聽 見 狗 咬 .
I heard the dog bark.
YǍO4 舀 (TV) scoop up and bail
out liquid. yǎo-shuǐ 舀 水 bail
out the water.
YÀO2 藥 (N) (1) medicine. chī-yào

Y

吃藥 take medicine orally.
shàng-yào 上藥 apply medicine externally. (2) chemical compound. dúyào 毒藥 poison. huǒyào 火藥 gunpowder. (TV) poison something or someone. Bǎ-ta-yàosi-le. 把他藥死了 . He was poisoned to death.

YÀO₁ 要 (TV) (1) want. Nǐ-yào-shénma? 你要甚麼 ? What do you want? (2) ask for. Gēn-ni-mǔqin-yào. 跟你母親要 . Ask your mother for it. (3) accept. Tā-gěi-nǐ, nǐ-yàole-méiyou? 他給你，你要了沒有 ? He gave it to you. Did you take it? (4) order food (in a restaurant). Wǒ-yào-le-yíge-zhájī. 我要了一個炸鷄 . I ordered a fried chicken.
(AV) (1) about to. Wǒ-gēge yào-zǒu-le. 我哥哥要走了 . My older brother is about to leave here. (2) need to, should. Nǐ-yào-nǔlì. 你要努力 . You should work hard. (3) want, desirous of. Wǒ-yào-xué-kāi-chē. 我要學開車 . I want to learn to drive. (AD) (con. yàoshi 要是). if. Nǐ-yào-qù, wǒ-jiu-bu-qù. 你要去，我就不去 . If you go, I won't go. (B) important. yàodiǎn 要點 important point. yàorén 要人 important person.

YÁOBǍI₅ 搖擺 (IV) swing to and fro. Nèige-shùzhīzi láihuíde-

yáobǎi. 那個樹枝子來回的搖擺 . That tree branch swings back and forth.

YÀOBÙRÁN₁ 要不然 (MA) otherwise. Nǐ-gǎnkuài-qù, yào-burán-jiu-wǎn-le. 你趕快去，要不然就晚了 . You have to go immediately, otherwise you would be late. Tā-búshi-dǎ-pái jiùshi-hē-jiǔ yàoburán-jiu-shuì-jiào. 他不是打牌就是喝酒要不然就睡覺 . If he's not playing cards, he's drinking; otherwise he's sleeping.

YÀOCHǍNG₄ 藥廠 (N) medicine factory. (M: jiā 家).

YĀODÀI₄ 腰帶 (N) waist belt. (M: gēn 根 , tiáo 條).

YÀODE₃ 要得 (RV) (lit. can be kept) good, desirable. yàobude 要不得 no good.

YÀODIǍN₃ 要點 (N) essential point, main point. Zuò-shì děi-zhuāzhu-yàodiǎn. 作事得抓住要點 . In working you must grasp the essential points.

YÀO-FÀN₃ 要飯 (VO) (lit. ask for food) beg (to maintain one's existence). (syn. tǎo-fàn 討飯). Tā-yàole-sānnián-fàn-le. 他要了三年飯了 . He has been a beggar for three years.

YÀOFÀNDE₄ 要飯的 (N) beggar.

YÀOFÁNG₃ 藥房 (N) drug store pharmacy. (M: jiā 家).

Y

YÀOFĀNGR₃ 药方兒 (N) prescription (for medicine).(M: zhāng 张). kāi-yàofāngr 開药方兒 write a prescription.

YÁOHE₅ 吆喝 (IV) call or cry out as a hawker does.

'YÁOHUÀNG₄ 搖晃 see HUÀNG(YOU) 晃摇 .

YÀOJǏN₁ 要緊 (SV) important. bu-tài-yàojǐn 不太要緊 not very important.

YÁOLÁN₄ 摇籃 (N) rocking cradle.

YÀOLǏNG₄ 要領 (N) main point. Tā-shuōle-bàntiān méi-dé-yào-lǐng. 他說了半天沒得要領 . He talked for quite a while but didn't get to the point.

YÀO-MÌNG₂ 要命 (VO) (1) demand one's life. Zǎowǎn-wǒ-yào-nǐde-mìng. 早晚我要你的命 . Sooner or later I'll get you. (2) make things difficult for someone. Nǐ-yào-wode-mìng-a! 你要我的命啊 ! fig. You just want to kill me!

(SV) terrible. Tā-bènde-yàomìng. 他笨的要命 . He is terribly stupid. Nèijiàn-shìqing jēn-yàomìng. 那件事情真要命 . That matter is terrible.

YÀOPIÀNR₃ 药片兒 (N) medicine tablets. (M: kē 顆 , lì 粒).

YÀOPÙ₃ 药鋪 (N) old fashioned Chinese medical herb store. (M: jiā 家).

YÀOQIÁNG₄ 要強 (SV) desirous of getting ahead. Tā-hěn-yào-qiáng. 他很要強 . He is very industrious in trying to get ahead.

'YĀOQǏNG₅ 邀請 (TV) invite. Wǒ-bu-xiǎng-'yāoqǐng-ta. 我不想邀請他 . I'm not planning to invite him.

YĀOQIU₂ 要求 (TV) request, demand. Tā-yāoqiu-wo-gěi-ta-jiā-xīn. 他要求我給他加薪 . He asked me to give him a raise (salary). (N) request, demand. Wǒ-bu-néng-jiēshòu nǐde-yāoqiu. 我不能接受你的要求 . I can't accept your demands.

YÀOSHI₃ 鑰匙 (N) key (for a lock). (M: bǎ 把).

YÀOSHI₁ 要是 (MA) if, in case. (syn. rúguǒ 如果). Yàoshi-nǐ-bulái, wǒ-jiu-bu-qù. 要是你不來我就不去 . If you don't come, I won't go.

YÀOSHUǏR₃ 药水兒 (N) liquid medicine.

YÀOSǏ₃ 要死 used after de 的 , serves as a compliment of a descriptive sentence, extremely. Wǒ-lèide-yàosǐ. 我累得要死 . I am extremely tired.

YÀOWÁNR₄ 药丸兒 (N) medicine pill. (M: kē 顆 , lì 粒).

YÀO-YÁ₂ 咬牙 (VO) (1) clench one's teeth as an expression of hatred or as an aid to endure suffering. Yì-yǎo-yá, yě-jiu-guòqu-le. 一咬牙，也

Y

就過去了. Once you clench your teeth it will be over. (2) grind one's teeth. Tā-shuì-jiào yǎo-yá. 他 睡 覺 咬 牙. He grinds his teeth when he sleeps.

YÁOYAN₃ 謠言 (N) rumor. zào-yáoyan 造謠言 start a rumor.

YÁOYǏ₄ 搖椅 (N) rocking chair. (M: bǎ 把).

YĀOZI₄ 腰子 (N) kidney.

YÀOZI₄ 瘧子 (N) malaria. fā-yàozi 發瘧子 have malaria.

YĀPIÀN(YĀN)₅ 鴉片（烟）(N) opium. chōu-yāpiàn(yān) 抽鴉片（烟）smoke opium.

YĀPO₂ 壓迫 (TV) oppress, pressure. Nǐ-buyīnggāi-yāpo-ta. 你 不 應 該 壓 迫 他. You shouldn't oppress him. (N) oppression, pressure. Wǒ-shòubuliǎo-zhèizhǒngde-yāpo. 我 受 不 了 這 種 的 壓 迫. I can't stand this kind of oppression.

YÁQIĀNR₄ 牙籤兒 (N) toothpick. (M: gēn 根).

YÁR₅ 芽兒 (N) sprout. dòu-yár 豆芽兒 bean sprout. zhǎng-yár 長芽兒 to sprout.

YÁSHUA(ZI)₄ 牙刷（子）or YÁSHUĀR 牙刷兒 (N) toothbrush. (M: bǎ 把).

YÁSHUĀR₄ 牙刷兒 see YÁ-SHUĀ(ZI) 牙刷（子）.

YÁYǏ₃ 牙醫 (N) dentist.

YĀ-YÙN₅ 壓韻 (VO) rhyme. Xīn-shī bu-yídìng-děi-yā-yùn. 新 詩 不 一 定 得 壓 韻. New poetry does not necessarily have to rhyme.

YĀZI₃ 鴨子 (N) (1) duck. (M: zhī 隻). (2) Peip. foot. (M: zhī 隻).

YÀZHOU₃ 亞洲 (PW) Asia.

YĒ₄ 咽 (TV) choke by eating too fast. Tā-chīde-tài-kuài yēzhao-le. 他 吃 得 太 快. 咽 着 了. He ate too fast and choked.

YĒ₄ 擤 (TV) (1) tuck in. Bǎ-chèn-shān yēzai-kùzi-li. 把 襯 衫 擤 在 褲 子 裏. Tuck the shirt into the pants. (2) stuff in. Kǒudàirli yēmǎnle-dōngxi. 口 袋 兒 裏 擤 滿 了 東 西. The pocket is full of things.

YĚ₃ 野 (SV) (1) wild, untamed. Nèige-háizi-yějíle. 那 孩 子 野 極 了. That child is really wild. (2) uncivilized, crude. Tā-shuō-huà zhēn-yě. 他 說 話 真 野. He speaks very crudely. (IV) gallivant around. Nǐ-shàng-nǎr-yěqu-le? 你 上 那 兒 野 去 了? Where have you been gallivanting to?

YĚ₁ 也 (AD) (1) also, too. Nǐ-qù wǒ-yě-qù. 你 去 我 也 去 You go and I'll go too. Tā-niàn-shū yě-jiāo-shū. 他 念 書 也 教 書. He studies and also teaches. Tā-mài-shū yě-mài-bào. 他 賣 書 也 賣 報. He sells books and also newspapers. (2) and also, besides. Dōngxi-hǎo yě-bu-guì.

東西好也不貴. It's good stuff, and also it is not expensive. Nǐ-zěnma-yě-bu-shuì jiào-a? 你怎麼也不睡覺啊? Besides that, why don't you go to bed? Wǒmen-yě-bu-zhīdào tā-shi-shéi. 我們也不知道他是誰. Besides, we don't know who he is.

used after a nominal expression with a stressed question word, the question word with yě 也 means every-, any-. Tā-'shénma-dōngxi yě-bu-chī. 他甚麼東西也不吃. He doesn't eat anything. Tāmen-shéi-ye-bu'guǎn-shéi. 他們誰也不管誰. Nobody bothers with one another.

used after a verbal expression with a stressed question word, the question word with yě 也 means no matter, it doesn't matter. Tā-shuō-shénma wǒ-ye-shuō-hǎo. 他說甚麼我也說好. It doesn't matter what he will say, I'll say that it's good.

used after a verbal or nominal expression with or without lián 連 or jiùshi 就是, even. Wǒ(-lián)-'yìmáo-qián yě-méi-yǒu. 我（連）一毛錢也沒有. I don't have even a dime. Wǒ(-jiùshi)-yǒu-qián yě-bu-néng-géi-ni. 我（就是）有錢也不能給你. Even if I had the money, I could not give it to you. Nǐ(-jiùshi-)

'shuō-ye-méi-yòng. 你就是說也沒用. Even if you say it, it is useless.

used after a verbal expression which is then repeated after yě 也, alone, by itself. Chī-ye-bǎ-nǐ-chīqióng-le. 吃也把你吃窮了. Eating alone can make you poor. È-ye-bǎ-nǐ-èsi-le. 餓也把你餓死了. The hunger alone will kill you.

(S) YĚ... YĚ... 也...也... (1) also, too. Zhèige-yě-hǎo, nèige-yě-hǎo. 這個也好, 那個也好. This is good, that is good too. (2) both ...and.... Tā-yě-cōngming, yě-hǎokàn, wèi-shénma-méi-yǒu-nánpéngyou? 他也聰明, 也好看, 為甚麼沒有男朋友? She is both intelligent and pretty, but why doesn't she have a boy friend? (cf: YÒU... YÒU... 又...又...).

YÈ₁ 夜 (M) night. Wǒ-zuòle sān-tiān-sānyè cai-zuòwán. 我作了三天三夜才作完. I worked for three days and three nights to complete the job.

YÈ₃ 頁 (M) (1) leaf of a book or album (Chinese books are numbered by leaves instead of pages). (2) page of a book. Tā-kànle-èrshi-duō-yè-shū. 他看了二十多頁書. He has read over twenty pages of the book.

Y

(B) leaf (of a book or an album). huóyè-běnzi 活頁本子 loose-leaf note book.

YÈBĀN₃ 夜班 (N) night work, night shift.

YĚCĀN₃ 野餐 (N) picnic. (IV) go on a picnic.

YĚDÌ₃ 野地 (N) uncultivated land.

YĚJĪ₃ 野鷄 (N) (1) pheasant.(M: zhī 隻).(2) street-walker.

YÈLǏ₁ 夜裏 (TW) night. Tāmen-yèli-zuò-shì. 他們夜裏做事 . They work at night.

YĚMÁN₃ 野蠻 (SV) (1) uncivilized, barbarous. Zhèixie-dou-shi-yěmán-mínzú. 這些都是野蠻民族 . These are all uncivilized peoples. (2) rude. Tā-duì-shéi dou-hěn-yě-mán. 他對誰都很野蠻 . He is rude to everyone.

YÈR₂ 葉兒 or YÈZI 葉子 (N) leaf (of a plant).

YĚSHÒU₃ 野獸 (N) wild animal. (M: zhī 隻).

YĒSŪ₁ 耶穌 (N) Jesus. Yēsū-jīdū 耶穌基督 Jesus Christ.

YĒSŪJIÀO₂ 耶穌教 (N) Christianity (Protestant). (cf: JĪDŪ-JIÀO 基督教).

YÈTǏ₄ 液體 (N) liquid.

YĚWÀI₄ 野外 (PW) wilderness. Yěwài yǒu-hěn-duō-cǎo. 野外有很多草 . There is a lot of grass in the wilderness. Yěwài méi-you-fángzi. 野外沒有房子 . There aren't any houses in the wilderness.

YÈWÙ₃ 業務 (N) business activities (of an organization). Tā-men-gōngsīde-yèwu hěn-fādá. 他們公司的業務很發達 . Their company's business activities are very prosperous. Zhèige-bùmén-de-yèwu shi-shénma? 這個部門的業務是甚麼 ? What are the activities of this department?

YÈXIÀO₄ 夜校 (N) night school.

YÈXIĀOR₅ 夜消兒 (N) midnight snack. (M: dùn 頓). (syn. xiāoyè 消夜).

YĚXĪN₃ 野心 (N) covetousness, ambition. Tāde-yěxīn-hěn-dà. 他的野心很大 .His ambition is great.

YĚXǓ₁ 也許 (MA) maybe, perhaps. (syn. huòxǔ 或許 , huò (zhe)shi 或(者)是). Wǒ-yěxǔ-qù. 我也許去 . Perhaps I will go.

YÉYE₃ 爺爺 (N) grandfather (father's father). (syn. zǔfu 祖父).(M: wèi 位).

YÈYÚ₅ 業餘 (B-) in addition to one's occupation or outside one's profession. yèyú-zuòjiā 業餘作家 amateur writer. Zhòng-huār shi-wó-yèyúde-xiāo-qian. 種花兒是我業餘的消遣 . Growing flowers is my after work pastime.

YĒZI₄ 椰子 (N) coconut.

YÈZI₂ 葉子 see YÈR 葉兒 .

YĪ₁ 一 The tone of yi is level when used as an isolated syllable, in counting, before a toneless syllable or as a last syllable; the tone may be changed into rising tone when yi is followed by a syllable with a falling tone or into falling tone when yi is followed by a syllable with a level, rising or low tone. (NU) (1) one. (with a M used directly after SP, TV, IV, AV, SV or de 的, the unstressed yi 一 is often dropped.) one. yī-jiǔliùqī 一九六七 1967. Yī, èr, sān. 一,二,三. One, two, three. Yīde-fāng-shi-yī. 一 的 方 是 一. The square of one is one. èrshi-yī 二十一 twenty-one. yícì 一次 once. yìtiān 一天 one day. yìnián 一年 one year. yìběn 一本 one volume. zhèi(yi)ge 這(一)個 this one. Wǒ-Yǒu(yi)-ge-péngyou. 我有(一)個朋友. I have a friend. Tā-shi-hěn-cōngming-de(yi)-ge-rén. 他是很聰明的(一)個人. He is a very brilliant man. (2) first. dìyī 第一 first. yìlóu 一樓 first floor. yíhào 一號 number one or the first day of a month. (3) same. Tā-men-sānge-ren yìtiáo-xīn. 他們三個人一條心. The three of them have one mind. (4) all, whole. yìwūzi-rén 一屋子人 a roomful of people. Wǒ-yìtiān méi-chū-mén. 我一天沒出門. I didn't go out all day. Yìdōngtian-méi-xià-xuě. 一冬天沒下雪. It didn't snow all winter. (5) used in a series of NU-M structures, each, every. Liǎngmáo-wǔ yí-gè. 兩毛五一個. Twenty-five cents each. Yíge-ren-wǔkuai-qián. 一個人五塊錢. Five dollars for each person. (6) used repeatedly in a series of NU-M structures, each... one.... Tāmen yíge-ren yǒu-yíge-zhúyi. 他們一個人有一個主意. Each one of them has an idea. or Different people have different ideas.

(AD) (1) used in the first of two clauses, once. Tā-yì-shuō wǒ-cai-míngbai. 他一說我才明白. After he once mentioned it, then I understood. Tā-tái-tóu-yí-kàn, tiān-hēi-le. 他抬頭一看天黑了. Once he raised his head to look, then (he realized that) the sky had grown dark. Ràng-tā-yì-shuō, shénma-dou-bu-nán. 讓他一說,甚麼都不難. Let him mention it just once and it will all sound easy. (2) used in the middle of a reduplicated verb, a little, a little while. cā-yica 擦一擦 wipe a little. děng yideng 等一等 wait a little while. (cf: YI...JIÙ... 一...就..., YI...YI... 一...一...).

YĪ₄ 醫 (TV) treat an illness or a patient. yī-bìng 醫病 treat an illness.

(N) medicine (as a field of study or a profession). Tā-shi-xué-

Y

yī-de. 他是學醫的. He studies medicine. (B) (1) healing art, medicine. yīkē 醫科 medical course in a school. (2) medical doctor. shòuyī 獸醫 veterinarian. xīyī 西醫 western style doctor.

YĪ₃ 依 (TV) comply with theory, principle, law or one's wishes. Nàma-wǒmen-jiu-yī-nǐ. 那麼 我們就依你. In that case, we'll comply with your wishes.

YÍ(R)₅ 姨 (兒) or YÍMǓ 姨母 (N) aunt (mother's sister).

YǏ₂ 以 (B) followed by L to form PW or TW, from a certain point on (time or place). yǐdōng 以東 to the east (from here). zhèi-tiao-xiàn-yǐzuǒ 這條線以 左 to the left of this lone. chī-fàn-yǐqián 吃飯以前 before eating. (S) (1) YǏ...LÁI...以...來 ..., in terms of. yǐ-jiàqian-lai-shuō 以價錢來說 talk in terms of price. (2) YǏ...WÉI ...以...為... take something as. yǐ-zhèige-wéi-biāo-zhun 以這個為標準 take this as a standard. (3) YǏ... ÉRLÙN 以...而論, discuss something in terms of... YǏ-dìweì'-érlùn, nà-shi-tāde-dì-wei-gāo. 以地位而論. 那是他的地位高. If we talk about it in terms of position, his position is higher. (CV) by means of, using, with, according to. Yǐ-yīngchǐ-suàn.

以英尺算. Compute it by the foot. yǐ-měijīn-huán 以 美金還 pay back with American money.

YǏ₂ 億 (M) one hundred million. liùyì-rénkǒu 六億人口 a population of 600,000,000. (cf: WÀNWÀN 萬萬).

YǏBA₃ 尾巴 or WĚIBA 尾巴 (N) (1) tail (of an animal). (M: tiáo 條). gǒu-yǐba 狗尾巴 dog's tail. (2) tail-end. Zhuò-shì bié-liú-yǐba. 作事别 留尾巴. In doing work, don't leave out the tail-end.

YǏBĀN₂ 一般 (B-) general, common. yìbān-rén 一般人 common people. yibān-lai-shuō 一般來說 generally speaking. (AD) or YIBIĀNR 一邊兒 used before SV, equally, the same. yìbān-cháng 一般長 the same length. (cf: YÍYÀNG 一樣).

YÍBÀN(R)₁ 一半 (兒) (NU-M) half. Tā-fēngeǐ-wo-yibàn(r) 他 分給我一半(兒). He shared half (of it) with me. Tā-shuō-de yíbàn(r)-duì yíbàn(r)-'bú-duì. 他說的一半 (兒)對一半(兒)不 對. Half of what he said is right and half is wrong.

YÍBÈI₂ 一倍 (NU-M) double. Tāde-qián shi-wǒde-yíbèi. 他 的錢是我的一倍. His money is double that of mine. Tāde-qián-bǐ-wǒde-duō-yibèi. 他的錢比我的

多一倍. He has twice as much money as I do. Xiànzài-mài kéyi-dé-yíbèide-lìqian. 現在賣可以得一倍的利錢. If you sell it now, you can double the profit. (See: BÈI 倍).

YÍBÈIZI₃ 一輩子 (N) lifetime. (MA) all one's life. (syn. yìshēng 一生). Tā-yìbèizi méi-hē-guo-jiǔ. 他一輩子沒喝過酒. All his life he has never had liquor.

YÌBIĀNR₁ 一邊兒 (AD) (1) or YIBĀN 一般 used before SV, equally, the same. Tāmen-liǎngge-rén yìbiānr-gāo. 他們兩個人一邊兒高. They both are the same height. (2) used repeatedly, do something while doing something else, on one hand. Tā-yìbiānr-chīfàn, yìbiānr-kàn-shū. 他一邊兒吃飯, 一邊兒看書. He reads a book while eating. (PW) on one side. Tā-zhànzai-yìbiānr méi-shuō-huà. 他站在一邊兒沒説話. He is standing to one side without saying anything. Tā-zài-dāngzhōng, yìbiānr shì-Zhāng-xiansheng, yìbiānr shì-Lǐ-xiansheng. 他在當中, 一邊兒是張先生, 一邊兒是李先生. He is in the middle, on one side is Mr. Chang and on the other side is Mr. Li. (cf: YÍYÀNG 一樣, YÌFĀNGMIAN 一方面, YI-MIÀNR 一面兒).

YÍCHĂN₃ 遺產 (N) inheritance. yíchănshuèi 遺產稅 inheritance tax. Tā-fùqin-liúxia-bu-shăode-yíchăn. 他父親留下不少的遺產. His father left quite a large inheritance.

YÍCHÁNG₄ 異常 (AD) extremely, unusually. yìcháng-gāoxìng 異常高興 extremely happy.

YÌCHU₃ 益處 (N) advantage, benefit. Wǒ-kàn-nèiben-shū, déle-bu-shăo-de yìchu. 我看那本書得了不少的益處. I received quite a few benefits from reading that book. (See: HĂOCHU 好處).

YÍCHUÁN₃ 遺傳 (TV) transmit, pass something down in a family. Zhèi-zhǒng-bìng buyíchuán. 這種病不遺傳. This disease is not hereditary. (N) heredity.

YICÌ...YICÌ...₃ 一次...一次... or YIHUI...YIHUI... 一回...一回...(S) everytime. Wǒ-'qù-yici-Niǔyue bìng-yici. 我去一次紐約病一次. Everytime I go to New York I get sick.

YÍDÀI₃ 一帶 (NU-M) region, area. Niǔyuē-yídài 紐約一帶 New York area. zhèi-yídài-dìfang 這一帶地方 this area.

YÌDÀLI₃ 意大利 (PW) Italy. (cf: YIGUO 意國).

YÍDÀN₄ 一旦 (MA) once.

Y

Yídàn tā-dāying-le, jiu-yídìng-zuò. 一旦他答應了就一定作. Once he has promised, then he will definitely do it.

YÌDIĂNR₁ 一點兒 (NU-M) a little. Géi-wo-yidianr. 給我一點兒. Give me a little. Tā-yìdiănr dōu-bu-chī. 他一點兒都不吃. He won't eat even a little. Yìdiănr-yìdiănr-de-zuò. 一點兒一點兒的作. Do it little by little. Zhèige-bǐ-nèige gānjing-yidianr. 這個比那個乾淨一點兒. This is a little cleaner than the other.

YÍDÌNG₁ 一定 (AD) (1) certainly, definitely. Wŏ-yídìng-lái. 我一定來. I'll certainly come. (2) must be, must have. Tā-yídìng-zhīdào. 他一定知道. He must have known it. (SV) certain, definite, sure. A: Míngtiān-lái-a! B: Yídìng-yidìng. A: 明天來啊! B: 一定一定. A: Come tomorrow! B: I certainly will. Nà-shi-yídìng-de. 那是一定的. That's for sure.

YÍDÒNGR₅ 一動兒 see YÍLÁI 一來 (MA).

YÌFĀN₄ 一番 (NU-M) one occurrence of something. biăoyan-yi-fān 表演一番 perform once. Nín-zhèi-yìfān-huà hĕn-yŏu-lǐ. 你這一番話很有理. This talk of yours is very reasonable.

YÌFĀNGMIAN₂ 一方面 (MA) on one hand. Tā-yìfāngmian-yào-niàn-shū, yìfāngmian-you yào-zuò-shì. 他一方面要念書一方面又要作事. On one hand he wants to study, on the other he wants to work. (cf: YÌBIĀNR 一邊兒, YÍMIÀNR 一面兒).

YĪFU₂ 衣服 (N) clothes. (syn. yīshang 衣裳). (M: jiàn 件, shēn 身, tào 套). chuān-yīfu 穿衣服 wear clothes. tuō-yīfu 脫衣服 take off clothes.

YÍFU₅ 姨父 (N) uncle (mother's sister's husband).

YÍGÀI₁ 一概 (AD) without exception. Qiànde-zhàng-tā-yígài-bùhuán. 欠的賬他一概不還. He refuses to pay his debts without exception.

YÍGEJINR₅ 一個勁兒 (AD) constantly. Tā-yígejìnr-de-gēn-wo-dăo-luàn. 他一個勁兒的跟我搗亂. He constantly makes trouble for me.

YÍGÒNG₁ 一共 or ZŎNGGÒNG 總共 (AD) used in referring to numbers, altogether, in all, all told. Yígòng-'jǐkuài-qián? 一共幾塊錢? Altogether how many dollars?

YĪGUĀN₄ 醫官 (N) military medical officer.

YĪGUÌ₄ 衣櫃 (N) clothes closet, wardrobe.

YĪGUO₂ 意國 (PW) Italy. (cf: YÌDÀLÌ 意大利).

YĬHÒU₁ 以後 (TW) (1) afterward.

Y

Yǐhòu shéi-lái-le? 以 後 誰
來 了 ? Who came afterward?
(2) the future. Nà-shi-yǐhòude-
shì. 那 是 以 後 的 事 .
That's something for the future.
Yǐhòu bu-huì-bǐ-xiànzài-hǎo. 以
後 不 會 比 現 在 好 .
The future won't be better than
the present. (3) used after NU-
M, N, TW or a clause, indicates
a period of time, after. liǎngge-
lǐbài-yǐhòu 兩 個 禮 拜 以
後 after two weeks. wǒ-shēng-
ri-yǐhòu 我 生 日 以 後
after my birthday. xīngqīsān-yǐ-
hòu 星 期 三 以 後 after
Wednesday. Tā-láile-yǐhòu wǒ-
men-jiu bù-shuō-le. 他 來 了
以 後, 我 們 就 不 說
了 . After he came, we didn't
talk about it any more. Niàndao-
dìwǔkè-yǐhòu jiu-róngyi-le. 念
到 第 五 課 以 後 就
容 易 了 . It will be easy
after we reach the fifth lesson.
(PW) used after N, behind something. Zhèidao-qiáng-yǐhòu ké-
yi-zhòng-cài. 這 道 牆 以
後 可 以 種 菜 . Behind
this wall you can plant vegetables.
YÌHUǏR₁ 一 會 兒 (NU-M) a
short while. Tā-yìhuǐr-lái. 他
一 回 兒 來 . He will come
in a short while. Tā-zài-zhèr-
de-gōngfu bu-dà, jiu-yihuǐr. 他
在 這 兒 的 工 夫 不
大, 就 一 會 兒 . He
wasn't here long, only a short
while.
YÌHUÍ... YÌHUÍ...₃ 一 回 ...

回 ... see YÍCÌ...YÍCÌ... 一
次 ... 一 次 ....
YÍHUO₃ 疑 惑 (syn. yíxīn 疑
心) (TV) suspect. Wǒ-yíhuo
tā-shì-nèige-zéi. 我 疑 惑
他 是 那 個 賊 . I sus-
pect that he is the thief.
(N) suspicion. Wǒ-méi-you-
shenma-yíhuo. 我 沒 有 甚
麼 疑 惑 . I don't have any
suspicions.
YǏJÍ₂ 以 及 used to join coordinate expressions, and, as
well as, even including. Yīngwén, Déwén, yǐjí-Fàwén tā-dou-
huì. 英 文, 德 文, 以 及
法 文, 他 都 會 . He
knows English and German, as
well as French.
YĪJÍ₂ 埃 及 see ĀIJÍ 埃 及 .
YÌJIAN₁ 意 見 (N) (1) opinion.
fābiǎo-yìjian 發 表 意 見
express an opinion. tí-yìjian
提 意 見 put forth an opin-
ion. Wǒ-méi-you-yìjian. 我 沒
有 意 見 . I have no opinion.
(2) differing opinion. nào-yìjian
鬧 意 見 fight over different
opinions. Dōu-duì-ta-yǒu-yìjian.
都 對 他 有 意 見 .
Everybody is opposing him
(because of different opinions).
YÌJIĀZI₁ 一 家 子 (N) (1) a
family. (2) the same family or
clan. Tāmen-shi-yijiāzi. 他
們 是 一 家 子 . They
belong to the same family.
YǏJING₁ 已 經 (AD) already.
Tā-yǐjing-lái-le. 他 已 經
來 了 . He already came.

Y

YĪ...JIU...₁ 一...就...(S)
(1) as soon as. Tā-yí-kàn jiu-
míngbai-le.他 一 看 就 明
白 了 . As soon as he saw he
understood it. Wǒ-yì-tǎngxia jiu-
shuìzháo-le. 我 一 躺 下
就 睡 着 了 . As soon as
I laid down I fell asleep. (2)
once something happens, then
something else will always be
the consequence. Wúlùn-shì-shéi,
yì-dé-zhèige-bìng, jiu-suàn-
wán-le. 無 論 是 誰, 一
得 這 個 病, 就 算 完
了 . It doesn't matter who,
once he gets this sickness, he's
finished. Tā-yì-chūqu jiushi-
sāntian. 他 一 出 去 就
是 三 天 . Once he goes out
it always takes three days. (3)
with stress on yi 一 , indicates
getting the result with only one
attempt. Wǒ-'yì-cāi jiu-cāizhao-
le. 我 一 猜 就 猜 着
了 . I guessed only once and
got it right. (cf: YĪ 一 , YĪ...
YĪ... 一...一...).

YÌJUÉ₃ 議決 (TV) decide by
voting. Jīntian-kāi-huì yìjuéle-
sānjian-dà-shì. 今 天 開 會
議 決 了 三 件 大 事 .
At today's meeting we decided
three big matters.

YĪKAO₃ 依靠 see YĪKAO 倚
靠 .

YĪKAO₃ 倚靠 or YĪKAO 依靠
(TV) depend on. Méi-yǒu-nǐ wǒ-
yīkao-shéi-ne? 没 有 你 我
倚 靠 誰 呢 ? Without you,
whom can I depend on?

(N) someone or something to
be leaned on. Tā-fùqin-sǐ-le.
Tāmen-dōu-méi-you-yīkao-le.
他 父 親 死 了, 他
們 都 没 有 倚 靠 了.
His father died. They no longer
have anyone to lean on. (cf:
YĪLÀI 倚賴).

YÍKUÀIR₁ 一塊兒 (PW) to-
gether, the same place or time.
Nèixie-dōngxi dōu-fàngzai-yí-
kuàir. 那 些 東 西 都 放
在 一 塊 兒 . Put those
things in the same place. Tā-
men-yíkuàir-shuō. 他 們 一
塊 兒 說 . They speak at
the same time.

YĪLÁI₂ 一來 (MA) in the first
place. Yīlai-tài-guì, zàishuō,
yě-bu-hǎokàn, suóyi-bié-mǎi.
一 來 太 貴, 再 "說, 也
不 好 看, 所 以 別 買 .
In the first place it's too expensive, and again it's not good-
looking, so don't buy it.

YĪLÀI₃ 依賴 see YĪLÀI 依賴 .

YĪLÁI₁ 以來 (-B) (1) preceded
by NU-M expressions of time,
during all of a certain period of
time. Jèi-liǎngnian-yǐlái, wǒ-
dōu-zhùzai-jèr. 這 兩 年
以 來 我 都 住 在 這
兒 . I lived here during these
past two years. (2) used after
a clause or TW, with or without
zìcóng 自從 or cóng 從 pre-
ceding the clause or TW, since
some occurrence or a given
date of some time ago. (Cóng-)
wǒ-bì-yè-yǐlái jiu-méi-zuòguo-

Y

shì. (從) 我畢業以來
就沒做過事. Since I
graduated I haven't worked. (Zì-
cóng-) yĭjiŭwŭwŭ-yĭlái wŏ-jiu
bu-hē-jiŭ-le. 自從) 一九五五
以來, 我就不喝酒了.
I haven't drunk any alcholic beverage since 1955.

YĬLÀI₃ 倚賴 or YĬLÀI 依賴
(TV) be dependent on. Yíge-rén
bùneng-lăo-yĭlài-biéren. 一個
人不能老依賴別
人. One can't always be dependent on others. (cf: YĬKAO
倚靠).

YĬLÁI₂ 一來 or YÍDÒNGR 一
動兒 (MA) at the slightest
provocation. Tā-tàitai yìlái-jiu-
kū. 他太太一來就
哭. His wife cries easily. Yì-
lai tā-jiu-gēn-wo-yào-qián. 一
來他就跟我要錢.
He asks for money from me
very often.

YÌLÁI₃ 一來 used after SP such
as zhèi 這, nèi 那, zènma 這
麼, zhènma 這麼, nènma
那麼 , etc., and followed by
another clause, do something
once in a certain way. Wŏmen-
zènma-yìlái, tā-jiu-méi-fázi-le.
我們這麼一來他
就沒法子了. Once we
do it this way, he will have no
way out. Zhèi-yàngr-yìlái, shì-
qing-jiu-bu-hăobàn-le. 這樣
一來, 事情就不好
辦了. Once it is done this
way, it is difficult to handle.

YĬLÁI...ÈRLÁI...₃ 一來 ...

二來 ...(S) used for giving
reasons, in the first place...
and in the second place. Yĭlái
wŏ-méi-you-qián, èrlái wŏ-
méi-you-gōngfu. 一來我
沒有錢, 二來我沒
有工夫. In the first place
I don't have the money, secondly,
I don't have the time.

YÍLÈI₃ 一類 (NU-M) (1) one
kind. Yŏu-yílèi-ren wŏ-bu-xi-
huan. 有一類人我不
喜歡. There is one kind of
person I don't like. (2) the
same kind. Zhèi-liăngge bú-shi-
yílèi. 這兩個不是一
類. These two are not the
same kind.

YĬLĬ₄ 以裏 see YĬNÈI 以內.

YÌLÌ₄ 毅力 (N) firm attitude to
get something accomplished.
Tā-zuò-shì hĕn-you-yìlì. 他
作事很有毅力. He
has a firm determination in
doing things.

YÌLIÁN₄ 一連 (AD) used before
NU-M, continuously, in a series. Tā-yìlián-sāntiān méi-
chī-fàn. 他一連三天
沒吃飯. He didn't eat for
three days (continuously).

YÌLIÁNCHUÀN₅ 一連串 (NU-
M) a series of. Tā-jīngguole-
yiliánchuàn-bu-yùkuaide-shì-
qing. 他經過了一連
串不愉快的事情
He has gone through a series of
unhappy events.

YĪLIÀOR₄ 衣料兒 (N) mate-
rial, yardgoods (for making

Y

clothes).

YĪLIÚ₃ 一流 (NU-M) (1) (con.
dìyīliú 第一流). top quali-
ty, first class. yīliú-lǚguǎn 一
流旅馆 first class hotel.
(2) same category, same kind.
Zhèiliǎngge shi-yìliú. 這兩
個是一流 . These two
are in the same category.

YĪLÙ₃ 一路 (NU-M) (1) one
kind. (2) the same kind. Tāmen-
búshi-yílùde. 他們不是
一路的 . They are not the
same kind. (cf: YĪLÈI 一類).

YĪLÙ₂ 一律 (SV) uniform,
Zhèrde-fángqian bù-yílù. 這兒
的房錢不一律 . The
rents here are not the same.
(AD) uniformly. Tāmen-yílù-
chuān-bái-yīfu. 他們一律
穿白衣服 . They are
uniformly dressed in white
clothes.

YĪLÙN₃ 議論 (TV) discuss,
talk about. Wǒmen-yìlùnle-bàn-
tiān méi-you-jiéguǒ. 我們議
論了半天沒有結
果 . We have discussed it for
quite a while with no result.
(N) discussion. Yìlun-hěn-duō.
議論很多 . There were
many discussions.

YĪLÙPÍNG'ĀN₂ 一路平安
used to bid farewell, (lit. be
peaceful all the way) Have a nice
trip.

YĪMIÀNR₄ 一面兒 (NU-M) one
side. Tā-shuō-de shì-yímiànr-lǐ.
他說的是一面兒
理 . What he said only covered

one side of the reason.
(AD) used repeatedly, do something while doing something else.
Tā-yímiànr-chī-fàn yímiànr-
kàn-bào. 他一面兒吃
飯一面兒看報 . He
reads the newspaper while he
is eating. (cf: YĪBIĀNR 一邊
兒 , YĪFĀNGMIAN 一方面).

YĪMÍN₃ 移民 (TV) immigrate,
emigrate. Zhèngfǔ zhèng-jìhua
xiàng-Nánměi-yímín. 政府
正計劃向南美移
民 . The government is
planning to emigrate some people to South America.
(N) immigrant, emigrant. Wǒ-
shì-yíge-yímín. 我是一個
移民 . I'm an immigrant.

YĪMÓYIYÀNG₃ 一模一樣
(SV) exactly the same. Zhèi-
liǎngge yìmóyiyàng. 這兩
個一模一樣 . These
two are exactly the same.

YĪMŬ₅ 姨母 see YÍ(R) 姨
(兒).

YĪN₄ 音 (N) (1) sound (in
phonetics). (2) note (in music).

YĪN₁ 陰 (SV) (1) cloudy (of weather). (opp. qíng 晴). Tiān-yòu-
yīn-le. 天又陰了 . The
sky has gotten cloudy again. (2)
crafty, devious. Wǒmende-jīng-
lǐ hěn-yīn. 我們的經理
很陰 . Our manager is very
crafty.
(TV) deceive. Nǐ-kě-bié-yīn-wo.
你可別陰我 . Don't
deceive me.
(B-) (1) lunar. (opp. yáng 陽).

yīnlì 陰曆 lunar calendar. (2)
the other world. yīnjiān 陰間
Hades. (3) secret, concealed.
yīnmóu 陰謀 plot, scheme.
(4) negative. (opp. yáng 陽).
yīnjí 陰極 negative pole. (5)
shade, shadow. yīnyǐng 陰影
shade. shùyin 樹陰 shade of
a tree.

YĪN₃ 銀 (B) (1) silver (the material). yínqi 銀器 sliverware.
(2) money. yínháng 銀行 bank.
(3) silvery. yínsè 銀色 silver
color. yínpíxié 銀皮鞋
silver-colored shoes.

YĬN₄ 癮 (N) craving, yen. yǒu-
yǐn 有癮 have a craving for.
shàng-yǐn 上癮 become addicted. guò-yǐn 過癮 satisfy
the craving or yen for. Tāde-
yēn-yǐn hěn-dà. 他的烟
癮很大 . His craving for
tobacco is very great.

YĪN₂ 印 (TV) print, make an impression. yìn-yìbǎi-zhāng 印
一百張 print one hundred
copies.
(N) (1) seal, stamp. (M: kē 顆).
gàiyìn 蓋印 affix a seal or a
stamp. (2) imprint, mark, trace.
shǒu-yìn 手印 fingerprint.

YĪNCǏ₂ 因此 (MA).therefore,
hence. Tā-bugòu-zīge, yīncǐ
wǒ-méi-qǐng-ta. 他不夠資
格,因此我沒請他
He is not qualified, therefore
I didn't hire him.

YĪNDU₂ 印度 (PW) India.
YĪNDUNÍXĪYÀ₃ 印度尼西
亞 (PW) Indonesia. (syn. Yìnní

印尼).
YĪNDUYÁNG₅ 印度洋 (PW)
Indian Ocean.
YǏNEI₂ 以內 or YǏLǏ 以裏
(-B) (1) used after a noun, inside of, within certain stated
confines or limits. xuéxiào-
yǐnèi 學校以內 inside
the school. (2) used after NU-
M, less than, within a given
figure. wǔkuài-qián-yǐnèi 五
塊錢以內 less than five
dollars.

YĪNG₅ 應 (TV) agree to do something for someone. Nǐ-yīngle,
jiu-děi-gěi-ren-zuò. 你應
了,就得給人作
Since you agreed you must do
it for them.

YĪNG₅ 鷹 (N) eagle, hawk, fal-
con or any bird of the eagle
family. (M: zhī 隻).

YĪNG₃ 英 (B-) England, the United Kingdom, Great Britain.
Yīngguo 英國 England. Yīng-
wén 英文 English language.

YÍNG₄ 營 (N) (1) camp. xiàlìng-
yíng 夏令營 summer camp.
(2) battalion. yíngzhǎng 營長
battalion commander.
(M) battalion. yìyíng-rén 一
營人 one battalion of soldiers.
(B) manage, operate (business).
gūngyíng-shìyè 公營事業
government operated business.

YÍNG₂ 贏 (TV) win (in a game).
(opp. shū 輸). Tāmen-dǎ-qiú,
shéi-yíng-le? 他們打球,
誰贏了 ? Who won the
game they were playing? Nǐ-

Y

yíngle-duōshao-qián? 你赢
了多少錢? How much
money did you win?

YÌNG₄ 應 (TV) bear out (a prediction or a forecast). Zhēn-yìngle-
tade-huà-le. 真應了他
說的話了. His words
were really borne out.

YÌNG₁ 硬 (SV) (1) hard (not soft).
Zuànshí shi-zuì-yìng-de-dōngxi.
鑽石是最硬的東
西. A diamond is the hardest
thing. (2) stiff. Zhèige-zhǐ-hézi
bugòu-yìng. 這個紙盒子
不夠硬. This cardboard
box is not stiff enough. (3) unyielding. Tāde-kǒuqi-hěn-yìng.
他的口氣很硬. He
speaks in an unyielding manner.
(AD) do something at will with
no respect for reason or conse-
quences. Tā-yìng-bǎ-wǒde-chē
kāizǒu-le. 他硬把我的
車開走了. He drove my
car away without my permission.
Tā-yìng-bu-chéngrèn. 他硬
不承認. He denied it ob-
stinately.

YÌNGBÀNG₄ 英磅 (N) English
pound (money).

YÌNGCHǏ₃ 英尺 (M) foot (unit
of measurement). sānyīngchǐ
三英尺 three feet.

YÌNGCHOU₃ 應酬 (TV) do something as a social obligation or
for the sake of courtesy, such as
going to a party, entertaining
guests, making some remarks
or doing something to please
someone, etc. carry on social

intercourse. Wèile-yìngchou-
tade-fùqin, wǒ-mǎile-ta-yì-
zhang-huàr. 為了應酬
他的父親,我買了
他一張畫兒. As a
social obligation to his father
I bought one of his paintings.
Wǒ-bu-yànyi-gēn-ren yìngchou.
我不願意跟人應
酬. I don't like to carry on
social intercourse.
(N) social intercourse. Wǒ-jīn-
tian-yǒu-yíge-yìngchou. 我今
天有一個應酬. I
have a social engagement today.

YÌNGCÙN₃ 英寸 (M) inch.
liǎngyīngcùn 兩英寸 two
inches.

YÌNGDĀNG₁ 應當 (AV) ought
to, should. (syn. yīnggāi 應
該). Nǐ-yīngdāng kànkan-dài-
fu. 你應當看看大
夫. You should see a doctor.
A: Xièxie-nín-bāng-máng. B:
Nà-shi-yīngdāng-de. A: 謝謝
您幫忙. B: 那是應
當的. A: Thank you for
helping. B: That's just something I should do. A: Wǒmen-
qǐng-ta-ba. B: Wǒ-xiǎng yīngdāng. A: 我們請他吧.
B: 我想應當. A: Let's
invite him. B: I think we should.

YÌNGFU₃ 應付 (TV) deal with
a person or a situation, cope
with. Wǒ-búhuì-yìngfu-rén. 我
不會應付人. I am
not good in dealing with people.
Zhèi-zhǒng-qíngxing tā-yìngfu-
buliǎo. 這種情形他

Y

應付不了. He cannot cope with this kind of situation.

YĪNGGAI₁ 應該 (AV) ought to, should. (syn. yīngdāng 應當). Nǐ-yīnggai-qù. 你應該去 You should go. Tā-zěnma-méi-gěi-qián? Zhēn-shi-bu-yīnggai. 他怎樣沒給錢? 真是不應該. Why didn't he pay? He really shouldn't.

YĪNGGUO₁ 英國 (PW) England, the United Kingdom, Great Britain.

YÍNGHE₄ 迎合 (TV) meet or suit certain requirements and needs. Zào-wányìr děi-yínghé-xiǎoháirde-xīnlǐ. 造玩藝兒得迎合小孩兒的心理. In manufacturing toys one must meet the desires of children. Tā-bu-néng-yínghé-shídàide-xūyào. 他不能迎合時代的需要. He cannot meet the needs of the situation.

YĪNGHUA₄ 櫻花 (N) cherry blossom. (M: duǒ 朵, kē 棵).

YÍNGHUǑCHÓNGR₅ 螢火蟲兒 (N) firefly, glowworm.

YÍNGJIE₅ 迎接 (TV) receive or welcome someone. Nǐmen-dōu-qù-chēzhàn yíngjie-ta-qu-ma? 你們都去車站迎接他去嗎? Are you all going to the station to welcome him?

YĪNGLǏ₂ 英里 (M) mile. yìyīng-lǐ 一英里 one mile. (N) mile. yíge-yīnglǐ 一個英里 one mile.

YĪNGR₃ 影兒 or YĪNGZI 影子 (N) (1) shadow. Qiángshang-yǒu-yige-yīngr. 牆上有一個影兒. There is a shadow on the wall. (2) image, reflection from a mirror or mirrorlike object. jìngzi-li-de-yīngr 鏡子裏的影兒 reflection in a mirror. (3) vague image. Xiàngpiānr-bu-qīngchu jiu-yǒu-yìdiǎnr-yīngr. 像片兒不清楚就有一點影兒. The photograph is not clear, there is only a vague image on it. Wǒ-dōu-wàng-le. Yìdiǎn-yīngr yě-méi-yǒu-le. 我都忘了. 一點兒影兒也沒有了. I forgot completely. It doesn't leave even a vague image.

YĪNGTAO₃ 櫻桃 (N) cherry (fruit). (M: kē 顆).

YĪNGWÉN₁ 英文 (N) English language or literature. shuō-yīngwén 說英文 speak English.

YĪNGWǓ₅ 鸚鵡 (N) parrot, parakeet, cockatoo or any bird of the parrot family. (M: zhī 隻).

YĪNGXIANG₁ 影響 (TV) influence, affect. Wǒ-méi-xǐngdào huì-yíngxiang-tā. 我沒想到會影響他. I didn't think it could affect him. (N) influence, effect. Nèijian-shìqing-duì-wǒ méi-yíngxiang. 那件事情對我沒影響. That matter has no

Y

effect on me. Tā-líkai-le, wǒ-men-shòule-hěn-dà-de-yíng-xiang. 他 離 開 了, 我 們 受 了 很 大 的 影 響. He has left, the influence on us has been very great.

YĪNGXIONG₂ 英 雄 (N) hero.

YÍNGYǍNG₃ 營 養 (N) nourish-ment, nutritional value. Tāmen-chī-de-tài-shǎo, suóyi-yíngyǎng-bú-gòu. 他 們 吃 的 太 少, 所 以 營 養 不 够. They eat too little, therefore they are undernourished.

YĪNGYǑNG₅ 英 勇 (SV) brave.

YĪNGYÒNG₃ 應 用 (TV) use in actual practice, apply. Wǒmen-xiànzài hái-bunéng-yīngyòng-xīnde-lǐlùn. 我 們 現 在 還 不 能 應 用 新 的 理 論. We can't apply the new theory yet. (N) application.

YǏNGZI₅ 影 子 <u>see</u> YǏNGR 影 兒.

YÍNHÁNG₁ 銀 行 (N) bank (<u>mon-ey-handling institution</u>). (M: jiā 家).

YĪNIÁNDÀOTÓU₃ 一 年 到 頭 (MA) all year round. Tā-yìnián-dàotóu dōu-hěn-máng. 他 一 年 到 頭 都 很 忙. He is very busy all year round.

YĪNJIÉ₄ 音 節 (N) syllable.

YĪNLÌ₅ 陰 曆 (N) lunar calendar. (<u>opp</u>. yánglì 陽 曆).

YĪNLIÁNGR₄ 陰 涼 兒 shady and cool place.

YĪNLIÀO₅ 飲 料 (N) beverages.

YǏNMÁN₅ 隱 瞞 (TV) conceal

information. Nǐ-yǐnmánbuliǎo-nide-mìmì. 你 隱 瞞 不 了 你 的 秘 密. You can't hide your secret.

YĪNMÓU₄ 陰 謀 (N) crafty plan, plot, scheme.

YĪNMÙ₃ 銀 幕 (N) motion pic-ture screen.

YÌNNÍ₃ 印 尼 (PW) Indonesia. (<u>syn</u>. yìndùníxīyà 印 度 尼 西 亞).

YĪNQIN₃ 殷 勤 (SV) attentive <u>to someone's personal needs</u>. Tā-fúshi-bìngren hěn-yīnqin. 他 服 侍 病 人 很 殷 勤. She is very attentive to taking care of the patients. (N) attentiveness to <u>someone's personal needs</u>. xiàn-yīnqin 獻 殷 勤 pay special atten-tion to <u>someone's personal needs with an ulterior motive in mind.</u>

YǏNQÍNG₃ 引 擎 (N) (1) engine. (2) motor.

YÌNR₃ 印 兒 (N) mark, trace. jiǎo-yìnr 腳 印 兒 foot-prints. Méi-cāgānjing, hái-yǒu-hǎoxiē-yìnr-ne. 沒 擦 乾 淨, 還 有 好 些 印 兒 呢. It isn't wiped clean, there are still lots of marks.

YÌNSE₄ 印 色 <u>or</u> YÌNSHAI 印 色 (N) <u>a kind of</u> red ink, mixed with raw silk, <u>used for making imprints of a stamp or seal, similar to a stamp pad.</u>

YÌNSHAI₄ 印 色 <u>see</u> YÌNSE 印 色.

YǏNSHÍ₄ 飲 食 (N) (<u>lit</u>. drink

Y

and eat) food intake, diet. Shēn-
ti-bu-hǎo, děi-zhùyi-yǐnshí. 身
體 不 好, 得 注 意 飲
食. When one's health is not
good, one must pay attention to
the diet.

YÌNSHUĀ₄ 印 刷 (N) process of
printing. Wǒmen-bu-guǎn-yìn-
shuā. 我 們 不 管 印 刷.
We don't take care of the printing.

YÌNSHUĀJĪ₄ 印 刷 機 (N)
printing machine.

YÌNSHUĀPǏN₄ 印 刷 品 (N)
printed matter.

YÌNSHUĀSUǑ₃ 印 刷 所 (N)
print shop.

YĪN-TIĀN₂ 陰 天 (VO) cloudy
day. (opp. qíng-tiān 晴 天).
Jīntian yīn-tiān. 今 天 陰 天.
It's cloudy today.

YĪNWEI₁ 因 為 (MA) because.
Yīnwei-wǒ-méi-qián, suóyi-wǒ-
méi-qù. 因 為 我 沒 錢,
所 以 我 沒 去. I didn't
go because I didn't have any
money. Míngtian-wǒ-bú-qù-le,
yīnwei-wǒ-yǒu-shìh. 明 天 我
不 去 了, 因 為 我 有
事. I won't go tomorrow because I have another engagement.

YĪNXIǍN₅ 陰 險 (SV) crafty,
devious. Zhèige-rén yīnxiǎn. 這
個 人 陰 險. This person
is crafty.

YÌNXIANG₃ 印 象 (N) impres-
sion in the mind. Wǒ-duì-tāde-
yìnxiang-búcuò. 我 對 他 的
印 象 不 錯. My impres-
sion of him is fairly good. Nèr-

wǒ-qùguo-yícì, kěshi-méi-liú-
xia-shénma-yìnxiang. 那 兒
我 去 過 一 次, 可 是
沒 留 下 甚 麼 印 象.
I went there once but it didn't
leave any impression on me.

YĬNYOU₃ 引 誘 (TV) lead into
temptation. Tā-ná-qián-yǐnyou-
ta. 他 拿 錢 引 誘 他.
He used money to tempt him.
(N) temptation.

YĪNYUE₁ 音 樂 (N) music. tīng-
yīnyue 聽 音 樂 listen to
music.

YĪNYUEDUÌ₄ 音 樂 隊 (N)
band, orchestra.

YĪNYUEHUÌ₃ 音 樂 會 (N)
concert.

YĪNYUEJIĀ₃ 音 樂 家 (N)
musician.

YÍNZI₂ 銀 子 (N) (1) silver.
Yínzi-shi-yizhǒng-jīnshu. 銀
子 是 一 種 金 屬 Silver
is a metal. (2) silver money.
(M: liang 兩).

YÍQÌ₃ 一 氣 (AD) in one breath,
in one gulp. Wǒmen-yíqì-zuò-
wán-ba! 我 們 一 氣 作
完 吧 ! Let's finish it at one
stroke!
(NU-M) used after a V, exert
a concentrated effort for a
while. dàchī-yíqì 大 吃 一
氣 eat heartily for a while.

YÍQÌ₄ 儀 器 (N) apparatus.

YÌQÌ₅ 義 氣 (N) righteousness.
Tā-hěn-jiǎng-yìqi. 他 很 講
義 氣. He is very righteous.

YÌQÍ₄ 一 齊 (AD) in unison, together, all at the same time.

Y

Wǒmen-yìqí-zǒu-ba! 我們一
齊走吧！Let's go together!

YÌQǏ₃ 一起 (PW) the same
place or time, together. (syn.
yíkuàir 一塊兒). Tāmen-
dōu-zài-yìqǐ. 他們都在
一起. They are all at the
same place. Wǒmen(-zai)-yìqǐ-
zuò-shì. 我們（在）一起
作事. We work together.

YǏQIÁN₁ 以前 (TW) (1) in the
past, formerly, previously. Yǐqián wǒ-bù-chōu-yān. 以前
我不抽煙. Formerly,
I didn't smoke. (2) the past. Yǐ-
qián-shi-yǐqián, xiànzài-shi-
xiànzài. 以前是以前,
現在是現在. The past
is the past and the present is the
present. (3) used after NU-M,
N, TW or a clause, indicates a
period of time, before. liǎngge-
lǐbài-yǐqián 兩個禮拜以
前 two weeks before. Shèngdàn-
jié-yǐqián 聖誕節以前
before Christmas. Shuì-jiào-yǐ-
qián děi-shuā-yá. 睡覺以
前得刷牙. You must
brush your teeth before sleeping.
(PW) used after N, in front of
something. Zhèi-sānzhang-zhuō-
zi-yǐqián bu-néng-fàng-dōngxi.
這三張桌子以前
不能放東西. Nothing
can be put in front of these three
tables.

YÍQIÈ₂ 一切 (N) often used with
dōu 都, everything. Yíqiè dōu-
hěn-hǎo. 一切都很好.
Everything is very good. Tā-bú-

gù-yíqiè. 他不顧一切.
He disregards everything.

YÌQÚN₁ 一群 (NU-M) a crowd
of, a group of. yìqún-rén 一
群人 a crowd of people.

YǏSÈLIÈ₃ 以色列 (PW)
Israel.

YĪSHANG₁ 衣裳 (N) clothes.
(syn. yīfu 衣服). (M: jiàn
件, tào 套). chuān-yīshang
穿衣裳 wear clothes. Wǒ-
dìng-zuòle-yitao-yīshang. 我
定作了一套衣裳.
I had a suit of clothes made to
order.

YǏSHÀNG₁ 以上 (TW) (1) what
preceded, before this point. Wǒ-
yǐshàng-jiǎngde nǐmen-dōu-
dǒng-ma? 我以上講的
你們都懂嗎？ Have
you understood what I've explained so far? (2) used after a
noun, above. zhèitiao-xiàn-yǐ-
shàng 這條線以上
above this line. Sāncéng-lóu-
yǐshàng-de-fángzū jiu-guì-le.
三層樓以上的房
租就賣了. Above the
third floor the rent will be more
expensive. (3) used after NU-M,
more than, over. èrshi-rén-yǐ-
shàng 二十人以上 over
twenty people.

YÌSHĒN₃ 一身 (NU-M) (1) all
over the body. yìshēn-dǔ 一身
土 dirt all over the body. (2)
for clothes, suit. yìshēn-xīn-
yīshang 一身新衣裳 a
new dress.

YĪSHENG₁ 醫生 (N) medical

doctor. (<u>syn.</u> dàifu 大夫).
(M: wèi 位).

YÌSHĒNG₄ 一 生 (MA) for <u>one's</u>
whole life. (<u>syn.</u> yíbèizi 一 輩
子). Tā-yìshēng méi-qiàngwo-
biérén-de-qián. 他 一 生 没
欠 過 别 人 的 錢. He
hasn't owed people money all
his life.

YÌSHI₃ 儀 式 (N) ceremony.
zōngjiào-yíshi 宗 教 儀 式
religious ceremony. jǔxíng-yíshi
舉 行 儀 式 hold a cere-
mony.

YÌSHÍ₂ 一 時 (MA) (1) in a moment of. Zuótian wǒ-yìshí-gāo-
xìng, jiu-mǎi-le. 昨 天 我
一 時 高 興 就 買 了.
Yesterday, in a moment of high
spirits, I bought it. (2) for a
while. Tāmen-yìshí hái-bunéng-
mǎi. 他 們 一 時 還 不
能 買. They are not able to
buy it for a while.

YÌSHÌJIE₄ 一 世 界 (NU-M) all
over the place. Tā-nòngle-yíshì-
jie-mòshuǐr. 他 弄 了 一 世
界 墨 水 兒. He spilled
ink all over the place.

YÌSHU₂ 藝 術 (N) art. Tā-bu-
dǒng-yìshu. 他 不 懂 藝
術. He doesn't understand art.
(SV) artistic. Zhèi-jiān-wūzi bù-
zhì-de hěn-yìshu. 這 間 屋
子 佈 置 的 很 藝 術.
The decoration of this room is
very artistic.

YÌSHUJIĀ₃ 藝 術 家 (N) artist.
(M: wèi 位).

YÌSI₁ 意 思 (N) (1) meaning, what

one means. Zhèiju-huà shi-
shénma-yìsi? 這 句 話 是
甚 麼 意 思 ? What is the
meaning of this sentence? Wǒ-
bu-dǒng-tāde-yìsi. 我 不 懂
他 的 意 思. I don't un-
derstand what he meant. (2)
intention. Tāde-yìsi hěn-hǎo.
他 的 意 思 很 好. His
intention is pretty nice. Wǒ-
yǒu-yìsi gēn-ta-tántan. 我 有
意 思 跟 他 談 談. I
have the intention of talking with
him. Tā-'méiyou-nèige-yìsi.
他 没 有 那 個 意 思.
He doesn't mean it that way. <u>or</u>
He doesn't have that intention.
Nǐ-shi-shénma-yìsi? 你 是
甚 麼 意 思 ? <u>or</u> Nǐde-
yìsi-shi-shénma? 你 的 意
思 是 甚 麼 ? What do you
mean? or What's your intention?
(3) idea. Wǒde-yìsi gen-nǐde-
yíyàng. 我 的 意 思 跟
你 的 一 樣. My idea is
the same as yours. Tā-na-yìsi
shi-jiào-nǐ-bié-zuò. 他 那
意 思 是 叫 你 别 作.
His idea is to tell you not do it.
Nǐ-yǒu-shénma-yìsi, gǎnjǐn-
shuō. 你 有 甚 麼 意 思,
趕 緊 説. What kind of idea
do you have, hurry up and say
it. Nà-shi-Lǐ-xianshengde-yìsi.
那 是 李 先 生 的 意
思. That's what Mr. Li meant.
or That is Mr. Li's idea. (4)
<u>feelings</u> of appreciation or grat-
itude. Sònggei-ta-yìdiǎnr-lǐwu,
biǎoshi-biaoshi-wǒde-yìsi. 送

Y

給 他 一 點 兒 禮 物, 表 示 表 示 我 的 意 恩 . Give him a little gift in order to express my feelings. (See: YǑU-YÌSI 有 意 思 , BÙHǍOYÌSI 不 好 意 思).

YÌSÌR₅ 一 死 兒 (AD) insistently, stubbornly. Tā-yìsǐr-yào-qù. 他 一 死 兒 要 去 . He insists on going.

YÌTIĀN(DÀOWǍN)₃ 一 天 (到 晚) (AD) from morning till night, all day long. Tā-yìtiān-(dàowǎn) niàn-shū. 他 一 天 (到 晚) 念 書 . He studies from morning till night.

YÌTÓNG₅ 一 同 (AD) together. Wǒmen-yìtóng-zuò-shì. 我 們 一 同 作 事 . We work together.

YǏWÀI₃ 以 外 (-B) (1) used after a noun, outside of, beyond certain stated limits or confines. gōngyuán-yǐwài 公 園 以 外 outside the park. (2) used after NU-M, more than, over a given figure. èrshi-rén-yǐwài 二 十 人 以 外 over twenty people. (3) used after a noun or a clause, with or without chúqu 除 去 or chúle 除 了 ,besides. Chī-yào-yǐwài hái-děi-dǎ-zhēn. 吃 藥 以 外 還 得 打 針 . Besides taking medicine, it is still necessary to get on injection.

YÌWÀI₃ 意 外 (N) unanticipated happening (usually unpleasant), accident. Yòu-chūle-yìwàide-shìqing-le. 又 出 了 意 外 的 事 情 了 . Something

unanticipated happened again. Wànyī-yǒu-ge-yìwài, zěnma-bàn? 萬 一 有 個 意 外 , 怎 麼 辦 ? In case something unexpected happens, what do we do?

YǏWǍNG₃ 已 往 (TW) the past, before. Yǐwǎng tā-cháng-lái. 已 往 他 常 來 . He used to come often before. Yǐwǎngde-shì búyòng-xiǎng-le. 已 往 的 事 不 用 想 了 . There is no need to think of affairs of the past.

'YǏWÉI₂ 以 為 (TV) (1) assume, think incorrectly. Wǒ-'yǐwéi-xià-yǔ-le, yuánlái-méi-xià. 我 以 為 下 雨 了, 原 來 沒 下 . I thought it was raining, but it turned out that it wasn't. (2) usually followed by a pause, it is someone's opinion. Wǒ-'yǐwéi nǐ-yīnggāi-chuān-hóngde. 我 以 為 你 應 該 穿 紅 的 . I think you should wear a red dress. (cf: DǍNG 當).

YÍWÈN₄ 疑 問 (N) doubt, question. Méi-yǒu-yíwèn. 沒 有 疑 問 . No doubt.

YÌWU₄ 義 務 (N) duty, responsibility. jìn-yìwu 盡 義 務 fulfill a duty. Jiàoyu-zǐnǚ shì-fùmǔde-yìwu. 教 育 子 女 是 父 母 的 義 務 . To educate the children is the duty of the parents. (AD) without pay, free. Tā-yì-wu-gěi-ren-kàn-bìng. 他 義 務 給 人 看 病 . He

Y

treats patients free.

YĬXIÀ₁ 以 下 (TW) (1) what follows, after this point. Wǒ-yǐxià jiu-bù-shuō-le. 我 以 下 就 不 說 了 . What follows I won't tell. (2) used after a noun, below, under. zhèige-dìfang-yǐxià 這 個 地 方 以 下 below this point. (3) used after NU-M, less than, under. wǔshikuài-qián-yǐxià 五 十 塊 錢 以 下 less than fifty dollars.

YÍXIA(R)₁ 一 下(兒) or YÍXIÀZI 一 下 子 (NU-M) (1) one instance of doing something. Wǒdǎle-ta-yixiar. 我 打 了 他 一 下 兒 . I gave him a blow. Nèige-mén tā-yíxiar jiu-kāikaile. 那 個 門 他 一 下 兒 就 開 開 了 . He opened that door on the first try. Zhèi-yixiàr tā-méi-bànfa-le. 這 一 下 兒 他 沒 辦 法 了 . After this action, he has no way out. (2) for a while. Dàowǒmen-jiā lai-zuò-yixiar. 到 我 們 家 來 坐 一 下 兒 . Please come over to our house for a while. Qǐng-jìnlai, wōmen-tán-yixiar. 請 進 來 我 們 談 一 下 兒 . Please come in, let's chat for a while.

YĬXIĀN₃ 以 先 (TW) (1) previously. Yǐxiān tā-'bú-shi-zhèiyàngr. 以 先 他 不 是 這 樣 兒 . Previously he wasn't like this. (2) used after a N or a clause, before. Chī-fàn-yǐxiān

xǐ-shǒu. 吃 飯 以 先 洗 手 . Prior to eating wash your hands. (cf: YĪQIÁN 以 前).

YÍXIÀNG₂ 一 向 (MA) have always been, have always. Tā-yíxiàng jiu-zènma-qióng. 他 一 向 就 這 麼 窮 . He has always been poor like this. Tā-yíxiàng-chī-Zhōngguo-fàn. 他 一 向 吃 中 國 飯 . He has always eaten Chinese food.

YÍXIÀZI₁ 一 下 子 see YÍXIÀR 一 下 兒 .

YÌXIĒ₃ 一 些 (NU-M) some, a little. Hái-yǒu-yixiē-dōngxi méi-bānlai. 還 有 一 些 東 西 沒 搬 來 . There are still some things that haven't been moved here. Zhèige-hǎo-yixie. 這 個 好 一 些 . This is a little better.

YÍXIN₂ 疑 心 (syn. yíhuo 疑 惑) (TV) suspect. Wǒ-yíxīn shì-'tā-shāde-tā-tàitai. 我 疑 心 是 他 殺 的 他 太 太 . I suspect that he's the one who killed his wife. (N) suspicions. Tā-yòu-qǐ-yíxīn-le. 他 又 起 疑 心 了 . He has suspicions again.

YĪXUÉ₃ 醫 學 (N) medicine (branch of study).

YÌYǍN₄ 一 眼 (MA) at a glance. Wǒ-'yìyǎn jiu-kànjian-ta-le. 我 一 眼 就 看 見 他 了 . I saw him immediately.

YÍYÀNG₁ 一 樣 (SV) be the same. Tā-gēn-ta-fùqin bu-yíyàng. 他 跟 他 父 親 不 一 樣 . He isn't the same as his father.

Y

(AD) (1) equally, to the same degree. Tāmen-liǎngge-rén yíyàng-gāo. 他們兩個人一樣高. The two of them are equally tall. (2) just the same, regardless. Tā-yǐwei-tā-hěn-cōngming, kěshi-yíyàng-shàng-dàng. 他以為他很聰明，可是也一樣上當. He thought he was very smart, but he was swindled just the same. (cf: YIBĀN 一般, YIBIĀNR 一邊兒).

YÌYI₃ 意義 (N) significance, meaning. méi-you-yìyi 沒有意義 no significance. Jīntian-kāi-huì yǒu-hěn-dàde-yìyi. 今天開會有很大的意義. There was great significance in today's meeting.

YÌYǑNGJŪN₃ 義勇軍 (N) voluntary troops.

YĪYUÀN₂ 醫院 (N) hospital.(M: jiā 家).

YÌYUÁN₄ 議員 (N) member of parliament, congressman, senator.

YÌYUÀN₄ 議院 (N) Congress, Parliament, Diet, etc.

YĪYUE₁ 一月 see YÍYUE 一月.

YĪYUE₁ 一月 or YÍYUE 一月 (TW) (lit. the first month of the year) January.

YÌZǍOR₄ 一早兒 (TW) early in the morning. Tā-yìzǎor jiu-lái-le. 他一早兒就來了. He came early in the morning.

YÍZHÈNR₂ 一陣兒 or YÍ-ZHENZI 一陣子 (NU-M)

moment, for a spell. Tā-yí-zhènr-kū, yizhènr-xiào. 他一陣兒哭，一陣兒笑. He cries for a while, then laughs. Tāde-dùzi yízhènr-yí-zhènrde-téng. 他的肚子一陣兒一陣兒的痛. His stomach aches off and on. Gāngcái hěn-bu-shūfu. Zhèi-yízhènr hǎo-yidianr. 剛才很不舒服，這一陣兒好一點兒. Just a moment ago it was very uncomfortable, but at this moment it is better. Tā-wúlùn-xǐhuan-shénma, jiu-shi-yízhènr. 他無論喜歡甚麼就是一陣兒. It doesn't matter what he likes, it's only for a spell.

YÍZHÈNZI₂ 一陣子 see YÍZHÈNR 一陣兒 .

YÍZHÌ₁ 一致 (SV) consistent, the same, in agreement. Tā-shuōde-huà qiánhòu-bù-yízhì. 他說的話前後不一致. What he said is not consistent.

(AD) all in the same way, all in agreement. Tāde-jiànyì dà-jiā-yízhì-fǎnduì. 他的建議大家一致反對. Everybody (in agreement) opposed his suggestion.

YÌZHÌ₄ 意志 (N) willpower, intent. Tāde-yìzhi-hěn-qiáng. 他的意志很強. He has strong willpower.

YÌZHÍ₁ 一直 (AD) (1) all the time up until a certain point of

time. Tā-yìzhí-méi-qù. 他一直没去 . He has not gone up until now. Tāmen-yào-yìzhí-tándao-liǎng-diǎn.他們要一直談到兩點 . They will talk up until two o'clock. (2) straight toward. Tāmen-yìzhí-wàng-dōng-fēi. 他們一直往東飛 . They fly straight to the east.

YÍZHŬ₃ 遺嘱 (N) last will. xiě-yízhŭ 寫遺嘱 write a will. Tā-méi-liúxia-yízhŭ. 他没留下遺嘱 . He didn't leave a will.

YÍZI₄ 胰子 (N) soap. (syn. féi-zào 肥皂). (M: kuài 塊).

YÍZI₁ 椅子 (N) chair. (M: bǎ 把).

YǑNG₄ 勇 (SV) brave, courageous.

YÒNG₁ 用 (TV) (1) use, utilize. (syn. shǐ 使). Nǐ-kéyi-yòng-wǒde-qìchē. 你可以用我的汽車 . You may use my car. Nǐ-yòng-zhèizhi-bǐ-ba. 你用這枝筆吧 . Use this pen, will you. (2) need. Nǐ-yào-yòng-duōshao-qián? 你要用多少錢 ? How much money do you need? Yòngbuzháo-nǐ-qù. 用不着你去 . There is no need for you to go. (3) polite form, have a smoke, drink, meal, etc. Qǐng-yòng-fàn. 請用飯 . (lit. Please have food.) Dinner is served. Nín-yòngguo-fàn-le-ma? 您用過飯了嗎 ? Have you eaten?

(CV) done with or by certain tools

or process, made of certain materials. (syn. shǐ 使). Tā-yòng-kuàizi-chī-fàn. 他用筷子吃飯 . He eats with chopsticks. Zhèige-shi-yòng-jīqi-zuò-de. 這個是用機器作的 . This is made by machine. Dāo-shi-yòng-gōng-zuò-de. 刀是用鋼作的 . The knife is made of steel.

(AV) need to, have to. Wǒ-yě-yòng-qiān-zì-ma? 我也用簽字嗎 ? Do I also need to sign?

(N) used with yǒu 有 or méi-you 没有 (con. yòngchu 用處). usefulness, utility. Duì-wǒ zhèige-fángzi méi-shenma-yòng. 對我這個房子没甚麼用 . For me, this house doesn't have too much use. Zhèijiu-huà hěn-yǒu-yòng.這句話很有用 . This sentence is very useful.

YÒNGCHU₁ 用處 (N) useful-ness, utility. Zhèige-zhuōzi yòngchu-hěn-duō. 這個桌子用處很多 . This table has many uses. Zhèige-méi-shenma-yòngchu.這個没甚麼用處 . This doesn't have much use. (See: YÒNG 用).

YÒNGFA₄ 用法 (N) way or method to use something. Zhèi-ge-zì-de-yòngfa hen-duō. 這個字的用法很多 . There are many ways to use this word.

Y

YŎNGGĂN₃ 勇敢 (SV) coura-
geous, brave, daring. Tā-hĕn-
yŏnggăn. 他很勇敢. He's
very brave.
(N) bravery.

YÒNG-GŌNG₁ 用功 (VO) put
in effort. Tā-duì-zhèijian-shì
yòngle-bushăo-gōng. 他對
這件事用了不少
功. He put a lot of effort into
this matter.
(SV) studious, hard-working.
Wŏmende-háizi dou-hĕn-yòng-
gōng. 我們的孩子都
很用功. All our children
are very diligent.

YŌNGHÙ₃ 擁護 (TV) support a
government, leader, back someone in doing something. Wŏmen-
yōnghù-ni-jìngxuăn-shĕngzhăng.
我們擁護你競選
省長. We are backing you
to run for governor.
(N) support, backing.

YŌNGJĬ₄ 擁擠 (SV) be crowded.

YŎNGJIŬ₄ 永久 (AD) perma-
nently, eternally, perpetually.
Nĭ-bunéng-yŏngjiŭ-bu-jiéhūn.
你不能永久不結
婚, You can't be a bachelor
forever.
(SV) permanent. Zhè-bu-shi-
yŏngjiŭde-bànfa. 這不是
永久的辦法. This is
not a permanent method.

YÒNG-LÌ₃ 用力 (VO) make an
effort, use strength. Nĭ-dĕi-
duō-yòng-yidianr-lì. 你得多
用一點兒力. You
must put in more effort. Nĭ-

yòng-lì-tuī. 你用力推
Push it hard (with strength).

YŎNGQI₂ 勇氣 (N) bravery,
courage. Tā-yŏngqi-bu-gòu.
他勇氣不夠. He is
not brave enough.

YŎNGQIAN₃ 佣錢 (N) money
accepted by a middleman in a
transaction, brokerage fee,
commission. Tā-bu-shĭ-yòng-
qian. 他不使佣錢. He
doesn't accept any commission.

YÒNGREN₂ 用人 (N) servant.

YÒNG-XĪN₁ 用心 (VO) apply
one's mind. use one's brain.
Nĭ-dĕi-yòng-yidianr-xīn. 你
得用一點兒心. You
have to use your head a little
bit. Nĭ-dĕi-yòng-xīn-liànxi. 你
得用心練習. You'd
better put your mind to it when
you practice. Tā-niàn-shū hĕn-
yòngxīn. 他念書很用
心. He applies himself very
much when he studies.

YŎNGYUĂN₂ 永遠 (MA) for-
ever, permanently. Wŏ-bu-
xiăng-yŏngyuăn-zhùzai-zhèr.
我不想永遠住在
這兒. I don't plan to live
here forever. Tāde-wènti yŏng-
yuăn-bu-néng-jiĕjué. 他的
問題永遠不能解
決. He can never solve his
problems.

YŎNGYUE₄ 踴躍 (SV) enthusi-
astic (of a group or a large
number of people). Jīntiande-
tīngzhòng hĕn-yŏngyue. 今天
的聽眾很踴躍.

Today the audience is enthusiastic and numerous.

(AD) do something enthusiastically (in a group or by a large
number of people). Dàjiā-dōu-
yŏngyuè-juān-qián. 大家都
踴躍捐錢 . All the peo-
ple donate enthusiastically.

YŌU₂ 唷 (I) (con. āiyōu 哎唷).
indicating surprise, gosh, oh
my. Yōu! Zhè-shi-zěnma-hui-
shì? 唷！這是怎麼回
事 ? Gosh! What is this all
about?

YÓU₁ 油 (TV) paint, varnish. Wŏ-
men-gāi-yóu-fáng-le. 我們
該油房子 . It's time to
paint our house.

(SV) cunning, slippery. Tā-hěn-
yóu. 他很油 . He is very
slippery.

(N) (1) oil (for cooking, fuel,
lubrication, etc.). yòng-yóu-
zhá 用油炸 fry it in oil.

(2) paint, varnish. shàng-yicéng-
yóu 上一層油 put on a
coat of paint. (cf: YÓUQĪ 油漆
QĪ 漆).

YÓU₂ 由 (TV) up to or rest with
someone. Năr-néng-shénma-shì-
dōu-lǎo-yóuzhe-nǐ-ne? 那兒
能甚麼事都老由
着你呢 ? How can every-
thing be up to you all the time?
Zhèige-shì yóubuliǎo-wŏ. 這個
事由不了我 . This
thing cannot rest with me.

(CV) (1) from (a time or a place).
Wŏ-yóu-jiāli-lái. 我由家
裏來 . I came from home.

(2) from (a point of view). yóu-
zhèi-fāngmian-shuō 由這
方面説 talk about it from
this angle. (3) via, through or
pass a place. Wŏ-yóu-Rìběn-
jīngguò. 我由日本經
過 . I passed by Japan. (4)
something done by a person.
Zhège-qián yīnggāi-yóu-wŏ-fù.
這個錢應該由我
付 . This money should be
paid by me. (cf: CÓNG 從).

YŎU₁ 有 (negated by méi 没 only,
never bù 不).

(TV) (1) have. Tā-yŏu-liǎngge-
nǚ'er. 他有兩個女兒 .
He has two daughters. Nǐ-yŏu-
gōngfu-meiyou? 你有工
夫没有 ? Do you have
time? Wŏ-yŏu-péngyou-bāng-
máng. 我有朋友幫
忙 . I have friends to help me.
Wŏ-méi-you-huà-shuō. 我没
有話説 . I have nothing to
say. (2) there is, there are.
Chéngli-yŏu-gōngyuán-meiyou?
城裏有公園没有 ?
Are there any parks in the city?
Yìnián yŏu-wŭshi-èrge-lǐbài.
一年有五十二個
禮拜 . There are fifty-two
weeks in a year. Zhèi-yàngr-
xiàqu bú-huì-yŏu-hǎo-jiéguŏ.
這樣下去不會有
好結果 . There won't be
good results if it continues
this way. Qìchē yŏu-hěn-duō-
zhŏng. 汽車有很多
種 . There are many kinds of
cars. Yŏu-yitiān, yŏu-yíge-ren

Y

zài-wàitou jiào-mén. 有 一 天 有 一 個 人 在 外 頭 叫 門. One day there was somebody outside knocking on the door. (3) used before a PR or a noun of person, indicates the person will take the responsibility. Búyong-hàipà, yǒu-'wǒ-zài-zhèr-ne. 不 用 害 怕, 有 我 在 這 兒 呢. Don't be afraid, I'm here to take care of everything. Yǒu-Zhāng-xian-sheng wǒmen-jiu-fàng-xīn-le. 有 張 先 生 我 們 就 放 心 了. Since Mr. Chang will take care of things, we won't have to worry. (4) used with le 了 implies pregnancy. Tā-yǒu-le. 他 有 了. She is expecting. (5) used before NU-M to indicate being approximate, about, approximately. Xuéxiào lí-zhèr-yǒu-yìyīnglǐ. 學 校 離 這 兒 有 一 英 里. The school is about one mile from here. Tā-yǒu-'liùchǐ-gāo. 他 有 六 尺 高. He is about six feet tall. Tā-yǒu-'sìshi-suì-le. 他 有 四 十 歲 了. He is about forty years old.

(CV) used with SV or AV which may be preceded by nènma 那 麼, zhènma 這 麼 or zènma 這 麼, as...as.... Tā-méi-you-nǐ-(nènma-)gāo. 他 沒 有 你(那 麼) 高. He is not as tall as you are. Yàoshi tā-yǒu-nǐ-zènma-ài-niàn-shū jiu-hǎo-le. 要 是 他 有 你

這 麼 愛 念 書 就 好 了. If he liked to study as well as you do, that would be good. Tā-yǒu-tā-dìdi-nènme-cōngming-ma? 他 有 他 弟 弟 那 麼 聰 明 嗎? Is he as intelligent as his younger brother?

followed by a noun to form a SV. yǒu-yìsi 有 意 思 interesting. yǒu-yíngxiang 有 影 響 influential.

YÒU₁ 又 (AD) (1) again (repetition of an action). Wǒ-yòu-dào-nàr-qù-le. 我 又 到 那 兒 去 了. I went there again. Yòu-yào-xià-yǔ-le. 又 要 下 雨 了. It will rain again. Tā-shuōle-yòu-shuō, wǒ-yǐ-jīng-tīnggòu-le. 他 說 了 又 說, 我 已 經 聽 夠 了. He said it over and over again, I heard enough. Tā-wèn-le-yícì-yòu-yícì. 他 問 了 一 次 又 一 次. He asked it again and again. (2) also. Tā-yào-mǎi-ròu, yòu-yào-mǎi-yú. 他 要 買 肉 又 要 買 魚. He wants to buy meat and he also wants to buy fish. Zhèige-hěn-hǎo, yòu-piányi. 這 個 很 好, 又 便 宜. This is very good, also cheap. (3) used before a negative expression to make a reason for not doing something more emphatic. Tā-búbì-qù. Tā-yòu-bú-huì-yú-yòng. 他 不 必 去. 他 又 不 會 游 泳. He better not go because he can't swim at all. Wǒ-yòu-mei-shuō-nǐ-bu-duì, nǐ-hébì-shēng-qì-ne? 我 又 沒 說 你 不 對, 你 何 必 生 氣 呢? I didn't say you were wrong, why should you be angry? Wǒ-yòu-méi-ná-nǐde-qián, wǒ-búbì-géi-ni-zuò-shì. 我 又 沒 拿 你 的 錢, 我 不 必 給 你 作 事. I didn't take your money, so I don't need to work for you. Tā-yòu-bú-shi-nǐ-bàba, wèi-shénma nǐ-děi-tīng-tāde? 他 又 不 是 你 爸 爸, 為 甚 麼 你 得 聽 他 的? He's not your father, why do you have to listen to him? (4) used in an interrogatory expression to make the question more emphatic. Zhèi-yàngr-zuò yòu-yǒu-shénma-hǎo-chu-ne? 這 樣 兒 作 又 有 甚 麼 好 處 呢? What benefit is there in doing it this way? Wǒmen-jiù-ràng-ta-qù, tā-yòu-néng-zěnmayàng? 我 們 就 讓 他 去, 他 又 能 怎 麼 樣? We just let him go, what can he do? (5) used to show a change from an original situation. Gángcái-tài-lěng, xiànzài-yòu-tài-rè-le. 剛 才 太 冷, 現 在 又 太 熱 了. Just a moment ago it was too cold, now it is too hot. Nǐ-shuō-yào-chī, géi-ni-nálai-le, nǐ-yòu-'bù-chī-le. 你 說 要 吃, 給 你 拿 來 了, 你 又 不 吃 了. You said you wanted to eat, I brought it

for you, and now you don't want it. Tā-shuō-de hǎoxiàng-duì, kěshi-zài-xiángxiang yòu-bú-duì. 他 說 的 好 像 對 可 是 再 想 想 又 不 對. When he said it, it seemed right, but when I thought about it, it wasn't right. (6) used between a whole number and a fraction, and. yī-you-èrfēnzhi-yī 一 又 二 分 之 一 one-and-a-half.

(S) YÒU 又 ... YÒU 又 ... (usually followed by suóyi 所 以), not only...but also.... Píngguo yòu-hǎochī-yòu-yǒu-yíngyǎng. 蘋 果 又 好 吃 又 有 營 養. Apples are not only delicious but also nutritious. (cf: ZÀI 再 , YĚ... YĚ... 也 ... 也 ...).

YÒU₁ 右 (L) right (not left). wàng-yòu-kàn 往 右 看 look to the right. yòuyàn 右 眼 right eye.

YÓUBĀO₄ 郵 包 (N) postal parcel. jì-yóubāo 寄 郵 包 mail a parcel.

YǑU-BǍWO₂ 有 把 握 (VO) (lit. have grasp) certain, sure. Zhèizhong-shì wǒ-yìdiǎnr-'bǎ-wo dou-méiyǒu. 這 種 事 我 一 點 兒 把 握 都 沒 有. I'm not the least bit sure about this kind of affair.

YÒUBIANR₁ 右 邊 兒 (PW) the right side. Yòubianr-yǒu yíliàng-qìchē. 右 邊 兒 有 一 輛 汽 車. There is a car on the right. Qìchēde-yòu-

Y

bianr pènghuài-le. 汽車的
右邊兒碰壞了. The
right side of the car is damaged.

YǑU-BÌNG₂ 有病 (VO) get sick.

YÓUBUDE₄ 由不得 (RV) (1)
cannot help oneself from doing
something, involuntarily. Wǒ-
yóubude-hěn-shēng-qì. 我由
不得很生氣. I can't
help being angry. (2) cannot be
up to or cannot rest with someone. Nà-yóubude-nǐ. 那由不
得你. That cannot be up to
you.

YÓUCHĀI₃ 郵差 (N) postman,
mailman.

YŌUCHOU₅ 憂愁 (SV) dis-
tressed, sad, melancholy. Nǐ-
hébi-zhènma-yōuchou? 你何
必這樣憂愁呢? Why
is it necessary for you to be so
sad?

(N) sadness, melancholy.

YŌUDÀI₃ 優待 (TV) treat someone in a favorite way. tèbié-yōu-
dài 特別優待 treat in an
especially favorite way. Tāmen-
hěn-yōudai-wo. 他們很優
待我. They treated me very
favorably.

YǑU-DÀOLI₃ 有道理 (VO)
have principles or ways in doing
things. Zhèige-rén yǒu-dianr-
dàoli. 這個人有點兒
道理. This person has some
principles in doing things.

(SV) reasonable, logical. Tā-
shuōde-huà hen-yǒu-dàoli. 他
說的話很有道理.
What he said is very reasonable.

YǑUDE₁ 有的 used before a
verb, have something to...
Jīntian-wǎnshang tā-zhēn-yǒu-
de-chī-le. 今天晚上
他真有的吃了. To-
night he really has something
to eat.

(N) some, someone. Yǒude-
hǎo, yě-yǒude-'bù-hǎo. 有的
好, 也有的不好.
Some are good, some are also
bad.

YǑU... DE₂ 有 ... 的 (S) there
are some that... Yǒu-zuò-chē-
de, yǒu-qí-mǎ-de, yě-yǒu-
zǒuzhe-de. 有坐車的,
有騎馬的,也有走
着的. There are those who
ride in a car, those who ride a
horse and those who walk.

YŌUDĚNG₅ 優等 (B) first
class, top quality. yōuděng-
xuésheng 優等學生
straight A student.

YÓUDĒNG₅ 油燈 (N) oil lamp.
(M: zhǎn 盞).

YǑUDESHÌ₂ 有的是 (TV)
have a lot of something. Tā-
yǒudeshì-qián. 他有的是
錢. He has a lot of money.

YŌUDIǍN₃ 優點 (N) good
point, good feature.

YǑU(YI)DIǍNR₁ 有(一)點
兒 (AD) somewhat, a bit. Tā-
yǒu(yi)diǎn-zhāo-jí. 他有
(一)點着急. He is
somewhat worried. Wǒ-yǒu(yi)-
diǎnr-bu-shūfu. 我有(一)
點兒不舒服. I am
a bit uncomfortable.

Y

YŎU-DÚ₃ 有毒 (VO) poisonous.

YÓU...ER...₄ 由...而... (S) from... to... yóu-'xiǎoxué-ér-'zhōngxué 由小學而中學 from primary school to high school.

YÓUFÈI₄ 郵費 (N) postage.

YŎU-FĒNBIE₂ 有分別 (VO) there is a difference. Zhèige-gen-nèige yǒu-hěn-dà-de-fēnbie. 這個跟那個有很大的分別. There is a great difference between this and that.

YÓUJÍDUÌ₄ 游擊隊 (N) guerrilla band.

YŎU-JĪNGSHEN₃ 有精神 (VO) have energy. Wǒ-méi-you-nèn-ma-da-jīngshen. 我沒有那麼大精神. I don't have that much energy. (SV) energetic, full of vitality. Zhèiwei-lǎo-xiansheng zhēn-yǒu-jīngshen. 這位老先生真有精神. This old gentleman is really energetic. Zhèi-zhāng-huàr yǒu-jīngshen. 這張畫兒有精神. This picture is full of life.

YŎU-JĪNGYAN₂ 有經驗 (VO) have experience. Wǒ-yǒu-yi-dinar-yīngyan. 我有一點兒經驗. I have a little experience. (SV) experienced.

YÓU(ZHÈNG)JÚ₁ 郵(政)局 (N) post office.

YÓULǍN₅ 遊覽 (TV) go sightseeing. Tāmen-qu-yóulǎn-xīhú-qu-le. 他們去遊覽西湖去了. They went sightseeing at Western Lake.

YŎU-LĬ₁ 有理 (SV) be in the right, right. Wǒ-juéde tā-yǒu-lǐ. 我覺得他有理. I think he is right. (VO) have a reason for something. Nǐ-yǒu-nǐde-lǐ, tā-yǒu-tāde-lǐ. 你有你的理, 他有他的理. You have your reasons and he has his.

YŌULIÁNG₅ 優良 (SV) excellent, superior.

'YŎU-LIǍNGSHǑUR₄ 有兩手兒 or 'YŎU-LIǍNGXIÀZI 有兩下子 (VO) be pretty good at something. Zuò-zhèi-zhòng-shì tā-'yǒu-liǎngshǒur. 作這種事他有兩手兒. He's pretty good at doing this kind of thing. (cf: 'YŎU-YISHǑUR 有一手兒).

'YŎU-LIǍNGXIÀZI₄ 有兩下子 see 'YŎU-LIǍNGSHǑUR 有兩手兒.

YŎU-LĬMAO₃ 有禮貌 (VO) have courtesy, courteous.

YǑUMÍNG₁ 有名 (SV) well-known, famous, prominent. Tā-zài-wàijiāojiè-hěn-yǒumíng. 他在外交界很有名. He is quite famous in diplomatic circles.

YŌUMO₂ 幽默 (SV) have a sense of humor, humorous. Tā-zhēn-yōumo. 他真幽默. He is really humorous. (N) humor.

Y

YÓUNÌ₄ 油膩 (SV) greasy, oily, fatty. Yóunìde-dōngxi bu-hǎo-xiāohua. 油膩的東西不好消化 . Greasy things are not easy to digest.

YÒUPÀI₃ 右派 (N) rightist elements.

YÓUPIÀO₁ 郵票 (N) postage stamp. (M: zhāng 張).

YÓUQÌ₂ 油漆 (N) paint, lacquer, varnish. (M: dào 道). shàng-yidao-yóuqī 上一道油漆 put on a coat of paint. (TV) paint. Tāmen-yóuqī-fángzi-ne. 他們油漆房子呢 . They are painting their house now. (cf: QĪ 漆 , YÓU 油).

YÓUQÍ(SHI)₂ 尤其 (是)(AD) especially. Wǒde-wūzi hěn-rè, yóuqí-xiàtian. 我的屋子很熱,尤其夏天 . My room is very hot, especially in the summer.

YŎU-QIÁN₁ 有錢 (VO) have money. Tā-yǒu-nènma-duō-qián-ma? 他有那麼多錢嗎 ? Does he have that much money? (SV) rich. Tā-zhēn-yǒuqián. 他真有錢 . He is really rich.

YŎU-QÙ₄ 有趣 (VO) interesting. Tā-shuō-de-huà yǒu-qù. 他說的話有趣 . What he says is interesting.

YŎUSHĒNGDIÀNYǏNG₅ 有聲電影 (N) sound film.

YŎUSHI HOU(R)₁ 有時候(兒) sometimes, at certain times. Tā-yǒu-shíhou-qù. 他有時候去 . He goes occasionally.

YÒUSHŎU₁ 右手 (N) right hand.

YŎU-SHÙR₃ 有數兒 (VO) (1) have a definite amount, know the exact amount. Nǐ-bié-ná-tade-qián, tāde-qián-yǒu-shùr. 你别拿他的錢,他的錢有數兒 . Don't take his money, it's all accounted for. (2) definite and limited amount. Wǒ-měiyuè-zhèngde-shì-yǒu-shùr-de-qián. 我每月掙的錢有數兒 . I earn a definite limited amount of money each month. (3) know something exactly. Zhèige-guì-bu-guì tā-xīnli-yǒu-shùr. 這個貴不貴他心裏有數兒 . (Even if he doesn't say it,) he knows exactly whether it's expensive or not.

YÓUTǑNG₄ 郵筒 (N) mail box (in the form of a cylinder).

YÓUXÌ₄ 遊戲 (IV) play. Tā-men-zài-yuànzili-yóuxi-ne. 他們在院子裏遊戲呢 . They are playing in the courtyard. (N) game, recreation. Zhè-bu-shi-yóuxi. 這不是遊戲 . This is not a game. (cf: WÁNR 玩兒).

YÓUXIĀNG₄ 郵箱 (N) mail box.

YŎUXIÀO₂ 有效 (SV) (1) effective. Nèige-yào hěn-yǒuxiào. 那個藥很有效 . That medicine is very effective. (2) valid. Nèitiao fǎlù hái-yǒuxiào-ma? 那條法律還有

Y

效 嗎 ? Is that law still valid?

YŎUXIE₃ 有 些 ' (AD) a little. Tā-yŏuxie-nánweiqíng. 他 有 些 難 為 情 . He is a little embarrassed.

(N) some. Tāde-shū yŏuxie-guì, yŏuxie-piányi. 他 的 書 有 些 貴 有 些 便 宜. Some of his books are expensive and some are cheap.

YŎU-XĪN₅ 有 心 (VO) have intention, intend. Wŏ-yŏu-xīn-jiào-ta-huíjiā. 我 有 心 叫 他 回 家 . I intend to tell him to return home.(cf: YŎUYÌ 有 意 , YŎU-YÌSI 有 意 思).

YÓUXÍNG₃ 遊 行 (IV) parade. Míngtian tāmen-yòu-yào-yóuxíng-le. 明 天 他 們 又 要 遊 行 了 . They will parade again tomorrow.

(N) parade. Míngtiande-yóuxíng rén-yídìng-hěn-duō. 明 天 的 遊 行 人 一 定 很 多 There will certainly be many people in the parade tomorrow.

YŎU-XÌNGQU₂ 有 興 趣 (VO) have interest in. Wŏ-duì-zhèi-zhŏng-shì hěn-yŏu-xìngqu. 我 對 這 種 事 很 有 興 趣 . I have a great deal of interest in this kind of affair.

YÓU-XÌNGR₅ 由 性 兒 (VO) do something at will or as one likes it. Nǐ-yóuxìngr-chī-ba. 你 由 性 兒 吃 吧 !You can eat as much as you like. Bú-néng-yóuzhe-nǐde-xìngr. 不 能 由 着 你 的 性 兒 . You can't do everything you want

to.

YŎUXIÙ₅ 優 秀 (SV) superior, outstanding. Tāmende-gōng-chéngshī-doū-hěn-yŏuxiù. 他 們 的 工 程 師 都 很 優 秀 . All of their engineers are very outstanding.

YŎU-XUÉWEN₂ 有 學 問 (VO) have learned knowledge, learned. Tā-yŏu-xuéwen. 他 有 學 問 . He is learned.

YŎU-YÁNJIU₂ 有 研 究 (VO) have done research on some subjects. Tā-duì-lìshǐ hěn-yŏu-yánjiu. 他 對 歷 史 很 有 研 究 . He has made a profound study of history.

YÓUYI₂ 猶 疑 (SV) hesitant. Wŏ-xiànzài hěn-yóuyi. 我 現 在 很 猶 疑 . I'm rather hesitant now. Nǐ-bié-yóuyi-le,jiu-nèn-ma-bàn-ba. 你 別 猶 疑 了,就 這 麼 辦 吧. Don't be hesitant any more, let's do it this way.

YŎUYÌ₄ 友 誼 (N) friendship. Tāmende-yŏuyi hěn-shēn. 他 們 的 友 誼 很 深. They have a very deep friendship.

YŎUYÌ₃ 有 意 (VO) (con. yŏu-yìsi 有 意 思). have intention, intend. Tā-yŏuyì-qǐng-yi-ge-shūji. 他 有 意 請 一 個 書 記 . He intends to hire a secretary.

(AD) intentionally, on purpose. Tā-yŏuyì-jiào-wo-nánweiqíng. 他 有 意 叫 我 難 為 情 . He embarrassed me on purpose.(cf: YŎU-XĪN 有 心).

Y

YÓUYÌHUÌ$_4$ 游藝會 (N) gathering <u>for entertainment (as a gala show in the army)</u>.

YÓUYÌN$_3$ 油印 (TV) mimeograph, duplicate. Tā-yóuyìnle-wǔbǎizhāng-chuándān. 他油印了五百張傳單. He mimeographed five hundred flyers.

'YǑU-YISHǑUR$_4$ 有一手兒 (VO) have an illicit relationship with.
(SV) be pretty good <u>at something</u>.
(cf: 'YǑU-LIǍNGSHǑUR 有兩手兒).

YǑU-YÌSI$_1$ 有意思 (VO) (1) have meaning <u>or</u> ideas. Nǐ-yǒu-shénma-yìsi, kuài-shuō. 你有甚麼意思,快說. What's your idea, hurry up and say it. (2) have intention, intend. Wǒ-yǒu-yìsi-mǎi-zhèige. 我有意思買這個. I intend to buy this.
(SV) interesting. Zhèige-gùshi zhēn-yǒuyìsi. 這個故事真有意思. This story is really interesting. (cf: YǑU-XĪN 有心).

YǑU-YITIĀN$_2$ 有一天 <u>used to introduce a sentence or a story</u>, on a certain day, at some time. Yǒu-yitiān-tā-lái-kàn-wǒ, wǒ-méi-zài-jiā. 有一天他來看我我沒在家. One day he came to see me but I wasn't home. Jiānglái-yǒu-yi-tiān, wǒ-děi-mǎi-yíge-qìchē. 將來有一天我得買一個汽車. One day

in the future I will have to buy a car.

YÓU-YǑNG$_2$ 游泳 (VO) swim. Wǒ-méi-yóuguo-yǒng. 我沒游過泳. I have never swum.

YǑU-YÒNG(CHU)$_2$ 有用(處) (SV) useful. Zhèiben-shū zhēn-yǒuyòng(chu). 這本書真有用(處). This book is really useful.
(VO) have use. Zhèige yǒu-hěn-duōde-yòng(chu). 這個有很多的用(處). This has many uses.

YÓUYǑNGCHÍ$_3$ 游泳池 (N) swimming pool.

YÓUYǑNGYĪ$_4$ 游泳衣 (N) swim suit. (M: jiàn 件).

YÓUYÚ$_5$ 由於 (MA) because, since, due to. Nèicì-shībài-shi-yóuyú-jīngji-de-guānxi. 那次失敗是由於經濟的關係. The failure that time was because of economic reasons.

YǑUYUÁN$_4$ 有緣 (SV) be fated <u>to meet</u>. Wǒmen-zhēn-yǒuyuán, yòu-pèngjian-le. 我們真有緣,又碰見了. It's fate for us, we meet again.

YŌUYUÈ$_5$ 優越 (SV) superior, outstanding. Bié-juéde-nǐ-bǐ-biéren-yōuyuè. 別覺得你比別人優越. Don't think you are superior to others.

YÒUZHÌ$_3$ 幼稚 (SV) childish, immature. Tā-shuō-de-huà tài-yòuzhi. 他說的話太幼稚. What he said is too

Y

childish.

YŎU-ZHÌSHI₄ 有 知 識 (VO)
have knowledge, knowledgeable.

YÒUZHÌYUÁN₃ 幼 稚 園 (N)
kindergarten. (M: suŏ 所).

YÚ₁ 魚 (N) fish. (M: tiáo 條).

YÚ₃ 於 (CV) for, toward, with
reference to. Zhèi-jiàn-shì yú-
wŏ méi-guānxi. 這 件 事 於
我 沒 關 係. This matter
is no concern of mine.

YŬ₁ 雨 (N) rain. (M: zhèn 陣,
chăng 場). xià-yŭ 下 雨 to
rain. Zhèi-zhèn-yŭ hĕn-lìhai.
這 陣 雨 很 利 害. This
spell of rain is terrific.

YÙ₄ 玉 (N) jade.

YUĀN₃ 冤 (SV) (1) be wronged,
cheated. Wŏ-hĕn-yuān. 我 很
冤. I feel that I've been
wronged. (2) not worth-while.
Dĕngle-liăngge-zhōngtóu kàn-
zhèige-diànyĭngr zhēn-yuān. 等
了 兩 個 鐘 頭 看 這
個 電 影 兒 真 冤. It's
not worth-while to wait two hours
for this movie.
(TV) cheat, fool, deceive. Nĭ-
bié-yuān-wo. 你 別 冤 我.
Don't fool me. (cf: YUĀNWANG
冤 枉).

YUÁN₃ 圓 (SV) round, circular.
Tāde-liăn hĕn-yuán. 他 的 臉
很 圓. He has a round face.

YUÁN₄ 元 (M) dollar. yìyuán-qián
一 元 錢 one dollar.

YUÁN₃ 員 (-B) (1) person who has
certain specific duties. jiàoyuán
教 員 teacher. (2) personnel.
rényuán 人 員 personnel. (3)

member of an organization.
huìyuán 會 員 club member.

YUĂN₁ 遠 (SV) far away, distant.
Nĭ-jiā lí-xuéxiào yuăn-buyuan?
你 家 離 學 校 遠 不
遠? Is it far from your home
to the school? Nĭ-lí-wo yuăn-
yidianr. 你 離 我 遠 一
點 兒. lit. or fig. Keep
your distance from me. Wŏmen-
líde-tài-yuăn. 我 們 離 得
太 遠. lit. or fig. We are
too far apart. Tā-gēn-nĭ chà-
de-hĕn-yuăn. 他 跟 你 差
得 太 遠. There is a great
(distance of) difference between
you and him.
(AD) by far. Tā-yuăn-bĭ-tā-jiĕ-
jie-piàoliang. 他 遠 比 他
姐 姐 漂 亮. She is far
more beautiful than her older
sister. Tā-yuăn-burú-nĭ. 他
遠 不 如 你. He is not as
good as you by far.

YUÁNCHAO₃ 元 朝 (TW) Yüan
or Mongol dynasty.

YUÁNDÀN₄ 元 旦 (TW) New
Year's Day.

YUĂNDŌNG₃ 遠 東 (PW) Far
East.

YUÁNGĂOR₃ 原 稿 兒 (N)
original draft of a manuscript.

YUÁNGÀOR₄ 原 告 兒 (N)
plaintiff.

YUÁNGU₁ 緣 故 (N) reason,
cause. shénma-yuángu 甚 麼
緣 故 what reason. Nà-shi-
yīnwei-ta-méi-xìngqu-de-yuán-
gu. 那 是 因 為 他 沒
興 趣 的 緣 故. That is

Y

because he is not interested.
(cf: YUÁNYĪN 原因).

YUÁNGUĪ₅ 圓規 (N) compass (for drawing circles).

YUÀNHEN₄ 怨恨 (TV) hate, spite. Wǒ-yìdiǎnr dou-buyuàn-hen-ta. 我一點兒都不怨恨他. I don't hate him at all.

YUÁN-HUÁNG₅ 圓謊 (VO) cover up a lie. Qǐng-nǐ-tì-wo-yuán-yíge-huǎng-ba. 請你替我圓一個謊吧! Please cover up a lie for me.

YUÁNJÍ₄ 原籍 (N) one's home town.

YUĀNJIA₅ 冤家 (N) rival, enemy, adversary.

YUÁNLÁI₂ 原來 (MA) (1) originally, at first. Wǒ-yuánlái-bù-chōu-yān, xiànzài-chōu. 我原來不抽烟, 現在抽. I didn't smoke at first, but now I do. (2) it turns out that... after all. Tā-yuánlái-'bú-shi-diànyǐngr-míngxīng-a. 他原來不是電影兒明星啊. It turned out that he was not a movie star after all.

YUÁNLIANG₂ 原諒 (TV) forgive. Wǒ-yǒngyuǎn-bu-néng-yuánliang-ta. 我永遠不能原諒他. I'll never forgive him. Qǐng-nín-yuánliang-wo. 請你原諒我. Please excuse me.

YUÁNLIÀO₄ 原料 (N) raw material.

YUÁNMǍN₃ 圓滿 (SV) satisfactory, right in all aspects. Jié-

guǒ hěn-yuánmǎn. 結果很圓滿. The result is satisfactory.
(AD) satisfactorily. yuánmǎn-jiějué 圓滿解決 solved satisfactorily. Huìyì yuánmǎn-bì-mù-le. 會議圓滿閉幕了. The meeting has been satisfactorily closed.

YUĀNQU₄ 冤屈 (SV) be wronged.

YUÁNSHǏ₄ 原始 (SV) primitive. yuánshǐ-shēnghuo 原始生活 primitive life. Nèige-mín-zú hěn-yuánshǐ. 那個民族很原始. That race is quite primitive.

YUÁNSHUÀI₄ 元帥 (N) commander-in-chief, marshal.

YUĀNWANG₃ 冤枉 (TV) do injustice to, wrong someone. Wǒ-méi-yuānwang-tā. 我沒冤枉他. I didn't wrong him.
(SV) (1) be wronged. Wǒ-juéde hěn-yuānwang. 我覺得很冤枉. I feel very wronged. (2) not worth-while. Kāi-wǔshi lǐ-dì chī-zhèi-zhǒng-fàn tài-yuānwang-le. 開五十里地吃這種飯太冤枉了. It's not worthwhile at all to drive fifty miles for food like this. (cf: YUĀN 冤).

!YUÀNWANG₄ 願望 (N) hope, wish.

YUÁNXIĀN₂ 原先 (MA) at first, previously. Yuánxiān wǒ-yě-bú-renshi-ta. 原先我也

Y

不認識他. At first I didn't know him either.

YUĀNYANG₅ 鴛鴦 (N) a kind of brightly colored Chinese water bird, the male and female of which are practically inseparable; often used to refer to married couples, mandarin ducks. (M: duì 對).

YUÀNYI₁ 願意 (AV) willing to, would like to. Wŏ-yuànyi-qù. 我願意去. I'm willing to go. Wŏ-yuànyi-zuò-tāde-chē. 我願意坐他的車. I would like to ride in his car. (cf: BÚYUÀNYÌ 不願意).

YUÁNYĪN₃ 原因 (N) reason, cause. Yuānyĭn hĕn-duō. 原因 很多. The reasons are many. (cf: YUÁNGU 緣故).

YUÁNZÉ₃ 原則 (N) principle. (M: tiáo 條). Zhèi-shi-yuánzéde-wènti. 這是原則的 問題. This is a matter of principle.

YUÀNZHĂNG₃ 院長 (N) head of an organization, the last syllable of which in Chinese is yuàn. yīyuànde-yuànzhăng 醫院的 院長 superintendent of a hospital. yánjiuyuànde-yuànzhăng 研究院的院長 dean of a graduate school.

YUÁNZHU 援助 (TV) help, aid. Wŏmen-yīngdāng-yuánzhutamen. 我們應當援助 他們. We ought to help them. (N) help, aid. Tāmen-débuzháo Mĕiguode-yuánzhu. 他們得 不着美國的援助

They cannot get American aid.

YUÁNZI₂ 園子 (N) (1) garden. (2) orchard. (3) Peip. theater.

YUÁNZĬ₃ 原子 (N) atom.

YUÀNZI₂ 院子 (N) courtyard.

YUÁNZĬBĬ₃ 原子筆 (N) ballpoint pen.

YUÁNZĬDÀN₃ 原子彈 (N) atomic bomb.

YUÁNZĬNÉNG₃ 原子能 (N) atomic energy.

YÙBÀO₄ 預報 (N) advance notice. tiānqì-yùbào 天氣 預報 weather forecast.

YÙBEI₁ 預備 (TV) prepare, get ready. (syn. zhŭnbei 準 備). Nĭ-dĕi-yùbei-yíliang-qìchē. 你得預備一輛 汽車. You have to have a car ready. Tā-yùbei-míngtianlái. 他預備明天來. He is preparing to come tomorrow. Nĭde-gōngke yùbeile-meiyou? 你的功課預備 了沒有? Did you prepare your lessons? (N) preparation.

YÙBÈN₅ 愚笨 (SV) stupid, slow in learning. (N) foolishness.

YÙCÈ₄ 預測 (TV) predict. méifázi-yùcè 沒法子預 測 no way to predict. (N) prediction.

YÚCHÌ₅ 魚翅 (N) shark fins (used as a delicacy).

YÚCHŬN₅ 愚蠢 (SV) stupid.

YÚCÌ₅ 魚刺 (N) fishbone. (M: gēn 根).

YÙDAO₄ 遇到 (RV) run into

Y

(a person or a situation). Yào-
shi-yùdao-zhèi-zhŏng-qíngxing
wŏ-jiu-méi-bànfa-le. 要是
遇到這種情形我
就沒辦法了. If we
run into this kind of situation,
then I won't know what to do.

YŬDIǍNR₄ 雨點兒 (N) rain-
drop.

YÙDÌNG₃ 預定 (TV) (l) plan
and decide something in advance.
Nǐ-yùdìng-shénme-shíhou-lái?
你預定甚麼時候
來? When do you plan to come?
(2) order or reserve in advance.
Wŏ-yùdìngle-liǎngzhāng-piào.
我預定了兩張票.
I reserved two tickets.

YUE₂ 約 (TV) invite, ask. Nǐ-
yuēle-ta-le-ma? 你約了他
了嗎? Did you invite him?
(cf: YĀO 邀).
(AD) (con. dàyuē 大約). approximately. Nèige-xuéxiào yuē-
yŏu-yìqiān-duo-xuésheng. 那
個學校約有一千
多學生. There are around
one thousand students in that
school.

YUE₁ 月 (N) month. liǎngge-yuè
兩個月 two months.
(B) moon. yuèguāng 月光
moonlight.

YUÈBING₅ 月餅 (N) mooncake
(round cake eaten during the
Mid-autumn Festival).

YUÈCHŪ₃ 月初 (TW) the first
few days of a month. Tā-xiàyuè-
yuèchū-lái. 他下月月初
來. He will come during the

first few days of next month.

YUÈDǏ₃ 月底 (TW) the end of
a month. Tāmen-yuèdǐ fā-xīn-
shuǐ. 他們月底發薪
水. They pay the salaries at
the end of the month.

YUĒDÌNG₄ 約定 (TV) agree to,
decide to. Wŏmen-yuēdìng
míngtian-qù-yěcān. 我們約
定明天去野餐. We
agreed to go on a picnic tomorrow.

YUÈDUÌ₃ 樂隊 (N) band, or-
chestra. (M: duì 隊).

YUÈFA₅ 越發 (AD) more than
before. Tā-yuèfa-piàoliang-le.
她越發漂亮了. She
is even prettier than before.

YUÈFÈNPÁI(R)₄ 月份牌(兒)
(N) calendar (chart not system).
(syn. rìlì 日曆).

YUÈFÙ₄ 岳父 (N) father-in-
law (wife's father).

YUÈGUO₅ 越過 (TV) surpass,
exceed. Tāmen yǐjing-yuèguo-
-wŏmen-qù-le. 他們已經
越過我們去了.
They have already surpassed us.

YUÈHUÌR₂ 約會兒 (N) pre-
arranged meeting, appointment,
date. dìng-yuēhuìr 定約會
兒 make an appointment or
make a date. Wŏ-jīntian yŏu-
yige-yuēhuìr. 我今天有
一個約會兒. I have
an engagement today.

YUÈJIHUĀR₅ 月季花兒
(N) rose. (M: duŏ 朶 , kē 棵).

YUÈJÌN₄ 躍進 (TV) proceed in
jumps, leap forward. Wŏmen-

Y

xiàngzhe-mùbiāo yuèjìn. 我們
向着目標躍進. We
leap forward to our goal.
(N) a jump-like development. dà-
yuèjìn 大躍進 Great Leap
Forward.

YUÈKĀN₃ 月刊 (N) monthly
(magazine). (M: běn 本).

YUÈLÁIYUE₂ 越來越 (AD)
getting more and more. Dōngxi
yuèláiyuè-guì. 東西越來
越貴. Things are getting
more and more expensive. Tā-
yuèláiyuè-xǐhuan-niàn-shū. 他
越來越喜歡念書.
He likes more and more to study.

YUÈLIANG₁ 月亮 (N) moon.

YUÈMŬ₄ 岳母 (N) mother-in-
law (wife's mother).

YUÈNÁN₃ 越南 (PW) Viet Nam.

YUÈPŬ₄ 樂譜 (N) music score,
sheet music.

YUÈQI₄ 樂器 (N) musical in-
strument. (M: jiàn 件).

YUÈSHÍ₄ 月蝕 (N) lunar eclipse.

YUÈTÁI₄ 月台 (N) platform,
ramp (of a train station).

YUÈYÁR₅ 月牙兒 (N) cres-
cent moon, quarter moon.

YUÈ...YUÈ...₂ 越...越...
(S) the more... the more....
Tā-yuè-zǒu yuè-kuài. 他越
走越快. The more the
walked the faster he went. Nǐ-
yuè-mǎi-yuè-guì. 你越買
越貴. The more you buy the
more expensive it is.

YŬFĂ₃ 語法 (N) grammar. (syn.
wénfǎ 文法).

YÙFÁNG₃ 預防 (TV) take
preventative measures against.
Wǒmen-děi yùfáng-liúxíng-gǎn-
mào. 我們得預防流
行感冒. We should take
preventative measures against
flu. Zhèi-zhong-shì bu-róngyi-
yùfáng. 這種事不容易
預防. It's not easy to take
preventative measures against
this kind of thing.
(N) prevention.

YÙFÁNGZHĒN₃ 預防針 (N)
preventative inoculation. dǎ-
yùfángzhēn 打預防針
give or receive a preventative
inoculation.

YÚGĀNR₅ 魚竿兒 (N) fishing
rod. (M: gēn 根).

YÙJIAN₃ 遇見 (RV) meet (ac-
cidentally), run into. (syn.
pèngjian 碰見). Míngtian
nǐ-yùdejiàn-ta-ma? 明天你
遇得見他嗎? By any
chance, will you meet him tomorrow? Wǒ-zuótian yùjian-
yijian-hěn-bu-yùkuai-de-shì-
qing. 我昨天遇見一
件很不愉快的事
情. Yesterday I ran into a
very unpleasant situation.

YÙKUAI₃ 愉快 (SV) (1) pleasant.
Zhèrde-huánjing hěn-yùkuai.
這兒的環境很愉
快. The surroundings here
are very pleasant. (2) happy.
Tā-kànzhe hěn-yùkuai. 他看
着很愉快. He looks
very happy.

'YÚLE₄ 娛樂 (N) amusement,
fun. Tā-juéde niàn-shū shi-yi-

Y

zhong-yúlè. 他覺得念書是一種娛樂. He feels that studying is a kind of amusement.

YÙLIÀO₃ 預料 (TV) predict. Wǒ-yùliào tā-yídìng-qù. 我預料他一定去. I predict that he will certainly go.

(N) prediction. Zhè-shi-wǒde-yùliào. 這是我的預料. This is my prediction.

YÙLÙN₄ 輿論 (N) public opinion. 'Yùlùn duì-ta-hěn-búlì. 輿論對他很不利. Public opinion is not in favor of him.

YÙMI₄ 玉米 or LĂOYÙMI 老玉米 (N) corn (the plant, the ear, or the kernel). (M: kē 棵, gè 個, lì 粒).

YŪN₃ 暈 (IV) faint. Tā-yūnguoqu-le. 他暈過去了. He fainted.

(SV) (1) or YÙN 暈 dizzy. tóu-yūn 頭暈 light-headed. Nǐ-hái-juéde-yūn-ma? 你還覺得暈嗎? Do you still feel dizzy? (2) reckless. Nèi-háizi tài-yūn-le. 那孩子太暈了. That child is reckless.

YÚN₃ 勻 (SV) be evenly distributed, even. Tāmende-qián fēn-de-hěn-yún. 他們的錢分的很勻. They divided that money evenly.

(TV) make space or time, spare money, etc. Nǐ-néng-yún-jǐfēn-zhōng gēn-wo-tántan-ma? 你能勻幾分鐘跟我談談嗎? Can you make a little time to talk with me?

YÙN₃ 熨 (TV) iron something to make it flat. (syn. lào 烙). yùn-yīshang 熨衣裳 iron clothes.

YÙN₃ 暈 (TV) have motion sickness. yùn-fēijī 暈飛機 airsick.

(SV) or YŪN 暈 dizzy. Zhuàn-de wǒ-zhí-yùn. 轉得我直暈. Spinning around so much made me dizzy.

YÙN₃ 運 (TV) ship, transport, convey goods, products, etc. yùn-huò 運貨 transport goods. Nǐ-bǎ-jiājiu yùndao-nǎr-qu-le? 你把傢俱運到那兒去了? Where did you ship your furniture?

YÙN₅ 韻 (N) rhyme.

YÚNCAI₂ 雲彩 (N) cloud. (M: kuài 塊, piàn 片).

YÙN-CHĒ₃ 暈車 (VO) be carsick. Tā-yòu-yùn-chē-le. 他又暈車了. He's carsick again.

YÙN-CHUÁN₃ 暈船 (VO) be seasick.

YÙNDONG₂ 運動 (IV) exercise. Wǒ-yào-sànsan-bu, yùndong-yundong. 我要散散步運動運動. I want to take a stroll to get some exercise.

(TV) work on someone to gain some advantage, such as a job, a raise in pay, a promotion, etc., pull strings. Tā-zhèng-yùndong-nèige-chāishi-ne. 他正運動那個差事呢. He's trying to get tnat job by pulling strings. Bié-xiǎng-yùndong wo, méi-yòng. 別 想 運 動 我，沒 用. Don't try to work on me, it's no use.

(N) (1) physical exercise. Dǎ-qiú shi-yizhǒng-yùndong. 打 球 是 一 種 運 動. Playing ball is a kind of exercise. (2) a movement (started to bring about change in society). fùnǔ-yùndong 婦 女 運 動 women's movement.

YÙNDÒNGCHĂNG₃ 運·動場 (N) athletic field.

YÙNDOU₄ 熨斗 (N) iron (for ironing clothes). (M: bǎ 把).

YÙNFÈI₃ 運費 (N) cost of freight, shipping fee.

YÙNHÉ₃ 運河 (N) canal. (M: tiáo 條).

YÚNNÁN₃ 雲南 (PW) Yúnnan province.

YÙNNIANG₅ 醞釀 (TV) brew, ferment (figuratively). Tāmen-zhèngzai-yùnniang-bà-gōng-ne. 他 們 正 在 醞 釀 罷 工 呢. They are fermenting a strike now.

YÙNQI₂ 運氣 (N) luck. Nǐ-yùnqi zěnmayàng? 你 運 氣 怎 麼 樣? How's you luck? Yùnqi bu-hǎo. 運 氣 不 好. Bad luck. (SV) lucky. Tā-zhēn-yùnqi. 他 真 運 氣. He is very lucky.

YÙNSHŪ₃ 運輸 (TV) transport, ship. Wǒmen-jiù-guǎn-yùnshū-qìyóu. 我 們 就 只 運 輸 汽 油. We transpor only pe-troleum.

(N) transportation (of goods). hángkōng-yùnshū 航空運輸 transportation by air.

YÙNSHŪJĪ₄ 運輸機 (N) cargo-carrying airplane. (M: jià 架).

YÚNXU₄ 允許 (TV) permit, allow. Nǐ-yúnxu-ta-qù-ma? 你 允 許 他 去 嗎? Do you allow him to go?

YÙNYONG₃ 運用 (TV) use, utilize. Nà-kàn-ni-zěnma-yùn-yong-le. 那 看 你 怎 麼 運 用 了. It all depends on how you use it.

(N) use, utilization.

YǓQI₄ 語氣 (N) tone of speech. Tīng-tāde-yǔqi, wǒ-jiu-zhǐdao-bu-xíng. 聽 他 的 語 氣，我 就 知 道 不 行. I knew it wouldn't do by listening to his tone of voice.

YǓQI₃ 與其 (MA) followed by a clause usually introduced by (hái-)bùrú(還) 不如, rather than. Nèige-qián yǔqi-gěi-tā, (hái-)bùrú-gěi wǒ. 那 個 錢 與 其 給 他，(還) 不 如 給 我. It would be better to give that money to me rather than to him.

YÙSÀI₄ 預賽 (N) preliminary contest.

YǓSĂN₃ 雨傘 (N) umbrella. (M: bǎ 把). dǎ-yǔsǎn 打 雨 傘 hold up an umbrella.

YÚSHÌ₃ 於是 (MA) then, there-upon. Yúshì tā-kū-le. 於 是 她 哭 了. Then she cried.

YÚSHÙ₅ 榆樹 (N) elm tree.(M:

Y

kē 標).

YÙSUÀN₃ 預算 (TV) make advance plans <u>or</u> calculations. Wǒ-yùsuàn děi-yòng-liǎngnián. 我 預算 得 用 兩年 . I calculated that it would take two years. (N) budget. Tāde-yùsuàn hái-méi-zuòhǎo. 他的 預算 還 沒 作 好 . He hasn't finished making out his budget yet.

YÙTOU₅ 芋頭 (N) taro.

YÚWǍNG₄ 魚網 (N) fish net. (M: zhāng 張).

YÙWANG₄ 慾望 (N) lust, desire.

YǓWÉN₃ 語文 (N) (1) (<u>con.</u> yǔ-yán-wénzì 語言文字). spoken and written language. (2) (<u>con.</u> yǔyán-wénxué 語言文學). language and literature.

YÙXIĀN₂ 預先 (MA) beforehand. Wǒmen-děi-yùxiān-mǎi-piào. 我們 得 預先 買 票 . We ought to buy the tickets beforehand.

YǓXIÉ₄ 雨鞋 (N) overshoes, galoshes. (M: zhǐ 隻 , shuāng 雙).

YÚXÌNG₄ 餘興 (N) an extra entertainment <u>which comes after the main activity</u>. Chīwán-fàn yǒu-shénma-yúxìng? 吃完飯 有 甚麼 餘興 ? What entertainment will there be after eating?

YǓYÁN₂ 語言 (N) language. Zhōngguo-yǔyán 中國語言 Chinese language. Yígòng-yǒu-duōshao-zhǒng-yǔyán? 一共 有 多少 種 語言 ? How many kinds of language are there altogether? (cf: YÁN-YǓ 言語).

YÙYÁN₅ 寓言 (N) fable.

YǓYÁNXUE₃ 語言學 (N) linguistics, philology. (M: mén 門).

YǓYĪ₃ 雨衣 (N) raincoat. (M: jiàn 件).

YǓYĪN₅ 語音 (N) sounds of a language.

YÙZHĪ₄ 預支 (TV) obtain in advance money due <u>at a later date</u>.

YǓZHÒU₃ 宇宙 (N) universe, cosmos.

Y

Z

ZÁ₃ 砸 (TV) pound, hammer, smash, break something. zá-hétao 砸核桃 break a walnut (by smashing). Ná-chuízi-záza. 拿鎚子砸砸. Pound it with the hammer. Bǎmén-zákai. 把門砸開. Smash the door open. Shítou-diàoxialai, bǎ-tade-tóu zá-le. 石頭掉下來, 把他的頭砸了. A stone fell down and crashed down on his head. Tā-bǎ-fànwǎn-zá-le. 他把飯碗砸了. He broke the rice bowl. or He lost his job.

(SV) be a failure or flop. Nèicì-wǒmen-chàng-xì, zhēn-zá-le. 那次我們唱戲, 真砸了. The time that we had a musical play it was a flop.

(RE) indicates that the result of the action was a failure. Tā-bǎ-shìqing bànzá-le. 他把事情辦砸了. His handling of the matter was a failure.

ZĀI₂ 栽 (TV) plant. zāi-huār 栽花兒 plant a flower.

ZĀI₃ 栽 (TV) (1) fall, tumble. Wǒ-zāidǎo-le. 我栽倒了. I have fallen. (2) fail in doing something and lose face. Tā-zāi-(gēntou)-le. 他栽(跟頭)了. He failed and lost face.

ZĀI₃ 宰 (TV) slaughter an animal. zǎi-niú 宰牛 slaughter a cow.

ZÀI₁ 在 (IV) exist, be alive. Zhāng-xiansheng hái-zài, tā-tàitai-bu-zài-le. 張先生還在, 他太太不在了. Mr. Chang is still alive, but his wife has passed away. Nǐde-fángzi hái-zài. 你的房子還在. Your house still exists.

(TV) (1) be at, in, on a place, at a time. Tā-zài-jiā, méi-zài-zhèr. 他在家, 沒在這兒. He is at home, not here. Tā-dìng-de-shíhou jiù-zài-míngtian-wǎnshang. 他訂的時候就在明天晚上. The time which he settled on is tomorrow evening. Nǐ-qù-zhǎo-ta-ba, tā-zhǔn-zài. 你去找他吧, 他準在. Go and look for him, he's certainly there. (2) depend upon, be up to someone to decide. Wǒmen-zěnma-bàn, jiu-zài-nǐ-le. 我們怎麼辦, 就在你了. How we act will be up to you. Nà-zài-nǐ-yǒu-duōshao-qián. 那在你有多少錢. That depends upon how much money you have. (3) according to. Zài-wǒ-kàn, nà-bu-yàojǐn. 在我

看，那不要緊. According-ing to the way I look at it, it is not important.

(CV) at, in, on a place, at a time. Wǒ-bu-xǐhuan-zai-fàng-guānr-chī-fàn. 我不喜歡在飯館兒吃飯. I don't like to eat in a restaurant. Tā-shì-zài-lái-yǐqián shuō-de. 他是在來以前說的. It was before he came that he said it.

(PV) at, in, on a place, at a time. Tā-zhùzai-wǒ-jiā-le. 他住在我家了. He lived in my house. Tā tǎngzai-dìxia-le. 他躺在地下了. He is lying on the floor.

(AD) (con. zhèngzai 正在). in the midst of doing something. Tā-zai-jiào-ni-ne. 他在叫你呢. He is calling you. Nǐ-zai-zuò-shénma? 你在作甚麼? What are you doing? (See: DE 的, ĀI 挨).

ZÀI₁ 再 (AD) (1) used in commands, suggestions or suppositional phrases, again. Yǒu-gōngfu, qǐng-zài-lái. 有工夫，請再來. When you have time, please come again. Yàoshi-zài-xià-yǔ, nà-hái-děi-gǎi-rìzi. 要是再下雨，那還得改日子. If it rains again, the date will have to be changed again. Wǒ-hái-dei-zài-qù-liang-ci. 我還得再去兩次. I have to go there several more times. Wǒ-bu-zài-hē-jiǔ-le. 我不再喝酒了. I'm not

going to drink again. (cf: HÁI 還 YÒU 又). (2) unstressed, preceded by an expression of time or condition to indicate a suggestion or command or a future happening, then. Chīle-fàn zai-zǒu-ba. 吃了飯再走吧. Let's eat and then leave. Míngtian zai-zuò. 明天再作. We'll do it tomorrow. (cf:CÁI 才).

(3) stressed, used before SV, more, -er. Yàoshi-'zài-guì wǒ-jiu-mǎi-buqǐ-le. 要是再貴我就買不起了. If it is more expensive, I can't afford it. Wǒ-méiyou-zài-dà-de. 我沒有再大的. I have nothing bigger. (4) furthermore, on top of that. Nǐ-bu-qù, wǒ-zai-bu-qù, nà-duóma-buhaoyìsi. 你不去，我再不去，那多麼不好意思. You're not going, furthermore I'm not going, how embarrassing that will be. Běnlái-qián-jiu-bu-gòu, nǐ-zai-mǎi-qìchē, nà-zěn-ma-bàn a? 本來錢就不夠，你再買汽車，那怎麼辦呢? In the first place there's not enough money, on top of that you want to buy a car, how can it be done?

ZÀI-CHĂNG₄ 在場 (VO) be at the place where something hap-pened. Chū-'shì-de-shíhou, tā-méi-zài-chǎng. 出事的時候，他沒在場. When the accident happened, he was not there.

ZÀIHU₁ 在乎 (TV) care about.

Wǒ-bu-zàihu-tā-gěi-qián-bu-gei. 我 不 在 乎 他 給 錢 不 給 . I don't care whether he gives money or not.

ZĀIHUANG₅ 災 荒 (N) famine. nào-zāihuang 鬧 災 荒 have a famine.

ZÀIHUÌ₃ 再 會 (TV) goodbye. (syn. zàijiàn 再見).

ZÀIJIÀN₁ 再見 (TV) goodbye. (syn. zàihuì 再會).

ZÀI...MÉIYOU-LE₂ 再 ... 没 有 了 (S) nothing more than... Tā-zài-ài-shuō-huà méiyǒu-le. 他 再 愛 説 話 没 有 了 . Nobody is more talkative than she. Nà-zài-hǎo méiyǒu-le. 那 再 好 没 有 了 .Nothing is better than that.

ZÀISĀN₃ 再 三 (MA) repeatedly. Tā-zàisànde-qǐng-wǒ-lái. 他 再 三 的 請 我 來 .He repeatedly asked me to come.

ZÀISHUŌ₁ 再 説 (TV) talk about it, see about it. Yǐhòu-zàishuō. 以 後 再 説 . We'll see about it later.
(MA) moreover, furthermore. Tā-hěn-cōngming, zàishuō-yě-yònggōng, súoyi xiānsheng-dōu-xǐhuan-ta. 他 很 聰 明 , 再 説 , 也 用 功 , 所 以 先 生 都 喜 歡 他 .He is brilliant,moreover, he works hard, therefore all the teachers like him.

ZÀIYEBU₂ 再 也 不 (S) never again. Wǒ-zàiye-bu-lai-le. 我 再 也 不 來 了 .I'll never come again.

ZÀIZHÒNGQÌCHĒ₃ 載 重 汽 車 (N) truck.(M: liàng 輛).

ZÁLUÀN₄ 雜 亂 (SV) be confused.

ZǍN₃ 攢 (TV) (1) collect (as a hobby). zǎn-yóupiào 攢 郵 票 collect stamps. (2) save money. zǎn-qián 攢 錢 save money. (cf: SŌUJI 搜集).

ZÀNCHENG₁ 贊 成 (TV) agree with, support someone's idea. (opp. fǎnduì 反對). Wǒ-zàn-cheng-ta. 我 贊 成 他 . I agree with him. Tāde-yìjian wo-zàncheng. 他 的 意 見 我 贊 成 . I support his opinion.

ZĀNG₁ 髒 (SV) dirty, filthy. (syn. āza 骯 髒 , āngzang 骯 髒). (opp. gānjing 乾 淨).

ZÀNG₄ 贜 (N) (1) booty, loot, stolen goods or money. fēng-zāng 分 贜 share the booty. (2) bribe taken by a government official. tān-zāng 貪 贜 take a bribe.

ZÀNMEI₄ 贊 美 (TV) praise. Rén-dou-zànmei-ta. 人 都 贊 美 他 . All the people praised him.

ZÁNMEN₄ 咱 們 (PR) Peip. we, us (includes the person or persons spoken to). Nǐ-gēn-wǒ zán-men-liangge-ren yíkuàir-qù. 你 跟 我 咱 們 兩 個 人 一 塊 兒 去 . You and I, the two of us will go together. (cf: WǑMEN 我 們).

ZĀO₃ 糟 (SV) (1) rotten (about to fall apart or break). Shéngzi-zāo-le. 繩 子 糟 了 .The rope is about to break. (2) (con. zāogāo 糟 糕). bad, be in a

Z

bad state, be a mess. Shìqing zǎo-le. 事情糟了. That matter turned into a mess. Zhēn-zāo. 真糟. It's really a mess.

ZÁO₄ 鑿 (TV) (1) chisel. záo-yige-dòng 鑿一個洞 chisel a hole. (2) hammer, pound. záo-mén 鑿門 pound on the door.

ZǍO₁ 早 (SV) (1) early.(opp. wǎn 晚). Bù-zǎo-le. 不早了. It's not early. A: Kuài-wánle-ba? B: Wán? Hái-zǎo. A: 快 完了吧? B: 完? 還早. A: Will it be finished soon? B: Finished? It's still early., (2) used as a greeting, good morn-ing. Wáng-xiānsheng, zǎo. 王 先生, 早. Good morning, Mr. Wang.
(RE) early. Wǒ-qǐzǎo-le. 我 起早了. I got up too early. or I get up early now.
(AD) (1) early. zǎo-shuì-zǎo-qǐ 早睡早起 early to bed, early to rise. Wǒ-zǎo-láile-yi-tian. 我早來了一天. I came one day too early. Míng-tian-zǎo-yidianr-lái. 明天 早一點兒來. Come a little earlier tomorrow. (2) ear-lier (before it was too late). Nǐ-wèi-shénma zǎo-bu-shuō? 你 為甚麼早不說? Why didn't you say it earlier (before it was too late)? Nǐ-zǎo-gàn-shénma-laizhe? 你早幹甚 麼來着? What were you doing before it was too late? (3) long ago. Wǒ-zǎo-jiu-tīngshuō-le. 我早就聽說了. I

heard it long ago. Yàoshi-yǒu-qián, wǒ-zǎo-mǎi-le. 要是 有錢我早買了. If I had the money, I would have bought it long ago.

ZÀO₅ 竈 (N) kitchen stove or range.

ZÀO₃ 造 (TV) (1) build. zào-fáng-zi 造房子 build a house. (2) make, manufacture. Nèige-gōngchǎng zào-shénma? 那個 工廠造甚麼? What does that factory produce? fig. zào-yáoyan 造謠言 start rumors.

ZǍOCHEN₁ 早晨 or ZǍO-SHANG 早上 (TW) morning.

ZǍOFÀN₁ 早飯 (N) (1) break-fast. (M: dùn 頓). (2) Peip. lunch. (M: dùn 頓).

ZÀO-FǍN₃ 造反 (VO) rebel or revolt against the government, behave in a rebellious manner. Tāmen-fǎnduì-zhèngfǔ, kěshi-bìng-méi-zào-fǎn. 他們反 對政府, 可是並沒 造反. They opposed the government but they didn't reb-el. Zhèixie-háizi yào-zào-fǎn. 這些孩子要造反. These children are going to re-bel.

ZÀOGĀO₂ 糟糕 (SV) (1) bad, be in a bad state, be a mess. Tā-de-qíngxing-zāogāo-tòule. 他 的情形糟糕透了. His situation is very bad. (2) What a mess! Zāogāo! Zhè-zěnma-bàn? 糟糕! 這怎 麼辦? What a mess! What can be done now?

ZÀOHUA₄ 造化 (N) good luck. yǒu-zàohua 有造化 have good luck. Nà-shi-nǐde-zàohua. 那是你的造化. That's your good luck.

ZĀOJIAN₃ 糟踐 see ZĀOTA 糟蹋

ZĂOJIU₂ 早就 (AD) long ago. Wo-zǎojiu-lái-le. 我早就 來了. I came long ago.

ZĀO-NÀN₅ 遭難 (VO) meet with misfortune.

ZÀO-NIÈ₅ 造孽 (VO) do some kind of wrong or evil thing. Shā-rén jiu-shi-zào-niè. 殺人; 就是造孽. To kill somebody is an evil thing.

ZĂOPÉN₃ 澡盆 (N) bathtub.

ZĂOR₅ 棗兒 (N) date (fruit).

ZĂOSHANG₁ 早上 see ZĀO-CHEN 早晨.

ZĀOTA₃ 糟蹋 or ZĀOJIAN 糟踐 (TV) (1) waste. Bié-zāota-zhǐ. 別糟蹋紙. Don't waste paper. (2) spoil, ruin. Tā-zuò-cài-méi-zuòhǎo, bǎ-ròu-dōu-zāota-le. 他作菜 沒作好,把肉都糟蹋了. He didn't cook it right, all the meat is spoiled. (3) insult. Tā-jing-zāota-rén. 他 竟糟蹋人. He always insults people.

'ZĂOWĂN₂ 早晚 (MA) sooner or later. Tā-zǎowǎn-dei-xué-huì-le. 他早晚得學 會了. He'll learn it sooner or later.

ZÁOZI₅ 鑿子 (N) chisel. (M:

bǎ 把).

ZÁSHUĂR₄ 雜耍兒 (N) variety show.

ZÁZHÌ₂ 雜誌 (N) magazine, periodical. (M: fènr 份兒). dìng-yifènr-zázhì 訂一份兒雜 誌 subscribe to a magazine.

ZÉBEI₄ 責備 (TV) reprimand, scold, rebuke. Bú-yao-jìng-zé-bei-biéren. 不要竟責備 別人. Don't always reprimand others.

ZÉI₂ 賊 (N) thief. dǎi-zéi 逮 賊 catch a thief. (AD) irritatingly. zéi-liàng 賊 亮 irritatingly shiny.

ZĒNGCHĂN₄ 增產 (VO) (con. zēnjiā-shēngchǎn 增加生 產). increase production.

ZĒNGDUŌ₅ 增多 (TV) increase.

ZĒNGJIĀ₂ 增加 (TV) increase, add to. Xuésheng zēngjiāle-hen-duō. 學生增加了很 多. The number of students has increased a great deal.

ZĒNGZHĂNG₄ 增長 (TV) increase. zēngzhǎng-zhīshi 增 長知識 increase one's knowledge.

ZĚNMA₁ 怎麼 (AD) how, in which way. Nǐ-shi-zěnma-lái-de? 你是怎麼來的? How did you come here? Zěn-ma-bàn? 怎麼辦? What can be done? Zhèige-'zěnma-hǎo-ne? 這個怎麼好 呢? In which way is this good? (MA) why. Zěnma-ni-bu-gào-song-ta? 怎麼你不告 訴他? Why don't you tell

him? Nǐ-zěnma-bu-qù? 你 怎
麼 不 去 ? Why aren't you
going?

used by itself at the beginning of
a sentence, what? (syn. zěnmazhe 怎麼 着). Zěnma? lián-
'nǐ-dou-bu-zhīdào. 怎 麼 ? 連
你 都 不 知 道 . What?
Even you don't know it.

used after a vocally stressed
negative expression, not very.
Nèige 'bù-zěnma-hǎo. 那 個
不 怎 麼 好 . That is not
very good.

when vocally stressed and followed by a phrase with dōu 都
or yě 也 , no matter, it doesn't
matter. Wǒ-'zěnma-shuō dou-
bu-duì. 我 怎 麼 説 都 不
對 . No matter how I said it,
it was always wrong. 'Zěnma-
piányi yě-dei-yìbǎikuai-qián. 怎
麼 便 宜 也 得 一 百
塊 錢 . No matter how cheap
it is, we still need one hundred
dollars.

used in two phrases repeatedly,
no matter how... Tā-'zěnma-
chàng zěnma-hǎotīng. 他 怎
麼 唱 怎 麼 好 聽 . It's
good to listen to, no matter how
he sings it.

used in reduplication, in a certain kind of way. Tā-cháng-shuō
tāde-qìchē zěnma-zěnma-piányi.
他 常 説 他 的 汽 車
怎 麼 怎 麼 便 宜 . He
often says that his car is cheap
in certain ways.

(SP) what kind of. Zhè-shi-zěn-

ma-yijiu-huà? 這 是 怎 麼
一 句 話 ? What kind of a
sentence is this?

(IV) do what. A: Zěnma-le?B:
Méi-zěnma. A: 怎 麼 了 ?
B: 沒 怎 麼 . A: What's hap-
pened? B: Nothing happened.
Zhè-zěnma-hǎo? 這 怎 麼
好 ? What can be done(to make
things better)?

ZĚNMA₂ 這麼 or ZHÈNMA 這
麼 (AD) this way. Zěnma-bàn-
ba. 這麼 辦 吧 . Let's do
it this way.

ZĚNMAYÀNG(R)₁ 怎 麼 樣 (兒)
(IV) (1) how is it. Zhèige zěnmayàng? 這 個 怎 麼 樣 ?
How is this one? Nǐ-juéde zěnmayàng? 你 覺 得 怎 麼
樣 ? How do you feel? A: Zěnmayàng? B: Hěn-hǎo. A: 怎 麼
樣 ? B: 很 好 . A: How are
things? B: Fine. (See: BUZĚN-
MAYÀNG 不 怎 麼 樣). (2)
what to do. (syn. zěnmazhe 怎
麼 着). Wǒ-qù, nǐ-zěnma-
yàng? 我 去, 你 怎 麼 樣 ?
I am going, what are you going
to do? Nǐ-shuō-zěnmayàng? 你
説 怎 麼 樣 ? (You say),
what should be done? Wǒ-dǎle-
ta-le, kěshi-yě-méi-zěnmayàng.
我 打 了 他 了, 可 是
也 沒 怎 麼 樣 . I gave
him a beating, but nothing happened. Nǐ-cāi-zěnmayàng? 你
猜 怎 麼 樣 ? (You) guess
what's happened? Nǐ-hái-yào-
zěnmayàng? 你 還 要 怎
麼 樣 ? What else do you want

Z

to do? Nǐ-néng-bǎ-ta-zěnma-yàng? 你 能 把 他 怎 麼 樣 ? What can you do to him? Yàoshi-tā-bu-qù nǐ-zěnmayàng? 要 是 他 不 去 你 怎 麼 樣 ? If he won't go what would you do? Wǒ-'zěnmayang dou-bu-duì. 我 怎 麼 樣 都 不 對 . It doesn't matter what I do, I am always wrong. (AD) how, in which way. Wǒmen-zěnmayangr-qù? 我 們 怎 麼 樣 兒 去 ? How are we going to go?

'ZĚNMAYÀNGR₁ 怎 麼 樣 兒 or ZHÈNMAYÀNGR 怎 麼 樣 兒 (IV) do something this way. Nǐ-kàn zěnmayàngr hǎo-bu-hao? 你 看 這 麼 樣 兒 好 不 好 ? Look, how about doing it this way? (AD) in this way, in this manner. Wǒ-zěnmayàngr-shuō-ba. 我 這 麼 樣 兒 説 吧 . Let me say it this way.

ZĚNMAZHE₂ 怎 麼 着 (IV) what to do. (syn. zěnmayàng 怎 麼 樣). Nǐ-shuō-zěnmazhe-ne? 你 説 怎 麼 着 呢 ? (You say) what should be done? Zěnmazhe dou-kéyi. 怎 麼 着 都 可 以 . It will be all right whatever it is.

used by itself at the beginning of a sentence, what? (syn. zěn-ma 怎 麼). Zhěnmazhe? Tā-gǎn-dǎ-rén! 怎 麼 着 ? 他 敢 打 人 ! What? He dares hit people!

ZÉREN₂ 責 任 (N) responsibility,

duty. fù-zéren 負 責 任 shoulder responsibility. jìn-zé-ren 盡 責 任 fulfill (one's) responsibility.

ZHĀ₂ 扎 (TV) (1) jab with a thin pointed instrument. zhā-yíge-yǎnr 扎 一 個 眼 兒 poke a hole. Tā-yòng-dāozi jā-rén. 他 用 刀 子 扎 人 . He stabbed someone with a knife. (2) Peip. embroider. Tā-huì-zhā-huār. 他 會 扎 花 兒 . She knows how to embroider(flower patterns). (cf: XIÙ 繡). (3) give or have Chinese needle therapy (acupuncture) or an injection. Zhā-zhēn néng-zhì-hěn-duōzhǒng-bìng. 扎 針 能 治 很 多 種 病 . Acupuncture can cure many kinds of illnesses. (4) lit. or fig. piercing to the ear. Zhèige-shēngyi zhā-ěrduo. 這 個 聲 音 扎 耳 朵 . His voice is very piercing. Tāde-huà zhā-ěrduo. 他 的 話 扎 耳 朵 . His words are sharp.

ZHÁ₂ 炸 (TV) fry. zhá-yú 炸 魚 fry fish or fried fish.

ZHÀ₂ 炸 (TV) (1) lit. or fig. ex-plode. Zhàdàn zhà-le. 炸 彈 炸 了 . The bomb has ex-ploded. Tā-yìtīng jiu-zhà-le. 他 一 聽 就 炸 了 . He ex-ploded as soon as he heard it. (2) bomb, bombard. zhà-fēijī-chǎng 炸 飛 機 場 bomb the air field. (3) crack (in glass or similar substances as a result of heat or cold). Jiǔ-bēi-zhà-le. 酒 杯 炸 了 . The wine cup

Z

has cracked.

ZHÀ(YI)₃ 乍 (一) (AD) at the very beginning of <u>doing something</u>, at first. Tāde-huà zhà(yi)ting, hěn-yǒu-lǐ. 他的話乍一聽很有理. When you first listen to him, it sounds very reasonable. Wǒ-zhà(yi)-lái-de-shihou, dōu-bu-shú. 我乍(一)來的時候都不熟. When I had just arrived here, nothing was familiar.

ZHÀDÀN₁ 炸彈 (N) bomb.

ZHĀI₁ 摘 (TV) (1) take off <u>of the head or hand, such as glasses, earmuffs, gloves; or some-where else on the body, such as jewelry, flowers or other adorn-ment.</u> (opp. dài 戴). zhāi-mào-zi 摘帽子 take off the hat. zhāi-yǎnjìngr 摘眼鏡兒 take off the eyeglasses. (cf:TUŌ 脫).(2) pick off <u>from a tree.</u> zhāi-huār 摘花兒 pick flowers. zhāi-píngguǒ 摘蘋果 pick apples. (3) take off <u>or</u> down <u>a flag or something hang-ing from a hook.</u> (opp. guà 掛). zhāi-huàr 摘畫兒 take down the painting.

ZHǍI₂ 窄 (SV) (1) narrow. (opp. kuān 寬). Zhèige-mén hěn-zhǎi. 這個門很窄. This door is very narrow. Tā-de-yǎnguāng tài-zhǎi. 他的眼光太窄 His view is too narrow. (2) concerned <u>or</u> upset over minor matters. (opp. kuān 寬). Tā-xīn-zhǎi. 他心窄. He is concerned (over

minor matters).

ZHÀI₂ 債 (N) debt (<u>money</u>). (M: bǐ 筆). qiàn-zhài 欠債 (<u>lit.</u> owe debt) be in debt. Wǒ-yǒu-yibì-zhài, hái-méi-huán. 我有一筆債,還沒還. I have a debt which has not yet been paid. (cf: ZHÀNG 賬).

ZHĀIYÀO₄ 摘要 (N) outline, abstract, summary.

ZHÀLANR₃ 柵欄兒 (N) fence. (M: dào 道).

ZHĀN₃ 沾 (TV) (1) touch, have physical contact. Xīn-xié hái-méi-zhān-dì-ne. 新鞋還沒沾地呢.(<u>lit.</u> The new shoes haven't touched the ground yet.) The new shoes haven't been worn yet. (2) have <u>something</u> stick <u>or</u> rub off onto <u>something else</u> through physical contact. Wǒ-shǒushang zhānle-yidianr-tǔ. 我手上沾了一點兒土. I got a little dirt on my hand.

ZHĀN₃ 粘 (TV) stick on <u>with paste, glue or other sticky sub-stances,</u> paste, glue. Bǎ-guǎng-gào zhānzai-qiángshang. 把廣告粘在牆上. Paste the advertisement on the wall. Zhèiliǎng-zhang-zhǐ zhānshang-le. 這兩張紙粘上了. These two sheets of paper are stuck together.

ZHǍN₅ 盞 (M) <u>for lamps, lan-terns or electric lights.</u>

ZHÀN₁ 站 (IV) stand. Nǐ-wàng-hòu-zhàn. 你往後站. Stand back. Zhàn-qilai. 站起

來 . Stand up. Nǐ-zhànzai-zhèr gàn-shénma? 你 站 在 這 兒 幹 甚 麼 ? What are you doing standing here? Wǒ-zhàn-le-yihuǐr-le. 我 站 了 一 會 兒 了 . I have stood for awhile. Wǒ-zhànzhe-ba. 我 站 着 吧 . Let me stand. Jiēshang-zhànzhe-hǎoxiē-rén. 街 上 站 着 好 些 人 . A great many people are standing on the street. Tā-bù-néng-zhànzai-wǒde-lìchang shuōhuà. 他 不 能 站 在 我 的 立 場 說 話 . He cannot speak from my standpoint. (M) station, depot, stop. Zài-guò-'sān-zhàn jiu-dào-le. 再 過 三 站 就 到 了 . We'll be there after three more stops. (N) station, depot, stop. huǒchē-zhàn 火 車 站 railroad station. Dàole-zhàn zài-shuō-ba. 到 了 站 再 說 吧 . We'll talk about it after we get to the station.

ZHÀN₃ 佔 (TV) (1) (con. zhànlǐng 佔 領). seize and occupy by military force. Dírén-bǎ-fēiji-chǎng-zhàn-le. 敵 人 把 飛 機 場 佔 了 . The enemy occupied the airfield. (2) take, occupy a place for use. Zhèi-jian-wūzi yǒu-ren-zhàn-le. 這 間 屋 子 有 人 佔 了 . This room is occupied by somebody. (3) occupy space or time. Zhèixie-dōngxi tài-zhàn-dìfang. 這 些 東 西 太 佔 地 方 . These things take up too

much space. Wǒ-jiāo-shū bǎ-shíhou-dou-zhàn-le. 我 教 書 把 時 候 都 佔 了 . All of my time is occupied by teaching. (4) constitute a certain portion or percentage. Zhèige-xué-xiào nǚshēng-zhàn-bǎifēnzhi'èr-shí. 這 個 學 校 女 生 佔 百 分 之 二 十 . In this school, female students constitute only twenty per cent of the total.

ZHÀNCHǍNG₄ 戰 場 (N) battlefield.

ZHÀNDÒU₅ 戰 鬥 (IV) fight a battle.

ZHÀNFÁNG₄ 棧 房 . (N) (1) warehouse (for merchandise). (2) old-fashioned small hotel, inn.

ZHÀNFÚ₅ 戰 俘 (N) prisoner of war.

ZHĀNG₃ 章 (M) chapter (of a book). diyīzhāng 第 一 章 the first chapter.

ZHĀNG₄ 張 (TV) open the mouth or hands. zhāng-zuǐ 張 嘴 open the mouth. bǎ-shǒu zhāng-kai 把 手 張 開 open the hand.

ZHĀNG₁ 張 (M) for things which have flat, extended surfaces. yì-zhāng-zhǐ 一 張 紙 a sheet of paper. yìzhāng-zhuōzi 一 張 桌 子 a table. yìzhāng-chuáng 一 張 牀 a bed.

ZHǍNG₃ 長 (-B) head of an organization. xiàozhǎng 校 長 head of a school, principal.

ZHǍNG₁ 長 (IV) grow. Tā-jīnnian zhǎngle-liǎngcùn. 他 今 年

長了兩寸. He has grown two inches this year. Wǒ-zhǎng-le-yisuì. 我長了一歲. I've grown a year older. Háizi dou-zhǎnggāo-le. 孩子都長高了. All the children have grown tall. Tāde-bízi zhǎngde-hěn-hǎokàn.他的鼻子長得很好看.Her nose is very pretty. (TV) (1) or SHĒNG 生 grow out of something, come out. Shù-zhǎng-yèzi-le. 樹長葉子了. The leaves have come out on the tree. Dàngāoshang zhǎng-méi-le.蛋糕上長霉了. The cake has become moldy. Guǒzi zhǎng-chóngzi-le. 果子長蟲子了.This fruit has worms. Tā-tóushang zhǎngle-yíge-bāo. 他頭上長了一個包. A boil developed on his head.(2) increase. zhǎng-xuéwen 長學問 increase one's learned knowledge. zhǎng-běnshi 長本事 increase one's ability. (3) older. Tā-bǐ-wǒ-zhǎng-liǎngsuì. 他比我長兩歲. He is two years older than I.

ZHǍNG₃ 漲 (IV) (1) go up, rise (of price). Dōngxide-jiàqian dōu-zhǎngle. 東西的價錢都漲了. All of the prices have gone up. (2) rise (of a river). Héli shuǐ-zhǎng-le. 河裏水漲了. The water in the river rose.

ZHÀNG₂ 賬 (N) (1) debt. (M: bǐ 筆). Bié-gǎi-zhàng. 別該賬. Don't get into debt. Tā-gēn-wo-yào-zhàng. 他跟我要賬. He asked me to repay my debt. Zhàng-dou-huánqīng-le. 賬都還清了. All of the debt was paid off. (cf: ZHÀI 債). (2) account. (M: bǐ 筆). jì-zhàng 記賬 keep record of an account or charge to an account. Tāde-zhàng bu-qīngchu. 他的賬不清楚. The figures in his account are messed up. (3) account book, ledger. (M: běn 本). Zhèibǐ-qián hái-méi-shàng-zhàng-ne. 這筆錢還没上賬呢.This sum of money has not been written in the book yet. Wǒ-qu-mǎi-yiběn-zhàng. 我去買一本賬. I'll go to buy an account book.

ZHÀNG₃ 漲 (IV) expand. Tiānqi-rè mùtou-jiu-zhàng-le. 天氣熱木頭就漲了.Wood expands in the hot weather.

ZHÀNG₄ 丈 (M) a unit of measure for length, ten Chinese feet. (See: CHǏ 尺).

ZHÀNG₃ 仗 (TV) depend upon. Wǒmen-děi-zhàngzhe-ta. 我們得仗着他. We have to depend on him.

ZHÀN-GǍNG₄ 站崗 (VO) guard a post, stand watch.

ZHǍNGBÈI₄ 長輩 (N) a person of the older generation, elder. Tā-shi-wǒmende-zhǎngbei. 他是我們的長輩. He is our elder.

ZHĀNGCHEN₃ 章程 (N) (1)

regulation, rule. (2) constitution of an organization. (3) printed regulations, such as in a school catalogue. (M: fènr 份兒).

ZHÀNGDĀNR₂ 賬單兒 or ZHÀNGDANZI 賬單子 (N) bill, invoice, statement. (M: zhāng 張).

ZHÀNGDĀNZI₂ 賬單子 see ZHÀNGDĀNR 賬單子 .

ZHÀNGFU₂ 丈夫 (N) (1) husband. (2) manly man. dà-zhàng-fu 大丈夫 a manly man. (cf: XIĀNSHENG 先生).

ZHĂNGGUÌDE₄ 掌櫃的 (N) manager of a store.

ZHĀNG-JIÀR₃ 漲價兒 (VO) raise prices. Dōngxi-lăo-zhăng-jiàr. 東西老漲價兒 . The prices of things are always going up. Yì-yŏu-ren-măi, ta-jiu-zhăngjiàr. 一有人買 他就漲價兒 . As soon as somebody wants to buy it, he raises the price.

ZHĂNGJÌN₃ 長進 (IV) make progress (in learning or experience).

(N) progress, improvement. Tā-niàn-shū yŏu-zhăngjin. 他念 書有長進 . There is improvement in his studying.

ZHÀNLĬNG₄ 佔領 (TV) seize and occupy by military force.

ZHĀNGLO₄ 張羅 (TV) (1) go around to take care of something. Tāmende-zhănlăn míngtiān-kāi-mù, wŏ-děi-qu gěi-tamen-zhăng-lo-zhanglo. 他們的展覽 明天開幕，我得去

給他們張羅張羅. Their exhibition will open tomorrow, I have to go around to take care of the details. (2) go around to try to get a loan. Wŏ-děi-chū-qu-zhānglo-yibĭ-kuănzi. 我得 先去張羅一筆款 子 . I have to go out to different places to get a loan.

ZHÀNGMŪNIÁNG₄ 丈母娘 (N) mother-in-law (wife's mother).

ZHĀNGNĂO₅ 樟腦 (N) camphor.

ZHÀNGREN₄ 丈人 (N) father-in-law (wife's father).

ZHĀN-GUÀ₅ 占卦 (VO) foretell by casting lots.

ZHĀN-GUĀNG₄ 沾光 (VO) share one's glory, accomplishments or benefit from someone's help. Wŏ-zhānle-nín-bushăode-guāng. 我沾了您不少的 光 . I have got quite a bit of benefit from your help.

ZHĂNGWO₄ 掌握 (TV) (1) seize, take hold of. zhăngwo-jīhui 掌 握機會 seize an opportunity. zhăngwo-quánli 掌握權利 seize power. (2) have a grasp of, master. Běipíng-huà-de-fāyīn tā-dou-néng-zhăngwo-le. 北平 話的發音他都能 掌握了 . He can completely master the sound system of Pekinese.

ZHĂNGZĬ₅ 長子 (N) eldest son.

ZHÀNGZI₅ 帳子 (N) bed curtain, mosquito net. Bă-zhàngzi-fàng-xialai. 把帳子放下來 . Put down the bed curtain.

ZHĀNG-ZUI₃ 張嘴 (VO) open

the mouth.

ZHÀNJIÀN₄ 戰艦 (N) warship,
battleship. (cf: ZHĪ 隻).

ZHĂNKĀI₄ 展開 (RV) open out,
spread, develop. Tāmende-shì-
yè-hái-mei-zhănkāi. 他們的
事業還沒展開. Their
enterprise still has not developed.

ZHĂNLĂN₂ 展覽 (TV) display,
exhibit. Bă-huàr náchulai zhăn-
lan-zhanlan. 把畫兒拿
出來展覽展覽. Take
the picture out to display it.
(N) exhibition. kāi-zhănlăn 開
展覽 have an exhibition.

ZHĂNLĂNHUÌ₃ 展覽會 (N)
exhibition.

ZHÀNLĬNG₃ 占領 (TV) occupy
a territory by military force.
Nèige-chéng ràng-díren-zhàn-
lĭng-le. 那個城讓敵
人佔領了. The city has
been occupied by the enemy.

ZHĀNMÀO₄ 氈帽 (N) felt hat.
(M: dĭng 頂).

ZHÀN-PIÁNYI₂ 佔便宜 (VO)
take advantage of someone. (opp.
chī-kuī 吃虧). Béi-lăo-xiăng
zhàn-wŏde-piányi. 別老想
佔我的便宜. Don't
always think of taking advantage
of me.

ZHĂN-QĪ₄ 展期 (VO) postpone.

ZHÀNSHÌ₅ 戰士 (N) warrior.

ZHÀNTÁI₄ 站台 (N) platform
(in a railroad or bus station).

ZHÀNZHĂNG₄ 站長 (N) station
master.

ZHÀNZHĒNG₃ 戰爭 (N) war.

ZHĀO₃ 招 (TV) (1) wave, beckon
(with the hand). Tā-xiàng-wo
zhāo-shŏur. 他向我招
手兒. He waved to me. (2)
recruit people. zhāo-bīng 招
兵 recruit soldiers. zhāo-xué-
sheng 招學生 recruit stu-
dents. (3) attract a large number
of people or things. zhāo-cāng-
ying 招蒼蠅 attract flies.
zhāo-măyĭ 招螞蟻 attract
ants. (4) cause an emotional
reaction in someone. Bié-zhāo-
nĭ-māma-shāng-xīn. 別招
你媽媽傷心. Don't
make your mother sad. Tā-bù-
zhāo-ren-xĭhuan. 他不招
人喜歡. He makes people
dislike him. Wŏ-zhāo-ni-le-ma?
我招你了嗎? Did I
bother you? (5) tease, provoke.
Bié-zhāo-nèige-háizi. 別招
那個孩子. Don't tease
that child. (6) pass a disease on
to someone. Tā-shāng-fēng. Nĭ-
bié-zhāoshang. 他傷風. 你
別招上. He has a cold.
Don't get it from him. (7) confess (in court). Bù-dă-ta, ta-bu-
zhāo. 不打他,他不招.
If you don't beat him, he won't
confess.

ZHĀO₄ 着 (IV) see ZHÁO 着 (3).
dial. used by itself, that's right.
Zhāo, zhāo, nín-shuō-de-duì.
着, 着, 您說的對.
That's right. What you said is
true.

ZHÁO₂ 着 (IV) (1) lighted, ignited.
Huŏ zháole. 火着了. The

fire is lit. Zháo-huǒ-le! 着 火 了 ! Fire! (2) fall asleep. Tā-tǎngxiale, hái-méi-zháo-ne. 他 躺 下 了, 還 没 着 呢. He has lain down, but has not yet fallen asleep. (3) or ZHAO 着 touch, have physical contact. zháo-dì 着 地 touch the ground.

(RE) (1) ignited, lighted. Yān diǎnzháo-le. 烟 點 着 了. The cigarette is lighted. (2) fall asleep. Tā-shuìzháo-le-méiyou? 他 睡 着 了 没 有 ? Has he fallen asleep? (3) <u>when not stressed in actual RV, indicates success in attaining or getting something.</u> Qián nǐ-názhaole-ma? 錢 你 拿 着 了 嗎 ? Have you got the money? Wǒ-diào-zhao-yitiáo-dà-yú. 我 釣 着 一 條 大 魚. I have caught a big fish. (4) <u>when stressed in actual RV, indicates some benefit has been obtained.</u> Zhèi-xià-zi nǐ-ke-mǎizháo-le. 這 下 子 你 可 買 着 了. This time, you really bought the right one. (5) <u>indicates to hit the target.</u> Tā-dǎ-niǎor méi-dǎ-zháo. 他 打 鳥 兒 没 打 着 He shot at the bird but missed. Zhēn-ràng-ni-shuōzháo-le. 真 讓 你 説 着 了. You really hit the nail on the head.

ZHǍO₁ 找 (TV) look for, find. Nǐ-zhǎo-shéi? 你 找 誰 ? Whom are you looking for? Wǒ-zhǎo-Lǐ-xiansheng shuō-huà. 我 找 李 先 生 説 話. I

want to talk to Mr. Li. Lǐ-xiansheng! Yǒu-ren-zhǎo! 李 先 生 ! 有 人 找 ! Mr. Li! Someone is looking for you! Nǐ-zhǎo-fángzi zhǎohǎo-le-meiyou? 你 找 房 子 找 好 了 没 有 ? Have you found a suitable house? Tā-zhǎobuzhǎo-shì. 他 找 不 着 事. He cannot find a job. Tā-jìng-zhǎo-róngyide-zuò. 他 竟 找 容 易 的 做. He always looks for the easy thing to do. Bié-jìng-zhǎo-piányi. 别 竟 找 便 宜. Don't always look to take advantage. Tā-na-shi zhǎo-huà-shuō. 他 那 是 找 話 説. That was because he was looking for something to say. Bié-zhǎo-bièniu. 别 找 别 扭. Don't look for anything unpleasant. Nǐ-bié-zhǎo-máfan. 你 别 找 麻 煩. Don't look for trouble. Bié-zhǎo-chár. 别 找 碴 兒. Don't pick on everything. Nǐ-shi-zhǎo-dǎ. 你 是 找 打. You are looking for a spanking.

ZHÀO₃ 照 (TV) (1) have a light shine on <u>something.</u> Tàiyang-zhào-wǒde-yǎnjing. 太 陽 照 我 的 眼 睛. The sun is shining in my eyes. Diàndēng bǎ-lù-zhàode-hěn-liàng. 電 燈 把 路 照 得 很 亮. The light is shining very brightly on the road. Yòng-shǒu-diàndēng zhào-yizhao. 用 手 電 燈 照 一 照. Shine the flashlight on it. (2) look at oneself

Z

(as in a reflection). Tā-xǐhuan-zhào-jìngzi. 他喜歡照鏡子. She likes to look at herself in a mirror. (3) take a picture or an X-ray. zhào-yi-zhang-xiàngpiānr 照一張像片兒 take a picture. zhào-zhèiduo-huār 照這朵花兒 take a picture of this flower. zhào-àikèsī-guāng 照愛克斯光 have an X-ray taken.

(CV) (1) according to. zhào-dào-li-shuō 照道理説 talk about it according to logic. zhào-wo-kàn 照我看 according to the way I look at it. Jiù-zhào-zhe-nǐde-yìsi-zuò-ba. 就照着你的意思作吧. Let's do it according to your ideas. (2) aiming at. Tā-zhào-zhe-nèige-lǎohǔ fàngle-yiqiāng. 他照着那個老虎放了一鎗. He fired a shot at that tiger after aiming at it.

ZHÀO₅ 罩 (TV) cover something with something in the form of an inverted bowl. Ná-zhàor-bǎ-cài-zhàoshang. 拿罩兒把菜罩上. Put a cover on the food.

ZHÁOBU₅ 找補 (TV) (1) add something to reach a certain amount. Yàoshi-bu-gòu, zai-zháobu-yidianr. 要是不够, 再找補一點兒. If it is not enough, add a little more. (2) touch up. Nǐ-yóude-nèige-zhuōzi děi-zài-zháobu-

zhaobu. 你油的那個桌子得再找補找補. The table which you painted needs to be touched up.

ZHÀOCHÁNG₃ 照常 (IV) go on as usual. Xuéxiàode-shì yíqiè-zhàocháng. 學校的事一切照常. Everything in the school is going on as usual. (AD) as usual. Wǒmen-zhào-cháng-shàng-kè. 我們照常上課. We go to classes as usual. or Classes are going on as usual.

ZHÀODAI₃ 招待 (TV) (1) enter-tain, be hospitable to. Tā-xǐ-huan-zhāodai-kèren. 他喜歡招待客人. He likes to entertain guests. Wǒmen-zěnma-zhāodai-ta-ne? 我們怎麼招待他呢? How are we going to entertain him? (2) take care of someone. Méi-rén-guòlai-zhāodai-wo. 没人過來招待我. Nobody came over to take care of me. (N) (1) usher. nǔ-zhāodài 女招待 waitress. (2) service, hospitality.

ZHÀOGU₂ 照顧 (TV) (1) take care of, look after something or someone. Jiālide-shìqing shéi-zhàogu? 家裏的事情誰照顧? Who takes care of the things in the home? (2) patronize a store. Qǐng-nín-duō-zhàogu. 請您多照顧. Please come in (and pa-tronize) more often. (cf: ZHÀO-LIAO 照料, ZHÀOYING 照

Z

應).

ZHÀOGUĂN₅ 照 管 (TV) look after, take care of <u>something</u> or someone

ZHĀOHU₄ 招 呼 (TV) (1) take care of <u>someone</u>. Tā-tài-lăo-le. Děi-yǒu-ren-zhāohu. 他太老了, 得有人招呼. He is too old. There must be someone to take care of him. (2) make some gesture <u>or</u> say <u>something</u> to show recognition <u>or</u> give a greeting. Tā-kànjian-wo-le, kě-shi-méi-zhāohu. 他看見我了, 可是没招呼. He saw me but didn't say hello. (3) send a message, inform. Wǒ-men-zǒu-de-shíhou, nǐ-zhāohu-ta-yixia. 我們走的時候, 你招呼他一下. When we are going to leave, you let him know.

(N) message. dǎ-zhāohu 打招呼 send a message <u>or</u> send a greeting.

ZHÁO-HUǑ₂ 着 火 (VO) catch on fire. Nèige-pùzi zháo-huǒ-le. 那個舖子着火了. That store caught on fire.

ZHÁO-JÍ₁ 着 急 (VO) (1) be excited and upset. (2) be worried, concerned. Nǐ-zhāo-shénma-jí? 你着甚麼急? What are you worrying about? <u>or</u> Why are you so excited?

(SV) (1) be excited and upset. Tā-tīngshuō-nǐ-bìngle hěn-zhāojí. 他聽説你病了很着急. He has learned that you are sick, he is very much

upset. (2) worried, anxious. Děng-liăngtian bu-yàojǐn, bié-zhāo-jí. 等兩天不要緊, 别着急. It doesn't matter if it takes a couple of days, don't be anxious.

ZHĀOJIA₅ 招 架 (TV) fend off. Wǒ-zhāojia-buzhù. 我招架不住. I cannot fend it off.

ZHÀO-JÌNGZI₂ 照 鏡 子 (VO) look at <u>oneself</u> in a mirror.

SHÀOJIÙ₃ 照 舊 (IV) (1) do <u>something</u> as before, follow old methods. A: Zěnma-bàn? B: Zhàojiù-ba. A: 怎麼辦? B: 照舊吧. A: How shall we do it? B: Let's do it the old way. (2) remain as before. Nèr-de-qíngxing hái-zhàojiù. 那兒的情形還照舊. The situation there is still the same. (AD) as before, as usual. Tā-zhàojiù-zuò-tade-shì. 他照舊作他的事. He does his work as usual.

ZHĀOKĀI₅ 召 開 (TV) call a meeting. zhāokāi-huìyì 召開會議 call a meeting.

ZHÀO-LÌ₄ 照 例 (VO) according to precedent. Zhào-lì bu-xíng-ma? 照例不行嗎? Do it the traditional way. Won't it do?

(AD) according to tradition. Wǒ-zhào-lì-bu-gěi-xiăofèi. 我照例不給小費. It's my custom not to give tips.

ZHÀO-LIÁNG₁ 着 涼 (VO) catch cold. Wǒ-zhāole-yidianr-liáng. 我着了一點兒涼.

Z

I caught slight cold. (cf: SHĀNG-FĒNG 傷風).

ZHÀOLIAO₃ 照料 (TV) take care of things. Jiālide-shì méi-ren-zhàoliao. 家裏的事沒人照料. Nobody is taking care of the things in the home. Shì-tài-duō, zhàoliao-buguolái. 事太多,照料不過來. There are too many things, I cannot get around to taking care of all of them. (cf: XHÀOGU 照顧, ZHÀOYING 照應).

ZHÁOLO₄ 着落 (N) whereabouts. Diūle-de-dōngxi hái-méi-you-zháolo. 丟了的東西還沒有着落. There's no trace of the things which were lost.

ZHĀOMÙ₅ 招募 (TV) recruit soldiers.

ZHĀOPAI₃ 招牌 (N) (1) sign of a shop indicating its type of business. (2) trade-mark. (cf: HUĀNGZI 幌子).

ZHÀOPIÀN₄ 照片 (N) photograph. (M: zhāng 張). (cf: XIÀNGPIĀNR 像片兒).

ZHĀOQÌ₅ 朝氣 (N) (lit. morning air) youthful vigor.

ZHÁO-QIÁN₂ 找錢 (VO) give back change (after receiving a large bill or coin). Wǒ-gěi-ta wǔkuai-qián, tā-zháo-gei-wo-yí-kuài. 我給他五塊錢,他找給我一塊. I gave him a five dollar bill and he gave me back one dollar change.

ZHĀOR₃ 招兒 (N) clever method or way, plan, idea. Tāde-zhāor hěn-duō. 他的招兒很多. He has a lot of ways. Méi-zhāor-le. 沒招兒了. No more ideas. Wǒ-děi-xiǎng-yíge-zhāor zhuàn-dianr-qián. 我得想一個招兒賺點兒錢. I must think up a way to make some money.

(M) (1) move, stroke, trick. Tā-huì-zènma-yizhāor. 他會這麼一招兒. He knows a trick like this. (2) step, move (of chess, checkers or certain board games). Zhèi-zhāor-qí-hěn-lìhai. 這招兒棋很利害. This move is terrific.

ZHÀOR₅ 罩兒 (N) cover (in the shape of an inverted bowl). dēng-zhàor 燈罩兒 lamp shade.

ZHĀOREN₅ 招認 (TV) confess to a legal authority.

ZHÁO-SHǑU₄ 着手 see ZHUÓ-SHǑU 着手.

ZHÀO-XIANG₁ 照像 (VO) (1) take a photograph. Tā-xiǎng-yào-gěi-wǒ zhào-xiàng. 他想要給我照像. He wants to take a photograph of me. (2) have a photograph taken. Wǒ-děi-zhào-yizhang-xiàng. 我得照一張像. I must take a photograph. or I must have my photograph taken. (cf: PĀI-ZHÀO 拍照).

ZHÀOXIÀNGJĪ₂ 照相機 (N)

camera. (M: jià 架).

ZHĂOXUN₅ 找尋 (TV) Peip.
pick on someone, give someone
a hard time. Nĭ-bié-zhăoxun-wo.
你别找尋我. Don't
pick on me.

ZHĂOYĂN₄ 招眼 (SV) (lit. attract the eye) conspicuous. Nèi-
jian-yīshang-tài-zhăoyăn. 那
件衣裳太招眼. That
garment is too conspicuous.

ZHÀO-YÀNGR₃ 照樣兒 (VO)
do something according to an
existing or old model. Búyong-
găi-le, hái-zhào-yuánláide-nèi-
ge-yàngr. 不用改了,還
照原來的那個樣
兒. Don't change it, we will
do it according to the original
way.
(AD) according to the model.
Wŏmen-kéyi-zhàoyàngr-zuò-yi-
ge. 我們可以照樣兒
作一個. We can make one
like it.

ZHÀOYING₃ 照應 (TV) take
care of or watch after something
or someone. Shìqing-tai-duō
wŏ-zhàoying-bu-guòlái. 事情
太多我照應不過
來. There's too much to do, I
can't get to it. Qĭng-nin-zhào-
ying-zhaoying-wŏde-háizi. 請
您照應照應我的
孩子. Please watch after my
child. (cf: ZHÀOGU 照顧,
ZHÀOLIAO 照料).

ZHĀR₄ 渣兒 (N) small pieces,
crumbs. diào-zhār掉渣兒drop
crumbs.

ZHĀSHI₄ 札實 (SV) solid (of
the abstract). Tāde-xuéwen-
hen-zhāshi. 他的學問
很札實. He is solid in
his knowledge.

ZHÀYÀO₃ 炸藥 (N) gunpowder.

ZHÁZHENG₅ 札掙 (IV) force
oneself to do something. Tā-
zházhengzhe-qĭlai-le. 他札
掙着起來了. He
forced himself to get up.

ZHE₁ 着 (P) (1) added to a TV
or IV, indicates that the action
or condition is going on or con-
tinuing. Nĭ-jìzhe. 你記着.
You remember. Nín-qĭng-zuò,
wŏ-yuànyi-zhànzhe. 您請坐,
我願意站着. Please
sit down, I would like to remain
standing. Zhuōzishang-fàngzhe-
hăoxiē-dōngxi. 桌子上放
着好些東西. There
are a lot of things lying on the
table. (2) added to a TV or IV,
forms adverbial or coverbial
expressions. Zhèijian-yīshang
wŏ-chuānzhe zhèng-héshì. 這
件衣裳我穿着正
合適. These clothes fit me
perfectly. Tā-názhe-shū shuì-
jiào. 他拿着書睡覺.
He went to sleep holding a book.
(3) added to a TV or IV which is
then repeated, forms adverbial
expressions. This indicates
that while one action is going on
some kind of change is expected.
Wŏde-qìchē zŏuzhe-zŏuzhe bu-
zŏu-le. 我的汽車走
着走着不走了. My

Z

car ran and ran when finally it stopped. Nèiliǎngge-háizi wánr-zhe-wánrzhe dáqilai-le. 那兩個孩子玩兒着玩兒着打起來了. Those two children were playing along when finally they started fighting. Xié wǒ-chuānzhe-chuānzhe chuānpò-le. 鞋我穿着穿着穿破了. I wore and wore my shoes when finally they wore out.

ZHĒ₃ 遮 (TV) (1) block out, screen off. Yúncai-zhēshang-tàiyang-le. 雲彩遮上太陽了. The clouds blocked out the sun. (2) cover up. Tā-yòng-biéde-huà gěi-zhēguoqu-le. 他用別的話給遮過去了. He used some other words to cover it up.

ZHĒ₄ 折 (TV) (1) turn upside down or over. zhē-gēntou 折跟頭 turn a somersault. (2) dump, pour or spill something by turn-ing the container upside down. Tā-méi-xiǎoxin bǎ-yiwǎn-cài, dōu-zhēzai-zhuōzi-shang-le. 他沒小心把一碗菜都折在桌子上了. He wasn't careful. He dumped a plate of food on the table. (3) go or come back. Tā-méi-zǒu-dào jiu-zhēhuilai-le. 他沒走到就折回來了. Be-fore he got there, he came back.

ZHĒ₄ 螫 (TV) sting. Mìfēngr-zhē-rén. 蜜蜂兒螫人. Bees sting people.

ZHĒ₂ 折 (TV) (1) fold; bend. Bǎ-

zhǐ-zhéshang. 把紙折上. Fold up the paper. (2) pay in collateral. zhé-zhàng 折賬 repay in collateral. Wǒde-qì-chē cái-néng-zhé-yìbǎikài-qián. 我的汽車才能折一百塊錢. My car can be worth only a hundred dollars in collateral.

ZHÉ₃ 折 (M) discount. dǎ-bāzhé 打八折 twenty per cent off (eighty per cent needs to be paid). (cf:DǍ...ZHÉ 打...折).

ZHÈ₁ 這 (SP) or ZHÈI 這 this, these. zhè-sānge 這三個 these three.

(N) or ZHÈI 這 used before a verb, this (referring to persons, things, events, etc.). Zhè-shi-shénma? 這是甚麼? What is this? Zhè-shi-zěnma-huì-shì? 這是怎麼回事? What is this all about? Nín-zhè-shi-gàn-shénma? 您這是幹甚麼? What are you doing this for?

(AD) (1) in this case, then, if so. Zhè-zěnma-bàn? 這怎麼辦? In this case, what can be done? Zhè-jiu-duì-le. 這就對了. In this case, it is right. Wǒ-zhè-cai-míngbai. 我這才明白. or Zhè-wǒ-cai-míngbai. 這我才明白. Then I under-stand. (2) used before a SV or a verb, how (exclamatory). Tā-shuō-de zhè-hǎotīng-a! 他說得這好聽啊! How nice it sounded when he talked

about it! Tā-zhè-chī-a! 他這
吃啊 ! How he ate! (cf: NÀ
那 , ZHÈI 這).

ZHĒGAI₅ 遮蓋 (TV) cover up.
(See: ZHĒ 遮).

ZHÈI₁ 這 or ZHÈ 這 (SP) this,
these. zhèi(yi)ge 這 (一) 個
this one. zhèi-sānge 這 三 個
these three.

(N) used before a verb, this ,
these. Zhèi-shi-'shéi-shuō-de?
這 是 誰 説 的 ? Who
said this?

ZHÈIGE₁ 這 個 used repeatedly
for hesitation, ah... Tā-jiào-
zhèige-zhèige...wǒ-xiǎng-bu-
qilái-le. 他 叫 這 個 這
個...我 想 不 起 來 了.
His name is ah... I cannot remember. (see: ZHÈI 這).

ZHÈIHUIR₃ 這 會 兒 (TW)
this moment right now.

ZHÈIYANGR₁ 這 樣 兒 (IV) do
something this way. Bié-zhèi-
yangr. 別 這 樣 兒 . Don't
do it this way.

(AD) in this way, in this manner.
Zhèiyangr-shuō, bu-hǎo. 這 樣
兒 説, 不 好 . It is not
good to say it this way. (See:
ZHÈI 這, YÀNGR 樣 兒).

ZHÈIJIĀNG₂ 浙 江 (PW)Chekiang
province.

ZHÈIJIU₁ 這 就 (AD) immediately.
Wǒ-zhèjiu-lái. 我 這 就 來 .
I'll come immediately.

ZHÉKOU₃ 折 扣 (N) discount.
(See: DĂ-ZHÉKOU 打 折 扣).

ZHELI₂ 這 裏 (PW) here. (syn.
zhèr 這 兒). Tāmen-dou-zài-

zhèli. 他 們 都 在 這 裏 .
They are all here.

ZHÉMO₄ 折 磨 (TV) lit. or fig.
torture. shòu-zhémo 受 折
磨 undergo torture. Bié-zhèn-
ma-zhémo-wo. 別 這 麼 折
磨 我 . Don't torture me like
this.

ZHĒN₃ 針 (N) (1) needle, pin.
(M: gēn 根). (2) injection,
shot. Nǐ-géi-wo-dǎ-shénma-zhēn?
你 給 我 打 甚 麼 針 ?
What kind of an injection will
you give me?

(M) (1) injection, shot. dǎ-yi-
zhēn 打 一 針 get or give
a shot. (2) stitch. féng-liang-
zhēn 縫 兩 針 sew a couple
of stitches.

ZHĒN₁ 真 (SV) (1) real, genuine,
true. (opp. jiǎ 假). zhēn-pízi
真 皮 子 real leather. Wǒ-
shuōde-dou-shi-zhēnde. 我 説
的 都 是 真 的 . Every-
thing I said is true. (2) clear.
Shū-shang-de-zì bu-zhēn. 書
上 的 字 不 真 . The
characters in the book are not
clear.

(AD) really. Zhēn-hǎo. 真 好
Really good.

(RE) in potential RV only,
clearly. tīngbuzhēn 聽 不 真
cannot hear clearly.

ZHÈN₄ 鎮 (N) rural market town.

ZHÈN₅ 陣 (N) disposition of
troops. shàng-zhèn 上 陣 go
to the battlefield.

ZHÈN(ZI)₄ 陣 (子) or ZHENR
陣 兒 (M) short period, spell.

Z

Xiàle-yizhèn-yǔ. 下了一陣雨 . There was a spell of rain.

ZHÈNDÌ₅ 陣地 (N) position in a battle area, battle formation.

ZHÈNDING₃ 鎮定 (TV) calm down. Bié-huāng, xiān zhènding-yixia. 別慌、先鎮定一下 . Don't be nervous, calm down first.

(SV) calm. Tā-tīngshuō-nèige-xiāoxi, háishi-hen-zhènding. 他聽說那個消息,還是很鎮定 . When he heard that news, he was still very calm.

ZHÈNDUÌ₄ 針對 (TV) pin-point. Wǒ-shi-zhènduì-tade-wènti huí-da-de. 我是針對他的問題回答的 . In answering him, I was pin-pointing his question.

ZHE(...)NE₁ 着 (...) 呢 (S) indicates in the midst of some action or state. Tā-zai-wàitou-zhànzhe-ne. 他在外頭站着呢 . He is standing outside. Mén-guānzhe-ne. 門關着呢. The door is closed. Nèige-shíhou fēijī-hái-fēizhe-ne. 那個時候飛機還飛着呢. At that time the airplane was still flying. Qiáng-shang-guàzhe-huàr-ne. 牆上掛着畫兒呢. The painting is hanging on the wall. Tā-kànzhe-bào-ne. 他看着報呢. He is reading the newspaper.

ZHE(DE)NE₄ 着 (的) 呢 (P)

used at end of a sentence after a SV or after a phrase with an AV, very, quite. kuài-zhe(de)ne 快着的呢 very fast. hǎokàn-zhe(de)ne 好看着(的)呢 very pretty.

ZHĒNG₃ 睜 (TV) open the eyes. Nǐ-zhēngkai-yǎn-kànkan. 你睜開眼看看 . Open your eyes and take a look.

ZHĒNG₄ 蒸 (TV) steam something in cooking. zhēng-fàn 蒸飯 steam rice or steamed rice. Fàn-shi-zhēngde-shi-zhǔde? 飯是蒸的是煮的? Is the rice steamed or boiled?

ZHĒNG₄ 爭 (TV) argue about, fight over. Wǒ-bu-gēn-tamen-zhēng. 我不跟他們爭 . I won't argue about it with them.

ZHĚNG₂ 整 (B-) whole, unbroken. Wǒde-wǎn bú-shi-pòde, shi-zhěngde. 我的碗不是破的是整的. My bowl is not the broken one, it is the unbroken one.

used before a M or between a NU-M, whole. Yǒu-méi-you-'zhěng-zhāng-de-zhǐ? 有沒有整張的紙? Are there any whole pieces of paper? Tā-gěile-wo-yì-'zhěng-kuài-dàngāo. 他給了我一整塊蛋糕 . He gave me a whole piece of cake.

used before or after a NU-M (N), exactly (so much or many). zhěng-sānnián 整三年 or sānnián-zhěng 三年整

exactly three years.

(AD) exactly. Tā-zhěng-qiàn-wo
yibǎikuai-qián. 他 整 欠 我
一 百 塊 錢 . He owes me
exactly one hundred dollars.

ZHĚNG₄ 整 (TV) (1) fix, repair.
Tā-bǎ-wǒde-biǎo zhěnghǎo-le.
他 把 我 的 表 整 好
了 . He repaired my watch. (2)
give someone a hard time. Tā-
men-bǎ-wǒ-zhěngde hěn-cǎn. 他
們 把 我 整 的 很 慘.
They gave me a very hard time.

ZHÈNG₂ 正 (opp. xié 斜 , wāi 歪,
piān 偏) (SV) (1) straight, level, upright. Zhèitiao-xiàn huà-
de bu-zhèng. 這 條 線 畫
得 不 正 . This line is not
drawn straight. Wǒmen-dei-zǒu-
zhèng-lù. 我 們 得 走 正
路 . We have to go by the main
road. or We have to go straight.
Zhèige-ren hěn-zhèng. 這 個
人 很 正. He is a very
proper man. Zhèige-yánse-bu-
zhèng. 這 個 顏 色 不 正 .
This color is off. (2) be centered.
(opp. wāi 歪). Zhèige-zhuōzi
bǎide-bu-zhèng. 這 個 桌 子
擺 得 不 正 . This table
is placed off center.

(TV) put something straight or
in the center. Nèige-zhōng guà-
wāi-le. Nǐ-bǎ-ta-zhèngguolai.
那 個 鐘 掛 歪 了, 你
把 他 正 過 來. This
clock is hung at an angle. Put
it straight.

(RE) straight, be centered. Nǐ-
zuòzhèng-le. 你 坐 正 了

Sit straight. Bǎ-nèizhang-
huàr guàzhèng-le. 把 那 張
畫 兒 掛 正 了 . Hang
that picture straight. or Hang
that picture in the center.

used before expressions which
indicate direction. zhèng-dōng
正 東 due east. zhèng-qián-
fāng 正 前 方 straight on.

ZHÈNG₃ 正 (B-) chief, main,
principal (in contrast to secondary). (opp. fù 副). Tā-shì-
zhèngxiàozhǎng, wǒ-shì-fùde.
他 是 正 校 長, 我 是 副
的 . He is the principal and
I am the vice principal.

ZHÈNG₁ 正 (AD) (1) (con. zhèngzai 正 在). in the midst of.
Tāmen-zhèng-chūlai. 他 們
正 出 來 . They are just
coming out. (2) exactly, just.
zhèng-héshì 正 合 適 Just
right. Tā-shuō-de zhèng-duì.
他 說 的 正 對 . He
said it just right.

ZHÈNGCE₂ 政 策 (N) policy
(political, economic, social,
etc.). Zhèngce hái-mei-dìng-
ne. 政 策 還 沒 定 呢
The policy has not yet been
decided.

ZHÈNGCHÁNG₃ 正 常 (SV)
normal. Zhè-shi-zhèngchángde-
bànfa. 這 是 正 常 的 辦
法 . This is the normal way
of doing it. Tā-yǒu-yidianr-bu-
zhèngcháng. 他 有 一 點
兒 不 正 常 . He is a
little abnormal.

ZHÈNGCHǍO₅ 爭 吵 (TV)

Z

quarrel.

ZHÈNGDANG₂ 正當 (SV) up-
right, proper (referring to behavior or a situation). Bú-
zhèngdangde-shìqing, bù-yīng-
dāng-zuò. 不正當的事
情, 不應當作. One
should not do anything which is
not proper. (cf: ZHÈNGJING 正
經, ZHÈNGPAI 正派).

ZHÈNGDǍNG₃ 政黨 (N) politi-
cal party.

ZHĚNGDUN₃ 整頓 (TV) rear-
range, reorganize (of an organization). Zhěnggèrde-xuéxiào
tài-luàn, děi-zhěngdun-yixia. 整
個兒的學校太亂,
得整頓一下. The
whole school is a mess, it needs
to be reorganized.

ZHĚNGFĒNG₅ 整風 (IV) rectify.
zhěngfēng-yùndòng 整風運
動 rectification movement.

ZHĒNGFÚ₄ 征服 (RV) compel
submission by force.

ZHÈNGFǓ₁ 政府 (N) govern-
ment.

ZHĚNGGÈR₁ 整個兒 (B) com-
plete, whole. Zhěnggèrde-shì-
jiè-dōu-luàn-le. 整個兒的
世界都亂了. The
whole world has become a mess.
Géi-wo-yíge-zhěnggèrde-júzi.
給我一個整個兒
的橘子. Give me a whole
orange.
(AD) completely. Tā-zhěnggèrde-
bùdǒng. 他整個兒的
不懂. He doesn't understand
at all.

ZHÈNGHǍO₃ 正好 (SV) just
right. Bù-duō bù-shǎo, zhènghǎo. 不多不少, 正好.
Not too much, not too little,
just right.
(MA) by a happy coincidence.
Zhènghǎo nèitian-wǒ-méi-shì.
正好, 那天我沒事.
By a happy coincidence I was
free that day.

ZHÈNGJING₂ 正經 (SV) (1)
proper, upright (referring to
behavior or a situation). Tāde-xíngwei bu-zhèngjing. 他
的行為不正經. His
behavior is not proper. (2) serious. Tā-bu-zuò-zhèngjing-
shì. 他不作正經事.
He doesn't do anything serious.
Nǐ-shuō-dianr-zhèngjingde. 你
說點兒正經的. Say
something serious.
(AD) seriously. Tā-bu-zhèng-
jing-zuò-shi. 他不正經
作事. He doesn't do any-
thing seriously. (cf: ZHÈNG-
DANG 正當, ZHÈNGPAI 正
派).

ZHÈNGJU₂ 證據 (N) proof
evidence. Ná-zhèngju-lai. 拿
證據來. Bring the evi-
dence.

ZHÈNGKE₄ 政客 (N) politician.

ZHĚNGLI₂ 整理 (TV) straighten
out, put in order. Wǒ-děi-zhéng-
li-zhengli-wūzi. 我得整
理整理屋子. I have
to straighten out my room. Shì-
qing-tai-luàn, méi-fázi-zhéngli-
le. 事情太亂沒法

Z

子整理了 . This matter
is too confused. There is no way
of straightening it out.

ZHĒNGLÓNG₅ 蒸籠 (N) steamer
(for cooking).

ZHĒNGLUN₄ 爭論 (TV) argue,
dispute. Nǐ-búbì-gen-ta-zhēng-
lun-nèixie-bu-yàojǐnde-shìqing.
你不必跟他爭論
那些不要緊的事
情 . Don't argue with him
about those trifling matters.

ZHÈNGMIAN₄ 正面 (AD) face-
to-face, head on. Wǒ-gēn-ta-
zhèngmian-chōngtuqilai-le. 我
跟他正面衝突起
來了 . I crashed with him
head on.

ZHÈNGMIÀNR₃ 正面兒 (PW)
correct side, right side. Zhèi-
bianr-shi-zhèngmiànr. 這邊
兒是正面兒 . This
side is the correct side.

ZHÈNGMÍNG₂ 證明 (TV) prove.
Wǒ-néng-zhèngming tā-bu-duì.
我能證明他不對 .
I can prove that he is wrong.
(N) proof, evidence. Wǒ-méi-
you-zhèngmíng. 我沒有證
明 . I don't have any proof.

ZHÈNG-MÌNG₅ 掙命 (VO)
struggle for existence.

ZHÈNG(ZAI)...NE₁ 正（在）...
呢 (S) in the midst of. Tāmen-
zhèng(zai)-chī-fàn-ne. 他們
正在吃飯呢 . They are
in the midst of eating.

ZHÈNGPAI₄ 正派 (SV) proper,
upright (of a person). Tā-hěn-
zhèngpai. 他很正派 . He

is very proper
(N) orthodox. Tāmen-dōu-shì-
zhèngpai, nèixie-shì-fǎnpài.
他們都是正派,那
些是反派 . They are all
orthodox, the others are un-
orthodox. (cf: ZHÈNGDANG 正
當, ZHÈNGJING 正經).

ZHĒNGQÌ₄ 蒸汽 (N) steam.

ZHĚNGQÍ₃ 整齊 (SV) neat,
orderly. Tāmen-dōu-chuānde-
hěn-zhěngqi. 他們都穿
得很整齊 . They are all
dressed very neatly.

ZHÈNG-QIÁN₃ 掙錢 (VO) earn
money (by working). zhèng-qián-
yǎng-jiā 掙錢養家 earn
money to support a family.(cf:
ZHUÀN 賺).

ZHĒNGQIU₅ 徵求 (TV) seek
out, in quest of. Wǒmen-děi-
zhēngqiu-tade-yìjian. 我們
得徵求他的意見 .
We must seek out his opinion.
Wǒ-yào-dēng-bào-zhēngqiu-yí-
ge-shūji. 我要登報徵
求一個書記 . I wish
to place an advertisement in the
paper for a secretary.

'ZHĒNGQŬ₃ 爭取 (TV) (1)
strive for. zhēngqǔ-shènglì 爭
取勝利 strive for victory.
zhēngqǔ-shíjiān 爭取時
間 try to gain time. (2) win
someone to one's own side. Wǒ-
men-děi-bǎ-nèijige-ren 'zhēng-
qǔguolai. 我們得把那
幾個人爭取過來 .
We must try to win those people
to our side.

Z

ZHÈNGQUÁN₃ 政權 (N) political power. duóqǔ-zhèngquán 奪取政權 usurp political power. Zhèngquán bu-zai-tade-shóuli. 政權不在他的手裏. The political power is not in his hands.

ZHÈNGQUE₂ 正確 (SV) accurate. Tāde-xiāoxi bu-zhèngque. 他的消息不正確. His information is not accurate.

ZHÈNGREN₃ 證人 (N) witness. zuò-zhèngren 作證人 be a witness.

ZHÈNGSHÍ₄ 證實 (TV) has been proved.

ZHÈNGSHÌ₂ 正式 (SV) formal. Zhè-shì-zhèngshide-shǒuxu. 這是正式的手續. This is the formal procedure.

(AD) formally. Tāmen-zhèngshì-tōngzhi-ni-le. 他們正式通知你了. They have informed you formally.

ZHĒNGTIĀN₂ 整天 (M) whole day. Wǒ-zuòle-yizhěngtiān-de-shì. 我作了一整天的事. I worked for a whole day.

(AD) (1) all day. Tā-zhēngtiān-bu-chūqu. 他整天不出去. He stays in all day long.

(2) always, all the time. Tā-zhēngtiān-bàoyuan. 他整天抱怨. She complains all the time.

ZHÈNGUI₄ 珍貴 (SV) precious, valuable.

ZHĒNGWǓ₁ 正午 (TW) noon.

ZHÈNGYAO₃ 正要 (AV) just about to do something. Wǒ-zhèngyao-chūqu. 我正要出去. I'm just about to go out.

ZHĚNGYÈ₂ 整夜 (M) all night. Háizi-kūle-yizhěngyè. 孩子哭了一整夜. The baby cried all night long.

(AD) all night long. Tā-zhěng-yède-kàn-shū. 他整夜的看書. He reads all night long. Wǒ-zhěngyè-méi-hé-yǎn. 我整夜沒合眼. I didn't close my eyes all night long.

ZHÈNGYÌ₄ 正義 (N) justice. Tāmen-dou-bu-jiǎng-zhèngyì. 他們都不講正義. None of them pays attention to justice.

ZHĒNGYUE₃ 正月 (TW) first month of the year of the lunar calandar.

ZHÈNGZAI₁ 正在 (AD) in the midst of. (See: ZHÈNG 正, ZHÈNG(ZAI)...NE 正(在)...呢).

ZHĒNGZHA₃ 掙扎 (IV) struggle. Kǔnshangde-láohu hái-zài-nèr-zhēngzha-ne. 捆上的老虎還在那兒掙扎呢. The bound tiger is still struggling to free himself. Yào-shi-búshi-wèile-shēnghuo, wèi-shénma-zài-shìjie-shang-zhēng-zha-ne? 要是不是為了生活，為甚麼在世界上掙扎呢. Why struggle in this would if not for a living.

Z

ZHÈNGZHI₁ 政治 (N) politics.

ZHÈNGZHIJIĀ₄ 政治家 (N) statesman.

ZHÈNGZHONG₃ 鄭重 (SV) serious, intent. Tāde-tàidu-hěn-zhèngzhong. 他的態度很鄭重. His attitude is very serious.
(AD) seriously, intently. Tā-hěn-zhèngzhongde gen-women-shuō. 他很鄭重的跟我們説. He spoke very seriously to us.

ZHĒNLĬ₂ 真理 (N) truths, principles. Tā-zài-jiàotáng-jiǎng-zhēnlǐ. 他在教堂講真理. He explains the truths in the church.

ZHĒNLIÁOSUŎ₄ 診療所 (N) clinic, small hospital.

ZHÈNMA₂ 這麼 see ZÈNMA 這麼.

'ZHÈNMAYÀNGR₁ 這麼樣兒 see 'ZÈNMAYÀNGR 這麼樣兒.

ZHÈNR₄ 陣兒 see ZHÈN(ZI) 陣 (子).

ZHĒNSHIDE₃ 真是的 used independently to show sympathy, that's really too bad.

ZHĒNTÀN₃ 偵探 (N) (1) private investigator. (2) spy.

ZHĚNTOU₄ 枕頭 (N) pillow.

'ZHĒNXIÀN₁ 針線 (N) (1) needle and thread. zhēnxian-hézi 針線盒子 sewing box. (2) needle work. zuò-zhēnxian 作針線 do needle work.

ZHÈNYĀ₅ 鎮壓 (TV) repress, put down an uprising. Zhèngfǔ-pài-bīng-lai-zhènyā-tamen. 政府派兵來鎮壓他們. The government sent troops to repress them.

ZHĒNZHENG₃ 真正 (B) real, genuine. Zhè-cai-shi-zhēnzhèngde hǎo-péngyou. 這才是真正的好朋友. This is a real good friend.
(AD) truly, really. Wǒ-zhēnzhèngde-míngbai-le. 我真正的明白了. I really understood it.

ZHĒNZHŪ₄ 珍珠 (N) pearl. (M: kē 顆).

ZHĒNZHUO₃ 斟酌 (TV) consider, weigh. Wǒmen-zhēnzhuo-zhenzhuo. 我們斟酌斟酌. Let's consider it. Qǐng-nín-zhēnzhuozhe-bàn-ba. 請您斟酌着辦吧. Please use your own judgment in doing it.

ZHĚNZI₄ 疹子 (N) measles. chū-zhěnzi 出疹子 have measles.

ZHĚR₃ 摺兒 see ZHĚZI 摺兒.

ZHÈR₁ 這兒 (PW)(1) here. (syn. zhèli 這裏 , zhèige-dìfang 這個地方). Tā-zài-zhèr. 他在這兒. He is here. Wǒ-zher-méi-zhǐ-le. 我這兒沒紙了. I have no paper here. Qǐng-nǐ-dào-wǒ-zher-lái-yixia. 請你到我這兒來一下. Please come here (to me) once. Xiǎng-dao-zher, jiu-juéde-shénma-dōu-míngbai-le. 想到這

Z

兒, 就覺得甚麼都明白了. In thinking up to this point, I felt I understood everything. (2) point of time, now. Nǐ-cóng-zhèr-béng-lí-wo. 你從這兒甭理我. Don't talk to me from now on.

ZHÉXUE₃ 哲學 (N) (1) philosophy (as a branch of learning). (2) philosophy.

ZHÉZHŌNG₃ 折衷 (IV) compromise. Wǒmen-zhézhōng-yi-xiazi. 我們折衷一下子. Let's compromise. Xiǎng-ge-zhézhong-bànfa. 想個折衷辦法. Let's think up a compromise.

ZHÉZI₄ 摺子 (N) (1) book or paper in accordion form. (2) bank book.

ZHÉZI₃ 摺子 or ZHER 摺兒 (N) wrinkle, crease, pleat. Yī-shangshang yǒu-hěn-duō-zhězi 衣裳上有很多摺子. The clothes are full of wrinkles. Tā-liǎnshang méi-you-zhězi. 他臉上沒摺子. She doesn't have any wrinkles on her face.

ZHĪ₃ 織 (TV) (1) weave. zhī-bù 織布 weave cloth. (2) knit. zhī-máoyī 織毛衣 knit a sweater. zhī-máoxiàn 織毛線 knit with yarn.

ZHĪ₁ 隻 (M) for birds, some animals, boats, one of certain paired things. yìzhī-niǎor 隻鳥兒 a bird. yìzhī-māo 一隻貓 a cat. yìzhī-chuán 一隻船 a boat. liǎng-zhī-

shǒu 兩隻手 two hands. yìzhī-xié 一隻鞋 one shoe.

ZHĪ₁ 枝 (M) (1) for long, thin, and inflexible objects. yìzhī-bǐ 一枝筆 one pen. yìzhī-yān 一枝烟 one cigarette. (2) for flowers with stems intact. yìzhī-méiguihuār 一枝玫瑰花兒 a (stem of) rose. (3) detachment of soldiers. yìzhī-bīng 一枝兵 a detachment of soldiers. (4) branch of a family. Tāmen-jiā yǒu-sānzhī. 他們家有三枝. There are three branches in their family. (5) watt. (syn. zhú燭). duōshao-zhī-guāng 多少枝光 how many watts?

ZHĪ₂ 直 (SV) (1) straight. Zhèi-tiao-lù hěn-zhí. 這條路很直. This road is very straight. (2) honest, straightforward (of a person). Zhèige-rén hěn-zhí. 這個人很真. This person is straightforward.

(TV) straighten. Zhèige-gùnzi wānle, zhíbuguòlái-le. 這個棍子彎了直不過來了. This stick is curved and cannot be straightened out.

(AD) (1) directly, straight. Wǒ-gēn-ni-zhí-shuō-ba. 我跟你直說吧. Let me tell you directly. Zhí-zǒu, bié-guǎ-wānr. 直走, 別拐彎兒. Go straight, don't make turns. (2) continuously, keep doing sometime. Tā-zhi-shuō tā-lái. 他直說他來. He kept saying that he would come.

ZHÍ₂ 值 (TV) worth <u>a certain</u> <u>amount of money.</u> Zhí-duōshao-qián? 值 多 少 錢 ? How much is it worth? (SV) worthwhile. Fèi-nènma-dà-de-shì, bù-zhí. 費 那 麼 大 的 事 不 值 . It isn't worthwhile to go through that much trouble.(cf: ZHÍDE 值 得).

ZHÍ₁ 紙 (N) paper. (M: zhāng 張).

ZHĬ₂ 指 (TV) (1) <u>lit or fig.</u> point at (<u>with the finger or a long and</u> <u>pointed object</u>). Tā-yòng-shǒu-zhǐzhe-nèige-zì. 他 用 手 指 着 那 個 字 . He pointed to the character with his finger. Bǎ-wǒde-cuòr gei-zhǐchulai-le. 把 我 的 錯 兒 給 指 出 來 了 . My mistakes are pointed out. (2) depend on. Wǒ-jiu-zhǐzhe-nǐ-le. 我 就 指 着 你 了 . I'll just depend on you. Tā-zhǐzhe-huà-huàr shēnghuo. 他 指 着 畫 畫 兒 生 活 . He depends on painting to make a living. (3) refer to. Tā-shì-zhǐ-zhe-nèijian-shì shuō-de. 他 是 指 着 那 件 事 說 的. When he said it, he referred to that matter.

ZHĬ₂ 只 (AD) only, just, exclu-sively. Wǒmen-zhǐ-néng-zhèi-yangr-zuò. 我 們 只 能 這 樣 作 . We can only do it this way. (See: BÙZHǏ 不 只).

ZHĬ₄ 止 (TV) stop <u>something</u>. Tā-

zhǐbuzhùde-dà-kū. 他 止 不 住 的 大 哭 . She cannot stop crying.

ZHÌ₃ 置 (TV) purchase <u>property,</u> <u>furniture, etc.</u> Tā-zhìle-yisuǒ-fángzi. 他 置 了 一 所 房 子 . He has bought a house.

ZHÌ₃ 治 (TV) heal, treat (<u>an</u> <u>illness</u>). Wǒde-bìng shi-tā-zhìhǎo-le-de. 我 的 病 是 他 治 好 了 的 . It was he who cured my illness.

ZHÌ₅ 質 (N) quality (<u>vs. quantity</u>). Tāmende-'chūchǎn liàng-gòu kěshi-zhì-buxíng. 他 們 的 出 產,量 夠,可 是 質 不 行 . As far as their pro-duction is concerned, the quan-tity is enough, but the quality is not satisfactory.

ZHÌ'ĀN₅ 治 安 (N) law and order,public security. Nèige-dìfangde-zhì'ān zěnmayàng? 那 個 地 方 的 治 安 怎 麼 樣 ? How is the law and order in that place? <u>or</u> Is that place safe?

'ZHÌBÀN₅ 置 辦 (TV) provide for, purchase <u>a large amount of</u> <u>something.</u> Nǐ-nüerde-jiàzhuang zhìbàn-le-ma? 你 女 兒 的 嫁 妝 置 辦 了 嗎 ?Did you provide the dowry for your daughter?

ZHÌ-BÙ₃ 織 布 (VO) weave cloth.

ZHÌBUJÌ₃ 至 不 濟 (MA) if worse comes to worst. Zhìbují-wǒ-kéyi-bǎ-biǎo-mài-le. 至

Z

不濟我可以把表
賣了. If worse comes to
worst, I can sell my watch.

ZHĬCHI₃ 支持 (TV) give sup-
port, give backing. Dàjiā-dōu-
zhíchi-ta. 大家都支持
他. Everybody supported him.

ZHĬCHU(LAI)₂ 指出（來）(RV)
point out. Tā-zhǐchu-wǒ-hěn-
duō-cuòr-(lai). 他指出我
很多錯兒（來）. He
pointed out many mistakes of
mine.

ZHÌ-CÍ₄ 致詞 (VO) give a
speech on a certain occassion.
Xiàozhǎng-zhì-cí-yǐhòu, dàjiā-
dou-gǔzhǎng. 校長致詞
以後,大家都鼓掌,
After the principal finished his
speech, everybody applauded.

ZHĪDAO₁ 知道 (TV) know, know
of. Nǐ-bu-zhǐdào. 你不知
道. You don't know. Ràng-ta-
zhǐdao-zhidao shì-zěnma-hui-
shì. 讓他知道知道
是怎麼回事. Let him
know what it is all about. Wǒ-
zhǐdao-ta, kěshi-méi-jiànguo.
我知道他,可是沒
見過. I know of him, but I
have never met him.

'ZHĬDĂO₃ 指導 (TV) direct,
guide. Qǐng-nín-'zhǐdǎo. 請您
指導. Please direct us. or
Please give us some advice.
(N) guidance. Méi-you-nínde-
'zhǐdǎo wǒmen-zuòbuhǎo. 沒有
您的指導我們作
不好. We cannot do it well
without your guidance.

ZHÍDE₂ 值得 (RV) worthwhile
to do something. zhíbude 值
不得 or buzhíde 不值得
it isn't worthwhile. Nèige-dìfang zhíde-qu-kànkan. 那個
地方值得去看看.
It's worthwhile to go to see
that place. (cf: ZHÍ 值).

ZHÍDE₄ 只得 see ZHĬHĂO 只
好

ZHĪDIÀN₄ 支店 (N) branch
store.

'ZHĬDIĂN₃ 指點 (TV) (1) point
with the finger. (2) used as a
polite way to ask for instructions,
point out. Qǐng-nín-zhídian-zhi-
dian. 請您指點指點.
Please point out what was wrong
and what has to be done.

ZHÌDU₁ 制度 (N) system (method or policy of political or social organizations). jīngji-zhìdu
經濟制度 economic sys-
tem. xuéxiàode-zhìdu 學校
的制度 school system.

ZHÌDUO₂ 至多 (MA) at most.
Wǒ-zhìduo-gěi-ta-yìbǎikuai-
qián. 我至多給他一
百塊錢. At most, I'll
give him one hundred dollars.

ZHĪFÁNG₅ 脂肪 (N) fat (on a
human body or an animal).

ZHÌFÚ₃ 制服 (N) uniform.(M:
tào 套).

ZHĪGŌNG₅ 職工 (N) (con. zhí-
yuán-gōngren 職員工人).
management and labor.

'ZHĬGUĂN₃ 只管 (MA) (lit. only
take care) just do something
without worrying. Nǐ-'zhǐguǎn-

gàosong-wo. 你只管告诉我. You just tell me and don't worry about anything else.

ZHǏHǍO₂ 只好 or ZHǏDE 只得 (AD) can only, have no choice but. Yàoshi-méi-you-fēijǐ, wǒ-zhǐhǎo-bu-qù. 要是没有飛機、我只好不去. If there is no airplane, the only thing I can do is not to go.

ZHǏHUǏ₃ 指揮 (TV) direct, command, conduct. zhǐhuǐ-yuè-duì 指揮樂隊 conduct an orchestra or a band. Tā-zài-qiánxiàn-zhǐhuǐ-jūnduì. 他在前線指揮軍隊. He commands an army at the front line.
(N) (1) command, instruction. Tā-bu-tīng-zhǐhuǐ. 他不聽指揮. He doesn't obey orders. (2) conductor of an orchestra or a band.

ZHǏJIA₄ 指甲 (N) nail (of finger or toe).

ZHǏJIÀGE₂ 支家哥 (PW) Chicago.

ZHǏJIÀO₂ 指教 (TV) (lit. point out and teach) instruct someone about something. Qǐng-nín-duō-zhǐjiào. 請您多指教. Please give more instructions.

ZHÍJIE₃ 直接 (SV) direct. (opp. jiānjiē 間接). Wǒmende-guānxi bùzhíjiē. 我們的關係不直接. Our relationship isn't direct.
(MA) directly. Wǒ-zhíjie-gēn-ta-shuō-ba. 我直接跟他說吧. Let me talk to him directly.

ZHÍJUÉ₃ 直覺 (N) intuition.

ZHÍLÌ₄ 智利 (PW) Chile.

ZHÌLIÁO₅ 治療 (TV) treat or cure a sickness. Wǒmen-miǎnfèi-zhìliáo-zhèizhǒng-bìng. 我們免費治療這種病. We treat this kind of illness free.

ZHĪMA₅ 芝蔴 (N) (1) sesame. (2) sesame seed. (M: lì 粒).

ZHÍMÍNDÌ₃ 殖民地 (N) colony.

ZHǏNÁNZHĒN₂ 指南針 (N) compass (for showing directions).

ZHÍNǙR₄ 姪女兒 (N) niece (brother's daughter).

ZHĪPEI₃ 支配 (TV) administer, dispose. Zhèibǐ-qián yóu-nǐ-zhīpei. 這筆錢由你支配. This money will be administered by you.

ZHĪPIÀO₂ 支票 (N) check (for money). (M: zhāng 張). zhī-piào-běnzi 支票本子 check-book. kāi-zhīpiào 開支票 write a check.

ZHÌQI₃ 志氣 (N) ambition.

ZHÍ-QIÁN₃ 值錢 (VO) worth money. zhí-duōshao-qián 值多少錢 worth how much money.
(SV) valuable. bù-zhí-qián 不值錢 worthless.

ZHÍR₄ 姪兒 or ZHÍZI 姪子 (N) nephew (brother's son).

ZHÍRÌ₄ 值日 (VO) be on duty (for a day). Jīntian shéi-zhírì?

Z

今天誰值日 ? Who is on duty today?

ZHÌSHǍO₂ 至少 (AD) at least. Zhìshǎo nǐ-děi-ràng-wo-gěi-xiǎofèi. 至少你得讓我給小費. At least, you must let me give the tips.

ZHÍSHĒNG(FĒI)JĪ₃ 直升 (飛) 機 (N) helicopter. (M: jià 架).

ZHĪSHI₂ 知識 (N) knowledge. qiú-zhīshi 求知識 seek knowledge. dé-zhīshi 得知識 obtain knowledge. zhǎng-zhīshi 長知識 increase knowledge.

ZHǏSHǏ₄ 支使 (TV) order people around. Tā-lǎo-ài-zhǐshǐ-rén. 他老愛支使人. He always likes to order people around.

ZHǏSHÌ₄ 指示 (TV) give instructions(from a superior to a subordinate). Qǐng-nín-zhǐshì. 請您指示. Please give instructions. (N)instructions (from a superior to a subordinate). Nín-yǒu-shén-ma-zhǐshì? 您有甚麼指示 ? What kind of instructions do you have ?

ZHǏSHÌ₂ 只是 (1) except, but only. Tā-dōu-hěn-hǎo zhǐshì-lǎn-yidianr. 他都很好只是懶一點兒. He's good in every way, the only thing is that he is a little lazy. Biéde-dōu-bu-xíng, zhǐshì-zhèi-yíge-hǎo. 別的都不行, 只是這一個好. All the others are not satisfactory,

but only this is good.

ZHĪSHIFÈNZǏ₄ 知識份子 (N) intellectual. Tā-shì-zhīshi-fènzǐ. 他是知識份子. He is an intellectual.

ZHÍSHUǍNG₃ 直爽 (SV) frank, straightforward (of a person).

ZHĪ-'SUǑYǏ₃ 之所以 used after the subject of a clause,with or without de-yuǎngu 的原故 at the end; usually followed by another clause introduced by yīnwei 因為 , the reason why. Wǒ-zhī-suǒyǐ-bu-gàosong-ni (-de-yuángu), shì-yīnwei-pà-ni-shēngqì. 我之所以不告訴你的原故, 是因為怕你生氣. The reason that I didn't tell you is because I was afraid that you might get angry. (cf: 'SUǑYǏ 所以).

ZHǏ-TÉNG₄ 止痛 (VO) relieve pain.

ZHǏTOU₃ 指頭 (N) finger or toe.

ZHǏWANG₃ 指望 (TV) hope and expect. Wǒ-zhǐwang-tā-bāng-máng, kěshi-ta-méi-lái. 我指望他幫忙,可是他沒來. I was hoping that he would help, but he didn't come. (N) hope. Méi-you-zhǐwang-le. 沒有指望了. There is no hope. (cf: PÀNGWANG 盼望 , XĪWANG 希望).

ZHǏWÉN₅ 指紋 (N) fingerprint. yìn-zhǐwén 印指紋 make a fingerprint.

ZHÌWEN₃ 質問 (TV) question, interrogate. Wǒmen-dei-zhìwen-ta. 我們得質問他. We have to question him.

ZHÍWU₄ 植物 (N) plant (generic term).

ZHÍWU₃ 職務 (N) duty (on a job). Nǐde-zhíwu shì-shénma? 你的職務是甚麼? What are your duties?

ZHÌXIANG₅ 志向 (N) goal or purpose of one's ambition.

ZHÍXÌNGZI₅ 直性子 (N) (1) frank nature. (2) person with a frank nature. Tā-shi-ge-zhí-xìngzi. 他是個直性子. He is a person with a frank nature.

ZHÌXU₂ 秩序 (N) order (of a social group). wéichi-zhìxu 維持秩序 maintain order. Tā-bu-shǒu-zhìxu. 他不守秩序. He doesn't observe the rules (of order). Huìchǎngde-zhìxu hěn-huài. 會場的秩序很壞. The order in the meeting place is very bad.

ZHǏYĀN₃ 紙烟 (N) cigarette. (syn. yānjuǎnr 烟捲兒, xiāngyān 香烟). (M: zhī 枝, bāo 包, tiáo 條).

ZHǏYÀO₁ 只要 or ZÍYAO 只要 (MA) if only. Zhǐyao-nǐ-gěi-qián, ta-shénma-dou-néng-bàn. 只要你給錢,他甚麼都能辦. If only you pay the money, he can do every-thing.

ZHÍYÈ₂ 職業 (1) profession. (2) job.

ZHÌYU₃ 至於 (CV) as far as

something is concerned, with regard to. Wǒ-míngtian-qù, zhìyu-tā-shénma-shíhou-qu, wǒ-jiu-bu-zhīdào-le. 我明天去,至於他甚麼時候去,我就不知道了. I'm going tomorrow, with regard to when he is going, I don't know.

ZHÍYUÁN₃ 職員 (N) member of a managerial staff in any large organization.

ZHÌYUÀN₃ 志願 (N) ambition, will.

ZHÌYUÀNJŪN₄ 志願軍 (N) army of volunteers.

'ZHÌZÀO₄ 製造 (TV) manufac-ture.

ZHǏZHĀNG₄ 紙張 (N) paper (generic term).

ZHÍZHAO₃ 執照 (N) official license or certificate. qǐng-zhí-zhao 請執照 apply for a license. lǐng-zhízhao 領執照 receive a license.

ZHĪZHŪ₄ 蜘蛛 (N) spider.

ZHIZHUWǍNG₅ 蜘蛛網 (N) spider web.

ZHÍZI₄ 姪子 see ZHÍR 姪兒.

ZHŌNG₄ 中 (L) (1) middle. jiào-shìzhōng 教室中 in (the middle of) the classroom. zhōngtú 中途 midway. Zhōngměi 中美 Central America. Tā-sānyue-'zhōng-lái. 他三月中來 He will come in the middle of March. (2) in, within a period of time. sānge-yuè-zhōng 三個月中 in three months.

Tā-'sānyue-zhōng-lai. 他 三 月 中 來 . He will come in March.

(S) ZHÈNG(ZAI)... ZHŌNG 正 (在)... 中 be in the process of... zhèng(zai)-jìnxíng-zhōng 正 在 進 行 中 in the process of proceeding. zhèng (zai)-bànlǐ-zhōng 正 (在) 辦 理 中 in the process of doing it.

(B) (1) Chinese. zhōngfú 中 服 Chinese clothes. Zhōng-měi 中 美 Chinese and America. (2) in between. zhōnglì 中 立 neutral. (3) used before certain verbs to form SV, be good to. zhōngkàn 中 看 be pleasant to watch.

ZHŌNG₁ 鐘 (N) (1) clock. (M: zuò 座). (2) bell. (M: kǒu 口). zìyóuzhōng 自 由 鐘 Liberty Bell. (3) time (as indicated by the clock; must be used after one of the following M: diǎn 點 , kè 刻 , fēn 分 , miǎo 秒). yìdiǎn-zhōng 一 點 鐘 one o'clock or one hour. yíkè-zhōng 一 刻 鐘 a quarter-hour. yìfēn-zhōng 一 分 鐘 one minute. yìmiǎo-zhōng 一 秒 鐘 one second.

ZHŌNG₃ 腫 (IV) swell up. Liǎn-zhōng-le. 臉 腫 了 . The face is swollen.

ZHŎNG₂ 種 (N) (1) race (of people). báizhǒngrén 白 種 人 white race. (2) species. Zhèi-shi-shénma-zhōngde-gǒu？ 這 是 甚 麼 種 的 狗 ? What

species is the dog? (M) kind. Wǒ-yǒu-liǎngzhǒng-bànfa. 我 有 兩 種 辦 法 . I have two kinds of methods. Zhèizhong-dōngxi méi-yòng. 這 種 東 西 沒 用 . This kind of thing is useless. Wǒ-yǒu-zènma-yizhong-'xiǎngfǎ. 我 有 這 麼 一 種 想 法 . I have a kind of way of thinking which is like this.

ZHÒNG₂ 種 (TV) (1) plant, sow. zhòng-dì 種 地 till the soil, farm. zhòng-shù 種 樹 plant trees. (2) inoculate for smallpox. zhòng-huǎr 種 花 兒 plant flowers or inoculate for smallpox. zhòng-niúdòu 種 牛 痘 inoculate for smallpox.

ZHÒNG₁ 重 (SV) (opp. qīng 輕) (1) heavy (in weight). (syn. chén 沈). Jīnzi hěn-zhòng. 金 子 很 重 . Gold is very heavy. Zhèige-zhuózi èrliǎng-zhòng. 這 個 鐲 子 二 兩 重 . This bracelet weighs two ounces. (2) heavy, emphasized. Tāde-kǒuyin hen-zhòng. 他 的 口 音 很 重 . His accent is heavy. Zhèizhang-huàr-shàng-de lán-yánse tài-zhòng-le. 這 張 畫 上 的 藍 顏 色 太 重 了 . The blue color in this painting has been emphasized too much. (3) serious. Tā-de-zéren-xīn hen-zhòng. 他 的 責 任 心 很 重 . He is very serious about his responsibilities. Tāde-bìng hěn-zhòng. 他 的 病 很 重 . His illness is very serious. Tā-bǎ-péngyou-kànde-hěn-zhòng. 他 把 朋 友 看 得 很 重. He gives a great deal of weight to friendship. (4) heavy, excessive. Wǒde-gōngzuo-tài-zhòng-le. 我 的 工 作 太 重 了. My work load is too heavy. Tāde-méimao hěn-zhòng. 他 的 眉 毛 很 重. His eyebrows are very heavy. Tā-sòng-de-lǐwu hěn-zhòng. 他 送 的 禮 物 很 重. The gift he gave is very expensive. (N) weight. Zhèikuài-tiě zhòng-shi-wǔbàng. 這 塊 錢 重 是 五 磅. The weight of this hunk of iron is five pounds. (TV) give importance to, emphasize. zhòng-gǎnqing 重 感 情 give importance to personal feelings.

(AD) severely, heavily. Wǒmen-děi-zhòng-fá-ta. 我 們 得 重 罰 他. We have to punish him severely.

ZHÒNG₃ 中 (TV) (1) hit (the target). Wǒ-dǎle-yiqiāng, kěshi-méi-zhòng. 我 打 了 一 鎗, 可 是 沒 中. I fired one shot but didn't hit it. (2) be struck by illness or be infatuated. Tā-zhòngle-shénma-bìng-le? 他 中 了 甚 麽 病 了? What illness was he struck with? (3) win a prize. Wǒ-zhòng-le-yìge-èrjiǎng. 我 中 了 一 個 二 獎. I won second prize.

(RE) hit the target, reach a goal.

Zhēn-ràng-ta-cāizhòng-le. 真 讓 他 猜 中 了. He really guessed it. Tā-yòu-méi-kǎozhòng. 他 又 沒 考 中. He didn't pass the examination again.

ZHÒNGBÀN₄ 重 辦 (TV) punish or fine severely. Wǒmen-děi-zhòngbàn-ta. 我 們 得 重 辦 他. We have to punish him severely.

ZHŌNGBIǍO₄ 鐘 表 (N) timepiece, clocks and watches. xiūli-zhōngbiǎo 修 理 鐘 表 repair clocks and watches.

ZHŌNGBÙ₄ 中 部 (PW) middle part. Měiguode-zhōngbù 美 國 的 中 部 the middle part of the U.S.A.

ZHÒNGDÀ₃ 重 大 (SV) important. zhòngdàde-ànzi 重 大 的 案 子 important case.

ZHŌNGDIǍNR₂ 鐘 點 兒 (N) (1) hour. (syn. xiǎoshí 小 時, zhōngtóu 鐘 頭). sānge-zhōng-diǎnr 三 個 鐘 點 兒 three hours. (2) period of time. An-zhōngdiǎnr-gěi-qián. 按 鐘 點 兒 給 錢. Pay according to the hour. (3) time (as indicated on the clock). Zhōngdiǎnr-hái-méi-dào-ne. 鐘 點 兒 還 沒 到 呢. The time is not up yet.

ZHÒNG-(NIÚ)DÒU₄ 種 (牛) 痘 (VO) vaccinate. Nǐ-zhòng-le-(niú)dòu-le meiyou? 你 種 了 (牛) 痘 了 沒 有? Did you have your vaccination yet?

ZHÒNG-DÚ₄ 中 毒 (VO) be

Z

poisoned. Tā-shi-zěnma-zhòng-de-dú? 他是怎麼中的毒? How was he poisoned?

ZHŌNGFAN₁ 中飯 (N) lunch. (M: dùn 頓).

ZHÒNG-FĒNG₄ 中風 (VO) have an apoplectic stroke. (N) apoplexy. Tā-dé-de shì-zhòng-fēng. 他得的是中風. What he got was apoplexy.

'ZHÒNGGŌNGYÈ₃ 重工業 (N) heavy industry.

ZHŌNGGUO₁ 中國 (PW) China.

ZHŌNGGUOHUÀ₁ 中國話 (N) Chinese spoken language. (M: jù 句). shuō-Zhōngguohuà 説中國話 speak Chinese. xué-Zhōngguohuà 學中國話 learn Chinese.

ZHŌNGGUOREN₁ 中國人 (N) Chinese person.

ZHŌNGHOU₄ 忠厚 (SV) honest and generous. Tā-duì-rén hen-zhōnghou. 他對人很忠厚. He is very honest and generous toward people.

ZHŌNGHUÁMÍNGUÓ₁ 中華民國 (N) (1) Republic of China. (2) denotes a certain year since the establishment of the Chinese Republic, starting with 1912. Zhōnghuáminguó-wǔshi-wǔnián 中華民國五十五年 the fifty-fifth year of the Republic, 1966.

ZHŌNGJIĀN₄ 中間 (PW) inside, middle. Zài-tāmen-zhōngjiān, yǒu-hěn-duōde-wènti. 在他們中間有很多的問題. There are a lot of problems among them. (cf: ZHŌNGJIÀNR 中間兒).

ZHŌNGJIÀNR₂ 中間兒 (PW) middle. (syn. dāngjiànr 當間兒, dāngzhōng 當中). Bǎ-zhuōzi-fàngzai-zhōngjiànr. 把桌子放在中間兒 Put the table in the middle. Zhōngjiànr-yǒu-rén-lā-qiàn. 中間兒有人拉縴. There's a broker in between. (cf: ZHŌNGJIĀN 中間).

ZHŌNGLÈI₃ 種類 (N) kind, category. Zhǒnglèi-hěn-duō. 種類很多. There are many kinds.

ZHŌNGLÌ₃ 中立 (IV) neutral. Wǒ-zhōnglì, shéi-ye-bu-xiàng-zhe. 我中立,誰也不向着. I am neutral, I am not for anybody. (N) neutrality. shǒu-zhōnglì 守中立 assumed neutrality.

ZHŌNGQIŪ(JIÉ)₄ 中秋(節) (TW) the Mid-Autumn Festival.

ZHŌNGR₄ 盅兒 (B) cup. jiǔ-zhōngr 酒盅兒 wine cup. (M) cup. Zánmen hē-yizhongr. 咱們喝一盅兒. Let's have a drink.

ZHŌNGR₃ 種兒 see ZHONGZI 種子

ZHÒNGSHĀNG₄ 重傷 (N) severe wound. shòu-zhòngshāng 受重傷 be badly wounded.

ZHŌNGSHĒN₄ 終身 (B) all of one's life, life-time. zhōngshēn-shìyè 終身事業 life-time career. zhōngshēn-dàshì 終身大事 marriage (the big affair of a life-time).

(AD) for one's whole life. Tā-xiǎng-zhōngshēn-bu-jià-le. 她想終身不嫁了. She doesn't want to marry during her life-time.

ZHŌNGSHÌ₄ 中式 (N) Chinese style.

ZHÒNGSHÌ₃ 重視 (TV) have high regard for someone, regard something as important, emphasize. Nǐ-búbi-zhòngshì-zhèiyàngrde-shìqing. 你不必重視這樣兒的事情. You don't have to pay special attention to this kind of thing.

ZHŌNGTÓU₁ 鐘頭 (N) hour. (syn. xiǎoshí 小時, zhōng-diǎnr 鐘點兒). liǎngge-bàn-zhōngtóu 兩個半鐘頭 two-and-a-half hours.

ZHŌNGWÉN₁ 中文 (N) Chinese language, Chinese written language. niàn-Zhōngwén 念中文 study Chinese. shuō-Zhōng-wén 説中文 speak Chinese. xué-Zhōngwén 學中文 learn Chinese.

ZHŌNGWǓ₁ 中午 (TW) noon.

ZHŌNGXĪ₃ 中西 (N) China and western countries.

ZHŌNGXĪN₃ 中心 (N) center, core. sīxiǎngde-zhōngxīn 思想的中心 core of thought. shāngyè-zhōngxīn 商業中心 center of commerce.

ZHŌNGXUÉ₁ 中學 (N) high school, middle school.

ZHŌNGYĀNG₃ 中央 (PW) the center. húde-zhōngyāng 湖的中央 the center of the lake. (AT) central. Zhongyāng-gōng-yuán 中央公園 Central Park.

ZHÒNGYÀO₂ 重要 (SV) important. Méiyou-bǐ-zhèige-gèng-zhòngyàode-le. 没有比這個更重要的了. There is nothing more important than this.

ZHŌNGYĪ₄ 中醫 (N) (1) Chinese medical science. Tā-xué-zhōng-yī. 他學中醫. He is studying Chinese medical science. (2) doctor (who practices Chinese medicine). Tā-shì-zhōngyī. 他是中醫. He is a doctor (of Chinese medicine).

ZHÒNGYI₄ 中意 (TV) like, be pleased with. Wǒ-zhòngyi-nèi-ge-hóngde. 我中意那個紅的. I like that red one.

(VO) fit one's taste, suit one's idea. Zhèige zhòng-nǐde-yì-ma? 這個中你的意嗎? Does this suit you?

ZHŌNGYÒNG₄ 中用 (SV) useful. bu-zhōngyòng 不中用 useless.

'ZHŌNGYÚ₄ 終於 (AD) finally. Wǒ-zhōngyú-děi-gěi-ta-qián. 我終於得給他錢. I finally must give him money.

ZHŎNGZHŎNG₃ 種種 (N) various kinds, all different kinds. Wǒ-xiǎngle-zhǒngzhǒngde-bànfa. 我想了種種的辦法. I have thought of all

Z

different kinds of methods.

ZHŎNGZI₃ 種子 <u>or</u> ZHŎNGR 種兒 (N) seed. (M: lì 粒, kē 顆). să-zhŏngzi 撒種子 scatter the seeds. xià-zhŏngzi 下種子 sow seeds.

ZHŎNGZÚ₃ 種族 (N) race (<u>of</u> <u>people</u>).

ZHŌU₄ 粥 (N) congee (<u>gruel made</u> <u>of rice or millet</u>). (syn. xīfàn 稀飯). hē-zhōu 喝粥 eat congee. áo-zhōu 熬粥 cook congee.

ZHŌU₄ 洲 (-B) continent. Měi-zhou 美洲 American cǒntinent. Àozhou 澳洲 Australian con-tinent.

ZHŌU₄ 州 (-B) state (<u>of the U.S.</u>). Niǔyuezhōu 紐約州 New York State. zhōulì-dàxué 州立 大學 state university. zhōu-zhǎng 州長 governor of a state.

ZHŌU₄ 周 (M) (1) number of times <u>around something.</u> rào-dìqiú-yizhōu 繞地球一周 go around the earth one time. (2) week. Kāi-xué yǐjing-sānzhōu-le. 開學已經三周了. It has been three weeks since school started.

ZHÒU₄ 皺 (SV) be wrinkled. Yī-shang-zhòu-le. 衣裳皺了. The clothes are wrinkled. (TV) wrinkle <u>the brow.</u> zhòu-méi 皺眉 knit one's brow.

ZHŌUCHAO₃ 周朝 (TW) Chou dynasty.

ZHŌUDAO₃ 周到 (SV) thorough, careful, meticulous (<u>in thinking</u>

or in action). Tā-xiăngde hěn-zhōudao. 他想的很周 到. He takes everything into consideration. Zhŭren-zhāode-hěn-zhōudao. 主人招待 得很周到. The host is very thorough in taking care of his guests.

ZHŌUKĀN₄ 週刊 (N) weekly. (M: qī 期).

ZHÒU-MEI₄ 皺眉 (VO) knit <u>one's</u> eyebrows, frown.

ZHŌUMI₄ 周密 (SV) careful, thoroughgoing (<u>in thinking or</u> <u>planning</u>). Tā-sīxiang-zhōumi. 他思想周密. He al-ways thinks thoroughly.

ZHŌUMÒ₄ 周末 (TW) week-end.

ZHŌUNIÁN₃ 周年 (M) anniver-sary, full year. èrzhōunián 二 周年 two full years. (B) anniversary. zhōunián-jì-niàn 周年紀念 commem-oration of an anniversary.

ZHŌUWEI₃ 周圍 (PW) the area around <u>something.</u> xuéxiào-zhōu-wéi 學校周圍 around the school. Zhōuwéi-dou-yǒu-shù. 周圍都有樹. There are trees around it.

ZHÒUWENR₄ 皺紋兒 (N) wrinkle. Tā-liǎn-shang méiyou-zhòuwénr. 他臉上沒有 皺紋兒. There aren't any wrinkles on his face.

ZHŌUXUAN₄ 周旋 (TV) deal with <u>or</u> speak with <u>people diplo-matically.</u> Zài-shèhui-shang nǐ-děi-gēn-ren-zhōuxuan. 在

Z

社 會 上 你 得 跟 人
周 旋 . In society you have to
deal diplomatieally with people.

ZHÒUYÈ₃ 晝 夜 (N) day and
night. Zhòuyè-bù-tíng. 晝 夜
不 停 . It doesn't stop day and
night.
(M) day and night. yízhòuyè 一
晝 夜 a whole day and a whole
night.

ZHŪ₃ 猪 (N) pig, hog. (M: kǒu
口 , tóu 頭). zhūròu 猪 肉
pork. zhūyóu 猪 油 lard. mǔ-
zhū 母 猪 sow. gōngzhū 公
猪 boar.

ZHÚ₃ 燭 (M) watt. (syn. zhī 枝).
wǔshizhú-de-diàndēng 五 十
燭 的 電 燈 fifty-watt bulb.

ZHǓ₃ 煮 (TV) boil. zhǔshuǐ 煮
水 boil water.

ZHÙ₄ 註 (TV) annotate, make an
explanatory note (in a book or
written material). zhù-xiǎo-
zhùr 註 小 註 兒 make an
explanatory note.

ZHÙ₁ 住 (IV)(1) live, reside. Nín-
zài-nǎr-zhù? 您 在 那 兒
住 ? Where do you live? Zuó-
tian-wǎnshang-nín-zhùzai-nǎr-
le? 昨 天 晚 上 您 住
在 那 兒 了 ? Where did
you stay last night? Wǒ-zhù-
xuéxiào. 我 住 學 校 . I
live at the school. Zhèi-fángzi
bu-néng-zhù-rén. 這 房 子
不 能 住 人 . People can't
live in this house.
(2) stop (rain, wind, snow, etc.).
Yǔ-zhù-le. 雨 住 了 . The
rain has stopped.

(TV) stop (hand, foot, mouth).
Wǒ-yìzhí-méi-zhù-jiǎo. 我 一
直 没 住 腳 . I haven't
stopped running all the time.
(RE) (1) indicates firmness of
action. Nǐ-zhànzhù-le. 你 站
住 了 . Stand firmly. Nǐ-
jìzhu. 你 記 住 . Keep it
firmly in mind. (2) indicates
bringing some action to a complete halt. Tā-bǎ-wo-wènzhu-
le. 他 把 我 問 住 了 .
He stumped me by asking that
question. Nǐ-zhànzhu. 你 站
住 . Stop (walking). Tā-jiao-
tàitai-gei guǎnzhu-le. 他 叫
太 太 給 管 住 了 . He
was completely controlled by
his wife. Wǒ-bǎ-ta-jiàozhu-le.
我 把 他 叫 住 了 . I
stopped him (by calling). Tā-
tōu-dōngxi jiào-ren-gei-zhuā-
zhu-le. 他 偷 東 西 叫
人 給 抓 住 了 . He was
caught while he was stealing.
(cf: DĀI 待).

ZHUĀ₃ 抓 (TV) (1) lit. or fig.
grasp. zhuā-yìbǎ-mǐ 抓 一 把
米 grasp a handful of rice.
zhuāzhu-yàodiǎn 抓 住 要
點 grasp the essential points.
(2) scratch. zhuā-yǎngyang 抓
痒 痒 scratch where it itches.
zhuā-nǎodai 抓 腦 袋 scratch
the head. Tā-ràng-māo-zhuā-le.
他 讓 貓 抓 了 . He was
scratched by a cat. (cf: NÁO
撓). (3) catch, arrest. Jǐng-
chá-zhuā-le-yíge-zéi. 警 察
抓 了 一 個 賊 . The

Z

police caught a thief. (4) find time. zhuā-dianr-gōngfu 抓點兒工夫 find a little time. (5) catch, get something or someone in a hurry. Wǒ-děi-chūqu zhuā-dianr-qián. 我得出去抓點兒錢. I have to go out to get some money. Bié-suíbiàn-xiā-zhuā. 別隨便瞎抓. Don't grasp blindly. Tā-zhāzhao-shen-ma-suàn-shenma. 他抓着甚麼算甚麼. He grasps whatever he can get.

ZHUĀI₄ 摔 (TV) fling, throw something at something. Ná-ní-zhuāi-ta. 拿泥摔他. Throw mud at him.

ZHUĂI₄ 跩 (IV) (1) waddle. Tā-zǒu-lù lǎo-zhuǎi. 他走路老跩. He waddles while he is walking. (2) (con. zhuǎi-wén 跩文). quote or use literary words in speech or writing unnecessarily. Béi-zhuǎi-le. 別跩了. Don't use bookish language.

ZHUÀI₄ 拽 (TV) pull, drag, hold with the hand. Tā-zhuàizhe-wǒ, bu-jiào-wo-zǒu. 他拽着我不叫我走. He is holding me and won't let me go. Tā-bǎ-wo-zhuàishailai-le. 他把我拽上來了 He pulled me up.

ZHUĀI-WÉN₅ 拽文 (VO) quote or use literary words in speech or writing unnecessarily. Tā-shuō-huà ài-zhuāi-wén. 他說話愛拽文. He likes to use literary words when he speaks.

ZHUĂN₃ 磚 (N) brick. (M: kuài 塊).

ZHUĀN₃ 專 (AD) exclusively, only (nothing else). Tā-zhuān-guǎn-zhèixie-shì. 他專管這些事. He takes care of these things exclusively. (SV) engrossed in, devoted to one thing. Tā-niàn-shū xīn-hen-zhuān. 他念書心很專. When he studies he is very engrossed.

ZHUĂN₂ 轉 (TV) (1) or ZHUÀN 轉 turn, make a turn. zhuǎn-yíge-wānr 轉一個彎兒 turn a corner. xiàng-hòu-zhuǎn 向後轉 turn around. (2) transfer, change to, turn into. Tāde-yìsi xiànzài-zhuǎndao-biéde-shìqingshang-qu-le. 他的意思現在轉到別的事情上去了. He changed his idea to another subject. Tā-zhuǎndao-lìngwài-yíge-xuéxiào-qu-le. 他轉到另外一個學校去了. He has transferred to another school. Wǒde-jīngji-qíngxing hái-méi-zhuǎnguolái-ne. 我的經濟情形還沒轉過來呢. My economic situation has not yet turned for the better. Děng-zhuǎnguo-nián-lai zài-shuō. 等轉過年來再說. Let's wait until next year. (3) forward a letter. Qǐng-nín-bǎ-zhèifeng-xìn zhuángei-ta. 請您把這封信轉給他.

Please forward this letter to him.
(AD) in turn. Tā-jiào-wǒ-bàn, wǒ-jiu-zhuǎn-tuō-nín-tì-ta-bàn. 他 叫 我 辦, 我 就 轉 托 您 替 他 辦. He asked me to do it, but I in turn ask you to do it.

ZHUÀN₃ 傳 (N) biography. (M: piān 篇).

ZHUÀN₂ 轉 (TV)(1) turn or revolve something in a circle. Tā-yòng-shǒu-zhuàn-nèige-lúnzi. 他 用 手 轉 那 個 輪 子. He turned the wheel with his hand. (2) or ZHUÁN 轉 turn, make a turn. zhuàn-wānr 轉 彎 兒 turn a corner. Tā-yòu-zhuànhuilai-le. 他 又 轉 回 來 了. He made a turn and came back. (IV) (1) go around. Tāmen-wéi-zhe-zhuōzi-zhuàn. 他 們 圍 着 桌 子 轉. They go around the table. Wǒ-dao-jiē-shang-qu-zhuànzhuan-qu. 我 到 街 上 去 轉 轉 去. I want to walk around in the streets. (2) revolve. Nèige-qiú zài-dìxia-zhuàn. 那 個 球 在 地 下 轉. That ball revolves on the ground.

ZHUÀN₂ 賺 (TV) (1) make money in business. (opp. péi 賠). Zuò-mǎimai jiu-děi-xiǎng-zhuàn-qián. 作 買 賣 就 得 想 賺 錢. If you are in business you have to think of making money. (2) dial. make money by working for salary or in business. Tā-

zài-gōngsī yíge-yuè-zhuàn-duō-shao-xīnshui? 他 在 公 司 一 個 月 賺 多 少 薪 水 ? How much is his monthly salary in the company? (cf: ZHÈNG QIÁN 掙 錢).

ZHUĀNCHĒ₄ 專 車 (N) special car (of a train). (M: liàng 輛).

ZHUǍNDÁ₄ 轉 達 (TV) pass on information. Jìshi-Zhāng-xiān-sheng-méi-zài, jiu-qǐng-nín-tì-wo-zhuǎndá-ba. 既 是 張 先 生 沒 在, 就 請 您 替 我 轉 達 吧. Since Mr. Chang is not here, please pass this information on to him.

ZHUĀNG₄ 椿 (M) for affairs, matters, etc. Zhèizhuāng-shì bu-hǎobàn. 這 椿 事 不 好 辦. This matter is not easy to handle.

ZHUĀNG₂ 裝 (TV) (1) load, pack. zhuāng-zǐdàn 裝 子 彈 load the gun with bullets. zhuāng-chē 裝 車 load the car. Bǎ-qián zhuāngzai-kǒudàirli. 把 錢 裝 在 口 袋 兒 裏. Put the money in the pocket. Xiāng-zi-xiǎo, dōngxi-duō, zhuāngbu-xià. 箱 子 小, 東 西 多, 裝 不 下. The trunk is too small to put this much stuff in. (2) install. zhuāng-diànhuà 裝 電 話 install a telephone.

ZHUĀNG₂ 裝 (TV) pretend to be, act the role of. Wǒ-zhuāng-bu-zhīdào. 我 裝 不 知 道. I'll pretend that I know nothing about it. Bǎ-zhèige bǎizai-zher, zhuāngzhuang-yàngzi. 把 這

Z

個 擺 在 這 兒, 裝 裝
樣 子. Put this one here to
make it look presentable.

ZHUÀNG₃ 撞 (TV) (l) bump into,
collide with, hit. zhuàng-chē
撞 車 have a car collision.
Qìchē-gēn-shù zhuàngshang-le.
汽 車 跟 樹 撞 上 了.
The car hit a tree. (2) strike
something. zhuàng-zhōng 撞
鐘 strike a bell. Tā-yòng·tóu
zhuàng-wo. 他 用 頭 撞 我.
He hit me with his head.

ZHUÀNG₄ 壯 (SV) strong (of a
human body). (opp. ruò 弱).
(TV) strengthen one's courage
or prestige. Hē-diǎnr-jiù zhuàng-
zhuang-dǎnzi.喝 點 兒 酒 壯
壯 胆 子. Drink some wine
and it will give you the courage.

ZHUĀNGBAN₅ 裝 扮 (TV) adorn,
dress up, make up (of a person).
Tā-bù-zhīdao-zěnme-zhuāngban.
她 不 知 道 怎 麼 裝
扮. She doesn't know how to
make up. Tā-zhuāngbancheng
yíge-lǎotàitai. 他 裝 扮 成
一 個 老 太 太. He dis-
guised himself as an old lady.

ZHUÀNGDĪNG₄ 壯 丁 (N) young
man ready for induction into the
army.

ZHUÀNGGUĀN₅ 壯 觀 (SV) spectacular. ˌChángchéng-hěn-zhuàng-
guān. 長 城 很 壯 觀. The
Great Wall is really spectacular.

ZHUĀNGJIA₄ 莊 稼 (N) (1) standing crop.Zhuāngjia-zhǎngde-hěn-
hǎo. 莊 稼 長 得 很 好.
The crops are growing very well.

(2) farming. zhòng-zhuāngjia
種 莊 稼 farm.

ZHUĀNGJIALǍOR₅ 莊 稼 老
兒 (N) farmer.

-ZHUÀNGKUANG₃ 狀 況 (N)
situation. (cf: JĪNGKUANG 景
況 ， QÍNGKUANG 情 況).

ZHUĀNG-SHǍ₄ 裝 傻 (VO)
pretend to be a fool.

ZHUĀNGSHI₄ 裝 飾 (TV) (1)
decorate. Tāde-kètīng zhuāng-
shide-hěn-hǎo. 他 的 客 廳
裝 飾 的 很 好. His
sitting room is very well decorated. (2) dress up, make up
(of a person). Nǐ-bu-zhuāngshi
yě-piàoliang. 你 不 裝 飾
也 漂 亮. You're beautiful
without dressing up.
(N) (1) adornment. (2) decoration.

'ZHUĀNGSHIPǏN₄ 裝 飾 品
(N) decoration.

ZHUĀNGSHU₄ 裝 束 or
ZHUĀNGSU 裝 束 (N) manner
or style of one's· dress.

ZHUĀNGSU₄ 裝 束 see
ZHUĀNGSHU 裝 束.

ZHUÀNGTAI₄ 狀 態 (N) (1) appearance, form. (2) situation,
condition.

ZHUĀNGZǏ₄ 莊 子 (N) Chuang-
tzu (the philosopher).

ZHUǍNJĪ₄ 轉 機 (N) indication
that things are turning for the
better. Shìqing-yǒule-zhǎngji-
le. 事 情 有 了 轉 機
了. Things have ·started to
turn for the better.

ZHUÀNJI₃ 傳 記 (N) biography.

(M: piān 篇).

ZHUĀNJIĀ₂ 專家 (N) specialist, expert.

ZHUĂNJIĀO₃ 轉交 (TV) forward a letter or something. Qǐng-nín-bǎ-zhèifēng-xìn zhuǎn-jiāogei Lǐ-xiānsheng. 請您把 這封信轉交給李 先生 . Please forward this letter to Mr. Li.

ZHUĀNLÌ₄ 專利 (IV) have a patent. Zhèizhǒng-yào yóu-wǒ-zhuānlì-shínián. 這種藥由 我專利十年 . I have had the patent for this medicine for ten years.

ZHUĀNMÀI₄ 專賣 (N) monopoly. yān-jiǔ-zhuānmài 烟酒專 賣 monopoly of tobacco and alcoholic beverages.

ZHUĀNMÉN₂ 專門 (AD) exclusively, especially, only (nothing else). Tā-zhuānmén-yánjiu-Zhōngwén. 他專門研究 中文 . He studies Chinese only.

(N) specialty. Zhè-shi-tāde-zhuānmén. 這是他的專 利 . This is his specialty.

ZHUĀNSHǏ₅ 專使 (N) special envoy, special ambassador.

ZHUĀNTUŌ₃ 轉托 (TV) ask someone to do something as a favor in other people's turn. Yīnwei-wǒ-méi-gōngfu, nǐ-nèi-jian-shì wǒ-zhuāntuō Lǐ-xian-sheng-le. 因為我沒工 夫,你那件事,我轉 托李先生了 . Because I don't have time, I have asked

Mr. Li to do it for you in my place.

ZHUǍN-WÁNR₃ 轉彎兒 (VO) (1) turn a corner. Zài-qiántou-lùkǒur zhuǎn-wánr. 在前頭 路口兒轉彎兒 . Make a turn at the street in front. (2) do something in a roundabout way. Wǒ-méi-zhíjiē-tuō-ta, wǒ-zhuǎnle-ge-wānr. 我沒直 接托他,我轉了個 彎兒 . I asked him in a roundabout way. Tā-gēn-wǒ-zhuǎnzhe-wānr-shuō. 他跟 我轉着彎兒說 . He beat around the bush with me.

ZHUĀNXĪN₃ 專心 (IV) concentrate, devote one's mind to. Tā-bu-néng-zhuānxīn. 他不 能專心 . He cannot concentrate.

(AD) diligently and single-mindedly. Nǐ-děi-zhuānxīn-niàn-shū. 你得專心念書 . You must study diligently.

ZHUĂN-XUÉ₂ 轉學 (VO) transfer to another school.

ZHUǍN-YǍN₄ 轉眼 (VO) (lit. turn one's eyes) blink one's eyes. zhuǎn-yǎn-de-gōngfu 轉 眼的工夫 a split-second. Yì-zhuǎn-yǎn jiu-yòu-guò-nián-le. 一轉眼就 又過年了 . As soon as you blink your eyes, it will be a new year again.

ZHUĀNZHÌ₃ 專制 (SV) dictatorial. Tā-tài-zhuānzhì. 他太 專制 . He is too dictatorial.

ZHUĀ-XIĀ₄ 抓瞎 (VO) not

Z

know what to do. Tā-zhuāle-xià-le. 他 抓 了 瞎 了. He doesn't know what to do.

ZHUĀZHU₃ 抓 住 (RV) grasp firmly. zhuāzhu-jīhuì 抓 住 機 會 grasp the opportunity. Yòng-shǒu-zhuāzhu. 用 手 抓 住. Grasp it with the hand.

ZHUĂZI₄ 爪 子 (N) claw. (M: zhi 隻).

ZHǓBÀN₄ 主辦 (TV) (1) direct or be in charge of doing something. Shéi-zhǔbàn-nèijian-shì? 誰 主 辦 那 件 事? Who is in charge of doing that? (2) sponsor a show, gathering, exhibition, etc. Zhèige-huì-shi-xuéxiào-zhǔbànde. 這 個 會 是 學 校 主 辦 的. This meeting is sponsored by the school.

ZHÙ- CÈ₃ 註 册 (VO) (lit. make a note in a book) register (for school). (cf: DĒNG-JÌ 登 記, GUÀ-HÀO 掛 號).

ZHÙCHU₃ 住 處 (N) place to live.

ZHÙCÍ₅ 祝 詞 (N) toast or speech of congratulation.

'ZHǓDÒNG₄ 主動 (N) initiative action. Wǒmen-děi-zhēngqǔ-'zhǔdòng. 我 們 得 爭 取 主 動. We have to struggle for initiative action.

(IV) initiate, take the initiative. Wǒmen-yīngdāng-'zhǔdòng. 我 們 應 當 主 動. We should take the initiative.

ZHǓFU₃ 囑 咐 (TV) give advice to make sure, impress something upon someone. Nǐ-'zhǔfu-zhǔfu-ta, ràng-ta-shǎo-shuō-huà.

你 囑 咐 囑 咐 他, 讓 他 少 説 話. You tell him to make sure that he doesn't talk too much.

ZHÙFÚ₅ 祝 福 (TV) wish happiness, bless. Wǒ-xiànzài-zhǔ-fú-nǐmen. 我 現 在 祝 福 你 們. Now I wish you happiness and blessings.

ZHǓGU₃ 主 顧 (N) customer, patron.

ZHǓGUĀN₃ 主 觀 (SV) subjective. (opp. kèguān 客 觀).

ZHUĪ₂ 追 (TV) (1) lit. or fig. chase after, pursue. Jǐngchá-zhuī-zéi. 警 察 追 賊. The policemen are chasing after the thief. Tā-zhuī Lǐ-xiaojie. 他 追 李 小 姐. He is chasing after Miss Li. Tā-tài-kuài, wǒ-zhuībushàng-ta. 他 太 快, 我 追 不 上 他. He is too fast, I cannot catch up with him. (2) search after, investigate. Wǒ-zhīdao-shi-shéi-tōude, kěshi wǒ-bu-xiǎng-zhuī-le. 我 知 道 是 誰 偷 的, 可 是 我 不 想 追 了. I know who stole it, but I don't think this matter should be looked into any further.

ZHUĪJIĀ₅ 追 加 (IV) supplement a budget. zhuījiā-yùswàn 追 加 預 算 supplement a budget.

ZHUĪQIÚ₄ 追 求 (TV) (1) seek for. zhuīqiú-zhēnlǐ 追 求 真 理 seek for the truth. (2) fig. chase after. Tā-zhuīqiú-Lǐ-xiaojie. 他 追 求 李 小

姐 . He's chasing after Miss Li.

ZHUĪZI₄ 錐子 (N) awl. (M: bǎ 把).

ZHUÌZI₅ 墜子 (N) (1) pendants. (2) earrings. (M: fù 付 , duì 對).

'ZHǓJIǍOR₃ 主角兒 see ZHǓJUÉR 主角兒

ZHǓJUÉR₃ 主角兒 or 'ZHU- JIǍOR 主角兒 (N) (1) lead- ing actor or actress. (2) princi- pal character in a play or story.

ZHÙMÍNG₄ 著名 (SV) famous. (syn. chūmíng 出名).

ZHǓN₂ 准 (TV) allow, permit. Bù-zhǔn-chōu-yān. 不准抽 烟 . No smoking. Nǐ-zhun-wo- qù, wǒ-jiu-qù. 你准我去 , 我就去 . If you allow me to go, I'll go.

ZHǓN₂ 準 (SV) accurate. Tā-dǎ- qiāng dǎde-hěn-zhǔn. 他打 鎗打得很準 . He is very accurate in shooting. Wǒ- de-biǎo-bu-zhǔn. 我的表 不準 . My watch is not ac- curate. Tāde-Zhōngguo-huà fā- yīn-hěn-zhǔn. 他的中國 話發音很準 . His Chinese pronunciation is very accurate.

(AD) definitely, for sure. Wǒ- zhǔn-zhǐdao tā-bu-huì. 我準 知道他不會 . I defi- nitely know that he doesn't know how to do it. Nǐ-chīle-zhèige- yào zhǔn-hǎo. 你吃了這 個藥準好 . After you take this medicine, you will def- initely be all right.

(RE) indicates being sure of doing something. Nǐ-kànzhǔn-le zai-mǎi. 你看準了 再買 . Don't buy it unless you're sure it's the right one.

ZHUNBEI₃ 準備 (TV) prepare. (syn. yùbei 預備). Wǒ-děi- 'zhǔnbei-zhǔnbei. 我得準 備準備 . I have to prepare a little.

(N) preparation.

ZHǓNQUE₂ 準確 (SV) accurate. Tāde-xiāoxi bu-zhǔnque. 他 的消息不準確 . His information is not accurate.

ZHUNR₄ 準兒 (N) used with yǒu 有 or mei 没 certainty, accuracy. Yīngdāng-zěnma-bàn wǒ-xīnli-yǒu-zhǔnr. 應當 怎麼辦我心裏有 準兒 . I know for sure how to handle this. Tā-méi-zhǔnr- lái-bu-lái. 他没準兒來 不來 . It's not certain wheth- er he will come or not.

ZHǓNSHÍ₄ 準時 (AD) on time, at the appointed time. zhǔnshí- chū-xí 準時出席 attend a meeting on time. Tā-shi-zhǔn- shí-dào-de. 他是準時 到的 . He arrived on time.

ZHǓNXǓ₅ 準許 (TV) allow, permit. Zhèr-zhǔnxǔ-he-jiǔ-ma? 這兒準許喝酒嗎? Is drinking allowed here?

(N) permission.

ZHUŌ₄ 捉 (TV) catch, capture. (syn. děi 逮 or dǎi 逮). Wǒ- men-zhuōzhu-liǎngge-zéi. 我 們捉住兩個賊 We

Z

caught two thieves.

ZHUŌ-MICÁNG₄ 捉迷藏 (VO) play blindman's buff, play hide and seek.

ZHUÓ-SHǑU₄ 着手 or ZHÁO-SHǑU 着手 (VO) start to work on something. Nèijian-shì bu-zhīdào yīngdāng-zěnma-zhuó-shǒu. 那件事不知道應當怎麼着手. I don't know how to start to work on that job.

ZHUÓZHÒNG₄ 着重 (TV) emphasize, stress, underscore. (syn. zhùzhòrg 注重). Zhèige-xuéxiào hěn-zhuózhòng-tǐyu. 這個學校很着重體育. This school emphasizes physical training.

ZHUŌZI₁ 桌子 (N) table (furniture). (M: zhāng 張).

ZHUÓZI₄ 鐲子 (N) bracelet, wristlet. (M: fù 副).

ZHǓQUÁN₃ 主權 (N) sovereignty.

ZHÙR₄ 註兒 (N) commentary, annotation, note (in a book or written material). jiā-xiǎo-zhùr 加小註兒 add some notes.

ZHǓREN₂ 主人 (N) host. Ràng-wo-zuò-zhǔren-ba. 讓我作主人吧. (lit. Let me act as a host) Let me pay the bill (of a party).

ZHǓRÈN₃ 主任 (N) chief executive officer, director.

ZHŪRÒU₃ 猪肉 (N) pork.

ZHÙ-SHŪ₅ 著書 (VO) write books.

ZHÚSǓN₅ 竹笋 (N) bamboo shoot.

ZHŪWÈI₃ 諸位 (N) used in addressing or speaking to a group of people. Zhūwei-zǎo. 諸位早. Good morning, everybody. Zhūwei-xiānsheng, zhūwei-tàitai. 諸位先生, 諸位太太. Ladies and Gentlemen.

ZHǓXÍ₃ 主席 (N) (1) chairman. (2) used with a surname as a title. Zhāng-zhǔxí 張主席 Chairman Chang.

ZHÙ-XIÀO₂ 住校 (VO) live at the school.

ZHǓYÀO₃ 主要 (SV) essential, major. zhǔyàode-wèntí 主要的問題 essential problems.

ZHÚYÌ₁ 主意 (N) (1) idea, plan. chū-zhúyi 出主意 suggest ideas. gǎi-zhúyi 改主意 change the mind. Nǐ-shi-shén-ma-zhúyi? 你是甚麼主意? What is your idea? (2) decision. dǎ-zhúyi 打主意 or ná-zhúyi 拿主意 make decisions. Wǒ-xīnli-yi-luàn jiu-méi-zhúyi-le. 我心裏一亂就沒主意了. As soon as I get confused, I cannot make a decision.

ZHǓYÌ₃ 主義 (N) doctrine, -ism. Sānmíng-zhǔyì 三民主義 The Three Principles of the People.

ZHÙ-YÌ₁ 注意 (VO) pay attention, be careful. Qǐng-nín-zhù-dianr-yì. 請您注點兒意. Please pay attention. (TV pay attention to, Nǐ-děi-zhùyì-ta. 你得注意他.

You must pay attention to him.

ZHÙ-(YI)YUÀN₃ 住（醫）院
(VO) be confined or live in a
hospital.

'ZHŬZHĀNG₃ 主張 (TV) advo-
cate, propose, favor (a proposal,
motion). Wŏ-zhŭzhāng kāi-huì-
tăolun. 我主張開會討
論. I propose that we discuss
it in a meeting.
(N) conviction. Zhèige-ren méi-
you-'zhŭzhāng. 這個人沒
有主張. He has no con-
victions.

ZHÙZHǏ₂ 住址 (N) address (of
a person).

ZHÙZHÒNG₂ 注重 (TV) em-
phasize, stress, underscore.
(syn. zhuózhòng 着重). Tā-
men-zhùzhòng-shìshí. 他們
注重事實. They empha-
size the facts.

ZHŪZI₄ 珠子 (N) (1) bead. (M:
kē 顆). (2) pearl. (M: kē 顆).

ZHÚZI₄ 竹子 (N) bamboo. (M:
kē 棵).

ZHÙZI₄ 柱子 (N) pillar, post.
(M: gēn 根).

ZǏ₃ 紫 (SV) purple. Tā-qì-de
liăn-dou-zǐ-le. 他氣得臉
都紫了. He was so angry
that his face turned purple.

ZÌ₁ 字 (N) (1) Chinese characters
(unit symbol of the Chinese writing system). Tā-rènshi-bushăo-
zì. 他認識不少字.
He knows quite a few characters.
(2) Chinese syllable. Tā-yíge-
zì-yíge-zì-de shuō-de-hěn-qīng-
chu. 他一個字一個

字的說得很清楚.
He pronounced it very clearly,
syllable by syllable. (3) word.
Zhèiben-Yīngwen-shū yŏu-sān-
wan-zì. 這本英文書
有三萬字 . There are
about thirty thousand words in
this English book.

ZÌBEN₃ 資本 (N) capital (funds).
Zuò-shēngyi dei-you-zīben. 作
生意得有資本 . If
you want to do business you
must have capital.

ZÌBENJIĀ₂ 資本家 (N)
capitalist.

ZÌBENZHŬYÌ₂ 資本主義
(N) capitalism.

'ZÌCHĂN₅ 資產 (N) property.

ZÌCHĂNJIĒJÍ₃ 資產階級
(N) capitalist class, propertied
class.

ZÌCÓNG(... YǏHÒU)₂ 自從（...
以後）(CV) ever since. Zì-
cóng-nèicì-tā-lái-(yǐhòu), wŏ-
jiu-méi-kànjian-ta. 自從那
次他來（以後）,我就
沒看見他 . Ever since
the last time he came I haven't
seen him.

ZÌDÀ₂ 自大 (SV) be conceited,
arrogant. Búyao-zìdà. 不要
自大 . Don't be conceited.

ZÌDÀN₃ 子彈 (N) bullet, car-
tridge. (M: fā 發 , lì 粒 , kē
顆).

ZÌDIĂN₂ 字典 (N) dictionary
(entries listed by characters or
by words). (M: ben 本 , bù 部).
Yīnwen-zìdiăn 英文字典
English dictionary. (cf: CÍDIĂN

Z

辭典).

ZÌDÒNG₃ 自動 (B-) automatic.

zìdòng-diàntī 自動電梯
automatic elevator.

(AD) voluntarily. (opp. bèidòng
被動). Tā-zìdòng-géi-wo-
wǔ-kuài-qián. 他自動給
我五塊錢 . He gave me
five dollars voluntarily.

ZÌGE₂ 資格 (N) qualification.
Tā-zīge-hen-gāo. 他資格
很高 . His qualifications are
very high. Wǒ-bu-gòu-zīge. 我
不夠資格 . I am not
qualified.

ZÌGĚR₄ 自個兒 (PR) Peip.
oneself. Tā-zìgěr-shuō-de. 他
自個兒說的 . He said
it himself. Nǐ-wèi-shénma bú-
wèn-nǐ-zìgěr? 你為甚麼
不問你自個兒 ?Why
don't you ask yourself? (cf: ZÌJǏ
自己).

ZÌHAO₃ 字號 (N) name of a
business establishment. Nèige-
pùzi shénma-zìhao? 那個
舖子甚麼字號 ?
What is the name of that store?

ZÌJǏ₂ 自己 (PR) oneself. Ràng-
ta-zìjǐ-shuō. 讓他自己
說 . Let him say it himself.
Wǒ-shì-zì'jǐ-lái-de.我是自
己來的 . I came by myself.
(cf: ZÌGĚR 自個兒).

ZIJIREN₃ 自己人 (N) people
belonging to the same group,
close friends. Zánmen-shi-zìjǐ-
ren.咱們是自己人
We are close friends.

ZÌJU₄ 字據 (N) personal

document, receipt, IOU, etc.
(M: zhāng 張).

ZÌJUÉ₅ 自覺 (IV) realize, be
aware of. Tāde-máobing tā-
bu-néng-zìjué. 他的毛病
他不能自覺 . He
cannot realize his own bad
habits.

ZÌLAIHUǑ₃ 自來火 (N) Peip.
cigarette lighter.(syn. dǎhuǒjī
打火機).

ZÌLAISHUǏ₂ 自來水 (N) tap
water, running water.

ZÌLAISHUIBǏ₂ 自來水筆
(N) fountain pen. (M: zhī 枝 ,
guǎn 管).

ZÌLIAO₄ 資料 (N) material,
data.

ZÌMǍN₄ 自滿 (SV) be self-
satisfied and conceited. Bú-
yào-zìmǎn. 不要自滿 .
Don't be conceited.

ZǏMEI₂ 姊妹 or JIEMEI 姐
妹 (N) sisters. Wǒmen-zǐ-
mei-sānge. 我們姊妹
三個 : There are three
sisters in our family, including
myself. Tāmen-zǐmei-liǎngge-
dōu-hěn-cōngming.他們姊
妹兩個都很聰明
The two sisters are both very
bright.

ZÌMÙ₄ 字幕 (N) subtitle of a
movie or projected slide.

ZÌMǓR₄ 字母兒 (N) alphabet.

'ZǏNǙ₄ 子女 (N) son and
daughter.

ZǏR₃ 子兒 Peip. (N) (l) seed.
cǎozǐr 草子兒 grass seed.
dǎ-zǐr 打子兒 bear seeds.

Z

(2) piece of a board game. diūle-yíge-zĭr 丟 了 一 個 子 兒 lost one piece.

(B) (1) egg (of poultry). jīzir 雞 子 兒 chicken egg. (2) bullet. qiāngzĭr 鎗 子 兒 bullet.

ZÌR₄ 字 兒 (N) Peip. (1) contract, lease, deed. (M: zhāng 張). lì-yizhāng-zìr 立 一 張 字 兒 signed a contract. (2) message. (M: zhāng 張). Gĕi-ta-liú-yizhang-zìr. 給 他 留 一 張 字 兒 . Leave him a message.

ZÌRAN₂ 自 然 (SV) natural, normal. Tāde-tàidu hen-zìran. 他 的 態 度 很 自 然 . His manner is very natural.

(MA) (1) of course, naturally. Tā-zìran-bu-kĕn. 他 自 然 不 肯 . Of course, he won't.

(2) naturally, by nature. Tā-dà-le, zìran-jiu-míngbai-le. 他 大 了 , 自 然 就 明 白 了 . When he grows up, he will understand it naturally.

ZÌRÁN₃ 自 然 (N) (1) natural science (as a subject in school). (2) nature. dà-zìrán 大 自 然 mother nature.

ZÌSHĀ₂ 自 殺 (IV) commit suicide.

ZÌSHI₃ 姿 勢 (N) bodily posture, stance (as in playing some athletic game or in dancing), form (as in a statue). Tāde-zīshi hĕn-hăokàn. 他 的 姿 勢 很 好 看 . His posture is very nice.

ZÌSĪ₂ 自 私 (SV) selfish.

'ZÌSŪN₄ 子 孫 (N) descendants.

ZÌWEIR₃ 滋 味 兒 (N) (1) flavor, taste. Zhèige-cài méiyou-zīweir. 這 個 菜 沒 有 滋 味 兒 . This food has no flavor. (2) fig. sensation, feeling. Tā-shuō-de-huà, wŏ-jué-de-bu-shi-zīweir. 他 說 的 話 , 我 覺 得 不 是 滋 味 兒 . I don't feel right about what he said. Wŏ-méi-chángguo-nèizhŏng-zīweir. 我 沒 嘗 過 那 種 滋 味 兒 . I have never tasted that kind of flavor. or I have never had that kind of sensation.

ZÌWŎ₄ 自 我 (AD) by oneself. Wŏmen zìwŏ-jièshào ba. 我 們 自 我 介 紹 吧 . Let's introduce ourselves. Wŏmen-zìwŏ-pīpíng. 我 們 自 我 批 評 . Let's criticize ourselve.

ZÌXÌ₃ 仔 細 (SV) careful, attentive. Tā-hĕn-zĭxi. 他 很 仔 細 . He is very careful.

(AD) carefully. Nĭ-zĭxi-xiáng-xiang. 你 仔 細 想 想 . You think carefully.

ZÌXÍ₃ 自 習 or ZÌXIŪ 自 修 (N) study hall (the class).

ZÌXÌN₃ 自 信 (IV) confident. Tā-bùgăn-zìxìn. 他 不 敢 自 信 . He doesn't dare to be confident.

(N) (con. zìxìnxīn 自 信 心). confidence. Tā méi-you-zìxìn. 他 沒 有 自 信 . He has no confidence.

ZÌXÍNGCHĒ₃ 自 行 車 (N)

Z

bicycle. (syn. jiǎotachē 腳踏
車). (M: liàng 輛). qí-zì-
xíngchē 騎自行車 ride a
bicycle.

ZÌXÌNXĪN₃ 自信心 (N) con-
fidence. Tā-zìxìnxīn hěn-qiáng.
他自信心很強. He
has great confidence.

ZÌXIŪ₂ 自修 (IV) study by oneself, be self-taught. Tā-méi-
shàngguo-xuéxiào, tā-yizhíde-
shi-zìxiū. 他没上過學
校, 他一直的是自
修. He has never been to
school, he has always been self-
taught.
(N) or ZÌXÍ 自習 study hall
(the class). (M: táng 堂). Jīn-
tian-xiàwu yǒu-yitáng-zìxiū. 今
天下午有一堂自
修. There is a study period
this afternoon.

ZĪYĂNG₃ 滋養 (N) nourishment.
(SV) nourishing. Niúnǎi-hěn-zī-
yang. 牛奶很滋養.
Milk is very nourishing.

ZÌYĂNR₄ 字眼兒 (N)(1) diction.
Tāde-zìyǎnr-hěn-qíngchu. 他
的字眼兒很清楚.
His diction is very clear. (2)
usage of words. Tā-hěn-jiǎngjiu-
zìyǎnr. 他很講究字
眼兒. He's very particular
about diction. or He is very
particular about how he·uses
words.

ZÌYĀO₁ 只要 see ZHǏYAO 只
要.

ZÌYÓU₁ 自由 (SV) free (unre-
stricted). Wǒmènde-gōngsī hěn-

zìyóu. 我們的公司
很自由. Our company is
very free.
(N) freedom, liberty. Zhè-shi-
wǒde-zìyóu. 這是我的
自由. This is my freedom.
(AD) freely. Nǐmen-kéyi-zìyóu-
huódòng-le. 你們可以
自由活動了. Now you
may do whatever you like.

ZĪYUÁN₃ 資源 (N) resources.

ZÌZAI₄ 自在 (SV) free and
comfortable.

ZÌZHÌ₄ 自治 (IV) govern itself.
Nèige-dìfang yǐjing-zìzhì-le.
那個地方已經自
治了. That place now gov-
erns itself.
(N) autonomy.

ZÌZHǏLǑUR₅ 字紙簍兒
(N) wastepaper basket.

ZÌZHIQŪ₄ 自治區 (N) au-
tonomous area.

ZÌZHǓ 自主 (IV) have the
authority to decide by oneself.
Tā-bù-néng-zìzhǔ. 他不能
自主. He cannot decide by
himself.

ZŎNG₃ 總 (TV) add together.
zǒngchilai-shuō 總說起
來 sum up.
(AD) (1) always. Tā-zǒng-zèn-
ma-shuō. 他總這麼說.
He always says it this way. (2)
anyway, in any event. Tā-zǒng-
bu-néng-bu-géi-ni-qián. 他
總不能不給你錢.
He'll have to pay you anyway.
Zuótian-lái-le zǒng-yǒu-yìbǎi-
ren. 昨天來了總有

一百人 . There must have been a hundred people who came yesterday anyway.

(B-) (1) main. zŏng-bànshichù 總辦事處 main office. (2) chief. zŏng-biānjí 總編輯 chief editor. (3) general. zŏng-bàgōng 總罷工 general strike.

ZŎNG'ÉRYÁNZHI₃ 總而言之 (MA) sum up, in one word.

ZŎNGGÒNG₃ 總共 see YÍGÒNG 一共 .

ZŎNGHÁNG₃ 總行 (N) principal business office.

ZŎNGHÉ₃ 綜合 (TV) synthesize. Bă-dàjiāde-yìjian zŏnghé-qilai. 把大家的意見綜合起來 . Put everybody's opinion together. (N) synthesis.

ZŎNGJI₄ 踪蹟 (N) trace, track.

ZŎNGJIÀO₂ 宗教 (N) religion. xìn-zŏngjiào 信宗教 believe in religion.

ZŎNGJIÉ₄ 總結 (TV) (1) bring to a total, add up. Bă-zhàng zŏngjié-yixia. 把賬總結一下 . Add up the account. (2) sum up, recapitulate. Qĭng-nĭ-bă-tāmende-yìsi zŏngjié-yixiar. 請你把他們的意思總結一下兒 . Please summarize their opinions. (N) summation. Zuò-yige-zŏngjié. 作一個總結 . Sum up.

ZŎNGJĪNGLĬ₃ 總經理 (N) general manager.

ZŎNGLĬ₃ 總理 (1) (con. zŏng-jīnglĭ 總經理). general manager. (2) premier, prime minister. (3) chief director of Kuomintang, usually referring to Dr. Sun Yat-sen.

ZŎNGPAI₅ 宗派 (N) sect, school of philosophy.

ZÒNGRAN₃ 縱然 (MA) even if. Nĭ-zòngran-gĕi-ta-qián, tā-ye-bu-yidìng-kĕn-zuò. 你縱然給他錢,他也不一定肯作 . Even if you pay him he may not be willing to do it. (See: JIÒUSHI 就是).

ZŎNGSĪLÌNG₃ 總司令 (N) commander-in-chief.

ZŎNGTŎNG₂ 總統 (N) president (of a country).

ZŎNGZHI₄ 總之 (MA) (con. zŏng'éryánzhi 總而言之). sum up, in one word.

ZŎU₁ 走 (IV) (1) walk. Háizi-gāng-huì-zŏu. 孩子剛會走 . The child just learned how to walk. (2) leave, depart. Wŏ-míngtian-zŏu. 我明天走 . I'll leave tomorrow. (3) move, go (of a boat, vehicle, machine, etc.). Zhōng-bu-zŏu-le. 鐘不走了 . The clock doesn't run. Zhèitiao-hé bu-néng-zŏu-chuán. 這條河不能走船 . No ship can sail on this river. (4) go by way of, take a route. Wŏmen-zŏu-nĕitiao-lù? 我們走那條路 ? Which way shall we take? (5) move, make a move (in a board game). Shéi-xiān-zŏu?

Z

誰 先 走 ? Who moves first?
(6) get together, have contact.
Tāmen-zǒude-hěn-jìn. 他們
走 得 很 近. They see
each other very often. (7) lose
<u>flavor, shape, pitch, color, etc.</u>
Zhèishuāng-xié zǒule-yàngzi-le.
這 雙 鞋 走 了 樣 子
了. This pair of shoes has lost
its shape. (8) <u>something bad</u>
happens accidentally. Diànxiàn
zǒule-huǒ-le. 電 線 走 了
火 了. The wire had a short-
circuit.
(RE) (1) away. Tā-bǎ-qìchē-
kāizǒu-le. 他 把 汽 車 開
走 了. He drove the car
away. (2) <u>indicates losing of</u>
<u>flavor, shape, pitch, etc.</u> Tā-
ba-diàozi chàngzǒu-le. 他 把
調 子 唱 走 了. He sings
out of tone.
ZÒU₄ 揍 (TV) <u>Peip.</u> hit, strike,
sock. Wǒ-zòu-ni. 我 揍 你.
I'll sock you.
ZǑU-DÀOR₄ 走 道 兒 (VO)
walk on the road. (cf: ZǑU-LÙ
走 路).
ZǑUDÚ₃ 走 讀 (IV) be a day-
student (<u>opposite to boarding stu-</u>
<u>dent</u>). Wǒ-bú-zhù-xiào, zǒudú.
我 不 住 校, 走 讀. I
don't live at school, I'm a day-
student.
ZǑU-FĒNG₄ 走 風 (VO) leak out
information. Bié-zǒule-fēng. 別
走 了 風. Don't leak out any
information.
ZǑULANG₄ 走 廊 (N) (1) veranda.
(2) a long roofed open corridor.

ZǑU-LÙ₃ 走 路 (VO) (1) walk
on the road. Tā-zǒu-lù zǒude-
hěn-kuài. 他 走 路 走 得
很 快. He walks very fast.
(2) take a route to go <u>somewhere.</u>
Zǒu-něitiáo-lù? 走 那 條
路 ? Which road are we taking?
(3) leave, go away. Nǐ-juéde-
jèr-bu-hǎo nǐ-kéyi-zǒu-lù. 你
覺 得 這 兒 不 好 你
可 以 走 路. If you feel
it's not good here, you can
leave. (cf: ZOU-DÀOR 走 道
兒).
ZǑU-SĪ₃ 走 私 (VO) smuggle.
Zhèixie-dōngxi dōu-shi-zǒu-sī
yùnjinlai-de. 這 些 東 西
都 是 走 私 運 進 來
的. All these things are
smuggled in.
ZÒU-YUÈ₅ 奏 樂 (VO) play
music.
ZǑU-YÙN₂ 走 運 (VO) have a
streak of good <u>or</u> bad luck. zǒu-
hǎo-yùn 走 好 運 be in good
luck. zǒu-bèi-yùn 走 背 運
be in bad luck.
(SV) lucky. Tā-zēn-zǒu-yùn.
他 真 走 運. He is really
lucky.
ZŪ₁ 租 (TV) rent. zū-qìchē 租
汽 車 rent a car. Bǎ-fángzi
zūchuqu. 把 房 子 租 出
去. Rent the house to him.
ZŪ₄ 組 (M) section <u>or</u> department
<u>of an organization.</u> Měi-yibān
fān-sānzǔ. 每 一 班 分 三
組. Every class is divided
into three sections.
(B) section, department, group.

Z

xiǎozǔ 小組 small group.

ZUĀN$_4$ 鑽 (TV) (1) worm into, enter a hole. zuān-kūlong 鑽窟窿 enter a hole. (2) fig. intrigue for a position, seek to advance oneself through flattery. Tā-zhēn-néng-zuān. 他真能鑽. He really can get himself ahead.

ZUÀN$_4$ 攥 (TV) grasp, hold fast, clench one's fist. zuàn-qiántou 攥拳頭 make a fist. Tā-shóuli-zuànzhe-yibǎ-piàozi. 他手裏攥着一把票子. He is holding a handful of bank notes.

ZUÀNSHÍ$_3$ 鑽石 (N) diamond. (syn. jīngāngshí 金鋼石, jīngāngzuànr 金鋼鑽兒). (M: lì 粒, kē 顆).

ZǓFÙ$_3$ 祖父 (N) grandfather (father's father). (syn. yéye 爺爺). (M: wèi 位).

ZǓGUÓ$_4$ 祖國 (N) (lit. ancestor country) fatherland.

ZUǏ$_1$ 嘴 (N) (1) mouth. (M: zhāng 張). bì-zuǐ 閉嘴 close one's mouth. Bǎ-zuǐ-zhāngkai. 把嘴張開. Open your mouth. (2) bill (of a bird).

ZUÌ$_3$ 罪 (N) (1) sin, crime, wrong. yǒu-zuì 有罪 be sinful, be convicted. fàn-zuì 犯罪 commit a crime. (2) suffering, suffer. shòu-zuì 受罪 suffer.

ZUÌ$_2$ 醉 (SV) drunk. Tā-zuì-le. 他醉了. He is drunk. (RE) drunk. Zhèige-jiu hēbuzuì. 這個酒喝不醉. One cannot get drunk with this wine. (TV) pickle things in wine. zuì-pángxie 醉螃蠏 pickle crabs in wine or pickled crabs.

ZUÌ$_1$ 最 (AD) (1) used before SV or AV, most, -est. zuì-dà 最大 biggest. Tā-zuì-xǐhuan-shuō-huà. 他最喜歡說話. He likes to talk the most. or He likes most to talk. (2) used before L or PW, farthest to or nearest a place. zuì-qiántou 最前頭 farthest to the front. zuì-zhàngtou 最上頭 farthest to the top.

ZUǏBA$_4$ 嘴巴 (N) (1) dial. mouth. (2) Peip. slap on the cheek. Dǎ-ta-yíge-zuǐba. 打他一個嘴巴. Slap him once on the cheek.

ZUǏBÈN$_4$ 嘴笨 (SV) not smart in talking, slow of speech. Tā-zuǐbèn. 他嘴笨. He doesn't speak smartly.

ZUǏCHÁN$_4$ 嘴饞 (SV) voracious, greedy.

ZUÌCHŪ$_2$ 最初 (MA) at the very beginning. Zuìchū tā-bu-yuànyi-qù. 最初他不願意去. At the very beginning he wasn't willing to go.

ZUǏCHÚN$_5$ 嘴唇 (N) lips (of the mouth). (M: piàn 片).

ZUÌ'È$_5$ 罪惡 (N) sin, badness, wrongdoing.

ZUÌGUOR$_4$ 罪過兒 (N) sin, guilt, crime. Wǒde-zuìguor bu-xiǎo. 我的罪過不小. My sins are not small.

ZUÌHǍO$_1$ 最好 (MA) it's best.

Wǒmen-zuìhǎo-míngtian-zǒu. 我們最好明天走. It's best that we go tomorrow.

ZUÌHÒU₂ 最後 (TW) at the very last, after all. Zhìhòu ta-háishi-qù-le. 最後他還是去了. He went after all. (PW) last (in position). Tā-zài-zuì-hòu. 他在最後. He is last. Zhè-shi-wǒ-zuìhòude-yiju-huà. 這是我最後的一句話. This is my last word.

ZUÌJÌN₂ 最近 (TW) most recently, the near future. Tā-zuì-jìn-méi-lái. 他最近沒來. Most recently he hasn't come. Zuìjìn wǒ-yào-dào-Zhōng-guo-qu. 最近我要到中國去. I'll go to China in the near future.

ZUÌMÍNG₄ 罪名 (N) (lit. name of crime) ground of charge, type of crime, class of offense. Gěi-ta-yige-shénma-zuìmíng? 給他一個甚麼罪名? On what grounds do you charge him?

ZUÌNIE₅ 罪孽 (N) (1) sin. (2) suffering.

ZUǏR₄ 嘴兒 (N) (1) nozzle, spout, mouth (of an object). chá-húzuǐr 茶壺嘴兒 spout of a teapot. (2) a part of an object held in the mouth. yān-zuǐr 煙嘴兒 cigarette holder.

ZUÌREN₄ 罪人 (N) (1) sinner, evildoer. (2) prisoner, criminal.

ZǓMǓ₃ 祖母 (N) grandmother (father's mother). (syn. nǎinai

奶奶). (M: wèi 位).

ZŪN₄ 尊 (B-) your (honorable)... zūn-xìng 尊姓 your honorable name. zūnfūrén 尊夫人 your wife.

ZŪN₅ 尊 (M) (1) for cannons (artillery). yìzūn-dàpào 一尊大炮 a cannon. (2) for stat-ues. yìzūn-fóxiàng 一尊佛像 a Buddhist statue.

ZŪNJÌNG₃ 尊敬 (TV) revere, respect (a person). Zhōngguo-ren-zūnjìng-lǎoren. 中國人尊敬老人. Chinese people respect elders. (SV) respectful. Rén-duì-ta hen-zūnjìng. 人對他很尊敬. People are very re-spectful toward him. (cf: ZŪN-ZHONG 尊重).

ZŪNZHONG₃ 尊重 (TV) re-spect (a person, behavior or opinion). Wǒmen-dou-zūnzhong-tāde-yìjian. 我們都尊重他的意見. We all respect his opinions. (SV) (1) respectable. Tā-zìjǐ-bu-zūnzhong, biéren-jiu-kàn-buqǐ-ta. 他自己不尊重, 別人就看不起他. If he is not respectable, others will look down on him. (2) respectful. (cf: ZŪNJÌNG 尊敬).

ZUǑ₁ 左 (L) left. zuǒ-shǒu 左手 left hand. cóng-zuǒ-dào-yòu 從左到右 from left to right. Wàng-zuǒ-zǒu. 往左走. Walk to the left. (SV) (1) be leftist. Tāmen-dōu-wàng-zuǒ-kàolǒng. 他們都 往左靠攏 . They are all leaning toward the left. (2) Peip. wrong, incorrect. Nà-jiu-zuǒ-le. 那就左了 . That will be wrong.

ZUÒ₁ 作 (TV) (1) do something, engage in something or a job. Tā-zuò-shénma-shì? 他作 甚麼事 ? What does he do? Wǒ-děi-zhǎo-ge-'shì-zuò. 我 得找個事作 . I have to look for a job to do. Tā-xiàn-zài-zuò-shēngyi. 他現在 作生意 . He is doing business now. (2) make, produce something. Wǒ-xiǎng-zuò-yige-zhuōzi. 我想作一個桌 子 . I want to make a table. Tā-huì-zuò-fàn, yě-huì-zuò-yīshang. 他會作飯, 也會作 衣裳 . He knows how to cook food and also knows how to make clothes. Zhèige-shi-yòng-shítou-zuò-de. 這個是用石 頭作的 . This is made of stone. Nèige-gēr shì-shéi-zuò-de? 那個歌兒是誰 作的 ? Who wrote that song? Tā-zuòle-yipian-wénzhang. 他 作了一篇文章 . He wrote an article. (3) serve as, function, be in the role of. Tā-zuòle-fùqin-le. 他作了父 親了 . He became a father. Nǐ-jiào-wo-zuò-xuésheng-de-zěnma-bàn? 你叫我作 學生的怎麼辦? What can you expect me, a student, to do? Wǒmen-qǐng-tā zuò-

dàibiǎo. 我們請他作 代表 . We asked him to be our representative. (4) celebrate an occasion. zuò-shēngr-作生日 have a birthday party.

(PV) used with verbs, such as dàng 當 , jiào 叫 , rèn 認 , kàn 看 , zhuāng 裝 etc. , as. Zhè-jiu-jiàozuo-húdu. 這就 叫作糊塗 . This is called muddleheadedness. Wǒ-ná-tā-dàngzuo-jiāli-de-rén. 我拿他當作家裏 的人 . I took him as a member of our family.

(S) NÁ...ZUO 拿...作 use... as.... Wǒ-ná-zhèijian-wūzi zuò-shūfáng. 我拿這間 屋子作書房 . I use this room as a study.

ZUÒ₁ 坐 (IV) (1) sit. Qǐng-zuò. 請 坐 . Please sit down. Wǒ-yuànyi-zhànzhe, nín-zuòxia-ba. 我願意站著, 您坐 下吧 . I like to stand, you sit down. Qǐng-jinlai-zuòzuo. 請進來坐坐 . Please come in and sit for a while. Wǒ-yǒu-shì, zuòbuzhù. 我有 事, 坐不住 . I am busy, I cannot sit for long. Nín-zuò-zai-nǎr-le? 您坐在那 兒了 ? Where did you sit? (2) seat a certain number of people. Wǒde-qìchē néng-zuò-wǔge-rén. 我的汽車能 坐五個人 . My car can seat five people.

(TV) travel by or on any

Z

conveyance except those which one straddles. zuò-fēijī 坐飛機 ride on an airplane. zuò-diàntī 坐電梯 ride the elevator. Wǒ-zuò-huǒchē-qù. 我坐火車去. I go by train.

ZUÒ₃ 座 (M) for buildings, mountains, or objects of a similar shape. yízuò-lóu 一座樓 a building. yízuò-fén 一座墳 one tomb. yízuò-zhōng 一座鐘 one clock. yízuò-shān 一座山 one mountain. yízuò-chéng 一座城 a city.

ZUÒ-BÌ₄ 作弊 (VO) do something for the purpose of cheating. Tā-kànjian-hěn-duo-xuésheng kǎoshìde-shíhou zuò-bì. 他看見很多學生考試的時候作弊. He saw a lot of students cheating during their examination.

ZUǑBIANR₁ 左邊兒 (PW) left side.

ZUÒ-DIÀNTĪ₃ 坐電梯 (VO) ride on an elevator.

ZUÒ-DŌNG₅ 作東 (VO) be the host. Míngtian women-qu-chī-fàn, wǒ-zuò-dōng. 明天我們去吃飯我作東. Tomorrow, when we go out to eat, I will be the host.

ZUÒ-DUÌ₄ 作對 (VO) oppose, be against. Bié-gēn-wo-zuò-duì. 別跟我作對. Don't oppose me.

ZUÒFA₂ 作法 (N) way of doing things.

ZUÒFANG₅ 作坊 (N) an old-fashioned shop to manufacture certain products.

ZUÒFÈI₄ 作廢 (IV) invalid, void. Zhèizhong-piàozi zǎojiu-zuòfèi-le. 這種票子早就作廢了. This kind of bank note was invalid long ago.

ZUÒ-GŌNG₂ 作工 (VO) work (usually physical labor).

ZUÒ-GUĀN₂ 作官 (VO) be a governmental official.

ZUÒ-HUÓ₄ 作活 (VO) do manual or physical work, such as carpentry, farming, needlework, etc.

ZUÒJIĀ₃ 作家 (N) writer, author.

ZUÒ-JIĂ₄ 作假 (VO) produce something fake to deceive somebody.

ZUÓLIAOR₄ 作料 (N) seasoning ingredient (for cooking).

ZUÒ-LĬBAI₂ 作禮拜 (VO) worship, attend services.

ZUÒ-MÈNG₂ 作夢 (VO) have a dream. Nà-jiu-gēn-zuòle-yi-chang-mèng-yiyàng. 那就跟作了一場夢一樣. That is just like having a dream.

ZUÓMO₄ 琢磨 (TV) think over. Nǐ-zuómo-zuómo. 你琢磨琢磨. You think it over.

ZUǑPÀI₃ 左派 (N) leftist.

ZUÒPIN₃ 作品 (N) work of art, including books, essays, paintings, sculpture, musical works, etc.

ZUÒ-QŬ₄ 作曲 (VO) compose music.

ZUÒR₃ 座兒 (N) (1) or ZUÒ-WEI 座位 seat. Méi-zuòr-le.

Z

没座兒了 No seats left.
(2) holder, base, stand (<u>as for</u>
<u>a vase</u>).
ZUÒ-RÉN₄ 作人 (VO) (<u>lit</u>. be
a human being) develop <u>one's</u>
character to behave properly
<u>toward other members of society</u>.
ZUÒ-SHÌ₁ 作事 (VO) work,
have a job. Tā-zài-nǎr-zuò-shì?
他在那兒作事?
Where does he work? Wǒ-méi-
zuò-shì. 我没作事. I
don't have a job.
'ZUǑSHǑU₁ 左手 (N) left hand.
ZUÒTÁNHUÌ₃ 座談會 (N)
discussion, forum.
ZUÓTIAN₁ 昨天 (TW) yester-
day.
ZUÒWEI₃ 坐位 or ZUÒR 座兒
(N) seat, place to sit. Nǐ-géi-
wo-zhàn-yige-zuòwei. 你 給
我佔一個坐位. Save
a seat for me.
ZUÒ-WÉN₃ 作文 (VO) write a
composition.
(N) (1) composition (<u>as a course</u>
<u>in a school</u>) (M: táng 堂). (2)
composition (<u>writing</u>). (M: piān
篇).
ZUÒ-ZÌ₃ 作戲 (VO) act in a
play.
ZUÒXIA₁ 坐下 (RV) sit down.
ZUÒYÈ₃ 作業 (N) homework.
ZUÒYONG₃ 作用 (N) (1) action
(<u>by some natural force</u>). qǐ-huà-
xué-zuòyong 起化學作
用 cause a chemical action. (2)
effect. Tā-zhèiyangr-bàn yǒu
duó-dà-zuòyong-ne? 他這樣
辨有多大作用呢?

How big is the effect in doing
it this way? (3) motive, under-
lying purpose, function. Tāde-
xíngdòng méiyou-zuòyong. 他
的行動没有作用.
There's no motive for his action.
ZUǑYÒU₃ 左右 (AD) either
way, anyhow. Tā-juéde zuǒ-
yòu-dou-buhéshì. 他覺得
左右都不合適.He
feels that neither way is satisfactory. Wǒ-zuǒyou-méi-shì.
我左右没事. I have
nothing to do anyhow.
(-B) (1) <u>used after a noun, in-</u>
<u>dicates a place around the noun</u>,
in the vicinity of. zài-pùzi-zuǒ-
yòu 在鋪子左右 in
the vicinity of the store. (2)
<u>used after NU-M</u>, around, about
<u>the given figure</u>. (syn. shàng-
xià 上下). sānshikuai-qian-
zuǒyòu 三十塊錢左
右 in the neighborhood of
thirty dollars.
ZUÒ-ZHÀN₄ 作戰 (VO) wage
war.
ZUÒZHĚ₃ 作者 (N) author.
ZUÒ-ZHǓ₂ 作主 (<u>lit</u>.be the
boss) (VO) (1) be in position to
decide <u>something</u>. Nǐ-zuòdeliǎo-
zhǔ-ma? 你作得了主
嗎? Are you in a position to
decide? (2) decide, make a decision (<u>to do certain things</u>).
Wǒ-tì-ni-zuò-zhǔ. 我替你
作主. Let me decide it for
you.
ZUÒZUO₃ 做作 (TV) act un-
naturally. Tāde-tàidu shì-zuò-

Z

zuo-de, bu-zìran. 他 的 態
度 是 做 作 的，不 自
然 . Her manners are very put
on and are not natural.

ZŪQIAN$_2$ 租 錢 (N) money used
in paying rent for anything.

ZŪQIÚ$_3$ 足 球 (N) (1) football,
soccer ball (the ball). (M: zhǐ
隻). (2) football, soccer (the
game). (M: chǎng 場). dǎ-zúqíu
打 足 球 play football. tī-
zúqiú 踢 足 球 play soccer
or kick the football.

ZŪXIĀN$_4$ 祖 先 (N) ancestors.

ZÚYĬ$_4$ 足 以 (AD) enough to,
sufficiently. Nà-yě-jiu-zúyi-
mǎnyì-le. 那 也 就 足 以
滿 意 了 . That will be e-
nough to be satisfied.

ZŪZHǍNG$_4$ 組 長 (N) head of a
section in which the last syllable
of the Chinese is zǔ 組 .

ZŬZHI$_1$ 組 織 (TV) organize.
Wǒmen-děi-zǔzhi-qilai. 我 們
得 組 織 起 來 . We must
be organized.

(N) (1) organization. Zhèi-shi-
shénma-zǔzhi? 這 是 甚 麼
組 織 ? What kind of organization is this? (2) the Organization (referring to the Communist
Party). Děi-xiàng-zǔzhishang-
qǐngqiú. 得 向 組 織 上
請 求 . (We) must request
it from the Party.

'ZŬZHĬ$_4$ 阻 止 (TV) stop someone from doing something. Yào-'
shi-tamen-yídìng-yào-zuò, méi-
ren-néng-'zhǔzhǐ-tamen. 要 是
他 們 一 定 要 作 '沒
人 能 阻 止 他 們 . If
they insist on doing it, nobody
can stop them.

ZŬZONG$_3$ 祖 宗 (N) ancestors.

Z

627

COMPARATIVE TRANSCRIPTION TABLE

Pinyin Yale Wade-Giles

Pinyin	Yale	Wade-Giles	Pinyin	Yale	Wade-Giles
a	a	a	ci	tsz	tz'u
ai	ai	ai	cong	tsung	ts'ung
an	an	an	cou	tsou	ts'ou
ang	ang	ang	cu	tsu	ts'u
ao	au	ao	cuan	tswan	ts'uan
			cui	tswei	ts'ui
ba	ba	pa	cun	tswun	ts'un
bai	bai	pai	cuo	tswo	ts'o
ban	ban	pan			
bang	bang	pang	da	da	ta
bao	bau	pao	dai	dai	tai
bei	bei	pei	dan	dan	tan
ben	ben	pen	dang	dang	tang
beng	beng	peng	dao	dau	tao
bi	bi	pi	de	de	te
bian	byan	pien	dei	dei	tei
biao	byau	piao	deng	deng	teng
bie	bye	pieh	di	di	ti
bin	bin	pin	dian	dyan	tien
bing	bing	ping	diao	dyau	tiao
bo	bwo	po	die	dye	tieh
bou	bou	pou	ding	ding	ting
bu	bu	pu	diu	dyou	tiu
			dong	dung	tung
ca	tsa	ts'a	dou	dou	tou
cai	tsai	ts'ai	du	du	tu
can	tsan	ts'an	duan	dwan	tuan
cang	tsang	ts'ang	dui	dwei	tui
cao	tsao	ts'ao	dun	dwun	tun
ce	tse	ts'e	duo	dwo	to
cen	tsen	ts'en			
ceng	tseng	ts'eng	e	e	e, o
cha	cha	ch'a	ei	ei	ei
chai	chai	ch'ai	en	en	en
chan	chan	ch'an	eng	eng	eng
chang	chang	ch'ang	er	er	erh
chao	chau	ch'ao			
che	che	ch'e	fa	fa	fa
chen	chen	ch'en	fan	fan	fan
cheng	cheng	ch'eng	fang	fang	fang
chi	chr	ch'ih	fei	fei	fei
chong	chung	ch'ung	fen	fen	fen
chou	chou	ch'ou	feng	feng	feng
chu	chu	ch'u	fo	fwo	fo
chuai	chwai	ch'uai	fou	fou	fou
chuan	chwan	ch'uan	fu	fu	fu
chuang	chwang	ch'uang			
chui	chwei	ch'ui	ga	ga	ka
chun	chwun	ch'un	gai	gai	kai
chuo	chwo	ch'o	gan	gan	kan
			gang	gang	kang

Pinyin	Yale	Wade-Giles	Pinyin	Yale	Wade-Giles
gao	gau	kao	ke	ke	k'e, k'o
ge	ge	ke, ko	ken	ken	k'en
gei	gei	kei	keng	keng	k'eng
gen	gen	ken	kong	kung	k'ung
geng	geng	keng	kou	kou	k'ou
gong	gung	kung	ku	ku	k'u
gou	gou	kou	kua	kwa	k'ua
gu	gu	ku	kuai	kwai	k'uai
gua	gwa	kua	kuan	kwan	k'uan
guai	gwai	kuai	kuang	kwang	k'uang
guan	gwan	kuan	kui	kwei	k'uei
guang	gwang	kuang	kun	kwun	k'un
gui	gwei	kuei	kuo	kwo	k'uo
gun	gwun	kun			
guo	gwo	kuo	la	la	la
			lai	lai	lai
ha	ha	ha	lan	lan·	lan
hai	hai	hai	lang	lang	lang
han	han	han	lao	lau	lao
hang	hang	hang	le	le	le
hao	hau	hao	lei	lei	lei
he	he	he, ho	leng	leng	leng
hei	hei	hei	li	li	li
hen	hen	hen	lia	lya	lia
heng	heng	heng	lian	lyan	lien
hong	hung	hung	liang	lyang	liang
hou	hou	hou	liao	lyau	liao
hu	hu	hu	lie	lye	lieh
hua	hwa	hua	lin	lin	lin
huai	hwai	huai	ling	ling	ling
huan	hwan	huan	liu	lyou	liu
huang	hwang	huang	long	lung	lung
hui	hwei	hui	lou	lou	lou
hun	hwun	hun	lu	lu	lu
huo	hwo	huo	luan	lwan	luan
			lun	lwun	lun
ji	ji	chi	luo	lwo	lo
jia	jya	chia	lü	lyu	lü
jian	jyan	chien	lüan	lywan	lüan
jiang	jyang	chiang	lüe	lywe	lüeh
jiao	jyau	chiao			
jie	jye	chieh			
jin	jin	chin	ma	ma	ma
jing	jing	ching	mai	mai	mai
jiong	jyong	chiung	man	man	man
jiu	jyou	chiu	mang	mang	mang
ju	jyu	chü	mao	mau	mao
juan	jywan	chüan	mei	mei	mei
jue	jywe	chüeh	men	men	men
jun	jyun	chün	meng	meng	meng
			mi	mi	mi
ka	ka	k'a	mian	myan	mien
kai	kai	k'ai	miao	myau	miao
kan	kan	k'an	mie	mye	mieh
kang	kang	k'ang	min	min	min
kao	kau	k'ao	ming	ming	ming

Pinyin	Yale	Wade-Giles	Pinyin	Yale	Wade-Giles
miu	myou	miu	qiang	chyang	ch'iang
mo	mwo	mo	qiao	chyau	ch'iao
mou	mou	mou	qie	chye	ch'ieh
mu	mu	mu	qin	chin	ch'in
			qing	ching	ch'ing
na	na	na	qiong	chyung	ch'iung
nai	nai	nai	qiu	chyou	ch'iu
nan	nan	nan	qu	chyu	ch'ü
nang	nang	nang	quan	chywan	ch'üan
nao	nau	nao	que	chywe	ch'üeh
ne	ne	ne	qun	chyun	ch'ün
nei	nei	nei			
nen	nen	nen	ran	ran	jan
neng	neng	neng	rang	rang	jang
ni	ni	ni	rao	rau	jao
nian	nyan	nien	re	re	je
niang	nyang	niang	ren	ren	jen
niao	nyau	niao	reng	reng	jeng
nie	nye	nieh	ri	r	jih
nin	nin	nin	rong	rung	jung
ning	ning	ning	rou	rou	jou
niu	nyou	niu	ru	ru	ju
nong	nung	nung	ruan	rwan	juan
nou	nou	nou	rui	rwei	jui
nu	nu	nu	run	rwun	jun
nuan	nwan	nuan	ruo	rwo	jo
nun	nwun	nun			
nuo	nwo	no	sa	sa	sa
nü	nyu	nü	sai	sai	sai
nüe	nywe	nüeh	san	san	san
			sang	sang	sang
ou	ou	ou	sao	sau	sao
			se	se	se
pa	pa	p'a	sen	sen	sen
pai	pai	p'ai	seng	seng	seng
pan	pan	p'an	sha	sha	sha
pang	pang	p'ang	shai	shai	shai
pao	pau	p'ao	shan	shan	shan
pei	pei	p'ei	shang	shang	shang
pen	pen	p'en	shao	shau	shao
peng	peng	p'eng	she	she	she
pi	pi	p'i	shei	shei	shei
pian	pyan	p'ien	shen	shen	shen
piao	pyau	p'iao	sheng	sheng	sheng
pie	pye	p'ieh	shi	shr	shih
pin	pin	p'in	shou	shou	shou
ping	ping	p'ing	shu	shu	shu
po	pwo	p'o	shua	shwa	shua
pou	pou	p'ou	shuai	shwai	shuai
pu	pu	p'u	shuan	shwan	shuan
			shuang	shwang	shuang
qi	chi	ch'i	shui	shwei	shui
qia	chya	ch'ia	shun	shwun	shun
qian	chyan	ch'ien	shuo	shwo	shuo

Pinyin	Yale	Wade-Giles	Pinyin	Yale	Wade-Giles
si	sz	szu	ya	ya	ya
song	sung	sung	yai	yai	yai
sou	sou	sou	yan	yan	yen
su	su	su	yang	yang	yang
suan	swan	suan	yao	yau	yao
sui	swei	sui	ye	ye	yeh
sun	swun	sun	yi	yi	i
suo	swo	so	yin	yin	yin
			ying	ying	ying
ta	ta	t'a	yong	yung	yung
tai	tai	t'ai	you	you	yu
tan	tan	t'an	yu	yu	yü
tang	tang	t'ang	yuan	ywan	yüan
tao	tau	t'ao	yue	ywe	yüeh
te	te	t'e	yun	yun	yün
teng	teng	t'eng			
ti	ti	t'i	za	dza	tsa
tian	tyan	t'ien	zai	dzai	tsai
tiao	tyau	t'iao	zan	dzan	tsan
tie	tye	t'ieh	zang	dzang	tsang
ting	ting	t'ing	zao	dzau	tsao
tong	tung	t'ung	ze	dze	tse
tou	tou	t'ou	zei	dzei	tsei
tu	tu	t'u	zen	dzen	tsen
tuan	twan	t'uan	zeng	dzeng	tseng
tui	twei	t'ui	zha	ja	cha
tun	twun	t'un	zhai	jai	chai
tuo	two	t'o	zhan	jan	chan
			zhang	jang	chang
wa	wa	wa	zhao	jau	chao
wai	wai	wai	zhe	je	che
wan	wan	wan	zhei	jei	chei
wang	wang	wang	zhen	jen	chen
wei	wei	wei	zheng	jeng	cheng
wen	wen	wen	zhi	jr	chih
weng	weng	weng	zhong	jung	chung
wo	wo	wo	zhou	jou	chou
wu	wu	wu	zhu	ju	chu
			zhua	jwa	chua
xi	syi	hsi	zhuai	jwai	chuai
xia	sya	hsia	zhuan	jwan	chuan
xian	syan	hsien	zhuang	jwang	chuang
xiang	syang	hsiang	zhui	jwei	chui
xiao	syau	hsiao	zhun	jwun	chun
xie	sye	hsieh	zhuo	jwo	cho
xin	syin	hsin	zi	dz	tzu
xing	sying	hsing	zong	dzung	tsung
xiong	syung	hsiung	zou	dzou	tsou
xiu	syou	hsiu	zu	dzu	tsu
xu	syu	hsü	zuan	dzwan	tsuan
xuan	sywan	hsüan	zui	dzwei	tsui
xue	sywe	hsüeh	zun	dzwun	tsua
xun	syun	hsün	zuo	dzwo	tso

COMPARATIVE TRANSCRIPTION TABLE

Wade-Giles   Pinyin   Yale

Wade-Giles	Pinyin	Yale	Wade-Giles	Pinyin	Yale
a	a	a	ch'u	chu	chu
ai	ai	ai	chua	zhua	jwa
an	an	an	chuai	zhuai	jwai
ang	ang	ang	ch'uai	chuai	chwai
ao	ao	au	chuan	zhuan	jwan
			ch'uan	chuan	chwan
cha	zha	ja	chuang	zhuang	jwang
ch'a	cha	cha	ch'uang	chuang	chwang
chai	zhai	jai	chui	zhui	jwei
ch'ai	chai	chai	ch'ui	chui	chwei
chan	zhan	jan	chun	zhun	jwun
ch'an	chan	chan	ch'un	chun	chwun
chang	zhang	jang	chung	zhong	jung
ch'ang	chang	chang	ch'ung	chong	chung
chao	zhao	jau	chü	ju	jyù
ch'ao	chao	chau	ch'ü	qu	chyu
che	zhe	je	chüan	juan	jywan
ch'e	che	che	ch'üan	quan	chywan
chei	zhei	jei	chüeh	jue	jywe
chen	zhen	jen	ch'üeh	que	chywe
ch'en	chen	chen	chün	jun	jyun
cheng	zheng	jeng	ch'ün	qun	chyun
ch'eng	cheng	cheng			
chi	ji	ji	e, o	e	e
ch'i	qi	chi	ei	ei	ei
chia	jia	jya	en	en	en
ch'ia	qia	chya	eng	eng	eng
chiang	jiang	jyang	erh	er	er
ch'iang	qiang	chyang			
chiao	jiao	jyau	fa	fa	fa
ch'iao	qiao	chyau	fan	fan	fan
chieh	jie	jye	fang	fang	fang
ch'ieh	qie	chye	fei	fei	fei
chien	jian	jyan	fen	fen	fen
ch'ien	qian	chyan	feng	feng	feng
chih	zhi	jr	fo	fo	fwo
ch'ih	chi	chr	fou	fou	fou
chin	jin	jin	fu	fu	fu
ch'in	qin	chin			
ching	jing	jing	ha	ha	ha
ch'ing	qing	ching	hai	hai	hai
chiu	jiu	jyou	han	han	han
ch'iu	qiu	chyou	hang	hang	hang
chiung	jiong	jyung	hao	hao	hau
ch'iung	qiong	chyung	hei	hei	hei
cho	zhuo	jwo	hen	hen	hen
ch'o	chuo	chwo	heng	heng	heng
chou	zhou	jou	ho	he	he
ch'ou	chou	chou	hou	hou	hou
chu	zhu	ju	hsi	xi	syi

Wade-Giles	Pinyin	Yale	Wade-Giles	Pinyin	Yale
hsia	xia	sya	k'o, k'e	ke	ke
hsiang	xiang	syang	kou	gou	gou
hsiao	xiao	syau	k'ou	kou	kou
hsieh	xie	sye	ku	gu	gu
hsien	xian	syan	k'u	ku	ku
hsin	xin	syin	kua	gua	gwa
hsing	xing	sying	k'ua	kua	kwa
hsiu	xiu	syou	kuai	guai	gwai
hsiung	xiong	syung	k'uai	kuai	kwai
hsü	xu	syu	kuan	guan	gwan
hsüan	xuan	sywan	k'uan	kuan	kwan
hsüeh	xue	sywe	kuang	guang	gwang
hsün	xun	syun	k'uang	kuang	kwang
hu	hu	hu	kuei	gui	gwei
hua	hua	hwa	k'uei	kui	kwei
huai	huai	hwai	kun	gun	gwun
huan	huan	hwan	k'un	kun	kwun
huang	huang	hwang	kung	gong	gung
hui	hui	hwei	k'ung	kong	kung
hun	hun	hwun	kuo	guo	gwo
hung	hong	hung	k'uo	kuo	kwo
huo	huo	hwo			
			la	la	la
i, yi	yi	yi	lai	lai	lai
			lan	lan	lan
jan	ran	ran	lang	lang	lang
jang	rang	rang	lao	lao	lau
jao	rao	rau	le	le	le
je	re	re	lei	lei	lei
jen	ren	ren	leng	leng	leng
jeng	reng	reng	li	li	li
jih	ri	r	lia	lia	lya
jo	ruo	rwo	liang	liang	lyang
jou	rou	rou	liao	liao	lyau
ju	ru	ru	lieh	lie	lye
juan	ruan	rwan	lien	lian	lyan
jui	rui	rwei	lin	lin	lin
jun	run	rwun	ling	ling	ling
jung	rong	rung	liu	liu	lyou
			lo	luo	lwo
ka	ga	ga	lou	lou	lou
k'a	ka	ka	lu	lu	lu
kai	gai	gai	luan	luan	lwan
k'ai	kai	kai	lun	lun	lwun
kan	gan	gan	lung	long	lung
k'an	kan	kan	lü	lü	lyu
kang	gang	gang	lüan	lüan	lywan
k'ang	kang	kang	lüeh	lüe	lywe
kao	gao	gau			
k'ao	kao	kau	ma	ma	ma
ke, ko	ge	ge	mai	mai	mai
k'e, k'o	ke	ke	man	man	man
kei	gei	gei	mang	mang	mang
ken	gen	gen	mao	mao	mau
k'en	ken	ken	mei	mei	mei
keng	geng	geng	men	men	men
k'eng	keng	keng	meng	meng	meng
ko, ke	ge	ge	mi	mi	mi

Wade-Giles	Pinyin	Yale	Wade-Giles	Pinyin	Yale
miao	miao	myau	p'iao	piao	pyau
mieh	mie	mye	pieh	bie	bye
mien	mian	myan	p'ieh	pie	pye
min	min	min	pien	bian	byan
ming	ming	ming	p'ien	pian	pyan
miu	miu	myou	pin	bin	bin
mo	mo	mwo	p'in	pin	pin
mou	mou	mou	ping	bing	bing
mu	mu	mu	p'ing	ping	ping
			po	bo	bwo
na	na	na	p'o	po	pwo
nai	nai	nai	pou	bou	bou
nan	nan	nan	p'ou	pou	pou
nang	nang	nang	pu	bu	bu
nao	nao	nau	p'u	pu	pu
ne	ne	ne			
nei	nei	nei	sa	sa	sa
nen	nen	nen	sai	sai	sai
neng	neng	neng	san	san	san
ni	ni	ni	sang	sang	sang
niang	niang	nyang	sao	sao	sau
niao	niao	nyau	se	se	se
nieh	nie	nye	sen	sen	sen
nien	nian	nyan	seng	seng	seng
nin	nin	nin	sha	sha	sha
ning	ning	ning	shai	shai	shai
niu	niu	nyou	shan	shan	shan
no	nuo	nwo	shang	shang	shang
nou	nou	nou	shao	shao	shau
nu	nu	nu	she	she	she
nuan	nuan	nwan	shei	shei	shei
nun	nun	nwun	shen	shen	shen
nung	nong	nung	sheng	sheng	sheng
nü	nü	nyu	shih	shi	shr
nüeh	nüe	nywe	shou	shou	shou
			shu	shu	shu
o, e	e	e	shua	shua	shwa
ou	ou	ou	shuai	shuai	shwai
			shuan	shuan	shwan
pa	ba	ba	shuang	shuang	shwang
p'a	pa	pa	shui	shui	shwei
pai	bai	bai	shun	shun	shwun
p'ai	pai	pai	shuo	shuo	shwo
pan	ban	ban	so	suo	swo
p'an	pan	pan	sou	sou	sou
pang	bang	bang	ssu, szu	si	sz
p'ang	pang	pang	su	su	su
pao	bao	bau	suan	suan	swan
p'ao	pao	pau	sui	sui	swei
pei	bei	bei	sun	sun	swun
p'ei	pei	pei	sung	song	sung
pen	ben	ben	szu, ssu	si	sz
p'en	pen	pen			
peng	beng	beng	ta	da	da
p'eng	peng	peng	t'a	ta	ta
pi	bi	bi	tai	dai	dai
p'i	pi	pi	t'ai	tai	tai
piao	biao	byau	tan	dan	dan

Wade-Giles	Pinyin	Yale	Wade-Giles	Pinyin	Yale
t'an	tan	tan	ts'u	cu	tsu
tang	dang	dang	tsuan	zuan	dzwan
t'ang	tang	tang	ts'uan	cuan	tswan
tao	dao	dau	tsui	zui	dzwei
t'ao	tao	tau	ts'ui	cui	tswei
te	de	de	tsun	zun	dzwun
t'e	te	te	ts'un	cun	tswun
tei	dei	dei	tsung	zong	dzung
teng	deng	deng	ts'ung	cong	tsung
t'eng	teng	teng	tu	du	du
ti	di	di	t'u	tu	tu
t'i	ti	ti	tuan	duan	dwan
tiao	diao	dyau	t'uan	tuan	twan
t'iao	tiao	tyau	tui	dui	dwei
tieh	die	dye	t'ui	tui	twei
t'ieh	tie	tye	tun	dun	dwun
tien	dian	dyan	t'un	tun	twun
t'ien	tian	tyan	tung	dong	dung
ting	ding	ding	t'ung	tong	tung
t'ing	ting	ting	tzu	zi	dz
tiu	diu	dyou	tz'u	ci	tsz
to	duo	dwo			
t'o	tuo	two	wa	wa	wa
tou	dou	dou	wai	wai	wai
t'ou	tou	tou	wan	wan	wan
tsa	za	dza	wang	wang	wang
ts'a	ca	tsa	wei	wei	wei
tsai	zai	dzai	wen	wen	wen
ts'ai	cai	tsai	weng	weng	weng
tsan	zan	dzan	wo	wo	wo
ts'an	can	tsan	wu	wu	wu
tsang	zang	dzang			
ts'ang	cang	tsang	ya	ya	ya
tsao	zao	dzau	yai	yai	yai
ts'ao	cao	tsau	yang	yang	yang
tse	ze	dze	yao	yao	yau
ts'e	ce	tse	yeh	ye	ye
tsei	zei	dzei	yen	yan	yan
tsen	zen	dzen	yi, i	yi	yi
ts'en	cen	tsen	yin	yin	yin
tseng	zeng	dzeng	ying	ying	ying
ts'eng	ceng	tseng	yu	you	you
tso	zuo	dzwo	yung	yong	yung
ts'o	cuo	tswo	yü	yu	yu
tsou	zou	dzou	yüan	yuan	ywan
ts'ou	cou	tsou	yüeh	yue	ywe
tsu	zu	dzu	yün	yun	yun

COMPARATIVE TRANSCRIPTION TABLE

Yale Wade-Giles Pinyin

Yale	Wade-Giles	Pinyin	Yale	Wade-Giles	Pinyin
a	a	a	chye	ch'ieh	qie
ai	ai	ai	chyou	ch'iu	qiu
an	an	an	chyu	ch'ü	qu
ang	ang	ang	chyun	ch'ün	qun
au	ao	ao	chyung	ch'iung	qiong
			chywan	ch'üan	quan
ba	pa	ba	chywe	ch'üeh	que
bai	pai	bai			
ban	pan	ban	da	ta	da
bang	pang	bang	dai	tai	dai
bau	pao	bao	dan	tan	dan
bei	pei	bei	dang	tang	dang
ben	pen	ben	dau	tao	dao
beng	peng	beng	de	te	de
bi	pi	bi	dei	tei	dei
bin	pin	bin	deng	teng	deng
bing	ping	bing	di	ti	di
bou	pou	bou	ding	ting	ding
bu	pu	bu	dou	tou	dou
bwo	po	bo	du	tu	du
byan	pien	bian	dung	tung	dong
byau	piao	biao	dwan	tuan	duan
bye	pieh	bie	dwei	tui	dui
			dwo	to	duo
cha	ch'a	cha	dwun	tun	dun
chai	ch'ai	chai	dyan	tien	dian
chan	ch'an	chan	dyau	tiao	diao
chang	ch'ang	chang	dye	tieh	die
chau	ch'ao	chao	dyou	tiu	diu
che	ch'e	che	dz	tzu	zi
chen	ch'en	chen	dza	tsa	za
cheng	ch'eng	cheng	dzai	tsai	zai
chi	ch'i	qi	dzan	tsan	zan
chin	ch'in	qin	dzang	tsang	zang
ching	ch'ing	qing	dzau	tsao	zao
chou	ch'ou	chou	dze	tse	ze
chr	ch'ih	chi	dzei	tsei	zei
chu	ch'u	chu	dzen	tsen	zen
chung	ch'ung	chong	dzeng	tseng	zeng
chwai	ch'uai	chuai	dzou	tsou	zou
chwan	ch'uan	chuan	dzu	tsu	zu
chwang	ch'uang	chuang	dzung	tsung	zong
chwei	ch'ui	chui	dzwan	tsuan	zuan
chwo	ch'o	chuo	dzwei	tsui	zui
chwun	ch'un	chun	dzwo	tso	zuo
chya	ch'ia	qia	dzwun	tsun	zun
chyan	ch'ien	qian			
chyang	ch'iang	qiang	e	e, o	e
chyau	ch'iao	qiao	ei	ei	ei

Yale	Wade-Giles	Pinyin		Yale	Wade-Giles	Pinyin
en	en	en		jau	chao	zhao
eng	eng	eng		je	che	zhe
er	erh	er		jei	chei	zhei
				jen	chen	zhen
fa	fa	fa		jeng	cheng	zheng
fan	fan	fan		ji	chi	ji
fang	fang	fang		jin	chin	jin
fei	fei	fei		jing	ching	jing
fen	fen	fen		jou	chou	zhou
feng	feng	feng		jr	chih	zhi
fou	fou	fou		ju	chu	zhu
fu	fu	fu		jung	chung	zhong
fwo	fo	fo		jwa	chua	zhua
				jwai	chuai	zhuai
ga	ka	ga		jwan	chuan	zhuan
gai	kai	gai		jwang	chuang	zhuang
gan	kan	gan		jwei	chui	zhui
gang	kang	gang		jwo	cho	zhuo
gau	kao	gao		jwun	chun	zhun
ge	ke, ko	ge		jya	chia	jia
gei	kei	gei		jyan	chien	jian
gen	ken	gen		jyang	chiang	jiang
geng	keng	geng		jyau	chiao	jiao
gou	kou	gou		jye	chieh	jie
gu	ku	gu		jyou	chiu	jiu
gung	kung	gong		jyu	chü	ju
gwa	kua	gua		jyun	chün	jun
gwai	kuai	guai		jyung	chiung	jiong
gwan	kuan	guan		jywan	chüan	juan
gwang	kuang	guang		jywe	chüeh	jue
gwei	kuei	gui				
gwo	kuo	guo		ka	k'a	ka
gwun	kun	gun		kai	k'ai	kai
				kan	k'an	kan
ha	ha	ha		kang	k'ang	kang
hai	hai	hai		kau	k'ao	kao
han	han	han		ke	k'e, k'o	ke
hang	hang	hang		ken	k'en	ken
hau	hao	hao		keng	k'eng	keng
he	ho	he		kou	k'ou	kou
hei	hei	hei		ku	k'u	ku
hen	hen	hen		kung	k'ung	kong
heng	heng	heng		kwa	k'ua	kua
hou	hou	hou		kwai	k'uai	kuai
hu	hu	hu		kwan	k'uan	kuan
hung	hung	hong		kwang	k'uang	kuang
hwa	hua	hua		kwei	k'uei	kui
hwai	huai	huai		kwo	k'uo	kuo
hwan	huan	huan		kwun	k'un	kun
hwang	huang	huang				
hwei	hui	hui		la	la	la
hwo	huo	huo		lai	lai	lai
hwun	hun	hun		lan	lan	lan
				lang	lang	lang
ja	cha	zha		lau	lao	lao
jai	chai	zhai		le	le	le
jan	chan	zhan		lei	lei	lei
jang	chang	zhang		leng	leng	leng

Yale	Wade-Giles	Pinyin	Yale	Wade-Giles	Pinyin
li	li	li	nyau	niao	niao
lin	lin	lin	nye	nieh	nie
ling	ling	ling	nyou	niu	·niu
lou	lou	lou	nyu	nü	nü
lu	lu	lu	nywe	nüeh	nüe
lung	lung	long			
lwan	luan	luan	ou	ou	ou
lwo	lo	luo			
lwun	lun	lun	pa	p'a	pa
lya	lia	lia	pai	p'ai	pai
lyan	lien	lian	pan	p'an	pan
lyang	liang	liang	pang	p'ang	pang
lyau	liao	liao	pau	p'ao	pao
lye	lieh	lie	pei	p'ei	pei
lyou	liu	liu	pen	p'en	pen
lyu	lü	lü	peng	p'eng	peng
lywan	lüan	lüan	pi	p'i	pi
lywe	lüeh	lüe	pin	p'in	pin
			ping	p'ing	ping
ma	ma	ma	pou	p'ou	pou
mai	mai	mai	pu	p'u	pu
man	man	man	pwo	p'o	po
mang	mang	mang	pyan	p'ien	pian
mau	mao	mao	pyau	p'iao	piao
mei	mei	mei	pye	p'ieh	pie
men	men	men			
meng	meng	meng	r	jih	ri
mi	mi	mi	ran	jan	ran
min	min	min	rang	jang	rang
ming	ming	ming	rau	jao	rao
mou	mou	mou	re	je	re
mu	mu	mu	ren	jen	ren
mwo	mo	mo	reng	jeng	reng
myan	mien	mian	rou	jou	rou
myau	miao	miao	ru	ju	ru
mye	mieh	mie	rung	jung	rong
myou	miu	miu	rwan	juan	ruan
			rwei	jui	rui
na	na	na	rwo	jo	ruo
nai	nai	nai	rwun	jun	run
nan	nan	nan			
nang	nang	nang	sa	sa	sa
nau	nao	nao	sai	sai	sai
ne	ne	ne	san	san	san
nei	nei	nei	sang	sang	sang
nen	nen	nen	sau	sao	sao
neng	neng	neng	se	se	se
ni	ni	ni	sen	sen	sen
nin	nin	nin	seng	seng	seng
ning	ning	ning	sha	sha	sha
nou	nou	nou	shai	shai	shai
nu	nu	nu ˅	shan	shan	shan
nung	nung	nong	shang	shang	shang
nwan	nuan	nuan	shau	shao	shao
nwo	no	nuo	she	she	she
nwun	nun	nun	shei	shei	shei
nyan	nien	nian	shen	shen	shen
nyang	niang	niang	sheng	sheng	sheng

Yale	Wade-Giles	Pinyin	Yale	Wade-Giles	Pinyin
shou	shou	shou	tsau	ts'ao	cao
shr	shih	shi	tse	ts'e	ce
shu	shu	shu	tsen	ts'en	cen
shwa	shua	shua	tseng	ts'eng	ceng
shwai	shuai	shuai	tsou	ts'ou	cou
shwan	shuan	shuan	tsu	ts'u	cu
shwang	shuang	shuang	tsung	ts'ung	cong
shwei	shui	shui	tswan	ts'uan	cuan
shwo	shuo	shuo	tswei	ts'ui	cui
shwun	shun	shun	tswo	ts'o	cuo
sou	sou	sou	tswun	ts'un	cun
su	su	su	tsz	tz'u	ci
sung	sung	song	tu	t'u	tu
swan	suan	suan	tung	t'ung	tong
swei	sui	sui	twan	t'uan	tuan
swo	so	suo	twei	t'ui	tui
swun	sun	sun	two	t'o	tuo
sya	hsia	xia	twun	t'un	tun
syan	hsien	xian	tyan	t'ien	tian
syang	hsiang	xiang	tyau	t'iao	tiao
syau	hsiao	xiao	tye	t'ieh	tie
sye	hsieh	xie			
syi	hsi	xi	wa	wa	wa
syin	hsin	xin	wai	wai	wai
sying	hsing	xing	wan	wan	wan
syou	hsiu	xiu	wang	wang	wang
syu	hsü	xu	wei	wei	wei
syun	hsün	xun	wen	wen	wen
syung	hsiung	xiong	weng	weng	weng
sywan	hsüan	xuan	wo	wo	wo
sywe	hsüeh	xue	wu	wu	wu
sz	ssu, szu	si			
			ya	ya	ya
ta	t'a	ta	yai	yai	yai
tai	t'ai	tai	yan	yen	yan
tan	t'an	tan	yang	yang	yang
tang	t'ang	tang	yau	yao	yao
tau	t'ao	tao	ye	yeh	ye
te	t'e	te	yi	yi, i	yi
teng	t'eng	teng	yin	yin	yin
ti	t'i	ti	ying	ying	ying
ting	t'ing	ting	you	yu	you
tou	t'ou	tou	yu	yü	yu
tsa	ts'a	ca	yun	yün	yun
tsai	ts'ai	cai	yung	yung	yong
tsan	ts'an	can	ywan	yüan	yuan
tsang	ts'ang	cang	ywe	yüeh	yue

CHARACTER INDEX

The number before the decimal point is the radical number; the number after the decimal point is the number of residue strokes. The number after the dash is the total number of strokes. The characters listed below are the first syllable of each entry.

18. 6-8	刷	shuā	20. 3-5	包	bāo	28. 9-11	参 cān
18. 7-9	剌	lá	20. 4-5	匈	xiōng		**29** 又
18. 7-9	前	qián	**21** 匕			29. 0-2	又 yòu
18. 7-9	剃	tì	21. 3-5	北	běi	29. 1-3	义 chā
18. 7-9	削	xiāo	21. 9-11	匙	chí	29. 2-4	及 jí
18. 8-10	剛	gāng	**22** 匚			29. 2-4	反 fǎn
18. 8-10	剔	tī	22. 5-7	匣	xiá	29. 2-4	友 yǒu
18. 9-11	剝	bāo	22. 8-10	匪	fěi	29. 6-8	叔 shū
		bō	22. 11-13	匯	huì	29. 6-8	受 shòu
18. 9-11	副	fù	**23** 匸			**30** 口
18. 9-11	剪	jiǎn	23. 2-4	匹	pǐ	30. 0-3	口 kǒu
18. 10-12	創	chuǎng			pī	30. 2-5	只 zhǐ
18. 10-12	割	gē	23. 9-11	區	qū	30. 2-5	叼 diāo
18. 10-12	剩	shèng	**24** 十			30. 2-5	召 zhāo
18. 12-14	劃	huà	24. 0-2	十	shí	30. 2-5	古 gǔ
18. 13-15	劇	jù	24. 1-3	千	qiān	30. 2-5	句 jù
18. 13-15	劍	jiàn	24. 2-4	升	shēng	30. 2-5	可 kě
18. 13-15	劈	pī	24. 2-4	午	wǔ	30. 2-5	另 lìng
19 力			24. 3-5	半	bàn	30. 2-5	史 shǐ
19. 0-2	力	lì	24. 6-8	卑	bēi	30. 2-5	司 sī
19. 3-5	功	gōng	24. 6-8	協	xié	30. 2-5	台 tái
19. 3-5	加	jiā	24. 7-9	南	nán	30. 2-5	右 yòu
19. 5-7	劫	jié	24. 10-12	博	bó	30. 3-6	吃 chī
19. 5-7	努	nǔ	**25** 卜			30. 3-6	吊 diào
19. 6-8	效	xiào	25. 3-5	占	zhān	30. 3-6	各 gè
19. 7-9	勁	jìn	25. 3-5	卡	qiǎ	30. 3-6	合 hé
19. 7-9	勉	miǎn	**26** 卩			30. 3-6	吉 jí
19. 7-9	勇	yǒng	26. 4-6	危	wēi	30. 3-6	叫 jiào
19. 9-11	動	dòng	26. 4-6	印	yìn	30. 3-6	名 míng
19. 9-11	務	wù	26. 5-7	即	jí	30. 3-6	向 xiàng
19. 10-12	勞	láo	26. 5-7	卻	què	30. 3-6	吐 tǔ
19. 10-12	勝	shèng	26. 6-8	卷	juǎn	30. 3-6	同 tóng
19. 11-13	勢	shì			juàn	30. 3-6	吆 yāo
19. 11-13	勤	qín	26. 7-9	卸	xiè	30. 4-7	呀 yā
19. 14-16	勳	xūn	**27** 厂			30. 4-7	吵 chǎo
19. 18-20	勸	quàn	27. 7-9	厚	hòu	30. 4-7	呈 chéng
20 勹			27. 8-10	原	yuán	30. 4-7	吹 chuī
20. 1-3	勺	sháo	27. 9-11	厠	cè	30. 4-7	吩 fēn
20. 2-4	勾	gōu	**28** 厶			30. 4-7	否 fǒu
20. 2-4	勻	yún	28. 3-5	去	qù	30. 4-7	告 gào

30.4-7	含	hán	30.7-10	哼	heng	30.12-15	嘿 hēi
30.4-7	吝	lìn	30.7-10	唧	jī	30.12-15	噘 juē
30.4-7	吸	xī	30.7-10	哭	kū	30.12-15	嘹 liáo
30.4-7	吞	tūn	30.7-10	哪	něi / nǎ	30.12-15	嘔 ou / ōu / óu / ǒu / òu
30.5-8	周	zhōu	30.7-10	哦	e		
30.5-8	咒	zhòu	30.7-10	唐	táng		
30.5-8	咕	gū	30.8-11	啊	a	30.12-15	噴 pēn
30.5-8	呵	hā	30.8-11	唱	chàng	30.13-16	嘴 zuǐ
30.5-8	和	hàn / hé / huò	30.8-11	啐	cuì	30.13-16	噸 dūn
			30.8-11	唎	lǎ	30.13-16	嚔 tì
30.5-8	呼	hū	30.8-11	啃	kěn	30.14-17	嚐 cháng
30.5-8	咖	kā	30.8-11	商	shāng	30.14-17	嚄 huò
30.5-8	命	mìng	30.8-11	啤	pí	30.14-17	嚇 xià
30.5-8	呢	ne	30.8-11	售	shòu	30.16-19	嚥 yàn
30.5-8	咻	wài	30.8-11	唯	wéi	30.17-20	嚼 jiáo
30.5-8	味	wèi	30.8-11	問	wèn	30.17-20	嚷 rǎng
30.5-8	咱	zá / zán	30.8-11	啟	qǐ	30.17-20	嚴 yán
30.6-9	哀	āi	30.9-12	喘	chuǎn	30.19-22	囉 luó
30.6-9	哆	duō	30.9-12	單	dān	30.21-24	囑 zhǔ
30.6-9	哎	āi / ái / ǎi / ài / ēi / éi / ěi / èi	30.9-12	喊	hǎn	**31** 口	
			30.9-12	喝	hē	31.2-5	四 sè / sì
			30.9-12	喚	huàn	31.2-5	囚 qiū
			30.9-12	喪	sàng	31.3-6	回 huí
			30.9-12	喂	wèi	31.3-6	因 yīn
			30.9-12	喜	xǐ	31.4-7	困 kùn
30.6-9	哏	gén	30.9-12	唾	tù	31.4-7	囤 tún
30.6-9	哈	hā	30.9-12	啞	yǎ	31.5-8	固 gù
30.6-9	咳	hāi / hài / ké	30.10-13	嗒	dā	31.8-11	國 guó
			30.10-13	嗯	en	31.8-11	圈 juàn / quān
30.6-9	咳	ké	30.10-13	嗎	ma		
30.6-9	哄	hǒng	30.10-13	嗓	sǎng	31.10-13	圍 wéi
30.6-9	品	pǐn	30.10-13	嗜	shì	31.10-13	園 yuán
30.6-9	哇	wa	30.10-13	嗆	qiàng	31.10-13	圓 yuán
30.6-9	咽	yàn	30.11-14	嘟	dū	31.11-14	圖 tú
30.6-9	咬	yào	30.11-14	喉	hóu	31.11-14	團 tuán
30.6-9	咧	lie	30.11-14	嘆	tàn	**32** 土	
30.7-10	哲	zhé	30.11-14	嘖	tsk	32.0-3	土 tǔ
30.7-10	啾	dí	30.12-15	嘲	cháo	32.3-6	在 zài
30.7-10	哥	gē	30.12-15	嘶	ss	32.3-6	地 di

40.4-7	完	wán	42.1-4	少	shǎo / shào	49.0-3	己	jǐ
40.5-8	宗	zōng	42.3-6	尖	jiān	49.1-4	巴	bā
40.5-8	定	dìng	**43**	尢		**50**	巾	
40.5-8	官	guān	43.3-6	尥	liào	50.2-5	布	bù
40.6-9	客	kè	43.9-12	就	jiù	50.2-5	市	shì
40.6-9	宣	xuān	**44**	尸		50.3-6	帆	fān
40.7-10	害	hài	44.1-4	尺	chǐ	50.4-7	希	xī
40.7-10	家	jiā	44.2-5	尼	ní	50.5-8	帘	lián
40.7-10	容	róng	44.4-7	局	jú	50.5-8	帖	tiě
40.7-10	宴	yàn	44.4-7	尿	niào / suī	50.6-9	帝	dì
40.8-11	宰	zǎi	44.4-7	屁	pì	50.7-10	師	shī
40.8-11	寂	jì	44.4-7	尾	wěi / yǐ	50.7-10	席	xí
40.8-11	寄	jì	44.5-8	屆	jié	50.8-11	常	cháng
40.8-11	宿	sù	44.5-8	居	jū	50.8-11	帶	dài
40.9-12	寓	yù	44.6-9	屎	shǐ	50.8-11	帳	zhàng
40.9-12	富	fù	44.7-10	展	zhǎn	50.9-12	幅	fú
40.9-12	寒	hán	44.12-15	層	céng	50.14-17	幫	bāng
40.10-13	寬	kuān	44.18-21	屬	shǔ	**51**	干	
40.11-14	寡	guǎ	**46**	山		51.0-3	干	gān
40.11-14	寧	nìng	46.0-3	山	shān	51.2-5	平	píng
40.11-14	實	shí	46.4-7	岔	chà	51.3-6	年	nián
40.12-15	審	shěn	46.5-8	岸	àn	51.5-8	幸	xìng
40.12-15	寫	xiě	46.6-9	炭	tàn	51.10-13	幹	gàn
40.13-16	憲	xiàn	46.7-10	島	dào	**52**	幺	
40.16-19	寶	bǎo	46.8-11	崗	gǎng	52.0-3	幺	yāo
41	寸		**47**	巛		52.1-4	幻	huàn
41.0-3	寸	cùn	47.3-6	州	zhōu	52.2-5	幼	yòu
41.6-9	封	fēng	47.3-6	巡	zún	52.6-9	幽	yōu
41.7-10	尅	ké	**48**	工		52.9-12	幾	jǐ
41.7-10	射	shè	48.0-3	工	gōng	**53**	广	
41.8-11	將	jiāng / jiǎng / jiàng	48.2-5	左	zuǒ	53.4-7	序	xù
41.8-11	專	zhuān	48.2-5	巧	qiǎo	53.5-8	店	diàn
41.9-12	尋	xín	48.2-5	巨	jiǔ	53.5-8	底	dǐ
41.9-12	尊	zūn	48.7-10	差	chā / chà / chāi	53.5-8	府	fǔ
41.11-14	對	duì				53.6-9	度	dù
41.12-15	導	dǎo				53.7-10	座	zuò
42	小		**49**	己		53.9-12	廊	láng
42.0-3	小	xiāo	49.0-3	己	yǐ	53.10-13	廚	chú
						53.11-14	廣	guǎng
						53.12-15	廠	chǎng

53.12-15	廢	fèi	60.12-15	徹	chè	61.9-13	想 xiǎng
53.12-15	廟	miào	60.12-15	德	dé	61.9-13	意 yì
54	廴		60.13-16	徼	jiǎo	61.9-13	愚 yú
54.5-8	延	yán	**61**	心		61.10-13	慌 huāng
54.6-9	建	jiàn	61.0-4	心	xīn	61.10-14	慶 qìng
55	廾		61.1-5	必	bì	61.10-14	態 tài
55.4-7	弄	nòng	61.3-6	忙	máng	61.11-14	慘 cǎn
		nèng	61.3-7	忌	jì	61.11-14	慚 cán
57	弓		61.3-7	忍	rěn	61.11-14	慣 guàn
57.0-3	弓	gōng	61.3-7	忘	wàng	61.11-14	慷 kāng
57.1-4	引	yǐn	61.3-7	志	zhì	61.11-14	慢 màn
57.4-7	弟	dì	61.4-7	快	kuài	61.11-15	憋 biē
57.5-8	弦	xián	61.4-8	忽	hū	61.11-15	慰 wèi
57.7-10	弱	ruò	61.4-8	念	niàn	61.11-15	憂 yōu
57.8-11	強	qiáng	61.4-8	忠	zhōng	61.12-15	慪 òu
57.8-11	張	zhāng	61.5-8	怪	guài	61.12-16	憑 píng
57.9-12	弼	zhōu	61.5-8	怕	pà	61.13-16	懊 ào
57.11-14	彆	biē	61.5-8	怯	qiè	61.13-16	懂 dǒng
57.12-15	彈	dàn	61.5-8	性	xìng	61.13-16	懈 xiè
		tán	61.5-9	急	jí	61.13-17	懇 kěn
57.19-22	彎	wān	61.5-9	思	sī	61.13-17	應 yīng
59	彡		61.5-9	怨	yuàn		yìng
59.4-7	形	xíng	61.5-9	怎	zěn	61.14-17	懦 nuò
59.8-11	彩	cǎi	61.6-9	恨	hèn	61.15-18	懶 lǎn
59.12-15	影	yǐng	61.6-9	恢	huī	61.15-19	懲 chéng
60	彳		61.6-9	恰	qià	61.16-19	懷 huái
60.4-7	彷	fǎng	61.6-10	恭	gōng	61.16-20	懸 xuán
60.5-8	彼	bǐ	61.6-10	恐	kǒng	61.19-23	戀 liàn
60.5-8	往	wǎng	61.7-10	悄	qiào		luàn
60.5-8	征	zhēng	61.7-11	您	nín	**62**	戈
60.6-9	待	dài	61.8-11	惦	diàn	62.2-6	成 chéng
60.6-9	後	hòu	61.8-11	情	qíng	62.3-7	戒 jiè
60.6-9	律	lǜ	61.8-12	悲	bēi	62.3-7	我 wǒ
60.6-9	很	hěn	61.9-12	惱	nǎo	62.4-8	或 huò
60.7-10	徑	jìng	61.9-12	愉	yú	62.10-14	截 jié
60.7-10	徒	tú	61.9-13	愛	ài	62.12-16	戰 zhàn
60.8-11	從	cóng	61.9-13	慈	cí	62.13-17	戴 dài
60.8-11	得	dé	61.9-13	惡	è	62.13-17	戲 xì
		děi	61.9-13	感	gǎn	62.14-18	戳 chuō
60.9-12	循	xún	61.9-13	惹	rě		
60.10-13	微	wēi					

64.11-14	撇	piě	64.17-20	攔	lán	68.7-11	斜	xié
64.11-14	摔	shuāi	64.17-20	攏	lǒng	68.9-13	斟	zhēn
64.11-14	摘	zhāi	64.18-21	攝	shè	69 斤		
64.11-14	摺	zhé zhě	64.18-21	攙	chān	69.0-4	斤	jīn
64.11-15	摩	mó	64.19-22	攤	tān	69.4-8	爷	fǔ
64.12-15	撣	dǎn	64.19-22	攢	zǎn	69.8-12	斯	sī
64.12-15	撲	pū	64.20-23	攥	zuàn	69.9-13	新	xīn
64.12-15	撐	chēng	64.20-23	攪	jiǎo	69.14-18	斷	duàn
64.12-15	撳	dèn	65 支			70 方		
64.12-15	撅	juē	65.0-4	支	zhī	70.0-4	方	fāng
64.12-15	撬	juē	66 攴			70.4-8	於	yú
64.12-15	摳	kōu	66.2-6	收	shōu	70.5-9	施	shī
64.12-15	撥	bō	66.3-7	改	gǎi	70.6-10	旁	páng
64.12-15	播	bō	66.3-7	攻	gōng	70.6-10	旅	lǚ
64.12-15	撤	chè	66.4-8	放	fàng	70.7-11	旋	xuàn
64.12-15	撮	cuō	66.5-9	故	gù	70.10-14	旗	qí
64.12-15	撈	lāo	66.5-9	政	zhèng	71 无		
64.12-15	撩	liāo	66.6-10	效	xiào	71.5-10	既	jì
64.12-15	撓	náo	66.6-10	致	zhì	72 日		
64.12-15	撒	sā	66.7-11	敗	bài	72.0-4	日	rì
64.12-15	撕	sī	66.7-11	教	jiāo jiào	72.2-6	旮	gā
64.13-16	擔	dān	66.7-11	救	jiù	72.2-6	早	zǎo
64.13-16	擋	dǎng	66.7-11	敏	mǐn	72.3-7	旱	hàn
64.13-16	擠	jǐ	66.8-12	敝	bì	72.4-8	昏	hūn
64.13-16	撿	jiǎn	66.8-12	敞	chǎng	72.4-8	明	míng
64.13-16	據	jù	66.8-12	敢	gǎn	72.5-9	昨	zuó
64.13-16	操	cāo	66.8-12	散	sǎn	72.5-9	春	chūn
64.13-16	擁	yōng	66.9-13	敬	jìng	72.5-9	昧	mèi
64.13-16	撞	zhuàng	66.10-14	敲	qiāo	72.5-9	是	shì
64.14-17	擱	gē	66.11-15	敵	dí	72.5-9	星	xīng
64.14-17	擦	cā	66.11-15	數	shù shǔ	72.6-10	晃	huàng
64.14-17	擰	níng nǐng	66.11-15	整	zhěng	72.6-10	晉	jìn
64.15-18	擴	kuò	66.11-15	徵	zhēng	72.6-10	晒	shài
64.15-18	擺	bǎi	67 文			72.6-10	晌	shǎng
64.15-18	撵	niǎn	67.0-4	文	wén	72.6-10	時	shí
64.15-18	擾	rǎo	68 斗			72.7-11	晚	wǎn
64.15-18	擲	zhì	68.0-4	斗	dǒu	72.7-11	晝	zhòu
64.15-19	攀	pān	68.6-10	料	liào	72.8-12	景	jǐng
						72.8-12	晾	liàng
						72.8-12	普	pǔ

72.8-12	暑	shǔ	75.4-8	東	dōng	75.8-12	棍	gùn
72.8-12	晴	qíng	75.4-8	果	guǒ	75.8-12	極	jí
72.8-12	替	tì	75.4-8	杯	bēi	75.8-12	棵	kē
72.9-13	暗	àn	75.4-8	松	sōng	75.8-12	棉	mián
72.9-13	暖	nuǎn	75.4-8	枕	zhěn	75.8-12	棚	péng
72.9-13	暈	yūn	75.4-8	枝	zhī	75.8-12	森	sēn
		yùn	75.4-8	柏	bǎi	75.8-12	棋	qí
72.10-14	暢	chàng			bó	75.8-12	棄	qì
72.11-15	暴	bào	75.5-9	查	chá	75.8-12	椅	yǐ
72.12-16	曉	xiǎo	75.5-9	架	jià	75.8-12	棗	zǎo
72.14-18	曠	kuàng	75.5-9	柳	liǔ	75.8-12	棧	zhàn
73 日			75.5-9	某	mǒu	75.8-12	植	zhí
73.2-6	曲	qū	75.5-9	柔	róu	75.9-13	楓	fēng
		qǔ	75.5-9	柿	shì	75.9-13	楞	lèng
73.3-7	更	gèng	75.5-9	相	xiāng	75.9-13	業	yè
73.6-10	書	shū	75.5-9	柱	zhù	75.9-13	楊	yáng
73.8-12	曾	céng	75.5-9	染	rǎn	75.9-13	榆	yú
73.8-12	最	zuì	75.6-10	案	àn	75.10-14	榜	bǎng
73.9-13	會	huì	75.6-10	柴	chái	75.10-14	概	gài
		kuài	75.6-10	根	gēn	75.10-14	構	gòu
74 月			75.6-10	格	gé	75.10-14	槐	huái
74.0-4	月	yuè	75.6-10	桂	guì	75.11-15	標	biāo
74.2-6	有	yǒu	75.6-10	核	hé	75.11-15	槽	cáo
74.4-8	朋	péng			hú	75.11-15	橫	héng
74.4-8	服	fú	75.6-10	栗	lì	75.11-15	樓	lóu
74.7-11	望	wàng	75.6-10	桃	táo	75.11-15	模	mó
74.8-12	期	qī	75.6-10	校	jiào			mú
74.8-12	朝	zhāo			xiào	75.11-15	樣	yàng
		cháo	75.6-10	栽	zāi	75.11-15	樂	yuè
75 木			75.6-10	桌	zhuō			lè
75.0-4	木	mù	75.6-10	框	kuàng	75.11-15	樟	zhāng
75.1-5	本	běn	75.7-11	桿	gǎn	75.11-15	樁	zhuāng
75.1-5	末	mò	75.7-11	梨	lí	75.12-16	橙	chéng
75.1-5	未	wèi	75.7-11	梢	shāo	75.12-16	機	jī
75.1-5	札	zhā	75.7-11	梳	shū	75.12-16	橘	jú
75.3-7	呆	ái	75.7-11	條	tiáo	75.12-16	樸	pū
75.3-7	材	cái	75.7-11	梯	tī	75.12-16	樹	shù
75.3-7	村	cūn	75.7-11	桶	tǒng	75.12-16	橋	qiáo
75.3-7	朵	duǒ	75.7-11	梧	wú	75.12-16	橡	xiàng
75.3-7	杏	xìng	75.8-12	棒	bàng	75.13-17	檢	jiǎn
75.4-8	板	bǎn	75.8-12	棺	guān			

75.14-18	檀	tán	**82** 毛		85.6-9	津	jīn
75.14-18	櫃	guì	82.0-4 毛	máo	85.6-9	活	huó
75.18-22	權	quán	82.8-12 毯	tǎn	85.6-9	洒	sǎ
.75.18-22	攖	yǐng	82.13-17 氈	zhān	85.6-9	洗	xǐ
76 欠			**83** 氏		85.7-10	洩	xiè
76.0-4	欠	qiàn	83.1-5 民	mín	85.6-9	洋	yáng
76.2-6	次	cì	**84** 气		85.7-10	浮	fú
76.8-12	欵	kuǎn	84.6-10 氧	yǎng	85.7-10	酒	jiǔ
76.8-12	欺	qī	84.6-10 氣	qì	85.7-10	浪	làng
76.9-13	歇	xiē	84.7-11 氫	qīng	85.7-11	涼	liáng
76.10-14	歌	gē	**85** 水		85.7-10	流	liú
76.11-15	歎	tàn	85.0-4 水	shuǐ	85.7-10	海	hǎi
76.12-16	歐	ōu	85.1-5 永	yǒng	85.7-10	消	xiāo
76.18-22	歡	huān	85.2-7 求	qiú	85.7-10	浴	yù
77 止			85.3-6 池	chí	85.8-11	淡	dàn
77.1-5	正	zhèng	85.3-6 江	jiāng	85.8-11	淋	lín / lún
77.2-6	此	cǐ	85.3-6 汗	hàn			
77.3-7	步	bù	85.4-7 沈	chén	85.8-11	混	hún / hùn / hǔn
77.4-8	歧	qí	85.4-7 沖	chōng			
77.4-8	武	wǔ	85.4-7 決	jué	85.8-11	淮	huái
77.5-9	歪	wāi	85.4-7 沒	méi	85.8-11	深	shēn
77.9-13	歲	suì	85.4-7 沙	shā	85.8-11	涮	shuàn
77.12-16	歷	lì	85.4-7 汽	qì	85.8-11	淺	qiǎn
77.14-18	歸	guī	85.5-8 波	bō / pō	85.8-11	淒	qī
78 歹			85.5-8 法	fá / fǎ / fa	85.8-11	清	qīng
78.2-6	死	sǐ			85.8-11	淘	táo
78.8-12	殖	zhí	85.5-8 況	kuàng	85.8-11	添	tiān
78.8-12	殘	cán	85.5-8 河	hé	85.8-11	淹	yān
79 殳			85.5-8 泥	ní	85.8-11	液	yè
79.5-9	段	duàn	85.5-8 泡	pào	85.8-11	淤	yū
79.7-11	殺	shā	85.5-9 泉	quán	85.9-12	測	cè
79.8-12	殼	ké	85.5-10 泰	tài	85.9-12	湊	còu
79.9-13	毀	huǐ	85.5-8 沿	yán	85.9-12	減	jiǎn
80 毋			85.5-8 油	yóu	85.9-12	渴	kě
80.1-5	母	mǔ	85.5-8 沾	zhān	85.9-12	涵	hán
80.3-7	每	měi	85.5-8 治	zhì	85.9-12	渾	hún
80.5-9	毒	dú	85.5-8 注	zhù	85.9-12	湖	hú
81 比			85.6-9 派	pài	85.9-12	溫	wēn
81.0-4	比	bǐ	85.6-9 洞	dòng	85.9-12	湯	tāng
					85.9-12	渣	zhā

109.8-13	睜	zhēng	112.11-16	磨	mó	115.10-15	稿	gǎo
109.9-14	瞄	miáo			mò	115.10-15	穀	gǔ
109.9-14	睡	shuì	112.11-16	磚	zhuān	115.11-16	積	jī
109.10-15	瞌	kē	112.14-19	礙	ài	115.12-17	穗	suì
109.10-15	瞎	xiā	**113**	示		115.14-19	穩	wěn
109.11-16	瞞	mán	113.0-5	示	shì	**116**	穴	
109.12-17	瞪	dèng	113.3-7	社	shè	116.2-7	究	jiū
109.12-17	瞭	liáo	113.4-8	祈	qí	116.3-8	空	kōng
109.12-17	瞧	qiáo	113.5-9	神	shén			kòng
109.14-19	矇	mēng	113.5-9	祝	zhù	116.4-9	突	tū
110	矛		113.6-11	祭	jì	116.4-9	穿	chuān
110.0-5	矛	máo	113.6-11	票	piào	116.7-12	窗	chuāng
			113.7-11	視	shì	116.7-12	窖	jiào
111	矢		113.8-13	禁	jìn	116.8-13	窟	kū
111.3-8	知	zhī	113.9-13	福	fú	116.9-14	窩	wō
111.7-12	短	duǎn	113.9-13	禍	huò	116.9-14	窯	yáo
111.8-13	矮	ǎi	113.13-17	禮	lǐ	116.10-15	窮	qióng
111.12-17	矯	jiǎo	**115**	禾		116.13-18	竅	qiào
112	石		115.2-7	私	sī	116.14-19	竈	zào
112.0-5	石	dàn	115.2-7	禿	tū	**117**	立	
		shí	115.3-8	秀	xiù	117.0-5	立	lì
112.4-9	砍	kǎn	115.4-9	科	kē	117.5-10	站	zhàn
112.4-9	砂	shā	115.4-9	秒	miǎo	117.6-11	章	zhāng
112.4-9	砌	qì	115.4-9	秋	qiū	117.6-11	竟	jìng
112.5-10	砲	pào	115.5-10	秤	chèng	117.7-12	童	tóng
112.5-10	破	pò	115.5-10	秘	mì	117.9-14	端	duān
112.6-11	砸	zá	115.5-10	秧	yāng	117.9-14	竭	jié
112.7-12	硫	liú	115.5-10	秩	zhì	117.15-20	競	jìng
112.7-12	硯	yàn	115.5-10	租	zū	**118**	竹	
112.7-12	硬	yìng	115.6-11	移	yí	118.0-6	竹	zhú
112.8-13	碰	pèng	115.7-12	程	chéng	118.4-10	笑	xiào
112.8-13	碗	wǎn	115.7-12	稜	léng	118.5-11	笨	bèn
112.9-14	碴	chá	115.7-12	稍	shāo	118.5-11	笛	dí
112.9-14	磁	cí	115.7-12	稅	shuì	118.5-11	符	fú
112.9-14	碟	dié	115.7-12	稀	xī	118.5-11	笤	tiáo
112.10-15	磅	bàng	115.8-13	稠	chóu	118.6-12	筆	bǐ
112.10-15	磕	kē	115.9-14	種	zhǒng	118.6-12	答	dá
112.10-15	碼	mǎ			zhòng	118.6-12	等	děng
112.10-15	碾	niǎn	115.9-14	稱	chèn	118.6-11	第	dì
112.10-15	確	què			chēng	118.6-12	筍	sǔn
			115.10-15	稻	dào			

118.6-12	筒	tǒng	120.1-7	糾	jiū	120.10-16	縣	xiàn
118.7-13	節	jié	120.3-9	紀	jì	120.10-16	緣	yuán
118.7-13	筷	kuài	120.3-9	紅	hóng	120.11-17	繃	bēng
118.7-13	筐	kuāng	120.3-9	約	yuē	120.11-17	繁	fán
118.8-14	管	guǎn	120.4-10	純	chún	120.11-17	縫	féng / fèng
118.8-14	算	suàn	120.4-10	紡	fǎng			
118.8-14	箝	qián	120.4-10	級	jí	120.11-17	繩	shéng
118.9-15	箭	jiàn	120.4-10	納	nà	120.11-17	縮	suō
118.9-15	篇	piān	120.4-10	紐	niǔ	120.11-17	總	zǒng
118.9-15	箱	xiāng	120.4-10	紗	shā	120.11-17	縱	zòng
118.9-15	範	fàn	120.4-10	素	sù	120.12-18	繞	rào
118.12-18	簡	jiǎn	120.4-10	索	suǒ	120.13-19	繫	jì
118.12-16	篩	shāi	120.4-10	紙	zhǐ	120.13-19	繮	jiāng
118.13-19	簽	qiān	120.5-11	絆	bàn	120.13-19	繳	jiǎo
118.13-19	簾	lián	120.5-11	累	lěi / lèi	120.13-19	織	zhī
118.13-19	簸	bò				120.14-20	辮	biàn
118.14-20	籌	chóu	120.5-11	細	xì	120.14-20	繡	xiù
118.14-20	籍	jì	120.5-11	終	zhōng	120.15-21	繼	jì
118.15-21	籃	lán	120.5-11	組	zǔ	120.15-21	續	xù
118.15-21	籤	qiān	120.6-12	統	tǒng	120.16-22	纏	chán
118.17-23	籠	lóng	120.6-12	給	gěi	120.17-23	纖	xiān
118.19-25	籬	lí	120.6-12	結	jié	[121]	缶	
[119]	米		120.6-12	絲	sī	121.3-9	缸	gāng
119.0-6	米	mǐ	120.6-12	紫	zǐ	121.4-10	缺	quē
119.4-10	粉	fěn	120.7-13	綁	bǎng	[122]	网	
119.5-11	粒	lì	120.7-13	絹	juàn	122.8-13	置	zhì
119.5-11	粘	zhān	120.7-13	綑	kǔn	122.8-13	罪	zuì
119.5-11	粗	cū	120.8-14	綢	chóu	122.9-14	罰	fá
119.8-14	精	jīng	120.8-14	綱	gāng	122.10-15	罷	bà
119.9-15	糊	hú	120.8-14	經	jīng	122.10-15	罵	mà
119.10-16	糕	gāo	120.8-14	綿	mián	122.14-19	羅	luó
119.10-16	糖	táng	120.8-14	網	wǎng	[123]	羊	
119.11-17	糨	jiàng	120.8-14	維	wéi	123.0-6	羊	yáng
119.11-17	糠	kāng	120.9-15	編	biān	123.3-9	美	měi
119.11-17	糞	fèn	120.9-15	緞	duàn	123.5-11	羞	xiū
119.12-18	糧	liáng	120.0-15	練	liàn	123.6-12	羨	xiàn
119.12-18	糟	zāo	120.9-15	綠	lǜ	123.7-13	義	yì
119.13-19	糯	zòng	120.9-15	緩	huǎn	123.7-13	群	qún
[120]	糸		120.9-15	線	xiàn	[124]	羽	
120.1-7	糸	xì	120.10-16	緊	jǐn	124.4-10	翅	chì

140.6-10	草	cǎo	140.16-20	蘋	píng		144 行
140.6-10	荒	huāng	140.17-21	護	hù	144.0-6	行 háng
140.6-10	荔	lì	140.17-21	蘭	lán		xíng
140.7-11	莊	zhuāng	140.18-20	藏	cáng	144.6-12	街 jiē
140.7-11	荷	hé	140.19-23	蘿	luó	144.9-15	衝 chōng
140.7-11	莫	mò		141 虎		144.10-16	衛 wèi
140.8-12	菜	cài	141.2-8	虎	hǔ		145 衣
140.8-12	菠	bó	141.5-11	處	chù	145.0-6	衣 yī
140.8-12	菲	fēi	141.5-11	虛	xū	145.2-8	表 biǎo
140.8-12	華	huá	141.7-13	號	hào	145.3-9	衫 shān
140.8-12	菊	jú	141.11-17	虧	kuī	145.4-10	衰 shuāi
140.8-12	菩	pú		142 虫		145.5-11	被 bèi
140.9-13	董	dǒng	142.3-9	虹	gàng	145.5-11	袍 páo
140.9-13	葫	hú	142.3-9	虼	gè	145.5-11	袖 xiù
140.9-13	落	là	142.4-10	蚊	wén	145.6-12	裁 cái
140.9-13	蔥	lào cōng	142.5-11	蛀	zhù	145.6-12	裂 liè
140.9-13	韭	jiǔ	142.5-11	蛋	dàn	145.7-13	裝 zhuāng
140.9-13	葡	pú	142.5-11	蛇	shé	145.7-13	補 bǔ
140.9-13	萬	wàn	142.5-11	蛆	qū	145.7-13	裏 lǐ
140.9-13	葉	yè	142.6-12	蛤	gé há	145.7-13	裙 qún
140.10-14	蒸	zhēng	142.6-12	蛐	qū	145.8-14	製 zhì
140.10-14	蒼	cāng	142.8-14	蜘	zhī	145.8-14	裹 guó
140.10-14	蓋	gài	142.8-14	蜻	qíng	145.9-15	複 fù
140.10-14	蒜	suàn	142.8-14	蜜	mì	145.10-16	褟 jiè
140.11-15	蔫	niān	142.9-15	蝗	huáng	145.10-16	褲 kù
140.12-16	著	zhù	142.9-15	蝎	xiē	145.10-16	褥 rù
140.12-16	薑	jiāng	142.9-15	蝦	xiā	145.14-20	襪 wà
140.13-17	薄	báo bò	142.10-16	螞	mǎ	145.16-22	襯 chèn
140.13-17	薪	xīn	142.10-16	螃	páng		146 西
140.14-18	藉	jiè	142.10-16	螺	shǐ	146.0-6	西 xī
140.14-18	蕭	xiāo	142.10-16	螢	yíng	146.3-9	要 yào
140.15-19	繭	jiǎn	142.11-17	蟄	zhē	146.13-19	霸 bà
140.15-19	藍	lán	142.11-17	螺	luó		147 見
140.15-19	藕	ǒu	142.12-18	蟲	chóng	147.0-7	見 jiàn
140.15-19	藤	téng	142.15-21	蠢	chǔn	147.4-11	規 guī
140.15-19	藝	yì	142.15-21	蠟	là	147.9-16	親 qīn
140.15-19	藥	yào	142.20-26	蠶	cán	147.13-20	覺 jué
140.16-20	蘆	lú		143 血		147.18-25	觀 guān
140.16-20	蘑	mó	143.0-6	血	xiě xuè		148 角
						148.0-7	角 jiǎo

157.6-13	路	lù
157.6-13	跳	tiào
157.7-14	踅	zhuài
157.7-14	跺	duò
157.8-15	踩	cǎi
157.8-15	踢	tī
157.8-15	踪	zōng
157.9-16	踹	chuài
157.9-16	蹄	tí
157.9-16	踴	yǒng
157.11-18	蹦	bèng
157.11-18	蹚	tāng
157.12-19	蹭	cèng
157.12-19	蹲	dūn
157.13-20	蹾	dūn
157.14-21	躍	yuè
158	身	
158.0-7	身	shēn
158.7-14	躲	duǒ
158.8-15	躺	tǎng
159	車	
159.0-7	車	chē
159.1-8	軋	yà
159.2-9	軌	guǐ
159.2-9	軍	jūn
159.4-11	軟	ruǎn
159.7-14	輕	qīng
159.8-15	輪	lún
159.8-15	輛	liàng
159.9-16	輸	shū
159.10-17	輿	yǔ
159.11-18	轆	lù
159.11-18	轉	zhuǎn zhuàn
159.14-21	轟	hōng
160	辛	
160.5-12	辜	gū
160.6-13	辣	là
160.9-16	辦	bàn
160.12-19	辭	cí
160.14-21	辯	biàn
161	辰	
161.6-13	農	nóng
162	辵	
162.3-7	迅	xùn
162.4-8	近	jìn
162.4-8	迎	yíng
162.6-10	追	zhuī
162.6-10	迷	mí
162.6-10	送	sòng
162.6-10	速	sú
162.6-10	退	tuì
162.6-10	逃	táo
162.7-11	造	zào
162.7-11	這	zhè zhèi zèn
162.7-11	逞	chěng
162.7-11	逗	dòu
162.7-11	逢	féng
162.7-11	逛	guàng
162.7-11	連	lián
162.7-11	通	tōng
162.8-12	逮	děi
162.8-12	進	jìn
162.8-12	透	tòu
162.9-13	運	yùn
162.9-13	逼	bī
162.9-13	遍	biàn
162.9-13	道	dào
162.9-13	達	dá
162.9-13	過	guò
162.9-13	遇	yù
162.9-13	遊	yóu
162.10-14	遞	dì
162.10-14	遠	yuǎn
162.11-15	遭	zāo
162.11-15	蓮	lián
162.11-15	適	shì
162.12-16	遮	zhē
162.12-16	遲	chí
162.12-16	選	xuǎn
162.12-16	遺	yí
162.13-17	避	bì
162.13-17	邁	mài
162.13-17	邀	yāo
162.13-17	還	hái huán
162.15-19	邊	biān
162.15-19	邋	lá
162.19-23	邏	luó
163	邑	
163.4-7	邦	bāng
163.4-7	那	něi nèi
163.4-7	那	nà
163.8-11	都	dōu
163.8-11	部	bù
163.9-12	郵	yóu
163.9-12	鄉	xiāng
164	酉	
164.3-10	配	pèi
164.5-12	酥	sū
164.7-14	酸	suān
164.8-15	醃	yān
164.8-15	醉	zuì
164.8-15	醋	cù
164.9-16	醒	xǐng
164.9-16	醞	yùn
164.11-18	醬	jiàng
164.17-24	釀	niàng
164.20-27	釅	yàn
165	釆	
165.13-20	釋	shì
166	里	
166.0-7	里	lǐ
166.2-9	重	chóng zhòng
166.4-11	野	yě
166.5-12	量	liáng liàng

167 金			167.14-22	鑛	kuàng	170.8-11	陪	péi	
167.0-8	金	jīn	167.14-22	鑰	yào	170.8-11	陰	yīn	
167.2-10	釘	dīng	167.15-23	鑑	jiàn	170.9-12	隊	duì	
167.2-10	針	zhēn	167.17-25	鑲	xiāng	170.9-12	階	jiē	
167.3-11	釣	diào	167.18-26	鑽	zuàn	170.9-12	陽	yáng	
167.4-12	鈔	chāo	167.18-26	鑷	niè	170.10-13	隔	gé jiē	
167.4-12	鈎	gōu	167.19-27	鑼	luó				
167.5-13	鮑	bào	167.19-27	鑿	záo	170.10-13	隘	xiàn	
167.5-13	鈴	líng	**168** 長			170.13-16	鄰	lín	
167.5-13	鉛	qiān	168.0-8	長	cháng	170.13-16	隧	suì	
167.6-14	銅	tóng			zhǎng	170.13-16	隨	suí	
167.6-14	銀	yín	**169** 門			170.13-16	險	xuǎn	
167.7-15	鋤	chú	169.0-8	門	mén	170.14-17	隱	yǐn	
167.7-15	鋁	lǚ	169.1-9	閂	zhuān	**172** 隹			
167.7-15	鋪	pū pù	169.2-10	閃	shǎn	172.2-10	隻	zhī	
167.7-15	銲	hàn	169.3-11	閉	bì	172.3-11	雀	qiāo	
167.7-15	銷	xiāo	169.4-12	閒	jiān	172.4-12	雇	gù	
167.8-16	錐	zhuī	169.4-12	開	kāi	172.4-12	集	jí	
167.8-17	錦	jǐn	169.4-12	閏	rùn	172.8-16	雕	diāo	
167.8-16	錯	cuò	169.4-12	閑	xián	172.9-17	雖	suí	
167.8-16	鋼	gāng	169.6-14	閨	guī	172.10-18	雙	shuāng	
167.8-16	鋸	jù	169.8-16	閣	kuò	172.11-19	離	lí	
167.8-16	錢	qián	169.8-16	悶	mèn	172.11-19	難	nán	
167.8-16	銹	xiù	169.10-18	闖	chuǎng	**173** 雨			
167.8-16	錫	xī	169.11-19	關	guān	173.0-8	雨	yǔ	
167.9-17	錘	chuí	**170** 阜			173.3-11	雪	xuě	
167.9-17	鍋	guō	170.4-7	阨	è	173.4-12	雲	yún	
167.10-18	鎮	zhèn	170.4-7	防	fáng	173.5-13	雹	báo	
167.10-18	鎳	niè	170.5-8	阻	zǔ	173.5-13	電	diàn	
167.10-18	鎗	qiāng	170.5-8	阿	ē	173.5-13	零	líng	
167.10-18	鎖	suǒ	170.5-8	附	fù	173.5-13	雷	léi	
167.11-19	鏟	chǎn	170.5-8	陀	túo	173.6-14	需	xū	
167.11-19	鏈	liàn	170.6-9	限	xiàn	173.7-15	霉	méi	
167.11-19	鏡	jìng	170.7-10	陣	zhèn	173.8-16	霍	huò	
167.12-20	鐘	zhōng	170.7-10	除	chú	173.8-16	霓	ní	
167.12-20	鐮	lián	170.7-10	陝	shǎn	173.9-17	霜	shuān	
167.13-21	鐳	léi	170.7-10	院	yuàn	173.12-20	霧	wù	
167.13-21	鐵	tiě	170.8-11	陳	chén	173.13-21	露	lòu lù	
167.13-21	鐲	zhuó	170.8-11	降	jiàng	173.16-24	靈	líng	
			170.8-11	陸	lù				

174	青		182	風	187.16-26	驢	lú
174.0-8	青 qīng		182.0-9	風 fēng		188	骨
174.8-16	靜 jìng		182.5-14	颱 tái	188.0-10	骨	gú
	175	非	182.6-15	颳 guā			gǔ
175.0-8	非 fēi		182.11-20	飄 piāo	188.4-14	骯	āng
175.7-15	靠 kào			183	飛	188.4-14	骰 shǎi
	176	面	183.0-10	飛 fēi	188.5-15	骷	kū
176.0-9	面 mìan			184	食	188.13-23	髒 zāng
	177	革	184.0-9	食 shí	188.13-23	體	tǐ
177.0-9	革 gé		184.4-12	飯 fàn		189	高
177.4-13	靴 xuē		184.5-13	飽 bǎo	189.0-10	高	gāo
177.6-15	鞋 xié		184.6-14	餅 bǐng		190	髟
177.6-15	鞏 gǒng		184.6-14	餃 jiāo	190.8-18	鬆	sōng
177.8-17	鞠 jū		184.6-15	養 yǎng	190.9-19	鬍	hú
177.9-18	鞭 biān		184.7-16	餐 cān		191	鬥
177.9-18	鞦 qiū		184.7-15	餓 è	191.5-15	鬧	nào
	178	韋	184.7-15	餘 yú	191.6-16	鬨	hòng
178.8-18	韓 hán		184.8-16	館 guǎn	191.14-24	鬪	dòu
	180	音	184.8-16	餛 hún	191.16-26	鬮	jiū
180.0-9	音 yīn		184.8-16	餡 xiàn		194	鬼
180.12-21	響 xiǎng		184.9-17	餿 sōu	194.0-10	鬼	guǐ
	181	頁	184.9-17	餵 wèi	194.4-14	魁	kuí
181.0-9	頁 yè		184.11-19	饅 mán		195	魚
181.2-11	頂 dǐng		184.12-20	饒 ráo	195.0-11	魚	yú
181.3-12	順 shùn		184.18-20	饞 chán	195.6-17	鮮	xiān
181.3-12	項 xiàng			185	首	195.7-18	鯉	lǐ
181.3-12	須 xū		185.0-9	首 shǒu	195.7-18	鯽	jì
181.4-13	預 yù		18	186	香	195.8-19	鯨	jīng
181.4-13	頓 dùn		186.0-9	香 xiāng	195.9-20	鱷	è
181.4-13	頑 wán			187	馬	195.13-24	鱗	lín
181.5-14	領 lǐng		187.0-10	馬 mǎ		196	鳥
181.7-16	頭 tóu		187.5-15	駐 zhù	196.0-11	鳥	niǎo
181.8-17	頰 ké		187.5-15	駕 jià	196.5-16	鴛	yuān
181.9-18	額 é		187.6-16	駱 luò	196.5-16	鴨	yā
181.9-18	題 tí		187.8-18	騎 qí	196.6-17	鴿	gē
181.9-18	顏 yán		187.9-19	騙 piàn	196.7-18	鵝	é
181.10-19	願 yùan		187.10-20	騰 téng	196.10-21	鷄	jī
181.12-21	顧 gù		187.11-21	騾 luó		197	鹵
181.13-22	顫 chàn		187.12-22	驕 jiāo	197.9-20	鹹	xián
181.14-23	顯 xiǎn		187.14-24	驚 jīng	197.12-23	鹽	yán

197.13-24 鹻 jiǎn

198 鹿

198.0-11 鹿 lù

198.9-19 麒 qí

199 麥

199.0-11 麥 mài

199.8-19 麴 qú

199.9-20 麵 miàn

200 麻

200.0-11 麻 má

200.3-14 麼 ma
　　　　　 mo

200.4-15 摩 mā

201 黃

201.0-12 黃 huáng

202 黍

202.5-17 黏 nián

203 黑

203.0-12 黑 hēi

203.4-16 默 mò

203.5-17 點 diǎn

203.8-20 黨 dǎng

207 鼓

207.0-13 鼓 gǔ

209 鼻

209.0-14 鼻 bí

210 齊

210.0-14 齊 qí

211 齒

211.0-15 齒 chǐ

211.5-20 齣 chū

212 龍

212.0-17 龍 lóng

A CATALOG OF SELECTED DOVER
BOOKS IN ALL FIELDS OF INTEREST

CONCERNING THE SPIRITUAL IN ART, Wassily Kandinsky. Pioneering work by father of abstract art. Thoughts on color theory, nature of art. Analysis of earlier masters. 12 illustrations. 80pp. of text. 5⅜ x 8½.   23411-8

ANIMALS: 1,419 Copyright-Free Illustrations of Mammals, Birds, Fish, Insects, etc., Jim Harter (ed.). Clear wood engravings present, in extremely lifelike poses, over 1,000 species of animals. One of the most extensive pictorial sourcebooks of its kind. Captions. Index. 284pp. 9 x 12.   23766-4

CELTIC ART: The Methods of Construction, George Bain. Simple geometric techniques for making Celtic interlacements, spirals, Kells-type initials, animals, humans, etc. Over 500 illustrations. 160pp. 9 x 12. (Available in U.S. only.)   22923-8

AN ATLAS OF ANATOMY FOR ARTISTS, Fritz Schider. Most thorough reference work on art anatomy in the world. Hundreds of illustrations, including selections from works by Vesalius, Leonardo, Goya, Ingres, Michelangelo, others. 593 illustrations. 192pp. 7⅛ x 10¼.   20241-0

CELTIC HAND STROKE-BY-STROKE (Irish Half-Uncial from "The Book of Kells"): An Arthur Baker Calligraphy Manual, Arthur Baker. Complete guide to creating each letter of the alphabet in distinctive Celtic manner. Covers hand position, strokes, pens, inks, paper, more. Illustrated. 48pp. 8¼ x 11.   24336-2

EASY ORIGAMI, John Montroll. Charming collection of 32 projects (hat, cup, pelican, piano, swan, many more) specially designed for the novice origami hobbyist. Clearly illustrated easy-to-follow instructions insure that even beginning papercrafters will achieve successful results. 48pp. 8¼ x 11.   27298-2

THE COMPLETE BOOK OF BIRDHOUSE CONSTRUCTION FOR WOOD-WORKERS, Scott D. Campbell. Detailed instructions, illustrations, tables. Also data on bird habitat and instinct patterns. Bibliography. 3 tables. 63 illustrations in 15 figures. 48pp. 5¼ x 8½.   24407-5

BLOOMINGDALE'S ILLUSTRATED 1886 CATALOG: Fashions, Dry Goods and Housewares, Bloomingdale Brothers. Famed merchants' extremely rare catalog depicting about 1,700 products: clothing, housewares, firearms, dry goods, jewelry, more. Invaluable for dating, identifying vintage items. Also, copyright-free graphics for artists, designers. Co-published with Henry Ford Museum & Greenfield Village. 160pp. 8¼ x 11.   25780-0

HISTORIC COSTUME IN PICTURES, Braun & Schneider. Over 1,450 costumed figures in clearly detailed engravings–from dawn of civilization to end of 19th century. Captions. Many folk costumes. 256pp. 8⅜ x 11¾.   23150-X

PIANO TUNING, J. Cree Fischer. Clearest, best book for beginner, amateur. Simple repairs, raising dropped notes, tuning by easy method of flattened fifths. No previous skills needed. 4 illustrations. 201pp. 5⅜ x 8½.   23267-0

HINTS TO SINGERS, Lillian Nordica. Selecting the right teacher, developing confidence, overcoming stage fright, and many other important skills receive thoughtful discussion in this indispensible guide, written by a world-famous diva of four decades' experience. 96pp. 5⅜ x 8½.   40094-8

THE COMPLETE NONSENSE OF EDWARD LEAR, Edward Lear. All nonsense limericks, zany alphabets, Owl and Pussycat, songs, nonsense botany, etc., illustrated by Lear. Total of 320pp. 5⅜ x 8½. (Available in U.S. only.)   20167-8

VICTORIAN PARLOUR POETRY: An Annotated Anthology, Michael R. Turner. 117 gems by Longfellow, Tennyson, Browning, many lesser-known poets. "The Village Blacksmith," "Curfew Must Not Ring Tonight," "Only a Baby Small," dozens more, often difficult to find elsewhere. Index of poets, titles, first lines. xxiii + 325pp. 5⅜ x 8¼.   27044-0

DUBLINERS, James Joyce. Fifteen stories offer vivid, tightly focused observations of the lives of Dublin's poorer classes. At least one, "The Dead," is considered a masterpiece. Reprinted complete and unabridged from standard edition. 160pp. 5³⁄₁₆ x 8¼.   26870-5

GREAT WEIRD TALES: 14 Stories by Lovecraft, Blackwood, Machen and Others, S. T. Joshi (ed.). 14 spellbinding tales, including "The Sin Eater," by Fiona McLeod, "The Eye Above the Mantel," by Frank Belknap Long, as well as renowned works by R. H. Barlow, Lord Dunsany, Arthur Machen, W. C. Morrow and eight other masters of the genre. 256pp. 5⅜ x 8½. (Available in U.S. only.)   40436-6

THE BOOK OF THE SACRED MAGIC OF ABRAMELIN THE MAGE, translated by S. MacGregor Mathers. Medieval manuscript of ceremonial magic. Basic document in Aleister Crowley, Golden Dawn groups. 268pp. 5⅜ x 8½.   23211-5

NEW RUSSIAN-ENGLISH AND ENGLISH-RUSSIAN DICTIONARY, M. A. O'Brien. This is a remarkably handy Russian dictionary, containing a surprising amount of information, including over 70,000 entries. 366pp. 4½ x 6⅛.   20208-9

HISTORIC HOMES OF THE AMERICAN PRESIDENTS, Second, Revised Edition, Irvin Haas. A traveler's guide to American Presidential homes, most open to the public, depicting and describing homes occupied by every American President from George Washington to George Bush. With visiting hours, admission charges, travel routes. 175 photographs. Index. 160pp. 8¼ x 11.   26751-2

NEW YORK IN THE FORTIES, Andreas Feininger. 162 brilliant photographs by the well-known photographer, formerly with *Life* magazine. Commuters, shoppers, Times Square at night, much else from city at its peak. Captions by John von Hartz. 181pp. 9¼ x 10¾.   23585-8

INDIAN SIGN LANGUAGE, William Tomkins. Over 525 signs developed by Sioux and other tribes. Written instructions and diagrams. Also 290 pictographs. 111pp. 6⅛ x 9¼.   22029-X

ANATOMY: A Complete Guide for Artists, Joseph Sheppard. A master of figure drawing shows artists how to render human anatomy convincingly. Over 460 illustrations. 224pp. 8⅜ x 11¼. 27279-6

MEDIEVAL CALLIGRAPHY: Its History and Technique, Marc Drogin. Spirited history, comprehensive instruction manual covers 13 styles (ca. 4th century through 15th). Excellent photographs; directions for duplicating medieval techniques with modern tools. 224pp. 8⅜ x 11¼. 26142-5

DRIED FLOWERS: How to Prepare Them, Sarah Whitlock and Martha Rankin. Complete instructions on how to use silica gel, meal and borax, perlite aggregate, sand and borax, glycerine and water to create attractive permanent flower arrangements. 12 illustrations. 32pp. 5⅜ x 8½. 21802-3

EASY-TO-MAKE BIRD FEEDERS FOR WOODWORKERS, Scott D. Campbell. Detailed, simple-to-use guide for designing, constructing, caring for and using feeders. Text, illustrations for 12 classic and contemporary designs. 96pp. 5⅜ x 8½. 25847-5

SCOTTISH WONDER TALES FROM MYTH AND LEGEND, Donald A. Mackenzie. 16 lively tales tell of giants rumbling down mountainsides, of a magic wand that turns stone pillars into warriors, of gods and goddesses, evil hags, powerful forces and more. 240pp. 5⅜ x 8½. 29677-6

THE HISTORY OF UNDERCLOTHES, C. Willett Cunnington and Phyllis Cunnington. Fascinating, well-documented survey covering six centuries of English undergarments, enhanced with over 100 illustrations: 12th-century laced-up bodice, footed long drawers (1795), 19th-century bustles, l9th-century corsets for men, Victorian "bust improvers," much more. 272pp. 5⅜ x 8¼. 27124-2

ARTS AND CRAFTS FURNITURE: The Complete Brooks Catalog of 1912, Brooks Manufacturing Co. Photos and detailed descriptions of more than 150 now very collectible furniture designs from the Arts and Crafts movement depict davenports, settees, buffets, desks, tables, chairs, bedsteads, dressers and more, all built of solid, quarter-sawed oak. Invaluable for students and enthusiasts of antiques, Americana and the decorative arts. 80pp. 6½ x 9¼. 27471-3

WILBUR AND ORVILLE: A Biography of the Wright Brothers, Fred Howard. Definitive, crisply written study tells the full story of the brothers' lives and work. A vividly written biography, unparalleled in scope and color, that also captures the spirit of an extraordinary era. 560pp. 6⅛ x 9¼. 40297-5

THE ARTS OF THE SAILOR: Knotting, Splicing and Ropework, Hervey Garrett Smith. Indispensable shipboard reference covers tools, basic knots and useful hitches; handsewing and canvas work, more. Over 100 illustrations. Delightful reading for sea lovers. 256pp. 5⅜ x 8½. 26440-8

FRANK LLOYD WRIGHT'S FALLINGWATER: The House and Its History, Second, Revised Edition, Donald Hoffmann. A total revision—both in text and illustrations—of the standard document on Fallingwater, the boldest, most personal architectural statement of Wright's mature years, updated with valuable new material from the recently opened Frank Lloyd Wright Archives. "Fascinating"—*The New York Times*. 116 illustrations. 128pp. 9¼ x 10¾. 27430-6

CATALOG OF DOVER BOOKS

THE STORY OF THE TITANIC AS TOLD BY ITS SURVIVORS, Jack Winocour (ed.). What it was really like. Panic, despair, shocking inefficiency, and a little heroism. More thrilling than any fictional account. 26 illustrations. 320pp. 5⅜ x 8½. 20610-6

FAIRY AND FOLK TALES OF THE IRISH PEASANTRY, William Butler Yeats (ed.). Treasury of 64 tales from the twilight world of Celtic myth and legend: "The Soul Cages," "The Kildare Pooka," "King O'Toole and his Goose," many more. Introduction and Notes by W. B. Yeats. 352pp. 5⅜ x 8½. 26941-8

BUDDHIST MAHAYANA TEXTS, E. B. Cowell and others (eds.). Superb, accurate translations of basic documents in Mahayana Buddhism, highly important in history of religions. The Buddha-karita of Asvaghosha, Larger Sukhavativyuha, more. 448pp. 5⅜ x 8½. 25552-2

ONE TWO THREE . . . INFINITY: Facts and Speculations of Science, George Gamow. Great physicist's fascinating, readable overview of contemporary science: number theory, relativity, fourth dimension, entropy, genes, atomic structure, much more. 128 illustrations. Index. 352pp. 5⅜ x 8½. 25664-2

EXPERIMENTATION AND MEASUREMENT, W. J. Youden. Introductory manual explains laws of measurement in simple terms and offers tips for achieving accuracy and minimizing errors. Mathematics of measurement, use of instruments, experimenting with machines. 1994 edition. Foreword. Preface. Introduction. Epilogue. Selected Readings. Glossary. Index. Tables and figures. 128pp. 5⅜ x 8½. 40451-X

DALÍ ON MODERN ART: The Cuckolds of Antiquated Modern Art, Salvador Dalí. Influential painter skewers modern art and its practitioners. Outrageous evaluations of Picasso, Cézanne, Turner, more. 15 renderings of paintings discussed. 44 calligraphic decorations by Dalí. 96pp. 5⅜ x 8½. (Available in U.S. only.) 29220-7

ANTIQUE PLAYING CARDS: A Pictorial History, Henry René D'Allemagne. Over 900 elaborate, decorative images from rare playing cards (14th–20th centuries): Bacchus, death, dancing dogs, hunting scenes, royal coats of arms, players cheating, much more. 96pp. 9¼ x 12¼. 29265-7

MAKING FURNITURE MASTERPIECES: 30 Projects with Measured Drawings, Franklin H. Gottshall. Step-by-step instructions, illustrations for constructing handsome, useful pieces, among them a Sheraton desk, Chippendale chair, Spanish desk, Queen Anne table and a William and Mary dressing mirror. 224pp. 8⅛ x 11¼. 29338-6

THE FOSSIL BOOK: A Record of Prehistoric Life, Patricia V. Rich et al. Profusely illustrated definitive guide covers everything from single-celled organisms and dinosaurs to birds and mammals and the interplay between climate and man. Over 1,500 illustrations. 760pp. 7½ x 10⅛. 29371-8

Paperbound unless otherwise indicated. Available at your book dealer, online at **www.doverpublications.com**, or by writing to Dept. GI, Dover Publications, Inc., 31 East 2nd Street, Mineola, NY 11501. For current price information or for free catalogues (please indicate field of interest), write to Dover Publications or log on to **www.doverpublications.com** and see every Dover book in print. Dover publishes more than 500 books each year on science, elementary and advanced mathematics, biology, music, art, literary history, social sciences, and other areas.